Complete Book
of C Programming

Barry M. Austell-Wolfson
Claudel Financial

R. Derek Otieno
DeVry Institute of Technology

Prentice Hall
Upper Saddle River, New Jersey   *Columbus, Ohio*

Library of Congress Cataloging-in-Publication Data

Austell-Wolfson, Barry M.
    Complete book of C programming / Barry M. Austell-Wolfson, R. Derek
  Otieno.
      p.   cm.
    ISBN 0-13-096093-4
    1. C (Computer program language)   I. Otieno, R. Derek.   II. Title.
  QA76.73.C15A97   2000
  005.13'3—dc21
                                                                                99-30447
                                                                                CIP

Publisher: Charles E. Stewart, Jr.
Production Editor: Alexandrina Benedicto Wolf
Production Coordination: Custom Editorial Productions, Inc.
Design Coordinator: Karrie Converse-Jones
Cover Art: FPG International
Cover Designer: Linda Fares
Production Manager: Matt Ottenweller
Marketing Manager: Ben Leonard

This book was set in Times Roman by Custom Editorial Productions, Inc., and was printed and bound by
The Banta Company. The cover was printed by Phoenix Color Corp.

10 9 8 7 6 5 4 3 2 1

ISBN: 0-13-096093-4

Prentice-Hall International (UK) Limited, *London*
Prentice-Hall of Australia Pty. Limited, *Sydney*
Prentice-Hall of Canada, Inc., *Toronto*
Prentice-Hall Hispanoamericana, S. A., *Mexico*
Prentice-Hall of India Private Limited, *New Delhi*
Prentice-Hall of Japan, Inc., *Tokyo*
Prentice-Hall (Singapore) Pte. Ltd., *Singapore*
Editora Prentice-Hall do Brasil, Ltda., *Rio de Janeiro*

Preface

WHY ANOTHER C BOOK?

Complete Book of C Programming serves as a textbook for students and a detailed reference for professional C users. Many other C texts provide merely an "overview" of C. After learning with these texts, our students find that they are unable to effectively program once they find themselves in a real-world setting. They can rarely find any answers by rereading their textbooks. There are also excellent reference texts. But these are short, terse affairs with few examples. They list bare principles without mechanics, detail, or illustration useful to the expert. Because of their scope, highly technical style, and argot, they are beyond the reach of the novice or even intermediate programmer.

This book provides a step-by-step approach to some of C's arcane problems. It shows:

- how C makes stealth-like conversions in simple addition, multiplication, and similar basic operations that can overflow your variables.
- how placement of structure templates vis-à-vis function declarations has significance.
- how actual arguments in function calls are automatically converted in certain cases and are converted in different ways in different contexts, and when conversion is forbidden and what type compatibility means.
- how the value representing the starting address of a local array you return from a function can be trashed immediately upon returning.
- the recursive nature of scope specifiers and type qualifiers in nonscalar variables.
- portability problems in file operations and bit manipulation.
- how to write a variable argument list function that calls another such function.

In some cases, the depth and level of detail may seem unduly exhaustive or even tedious, but it won't be when you have a problem in those areas. On a more practical level, we show you how to create attractive, even elegant, reports suitable for a business environment, as well as professional-looking screen layouts.

This book is intended for readers with no previous programming experience, but at the same time, those with extensive backgrounds in the computing field. It has been specifically designed to be used as a textbook in a typical C sequence in both two-year and four-year colleges. At the same time, it is meant to be useful as an advanced reference text in the more sophisticated computer information systems courses such as database programming. The programmer must interface with the database engine's application programmer interfaces, which demand mastery of pointers to all sorts of data types and functions.

However, to avoid overwhelming the novice on a first read-through, we have marked particularly esoteric topics as "Optional."

WHO BENEFITS FROM THIS BOOK

Who benefits from this book? Specifically,

- Students and novice programmers.
- C instructors and professional C programmers frustrated with the scope and depth of existing C texts.
- Those who want to transition to C++ programming at a level that prepares them to create C++ classes and work with foundation class libraries.
- Those who program in multiple environments and need to understand platform differences in how bytes are stored and bits are evaluated, how nonscalar variables are padded and aligned, and how files are treated.

OBJECTIVES OF THIS BOOK

This book sets out to:

- teach the reader how to design programs that are easy to read, debug, modify, and maintain.
- provide the reader with the ability to write portable and well-designed elementary, intermediate, and advanced Standard C programs in their entirety. These include both batch and interactive programs.
- familiarize the reader with information processing and systems concepts that will help them interact with users and systems analysts when designing programs.
- teach students useful techniques for maintaining and modifying older "legacy" programs. The chapter dealing with control-break logic and sequential file update is especially representative of this objective.

We have identified the following as attributes of "good" programs, and developed this standard that each program written in this book embraces, exemplifies, and illustrates: consistent usage, complete documentation, thorough error detection and correction, restriction of side effects (elements of data encapsulation within function level), modularity, and consistent identifier naming convention.

USING THIS BOOK AS A TEXTBOOK

We have taught several courses using drafts of this text. These courses have included quarter-long courses at two-year colleges and semester-long courses at four-year colleges and universities, as well as short courses for programmers in industry and large government organizations. We have found the following sequence effective:

- *Introduction to C programming* (the first programming course)—Chapters 1 to 9 for a course that meets twice a week for 15 weeks.
- *Intermediate/Advanced C programming* (continuation of the first course)—Chapters 10 to 17.
- *Advanced C programming and reference document* (continuation of the first two courses in C programming) or *Intermediate C programming for students in Electronics Engineering*—Appendixes A to E, K, and L.
- *Introduction to C programming* (those who have learned other languages such as COBOL, Visual Basic, and PASCAL). This can be offered as a course preceding Object Oriented Programming with C++ where the students will be taught how to write classes—Chapters 1 to 15. The instructor can easily bypass or spend less time on Chapter 11 without losing continuity.

STANDARD C

In 1978, Brian W. Kernighan and Dennis M. Ritchie published their now-revered classic work, *The C Programming Language* (Prentice Hall). The work was unofficially acknowledged by the programming community as the bible of the C language—to such an extent that the moniker "K&R C" was applied to programs and implementations that complied with the prescriptions in the text and its de facto standard. In 1983, a working group, established under the auspices of the American National Standards Institute (ANSI), began work on an official standard for the C language. The language standard was adopted by ANSI in December 1989. The *ANSI C Standard*, as it came to be called, made a number of modifications and extensions to K&R C. The most significant addition was the introduction of function prototypes to allow strict parameter type checking.

The International Standardization Organization (ISO), a senior organization to ANSI based in Switzerland, in conjunction with the International Electrotechnical Commission, adopted the ANSI C Standard with minor editorial changes; and ANSI readopted the same standard, now called the ISO C Standard. The official name for the standard is ISO/IEC 1989-1990. This international standard was expressly designed to promote the portability of C programs among a variety of data processing systems. It was intended for both code implementors and programmers who could use such code. The ISO C Standard was amended in April 1994 by the Joint Technical Committee on Information Technology of ISO in Technical Corrigendum 1; it was further amended in Technical Corrigendum 2 in April 1996. By and large the changes are merely clarifying ones. The ISO C Standard, as modified, is referred to as Standard C. We will refer throughout this book to code or implementations that conform to the international standard as *Standard C*.

In appendixes devoted to direct memory access on the PC, we necessarily use functions and deal with concepts not part of Standard C. Apart from that limited deviation, all the programs and examples in the book are meant to adhere strictly to Standard C and be completely portable on all systems.

OTHER MATERIALS

Answers to review questions and programming assignments at the end of each chapter are contained in a Teacher's Manual available from Prentice Hall. At the back of this book is a CD containing a "lite version" of the *CodeWarrior* C compiler. *CodeWarrior* is an integrated development environment that supports both Mac and Windows 95/98/NT. It is used heavily by games writers and others because of its developmental tools. The CD also contains all programs found in the book, along with supporting files; source codes, including files and graphic images related to the Graphics Mode and Mouse appendix; and miscellaneous additional source-code utilities and explanatory text. The materials available on the CD can also be accessed online at www.atl.devry.edu/dotieno.

ACKNOWLEDGMENTS

Very special thanks to our copyeditor, Elizabeth Judd, who helped transfigure our sometimes turgid computer argot into a tight, readable whole and gave us wonderful English usage and grammar instruction along the way; to one of our reviewers, Gerald Flynn, SUNY (Farmingdale), who made dozens of insightful, thought-provoking, witty, and astute comments, suggestions, and corrections; and to Dr. Vladimir U. Romanov, Research Computer Center of Moscow State University, author of several Russian-language graphics books, who assisted greatly in writing the graphics appendix.

We thank William Stencel who read parts of the manuscript, made useful suggestions, and assisted in writing some chapter summaries; Drew Flowers, who also assisted with several chapter summaries; and Zelena Rockingham, who generated many of the graphics figures for the first chapter and coordinated the efforts of the students who worked on certain chapter summaries, programming exercises, and various other tasks. Getting the students involved gave us a unique perspective, thereby making this book representative of the needs and interests of a wide variety of students. Special thanks also go to Rich Grillo of National Data Corporation, who provided the much-needed industry perspective, especially in the area of EDI programming.

We would like to thank the following reviewers for their valuable suggestions: Shakil Aktar, Central Michigan University; Zhiging Liu, Indiana University; and Robert Snapp, University of Vermont.

The authors are indebted to the following students for their participation in this project: Shawn Yates, Joseph Carl Barnett, III, Mark Glazer, Christine Marie Cook, Heike Braxston, Gerrit Dwayne Van Vranken, Christopher McDowell, Jim Dorin, Dale Babcock, Irvin and Linda Bunts, and Evi Green, EIC.

We are indebted further to Jennifer Austell-Wolfson for her assistance in editing and word processing, and to the staff at Custom Editorial Productions for their efforts in coordinating the publication of the book. Thanks in particular to Laura Citro, project editor, and to Tammy Haskins, production specialist.

Finally, we acknowledge the support of our families during the long hours of work on this project: Jennifer Austell-Wolfson and Harwood Wolfson; and Betty Norman Otieno and Joseph, Joshua, Lillian, and Benjamin Otieno.

COMMENTS AND SUGGESTIONS

We appreciate any corrections, comments, or suggestions readers might have. Please contact R. Derek Otieno (dotieno@faculty.atl.devry.edu) regarding the programming exercises and ACE Billing project at the end of each chapter, and Barry Austell-Wolfson (wolfson@claudel.com) regarding any other aspect of the book. We will acknowledge any input in future editions, unless you wish to remain anonymous.

Brief Contents

Contents

15 Dynamic Data Structures and Memory Allocation 674

16 Working with the System 725

Complete Book
of C Programming

CHAPTER 1

Building Blocks

OBJECTIVES

- To learn exactly what a computer program is and how it is written and compiled
- To understand what a computer program does, learn how a computer executes a set of instructions, and find out what sort of instructions a computer can be made to carry out
- To understand the differences among the various programming languages and some of the attributes of C in particular
- To learn about different types of programs, such as operating system programs and application programs, and to understand the difference between batch and interactive processing
- To learn a proper methodology for designing, writing, and debugging programs
- To understand the basic principles of structured programming

NEW TERMS

algorithm	file	RAM
batch processing	functions	record
byte	hardware	redirection
character	hierarchy chart	registers
comments	initialize	requirements document
compile-time error	input	run-time errors
compiled language	interactive processing	sequential construct
compiler	iterative construct	source code
compiling	module	structured programming
conditional construct	object code	stub
CPU	output	syntax error
database	portability	top-down design
executable code	program	volatile memory
field	pseudocode	

This book is about programming in Standard C language. A ***program*** is a set of instructions

- that form a computerized solution to a problem.
- initially written by a programmer in ordinary text.
- converted to a language understood by a computer.
- carried out or "executed" by the computer.

The instructions written by the programmer and the version of the instructions executed by the computer are in a special format with lots of strange words, signs, and symbols known to only a select few—just like a spy's secret code—and so they are both called *code*. The text version is the ***source code;*** the computer's version is the ***executable code.*** You are about to become one of the select few.

Figure 1.1 *Building Blocks of Programming*

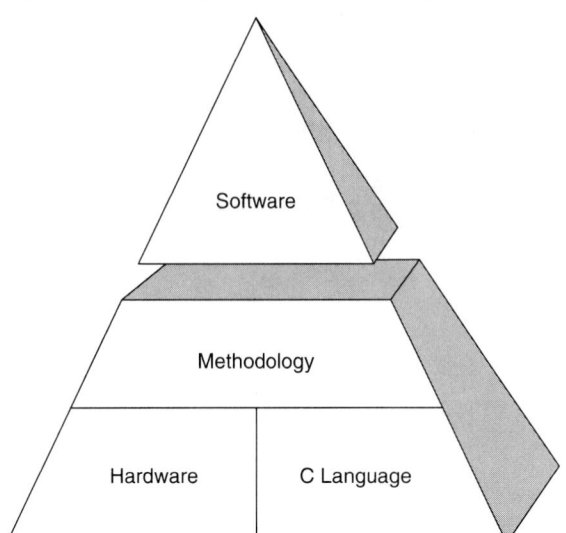

A simple problem suitable for a programming solution would be calculating employees' weekly paychecks based on the number of hours worked, the rate of pay, the amount of certain withholdings, and so on. But before we start writing a programming solution to such a problem, we must first have a basic understanding of the three building blocks in the first figure, Figure 1.1.

Why do we need to discuss computer hardware? You can't learn to fly a jet airplane without knowing that the plane has a motor that runs on fuel and pushes air out turbines causing the plane to move forward, and that it has wings, and that air pressure moving against the wings causes the plane to move upward. Nearly all computer programs involve retrieving data, manipulating the data, and sending the results somewhere. What is retrieved is called ***input;*** what is sent is called ***output.*** We must at least know what basic components of the computer are involved in both ends of this process, just as we must know a little about an airplane's fuel requirements and wing operation before flying one. We need to know how data is stored, how instructions are processed, how we can speed up the operation of the program, and what limits the hardware imposes on our instructions.

"All right, all right. So we'll look at the hardware. Then will you teach us the arcane secrets of C, so we can start coding?" Not so fast. If you were about to build your "dream house," would you let a pack of apprentice carpenters loose on the job without even discussing your wishes or pocketbook, or without having a carefully thought-out and reviewed set of architectural drawings and plans and specifications? Would you say, "They know how to pound nails, so they'll figure it out; if it's not to my liking, we can always change it later"?

Before you start writing a set of instructions for the computer, and even before we discuss programming languages, we must understand the basic methodology of attacking a programming problem. We have to build a program in a logical, methodical, organized fashion, designed not only to produce results but also to produce consistently accurate results, be understood by other programmers working as part of a team on the problem, and be easily changed and maintained. This is the second building block we will cover in this chapter: programming methodology.

Finally, we address the programming language's syntax in the context of the text portion of the programmer's job, the source code. Most of this book is devoted to this final building block.

In this first chapter, we will look at a simple program and then even write the working framework of a somewhat more complex one.

1.1   HARDWARE

Notwithstanding C3PO, R2D2, Lt. Commander Data, and HAL, a computer does not think. A computer is little more than a fast abacus with wires and a large internal closet for storing its results. It does neither more nor less than precisely what the programmer instructs it to do.

Figure 1.2 *Components of a Computer System*

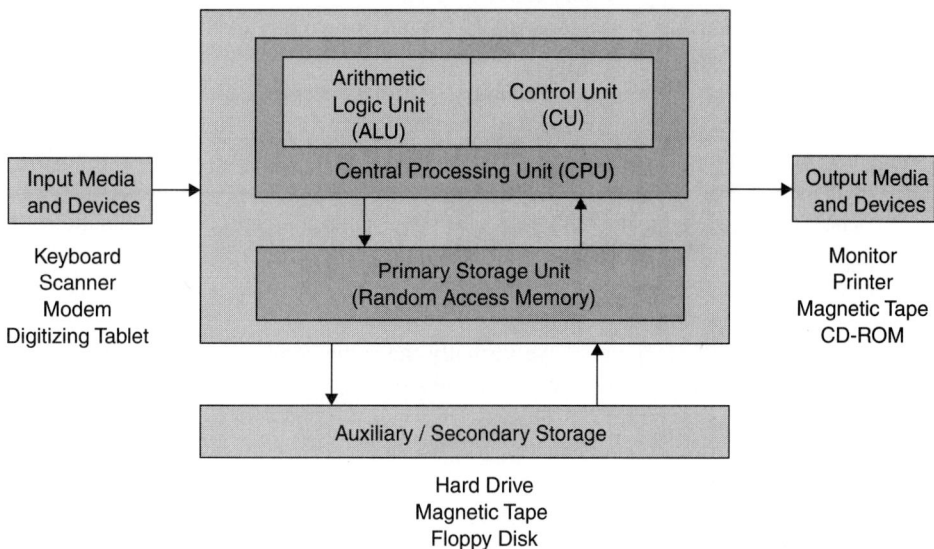

At times—particularly when you are a novice programmer—this single-mindedness can be frustrating. If you use "=" in an instruction to the computer when you meant to use "==", the computer doesn't speak up and tell you that it's obvious you have made an error. It's as though you had a faithful, unquestioning servant. You instruct your servant to burn the old Rubens when you meant to say the old ribbons, and two minutes later, your priceless 17th-century painting is in ashes.

Despite computers' ability to tackle immense and complex problems, the basic tasks they can perform are limited. These tasks can be grouped into three categories, each of them by themselves simple operations:

- Arithmetic operations (addition, subtraction, multiplication, and division)
- Comparison operations (determining whether a given value is greater than, equal to, or less than another value)
- Storage and retrieval operations (such as saving data on a disk so that it can be used later, perhaps on another computer)

Computers are useful to people because of their ability to perform these simple tasks accurately and quickly—very quickly. But it takes programming effort to utilize these basic operations so that the computer can be made to perform useful functions. The computer has to be precisely instructed on what operations to carry out and in what order. Without detailed instructions, the computer is just a useless heap of circuits and nuts and bolts.

1.1.1   Basic Computer Components

All computers, regardless of size and complexity, have three basic components: the central processing unit (CPU), the primary storage unit, and peripherals. Some of the peripherals, such as the hard drive, store data; others, such as printers, terminals, and modems, are nonstoring input/output devices. These basic components are individually or collectively called *hardware.* Figure 1.2 illustrates the relationships among the main hardware components.

Storage, or memory, is the place where data is kept. Primary storage is housed within the processor unit; secondary storage or memory resides elsewhere. The distinction is not only one of location but also of duration. Data in primary memory disappears once the computer is turned off. Accordingly, primary memory is called *volatile memory.* Data in secondary memory, on the other hand, remains intact until it is explicitly altered or removed. If you turn your computer off, the data on the computer's hard drive or a floppy diskette or tape does not disappear. The same data is there in the same state when you turn the computer on again.

Primary memory is also commonly referred to as random access memory or **_RAM._** When owners of personal computers (PCs) refer to their PCs as being so many megabytes of RAM, they are referring to their computer's primary memory capacity. That capacity is measured in how many characters (or their numeric equivalent) the computer is able to fit into its primary memory. The location for a single character is called a **_byte._**

Data is transferred from the peripherals to primary memory. Data may come from a noninteractive secondary storage medium such as a file on the hard drive, or it may come interactively from a device such as the keyboard. Data in primary memory must in turn be transferred to the CPU for processing in memory locations within the CPU called **_registers._**

The **_CPU_** is the component that performs all the computer's processing functions. It is often referred to as the "brain" of the computer. The CPU has two major components: the control unit and the arithmetic/logic unit. Registers are located within the arithmetic/logic unit. The control unit directs the transfer of data from primary memory to the registers.

Even though all computers have virtually the same components, the individual components vary considerably from one type of system to the next. Nevertheless, as long as we adhere to Standard C, the same C program that runs on the MS-DOS and Windows for PC platforms can be compiled to run on UNIX platforms, or Macintosh platforms, or OS/MVS for IBM mainframes, or VMS for DEC computers.

The ability of a program's instructions to operate without modification on any computer system, and to operate in the same predictable way no matter what system is used, is called **_portability._** Since Standard C is strong in the virtue of portability, we will find that the way a Standard C program handles interaction with input and output devices, and how memory is allocated and used in programs, is opaque (or inaccessible) to the programmer. In other words, Standard C instructions cause the computer to carry out operations without the programmer having to bother with the details of how all that is done, and without having to worry that certain instructions will cause different behavior in different computer environments.

One way Standard C promotes portability is that it allows the computer's own operating system to handle its interfaces to the various peripheral devices. Standard C also takes advantage of the operating systems' ability to read input from a file instead of the keyboard. In the UNIX, DOS, and some other environments, this capacity is called **_redirection_**. The ability to redirect data from one device to another automatically, behind the scenes, makes it possible for a beginner in Standard C to write programs that read from files and write to files without having to deal with the intricacies of file pointers, buffers, and opening and closing files. The ability to redirect also makes it possible to write a program that can either read data from a file and write output to a file, or if invoked another way, read from the keyboard and direct its output to the screen—all without any changes to the program.

1.2   PROGRAMS

Generically speaking, there are two types of programs—application programs and operating system programs. We can refer to both types as _software_. Either type can be executed in one of two ways (or a mixture of these): batch or interactive. Although we will follow the same basic method in designing and implementing all our programs, the relative emphasis on some steps in the programming process will differ depending on which program type or execution method we are dealing with.

We will first briefly discuss the two types of programs and their methods of execution. Then we will examine the basic units that data is organized into before moving on to carefully treat programming methodology.

Programs also differ in the type of language they are written in. They may be written in either of two types of programming languages: compiled or interpreted. In a **_compiled language,_** the entire source code is translated into executable machine-language code just once. This process is managed by software called a **_compiler._** Some examples of compiled languages include C, COBOL, Pascal, and FORTRAN.

Interpreted language instructions are translated into machine language every time the program is run. Examples of interpreted languages include SNOBOL4, LISP, and earlier versions of Visual Basic.

1.2.1   Types of Programs and Execution Methods

Operating system programs control the overall operations of the computer. Application programs perform tasks required by users. In our book, we deal almost exclusively with application programs. Most of the problems will draw on business as well as on science and engineering applications.

In *batch processing,* the user does not interact directly with the computer during program execution. Instead, several user programs are grouped, or batched, and processed one right after another in a continuous stream to complete a business process. For example, a daily order-entry system may involve three steps: (1) merge the data from all the locations, regions, or branches, (2) separate the data into valid data and invalid data, and (3) produce reports. A batch process may also be a single program that uses batched input data—for example, a payroll program that produces a paycheck for every employee.

By contrast, *interactive processing* involves communication between the computer and the end user through an input device such as a keyboard-and-mouse combination. During interactive processing, results may be sent to the terminal or screen for the end user to act on. Getting credit authorization or using an electronic teller at a bank would be an example of interactive processing.

1.2.2   Data Organization

Working from the most basic unit of data to the most complex, just as though we were moving from describing electrons to atoms to molecules to compounds, or from cities to counties to states to countries to continents, our data units can be described as follows:

- *Character*. A character is the most basic unit of data organization. In this context, a character includes anything that can be typed on the keyboard. A character (or its numeric equivalent) corresponds to a single byte of data.
- *Field*. A field is a set of characters grouped together to form a meaningful unit of data. A field would often be a variable or identifier name in our programs. Examples could include name, age, or salary.
- *Record*. A record is a group of related fields. For example: an employee record may have name, social security number, hire date, promotion date, birth date, rate of pay, and hours worked fields.
- *File*. A file is a group of related records.
- *Database*. A database is a set of related and integrated files.

1.3   COMPUTER PROGRAMMING METHODOLOGY AND THE DESIGN PROCESS

What is computer programming? What it is *not*—contrary to common misconception among novice programmers and students—is churning out reams of code without much thought to planning, design, and maintainability. We define it rather as the entire series of steps involved in solving a problem using the computer. Writing code is but one of the steps.

Although there is some difference of opinion among programming theorists as to precisely how many steps there are in the programming process, we find it clearest to detail eight separate steps:

1. Define the problem.
2. Analyze the problem.
3. Design the logic.
4. Write the program using the language of choice—in our case, Standard C.
5. Key in the program using a suitable text editor.
6. Test and debug the program.
7. Gather and compile the documentation.
8. Maintain the program.

1.3.1   Step 1: Define the Problem

In practice, the programming process starts with an end-user request. The end user may be a specific department within a company such as billing, or a particular target group identified by a marketing organization. Often the end-user request is not well defined. In some cases, the problem presented is not even worthy of a programming solution.

In large part, we leave problem definition to books dealing with systems analysis. In this book, we will start in most cases with a defined problem.

1.3.2   Step 2: Analyze the Problem

Analysis is the process of determining *what* needs to be done before deciding *how* it should be done. The determination is memorialized in what is called a requirements document. The ***requirements document*** is the formal statement of the problem. It becomes a type of contract between the users and the programmers regarding what must be delivered.

Several players are usually involved in problem analysis: programmers (also known as developers), systems analysts, and end users. Together these three produce the requirements document.

1.3.3   Step 3: Design the Logic

The design phase is the first one in which the programming issues are addressed. Here are all the steps you should take during this phase.

1. *Study the requirements document carefully.* Be sure that you fully understand it. As you read the problem, you must be sure you have identified all the input requirements, processing requirements, and output requirements. The three requirements are sometimes collectively referred to as *IPO*, an acronym for input, processing and output. Once you have fully grasped these requirements, you are a long way toward having a handle on the programming problem.

The IPO requirements are generally depicted on system flowcharts (Figure 1.3). These flowcharts show the flow of data into and out of the program. System flowcharts should be distinguished from the logic flowcharts we will discuss below.

Figure 1.3   *System Flowchart*

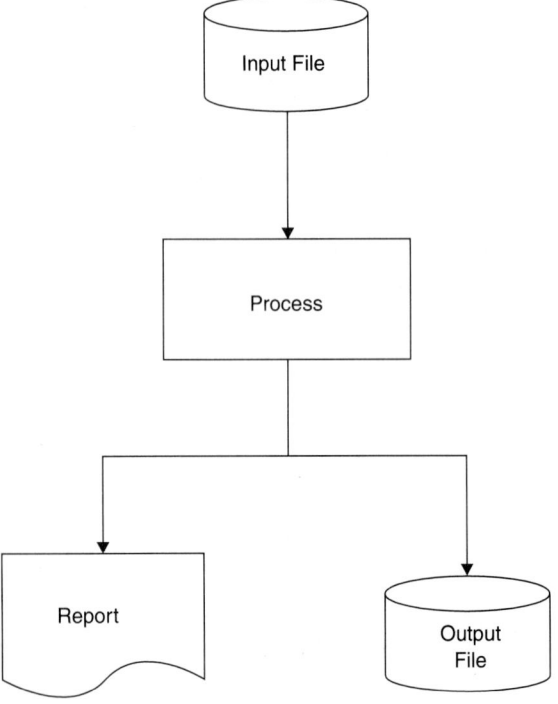

Table 1.1 *Sample Record Layout*

Member File Record Layout			
Field Name	**Size**	**Type**	**No. of Decimal Positions if Numeric**
memberLastName	15	Alphanumeric (char)	
memberInitials	2	Alphanumeric (char)	
numberOfCharges	2	Alphanumeric (digits)	
specialMemberFeeFlag	1	Alphanumeric (char)	
discount	4	Alphanumeric (digits)	
averageCharges	4	Alphanumeric (digits)	

Input requirements are often gleaned from a record layout specifying which fields to read as well as their data types and other pieces of information. Table 1.1 shows a sample record layout.

Processing requirements involve calculations and decisions, and actions based on the data and calculations. If a teacher has to compile grades for all the students in a class, calculations would include taking a sum of each test and then finding an average. If the average is between certain levels, a specific letter grade is assigned.

Output requirements, such as report titles, column headings, data and calculated items to appear in the report, and the format for each of these, are often set forth in a printer spacing chart. A sample is found in Figure 1.4.

2. *Create sample data to use in testing the stated problem.* Being able to create sample data is a good indication that you have understood the problem. If you cannot create sample data, perhaps you need a clearer understanding of the problem. You may need to consult the person who wrote the problem: your professor, or the systems analyst if this is a job environment.

Figure 1.4 *Printer Spacing Chart*

```
        Program ID:          Fig 1-4
        Program Title:       ACE MEMBERSHIP BILLING SYSTEM
        Programmer:          AUSTELL-WOLFSON & OTIENO
        Chart Title:         ACE PRINTER SPACING CHART
```

1	PROGRAM NAME:	XXX				
2	AUTHOR:	XXXXXXXXXXXXXXXX				
3						
4			ACE BILLING SYSTEM MONTHLY REPORT			
5	- -					
6						
7	CUSTOMER NAME	CHARGES	BILL	SPECIAL FEE	ACT FEE	DISCOUNT	TOT
8	XXXXXXXXXXXXXXX	99	$$.$$9	$$9.99	$.$$9.99	$.$$9	$$.$$
9	XXXXXXXXXXXXXXX	99	$$.$$9	$$9.99	$.$$9.99	$.$$9	$$.$$
10	XXXXXXXXXXXXXXX	99	$$.$$9	$$9.99	$.$$9.99	$.$$9	$$.$$
11	XXXXXXXXXXXXXXX	99	$$.$$9	$$9.99	$.$$9.99	$.$$9	$$.$$
12						
13	. . . .					
14	ACE CLUB TOTALS		$$$$.$$9	$$$.$$9	$$$.$$9.99	$$$.$$9	$.$$$.$$
15						

3. *Using paper and pencil, process the data manually.* This will further establish that you conceptually understand the problem and can solve it for a limited set of data.

4. *List all the tasks involved in solving the problem.* This should be the articulation of the manual process you have just gone through, broken into individual tasks.

5. *Group these tasks into logical groups.* At the highest, overall level, the groups should include initialization, processing, and termination. Under the initialization group, you would have all the tasks that must be done at the beginning, and only once. This often includes opening files, if any, and assigning initial values to variables (as we discuss later, a variable is a work area in memory that we use to store a piece of data). Identify which variables to ***initialize*** (assign beginning values to) by studying the processing that must take place, the input you are given, and the output to be produced. For example, you are given a problem requiring you to print the average of a list of numbers. Once you have examined the processing that you must do, you find that you must set up an accumulator that needs to be initialized to zero. You see, your knowledge of the output to be produced guided you in determining the additional variable to declare and initialize.

6. *Arrange these logical groups into their hierarchical sequence, starting with the highest-level modules.* The various group levels are in the nature of an outline. There are main topics and subtopics and sub-subtopics and so on. The main topics are at what programming theorists would call the "highest level." The method of working from main to subtopics is also referred to as ***top-down design*** or stepwise refinement. We successively break each discrete program piece or ***module*** into its respective detailed modules and submodules.

By coding modules in this top-down manner, the overall organization of the program is given primary attention. Details for minor modules are deferred. These are coded last. This top-down approach is analogous to writing a term paper, or even writing this book. First, an outline with major headings only is developed. The outline gets more and more detailed after the main organization or structures have been established.

A number of tools are used to design and organize the system. We will use these tools extensively throughout this book: hierarchy charts, pseudocode, algorithms, and flowcharts.

A ***hierarchy chart***—otherwise called a Visual Table of Contents (VTOC) or structure chart—graphically represents the organizational relationships among discrete program modules. In C, program pieces or modules are called ***functions.*** Figure 1.5 shows a hierarchy chart with the various program modules.

Flowcharts, pseudocode, and algorithms are all tools that show the actual flow of the logic of a module, while a hierarchy chart simply shows the modules themselves and their levels in the structure. An example of pseudocode for a programming problem dealing with a billing system described at the end of this chapter is found in Figure 1.18.

Flowcharts and pseudocode both express the logic of a program. Therefore, only one of them is needed for any given problem. In our book, we will primarily use pseudocode. At times, flowcharts will be used along with pseudocode to afford greater clarity. ***Pseudocode*** uses ordinary everyday language in a structured way.

Figure 1.5 *Hierarchy Chart*

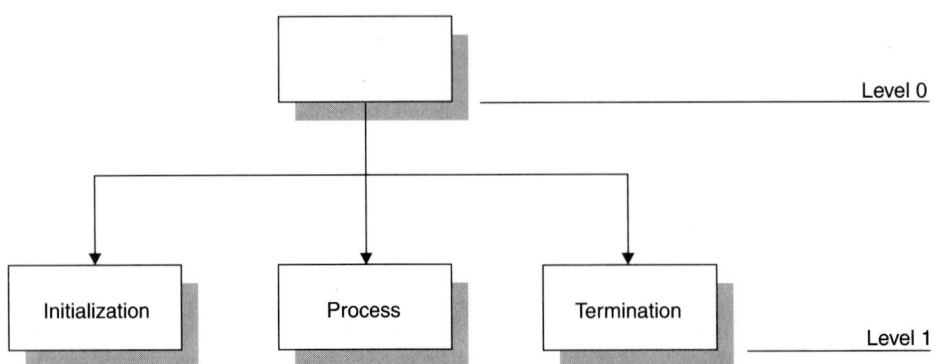

An *algorithm* is broadly defined as a step-by-step procedure for solving a problem or accomplishing some end. The algorithm encompasses a finite number of steps, though one or more of the steps may involve repetition of an operation. A simple example of an algorithm is the procedure for finding the average of three numbers:

Step 1: Set the sum to zero.
Step 2: Get the first number.
Step 3: Add the first number to the sum.
Step 4: Get the second number.
Step 5: Add the second number to the sum.
Step 6: Get the third number.
Step 7: Add the third number to the sum.
Step 8: Divide the sum by three.

We can generalize this algorithm: steps 2 and 3 can be repeated for any number of values.

1.3.4 Step 4: Write the Program Using the Language of Choice

In our case, we use Standard C programming language. Nearly this whole book is devoted to this step. We will introduce features of Standard C and then write programs that employ these features. We will work on the basic program design from the start. However, our initial method of solving the problem will necessarily be rudimentary. As we progress to later chapters, our knowledge base of Standard C will have increased dramatically, allowing us to develop ever more complete and sophisticated solutions.

1.3.5 Step 5: Key in the Program Using a Suitable Text Editor

Most of the C compilers available in the PC environment use an Integrated Development Environment (IDE), which allows the programmer to key in, assemble, and run the program. We refer readers to the compiler manual appropriate for their programming environment. See also the more extensive discussion of editors below.

For many novice programmers, it may actually be better to write any initial coding manually with paper and pen. That way, the details of the programming environment and syntax do not interfere.

1.3.6 Step 6: Test and Debug the Program

The testing and debugging phase has two parts: debugging and desk-checking.

Debugging.   In the debugging process, the programmer corrects all errors in the program. There are two types of errors—syntax errors and logic errors. A *syntax error* (also referred to as a *compile-time error*) is an error that results when an instruction violates the programming language rules. For example, in C, statements must be terminated with semicolons. If you forget to put one at the end of a statement, you have a syntax error.

When the compiler finds even one such error in a program statement, it does not translate the rest of the statements into executable code. It does, however, continue to check each of the remaining statements and issue syntax error messages accordingly. Since testing requires an executable program, no testing can take place as long as the syntax errors remain.

Sometimes your instructions are technically in compliance with Standard C rules, but the compiler senses that you really may have meant to say something else. In that case, the compiler issues a warning, not an error message. For instance, where your statement is something like

```
if (a = b)
```

in nine cases out of ten, you mean to say

```
if (a == b)
```

Since both are syntatically correct, the computer warns you of a *potential* error. Warnings do not prevent translation of the source code into executable code.

If you really mean to say what you said, you might modify the statement to make it conform to more common usage, or you might just leave it as it is but add an explanation to your code that says, "Yes, though this statement or expression is unusual, it is what I intended and here's why: . . . " These explanations are called *comments*. We will discuss them below.

Logic errors can be of at least two different types. One is a pure logic error. The classic case is the fence-post problem. You have 100 feet to cover with fence posts and you must place each post 10 feet apart. If you simply divide the total number of feet by the number of feet between posts, you have failed to consider that there is an extra post on one side.

The other kind of logic error could be called a program operation error. Since most of these are fairly esoteric, we will defer explanation of this sort of error to a later time.

Some logic errors cause abnormal program behavior during execution, resulting in the program terminating prematurely. A common error of this nature is division by zero. We call such errors *run-time errors*. On the other hand, some logic errors do not affect the completion of the program but produce incorrect results. Or they may produce results that are sometimes correct and sometimes incorrect. This latter type of error may be the most difficult to catch and correct.

Desk-Checking. In desk-checking, the programmer manually executes the program using test data. This process should be first accomplished with pseudocode or a flowchart, then repeated with a completed program. Testing representative sample data against the pseudocode allows the programmer to check and validate the correctness of the logic of the problem's solution. It is useful to desk-check with pseudocode because the programmer is able to concentrate on logic alone, not on the implementation details demanded by the language's syntax.

When the programmer does the same desk-checking against a completed program, the focus can now shift to the implementation details; desk-checking against the pseudocode has already validated the logic. A thorough desk-checking is perhaps the best defense against logic errors.

1.3.7   Step 7: Gather and Compile the Documentation

The programmer must provide both technical documentation and user documentation.

Technical Documentation. Technical documentation should be sufficient to allow any programmer—the one who wrote the program or others—wishing to make changes to do so without diminishing the program's capabilities or altering it in unintended ways. Technical documentation consists of

- Problem specification
- Hierarchy chart
- Pseudocode for each module in the hierarchy chart
- Input record layouts
- Output record or report layouts (typical printer spacing charts)
- System flowcharts

In addition to the separate pieces of technical documentation, much documentation should be found within the program itself. The programmer should include detailed explanations—called ***comments***—throughout the code, explaining the various steps of the program. As we will show later in the chapter, comments are part of the text version of the program, but they are discarded when the text version is translated to the executable program.

User Documentation. User documentation is what is commonly referred to as a *user's manual*. These are the instructions the end user needs in order to use the application. The size of this manual is often dictated by the magnitude and complexity of the application.

1.3.8   Step 8: Maintain the Program

As the needs of the business for which programs were written change, programs in production must often be changed. Program maintenance is drastically simplified if the first seven steps are done properly and documented adequately.

1.4   STRUCTURED PROGRAMMING METHODOLOGY

So far, we have defined programming and simply listed the steps involved in programming. Now we will discuss in detail proven methods of actually designing the programs.

We will use structured programming methodology. ***Structured programming*** is a program implementation technique that systematizes and organizes the entire cycle of program design, coding, and testing. The ultimate goal of this technique is to develop correct, reliable programs by preventing errors and facilitating debugging. Structured programming embraces three philosophies:

- Top-down design
- Independent program modules
- Structured coding principles

1.4.1   Top-Down Design

The most difficult aspect of programming is learning to organize solutions into clear, concise sequences of events. It is not uncommon to see a student freeze before starting to write a program. Top-down design gives everyone—beginners and experienced programmers alike—a starting point.

Using top-down design in solving a problem involves proceeding from the general to the specific. In effect, the problem is gradually broken into smaller and smaller subproblems.

1.4.2   Independent Program Modules

Once the problem has been broken into its most basic units, a solution is formulated for each unit. A hierarchy chart is used to show how these modules relate to one another to form a complete solution.

1.4.3   Structured Coding Principles

Structured coding involves constructing programs with only three types of constructs: sequential, conditional, and iterative. Figure 1.6 shows flowchart symbols used to graphically represent these constructs.

In a ***sequential construct,*** statements are executed one after the other. Figure 1.7 shows a flowchart depiction and a pseudocode depiction of the sequential construct.

In a ***conditional construct,*** we test to decide which statement to execute next. There are three conditional constructs:

- IF-THEN
- IF-THEN-ELSE
- CASE/SWITCH

Figure 1.6 *Flowchart Symbols*

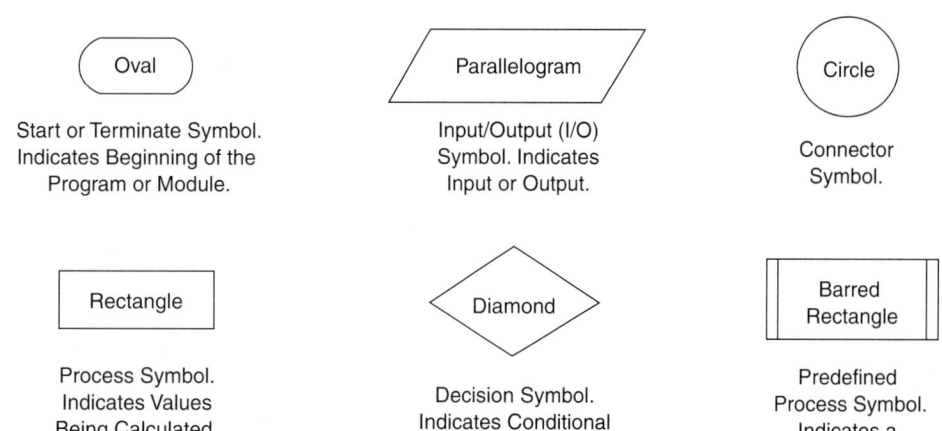

Oval
Start or Terminate Symbol.
Indicates Beginning of the
Program or Module.

Parallelogram
Input/Output (I/O)
Symbol. Indicates
Input or Output.

Circle
Connector
Symbol.

Rectangle
Process Symbol.
Indicates Values
Being Calculated
and Assigned.

Diamond
Decision Symbol.
Indicates Conditional
Constructs.

Barred
Rectangle
Predefined
Process Symbol.
Indicates a
Module.

Figure 1.7   *Sequential Construct: Flowchart and Pseudocode*

Sequence

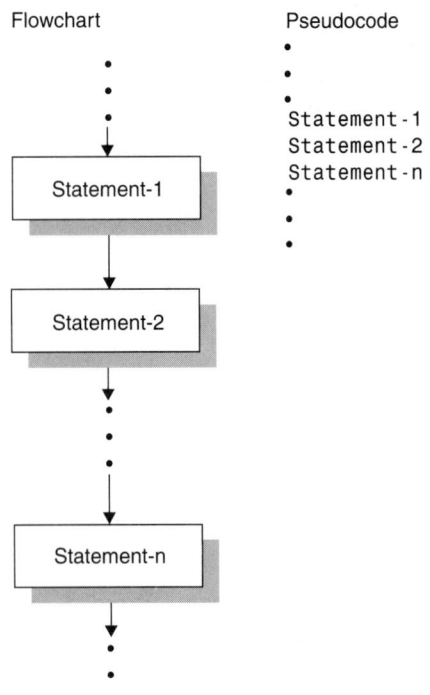

Figures 1.8 to 1.14 show flowchart and pseudocode depictions of each construct. The last of these constructs, the case/switch, is sometimes referred to as *multiway branching.*

In an ***iterative construct,*** one or more statements are repeatedly executed until a specific condition is met. There are two forms of iterative constructs—the while loop and the do while loop. In C, there is a third construct, called the for loop, that is a variation of the while loop. The for loop has built in initialization before the condition testing, and a built-in update mechanism after the condition testing.

Note that these constructs can and often are nested within one another, as Figure 1.14 illustrates.

Figure 1.8   *IF-THEN: Flowchart and Pseudocode*

Selection
if-then Construct

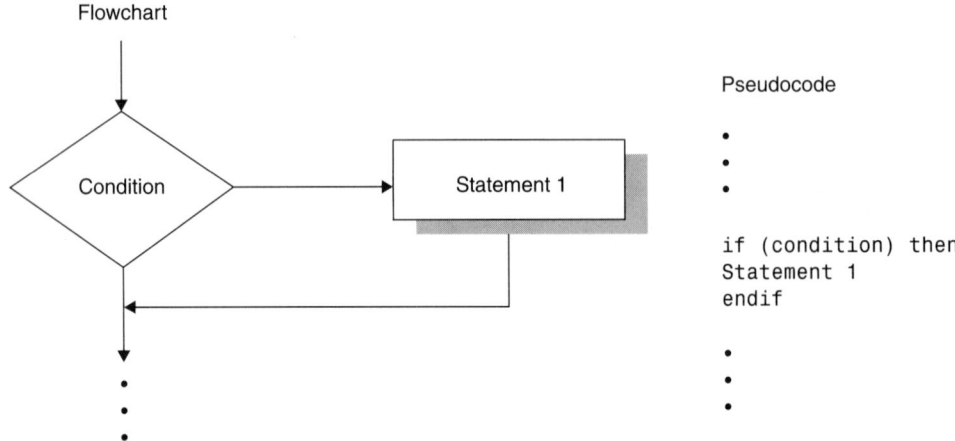

Figure 1.9 *IF-THEN-ELSE: Flowchart and Pseudocode*

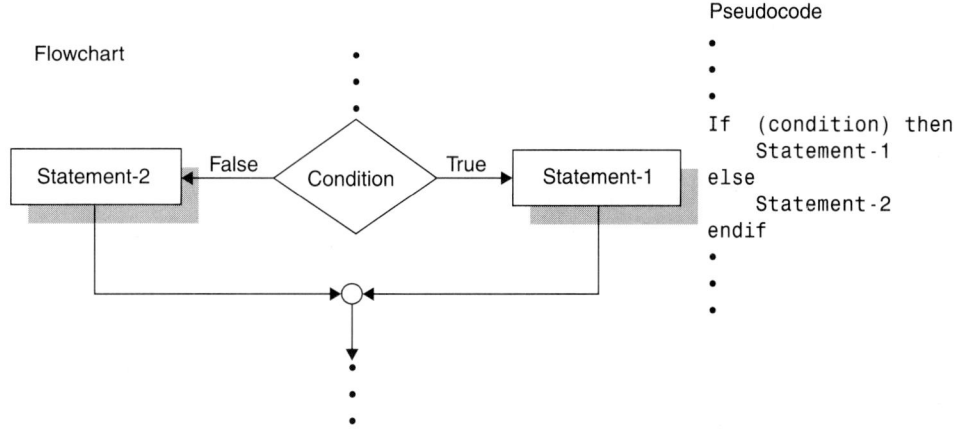

Selection
if-then-else Construct

Figure 1.10 *CASE/SWITCH: Flowchart and Pseudocode*

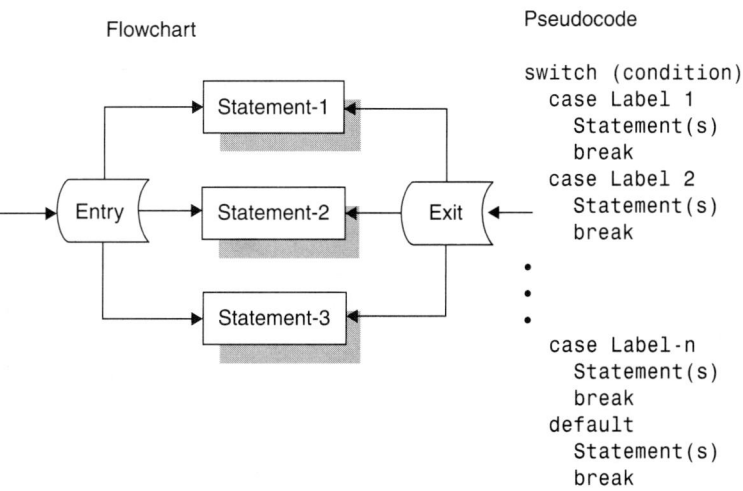

Selection
case/switch Construct

Figure 1.11 *WHILE Loop: Flowchart and Pseudocode*

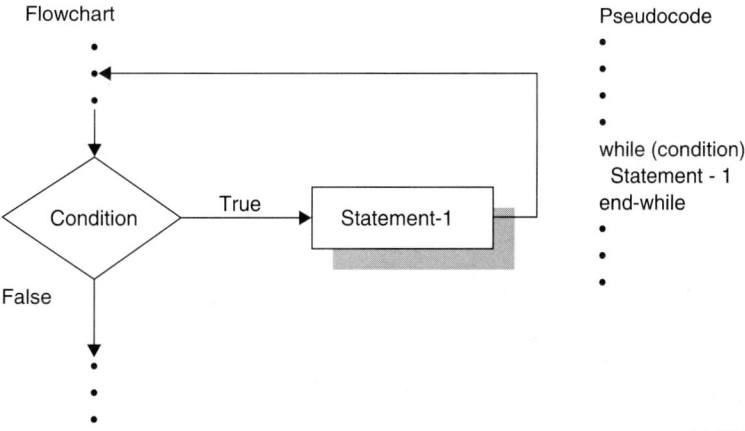

Repetition
while Construct

Figure 1.12   *DO WHILE Loop: Flowchart and Pseudocode*

Repetition
do/while Construct

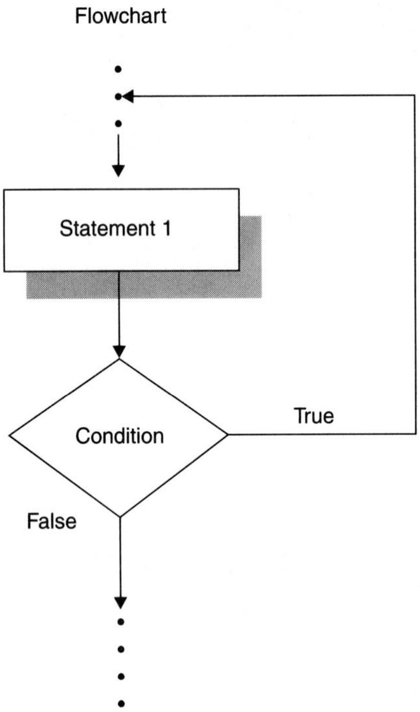

Flowchart

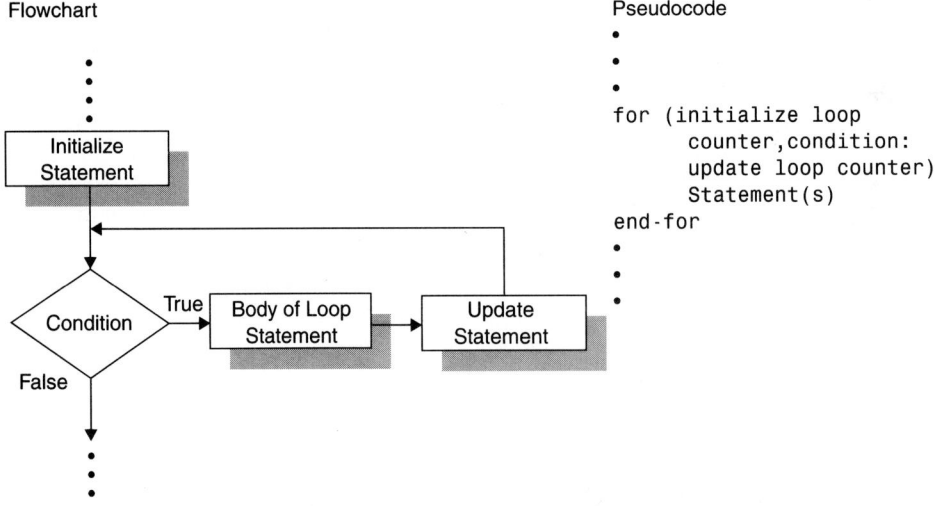

```
Pseudocode
•
•
•
do
   Statement-1
while (condition)
•
•
•
```

Figure 1.13   *FOR Loop: Flowchart and Pseudocode*

Repetition
for Construct

Flowchart

```
Pseudocode
•
•
•
for (initialize loop
     counter,condition:
     update loop counter)
     Statement(s)
end-for
•
•
•
```

Figure 1.14 *Nested Constructs*

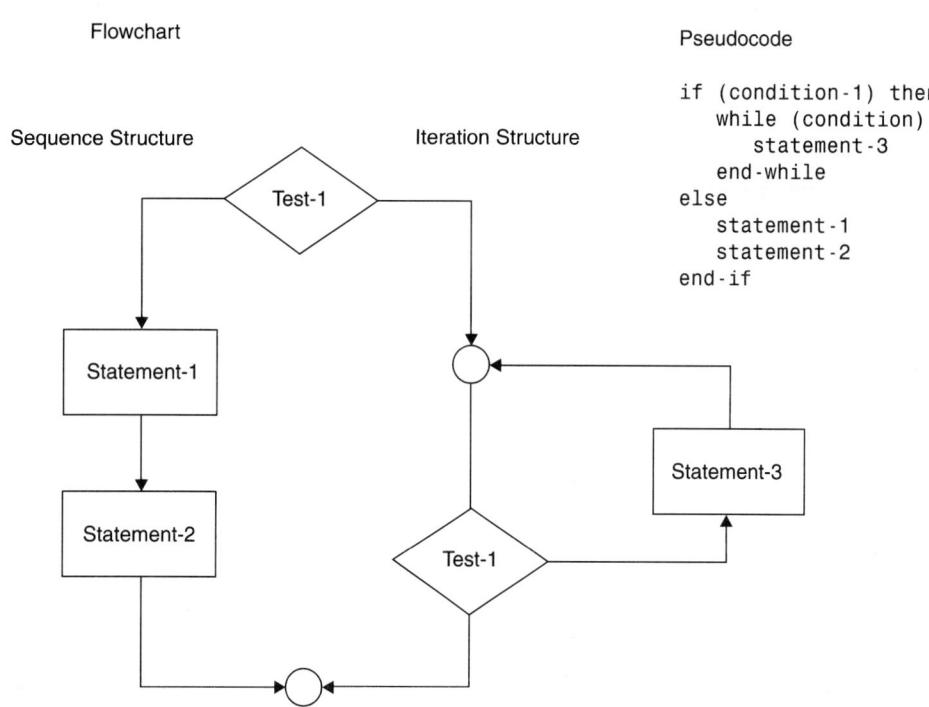

1.5 **APPLICATION: PROGRAMMING SPECIFICATIONS**

The following example is used to illustrate the design step of programming development methodology. Although the example represents a typical business application, the methodology applies to any type of program to be developed.

Program Name: ACE Club Membership Billing Program.

Program Specification: Process a file of club member records, compute and print bills for each member, and print the total amounts for all members.

Input Record Layout: Member data records are kept in a file. Each of these records is on a single line of the file. Each record contains six fields, as shown by the record layout in Table 1.2.

Input File(s): In this case, we have a single input file. This is a sample of what is contained in the file.

```
Austell-WolfsonBA05 00003500
Otieno      DE12Y01206000
VanVranken  GE08Y00804230
Yates       SY17Y11708200
Cook        CH03 00004100
Stencil     BI10Y10108150
Rockingham  ZE23Y12309300
Zindar      SY04 00006200
McDowell    CH19 10008420
Grilo       RI17 01703500
Braxkston   HE18Y01807400
Pope        SC22Y12208590
Hardin      GA02 00004060
```

Table 1.2 *Member File Record Layout*

Member File Record Layout			
Field Name	**Size**	**Type**	**No. of Decimal Positions if Numeric**
memberLastName	15	Alphanumeric (char)	
memberInitials	2	Alphanumeric (char)	
numberOfCharges	2	Alphanumeric (digits)	
specialMemberFeeFlag	1	Alphanumeric (char)	
discount	4	Alphanumeric (digits)	
averageCharges	4	Alphanumeric (digits)	

```
Sonby          TO32 10008030
Murphy         RY26Y12608420
Bate           ST05Y00506320
Murray         GE28 02804780
Franklin       LO01 00002500
Meyers         JA24Y12408430
Kirk           JT12 10009360
```

Report Layout: Figure 1.15 shows the required report layout.

Processing Requirements:
1. Print a suitable heading at the beginning of the report, as shown in the report layout.
2. Read a file of member records.
3. Process each record read by
   - computing an individual bill, equal to the sum of charges, special membership fee, and activity fee, minus discounts (if any), by
     - calculating the bill due, at a rate of $200 per activity.
     - billing the member $250 for the special membership fee, if there is a Y in the special membership fee field.

Figure 1.15 *Report Layout*

```
Program Name: ACECHxx.EXE                              Page: xx
   Run Date: 12/10/2000         Ace Billing



Customer Name       Charges Bill   Mbr Fee   Act Fee    Disc Total Bill


xxxxxxxxxxxxxxx xx xx  $xxxx.xx  $xxxx.xx  $xxxx.xx  $xxxx.xx  $xxxxx.xx
```

- computing the activity fee based on the number of charges made according to the following schedule:

ACTIVITY FEE	CHARGES
$750	6 or fewer
$500	7–12
$250	More than 12

- awarding discounts equal to the amount in the incoming record if, and only if, the average bill is greater than $2500.
- incrementing the ACE Club totals for charges, special membership fee, activity fee, discounts, and overall total.
4. Print a detail line for each record.
5. Print a total line for the entire club at the end of the report.

1.6   APPLICATION: SOLUTION

We use structured design to solve this problem. Accordingly, we begin at the overview level (Figure 1.16).

The first level is PREPARE ACE BILLING REPORT. This level simply represents the overall problem. The next level is somewhat generic to all problems; it is three-tiered (Figure 1.17).

If we perform all the necessary initialization, process every member record according to the processing requirements, and perform appropriate termination steps, we will have solved the entire problem. We continue this process of subdividing each module further and further until we now have the completed solution, diagrammed as shown in Figure 1.18.

Figure 1.16   *Top Program Level*

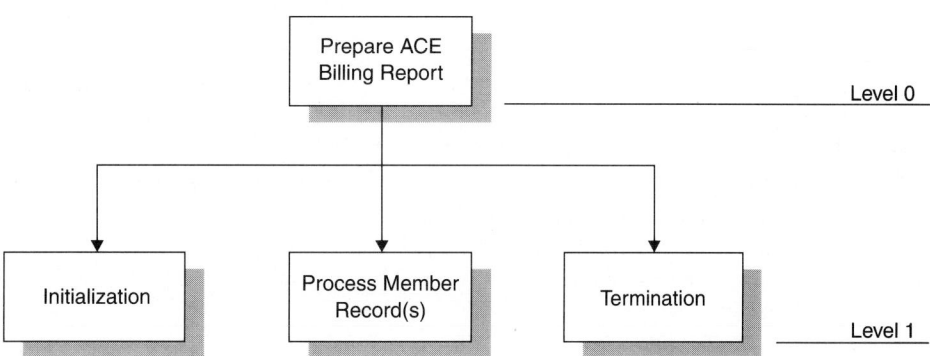

Figure 1.17   *Top Two Program Levels*

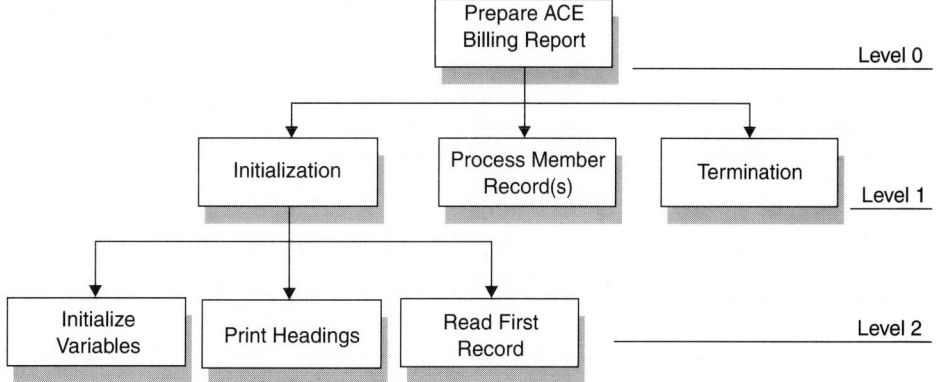

Figure 1.18   *Program Hierarchy Chart*

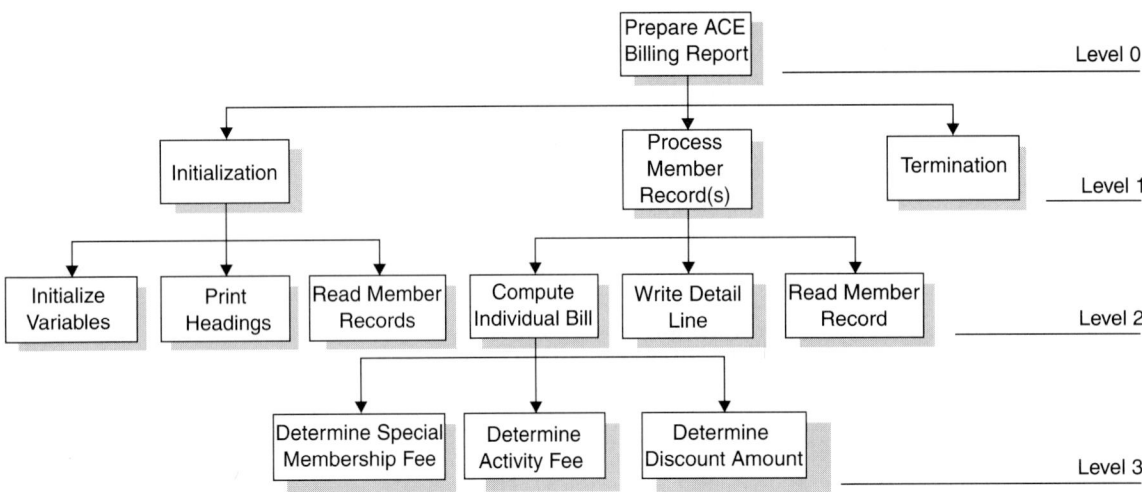

Our next step is to develop the logic for each of the modules identified in our hierarchy chart. This logic may be expressed using pseudocode or a flowchart. The pseudocode version is illustrated in Figure 1.19.

The actual implementation of these flowcharts/pseudocodes will be done in subsequent chapters as we present more features of Standard C.

Figure 1.19   *Pseudocode for ACE Billing Program*

```
MAIN LINE LOGIC
   Initialization
   While (Not end of file)
     Process Member Record
   End while
   Termination

Initialization Module
   Initialize Variables
   Print Headings
   Read Member Record
Termination Module
   Write ACE Club Totals

Initialize Variables Module
   Special Membership Fee = 0
   Activity Fee = 0
   Discount Amount = 0
   Club Totals = 0

Print Headings Module
   Print the headings according to the report layout

Process Member Record Module
   Compute Individual Bill
   Write Detail Record
   Read the Next Member Record

Compute Individual Bill Module
   Determine Special Membership Fee
   Determine Activity Fee
```

Figure 1.19   *(continued)*

```
   Determine Discount Amount
   Charge Amount = Number of Charges * 200
   Total Individual Bill = Charge Amount + Special Membership Fee +
      Activity Fee - Discount
   Ace Club Totals = Ace Club Totals +  Total Individual Bill

Determine Special Membership Fee Module
   If Special Membership = 'Y'
      Special Membership Fee = 2500
   Else
      Special Membership Fee = 0
   End if

Determine Activity Module
   If Number Of Charges  <= 6
      Activity Fee = 250
   End if

   If Number of Charges  >  6 and Number Of Charges <= 12
      Activity Fee = 500
   End if

   If Number Of Charges  > 12
      Activity Fee = 750
   End if

Determine Discount Amount Module
   If Average Bill > 2500
      Discount  = Discount Amount
   Else
      Discount = 0
   End if
```

1.7   C LANGUAGE INTRODUCTION: THE SOURCE CODE

Now that we have examined hardware components and programming methodology, we turn to the programming language itself. We will start by examining the source code and its basic components. We will also write, compile, and execute our first C program. Finally, we will implement as much of the ACE Billing program as we can based on the amount of C covered.

The source code is a set of instructions, written by you, the programmer, in the computer language's syntax. Most of the material in this book will deal with what you must write in the source code to accomplish specified programming tasks.

Let's start with a simple task, adding two numbers. In an imaginary computer language, this might constitute a source code: "First, kindly ask the user to type in two numbers on the keyboard; next, please add them; finally, would you be so good as to let the user know by way of the computer monitor what their sum is." In C, a no-frills source code to accomplish the same thing would look like this:

 **Listing**   **1.1 add.c**

```
/* add.c */

/* basic intro to C program */

#include <stdio.h> /* standard C header file */
```

```
int main(void) /* function where program execution starts */
{
/* declaration of three variables of type int */
   int firstValue, secondValue, sum;

   /* give user instructions on the screen */
   printf("Enter two numbers\n");
   printf("Press [Enter] after each\n");

   /* get input from keyboard and store it */
   scanf("%d%d", &firstValue, &secondValue);

   /* add the two numbers and store result */
   sum = firstValue + secondValue;

   /* write the two input numbers and the total on the screen */
   printf("\nTotal of %d plus %d is %d\n", firstValue, secondValue, sum);

   return 0;
}
```

 Execution of add.c begins with the function called main().

Program execution always begins with execution of the function called main(). **A C program contains one or more functions, one of which must be** main().

We will devote a lengthy chapter to functions, Chapter 8. Briefly, a function is a block of statements designed by the programmer to perform a discrete task. Here, that task is calculating the sum of two numbers. These functions are the "modules" we have been discussing all along. In Chapter 8, we will also explain why we conclude add.c's main() function with a return 0 statement.

We first reserve computer memory space to house three values. We do this by declaring three variables named firstValue, secondValue, and sum. A variable is no more than a name we humans give the memory space the computer reserves for us to house a value.

We then make the following appear on the computer screen:

```
Enter two numbers
Press [Enter] after each one
```

and the user responds with something like

```
16
78
```

The line that starts with scanf() causes the user's two responses to be stored in the memory space set aside for the variables firstValue and secondValue. We then add these two values and store the result in the memory space set aside for the variable sum. The final line sends the result to the screen. (The statements that start with scanf() and printf() are discussed in much greater detail in later chapters.)

```
Total of 16 plus 78 is 94
```

Aren't computers smart?

Some of the "frills" we omitted would include things like error-checking. If the user types a word instead of a number, or types a number too high or too low in the context of the program, the program needs to be able to say so, and to then go back and be ready to accept fresh input on another user attempt.

We could also glamorize what the user sees on the screen. The way the program works now, the input and output just scrolls up the screen in whatever the default color foreground-background combination of the computer is—most likely gray letters on a black or green background. We could put the data in attractive colors, carefully arranged in fixed places on the screen and enclosed in color-coordinated windows or lined borders.

Figure 1.20 *Source Code Components*

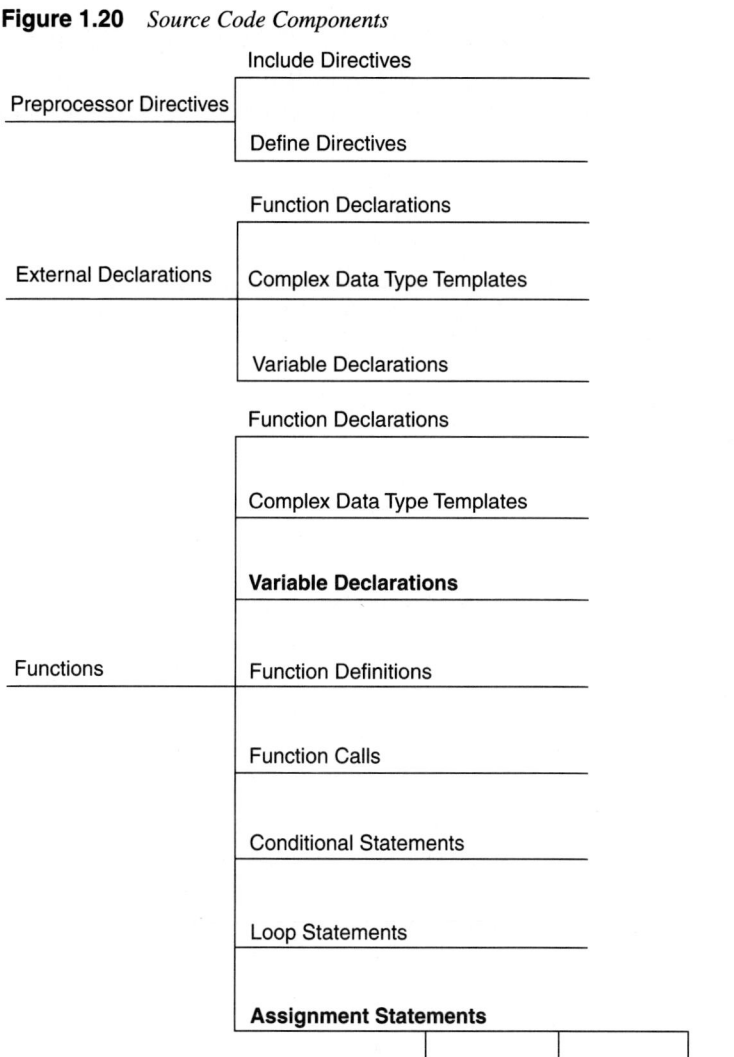

We could also enhance the input/output mechanism. The numbers might be read in from a file rather than from the keyboard and the results printed to a file or to the printer rather than to the screen. The program might provide for successive input-result cycles until users signal they're finished, or the end of the file is reached if input comes from a file. All this comes in later chapters and in the appendixes.

1.7.1 Source Code Components

Structurally, a C source code has the chief components shown in Figure 1.20.

In the next two chapters, we will cover the items highlighted in Figure 1.20. We will take a look at the two basic elements of a simple source code: the variables that house the values we input and manipulate, the operators that link the variables in defined ways, and the statements in which we declare variables and assign them values.

Before we cover that material, it would be helpful to go over some mechanics of how the source code is put together and then see what happens to it after it is.

1.7.2 A Little Ado about Nothing: Comments and Spaces

The text between each bookend-like pair of /* and */ in add.c is called a comment. Comments are part of the source code, but they are ignored during program execution; in fact, as we have noted, comments are not even included in the machine-language version of the program the computer reads when it executes the program.

There are two ways of writing comments. The only method permitted by Standard C is the one used in add.c: to enclose the comment with a /* at its start and a */ at its end. This allows you to extend your comments over more than one line.

The other way is to use double slashes. Everything after the double slashes is a comment, but only to the end of the source code line on which the double slashes occur. The double slash method is expressly allowed by C++, and consequently will work in combined C/C++ compilers. Since this latter method is otherwise nonstandard, exclusive use of the former "bookend" form of comment is preferred. We mention the alternative method only because you might see it in other programmers' code.

Here are a few short examples of comments:

```
v1 = 3; /* I'm a comment */
v2 = 5; /* How do you do. Allow me to introduce myself.
            I am a comment */
sum = v1 + v2; // Me too! Strictly a nonstandard one-liner
```

1.7.3   Why Comments?

The principal purpose of comments is to explain to the programmer who wrote the source code, or to others who might look at it, what exactly the source code is doing at any given point. You might remember this afternoon precisely why you wrote a particular thing in your code this morning or what a complex bit of code means, but without comments you could spend hours reconstructing your logic when you look at the same code several weeks or months from now in order to modify it. *The liberal use of comments throughout your code is encouraged.*

Comments can be short

```
int firstValue, secondValue, sum; /* declare
            variables to house input and result */
```

or they can be long, detailed explanations of code:

```
for (i = 0; i < length * 2; i++)
{
/*
Border between primary screen and screen window. We want the color for this row
split between the two. We need the bottom-half character, ■, with the primary
screen's background color as its foreground color and the window's background color
as its background color: to do this, shift the window color to the right 4 bits and
OR it with the primary color shifted first right and then left to wipe out the
background color but preserve the foreground. We need the top-half character with
the window's background color as its foreground and black as its background: to do
this, just shift the bits 4 to the right, leaving all zeros in the background.
*/
   cpc('■', ((primary >> 4) << 4) ¦
      (window >> 4), row - 1, 40 - length + i);
   cpc('■',
      (window >> 4), row + 1, 40 - length + 1 + i);
};
```

(To give a complicated comment, we used a complicated example. You aren't expected to understand what's going on in this bit of code. If you find it enticing, be patient; we'll do this sort of thing later in this book. If not, perhaps you should consider a career in law or accounting instead of in programming.)

Each program and each function should have an ID comment block. Each block of code should be preceded by at least one line of comment. Figure 1.21 provides an example of a program ID comment block.

In this book, we will generally omit program ID comment blocks and either omit or shorten function ID comment blocks. We do so to save space and because the code is accompanied by a detailed explanation in most cases. You should not omit these ID blocks from your programs.

Fig 1.21 *ID Comment Block*

Comment Block

```
/********************************************************************/
/*      Program Name:  add.c                                     */
/*        Author:  Austell-Wolfson and Otieno                    */
/*        Date:  09/29/00                                        */
/*                                                               */
/*      Purpose:                                                 */
/*        Briefly state what the program has been written to do. */
/*                                                               */
/*      Technique:                                               */
/*        Give a narrative, or a high-level algorithm            */
/*        of how the purpose is achieved.                        */
/*                                                               */
/*      Input:                                                   */
/*        Discuss the input requirements of this program.        */
/*        Be sure to give an example of how this input is        */
/*        to be provided.                                        */
/*                                                               */
/*      Output                                                   */
/*        Any special information about the output,              */
/*        e.g., volume, required medium or device.               */
/*                                                               */
/*      Modifications                                            */
/*        Date and description of modifications, as well as      */
/*        name of the programmer making each modification.       */
/********************************************************************/
```

You might also use comments to mark the end of a block of code where there are so many levels of indentation that it is difficult to see clearly which lines of code go in which block:

```
while (one != two)
{
   while(scanf("%d", &max) == 1)
   {
      if (one < max)
      {
         if (one > min)
         {
            lots of code here
         } /* end inner if block */
         lots of code here
      } /* end outer if block */
      else
      {
         lots of code here
      }
   } /* end inner while loop */
   lots of code here
} /* end outer while loop */
```

1.7.4   Commenting Out Code: Nested Comments

Sometimes you might want to see temporarily how your code runs without a particular group of lines in it, or with that group of lines replaced by an alternative block of code. You can accomplish this without actually deleting the lines from the source code file by commenting the lines out—that is, putting /* immediately before and */ immediately after the section.

As a general rule, you may not comment out a block of code that contains comments internally. However, Borland C and a few other compilers allow you to select an option that permits your source code to nest comments. Again, since this usage is nonstandard, it may be wise to avoid it. (See Chapter 11 for more standard methods of effectively commenting out code containing internal comments by conditional compilation.)

1.7.5   Spaces

Apart from

- spaces required to set off one variable name or keyword (see Chapter 2) from another
- a couple of special rules for lines starting with **#** (see Chapter 11)
- splitting into two lines what `printf()` sends to the screen (see Chapter 3)

you may use as much or as little spacing as you wish. The computer ignores the spaces. Thus,

```
a = c * (d - 1);
```

is the same to the computer as

```
a=c*(d-1);
```

and

```
setcurs(row, col); readline_here(len, temp); cps(temp,
    color, row, col);
```

is the same as

```
setcurs(row, col);
readline_here(len, temp);
cps(temp, color, row, col);
```

In fact the following mess is the same to the computer as the first listing, `add.c`:

```
#include<stdio.h>
int main(void){int firstValue,secondValue,sum;printf
("Enter two numbers:\n");printf(
"Press [Enter] after each\n");scanf(
"%d%d",&firstValue,&secondValue);sum=firstValue
+secondValue;printf(
"\nTotal of %d plus %d is %d",firstValue, secondValue,sum);return 0;}
```

1.7.6   Recommended Spacing Practices

You are free to make your code as visually readable or unreadable as you choose. However, we recommend the following practices to you:

- *Put no more than one statement per line.* (The semicolon marks the end of a statement.)
- *Add an extra line space to separate groups of conceptually related statements.*
- *Align the opening and closing braces of a block of code on the code fragment that governs it, indent the block of statements, and do the same for each block within a block.*

```
int main(void)
{
    code here
}
```

Notice how the `i` in `int` is horizontally aligned with the opening and closing braces of the block of code. Even a simple program like `add.c` has a level of indentation: all the statements within `main()` are indented one level.

The default setting in the Borland C or Microsoft C editor is a tab stop every eight spaces. You may well find that eight spaces indentation per level results in too many statements being split in order to fit on the screen. Most programmers change the default and use two, three, or four instead.

- *Limit each line to 80 characters.*

You are permitted to exceed the 80-character per line screen width for writing your code. However, extending code beyond the right screen boundary will decrease screen readability considerably. Also, if you print out a hard copy of your source code, you will lose the part that extends beyond the screen if your printer does not have a wide carriage.

You are not limited to a single line per code statement. Indeed, assuming you choose to confine your code within the screen's boundaries, you will be often obliged to split up long lines, particularly those found at several indentation levels in.

Since the compiler generally ignores spaces, it normally makes no difference where you split your source code lines. There are exceptions:

- **Text beginning with #—called *preprocessor directives*—must be on a single line. (See Chapter 11.)**
- **Material surrounded by a pair of double quotes—called *literal strings*—may not be split between lines. (See Chapter 7.)**
- **Variable names or C keywords or operators, consisting of more than a single character may not be split between lines.** For instance if you have a variable named `indivisible`, you may not put *in* on one line and *divisible* on the next line. (Keywords and operators will be covered in Chapters 2 and 3.)

Even in these three cases, where line splitting is not allowed, you can use a backslash at the end of a line to have the compiler concatenate the two lines and treat them as one logical line. You can do this over more than two physical lines to create a single logical line out of several lines. You can even split keywords or variables. For instance, the following would be bizarre but permissible:

```
in\
t mai\
n(vo\
id)
```

In any event, Standard C requires only that the compiler support at least 509 characters in a single line (as concatenated with any backslashes). Even though some compilers allow far more, for reasons of portability, you should limit your lines to 509 characters. (For reasons of style, as we said, you should limit yourself to 80 characters per line.)

Normally, you will split single statements that exceed 80 characters at spaces between keywords or variable names, at commas, or before or after C operators such as **+** or **−**. For example:

```
place_char('$', C((fore + (1 << 7)),back),
    page_start_row + back * 2, table_lcol + fore * 2 + 1);


sprintf(temp, "  %s  ", i == 0 ?
    "Information Page" : i == 1 ?
    "Data Page        " : i == 2 ? "Select Colors   " :
    "Exit            ");
```

As a matter of convention, as in the last example, the second and any succeeding lines of the same statement are indented one level further in than the statement's first line.

1.7.7 Typing in and Naming Your Source Code

To type the source code, you normally use the editor that comes with your compiler. However, you may use any other editor that saves files as ASCII text. You could, for instance, use the Microsoft C editor or the editor provided with DOS to create a source code to be compiled by Borland C. The Borland C and Microsoft C editors both have search and search-and-replace commands, which allow you to find every instance in your source code of a group of characters or to locate them and replace them with another set of characters (the latter of which may be just a blank if you want to simply eliminate each occurrence of a character or group of characters).

Neither of these compiler editors has the power that macros in a sophisticated word processing program such as WordPerfect or Microsoft Word would afford. You may use one of these word processing programs to create your source code as long as it has a utility that allows it to store a file as flat ASCII text—that is, without the special characters word processing programs use to indicate such features as tabs, margin settings, fonts, and document creation formats. Nevertheless, the practice is to be discouraged. Word processors are not self-contained integrated C development environments, so for instance they will not highlight potential syntax errors (some compilers put keywords in one color, integer variables in another, and so on). For another thing, there is not always a perfect translation of characters from the word processor to ASCII text. For example, some word processors will alter the paired apostrophes or double quotes you wrote into printer's left and right apostrophes and double quotes without telling you it is doing that; these do not get properly translated.

1.7.8   Including Other Files

Your source code file includes the contents of any other files you indicate through an include directive, just as though you manually typed in each line of those outside files at the point where the include directive is found in your source code. All include directives start with #include and conclude with the name of a file. In add.c, for instance, we bring the entire contents of stdio.h, a file that deals with *ST*an*D*ard *I*nput and *O*utput.

```
#include <stdio.h>
```

Those included source codes can be your own files, Standard C files, or those of a third-party vendor. In add.c, the file included, stdio.h, is a Standard C file. We will discuss include directives extensively, and what is generally found in these included files, in Chapter 11.

1.7.9   Permissible Names

The name of the first source code file we looked at is add.c. In naming programs, the programmer must comply with the particular operating system's file naming conventions and restrictions. For example, for programs to be run on DOS-based machines, the source code file name must follow the usual DOS conventions as to length of base name and extension (8 and 3, respectively) and allowable characters, namely, the letters of the alphabet, the digits 0 to 9, and any of the following: ~ ! @ # $ & ( ) { } ' _

By convention, the source code carries a .c extension—for instance, add.c. However, despite what you might read in some C books, you are free to use any other extension, or none at all if you choose, although the .c extension is well-nigh universally used by C programmers and you should certainly comply with the convention. If you fail to specify an extension and do not indicate you want none by putting a period at the end of the base name (add.), most C editors will add .c automatically when you save the file for the first time (.cpp in some combination C/C++ compilers such Borland C++ unless you change the default).

1.7.10   From Human-Readable to Machine Language

The compiler (Borland C, Microsoft C, or whatever else you use) takes the source code, with its human-readable letters and punctuation, and transforms it into a machine-language version. The process is called *compiling* and the resulting code is called *object code.* If you make no contrary specification—and you rarely would—the compiler will assign the object code a file name with the same base name as the source code's, with a .obj extension: add.obj for our mini-source code example here.

When you first begin programming, your program will consist of a single source code. As your programming becomes more sophisticated and longer and more complex, your program may contain several source codes. Each of the source codes in a program is compiled separately into its own object code. You specify these additional source code files by listing them in a *project file.* We cover the mechanics of multiple-source code programs in Chapter 17. Until then, we will limit programming examples to single-source code programs.

1.7.11   Libraries and Linking

After the compilation is complete, the resulting object code for your source code and those compiled from any other source codes that make up your program are linked with precompiled groups of functions called *libraries*—a Standard C library and any of your own or third-party vendors' libraries (the

Figure 1.22 *Creation of Executable Code*

latter are sometimes called *toolkits;* you will learn how to create your own library in Chapter 17). The result is the running version of the program, called the ***executable code*** (Figure 1.22).

1.8   APPLICATION: ACE BILLING PROGRAM

Now that we have finally discussed all the building blocks of programming, we are ready for our first programming problem. But before we jump in, we must make some minor accommodations.

When we presented structured design programming methodology, we introduced the concept of a module or function. There are two types of function: standard functions supplied by the C compiler, and user-defined functions written by the programmer. The printf() and scanf() functions we used earlier in add.c are two common Standard C functions, and we will discuss them in detail in Chapter 3.

However, we cannot cover functions in detail until much later in the book. Functions are not fully discussed until Chapter 8. The main thing we ignore until then is the concept of transmitting values to the functions—a process called *passing parameters.*

An example will illustrate. The principal task of add.c was to add two variables' values and store the sum in a third variable. We could have created a separate function to handle that discrete task.

Listing 1.2 add_func.c

```
/* add_func.c */

  /* add.c with a function for addition */

  #include <stdio.h> /* Standard C header file */

  int add(int numOne, int numTwo);
  int main(void) /* function where program execution starts */
  {
      int firstVal, secondVal, sum; /* declare 3 variables of type int */

      /* give user instructions on the screen */
      printf("Enter two numbers\n");
      printf("Press [Enter] after each\n");
```

```
    /* get input from keyboard and store it */
    scanf("%d%d", &firstVal, &secondVal);

    /* add the two numbers and store result */
    sum = add(firstVal, secondVal);

    /* write the two input numbers and the total on the screen */
    printf("\nTotal of %d plus %d is %d", firstVal, secondVal, sum);

    return 0;
}

int add(int numOne, int numTwo)
{
    return numOne + numTwo;
}
```

The function add() is composed of the following portion of add_func.c:

```
int add(int numOne, int numTwo)
{
    return numOne + numTwo;
}
```

This entire block of text is called the add() function's definition. We have passed two values to the add() function. This is what we referred to above as *passing parameters*. In turn, add() returns a single value to the function that invoked or "called" it, main(). This value has a certain type, int, noted by placing this C keyword immediately before the name of the function. The line above main()

```
int add(int numOne, int numTwo);
```

is called the function's *prototype*. The prototype alerts the compiler to how many values are passed to the function and what their type is, as well as to what the type of the value returned is. This "heads-up" is given before the compiler has the benefit of seeing the function definition. In this way, when the compiler sees the statement in main()

```
sum = add(firstVal, secondVal);
```

it is able to either confirm that the statement has the correct number and types of parameters or else issue an error message—and it can make this assessment despite the fact that the function definition comes later in the source code.

In the first seven chapters, we will not pass any values to functions. If the functions use the values of any variables, they will be what are known as *global variables*. As we explain in later chapters, these are variables the values of which are known to and accessible to all functions without their values being passed to the functions.

Note that this extensive use of global variables is not good practice, and we will discontinue it after Chapter 7. We have chosen this approach so that we can apply the concept of modular design right from the beginning.

In fact, since we will not have discussed variables fully until Chapter 2, the programming exercise that follows immediately does not even use them.

Still, to comply with the top-down methodology, it is necessary to create functions from the outset. In this first chapter, we stay at the very uppermost level. We ignore all details of the functions' implementation. All we use is a function skeleton, called a ***stub.*** The purpose of a stub is solely to show us that the function has been executed and to demonstrate that the overall flow of program logic is correct. Even after you understand all the intricacies of functions, you should start coding with stubs only.

Listing 1.3, acech01.c, is a *complete* program since it has a body for every module in the hierarchy chart of Figure 1.18, and runs and produces results, yet it is *incomplete* in that all the functions but one have not been implemented. The acech01.c program, our first pass at solving the ACE Billing application, has many features that have not been presented yet. We would, however, like you to be able to follow the program at a high level. Look at the output produced and map it with program flow.

Program flow begins with the first statement of the main() function, and execution continues statement by statement. However, when a function is called by mentioning its name, program flow shifts to that function; the function's statements are executed; then program flow returns to main() at the statement following the function's call, and so on until the end of main() is reached.

 **Listing** **1.3 acech01.c**

```c
/* +----------------------------------------------------------------+
   +   Program Name: acech01.c
   +      Author(s): Austell-Wolfson and Otieno
   +      Date: 04/10/2000
   +   Purpose:
   +      This program implements the Ace billing program.
   +   At this point the modules can only be written as
   +   stubs because we have not yet learned enough C to
   +   further implement the stubs.
   +
   +   Process:
   +   At this point, all we can do is print the headings
   +   and print stubs for the rest of the functions.
   +   Functions will be developed in subsequent chapters.
   +----------------------------------------------------------------+
*/

#include <stdio.h>

void initialization(void); /* prototype - discussed in Chapter 8 */
void processMemberRecord(void);
void termination(void);
void initializeVariables(void);
void printHeadings(void);
void readMemberRecord(void);
void computeIndividualBill(void);
void writeDetailLine(void);
void determineSpecialFee(void);
void determineActivityFee(void);
void determineDiscountAmt(void);

int main(void)
{
   initialization();
   processMemberRecord(); /* No loop logic yet - Chapter 5 */
   termination();
   return 0;
}

void initialization(void)
{
   initializeVariables();
   printHeadings();
   readMemberRecord();
   printf("initialization function has executed successfully\n");
}

void processMemberRecord(void)
{
   computeIndividualBill();
   writeDetailLine();
   readMemberRecord();
   printf("processMemberRecord function has executed successfully\n");
}
```

```c
void termination(void)
{
   printf("termination function has executed successfully\n");
}

void initializeVariables(void)
{
   printf("initializeVariables function has executed successfully\n");
}

void printHeadings(void)
{
   printf("+--------------------------------------------------"
          "----------------------+\n");
   printf("+                                                  "
          "                       +\n");
   printf("+    Program Name: ACECH01.EXE                     "
          "          Page:  1    +\n");
   printf("+         Run Date: 12/10/2000         Ace Billing "
          "                       +\n");
   printf("+                                                  "
          "                       +\n");
   printf("+                                                  "
          "                       +\n");
   printf("+--------------------------------------------------"
          "----------------------+\n");
   printf("+                                                  "
          "                       +\n");
   printf("+ Customer Name  Charges  Bill       Mbr Fee    Act Fee"
          "    Disc    Total Bill +\n");
   printf("+--------------------------------------------------"
          "----------------------+\n");
   printf("+                                                  "
          "                       +\n\n");
}

void readMemberRecord(void)
{
   printf("readMemberRecord function has executed successfully\n");
}

void computeIndividualBill(void)
{
   determineSpecialFee();
   determineActivityFee();
   determineDiscountAmt();
   printf("computeIndividualBill function has executed successfully\n");
}

void writeDetailLine(void)
{
   printf("writeDetailLine function has executed successfully\n");
}

void determineSpecialFee(void)
{
   printf("determineSpecialFee function has executed successfully\n");
}
```

```
void determineActivityFee(void)
{
    printf("determineActivityFee function has executed successfully\n");
}

void determineDiscountAmt(void)
{
    printf("determineDiscountAmt function has executed successfully\n");
}
```

The output of this program is shown below. It reflects the order of the function calls.

```
initializeVariables function has executed successfully
+--------------------------------------------------------------------+
+                                                                    +
+   Program Name: ACECH01.EXE                            Page:  1    +
+       Run Date: 12/10/2000          Ace Billing                    +
+                                                                    +
+                                                                    +
+--------------------------------------------------------------------+
+                                                                    +
+ Customer Name  Charges  Bill      Mbr Fee    Act Fee   Disc   Total Bill +
+--------------------------------------------------------------------+
+                                                                    +
```

```
readMemberRecord function has executed successfully
initialization function has executed successfully
determineSpecialFee function has executed successfully
determineActivityFee function has executed successfully
determineDiscountAmt function has executed successfully
computeIndividualBill function has executed successfully
writeDetailLine function has executed successfully
readMemberRecord function has executed successfully
processMemberRecord function has executed successfully
termination function has executed successfully
```

Now let's take a look at what makes up a source code in the next chapter.

Chapter Summary

1. A program is a set of instructions that form a computerized solution to a problem, written initially as ordinary text, then converted to a language understood by a computer, and finally executed by the computer.

2. The building blocks to successful programming involve understanding the hardware, understanding programming methodology, and finally, learning to write the source code.

3. The basic function of computers falls into three categories: arithmetic operations, comparison operations, and storage and retrieval operations.

4. All computers have three basic components: the central processing unit (CPU), the primary storage unit, and peripherals.

5. Data is held in the storage units of a computer. Primary storage, often called volatile memory or RAM, is housed within the CPU, or central processing unit. Data in secondary memory, such as a computer's hard drive, remains intact until it is altered or removed.

6. In batch processing, several programs are carried out at one time in a continuous stream without any input from the user; interactive processing involves communication between the user and the program at run time.

7. One of the main advantages of C programming is that it is portable. Portability is the ability of a program's instructions to operate without modification on any computer system and to operate in the same predictable way no matter what system is used.

8. Programs can be written in either a compiled language, in which the program is translated into machine language only once, or interpreted, in which the code is translated into machine language at run time.

9. The programming process consists of eight basic steps:
   - Define the problem.
   - Analyze the problem.
   - Design the logic.
   - Write the program using the language of choice.
   - Key in the program using a suitable text editor.

- Test and debug the program.
- Gather and complete the documentation.
- Maintain the program.

10. In designing the logic of a program, I/O requirements are depicted in system flowcharts. Input is often documented in record layouts, and output is documented in printer spacing charts.

11. A hierarchy chart or structure chart graphically represents the organizational relationships among discrete program modules.

12. In debugging a program, one encounters syntax errors, which are grammatical errors in writing the program language, and logic errors.

13. Logic errors consist of pure logic errors and program operation errors. When such errors cause premature program termination, they are called run-time errors.

14. Structured programming is a program implementation technique that systematizes and organizes the entire cycle of program design, coding, and testing. This is achieved by utilizing top-down design, independent program modules, and structured coding principles.

15. Top-down design programming involves starting with a main task or topic and breaking it into smaller subtasks until it is broken into its most basic units.

16. Once the task is broken into its most basic units, a solution called a module is formulated for each unit. The relationship between all of the modules is depicted in a hierarchy chart.

17. C calls modules *functions*. A function is a block of statements designed by the programmer who wrote them to perform a discrete task.

18. All structured coding involves only three types of constructs: sequential, in which statements are executed one after the other, conditional, in which the program executes from a choice of statements, depending on tested conditions, and iterative, in which one or more statements are repeatedly executed until a specific condition is met.

19. Source code is a set of instructions, written by the programmer, in the computer language's syntax.

20. Placing comments in source code helps explain what the source code is doing and the reason it was written that way. Comments can also be used to temporarily remove sections of code from the compilation process without deleting the actual source text.

21. Spacing makes the code more readable and provides formatting for the code text. Some good spacing practices are putting only one statement on one line, putting a double space between groups of similar code lines, and limiting each line to 80 characters.

Review Questions

1. An advanced computer can sense the wishes of the programmer and perform the necessary tasks even if it receives the wrong instructions. True or false?
2. What is a computer program?
3. What are the programmer's text version and the computer's machine-language version of the program respectively called?
4. What are retrieving and sending data on the computer respectively called?
5. What are three categories of basic tasks that a computer can perform?
6. Which is the most readily accessible by the computer: registers, RAM, or secondary storage?
7. Is C a compiled or interpreted language?
8. What is meant by *portability* in relation to programming languages?
9. List the steps of a good programming methodology and design process.
10. What is meant by *top-down* programming?
11. What does a flowchart do?
12. What sort of error results when an instruction violates the programming language rules?
13. What is a *function* in the C programming language?
14. The compiler always disregards spaces in the text version of a computer program. True or false?
15. List two techniques for simplifying the design of a C program and facilitating debugging.
16. A C program that compiles without any syntax errors will always run properly.
17. Define *programming*.
18. Define *compiler*.
19. Define *source program*.
20. Define *object program*.
21. Define *executable program*.
22. What is the meaning of the term *structured programming*?
23. Define *field* and give an example.
24. Define *record* and give an example.
25. Define *file* and give an example.
26. Explain the difference between *hardware* and *software* and give an example of each.
27. Define *register*.
28. What is *volatile memory*?
29. What is a *program stub*?
30. Explain *batch processing* and give an example.
31. Explain *interactive processing* and give an example.
32. Explain the difference between a *syntax error* and a *compile-time error*.
33. List three programming constructs presented in this chapter.

Programming Exercises

The problems given in this chapter are complete programming assignments. You are to apply the programming methodology principles presented in the chapter to solve these problems. Remember the definition we gave to programming: the entire series of steps involved in solving a problem using the computer. Many of these steps can be done before you know any computer language. At this point all we expect of you is to be able to

- think through the solution to these problems.
- identify the modules that, once implemented, will solve the problem.
- prepare a hierarchy chart of all the modules.
- prepare pseudocode/flowchart for each module in the hierarchy chart.
- write the program stubs in the same way as we did with the ACE Billing system application.

Later chapters will be asking you to implement pieces of these modules as your knowledge of Standard C increases.

Programming Assignment 1.1: Billing

Program Description

Write a Billing program that reads the following data from an order file: product name, product description, product cost per item, and the quantity of items ordered. The program is to calculate the extended cost for each product and apply the appropriate percentage discount against the total extended cost according to the accompanying table. The extended cost is the product of the cost and the quantity. If the customer does not qualify for a discount, then only print the message "Thank you for your business" at the bottom of the report.

Input: Input record layout and sample input data (see Table P1.1A).

Table P1.1A   *Input for Programming Assignment 1.1*

Customer Order File			
Field Name	**Size**	**Type**	**No. of Decimal Positions**
Product Number	6	String (Alphanumeric)	
Product Description	25	String (Alphanumeric)	
Quantity	5	Numeric (up to 32,000)	
Cost per item	8	Numeric (up to 999,999,99)	2

Sample Data: (see Tables P1.1B and P1.1C on page 34).

Table P1.1B   *Sample Product Data for Programming Assignment 1.1*

Product Number (6 chars)	Product Description (20 chars)	Cost	Quantity
TZ3232	Dining room set	220.95	1
RX9935	Sofa	322.43	2
WS2300	Loveseat	199.99	1
ER3401	Bookshelf	149.99	4
HD5641	Coffee table	99.99	2

Table P1.1C   *Sample Discount Ranges for Programming Assignment 1.1*

Discount Range and Percent Discount for Each Range	
Range of Extended Cost	*Percent Discount*
$1,000 – $5,000	Your order has been discounted 5%
$5,000.01 – $10,000	Your order has been discounted 7%
$10,000+	Your order has been discounted 10%

Output: (see Figure P1.1)

Figure P1.1   *Output for Programming Assignment 1.1*

```
Program Name: PA1-1                              Page: 1
Author: Your Name                    Run Date: 12/19/2000
----------------------------------------------------------
              Billing Invoice for Acme Retail
----------------------------------------------------------
Product     Product                            Extended
Number      Description     Cost    Quantity   Cost
----------------------------------------------------------
TZ3232      Dining room set 220.95  1               220.95
RX9935      Sofa            322.43  2               644.86
WS2300      Loveseat        199.99  1               199.99
ER3401      Bookshelf       149.99  4               599.96
HD5641      Coffee table     99.99  2               199.98
                                 Order Total:  $1,865.74

Your order has been discounted 5%. Thank you for your business.
```

Programming Assignment 1.2: VP's Payroll Report

Program Description

The new vice president would like to see a list of all the employees in her department—their social security numbers, titles, salaries, and the combined total of all their salaries. Write a program that reads and displays the data given according the input record layout specified. The program should also print a message as determined by the range in which the total salary falls. Change the values of the salaries so you can see each message. The parameters and input are shown in Tables P1.2A and P1.2B, respectively; the sample data and output report format are shown in Figures P1.2A and P1.2B, respectively.

Table P1.2A   *Parameters for Programming Assignment 1.2*

Salary Ranges and Appraisals	
Salary Range	*Appraisal*
$0 – $200,000	Excellent work, the department is under budget
$200,000 – $210,000	The department is over budget; cut back on unnecessary expenses
$210,000+	The department is seriously over budget; see your manager

Input: Input record layout and sample input data (see Table P1.2B)

Table P1.2B *Input for Programming Assignment 1.2*

Payroll File Record Layout			
Field Name	**Size**	**Type**	**No. of Decimal Positions**
Social Security Number	9	String	
Employee name	20	String	
Employee title	25	String	
Employee salary	6	Numeric (999,999.99)	2

Sample Data: (see Figure P1.2A)

Figure P1.2A *Sample Data for Programming Assignment 1.2*

```
Kathy Ray          123456798     Executive     $60,000
Vicki Anderson     985673456     CPA           $30,000
John Jameson       783452167     Clerk         $21,000
Paul Estes         125346783     Clerk         $18,000
Kim Alliantz       567823561     Manager       $40,000
```

Output Report: (see Figure P1.2B)

Figure P1.2B *Output Report for Programming Assignment 1.2*

```
Payroll Salary Report
-----------------------------------------------------------------
Employee Name(20)      Social Security
                       Number          Title(15)    Salary
-----------------------------------------------------------------
Kathy Ray              123456798       Executive    $60,000
Vicki Anderson         985673456       CPA          $30,000
John Jameson           783452167       Clerk        $21,000
Paul Estes             125346783       Clerk        $18,000
Kim Alliantz           567823561       Manager      $40,000
Total                                               $169,000
Excellent work, the department is under budget.
```

Programming Assignment 1.3: Payroll Processing

Program Description

Write a C program to process the weekly payroll of the Otieno-Omaya Consulting Services (OCS). For each employee of OCS, your program will compute the gross pay, deductions, and net pay. This information is to be clearly printed in the output along with certain summary information for the entire payroll.

Each week OCS enters data for each employee that includes the information in Table P1.3.

Using this information, your program should carry out the following computations:

1. Gross pay: regular pay for the first 40 hours and time and a half beyond that up to a limit of 74 hours in a given week.
2. Deductions:

   Nomenclature:

   g represents gross pay

Table P1.3 *Employee Data for Programming Assignment 1.3*

OCS Payroll File Record Layout			
Social Security Number	9	String (digits)	
Hourly pay rate	5	Number	2
Number of exemptions	2	Number (0-19)	
Health insurance code	1	Number (1-4)	
Hours worked	5	Number (999.99)	2

t represents taxable pay.

e represents the number of exemptions.

a. Federal income tax withholding is defined as

```
t = g - 14.0 * e - 11.0
withholding = t * (0.14 + 2.3 * 0.0001 * t)
```

b. State income tax withholding is defined as 38% of the amount withheld for federal income tax.

c. Social security tax is $16.70 or (7.7% of g), whichever is smaller.

d. Health insurance

   1—No coverage.

   2—Employee coverage ($8.00 per week).

   3—Family coverage ($17.50 per week).

   4—Major medical coverage ($18.00 per week).

3. Net pay: gross pay less all deductions.

For each employee, your program should produce an output report in a legible format with each item clearly labeled.

After the last employee has been processed, your program should print a summary report that includes the number of employees processed, total gross pay, total deductions of each type, and total net pay.

Your program must be capable of processing an arbitrary number of data records and should perform the following data validation:

■ If deductions exceed gross pay? The net pay should be zero.

■ If taxable pay is negative? The tax should be zero.

Without making this file unreasonably large, design it so that it will test all the features of your algorithm. For example, you should include some invalid data in the file just to show how your program will handle it. When a record with invalid data is encountered, a message should be written to the output file citing the invalidity, and processing of that record should halt. Your program should then go on to the processing of the next input record in the file.

Design the output of your program to your own taste, but keep readability, pleasant appearance, and completeness in mind in doing so.

Programming Assignment 1.4: UNIX System Administration

Program Description

A user account on a UNIX system has many elements. These are some of them:

■ Username: a unique login name

■ UID: an ID number that equates to a username

■ GID: each user is a member of a primary group; groups have ID numbers

■ Full Name: the full name of the user

■ Home directory: a private area on disk for each user

■ Shell: the user's default command environment

Some of these elements must be validated from preestablished list of values. The UID is to be obtained from the UID file that has the next UID number. Your program must update that number with a new one that is greater by 1. The GID, Home Directory, and Shell must be validated from system-maintained tables (see Tables P1.4A to P1.4C).

Table P1.4A *System Table for Programming Assignment 1.4: GID Table*

GID Table	
GID	*Group name*
11	Admin
12	Accounting
13	Marketing
14	End-Users
15	Managers
16	Shipping
17	MIS
18	Sales
19	Guest
20	Development

Table P1.4B *System Table for Programming Assignment 1.4: User's Default Directories*

User's Default Directories
/home/faculty
/home/student
/home/admin
/home/infoSys
/users/assistants
/users/faculty/research

Table P1.4C *System Table for Programming Assignment 1.4: User's Default Command*

User's Default Command Environment
/usr/bin/ksh
/usr/bin/cshx
/usr/bin/sh
/usr/bin/cah

Write a program that reads the following fields: User Name, GID, Full name, Home directory, and the default shell environment. The program must check to make sure that GID, Home directory, and the default shell environment are all valid according to the system tables. The program is to produce the report given in the accompanying figure. Most implementations of UNIX require a certain format for a user name. Validate the user name to ensure it is between 2 and 8 characters in length.

Input: Enter data interactively

Output: (see Figure P1.4)

Figure P1.4   *Output for Programming Assignment 1.4*

User Name	User ID	Group ID	Full Name	Shell
bjohnson	203	15	Bill Johnson	/usr/bin/ksh
gvanvranken	203	16	Gerrit	/usr/bin/ksh
cmcdowell	203	17	Bill Johnson	/usr/bin/ksh
bjohnson	203	15	Bill Johnson	/usr/bin/ksh

Programming Assignment 1.5: UNIX System Administration

Program Description

Write a program that reads the data from a file having the fields user name, UID, group name, and shell and that produces the report sorted by GID (Group ID); see Figure P1.5A. In addition, you are to count the number of occurrences of each GID and produce the report shown in Figure P1.5B.

Input: UNIX account file

Output: (see Figures P1.5A and P1.5B)

Figure P1.5A   *Output for Programming Assignment 1.5: Sorted User Table*

User Name	User ID	Group	Full Name	Shell
bjohnson	203	manager	Bill Johnson	/usr/bin/ksh
trolling	207	INVALID	Tonya Rollings	/usr/bin/cshX
janderso	204	accounting	Jane Anderson	/usr/bin/sh
kriddle	201	manager	K. Riddle	/usr/bin/ksh
pmasters	999	INVALID	Paul Masters	/usr/bin/kshX
jhu	323	development	Jim Hu	/usr/bin/sh

Figure P1.5B   *Output for Programming Assignment 1.5: Group ID Occurrence Table*

Groups	Members
admin	0
accounting	1
marketing	0
users	0
manager	2
development	2
shipping	0
mis	0
sales	0
guest	0

Programming Assignment 1.6: UNIX System Administration

Program Description

The UNIX file /etc/passwd stores information about each user. This information must be formatted in a specific way for users to be able to log in. A typical line in the file looks like this:

- srobbind:x:325:15:Suzie Robbindra:/home/srobbind:/usr/bin/sh

These fields are colon delimited and break out as follows:

- User name
- Password
- UID

- GID
- Comment (Full name goes here)
- User's home directory
- User's default shell

Write a program that prompts the user for this information. As the data for these fields is entered, the program is to write a record delimited by a colon after each field to the `/etc/passwd`. This record is printed to standard output.

Be sure to validate the user name (must be between 2 and 8 characters), UID (from a control file), and GID against the table values given in Programming Assignment 1.5.

Programming Assignment 1.7: UNIX System Administration

Program Description

One job of a system administrator is to ensure that no single user is hogging all the disk space. Write a program that divides the disk space equally among users, lists the amount of space each user is occupying, and creates a "disk hog" report listing anyone using more than their "fair share."

Input: Interactively enter the total disk space—for example 3000 MB.

Get the user IDs in the system and the amount of disk space, in millions of bytes, that they are using. For example:

```
bjohnson    10
trolling    53
janderso    268
kriddle     154
pmasters    312
jhu         285
jvictores   196
keddenfi    210
shedding    362
jtonguet    57
gvanvran    129
cmcdowe     318
jxbc        412
ljones      121
tjones      8
gwarshin    59
```

Calculate allowed usage as the average of the total number of bytes available divided by the number of users in the system.

The number of bytes by which each user is over their allowed usage is the difference between the number of bytes of allowed usage minus the number of bytes in actual use. The percentage by which each user is over their allowed usage is the quotient of the number of bytes by which each user is over their allowed usage and the number of bytes of allowed usage times 100.

Output: (see Figure P1.7)

Figure P1.7 *Output for Programming Assignment 1.7*

```
                    Disk Hog Report

Number of users:

Allowed usage              MB
Total Usage                MB
Free Space                 MB

Disk Hogs

Username      Bytes Used    Bytes Allowed    Bytes Over    % Over
------------------------------------------------------------------------
```

Programming Assignment 1.8: Science and Engineering (Chemical Engineering)

Program Description

Combustion Engineering, Inc. produced "Steam Tables: Properties of Saturated and Supersaturated Steam." These tables are widely used in performing many chemical engineering calculations. Given below is a sample of such steam tables. These steam tables are updated regularly from a file whose accuracy has been carefully verified or from information generated by a mathematical model. In either case, your program is to produce a report that publishes these values:

- V = specific volume (ft.)^3/ (lb.$_m$)
- H = specific enthalpy (Btu)/ (lb.$_m$)
- S = specific entropy (Btu)/ (lb.$_m$) (R)
- l (in. Hg) at 32 ($^\circ$F) = 0.4912 (psia)

Saturated Steam: (see Table P1.8)

Table P1.8 *Properties of Saturated Steam for Programming Assignment 1.8*

	Absolute Pressure		Specific Volume			Enthalpy			Entropy	
Temp	Psia	In. Hg (32°F)	Sat. Liquid V_f	Evap. V_{fg}	Sat. Vapor V_g	Sat. Liquid H_f	Sat. Vapor H_{fg}	Sat. Vapor. H_g	Sat. Liquid S_f	Sat. Vapor S_g
32	0.0886	0.1806	0.01602	3305.7	3305.7	0.00	1075.1	1075.1	2.1885	2.1865
34	0.0961	0.1957	0.01602	3060.4	3060.4	2.01	1074.0	1074.0	2.1755	2.1796
36	0.1041	0.2120	0.01602	2836.6	2836.6	4.03	1072.9	1072.9	2.1645	2.1727
38	0.1126	0.2292	0.01602	2632.2	2632.2	6.04	1071.7	1071.7	2.1533	2.1655
40	0.1217	0.2478	0.01602	2445.1	2445.1	8.05	1070.5	1070.5	2.1423	2.1517
42	0.1315	0.2677	0.01602	2271.8	2271.8	10.06	1069.3	1069.3	2.1314	2.1449
44	0.1420	0.2891	0.01602	2112.2	2112.2	12.06	1068.2	1068.2	2.1207	2.1384
46	0.1532	0.3119	0.01602	1965.5	1965.5	14.07	1067.1	1067.1	2.1102	2.1317
48	0.1652	0.3364	0.01602	1829.9	1829.9	16.07	1078.6	0.0162	2.1423	2.1252

Input Data:

```
32 0.0886 0.1806 0.01602 3305.7 3305.7 0 1075.1 1075.1 2.1885 2.1865
```

Output Report Layout: (see Figure P1.8 on page 41)

Programming Assignment 1.9: Science and Engineering (Compiler Construction)

Program Description

ANSI C language may be used to write a compiler for another language such as Pascal. For example, the following are Pascal assignment statements. Some are valid; others are not. Write a program that checks the syntax of these statements. (See Table P1.9 on page 41.)

Input data: Pascal assignment statements

Output Report: (see Figure P1.9 on page 41)

Figure P1.8   *Output Report Layout for Programming Assignment 1.8*

```
--------------------------------------------------------------------------------
Program Name:PA1-8                                                       Page: 1
Author: Your Name                                          Run Date: 12/19/1998
--------------------------------------------------------------------------------
Steam Tables: Properties of Saturated and Supersaturated Steam
--------------------------------------------------------------------------------
```

V = specific volume (ft)^3/ (lb$_m$)
H = specific enthalpy (Btu)/ (lb$_m$)
S = specific entropy (Btu)/ (lb$_m$) (R)
(in. Hg) at 32 (°F) = 0.4912 (psia)

```
--------------------------------------------------------------------------------
Saturated steam
--------------------------------------------------------------------------------
```

Temp	Psia	In Hg	Sat. Liquid	Evap Vfg	Sat. Vapor	Sat. Liq	Sat. Vapor	Sat. Liq	Sat. Vapor	Sat. Vapor
32	0.0886	0.1806	0.01602	3305.7	3305.7	0	1075.1	1075.1	2.1885	2.1865

Table P1.9   *Pascal Assignment Statements for Programming Assignment 1.9*

B := 100;	Valid Statement
B = 100;	Invalid (= must be an assignment operator: :=)
B := 100	
A := B;	Valid Statement
C := 200;	Valid Statement
B := B * 10 - C;	Valid Statement
Radius := 100;	Valid Statement
Circumference := 2 * Pi * Radius;	Valid Statement
Area Of Circle := 2 * Pi * Radius * Radius;	Invalid (Invalid identifier)
Area := 2 * Pi * Radius * Radius;	Valid Statement
Programming := Data_Structures + Algorithms;	Valid Statement
100 := 20 + Alpha;	Invalid Statement
Sum := Sum New_Data_Value;	Invalid Statement (bad expression)
Sum := Sum + New_Data_Value;	Valid Statement
Sum := Sum + New_Data_Value	Invalid Statement (missing ;)

Figure P1.9   *Output Report for Programming Assignment 1.9*

```
Program Name: PA1-9                                          Page: 1
Author: Your Name                                Run Date: 12/19/2000
--------------------------------------------------------------
                PASCAL Assignment statement checking
--------------------------------------------------------------
```

Programming Assignment 1.10: Science and Engineering (Mathematics—The Game of Life)

Program Description: (see Figure P1.10A)

Figure 1.10A   *Program Description for Programming Assignment 1.10*

NW	N	NE
W	Life Form	E
SW	S	SE

The "Game of Life" was developed by mathematician John Conway. You are to write a program that plays this game. In this programming exercise, we describe the game in a way that it can be programmed. In Figure P1.10A, we have labeled each neighbor according to its geographic location relative to the "Life Form." *NW* stands for northwest, *SE* stands for southeast, and so on. Each cell changes depending on its eight neighbors, each of which has eight neighbors in turn. Thus every cell is linked to every other cell through a chain of neighbors. This feature makes "The Game of Life" extremely interesting and entertaining and mathematically intriguing. Many generations of cells must change state before cells can alter one another from across the cellular region.

A cell becomes occupied by giving birth to an individual. That is, a birth yields an occupied cell. All deaths and all births for a given generation occur simultaneously. The rules for playing the game are as follows:

- Births: Each empty cell surrounded by exactly three occupied cells is a birth cell.
- Deaths: Each occupied cell with four or more neighboring occupied cells dies from overpopulation. Every occupied cell with one or no neighboring cells dies from isolation.
- Each occupied cell with two or three neighboring occupied cells survives to the next generation.

Input Data: Locations of life forms, the size of the grid (universe), and the number of generations.

Output Report: (see Figure P1.10B)

Figure P1.10B   *Output Report for Programming Assignment 1.10*

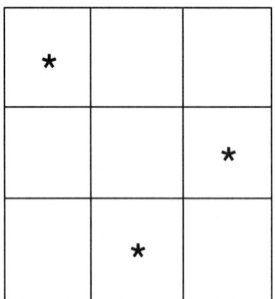

Programming Assignment 1.11: Distribution/Packaging/Shipping

Program Description

Read data from a file and generate the following distribution/packing/shipping slip for each order. The data is provided according the input record layout given in Table P1.11 on page 43.

Input: Order file

Output: (see Figure P1.11 on page 44)

Table P1.11 *Input Record Layout for Programming Assignment 1.11*

OCS Order File Layout		
Field Name	*Size*	*No of Decimal Places*
Company Name	30	
Address Line 1	30	
Address Line 2	30	
City	25	
State	2	
Zip Code	9	
Country	3	
Phone Number	13	
Invoice Number	6	
Invoice Date	6	
Ship to Name	30	
Ship to Address Line 1	30	
Ship to Address Line 2	30	
Ship to City	25	
Ship to State	2	
Ship to Zip Code	9	
Ship to Country	3	
Ship to Phone Number	13	
Customer Number	6	
Ship Via	6	
F.O.B.	6	
Terms	20	
Purchase Order Number	10	
Salesperson	15	
Order Date	6	
Sales Order	5	
Quantity Ordered	4	
Shipped Quantity	4	
Quantity Back Ordered	4	
Item Number	6	
Item Description	30	

Figure P1.11   *Output for Programming Assignment 1.11*

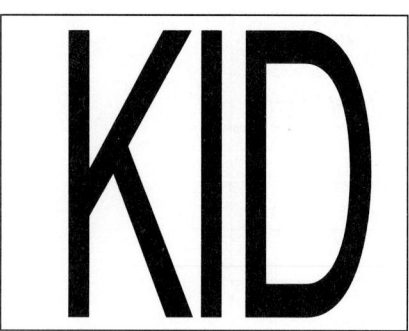

Packing Slip

Invoice 71463598
Invoice Date 12/23/00

Kiddie Litter
15800 Freemanville Road
Atlanta, GA 30033
Telephone: 404-275-2127
Fax: 404-475-5891

Ship to:

Betty Norman Otieno
Eastgate Congregation
2995 Wildhare Lane
Orange, GA 32939

Customer No	Ship via	Status	Terms	P.O. No.	Cust Rep	Order Date	Sales Order
155868	UPS Std.	OK	Net 30	BO1223981	BARB	12/19/00	13782

Order Qty.	Shipped Qty	Backorder Qty	Description			
1	1	0	4863	Dated Preschool (April-June)		
1	1	0	4893	Dated Tea, Pre-Junior (April-June)		
1	1	0	SO	<<<Small Order Fee>>>		
1	1	0	SHIP	Default Ship Method		

Page   1

Programming Assignment 1.12: Invoicing

Program Description

Read data from a file and generate the following invoicing slip for each order. The data is provided according the input record layout given in Table P1.12.

Table P1.12 *Input Record Layout for Programming Assignment 1.12*

OCS Order File Layout		
Field Name	*Size*	*No of Decimal Places*
Company Name	30	
Address Line 1	30	
Address Line 2	30	
City	25	
State	2	
Zip Code	9	
Country	3	
Phone Number	13	
Invoice Number	6	
Invoice Date	6	
Ship to Name	30	
Ship to Address Line 1	30	
Ship to Address Line 2	30	
Ship to City	25	
Ship to State	2	
Ship to Zip Code	9	
Ship to Country	3	
Ship to Phone Number	13	
Customer Number	6	
Ship Via	6	
F.O.B.	6	
Terms	20	
Purchase Order Number	10	
Salesperson	15	
Order Date	6	
Sales Order	5	
Quantity Ordered	4	
Shipped Quantity	4	
Quantity Back Ordered	4	
Item Number	6	
Item Description	30	
Discount	3	
Tax Indicator	1	
Unit Price	5	2

Input: Order file or interactively

Output: (see Figure P1.12)

Figure P1.12 *Output for Programming Assignment 1.12*

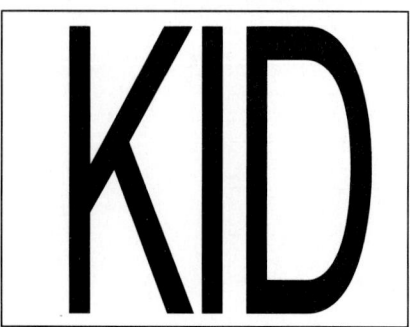

Packing Slip

Invoice 71463598
Invoice Date 12/23/00

Kiddie Litter
15800 Freemanville Road
Atlanta, GA 30033
Telephone: 404-275-2127
Fax: 404-475-5891

Bill to:

Betty Norman Otieno
Eastgate Congregation
2995 Wildhare Lane
Orange, GA 32939

Ship to:

Betty Norman Otieno
Eastgate Congregation
2995 Wildhare Lane
Orange, GA 32939

Customer No	Ship via	Status	Terms	P.O. No.	Cust Rep	Order Date	Sales Order
155868	UPS Std.	OK	Net 30	BO1223981	BARB	12/19/00	13782

Order Qty.	Shipped Qty	Backorder Qty	Description	Discount %	Tax	Unit Price	Extended Price
1	1	0	4863 Dated Preschool (April-June)		N	1.65	1.65
1	1	0	4893 Dated Tea, Pre-Junior (April-June)		N	1.85	1.85
1	1	0	SO <<<Small Order Fee>>>		N	1.00	1.00
1	1	0	SHIP Default Ship Method	100%	N	3.00	0.00

Invoices must accompany returns
Thank you for your order!

Nontaxable Subtotal	4.50
Taxable Subtotal	0.00
Tax	0.00
Total Invoice	**4.50**
Last Payment	0.00
Balance Due	**4.50**

Programming Assignments 1.13 to 1.18:
Electronic Data Interchange (EDI)

Electronic Data Interchange, commonly referred to by its acronym, EDI, is the computer-to-computer transfer of business transaction information using standard, industry-accepted message formats. Often, companies' dealings with one another involve massive amounts of data interchange. They may send each other purchase orders, invoices, requests for proposals, acknowledgments, and many other forms of transaction documentation. If there were no uniform standard for interchanging this data, companies would duplicate much of the data entry made at the other end.

The Department of Defense, for instance, deals with several hundred thousand different suppliers. With a uniform standard for data interchange, these suppliers can all simply transmit files in the agreed-on format.

Our problem will focus on the insurance claims information process. It comes from a real-life problem.

EDI Scenario Overview

An electronic claims clearinghouse is a data processing center that takes all the insurance claim information from a doctor's office or hospital, separates it by insurance carrier, and sends it electronically to the insurance carriers formatted to each carrier's specifications. Below is a sample matrix, detailing the format that claims could be received in. Each claim is terminated by an end-of-line sequence (\n).

Sample Inbound Format: (see Table P1.13A)

Table P1.13A *Sample Inbound Format for Programming Assignments 1.13 to 1.18*

Field Name	Description	Required	Positions	Length
Record ID	Always "AA0"	YES	1-3	3
Account No.	Account no of submitter	YES	4-10	7
Carrier ID	ID No of carrier to which this claim is to be sent.	YES	11-15	5
Software Brand	Name of software used to create this file.	YES	16-35	20
Software Version	Version of software named above.	YES	36-39	4
Provider ID	ID NO of billing provider	YES	40-46	7
Tax ID	Tax ID of billing provider	YES	47-55	9
Company Name	If hospital or nursing home, company name.	Conditional	56-75	20
Provider Last Name	If individual doctor, last name of doctor.	Conditional	76-90	15
Provider First Name	If individual doctor, first name of doctor.	Conditional	91-102	12
Provider Middle Ini	If individual doctor, middle initial of doctor	NO	103-103	1
Patient Last Name	Last Name of Patient	YES	104-118	15
Patient First Name	First Name of Patient	YES	119-130	12
Patient Middle Ini	Middle Initial of Patient	NO	131-131	1
Patient SSN	Social Security No of Patient	YES	132-140	9

(continues on the next page)

Table P1.13A   *(continued)*

Field Name	Description	Required	Positions	Length
Patient Date of Birth	Date patient was born. (YYYYMMDD)	YES	141-148	8
Diagnosis Code	Diagnosis of patient's condition	YES	149-153	5
Insured Last Name	Last Name of Insured	YES	154-168	15
Insured First Name	First Name of Insured	YES	169-180	12
Insured Middle Ini	Middle Initial of Insured	NO	181-181	1
Insured ID	Insured's Policy No (Must be two alpha characters followed by 7 numeric characters. ("DE3344556")	YES	182-190	9
Insured Date of Birth	Date insured was born. (YYYYMMDD)	YES	191-198	8
Patient Relation to Insured	01-Self, 02-Spouse, 03-Child.	YES	199-200	2
Claim Charge	Amount to be paid on this claim (Decimal is implied. Example $100.00 would be 0010000)	YES	201-207	7
Reserved for future use	Filler	NO	208-220	13

Below is a sample matrix, detailing the format that claims could be sent to an insurance carrier in. Each claim is exactly 180 bytes long and has no separator.

Sample Outbound Format: (see Table P1.13B)

Table P1.13B   *Sample Outbound Format for Programming Assignments 1.13 to 1.18*

Field Name	Description	Required	Positions	Length
Record ID	Always "T00"	YES	1-3	3
Provider ID	ID NO of billing provider	YES	4-10	7
Tax ID	Tax ID of billing provider	YES	11-21	9
Company Name	If hospital or nursing home, company name.	Conditional	22-41	20
Provider Last Name	If individual doctor, last name of doctor.	Conditional	42-56	15
Provider First Name	If individual doctor, first name of doctor.	Conditional	57-68	12
Provider Middle Ini	If individual doctor, middle initial of doctor	NO	69-69	1
Insured Last Name	Last Name of Insured	YES	70-84	15
Insured First Name	First Name of Insured	YES	85-96	12

Table P1.13B   *(continued)*

Field Name	Description	Required	Positions	Length
Insured Middle Ini	Middle Initial of Insured	NO	97-97	1
Insured ID	Insured's policy No (Must be two alpha characters followed by 7 numeric characters. ("DE3344556")	YES	98-106	9
Insured Date of Birth	Date insured was born. (YYYYMMDD)	YES	107-114	8
Patient Relation to Insured	01-Self, 02-Spouse, 03-Child.	YES	115-116	2
Patient Last Name	Last Name of Patient	YES	117-131	15
Patient First Name	First Name of Patient	YES	132-143	12
Patient Middle Ini	Middle Initial of Patient	NO	144-144	1
Patient SSN	Social Security No of Patient	YES	145-153	9
Patient Date of Birth	Date patient was born. (YYYYMMDD)	YES	154-161	8
Claim Charge	Amount to be paid on this claim (Decimal is implied. Example $100.00 would be 0010000)	YES	162-168	7
Reserved for future use	Filler	NO	169-180	12

Programming Assignment 1.13: EDI

Write a program that parses data from the sample inbound file above and produces a report of fields and data in each field.

Programming Assignment 1.14: EDI

Write a program that parses data from the sample outbound file above and produces a report of fields and data in each field.

Programming Assignment 1.15: EDI

Write a program that does limited data validation.

- Check for blank fields in fields that require data.
- Make sure patient relation to insured is one of the designated values.
- Make sure Insured ID follows the prescribed format: two alpha characters followed by seven numeric characters.
- Make sure the dates are valid dates.

Programming Assignment 1.16: EDI

Write a program that creates a report of accepted/rejected claims for submitter.

Programming Assignment 1.17: EDI

Write a program that separates accepted claims by carrier ID.

Programming Assignment 1.18: EDI

Write a program that reformats claims from inbound format to outbound format.

Programming Assignment 1.19: Inventory

Program Description

Write a program that reads the inventory file and produces three complete inventory reports. The program is to validate the data read according to the validation criteria listed below and produce the three reports specified below. In addition, track the number of entries for each manufacturer.

Validation Criteria

- The part number must be between 0 and 2500, exclusively.
- The manufacturer ID is between 10 and 21, exclusively.
- Get the manufacturer's name from the table based on the ID read in.

Reports

- A list of all inventory items with the invalid ones tagged as INVALID
- A list of all valid inventory items
- A list of all the invalid inventory items
- A report tallying all the part numbers from each manufacturer

The input record layout is shown in Table P1.19

Table P1.19 *Input Record Layout for Programming Assignment 1.19*

OCS Inventory File		
Field Name	*Size in Bytes*	*No of Decimal Places*
Part Number	4	
Manufacturer ID #	2	
Manufacturer Name	25	
Description	50	
Quantity on Hand	4	
Quantity on Order	4	
Date Ordered	6	
Expected Delivery Date	6	

```
Valid Manufacturer ID table:
11      Specific Motors
12      Chevrolb
13      Mazduh
14      Fired
15      Jupiter
16      Honduh
17      Adams
18      Volkscart
19      Limburger
20      Nissoff
```

The report should look like Figure P1.19.

Figure P1.19 *Report for Programming Assignment 1.19*

```
Part Number    Man ID   Manufacturer      Description    Qty
-----------------------------------------------------------------
7285           11       Specific Motors   Brake Pad      152
3207           14       Fired             Rear vw mir    9
4114           17       Adams             Tralr Htch     3
3229           14       Fired             Gas Cap        21
2341           21       INVALID           *******
```

Programming Assignment 1.20: General Category (Programa Pro Rata)

Program Description

You have a flat tire and it must be replaced, but all is not lost—the tire is unconditionally guaranteed (on a pro rata basis). You are to write a program that calculates the cost of replacing the tire. The cost is based on the percentage of the tread used (the amount of tread worn away divided by the tread depth when the tire was new), times the price of a new tire, plus a charge for mounting and balancing plus state tax. Your program is to read five values from standard input representing

- the tread depth now (e.g., 3mm).
- the tread depth when the tire was new (e.g., 9mm).
- the price of a new tire (e.g., $21.00).
- the mounting and balancing charge (e.g., $2.50).
- the state tax rate (program useful in any state) (e.g., 4%).

Your program must print out this data immediately after reading it so that you can be sure the proper values were read. It should then compute and print the total cost of replacing the tire.

Here is an example. If the tread depth now is 3 mm and the tread depth of the tire when new was 9 mm, then 6 mm of the tread has been used, so I must pay 6/9 = 0.67 or 67% of the cost of the new tire. Say the new tire costs $21.00 (a Kmart special), mounting and balancing are $2.50, and the state tax is 4%. Then my total cost is $17.16, as Figure P1.20 shows.

Figure P1.20 *Calculation of Total Cost for Programming Assignment 1.20*

```
  6 / 9 = 0.67
                      21.00      cost of new tire
                    x  0.67      percentage of tread used
                    _____
                      14.00      cost based on percentage
                    x  2.50      mounting and balancing charge
                    _____
          16.5        16.50      subtotal
        x  0.04        0.66      state tax
        _____
           0.66       17.16      total cost
```

Programming Assignment 1.21: General Category (Nation's Economy)

Program Description

One of the benefits gained from a disastrous peanut crop in recent years was the realization by some of the nation's leading economists that the cost of a peanut butter and jelly sandwich is an excellent indicator of the consumer'splight. Your assignment is to write a program that could be used to monitor the fluctuations in this crucial indicator. Assume that the national standard peanut butter and jelly sandwich uses the following amounts of ingredients:

- Peanut butter   0.8 ounce
- Jelly   0.3 ounce
- Bread   1.6 ounces (two slices)

Using this information, your program should

1. Read in data, which give weight and cost of a jar of peanut butter, a jar of jelly, and a loaf of bread. You should set up your data file so that it has three lines, each containing the weight and cost. Be sure to "echo-check" the data as it reads.
2. Compute the cost of
   a. Peanut butter per sandwich
   b. Jelly per sandwich
   c. Bread per sandwich
   d. The whole sandwich
3. Write out (labeled) each of the costs computed in (2) above.

You may test your program with any data you wish, but for the sake of convenience in grading, please hand in a test of the program against the following data:

1. A 40-ounce jar of peanut butter costs $4.59.
2. A 32-ounce jar of jelly costs $0.89.
3. A 24-ounce loaf of bread costs $0.71.

Programming Assignment 1.22: General Category (Police Department)

Program Description

The Snellville Police Department has accumulated information on speeding violations over a period of time. The department has now divided the town into four zones and wishes to have statistics on speeding violations by zone. For each violation an entry is made in a data file containing the following information:

- Vehicle registration number (eight-digit code)
- Driver's social security code (nine-digit code)
- Zone in which offense occurred (1–4)
- Speed limit in miles per hour (integer)
- Actual speed recorded in mph (integer)

Write a program to produce two reports. First, give a listing of speeding fines collected, where the fine is calculated as the sum of court costs ($35.00) plus $1.25 for every mile per hour by which the speed limit was exceeded. This listing should be in the form of a table with the following headings:

Speed Violations

Vehicle Registration	Driver's SS#	Speed Recorded	Speed Limit	Zone	Fine Charged

This table is to be followed by a second table in which an analysis of violations by zone is given. For each of the four zones, give the number of violations processed and the average fine. The headings for this second table should be as follows:

Analysis of Violations by Zone

Zone	Number of Violations	Average Fine

Test your program on the list of traffic violations given Table P1.22.

Table P1.22 *List of Traffic Violations for Programming Assignment 1.22*

Vehicle Registration	Driver's SS#	Zone	Speed Recorded	Speed Limit
45631288	489376281	2	34	25
83792910	362917490	2	48	35
87378264	284940083	1	73	55
48433782	205849437	4	80	55
91999237	583889239	4	62	45

Programming Assignment 1.23: Science and Engineering (Numerical Palindrome)

Program Description

A palindrome is the same text reading backward and forward: "a man, a plan, a canal, Panama." A numerical palindrome is a number that is the same forward and backward. One can create a numerical palindrome by following a simple algorithm:

- Start by taking a number.
- If the number is not a palindrome, reverse the number and add the number to its reversal.
- Repeat the preceding step until you get your palindrome.

For example, the number 101 is a palindrome but 561 is not. Let's apply the above algorithm to the 561 number. Here are the steps:

Step 1: Reverse the number and add: 165 + 561 = 726. However, 726 is not a palindrome.
Step 2: Reverse the new number and add the reversal of the new number to the new number:
627 + 726 = 1353. But 1353 is also not a palindrome.
Step 3: Reverse the new number and add the reversal of the new number:
3531 + 1353 = 4884. Success! It took us three repetitions to produce a palindrome—4884—with this algorithm.

Write a program that reads a positive number, produces a palindrome, and prints the number of reversals required.

Programming Assignment 1.24: General Category (Character Observation)

Program Description

Write a C program that reads in a series of records and computes the frequency of all the characters in the character set. The program should read in data until the end of file is reached and produce as output the following report:

```
Character   Count   Percentage
    U        9999     999.99
    +        9999     999.99
    a        9999     999.99
    A        9999     999.99
Totals       9999     999.99
```

Programming Assignment 1.25: Science and Engineering (Ackerman's Function)

Program Description

Ackerman's function $A(m,n)$ is defined as follows:

$$A(m,n) = \begin{cases} n+1, \text{ if } m = 0 \\ A(m-1,1), \text{ if } n = 0 \\ A(m-1, A(m,n-1)), \text{ otherwise} \end{cases}$$

Write a C program to evaluate this function and print out the result. Test your program on $A(3,2)$.

Programming Assignment 1.26: Science and Engineering (Binomial Coefficients)

Program Description

Binomial coefficients are common in mathematics. They are defined as

$$\left(\frac{n}{m}\right) = \frac{n!}{m!\,(n-m)!}$$

Where

$$n! = 1 * 2 * 3 * \ldots * (n-1) * n \text{ or}$$
$$n! = n * (n-1) * (n-2) * (n-3) * \ldots * 2 * 1$$

binomial coefficients can be computed by using the following relation:

$$\left(\frac{n}{m}\right) = \left(\frac{n-1}{m}\right) + \left(\frac{n-1}{m-1}\right)$$

Write a C program to evaluate the binomial coefficients.

Programming Assignment 1.27: Electronics (ZEI)

Program Description

As an engineer at Zindar Engineering Inc. (ZEI), you have received an order to write code for a microprocessor that will process commands it receives. You will have to write C functions that interpret the commands and react accordingly. There will be many of these processors with the same code in them running at once, so each processor will have its own address, which starts out as 0. Because the processor used is one of the widely available 8-bit processors, the largest variable type you can use is a char (signed or unsigned).

The processor will have two primary functions. The first is to store and retrieve data sent to it. The second is to use LEDs to indicate the status of the processor. Each processor will be able to store ten 1-byte values in its memory. The values will be assigned and retrieved in response to the commands shown below. There will be four LEDs that will be turned off and on in response to the commands, as shown below.

Commands will be received as 2 bytes (referred to as a *word*). For the processor to react to a command, the first byte must be equal to the address of the processor. After a processor determines a command is meant for it, the command byte will be decoded. The first 4 bits (referred to as the *most significant nibble* or *MSN*) will contain the command code. The second nibble (*least significant nibble* or *LSN*) will contain any additional data required. Table P1.27A shows what the second byte of each command looks like.

Table P1.27A   *Second-Byte Command Table for Programming Assignment 1.27*

MSN	Hex	Function Description	Auxiliary Data Use (LSN)
0001	1	Reply with Address	None
0010	2	Reply with Address + LED status	None
0011	3	Reply with data #x	Specify data number (0–9)
0100	4	Turn off LED x	Specify LED (flag style)
0101	5	Turn on LED x	Specify LED (flag style)
0110	6	Toggle LED x	Specify LED (flag style)
0111	7		
1000	8	Clear data #x	Specify data number (0–9)
1001	9	Store low-order nibble	Provide low-nibble value
1010	A	Store high-order nibble	Provide high-nibble value
1011	B	Locate low-order nibble	Provide low-order nibble to find
1100	C	Locate high-order nibble	Provide low-order nibble to find
1101	D		
1110	E	Increment address by x	Specify value to add to address
1111	F	Decrement address by x	Specify value to subtract from address

Responses

Any commands that require a response (0001,0010,0011,1100) will generate an output. The output will be 2 bytes. The first byte will always be the address of the processor; the second will be the requested data.

Response Table: (see Table P1.27B)

Table P1.27B   *Response Table for Programming Assignment 1.27*

Command	2nd Byte of Response
0001	Blank (zeros)
0010	1st nibble = 0, 2nd nibble = LED states
0011	Data held in element requested
1100	Element number where data matches

Data Commands

When data is stored, it is stored in the next available element in the memory array (10 available locations) starting with index 0 and going to index 9. If data is stored after the array is full, the value is stored in 9 and all the other values are shifted, so that the value that was in 0 is now lost.

The store low-order nibble will always come first and will always be followed by a store high-order nibble. The high-order nibble must be multiplied by 16, then added to the low-order nibble to get the whole value to be stored. For example, the result of the following two commands is to store decimal 35 (0010 0011) in the next available memory location:

```
{Address}   0101 0011   Stores the low-order value of 0011 (decimal 3)
{Address}   0110 0010   Stores the high-order value of 0010 (decimal 2)
```

where address is the address of the processor to execute the commands.

A search command is similar to a store command, except that the values are kept in a temporary location, not in the data array. Once the high nibble is received, the processor should search its array to see if the value specified by the search data matches any of the array elements. If it does, the index of the first element to match should be sent in a reply message.

Reminder: Clear any temporary values used to store or calculate the separate nibbles.

LED Commands

The LEDs are accessed by writing their state (1 = on; 0 = off) to a specific memory location. For the sake of this exercise, you can just use pointer to a char variable. Each LED is represented by a bit within that variable. To manipulate any one LED, you must use bit operations. When changing the state of one LED, be careful not to alter the state of the other LEDs. Table P1.27C shows how each LED can be accessed. Commands can have more than one bit, indicating the operation should be carried out on more than one LED. The following commands would turn on LED-3, then request the state of the LEDs. The response is shown in bold.

```
{Address}   0101 0100   Turns on LED-3
{Address}   0010 0000   Request state of LEDs

{Address}   0000 0100   All LEDs off except LED-3
```

where address is the address of the processor to execute the commands.

Table P1.27C   *LED Access Command Table for Programming Assignment 1.27*

LED Number	Bit Number	Hex Value
LED-0	0	1
LED-1	1	2
LED-3	3	4
LED-4	4	8

Test Program

What you must do now is write a test program for a PC that will allow a user to manually type in the codes of the commands they wish to issue. For the test program, the computer will be the only processor running, but it still needs to store and update its address as commanded. The user should be able to select binary or hex. The transactions shown below provide an example of a test session:

```
ZEI processor testing software
bxxxxxxxxxxxxxxxx (16 bits) for binary input
hxxxx (4 nibbles) for hexadecimal input
spaces are ignored
```

```
Enter your command >h 00 20
                              response: h0000
Enter your command >b 00000000 00100000
                              response: b0000000000000000
Enter your command >h 00 E5
                              response:
Enter your command >h 00 20
                              response:
Enter your command >h 05 20
                              response: h0500
Enter your command >h 05 54
                              response:
Enter your command >h 05 20
                              response: h0504
Enter your command >h 05 93
                              response:
Enter your command >h 05 A2
                              response:
Enter your command >h 05 30
                              response: h0523
Enter your command >Q
                    ----PROGRAM TERMINATED----
```

CHAPTER 2

Using Variables

OBJECTIVES

- To understand the basic data types and their composition and range
- To learn C's keywords
- To understand memory reservation for variables
- To learn the syntax of variable declaration, initialization, and assignment
- To learn the difference between variables and constants and between floating point numbers and integers

- To become familiar with the concepts of octal, hexadecimal, and binary number representation
- To understand how computers handle characters and what character encoding is

NEW TERMS

arithmetic type	floating point type	signed type
assignment statement	hexadecimal notation	significand
binary notation	initialization	statement
case sensitive	integer type	unsigned type
constant	keyword	variable
declaration	octal notation	

A ***variable*** represents a specific location in the computer's random access memory or RAM. A variable's value is stored at that location. Variables are the nuts and bolts of the program. The program creates variables, assigns them values, and then changes the values according to a set of instructions. For example, in add.c in Chapter 1, we created three variables, assigned values to two of them by user input, added those values, and stored the sum in the third variable.

The values that get stored into the variables are called ***constants.*** Constants, in general, are no different from the numbers you've seen since early grammar school: 28, 188, 23.75, and so on. In later chapters, you will learn

- how to make variables *act* like constants, in that the initially assigned values cannot be changed during the life of the program.
- how to use manifest constants—names that *look* like variables, but that are removed by the computer before program execution and replaced with the constants they represent.
- how to create string constants—constants ostensibly made up of letters instead of numbers.

But for now, when we talk about constants, we just mean garden variety numbers.

Variables have both names and types. For each variable name, the computer assigns a *location*—also called an *address*—in RAM. To the computer, the variable's name *is* its address. When we compile our source code, the variables we create by name are transformed into mere instructions to reserve nameless memory locations. In add.c in the last chapter, our instructions get translated into something like the following: reserve three memory locations; place values into locations 1 and 2; place the sum of the values stored in location 1 and location 2 into location 3.

The type tells the computer how to store the value of a variable at its assigned address and how much space to reserve starting at that address. We reserve a memory location in the first place by ***declaration*** of a variable type and name.

2.1   VARIABLE NAMES

You are somewhat more limited in what characters you can use for variable names than for source code file names. Variables names can contain any letter of the alphabet (either uppercase or lowercase), the underscore character, and the digits 0 to 9. The first character cannot be a digit.

Here are some good and bad examples of variable names. Each is preceded by a type designation, which we'll explain shortly.

```
int tuition; /* ok */
long john_silver; /* ok */
long night2; /* ok */
short 1night_stand; /* illegal: first character digit */
short money$; /* illegal character $ */
short long: /* illegal: keyword */
long distance call; /* illegal: space character */
unsigned prenuptial-agreement; /* illegal character - */
int _score; /* ok, but bad idea */
```

 The last example, _score, is a legal but risky variable name. *Your C library often uses variables that have an underscore as the first character. If you avoid this usage, you don't run the risk of a conflict between a system variable and your own.*

2.1.1   Case Sensitivity and Significant Characters

 C variables are case sensitive.

When we say that variables in C are ***case sensitive,*** we mean, for instance, that the variables Total, TOTAL, and total will be read by C as three completely different variables. That is, they will be assigned three separate memory locations—if you are silly enough to use all of them in one program. Most C programmers use all lowercase letters for variables and all uppercase letters for manifest constants (constants masquerading as variables; see Chapter 11). Some C programmers have adopted the programming style of initial caps for the start of each separate internal word in a variable name:

```
long wayHome;
```

Often programmers capitalize the very first letter of global variables. Basically, local variables are those declared within a function or smaller block, whereas global variables are those declared outside any function. (See Chapter 10 for a more complete explanation of the difference and its significance.)

Standard C requires compilers to recognize at least the first 31 characters of a variable name in distinguishing among local variables and at least the first 6 in distinguishing among global variables. Standard C allows the compiler to ignore case in distinguishing among global variables—an exception to the case sensitivity rule stated above.

These limits, particularly the rather stingy one for global variables, were adopted as part of Standard C as a nod to older compilers that are far more restrictive than more modern ones. Many compilers recognize more than the minimum number of characters, especially as to the miserly global variable character number, and most recognize uppercase letters in a name as different from uppercase with respect to global variables. However, for maximum portability, it is best not to depend on more. You may use more than this minimum number of characters for a variable name, but the compiler may ignore characters beyond the minimum number. For instance, if two local variable names of 40 letters each have the same first 31 characters but differ past that point, the compiler is permitted to treat them as the same variable.

In general, longer variable names, with words separated by underscores or with capital letters at the beginning of each word, are more readable than short cryptic ones.

```
int MinHrsPerWeek /* descriptive */
int mxhw, mnhw; /* cryptic */
```

The 31-character minimum should give you plenty of leg room for a descriptive variable name.

2.1.2   Keywords

Certain words are *keywords,* reserved by C. You may not use them as variable names. C's keywords are listed in Table 2.1. We will discuss all these terms in the course of this book. (Note that the pointer modifiers are PC specific; they are not part of Standard C.)

Table 2.1   *Keywords*

Category	Keyword
Scope	auto
	const
	extern
	static
Type Qualifiers	register
	volatile
Flow	break
	case
	continue
	default
	do
	else
	for
	goto
	if
	return
	while
Defined Types	char
	double
	float
	int
	long
	short
	signed
	unsigned
	void
Derived Types	enum
	struct
	union
Pointer Modifiers	far
	huge
	near
Miscellaneous	sizeof
	typedef

You can, if you wish, however, use keywords as *part* of a variable name:

```
int union; /* illegal */
int unionDues; /* OK */
```

2.2   VARIABLE TYPES

C uses a different method and different amounts of memory to store different types of data. ***Arithmetic types*** are grouped into two major categories: ***integer types*** and ***floating point types.*** (The third category of arithmetic types is enum. These three arithmetic types plus pointer types are called *scalar variable types.* See Chapter 13 for a more complete discussion of these and the other type categories and Chapter 7 for a discussion of pointers.)

Integer types are for whole numbers, whereas floating point types house numbers that can have a fractional component. Within those two major categories are the following subcategories shown in Figure 2.1.

Standard C gives you alternative ways of writing the same integer types. You can use the keyword signed in place of signed int and the keyword unsigned instead of unsigned int. You can, and generally would, also use short instead of short int and long in place of long int.

As you can see, each integer type comes in two flavors, signed and unsigned. Types that are signed can accommodate negative values; unsigned cannot. There is no such differentiation for floating point types. Each of the three floating point types can hold both negative and positive values.

The default for all int types (short int, int, and long int) is signed, so if you declare a short, int, or long without more, it will be signed, exactly as though you had written the alternative respective formulations signed short, signed int, or signed long. To make any of these unsigned, you have to place the word unsigned before short or int or long.

The default for char is implementation specific. Implementations are permitted to treat char in one of three ways: as a signed char, as an unsigned char, or as a mixture. The hybrid char can hold only positive values, but for purposes of automatic conversions (for example, when assigning the value of a char to a variable of another type; see Chapter 13), it is deemed a signed char. Some compilers, such as Borland C, permit the programmer to elect either signed char or unsigned char as the default for char.

In light of the foregoing, all of the type names on the same line in Table 2.2 are identical types.

Figure 2.1   *Integer and Floating Point Types*

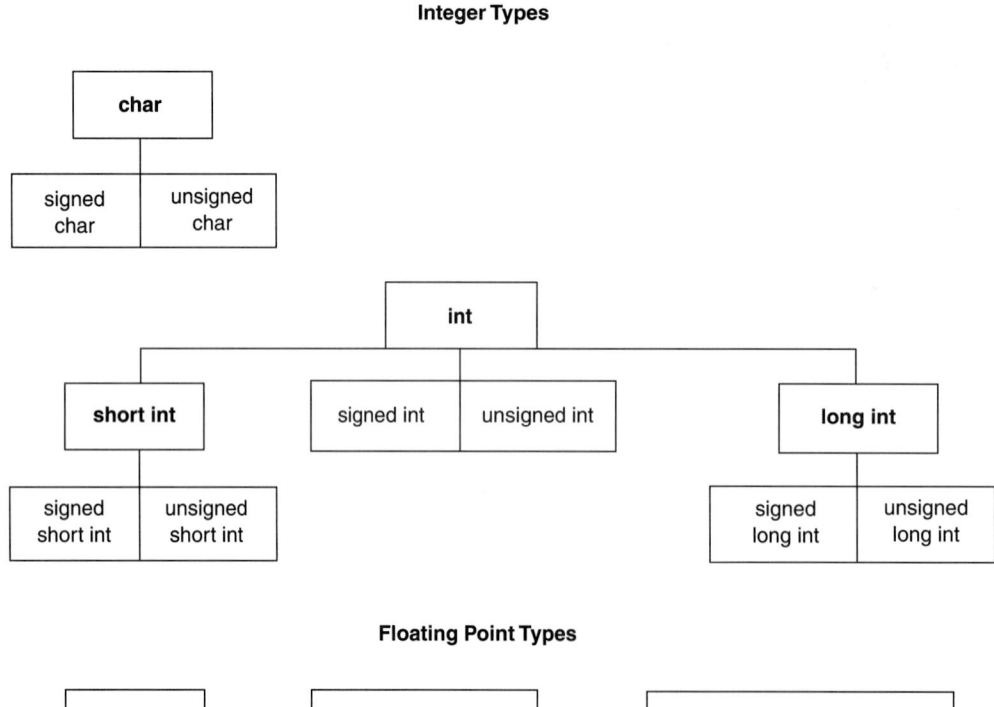

Table 2.2 *Identical Type Declarations*

signed short int	signed short	short int	short
unsigned short int	unsigned short		
signed int	signed	int	
unsigned int	unsigned		
signed long int	signed long	long int	long
unsigned long int	unsigned long		

2.3 BITS AND BYTES

Imagine that your computer's primary memory is a somewhat unusual type of real estate development. It consists of an extremely long row of at least a million buildings, all on one side of a very, very long street. The address of the first lot is 0, that of the next is 1, that of the one after that is 2, and so on. Some of the lots have homes on them; the others have commercial buildings.

Now, the people who own buildings in this development can name their buildings: "Billie Bob Restaurant," "Red-Roof Georgian," and the like. And their friends and clients can send them mail addressed to those descriptive names, but before the post office gives the mail to the mail carriers, it erases the descriptive name and writes the house number in its place.

Building owners are entitled to use more than one lot for a building. Residential owners can have a single-plot building, a duplex, or a quadraplex; commercial owners' buildings can cover four, eight, or ten lots. In all cases, the address the post office writes in for a multilot building is the address of the lowest lot number the building is on.

On the computer, each of these lots is called a *byte*. Each byte has its own address in the computer's memory, just as each lot has its own address in the post office's book. On a particular computer system, each of the variable types has a designated number of bytes. Standard C does not specify the number of bytes for each type, but it does lay down certain rules. For integer types, a char must be a single byte, an int must have at least as many bytes as a short, and a long must have at least as many bytes as an int. On a PC, both a short and an int have 2 bytes and a long has 4. On many other systems, a short is 2 bytes and an int is 4 bytes. On a PC, therefore, there is no difference in the number of bytes and range of values between a short and an int; on other systems, there may be. Whatever the variable's type, its address in RAM is considered the address of the first byte it occupies.

Actually, by specifying minimums for ranges, detailed in the next section, Standard C does in effect specify minimum byte sizes. Since an unsigned short and an unsigned int must be able to hold at least 65,535 and an unsigned long must be able to hold at least 4,294,967,295, it follows from the rules discussed in Chapter 12 that a short and an int must have at least 2 bytes and a long must have at least 4 bytes—assuming, as is nearly always the case for all computer types, that a byte has 8 bits.

There are no byte-size rules for floating point types, but the programmer can assume the same sort of arrangement, namely, that a double will be at least as big as a float, and a long double will be at least as big as a double. On a PC, a float has 4 bytes, a long has 8 bytes, and a long double has 10 bytes.

2.3.1 The Value of Bits

Even though a floating point variable may take up the same number of bytes as an integer variable (say, a long and a float on a PC), they are as different as a sprawling ranch house and a skyscraper on the same four lots. A long is a comparatively simple affair; a float is not.

Each byte is made up of bits. On the PC and most other computer systems, a byte has 8 bits. However, on a *very* small number of computers, there are 7 or 9 bits, or even some other number. No matter which variable type we're talking about, each of these bits can have a value of only 0 or 1.

The way the bytes' group of bits is interpreted to determine the variable's value for integer variables is much different from the interpretation scheme for floating point variables. The method also differs slightly among integer variable types depending on whether the variable is a *signed type* (one that can have positive or negative integer values) that happens to be given a negative value on the one hand, or whether it is either an *unsigned type* (one that can hold only positive values) or a signed type that happens to have a positive number on the other hand. The precise method of determining value from the respective bits' values for different types is covered in detail in Chapter 12. Once you read that chapter, you will have a better understanding of Table 2.3, showing the smallest and largest possible values for the respective types (a negative number with a larger absolute value is considered smaller than one with a smaller absolute value; –99 is smaller than –3).

What Standard C means by "minimum" in the context of lowest and highest values can be clarified as follows. An int must have a lowest possible value of at least –32,767. Its actual lowest value can be *lower* than that. For instance, on a two's complement system, as explained in Chapter 12, its lowest possible value will be –32,768. On a machine that uses two's complement and has a 4-byte int, its lowest possible value will be –2,147,483,648. But its lowest possible value has to be *at least* as low as –32,767. Likewise, an int must have a highest possible value of at least 32,767. Its actual highest possible value can be a *higher* value than that (for example, it will be 4,294,967,295 if it has 4 bytes), but its highest possible value has to be at least that high.

2.3.2   Floating Point Format and Range

In C, very large or very small floating point constants are commonly expressed in the source code in exponential notation: the values are represented as a floating point number of between 1 and 10, raised to an integral power of 10. The method is the same as the scientific notation commonly used in scientific or engineering applications, but the syntax is slightly different. For example:

```
Decimal                   Exponential    Scientific
Notation                  Notation       Notation

3,200,000,000,000.00      3.2e15         3.2 x 10^15
            0.0000724     7.24e-5        7.24 x 10^-5
```

(Do not confuse e here, which stands for exponent of 10, with e, the base of natural logarithms—a number with a value of approximately 2.718.) You can use either the decimal notation or the exponential notation for floating point constants. See Section 2.7 for the format rules for decimal and exponential notation in C.

Table 2.3   *Range for Integer Types: Standard C Minimums and PC Range*

Type	Standard C Minimums	Range
signed char	–127 to 127	–128 to 127
unsigned char	0 to 255	0 to 255
signed short	–32,767 to 32,767	–32,768 to 32,767
unsigned short	0 to 65,535	0 to 65,535
signed int	–32,767 to 32,767	–32,768 to 32,767
unsigned int	0 to 65,535	0 to 65,535
signed long	–2,147,483,647 to 2,147,483,647	–2,147,483,648 to 2,147,483,647
unsigned long	0 to 4,294,967,295	0 to 4,294,967,295

Table 2.4 *Required Standard C Minimum and Typical Floating Point Values*

Type	# Decimal Digits Precision		Number of Bytes		Standard C Minimum Range		PC System Range	
	C Min	PC	C Min	PC	Smallest Positive	Largest Positive	Smallest Positive	Largest Positive
float	6	6	none	4	e^{-37}	e^{37}	$1.17549e^{-38}$	$3.40282e^{38}$
double	10	15	none	8	e^{-37}	e^{37}	$2.22507e^{-308}$	$1.79769e^{308}$
long double	10	19	none	10	e^{-37}	e^{37}	$3.36210e^{-4932}$	$1.18973e^{4932}$

Table 2.4 for floating point numbers includes not only a range for each of the three types, but also the number of digits of precision. The floating point types have an enormous range, but within that range if a value has more than a certain number of digits, the ones past the type's precision get lost in the shuffle. So, for instance, if you try to store 0.123456789 into a `float`, you may get only 0.123457.

Note that the C Standard does not guarantee that a `long double` will have greater precision than a `double`, nor is `double` or even `long double` guaranteed to have a greater range than `float`.

The ranges for negative values are the same as for positive values. For example, a `float` has a range from $-1.17549e^{-38}$ to $-3.40282e^{38}$ as well as from $1.17549e^{-38}$ to $3.40282e^{38}$.

2.4   LETTERS AND OTHER NUMBERS

So much for numbers. What about letters and other characters such as + or – or #? Well, they really do not exist as such. What the computer does is take a value stored as an integer and treat that value as a certain character according to a predetermined encoding system. Each number from 0 to 255 (the largest integer we can represent with a single byte of 8 bits) corresponds to a designated letter or character.

The two most common encoding systems are the American Standards Code for Information Interchange (ASCII), used by the PC and most minicomputers, and Extended Binary-Coded Decimal Interchange Code (EBCDIC), used chiefly by mainframes. There is also Baudot Code, used in telecommunications. The complete listing of which characters correspond to which numbers under ASCII and EBCDIC is found in Appendix F.

The standard ASCII character set contains 128 characters, with corresponding values between 0 and 127. IBM-compatible PCs also support an extension of the ASCII character set to values between 128 and 255. Appendix F includes this extension. It also contains printed characters assigned by IBM to the nonprinting control characters (those with values between 0 and 31). Some of these characters will show up on the computer screen if they are sent there. On a printer, those characters may cause certain actions to be taken (for example, on a PC, sending a character with a value of 12 to the screen will cause ♀ to appear; sending this formfeed character to the printer will cause it to eject the current page).

What this means is that to the computer, there really is no such thing as a character. A character is simply a numerical value that we can direct the computer to print to the screen or the printer as though it were a character.

ASCII assigns capital letters of the alphabet to the numbers starting just after 64 (bit 6 on) and lowercase letters to the numbers starting just after 96 (bits 5 and 6 on). When we have the number 65, we can direct the computer to *depict* it as 65 or as A. The character representation of the digits 0 to 9 is ASCII 48 to 57. Be careful not to confuse this character depiction—for the screen, printer, or file—of the numbers with the numerical values themselves. The character 1 is the value 49, not the value 1.

2.4.1   Character Assassination

We have called Section 2.4 "Letters and Other Numbers" to emphasize the difference between the way people view letters and numbers and the way the computer does. Whether a variable should be declared as int or char should depend on storage requirements and the probable value range of the variable rather than on whether the data represents numbers or letters. Thus, if a variable represents the number of days in a particular month or the number of columns on a video monitor, char will do fine even though we are dealing with a number. Using int would just waste storage space. *You can profitably use* char *to store data representing numerical values as such where saving memory is a consideration.* In Chapter 13, we will show you how you can even store values in individual bits or groups of bits called *bit fields*.

Conversely, storage requirements may dictate type. If we are printing a character with a corresponding numerical value beyond 127—say, drawing a box using +) , * . and – (ASCII 218, 196, 191, 179, 192 and 217; see Appendix F)—we need to select int or unsigned char. A signed char could not fit those numbers.

 On the other hand, *in programs of modest size, where memory size is not a consideration, it may make more sense to use* int *even for small numbers.* That way, you will avoid confusing an outsider who looks at your program and associates char with characters only and int with integer numbers only—a not-astonishing semantic connection. Also, you may find using char to store small integer numbers a nuisance when you use a programming device called the *debugger* to find errors in your program. When you ask the debugger to give you the value of a char, it gives you the character equivalent of the number. Thus, it will tell you that your screen column width variable now has a value of P (assuming ASCII notation) rather than 80. Though you can use a trick to make the debugger show the numerical value, there's an extra step involved. For those reasons and because most programmers are in the habit of "char = character" and "int = number," throughout this book we will generally use char for characters and int for numbers even if we expect the numbers to be small values.

2.5   VARIABLE DECLARATION STATEMENTS

A *statement* is a complete instruction to the computer.

 In C, statements are terminated by semicolons.

As you see from Figure 1.20, there are different kinds of statements: variable declaration statements, function statements, complex data type declaration statements, assignment statements, and control statements. In this chapter, we will discuss only variable declaration statements and assignment statements.

A cardinal rule of C is

 You cannot use a variable before you have declared it.

Variable declaration statements assign a name and type to one or more variables. To the computer, assigning a name means allocating a specific memory location to the variable. Each address corresponds to a single byte in memory. The variable type portion of the declaration tells the computer how many bytes to reserve starting at that address. Here are examples of declaration statements:

```
int num;
char ch;
float production;
float hours;
float downtime;
```

You can make multiple declarations of the same variable type in one statement as long as you separate the variable names by commas. The type keyword is not repeated. The following statement is equivalent to the last three statements in the preceding example:

```
float salary, hours, downtime;
```

You can also assign a value to a variable at the time you declare it:

```
int i = 0;
```

This combination declaration and assignment is sometimes referred to as ***initialization.***

Just as you can make multiple declarations of the same type variable in one statement, you can combine more than one initialization in one statement. Again, they must be separated by commas:

```
char small = 'a', uc = 'A', num = '1';
```

In fact, you can combine nonassigning declarations with initializations in the same statement:

```
int horses, cows = 3; /* sloppy practice */
```

 Combining nonassigning declarations with initializations in the same statement is sloppy practice, however. It is too easy to misread this statement as assigning 3 to both horses and cows. At the other extreme, some programmers insist on a separate statement for each variable declaration:

```
int a;
int b;
int c;
int d;
```

 This practice tends to make the hard copy of the source code rather long. However, *a separate declaration statement for each variable is justified if a comment needs to be inserted to explain just what purpose the variable serves in the course of a program.*

```
float totRegHrs; /* # of nonovertime hrs worked by
                    clerical shift in current month */
```

 A sound middle ground: *declaration statements should group like sets of variables.* Take the following example, some of which includes forms we won't cover until later chapters:

```
int a, b, num; /* simple declaration of ints */
int c = 0, d = 3, e = 4; /* initialization of ints */
int *p1, *p2; /* simple declaration of pointers to int */
int hours[5], salary[5]; /* simple declaration of array of ints */
int customers[3] = {15, 2, 25}; /* initialization of
                                   array of ints */
```

We could have made all those declarations in a single declaration statement, using the keyword int only once. However, grouping the variables in separate statements is much clearer.

You can generally use a variable that has already been assigned and declared in an initialization statement as part of the initialization of another variable:

```
int num = 4;
int val = num + 2; /* permissible usage */
```

However, all assigning values in an initialization must be constants where the variable they are assigned to is one of static duration (see Chapter 10) or an array, structure, or union variable (see Chapters 6 and 13).

 All declaration statements must precede any nondeclaration statements within the same function.

```
int num;
num = 7;
int val = 3; /* error! */
```

2.6   ASSIGNMENT STATEMENTS

Assignment statements are the working part of the program. In assignment statements, values are stored in the locations reserved for variables.

 The left side of the assignment statement must be a single variable.

```
int width;
width = 12; /* OK */
length + 13 = 5; /* error! */
```

Except for the types of initializations where only constants may be used, listed above, what's assigned to a variable—what goes on the right side of the assignment statement—can be any combination of variables and constants (and, as you will see when we get to functions in Chapter 8, even function calls' return values):

```
totHours = (52 * hours * days) - (sickDays * 5);
salary = 12 * totHours;
```

However, what's assigned is evaluated to a single numerical value before anything is placed in memory at the address corresponding to the variable name.

The variable you're assigning a value to can appear on both sides of the assignment statement:

```
int hours = 4;
hours = hours + 3;
```

This device is quite common. Initially, hours has a value of 4; after the second statement, it has a value of 7. Remember, this is an assignment statement, not an algebraic equation where both sides must be equal. In C, the = is an assignment operator, not an equal sign.

2.7   ASSIGNING CONSTANTS—FLOATING POINT

 When assigning constants to floating point variables, you must use a decimal point, even if the number you're assigning is an integer.

```
double dutch = 333.25;
double team = 6./9.;
double mint = 0.003478;
double take = .0375;
```

Your failure to include a decimal point in assigning an integer value to a floating point variable may result in an erroneous calculation. For instance, omitting the decimal points in the team example above would incorrectly produce a value of zero. (See Chapter 13 for the reason that is so.) You will not be warned or given an error message—just erroneous results. Thanks for nothing.

There is one exception to the rule that a decimal point must be included in assigning a value to a floating point variable. If you use exponential format, no decimal point is required in the part that precedes the exponent portion.

The part of the constant other than any exponent portion is sometimes referred to as the *significand* part. Within the significand part, the parts are sometimes referred to as the *whole-number* part and the *fractional* part.

2.7.1   Exponential Format

You may also use the exponential format in assigning floating point values, even if the numbers are not particularly small or large.

```
double orNothing = 2.3e29;
double trouble = -3.172e3;
```

You may not, however, use octal or hexadecimal notation (see Section 2.8.1) in assigning floating point numbers.

In the exponential format, you may use uppercase E instead of lowercase e:

```
float sunMiles = 93.e6; /* 93 million miles */
float protonCharge = 1.6E-19;
```

Note from the distance-to-the-sun example that while by convention, the exponential format, like the scientific format, consists of a floating point number from 1 to 10 plus an exponent, this is not required. But, the exponent portion of a number in exponential format must be an integer in decimal format:

```
float chocolate = 4.37e17.2; /* error! */
```

You may include a zero before an exponent, but that is not required (even though, as we will see in the next chapter, a minimum two-digit exponent format is how the exponent portion is printed when you send its value in text form to the screen or elsewhere, so you will see a leading zero if the exponent is less than an absolute value of 10). Both these alternatives are valid:

```
double dover = 3.8e03;
double back = 2.2e2;
```

If the exponent is a positive number, you may include the + sign, though normally you would omit the sign unless it is negative:

```
double standard = 1.1e3;
double talk = 12e+3;
```

The `talk` example is not deficient. As we noted earlier, in assigning floating point constants, you need either a decimal point *or* an exponent part. Of course, you could have inserted a period after the 12 or a period followed by a zero for more clarity. On the other hand, having an exponent part does not excuse you from having either a whole-number part or a fractional part. The following is not permitted:

```
double duty = e2; /* error! */
```

In summary, we can slightly restate our earlier rule formulation for assigning constants to floating point variables:

You must have either a whole-number part or a fractional part, and either a decimal point or an exponential part to a floating point constant.

No spaces are allowed in the exponential format:

```
double vision = 1.3  e 12; /* two errors! */
```

2.7.2   Floating Point Constant Type Rules

Like variables, constants have types. The significance of a constant's type will become more apparent when we have discussed automatic type conversions in Chapter 13.

Without any suffix, a floating point constant is of type `double`, no matter what its format—decimal or exponential. A floating point constant is always treated as positive. If the number starts with a minus sign, the minus sign is treated as a unary sign operator (see Section 4.4) rather than as part of the constant.

Standard C allows you to alter a floating point constant's type and designate it as `float` or `long double` by adding an F (or f) or L (or l) at the end, respectively, with no intervening spaces between the number and the suffix. For instance, the following value will be stored as a `float` even though it has been assigned to a `double`:

```
double yourPleasure = 87.23e17F;
```

Adding a suffix this way has significance in several contexts. First, the value is stored differently from the way it would have been without the suffix. Contrast the following two assignments of the same value, one with a suffix and the other without:

```
double deception = .000034F;
deception = .000034;
```

Here's how the bits of `deception` look after each of those two assignments on a system where `float` has 4 bytes and `double` has 8.

```
.000034F: 001111110000 00011101001101100111001000000000000000000000000000000000
.000034:  001111110000 00011101001101100111000110101100000101001100011000110
```

In the first case, some of the least significant bits are ignored in assigning value. (See Chapter 12 for an explanation of the bit configuration for floating point types.)

Furthermore, forcing a floating point constant to be treated as a `long double` by appending L (or l) is important where the constant is an argument to a variable argument function such as `printf()` and an argument of `long double` is expected. (See Chapter 8 for an explanation of this somewhat recondite concept.)

2.8   ASSIGNING CONSTANTS—INTEGERS

For integer types you can assign integers either as numbers or as the character equivalent of numbers. Each of those two methods in turn permits alternative methods.

2.8.1   Assigning Integers as Numbers—Decimal, Octal, and Hexadecimal Notation

You may assign integers in decimal format:

```
int num = 105;
char val = 102;
```

You can also use *hexadecimal notation* or *octal notation.* The following assignments are all identical in resulting value:

```
int num;
num = 105; /* decimal notation */
num = 0x69; /* hexadecimal */
num = 0151; /* octal notation */
```

Octal notation is the representation of a number in base 8; hexadecimal is in base 16. Each digit from the right represents a successively higher power of 8 or 16, just as each digit represents a successively higher power of 10 in decimal notation and a successively higher power of 2 in *binary notation,* the notation the computer uses internally to store all values.

Octal numbers are written with a 0 followed by the octal digits. Hexadecimal numbers are written with a 0x (or 0X) followed by the hexadecimal digits. Hexadecimal digits 10 to 15 are represented by the letters A to F (or a to f). (See Chapter 12 for a more complete discussion of octal and hexadecimal numbers.)

Regardless of whether you use decimal, octal, or hexadecimal notation for assignment, the computer stores the number in binary—both integer and floating point numbers. Nonetheless, you cannot use binary notation in making an assignment:

```
int num = 01100101; /* interpreted as octal */
long line = 11010010; /* interpreted as decimal */
```

2.8.2   Assigning Constants to long Variables

With a long, you must put the letter L after the number in assigning constants:

```
long ago = 16L;
unsigned long memory = 3087007L; /* start of PC video memory */
long time = 1193180L; /* number of computer cycles per second on a PC */
```

You can also use octal notation or hexadecimal notation. The following assignments store exactly the same values as the preceding three:

```
long ago = 0x10L;
unsigned long memory = 0xB8000000L;
long time = 04432334L;
```

In place of a capital L in all these cases, you may use a lowercase l, but since it is easily confused with the number 1, we do not recommend it.

 Failure to append an L to a constant assigned to a long *can lead to incorrect results.* Such a failure will not always cause a problem. If you make a simple assignment of a constant to a long without adding an L

```
long num = 365;
```

and then print the variable, you will find it to have been properly assigned. Under the rules discussed in the next section, the constant has a type of int, and under the conversion rules on assignment discussed in Chapter 13, this int is automatically converted to a long on assignment. However, if you assign several values without the proper suffix, you may have trouble. For example, if we print out the value of `val` following this assignment

```
long val = 365 * 24 * 60;
```

we get 1312 instead of 525,600. The three constants all have type `int` and this type can hold only 32,767 (see Figure 2.4). The odometer effect discussed in Section 2.8.4 causes the value to cycle 16 times from 0 to 32,767, with 1312 left over. This is the end value assigned to `val`. Although, as you will see in Chapter 13, the value on the right side of the assignment operator gets converted to the type of the variable on the left, conversion occurs only after full evaluation on the right—too late to save the day here.

Likewise, if you pass a single constant as an argument to a function that took a `long` as a parameter without appending the L, there would generally be no problem. (Functions and passing arguments are discussed in Chapter 8.) Again, under the conversion rules discussed in Chapter 13, the argument would be converted to the type of the function's parameter. However, if you passed 365 * 24 * 60 as above, we would run into the same problem: the damage is done before the argument is even passed and converted. Also, certain functions, called *variable-argument functions,* do not convert their variable arguments. The `printf()` function, discussed in the next chapter, is such a function. So the following statement would give the wrong value for both of its constant arguments:

```
printf("%ld %ld\n", 223, 365);
```

```
23920863 22740992
```

We would have the same problem trying to print as a `long double` a floating point constant that does not have an L appended to it.

```
printf("%.Lf\n", 1.0e6);
printf("%.Lf\n", 1.0e6L);
```

The results:

```
0
1000000
```

2.8.3   Integer Constant Type Rules

As we explained above, all constants have types. In the absence of explicit typing with a suffix, the following rules apply:

- **All character constants have type** `int`.
- **A decimal integer constant (for example, 99) without any suffix has the first of the following types big enough to house its value:** `int`, `long`, `unsigned long`.
- **A hexadecimal or octal integer constant (like 077 or 0x23) without any suffix has the first of the following types big enough to house its value:** `int`, `unsigned`, `long`, `unsigned long`.

Observe that, for instance, on a system where `int` is only 2 bytes, values from 32,768 through 65,535 (too big for an `int`) will have type `long`, but the same values in octal or hexadecimal notation will have type `unsigned`.

Using a suffix of U (or u) forces a constant to be treated as an `unsigned int` if the value is small enough to fit there; otherwise, its type with this suffix will be `unsigned long`:

```
int num = 17U;
```

Using a suffix of L (or l) forces a constant to be treated as a `long` if it fits there, or as an `unsigned long` if it does not. Using a suffix of L (or l) *with* U (or u) in any order after a number forces it to be treated as an `unsigned long`:

```
long in_the_tooth = 0x98A3LU;
long john_silver = 11723uL;
```

As we saw above, for integer constants without suffixes, treatment varies depending on whether we have decimal notation on the one hand, or octal or hexadecimal on the other; for integer constants *with* any of these suffixes (U, u, L, l, or any combination of U or u and L or l), the rules above for which type results apply uniformly to all notations.

As with floating point constants, negative integer constants are treated as positive values, preceded by a unary sign operator.

2.8.4   Overflow

If you assign to any integer type a value that exceeds its maximum range (see Table 2.3 for the respective ranges), you get an effect like a car odometer. If your car odometer passes 99,999, it starts over again at 0. With the computer, once you pass the top value for a particular type, it jumps down to the lowest possible value and then starts up again. If the type is a `signed` type, this means that the next number after the highest possible value will be the smallest possible negative number—that is, the one with the largest absolute value. Let's take `signed int` as an example. (See Figure 2.2.) We assume that this type has 2 bytes.

Table 2.5 shows how some sample numbers are stored into `signed int` variables.

The computer gives you no warning of this odometer effect; it just stores the wrong value.

2.8.5   Assigning Character Constants to Integer Types

We can assign characters (really the number equivalent of characters) to an integer variable by assigning its corresponding numerical value in decimal, octal, or hexadecimal notation, as we've seen.

Figure 2.2   *The Odometer Effect of Overflow*

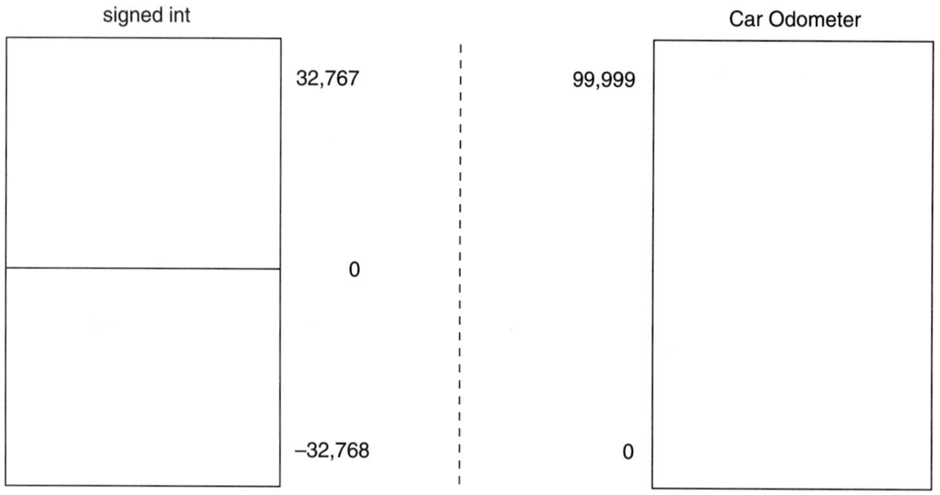

signed int

32,767

0

−32,768

Car Odometer

99,999

0

Table 2.5   `signed int`*: Sample Values*

Number Assigned	Value Stored
32767	32767
32768	−32768
32769	−32767
50000	−15536
65535	−1
65536	0
65537	1

The following statements each assign the numerical equivalent of the letter A to ch, assuming ASCII character encoding:

```
char ch;
ch = 65;
ch = 0101; /* octal equivalent */
ch = 0x41; /* hexadecimal equivalent */
```

As an alternative you may assign the character representation enclosed in single quotes:

```
int ch;
ch = 65;
ch = 'A'; /* same result as last statement assuming ASCII notation */
ch = 187;
ch = '7' /* same as last statement assuming ASCII notation: use Alt + keypad on PC */
```

In fact, this single-quote method is more portable since it does not assume ASCII or any other character encoding.

You will not find 7 on your keyboard. On a PC, to make your editor show ASCII characters beyond 127, such as 7, you must hold down the Alt key, type in the three digits that make up the ASCII value, and release the Alt key. This only works with the keypad. It makes no difference whether NUM LOCK is on or off.

A table of ASCII and EBCDIC values assigned to represent the various characters is found in Appendix F. Be careful in assigning a character beyond 127 in the table. If you want to use a char to store the character, you must use unsigned char.

Since assigning a value with a character in single quotes is the same as assigning its numerical equivalent, the following usage is permitted:

```
char ch = 'B' + ('a' - 'A');
ch = 66 + (97 - 65); /* same as last statement assuming ASCII character encoding */
ch = 66 + ('a' - 65); /* same again, with identical assumption */
```

The result is 'b' or 98. You may observe that adding ('a' – 'A') to an uppercase letter will yield the same letter in lowercase; conversely, subtracting ('a' – 'A') from a lowercase letter will produce the corresponding uppercase letter. (These results assume the computer uses ASCII character encoding. For maximum portability, use toupper() and tolower() to convert to uppercase and lowercase respectively. See Chapter 9.)

We may likewise do the following:

```
char ch = '3' - '1';
ch = '3' - 1;
```

The first statement assigns 2 to ch; the second assigns the encoded value of '2' (these statements work in either ASCII or EBCDIC since the digits are sequentially stored in both; characters are not stored sequentially in EBCDIC).

 Incidentally, although using a combination of left- and right-hand single quotes around a character may look prettier to you, *the compiler recognizes only the right-hand single quotation mark in assigning character constants.*

```
char ch = 'a'; /* error */
char ch = 'a'; /* OK */
```

2.8.6 Assigning Character Constants to Integer Types: Escape Sequences and Nonprinting Characters

A few characters are nonprinting. When the printer—or in some cases the screen—encounters them, they result in some action being taken. To assign these nonprinting characters to variables, you may use their numerical equivalent:

```
char ch = 9; /* assign tab character to ch in ASCII */
```

Table 2.6 *Nonprinting Characters*

Decimal Value	Escape Sequence	Action
7	\a	beep
8	\b	backspace
12	\f	formfeed
10	\n	newline
13	\r	carriage return
9	\t	horizontal tab
11	\v	vertical tab

Since by hypothesis, these characters are nonprinting, the second assignment technique of enclosing the character representation in single quotes is not available. Instead, you can use escape sequences—a backslash followed by a letter without an intervening space—as an alternative. Table 2.6 shows the special nonprinting characters and their corresponding numerical value in ASCII character encoding, escape sequence, and action.

You enclose the backslash-letter combination in single quotes in making an assignment. For example:

```
char ch = '\t'; /* assign tab character to ch */
```

We will explain the respective actions of these nonprinting characters more fully in the next chapter. Briefly, the formfeed character causes the printer to eject the current page and advance to the next page. The newline character advances the printer or screen cursor to the next line; the carriage return character puts the printer or screen cursor at the beginning of the current line. The character generated by pressing the Enter key on the keyboard is a newline.

2.8.7   Numeric Escape Sequences

You can also use escape sequences as an alternative means of assigning *printable* characters. You may use octal or hexadecimal notation in these escape sequences—no decimal notation. The format is \n, \nn, or \nnn for octal notation and \xn or \xnn for hexadecimal. Since the compiler has a \ to alert it to the fact that an octal or hexadecimal number is coming, the zero that precedes the nonescape sequence assignment of octal and hexadecimal numbers is omitted.

Here are six ways to assign the same value (assuming ASCII character encoding insofar as the value equivalency is concerned)—four using methods we've covered earlier and two with escape sequences:

```
char ch;
ch = 65;
ch = 0101;
ch = 0x41;
ch = 'A';
ch = '\101';
ch = '\x41';
```

2.8.8   Special Character Assignment

For certain printing characters, you must insert a \ after the initial single quote and before the character when you use the paired-single quote method of assignment or when these characters appear inside string constants (see Chapter 7). These characters are listed in Table 2.7. Thus for instance:

```
char ch = '\''; assign single quote to ch
```

Table 2.7 *Special Character Assignment*

Character	Format
backslash	'\\'
double quote	'\"'
single quote	'\''
question mark	'\?'

However, the double quote mark does not require a backslash in character constants

```
char ch = '"';
```

and the single quote does not need a backslash in string constants

```
char saying[] = "top o' the morning";
```

But, you *may* include a backslash in each of these two cases, so there is little reason for you to remember these two exceptions other than for the purposes of recognizing that there is no error if you see either case without a backslash.

2.9 APPLICATION: ACE BILLING PROGRAM

In the ACE Billing program, we make use of our new ability to declare variables and assign them values.

 **Listing 2.1 acech02.c**

```
/*
   +--------------------------------------------------------------------+
   + Program Name: acech02.c
   +    Author(s): Austell-Wolfson and Otieno
   +         Date: 12/10/2000
   + Purpose:
   +    This program implements the ace billing program.
   +    We have learned how to declare variables that hold single
   +    values. We have also learned how to assign values to these
   +    variables. We now apply these capabilities in this program.
   +
   +    Process:
   +    At this point, we print the headings, declare variables,
   +    assign values to the variables where applicable, and execute
   +    the stubs for the rest of the functions.
   +--------------------------------------------------------------------+
*/

#include <stdio.h>
void initialization(void); /* Prototype - discussed in Chapter 8 */
void processMemberRecord(void);
void termination(void);
void initializeVariables(void);
void printHeadings(void);
void readMemberRecord(void);
void computeIndividualBill(void);
void writeDetailLine(void);
void determineSpecialFee(void);
```

```c
void determineActivityFee(void);
void determineDiscountAmt(void);

/*
  +----------------------------------------------------------------+
  + Declare variables outside of main function so that all the other
  + functions will have access to them. Doing this gives these
  + variables global scope and therefore allows us to develop and
  + work with modules this early. We will discontinue this practice
  + once functions have been discussed.
  +----------------------------------------------------------------+
*/

char  SpecialMembershipFlag = 'Y';
float Discount = 0.0;
float AverageBill = 0.0;
float MembershipFee = 0.0;
float ActivityFee = 0.0;
float DiscountAmount = 0.0;
float ClubTotals = 0.0;
float ChargeAmounts = 0.0;
float NumberOfCharges = 0.0;
float TotalIndividualBill = 0.0;
float SpecialMembershipFee = 0.0;
float AceClubTotals = 0.0;

int main(void)
{
    initialization();
    processMemberRecord(); /* No loop logic yet. Not until chapter 5 */
    termination();
    return 0;
}

void initialization(void)
{
    initializeVariables();
    printHeadings();
    readMemberRecord();
    printf("Initialization function has executed successfully\n");
}

void processMemberRecord(void)
{
    computeIndividualBill();
    writeDetailLine();
    readMemberRecord();
    printf("ProcessMemberRecord function has executed successfully\n");
}

void termination(void)
{
    printf("Termination function has executed successfully\n");
}

/*
  +----------------------------------------------------------------+
  + We set up a function that would allow us to reinitialize
  + commonly used program variables. While this approach may seem
  + redundant and too modular, in fact it serves to
  + overcome a common problem. Often as the program grows in
  + complexity, there is a need to reinitialize certain variables.
```

```
                + Unless this is done in an organized, uniform fashion, what
                + often happens is that only some variables are reinitialized,
                + or variables are initialized in a different fashion at
                + different points in the program. This problem is particularly
                + acute if more than one programmer is working on the project.
                +----------------------------------------------------------------+
      */
      void initializeVariables(void)
      {
         SpecialMembershipFlag = 'Y';
         Discount = 0.0;
         AverageBill = 0.0;
         MembershipFee = 0.0;
         ActivityFee = 0.0;
         DiscountAmount = 0.0;
         ClubTotals = 0.0;
         ChargeAmounts = 0.0;
         NumberOfCharges = 0.0;
         TotalIndividualBill = 0.0;
         SpecialMembershipFee = 0.0;
         AceClubTotals = 0.0;
         printf("InitializeVariables function has executed successfully\n");
      }


      void printHeadings(void)
      {
         printf("+--------------------------------------------------------"
                "-----------------------+\n");
         printf("+                                                         "
                "                       +\n");
         printf("+    Program Name: ACECH02.EXE                            "
                "         Page:  1    +\n");
         printf("+       Run Date: 12/10/2000                Ace Billing    "
                "                       +\n");
         printf("+                                                         "
                "                       +\n");
         printf("+                                                         "
                "                       +\n");
         printf("+--------------------------------------------------------"
                "-----------------------+\n");
         printf("+                                                         "
                "                       +\n");
         printf("+ Customer Name  Charges  Bill        Mbr Fee    Act Fee"
                "    Disc    Total Bill +\n");
         printf("+--------------------------------------------------------"
                "-----------------------+\n");
         printf("+                                                         "
                "                       +\n\n");
      }


      void readMemberRecord(void)
      {
         printf("ReadMemberRecord function has executed successfully\n");
      }


      void computeIndividualBill(void)
      {
         determineSpecialFee();
         determineActivityFee();
         determineDiscountAmt();
         printf("ComputeIndividualBill function has executed successfully\n");
      }
```

```
        void writeDetailLine(void)
        {
           printf("WriteDetailLine function has executed successfully\n");
        }

        void determineSpecialFee(void)
        {
           printf("DetermineSpecialFee function has executed successfully\n");
        }
        void determineActivityFee(void)
        {
           printf("DetermineActivityFee function has executed successfully\n");
        }

        void determineDiscountAmt(void)
        {
           printf("DetermineDiscountAmt function has executed successfully\n");
        }
```

2.9.1   Output

```
InitializeVariables function has executed successfully
+------------------------------------------------------------------------+
+                                                                        +
+   Program Name: ACECH02.EXE                              Page:  1      +
+       Run Date: 12/10/2000           Ace Billing                       +
+                                                                        +
+                                                                        +
+------------------------------------------------------------------------+
+                                                                        +
+ Customer Name  Charges  Bill      Mbr Fee    Act Fee    Disc   Total Bill +
+------------------------------------------------------------------------+
+                                                                        +

ReadMemberRecord function has executed successfully
Initialization function has executed successfully
DetermineSpecialFee function has executed successfully
DetermineActivityFee function has executed successfully
DetermineDiscountAmt function has executed successfully
ComputeIndividualBill function has executed successfully
WriteDetailLine function has executed successfully
ReadMemberRecord function has executed successfully
ProcessMemberRecord function has executed successfully
Termination function has executed successfully
```

Chapter Summary

1. A variable represents a specific location in the computer's random access memory or RAM that can hold a value.
2. Variables have both names and types. For each variable name, the computer assigns a specific address in memory. The type tells the computer how to store the value of the variable and how much memory to reserve at that address.
3. Variable names can contain any letter of the alphabet (both cases), the underscore character, and the digits 0 to 9. The

name cannot begin with a digit. Since variable names defined by the system often begin with an underscore character, it is best to avoid beginning with this character either.
4. Variables are case sensitive, meaning that uppercase and lowercase letters spell completely different names.
5. Although variable names can be any length, Standard C compilers are permitted to recognize as few as the first 31 characters of local variables and as few as the first 6 char-

acters of global variables. Any uniqueness in the variable name must be within the part of the name recognized.

6. You cannot use C keywords for variable names.

7. Variables generally have two types that can be used in arithmetic computations: integer types (variables with whole numbers) and floating point types (variables having a fractional component or decimal point). The type designated as char holds a value represented by 1 byte.

8. To store lengthy numbers more efficiently in memory, C divides integer variables according to the number of bytes each number takes in memory: char, short, int, and long. The int type has a size falling between short (smaller or equal to int) and long (greater than or equal to int).

9. Each integer type also can be either signed, which can accommodate negative values, and unsigned, which can accommodate only positive values. The default for all int types is signed.

10. Floating point variables are of three types: float, double, and long double. The range for each type varies in terms of precision (the number of digits to the right of the decimal point), and the number of bytes.

11. Letters and other printable characters are actually stored in memory as a numeric value. PCs and some other computers use a coding standard called ASCII, and mainframes usually use a coding standard called EBCDIC.

12. A programmer creates a variable and gives it a value by specific C commands, called statements. The statement that gives a name and type to a variable is called a declaration. The statement that gives a value to a variable is called an assignment.

13. Assigning a name allocates a specific memory starting address, and assigning a type tells the computer how many bytes to reserve at that starting address and how to evaluate the bytes.

14. If you assign a value at the time you declare a variable, it is called initialization. It is good practice to declare like groups of variables in a single statement.

15. When coding an assignment statement, the variable name goes on the left side and the value assigned goes on the right.

16. One assigns a value to a floating point variable either by using a decimal point (indicating which is the whole number and which is the fractional part), or by exponential notation (indicating the size or power of the number times 10), or both.

17. For integer types, you can assign integers either as numbers or as the character equivalent of numbers. This can either be in decimal notation (ordinary numbers with a base 10), hexadecimal notation (the representation of numbers in base 16), or octal notation (the representation of numbers in base 8).

18 When assigning a number to long variables, you must place an L after the number on the right side of the equation to ensure that the variable will have sufficient places to hold the number.

19. Constants have types as well as variables. A programmer should keep in mind both the constant's type and the variable's type when storing or assigning a constant to a variable. Unless otherwise specified, constants are typed by these rules:

   ■ All character constants have type int.
   ■ A decimal integer constant without a suffix will fall into the smallest int type in which it will fit: int, long, or unsigned long.
   ■ A hexadecimal or octal integer constant without a suffix will fall into the smallest int type in which it will fit: int, unsigned, long, or unsigned long.

20. Characters are assigned to an integer variable by assigning its corresponding numerical value in decimal, octal, or hexadecimal notation. Characters can also be assigned by enclosing the character representation (the actual letter or other symbol) in single quotes.

21. Because some characters do not print but control printer and other computer functions (generally the first 32 characters in the ASCII character set), these can be assigned by either the numerical equivalent or a standardized "escape sequence" enclosed in single quotes (a backslash followed by a letter).

22. Certain characters, such as backslashes and quotes, must be assigned by inserting a / after the initial quote and before the character.

Review Questions

1. In the C programming language, could the words total, TOTAL, Total, and totaL refer to the same variable, or would they all be different variables?

2. Can the first character in a variable name be a digit?

3. Write the following number in exponential notation: 0.00000968.

4. Is it necessary to include a decimal point when assigning a value to a floating point variable? Explain.

5. After you assign a hexadecimal number to a variable, what notation does the computer use to store the value? What about a decimal number? What about an octal number?

6. Can a number be assigned to a variable in binary notation?

7. What letter must be added to the end of a constant when assigning a value to a long variable?

8. Identify the following variable names as valid or *not* valid:
   a. Cprogram
   b. C programs
   c. Lotus123
   d. 123Lotus
   e. Excel
   f. automechanic
   g. auto
   h. int
   i. case

9. Indicate which of the following declarations are valid or invalid. Assume that they will all be declared in the same program.
   a. `int Cprogram;`
   b. `int Cprogram;`
   c. `int auto;`
   d. `float Cprograms;`
   e. `int float Lotus123;`
   f. `int localfloat;`
   g. `char 123Lotus;`
   h. `unsigned Windows 98;`
   i. `long unsigned xyz;`
   j. `unsigned long lease;`

10. What is the effect of variable declaration? In other words, what happens when you declare a variable?

11. What is the difference between a variable and a constant?

12. Write the equivalent C assignment statements representing the following mathematical expressions:
   a. $y = 10x^2 + 15x + 100$ (assume y and x are declared as floating point variables)
   b. $z = \mu u + 1 / 2\sigma$
   c. $y = \pi(1 + x)^2 / ((1 + x)^2 - 1)$

13. Which of the following are valid C constants? If invalid, state why.
   a. −3456
   b. +1234
   c. False
   d. Maximum
   e. 100,123
   f. −6.000000
   g. −5.
   h. $3 + 100\pi$
   i. 123e17
   j. −123e−17

   k. 1.034e45.5
   l. 1.e10
   m. −0.0
   n. ' '
   o. '1'
   p. "character"
   q. 10^{35}

14. Declare variables with the appropriate data types and assign them the scalar values in the previous question (numeric and character constant examples only—exclude (c), (d), (h) and (p)).

(In questions 15 and 16, assume that what is to the left of a / is divided by what is to its right.)

15. Evaluate the results of the following expressions based on these values:

   $a = 1.0, b = 7.0, c = 5.5, d = 35, e = 12, f = 14,$
   $g = 1, h = 0$

   a. `c / d / 5 * f`
   b. `-a * b/c * d`
   c. `(d - 32 * e) * g + h`

16. What is the result of evaluating the following: 6/9?

17. What must we do to get the result of the previous question to be 0.66666?

18. What is the result of 6.0 / 9?

19. Give the range of values and number of bytes for `char`, `int`, and `float` in your programming environment.

20. Evaluate the following C expressions. Assume ASCII character encoding.
   a. Given that `int a = 10`, what is the value of a = a + ('Z' − 'A')
   b. `char ch = 'A';` what is `ch = ch + 1;`?
   c. `char ch = 'A';` what is `ch = ch + 24;`?

Programming Exercises

The specifications of the programming assignments were introduced in Chapter 1, at which time you were to

- think through the solution to these problems.
- identify the modules that, once implemented, will solve the problem.
- prepare a hierarchy chart of all the modules.
- prepare pseudocode/flowchart for each module in the hierarchy chart.
- write the program stubs the same way we did with the ACE Billing system application.

In Chapter 2, the concept of a program variable or identifier declaration was presented—especially scalar variables, along with the variety of data types with which they may be associated. A scalar variable is one that can only hold a single value at a time. These programming assignments provide you an opportunity to build on the design that you did after Chapter 1. At this point we ask that you declare all your variables outside of `main()`, similar to what we did in the application section, so that all the other modules will have access to them. Let's continue to produce the indicated headings as a part of our output. Follow the example shown in Section 2.9. We have designed these programs so that they build on the work done in previous chapters until the original problem is completely solved. We have also tried to point out how much you should be able to do here to help you along.

Programming Assignment 2.1: Billing

Program Description

Declare some variables that you think you might use in Billing programs. For example:

```
int InvoiceNumber;
int ProductNumber;
```

```
float Cost;
float Extension;
```

Programming Assignment 2.3: Payroll

Program Description

Declare some variables that you think you might use in Payroll programs. For example:

```
float Salary;
float HoursWorked;
int EmployeeNumber;
```

Programming Assignment 2.4 to 2.7: UNIX System Administration

Program Description

Continuing from the program we described in Chapter 1, Programming Assignment 1.4, create variable names for the UID and the GID. We will use these variables in subsequent chapters. Write some program statements that would assign values to these variables.

Programming Assignment 2.8: Science and Engineering (Chemical Engineering)

Program Description

This is a continuation of Programming Assignment 1.8. Declare some or all of the variables you have already identified.

Programming Assignment 2.9: Science and Engineering (Compiler Construction)

Program Description

This is a continuation of Programming Assignment 1.9. Declare some of or all of the variables you have already identified.

Declare nine character variables and assign the following values to them:

'B', ' ', ':', '=', ' ', '1', '0', '0', ';'.

You will modify and develop this further as you learn more Standard C.

Programming Assignment 2.10: Science and Engineering (Mathematics—The Game of Life)

Program Description

This is a continuation of Programming Assignment 1.10. Declare variables that can hold the coordinates of a life form, as well as a variable that can hold a life entity, and await additional information about Standard C before implementing the rest of the logic.

Programming Assignment 2.11: Distribution/Packaging/Shipping

Program Description

Identify and declare all the scalar variables for solving this problem, or simply declare the variables you have already identified in Chapter 2. Be sure to write the headings for the report that you can do based on the information you have accumulated to this point.

Programming Assignment 2.12: Invoicing

Program Description

Identify and declare all the scalar variables for solving this problem, or simply declare the variables you have already identified in Chapter 2. Be sure to write the headings for the report that you can do based on the information you have accumulated to this point.

Programming Assignment 2.13 through 2.18: EDI Claims Report

Program Description

Write a program ID block for a program that will show how many total claims are accepted and rejected, and the dollar amounts charged for each claim status.

Declare integer variables for the total accepted claims, total rejected claims, and total claims overall. Also declare floating point variables for the accepted dollar amount, rejected dollar amount, and total dollar amount.

Programming Assignment 2.19: Inventory

Program Description

Continuing from the program that we described in Chapter 1, Programming Assignment 1.19, create variable names for the Part Number, Quantity on Hand, and Quantity on Order. We will use these variables in subsequent chapters. Write some program statements that would assign values to these variables.

Programming Assignment 2.20: General Category (Programa Pro Rata)

Program Description

This is a continuation of Programming Assignment 1.20.

Declare variables of proper types to hold the following values:

- Tread depth now
- Tread depth when the tire was new
- Price of a new tire
- Mounting and balancing charge
- State tax rate (program useful in any state) (for example, 4%)

Programming Assignment 2.21: Nation's Economy

Program Description

This is a continuation of Programming Assignment 1.21. Declare variables of proper types to hold the following values. Be sure to declare any other variables you know you will need in order to complete the calculations:

- Weight of a jar of peanut butter
- Weight of a jar of jelly
- Weight of a loaf of bread
- Cost of a jar of peanut butter
- Cost of a jar of jelly
- Cost of a loaf of bread

Programming Assignment 2.22: Police Department

Program Description

This is a continuation of Programming Assignment 1.22.

Declare variables of proper types to hold the values you have identified as needed for input, calculations, and output.

Programming Assignment 2.27: Electronics

Program Description

Declare some of the variables the test program will require. Remember that you want to make the most efficient use of storage space as possible, so consider what type of variable is required for each value to be stored. Some possible variables include ones that will store

- LED status (or equivalent value)
- Data stored in micro (just 1 byte for now)
- User's command input

CHAPTER 3

Introduction to I/O

OBJECTIVES

- To be able to accomplish simple data input and output
- To learn about special nonprinting action characters
- To understand the concept of an input and output stream

- To understand buffering and to learn the difference between buffered and unbuffered input and output
- To learn some of the secrets of proper report layout

NEW TERMS

field-width modifier	formatted I/O	reading
flag	precision modifier	writing

In this chapter, we will cover formatted input from and output to what are referred to as the "standard" input and output devices—the keyboard for input and the screen for output. Formatted input and output are referred to as *formatted I/O* for short. For sending formatted output to the screen, we will use the printf() function; for obtaining formatted input from the keyboard, we will use the scanf() function. Sending output to a device such as the screen or to a file is sometimes referred to as *writing,* and obtaining input from a device such as the keyboard or a file is sometimes referred to as *reading.*

In later chapters, we will take a look at functions that print to a file (fprintf()) and read input from a file (fscanf()) and that write to a location in the computer's random access memory (sprintf()) and read input from a location in memory (sscanf()). We will also show you how to use the simpler printf() and scanf() functions for I/O to and from a file by redirecting standard input or standard output from the keyboard and screen to a file.

The printf() function takes values of variables and converts them to characters (for example, the value 7.327 stored in RAM on a bit level in binary is converted to characters such as "7.327" or "7.327000" or "7.33") with the aid of formatting commands given to it by the programmer. The scanf() function does the reverse: it takes values in character form and with the aid of similar formatting commands, converts these character groups into values to be stored in variables in memory, the addresses of which the programmer also gives it. These formatting commands and the nature of the work performed by the two reading and writing partner functions are the reason they are called *formatted* input and output functions.

3.1   THE `printf()` FUNCTION

The `printf()` function has two elements: a format string and an argument list.

```
int one = 5, two = 7;
printf("The sum of %d and %d is %d", one, two, one + two);
```

The format string is enclosed in double quotes (in later chapters, we will see an exception to this rule) and is separated from the argument list by a comma. If more than one argument exists, as in this example, the arguments are separated by commas.

The format string is printed out on the standard output device (the video display unless redirected; see Chapters 14 and 16) character by character until what is called a *conversion specifier* is encountered. At that point, the value of the next variable, constant, or expression in the argument list is printed, in the format indicated by the conversion specifier. The process continues in the same way until the end of the format string. In the example above, there are three `%d` conversion specifiers, corresponding to the three arguments in the argument list. So first "The sum of" is printed, then "5", then "and", then "7", then "is", then "12".

```
The sum of 5 and 7 is 12
```

All conversion specifiers begin with `%` and end with one or two letters that indicate the type to be printed, as shown in Table 3.1.

Note from this list that there is no separate specifier for `float`. Both `float` and `double` are printed as `double`. Also, while we've listed the specifiers for `short` and `unsigned short`, those specifiers are no different than the `int` specifiers on a PC, since a `short` is no different there than an `int`, though they may differ in other environments.

The `%d` specifier is identical to the `%i` specifier; `%d` is generally used. The `%i` specifier is a Standard C addition, created for symmetry with the `scanf()` specifiers. As a result of this addition, data can be

Table 3.1   `printf()` *Conversion Type Specifiers*

Specifier	Output Format
Basics	
%c	character
%s	string
%d or %i	int
%u	unsigned int
%f	double
Type Size Variations	
%ld	long
%lu	unsigned long
%hd	short
%hu	unsigned short
%Lf	long double
Format Variations: Octal/Hexadecimal and Exponential	
%o	unsigned int—octal notation
%x or %X	unsigned int—hex notation
%e	double—exponential format
%g	%f or %e, whichever output is shorter
Special Cases	
%p	pointer address value
%n	# of characters printed to that point

read in and written out with the same specifier if the `%i` specifier is being used with `scanf()` to obtain input. As we will see later, the `%d` and `%i` specifiers are different from one another with `scanf()`.

Here are some examples from the most commonly used set of specifiers:

```
printf("The first letter in the alphabet is %c\n", 65);
printf("The second is %c\n", 'B');
printf("%d is an integer\n", 822);
printf("%f is a floating point number\n", 822.75);
printf("My name is %s; hers is %s\n", "Lemmy", "Ida");
```

```
The first letter in the alphabet is A
The second is B
822 is an integer
822.750000 is a floating point number
My name is Lemmy; hers is Ida
```

Note that these specifiers determine how data is *displayed*, not how it is *stored*. The first example will print A at the end only if the system uses ASCII character encoding. In the second example, a B will print at the end no matter what character encoding system is in use.

3.1.1   %c and New Kids on the Block: Strings and Pointers

The `%c` conversion specifier prints a `char`, `short`, or `int` argument value, passed as an `int` and converted for printing to `unsigned char`, as a single character, according to the computer's character-encoding system. The ASCII character-encoding system, used on the PC, and EBCDIC, used on most mainframes, are depicted in Appendix F.

The argument can be in any of those formats discussed in Section 2.8.5: an integer variable of type `char`, `short`, or `int`; a constant in decimal, octal, hexadecimal notation; the character representation of an integer value enclosed in single quotes; or an escape sequence enclosed in single quotes. Assuming the system is using ASCII character encoding (where the value 65 is depicted as an uppercase A, the following code fragment

```
char ch = 65;
int num = 65;
printf("Some characters: %c \t%c %c %c %c %c %c %c",
   ch, num, 65, 0101, 0x41, 'A', '\101', '\n', '\x41');
```

produces this output:

```
Some characters: A    A A A A A
 A
```

The `%s`, `%p`, and `%n` specifiers present concepts we are not yet familiar with. As we will learn in Chapter 7, a string—corresponding to the `%s` specifier—is a series of bytes, each interpreted as characters, terminated (in memory, not in the printed-out string) by an extra byte with a value of 0 (also called the NULL character) to show the computer where the string ends.

The `%s` specifier causes the string argument corresponding to it to be printed from its start to the NULL character that terminates it. The NULL character is not printed:

```
char *prog = "C program"; /* one way to declare a string */
printf("%s program run.\n%s run.\n%s. . . %s\n",
   "C", prog, "Run program run.\n", "Please!");
```

```
C program run.
C program run.
Run program run.
. . . Please!
```

The first `%s` causes the first argument, the single-letter string "C", to print; then the space character and the following characters, "program run.", are printed; then the newline character, which moves printing to the next line, is printed; then the next `%s` specifier causes the value of the argument prog, "C Program" to print; then the characters "run." are printed; another newline character causes printing to move to the next line; the next `%s` specifier causes the argument "Run program run.\n", which includes a newline character, to print; then "..." is printed; then the final `%s` specifier causes "Please!" in the argument list to print; and finally a newline moves printing to the next line. *(It is nearly always a good idea to terminate each* `printf()` *statement with a newline character, so that any following* `printf()` *or other writing statement does not get stuck onto the tail end of the previous statement.)*

The `%n` specifier tells us how many characters were printed by a `printf()` statement up to the point of the specifier. However, nothing is printed out by the statement that contains it; rather, the result is stored in an `int` variable you place as an argument. For reasons we will explain when we get to pointers, you place an & in front of the variable in the argument list for a `%n` specifier:

```
printf("\nTell me %s%n;\nafter that, I don't care: ",
    "how many characters printed out so far", &number);
printf("%d\n", number);
```

```
Tell me how many characters printed out so far;
after that, I don't care: 46
```

The `%p` specifier is used to print the value of a pointer. A pointer is a variable whose value is the address of another variable. We defer discussion of the `%p` conversion specifier until we deal with pointers in Chapter 7.

3.2   NONPRINTING CHARACTERS—ESCAPE SEQUENCES

You might wonder what happened to \n in each of the examples. The \n is a nonprinting character. There are a series of \-letter combinations—called escape sequences—that cause the printer or screen to take some specified action rather than print a character. Table 3.2, repeated from Chapter 2, shows the special nonprinting characters and their corresponding action.

The formfeed character (\f) causes the printer to eject the current page and advance to the next page. The formfeed character effects no action on the screen; all you get is the female biological symbol, ♀, assuming the system uses ASCII character encoding and follows the IBM designations for nonprinting characters with values between 1 and 31—without the accompanying action.

The newline character (\n) advances the printer or screen cursor to the next line at the same column; the carriage return character (\r) puts the printer or screen cursor at the beginning of the current line. The action generated by the [Enter] key on the keyboard is a newline.

The horizontal tab character (\t) moves the printer to the next horizontal tab stop, generally at columns 8, 16, 24, 30, and so on (with the first column being column 0). The vertical tab character (\v) moves the printer to the next vertical tab; however, most printers just ignore the vertical tab.

Table 3.2 *Nonprinting Characters*

Escape Sequence	Action
\a	beep
\b	backspace
\f	formfeed
\n	newline
\r	carriage return
\t	horizontal tab
\v	vertical tab

The backspace character (\b) moves the printer or the screen cursor back one character. With some printers, you can use the carriage return or backspace characters to overstrike the same space:

```
/* carriage return at end */
printf("I'd like this underlined, please.\r");
printf("___ ____ ____ _____  _____\n");
/* backspaces here */
printf("This too.\b\b\b\b\b\b\b\b____ ___\n");
```

<u>I'd</u> <u>like</u> <u>this</u> <u>underlined</u>, <u>please</u>.
<u>This</u> <u>too</u>.

However, on the screen in most environments, this normally will simply cause the new characters to replace the old:

___ ____ ____ _____ _____.

____ ___.

Also, we should note that not all printers support the backspace and carriage return characters in this fashion. Nor do all printers support ASCII characters beyond 127 or support them without some special escape sequence first being sent to enable their being printed.

These nonprinting characters can appear at any place in the format string or in a string or character constant argument, either singly or (except for character constant arguments) in combination:

```
printf("\t\t\tTab over; then print a newline\n");
printf("%sTwo tabs and then a newline%s", "\t\t", "\n");
printf("%c%cTabs and newline another way%c",
    '\t', '\t', '\n');
printf("start over\nstart over\nstart over\n"
    "\tstart over and in\n");
printf("\nalign:\t\t%s\t%3.1f\n\t\t%s\t%3.5f\n",
    "one", 299.48484, "seven", 29.33);
```

```
                Tab over; then print a newline
          Two tabs and then a newline
          Tabs and newline another way
start over
start over
start over
    start over and in

align:    one     299.5
          seven   29.33000
```

As you see, in the argument list, characters are enclosed with apostrophes and strings are enclosed with double quotation marks; neither is so enclosed within the format string. The following listing demonstrates the use of the backspace, tab, and carriage return for screen input and output. We obtain a user response from the keyboard/screen with the scanf() function covered later in the chapter.

 **Listing 3.1 backup.c**

```
/* backup.c */

/* demonstrate \b\t\r */

#include <stdio.h>

int main(void)
{
    float hourly;
```

```
    printf("\nEnter your hourly salary: ");

    /* set cursor to start of underlining */
    printf(" $_____\b\b\b\b\b");
    scanf("%f", &hourly);

    /* leave space at beginning of line */
    printf("\t\tyou earn %.2f a month.",
        hourly * 40. * 52. / 12.);
    printf("\rAs I figure it,\n"); /* now go back & fill in space */
}
```

The first `printf()` statement prints the following output to the screen:

`Enter your hourly salary:`

Since the format string is not terminated by a newline character, the next `printf()` statement picks up on the screen just where the first one left off, with this as the result:

`Enter your hourly salary: $_____`

The backspace characters move the cursor back to the spot directly after the dollar sign but do not write over the underline characters. After a response, the screen looks like this:

`Enter your hourly salary: $12.50`

The characters typed in have obliterated the underline characters. (If the output were redirected to a printer, the 12.50 would now be underlined.)

The newline and two tab characters cause the cursor to move to the next line and then move over 16 spaces, where the result is printed:

`            you earn $2166.67 a month.`

The final `printf()` statement moves the cursor to the start of the same row, where it prints "As I figure it", leaving the screen looking like this:

`Enter your hourly salary: $12.50`
`As I figure it, you earn $2166.67 a month.`

3.2.1   Backslash Notation for Printing Characters

You must use the backslash notation inside the format string, or in string or character arguments for certain *printing* characters as well, namely, the single quote, double quote, question mark, and backslash characters. Otherwise, the compiler would confuse the character with some other action the character can represent—for instance, the double quote character's closing off the string:

```
printf("The man said \"My nickname is \'Luke\'\"\n"
    "\"What's yours\?\"\n");
printf("Use the file named \"c:\\tc\\output\" or else %s\n",
    "\"c:\\tc\\printout\"");
```

```
The man said "My nickname is 'Luke'"
"What's yours?"
Use the file named "c:\tc\output" or else "c:\tc\printout"
```

There are two exceptions to this superfluous backslash rule: the double quote mark does not require a backslash in character constants

```
char quote = '"';
```

and the single quote does not need a backslash in string constants

```
char reference[] = "heap o' junk";
```

Table 3.3 *Special Character Printing*

Print Character	Format
backslash	\\
double quote	\"
single quote	\'
question mark	\?
percent sign	%%

However, you *may* include a backslash in either of these two cases, so there is little reason for you to remember the two exceptions other than to recognize that there is no error if you see either example without a backslash.

To print out a percent sign, you must precede the percent sign with another percent sign. This stops the compiler from mistaking the percent sign for a `printf()` or `scanf()` specifier. Table 3.3 shows the characters that require either a backslash or a percent sign before them in order to print properly.

3.3   ARGUMENT EVALUATION; MATCHING SPECIFIERS AND ARGUMENTS

The `printf()` function is flexible. You may use constants, variables, or constant-variable expressions in the argument list. In all cases, each argument is evaluated and then its value is assigned to the corresponding specifier for printing:

```
int whole = 18;
float fraction = .3592, real = 19.27;
printf("You can make boxes with funny characters"
    " like %c %c %c %c %c %c\n",
    '6', '7', 'L', '9', '=', '**'); /* character constants */
printf("Plus ça change, plus c'est %s.\n",
    "la même chose"); /* string */
printf("%d is an integer\n", 993); /* integer constant */
printf("%f is a floating point constant\n",
    923.7823); /* floating point constant */
printf("fraction: %f\n", fraction); /* variable */
printf("The third letter of the alphabet is %c\n",
    'A' + 2); /* constant expression */
printf("%f is one result\n",
    real - fraction); /* variable expression */
printf("%d is another result\n",
    (whole / 3) + (5 * 2)); /* variable/constant expression */

You can make boxes with funny characters like 6 7 L 9 = **
Plus ça change, plus c'est la même chose.
993 is an integer
923.782300 is a floating point constant
fraction: 0.359200
The third letter of the alphabet is C
18.910800 is one result
16 is another result
```

You may print strings without any conversion specifiers or arguments. Some of the last examples could be rewritten like this:

```
printf("You can make boxes with funny characters"
    " like 6 7 ∟ 9 = ⌐\n");
printf("Plus ça change, plus c'est la même chose.\n");
printf("993 is an integer\n");
```

That being so, you might wonder why we bothered with the more complex formulation above. You will see the answer when you get to conversion specifier modifiers later in this chapter.

As you can see, the printf() function causes the format string to be printed character by character until a conversion specifier is encountered. Then the first argument in the argument list is evaluated and printed in a format corresponding to the first conversion specifier. Then the next characters in the format string are read and printed until the second conversion specifier is reached, at which point the second argument in the argument list is evaluated and printed in a format corresponding to the second conversion specifier, and so on.

The argument list is read from left to right as the conversion specifiers are encountered. *You must take great care that each conversion specifier has a corresponding argument and vice versa, as well as making sure that the arguments are in the same order as the conversion specifiers they correspond to and that the types of the specifiers and those of the arguments correspond.*

Since printf() is a function that takes a variable number of arguments (see Chapter 8), the compiler is not able to warn you if the number of conversion specifiers and arguments is not the same. A mismatch can lead to unwanted or even disastrous results.

Assuming the types of the specifiers and arguments match, if there are insufficient arguments for the format string's conversion specifiers, the behavior is undefined. Often the result is the computer locking up, as unsatisfied conversion specifiers gobble up bytes from the memory area where the addresses of the next instructions to be executed are found. If the conversion specifiers are exhausted while arguments remain, the superfluous arguments are evaluated (so if an argument performs some incidental operation, the operation is performed), but discarded. In the first case, there may be untold havoc; in the second, you may not know data has been discarded. Choose your poison.

If there is a type mismatch between conversion specifiers and arguments, all manner of strange things can happen. For example, assuming that on a particular system an int is 4 bytes and a long and a double are both 8, with this code fragment

```
double dipping = 2222.22;
long about_now = 1000000L;
int tern = 200;
printf("%ld %d %d\n", dipping, about_now, tern);
```

the computer places onto a variable memory pool called the *stack* 8 bytes each for dipping and about_now and 4 for tern. The first conversion specifier, %ld, uses the correct number of bytes for dipping, but then it figures out what value those bytes would have if they collectively comprised a long. Since the way the bytes of a long are interpreted is completely different from the way the bytes of a double are interpreted (see Chapter 12), some very strange result is printed. The next two %d specifiers each take half of about_now's 8 bytes and interpret them separately as though they were int values. This time, the way bytes are interpreted is the same, but they are the wrong bytes. Finally, even though the last conversion specifier, %d, correctly matches the last argument, tern, the computer never gets that far. The variable in the last argument is ignored.

There are a few exceptions to the requirement for matching the conversion specifier and corresponding argument type. The exceptions derive from automatic type conversions that occur in variable argument functions such as printf(). The types char, unsigned char, and short are all automatically converted to int; unsigned short is automatically converted to either unsigned int or signed int; and float is automatically converted to double. (See Chapter 8 for a complete discussion of variable argument functions and these conversions.)

Therefore, you may use any of the int specifiers—%d and %i, %o, %x, and %X, and %c, for char, unsigned char, and short as well as for int, of course; and you may use a %f specifier for float as well as for double. So, for instance, when you pass a char for a %d specifier, inside the printf() function, the char value is converted to however many bytes an int is in the system, and when the %d specifier looks about for that many bytes to snack on, it finds the correct bytes and everything is kept in synch.

Yes, we did say that a %c specifier is an int specifier, even though it prints values as characters.

3.4   INTEGER AND FLOATING POINT TYPE SIZE VARIATIONS

In the second part of Table 3.1, we listed type size variations to the basic %d and %f conversion specifiers. Some examples:

```
signed statement = -5287;
unsigned will = 5287;
long number = -23247235L;
unsigned long letter = 23247235Lu;
short beer = -387;
unsigned short codicil = 387;
long double indemnity = 17.23;
printf("signed: %d, unsigned: %u\n", statement, will);
printf("long: %ld, unsigned long: %lu\n", number, letter);
printf("short: %hd, unsigned short: %hu\n", beer, codicil);
printf("long double: %Lf\n", indemnity);

signed: -5287, unsigned: 5287
long: -23247235, unsigned long: 23247235
short: -387, unsigned short: 387
long double: 17.230000
```

(On the PC, all these short-specific specifiers would have the same effect as the corresponding specifiers without the h.)

3.4.1   Type Size Variation Format

In Chapter 2, you saw that when assigning constants to variables, you can use either L or l to assign a long and any combination of L or l and U or u to assign an unsigned long and either F or f to assign a float. The printf() function conversion specifiers do not have this case flexibility for printing. The only permitted letters are shown in Table 3.4.

Be careful to follow this format exactly. Certain other combinations produce obviously incorrect results, but others just print wrong results that may pass for correct if you are not watching carefully:

```
printf("%ld\n", 95235L); /* correct */
printf("%LD\n", 95235L); /* obviously incorrect result */
printf("%Ld\n", 95235L); /* not so obviously incorrect: 'L' ignored: overflow */

95235
%LD
29699
```

Table 3.4 *Specifiers for* short, long, long double

Type	Specifiers
short	%hd, %hi, %ho, %hx, %hX
unsigned short	%hu
long	%ld, %li, %lo, %lx, %lX
unsigned long	%lu
long double	%Lf, %Le, %LE, %Lg, %LG

Table 3.5 `printf()` *Conversion Specifiers vs. Constants*

Type	Specifier	Constant
short	%hd	
unsigned short	%hu	
long	%ld	L or l
unsigned long	%lu	LU, UL, lu, ul, Lu, lU, Ul, or uL
float	%f	F or f
double	%f	
long double	%Lf	L or l

Table 3.5 provides a comparison of the `printf()` specifiers and corresponding constant assignment formats for the same types.

3.5   OCTAL AND HEXADECIMAL

When you assign integer constants, you can use octal or hexadecimal notation instead of decimal. You signal to the computer that your digits are octal by placing a zero in front of them, and that the digits are hexadecimal by placing a 0x or 0X in front of them:

```
int num = 65;
num = 011;
num = 0x41;
```

Likewise, when you print an integer value, you may direct printing in either of these alternative notations. For octal, you use a `%o` specifier, and for hex, `%x`. Note that the octal specifier is a lowercase letter, not the zero you use to assign constants to variables.

If you just use `%o` or `%x`, without the # flag discussed below, `printf()` will print the octal or hexadecimal digits without any preceding 0 or 0x:

```
printf("decimal 15 is octal %o\n", 15);
printf("decimal 44 is hexadecimal %x\n", 44);

decimal 15 is octal 17
decimal 44 is hexadecimal 2c
```

If you use `%X` instead of `%x`, you get uppercase "digit" letters instead of lowercase if there are any letters in the hex representation of the value:

```
printf("decimal 44 is hexadecimal %X\n", 44);

decimal 44 is hexadecimal 2C
```

You can also print out `long` or `short` values in octal or hexadecimal notation using the specifiers indicated in Table 3.6.

The difference between X and x is the same as in the immediately preceding example.

You may use the alternative octal and hexadecimal `%o` and `%x` or `%X` formats only to print positive integer values. For negative integer values, you must use the `%d` or equivalent `%i` specifier. Octal and hexadecimal notation are used chiefly for the convenient correspondence between a hexadecimal digit and four binary digits and between an octal digit and three binary digits. That correspondence loses its

Table 3.6 `printf()` `long` *and* `short` *Octal and Hex Conversion Specifiers*

Type	Notation	Specifier
short	octal	%ho
short	hex	%hx, %hX
long	octal	%lo
long	hex	%lx, %lX

significance for negative numbers, where one of the bits is used for sign. (See Chapter 12 for an explanation of the above correspondence and negative numbers.)

3.6 EXPONENTIAL NOTATION

Just as you may assign floating point constants in exponential format, so may you print out floating point values in this alternative format with the `%e` conversion specifier. The format of the `%e` specifier output is

`[-]d.ddde±dd`

where there is always one digit to the left of the decimal point and as many to the right as any precision modifier specifies (with six as the default if none is specified—see below for a discussion of precision modifiers), and the exponent is always expressed in two digits and with a sign:

```
float floater = 178355.46;
printf("floater in decimal format: %f\n", floater);
printf("floater in exponential format: %e\n", floater);
printf("%e\n", 1.0)

floater in decimal format: 178355.453125
floater in exponential format: 1.783555e+05
1.000000e+00
```

The `%g` specifier prints either in `%f` format or `%e` format (except, as discussed below, for a slight difference in the meaning of the precision modifier and treatment of trailing zeros, as between the `%g` specifier on the one hand and the `%f` and `%e` specifiers on the other). If the value is less than $1.0e^{-5}$, the exponential format is used. Otherwise, except as indicated below for very large values, a `%f` style is used:

```
printf("%g %g\n", 0.00012512345, 0.000012512345);

0.00012512345 1.2512345e-05
```

If the result is so large that the full value cannot be printed within the specified precision, the exponential format is used. Otherwise a `%f` style is used:

```
printf("%.7g %.8g\n", 12345678., 12345678.);
printf("%.5g %.6g %g\n", 123456., 123456., 123456.);

1.234568e+07 12345678
1.2346e+05 123456 123456
```

With a `%g` specifier, trailing zeros are eliminated from the fractional portion, whichever style happens to be used. If the result has no digits after the decimal point, the decimal point is also eliminated.

```
printf("%g %f %g %f\n", 1.25, 1.25, 1.0, 1.0);

1.25 1.250000 1 1.000000
```

A `%E` specifier simply causes the printer to use a capital E in the output rather than a lowercase e:

```
float upper_case = 178355.46;
printf("upper_case: %E\n", upper_case);


upper_case: 1.783555E+05
```

Likewise, `%G` will print a capital E instead of lowercase e if the exponential format is the resulting format.

The specifiers `%Le`, `%LE`, `%Lg`, and `%LG` for a `long double` are the same as `%e`, `%E`, `%g`, and `%G`, respectively, for a `double`. You may not use a lowercase l in place of L in any of those.

3.7   MODIFIERS

As we've seen, each conversion specifier begins with a `%` and ends with a conversion character or pair of characters to indicate the type. You can insert what are called *modifiers* immediately after the `%` and before the conversion type specifier to:

- indicate the *minimum* print space to be reserved to print an item—called a ***field-width modifier.***
- indicate whether, if the item does not fill up that whole space, it is to be padded in front or behind with space characters (so as to right- or left-align the item in the space, respectively), zeros, a plus or minus sign, or other characters—called a ***flag.***
- indicate, for floating point types, how many decimal places are to be printed; for strings, the *maximum* number of characters to be printed; and for integer types, the *minimum* number of digits to appear—called a ***precision modifier.***

3.7.1   Field-Width Modifier

The field-width modifier is entered as a decimal integer. It determines the *minimum* width of the field. If the number requires a larger field to print (for example, we specify a field width of 2 to print out 387), the field width will be expanded to print the entire number or string rather than truncating it. If the field-width modifier is larger than the number or string requires, the excess space is padded with leading blanks (trailing spaces if the left justification flag, discussed below, appears in the specifier):

```
printf("%25s\n", "oblivious");
printf("%3s\n", "perspicacious");
printf("%25d\n", 17);
printf("%3d\n", 28383);
printf("%25f\n", 18.398399);
printf("%3f\n", 18.398399);


                oblivious
perspicacious
                       17
28383
                18.398399
18.398399
```

A common use of the field-width modifier is to right-align a column of numbers or strings of differing lengths and thereby ensure an equal amount of space is taken up by a column in a multicolumn printout. Let's say we wanted to produce a report in the following format:

```
                                 Delta:
                         Age in   Left-   Normal   Total
Mean Age Groups  YY-MM   Level    Right   Modes    Score

_____  _____   _____    _____   _____    _____


Mean for 5 years  5-2    29.80    6.93    15.27    52.00
   Subject's score        18      28      88       77
```

```
Mean for 6 years     6-5    18.83    7.30    5.70   31.83
  Subject's score             34     488      49       8

Mean for 7 years     7-8    12.29    7.23    2.06   21.62
  Subject's score            999      88              99
```

The following would do that in an orderly, organized fashion:

```
printf("%21s%7s%9s%9s%9s%9s\n", "","",
   "", "Delta:", "", "");
printf("%21s%7s%9s%9s%9s%9s\n", "",
   "Age in", "", "Left-", "Normal", "Total");
printf("%21s%7s%9s%9s%9s%9s\n", "Mean Age Groups",
   "YY-MM", "Level", "Right", "Modes ", "Score");
printf("%21s%7s%9s%9s%9s%9s\n\n", "_____",
   "_____", "_____", "_____", "_____", "_____");
printf("\n%21s%7s%9s%9s%9s%9s\n", "Mean for 5 years",
   "5-2", "29.80", "6.93", "15.27", "52.00");
printf("%21s%7s%9d%9d%9d%9d\n", "Subject's score", "",
   18, 28, 88, 77);
printf("\n%21s%7s%9s%9s%9s%9s\n", "Mean for 6 years",
   "6-5", "18.83", "7.30", "5.70", "31.83");
printf("%21s%7s%9d%9d%9d%9d\n", "Subject's score", "",
   34, 488, 49, 8);
printf("\n%21s%7s%9s%9s%9s%9s\n", "Mean for 7 years",
   "7-8", "12.29", "7.23", "2.06", "21.62");
printf("%21s%7s%9d%9d%9d%9d\n", "Subject's score", "",
   999, 88, 0, 99);
```

 There are a couple of things to note in this example. *First, a blank string, "", will print out spaces in the number indicated by the field-width modifier. Second, you can use the same field-width modifiers from row to row even though the types are different; the whole thing still lines up fine.*

The field width is the space reserved for all printing characters: any sign, any 0 or 0x or 0X prefix for octal or hexadecimal numbers printed with the # flag discussed below, the digits (both those to the left and to the right of the decimal point for floating point numbers), any letters for hexadecimal numbers, the decimal point for floating point numbers, and all the components of the exponent portion of the %e specifier or the %g specifier where the resulting print out is %e format:

```
printf("\n12345678\n%8.1f\n%8.1f\n%8.1f",
   -1234.5, -12345.6, -123456.7);
```

```
12345678
 -1234.5
-12345.6
-123456.7
```

The second output lines up in the eight-space field with a single leading space: there are seven total characters in the output. The third output also lines up, this time without any leading space since there are exactly eight characters in the output. The final output does not line up: there are nine characters for an eight-character field.

3.7.2   Precision Modifier

The precision modifier is given as an integer following a decimal point—for example, %.2f. The precision modifier has a different significance for different types.

Precision Modifier for Integer Types.   For integer specifiers (other than the %c specifier, where it has no relevance), the precision modifier dictates the *minimum* number of digits to display. If the value to be printed will not fill up the entire field, the start of the field is padded with leading 0s:

```
printf("%.4d\n", 12345);
printf("%.4d\n", 12);
```

```
12345
0012
```

The precision modifier is handy for equalizing date printouts:

```
printf("%.2d/%.2d/.2%d\n", day1, month1, year1);
printf("%.2d/%.2d/.2%d\n", day2, month2, year2);
```

```
03/12/00
11/02/00
```

Precision Modifier for Floating Point Types. For floating point types—its most common use—the precision modifier dictates the number of digits to be printed to the right of the decimal point (see below for a slight difference for the %g specifier). If there are fewer post-decimal point digits in the value than the number specified, zeros are added to the right of the last post-decimal point digit. If there are more, the value printed is rounded to the specified decimal place:

```
printf("%.2f\n", 17.835835);
printf("%.2f\n", 18.1);
```

```
17.84
18.10
```

A %.f or a %.0f specifier will print an integer number only, without any decimal point (unless, as to the decimal point, the # flag—discussed later—is present):

```
printf("%.f\n", 17.835835);
printf("%.0f\n", 17.835835);
```

```
18
18
```

If the value to be printed is less than 1, a %f specifier will print a zero before the decimal point:

```
printf("%f\n", .93954);
```

```
0.939540
```

In the absence of any precision modifier, a %f will print six digits after the decimal point:

```
printf("%f\n", 17.23);
```

```
17.230000
```

Unlike the %f and %e specifiers, the precision modifier in a %g specifier indicates the number of total significant digits (this does not include the decimal point, just digits to the left and right of it), not just the number of decimal digits. The precision modifier default is six for the %g conversion specifier, just as it is for %f and %e (though the meaning is, as we say, slightly different):

```
printf("%e \t%g\n", 0.000012512345, 0.000012512345);
printf("%.5f \t%.5g\n", 1.234567, 1.234567);
```

```
1.251235e-05    1.25123e-05
1.23457         1.2346
```

Precision Modifier for Strings. With strings, the precision modifier indicates the *maximum* field width. If the string is longer than this number, it is truncated:

```
printf("%s\n", "squeeze me in, please!");
printf("%.10s\n", "squeeze me in, please!);
```

```
squeeze me in, please!
squeeze me
```

What this also means is that if the argument corresponding to a %s specifier has no NULL character to terminate it, printing will work fine as long as the number of characters specified in the precision modifier does not exceed the memory area reserved for the argument:

```
char not_a_string[4] = {'N', 'o', 't', '!'}; /* no room for
                terminating NULL, so not a string */
printf("%.4s\n", not_a_string);
```

```
Not!
```

Without that saving feature here, the %s specifier would cause printing to continue until a NULL character happened to be reached by chance somewhere in memory. (In Chapter 7, we will explain how to create strings and why this is not one.)

3.7.3   Using Both Field-Width and Precision Modifiers Together

The field-width and precision modifiers may be—and often are—both found in one specifier. For instance, a %6.2f specifier will right-align a column of floating point numbers and ensure the numbers line up on the decimal point:

```
printf("%6.2f%6.2f%6.2f%6.2f\n", 19.299, 19.2, 93.0, 89.);
printf("%6.2f%6.2f%6.2f%6.2f\n", 299.9, 9.222, .098, 1.22);
printf("%6.2f%6.2f%6.2f%6.2f\n", 1.01, .21, .1, 89.01);
printf("%6.2f%6.2f%6.2f%6.2f\n", 2.99, 9., 3.1, 9.111);
```

```
 19.30 19.20 93.00 89.00
299.90  9.22  0.10  1.22
  1.01  0.21  0.10 89.01
  2.99  9.00  3.10  9.11
```

Remember, however, that the field-width modifier provides a *minimum* width only. The alignment scheme we've shown here works only to the extent the values do not require a larger field. Otherwise, the columns will not be aligned:

```
printf("%6.2f%6.2f%6.2f%6.2f\n", 1234429.299,
   19.2, 93.0, 89.);
printf("%6.2f%6.2f%6.2f%6.2f\n", 299.9, 2345669.222,
   .098, 1.22);
printf("%6.2f%6.2f%6.2f%6.2f\n", 1.01, .21,
   2223342.1, 89.01);
printf("%6.2f%6.2f%6.2f%6.2f\n", 2.99, 2222229.,
   3.1, 2222229.111);
```

```
1234429.30 19.20 93.00 89.00
299.902345669.22  0.10  1.22
  1.01  0.212223342.10 89.01
  2.992222229.00  3.102222229.11
```

Don't make the mistake of assuming the field width is the total of the digit before and the digit after the decimal point in a specifier that has both a field width and a precision modifier. A %5.2f specifier reserves a minimum field width of five (counting the decimal point as one of the five), not seven or eight. Thus, the following two columns of numbers will not line up:

```
printf("%5.2f%5.2f\n", 12345.67, 23456.78);
printf("%5.2f%5.2f\n", 123.45, 234.56);
```

```
12345.67 23456.78
123.45 234.56
```

3.7.4   Variable Field-Width/Precision Modifier

You can use a * in place of an integer for the field-width or precision modifiers or both, to allow you to place the value of those modifiers as variables in the argument list. You place the variables or variable expressions corresponding to the field-width and precision modifiers immediately before the spot in the argument list that corresponds to the conversion specifier for this item:

```
int width = 14, precision = 6;
double test = 123456.123456;
printf("%*.*f\n%*.8f\n", width, precision, test,
    width + 2, test);
width = precision = 2;
printf("%d/%d%d\n", 1, 2, 99);
printf("%*.*d/%*.*d/%*.*d\n", precision, width, 1,
    precision, width, 2, precision, width, 99);
```

```
   123456.123456
      123456.1234560000
1/2/99
01/02/99
```

Here, the values corresponding to each * are hardwired. Of course, in your program the values corresponding to the * could differ depending on the results of the program to that point or they could be derived interactively by user input or from a file.

A negative field width is taken as the left-justification flag, -, discussed below, followed by a positive field width. That is the result even if the field width is derived from a * modifier, where a negative argument is more likely inadvertent (otherwise, you would have probably just put a - explicitly in the conversion specifier). A negative precision modifier causes the precision modifier to be ignored altogether:

```
int num = -5;
printf("\n1234567890\n%*.*d xxxx\n", num, num * 2, 123);
printf("%5.4d xxxx\n", 123);
```

```
1234567890
123   xxxx
 0123 xxxx
```

With the %d specifier in the first example, the –5 corresponding to the field-width modifier is taken as left-justify and reserve five spaces. The –10 argument (num * 2) corresponding to the precision modifier is ignored. The %d specifier in the second example is shown just for contrast. Both modifiers are given the indicated effect: a field of five is reserved and within that field, a minimum of four characters are specified, so a leading zero is prepended to the three-character number.

3.7.5   Flags

Table 3.7 lists the flags and their meanings.

Table 3.7 printf() *Flags*

Flag	Meaning
–	Left-hand justified within the field.
+	Results of signed specifiers are displayed with a + if positive and a – if negative.
[space]	Results of signed specifiers are displayed with a leading space if positive and a – if negative.
#	Displays a leading 0 for %o and a leading 0x or 0X for %x or %X. For all floating point specifiers, ensures that a decimal point is displayed even if no digits follow the decimal point. For %g and %G, trailing zeros are not eliminated.
0	For all numeric specifiers, pads field with leading zeros if the number itself does not take up entire field width.

3.7.6   The − Flag

If a − flag is used and the value printed requires less space than the specified field width, the padded spaces are placed to the right of what's printed rather than to the left. In other words, the text is left-justified, printing at its extreme left side. The − flag can be used to left-align a series of printed items:

```
printf("%-12s%-12s\n", "Peters,", "Rob");
printf("%-12s%-12s\n", "Melendez,", "Marguerite");
printf("%-12s%-12s\n", "Doe,", "Crawford");
```

```
Peters,     Rob
Melendez,   Marguerite
Doe,        Crawford
```

3.7.7   The + and [space] Flags *(Optional)*

A + flag, used with numeric signed integer specifiers or with floating point specifiers, causes numbers to be displayed with a plus sign if the number is positive; a " " (for example, % d) used with those specifiers causes numbers to be displayed with a leading space rather than a plus sign if positive:

```
printf("%+d %+d %+d\n", 88, -988, 23);
printf("% d % d % d\n", 88, -988, 23);
```

```
+88 -988 +23
 88 -988  23
```

The % d specifier in this example would ensure that an equal amount of space is reserved for numbers in the same magnitude range but with differing signs.

The + and " " flags have no meaning for unsigned numeric specifiers (%u, %o, %x, %X, and all their short and long varieties) or for nonnumeric or nonprinting specifiers (%c, %s, %p, %n).

3.7.8   The zero Flag

A 0 flag, used with numeric specifiers (floating point or integer, not including %c), pads the field with leading zeros if the number itself does not take up the entire field width.

```
printf("%9.2f %9.2f\n", 890.33, 9.3);
printf("%09.2f %09.2f\n", 890.33, 9.3);
```

```
   890.33      9.30
000890.33 000009.30
```

The 0 flag is useful for date notation:

```
int month = 9, day = 1, year = 93;
printf("%02d/%02d/%02d\n", month, day, year);
```

```
09/01/93
```

The 0 flag is also useful in creating a file that interfaces between two applications when one of the applications requires fixed-length numeric fields (such as COBOL record layouts).

For integer type specifiers, you can generally produce the same result with a precision modifier as with the 0 flag:

```
int month = 9, day = 1, year = 93;
printf("%.2d/%.2d/%d\n", month, day, year);
```

```
09/01/93
```

However, in some circumstances, the result will not be precisely the same. The distinction is somewhat subtle. Take a modified version of one of our previous examples:

```
printf("\n1234567890\n%5.4d xxxx\n", 123);
printf("%05d xxxx\n", 123);
```

```
1234567890
 0123 xxxx
00123 xxxx
```

The entire five-character field specified by the field-width modifier in the first conversion specifier is not padded with zeros, but only has the single space required to make the three-character number equal the four digits specified as the minimum *characters* to print by the precision modifier in the same specifier.

3.7.9   The # Flag *(Optional)*

The # flag displays a leading 0 for the %o octal specifier and a leading 0x or 0X for the hexadecimal specifiers (for %x and %X, respectively):

```
printf("%o %x %X\n", 98, 7287, 29379);
printf("%#o %#x %#X\n", 98, 7287, 29379);
```

```
142 1c77 72C3
0142 0x1c77 0X72C3
```

For floating point specifiers (%f, %e, and %g and all their long double and uppercase-letter versions), the # flag causes a decimal point to be printed if the precision specified is 0 (including where there is a decimal point in the conversion specifier and no precision number, which is taken as 0 precision):

```
printf("%.f %#.f\n", 899., 899.);
```

```
899 899.
```

For the %g and %G specifiers, the # flag also means that trailing zeros will *not* be eliminated.

The # flag is not relevant to the %d, %i, or %u conversion specifiers, or their short or long varieties, or to %c or %s.

3.7.10   Multiple Modifiers

You can use more than one modifier at once. If you do, you must put them in the order: flag, field width, precision. If you use more than one flag, the order is not material:

```
printf("%12.2f%12.2f%12.2f\n", 2311.33, -33.2, 29393.);
printf("%+12.2f%+12.2f%+12.2f\n", 2311.33, -33.2, 29393.);
printf("%-+12.2f%-+12.2f%-+12.2f\n", 2311.33,
   -33.2, 29393.);
printf("%12X\n", 29379);
printf("%-#12X\n", 29379, 29379);
```

```
    2311.33      -33.20     29393.00
   +2311.33      -33.20    +29393.00
+2311.33    -33.20       +29393.00
      72C3
0X72C3
```

3.8   LONG FORMAT STRINGS

Normally, since the compiler ignores spaces, you can split a long statement between two or more lines anywhere in the statement, as long as you do not split variable or function names, or C keywords or multicharacter operators:

```
total_commissions = (lexington_office +
   newport_office + genoa_office) * .10 +
   (paris_office + london_office) * .12;
```

If your `printf()` statement can be split at any comma or other operator in the argument list, you have no problem:

```
printf("The first letters in the alphabet are %c %c %c %c %c\n;"
    'a', 'b', 'c', 'd', 'e');
```

You cannot be so cavalier with format strings or literal string arguments, however, because the spaces between the opening and closing quotation marks are read literally. The pair of quotation marks must both be on the same line. If you have a long literal string, you have a problem with this rule—whether it be with `printf()`, or, as we will discuss in later chapters, with some of the other Standard C string functions such as `puts()`, or with your own homemade functions that take strings as arguments.

There are several solutions to this problem. The least desirable solution is just to extend the string beyond the 80-character screen width. However, using super-long lines extending beyond the screen width is a sloppy programming practice. Lines more than 80 characters long—a screen's worth—make your code hard to read and may lead to programming errors. There are more acceptable alternative solutions: logical line continuation, separate `printf()` statements, and string concatenation.

3.8.1   Logical Line Continuation

You can preserve the long line logically but break it up visually by the use of the backslash character:

```
printf("I believe I may possibly be of the opinion that \
perhaps we need decisiveness\n");
```

```
I believe I may possibly be of the opinion that perhaps we need decisiveness
```

The line continues at column 0, an exception to the normal rule of the compiler's disregarding indentation. Thus, if you indent line 2 of the previous example

```
printf("I believe I may possibly be of the opinion that \
    perhaps we need decisiveness\n");
```

you get this as the string:

```
I believe I may possibly be of the opinion that     perhaps we need decisiveness
```

You can inadvertently reproduce this defective example if your C editor automatically indents when you press the Enter key after indenting a line of code.

Even with logical line continuation via backslashes, Standard C requires only that implementations permit lines of at least 509 characters.

3.8.2   Separate `printf()` Statements

Another choice is to split the statement into separate `printf()` statements:

```
printf("I believe I may possibly be of the opinion that");
printf(" perhaps we need decisiveness\n");
```

```
I believe I may possibly be of the opinion that perhaps we need decisiveness
```

Don't forget to leave a space either at the end of the first `printf()` statement or, as we did here, at the beginning of the second.

3.8.3   String Concatenation

Perhaps the most common approach is to use string concatenation. You close off the open quotation marks with close quotation marks and use another set of quotation marks on the next line or lines:

```
printf("I believe I may possibly be of the opinion that"
    " perhaps\n\twe need decisiveness.\n");
printf("There are %d reasons why we need more mirth and %d"
    " reasons\n\twhy we need less.\n", 5, 5);
```

```
printf("Don't forget about the extra"
   "space between lines.\n");
```

```
I believe I may possibly be of the opinion that perhaps
    we need decisiveness.
There are 5 reasons why we need more mirth and 5 reasons
    why we need less.
Don't forget about the extraspace between lines.
```

Literal strings (those surrounded by double quotes) with nothing between them but spaces or newlines are automatically concatenated (stuck together as though they were one string). This is so for strings on the same line as well as those on different lines:

```
printf("This " "is " "all " "one very long "
   "string.\n");
```

```
    This is all one very long string.
```

In Chapter 11, we will see the utility of this concept for multiple strings on a single line.

3.9   THE scanf() FUNCTION

The printf() function takes numerical and string data and converts it to characters to print on the screen (unless standard output has been redirected to some other location, as discussed in Chapter 14 or 16). The scanf() function does just the opposite. It takes character input from the keyboard (unless standard input has been redirected) and converts the input to values, which it then assigns to variables that you, as the programmer, select.

The scanf() function's format is similar to printf()'s; there is a format string with conversion specifiers and an argument list:

```
int num, int val;
scanf("%d%d", &num, &val);
```

Like printf(), the format string is enclosed by quotation marks and separated from the argument list by a comma. The items in the argument list are separated from one another by commas, just as with printf(). There are significant differences in substance, however. With printf(), the argument list can contain variables, constants, or variable-constant expressions. With scanf(), the list contains only the addresses of variables into which text, after having been read in and converted by scanf(), is stored.

To make the argument an address of a variable, you put the address operator, &, in front of the variable name. You may not insert a space between the & and the variable. In the example above, scanf() takes the character input the user types in, converts the first part to a value and stores it at the address of the variable num, and converts the second part to a value and stores that value at the address of the variable val.

With strings, we omit the &, since, as you will see in a later chapter, a string *is* an address:

```
scanf("%s", name);
```

3.9.1   The Input Mechanism

The scanf() function itself does not signal the user that it awaits input. It just halts program execution until the user types characters on the keyboard and signals completion by pressing the [Enter] key. For this reason, common practice is to alert the user to input data by a printf() statement or similar means:

```
printf("Type an integer number and press enter");
scanf("%d", &num);
```

Later in the book, you will learn more sophisticated methods for reading user input, but for now, we will have to use the somewhat unwieldy combination printf()-scanf() statements for input. Even though you will not often use scanf() once your programs become more sophisticated, the study of scanf() is important. You will still continue to use fscanf() to read data from a file; the fscanf() function is identical to scanf() save for the addition, just before the format string, of a variable that indicates the file to be read:

```
fscanf(rfile, "%d", &num);
```

You will also have occasion to use sscanf() to read data from a string in memory. (See Chapter 14 for a discussion of fscanf() and Chapter 9 for sscanf().)

3.10   CONVERSION SPECIFICATIONS

Conversion type specifiers for scanf() are similar to those for printf(), as Table 3.8 illustrates.

The fact that these specifiers are similar but not identical to those for printf() can lead to confusion:

- With printf(), there is no specifier for float: both float and double print as double. With scanf(), there are separate specifiers: %f for float and %lf for double.
- With printf(), the %d specifier is identical to the %i specifier; with scanf(), the %d specifier accepts decimal integer input only, whereas the %i specifier accepts decimal, octal, or hexadecimal input.

Table 3.8   scanf() *Conversion Type Specifiers*

Specifier	Input
Basics	
%c	character
%s	string
%d	int—decimal notation only
%u	unsigned—decimal notation only
%f, %e, %E, %g, %G	float—decimal or exponential format
Type Size Variations	
%hd	short—decimal only
%hu	unsigned short—decimal only
%hi	short—decimal, octal or hexadecimal
%ho	unsigned short—octal only
%hx	unsigned short— hexadecimal only
%ld	long—decimal only
%lu	unsigned long—decimal only
%li	long—decimal, octal or hexadecimal
%lo	unsigned long—octal only
%lx	unsigned long—hexadecimal only
%lf, %le, %lE, %lg, %lG	double
%Lf, %Le, %LE, %Lg, %LG	long double
Base Variations: Octal/Hexadecimal	
%i	int—decimal, octal or hex
%o	unsigned—octal notation only
%x	unsigned—hex notation only
Special Cases	
[. . .]	read until find character not within braces
[^. . .]	read until find character within braces
%p	pointer address value
%n	# of characters input to that point

Table 3.9 `printf()` *vs.* `scanf()` *vs. Constants*

Type	scanf() Specifier	printf() Specifier	Constant
short	%hd	%hd	
unsigned short	%hu	%hu	
long	%ld	%ld	L or l
unsigned long	%lu	%lu	LU, UL, lu, ul, Lu, lU, Ul, or uL
float	%f	%f	F or f
double	%lf	%f	
long double	%Lf	%Lf	L or l

- With `printf()`, there is no way to print negative values in octal or hexadecimal format. With `scanf()`, negative octal or hexadecimal notation numbers can be read in with a `%i` specifier.
- With `printf()`, the two versions of the hexadecimal specifier, `%x` and `%X`, differ with respect to case of letter digits. With `scanf()`, there is no difference between `%x` and `%X`; they both recognize uppercase or lowercase letters a–f or A–F as hexadecimal digits.
- With `printf()`, the `%f`, `%e`, and `%g` specifiers have different formats from one another; and the uppercase counterparts `%E` and `%G` print an uppercase E for the exponent rather than e (assuming the result of a `%G` specifier is the exponential format). With `scanf()`, there is no difference whatsoever among these six specifiers. They all recognize exponent and nonexponent floating point format, and if the exponent form appears in input, any of them recognize either E or e.
- Both `printf()` and `scanf()` have the `*` modifier. But the meaning and purpose for `scanf()` is completely different from its meaning and purpose for `printf()`. The difference can be highly confusing (not to mention that the same flexible asterisk character is also used to signify multiplication and, as you will see in later chapters, for pointer notation).
- For `printf()`, a field-width modifier indicates the *minimum* print *space* to be reserved to print an item. With `scanf()`, the field-width modifier specifies the *maximum* number of *characters* to be read. Unlike `printf()`, `scanf()` does not provide for precision specification. You cannot issue any direction such as "for this next floating point specifier, read only for two decimal places after the period," or "read the whole business and then round off to the third decimal place."
- With both `printf()` and `scanf()`, the format string may contain characters in addition to the specifiers (including their modifiers). However, it is more common to find additional characters in a `printf()` statement than not; additional characters are not often found in a `scanf()` statement and their effect is a good deal different there.

Table 3.9 presents a summary of letter notations in three different contexts.

3.11   MECHANICS OF `scanf()`

You can combine more than one input in a single `scanf()` statement. The following example provides for input of an integer value and two floating point values:

```
int employees;
float salary, hours;
scanf("%d%f%f", &employees, &salary, &hours);
```

If `scanf()` reads character by character and if one `scanf()` statement can contain several conversion specifiers, how does the computer know when to stop assigning the characters to one variable and start assigning them to the next? The answer lies in what is called "whitespace"—defined to include a space character, tab character, newline character, carriage return character, or formfeed character.

The processing of each conversion specifier is accomplished in a three-step process. First, all leading whitespace characters, if any, are read and discarded. Characters following any whitespace are read until the next whitespace is encountered. Finally, scanf() converts characters read in between whitespaces to a value and stores the value in the variable that corresponds to the conversion specifier. If the conversion specifier is a %s, a terminating \0 is added to make the series of character values a string, something that will become more meaningful to you after we discuss strings in Chapter 7. The whitespace that terminated character reading is placed back into the input stream, not discarded as it is at the front end.

Let's use the preceding example, with employees, salary, and hours, as an illustration. Say the user types in the following (moving from one line to the next indicates that the user has pressed the Enter key, generating a newline character):

```
12
345.90
49.1231
```

The following processing occurs with the respective conversion specifiers:

1. There is no initial whitespace in this example. Therefore, the computer reads in the 1 and 2 before stopping at the newline character. The 1 and 2 are read as "12", converted to the value 12, and stored in employees. The newline character is placed back into the input stream.

2. The newline character—placed back into the input stream after terminating the first round of character reading—is read and discarded and the computer reads in 345.90 until stopping at the newline character following the zero. The characters in 345.90 are converted to the value 345.9 and that value is assigned to salary. The newline is placed back into the input stream.

3. The newline is read and discarded and the computer reads in 49.1231 and stops at the newline. The characters 49.1231 are converted to the value 49.1231 and the value stored in hours. The newline is placed back into the input stream to be read by any subsequent scanf() statement or any other function that reads from standard input.

Since spaces are whitespace, too, the following input, with one or more spaces between each entry, would produce the very same result

```
12 345.90 49.1231
```

as would

```
12          345.90
49.1231
```

where the user pressed Tab between the first and second inputs.

Nothing is sent to the computer for processing until the Enter key is pressed. Meanwhile, the user can change what is to be sent for processing by backspacing and typing over incorrect input.

3.11.1 Exceptional Cases

There are several exceptions to the procedure just described and illustrated. The computer will read and store whitespace just like it was any normal character

- if the conversion specifier is %c. There is an exception to this exception, discussed below.
- in certain cases with a %[. . .] or a %[^. . .] specifier.

Conversely, the computer will stop even before encountering whitespace if

- it reads a character not appropriate for the particular conversion specifier (such as a nondigit character for a %d specifier).
- characters are inserted into the format string between conversion specifiers and those characters are not encountered at that point in the input stream.
- a modifier is used in the conversion specifier to dictate the maximum number of characters that can be read for that specifier and that number of characters is read before coming to whitespace.
- in certain cases with a %[. . .] or a %[^. . .] specifier.

3.12   THE %c CONVERSION SPECIFIER

With a %c specifier, scanf() reads the next character (or, as we will see below, the next specified number of characters if the c is preceded by an integer, as in %20c), even if it is whitespace. When the %c specifier is used, whitespace is read in just like any other character, not discarded. However, if you insert a space just before the %c specifier (before the %, not between it and the c), the whitespace is skipped just as for other conversion specifiers. Contrast two examples. Here's the first:

```
int i;
char c1, c2;
scanf("%d%c%c", &i, &c1, &c2);
printf("%d %c%c\n", i, c1, c2);
printf("%d\n", c1); /* show c1 is a newline */
```

Here, if we enter

```
25
x
```

we get the following output:

```
25
x
10
```

The 2 and 5 are read by the %d specifier and the value stored in i. The newline character after the 5 is placed back into the input stream, where it is read and stored by the %c specifier in c1. The following character, x, is read by the next %c specifier and stored in c2.When we direct printing of i, c1, and c2, all we get for c1 is a newline, causing the x to be printed on the line after 25. To prove that is what is stored in c1, we direct printing of the decimal value of c1 in the next statement. We get the number 10, the value of the newline character (assuming ASCII character encoding).

On the other hand, if we put spaces before the %c specifiers

```
scanf("%d %c %c", &i, &c1, &c2);
printf("%d %c %c\n", i, c1, c2);
```

and we enter

```
25
a
b
```

we get acceptable output:

```
25 a b
```

3.13   CHARACTERS BETWEEN CONVERSION SPECIFIERS

The result in the second half of the preceding example does not derive from any inherent properties of the %c specifier. The %c specifier continues to read and accept whitespace as well as non-whitespace input. Rather the result was occasioned by the following rule:

 Placing a whitespace character anywhere in the format string causes all whitespace to be read and discarded at that point.

If several consecutive whitespace characters appear in the format string, the effect is just as though only one had appeared, so placing more than one consecutive whitespace character there is probably inadvertent on the part of the programmer.

If what follows a whitespace character in the format string is a conversion specifier for any numerical input—all of which read and discard all whitespace before starting the read–convert to value process—placing a whitespace character has accomplished nothing that would not have happened anyway. However, there is an instance, other than before a %c specifier, where inserting a whitespace character in the format string can change the result. That instance is before a character in the format string that is between conversion specifiers.

 If a character is placed in the format string between conversion specifiers, the character, when encountered in the input stream, is read and discarded.

We can make use of this rule to simplify user input. For instance, if we want the user to input a date—month, day and year—and we want the ability to store the month, day, and year separately as numerical values so we can easily manipulate them later, we could ask for three separate inputs:

```
printf("input the month number (mm)\n");
scanf("%d", &month);
printf("input the day (dd)\n");
scanf("%d", &day);
printf("input the year (yy)\n");
scanf("%d", &year);
```

or

```
printf("input the month number, day and year,"
  " pressing the enter key after each");
scanf("%d%d%d", &month, &day, &year);
```

We can, however, simplify things by asking for a single combination input:

```
printf("input the date (format: mm/dd/yy)");
scanf("%d/%d/%d", &month, &day, &year);
printf("%d/%d/%d", month, day, year);
```

Note the two / characters in the format string to gobble up the anticipated extraneous input. Thus, with input of

```
10/11/99
```

we get output of

```
10/11/99
```

We could also have used the following statement to accomplish the same thing:

```
char ch;
scanf("%d%c%d%c%d", &month, &ch, &day, &ch, &year);
printf("%d/%d/%d", month, day, year);
```

This alternative would also have the advantage of permitting the user to enter a date either in the format mm-dd-yy or the specified mm/dd/yy.

If we want to provide for the possibility that the user in this date-entry exercise might enter spaces between the date elements, we can place a space before the /:

```
scanf("%d /%d /%d", &month, &day, &year);
```

Then if the user types in

```
10  / 11 / 99
```

we still get the same result. We don't need a space *before* the %d specifiers since the numerical input specifiers gobble up starting whitespace by themselves.

3.13.1 Failure to Encounter Character in Format String

 If there is no whitespace in the input stream at the point where a whitespace in the format string is encountered, the whitespace in the format string is ignored.

Thus, with the last formulation, input of any of the following would produce the same result:

```
10 / 11 / 99
10/11/99
10/11 / 99
```

Great care must be taken when placing a character other than a whitespace character between conversion specifiers in the format string.

 If a character, other than a whitespace character, in the format string between conversion specifiers is not encountered in the input stream at the point where the character is reached in the format string, there will be a reading failure.

Later in the chapter, we will discuss just what happens in the event of failure and in what other circumstances inappropriate characters can cause failure.

3.14   MODIFIERS

Just as with `printf()`, you may place modifiers between the `%` and the conversion type letter. You may use a `*` or a field-width modifier. If you use both, the `*` must come first. The complete order of what may come after the `%` is as follows:

- An optional assignment suppression character, `*`
- An optional maximum field width
- An optional type size specification: lowercase h or l, indicating `short` or `long`, respectively, for any of the integer numeric specifiers or the `%n` specifier; or L, indicating `long double`, for any of the floating point specifiers
- The conversion specifier letter itself, c, s, d, i, o, u, x, X, f, e, E, g, or G (or the [. . .] construction)

Here is an example using all of these : `%*8ld`, indicating that no more than the next eight characters (accepting as valid only the decimal digits and any preceding sign) are to be read in as a `long`, and then discarded rather than stored anywhere.

3.14.1   The * Modifier (Assignment Suppression Character)

The `*` has a much different purpose from its use with `printf()`, where it acts as a placeholder for variables in the argument list for the field-width and precision modifiers. With `scanf()`, the asterisk directs reading of characters and then discarding them rather than storing them in the next argument list variable. In the `scanf()` context, the `*` is sometimes referred to as the *assignment suppression character*.

For instance, in one of our previous examples, where we read in a date,

```
char ch;
scanf("%d%c%d%c%d", &month, &ch, &day, &ch, &year);
printf("%d/%d/%d", month, day, year);
```

we stored in ch the / or – input that was read by the `%c` specifiers, and then just ignored ch when we printed the whole business. We can accomplish the same thing without using a trashbin variable this way:

```
scanf("%d %*c%d %*c%d", &month, &day, &year);
```

The ones skipped are omitted from the argument list.

Likewise,

```
printf("Input month, day & year\n");
scanf("%d %*d%d", &month, &year);
```

would cause the day input to be read and discarded. Of course, here we could have just altered the user prompt to ask for a month and year only, eliminating the necessity for a `%*d` specifier. However, this example would be useful were we using `fscanf()` to read from a file where we know the file contains month, day, and year data and where we have no interest in the day data. (See Chapter 14 for a discussion of `fscanf()`.)

3.14.2   Field-Width Modifier

The field-width modifier indicates the *maximum* input field width—the opposite from its usage with `printf()`. Input stops at the earlier of the first whitespace character (assuming the specifier is not `%c`) or when as many characters as the field width are read in. The following code, input, and output result are illustrative:

```
scanf("%3d%3d%3d", &i1, &i2, &i3);
printf("%d %d %d\n", i1, i2, i3);
```

111222333444

111 222 333

The first `%3d` specifier stops the reading of the input stream after the third character. The next `%3d` specifier takes up at the first 2 and reads through the last 2. The final `%3d` specifier starts at the first 3 and stops at the last 3, leaving the "444\n" in the input stream. Absent the modifier, the first specifier would have caused the entire numerical value to be read and stored in `i1` (causing an odometer-like overflow).

Again, the user would not normally type input manually in such a compressed format. The use is chiefly with files. It would be common to store records of data in a text file, with each line containing a single record. Each record would in turn be composed of fields: say a part record consisting of a manufacturer's part number, the company's internal tracking number, wholesale price, retail price, a text description of the part, and so on. To save space and achieve uniformity, the characters for each field might be allocated a specified number of characters, with no spaces between fields. In the part example, something like the following symbolically might be in the file:

MMMMMMMCCCCCCCCCCCWWWWWRRRRRTTTTTTTTTTTTTTTTTTTTTTTTTT

The record file would be read back in using `fscanf()`, with field-width modifiers in the respective conversion specifiers.

With the `%c` specifier, a default field width of 1 is assumed if the field-width modifier is omitted. With all other conversion specifiers, input will be read until whitespace or an inappropriate character is encountered if there is no field-width modifier.

Initial whitespace that is discarded by the specifier does not count toward the maximum field width. For instance:

```
printf("Type social security #: format \"123-45-6789\"\n");
scanf("%11s", ssn);
printf("%s\n", ssn);
```

[two tabs] 346-40-4095 and that's not all
346-40-4095

However, if the specifier were `%c` or `[. . .]`, which do not skip whitespace, the initial whitespace would count as part of the input field.

Input for the `%x`, `%X`, or `%o` specifiers may or may not be preceded by a 0, or 0x, or 0X, respectively; and octal or hexadecimal input for the `%i` specifier must have such prefixes. If input does have prefixes, the prefixes are counted toward the field width. Any sign, decimal point, the letter e or E, and so on for any numerical specifier also counts:

```
scanf("%3x", &num);
scanf("%3x", &val);
printf("num: %d val: %d\n");
11
```
    0x11
num: 11 val: 1

In the first case, both characters are read and the specifier stops at the newline. Input does not continue for this specifier: the field width is a maximum, not a minimum. The next statement's specifier reads and discards the leftover newline, then reads in only the next three characters, stopping at the first 1.

Since `scanf()` stops at the *earlier* of field width or whitespace, you cannot use a large field width to force `scanf()` with a `%s` specifier to read more than one word into an array, as the following true story shows.

The Town of Solemn, Nebraska, had fallen on hard times. The Singer Sewing Machine Company, which constituted the lifeblood of the town, had just relocated its plant to California. A shy young machine operator, one Madonna McGillicuty, who was now out of a job, presented herself at the local unemployment office. She input her employment application on a computer, the program having been written by a novice C programmer:

```
printf("Enter name:\n" );
scanf("%81s", name);
printf("Enter occupation:\n");
scanf("%81s", occupation);
```

She dutifully responded:

```
Madonna McGillicuty
Singer Sewing Machine operator
```

The following week, she received a telegram:

> Madonna:
>
> Lead singer, religious spoof musical movie left to join convent. Need you urgently Hollywood Monday. Bring trashy clothes. Love your name! Stop.
>
>   Martin Scorsese

The rest, as they say, is history. No matter what the user does, there is no way to input a first and last name into a single variable with scanf() and a %s specifier. Later in the chapter, we will show you one way of accomplishing this job, with a [. . .] specifier. In Chapter 9, we will show you a far simpler, more efficient method, using the gets() function.

Meanwhile, now that we've gone over the rules for scanf(), we will show you some simple examples of each conversion specifier. Then we will examine scanf()'s termination characteristics.

3.15   CONVERSION SPECIFIER EXAMPLES

We will use the following declarations for the code fragments throughout this section:

```
char c1, c2;
char s[20];
int i1, i2, i3;
unsigned u1;
short little1, little2, little3;
unsigned short ulittle;
long big1, big2, big3;
unsigned long ubig;
float f1, f2, f3;
double big_f;
long double huge_f;
```

3.15.1   The %c and %s Conversion Specifiers

Both the %c and %s specifier read input for storage starting at the address of a char. The following code is illustrative:

```
scanf("%c%s", &c1, s);
printf("%c %s\n", c1, s);
```

O Sue

O Sue

Normally, the %c specifier is used to read a single character only, but as we've seen, if it has a field-width modifier, it will read the number of characters indicated by the field-width modifier. Both the %c and %s specifiers will cause byte values to be placed in memory character by character starting at the address corresponding to the specifier in the argument list. So the %c specifier and the %s specifier have features in common. However, these two specifiers have significant differences as well:

- The %c specifier reads whitespace and other characters without differentiation in reading effect. The %s specifier skips over and discards any leading whitespace, and, assuming it has read in non-whitespace characters, stops if it encounters whitespace and puts it back into the input stream.

- The %s specifier stops only if it encounters nonleading whitespace or a newline character, or if a number of characters (not counting any leading whitespace) equal to any field-width modifier have been read (or, as with any specifier, if it reaches the end of the file). The %c specifier reads in only a single character unless it has a field-width modifier; if it has a field-width modifier, it stops only when it reads that many characters in—not stopping for a newline character or whitespace. *The %s specifier without a field-width modifier can be dangerous, because the memory area reserved beginning at the address corresponding to the specifier in the argument list may not be large enough to hold all the characters read in, thus potentially writing over memory areas reserved by other variables.* The unmodified %c specifier does not pose this danger.

- In all cases—even where reading is stopped because as many characters as is indicated by any field-width modifier have been read—the %s specifier causes a terminating '\0' to be placed after the characters read in as though such a character were found in the input stream just before the newline that terminates the read. This terminating NULL character makes the variable that starts at the address that corresponds to the %s specifier a C string, a concept we will examine in Chapter 7. The %c specifier does not place any terminating NULL.

3.15.2   Suffixes and Numeric Conversion Specifiers

As we have seen, you can use suffixes on assignment of constants to integer and floating point variables:

```
unsigned check = 10U;
long hand = 2000000L;
unsigned long haul = 3000000LU;
float age = 23.3F;
long double up = 233333.3e343L;
```

None of these suffixes are recognized as valid input by any of the scanf() numeric conversion specifiers. If input matching any of the above examples were read by any of these specifiers, reading would end at the suffix letter, and the letter would be placed back into the input stream.

3.15.3   The %d and %u Conversion Specifiers

The %d specifier reads in integer input in decimal notation only, for storage into an int. The %u specifier does the same for storage into an unsigned int. The following code fragment, input, and output are illustrative:

```
scanf("%d%u", &i1, &u1);
printf("%d %u\n", i1, u1);
```

```
-63 63
```

```
-63 63
```

Any input, other than whitespace or a leading sign, that is not a digit causes the %d and %u specifiers to stop reading.

3.15.4   The %i Conversion Specifier

The %i specifier reads in integer input in decimal, octal, or hexadecimal notation for storage into an int. Input in octal notation must commence with a 0; input in hexadecimal notation must commence with a 0x or 0X. Of course, whether the number input is in decimal, octal, or hexadecimal notation, the result is stored in binary and can be printed back out in any of the three formats:

```
scanf("%i%i%i", &i1, &i2, &i3);
printf("%d %#o %#x\n", i1, i2, i3);
printf("%d %d %d\n", i1, i2, i3);
```

```
63 077 0x3f

63 077 0x3f
63 63 63
```

3.15.5   The %o and %x Conversion Specifiers

The %o specifier reads in integer input in octal notation for storage into an unsigned int; the %x specifier does the same for integer input in hexadecimal notation. Since these conversion specifiers warn the computer that input in octal or hexadecimal digits is coming, there is no need to start the number with a 0 for octal or a 0x or 0X for hexadecimal. However, the specifiers accept any of those forms as well. For instance, the %x specifier will accept any of the following formats of the same value: 0xFF, 0XFF, ff, FF, 00ff. Some examples:

```
scanf("%o%o", &i1, &i2);
printf("%#o %#o\n", i1, i2);
scanf("%x%x%x", &i1, &i2, &i3);
printf("%#x %#x %#x\n", i1, i2, i3);
printf("%d %d %d\n", i1, i2, i3);

077 77
077 077

3f 0X3F 0x3f
0x3f 0x3f 0x3f
63 63 63
```

There is no difference between the %x and %X specifier: either reads lowercase a–f and uppercase A–F as hexadecimal digits.

3.15.6   Integer Type Size Variations

The %hd, %hi, %hu, %ho, and %hx, and the %ld, %li, %lu, %lo, and %lx specifiers do the same things as their respective cousins without the h or l, for storage into short or unsigned short, as the case may be, or long or unsigned long, respectively. (On a PC, all the short-specific specifiers would have the same effect as the corresponding specifiers without the h.)

```
scanf("%hd%hu", &little1, &ulittle);
printf("%hd %hu\n", little1, ulittle);
scanf("%hi%ho%hx", &little1, &little2, &little3);
printf("%hd %hd %hd\n", little1, little2, little3);
scanf("%ld%lu", &big1, &ubig);
printf("%ld %lu\n", big1, ubig);
scanf("%li%lo%lx", &big1, &big2, &big3);
printf("%ld %ld %ld\n", big1, big2, big3);

-63 63
-63 63

63 077 0x3f
63 63 63

-16777215 16777215
-16777215 16777215

16777215 077777777 0xffffff
16777215 16777215 16777215
```

As we have indicated, not only is it not required to follow keyboard input to be stored in a long variable with an L or l, as you do with assigning constants, but this is not permitted. The same goes for any of the other constant suffixes. The extra letter or letters will stop the read by the specifier and be thrown back into the input stream just as any other letter would:

```
scanf("%ld%c", &big1, &c1);
printf("%lu %c\n", big1, c1);
```

122L

122 L

3.15.7 Floating Point Conversion Specifiers

The `%f`, `%lf`, and `%Lf` specifiers input floating point numbers for storage into a `float`, `double`, and `long double`, respectively:

```
scanf("%f%lf%Lf", &f1, &big_f, &huge_f);
printf("%f %f %Lf\n", f1, big_f, huge_f);
```

123.456 123.456 123.456

123.456001 123.456000 123.456000

Any of these will accept input in normal decimal format or in exponential format—both e and E forms:

```
scanf("%f%f%f", &f1, &f2, &f3);
printf("%f %f %f\n", f1, f2, f3);
```

1.23456e2 1.23456E2 123.456

123.456001 123.456001 123.456001

Any spaces improperly inserted in the exponential form input should result in erroneous readings, as should any other failure to comply with the rules for assigning constants to floating point variables (see Chapter 2):

```
1.2 e 12 /* spaces not allowed */
e3 /* no significand: must have whole-number or fractional part */
12e /* exponent part must have an integer following it */
2323 /* no decimal point or exponent part */
```

Some of these will work on some compilers, but since such a result would not be Standard C, you cannot count on it.

You may also use `%e`, `%E`, `%g`, or `%G` in place of `%f`; `%le`, `%lE`, `%lg`, or `%lG` in place of `%lf`; or `%Le`, `%LE`, `%Lg`, or `%LG` in place of `%Lf`. With `scanf()`, unlike with `printf()`, these specifiers are absolutely identical to `%f`, `%lf`, and `%LF`, respectively. Since they do nothing different from the specifiers they could replace, there seems little point worrying about them, other than to know that if you see them in code, they are valid specifiers. Or perhaps you might find it convenient or in some sense symmetrical to use, say, a `%g` input specifier where you are using `%g` to print the value with `printf()` once input with `scanf()`.

3.15.8 The %[. . .] and %[^. . .] Conversion Specifiers *(Optional)*

These two conversion specifiers are the flip side of one another. The `%[. . .]` specifier reads input until it encounters a character not contained within brackets; the `%[^. . .]` specifier reads only as long as none of the characters within the brackets is encountered. In either case, once a nonconforming character is encountered, character reading stops, the characters read are stored in the string given as the argument, and the nonconforming character is put back into the input stream. Note that the ellipsis (. . .) is not part of the specifier; it is just to tell you that you must place a list of one or more characters at that point.

With those two specifiers, there is no question of whitespace as such. The tab, space, or newline characters are treated just like any other characters. Let's look at an example:

```
scanf("%[^$,.1234567890]", str); /* stop at any number, $, period or comma */
printf("%s\n", str);
scanf("%[$,.1234567890]", str); /* read until nonmonetary input */
printf("%s\n", str);
scanf("%[abcdefghijklmnopqrstuvwxyzABCDEFGHIJKLMNOPQRSTUVWXYZ ']",
   str); /* read until input is not ltr, space, apostrophe */
printf("%s\n", str);
scanf("%[^abcdefghijklmnopqrstuvwxyzABCDEFGHIJKLMNOPQRSTUVWXYZ!]",
   str); /* stop at any letter or exclamation point */
printf("%s\n", str);
```

Have any money?$1,000,000That's not hay$1,000,000!

```
Have any money?
$1,000,000
That's not hay
$1,000,000
```

The first statement's conversion specifier reads characters only until it comes to a digit, a $, or a period. It reads "Have you any money?" and then stops when it gets to a dollar sign. The "Have you any money?" characters read are stored in the string str and the dollar sign is put back into the input stream. The next statement does just the opposite: it reads only so long as the characters are the digits, dollar sign, comma, or period. It reads the "$1,000,000" and then stops when it gets to the T. The "$1,000,000" is stored in str and the T is put back into the input stream.

To allow for reading of the full sentence, "That's not hay," we have to include the space character and the apostrophe in the allowable set of characters in the next statement. The conversion specifier in this statement reads until it comes to a character that is not an uppercase or lowercase letter or a space or apostrophe. This statement does essentially the same thing as the first statement, which reads any character but numbers. We read the sentence in, stop at the dollar sign, store the sentence into str, and put the dollar sign back into the input stream. The last statement does the opposite, reading until it gets to letter input or the exclamation point.

Notice that with this somewhat elaborate scheme, we were able to store a sentence of more than one word into a string. We could have solved the novice programmer's Madonna problem, discussed earlier in the chapter, this way:

```
printf("Enter name:\n");
scanf("%[^\n]", name);
printf("Enter occupation:\n");
scanf("%*c%[^\n]", occupation);
printf("%s\n%s\n", name, occupation);
```

Madonna McGillicuty
Singer Sewing Machine operator

```
Madonna McGillicuty
Singer Sewing Machine operator
```

We will see a much easier way to do this, with the gets() function, in Chapter 9.

These conversion specifiers provide a third alternative method for the date input exercise we discussed earlier:

```
scanf("%d%[ -/]%d%[ -/]%d", &month, str, &day, str, &year);
printf("%d/%d/%d\n", month, day, year);
scanf("%d%[ -/]%d%[ -/]%d", &month, str, &day, str, &year);
printf("%d/%d/%d\n", month, day, year);
scanf("%d%[ -/]%d%[ -/]%d", &month, str, &day, str, &year);
printf("%d/%d/%d\n", month, day, year);
```

The %[-/] specifiers gobble up any spaces, hyphens, or slashes between date input and store them in a string trashbin, str. Now, for any of the following input

```
8/11/48
8-11-48
8 - 11 - 48
8 11 48
```

we get output of "8/11/48". This formulation proves to be the most flexible of all.

You can also use the %[. . .] specifier to gobble up trailing whitespace tossed back into input by an earlier specifier and lurking for a later specifier. Let's take a modified version of a previous example. Say we wanted to read in a number and a letter:

```
int num;
char ltr;
printf("Type a number\n");
scanf("%d", &num);

printf("Now type a letter\n");
scanf("%c", &ltr);
printf("num: %d  ltr: %c\n", num, ltr);
```

If we type "1" and then "a", here's all we get, however.

```
1
```

The computer doesn't even stop after the second printf() statement to allow us to enter a letter. The newline character generated when we pressed Enter the first time was read and placed back into the input stream by the %d specifier in the first scanf() statement. The extraneous newline is read and stored by the %c specifier in the second scanf() statement since this specifier does not skip over leading whitespace.

We can cure the problem by inserting the following statement after the first scanf() statement:

```
scanf("%*[ \t\n]");
```

This statement reads in (and because of the *, discards) all spaces, tabs, and newlines left over from the last input.

Note that if the second scanf() statement had a numeric specifier or a %s specifier, no problem would be encountered by the leftover newline. However, successive numeric specifiers present the problem of undigested letter input halting an entire series of numeric specifiers, as we discuss in the next section.

On a somewhat picky level: any [between the opening and closing [and], as well as any ^ not immediately following the opening [is considered part of the set of characters to match.

Any characters read in a %[. . .] or %[^. . .] specifier are stored one by one starting at the address in the argument list corresponding to the specifier—unless the specifier contains a *, in which case, the input is discarded. Like the %c specifier and unlike the %s specifier, no terminating NULL is added to the input read.

The field-width modifier has no application to the %[. . .] or %[^. . .] specifiers, so as with the %s specifier without a field-width modifier, you have the potential danger of the these specifiers storing past reserved memory unless you use the * to discard the input.

3.15.9   %n and %p

The %n specifier is not much used. No input is read by the specifier. The specifier causes the number of characters read in so far by the current scanf() statement to be stored in the variable the address of which corresponds to the specifier in the argument list. This variable must be an int (or short or long if the h or l size modifiers are used).

The %p specifier reads in a memory address in an implementation-specific format (generally the same format as it is written by the %p printf() specifier). We will defer further discussion of this specifier until we deal with pointers in Chapter 7.

3.16   WHAT STOPS scanf()

Unless the conversion specifier is %c or %s, the characters read from the input stream, after any initial discarded whitespace, must be a digit or a sign character (+ or –), or a character appropriate for the particular conversion specifier—for instance, for %x, a leading sign and 0x or 0x, and digits or the characters A–F or a–f. If a nonconforming digit is encountered, scanf() assumes that input for this specifier and variable has concluded and it puts the nonconforming character back in input.

If the *first* non-whitespace character a conversion specifier encounters is a nonconforming character, the scanf() statement halts completely, and places the offending character back in the input stream. No value is assigned to the variable corresponding to the specifier where the problem was encountered. Furthermore, if the scanf() statement containing that specifier also has other specifiers, this failed read will terminate the balance of the scanf() statement.

The same result follows if we insert a character (other than the space character) between conversion specifiers and the input at that point does not find the character. In our earlier example,

```
scanf("%d  /%d  /%d", &month, &day, &year);
```

if the input does not contain a slash after the first number and after the second, it will fail and terminate at that point.

The scanf() function's property of only accepting certain types of input for certain conversion specifiers can be a trap for the unwary. Suppose you use a %d specifier. If the first character is a letter instead of a digit, scanf() not only stops reading characters for this variable, but also places the letter back in the input stream. If you have succeeding scanf() statements, all with %d or %f or other numeric specifiers, each of these will fail because the offending letter is still first in the input stream (unless the letter happens by coincidence to be a–f or A–F and you come upon a %x or %X specifier, a still not very desirable result).

Conversely, the difference between the %c specifier's not skipping over whitespace and other specifiers' discarding leading whitespace can cause problems for the programmer who is not careful to take the difference into account. The most common oversight is the failure to take the newline character into account where a scanf() statement with a %c specifier follows another scanf() statement.

Even more than with printf(), with scanf() you must make absolutely certain that the conversion specifiers match the corresponding argument types, and that the number of conversion specifiers match the number of arguments in the argument list. If there are insufficient arguments for the format string, the behavior is undefined. If there are more arguments than conversion specifiers, the excess arguments are evaluated but otherwise ignored—without warning of any kind.

Let's test our understanding of the mechanics of scanf() with a multiple-input example. But first, we will describe the behavior of scanf() with regard to termination of a specifier's job and that of the scanf() statement as a whole.

3.16.1   Stopping and Skipping to Next Field, and Termination

The scanf() function stops scanning and storing the current input field and moves on to the next one in any of the following cases:

- The number of characters specified by any field-width modifier has been read.
- The next character is incompatible with the current specifier (such as a letter for a %d specifier) in an instance where acceptable characters have already been read in by the specifier. This includes the case where the next character is one of the characters in the set of a %[. . .] specifier, or is not one of those in the inverted set for a %[^ . . .] specifier.

A scanf() function call terminates altogether in any of the following cases:

- The next character (other than any whitespace to be discarded) is incompatible with the current specifier in an instance where no acceptable characters have yet been read in by the specifier.
- The next character conflicts with a corresponding non-whitespace character in the format string.
- The next character is EOF, signaling that the end of the input file has been reached. (This will occur, for instance, when a disk file has been redirected to standard input, so that scanf() reads from a file not the keyboard/screen. (See Chapters 14 and 16.)
- The end of the format string has been reached.

3.16.2   Heterogeneous Multiple Input Example

Assume that we have the following input:

```
2. quarts of oil
-12.8degrees Celsius
lots of luck
10.0LBS     of
dirt
100ergs of energy
```

with the following declarations:

```
float quant;
char units[21], item[21];
```

and the following two statements, repeated five times:

```
scanf("%f%20s of %20s", &quant, units, item);
scanf("%*[^\n]");
```

Here are the results of printing only the variables successfully assigned values on each call:

```
quant: 2.0      units: quarts     item: oil
quant: -12.8    units: degrees
[nothing assigned]
quant: 10.0     units: LBS        item: dirt
[nothing assigned]
```

In the first statement, the `%f` specifier reads 2, and stores it as a value, stops at the space, and places it back. The `%20s` reads in and discards the leftover space, reads in "quarts", and stops at the space and replaces it. The space in the format string gobbles up the leftover space; the o and f in the format string gobble up the next "of" in input; the space in the format string gobbles up the next space in input. The final `%20s` specifier stores "oil" and stops at the newline and replaces it. The next `scanf()` statement, with the `%*[^\n]` specifier, reads and also rejects and replaces the newline.

In the second set of statements, the `%f` specifier reads and discards the leftover newline, reads and stores –12.8 as a value, and stops and replaces the d in input. The `%20s` reads "degrees", including the replaced d, and stops and replaces the space character in input. The space in the format string reads and discards the leftover space. The o in the format string stops when it reads C, since that is not an o; the C is replaced in input. This time, the `%*[^\n]%` specifier reads and, owing to the *, discards all leftover input until but not including the newline. Notice that we have altered the final specifier from our earlier example. There the purpose was to gobble up the trailing newline. Here, we want to get rid of *all* extraneous input. There is no problem leaving a newline for the next statement here: it is a `%f` so it will just read and discard the leftover newline. By including the newline in the `%*[^\n]`'s character set, we are sure that we will read and discard everything but the final newline: we know that a newline terminates this line of input.

The next set of statements have no luck at all. The `%f` specifier chokes on the first character l, terminating the entire `scanf()` statement. The `%*[^\n]` specifier comes to our rescue and reads and discards the rest of the input line up to the newline, which it places back into input.

The `%f` specifier in the fourth set of statements and input line reads in "10.0" and stores this value, then stops at the L. It does not treat the L as a `long double` suffix. The `%20s` specifier reads in LBS, including the leftover L, and stops and replaces the newline. The space in the format string reads and discards all the spaces or tabs in input between "LBS" and "item". The o and f read and discard the same characters in input. The final `%20s` specifier in the statement reads and discards the newline still remaining unread, reads and stores "dirt", and reads and stops at the newline, replacing it in input.

The `%f` in the final set of statements fails on reading "100e" since this is not in proper floating point format. It takes the e as the start of an never-to-be completed exponential portion. This last failure might have gotten by some compilers, but the meaning of the input—100 ergs—would not be properly translated in any event.

Incidentally, you will see later that we would have normally coded this problem with a single set of paired `scanf()` statements, not five. Just to give you a preview, we would have normally written something along these lines, after having declared an `int` variable, `count`. This structure would handle any number of input lines:

```
while (!feof(stdin) && !ferror(stdin))
{
   count = fscanf(stdin, "%f%20s of %20s",
      &quant, units, item);
   if (count)
      printf("quant: %.1f\tunits: %s\titem: %s\n", quant,
         count > 1 ? units : "\t", count == 3 ? item : "");
   printf("count = %d\n", count);
   fscanf(stdin, "%*[^\n]");
}
```

3.17   THE `getchar()` AND `putchar()` FUNCTIONS

The `getchar()` function does the same job as `scanf()` with a `%c` specifier that has no field-width modifier: it gets the next character from the standard input stream (the keyboard, unless we redirect—see Chapters 14 and 16). Likewise, the `putchar()` function does the same job as `printf()` with a `%c` specifier: it writes the character you specify to the standard output stream (the screen, unless we redirect):

```
char ch;
scanf("%c", &ch);
printf("%c", ch);

/* next two do the same as two above */
ch = getchar();
putchar(ch);
```

The `getchar()` and `putchar()` functions are less complex than `scanf()` and `printf()`, more tailored to doing one simple task—retrieving or printing a single character. Accordingly, they have less "overhead"—that is, they take up less programming space and are quicker to execute than `printf()` and `scanf()`. For example, executable codes for a one-line program to read or write a single character, in Borland C with debugging off, are the following sizes:

single `printf()` statement:	6128 bytes
single `putchar()` statement:	4548 bytes
single `scanf()` statement:	6706 bytes
single `getchar()` statement:	4530 bytes
no statements at all:	3858 bytes

On our system, writing a single character 500,000 times to a file with `printf()`'s cousin, `fprintf()`, took 0.93 seconds, compared to 0.27 seconds for `fputc()`, the file analog to `putchar()`; reading a single character 500,000 times with `fscanf()` took 1.59 seconds, versus only 0.44 seconds with `fgetc()`. The `fprintf()`, `fputc()`, `fscanf()`, and `fgetc()` functions do for a specific named input or output stream (normally a file) what their analogs do for standard input and output. (See Chapter 14.)

Notice that the `getchar()` function has nothing within its parentheses. We can store the character it retrieves from standard input with an assignment statement

```
ch = getchar();
```

or we can just retrieve the character and discard it, without storing its value anywhere:

```
getchar();
```

We can compare this difference to `scanf()` examples we've seen:

```
scanf("%c", &ch);
scanf("%*c");
```

In the first statement, we retrieve a character and store it in `ch`; in the second, we retrieve and ignore what we've read.

We can use an unassigning `getchar()` statement to pause in the middle of program execution. For instance, if the user enters invalid data, we can send an error message to the screen, at the end of which will be the directive to press a key to continue:

```
. . .
printf("Error: Unable to open file\n"
   "Press the Enter key to continue");
getchar();
. . .
```

Once the user has read the message and pressed Enter, we can then wipe the message out and continue with the program. You can also use this device to observe program output as you develop a program, particularly if your program paints screens. However, it is probably simpler to set a breakpoint or run the program to the cursor, using the techniques described in your compiler's manual, assuming the C implementation you use has these features.

Just as with `printf()` and a `%c` specifier, we can use `putchar()` to send nonprinting characters to the screen:

```
putchar('\n');
putchar('\t');
```

The same rules apply for the printing of special characters:

```
putchar('\\'); /* print a backslash */
putchar('\"'); /* print a double quotation mark */
```

As with `printf()` and a `%c` specifier, you can print the character representation of a number:

```
putchar(99); /* print the letter 'c' if ASCII encoding */
```

3.18 THE `scanf()` AND `getchar()` FUNCTIONS: SAME INPUT STREAM

Characters read and discarded by one `scanf()` statement are available not only for succeeding `scanf()` statements but also for `getchar()`, `gets()` (see Chapter 9), and any other buffered functions that read from the standard input stream. This property can lead to error if you are not careful.

For example, the following code will not stop for the user to press a key at the `getchar()` statement:

```
printf("Type file name\n");
scanf("%s", filename);
. . .
printf("Error: Unable to open file\n"
   "Press the Enter key to continue\n");
getchar();
printf("Oops! Too slow. We had to continue without you");
. . .
```

The `getchar()` statement will read the newline discarded by the `scanf()` statement instead of waiting for more user input. Any of the following statements in place of the `getchar()` statement would suffer the same ignominious fate:

```
gets(filename);
fread(filename, 1, 1, stdin);
scanf("%c", filename);
```

(The `gets()` and `fread()` I/O functions are covered in later chapters.)

One remedy would be to alter the `scanf()` statement to gobble up the anticipated newline character:

```
scanf("%s%*c", name);
```

Once the program terminates, the input and output streams terminate. Remaining unread input stream data is not left over for a new program execution.

3.19   BUFFERING—getchar() vs. getch() vs. getche()

In the scanf() examples above, you observed that no input is sent to the computer for processing until the Enter key is pressed. This procedure is known as *buffered* input. The characters are stored in a temporary storage area called a *buffer* until the Enter key is pressed or until the buffer is full, if that happens earlier.

Buffering allows for more efficient data transfer. It also allows the user to correct errors by backspacing before finally sending the desired input for processing. On the other hand, sometimes buffering is a nuisance. You've already seen what a nuisance it is to have to deal with the newline character generated by pressing the Enter key to send data for processing. The newline character becomes part of the input stream and if, for example, the next statement is a scanf() statement with a %c specifier, you must do something to gobble up the newline before you get to that specifier. A function that did not avail itself of buffering might be more convenient in certain situations.

An unbuffered input-reading function could serve another purpose. Later on, as our programs become more sophisticated, you'll see that we often need immediate response without having to wait for the Enter key to be pressed to register user intentions—as where pressing Alt P signals that the user wants the results of what has been entered printed out, or pressing Page Down moves the user to another screen of data, or "Just press the letter of the option you wish" allows a selection to be made from a number of options in a menu.

On a PC, for both these purposes, we can use getch(). The getch() function, like getchar(), retrieves the next character from standard input. The difference is that getch() is unbuffered. As a key is pressed, getch() processes it without waiting for the Enter key to be pressed:

```
char ch;
printf("Type a character, any character.\n"
   "Just don't tell me what it is: ");
ch = getch();
printf("\nAh Ha! You typed in %c", ch);


Type a character, any character.
Just don't tell me what it is:
Ah Ha! You typed in z
```

If you type this into a source code and run it, you'll notice the second statement appears on the screen just as soon as you press a key.

The character typed is not written on the screen. There is another function, getche(), that does the same thing as getch(), except that it also causes the character typed in to be written to the screen, or "echoed"—hence the e on the end of its name. The getche() and getch() functions, unlike the others we covered in this chapter—printf(), scanf(), getchar(), and putchar(), which are all contained in stdio.h—are found in the include file, conio.h (short for *CON*sole *I*nput/*O*utput). Compare the two functions in the following program.

(Note that conio.h and the getch() and getche() functions are strictly for the DOS environment. None of this is part of Standard C.)

 **Listing**   **3.2 getche.c**

```
/* getche.c */

/* illustrate difference between getch and getche - DOS only */

#include <stdio.h>
#include <conio.h> /* getch, getche: DOS only */

int main(void)
{
   char ch;
```

```
       printf("Type a character, any character.\n"
          "Just don't tell me what it is: ");
       ch = getch(); /* don't echo character */
       printf("\nAh Ha! You typed in %c\n", ch);
       printf("Type a character, any character.\n"
          "Just don't tell me what it is: ");
       ch = getche(); /* echo character */
       printf("\nOops! I saw that. You typed in %c\n", ch);
       return 0;
    }
```

```
Type a character, any character.
Just don't tell me what it is:
Ah Ha! You typed in z

Type a character, any character.
Just don't tell me what it is: A
Oops! I saw that. You typed in A
```

The getch() function does not process leftovers in the input stream. Since getch() is unbuffered, any input put back into the input stream by scanf() would be read by a succeeding call to getchar(), as we have observed, but not by a succeeding call to getch(). For that reason, and because getch() obviates the need for the user to press ⌨Enter to register a key press, getch() is a better choice to halt the program pending a user key press, provided the program will be run only on a DOS machine. We can amend our earlier example:

```
printf("Error! Unable to open file\n"
    "Press any key to continue\n");
getch();
```

3.19.1   Unbuffered Output

On many computers (including the PC), output to standard output is also buffered. Nothing is sent to standard output until the user presses the ⌨Enter key. With other systems, each character is written to the screen right after it is typed. For example, with the following code fragment

```
int ch;
while((ch = getchar()) != EOF)
    putchar(ch);
```

on a PC, a program run might look like this:

My output is buffered. Reflect before pressing Enter^Z
My output is buffered. Reflect before pressing Enter

However, on some systems, a run might look like this:

wWeellll,,   mmyy   ssttaannddaarrdd   oouuttppuutt   iiss   nnoott
bbuuffffeerreedd..   II   ssiimmppllyy   ccaannnnoott   wwaaiitt   tthhaatt
lloonngg..

On some systems, you can use system commands to alter the default state of affairs. For instance, the following program duplicates the getch() and kbhit() functions for UNIX. (See Appendix C for a discussion of kbhit() and Chapter 16 for a discussion of system().)

 **Listing 3.3 get_unix.c**

```
/* get_unix.c */

/* UNIX equivalent to DOS compilers' getch() and kbhit() */

#include <stdio.h>
```

```c
#include <sys/filio.h>
#include <stdlib.h> /* system() */

int kbhitUnix(void)
{
    int charsAvailable = 0; /* ## of chars available for reading */
    ioctl(0, FIONREAD, &charsAvailable);
    return charsAvailable;
}

int main(void)
{
    int ch, i = 1000000;
    system("stty raw -echo");
    printf("Type a letter, any letter . . . ");
    while (i--) /* don't wait forever for keypress */
        if (kbhitUnix())
    {
        ch = getchar();
        printf("I bet you typed a%s %c\n", (ch != 'a' && ch != 'e'
            && ch != 'i' && ch != 'o' && ch != 'u') ? "" : "n", ch);
        break;
    }

    return 0;
}
```

3.20   APPLICATION: ACE BILLING PROGRAM

Input is given below; for output, see Figure 3.1.

3.20.1   Input

```
Austell-WolfsonBA05 00003500
Otieno          DE12Y01206000
VanVranken      GE08Y00804230
Yates           SY17Y11708200
Cook            CH03 00004100
Stencil         BI10Y10108150
Rockingham      ZE23Y12309300
Zindar          SY04 00006200
McDowell        CH19 10008420
Grilo           RI17 01703500
Braxkston       HE18Y01807400
Pope            SC22Y12208590
Hardin          GA02 00004060
Sonby           TO32 10008030
Murphy          RY26Y12608420
Bate            ST05Y00506320
Murray          GE28 02804780
Franklin        LO01 00002500
Meyers          JA24Y12408430
Kirk            JT12 10009360
```

 **Listing** **3.4 acech03.c**

```
/* +----------------------------------------------------------------+
   +   Program Name: acech03.c
   +     Author(s): Austell-Wolfson and Otieno
```

```
   +          Date: 12/10/2000
   +  Purpose:
   +    This program implements the ace billing program.
   +    We have learned how to:
   +        declare variables that hold single values and assign them
   +        values. We have also learned how read and write through
   +        scanf() and printf(). We now apply these capabilities in
   +        this program.
   +
   +  Process:
   +    At this point, we print the headings, declare variables, and
   +    assign values to the variables where applicable. We can read
   +    data from standard input and write data to standard output. We
   +    do this in the appropriate functions and execute the stubs for
   +    the rest of the functions. We encourage the user to run this
   +    program using the file acech03.dat as its standard input
   +    source, because the program has been written to read data
   +    according to the prescribed input record layout. In PC and
   +    UNIX platforms this is achieved through redirection. For
   +    example: acech03.exe < acech03.dat > acech03.rpt,
   +        where acech03.rpt is the standard output.
   +    Logic construction would be slightly different if we were to
   +    enter the data interactively and produce the same report.
   +----------------------------------------------------------------+
*/
#include <stdio.h>
void initialization(void); /* Prototype - discussed in Chapter 8 */
void processMemberRecord(void);
void termination(void);
void initializeVariables(void);
void printHeadings(void);
void readMemberRecord(void);
void computeIndividualBill(void);
void writeDetailLine(void);
void determineSpecialFee(void);
void determineActivityFee(void);
void determineDiscountAmt(void);


/* +----------------------------------------------------------------+
   +  Declare variables outside of main() function so that all the
   +  other functions will have access to them. Doing this gives
   +  these variables global scope and therefore allows us to develop
   +  and work with modules this early. We will discontinue this
   +  practice once functions have been fully discussed.
   +
   +----------------------------------------------------------------+
*/

char  SpecialMembershipFlag = 'Y';
float MembershipFee = 0.0;
float ActivityFee = 0.0;
float DiscountAmount = 0.0;
float ChargeAmount = 0.0;
float TotalIndividualBill = 0.0;
float AceClubTotals = 0.0;
float Charges = 0.0;
int   Discount = 0;
int   AverageCharges = 0;
int   NumberOfCharges = 0;
```

```c
int main(void)
{
    initialization();
    processMemberRecord(); /* No loop logic yet. Not until Chapter 5 */
    termination();
    return 0;
}

void initialization(void)
{
    initializeVariables();
    printHeadings();
    readMemberRecord();
}

void processMemberRecord(void)
{
    computeIndividualBill();
    writeDetailLine();
    printf("|                                                            |\n");
    printf("|------------------------------------------------------------|\n");
    printf("| ProcessMemberRecord function has executed successfully      |\n");
}

void termination(void)
{
    printf("| Termination function has executed successfully              |\n");
    printf("|                                                            |\n");
    printf("|_____|\n");
}

void initializeVariables(void)
{
    SpecialMembershipFlag = 'Y';
    Discount = 0;
    AverageCharges = 0;
    MembershipFee = 2500.0;
    ActivityFee = 250.0;
    DiscountAmount = 0.0;
    ChargeAmount = 0.0;
    NumberOfCharges = 0;
    TotalIndividualBill = 0.0;
    AceClubTotals = 0.0;
}

void printHeadings(void)
{
    printf("|------------------------------------------------------------|\n");
    printf("|                                                            |\n");
    printf("|    Program Name: ACECH03.EXE                      Page:  1  |\n");
    printf("|      Run Date: 12/10/2000          Ace Billing             |\n");
    printf("|                                                            |\n");
    printf("|                                                            |\n");
    printf("|------------------------------------------------------------|\n");
    printf("|                                                            |\n");
    printf("| Customer Name  Charges  Bill    Mbr Fee   Act Fee   Disc   Total Bill |\n");
    printf("|_____|\n");
```

```
    printf("|                                                          |\n");
}

void readMemberRecord(void)
{
/* +------------------------------------------------------------+
   +  Notice the use of the * modifier in scanf() function. We are
   +  using it to skip the two fields we cannot yet read, namely,
   +  the customer name and initials. This is a very common use of
   +  this feature. C is being used more and more to read and process
   +  files created by COBOL programs. These files often have many
   +  fields that are not useful to some programs, while imperative
   +  for other programs accessing the same file.
   +------------------------------------------------------------+
*/
    scanf("%*15c%*2c%2d%c%4d%4d", &NumberOfCharges,
        &SpecialMembershipFlag, &Discount, &AverageCharges);
}

void computeIndividualBill(void)
{
    Charges = 200 * NumberOfCharges;
    determineSpecialFee();
    determineActivityFee();
    determineDiscountAmt();

    TotalIndividualBill = Charges + MembershipFee + ActivityFee;
    TotalIndividualBill = TotalIndividualBill - DiscountAmount;
    AceClubTotals = AceClubTotals + TotalIndividualBill;
}

void writeDetailLine(void)
{
/* +------------------------------------------------------------+
   +  Notice that we employ the * modifier to help us format our report.
   +  Since we have not covered strings, we have elected to omit/skip
   +  the customer name(s) altogether. We do so for both input and
   +  output. Notice how the modifier * is used differently with
   +  scanf() and printf().
   +------------------------------------------------------------+
   */

    printf("| ");
    printf("%*s %*s  %2d  $%8.2f  $%8.2f  $%8.2f  $%5.f  $%9.2f",
        15, " ", 2, " ", NumberOfCharges, Charges, MembershipFee,
        ActivityFee, DiscountAmount, TotalIndividualBill);
    printf(" |\n");
}

void determineSpecialFee(void)
{
/* +------------------------------------------------------------+
   +  Determining special membership fees involves using "if-then"
   +  statements, which we have not yet covered. We therefore use a
   +  fixed fee to keep things moving. We will add these modifications
   +  once the decision type constructs have been presented.
   +------------------------------------------------------------+
```

```
    */

    MembershipFee = 2500.0;
}

void determineActivityFee(void)
{
/* +----------------------------------------------------------+
   +  Determining activity fees involves using "if-then" statements,
   +  which we have not yet covered. We therefore use a fixed fee to
   +  keep things moving. We will add these modifications once the
   +  decision type constructs have been presented.
   +----------------------------------------------------------+


    ActivityFee = 250.0;
}
void determineDiscountAmt(void)
{
/* +----------------------------------------------------------+
   +  Determining Discount amount involves using "if-then" statements,
   +  which we have not yet covered. We therefore use the Discount
   +  amount even though it may not apply so as to keep things moving.
   +  We will add these modifications once the decision type constructs
   +  have been presented.
   +----------------------------------------------------------+
    */
    DiscountAmount = Discount;
}
```

3.20.2   Output

Figure 3.1   *Output for ACE Billing Program*

```
 Program Name: ACECH03.EXE                              Page:  1
     Run Date: 12/10/2000           Ace Billing


 Customer Name  Charges  Bill       Mbr Fee    Act Fee    Disc    Total Bill

                    5  $ 1000.00  $ 2500.00  $  250.00  $    0  $  3750.00

 ProcessMemberRecord function has executed successfully
 Termination function has executed successfully
```

Chapter Summary

1. The standard input and output devices are normally the keyboard and screen, respectively. The printf() function sends formatted output to the screen, and the scanf() function obtains formatted input from the keyboard.

2. The `printf()` function has two elements: a format string and an argument list.
   - The format string is enclosed in double quotes and contains the data being sent to output. The format string can contain "formatting codes" called conversion specifiers. These specifiers begin with a % and contain one or two letters.
   - The argument list contains one or more variables, constants, or expressions separated by commas that are pulled in by conversion specifiers in the format string.
   - When the program is run, each conversion specifier in the format string is replaced with the value of a corresponding variable, constant, or expression in the argument list.
   - The conversion specifier not only replaces itself with the variable's value, it converts the value to the proper type (such as integer, floating point), format (such as hexadecimal notation, octal notation), or other characteristic.

3. The basic conversion type specifiers for `printf()` are
   - `%c`   character
   - `%s`   string
   - `%d` or `%i`   int
   - `%u`   unsigned int
   - `%f`   double

4. The `%c` specifier prints a `char`, `short`, or `int` argument value. The argument can be (1) an integer variable of the type `char`, `short`, or `int`, (2) a constant in decimal, octal, or hexadecimal notation, (3) the character representation of an integer value enclosed in single quotes, or (4) an escape sequence.

5. Nonprinting characters or escape sequences that cause the printer or screen to take some specified action can be designated by a backslash character and a letter (such as \a). Some of these are \f, the formfeed character, \n, which advances the printer or screen cursor to the next line, and \b, the backspace character.

6. The number of specifiers and the number of arguments must be the same. If there is a mismatch in the number of specifiers and the number of arguments, the program will compile but will execute unpredictably.

7. Normally you should also match specifier and argument types. You can, however, intermix certain types, because in `printf()`, certain types are all automatically converted to a single type. The types `char`, `unsigned char`, and `short` are automatically converted to `int`; `unsigned short` is automatically converted to `unsigned int` or `signed int`; and `float` is automatically converted to `double`.

8. In `printf()`, conversion specifiers can also indicate that you are using octal or hexadecimal instead of decimal notation, and they can print out floating point constants in exponential format with the use of the `%e` specifier.

9. The `printf()` function allows conversion modifiers to control spacing or precision in the printout. These modifiers are three major types: (1) field-width modifiers, (2) flags, and (3) precision modifiers.

10. The field-width modifier is a decimal integer and determines the minimum width of the field. The field size increases to fit the value size. If the value size is smaller, the excess space is padded with leading blanks, unless a flag modifier indicates otherwise.

11. In `printf()`, the precision modifier, designated as an integer following a decimal point, performs different functions depending on the type:
    - For integers, it dictates the minimum number of digits to display, and if the value is smaller, the extra space is padded with zeros.
    - For floating points, the precision modifier indicates the number of digits to the right of the decimal point. If the value has fewer digits to the right of the decimal point than the modifier, it adds zeros to the right to fill in the remaining digits. If the value has more digits than the specifier, the value is rounded so that its digits match that of the modifier.

12. You can replace the actual digits in the field-width or precision modifier with an *, and place the actual value as a variable in the argument list.

13. Flags determine whether a value in a field is left- or right-justified. They also control formatting of signed integers, display the decimal point in floating point values (even if no digits follow the decimal point), and pad a field with leading zeros if the value has fewer digits than the field length.

14. Modifiers must be placed in the following order: flag, field width, and precision.

15. When coding, you can split a long statement over two or more lines, as long as you do not split variable or function names, C keywords, or multicharacter operators. Long strings enclosed in quotes can be split over two or more lines by (1) using a backslash character at the end of each break in the line, (2) putting each part of the string in separate `printf()` statements, and (3) enclosing each separate line of the string in its own quotation marks.

16. The `scanf()` function takes character input from the keyboard and converts it to values, which it then assigns to variables the programmer selects. Like `printf()`, `scanf()` has a format string enclosed in quotes and an argument list separated by commas.

17. The `scanf()` argument list does not contain variables or constants, but rather the addresses of the respective variable or constant. To indicate that you are referring to the address of a variable rather than to the name in an argument, the name is preceded by the & symbol.

18. Although the conversion specifiers for `scanf()` are similar to `printf()`, some of the major differences are:
    - The `scanf()` function has separate specifiers for `float` (`%f`) and `double` (`%Lf`), while `printf()` treats `float` the same as `double`.
    - The `%d` and `%i` specifiers accept decimal, octal, and hexadecimal input in `printf()`, but in `scanf()`, the `%d` specifier accepts decimal input only. Also, `scanf()` allows negative values in octal or hexadecimal input, while `printf()` does not print negative values in these formats.
    - With `scanf()`, the specifiers `%e`, `%f`, and `%g` (and their uppercase counterparts) are treated all the same, whereas the formats are different in `printf()`.
    - In `scanf()`, the field-width modifier specifies the maximum number of characters to be read, while in `printf()`, the modifier indicates the minimum space

19. When evaluating input, scanf() places each portion of the input separated by whitespace into a separate variable. The term *whitespace* means a space, tab, newline character, carriage return, or formfeed.

20. Placing a whitespace character anywhere in the format string causes all whitespace to be read and discarded at that point. If a character is placed in the format string between conversion specifiers, the character, when encountered in the input stream, is also read and discarded.

21. Just as with printf(), you may place modifiers between the % and the conversion type letter. The asterisk, normally used as a field-width or precision modifier placeholder in printf(), acts as a suppression character in scanf(). Any input corresponding to a specifier containing an asterisk is discarded after being read and is not stored in any variable.

22. In scanf(), the field-width modifier indicates the maximum input field width—the opposite of its usage with printf(). Since scanf() stops at the earlier of field width or whitespace, you cannot input more than one word in a single field using this function.

23. Specifiers for scanf() vary according to input:

   - Integer input types   The %d (decimal input only), %u (unsigned decimal input), and %i (decimal, octal, or hexadecimal input).

   - Integer type size   Specifiers beginning with %h accept short or unsigned short; those beginning with %l accept long or unsigned long, respectively.

   - Floating point   %f, %lf, and %Lf specifiers input floating point numbers for storage into a float, double, and long double, respectively.

   - Bracketed   A specifier enclosing a letter in brackets "delimits" the string by "cutting off" the input when that character is encountered. Conversely, a bracketed specifier containing a ^ in front of the characters inside the brackets "delimits" the string as soon as any character *not* found inside the brackets is encountered.

24. Common pitfalls when using the scanf() statement include the following:

   - The input type must match the specifier type. The scanf() function not only terminates, but since it places the improper character back into the input stream, it can cause a "domino" effect, terminating many scanf() statements following it.

   - Certain scanf() specifiers, such as %c, retain the whitespace along with the other input, when a programmer may not intend such.

25. The getchar() and putchar() functions are "streamlined versions" of the scanf() and printf() functions and operate on a single character.

26. In the scanf() and getchar() functions, no input is normally sent to the computer for processing unless the Enter key is pressed. This is called buffered input. When unbuffered input is desired (input that doesn't have to wait in a buffer for the Enter key), you can use the getch() function in a DOS environment. The getche() function works the same as getch() but also displays the character on the screen.

27. Tables 13.10 and 3.11 summarize the printf() and scanf() conversion specifiers and give examples of each.

Table 3.10 printf() *Conversion Specifier Summary*

	Description	Flags	Size	Sample Specifier	Sample Argument	Sample Output	Argument Type
c	character	–					char, short, int
				%cx	'd'	dx	
				%10cx	'd'	d x	
				%-10cx	'd'	dx	
s	character string	–					char *
				%sx	"hand"	handx	
				%10sx	"hand"	hand x	
				%5.3sx	"hand"	hanx	

○ denotes space

Table 3.10   *(continued)*

	Description	Flags	Size	Sample Specifier	Sample Argument	Sample Output	Argument Type
				%-10sx	"hand"	handx	
				%10sx	""	x	
d, i	integer in signed decimal notation	– + # 0 ◯					char, short, int
				%dx or %ix	-36	-36x	int
				%10dp	-36	-36p	int
				%-10dp	-36	-36 p	int
				%+5d	30	+30	int
				%05d	30	00030	int
				p%5.4d	123	p 0123	int
				% 5dp	123	123p	int
			h	%hd	'b'	98	char
			h	%hd	98	98	short
			l	%ld	-200000L	-200000	long
			l	%+ld	200006L	+200006	long
			l	%9ldp	200006L	200006p	long
u	integer in unsigned decimal notation	– + # 0					unsigned int, unsigned char, unsigned short
				%u	36000L	36000	unsigned int
				%9up	36000L	36000p	unsigned int
				%-9up	36000L	36000 p	unsigned int
				%09u	36000L	000036000	unsigned int
			l	%lu	199006L	199006	unsigned long
o	integer in unsigned octal notation	– + # 0					unsigned int, unsigned short, unsigned char
				%o	30	36	unsigned int
				%5op	30	36p	unsigned int

◯ denotes space

(continued on next page)

Table 3.10   *(continued)*

Description	Flags	Size	Sample Specifier	Sample Argument	Sample Output	Argument Type
			%-5op	30	36 p	unsigned int
			%05o	30	00036	unsigned int
			%#5op	30	036p	unsigned int
		h	%ho	'b'	142	unsigned char
		h	%ho	89	131	unsigned short
		l	%lo	199006L	563066	unsigned long
x, X	integer in unsigned hexadecimal notation	− + # 0				unsigned int, unsigned short, unsigned char
			%x	30	1e	unsigned int
			%Xp	30	1Ep	unsigned int
			%5xp	30	1ep	unsigned int
			%-5xp	30	1e p	unsigned int
			%#xp	30	0x1e	unsigned int
		h	%hx	'b'	62	unsigned char
		h	%hx	130	82	unsigned short
		l	%lx	200006L	30d46	unsigned long
f	floating point in format i.ffffff	− + # 0 ○				float, double, long double
			%f	200.258	200.257996	float
			p%12f	200.258	p 200.257996	float
			p%12.2f	200.258	p 200.26	float
			%-12.2fp	200.258	200.26 p	float
			p%+12.2f	200.258	p +200.26	float
			p%#12.2f	200	p 200.00	float
		L	%Lf	3000.30034423	3000.300344	long double
e,E	floating point in format i.ffffe±xx	− + # 0 ○				float, double, long double
			%e	200.258	2.00258e+02	float

○ denotes space

Table 3.10 *(continued)*

	Description	Flags	Size	Sample Specifier	Sample Argument	Sample Output	Argument Type
				%E	200.258	2.00258E+02	float
				p%12e	200.258	p 2.00258E+02	float
				p%12.2e	200.258	p 2.00e+02	float
				%-12.2e	200.258	2.00e+02 p	float
				p%+12.2e	200.258	p +2.00e+02	float
				p%#12.2e	200	p 2.00e+02	float
			L	%Le	3000.30034423	3.000300e+03	long double
g,G	floating point in e or f format, whichever is shorter	– + # 0 ◯					float, double, long double
				%g	200.258	200.258	float
				p%7.3g	3000.30034423	p 3e+03	float
			L	p%Lg	3000.30034423	3000.30	long double
			L	p%#10.3Lg	3000.30034423	p 3.00e+03	long double
			L	p%+10.3Lg	3000.30034423	p +3e+03	long double
			L	%-10.3Lgp	3000.30034423	3e+03 p	long double
p	address					implementation dependent	void *
				%p	&a	388F:27DE	pointer to int var
n	no of chars written so far is stored in variable whose address is passed						int *, short *, long *
				123%n	&a	(no output - integer variable "a" contains value of 3)	int *
				1233%ln	&b	(no output - long variable "b" contains value 4)	long *
				1232%hn	&c	(no output -short variable "c" contains value 4)	short *

◯ denotes space

Table 3.11 `scanf()` *Conversion Specifier Summary*

	Description	Type Size	Sample Specifier	Sample Input	Argument Type
c	one character (more if field width modifier)		%c %5c	a abcde999	char *
s	characters until whitespace; add NULL		%s %5s%3s	Jones JonesBob	char *
[chars]	characters as long as within list		%[$1234567890.,]	$9,999.99	char *
[^chars]	characters as long as not within list		%[^\n]	Bob Jones	char *
d	decimal integer		%d	–65	int *
			%2d%2d%2d	120298abc	
		hd	%hd	65	short *
		ld	%ld	8888888	long *
o	octal integer with or without leading 0		%o %o	101 0101	unsigned *
		ho	%ho	101	unsigned short *
		lo	%lo	011111111	unsigned long *
x, X	hex integer with or without leading 0x or 0X		%x %x %x	41 0x41 0X41	unsigned *
		hx, hX	%hx, %hX	0x41	unsigned short *
		lx, lX	%lx, %lX	FFFFFFFFFFFF	unsigned long *
i	decimal integer, octal integer with leading 0, or hex integer with leading 0x or 0X		%i %i %i %i	65 0101 0xFE 0Xa8ae	int *
		hi	%hi	65	short *
		li	%li	–8888888	long *
u	decimal integer		%u	65	unsigned *
		hu	%hu	65	unsigned short *
		lu	%lu	8888888	unsigned long *
f, e, E, g, G	floating-point number in exponent format or not		%f %e %g	1.234e–2 1.234 .1234e+02	float *
		lf, le, lE, lg, lG	%lf %lG	1.23456789 1.23456e98	double *
		Lf, Le, LE, Lg, LG	%Lf %Le	1.234567e233 12345678.901	long double *
p	address in memory			(implementation dependent)	void *

○ denotes space

Table 3.11   *(continued)*

	Description	Type Size	Sample Specifier	Sample Input	Argument Type
n	(number of characters read so far; nothing read by this specifier)			(none)	int *
		hn			short *
		ln			long *

○ denotes spaces

Review Questions

1. What character combination forms a nonprinting character that orders the program to start a new line?
2. What character can be inserted into a line of source code in order to break it into two shorter lines that get pasted back together on compilation?
3. If a `printf()` statement in a program has three conversion specifiers, how many arguments would it have to have? Explain.
4. For integer types, what aspect of formatting does the precision modifier in `printf()` control?
5. What does the `printf()` precision modifier for floating points control?
6. What effect does the `printf()` flag '0' have?
7. If a `printf()` statement contains modifiers for field width, precision, and a flag, what order, if any, should the modifiers appear in?
8. How can you make `scanf()` prompt the user to enter characters from the keyboard?
9. How is the user ordinarily prompted to enter keyboard input to a `scanf()` statement?
10. What is the difference between the field-width modifier in a `printf()` statement and the field-width modifier in a `scanf()` statement?
11. What does the function `getchar()` do?
12. Give the generic syntax for the `printf()` function. Explain and give an example.
13. Give the generic syntax for the `scanf()` function. Explain and give an example.
14. Write a single `printf()` statement for each of the following problems so that it gives the stated output:
    a. This is "MY" line.
    b. You said "This is "MY" line" Don't you remember?
    c. The first time you said yes.
       The second time you said no.
        The third time you said yes. Which is it?
15. Write a separate `printf()` statement for each sentence and beep at the end of each sentence. Your series of `printf()` statements must keep the output all on the same line.

    The first time you said yes. The second time you said no. The third time you said yes. Which is it?

16. Write a `scanf()` statement that reads the following values from the specified input line:

    `George Washington12341002300`

    Skip the name field entirely, read 1234 into `studentId`, then read 100 into `examAverage`, then read 2 into `numberOfExams`, and finally read 300 into `finalExam`.
17. Write `printf()` statements that display the result of the preceding question as follows:

    `Student ID: 1234`
    `Exam Average: 100`
    `Final Exam Score: 300`
18. What would each of the following code segments produce?

    ```
    int price = 1000;
    int numOfCharsPrinted;
    unsigned int hexNum = 0x123456cd;
    double bigNumber = 200.149289f;
    int bigInt = 12345;
    float pi = 3.141593;
    double radius = 5.5E+5;
    ```

    a. `printf("%c%d\n", '$', price);`
    b. `printf("Name = %s\nPart of Name? ="`
       `"%5s\n what about now? = %.5s\n",`
       `"George Washington",`
       `"George Washington",`
       `"George Washington",`
       `numOfCharsPrinted);`
    c. `printf("hexNum = %x, %6X\n", hexNum,`
       `hexNum);`
    d. `printf("bigNumber values:\n%f\n%.2f\`
       `n%.6f\n", bigNumber,bigNumber,`
       `bigNumber);`
    e. `printf("bigInt values:\n¦%d¦\n¦%07d¦"`
       `"\n%¦-10d\n¦", bigInt, bigInt,`
       `"bigInt);`
    f. `printf("Area of circle with a radius "`
       `" of %f is %f\n", radius, pi * radius *`
       `radius);`

Programming Exercises

The specifications of the programming assignments were introduced in Chapter 1, at which time you were to

- think through the solution to these problems.
- identify the modules that, once implemented, will solve the problem.
- prepare a hierarchy chart of all the modules.
- prepare pseudocode/flowchart for each module in the hierarchy chart.
- write the program stubs the same way we did with the ACE Billing system application.

In Chapter 2, the concept of a program variable or identifier declaration was presented—especially scalar variables along with the variety of data types with which they may be associated. A scalar variable is one that can only hold a single value at a time. These programming assignments provide you an opportunity to build on the design that you did after Chapter 1. At this point, we ask that you declare all your variables outside of main(), similar to what we did in the application section, so that all the other modules will have access to them. Let's continue to produce the indicated headings as a part of our output. Follow the example shown in Section 3.20. We have designed these programs so that they build on the work done in previous chapters until the original problem is completely solved. To help you along, we have also tried to point out how much you should be able to do here.

By now you have learned how to (1) declare scalar variables, (2) assign values to these variables through assignment statements as well as through read statements (scanf()), and (3) print the variables' values to standard output devices such as the screen or a redirected file. We urge you to continue developing what you started in Chapter 1. If you have not started, we recommend that you start by applying the methodology presented in that chapter.

Programming Assignment 3.1: Billing

Program Description

Write a program that declares three variables—Cost, Quantity, and Extended Cost—according to their respective data types, calculates the extended cost, and prints the first line of the report as shown below. The Product Number and Product Descriptions may be hard-coded for now since we have not yet learned to deal with strings.

Input: Cost and Quantity

Output: (see Figure P3.1)

Figure P3.1   *Output for Programming Assignment 3.1*

Program Name: PA3-1				Page: 1
Author: Your Name				Run Date: 12/19/2000
Billing Invoice for Acme Retail				
Product No.	Product Description	Cost	Quantity	Extension
TZ3232	Dining room set	220.95	1	220.95

Programming Assignment 3.2: VP's Report (Payroll)

Program Description

The new vice president would like to see a list of all the employees in her department, their titles, salaries, and the combined total of all their salaries. Write a program that displays the following information. Use the printf() formatting capabilities presented in this chapter as well as in Appendix F-4, with the box characters, to produce this report.

Input: None; hard-code the values in the program.

Output: (see Figure P3.2)

Figure P3.2 *Output for Programming Assignment 3.2*

Program Name: PA3-2		Page: 1
Author: Your Name		Run Date: 12/19/2000
Payroll Report for the New Vice President		
Name (20)	Title (15)	Salary (9)
Kathy Ray	Executive	$60,000
Vicki Anderson	CPA	$30,000
John Jameson	Clerk	$21,000
Paul Estes	Clerk	$18,000
Kim Alliantz	Manager	$40,000
Total		$169,000

Programming Assignment 3.3: OCS Payroll

Program Description

This is a continuation of Programming Assignment 1.3. Declare all the variables needed to solve this problem, including Social Security Number, Hourly Pay Rate, Number of Exemptions, Health Insurance Code, and Hours Worked. Perform all the calculations needed for a single employee that do not require making any decisions and print out the designed report for one employee. Read all the data needed from the keyboard.

Input: Prompt from the keyboard and enter required data for calculations.

Output: (see Figure P3.3)

Figure P3.3 *Output for Programming Assignment 3.3*

Program Name: PA3-3	Page: 1
Author: Your Name	Run Date: 12/19/2000
OCS Payroll Report	

Programming Assignment 3.4 to 3.7: UNIX System Administration

Program Description

Write a program that prompts the user for UID (User ID) and GID (group ID) and prints the formatted report shown below. Use tabs to separate column fields and left-justify all fields. For now, Username, Full Name, and Shell will have to be hard-coded into the printf() statement.

Input:

```
Enter UID (User Id): 203
Enter GID (Group Id): 15
```

Output: (see Figure P3.4 on page 134)

Figure P3.4 *Output for Programming Assignments 3.4 to 3.7*

Program Name: PA3-4				Page: 1
Author: Your Name				Run Date: 12/19/2000
UNIX System Administration Report				
User Name	User ID	Group ID	Full Name	Shell
bjohnson	203	15	Bill Johnson	/usr/bin/ksh

Programming Assignment 3.8: Science and Engineering (Chemical Engineering)

Program Description

Write a program that declares all the variables needed by this problem and prompt the user to enter these values. Take the values entered and print out the first line of the table. Be sure to use the formatting features of printf() function along with Appendix F-4's table characters.

Input Data:

```
Enter the temperature:
Enter the absolute pressure in Pounds Per Inch (Psia):
Enter the absolute pressure in (Hg):
Enter specific volume saturated liquid pressure in (Hg):
Enter specific volume evaporation pressure (in Hg):
Enter specific volume saturated vapor pressure (in Hg):
Enter enthalpy saturated liquid pressure (in Hg):
Enter enthalpy saturated vapor pressure (in Hg):
Enter enthalpy saturated liquid pressure (in Hg):
Enter entropy saturated vapor pressure (in Hg):
```

Output Report Layout: (see Figure P3.8)

Figure P3.8 *Output Report Layout for Programming Assignment 3.8*

Program Name: PA3-8 Author: Your Name									Page: 1 Run Date: 12/19/2000	
Steam Tables: Properties of Saturated and Supersaturated Steam										
Temp	Psia	In Hg	Sat. Liq.	Evap Vfg	Sat. Vapor	Sat. Liq.	Sat. Vapor	Sat. Liq.	Sat. Vapor	Sat. Liq.
32	0.0886	0.1806	0.01602	3305.7	3305.7	0	1075.1	1075.1	2.1885	2.1865

Programming Assignment 3.9: Science and Engineering (Compiler Construction)

Program Description

Use printf() and the additional information from Appendix F to produce the hard-coded report in Figure P3.9.

Output Report: (see Figure P3.9)

Figure P3.9 *Output Report for Programming Assignment 3.9*

Program Name:PA3-9	Page: 1
Author:Your Name	Run Date: 12/19/2000
PASCAL Assignment Statement Checking	
B := 100;	Valid Statement
B = 100;	Invalid (= must be an assignment operator: :=)
B := 100	
A := B;	Valid Statement
C := 200;	Valid Statement
B := B * 10 - C;	Valid Statement
Radius := 100;	Valid Statement
Circumference := 2 * Pi * Radius;	Valid Statement
Area Of Circle := 2 * Pi * Radius * Radius;	Invalid (Invalid identifier)
Area := 2 * Pi * Radius * Radius;	Valid Statement
Programming := Data_Structures + Algorithms;	Valid Statement
100 := 20 + Alpha;	Invalid statement
Sum := Sum New_Data_Value;	Invalid statement (bad expression)
Sum := Sum + New_Data_Value;	Valid statement
Sum := Sum + New_Data_Value	Invalid statement (missing ;)

Programming Assignment 3.10: Science and Engineering (Mathematics—The Game of Life)

Program Description

This programming assignment is a continuation of Programming Assignment 1.10. You are to declare enough variables to hold three pairs of coordinates where life forms will be placed according to the grid shown below and a character variable to hold the actual life form. Prompt the user for the coordinate values, read them, and then draw the grid similar to the one given below, showing the actual locations of the life forms.

Processing:

1. Create three pairs of coordinates consisting of row and column. Each pair of coordinates represents the location of a life form.

2. Create a character variable to represent the life form and assign a value to the life form variable, say *. Do not use a blank character for the life form because then that life form will be invisible.

3. Assign a value to the row and a value to the column by prompting the user for these values. Read and store the first pair of values into the first pair of coordinate variables. Do the same for the second and third pairs.

4. Print out the values of these variables as shown under "Output Report."

Input data:

```
Enter coordinates for First Life form(e.g., 1 2) :
Enter coordinates for Second Life form(e.g., 2 1):
Enter coordinates for Third Life form(e.g., 0 0) :
```

Output Report: (see Figures P3.10A and P3.10B)

Figure P3.10A *Output Report for Programming Assignment 3.10: Heading*

Program Name: PA3-10	Page: 1
Author: Your Name	Run Date: 12/19/2000
Life in Another Universe	

Figure P3.10B *Output Report for Programming Assignment 3.10: Coordinates*

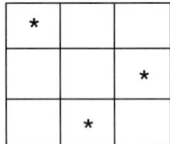

Programming Assignment 3.11: Distribution/Packaging/Shipping

Program Description

- Design and print the packaging slip given below.
- Hard-code the publisher's name and address.
- Hard-code the ship to address.
- Hard-code all the other values.
- Print the following values entered by the user: invoice number, invoice date, customer number, order date, sales order number, quantity ordered, quantity shipped, and back-order quantity.

Input:

```
Enter the Invoice Number: (5-digit number)
Invoice Date (Month):
Invoice date (Day):
Invoice Date (Year):
Enter Sales Order Number: (5-digit number)
Customer Number: (6-digit number)
Order Date (Month):
Order date (Day):
Order Date (Year):
Enter Quantity Ordered:
Enter Quantity shipped:
Enter Back Order Quantity:
```

   Declare enough variables to hold the above data items. Read data into these variables and then use their values in creating the distribution/packing/slip. Hard-code string values that we cannot yet read.

Programming Assignment 3.12: Invoicing

Program Description

Design and print the invoice given below.
- Hard-code the publisher's name and address.
- Hard-code the bill to address.
- Hard-code the ship to address.
- Hard-code all the other values.
- Print the following values entered by the user: invoice number, invoice date, customer number, order date, sales order number, quantity ordered, quantity shipped, and back-order quantity.

Input:

```
Enter the Invoice Number: (5-digit number)
Invoice Date (Month):
Invoice date (Day):
Invoice Date (Year):
Enter Sales Order Number: (5-digit number)
Customer Number: (6-digit number)
Order Date (Month):
Order date (Day):
Order Date (Year):
Enter Quantity Ordered:
Enter Quantity shipped:
Enter Back Order Quantity:
Enter tax percentage:
Enter the unit price:
Enter extended price:
```

Declare enough variables to hold the above data items. Read data into these variables and then use their values in creating the invoice. Hard-code string values that we cannot yet read.

Programming Assignment 3.13 to 3.18—EDI Claims Report

Program Description

A major service provided by a claims clearinghouse is the editing of the insurance claim data to ensure all of the data is in the correct place and in the correct format before being sent to the insurance company. This concept will be pursued in more detail in future chapters, but for now, write a program that displays a Claim Edit Notice as it would be sent to a customer. Model your display after the sample below. Use the formatting features presented in Chapter 3 as well as in Appendix F-4, with the box characters, to produce this report verbatim. In other words, use a series of printf() statements to produce this report. In later chapters, you will be able to produce the same report, but then it will reflect the actual data from the keyboard or from a file.

Input: None

Output: (see Figure P3.13)

Figure P3.13 *Output for Programming Assignments 3.13 to 3.18*

```
Program Name: PA3-13                                    Page: 1
Author: Your Name                          Run Date: 12/19/2000
                    EDI Claims Program

Submitter: AA12124 - Smith, Jack D
Claim Editing Notice

Provider No.      Patient Name              Status

3445433           Simmons        Paul            ACCEPT
3445433           Carr           Gene            ACCEPT
3445433           Criss          Vincent         REJECT
**Invalid Patient Relation to Insured: 88**
3334434           Kraizee        Guy             ACCEPT

        ********************End of Report******************
```

Programming Assignment 3.19: Inventory

Program Description

Write a program that prompts the user for Part Number and Quantity On Hand and prints the formatted report shown in Figure P3.19. Use tabs to separate column fields and left-justify all fields. For now, manufacturer's name and product descriptions will have to be hard-coded into the printf() statement.

Input:

```
Enter Part Number: 7285
Enter Quantity On Hand: 152
```

Output: (see Figure P3.19)

Figure P3.19   *Output for Programming Assignment 3.19*

Program Name: PA3-19			Page: 1
Author: Your Name			Run Date: 12/19/2000
Inventory Report of Quantity on Hand and Quantity Ordered			
Part Number	Manufacturer	Description	Qty on Hand
7285	Specific Motors	Brake Pad	152

Programming Assignment 3.20: General Category (Programa Pro Rata)

Program Description

This is a continuation of Programming Assignment 1.20. We have now covered enough Standard C for you to write a complete program that solves this problem for a single customer.

Input:

```
Enter the tread depth now:
Enter the tread depth when the tire was new:
Enter the price of a new tire:
Enter the mounting and balancing charge:
Enter the state tax rate:
```

Output: (see Figure P3.20 on page 139)

Programming Assignment 3.21: Nation's Economy

Program Description

This is a continuation of Programming Assignment 1.21. You now have all the Standard C knowledge needed to completely solve this problem for one set of data.

Output: (see Figure P3.21on page 139)

Programming Assignment 3.22: Police Department

Program Description

This is a continuation of Programming Assignment 1.22.

Declare variables of proper types to hold the values you have identified as needed for input, calculations, and output. Format the report according to the specifications and then print one line of the report.

Input:

```
Enter vehicle registration number (eight digit code):
Enter driver's social security code (nine digit code):
Enter zone in which offense occurred (1-4):
Enter speed limit in miles per hour (integer):
Enter actual speed recorded in mph (integer):
```

Output: (see Figure P3.22)

Figure P3.20 *Output for Programming Assignment 3.20*

Program Name: PA3-20		Page: 1
Author: Your Name		Run Date: 12/19/2000
Programma Pro Rata		
The tread depth now:		
The tread depth when the tire was new:		
The price of a new tire:		
The mounting and balancing charge:		
The state tax rate:		
6 / 9 = 0.67		

21.00	cost of new tire	
x 0.67	percentage of tread used	
14.00	cost based on percentage	
+ 2.50	mounting and balancing charge	
16.50	16.50	subtotal
x 0.04	0.66	state tax
0.66	17.16	total cost

Figure P3.21 *Output for Programming Assignment 3.21*

Program Name: PA3-21	Page: 1
Author: Your Name	Run Date: 12/19/2000
Nation's Economy	

Figure P3.22 *Output for Programming Assignment 3.22*

Program Name: PA3-22	Page: 1
Author: Your Name	Run Date: 12/19/2000
Speeding Violations	

Programming Assignment 3.27: Electronics

Program Description

Write a program that prompts the user in the same way specified under the "Test Program" section of Programming Assignment 1.27. At this time, the program will read a decimal number and print a hexadecimal number and vice versa, as shown in the sample below:

Input/Output:

Output: (see Figure P3.27)

Figure P3.27 *Output for Programming Assignment 3.27*

```
Program Name: PA3-27                                        Page: 1
Author: Your Name                             Run Date: 12/19/2000

                    Electronics Progress Report

```

```
ZEI processor testing software
    bxxxxxxxxxxxxxxxx (16 bits) for binary input
    hxxxx (4 nibbles) for hexadecimal input
    spaces are ignored

Enter your command (a hexadecimal number) > FF
    response:  257
Enter your command (a decimal number) > 257
    response:  FF
```

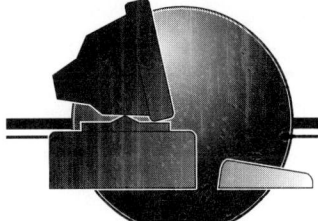

CHAPTER **4**

Expressions, Operators, and Type Conversion

OBJECTIVES

- To learn the values of various types of expressions
- To become familiar with unary and binary operators in general, and arithmetic and combination arithmetic-assignment operators in particular
- To become familiar with the concepts of operator precedence and associativity

- To learn several shorthand ways to increment and decrement variables by a specified integer value, both before and after evaluation of the balance of a statement
- To become familiar with the `sizeof` operator
- To learn the basics of type casting and conversion

NEW TERMS

binary operator	integer division	promotion
cast operator	modulus operator	rule of associativity
comma operator	operand	rule of precedence
decrement operator	operator	`sizeof` operator
demotion	postfix	unary operator
increment operator	prefix	

Variables and constants are linked together by what C calls operators. In Standard C, an **operator** generally specifies an operation to be performed that produces a value. An **operand** is an entity on which an operator acts. So in the statement

```
num = val + 2;
```

both = and + are operators, and num, val and 2 are their operands.

There are several types of operators: assignment, mathematical, logical, relational, and bitwise. We will leave discussion of logical and relational operators to the next chapter, and bitwise operators to a later chapter.

We've already seen the assignment operator. The assignment operator computes what is to its right and assigns that value to the variable to its left. Once we show you the mathematical operators, we will discuss the combination assignment-mathematical operators.

4.1 MATHEMATICAL OPERATORS

With one exception, C's mathematical operators perform the same functions as the + and − signs and as the × and ÷ signs we learned in grammar school. C has the mathematical operators given in Table 4.1; the operators perform the operations listed next to the respective operators.

Table 4.1 *Mathematical Operators*

Operator	Name
+	addition operator
–	subtraction operator
*	multiplication operator
/	division operator
%	modulus operator (remainder of division)

Unlike some computer languages, which use such characters as ^ (BASIC) or ** (FORTRAN, PL/1, and COBOL 85 in its compute statements) for the purpose, there is no separate operator for powers. In Chapter 8, on functions, we will show you how to use a Standard C function that performs that task, as well as how to make your own powers function.

4.1.1   Mathematical Operators and Integer Division

The standard arithmetic operators, +, –, *, and /, will be obvious to you:

```
int num = 10, val = 20;
num = val + 3; /* addition operator: num is now 23 */
val = num - val; /* subtraction operator: val is now 3 */
num = num * 3; /* multiplication operator: num is now 69 */
val = 24 / 5; /* division operator: val is now 4 */
```

The last statement requires some looking at. When you divide one integer into another, the result is the whole number of times the second number divides into the first, hence the result of 4 above. The answer is truncated rather than rounded. This truncation phenomenon is sometimes referred to as *integer division.*

When you divide one floating point number into another, you get the untruncated results you expect. For this purpose, floating point numbers include integers in floating point format—that is, whole numbers followed only by a decimal point:

```
24 / 5  =  4
25 / 5  =  5
24. / 5. =  4.8
24 / 5. =  4.8
```

In the last case, we had mixed integer and floating point division. As you can see, the result is not truncated. The integer, which has type int, is converted to a floating point number with type double prior to division (see Chapter 13). It wouldn't make any difference which number had been in floating point format and which in integer format. It is better practice to use a decimal point on all floating point type assignments, however.

Just one caveat on integer division. Everything works as advertised if both numbers are positive. However, if either is negative, Standard C permits an implementation to either round up or down to the nearest integer. If you have an integer division situation and there is a chance one of the values might be negative, it might be safer to test whether either is negative; if one or both are negative, you can temporarily convert both to positive values and after the integer division, alter the sign if one but not both are negative.

Integer division is usually employed in certain kinds of counting problems, in which the arguments are almost always positive; the extension to negative arguments may largely be only for mathematical completeness. The problem will rarely arise in a real programming task. But if the problem ever does arise in your application, it could be the most important one in the world to you at the time.

The integer remainder of integer division is referred to as the *modulus*. For example, the modulus of 10 / 12 is 2. C has an operator you can use to preserve or determine this remainder: the *modulus operator*, discussed in the next section.

4.1.2   Modulus Operator

The new kid on the block (unless your grammar school was a lot fancier than ours) is the ***modulus operator.*** The modulus operator is used only in calculations involving two integers. It tells us what the remainder is (what whole number is left over) when the integer to its left is divided by the integer to its right:

```
int val = 12, num = 5;
int remainder;
remainder = val % num;
```

Here, remainder has a value of 2. If the integer value to the left of the modulus operator is evenly divisible by the integer value to the right, the result is 0.

When would we ever use this unusual operator? Lots of situations. For instance, if we want to check whether a variable in our program is even or odd at some particular point in the program, we can ask whether that variable % 2 is 0 (it's even) or 1 (it's odd). We could use the modulus operator to help us print a neat table of numbers by printing a carriage return every eighth number (if number_counter % 8 is 0, print a newline character). We could use the modulus operator to test whether a variable used to store the calendar year represents a leap year: if year % 4 is 0, it's a leap year, unless it's a centennial (year % 100 is 0) that is not also a millennium (year % 1000 is 0).

The modulus operator may be used only where both values to either side of it are integers. Any integer type will do. (See the next section for a discussion of the modulus operator in cases where one or both values are negative.)

The same caveat on negative integers discussed in the preceding section on integer division applies to the modulus operator. Standard C requires that the result of applying the modulus operator for x%y equal x - (x%y)*y: in other words, the result of modulus operation on negative values must correspond to the way the implementation handles integer division with one or more negative values.

4.2   ASSIGNMENT-MATHEMATICAL OPERATOR COMBINATIONS

You will often have occasion in your programs to increase or decrease the value already assigned to a variable:

```
int num = 5;
num = num + 6;
```

From the computer's point of view, you aren't increasing num's value by 6. You are adding 6 to another number—which happens to be the value you retrieve from num—and storing the result of the calculation in num.

Nevertheless, C allows you to use a syntax that parallels the way humans see this exercise. The alternative syntax is also more compact:

```
num += 6;
```

You can combine any of the other mathematical operators with the assignment operator for a similar effect:

```
int num = 5;
num -= 2; /* same as num = num - 2: num is now 3 */
num *= 8; /* same as num = num * 8: num is now 24 */
num /= 2; /* same as num = num / 2: num is now 12 */
num %= 7; /* same as num = num % 7: num is now 5 */
```

4.3   INCREMENT AND DECREMENT OPERATOR

Not only will you often have occasion to increase or decrease the already-stored value of a variable, but you will find in particular that frequently you will increase or decrease the value by 1. You will note this especially once we cover loops in Chapter 5.

You have already seen two ways of increasing or decreasing the value of a variable by 1:

```
int num = 5;
num = num + 1;
num += 1;
num = num - 1;
num -= 1;
```

C offers an even more compact syntax:

```
num++; /* same as num += 1 or num = num + 1 */
num--; /* same as num -= 1 or num = num - 1 */
```

The ++ is called the ***increment operator;*** the -- is referred to as the ***decrement operator.***

4.3.1   Postfix vs. Prefix

C gives you the choice of executing a statement and then incrementing or decrementing a variable by 1 or the opposite—incrementing or decrementing a variable by 1 and then executing the statement in which the variable is contained. In the former case, we place the operator after the variable: this is called *postfix.* In the latter case, the operator comes just in front of the variable: this is called *prefix.* Consider the following:

```
int num;
int val = 7;
num = val++; /* postfix */
val = ++num; /* prefix */
```

After the first increment statement, num has a value of 7 but val has a value of 8. First the assignment is made and *then* val is incremented. On the other hand, both val and num have values of 8 after the next statement. *First* num is incremented and then the assignment is made.

     Avoid applying the increment or decrement operator to a variable that occurs more than once in a single statement.

```
val = num / 2 + --num;
```

It is clear that the second num will be decremented before it is added to num/2. But there is no way of knowing whether your compiler will use the decremented or undecremented value in calculating num / 2.

Lest you think otherwise, let us point out that surrounding the postfix-incremented variable with parentheses does not force it to be incremented before the balance of the statement is executed.

```
int num = 5, val = 7;
num = 1 + (val++);
```

After the second statement, num has a value of 8, not 9. The second statement is identical to

```
num = 1 + val++;
```

The parentheses do nothing.

What about this one:

```
k = m+++n;
```

Does the compiler treat this statement as

```
k = m + (++n);
```

or

```
k = (m++) + n;
```

and would it make any difference if we inserted a space after the first or second + (C's usual practice of ignoring spaces notwithstanding)?

Why worry about it? Just use parentheses or, better, split the statement into two separate statements (see Review Question 10b). Just be aware of the potential problem.

All right, you insist on knowing. Standard C requires implementations to parse code into the largest sequence of characters that make up a token. Take the following code fragment:

```
int x = 1, y = 3;
int num = x+++++y;
```

According to the rule just stated, the second statement must be parsed as

```
int num = x++ ++ +y;
```

even though the resulting statement will not compile without error, and even though the statement parsed as follows would:

```
int num = x++ + ++y;
```

If we rewrite the statement this way, the compiler does indeed respect the spacing, compiles without error, and produces the result we expect: values of 5, 2, and 4 for num, x, and y, respectively.

Going back to the somewhat simpler question we posed, we can see that spacing can alter the result despite the general notion that spacing is ignored:

```
int x = 1, y = 3;
int num = x++ + ++y;
num = x+++y; /* parsed as x++ +y */
num = x+ ++y; /* parsed just as it looks */
```

If we printed values for the three variables after each assignment statement, we would get values for num, x, and y, respectively, of 5, 2, and 4; 6, 3, and 4; and 8, 3, and 5.

You may theoretically use the increment or decrement operator with floating point variables as well as with integer types, though you will rarely have occasion to do so. As discussed in Chapters 7 and 9, you may, and often will, use the increment and decrement operators in connection with pointers. However, you may not apply either operator to a constant: remember that num++ is merely shorthand for num = num + 1, a formulation that makes no sense for a constant:

```
float total = 5.;
total++; /* OK, though very uncommon usage */
total = 6.++; /* error! */
```

4.4   UNARY SIGN OPERATORS

The mathematical operators are **binary operators:** each links something to its left and to its right with some action. There are also **unary operators,** which operate on a single variable or constant. We will cover two of them here.

The minus sign is used to change the value of the variable or constant it precedes from negative to positive or vice versa:

```
int num;
num = -12;
val = -num;
```

You may also use the plus sign as a unary operator

```
num = +12;
```

but this operator generally has no real effect. For an exception, see the next section.

4.5   OPERATOR PRECEDENCE AND ASSOCIATIVITY

What is assigned to num in the following statement:

```
num = 2 + 6 * 3 + 2;
```

When you have a number of operators in the same statement, the **rules of precedence** dictate the order in which the operations are processed. This statement assigns 22 rather than 40 to num because the * operator, like the / operator, has precedence over the + operator and the - operator.

What then of the following:

```
num = 12 / 4 * 3;
```

The processing order where operators have the same precedence is governed by the ***rules of associativity***—either left to right or right to left. Since the * and / operators associate from left to right, this statement assigns 9 to num, not 1.

We confess to finding the rules of precedence and associativity tedious. Worse, we feel that an attempt to master the rules and apply them from memory is dangerous. Why take a chance on an incorrect result when there is a safer solution? *All questions of precedence and associativity can, and we believe should, be finessed by a liberal application of parentheses to leave our programming intentions free from doubt.* We could, for example, rewrite our two previous examples this way

```
num = 2 + (6 * 3) + 2;
num = (12 / 4) * 3;
```

or this way

```
num = (2 + 6) * (3 + 2);
num = 12 / (4 * 3);
```

depending on our intentions.

Nevertheless, for those of you passionately interested in the question, we have included a precedence/associativity chart as Appendix J. Note that all operators associate from left to right except for the following, some of which we cover in later chapters:

- All unary operators
- The conditional operator
- The assignment operator and combination assignment-mathematical and assignment-bitwise operators

Now that we have discussed precedence, we can examine one example in which the unary + operator has a purpose:

```
unsigned long total, subtotal = 100L, offset = 100L,
  max = ULONG_MAX; /* maximum unsigned long value */
total = subtotal + +(max - offset);
```

Since the unary + operator has a higher precedence than the binary + operator, the unary + operator forces evaluation of (max - offset), and addition of the result to subtotal. This may be desirable if, as here, you are worried that adding max to subtotal first will result in integer overflow (see Chapter 2). The following statement will not produce the same desired result:

```
total = subtotal + (max - offset);
```

Though you should use parentheses prolifically, the compiler will ignore all those that override the rules of precedence. In this example, since the binary + operator and binary – operator have the same precedence, the compiler will ignore the parentheses. Since the binary + and – operators associate left to right, the evaluation order is subtotal + max and then - offset. (Notwithstanding the supposed evaluation order, however, on many compilers, the second formulation will work without overflow.)

4.6   COMBINING ASSIGNMENTS AND STATEMENTS WITH ASSIGNMENT OPERATORS AND COMMA OPERATORS

You may have multiple assignments in the same statement:

```
int a = 5;
int b, c;
int num = 17;
a = b = c = num  + a;
```

 With multiple assignments in the same statement, the assignment is made right to left.

Thus c is first assigned a value of 22, then c's value is assigned to b, and last, b's value is assigned to a. The variables a, b, and c now all have a value of 22.

You can use the multiple-assignment device with the assignment operator–mathematical operator combinations:

```
num = val += quantity + sample;
```

Appendix J, covering the rules of precedence, indicates that the assignment operators (including the combination assignment operator-mathematical operators) have the very lowest priority and that they associate left to right. Therefore, this example is equivalent to

```
num = (val = val + (quantity + sample));
```

 However, this is a good example of bad programming style, where the coder tries to impress other programmers with how clever the coder is and how compact and cryptic the code is. *It is far clearer programming style to avoid combination assignment operator-mathematical operators in multiple-assignment statements.*

```
val = val + quantity + sample
num = val;
```

You can also group assignment statements by separating them with commas:

```
int a, b, c;
a = 5, b = 3, c = a + b;
```

In this case, the commas are called *comma operators*; they are not merely separators as they were in all previous examples.

 Where assignment or other expressions are separated by comma operators, they are evaluated from left to right.

So, expanding on the last example:

```
int a = 0, b = 1, c = 2;
a = 5, b = 3, c = a + b;
```

After these statements, the variable c has a value of 8, not 1.

Technically, the comma operator transforms the statements linked in this way into a single statement. As a result, where usage calls for braces to surround a set of statements, you may link the statements with commas and dispense with the braces. Apart from multiple parts of control statements, addressed in Chapter 5, however, this usage is rare; it is generally limited to instances where the statements are so closely intertwined that they essentially form a single statement. For an example, see the `bitflip()` function in Listing 8.20, `two_flip.c`. Nevertheless, there is nothing to prevent you from making extensive use of the comma operator to link separate statements into one. (See Chapter 5, relating to loops, for a further discussion of the comma operator.)

4.7   EXPRESSIONS

Each combination of variables or constants with operators constitutes an expression. Thus,

```
num = (val + 7) * (2 + 3)
```

is an expression, as are its components

```
(val + 7)
(2 + 3)
```

Placing a semicolon after an expression makes it a statement. However, only statements that cause the computer to make an assignment or take some other action are sensible statements worthy of inclusion in a program. Both the following are legitimate C statements that will engender no error message from the compiler

```
val + 7;
num = (val + 7) * (2 + 3);
```

but the first statement has no effect whatever and you will get a warning from the compiler.

There are a couple of important points to make about assignments.

You may make an assignment within an expression.

```
int num, val;
num = (val = 7 + 3) * 2;
val = 17 + (num += 32);
```

In the first statement, `val` is assigned a value of 10 and `num` a value of 20. In the second, `num` is assigned a value of 52 and `val` a value of 69. The result is the same as if you had used a less compact form:

```
val = 7 + 3;
num = val * 2;
num = num + 32;
val = 17 + num;
```

Why is this so?

In C, every expression has a value. The value of an expression in which an assignment is made is the value assigned.

The practice of making assignments within expressions, though not uncommon, is not recommended, especially if you are not the only one looking at your code. The inner assignment is too easy to overlook, and it makes for code that is much more difficult to follow. But some programmers have a predilection for overly compact code, and as we will often do in this book, we will try to make sure you won't encounter anything you don't understand.

In Chapter 5, we will discuss relational expressions.

A relational expression has a value of 1 if it is true and 0 if it is false.

In that chapter, we will also continue the discussion, started in this chapter, of expressions separated by comma operators.

Expressions separated by comma operators have the value of the right-most expression.

4.8   THE `sizeof` OPERATOR

The `sizeof` *operator* tells us how many bytes a particular variable or variable type contains. For example, on a PC, given the declaration

```
int num;
```

the following two expressions would each have a value of 2:

```
sizeof(num)
sizeof(int)
```

This value is an unsigned integer constant and can be used in a statement the same way any constant could be. Its type is implementation defined. (To be specific, the value of a `sizeof` expression is whatever type the `typedef size_t` is defined to be in `sfddef.h`. A `typedef` is a nickname for a Standard C type. See Chapter 13.)

```
unsigned bytes, num, val;
bytes = sizeof(num) + sizeof(val);
```

But, you may ask, if we know how many bytes an `int` has, why not just replace those two expressions with 2s? First, because often calculation of the number of bytes will be more complex than in this simple example, especially when we learn in later chapters how to apply the `sizeof` operator to complex data types such as arrays and structures. Second, using `sizeof` makes the code more portable. An `int` may be 2 bytes on a PC but larger on another system.

The compiler does all that is necessary to evaluate at compile time the number of bytes in the operand of the `sizeof` operator. Though it would be poor programming style to do so, it would be possible to declare a new complex data type inside a `sizeof` expression. Such a declaration does not reserve any memory. The compiler must create the type to evaluate its size. However, any other attempted operations inside the `sizeof` operator are ignored:

```
int a = sizeof(enum seasons{spring, summer, fall, winter});
int b = sizeof(a++);
```

Initially the variable a is assigned the value of 2, the size of an `enum` (assuming `int` has 2 bytes). It is not incremented in the second statement, so it still has a value of 2. The attempted increment operation is ignored. See Chapter 13 for a description of declaration of the complex types `struct`, `union`, and `enum`.)

When you use the `sizeof` operator with a variable, you are not required to enclose the variable with commas. This is an operator, not a function call. However, when the operand is a type, you must use enclosing parentheses:

```
a = sizeof num + sizeof (val) + sizeof (int);
b = sizeof int; /* error */
```

For consistency, it is better style to use parentheses in all cases.

4.9   TYPE CONVERSIONS AND CASTING

Unlike some other programming languages, C permits you to use variables of different types in a single statement. When evaluating an expression such as a + b or c * d, in cases where one variable is of a different type from the other, the compiler makes a type conversion before evaluating the two together. In addition, if we assign the result to a third variable, there may be still another type conversion. Type conversion on assignment also takes place if we assign a single constant or variable to a variable of a different type. Here are the steps for mixed-type conversions.

The first evaluation takes place to the right of the assignment operator. In the first evaluation step, type conversion is accomplished in one or two steps. If any of the variables is a `signed char` or `unsigned char`, its value is converted to `int`. Next, the value of the variable with the lower type is converted to the type of the variable with the higher type, in the following ranking order from lowest to highest: `int`, `unsigned`, `long`, `unsigned long`, `float`, `double`, `long double`. Observe that this means that integer types will always be converted to floating point types if both are present.

This process is referred to as **promotion.** By using the largest type as the lowest common denominator, we prevent the data loss that often follows from the application of the following two **demotion** rules:

 Conversion Rule 1: When floating point types are demoted to integer types, they are truncated to the next lowest integer.

So 3.9 becomes 3. Therefore, by converting everything to floating point if any of the variables are floating point, we avoid the loss of data that would result from, say, multiplying 3.5 by 2 if we were to convert 3.5 to 3 before multiplying by 2.

 Conversion Rule 2: Converting a longer integer type to a shorter type truncates the higher-order bytes and leaves the lower-order bytes unchanged.

Take the following example:

```
long memory = 131072L; /* 2^17 */
unsigned letter = 256; /* 2^8 */
unsigned epistle = memory / letter;
```

If `memory` were demoted to `unsigned`, we would get a result of 0, since the two least significant bytes of `memory` contain all zeros (see Chapter 12). But by promoting the `letter` value to `long` instead, we get the correct result of 512.

In the second step, we assign the result of a mixed type combination.

 The final result of the right side of the assignment operator is converted to the type of the variable being assigned a value.

This process can result in either promotion or demotion, depending on the type of the variable on the left side of the assignment operator. Be careful in such a case: a lower-ranking variable may not be large enough to hold the result. Note the two demotion rules above.

The same conversion occurs when we assign a single constant or variable to a variable of a different type.

In addition to the conversions discussed above, there are also type casts, discussed below and in Chapter 13, and automatic conversions with operands of certain unary operators and with arguments and return values in function calls, both discussed in Chapter 13 as well. Restrictions on the conversions discussed above are also treated in that chapter. Attempted conversion of certain types into certain other types is not permitted.

4.9.1   Type Casting—Cast Operators

As with the rules of precedence, it is wisest not to leave your program results dependent on the vagaries of the rules of type conversion. With precedence, we make our intentions clear with judicious use of parentheses. With type conversion, we make our intentions clear with type casting.

To type cast, you precede the object you want treated as a particular type with the type enclosed in parentheses. The parentheses and type together constitute a *cast operator.* There are restrictions on conversion of certain types to certain other types. (See Chapter 13 for the restrictions.)

In some instances you will want a result different from what the default rules of type conversion would produce. Say, for instance, you wanted to calculate how much (in dollars and cents) of a company's profits each share of its stock would be entitled to:

```
float dividend;
long profits = 100000L, shares = 125000L;

dividend = (float) profits / (float) shares;
```

Absent this type cast, integer division would produce a result of zero. (Make sure you understand why only a single type cast to either long variable would have sufficed for both shares and profits to be converted to float.)

In an appropriate case you may want to use the cast operator even where there is only a single variable to the right of the assignment operator. For example, to convert from centimeters to inches and feet:

```
double centimeters = 72.3, inches;
int feet;

inches = centimeters / 2.54;
feet = (int) (inches / 12);
inches -= (double) feet * 12.;
```

In the second assignment statement, we intentionally make use of the second rule of demotion above: we truncate down to the nearest integer number of feet. In the final assignment statement, use of the cast operator is probably unnecessary, since using a floating point constant will force promotion of feet to a double; and, in any case, even if we had made the constant an integer by omitting the period following it, the integer result of multiplying the int variable by an integer-type constant would be promoted to double on assignment. However, type casting here avoids any uncertainty and also shows that the programmer is not unaware of hidden promotion or demotion operations. Even with the type casting, comments to each statement would be recommended.

You can also use type casting to manipulate and check the values in your program. For instance, to isolate the value of the low-order byte in a long value:

```
long time = 131073; /* 2^17 + 1 */
char low_byte = (char)time;
```

Here, we get a value of 1 for first, the value of the least significant byte of time.

You can type cast a result as well as individual values:

```
double secs = .025;
unsigned long beginning, end;

beginning = 181871L;
end = beginning + (unsigned long)(secs * 1193180./65536.);
```

You can also nest type casts:

```
double secs = .0125;
long ticks = 1193180L, num = 65536L;
unsigned long beginning, end;
end = beginning + (unsigned long) (secs * ((double) ticks /
    (double) num));
```

 Type casting can occasionally save time by preventing unnecessary conversions. For instance, say we wanted to add the integer portion of a floating point variable's value to an integer variable. The following

```
float hrsWorkedOT;
int normalHrs, totHrs;

totHrs = normalHrs + (int)hrsWorkedOT;
```

is faster than

```
totHrs = normalHrs + hrsWorkedOT;
```

since only one type conversion is made rather than two.

Sometimes you will want to use type casting just for the sake of clarity and documentation—for example, with

```
int num;
float val = 7.3;
num = val;
```

num will be assigned a value of 7. But we ensure this result, and at the same time tell anyone else reading our code that the truncation is intentional, this way:

```
/* rounding down intentionally -
    rules of conversion probably do it without type cast */
num = (int) val;
```

Likewise, in the first example in this section,

```
dividend = (float) profits / (float) shares;
```

we could have omitted either of the two type casts: under the rules of promotion discussed in the last section, the single uncast long value would be promoted to the higher-ranking type float. But including both type casts is clearer.

Chapter Summary

1. Variables and constants are linked together by operators. In Standard C, an operator generally specifies the operation to be performed that produces a value, and an operand is the entity on which an operator acts.

2. The types of operators are assignment, mathematical, logical, relational, and bitwise.

3. Mathematical operators perform the four standard arithmetic operations: add, subtract, multiply, and divide. A fifth operator, called the modulus operator, gives the remainder when an integer number is divided by another.

4. The division operator, when one integer is divided by another, results in the whole number of times the second number divides into the first (the result when the quotient is a whole number and a remainder). This operation, which truncates rather than rounds the whole number, is called integer division.

5. Mathematical operators used in combination with the assignment operator, =, can be used to reassign a value to a variable by performing a mathematical operation on it and replacing the original value with the result (for example, num += 6 is the same as num = num + 6).

6. Similarly, variables can be incremented or decremented by 1 by placing ++ or -- immediately after the variable name. (For instance, num++ is the same as num += 1 and is the same as num = num + 1.) This is useful in executing loops or similar statements in which the number is incremented each time the statement is executed.

7. Placing the operators before or after the variable name changes the way the variable is executed in statements. When placed before, the increment takes place first, and the incremented value—not the initial value—is used in the statement. When placed after, the initial value is used in the statement, and the increment is done after execution.

8. Binary operators act on two or more numbers or variables, to the left and right of the operator, while unary operators act only on a single value or variable.

9. When you have a number of operators in the same statement, the rules of precedence dictate the order in which the operations are processed, such as division and multiplication being performed before addition and subtraction. When operators have the same precedence, they are governed by rules of associativity, either left to right, or right to left.

10. Rather than rely on rules of precedence and associativity, it is better to liberally use parentheses to group expressions in the desired manner.

11. You can combine multiple assignments in the same statement. The assignment is made from right to left.

12. Each combination of variables or constants with an operator constitutes an expression. Although technically placing a semicolon after any expression makes it a statement, only statements that assign or take some other action have any effect.

13. Although you may make an assignment within an expression that is part of another assignment, it is best to avoid this practice, since it is easy to overlook the inner assignment when debugging.

14. A relational expression has a value of 1 if it is true and 0 if it is false.

15. The `sizeof` operator indicates how many bytes a particular variable or variable type contains. This is useful in determining the size of complex variables and arrays, and it makes the code more portable. The same variable type may be a different number of bytes on different operating systems.

16. Unlike other programming languages, C allows you to use variables of different types in a single statement. When an expression contains different types, the compiler makes a type conversion before evaluating the two together, and may make a conversion if the variables or constants are assigned to another variable type.

17. Variables are first converted according to a process called promotion:
   - If any of the variables is a `signed` or `unsigned` `char`, it is converted to `int`.
   - The value of the variable with the smaller type is converted to the type of variable with the largest size. This prevents the larger variables from being truncated to a smaller size.

18. Second, if the conversion is part of an assignment, the final result of the right side of the assignment (the value being assigned) is converted to the variable type that it is being assigned to.

19. A programmer can control how variables are converted by designating variables to be a certain type. This is done by placing the variable type in parentheses in front of the variable name—a process called type casting.

Review Questions

1. In the following expression, which elements are operators, and which are operands?

   $a = b + 10$

2. What does the modulus operator (%) do?

3. What is the difference between an arithmetic result that is rounded and one that is truncated?

4. Does the increment (++) operator go immediately before or after the variable it increments? Can you use this operator on a constant?

5. What is the difference between a unary and a binary operator?

6. The process of promotion refers to what?

7. Evaluate the following C expressions:
   a. `a = b = c = 2 * 3 - 6 * 2;`
   b. `12 % 2`
   c. `123457 % 2`
   d. `17 % 3`
   e. `15 % 3`
   f. `24 % 5 + 7 * 4 /7`
   g. `(3 + 2) * 4 % (6 + 3)`
   h. `3 + 2 * 4 % 6 + 3`
   i. `3 + (2 * 4) % 6 + 3`

8. Rewrite the following expressions as the example demonstrates.

   Example:
   ```
   sum += newValue;
   ```
   Equivalent to: `sum = sum + newValue;`

   a. `k += 10;`
   b. `k -= 10;`
   c. `k *= 10;`
   d. `k -= -10;`
   e. `k /= 10;`
   f. `k %= 2;`
   g. `k %= 3;`

9. Are the following valid C statements? Explain your answer.
   a. `10 += k;`
   b. `300 = k + 50;`
   c. `3.141529 * 5 = 632.56;`

10. Rewrite the following statements using two separate statements for each:
   a. `k = m + n++;`
   b. `k = m + ++n;`
   c. `k = m - n--;`
   d. `k = m - --n;`
   e. `k = m - ++n;`

11. Execute the program in Figure 4.1 by hand and show the results.

12. Type in the program of Review Question 11, execute it, study the results, and add comments to the program explaining what is going on, based on your understanding as well as on the results.

13. Execute the program in Figure 4.2 by hand and explain your results.

Figure 4.1 *Program for Review Question 11.*

```
#include <stdio.h>
/*
  +-------------------------------------------------------------------+
  +        Purpose:
  +        This program has purposefully withheld comments so that you
  +        can be tested on what it does. Adding comments to it is a
  +        part of your assignment.
  +        Caveats:
  +        This exercise is designed to help you see how these operators
  +        work in various settings. It is simply a teaching exercise.
  +        The examples here and in Review Question 13 are NOT examples of good
  +        programming. They are meant to test your theoretical grasp
  +        of the operators and to prepare you for other programmers'
  +        cryptic code.
  +        The problem is also meant to highlight unanticipated side
  +        effects and results. In all these cases, parentheses should be
  +        used or the statements should be split into two separate statements.
  +-------------------------------------------------------------------+
*/

int main(void)
{
  int a;
  int b;
  int c;
  int d;

  a = 0;
  b = 0;
  c = a++ + ++a;
  printf("11(a):\na = %d\nb = %d\nc = %d\n", a, b, c);

  d = a *= c++ + ++b + 3;
  printf("11(b):\na = %d\nb = %d\nc = %d\nd = %d\n",
     a, b, c, d);

  b = b++;
  printf("11(c):\nb = %d\n", b);

  printf("11(d):\n");
  printf("First b = %d\nSecond b = %d\n", --b, --b);
}
```

Figure 4.2 *Program for Review Question 13.*

```
#include <stdio.h>
/*
  +-------------------------------------------------------------------+
  +        See comment block to Review Question 11 for purpose and caveats
  +-------------------------------------------------------------------+
*/

int main(void)
{
  char  ch1;
  char  ch2;
  char  ch3;
  int   intNum1;
  int   intNum2;
  int   intNum3;
  float floatNum1;
```

```
        float floatNum2;
        float floatNum3;
        long  longNum;

        ch1 = 'x';
        intNum1 = ch1 = ch1 - 'a' + 'A';
        ch3 = intNum1;
        printf("13(a)\n");
        printf("    ch1 = %c Also equivalent to %d\n", ch1, ch1);
        printf("intNum1 = %d Also equivalent to %c\n", intNum1, intNum1);
        printf("    ch3 = %c Also equivalent to %d\n", ch3, ch3);

        intNum1 = 430;
        ch2 = intNum1;
        ch3 = intNum1 + 1;
        printf("13(b)\n");
        printf("intNum1 = %d Also equivalent to %c\n", intNum1, intNum1);
        printf("    ch2 = %c Also equivalent to %d\n", ch2, ch2);
        printf("    ch3 = %c Also equivalent to %d\n", ch3, ch3);

        floatNum1 = 400;
        floatNum2 = 450 * floatNum1;
        intNum3 = 2.5 * 8;

        intNum1 = floatNum1/450;
        floatNum3 = floatNum1/450;
        printf("13(c)\n");
        printf("  intNum1 = %d \n", intNum1);
        printf("floatNum1 = %f \n", floatNum1);
        printf("floatNum2 = %f \n", floatNum2);
        printf("floatNum3 = %f \n", floatNum3);

        longNum = 70000L;
        intNum1 = longNum;

        printf("13(d)\n");
        printf("intNum1 = %d Also equivalent to %x in hexadecimal\n",
            intNum1, intNum1);
        printf("longNum = %ld\n", longNum);
        printf("longNum = %lx in hexadecimal\n", longNum);
}
```

Programming Exercise

PROGRAMMING ASSIGNMENT 4.20:
GENERAL CATEGORY (PROGRAMA PRO RATA)

Program Description

Rewrite Programming Assignment 3.20, using integer variables for all input data and relying on type casting to get the correct results. This is especially important when doing integer division and you expect to get floating point results.

Output: (see Figure P4.20)

Figure P4.20 *Output for Programming Assignment 4.20*

Program Name: PA4-20	Page: 1
Author: Your Name	Run Date: 12/19/2000
Programma Pro Rata	

CHAPTER 5

Loops and Conditional Statements

OBJECTIVES

- To become familiar with logical operators, relational operators, and the conditional operator, and to learn how to use them
- To understand the concept of conditional execution of a statement or block of statements

- To write conditional statements in four different basic formats, and to appreciate what form of conditional statement is best for a particular context
- To learn how to short-circuit execution of conditional statements

NEW TERMS

conditional operator	null statement
logical operator	relational operator

In this chapter, we will look at conditional execution of a statement or block of statements. We will look at the `if` statement, where a statement or block of statements is executed only if the preceding conditional expression is true. We will look at the `switch` statement, where the program chooses one from among a list of statements or blocks of statements. Finally, we will look at `for` loops and `while` loops, where the program executes a statement or block of statements a certain number of times or while a specified condition exists.

5.1   `if` STATEMENTS

Often you will want to have the program execute a statement or block of statements only if a certain condition exists when you reach that point. In C, conditional execution is achieved by an `if` statement. In addition to containing the keyword `if`, the `if` statement has a condition (consisting of one or more logical or other expressions) and a body. The syntax of an `if` statement is as follows:

```
if statement - single statement body

  if (condition)
    statement;

if statement - compound statement body

  if (condition)
  {
    one or more statements;
  }
```

 There is no semicolon after the closing parenthesis of a conditional statement.

The condition following the keyword `if` *must* be enclosed in parentheses.

The `if` statement body can be a single statement or a series of statements. If it is a series of statements, the statements are enclosed in braces. If the condition is true, all the statements within the braces are executed; otherwise none is. There is no semicolon following the closing brace:

```
if (hours > 40.0)
{
    regularPay = 40.0 * hourlyRate;
    overtimePay = (hours - 40.0) * hourlyRate * 1.5;
    totalPay = regularPay + overtimePay;
}
```

With a single-statement body, many programmers use the following format:

```
if (condition) statement;
```

However, the format of placing the ensuing statement on a different line,

```
if (condition)
    statement;
```

is preferable. If you use this recommended format and are stepping through a program in debug mode, you will get to the second line only if the `if` condition is true; otherwise the line will be skipped. Thus, you will know whether the condition is true at that point or false by whether the line is skipped or not. If, however, you use the combination format, this visual method of distinguishing true from false will not be available.

Some programmers go a step further and enclose even a single statement body in braces for clarity:

```
if (condition)
{
    statement;
}
```

To save space, in this book we have not generally used this format. However, the end-of-chapter programming applications do use it. We highly recommend the format, both here and in `while` and other logic constructs.

5.1.1   Relational Operators

The conditional expression portion of the `if` statement generally uses one or more of C's ***relational operators,*** as in the previous example, which asks whether `little` is less than `big`

```
if (little < big)
. . .
```

Those operators and their meanings are listed in Table 5.1.

Table 5.1 *Relational Operators*

Operator	Meaning
==	Is equal to
!=	Is not equal to
>	Is greater than
>=	Is greater than or equal to
<	Is less than
<=	Is less than or equal to

Here are examples that use each of the relational operators (to simplify things, we've made every other example true):

```
int little = 4, small = 4, big = 8; /* used for all examples */
if (little == small) /* true */
    printf("little equals small\n");
if (little == big) /* false */
    printf("little equals big\n");

little equals small

if ( 3 != small) /* true */
    printf("3 is not equal to small\n");
if (small != 4) /* false */
    printf("small is not equal to 4\n");

3 is not equal to small

if (5 > 4) /* true */
    printf("5 is greater than 4\n");
if (2 > 10) /* false */
    printf("2 is greater than 10\n");

5 is greater than 4

if ((little * 3) >= (small / 2)) /* true */
    printf("little times three is greater than or equal to half of small\n");
if ((little - 4) >= (small + 4)) /* false */
    printf("little minus 4 is greater than or equal to small plus 4\n");

little times three is greater than or equal to half of small

if (small < big) /* true */
    printf("small is less than big\n");
if (big < small) /* false */
    printf("big is less than small\n");

small is less than big

if (little <= small) /* true */
    printf("little is less than or equal to small\n");
if (big <= little) /* false */
    printf("big is less than or equal to little\n");

little is less than or equal to small
```

5.1.2   Evaluating Expressions without Relational Operators

You can also test an expression that does not contain a relational operator.

 An expression evaluates to false if it has a value of zero. Otherwise, it evaluates to true—even if its value is negative.

```
int little = 4, small = 4, big = 8;
if (little - small) /* 0 */
    printf("test 1 is true\n");
if (big - little) /* 4 */
    printf("test 2 is true\n");
if (little) /* 4 */
    printf("test 3 is true\n");
if (little - big) /* -4 */
    printf("test 4 is true\n");
```

```
test 2 is true
test 3 is true
test 4 is true
```

You can see what this true-false rule of zero being the litmus test for falsity does: it gives us a shorthand way of asking whether something is equal to zero. Each of these four examples could (and probably should) have been written in a less compact way. Take the first example. The following two statements are equivalent:

```
if (little - small)
    printf("test 1 is true\n");
if ((little - small) != 0)
    printf("test 1 is true\n");
```

As an example, the following statement would decrement the page number variable `pagenum`, but only if the page were not already page 1:

```
if (pagenum - 1)
    pagenum--;
```

This is a shorthand way of writing either of the two following formulations:

```
if (pagenum - 1 != 0)
    pagenum--;
if (pagenum > 1)
    pagenum--;
```

Theoretically, you could place a constant alone as the condition. The expression would be true unless the constant were 0. Thus, the following condition would be true:

```
if (1)
    little--;
```

There is little reason to use this device of inserting a constant within the conditional portion of the `if` statement, however; you could omit the `if (1)` and have the same result. Nonetheless, you will find the always-true device useful in connection with `while` loops, covered later in this chapter. Also, the `if(constant)` device may make sense where `constant` is a manifest constant the value of which might be 0 or some other number (see Chapter 11 for an explanation of manifest constants).

```
if (DECREMENTING)
    little--;
```

You could also use the `if (1)` construction as part of the program creation-debugging stage. You could exclude or include a block of statements to isolate these statements' effect by alternatively using 0 or 1 as the condition:

```
if ([0 or 1])
{
    lots of statements here;
}
```

Using this device rather than commenting out the code fragment allows you to circumvent the rule against nested comments. But you have to be careful with placing the beginning and ending braces and with removing them when debugging is through.

5.1.3   More on the Value of Expressions—Misuse of == and =

 In C, each expression has a value.

In the last chapter, we learned that the value of an assignment expression as a whole is the value assigned. Thus, the statement

```
num = 3 + (val = 3);
```

would result in `val` having a value of 3 and `num` having a value of 6, the reason being that the expression

```
val = 3
```

has a value of 3.

A relational expression that evaluates to true has a value of 1; one that evaluates to false has a value of 0.

This is the converse of the rules that an expression with a value other than zero is true and one with a value of zero is false. Thus, following the statement

```
num = 3 + (val == 3);
```

num would have a value of 4 if val is 3 and 3 if it is something other than 3. And since this statement is a perfectly legitimate C statement, it would result in neither an error nor a warning message. This is so even though the construction is an unlikely one, the more likely construction being

```
num = 3 + (val = 3);
```

as in the example above, as a compact way of writing

```
val = 3;
num = 3 + val;
```

Incidentally, we think this sort of compact usage, though all too common, is to be discouraged; the second construction is far clearer. If you really want to achieve the result of these two statements,

```
if (val == 3)
   num = 4;
else
   num = 3;
```

use them and not the single-line cryptic statement in the first example.

Mistakenly using the relational equality operator == in place of the assignment operator = in this situation would not be altogether uncommon. Far more common, however, is the reverse—inadvertently using the assignment operator instead of the relational equality operator inside an if statement in the highly mistaken notion that an assignment operator is equivalent to "let *x* equal *y*".

Let's take an example. Since the value of an assignment statement is the value assigned, the statement

```
if (val = 3)
   num = 3;
```

will assign a value of 3 to num even if val has a value other than 3. The expression

```
val = 3
```

has a value of 3, and since 3 is a nonzero value,

```
if (3)
```

evaluates to true. This statement will not generate an error message since it is permitted C usage, though you will get a warning from some compilers, "Possibly incorrect assignment".

Just because you see an assignment operator inside the conditional expression of an if statement, it does not mean there is an error. Use of the assignment operator inside a conditional expression may be intentional. We will show you the most common application of that syntax in Chapter 8.

5.2   LOGICAL OPERATORS: MULTIPLE CONDITIONS

In algebra, the following expression

```
num < 8 < val
```

is taken to mean that num is less than 8 and val is greater than 8. This expression is valid in C, but it is almost certainly a mistake and in any event has a very different meaning. Under the rules of precedence, the < operator associates from left to right. Accordingly, the expression means

```
(num < 8) < val
```

Assuming val has a value of 2, the left-most expression evaluates to either 0 (if num is not less than 8) or 1 (if it is less than 8). In either event, val will have a greater value, and as a result, the right-most expression will incorrectly be evaluated to true.

Table 5.2 *Logical Operators*

Operator	Meaning
&&	and
¦¦	or
!	not

In C, you may indeed test for more than one condition at the same time. But you must use C's *logical operators* to establish the relationship between or among the conditions:

```
if (num < 8 && 8 < val)
```

There are three logical operators (Table 5.2). For example:

```
if ((big > small) && (small <= little))
    printf("both expressions are true\n");
```

Each relational test must stand on its own:

```
if ((big > small) && (big > little)) /* correct */
    big++;
if (big > small && > little) /* error! */
    big++;
```

 Where the && operator is used, *both* (all, if more than two subexpressions) subexpressions linked by the operator (or operators) must be true for the expression as a whole to be true. Where they are linked by ¦, the expression as a whole is true if *either* (any, if more than two) of the subexpressions is true.

```
if ((big > small) && (small <= little))
    printf("both expressions are true\n");
if ((small < big) ¦¦ (small > little))
    printf("at least one of these is true\n");
if (((small < big) ¦¦ (small > little)) && (small != 3))
    printf("at least one of the first two is true and the last is true\n");
if (small && big && (little < 6) &&
    ((small < big) ¦¦ (little < big)))
    printf("small and big are not zero and little is less than 6 and either small is
        less than big or little is less than big\n");
```

As you see, when the logical relationship gets complex, you need parentheses to preserve the logic. The following statements are not equivalent:

```
if (((small < big) ¦¦ (small > little)) && (small != 3))
    small += big;
if ((small < big) ¦¦ ((small > little) && (small != 3)))
    small += big;
if ((small < big) ¦¦ (small > little) && (small != 3))
    small += big;
```

The first statement is true if either of the first two subexpressions is true and the third is true. The second statement is true if either the first subexpression is true or both of the last two subexpressions are true. The third statement leaves to the vagaries of the rules of precedence which of these two approaches we meant to use.

Sometimes the logic becomes so complex that it becomes difficult mechanically to follow where we need to place open and close parentheses. Borland C gives you an easy-to-use tool to pin these down. If you put your cursor on an open or close parenthesis and type `Ctrl` `Q` `[`, your cursor will be placed on the parenthesis that, to the compiler, matches the parenthesis you started on. The same device works for open and close braces, brackets, and comments.

5.2.1   Evaluation Rules for Logical Expressions

Two important principles in C:

 Logical expressions are evaluated from left to right.
As soon as a logical subexpression is found that ensures that the expression as a whole will be true or false, evaluation stops.

From these principles, we can make the following observations:

- If subexpressions are linked by ¦¦, the computer will stop evaluating once it reaches one that evaluates to true.
- If subexpressions are linked by &&, the computer will stop evaluating once it reaches one that evaluates to false.

These companion rules save program execution time. If subexpressions are linked by ¦¦ and the first is true, the expression as a whole will evaluate as true no matter what the others evaluate to. If subexpressions are linked by && and the first is false, the expression as a whole will evaluate to false no matter what the subsequent ones evaluate to.

But the rules have other important consequences. For example, the following construction prevents the computer from halting because of an attempted division by zero:

```
if ((num != 0) && (val / num > 10))
    val *= 2;
```

Look at the following examples:

```
if (small > 4 && --big < 8)
    small--;

if (++little > 6 ¦¦ --big < 8)
    small--;
```

In the first statement, if small is not greater than 4, not only will small not be decremented; the less obvious result is that big will not be decremented either since its subexpression is not evaluated. Likewise, in the second statement, if little, as first incremented, is greater than 6, big will not be decremented.

Similarly, in the following statement from Listing 15.12, bin_sort.c, there is no danger of untoward side effects despite having the increment and decrement operator applied to variables used twice each in the same statement:

```
do
{
. . .
} while (left > right && ++left <= --right);
```

5.3   THE ! OPERATOR

The ! operator simply reverses an expression's logic: the expression is true if the subexpression it modifies is false and vice versa. Let's say you ask the user to select a number from a menu selection of nine items numbered from 1 to 9. You could flag incorrect user input this way:

```
ch = getchar();
if (!(ch >= '1' && ch <= '9'))
    printf("Error: you must enter digits only; try again");
```

If a digit is entered, the interior expressions will both be true, which makes the expression as a whole false in view of the ! operator. Consequently the error-message statement will not be executed. (In a real-life application, these two statements would be embedded in a looping construct wrapper, so that the message would repeat until a correct entry were made.)

The ! operator is also useful in testing for a single condition. We've already seen a compact way of asking whether something is not equal to zero:

```
if (big - little)
   big--;
```

With the ! operator we can ask the converse question—that is, it gives us a shorthand way of asking whether something *is* equal to 0:

```
if (!(big - little))
   big--;
if (!little)
   little = 2;
```

The following statements are equivalent to the last two:

```
if ((big - little) == 0)
   big--;
if (little == 0)
   little = 2;
```

5.4   ALTERNATIVES: `if . . . else if . . . else`

You can direct the computer to execute a statement or block of statements if a condition exists, or to execute another statement or block of statements if the condition does not exist. This is done by use of the `else` statement:

```
if (grade >= 70)
   printf("You passed\n");
else
   printf("You failed\n");
```

If the `if` statement's conditional expression condition evaluates to true, the body of the `if` statement is executed; otherwise the body of the `else` statement is executed.

You may have more than one `if` statement before the default `else` statement. Each `if` statement after the first is an `else if` statement:

```
printf("Grade: ");
if (grade >= 90)
   printf("A\n");
else if (grade > 80)
   printf("B\n");
else if (grade > 70)
   printf("C\n");
else if (grade > 60)
   printf("D\n");
else
   printf("F. See you next semester.\n");
```

In an appropriate case, you may leave off the final `else` statement. In other words, no default case is appropriate:

```
if (sales > 1000)
   bonus = 10;
else if (sales > 900)
   bonus = 9;
else if (sales > 800)
   bonus = 8;
```

What we have in the `if . . . else if . . . else if` construction is a series of statements, only one of which may be executed; if none of the conditions is met, all the statements will be ignored. In the `if . . . else if . . . else if . . . else` construction, one statement or block of statements will be executed no matter what.

Note that the following

```
if (letter == 'a')
   printf("It's a vowel\n");
else if (letter == 'e')
   printf("It's a vowel\n");
else if (letter == 'i')
   printf("It's a vowel\n");
else if (letter == 'o')
   printf("It's a vowel\n");
else if (letter == 'u')
   printf("It's a vowel\n");
```

is identical to this alternative formulation:

```
if (letter == 'a')
   printf("It's a vowel\n");
if (letter == 'e')
   printf("It's a vowel\n");
if (letter == 'i')
   printf("It's a vowel\n");
if (letter == 'o')
   printf("It's a vowel\n");
if (letter == 'u')
   printf("It's a vowel\n");
```

However, the first formulation is far more efficient. Once the computer finds a condition that evaluates to true, it does not bother to evaluate any subsequent `if else` conditions.

Depending on the logic of a program segment, there may be a substantive difference between a series of `if` statements and a corresponding chain of `if else` statements—for instance, in a student's programming effort for a ticktacktoe game. The following was meant to "toggle" between player X and player O:

```
if (player == 'X')
   player = 'O';
if (player == 'O')
   player = 'X';
```

This formulation doesn't work (do you see why?). What follows does:

```
if (player == 'X')
   player = 'O';
else
   player = 'X';
```

Like the `if` statement, the `else` and `else if` statement can be compound:

```
if (sides == 3)
{
   printf("Triangle\n");
   perimeter = a + b + c;
}
else if (sides == 4)
{
   printf("Quadrangle\n");
   perimeter = a + b + c + d;
}
else
{
   printf("Pentagon\n");
   perimeter = a + b + c + d + e;
}
```

It may be clearer not to think of the `else if` construction as a separate construction. Instead, it can be viewed simply as an `if` statement following an `else` clause, rather than as a nonconditional statement following an `else if` clause.

5.5   NESTING if STATEMENTS

In C, if statements, else if statements, or else statements can be nested. That is, for example, an if statement can be the body or one statement in the body of another if statement or else if statement or else statement. We see an illustration in Listing 5.1, if_date.c, which tests to see whether a date entered interactively is valid.

 **Listing 5.1 if_date.c**

```c
/* if_date.c */

/* nested ifs: determine whether date entered interactively is valid */

#include <stdio.h>

int main(void)
{
    int month, day, year;
    int error = 0;

    printf("Enter date \"mm/dd/yyyy\": ");
    scanf("%d %*c%d %*c%d", &month, &day, &year);

    if (month < 1 || month > 12 || day < 1 || day > 31)
        error = 1;
    else if (month == 2) /* test for 28 or 29-day max in Feb */
    {
        if /* test for leap year */

        (((year % 4 /* yr not divisible by 4: nonleap yr */
        /* centennial that is not also millennium: nonleap yr */
        || (year % 100 == 0  && year % 1000)) && day > 28) /* end leap-yr test */
        || day > 29) /* if first test false, must be leap yr */
        error = 1;
    }
    else if (month == 4 || month == 6 || month == 9 || month == 11)
    {
        if (day > 30) /* > 30 days & not Sep, Apr, Jun or Nov */
            error = 1;
    }

    if (error)
        printf("%d/%d/%d is an invalid date\n", month, day, year % 100);
    else
        printf("The date is %d/%d/%d\n", month, day, year % 100);
}
```

    When nesting conditional statements, take care to use braces to clarify which conditional statement goes with which.

    An else goes with the most recent if unless braces indicate otherwise.

Take the following program fragment as a deficient example:

```c
scanf("%d", &temperature);
if (temperature > 60)
    if (temperature < 90)
        printf("The weather is pleasant");
else
    printf("It's cold out");
```

Let's test this code out:

```
100
It's cold out
```

Oops! Not a very sensible result. What's going on here? We've used indenting in the fragment to make it *look* as though the else statement goes with the first if statement. But remember, the compiler ignores spacing. It treats the else statement as coupled with the second if statement, not the first. The code fragment should be rewritten like this:

```
if (temperature > 60)
{
   if (temperature < 90)
      printf("The weather is pleasant");
}
else
   printf("It's cold out");
```

You may have noticed that we enclosed the inner if statement of the first else statement in if_date.c in braces even though it is not a compound statement. Had we not done so, the next else if statement would have been incorrectly connected to the inner if statement. Then, if the month were not 2, we would incorrectly skip over the tests for the other months.

5.5.1   Nesting vs. Relational Operators

In many cases, you will have the choice between nesting if statements and using relational operators to combine the conditions. Which you choose is purely a matter of personal preference. Take a fragment from if_date.c as an example:

```
else if (month == 2)
{
   if ((year % 4 || (year % 100 == 0  && year % 1000) && day > 28) || day > 29)
      error = 1;
}
else if (month == 4 || month == 6 || month == 9 || month == 11)
{
   if (day > 30)
      error = 1;
}
```

We could rewrite the code like this:

```
else if (month == 2 && (((year % 4 || (year % 100 == 0
   && year % 1000) && day > 28) || day > 29)))
      error = 1;
else if ((month == 4 || month == 6 || month == 9 || month == 11) && day > 30)
      error = 1;
```

or even more compact:

```
else if (month == 2 && (((year % 4 || (!(year % 100) && year % 1000) && day > 28)
   || day > 29))) || ((month == 4 || month == 6 || month == 9 || month == 11)
   && day > 30)
      error = 1;
```

but you can see that the code starts to get a little hard to follow. In this example, the middle try is probably a good compromise between efficiency and complexity.

Now we will look at two alternative formulations to if statements: the conditional operator and the switch statement.

5.6   CONDITIONAL OPERATOR

C's **conditional operator** makes available a shorthand way of expressing an if . . . else statement pair. The structure is "if the test condition is true, use the first expression; otherwise use the second one." Here is the format:

```
(test condition) ? expression 1 : expression 2;
```

For instance,

```
max = (x > y) ? x : y;
```

sets max to the greater of x or y. If x is greater than y, max is set to x and the second expression is ignored; otherwise the first expression is ignored and max is set to y. This formulation is in lieu of the if . . . else formulation:

```
if (x > y)
    max = x;
else
    max = y;
```

The following program calculates how many employees a plant needs to hire to assemble a special order of computers, to be produced within one week, where one employee can assemble 40 computers a week. The plant union does not allow part-time help.

 **Listing 5.2 workers.c**

```
/* workers.c */

/* conditional operator example */

#include <stdio.h>

int main(void)
{
    int workers, computers;

    printf("Enter number of computers to be assembled: ");
    scanf("%d", &computers);

    workers = computers / 40 +

    /* add extra worker, but not if computers is evenly divisible by 40 */
        ((computers % 40 == 0) ? 0: 1);

    printf("\nPlant must hire %d worker%s", workers, workers == 1 ? "": "s");
}
```

The program calculates how many workers you need by simply dividing the number of machines by the number of machines one worker can assemble in one week. Because computers is an int, computers / LOAD is truncated down to the nearest integer. For example, if the order is for 90 computers, the result is 2. Since we cannot hire part-time help, we need to add an extra worker to handle the extra 10 computers. However, if computers is evenly divisible by LOAD, we don't need to hire one extra worker. The expression

```
(computers % 40 == 0) ? 0: 1
```

takes care of that problem. If computers is evenly divisible by LOAD, we add 0; otherwise we add 1.

As you can see from the last line of workers.c, you can even insert the conditional operator in the argument list of a printf() statement. If the number of workers needed is one, the %s specifier takes on a blank, so that "worker" is printed; otherwise, it takes on an "s", with the result that "workers" is printed.

5.6.1   Nesting Conditional Operators

Both the examples of the conditional operator in workers.c show how flexible the conditional operator is; you can insert it right in the middle of a statement as an expression or argument. You can also nest conditional operators, just as you can nest if statements. For an example, let's look at a program that calculates federal income taxes. The program, unclesam.c, is premised on the following tax rates:

First $30,000 of income: 15%
Next $110,000 of income: 33%
Next $110,000 of income: 36%
All income above $250,000: 39.6%

Listing **5.3 unclesam.c**

```
/* unclesam.c */

/* nested conditional operators */

#include <stdio.h>

#define LOW_RATE .15 /* up to MID */
#define MID_RATE .31 /* from MID to HIGH */
#define HIGH_RATE .36 /* from HIGH to SUPER */
#define SUPER_RATE .396 /* over SUPER */

#define MID 30000.
#define HIGH  140000.
#define SUPER 250000.

int main(void)
{
   float income = 0., tax = 0.;

   printf("Enter annual income\n");
   scanf("%f", &income);

   tax = LOW_RATE * (income <= MID ? income: MID);
   tax += MID_RATE * (income < MID ? 0: income <= HIGH ? income - MID: HIGH - MID);
   tax += HIGH_RATE * (income < HIGH ? 0: income <= SUPER ?
     income - HIGH: SUPER - HIGH);
   tax += SUPER_RATE * (income <= SUPER ? 0: income - SUPER);
   printf("Income: %.f\nTax: %.f\nRead it and weep\n\n\n", income, tax);
}
```

The lines such as

```
#define LOW_RATE 0.15
```

are what are known as define directives. The characters LOW_RATE are replaced with letters 0.15 as the first step of compiling, just as a word processor's search-and-replace function would do. (We cover this mechanism in Chapter 11.)

The program first calculates tax on the first $30,000 of income. The variable tax is set to LOW_RATE times

```
income <= MID ? income : MID
```

If total income is under the ceiling for the first rate, we multiply the low rate by total income; otherwise we multiply by the first rate ceiling amount.

Then we increment the tax calculated on the first $30,000 by the tax on the next $110,000 of income. That is equal to MID_RATE times

```
(income < MID ? 0: income <= HIGH ? income - MID: HIGH - MID)
```

We could have written the same statement in much lengthier fashion with if statements:

```
if (income <= MID)
   increment = 0;
else if (income <= HIGH)
   increment = income - MID;
else
   increment = HIGH - MID;
tax += increment * MID_RATE;
```

In other words, if total income is less than the ceiling for the lowest rate, don't add anything. Otherwise, if total income is less than the ceiling for the second rate, add that rate times the difference between the first and second rate ceilings. Otherwise, multiply the second rate by the second rate ceiling minus the first rate ceiling. The same sort of logic is used for the next two levels.

The nested conditional operator is somewhat difficult to read. We recommend that if you nest conditional operators, you do not go beyond single nesting, as in `unclesam.c`.

5.6.2   Logical Operators in Conditional Operator Expressions

The conditional portion of the conditional operator expression can contain logical operators (`&&`, `¦¦`, `!`) as well as relational operators, as the final statement of `min_sec.c` shows.

 **Listing 5.4 `min_sec.c`**

```
/* min_sec.c */

/* split seconds into minutes & seconds: conditional &
   modulus operators */

#include <stdio.h>

int main(void)
{
    int tot_seconds, minutes, seconds;

    printf("\nEnter number of seconds: ");
    scanf("%d", &tot_seconds);
    minutes = tot_seconds/60;
    seconds = tot_seconds % 60;
    printf("%d seconds is %d minute%s and %d second%s\n", tot_seconds, minutes,
        (minutes > 1 ¦¦ !minutes) ? "s": "", seconds, (seconds > 1 ¦¦ !seconds) ? "s": "");
}
```

Integer division takes care of calculating the number of minutes. The statement

```
minutes = tot_seconds / 60;
```

calculates the integral number of times 60 can be divided into `tot_seconds`; the remainder is truncated. The discarded remainder number of seconds is calculated with the help of the modulus operator.

We use the conditional operator to print an s at the end of "minute" and "second" if the number of either is 0 *or* more than 1. Otherwise, we omit the s.

```
(minutes > 1 ¦¦ !minutes) ? "s": ""
```

As you know, `!minutes` is the same as saying `minutes != 0`. And, as you may already have perceived, had we not been trying to illustrate this point about the use of logical operators with the conditional operator, we could have simplified the statement we just looked at like this:

```
printf("%d seconds is %d minute%s and %d second%s\n", tot_seconds, minutes, minutes
    != 1 ? "s" : "", seconds, seconds != 1 ? "s" : "");
```

5.7   THE `switch` STATEMENT

As we have discussed, if you want the program to choose from one of several alternatives, you can use the `if . . . else if . . . else if . . . else` construction. However, if there are quite a number of choices, that construction can become cumbersome. C offers a streamlined alternative, the `switch` statement. The format, however, is somewhat complex:

```
switch (integer variable, integer variable
    expression or integer variable/constant expression)
{
    case integer constant or integer constant expression:
        statement(s);
        break;
    case integer constant or integer constant expression:
        statement(s);
```

```
      break;
   default: statement(s);
}
```

There is no semicolon after the `switch` comparison expression. Nor is there any after the closing brace. A simple example:

```
char ch = getchar();
switch(ch)
{
   case 'a':
      printf("You typed an \'a\'");
      break;
   case 'e':
      printf("You typed an \'e\'");
      break;
   case 'i':
      printf("You typed an \'i\'");
      break;
   case 'o':
      printf("You typed an \'o\'");
      break;
   case 'u':
      printf("You typed a \'u\'");
   break;
   default: printf("You didn't type a lower case vowel");
}
```

Note that you need not enclose the statement or statements associated with a particular `case` with braces even though they are compound, but you could add them for clarity if you want. The integer variable or integer variable expression following the keyword `switch` *must* be enclosed in parentheses. The integer constant or integer constant expression following the keyword `case` doesn't have to be enclosed in parentheses, but you can use them for clarity if you want.

When the program encounters the `switch` statement, it jumps to the `case` whose value is equal to that of the variable or variable expression within the `switch` comparison expression. In the last example, if the user types in 'o', the program jumps to the `case 'o'` statement and prints

```
You typed an o
```

A common application of the `switch` statement is handling interactive menu choices, where users must select a number or letter to indicate which of the choices presented on the screen they wish.

5.7.1   The `switch` Comparison Expression

The `switch` comparison expression should be an integer variable or variable-constant expression. (Actually, you could in theory use an integer constant in the switch comparison expression, but that wouldn't make much sense unless the constant is a manifest constant you can alter prior to running the program; see Chapter 11). If you use a single variable as the `switch` comparison expression, the variable must be of integer type. This includes `char`, so using the `char` variable `ch` in the example above within the `switch` comparison expression is fine. If you use an expression within the comparison expression, each individual element must be either an integer type variable or an integer constant.

Listing 5.5 illustrates the use of a variable-constant expression in a `switch` comparison expression.

 **Listing** **5.5 `switch_x.c`**

```
/* switch_x.c */

/* switch expression can be variable-constant expression */

#include <stdio.h>

int main(void)
```

```
{
    char ch;
    printf("Type a letter and press [Enter] ");
    ch = getchar();
    printf("You typed ");

    /* Test uppercase letter as though it were lowercase.
       ASCII only; otherwise use switch(tolower(ch)) */
    switch(ch + ((ch >= 'A' && ch <= 'Z') ? ('a' - 'A') : 0))
    {
        case 'a': printf("an \'a\'"); break;
        case 'e': printf("an \'e\'"); break;
        case 'i': printf("an \'i\'"); break;
        case 'o': printf("an \'o\'"); break;
        case 'u': printf("a \'u\'"); break;
        default:
        printf("\'%c\', a character that is not a vowel", ch);
    }
    printf("\n");
}
```

The `switch` comparison expression here tests uppercase letters as though they were lowercase. Any uppercase letter (a value between A and Z) is converted to lowercase by adding the difference in numerical values between lowercase a and uppercase A. As the comment indicates, this device works only with ASCII character encoding. Using the `tolower()` function discussed in Chapter 9 would be more portable.

5.7.2   *case* "Labels"

The `case` labels must be constants, not variables or constant-variable expressions. And, of course, since the program attempts to match the `switch` variable with the `case` constants and since the `switch` variable must be of integer type, each `case` constant must also be an integer. Actually, the `case` label may be an expression as long as each of its components is an integer *constant* and the expression evaluates to a single integer constant. The `case` labels may not contain any references to variables. You will get an error message if you try to sneak a variable in. Allowable constants include integer constants, character constants, enumeration constants (see Chapter 13), and the `sizeof` operator with any operand, even a variable or type. Despite the deceptive terminology, a `const`-qualified variable, discussed in Chapter 10, is not a constant.

The `case` constants (as evaluated, if there are any constant expressions) must each be unique. They don't have to be in any particular order; they just can't have duplicate values:

```
char ch = getchar();
switch(ch)
{
    case ('e'):
        printf("You typed an \'e\'");
        break;
    case ('a'):
        printf("You typed an \'a\'");
        break;
    case ('f' - 1): /* error! evaluates to 'e' – not allowed */
        printf("You typed an \'e\'");
        break;
}
```

Standard C requires a compiler to support at least 257 `case` labels. That gives you one for each possible value of an `unsigned char` plus one for the `default` label. If you have more than that, you could stack `switch` statements and include a sentinel variable in each case, so your program knows to enter or skip any subsequent `switch` statements. Also, the 257 `case` label limit does not include `case` labels in any nested `switch` statement.

Incidentally, what we have called a case label is, for example, case 'a' or case 1. Don't let the word *label* mislead you into thinking the constant may only be a letter. Numbers are perfectly acceptable despite this nomenclature. In fact, the letter in single quotes is really a number in disguise anyway. Don't confuse case "labels" with labels for goto statements discussed at the end of this chapter, which are true word labels.

5.7.3 Mechanics of the `switch` Statement— the `default` Label and the `break` Statement

After the program evaluates the switch comparison expression, it jumps to the case whose label's value corresponds to the switch comparison expression's value. Once there, the program executes all statements in the switch body until it comes to a break statement.

If none of the labels' values match the switch comparison expression value, the program jumps to the default label and executes the statements there. The default label and statements are optional. If there is no match and no default label, the program jumps to the first statement after the switch body.

You might use a default label and accompanying statements to print out an error message or exit the program or return from the function if that point is reached, contrary to your expectations. For example:

```
switch(val)
{
    case 1: num = val; break;
    case 2: num = val * 2; break;
    case 3: num = val / 2; break;
    default: printf("This can't happen. Error!\n");
        exit(1); /* causes entire program to terminate */
}
```

You can also use the default label and statements as a catchall—for instance, where you expect val to be in the range of 1 to 100:

```
switch(val)
{
    case 1: num = val; break;
    case 3: num = val + 1; break;
    default: num = val + 100;
}
```

Here, you want to make num equal to val + 100 in every case but those in which val is 1 or 3.

Absent the error or catchall situation, there is generally no reason to use a default label. If you do not have one, there is also no technical reason why you need a break statement after the last case's code:

```
switch(val)
{
    case 1: num = val; break;
    case 3: num = val + 1;
}
```

 However, *it is good practice to put a break statement after the final case's code. That way, if you add another case at the end later, as often happens, you will not inadvertently let one case run into another.*

Which brings us to the next point:

 If there is no break statement between one case label and the next, program execution continues until a break is encountered.

```
char ch = getchar();
switch(ch)
{
    case 'a': printf("You typed an \'a\'");
    case 'e': printf("You typed an \'e\'");
```

```
        case 'i': printf("You typed an \'i\'");
        case 'o': printf("You typed an \'o\'");
        case 'u': printf("You typed a \'u\'");
        default: printf("You didn't type a lowercase vowel");
    }
```

If we type an a, the program prints

```
You typed an 'a'
You typed an 'e'
You typed an 'i'
You typed an 'o'
You typed a 'u'
You didn't type a lowercase vowel
```

Oops.

Often, however, the absence of a break statement between case labels is deliberate. One common example of this deliberate absence of break statements is the use of multiple labels for the same set of statements. We can rewrite the if_date.c program from earlier in this chapter for an illustration.

 **Listing 5.6 gooddate.c**

```
/* gooddate.c */

/* determine date validity: multiple switch cases */

#include <stdio.h>

int main(void)
{
    int month, day, year;
    int error = 0;

    printf("Enter date \"mm/dd/yyyy\": ");
    scanf("%d %*c%d %*c%d", &month, &day, &year);

    if (month < 1 || month > 12 || day < 1)
        error = 1;
    else switch(month)
    {
        case 1: case 3: case 5: case 7: case 8: case 10: case 12:
            if (day > 31)
            error = 1;
            break;
        case 4: case 6: case 9: case 11:
            if (day > 30)
            error = 1;
            break;
        /* Feb leap yr: divisible by 4
           unless nonmillennium centennial */
        case 2:
            if (day > ((year % 4) || (!(year % 100) && (year % 1000)) ? 28: 29))
            error = 1;
            break;
    } /* end switch */

    if (error)
        printf("%d/%d/%02d is an invalid date\n",
            month, day, year % 100);
    else
        printf("The date is %d/%d/%02d\n", month, day, year % 100);
}
```

We can use the absence of `break` statements to accomplish more than simply allowing for multiple labels for the same statement or statements. For instance:

```
switch(operand)
{
    case DECREMENT3: num--; /* absence of break here & next statement intentional */
    case DECREMENT2: num--;
    case DECREMENT1: num--; break;
    case INCREMENT3: num++; /* absence of break here & next statement intentional */
    case INCREMENT2: num++;
    case INCREMENT1: num++; break;
}
```

 As we have done, *if you do leave out a break statement deliberately, be sure to indicate that fact by comment so it does not appear to be an inadvertent error.*

Note that the mechanics of the `switch` statement do not mandate that the default come last or that the cases be at the top level inside the braces:

```
switch(num)
{
    default:
        if (num >= 15 && num <= 35)
            case 1: case 3: case 5:
            num += 20;
        else if (num <= -15 && num >= -35)
            case -5: case -3: case -1:
            num -= 20;
        else num = 0;
}
```

What happens here is that if num is 1, 3, or 5 *or* between 15 and 35, 20 is added to it; if it is –5, –3, –1 *or* between –15 and –35, 20 is subtracted; otherwise num is zeroed out. However, we strongly recommend that only case or default labels appear at the top level and that the default case be last, even if it takes a couple of extra lines to do so:

```
switch(num)
{
    case 1: case 3: case 5:
        num += 20;
        break;
    case -5: case -3: case -1:
        num -= 20;
        break;
    default:
        if (num >= 15 && num <= 35)
            num += 20;
        else if (num <= -15 && num >= -35)
            num -= 20;
        else num = 0;
}
```

5.8   `switch` vs. `if . . . else`

In many cases, you have no choice but to use the `if . . . else` construction where you need a choice among various alternative tests. If your choice is based on a `float` variable, you may not use `switch`. Nor can you use `switch` unless you are evaluating whether one of several choices is equal to a variable's value. No relationship other than equality can be tested with `switch`. Thus, the following construction is not amenable to the `switch` statement

```
if (hours < 1000)
    rate = 2;
else if (hours < 2000)
```

```
   rate = 3;
else if (hours < 3000)
   rate = 4;
else rate = 5;
```

since the relationship is not equality.

Short of these limitations, *if you can use* `switch` *and the choices are more than a few, you should use it instead of* `if . . . else`. *The construction is more efficient and compact.* For example, we took a simple `switch` statement with 17 different choices and looped millions of times and then coded the identical task with a series of `if . . . else`. The `switch` version has a somewhat smaller code and ran more than five times faster.

If you have a few specific choices and some ranges as well, you can just mix the cases with `if` statements as the default case, as we did in the last example in the previous section.

5.9   LOOPS

Sometimes we want the program to execute a certain statement or block of statements while a specified condition exists only, or a specified number of times. We do this by the use of `while` loops, `do-while` loops, or `for` loops. The syntax of the three loop forms is as follows:

```
while loop - single statement body:

   while (conditional expression)
      statement;

while loop - compound statement body:

   while (conditional expression)
   {
      more than one statement;
   }

do-while loop - single statement body:

   do statement
      while (conditional expression);

do-while loop - compound statement body:

   do
   {
      more than one statement;
   }
      while (conditional expression);

for loop - single statement body:

   for (initialization statement(s); conditional expression; update statement(s))
      statement;

for loop - compound statement body:

   for (initialization statement(s); conditional expression; update statement(s))
   {
      more than one statement;
   };
```

5.10   while LOOP

Let's look at the format of the while loop again:

```
while (conditional expression)
   statement;

while (conditional expression)
{
   more than one statement;
}
```

The loop consists of a conditional expression, which governs whether to continue executing the loop body statement or statements, and a loop body whose statement or statements are executed each loop iteration until the condition evaluates to false. Notice that there is no semicolon after the conditional expression.

We can use the while loop to automate the counting of vowels in user input, for example. We keep counting vowels until the user presses the [Esc] key. For the signaling of program termination, you want to use a key that the user would not type in during the normal operation of the program. The press of the [Esc] key is a common method of program termination in commercial programs. In Appendix A you will see how, on a PC, to make your program sense presses of [Alt] and [Ctrl] in combination with other keys and the function keys. Then you could ask the user to, for instance, press [Alt] and [X] to exit.

 Listing 5.7 vowelnum.c

```c
/* vowelnum.c */

/* demonstrate while loop: count vowels in user input */

#include <stdio.h>
#include <conio.h> /* getche(): DOS only */

#define ESC 27

int main(void)
{
   char ch;
   int a, e, i, o, u;

   a = e = i = o = u = 0;
   printf("Type in some text for vowel counting\n"
    "Press [ESC] key to quit\n");

   ch = getche();
   while (ch != ESC)
   {  /* convert lowercase to uppercase: ASCII only */
      if (ch >= 'a' && ch <= 'z')
         ch -= 'a' - 'A';
      switch(ch)
      {
         case 'A': a++; break;
         case 'E': e++; break;
         case 'I': i++; break;
         case 'O': o++; break;
         case 'U': u++; break;
         default: break;
      } /* end switch */
      ch = getche();
   } /* end while */
```

```
    printf("\nNumber of vowels entered:  a   e   i   o   u\n"
       "\t\t\t %3d %3d %3d %3d %3d", a, e, i, o, u);
}
```

First we obtain a value for `ch` outside the `while` loop. The first time through, we test whether `ch` has a value of 27 (the `define` directive substitutes 27 for ⌈Esc⌉ on a system that uses ASCII encoding; see Appendix F). If it does, we end the loop. Otherwise, we proceed to the `switch` statement for vowel counting. At the end of the loop, we get fresh user input and start a new loop iteration.

We used `getche()` rather than `getchar()` because `getchar()` requires us to press the ⌈Enter⌉ key to register whatever line we've typed in. That requirement would conflict with using ⌈Esc⌉ to signal program termination. Pressing the ⌈Esc⌉ key causes the line to be voided out, so that if we pressed ⌈Esc⌉ and then ⌈Enter⌉, all we would send to the computer is a carriage return character. The disadvantage to this approach is that any character typed in is sent for processing, without the ability to correct errors.

We could have eliminated the lowercase-to-uppercase conversion line and included dual `case` labels—for example,

```
case 'a': case 'A': a++; break;
```

The `getche()` function is a DOS compiler-only function. To achieve the same effect on a UNIX machine, see Listing 3.3, `get_unix.c`. For platforms other than UNIX or DOS, we can use the following program. Here we instruct the user to press ⌈Enter⌉ to quit; we use `getchar()` instead of `getche()` and use the `tolower()` function described in Chapter 9 to convert each letter to lowercase.

 **Listing 5.8 vowelgen.c**

```
/* vowelgen.c */

/* generic non-DOS vowelnum.c */

#include <stdio.h>
#include <ctype.h> /* tolower() */

int main(void)
{
   char ch;
   int a, e, i, o, u;

   a = e = i = o = u = 0;
   printf("Type in some text for vowel counting\n"
      "Press [Enter] key to quit\n");

   while ((ch = getchar()) != '\n')
   {
      switch(tolower(ch))
      {
         case 'a': a++; break;
         case 'e': e++; break;
         case 'i': i++; break;
         case 'o': o++; break;
         case 'u': u++; break;
         default: break;
      } /* end switch */
   } /* end while */

   printf("\nNumber of vowels entered:  a   e   i   o   u\n"
      "\t\t\t %3d %3d %3d %3d %3d", a, e, i, o, u);
}
```

5.10.1   A `scanf()` Loop Example

Here we use a different method of loop termination. This simple program asks the user to input a number of centimeters for conversion to feet and inches.

 **Listing** **5.9 scan_met.c**

```
/* scan_met.c */

/* convert centimeters to ft & inches with while loop */

#include <stdio.h>

int main(void)
{
    float centimeters, inches;
    int feet, items_read;

    printf("Centimeter to feet/inches conversion\n\n"
        "Enter length in centimeters\n"
        "Type any letter to quit\n");
    items_read = scanf("%f", &centimeters);
    while (items_read == 1)
    {
        inches = centimeters / 2.54;

        /* use integer division to truncate down */
        feet = (int)inches / 12;
        inches -= (float)feet * 12.;
        printf("%.2f centimeters is %d\' %.2f\"\n\n", centimeters, feet, inches);
        printf("Enter length in centimeters\n"
            "Type any letter to quit\n");
        items_read = scanf("%f", &centimeters);
    }
}
```

As you will see in Chapter 8, some functions return a value. The `scanf()` function returns the number of items successfully read in. Here, that value is assigned to the variable `items_read`. If a number is input where the `scanf()` specifier is a `%d` or `%f`, the number 1 gets stored in `items_read`. If a letter is typed in as a response to one of these specifiers rather than in response to a `%s` or `%c` specifier, `scanf()` fails to input any data and a 0 gets stored in `items_read`.

The program continues converting the centimeter input until the user types in a letter (or any other nonnumerical characters) instead of a number. At that point the conditional expression

```
while (items_read == 1)
```

becomes false and the loop ends. Meanwhile, each statement in the loop body is executed: the prompt statement, `scanf()` input, mathematical calculation statements, and result-printing statement.

5.10.2   Shortening the Condition Evaluation Mechanism

In C, as we've seen, each expression has a value. The expression

```
items_read = scanf("%f", &centimeters)
```

as a whole has the value equal to what is to the right of the assignment operator.

We can use these principles to streamline the condition evaluation in `scan_met.c`. Here's the operative portion of the loop in `scan_met.c`:

```
items_read = scanf("%f", &centimeters);
while (items_read == 1)
{
    . . .
    items_read = scanf("%f", &centimeters);
}
```

This three-line code fragment could be shortened to a single line:

```
while ((items_read = scanf("%f", &centimeters)) == 1)
```

What happens is that first the scanf() expression stops the program and waits for user input; the input is stored in centimeters; scanf() returns the number of items read in correctly (1 or 0 here); that number is assigned to items_read; the condition of whether the entire items_read statement is equal to 1 is then evaluated in the context of the while loop; if the test evaluates to true, the loop continues, and if not it stops. And all this is done with one statement.

We make use of the return value of scanf(), the number of items successfully read in, but since we don't need to store the result, we could omit the use of any variable to capture the return value. Then we could make the code even more compact:

```
while (scanf("%f", &centimeters) == 1)
```

In fact, since the return value of the scanf() call in this instance will be either 0 if unsuccessful or 1 if successful, we can shorten further:

```
while (scanf("%f", &centimeters))
```

You could not use this final bit of shortening if you were reading in more than one variable at a time; in that case, the result could be more than 0 and less than the maximum number of items to be read in. Thus

```
while (scanf("%f%f", &centimeters, &kilograms) == 2)
```

could not be shortened any further.

Nor could you use the most shortened form if you have redirected input from the screen to a file (see Chapters 14 and 16). On reaching the end of the file, scanf() would return a negative value—which would evaluate to true here.

Listing 5.10 shows what the compact version of scan_met.c looks like.

 **Listing 5.10 metric.c**

```c
/* metric.c */

/* convert centimeters to feet & inches (short version of
   scan_met.c) */

#include <stdio.h>

int main(void)
{
    float centimeters, inches;
    int feet;

    printf("Centimeter to feet/inches conversion\n\n"
        "Enter length in centimeters\n"
        "Type any letter to quit\n");
    while (scanf("%f", &centimeters))
    {
        inches = centimeters / 2.54;
        feet = (int)inches / 12;
        inches -= feet * 12;
    printf("%.2f centimeters is %d\' %.2f\"\n\n", centimeters, feet, inches);
    printf("Enter length in centimeters\n"
        "Type any letter to quit\n");
    }
}
```

5.10.3   Precedence of Relational Operator over Assignment Operator

We can make the same simplifying changes to vowelnum.c. Here are the operative statements:

```
ch = getche();
while (ch != ESC)
{
```

```
. . .
ch = getche();
}
```

We can replace these three statements with a single one:

```
while ((ch = getche()) != ESC)
```

Note that we have enclosed the expression

```
ch = getche()
```

in parentheses. Likewise note the inner parentheses in one of the examples above:

```
while ((items_read = scanf("%f", &centimeters)) == 1)
```

What if we omitted these extra parentheses?

```
while(ch = getche() != ESC)
```

Under the rules of precedence, the relational operators take priority over the assignment operator (see Appendix J). So the compiler reads the last statement as though it were

```
while(ch = (getche() != ESC))
```

The value assigned to ch would thus be the value of the logical expression

```
(getche() != ESC)
```

Since, as we saw earlier in the chapter, logical expressions have a value of 1 if true and 0 if false, ch would be assigned a value of 1 for any key but the ⌨Esc key—not the result we want.

5.11   for LOOP

The while loop contains only a condition evaluation expression and a loop body. A for loop contains three components in addition to the loop body: an initialization statement (or statements), a condition evaluation expression, and an update statement (or statements), in that order. The components are separated by semicolons:

```
for (initialization statement(s);
    conditional expression; update statement(s))
        statement;

for (initialization statement(s); conditional expression;
    update statement(s))
{
    more than one statement;
};
```

The for loop is processed in this manner:

1. The initialization component (really a complete assignment statement) is first executed. This is done only once, not during each loop iteration.
2. The condition is evaluated. The evaluation is done at the start of each iteration.
3. If the conditional expression evaluates to true:
   a. The statement or statements that form the body of the loop are executed.
   b. The update statement or statements are then executed.
   c. The program returns to step 2 for evaluation.
4. If the conditional expression evaluates to false, processing proceeds to the first statement after the loop body.

5.11.1   A Simple for Loop Example

Let's look at a simple example. The following listing, ascii_10.c, uses a for loop to print out the ASCII character representation of decimal integers from 33 to 255.

 **Listing** `5.11 ascii_10.c`

```c
/* ascii_10.c */

/* print out ascii/decimal table with for loop */

#include <stdio.h>

int main(void)
{
   int i;

   /* skip first 32 characters */
   for (i = 33; i < 256; i++)
   {
      /* 10 to a line; then new line */
      if (!((i - 33) % 10))
         putchar('\n');
      printf("%3d %c  ", i, i);
   }
}
```

The output is shown in Table 5.3.

Note that where the loop body consists of more than one statement, it is enclosed in braces. There is no semicolon after the evaluation component, nor after the end of the closing brace.

Table 5.3   *Output for Listing 5.11,* `ascii_10.c`

33	!	34	"	35	#	36	$	37	%	38	&	39	'	40	(	41	)	42	*
43	+	44	,	45	-	46	.	47	/	48	0	49	1	50	2	51	3	52	4
53	5	54	6	55	7	56	8	57	9	58	:	59	;	60	<	61	=	62	>
63	?	64	@	65	A	66	B	67	C	68	D	69	E	70	F	71	G	72	H
73	I	74	J	75	K	76	L	77	M	78	N	79	O	80	P	81	Q	82	R
83	S	84	T	85	U	86	V	87	W	88	X	89	Y	90	Z	91	[	92	\
93	]	94	^	95	_	96	`	97	a	98	b	99	c	100	d	101	e	102	f
103	g	104	h	105	i	106	j	107	k	108	l	109	m	110	n	111	o	112	p
113	q	114	r	115	s	116	t	117	u	118	v	119	w	120	x	121	y	122	z
123	{	124	¦	125	}	126	~	127	⌂	128	Ç	129	ü	130	é	131	â	132	ä
133	à	134	å	135	ç	136	ê	137	ë	138	è	139	ï	140	î	141	ì	142	Ä
143	Å	144	É	145	æ	146	Æ	147	ô	148	ö	149	ò	150	û	151	ù	152	ÿ
153	Ö	154	Ü	155	¢	156	£	157	¥	158	Pt	159	ƒ	160	á	161	í	162	ó
163	ú	164	ñ	165	Ñ	166	ª	167	º	168	¿	169	⌐	170	¬	171	½	172	¼
173	¡	174	«	175	»	176	░	177	▒	178	▓	179	│	180	┤	181	╡	182	╢
183	╖	184	╕	185	╣	186	║	187	╗	188	╝	189	╜	190	╛	191	┐	192	└
193	┴	194	┬	195	├	196	─	197	┼	198	╞	199	╟	200	╚	201	╔	202	╩
203	╦	204	╠	205	═	206	╬	207	╧	208	╨	209	╤	210	╥	211	╙	212	╘
213	╒	214	╓	215	╫	216	╪	217	┘	218	┌	219	█	220	▄	221	▌	222	▐
223	▀	224	α	225	ß	226	Γ	227	π	228	Σ	229	σ	230	µ	231	τ	232	Φ
233	θ	234	Ω	235	δ	236	∞	237	φ	238	ε	239	∩	240	≡	241	±	242	≥
243	≤	244	⌠	245	⌡	246	÷	247	≈	248	°	249	·	250	•	251	√	252	ⁿ
253	²	254	■	255																

The loop starts off by initializing our loop counter variable, i, to 33. We started just after the space character, ASCII 32; characters up to that point are nonprinting (see Appendix F, and isprint(), described in Chapter 9). Next, the program evaluates the test condition, namely, whether i is less than 256.

Since at this point, the test evaluates to true (33 is less than 256), the body of the loop is executed statement by statement. First a printf() statement is executed. The %3d specifier prints out the decimal representation of the loop counter, i. We use the 3 as part of the specifier in order to right-hand justify the numbers. The largest number we're going to be printing has three digits. The printf() statement then prints a space, the character representation of the loop counter (the %c specifier), and two more spaces.

The next statement contains a conditional expression—good practice for newly acquired skills. The expression

```
if (!((i - 32) % 10))
```

is the same as saying

```
if ((i - 32) % 10 == 0)
```

This tests for whether the loop counter is evenly divisible by 10—something that happens every 10 iterations. At that time, we print a newline character. The effect is to print 10 sets of decimal numbers and ASCII equivalents each line.

On the first iteration, this conditional expression evaluates to false, so the putchar() function is skipped and only the number-character combination "33 !" is printed. That completes the loop body. Now the update expression, i++, is executed. That makes i have a value of 34.

We continue like this until the end of the loop in which i has a value of 255. At that time, the update expression execution causes i to have a value of 256 and the loop's conditional expression evaluates to false, ending the loop.

5.11.2   Using Variables to Determine the Number of Loops

In our first for loop example, we used constants to determine how many loop iterations to go through. This need not be so, as mortgage.c shows. This program takes input of a loan amount, interest rate, and loan term. It then calculates the monthly payment and prints out an amortization schedule. You can use mortgage.c to figure out whether you should refinance your home loan.

 **Listing 5.12 mortgage.c**

```
/* mortgage.c */

/* prints out a mortgage amortization schedule with for loops */

#include <stdio.h>
#include <math.h> /* pow */

int main(void)
{

    double rate, balance, interest, principal, payment, interest_factor;
    int months, start_mon, start_yr;
    int month_num;

    printf("Mortgage amortization program\n\n");
    printf("Enter principal amount without commas: ");
    scanf("%lf", &balance); /* original principal balance */
    printf("\nEnter years to repay loan: ");
    scanf("%d", &months);
    months *= 12; /* number of months in loan term */
    printf("\nInput annual interest rate as a percentage: ");
    scanf("%lf", &rate);
    printf("\nEnter mortgage start month & year - MM (or M) YY (or YYYY): ");
    scanf("%d%d", &start_mon, &start_yr);
```

```
/* convert to monthly decimal from annual percent */
rate /= 1200.;

/* pmt: p * i / (1 - (1 + i)^-n): split into 2 parts for simplicity: */
interest_factor = 1./pow(1. + rate, (double)months);
payment = (balance * rate) / (1. - interest_factor);
printf("\n\n\tMonth    Date      Balance  Payment  Principal  Interest\n");
for (month_num = 0; month_num < months; month_num++)
{
    /* print prior month's balance before recalculating new bal this month */
    printf("\t%4d   %02d/01/%02d", month_num + 1,
    /* % 12 + 1: cycle from 1 to 12 */
       (start_mon + month_num - 1) % 12 + 1,
       (start_yr + (start_mon + month_num - 1) / 12) % 100);
    printf("  %10.2f", balance);
    interest = balance * rate;
    principal = payment - interest;
    balance -= principal;
    printf("  %8.2f  %8.2f  %8.2f\n", payment, principal, interest);
}
}
```

The payment calculation is made by the following formula:

$$principal = (principal * interest\ rate) / (1 - ((1 + interest\ rate)^{-term})))$$

To make the code easier to follow, we split the calculation into two statements, storing what follows the "1 -" in the denominator in a separate variable:

```
interest_factor = 1 / pow(1. + rate, months);
```

As you may remember from high school algebra, x^{-n} is the same as $1/x^n$.

We have used a Standard C function pow() to raise a value to a power. The pow() function prototype is contained in math.h and so the program here includes that Standard C header. As Plauger points out in his *The Standard C Library*, the pow() function, which raises x to the y power, is easily the most complex of the Standard C math functions, and that's saying something. It has to do lots of error and overflow and underflow checking, deal with a broad assortment of special cases (negative powers and fractional powers, to name a couple), and endeavor to develop a precise result for a broad range of argument values. Here, we have a very simple case: a number raised to an integer power. In such a case, you may be better off creating your own function instead of using the Standard C one. Yours would probably work much faster. In this program, where you use the power function only once, the difference wouldn't even be noticeable. But if you had another application where you did hundreds or thousands of the same calculation, that would be another story. In any case, we try our hand at a home-made power function in Chapter 8.

For each month of the loan term, we calculate how much of this month's payment is interest and how much is principal. Interest is equal to the current balance times the monthly interest rate:

```
interest = balance * rate;
```

After we calculate how much interest is, we can then determine how much of the payment is principal by just subtracting the interest from the payment:

```
principal = payment - interest;
```

In turn, once we determine how much the principal component of the payment is, we just subtract that amount from the current balance to derive the remaining balance:

```
balance -= principal;
```

Notice that we have split the nondate portion of the printing within the loop into two parts. First we print out the loan balance. This is really the balance at the end of the previous month, as calculated in the prior loop. Then we calculate the interest and principal components of this month's payment, print them out, and calculate the new balance, to be printed out in the next loop.

Table 5.4 shows what that new Jaguar would set you back at a $45,000 sticker price at 11% on a three-year loan:

Notice how we used the modulus operator and integer division to keep track of the month and year. For the month:

```
(start_mon + month_num - 1) % 12 + 1
```

Table 5.4 *Amortization Table for Three-Year $45,000 Loan at 10% Interest*

Month	Date	Balance	Payment	Principal	Interest
1	12/01/00	45000.00	1473.24	1060.74	412.50
2	01/01/01	43939.26	1473.24	1070.47	402.78
3	02/01/01	42868.79	1473.24	1080.28	392.96
4	03/01/01	41788.51	1473.24	1090.18	383.06
5	04/01/01	40698.33	1473.24	1100.17	373.07
6	05/01/01	39598.16	1473.24	1110.26	362.98
7	06/01/01	38487.90	1473.24	1120.44	352.81
8	07/01/01	37367.46	1473.24	1130.71	342.54
9	08/01/01	36236.76	1473.24	1141.07	332.17
10	09/01/01	35095.68	1473.24	1151.53	321.71
11	10/01/01	33944.15	1473.24	1162.09	311.15
12	11/01/01	32782.06	1473.24	1172.74	300.50
13	12/01/01	31609.32	1473.24	1183.49	289.75
14	01/01/02	30425.83	1473.24	1194.34	278.90
15	02/01/02	29231.50	1473.24	1205.29	267.96
16	03/01/02	28026.21	1473.24	1216.34	256.91
17	04/01/02	26809.87	1473.24	1227.49	245.76
18	05/01/02	25582.39	1473.24	1238.74	234.51
19	06/01/02	24343.65	1473.24	1250.09	223.15
20	07/01/02	23093.56	1473.24	1261.55	211.69
21	08/01/02	21832.01	1473.24	1273.12	200.13
22	09/01/02	20558.89	1473.24	1284.79	188.46
23	10/01/02	19274.11	1473.24	1296.56	176.68
24	11/01/02	17977.54	1473.24	1308.45	164.79
25	12/01/02	16669.10	1473.24	1320.44	152.80
26	01/01/03	15348.65	1473.24	1332.55	140.70
27	02/01/03	14016.11	1473.24	1344.76	128.48
28	03/01/03	12671.35	1473.24	1357.09	116.15

(continued on the next page)

Table 5.4   *(continued)*

Month	Date	Balance	Payment	Principal	Interest
29	04/01/03	11314.26	1473.24	1369.53	103.71
30	05/01/03	9944.73	1473.24	1382.08	91.16
31	06/01/03	8562.65	1473.24	1394.75	78.49
32	07/01/03	7167.90	1473.24	1407.54	65.71
33	08/01/03	5760.36	1473.24	1420.44	52.80
34	09/01/03	4339.92	1473.24	1433.46	39.78
35	10/01/03	2906.46	1473.24	1446.60	26.64
36	11/01/03	1459.86	1473.24	1459.86	13.38

Using % 12 will cause values incrementing by 1 to cycle from 0 through 11. Adding 1 to the result (%
12 + 1) produces 1 through 12. We subtract 1 from the month number to offset the extra 1.

For the year:

```
(start_yr + (start_mon + month_num - 1) / 12) % 100)
```

Dividing the integer expression start_mon + month_num - 1 by an integer constant of 12 gives us an
additional year only every 12 months. The % 100 produces a two-digit year formulation.

Note that, for simplicity, we have omitted error-checking. In a real-life application, you would have
extensive error-checking of all input data to ensure proper ranges and formats.

5.11.3   Floating Point Loop Counters

In mortgage.c, we compared an integer type variable to another integer type variable to determine
whether to continue processing the loop. You may also use floating point variables and numbers, although this is far less common. We can see an example in Listing 5.13, tempconv.c. The program converts Fahrenheit temperatures to their Celsius equivalents over a specified range of temperatures. The
increment can be a fraction of a degree if the user so specifies.

 **Listing   5.13 tempconv.c**

```c
/* tempconv.c */

/* for loop with floating point increment to convert Fahrenheit to Celsius */

#include <stdio.h>

int main(void)
{
    float high, low, increment;
    float i;

    printf("Enter temperature range in degrees Fahrenheit\n"
        "Low temperature: ");
    scanf("%f", &low);
    printf("High temperature: ");
    scanf("%f", &high);
    printf("Specify increment in degrees Fahrenheit or fractional degrees: ");
    scanf("%f", &increment);
    printf("\tFahrenheit\tCelsius\n");
```

```
      printf("\t----------\t-------\n\n");
      for (i = low; i <= high + .0001; i += increment)
         printf("\t  %5.2f  \t%5.2f\n", i, (5./9.) * (i - 32.));
   }
```

You have to pay particular attention to your conditional expression component when you use floating point numbers there. The stored (binary) floating point number is only a close approximation of the decimal value you want assigned. If we changed the conditional expression to

```
for (i = low; i <= high; i += increment)
```

here's the output we'd get from an input of 32 to 34 as the range and .2 as the increment:

Fahrenheit	Celsius
32.00	0.00
32.20	0.11
32.40	0.22
32.60	0.33
32.80	0.44
33.00	0.56
33.20	0.67
33.40	0.78
33.60	0.89
33.80	1.00

What happened to the last expected conversion of 34°? If we started at 32 and incremented by .2, why did i <= high evaluate to false when we added .2 to 33.8? If we alter the printf() statement in the loop to print out the value of i during each loop, we see the problem:

32.000000	32.00	0.00
32.200001	32.20	0.11
32.400002	32.40	0.22
32.600002	32.60	0.33
32.800003	32.80	0.44
33.000004	33.00	0.56
33.200005	33.20	0.67
33.400005	33.40	0.78
33.600006	33.60	0.89
33.800007	33.80	1.00

The lesson is that you always should give yourself a cushion if you must use comparisons of values with floating point numbers.

In an appropriate case, you can avoid the potential problem caused by the imprecision of floating point numbers by converting to integer numbers. For example, to print a Fahrenheit-Celsius temperature conversion table from 32° to 34° Fahrenheit, in .2-degree increments:

```
int i;
for (i = 32 * 10; i <= 34 * 10; i += 2)
   printf("\t%5.2f\t%5.2f\n", (float)i / 10., (5./9.) * (((float)i / 10.) - 32.));
```

5.11.4   Omitting the Initialization or Update Component of a for Loop

You may omit the initialization component or update component of the for statement. However, the semicolons must be retained:

```
if (val % 2 != 0)
   i = 2;
else
   i = 4;
```

```
for (; i < 10; i++) /* initialization omitted */
   val += i;

for (i = 0; i < 27;) /* update omitted */
{
   val += i;
   if (val % 2 == 0)
      i++;
   else
      i += 2;
}
```

You actually could omit both the initialization and update components, but then the `for` loop would be exactly like the `while` loop and you might as well in that case use a `while` loop instead.

```
for (; scanf("%f", &centimeters);)
   inches = centimeters / 2.54;
```

is the same as

```
while (scanf("%f", &centimeters))
   inches = centimeters / 2.54;
```

5.11.5   The Missing Body

You can even have a `for` loop or a `while` loop with no body:

```
for (i = 0; i < 27; printf("month is %d\n", i++));
```

All the work is done in the update component. Note that in this case, there is a semicolon following the final parenthesis. However, the semicolon at the end of a missing-body loop can be difficult to spot when debugging a program. Using a pair of empty braces makes the missing body explicit:

```
for (i = 0; i < 27; printf("month is %d\n", i++))
{
   /* no body */
}
```

You can use loops without bodies to delay program execution:

```
for (i = 0; i < 30000; i++);

i = 300000;
while (i--);
```

The time it takes this statement to execute will vary depending on the machine it's run on. See Chapter 16 for a more measurable way of delaying program execution.

The fact that a loop may legally be written without a body means that if you inadvertently insert a semicolon after the loop parentheses, you will introduce an error not signaled by the compiler. The following

```
int i = 0;
while (i++ < 13);
   printf("month is %d\n", i);
```

will print but one line:

```
month is 14
```

5.11.6   Increment Operator in the Condition Evaluation Component

If you use the increment (or decrement) operator to update in the condition evaluation component, the variable being incremented will be incremented during the loop iteration in which the test fails, even though the body of the loop is not executed:

```
for (i = 0; i < 3; i++)
   printf("i is %d\n", i);
printf("i is now %d\n", i);
```

The last `printf()` statement shows `i` to be 3, not 2. The fact that a variable is incremented postfix on evaluation does not prevent the final incrementing. The output for

```
i = 0;
while (i++ < 3)
    printf("i is %d\n", i);
printf("i is now %d\n", i);
```

is

```
i is 1
i is 2
i is 3
i is now 4
```

The condition evaluation component is completed before proceeding either to execute the loop body or move to the next statement past the loop.

5.11.7 Updating: Avoiding Infinite Loops

We have called the third component of the `for` statement the update component, because that typically is its function. However, as you have seen, you may put any statement in this third part, whether it serves to update or not. If you use the third component for a purpose other than updating, or omit the third component altogether, you must be careful to include an updating mechanism as part of either the evaluation component

```
val = 0;
for (i = 0; i++ < 25; val += 5)
    printf("val is %d\n", val);
```

or the body:

```
val = 5;
for (i = 0; i < 50; val += 5)
{
    printf("val is %d\n", val);
    i = val * 2;
}
```

Be careful not to set up a condition evaluation component that can never become false, locking up the program in an infinite loop:

```
for (i  = 0; i < 20; i--)
    . . .
```

On the other hand, a common use of `while` loops is an intentionally infinite loop. Loop termination is done within the loop body:

```
while (1)
{
    val *= num;
    if (val > 30000)
        break;
    scanf("%d", &length);
    sum += length;
    if (sum > 1000 || length > 100)
        break;
}
```

In many cases, you *could* rewrite the code so that the loop termination occurs within the condition evaluation component; it's just that it's often simpler to code it the other way. In other cases, such as the most recent example, it is not really feasible to use a noninfinite loop. The occasions for breaking the loop occur in different points in the loop. See later in the chapter for an explanation of the `break` statement. (Note that the multiple-exit point aspect of this loop example is inconsistent with top-down modular programming development principles. A different approach may be warranted in such a case, rather than simply using alternative syntax.)

Some programmers prefer this alternative format to the `while(1)` infinite loop mechanism:

```
for (;;)
    . . .
```

5.11.8   Multiple Initialization, Evaluation, and Update—the Comma Operator

The initialization component of the `for` statement may have multiple initializations. Each of the initializations is separated by comma operators. The following program calculates first-class postage rates (possibly, alas, out of date by the time you read this).

 Listing **5.14 stamps.c**

```
/* stamps.c */

/* use for loop to calculate postage rates on first class stamps */

#include <stdio.h>

int main(void)
{
    int ounces;
    float postage;

    printf("Ounces  Cost\n");
    printf(" ——     ——\n");

    for (ounces = 1, postage = 0.33; ounces <= 16; ounces++)
    {
        postage += 0.22;
        printf("%4d    $%1.2f\n", ounces, postage);
    }
}
```

The result is just the same as though we had separate assignment statements separated by semicolons:

```
ounces  = 1;
postage = 0.33;
for (; ounces <= 16; ounces++)
{
  postage += 0.22;
  printf("%4d    $%1.2f\n", ounces, postage);
}
```

The ability to have multiple initializations separated by comma operators is a consequence of the initialization component's being effectively a complete assignment statement. Remember that you can, in effect, combine multiple assignment statements into a single statement by separating the statements with comma operators.

Along the same lines, you can use the same assignment devices in the initialization as you can elsewhere in any assignment statement. For example:

```
for (day = month = months = 0; months < 12; months++)
    . . .
```

The update component of the `for` loop may also have multiple parts. Again, the parts are separated by comma operators:

```
for (total = count = 0; count < 10; total += count, count++)
  printf("total: %d\n", total);
```

There is no problem knowing whether `count` will be incremented prior to being added to `total` or not. Remember:

 Expressions separated by comma operators are evaluated from left to right.

The `partial.c` program illustrates multiple initialization and update. The program determines the number `num` of terms of the harmonic series

```
1 + 1/2 + 1/3 + 1/4 + . . .
```

for the partial sum `sum` that first exceeds 3, 5, 7, 9, 11, and 13.

 **Listing 5.15 partial.c**

```c
/* partial.c */

/* calculate # of terms in partial sum of a #: multiple
   initialization, update */

#include <stdio.h>

int main(void)
{
    int target;
    long num;
    double sum;

    printf("target terms    sum\n\n");

    /* do from 3 through 13 */

    for (target = 3, num = 0L, sum = 0.; target < 14;
        target += 2, num = 0L, sum = 0.)
    {
        while (sum <= target)
            sum += (1./++num);
        printf("%2d %7ld %10f\n", target, num, sum);
    }
}
```

The output:

```
target   terms      sum

    3      11     3.019877
    5      83     5.002068
    7     616     7.001274
    9    4550     9.000208
   11   33617    11.000018
   13  248397    13.000001
```

It is interesting to observe that initialization for the `while` statement is done in both the so-called initialization and update components of the `for` statement, and that updating for the `while` statement occurs in the `while` loop body.

The condition evaluation component of the `for` loop or `while` loops can be multiple, but here the syntax is more complex. You can't just separate multiple conditions by comma operators because the computer would not know whether the logical relationship between or among the multiple conditions is "and" or "or". Here, you must use logical operators, not comma operators:

```c
for (total = 0, count = start; count < end && total < 100; count++)
    total += count;

for (total = 0, count = start; count < end || (total > 100 && count > 50); count++)
    total += count;
```

That is not to say that you can't ever separate expressions in the condition component of a `for` or `while` statement. You can; it's just that only the value of the right-hand member of such expressions will determine whether the condition is met or not. Remember:

 The value, as a whole, of expressions separated by comma operators is the value of the right-hand member.

For example:

```
int sum = 0;
int i;
while (scanf("%d", &i), i > 0)
    sum += i;
```

This code fragment computes the sum of positive integers entered on the keyboard until termination is signaled by a zero or negative integer. Under the rule governing evaluation order of expressions separated by commas, the scanf() call is evaluated first, resulting in user input. Then the second expression is evaluated and its value alone is used to determine whether to continue looping.

This construction of comma operator-separated expressions in the condition component of a loop is useful only where, as here, all expressions but the right-most expression serve an independent purpose or cause some independent action other than determining whether to continue the loop; their values are completely ignored for that latter purpose.

5.11.9   Varying the for Loop Update

In a good number of cases, your for statement will contain an update expression that you simply increment by 1 by means of the increment operator. There are many other ways to update, however. For instance, you can increment by a multiple of some number other than 1. The following program, rate.c, uses a series of for loops to calculate the interest rate on a loan of a specified principal amount, term and monthly payment.

When we calculate the monthly payment from a given principal amount, term, and interest rate, we use the formula we saw earlier in mortgage.c:

$$principal = (principal * interest\ rate) / (1 - ((1 + interest\ rate)^{-term}))$$

But there is no formula to calculate interest rate from a given principal, term, and payment. The way we derive interest rate is iteratively—by a series of successive guesses. We guess at the interest rate and see how the payment we calculate from this guess matches the target payment.

 **Listing** **5.16 rate.c**

```
/* rate.c  */

/* calculate interest rate with floating point
   increments in for loops */

#include <stdio.h>
#include <math.h> /* pow */

int main(void)
{
    float principal, payment;
    float years, months;
    float i, j;

    printf("Input the following, pressing [Enter] after each:\n");
    printf("Principal amount: ");
    scanf("%f", &principal);
    printf("Monthly payment: ");
    scanf("%f", &payment);
    printf("Term in years: ");
    scanf("%f", &years);
    months = years * 12.;

    /* increment % by 1 until payment is too high */
    for (i = 1.; i < 20.; i += 1.)
        if (((principal * i/1200.)/(1. - (1./pow(1. + i/1200., months)))) > payment)
        break;
```

```
                  /* go to next lower % and now increment by .1, etc. */
                  for (j = i - 1; j < i; j += .1)
                      if (((principal * j/1200.)/(1. - (1./pow(1. + j/1200., months)))) > payment)
                      break;
                  for (i = j - .1; i < j; i += .01)
                      if (((principal * i/1200.)/(1. - (1./pow(1. + i/1200., months)))) > payment)
                      break;
                  for (j = i - .01; j < i; j += .001)
                      if (((principal * j/1200.)/(1. - (1./pow(1. + j/1200., months)))) > payment)
                      break;
                  printf("Annual interest rate is %.3f%%\n", j - .001);
              }
```

The program starts with a guess of 1% interest and increments 1% each loop until the payment calculated from the guess rate exceeds the target payment. (See later in the chapter for an explanation of the `break` mechanism.) Then it backs the guess rate down by the last 1% increment. After that it starts another loop, this time incrementing each loop 1/10%. Then we repeat the same process, incrementing by 1/100% each loop, then by 1/1000%.

You can also increment by an expression that may not evaluate to the same increase each loop:

```
for (i = 0; i < 10; i += val)
    val = i / 2;
```

Your update can increase geometrically rather than mathematically:

```
for (i = 0; i < filenum; i *= 10)
```

Likewise, your *evaluation condition* can be structured to increase geometrically, as the following program, `prime.c`, shows. The program checks whether an entered integer is a prime number—that is, is not evenly divisible by any integer other than 1.

 **Listing** **5.17 prime.c**

```
/* prime.c */

/* determine whether # is prime: evaluation condition
   increases geometrically */

#include <stdio.h>
#include <limits.h> /* ULONG_MAX: largest unsigned long value */

int main(void)
{
   unsigned long divisor, num;
   int prime;

   printf("Enter an positive integer < %lu for prime number testing: ", ULONG_MAX);
   scanf("%lu", &num);

   for (prime = 1, divisor = 2LU; (divisor * divisor) <= num && prime; divisor++)
      if (!(num % divisor))
   /* not a prime number if evenly divisible by another */
         prime = 0;
   printf("%lu is %sa prime number\n", num, prime ? "" : "not ");
}
```

(See whether you can figure out why we only need to test up to `divisor * divisor` rather than up to `num`.)

You can also decrement, both mathematically and geometrically:

```
for (i = 10; i > 0; i--)
    printf("i is now %d\n", i);

for (i = 256; i > 2; i /= 2)
    . . .
```

5.11.10   Taking Stock of the `for` Loop Mechanism

Typically, what we've called the initialization component of the `for` statement contains one or more assignment statements that serve as the starting point for the loop. *Typically*, what we've called the update component contains one or more assignment statements that increment or decrement the value of a loop counter whose value governs the evaluation of the conditional expression component. But neither of these need be so.

You can use the first expression of the `for` statement for something altogether different from initializing and the last expression for something that has nothing to do with updating the loop counter:

```
for (printf("Enter a number\nType 10 to quit\n"); num != 10;
     printf("You entered a %d\nEnter another or type 10 to quit\n", num),
     scanf("%d", &num));
```

Even the term *loop counter* incorrectly implies that there is *always* some variable in the condition evaluation expression that is incrementing or decrementing in some arithmetic or geometric fashion.

Remember what happens in the `for` loop:

- The first expression is executed at the start of the process.
- At the beginning of each iteration, the second `for` statement expression is evaluated. If true, the body of the loop is executed.
- Before going back and evaluating the second `for` statement expression, the final `for` statement expression is executed.

This process is what defines the `for` loop. It is useful to appreciate that the first expression is generally used to initialize and the last to update. However, if you understand the mechanics of the process, you will be able to make the use of the `for` loop much more flexible.

5.12   `do-while` LOOPS

The `for` loop and `while` loop test for the existence of a condition before either processing the loop body if the condition evaluates to true, or terminating the loop if it is false. The `do-while` loop first executes the loop body on each iteration, then *after* doing so tests the condition and terminates the loop if the condition is not met. For example:

```
do
{
   scanf("%d", &num);
   printf("number input is %d\n", num);
}
while (num > 1);
```

One thing this means is that the loop body will always be executed at least once.

Note that where the body consists of more than one statement in a block, the braces come directly after "do" and before "`while`".

 With the `do-while` loop, there *is* a semicolon after the condition evaluation component, unlike the case of `for` loops and `while` loops. Conversely, where the loop body is a single statement, there is no semicolon after the body.

```
do
   scanf("%d", &num)
      while (num);
```

5.13   CHOOSING YOUR LOOP

The `do-while` loop is much less commonly used than `while` loops or `for` loops. In most cases, you will want to evaluate the test condition before executing even one iteration. Assuming the situation you're looking at is not one of those appropriate for the `do-while` loop, you must choose between the `for` loop and the `while` loop.

Generally, almost any loop can be written as either a `while` loop or a `for` loop. The `for` loop lends itself more naturally to the situation in which you must loop a fixed number of times. The `while` loop, on the other hand, lends itself to cases in which the condition you test for depends on extraneous, nonmathematical factors—for example, an interactive program where the user enters an indeterminate amount of data and then signals termination of input by a certain key or certain type of entry, or a file-reading program where you read until the end of the file is reached or a specific character is encountered.

By far the most common use of `for` loops is in conjunction with arrays. We will see some examples in the next chapter.

5.14 PERIODIC CHANGE AND CYCLING WITH / AND %

If we want to increment or decrement a variable only every so many loop iterations, we can use the `/` operator and our understanding of integer division. For example:

```
int i, intensity;
for (i = 0; i < 2000; i++)
   intensity = i / 8;
```

Because of the way integer division works, the variable `intensity` will increment only every eight loop iterations.

If we want to cycle from one value to another, we can use the `%` operator. For example:

```
for (i = 0; i < 2000; i++)
{
   foreground_color = 30 + (i % 8);
   ch = 'A' + (i % 26);
   choice = (choice + 1) % 6;
}
```

The variable `foreground_color` will cycle from 30 through 37 and back. The variable `ch` will cycle from A through Z and back (assuming we have ASCII character encoding). The variable `choice` will cycle from 0 through 5 and back. The modulus operator will cycle or rotate us from 0 through 1 less than the number to the right of the modulus operator.

You can use both operators in combination:

```
for (i = 0; i < 2000; i++)
   background_color = 40 + ((i / 16) % 8);
```

This will change `background_color` every 16 iterations. Each time a change is made, `background_color` will increment from 40. However, when `background_color` gets to 47, the next change will be back to 40. See Listing D.1, `scrn_spd.c`, for an illustration of these concepts and an explanation of the significance of the code in the above examples. See also, Listing 5.12, `mortgage.c` for a simpler example.

These examples help answer a question frequently asked by students, namely, "Why do we have such a wacky operation as integer division or such weird operators as the modulus operator in the first place?" The examples put the `/` and `%` operators in a context in which the division is not being done for the commonplace mathematical reason.

5.15 NESTED LOOPS

Any of the loop types can have as its body or as part of its body another loop. This is referred to as *nesting* of loops. A nested `for` loop is used quite often. The following program, `box.c`, uses one to create a rectangle of interactively determined dimensions on the screen.

 **Listing** **5.18 box.c**

```
/* box.c */

/* draw a rectangle on the screen with nested for loops */

#include <stdio.h>
```

```
int main(void)
{
   int width, height, rows, cols;

   printf("Type width and box height: ");
   scanf("%d%d", &width, &height);
   putchar('\n');
   for (rows = 0; rows < height && rows < 24; rows++)
   {
      for (cols = 0; cols < width && cols < 79; cols++)
         putchar('$'); /* ASCII 219 */
      putchar('\n'); /* to next screen row */
   }
}
```

The outer loop moves from row to row. The inner loop goes column to column in a row, printing as many full-box characters as are input (up to 80—the maximum number of columns on the screen in text mode).

5.15.1   Mixing and Matching Nested Loops

The next program, calendar.c, has a for loop that houses a nested switch statement and two for loops. The program prints out a calendar for an input year. The outer for loop cycles through the months of the year. For each of those months, the switch statement tells us how many days in the month, the first inner for loop positions the first day of the month, and the second inner for loop handles the actual printing of the individual days.

 **Listing** **5.19 calendar.c**

```
/* calendar.c */

/* print a calendar for inputted year, using nested loops & switch */

#include <stdio.h>

int main(void)
{
   int year;
   int start_day; /* Sunday: 0, Monday: 1, etc. */
   int month, days, day;

   printf("Calendar year: ");
   scanf("%d", &year);
   printf("%d\n\n", year);
   start_day = (year + (year - 1)/4 - (year - 1)/100 + (year - 1)/400) % 7;

   for (month = 1; month <= 12; month++, start_day =
      (start_day + days) % 7)
   {
      printf("\n\n");

      /* print month label & determine number of days in month */
      switch (month)
      {
         case 1: case 3: case 5: case 7: case 8: case 10: case 12:
            switch(month)
         {
            case 1: printf("January"); break;
            case 3: printf("March"); break;
```

```
            case 5: printf("May"); break;
            case 7: printf("July"); break;
            case 8: printf("August"); break;
            case 10: printf("October"); break;
            case 12: printf("December"); break;
        }
        days = 31;
        break;
    case 2:
        printf("February");
    /* leap year if year evenly divisible by 4 except
        centennial that is not also millennium */
        days = year % 4 || (year % 100 && !(year % 1000)) ? 28: 29;
        break;
        default:
        switch(month)
        {
            case 4: printf("April"); break;
            case 6: printf("June"); break;
            case 9: printf("September"); break;
            case 11: printf("November"); break;
        }
        days = 30;
        break;
    } /* end outer switch */

    printf("\n\n\tSun\tMon\tTues\tWed\tThurs\tFri\tSat\n\t");

    /* position first day of month */
    for (day = 0; day < start_day; day++)
        putchar('\t');

    /* print out days in proper place */
    for (day = 1; day <= days; day++)
    {
        printf("%2d", day);
        if ((day + start_day) % 7)
            putchar('\t');
        else
            printf("\n\t");
    }
    } /* end for month is 1 to 12 */
}
```

The inner loop can in theory itself contain a nested loop, and so on, but nesting beyond a few levels is unusual. Nevertheless, Standard C requires compilers to support at least 15 levels of compound statements, iteration control statements, and selection control structures.

5.16   USING continue AND break: LOOP SHORT-CIRCUIT

The continue and break statements allow you to break out of a loop or loop iteration prematurely. The continue statement discontinues the current loop iteration and jumps to the next one. The break statement terminates the loop altogether. Both types of statements can be used with any of the three loop varieties, while, do-while, and for. The three loop types are also prematurely terminated by a return statement inside a function. (See Chapter 8.)

We take a look at a game of craps to illustrate both continue and break. The game is somewhat simplified. If you roll a 7 or an 11 initially, you win. Otherwise, you have to match the same roll before getting 7 or 11. We ignore special rules for snake eyes and boxcars.

 **Listing** **5.20** craps.c

```c
/* craps.c */

/* game of craps to illustrate continue & break */

#include <stdio.h>
#include <conio.h> /* getch */
#include <time.h> /* clock */

int main(void)
{
   unsigned first, second;
   unsigned long wager;
   unsigned long bankroll = 50000LU;

   printf("Specify an amount to bet (you have %lu to bet with)\n", bankroll);
   printf("Type a letter to quit while you're ahead\n");

   while (scanf("%lu", &wager)) /* quit on letter */
   {
      if (wager > bankroll)
      {
         printf("Sorry, Bub. That exceeds your bankroll\n\n");
         printf("Specify an amount to bet (you have %lu to bet with)\n", bankroll);
         printf("Type a letter to quit while you're ahead\n");
         continue;
      }
      printf("Press any key to roll dice\n");
      getch(); /* pauses program to allow user to read message */

      /* clock returns number of computer's clock ticks
         since program start */
      first = ((unsigned)clock() % 11) + 2; /* from 2 to 12 */
      printf("Your first roll was a%s %d\n", first == 8 || first == 11 ? "n": "", first);
      if (first == 7 || first == 11)
      {
         printf("That's a winner!\n\n");
         bankroll += wager;
         printf("Specify an amount to bet (you have %lu to bet with)\n", bankroll);
         printf("Type a letter to quit while you're ahead\n");
         continue;
      }

      /* keep getting second dice roll until match or 7 or 11 */
      do
      {
         printf("Press any key to roll dice\n");
         getch();
         second = ((unsigned)clock() % 11) + 2;
         printf("You threw a%s %d\n", second == 8 || second == 11 ? "n": "", second);
      } while (second != first && second != 7 && second != 11);
      printf("\n%d and %d\n", first, second);

      if (second == first)
      {
         bankroll += wager;
         printf("That's a winner!\n\n");
      }
      else
      {
         bankroll -= wager;
```

```
        printf("You lose! Honk!\n\n");
    }

    /* quit if no money left or if winnings too high */
    if (!bankroll)
    {
        printf("Busted! Pay your hotel bill and get out of town\n");
        break;
    }

    if (bankroll > 2000000LU)
    {
        printf("You broke the bank. Proceed to IRS notification window\n");
        break;
    }

    printf("Specify an amount to bet (you have %lu to bet with)\n", bankroll);
    printf("Type a letter to quit while you're ahead\n");
} /* end while */
}
```

To generate a relatively unpredictable number for each roll of the dice, we determine the number of the computer's clock ticks since the program's start with the clock() function, discussed in Chapter 16. On a PC there are about 18.2 ticks per second.

There is a standard C function, rand(), which supposedly generates random numbers, but we've chosen not to use that. The rand() function, the prototype for which is found in stdlib.h, is more correctly called a pseudo-random number generator. The numbers generated are random, sure enough, but you get exactly the same sequence of numbers from the first call on. So every time you start your program, you'd get the same supposedly random numbers. You could use srand(seed) to "seed" the random number generator: using the argument time(NULL), you get an essentially "random" seeding each time you run the program. However, the time() function is accurate only to the nearest second (see Chapter 16). Therefore, in this application, it would be too easy with that formulation to produce the same result repeatedly by waiting a precise number of seconds. Even the method we've chosen is "pseudo-random" because a deterministic method cannot perfectly simulate a nondeterministic event.

We get "dice roll" numbers of between 2 and 12 with the modulus operator. A number % 11 gives us numbers of between 0 and 10; adding 2 to that gives us the required range of 2 to 12:

```
second = ((unsigned)clock() % 11) + 2;
```

Actually, our program produces results that are not statistically valid. We generate a dice throw between 2 and 12, all equally likely the way we've coded. This is *not* the case in the real world: 7 has a higher likelihood of occurring than 2 or 11, for example (4 and 3, 3 and 4, 2 and 5, 5 and 2, 6 and 1, 1 and 6 for 7, versus only 1 and 1 for 2). We could generate an event for each die (1 through 6) and sum the results:

```
die1 = ((unsigned)clock() % 6) + 1;
die2 = ((unsigned)clock() % 6) + 1;
toss = die1 + die2;
```

However, though that formulation is statistically satisfying, the second number in this context is predictable given the first number—the computer is too quick. We leave it to you to craft a more nearly perfect solution.

The operative part of the program is one long while loop. We keep looping every time a new wager amount is input. If a letter is typed in, scanf() returns 0 and the loop, and the program, stop. Meanwhile, we first test to see whether the amount bet is within the user's remaining purse. If not, we print out a warning message, prompt the user to make another bet, *and* then skip the rest of the loop—which consists of rolling dice—by a continue statement. In a non-DOS environment, you would replace getch() with getchar() and alter the user directions accordingly.

Assuming we pass that first check, we then get our first dice roll number. We tell the user what it is, using the % operator to keep us grammatically correct: "an 8" and "an 11" for numbers beginning with vowels and "a 9," and so on, for the rest. If the number is 7 or 11, we add the amount of the bet to the user's pot of money and again skip over the rest of the loop with a `continue` statement.

Otherwise, we keep rolling the dice until we either get a match or a 7 or 11. We have to *first* roll the dice before making the test in this inner loop's conditional expression. To do this, we use a `do-while` loop rather than the more common do loop. If we find the first roll matches the second, we add the bet to the kitty. If the resulting pot of money is greater than $2 million, we exit from the loop altogether by a `break` statement. Likewise, if the second roll is a 7 or 11, we decrement the pot by the bet; if that wipes the user out, we end the loop with a `break`.

5.16.1   Loop Resumption Point

When you use `continue` inside a `while` loop, program flow moves to the conditional evaluation expression. When you use `continue` with a `for` loop, the program first executes the update expression and *then* moves to the condition evaluation component.

Where you have a `while` loop in which the condition evaluation expression does not contain an update mechanism, you have to take care to place the `continue` statement after the update statement in the loop body unless it is your intention not to update if the `continue` statement is executed.

5.16.2   Using `continue` and `break` in Nested Loops

 With nested loops, the `continue` statement and `break` statement operate only on the loop of which they are a part.

```
for (skip = finished = 0, i = start; i < end; i+= 2)
{
    for (j = 0; j < num; j++, skip = 0);
    {
        if (num > val)
            break; /* terminates inner loop only */
        if (num == 999)
        {
            finished = 1;
            break;
        }
        if (num % 50 == 0)
        {
            skip = 1;
            continue;
        }
        if (num % 5 == 0)
            continue; /* to next iteration of inner loop */
        val *= num - 3;
    }
    if (finished)
        break; /* terminates outer loop */
    if (skip)
        continue; /* to next iteration of outer loop */
    val--;
}
```

If the first `if` statement within the inner `for` loop is true, only the inner for loop is terminated. The same would appear to be true for the next `if` statement. However, setting the variable `finished` to 1 causes another `if` statement just after the inner loop to break the outer loop as well. The same dichotomy is used in the next two `if` statements of the inner `for` loop with `continue`.

Those from a "structured programming" conservative base may wince at such code. With the exception of the `switch`, where `break` is unavoidable, both `break` and `continue`, they say, ought to be considered "personae non grata" in good programs, arguing that a little bit of thought and careful planning will show that almost any code segment can be rewritten without resort to these two. Nevertheless, we are able to use those constructs precisely because C is rich and flexible enough to provide those features *without* compromising structured programming principles. On the other hand, the constructs can be abused. They should not be seen as a lazy substitute for modular design and functionality. Likewise for goto statements. Most books rightly condemn the goto statement (see the discussion later in this chapter). Even though the goto statement can be of great utility in the appropriate situation, they shy away from recommending the construct in any case for fear of abuse by novice programmers.

5.16.3   Using `continue` as a Placeholder for a Null Statement

A loop without any body is useful in several situations. Earlier we saw an example of a loop without a body for the purpose of delaying program execution:

```
for (i = 0; i < 2500000; i++);
```

Another example of a bodyless loop would be skipping over all input that is not whitespace or a digit to get to character input:

```
while (scanf("%d", &dummy));
```

A third example would be skipping over all input from the first character to the end of a line of input. This would be useful in cases where the program calls for a single letter to be input, but the user might type in a whole word by mistake.

```
while (getchar() != '\n');
```

We illustrate this third example in the following program, gender.c, where the user is instructed to read a list of names and indicate by typing f or m whether the name is female or male.

 **Listing** 5.21 **gender.c**

```
/* gender.c */

/* use continue to gobble up input past first letter */


#include <stdio.h>

int main(void)
{
    char ch;
    int males = 0, females = 0;

    printf("Enter \"f\" for female or \"m\" for male\n"
        "Enter \"q\" instead to quit\n");

    while ((ch = getchar()) != 'q' || ch != 'Q')
    {
        if (ch == 'm' || ch == 'M')
            males++;
        else if (ch == 'f' || ch == 'F')
         females++;
        else
        {
            while (getchar() != '\n')
                continue;
            printf("Error: must enter either"
                " \"f\" or \"m\"\nTry again\n");
            continue;
        }

        /* gobble up input through newline */
        while (getchar() != '\n')
            continue;

        printf("Enter \"f\" for female or \"m\" for male\n"
```

```
            "Enter a number instead to quit\n");
        }
        printf("%d male%s and %d female%s in list\n", males, males == 1 ?
            "" : "s", females, females == 1 ? "" : "s");
    }
```

The statement

```
while (getchar() != '\n');
```

reads characters from the input stream up to and including the newline character generated by pressing the Enter key. Therefore, if the user types "female" instead of just f, the "emale\n" that is left over after the outer while statement processes the f gets read and discarded. Absent this device, each of the remaining characters would be read and processed by the outer while statement. That would cause the error message to be triggered six times.

Note that the two statements

```
while (getchar() != '\n')
    continue;
```

could be collectively replaced with

```
fflush(stdin);
```

(See Chapter 14.)

We call what follows the for statement and the while statement in these three examples a *null statement*. You can also have a null do while construction

```
do ;
    while (getchar() != '\n=);
```

but generally a while loop is used in this situation.

 When you have a null statement, it is a good idea to use continue *to clarify your intentions, particularly if other programmers will be looking at your code.*

```
for (i = 0; i < 25000; i++)
    continue;

while (scanf("%d", &dummy))
    continue;

while (getchar() != '\n')
    continue;
```

 The fact that a null statement is permissible makes conditional compilation useful in some situations.

```
while (x++ < 25)
#if defined DATASTORE
{
    lots of statements
}
#else
    continue;
```

(See Chapter 11 for an explanation of conditional compilation.)

5.16.4   Using continue and break with switch Statements

If you have a switch statement nested within a for or while loop, you cannot use break within the switch statement body to terminate the loop. The break statement, as you have seen, has a particular significance in the switch statement body. You must use some other device to terminate the loop:

```
int keepLooping = 1;
while (scanf("%d", &num) && keepLooping)
{
```

```
        switch(num)
        {
           case 0:
              val--;
              break;
           case 13:
              keepLooping = 0;
              break;
        }
     }
```

On the other hand, since the `continue` statement has no independent meaning for the `switch` statement body, you can use it to move to the next iteration of a `for` or `while` loop:

```
while (scanf("%d", &num))
{
     switch(num)
     {
        case 0:
           val--;
           continue;
           break;
        case 13:
           continue;
           break;
     }
     val++;
}
```

5.17   THE goto STATEMENT

The `goto` statement causes a jump to a specified location in the code. Its syntax is as follows:

goto *label;*

Once the program encounters the `goto` statement, it moves to wherever in the code it finds the label followed by a colon:

label:

The `goto` statement should rarely be used. In fact, it is considered the height of poor programming technique. Jumps here and there in the code make the program hard to follow, indicate poor organization and coding style, and pave the way for error.

There is one recognized exception: when you need to get out of heavily nested loops quickly. Most often, this need arises on the discovery of an error condition. For example:

```
while (condition)
{
     while (another condition)
     {
        for (i = start; i < end; i++)
        {
           scanf("%f", &num);
           if (num > 999.9)
           {
              printf("Error: input out of range\n");
              goto error;
           }
        }
     }
}
error:
```

If you were to use a `break` statement at the point of error here, that would terminate only the `for` loop, not the inner or outer `while` loop.

Both the `goto` **statement and the corresponding label must be found within the same function.**

5.18   APPLICATION: ACE BILLING PROGRAM

Now that you understand loops, we will make use of them in the ACE Billing program. We can use the looping construct to efficiently process as many records as we have. We can use a loop to read the customer name a character at a time, though we will not have learned how to handle complete strings until Chapter 9.

At this point, we recommend that you run this program using the file `acech03.dat` as the standard input source. The `acech05.c` program has beeen written to read data accoring to that input record layout. In PC and UNIX platforms, reading in this fashion is achieved through redirection. For example:

```
acech05.exe < acech05.dat > acech05.rpt
```

where `acech05.rpt` is the standard output.

(See Chapter 16 for a more complete explanation of redirection.) It is beyond the scope of this chapter to write this program to receive the data interactively and still produce the same report format. Doing so would require us to store all the data into an array before printing out all the results. Otherwise, the input prompts would intermingle with the output report, and that would be a mess.

5.18.1   Input

Same as in Chapter 3 for `acech03.c`.

 **Listing 5.22 acech05.c**

```
/*
   +------------------------------------------------------------------+
   +    Program Name: acech05.c
   +       Author(s): Austell-Wolfson and Otieno
   +            Date: 12/10/2000
   +    Purpose:
   +        This program implements the ace billing program.
   +        We have learned how to:
   +            declare variables that hold single values and assign
   +            them values. We have also learned how to read and
   +            write through scanf() and printf(). We now apply
   +            these capabilities in this program.
   +
   +    Process:
   +        At this point, we print the headings, declare variables, and
   +        assign values to the variables where applicable. We can
   +        read data from standard input and write data to standard
   +        output.
   +        After Chapter 5:
   +            We can now set up a loop to process as many records as
   +            we have. We can also use the looping construct to read
   +            the customer name one character at a time even though we
   +            have not learned how to handle complete strings.
   +------------------------------------------------------------------+
*/
#include <stdio.h>

void initialization(void); /* Prototype - discussed in Chapter 8 */
void processMemberRecord(void);
void termination(void);
void initializeVariables(void);
void printHeadings(void);
```

```
void readMemberRecord(void);
void computeIndividualBill(void);
void writeDetailLine(void);
void determineSpecialFee(void);
void determineActivityFee(void);
void determineDiscountAmt(void);

/*
    +------------------------------------------------------------------+
    +
    +   Declare variables outside of main() function so that all the
    +   other functions will have access to them. Doing this gives
    +   these variables global scope and therefore allows us to
    +   develop and work with modules this early. We will discontinue
    +   this practice once functions have been fully discussed.
    +
    +------------------------------------------------------------------+
*/

char  SpecialMembershipFlag = 'Y';
float MembershipFee = 0.0;
float ActivityFee = 0.0;
float DiscountAmount = 0.0;
float ChargeAmount = 0.0;
float TotalIndividualBill = 0.0;
float AceClubTotals = 0.0;
float Charges = 0.0;
int   Discount = 0;
int   AverageCharges = 0;
int   NumberOfCharges = 0;
int   ReadStatus = 0;
float TotalAceClubTotals = 0.0;
float TotalCharges = 0.0;
int   TotalDiscount = 0;
int   TotalAverageCharges = 0;
int   TotalNumberOfCharges = 0;
float TotalTotalIndividualBill = 0.0;
float TotalMembershipFee = 0.0;
float TotalActivityFee = 0.0;
float TotalDiscountAmount = 0.0;

int main(void)
{
/*
    +------------------------------------------------------------------+
    +
    +   Observe that:
    +   1. scanf() returns the number of items that it has
    +      successfully read.
    +      For example:
    +      ReadStatus = scanf("%2d%c%4d%4d\n", &NumberOfCharges,
    +         &SpecialMembershipFlag, &Discount, &AverageCharges);
    +      ReadStatus == 4 if the above statement successfully reads
    +      4 items. We use that knowledge to construct a condition for
    +      our loop. We could have chosen to check for the end of
    +      file, instead of a successful read.
    +   2. initialization() function called the function to read
    +      the first set of values. This was necessary so that the
    +      condition of the loop would be meaningful. In other words,
    +      ReadStatus would not have a meaningful value if you had
    +      not done the first read. Since we have chosen this method,
```

```
    +        it follows that we must also read the next item at the
    +        end of the loop. In this case, processMemberRecord() would
    +        perform a read operation prior to returning control back
    +        to main(). We chose this approach because it keeps all the
    +        details within the respective modules.
    +    3. We could have used scanf() directly on the while condition
    +        and eliminated one module. This could be done as follows:
    +        while ((scanf("%2d%c%4d%4d\n", &NumberOfCharges,
    +            &SpecialMembershipFlag, &Discount, &AverageCharges)) == 4)
    +
    +-----------------------------------------------------------------+
*/
initialization();
while (4 == ReadStatus)
{
   (processMemberRecord());
}

/*
    +-----------------------------------------------------------------+
    +
    +    This is the one module that we have not used very much.
    +    It is still a good idea to have it because when we start
    +    opening files and discussing control-break logic,
    +    we will definitely use it.
    +
    +-----------------------------------------------------------------+
    */

   termination();
   return 0;
}

void initialization(void)
{
   initializeVariables();
   printHeadings();
   readMemberRecord();
}

void processMemberRecord(void)
{
   computeIndividualBill();
   writeDetailLine();
   readMemberRecord();
}

void termination(void)
{
   printf("%*s—   ——   ——   ——   —   ——   |\n",
      18, " ");
   printf("| ACE Club Totals    %3d $%8.2f $%8.2f $%8.2f $%5.f $%9.2f |\n",
      TotalNumberOfCharges, TotalCharges, TotalMembershipFee, TotalActivityFee,
      TotalDiscountAmount,TotalTotalIndividualBill);
   printf("|_____|\n");
}

void initializeVariables(void)
{
   SpecialMembershipFlag = 'Y';
   Discount = 0;
```

```
   AverageCharges = 0;
   MembershipFee = 2500.0;
   ActivityFee = 250.0;
   DiscountAmount = 0.0;
   ChargeAmount = 0.0;
   NumberOfCharges = 0;
   TotalIndividualBill = 0.0;
   AceClubTotals = 0.0;
   ReadStatus = 0;
}

void printHeadings(void)
{
   printf("┌──────────────────────────────────────────────────────────┐\n");
   printf("│                                                            │\n");
   printf("│   Program Name: ACECH05.EXE                      Page:  1  │\n");
   printf("│      Run Date: 12/10/2000            Ace Billing           │\n");
   printf("│                                                            │\n");
   printf("│                                                            │\n");
   printf("├──────────────────────────────────────────────────────────┤\n");
   printf("│                                                            │\n");
   printf("│Customer Name  Charges  Bill      Mbr Fee   Act Fee   Disc    Total Bill │\n");
   printf("├──────────────────────────────────────────────────────────┤\n");
   printf("│                                                            │\n");

}

void readMemberRecord(void)
{
   int  nameChar;  /* holds the customer name character from input */
   int  k;         /* a loop counter */

   /*
   +------------------------------------------------------------+
   +
   +   We implement a loop to read the customer name one character at
   +   a time and print it out for the entire length of a customer
   +   name and initials. Later on after discussing arrays, we will
   +   be able to store all the characters that make up the customer
   +   name in an array.
   +
   +------------------------------------------------------------+
   */

   /* Read and write all the characters in the customer name */

   printf("│ ");
   nameChar = getchar();
   for (k = 0; ((k < 15) && (nameChar != EOF)); k++)
   {
      putchar(nameChar);
      nameChar = getchar();
   }

   /* Print the two spaces that separate the customer name
      from initials before reading and printing the initials. */

   printf("  ");

   /*
      Read and print the first initial character. Make sure that the
```

```
         end-of-file condition is handled correctly.
    */

    if (nameChar != EOF)
    {
       putchar(nameChar);
       nameChar = getchar();
    }

    /* Read and print the next initial character. */

    if (nameChar != EOF)
    {
       putchar(nameChar);
       nameChar = getchar();
    }

    /*
       +----------------------------------------------------------------+
       +
       +     Read the rest of the data items/fields from the input data
       +     stream. The input data stream is assumed to be a file of
       +     a particular record layout. This file is read through the
       +     mechanism that your operating system has provided to handle
       +     standard input from a file instead of a keyboard.
       +
       +----------------------------------------------------------------+
    */

    ReadStatus = scanf("%2d%c%4d%4d\n", &NumberOfCharges,
       &SpecialMembershipFlag, &Discount, &AverageCharges);
}
void computeIndividualBill(void)
{
    Charges = 200 * NumberOfCharges;
    TotalCharges += Charges;
    TotalNumberOfCharges += NumberOfCharges;
    determineSpecialFee();
    determineActivityFee();
    determineDiscountAmt();

    TotalIndividualBill = Charges + MembershipFee + ActivityFee -
       DiscountAmount;
    AceClubTotals += TotalIndividualBill;
    TotalTotalIndividualBill += TotalIndividualBill;
    TotalMembershipFee += MembershipFee;
    TotalActivityFee += ActivityFee;
    TotalDiscountAmount += DiscountAmount;
    TotalAceClubTotals += AceClubTotals;
}

void writeDetailLine(void)
{
    printf(" %2d  $%8.2f  $%8.2f  $%8.2f  $%5.f  $%9.2f",
       NumberOfCharges, Charges, MembershipFee,
       ActivityFee, DiscountAmount, TotalIndividualBill);
    printf(" |\n");

}

void determineSpecialFee(void)
{
/*
```

```
    +----------------------------------------------------------------+
    +
    +  Tip: It is a good idea to use ('Y' == SpecialMembershipFlag)
    +  construction instead of (SpecialMembershipFlag == 'Y')
    +  because it affords an added safeguard against writing the
    +  following by mistake: (SpecialMembershipFlag = 'Y'), which is
    +  syntactically correct but has a completely different meaning.
    +  SpecialMembershipFlag = 'Y' is an assignment statement that
    +  assigns a value of 'Y' to the variable SpecialMembershipFlag.
    +  If used in a conditional construct, it assigns the
    +  value of 'Y' as it is supposed to, but it also evaluates to
    +  true. The reason is that according to
    +  Standard C, anything that is not zero or NULL is considered
    +  true. If we follow the convention of
    +  ('Y' == SpecialMembershipFlag), we could not write
    +  ('Y' = SpecialMembershipFlag) by mistake and get away with it
    +  because the compiler will immediately alert us that we are
    +  attempting to assign a value to a constant (or a non-Lvalue).
    +  We would immediately know that we meant to use "==", which is
    +  an equality operator, as opposed to "=", which is an assignment
    +  operator.
    +
    +----------------------------------------------------------------+
*/

    if ('Y' == SpecialMembershipFlag)
    {
       MembershipFee = 2500.0;
    }
    else
    {
       MembershipFee = 0.0;
    }
}
void determineActivityFee(void)
{
    if (NumberOfCharges <= 6)
    {
       ActivityFee = 250.0;
    }

    if ((NumberOfCharges > 6) && (NumberOfCharges < 12))
    {
       ActivityFee = 500.0;
    }

    if (NumberOfCharges > 12)
    {
       ActivityFee = 750.0;
    }
}

void determineDiscountAmt(void)
{
    if (AverageCharges > 2500)
    {
       DiscountAmount = Discount;
    }
    else
    {
       DiscountAmount = 0;
    }
}
```

Figure 5.1   *Output for* `acech05.exe`

```
┌─────────────────────────────────────────────────────────────────────────────┐
│                                                                               │
│  Program Name: ACECH05.EXE                                      Page:  1      │
│      Run Date: 12/10/2000              Ace Billing                            │
│                                                                               │
│                                                                               │
│                                                                               │
│  Customer Name  Charges  Bill      Mbr Fee     Act Fee     Disc     Total Bill│
│                                                                               │
│                                                                               │
│  Austell-Wolfson  BA  5  $ 1000.00  $    0.00  $  250.00  $    0  $  1250.00  │
│  Otieno           DE  2  $  400.00  $ 2500.00  $  250.00  $  120  $  3030.00  │
│  VanVranken       GE  8  $ 1600.00  $ 2500.00  $  500.00  $   80  $  4520.00  │
│  Yates            SY  7  $ 1400.00  $ 2500.00  $  500.00  $ 1170  $  3230.00  │
│  Cook             CH  3  $  600.00  $    0.00  $  250.00  $    0  $   850.00  │
│  Stencil          BI  0  $    0.00  $ 2500.00  $  250.00  $ 1010  $  1740.00  │
│  Rockingham       ZE  3  $  600.00  $ 2500.00  $  250.00  $ 1230  $  2120.00  │
│  Zindar           SY  4  $  800.00  $    0.00  $  250.00  $    0  $  1050.00  │
│  McDowell         CH  9  $ 1800.00  $    0.00  $  500.00  $ 1000  $  1300.00  │
│  Grilo            RI  7  $ 1400.00  $    0.00  $  500.00  $  170  $  1730.00  │
│  Braxkston        HE  8  $ 1600.00  $ 2500.00  $  500.00  $  180  $  4420.00  │
│  Pope             SC  2  $  400.00  $ 2500.00  $  250.00  $ 1220  $  1930.00  │
│  Hardin           GA  2  $  400.00  $    0.00  $  250.00  $    0  $   650.00  │
│  Sonby            TO  2  $  400.00  $    0.00  $  250.00  $ 1000  $  -350.00  │
│  Murphy           RY  6  $ 1200.00  $ 2500.00  $  250.00  $ 1260  $  2690.00  │
│  Bate             ST  5  $ 1000.00  $ 2500.00  $  250.00  $   50  $  3700.00  │
│  Murray           GE  8  $ 1600.00  $    0.00  $  500.00  $  280  $  1820.00  │
│  Franklin         LO  1  $  200.00  $    0.00  $  250.00  $    0  $   450.00  │
│  Meyers           JA  4  $  800.00  $ 2500.00  $  250.00  $ 1240  $  2310.00  │
│  Kirk             JT  2  $  400.00  $    0.00  $  250.00  $ 1000  $  -350.00  │
│                         ────────   ─────────  ─────────  ──────  ──────────  │
│  ACE Club Totals     88  $17600.00  $25000.00  $ 6500.00  $11010  $ 38090.00  │
│                                                                               │
└─────────────────────────────────────────────────────────────────────────────┘
```

5.18.2   Output

The output is shown in Figure 5.1.

Chapter Summary

1. The `if` statement and `for` and `while` loops provide for conditional execution of a statement or a block of statements.
2. With the `if` statement, statements are executed only if the conditional expression is true; with the `switch` statement, the program chooses one block of statements; with `for` loops and `while` loops, the program executes a block of statements while a specified condition exists.
3. The conditional expression portion of the `if` statement generally uses C's relational operators: `==` (equal to), `!=` (not equal to), `>` (greater than), `>=` (greater than or equal to), `<` (less than), `<=` (less than or equal to).
4. In C, each expression has a value.
5. A relational expression that evaluates to true has a value of 1; one that evaluates to false has a value of 0.
6. Normally, use of the `=` inside the parentheses of an `if` statement indicates inadvertent use of the assignment operator in place of the `==` relational operator.
7. You use logical operators to establish the relationship among conditions in an `if` statement to test for more than one condition at the same time; each test must stand on its own.
8. The logical operators are && (and), ¦¦ (or), and ! (not).
9. Logical expressions are evaluated from left to right.
10. If subexpressions are linked by ¦¦, evaluation stops at the first one that evaluates to true; if they are linked by &&, evaluation stops at the first that evaluates to false.
11. The `else` statement allows the program to execute one program block or another (the latter of which may also be conditional).
12. The `if`, `else`, and `else if` statements can be compound or nested. Braces should be used to clarify which conditional statement goes with which. An `else` goes with the most recent `if` unless braces indicate otherwise.

13. You generally can use combinations of relational operators to achieve the same purpose as nested `if` statements.

14. The conditional operator is a compact way of expressing an `if . . . else` statement pair: "if the test condition is true, use the first expression, otherwise use the second one."

15. Program flow jumps to the `case` matching the `switch` expression.

16. The `switch` expression must be of integer type; `case` labels must be constants and must evaluate to unique values.

17. The program executes all statements in the chosen `switch` body until it comes to a `break` statement; if there is no break statement between one `case` label and the next, execution continues until a `break` is encountered.

18. If there is no matching `case`, program flow moves to the `default` label, or to the first statement after the `switch` body if there is none.

19. The `switch` statement produces smaller and faster code than the `if` statement.

20. Since relational operators take priority over the assignment operator, omitting the inner set of parentheses in this example will not give a correct result:

```
while((ch = getche()) != ESC)
```

21. In addition to the loop body and condition evaluation expression comprising `while` and `do-while` loops, the `for` loop contains initialization and update components.

22. Using `variable % mod + more` in a loop that increments by 1 each iteration causes values to cycle from `0 + more` through `mod + more - 1`. Using the division operator in the same situation with `variable / divisor` causes values to increase by 1 each `divisor` iteration, provided both numerator and divisor are integer.

23. You may omit any or all of the three components of the `for` statement. However, the two semicolons must be retained.

24. You can have a `for` loop or a `while` loop with no body—called a null statement. The null statement is used to delay program execution and conditional compilation and for other purposes. If you inadvertently insert a semicolon after the loop parentheses, you will introduce an error not signaled by the compiler.

25. If you use the increment or decrement operator to update in the condition evaluation component of a loop construction, the variable being incremented will be incremented during the loop iteration in which the test fails, even though the body of the loop is not executed.

26. The initialization and components of the `for` statement may have multiple initializations, each initialization is separated by comma operators. For multiple conditions, normally you must use logical operators, not comma operators.

27. The `do-while` loop first executes the loop body on each iteration and then tests the condition; the loop body will always be executed at least once.

28. Any of the loop types can be nested with one another or with `switch` statements.

29. The `continue` statement discontinues the current loop iteration and jumps to the next one. The `break` statement terminates the loop. Loops and `switch` statements are also prematurely terminated by a `return` statement inside a function.

30. When you use `continue` inside a `while` loop, program flow moves to the conditional evaluation expression. When you use `continue` with a `for` loop, the program first executes the update expression and *then* moves to the condition evaluation component.

31. With nested loops, the `continue` statement and `break` statement operate only on the loop of which they are a part.

32. If you have a `switch` statement nested within a `for` or `while` loop, you cannot use `break` within the `switch` statement body to terminate the loop; you can use `continue` to move to the next iteration, however.

33. The `goto` statement causes a jump to wherever in the code it finds the corresponding label provided the label is within the same function as the `goto` statement.

Review Questions

1. Does a single equal sign = have the same functionality as a double equal sign? What is the difference, if any?

2. List the three logical operators in the C language.

3. If an expression contains the logical operator ¦¦ (or), and the program establishes one of the conditions to be true, will it still test the second condition, or will it stop right there?

4. If an expression tests whether a variable is equal to 2, what will the expression test for if we change it by adding the ! (not) operator?

5. If the first condition of an `if-else` statement is true, does the `else` statement get executed?

6. Can a variable be used for a case label?

7. Can a `switch` statement test whether one value is greater than another? Can `switch` statements be used with float values?

8. Name one component that could be useful in a loop if you want the loop to only execute a certain number of times.

9. Is it true or false that the initialization component of a `for` loop statement is executed with each iteration of the loop?

10. The `do-while` loop tests the condition after executing the loop body (True or False).

11. Name one situation in programming where it is considered acceptable to use a `goto` statement.

12. Use an `if` statement to print out the correct letter grade based on the value of `courseAverage` and the following grading scale:

90–100	A
80–89	B
70–79	C
60–69	D
0–59	F

13. Use an `if-else` statement to do Review Question 12.

14. Use a `switch` construct to do Review Question 12.

15. Write a piece of code to identify a letter of the alphabet as: a consonant, a vowel, or not a valid letter. Use the `switch` construct to solve this problem. A vowel is any of the following letters of the alphabet: A, E, I, O, U: Assume that only uppercase letters are valid. (In Chapter 9, we will show you how to conveniently test for both uppercase and lowercase input.)

16. Write the pseudocode for the `while` statement. Identify which part is evaluated first. Specify what must be done to avoid an infinite loop.

17. Show the output of the following source code segments:
    a.
    ```
    k = 0;
    sum = 0;
    while (k < 5)
    {
      k++;
      sum += k;
      printf("Sum = %d   k = %d\n", sum, k);
    }
    ```
    b.
    ```
    k = 0;
    sum = 0;
    while (k < 5);
    {
      k++;
      sum += k;
      printf("Sum = %d   k = %d\n", sum, k);
    }
    ```
    c.
    ```
    k = 0;
    sum = 0;
    while (k++ < 5);
    {
      sum += k;
      printf("Sum = %d   k = %d\n", sum, k);
    }
    ```
    d.
    ```
    k = 5;
    while (k > 1)
        printf("Value of k is %d\n", k);
        k--;
    ```
    e.
    ```
    while (printf("k = 5") > 1);
    ```

18. Write the pseudocode for the `for` statement. Identify which part is evaluated first and which parts are repeated for the duration of the loop. Specify what must be done to avoid an infinite loop.

19. Show the output of the following program segments:
    a.
    ```
    for (k = 0, sum = 0;k < 5;k++)
    {
       sum += k;
       printf("Sum = %d   k = %d\n", sum, k);
    }
    ```
    b.
    ```
    k = 3;
    for (;k > 0; k--)
    {
       printf("Please, do it again\n");
    }
    ```
    c.
    ```
    for (col = 1, printf("      "); col <= 12;
         printf("%3d ", col), col++);
    ```
    d.
    ```
    for (row = 1; row <= 12; row++)
    {
       for (col = 1, printf("\n%4d ", row);
       col <= 12; col++)
       {
          printf("%3d ", row * col);
       }
    }
    ```
    e.
    ```
    for (;;)
    {
       printf("Please, Choose Menu item\n");
    }
    ```

20. Write the pseudocode for the `do-while` loop. Identify which part is evaluated first, which part is evaluated last, and the condition under which the loop will terminate.

21. Write a program to calculate and print out the product of the odd numbers from 1 to 15.

22. Write a program to calculate and print the product of the even numbers from 1 to 15.

23. Write a program to count the number of odd numbers as well as the number of even numbers between 1 and 100. Print those counts as well as the respective averages of the even and odd numbers.

Programming Exercises

The specifications of the programming assignments were introduced in Chapter 1, at which time you were to

- think through the solution to these problems.
- identify the modules that, once implemented, will solve the problem.
- prepare a hierarchy chart of all the modules.
- prepare pseudocode/flowchart for each module in the hierarchy chart.
- write the program stubs the same way we did with the ACE Billing system application.

By now you have learned how to declare scalar variables, assign values to these variables through assignment statements as well as through read statements `scanf()`, and print the values to these variables onto the standard output devices such as the screen or a redirected file. We have also covered all the control structures available in Standard C . Therefore, you have all the logical constructs—selection, iteration, and sequence—needed to solve any problem. We urge you to continue developing what you started in Chapter 1. If you have not started, we recommend that you start by applying the methodology presented in that chapter. We have helped you get started with some of the programming assignments by specifying only what can be done by this time.

Programming Assignment 5.1: Billing (batch processing)

Program Description

Use the Billing program from the previous chapter as the basis for a program that determines whether the customer will be eligible for a discount on his or her order according to the total cost of the merchandise ordered. Discount the total an appropriate amount. If the customer does not qualify for a discount, print only "Thank you for your business" at the bottom of the report.

Input: Use the input record layout given in Programming Assignment 1.1.

Output: Use the output report layout given in Programming Assignment 1.1.

Programming Assignment 5.2.1: Payroll Report (batch processing)

Program Description

Write the program that reads the data for this problem from a file using the standard input file redirection technique demonstrated in Section 5.18. You may need to resort to reading the character strings one character at a time and printing it before moving on to the next character.

Input: Use the input record layout given in Programming Assignment 1.3

Output: Use the output report layout given in Programming Assignment 1.3

Programming Assignment 5.2.2: Payroll Report (interactive processing)

Program Description

When we write the interactive version of this program, we must confine ourselves to scalar variables since we have not learned how to handle strings yet. Therefore, the type of report we can produce is limited to the summary of the total number of employees and the total salary for that department.

Input: Enter employee salary.

Output: (see Figure P5.2)

Figure P5.2   *Output for Programming Assignment 5.2.2*

Department Totals
The total number of employees:
The total salary of all employees:

Programming Assignment 5.3.1: OCS Payroll (batch processing)

Program Description

This is a continuation of Programming Assignment 1.3. You have learned enough Standard C to write a complete functioning program for this problem.

Input: Use the OCS payroll file record layout given in Programming Assignment 1.3

Output: Use the output report layout given in Programming Assignment 1.3.

Programming Assignment 5.3.2: OCS Payroll (interactive processing)

Program Description

This is a continuation of Programming Assignment 1.3. You have learned enough Standard C to write a complete functioning program for this problem. Write an interactive that presents a menu to the user (see Figure P5.3 on page 212) and then acts on their menu selection.

Design your own data entry screen to prompt the user for all the data required by the problem. Once the user selects menu item 1, the user is prompted for the rest of the data needed to calculate the employee's net pay.

Figure P5.3 *Menu for Programming Assignment 5.3.2*

```
OCS Payroll Systems
1.        Enter Data on the current employee
2.        Print data on the current employee
3.        Exit the system
```

Output: Design your own output report.

Programming Assignment 5.5: UNIX System Administration (batch processing)

Program Description

Write a program that reads a file in which fields are delimited by ":" and produces the report given below. The User Name cannot exceed 8 characters, the UID (User ID) and GID (Group ID) are both integers, the Full Name is limited to 25 characters, and the Shell is limited to 30 characters.

Input: As below; also on disk as pa3-5.dat.

```
bawolfso:104:500:Barry Austell-Wolfson:/usr/bin/ksh
jawolfso:105:500:Jennifer Austell-Wolfson:/usr/bin/ksh
jmnotieno:103:510:Joseph Mac-Omaya Otieno:/usr/bin/ksh
jrotieno:106:510:Joshua Raymond Otieno:/usr/bin/Csh
bnotieno:107:510:Benjamin Norman Otieno:/usr/bin/ksh
ldotieno:108:510:Lillian Danae Otieno:/usr/bin/ksh
```

Output: (see Figure P5.5)

Figure P5.5 *Output for Programming Assignment 5.5*

Program Name: PA3-5				Page: 1
Author: Your Name				Run Date: 12/19/2000
UNIX system administration report				
User Name	User ID	Group ID	Full Name	Shell
bjohnson	203	15	Bill Johnson	/usr/bin/ksh

Programming Assignment 5.8: Science and Engineering (Chemical Engineering—batch processing)

Program Description

[You can now generate the table by reading the data from a file.]

Input Data: Steam data file.

■ All the numbers are separated by at least one space.

Output Report Layout: The same output report layout specified in Programming Assignment 1.8.

Programming Assignment 5.9: Science and Engineering (Compiler Construction)

Program Description

Write the program that reads these Pascal statements one character at a time, analyzes them, and declares the statement as "Invalid Statement" or "Valid Statement."

The syntax diagram for the Pascal constructs shown in Figure P5.9 would prove useful.

Figure P5.9 *Syntax Diagram for Programming Assignment 5.9*

Assignment Statement:

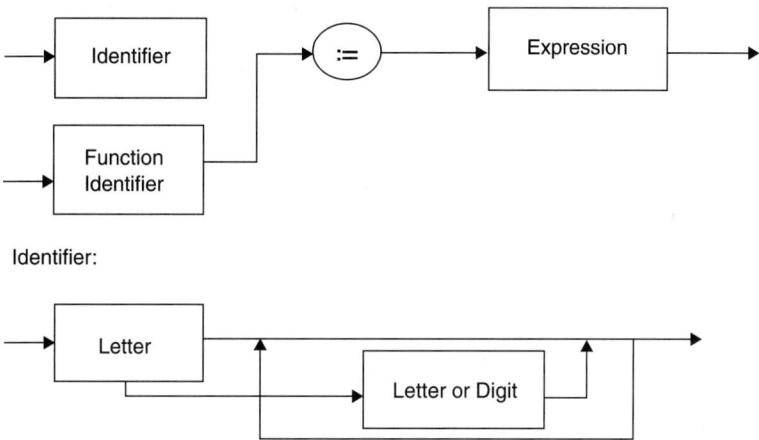

Identifier:

Fully implement this program. We have provided you with finite state automation figures in Figure P5.9 to help you in constructing the logic for syntax validation.

Input data:

```
B := 100;
B = 100;
B := 100
A := B;
C := 200;
B := B * 10- C;
Radius := 100;
Circumference := 2 * Pi * Radius;
Area Of Circle := 2 * Pi * Radius * Radius;
Area := 2 * Pi * Radius * Radius;
Programming := Data_Structures + Algorithms;
100 := 20 + Alpha;
Sum := Sum New_Data_Value;
Sum := Sum + New_Data_Value;
Sum := Sum + New_Data_Value
```

Output Report: Use the output report layout specified in Programming Assignment 3.9.

Programming Assignment 5.10: Science and Engineering (Mathematics—The Game of Life)

Program Description

Write a program that repeatedly

- prompts the user for the size of the grid.
- validates the input by making sure that the size specified does not exceed the screen dimensions.
- prompts the user for the number of generations.

The program uses this data to draw the square grid as many times as the number of generations specified. Each grid is to be filled with life forms in the diagonal cells starting from the northeast cell to the southeast cell for odd generations. The grid is to be populated with life forms in the diagonal cells starting from the northeast cell to the southwest cell for even generations. The program repeatedly asks the user for another grid size after drawing the previously requested grid until a grid size of zero is entered, at which point the program terminates.

Input Data:

```
Enter size of the grid (between 3 and 8, inclusively):
Enter the number of generations:
```

Output Report: Use the same report layout headings given for Programming Assignment 3.10. The formats of the reports themselves are shown in Figures P5.10A to P5.10D.

Figure P5.10A *Programming Assignment 5.10—Generation 0: Grid Size of 3*

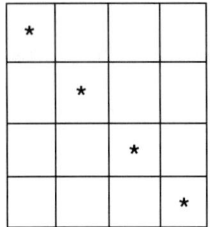

Figure P5.10B *Programming Assignment 5.10—Generation 1: Grid Size of 3*

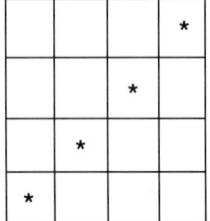

Figure P5.10C *Programming Assignment 5.10—Generation 0: Grid Size of 4*

Figure P5.10D *Programming Assignment 5.10—Generation 1: Grid Size of 4*

Programming Assignment 5.11.1: Distribution/ Packaging/Shipping (batch processing)

Program Description

Write the program to read data specified according to the input record specifications of Programming Assignment 1.11.

Input: You create, or use pa5-11.dat on disk.

Output: Produce the packing slip indicated in Programming Assignment 1.11.

Programming Assignment 5.11.2: Distribution/ Packaging/Shipping (interactive process)

Program Description (see Figure P5.11 on page 215)

Input: Prompt users for the following information when they select menu item 1.

```
Invoice number (5-digit number):
Invoice Date (mm/dd/yy) format:
```

Figure P5.11 *Program Description for Programming Assignment 5.11.2*

```
                OCS Publishing Distribution
1.        Enter data and accept specified defaults
2.        Print the Distribution Slip that is currently
          in the system
3.        Exit the system

Note: By using this system, you are accepting all the
system defaults.
```

```
Customer Number (6-digit number):
Order date (mm/dd/yy) format:
Sales Order number (5-digit number):
```

Output Report Layout: Use the packing slip specified above.

Programming Assignment 5.12: Invoicing (batch processing)

Program Description

Write the program to read data specified according to the input record specifications of Programming Assignment 1.12.

Input: You create, or use pa5-12.dat on disk.

Output: Produce the Invoice specified in Programming Assignment 1.12.

Programming Assignment 5.16.1: EDI Claims Report (batch processing)

Program Description

Write a program that requests the Claim Number, Provider Number, Patient Last Name, Patient First Name, Charge, and Status for an unlimited number of claims. A zero entered for the Claim Number should indicate that data entry is complete.

This time, use an integer for the Status, and have the user enter 1 for accepted and 0 for rejected. Your program should then be able to calculate the total accepted charges, the total rejected charges, and the overall total charges.

Use the data below to test your program; also test the program with data of your own. Make sure your program can handle an invalid charge entry. Have the user reenter the charge until a valid number is entered.

Also notice that even though you had the user enter 0 or 1 for the claim status, the report still shows the more user-friendly ACCEPT or REJECT.

To produce this report using the knowledge base we have through Chapter 5, it is necessary to read the data from a file using redirection. You may use the same technique covered in Section 5.18.

Tables P5.16A1 and P5.16B1 show the input record layouts and Figure P5.16A1 shows the output report layout for this programming assignment.

Table P5.16A1 *Input Record Layout for Programming Assignment 5.16.1: Claims Submitter Record*

Claims Submitter Record Layout			
Field Name	**Size**	**Data Attribute**	**No. of Decimal Positions**
SubmitterId	7	Char	
SubmitterLastName	20	Char	
SubmitterFirstName	15	Char	

Table P5.16B1   *Input Record Layout for Programming Assignment 5.16.1: Claims Record*

Claims Record Layout			
Field Name	*Size*	*Attribute*	*No. of Decimal Positions*
Claim Number	2	Integer	
Provider Number	7	long	
Patient Last Name	20	char	
Patient First Name	15	char	
Charge	5	float	2
Status	1	char (0 or 1)	

Figure P5.16A1   *Output Report Layout for Programming Assignment 5.16.1*

```
    **********************************************************
    Submitter: AA12124 - Smith, Jack D
    Claim Editing Notice

    Claim   Provider   Patient Name            Charge   Status
    No.     No.
    1       3445433    Simmons     Paul         60.00   ACCEPT
    2       3445433    Carr        Gene         45.00   ACCEPT
    3       3445433    Criss       Vincent      80.00   REJECT
    4       3334434    Kraizee     Guy         100.00   ACCEPT
                       Total Accept Charges: xxx.xx
                       Total Reject Charges: xxx.xx
                             Total Charges: xxx.xx
    ***********************End of Report***********************
```

Programming Assignment 5.16.2: EDI Claims Report (interactive process)

Program Description

Write a program that prompts the user for the following data from the keyboard: Charge and Status. The program is to determine whether the claim is accepted or rejected and is to accumulate the total charges rejected, the total charges accepted, and the net of all the charges. The program is to continue prompting for data until the user signals the end of file (for example, press `Ctrl` `Z` or `F6` on the PC and `Ctrl` `D` in UNIX).

Input Data:

```
Enter the Charge Amount:
Enter the Charge Status:
```

Output: (see Figure P5.16A2)

Figure P5.16A2   *Output for Programming Assignment 5.16.2*

```
                    Total Accept Charges: xxx.xx
                    Total Reject Charges: xxx.xx
                          Total Charges: xxx.xx
    ***********************End of Report***********************
```

Programming Assignment 5.20.1: Programa Pro Rata (batch process)

Program Description

This is a continuation of Programming Assignment 1.20. Modify the program so that it reads data from all the branch offices according to the format given below, calculates the prorated cost for each tire for each customer, and prints the result for each customer.

Input Record Layout: (see Table P5.20A1)

Table P5.20A1 *Input Record Layout for Programming Assignment 5.20.1*

OCS Tire Services			
Field Name	*Size*	*Attribute*	*No. of Decimal Positions*
Tread depth now			
Tread depth when new			
Price of a new tire			
The mounting and balancing charge			
The state tax rate			

Input Data: You create, or use pa5-20-1.dat on disk.

Output Report Layout: Use the output report layout specified in Programming Assignment 1.20

Programming Assignment 5.20.2: Programa Pro Rata (interactive process)

Program Description

This is a continuation of Programming Assignment 1.20. Modify the program so that it reads data from all the branch offices according to the format given in Figure P5.20A2 and calculates the prorated cost for each tire for each customer and prints the result for each customer.

Figure P5.20A2 *Input for Programming Assignment 5.20.2*

```
            OCS Tire Service Center

1.    Enter data about your tire
2.    Calculate and print the pro-rated cost
3.    Exit the system
```

Input: (see Figure P5.20A2)

Prompt users for the following information when they select menu item 1:

- Tread depth now (e.g., 3 mm)
- Tread depth when the tire was new (e.g., 9 mm)
- Price of a new tire (e.g., $21.00)
- Mounting and balancing charge (e.g., $2.50)
- State tax rate (program useful in any state) (e.g., 4%)

Output: Use the same output report layout specified in Programming Assignment 1.20.

Programming Assignment 5.21: Nation's Economy (batch processing)

Program Description

This is a continuation of Programming Assignment 1.21. Modify the program to read the data from a standard file having the following format or record layout:

- Weight of a jar of peanut butter
- Weight of a jar of jelly
- Weight of a loaf of bread
- Cost of a jar of peanut butter
- Cost of a jar of jelly
- Cost of a loaf of bread

The file is a typical input file for a Standard C program. All the numbers are separated by at least one whitespace.

Output Report Layout: Use the same output report layout you designed for Programming Assignment 1.21.

Programming Assignment 5.22: Police Department (batch processing)

Program Description

This is a continuation of Programming Assignment 1.22. Write the program to read the data from the standard input file and produce the report for the City of Snellville.

Input Record Layout: Each of the data items is separated by at least one whitespace. The layout is free-form.

Output: Same as the one specified in Programming Assignment 1.22.

CHAPTER 6

Arrays

OBJECTIVES

- To learn the difference between scalar and aggregate data types
- To learn how to create and initialize an aggregate data type composed of elements of the same scalar data type
- To become familiar with differences in methods of partial array initialization
- To learn to access, manipulate, and print data stored in arrays
- To see how arrays can be automatically sized and understand the inalterable aspect of array sizing
- To see the effect of exceeding array boundaries
- To learn what the `sizeof` operator produces when applied to nonscalar data types
- To become familiar with multidimensional arrays and see how they are stored in memory
- To see how to use loops to traverse arrays and sort with them
- To see how to use nested loops to traverse multidimensional arrays in different ways

NEW TERMS

array	multidimensional array	selection sort
bubble sort	one-dimensional array	subscript
element	row/column major addressing	
index	scalar variable	

Suppose you wanted to store, evaluate, and manipulate a single piece of data such as high temperature or total traffic flow or total gross revenue for each day during an entire calendar year. You *could* create a separate variable for each day:

```
int jan1, jan2, jan3 . . .
```

Then, whether you read in data from a file or from the keyboard, you would need 365 separate input statements. You would need 365 separate statements to manipulate the data and 365 conversion specifiers and arguments to print it out. What a mess! Fortunately, there is an easier way—arrays.

The variables we have discussed to this point have been what we call *scalar variables.* When we declare an int

```
int num;
```

we reserve 2 bytes in the computer's memory that we can access by simply using the variable's name (the computer, of course, treats this name as just an address):

```
num = 5;
```

Figure 6.1   *Memory Reservation in Array: Initialization or Separate Assignment Statements*

31	28	31	30	31	30	31	31	30	31	30	31
days[0]	days[1]	days[2]	days[3]	days[4]	days[5]	days[6]	days[7]	days[8]	days[9]	days[10]	days[11]

Figure 6.2   *Memory Reservation on a Bit Level*

0	0	0	0	0	0	0	0

high-order byte

0	0	0	1	1	1	1	1

low-order byte

An *array* is an example of an aggregate, rather than scalar, data type. With one declaration, we reserve a whole block of memory, the block consisting of a series of data objects of the array's type in contiguous memory locations. For example, when we declare the array

```
int days[12];
```

we reserve 24 contiguous bytes in RAM (assuming a PC or other platform with 2 bytes for an `int`)—space enough for 12 `ints`. Each of these individual `ints` is referred to as an *element* of the days array.

Likewise, when we declare

```
long double molecule_size[20];
```

we reserve 200 contiguous bytes (assuming a PC or other platform with 10 bytes per `long double`), with 20 `long double` variables that we can then access by array name and element number rather than by individual name.

When we assign values to elements of the array, either in the declaration statement,

```
int days[12] = {31, 28, 31, 30, 31, 30, 31, 31, 30, 31, 30, 31};
```

or by separate assignment statement,

```
days[0] = 31;
```

we place values into those bytes reserved by the array declaration. Figures 6.1 and 6.2 show how the array looks in memory after these assignments.

6.1   ARRAY DECLARATION

We declare an array with a type, a variable name, and the number of array elements, enclosed in brackets.

```
long byte_count[10];
```

The number in brackets following the array name is called a *subscript* or *index.* In the declaration, the subscript number tells the compiler how many spaces in memory to reserve.

 In the array declaration, the subscript must not contain any variables, only a constant or constant expression.

```
int contribution[365]; /* OK */

float salaries[MAX_EMPLOYEES * 2]; /* manifest constant and constant: OK */

int num = 5;
int val[num]; /* variable: error! */
```

Allowable constants include integer constants, character constants, enumeration constants (see Chapter 13), and the `sizeof` operator with any operand, even a variable or type:

```
int quantity;
int num[20];
int val[sizeof(num) / sizeof(quantity)];
```

Even though num is a variable, the compiler knows before program execution what its size in bytes is. The following would be identical to the last line above:

```
int val[sizeof(num) / sizeof(int)];
```

Two rules to mention at this point:

 The sizeof operator, applied to an array name, gives the number of bytes in the entire array. Once declared, the size of the array cannot be changed.

See Chapter 15 for changeable on-the-fly memory block reservations.

As with scalar variables, you can combine declarations into a single statement, either with other array variables or with scalar variables of the same type:

```
int num, val[5]; /* scalar and array int variables */
float hours[3], minutes[3], seconds[3];
```

However, we recommend against this practice for reasons of clarity.

6.2 ASSIGNMENT OF ARRAY ELEMENTS

We saw earlier that when used in connection with an array declaration, the bracketed subscript number following the array name tells the computer how many elements the array contains, and hence how many total contiguous bytes of memory to reserve. In any other context, the subscript has a different meaning. Anywhere else, the subscript number is a means of specifying a particular array element, either to assign it a value or to use its value:

```
int foreground[8]; /* declaration */
foreground[4] = 37; /* assignment of element */
color = foreground[4] + (background[4] * 16); /* use of element in assignment */
```

 The first element of an array has a subscript of 0, not 1.

Thus, max_days[3] refers to the fourth, not the third, element of the following max_days array:

```
int max_days[12]; /* declaration of 12-int array */
max_days[0] = 31; /* assign 1st element */
max_days[4] = 31; /* assign 5th element */
max_days[12] = 31 /* incorrect! outside array boundaries */
```

6.2.1 Exceeding Array Boundaries

You might suspect that the final statement in the last example would generate some sort of compiling error or run-time error. If so, you would be wrong. The computer in this case would blithely and without complaint store the value 31 in whatever 2 bytes happened to be after the last element of the array. To convince the skeptical among you, we've included a short program that demonstrates this surprising behavior, too_far.c.

 **6.1 too_far.c**

```
/* too_far.c */

/* no error-checking on out-of-bounds array assignment */

#include <stdio.h>

int main(void)
{
    int i;
    int second[3] = {4, 5, 6};
    int first[3] = {1, 2, 3};
```

```
    printf("&first[2]: %u\n", &first[2]);
    printf("&first[3]: %u\n", &first[3]); /* same address as next 1 */
    printf("&second[0]: %u\n", &second[0]);

    for (i = 0; i < 3; i++)
    {
    /* assign values to first[3], first[4], first[5] */
       first[3 + i] = 7 + i;

    /* now see second[ ] values */
       printf("second[%d] = %d\n", i, second[i]);
    }
    second[-1] = -99;
    printf("second[-1] = %d and first[2] = %d\n", second[-1],
       first[2]);
}
```

Here's the output on our system:

```
&first[2]: FFEE
&first[3]: FFF0
&second[0]: FFF0
second[0] = 7
second[1] = 8
second[2] = 9
second[-1] = -99 and first[2] = -99
```

As you can see from the addresses of first[2] (the last element of the first array) and second[0], the computer has stored the two arrays right next to one another (see Appendix B, on memory, to see why this is so). To the extent then that the designations first[3], first[4], and first[5] are valid despite their all being past the array boundaries, they would be the same address locations as second[0], second[1], and second[2]. Assigning values to first[3], first[4], and first[5] would be the same as assigning them to the three elements of second. And that's just what happens. When we assign values to elements of first beyond its boundaries, the computer doesn't bat an electronic eye. As you can see from the last pair of statements, the same goes for negative subscripts—which, by the way, are permitted in Standard C.

(Note that the above result is compiler dependent. Try testing this on yours. The result turns on whether one array is stored in memory right after the other and on the order in which they are assigned memory locations.)

There will be times when you want to go beyond the bounds of the array and intentionally do something like what we did in too_far.c. That's why C allows this usage. For example, you will see a legitimate use for negative subscripts when we cover pointers in Chapter 7—we can set a pointer to the middle of an array and then access an earlier element by a negative subscript, applying array notation to the pointer. Be wary of this! As one of our reviewers wisely pointed out, some things in programming, as in life, should not be done even though they can be done. Apart from the limited use in array subscripts as alternative notation for pointers, negative subscripts should be considered "armed and dangerous."

But if your source code unintentionally exceeds the array's limits, you may have a devil of a time finding the error. If you suspect this problem, you can pinpoint the error with your compiler's debug or inspect utility. But you often will be totally unsuspecting of this sort of error. You may end up overwriting program data, or even code. As is often the case with C, you are given plenty of rope to hang yourself with.

The typical example of inadvertently exceeding the array boundaries, and a common error, is assigning a value just past the final array element. The error generally arises from forgetting that with, for example,

```
int num[10];
```

the final element is num[9], not num[10]. Or it is caused by careless loop counters:

```
int num[10];
for (i = 0; i <= 10; i++)
. . .
```

This common error is referred to as the "fence-post error"—the name arising from the oft-incorrectly given answer to the riddle "How long is a fence that has 10 fence posts, each 10 feet apart?"

6.3 USE OF ARRAY ELEMENTS

You can place the value of an array element into another element of the same or a different array by assignment, just as you can with any variable:

```
int num[2], val[2];
num[0] = num[1] = 2;
val[0] = num[1];
```

In fact, once the array declaration has been made and a value assigned to an element, either at the time of declaration or later by separate assignment statement, you can use the element in the same fashion as you could any variable of the same type:

```
val[5] = num[3] * 2;
quantity = val[5]/num[3] + 17;
```

6.4 USING A for LOOP FOR ARRAY TRAVERSAL

Listing 6.1, too_far.c, illustrates the use of a for loop as a means of traversing an array. This usage is extremely common. We can initialize the loop counter to 0 (the first element), and then use the increment operator to continue through the loop until we reach the final element. For instance:

```
int temperature[7];
int i;

for (i = 0; i < 7; i++)
{
   scanf("%d", &temperature[i]);
   printf("Temperature on day %d: %d\n", i + 1, temperature[i]);
}
```

Remember that the last element of this array is temperature[6]. That is why the for loop counter is set to run from 0 until i is *less than* 7. Alternatively, we could have written the loop this way:

```
for (i = 1; i <= 7; i++) /* or i=1; i<8; or i=0; i<=6 */
{
   scanf("%d", &temperature[i - 1]);
   printf("Temperature on day %d: %d\n", i, temperature[i - 1];
}
```

We favor the "0 . . . <" formulation over the "1 . . . <=" or "0 . . . <=" formulations, but whichever you choose, use the same one consistently in all your coding to avoid mistakes.

Let's take a programming example that uses a for loop to traverse an array. The listing, datearry.c, is a more efficient version of the date-checking programs we've already seen: Listing 5.1, if_date.c, which uses if statements, and Listing 5.6, gooddate.c, which uses switch statements to accomplish what we do with arrays here.

 **Listing 6.2 datearry.c**

```
/* datearry.c */

/* use arrays to determine whether date entered interactively is valid */

#include <stdio.h>

int main(void)
{
```

```
    int max_days[13] = {0, 31, 29, 31, 30, 31, 30, 31, 31, 30, 31, 30, 31};
    int month, day, year;
    char error = 0;

    printf("Enter month (MM), day (DD) and year (YYYY)\n"
       "Pressing the [Enter] key after each\n");
    scanf("%d%d%d", &month, &day, &year);

    if (month < 1 || month > 12)
       error = 1;
    else
    {
       if (month == 2)
          if ((year % 4) || (!(year % 100) && (year % 1000)))
             max_days[1] = 28;
       if (day < 1 || day > max_days[month])
          error = 1;
    }

    if (error)
       printf("%d/%d/%02d is an invalid date\n", month, day, year % 100);
    else
       printf("The date is %d/%d/%02d\n", month, day, year % 100);
}
```

Note that we could have written the array this way:

```
int max_days[12] = {31, 29, 31, 30, 31, 30, 31, 31, 30, 31, 30, 31};
. . .
if (day < 1 || day > max_days[month - 1])
```

However, using up a couple of extra bytes to avoid the potential of forgetting to put "–1" in the indices and to allow us to view the problem in the commonsense everyday way is worth the tradeoff.

6.5   SORTING

We can make use of a nested for loop to not only traverse an array, but also at the same time, to sort its elements. Listing 6.3 uses a technique known as the **selection sort** to arrange in ascending order a series of numbers input by the user.

We proceed this way. We read the numbers into an array. Then we loop from the first array element to the last. For each such element, we compare its value to the value stored at each succeeding array element. That is, if we have a 20-element array, for the first iteration, we compare element 0 first to element 1, then to element 2, then to element 3, and so on through the last element, element 19. If the value of the comparison base element is less than the value we're comparing it to, we swap values (for example, if array element 0 is less than array element 4, element 0 is assigned the value of element 4 and vice versa).

After any such swaps, any further comparisons in the same iteration are made with the new lowest number. This way, in the first iteration, the lowest number is placed in array element 0; in the second iteration, the lowest of the remaining numbers is placed in element 1; and so on.

 **Listing** 6.3 **selectn.c**

```
/* selectn.c */

/* use simple selection sort with nested for loop to
   sort input numbers */

#include <stdio.h>

#define MAX 20
```

```
int main(void)
{
   int entries = 0; /* number of values input */
   int temp;
   int value[MAX];
   int i, j;

   printf("Type in up to %d integer numbers\n Type a letter to quit\n", MAX);
   while(scanf("%d", &value[entries]))
      if (entries++ > MAX)
         break;

   for (i = 0; i < entries - 1; i++) /* for each # but last */
      for (j = i + 1; j < entries; j++) /* from # after that to the last # */

      /* if lower value found, swap with current minimum value */
         if (value[j] < value[i])
         {
            temp = value[i];
            value[i] = value[j];
            value[j] = temp;
         }

   /* print sorted numbers */
   printf("Numbers sorted in ascending order:\n");
   for (i = 0; i < entries; i++)
      printf("%d  ", value[i]);
}
```

With only a slight alteration, you can sort in descending rather than ascending order: simply replace

```
if (value[j] < value[i])
```

with

```
if (value[j] > value[i])
```

You can make the process more efficient, and depending on the data, reduce the number of comparisons by using a ***bubble sort*** instead of a selection sort. In addition to the following listing for an example of bubble sorting, see Listing 6.7, acech06a.c.

 **Listing** **6.4 bubble.c**

```
/* bubble.c */

/* use simple bubble sort with nested for loop to sort input numbers */

#include <stdio.h>

void main(void)
{

   int list[10] = {99, -3, 4, 32, 8, 7, 38, 83, 478, 3};
   int k, temp;
   int more = 1;

   printf("unsorted list: ");
   for (k = 0; k < 10; k++)
   printf("%d ", list[k]);
   putchar('\n');

   while (more)
```

```
    {
        more = 0;
        for (k = 0; k < 9; k++)
        {
            if (list[k] > list[k + 1])
            {
                more = 1;
                temp = list[k];
                list[k] = list[k + 1];
                list[k + 1] = temp;
            }
        }
    }

    printf("\nsorted list: ");
    for (k = 0; k < 10; k++)
        printf("%d ", list[k]);
    putchar('\n');
}
```

As soon as we cover other topics, you can make the sorting in selectn.c and bubble.c more sophisticated. Once you learn how to create functions (Chapter 8), you can turn this program into a sort function to which you could pass the number of items to sort and whether to sort in ascending or descending order. Once we cover strings in Chapter 9, you could sort names or addresses or other such items as well as numbers. Once we discuss file operations in Chapter 14, you can provide for the input to sort to be read from a file rather than entered interactively.

On the other hand, you may not want to get carried away with enhancing the sorting mechanisms found in selectn.c and bubble.c. The algorithms that underlie these two sorts are simple and easy to understand, but they are not efficient methods of sorting very large amounts of data. For such tasks, we will use linked lists and binary trees (see Chapter 15).

6.6   ARRAY INITIALIZATION

Assignment of array elements in the array declaration statement is made by surrounding the elements with braces and separating each element with commas:

```
int max_days[12] = {31, 28, 31, 30, 31, 30, 31, 31, 30, 31, 30, 31};
```

 Except at time of declaration, you cannot assign a value to more than one array element at a time.

You cannot use the brace assignment device, nor can you copy the values from one array into another array by a single assignment statement:

```
int num[5];
int val[5] = {6, 13, 23, 53, 33};
num[5] = {17, 9, 20, 5, 3}; /* error! can't use brace assignment postdeclaration */
num = val; /* error! */
num[5] = val[5]; /* ok, won't work; assigns whatever is 2 bytes past last
        element of num to whatever is 2 bytes past val */
num[4] = val[4]; /* ok, but only assigns value of last
                    element of num to last element of val */
for (i = 0; i < 5; i++)
    num[i] = val[i]; /* correct method! */
```

You can use the const keyword to create an array of data that the program cannot later alter (see Chapter 10 for a discussion of const):

```
const int days_per_month[12] = {31, 28, 31, 30, 31, 30, 31, 31, 30, 31, 30, 31};
```

6.6.1   Omitting the Subscript in an Initialization Statement

If you omit the subscript in an initialization statement, the compiler automatically sizes the array according to the number of elements between the braces. The following declaration is treated by the compiler precisely the same as the last `max_days` declaration above:

```
int max_days[] = {31, 28, 31, 30, 31, 30, 31, 31, 30, 31, 30, 31};
```

Here, the subscript represents the number of months in the year. Since you presumably know how many elements there are in this particular array, you may want to use a subscript number to promote clarity. However, if you just have a long list of elements, you may want to intentionally leave the subscript number out of the array declaration to avoid miscounting the number of elements. In that case, you can use the `sizeof` operator to carry you through a `for` loop:

```
int height[] = {22, 28, 34, 343, 322,
    103, 5, 19, 193, 99, 204, 303, 203, 2, 389, 202};
int i;
for (i = 0; i < sizeof(height) / sizeof(int); i++)
    printf("box %d has a height of %d centimeters\n", i + 1, height[i]);
```

As we noted earlier, the `sizeof` operator, applied to an array name, gives us the number of bytes in the entire array. Dividing that by the number of bytes each element takes up gives us the number of elements.

You may omit the subscript number only with a simultaneous declaration and assignment, not with a simple declaration alone:

```
long bow[]; /* error! */
```

6.6.2   Prohibited Element Initialization

 In the initialization of any of the elements of an array, you may use only constants or constant expressions.

```
int num[3] = {117 * 4, 320 / 4 + 2, 8};
```

Allowable constants include floating point constants, integer constants, character constants, enumeration constants (see Chapter 13), and the `sizeof` operator with any operand, even a variable or type.

 You may not include variables in the initialization of an array.

```
int val = 18;
int num[2] = {val, 13}; /* error! */
```

6.6.3   Partial and Excess Initialization

You may assign fewer than all the elements in the declaration statement. If you declare an array to be `static` or external (both of which concepts we will learn about in Chapter 10), each element not assigned in the declaration statement is initialized to zero. Otherwise, they will have whatever garbage value happens to be at the respective memory locations. Contrast Figure 6.3 with Figure 6.4.

```
static int num[8] = {3, 6, 4, 5, 7};
```

```
int val[8] = {3, 6, 4, 5, 7};
```

You may skip elements only at the end of the array, however. The following is illegal:

```
int num[8] = {3,, 4, 7, 8}; /* error! */
```

Figure 6.3 *Initialization of Static Array*

num

3	6	4	5	7	0	0	0

Figure 6.4 *Initialization of Nonstatic Array*

val

3	6	4	5	7	???	???	???

But C allows you to place a comma after the last item if you wish. Both of the following are valid:

```
int num[ ] = {1, 2, 3};
int num_comma[ ] = {1, 2, 3,};
```

We are torn between saying that the trailing comma style is a sloppy way to code and suggesting you use it because it might prevent problems if you later decide to add elements to your declaration. There is no problem with an array of scalar variables; if you try to add another value to `num` without inserting a comma after 3, you will get an error message:

```
int num[ ] = {1, 2, 3 4}; /* error! Expected ',' */
```

But because of string concatenation, the following error would not be caught (note the inadvertent absence of a comma between the third and fourth elements of the array):

```
char *string_array[ ] = {"one", "two", "three" "four"};
printf("%s", string_array[2]);
```

```
threefour
```

We will explain the array-of-strings concept in the next chapter.

You will get an error if you try to initialize with more values than there are elements in the array:

```
int val[3] = {1, 2, 3, 4}; /* error! */
```

The trailing comma does not count as an additional element. Thus, in the declaration of `num_comma` above, the following yields 3, not 4:

```
sizeof(num_comma) / sizeof(int)
```

6.7   MULTIDIMENSIONAL ARRAYS

All the preceding examples involved arrays with a single subscript. We call this a ***one-dimensional array***. You can also have ***multidimensional arrays.*** Arrays can have two, three, or even more dimensions, though use of more than three dimensions would be nearly as rare as travel through the figurative fourth dimension, time.

With a two-dimensional array, we have an array of arrays. That is, we have a series of arrays each of which contains subarrays as elements. For instance,

```
int num[5][4];
```

is a five-element array, each element of which consists of an array of 4 `ints`.

You can *think* of the two-dimensional array as being made up of rows and columns, with the first subscript representing the rows and the second representing the columns, as in Figure 6.5.

Figure 6.5 *Conceptual Visualization of Two-Dimensional Array*

num[0][0]	num[0][1]	num[0][2]	num[0][3]
num[1][0]	num[1][1]	num[1][2]	num[1][3]
num[2][0]	num[2][1]	num[2][2]	num[2][3]
num[3][0]	num[3][1]	num[3][2]	num[3][3]
num[4][0]	num[4][1]	num[4][2]	num[4][3]

Figure 6.6 *Actual Memory Layout of Two-Dimensional Array*

num[0][0]	num[0][1]	num[0][2]	num[0][3]	num[1][0]	num[1][1]	num[1][2]	num[1][3]	. . .

Actually, however, the computer stores all these elements as contiguous bytes, with one complete subarray following another. (See Figure 6.6.)

However you choose to visualize a two-dimensional array, you can see that the right-most subscript varies fastest. This structure, which is used for most but not all programming languages, is sometimes referred to as ***row/column major addressing.*** One consequence of the setup is that with the often-used device, an array of strings (discussed in the next chapter), the characters of each string are found one right after the other in memory, and one string comes right after another.

6.7.1 Multidimensional Arrays and the `sizeof` Operator

The `sizeof` operator, applied to the name of a two-dimensional array, gives us the number of bytes in the entire two-dimensional array. In this num example,

```
sizeof(num)
```

would have a value of 40 if each int is 2 bytes. The `sizeof` operator can also be applied to any of the subarrays, so that

```
sizeof(num[0])
```

would have a value of 8 if each int is 2 bytes, and

```
sizeof(num) / sizeof(num[0])
```

would tell us how many subarrays are in num.

6.7.2 Initialization of Two-Dimensional Array

In a two-dimensional array, assignment at declaration is made with double sets of braces:

```
int num[5][4] =
{
    {3, 17, 83, 3},
    {34, 34, 83, 8},
    {22, 3, 33, 251},
    {1, 13, 22, 131},
    {123, 1, 3, 3}
};
```

Note the commas between the sets of braces. Actually, we could have omitted the inside braces. With a single set of braces, the elements are just filled in sequence of memory location. The only difference comes if fewer than all elements in a subarray are initialized, a topic we now turn to.

6.7.3 Partial Initialization of Two-Dimensional Array

Apart from the double-brace method's allowing us to keep better track of which value goes in which row and column, the only difference between the single- and double-brace methods comes when we initialize with fewer than all array elements. Observe the difference between the following examples, and their depictions in Figures 6.7 and 6.8.

```
static int num[5][4] =
{
    {3, 3, 3, 3},
    {3, 3, 3},
    {3, 3},
    {3},
};
static int num[5][4] = {3, 3, 3, 3, 3, 3, 3, 3, 3, 3, 3};
```

Figure 6.7 *Initailization of Two-Dimensional Array: Double-Brace Method*

3	3	3	3
3	3	3	0
3	3	0	0
3	0	0	0
0	0	0	0

Figure 6.8 *Initailization of Two-Dimensional Array: Single-Brace Method*

3	3	3	3
3	3	3	3
3	3	3	0
0	0	0	0
0	0	0	0

(We used `static` in both cases to ensure unfilled elements are set to zero rather than to whatever random value is found at the respective memory location.)

If you use the double-brace method and put too many elements within any of the inner braces, you will get an error message. The extra elements do not simply get pushed down into the next row:

```
int num[3][3] =
{
    {5, 7, 9, 10}, /* error here */
    {2, 5},
    {3, 17, 83}
};
```

Whether you use the single- or double-brace method, the rule for partial initialization is the same as for one-dimensional arrays; omissions may occur only at the end:

```
int number[3][3] = {1, 2, 3, 4, 5, 6, 7, 8, 9}; /* OK */
int num_oops[3][3] = {1,, 3,, 5,, 7,, 9}; /* error! */
int num[3][3] = {8, 2}; /* OK */
int quantity[3][3] =
{
    {1, 9, 3},
    {3, 4, 8},
    {4, 6, 8}
}; /* OK */
int qty[3][3] =
{
    {1, 9, 3},
    {3},
    {4, 6}
}; /* OK */
int qty_oops[3][3] =
{
    {1,, 3}, /* error */
    {3, 5},
    {4, 6, 8}
};
int amt[3][3] =
```

```
{
   {0},
   {2, 5, 8}
}; /* OK */
int amt_oops[3][3] =
{
   {}, /* error */
   {1, 2, 3},
   {4, 6, 8}
};
```

Notice in particular the first subarray of the next-to-last example. You can use a single zero value as a temporary placeholder for a subarray whose elements will be assigned postdeclaration later in the program. When we come to strings (in Chapter 7 you will find that the same holds for an array of strings. *When you initialize fewer than all strings in an array of pointers to* char, *you can use blank strings (*" "*) as a temporary placeholder for uninitialized elements.*

```
char * menuItems[] =
{
   "Exit", "Text Demo", "PCX Demo", "", "Drawing Demo",
};
```

6.7.4   Nested for Loops and the Multidimensional Array

Just as a for loop is a common tool for traversing a one-dimensional array, so is the nested for loop frequently used to traverse a two-dimensional array:

```
int num[4][3] =
{
   {10, 11, 12},
   {20, 21, 22},
   {30, 31, 32},
   {40, 41, 42}
};

int row, col;

for (row = 0; row < 4; row++)
{
   for (col = 0; col < 3; col++)
      printf("%3d", num[row][col]);
   putchar('\n');
}
```

The output:

```
10 11 12
20 21 22
30 31 32
40 41 42
```

Since the two-dimensional array is really a contiguous series of bytes in memory, there are instances in which you can treat the entire business as a single-dimensional array. This treatment can allow for faster, more efficient manipulation of data. For example, the following program writes data diagonally across the array with a single for loop. The visual part of this program works only on a PC.

 **Listing** **6.5 skip.c**

```
/* skip.c */

/* treat two-dimensional array as one-dimensional */

#define ROWS 25
#define COLS 80
```

```
#include <stdio.h>
#include <string.h> /* movedata */
#include <dos.h> /* segread, struct SREGS */

int main(void)
{
   struct SREGS segs;
   unsigned video_seg;

   /* set to all 0's since static */
   static int screen[ROWS][COLS * 2];
   int i;
   int ch = 'A' + 0x4F00; /* 'A' in white on red */

   segread(&segs); /* determine program data segment address */
   video_seg = 0xB800;


   for (i = 0; i < ROWS * 2 * COLS; i += (COLS + 3) * 2)
      ((int *)screen)[i] = ch;

   /* copy entire screen array to video segment */

   movedata(segs.ds, (unsigned)screen, video_seg, 0, ROWS *
      COLS * 2);
}
```

On a PC, this program writes the letter A in white on red across the screen diagonally. (For the nonarray mechanics of the program, see Appendix C.) All you need to focus on here is

```
for (i = 0; i < ROWS * 2 * COLS; i += (COLS + 3) * 2)
   ((int *)screen)[i] = ch;
```

This statement starts at the beginning of the two-dimensional array, screen, and moves 86 bytes at a time in memory. Each time it does so, it effectively moves to the next row, three int columns to the right. Once we cover pointers in the next chapter, you'll see that we could have accomplished the same thing somewhat more straightforwardly this way:

```
int *ptr = (int *)screen;
for (i = 0; i < ROWS * 2 * COLS; i += (COLS + 3) * 2)
   *(ptr + i) = ch;
```

6.8   MORE THAN TWO DIMENSIONS

The same logic we saw for two-dimensional arrays can be extended to three-dimensional arrays, or—theoretically—four-dimensional or more. You can think of a three-dimensional array as being made up of pages or planes in addition to rows and columns. You can initialize with three levels of braces:

```
float revenues[2][3][4] =
{
   {
      {124.4, 133.3, 133.5, 133.3},
      {238.2, 233.3, 323.3, 133.3},
      {323.3, 438.3, 238.3, 398.3} /* comma or not OK */
   }, /* comma required here */
   {
      {123.4, 234.3, 233.3, 543.5},
      {293.3, 393.6, 393.5, 393.5},
      {933.9, 393.3, 393.3, 203.6} /* comma or not OK */
   } /* comma or not OK */
};
```

If you omit the comma in the place indicated above, you will get an error. As we mentioned earlier with single-array initialization, it is optional in the other three locations.

As with the two-dimensional array, you can omit any or all of the inner braces, though this is not recommended. The same rules for partial initializations apply.

6.9   THREE-DIMENSIONAL ARRAY APPLICATION

The following program illustrates the use of a three-dimensional array to analyze residential real estate sales volume for three offices of a real estate brokerage company over a three-year period.

 Listing **6.6 broker.c**

```c
/* broker.c */

/* 3-dimensional array example: 3 real estate offices over 3 yrs */

#include <stdio.h>

#define OFFICES 3
#define YEARS 3
#define MONTHS 12

int main(void)
{
    int office, year, month;
    int sales[OFFICES][YEARS][MONTHS] =
    {
      {
        {222, 122, 233, 132, 222, 112, 222, 321, 133, 882, 232, 222},
        {939, 393, 393, 393, 339, 292, 292, 229, 229, 992, 292, 200},
        {539, 939, 393, 339, 393, 339, 339, 439, 323, 322, 223, 919}
      },
      {
        {139, 939, 393, 339, 323, 238, 469, 486, 319, 382, 284, 399},
        {399, 339, 939, 339, 228, 282, 229, 898, 339, 399, 383, 388},
        {939, 388, 939, 669, 994, 383, 229, 688, 984, 458, 948, 498}
      },
      {
        {599, 440, 974, 484, 894, 408, 398, 348, 649, 698, 398, 346},
        {848, 194, 198, 398, 644, 394, 354, 394, 395, 694, 609, 606},
        {383, 838, 235, 552, 538, 583, 593, 538, 664, 644, 624, 664}
      }
    };
    long office_tot, year_tot, month_tot;
    int start_year = 2000;

    /* traverse office-year-month (annual totals for each office) */
    printf("\nResidential Real Estate Sales\n"
      "(In Thousands of Dollars)\n\n");

    /* calculate totals office by office */
    for (office = 0, office_tot = 0L; office < OFFICES; office++)
    {
        printf("\n\nOffice No. %d\n\n", office + 1);
        printf("\t Jan Feb Mar Apr May Jun Jul Aug Sep Oct Nov Dec Total\n");

        /* print monthly data & accumulate in year total */
        for (year = start_year, year_tot = 0;
        year < start_year + YEARS; year++)
        {
```

```
         printf("\n%d    ", year);
         for (month = 0; month < MONTHS; month++)
         {
             printf("%5d",
                 sales[office][year - start_year][month]);
             year_tot += (long)sales[office][year - start_year][month];
         }
         office_tot += year_tot;
         printf("%8ld", year_tot);
     }
     printf("\n%76s\n", "———");
     printf("%76ld\n", office_tot);
 }

/* traverse month-office-hear */
printf("\n\nMonthly Averages Company-Wide\n\n");
printf("\t Jan Feb Mar Apr May Jun Jul Aug Sep Oct Nov Dec\n\n\t");

/* calculate average monthly totals company-wide
   over entire period */
for (month = 0, month_tot = 0L; month < MONTHS;
month++, month_tot = 0)
{
   for (office = 0; office < OFFICES; office++)
      for (year = 0; year < YEARS; year++)
         month_tot += (long)sales[office][year][month];
   printf("%5u", (unsigned)(month_tot / (long)(OFFICES * YEARS)));
 }
}
```

Here's the output:

```
Residential Real Estate Sales
(In Thousands of Dollars)

Office No. 1

     Jan Feb Mar Apr May Jun Jul Aug Sep Oct Nov Dec Total

2000 222 122 233 132 222 112 222 321 133 882 232 222   3055
2001 939 393 393 393 339 292 292 229 229 992 292 200   8038
2002 539 939 393 339 393 339 339 439 323 322 223 919  13545
                                                      _____
                                                       24638


Office No. 2

     Jan Feb Mar Apr May Jun Jul Aug Sep Oct Nov Dec Total

2000 139 939 393 339 323 238 469 486 319 382 284 399   4710
2001 399 339 939 339 228 282 229 898 339 399 383 388   9872
2002 939 388 939 669 994 383 229 688 984 458 948 498  17989
                                                      _____
                                                       57209


Office No. 3

     Jan Feb Mar Apr May Jun Jul Aug Sep Oct Nov Dec Total

2000 599 440 974 484 894 408 398 348 649 698 398 346   6636
2001 848 194 198 398 644 394 354 394 395 694 609 606  12364
2002 383 838 235 552 538 583 593 538 664 644 624 664  19220
                                                      _____
                                                       95429
```

```
Monthly Averages Company-Wide

 Jan Feb Mar Apr May Jun Jul Aug Sep Oct Nov Dec

 556 510 521 405 508 336 347 482 448 607 443 471
```

Notice the different ways we can traverse the arrays to achieve varying breakdowns of the data. In the first part of the program, we used a three-tiered nested loop. The outer loop represents the first dimension (offices), the middle loop represents the second dimension (years), and the innermost loop, the third dimension (months). In the second part of the program, we traverse month-office-year.

6.10 APPLICATION: ACE BILLING PROGRAM

In Chapter 5, we were unable to read in the member names as such. Without having learned about arrays, we were constrained to read and write the names character by character. Aside from finding this cumbersome, we could not run the program interactively. We had to read in data from a file through redirection. It was beyond the scope of the last chapter to write the program to receive the data interactively and still produce the same report format: doing so would require us to store all the data into an array before printing out all the results. Otherwise, the input prompts would intermingle with the output report, and that would not look good.

In acech06.c and acech06a.c, below, we utilize arrays. We build up to the most efficient solution gradually. In acech06.c, we use an array to store the member names. However, we still have scalar variables to store each field. That configuration leaves us unable to sort the records. Notice that the sorting functions in that program are not implemented.

In acech06a.c, we move to two-dimensional arrays, insofar as member names are concerned. We have an array for each field; the member name is a two-dimensional array. Each array consists of one field for all members. In effect, you can think of each array for the various fields (name, initials, membership flag, activity fee, and so on) as consisting of a row. A complete record for a member then is in effect a column, cutting across all the field arrays but with the same subscript number in each array. Thus, for example, member 1's record consists of SpecialMembershipFlag[0], CustomerName[0][16], CustomerInitials[0][3], MembershipFee[0], ActivityFee[0], DiscountAmount[0], ChargeAmount[0], TotalIndividualBill[0], AceClubTotals[0], Charges[0], Discount[0], AverageCharges[0], and NumberOfCharges[0]. Member 4's record is composed of SpecialMembershipFlag[3], CustomerName[3][16], CustomerInitials[3][3], MembershipFee[3], ActivityFee[3], DiscountAmount[3], ChargeAmount[3], TotalIndividualBill[3], AceClubTotals[3], Charges[3], Discount[3], AverageCharges[3], NumberOfCharges[3], and so on.

Now we are able to use the arrays to sort. In this program, we will sort alphabetically by name. So if we want to swap member 1 (John Candy) with member 3 (Tom Able), we must switch each of those various fields from one set of arrays to the other. We use a temporary element in each array for that purpose.

We use the final element in each field array to store the total for all members for that particular field. We could also have declared a separate scalar variable for each of those fields. The choice is somewhat arbitrary. Each method has its advantages. Since we use the final element for totaling, we use the second-to-last element for temporary swapping.

As you can see, this is a quantum leap from what we could do after the last chapter. But the method of slicing through arrays and making sure we keep a member's record in synch is cumbersome. Once we cover structures in Chapter 13, the methodology will become far more efficient.

6.10.1 Input

```
Kirk          JT20Y80001000
Otieno        RD10Y80002100
Otieno        JM30Y80003200
Omaya         JO40Y80004300
O'Malley      AV50Y80005400
Valentino     RJ60Y80006500
McCrory       KY70Y80007600
Mandell       SR80 80008700
```

```
        Smith          LA90 80009800
        Solzhenitsyn   AS11 80008980
        Gorbachev      MA21Y80004899
        Kissinger      HA22 80009790
        Schlesinger    JM23Y80005460
```

 **Listing** **6.7 acech06.c and acech06a.c**

```c
/*
    +------------------------------------------------------------------+
    +  Program Name: acech06.c
    +     Author(s): Austell-Wolfson and Otieno
    +          Date: 12/10/2000
    +  Purpose:
    +     This program processes a file of ACE Club member records and
    +     computes and prints the total amounts for all club members.
    +
    +  Process:
    +    This program prints the prescribed headings for the report and
    +    processes each record by:
    +       computing the individual member bill, equal to the sum of
    +       member bill, membership fee, and activity fee, minus any
    +       discount amount. The members are charged a special
    +       membership fee of $2500 if indeed the person is a special
    +       member, indicated by a "Y" in the membership flag field. The
    +       activity fees is based on the number of activities each
    +       member requests. The more activities they request, the more
    +       they are charged. A discount amount is applied if the member
    +       has an average charge of over $8000 per bill.
    +
    +------------------------------------------------------------------+
*/
#include <stdio.h>

void initialization(void);
void processMemberRecord(void);
void termination(void);
void initializeVariables(void);
void printHeadings(void);
void readMemberRecord(void);
void computeIndividualBill(void);
void writeDetailLine(void);
void determineSpecialFee(void);
void determineActivityFee(void);
void determineDiscountAmt(void);
void sortByClubMemberNames(void);
void printSortedReport(void);


/*
    +------------------------------------------------------------------+
    +
    +  Declare variables outside of main() function so that all the
    +  other functions will have access to them. Doing this gives
    +  these variables global scope and therefore allows us to
    +  develop and work with modules this early. We will discontinue
    +  this practice once functions have been fully discussed.
    +
    +------------------------------------------------------------------+
*/
char  SpecialMembershipFlag = 'Y';
char  CustomerName[16];
char  CustomerInitials[3];
```

```
float MembershipFee = 0.0;
float ActivityFee = 0.0;
float DiscountAmount = 0.0;
float ChargeAmount = 0.0;
float TotalIndividualBill = 0.0;
float AceClubTotals = 0.0;
float Charges = 0;
int   Discount = 0;
int   AverageCharges = 0;
int   NumberOfCharges = 0;
int   ReadStatus = 0;

/*  Variables used for holding and accumulating grand totals */
float TotalMembershipFee = 0.0;
float TotalActivityFee = 0.0;
float TotalDiscountAmount = 0.0;
float TotalChargeAmount = 0.0;
float TotalTotalIndividualBill = 0.0;
float TotalAceClubTotals = 0.0;
float TotalCharges = 0;
int   TotalDiscount = 0;
int   TotalAverageCharges = 0;
int   TotalNumberOfCharges = 0;

int main(void)
{
    initialization();
    while (6 == ReadStatus)
    {
        processMemberRecord();
    }
    sortByClubMemberNames();
    printSortedReport();

    termination();
    return 0;
}

void initialization(void)
{
    initializeVariables();
    printHeadings();
    readMemberRecord();
}

void processMemberRecord(void)
{
    computeIndividualBill();
    writeDetailLine();
    readMemberRecord();
}

/*
   +------------------------------------------------------------------+
   +
   +    termination() is the one module we have not used very much.
   +    Having this function is still a good idea because it serves
   +    as a reminder to do those tasks that need to be done after
   +    all the records have been processed. In this case, we print
   +    grand totals for the entire club in termination when we know
   +    that all the member records have been processed.
```

```
    +    We will use it even more once we start opening and closing
    +    files and handling the likes of control-break logic.
    +
    +
    +------------------------------------------------------------------+
*/

void termination(void)
{
    printf("| s──   ──────   ──────   ──────   ────   ──────   |\n",
        19, " ");
    printf("| ACE Club Totals   %3d $%8.2f  $%8.2f  $%8.2f  $%5.f"
        $%9.2f   |\n", TotalNumberOfCharges, TotalCharges,
        TotalMembershipFee, TotalActivityFee, TotalDiscountAmount,
        TotalTotalIndividualBill);
    printf("|_____|\n");
}

void initializeVariables(void)
{
    int k; /* index of the characters in the Name array */

    SpecialMembershipFlag = 'Y';
    Discount = 0;
    AverageCharges = 0;
    MembershipFee = 2500.0;
    ActivityFee = 250.0;
    DiscountAmount = 0.0;
    ChargeAmount = 0.0;
    NumberOfCharges = 0;
    TotalIndividualBill = 0.0;
    AceClubTotals = 0.0;
    ReadStatus = 0;

    TotalMembershipFee = 0.0;
    TotalActivityFee = 0.0;
    TotalDiscountAmount = 0.0;
    TotalChargeAmount = 0.0;
    TotalTotalIndividualBill = 0.0;
    TotalAceClubTotals = 0.0;
    Charges = 0;
    Discount = 0;
    TotalAverageCharges = 0;
    TotalNumberOfCharges = 0;

    /*
    +------------------------------------------------------------------+
    +
    +    We initialize the customer name to hold NULL characters for
    +    each character position in the name. We do it this way for
    +    pedagogical reasons only. You will find that there are
    +    functions you may use to initialize character arrays
    +    in the strings chapter.
    +
    +------------------------------------------------------------------+
    */
    for (k = 0; k < 16; k++)
    {
        CustomerName[k] = '\0';
    }

    for (k = 0; k < 3; k++)
```

```
      {
         CustomerInitials[k] = '\0';
      }
   }
}

void printHeadings(void)
{
   printf("|                                                                    |\n");
   printf("|                                                                    |\n");
   printf("|    Program Name: ACECH06.EXE                            Page:   1  |\n");
   printf("|       Run Date: 12/10/2000            Ace Billing                  |\n");
   printf("|                                                                    |\n");
   printf("|                                                                    |\n");
   printf("|--------------------------------------------------------------------|\n");
   printf("|                                                                    |\n");
   printf("| Customer Name   Charges  Bill      Mbr Fee    Act Fee    Disc    Total Bill |\n");
   printf("|--------------------------------------------------------------------|\n");
   printf("|                                                                    |\n");
}
void readMemberRecord(void)
{
/*
      +-----------------------------------------------------------------+
      +
      +
      +    Read the rest of the data items/fields from the input
      +    data stream. The input data stream is assumed to be a file
      +    of a particular record layout. This file is read through
      +    the mechanism that your operating system has provided
      +    to handle standard input from a file instead of a keyboard.
      +    Now that we have learned about arrays, we can create an
      +    array to hold all the characters that make up the name. We
      +    could not do this before Chapter 6.
      +
      +-----------------------------------------------------------------+
*/

   ReadStatus = scanf("%15c%2c%2d%c%4d%4d\n", CustomerName,
      CustomerInitials, &NumberOfCharges, &SpecialMembershipFlag,
      &Discount, &AverageCharges);
}

void computeIndividualBill(void)
{
   Charges = 200 * NumberOfCharges;
   TotalCharges += Charges;
   TotalNumberOfCharges += NumberOfCharges;
   determineSpecialFee();
   determineActivityFee();
   determineDiscountAmt();

   TotalIndividualBill = Charges + MembershipFee + ActivityFee -
      DiscountAmount;
   AceClubTotals = AceClubTotals + TotalIndividualBill;

   TotalTotalIndividualBill += TotalIndividualBill;
   TotalAceClubTotals += AceClubTotals;
}

void writeDetailLine(void)
{
   printf("|%15.15s  %s %2d $%8.2f  $%8.2f  $%8.2f  $%5.f  $%9.2f", CustomerName,
      CustomerInitials, NumberOfCharges, Charges, MembershipFee, ActivityFee, DiscountAmount,
```

```
         TotalIndividualBill);
      printf("  |\n");
}
void determineSpecialFee(void)
{
   /* see comment to acech05.c re following construction */
   if ('Y' == SpecialMembershipFlag)
   {
      MembershipFee = 2500.0;
   }
   else
   {
      MembershipFee = 0.0;
   }

   TotalMembershipFee += MembershipFee;
}

void determineActivityFee(void)
{
   if (NumberOfCharges <= 6)
   {
      ActivityFee = 250.0;
   }

   if ((NumberOfCharges > 6) && (NumberOfCharges < 12))
   {
      ActivityFee = 500.0;
   }

   if (NumberOfCharges > 12)
   {
      ActivityFee = 750.0;
   }

   TotalActivityFee += ActivityFee;
}

void determineDiscountAmt(void)
{
   if (AverageCharges > 8500)
   {
      DiscountAmount = Discount;
   }
   else
   {
      DiscountAmount = 0;
   }

TotalDiscountAmount += DiscountAmount;
}

/*
   +----------------------------------------------------------------+
   +
   +    Since we have declared all fields as scalar variables, we are
   +    not able to sort the data. The last two sorting functions are
   +    not implemented. See acech06a.c for the array approach.
   +
   +----------------------------------------------------------------+
*/
```

```
void sortByClubMemberNames(void)
{
}
void printSortedReport(void)
{
}


/*
   +---------------------------------------------------------------+
   +  Program Name: acech06a.c
   +     Author(s): Austell-Wolfson and Otieno
   +          Date: 12/10/2000
   +  Purpose:
   +     This program processes a file of ACE Club member records and
   +     computes and prints the total amounts for all club members.
   +
   +  Process:
   +     This program prints the prescribed headings for the report and
   +     processes each record by:
   +       computing the individual member bill, equal to the sum of
   +       member bill, membership fee, and activity fee, minus any
   +       discount amount. Members are charged a special membership
   +       fee of $2500 if indeed the person is a special member,
   +       indicated by a "Y" in the membership flag field. The
   +       activity fees are based on the number of activities
   +       each member requests. The more activities they request, the
   +       more they are charged. A discount amount is applied if the
   +       member has an average charge of over $8000 per bill.
   +
   +---------------------------------------------------------------+
*/
#include <stdio.h>
#include <string.h>

void initialization(void);
void processMemberRecord(void);
void termination(void);
void printGrandTotals(void);
void initializeVariables(void);
void printHeadings(void);
void readMemberRecord(void);
void computeIndividualBill(void);
void writeDetailLine(void);
void determineSpecialFee(void);
void determineActivityFee(void);
void determineDiscountAmt(void);
void sortByClubMemberNames(void);
void printSortedReport(void);
void swapValues(void);

/* see comment to acech05.c re declaring variables outside main */
char  SpecialMembershipFlag[100];
char  CustomerName[100][16];
char  CustomerInitials[100][3];
float MembershipFee[100];
float ActivityFee[100];
float DiscountAmount[100];
float ChargeAmount[100];
float TotalIndividualBill[100];
float AceClubTotals[100];
float Charges[100];
```

```
int    Discount[100];
int    AverageCharges[100];
int    NumberOfCharges[100];
int    ReadStatus = 0;
int    CurrentPos; /* Holds current array position being processed */
int    ClubMember = 0; /* Holds the count of all club members.
                    It is also used to index the array of club
                    members; therefore its value starts at 0. */

int main(void)
{
   initialization();
   while (6 == ReadStatus)
   {
      processMemberRecord();
   }
   printGrandTotals();
   sortByClubMemberNames();
   printSortedReport();

   termination();
   return 0;
}

void initialization(void)
{
   initializeVariables();
   printHeadings();
   readMemberRecord();
}

void processMemberRecord(void)
{
   computeIndividualBill();
   writeDetailLine();
   readMemberRecord();
}

/*
   +----------------------------------------------------------------+
   +
   +    termination() is the one module we have not used very much.
   +    Having this function is still a good idea because it serves
   +    as a reminder to do those tasks that need to be done after
   +    all the records have been processed. In this case, we print
   +    grand totals for the entire club in termination when we know
   +    that all the member records have been processed.
   +    We will use it even more once we start opening and closing
   +    files and handling the likes of control-break logic.
   +
   +----------------------------------------------------------------+
*/
void termination(void)
{
   printGrandTotals();
}

void initializeVariables(void)
{
   int k;  /* Index to our CustomerName array */
   int rowCount;
```

```
   /*  end of declarations */

   ReadStatus = 0;

   for (k = 0; k < 100; k++)
   {
      SpecialMembershipFlag[k] = 'Y';
      Discount[k] = 0;
      AverageCharges[k] = 0;
      MembershipFee[k] = 0.0;
      ActivityFee[k] = 0.0;
      DiscountAmount[k] = 0.0;
      ChargeAmount[k] = 0.0;
      NumberOfCharges[k] = 0;
      TotalIndividualBill[k] = 0.0;
      AceClubTotals[k] = 0.0;
   }

   for (rowCount = 0; rowCount < 100; rowCount++)
   {
      for (k = 0; k < 16; k++)
      {
         CustomerName[rowCount][k] = '\0';
      }
   }

   for (rowCount = 0; rowCount < 100; rowCount++)
   {
      for (k = 0; k < 3; k++)
      {
         CustomerInitials[rowCount][k] = '\0';
      }
   }
}

void printHeadings(void)
{
   printf("┌──────────────────────────────────────────────────────────┐\n");
   printf("│                                                            │\n");
   printf("│   Program Name: ACECH06A.EXE                     Page:  1  │\n");
   printf("│       Run Date: 12/10/2000            Ace Billing          │\n");
   printf("│                                                            │\n");
   printf("│                                                            │\n");
   printf("├──────────────────────────────────────────────────────────┤\n");
   printf("│                                                            │\n");
   printf("│ Customer Name  Charges      Bill     Mbr Fee   Act Fee   Disc  Total Bill │\n");
   printf("├──────────────────────────────────────────────────────────┤\n");
   printf("│                                                            │\n");

}

void readMemberRecord(void)
{
/*
   +------------------------------------------------------------+
   +
   +    Read the rest of the data items/fields from the input
   +    data stream. The input data stream is assumed to be a file
   +    of a particular record layout. This file is read through
   +    the mechanism that your operating system has provided
   +    to handle standard input from a file instead of a keyboard.
```

```
   +   Now that we have learned about arrays, we can create an
   +   array to hold all the characters that make up the name. We
   +   could not do this before Chapter 6.
   +
   +----------------------------------------------------------------+
*/
   ReadStatus = scanf("%15c%2c%2d%c%4d%4d\n", CustomerName[ClubMember],
      CustomerInitials[ClubMember], &NumberOfCharges[ClubMember],
      &SpecialMembershipFlag[ClubMember], &Discount[ClubMember],
      &AverageCharges[ClubMember]);
}

void computeIndividualBill(void)
{
   Charges[ClubMember] = 200 * NumberOfCharges[ClubMember];
   Charges[99] += Charges[ClubMember];
   NumberOfCharges[99] += NumberOfCharges[ClubMember];
   determineSpecialFee();
   determineActivityFee();
   determineDiscountAmt();

   TotalIndividualBill[ClubMember] = Charges[ClubMember] + MembershipFee[ClubMember] +
      ActivityFee[ClubMember] - DiscountAmount[ClubMember];
   TotalIndividualBill[99] += TotalIndividualBill[ClubMember];
   AceClubTotals[99] += TotalIndividualBill[ClubMember];
}

void writeDetailLine(void)
{
   printf("| %15.15s  %s %2d  $%9.2f  $%8.2f  $%8.2f  $%5.f  $%9.2f",
      CustomerName[ClubMember], CustomerInitials[ClubMember],
      NumberOfCharges[ClubMember], Charges[ClubMember],
      MembershipFee[ClubMember], ActivityFee[ClubMember],
      DiscountAmount[ClubMember], TotalIndividualBill[ClubMember]);
   printf(" |\n");
   ClubMember++; /* Increase the number of club members */
}

void determineSpecialFee(void)
{
   /* see comment to acech05.c re following construction */
   if ('Y' == SpecialMembershipFlag[ClubMember])
   {
      MembershipFee[ClubMember] = 2500.0;
   }
   else
   {
      MembershipFee[ClubMember] = 0.0;
   }

   MembershipFee[99] += MembershipFee[ClubMember];
   }

void determineActivityFee(void)
{
   if (NumberOfCharges[ClubMember] <= 6)
   {
      ActivityFee[ClubMember] = 250.0;
   }

   if ((NumberOfCharges[ClubMember] > 6) &&
```

```
            (NumberOfCharges[ClubMember] <= 12))
      {
         ActivityFee[ClubMember] = 500.0;
      }

      if (NumberOfCharges[ClubMember] > 12)
      {
         ActivityFee[ClubMember] = 750.0;
      }

   ActivityFee[99] += ActivityFee[ClubMember];
      }

void determineDiscountAmt(void)
{
      if (AverageCharges[ClubMember] > 8500)
      {
         DiscountAmount[ClubMember] = Discount[ClubMember];
      }
      else
      {
         DiscountAmount[ClubMember] = 0;
      }

      DiscountAmount[99] += DiscountAmount[ClubMember];
}

void sortByClubMemberNames(void)
{
      int k; /* Loop index variable */

      int MorePasses = 1; /* Determines whether to make more passes
         during the bubble sort algorithm */

/*
      +------------------------------------------------------------------+
      +  Start loop that makes as many passes through the array of
      +  club member names as needed for the entire list to be sorted.
      +
      +------------------------------------------------------------------+
*/
      while (1 == MorePasses)
      {
/*
      +------------------------------------------------------------------+
      +  Turn it off so that if the data is sorted, no
      +  passes will be necessary. If, however, there was
      +  a single swap, MorePasses will be set to 1
      +  and the while loop repeats as it should.
      +
      +------------------------------------------------------------------+
*/
         MorePasses = 0;
         for (k = 0; k < ClubMember - 1; k++)
         {
            if (strcmp(CustomerName[k], CustomerName[k + 1]) > 0)
            {
               CurrentPos = k;
               swapValues(); /* swap all values in parallel arrays */
               MorePasses = 1;
            }
```

```
      } /* end of for loop */
   } /* end of while loop */
}

void printSortedReport(void)
{
   int k; /* Loop index variable */

   /* print the column headings for the sorted list of club members */
   printHeadings();

   for (k = 0; k < ClubMember; k++)
   {
      printf("| %15.15s  %s %2d  $%9.2f  $%8.2f  $%8.2f  $%5.f  $%9.2f", CustomerName[k],
         CustomerInitials[k], NumberOfCharges[k], Charges[k], MembershipFee[k],
         ActivityFee[k], DiscountAmount[k], TotalIndividualBill[k]);
      printf(" |\n");

   }
}

void swapValues (void)
{
/*
   +-----------------------------------------------------------------+
   +  We have set up our arrays to be larger than really
   +  necessary to hold all the club members. We use the
   +  position next to the last position in the array
   +  as a temporary holder for swapping purposes
   +  during the sort. The last position in the arrays
   +  is used to hold the grand totals. The rest of the
   +  logic in this program has been so structured to
   +  preserve these slots in the arrays.
   +
   +-----------------------------------------------------------------+
*/
int  tempPos;

/*
   +-----------------------------------------------------------------+
   +  Since the list has 100 items with 99 being the last slot
   +  and since we are using slot 99 to hold the final totals,
   +  slot 98 is used for swapping. Therefore, we can only use
   +  97 slots to hold actual member data.
   +
   +-----------------------------------------------------------------+
*/
  tempPos = 98;

   /* Swap the last name of club member */
   strcpy(CustomerName[tempPos], CustomerName[CurrentPos]);
   strcpy(CustomerName[CurrentPos], CustomerName[CurrentPos + 1]);
   strcpy(CustomerName[CurrentPos + 1], CustomerName[tempPos]);

   /* swap the customer initials */
   strcpy(CustomerInitials[tempPos], CustomerInitials[CurrentPos]);
   strcpy(CustomerInitials[CurrentPos],
      CustomerInitials[CurrentPos + 1]);
   strcpy(CustomerInitials[CurrentPos + 1], CustomerInitials[tempPos]);

   /* swap the total membership fee */
```

```
        MembershipFee[tempPos] = MembershipFee[CurrentPos];
        MembershipFee[CurrentPos] = MembershipFee[CurrentPos + 1];
        MembershipFee[CurrentPos + 1] = MembershipFee[tempPos];

        /* swap the total activity fee */
        ActivityFee[tempPos] = ActivityFee[CurrentPos];
        ActivityFee[CurrentPos] = ActivityFee[CurrentPos + 1];
        ActivityFee[CurrentPos + 1] = ActivityFee[tempPos];

        /* swap the total Discount amount */
        DiscountAmount[tempPos] = DiscountAmount[CurrentPos];
        DiscountAmount[CurrentPos] = DiscountAmount[CurrentPos + 1];
        DiscountAmount[CurrentPos + 1] = DiscountAmount[tempPos];

        /* swap the total charge amount */
        ChargeAmount[tempPos] = ChargeAmount[CurrentPos];
        ChargeAmount[CurrentPos] = ChargeAmount[CurrentPos + 1];
        ChargeAmount[CurrentPos + 1] = ChargeAmount[tempPos];

        /* swap the total individual bill */
        TotalIndividualBill[tempPos] = TotalIndividualBill[CurrentPos];
        TotalIndividualBill[CurrentPos] =
            TotalIndividualBill[CurrentPos + 1];
        TotalIndividualBill[CurrentPos + 1] = TotalIndividualBill[tempPos];

        /* swap the total ace club totals */
        AceClubTotals[tempPos] = AceClubTotals[CurrentPos];
        AceClubTotals[CurrentPos] = AceClubTotals[CurrentPos + 1];
        AceClubTotals[CurrentPos + 1] = AceClubTotals[tempPos];

        /* swap the total Charges */
        Charges[tempPos] = Charges[CurrentPos];
        Charges[CurrentPos] = Charges[CurrentPos + 1];
        Charges[CurrentPos + 1] = Charges[tempPos];

        /* swap the total Discount */
        Discount[tempPos] = Discount[CurrentPos];
        Discount[CurrentPos] = Discount[CurrentPos + 1];
        Discount[CurrentPos + 1] = Discount[tempPos];

        /* swap the total average Charges */
        AverageCharges[tempPos] = AverageCharges[CurrentPos];
        AverageCharges[CurrentPos] = AverageCharges[CurrentPos + 1];
        AverageCharges[CurrentPos + 1] = AverageCharges[tempPos];

        /* swap the total number of Charges bill */
        NumberOfCharges[tempPos] = NumberOfCharges[CurrentPos];
        NumberOfCharges[CurrentPos] = NumberOfCharges[CurrentPos + 1];
        NumberOfCharges[CurrentPos + 1] = NumberOfCharges[tempPos];
}

void printGrandTotals(void)
{
    printf("| %*s——  ———  ———  ———  ——  ——— |\n",
        19, " ");
    printf("| ACE Club Totals   %3d  $%9.2f  $%8.2f  $%8.2f  $%5.f  $%9.2f |\n",
        NumberOfCharges[99], Charges[99], MembershipFee[99], ActivityFee[99],
        DiscountAmount[99], TotalIndividualBill[99]);
    printf("|_____|\n\n");
}
```

6.10.2   Output

Figures 6.9 and 6.10 show the output.

Figure 6.9 *Output for* acech06a.exe

```
  Program Name: ACECH06A.EXE                                          Page:   1
     Run Date: 12/10/2000              Ace Billing



Customer Name   Charges         Bill    Mbr Fee      Act Fee     Disc   Total Bill


Kirk            JT 20    $   4000.00  $ 2500.00   $   750.00   $      0   $   7250.00
Otieno          RD 10    $   2000.00  $ 2500.00   $   500.00   $      0   $   5000.00
Otieno          JM 30    $   6000.00  $ 2500.00   $   750.00   $      0   $   9250.00
Omaya           JO 40    $   8000.00  $ 2500.00   $   750.00   $      0   $  11250.00
O'Malley        AV 50    $  10000.00  $ 2500.00   $   750.00   $      0   $  13250.00
Valentino       RJ 60    $  12000.00  $ 2500.00   $   750.00   $      0   $  15250.00
McCrory         KY 70    $  14000.00  $ 2500.00   $   750.00   $      0   $  17250.00
Mandell         SR 80    $  16000.00  $    0.00   $   750.00   $   8000   $   8750.00
Smith           LA 90    $  18000.00  $    0.00   $   750.00   $   8000   $  10750.00
Solzhenitsyn    AS 11    $   2200.00  $    0.00   $   500.00   $   8000   $  -5300.00
Gorbachev       MA 21    $   4200.00  $ 2500.00   $   750.00   $      0   $   7450.00
Kissinger       HA 22    $   4400.00  $    0.00   $   750.00   $   8000   $  -2850.00
Schlesinger     JM 23    $   4600.00  $ 2500.00   $   750.00   $      0   $   7850.00

ACE Club Totals    527   $105400.00  $22500.00   $  9250.00   $  32000   $ 105150.00
```

Figure 6.10 *Output for* acech06a.exe—*Sorted Alphabetically*

```
  Program Name: ACECH06A.EXE                                          Page:   1
     Run Date: 12/10/2000              Ace Billing



Customer Name   Charges         Bill    Mbr Fee      Act Fee     Disc   Total Bill


Gorbachev       MA 21    $   4200.00  $ 2500.00   $   750.00   $      0   $   7450.00
Kirk            JT 20    $   4000.00  $ 2500.00   $   750.00   $      0   $   7250.00
Kissinger       HA 22    $   4400.00  $    0.00   $   750.00   $   8000   $  -2850.00
Mandell         SR 80    $  16000.00  $    0.00   $   750.00   $   8000   $   8750.00
McCrory         KY 70    $  14000.00  $ 2500.00   $   750.00   $      0   $  17250.00
O'Malley        AV 50    $  10000.00  $ 2500.00   $   750.00   $      0   $  13250.00
Omaya           JO 40    $   8000.00  $ 2500.00   $   750.00   $      0   $  11250.00
Otieno          RD 10    $   2000.00  $ 2500.00   $   500.00   $      0   $   5000.00
Otieno          JM 30    $   6000.00  $ 2500.00   $   750.00   $      0   $   9250.00
Schlesinger     JM 23    $   4600.00  $ 2500.00   $   750.00   $      0   $   7850.00
Smith           LA 90    $  18000.00  $    0.00   $   750.00   $   8000   $  10750.00
Solzhenitsyn    AS 11    $   2200.00  $    0.00   $   500.00   $   8000   $  -5300.00
Valentino       RJ 60    $  12000.00  $ 2500.00   $   750.00   $      0   $  15250.00

ACE Club Totals    527   $105400.00  $22500.00   $  9250.00   $  32000   $ 105150.00
```

Chapter Summary

1. An array is an example of an aggregate data type. An array declaration reserves a block of contiguous memory locations for the array's elements.

2. We declare an array with a type, a variable name, and the number of array elements, enclosed in brackets. The number in brackets following the array name is called a subscript or index.

3. In the array declaration, the subscript must contain only a constant or constant expression. Likewise, array elements may be initialized only with constants.

4. Initialization of array elements is made by surrounding the elements with braces and separating each element with commas. Except at the time of declaration, you cannot assign a value to more than one array element at a time.

5. If you omit the subscript number in an initialization statement, the compiler automatically sizes the array according to the number of elements between the braces.

6. You may assign fewer than all the elements on initialization, provided all holes are at the end. You may not initialize with more values than there are elements in the array.

7. If you declare an array to be `static` or external, each uninitialized element is set to zero. Otherwise, they will have garbage values.

8. The first element of an array has a subscript of 0. Assigning a value just past the final array element is a common error.

9. The `sizeof` operator, applied to an array name, gives the number of bytes in the entire array. To determine the number of elements in an array, you can divide `sizeof(array)` by the number of bytes each element takes up.

10. Once declared, the size of the array cannot be changed.

11. Other than on array declaration, the subscript number designates an array element, either to assign it a value or to use its value. Negative subscripts are permitted.

12. You can use an array element in the same fashion as you could any variable of the same type.

13. The `for` loop is commonly used to traverse an array, and the nested `for` loop is used to traverse multidimensional arrays.

14. A two-dimensional array is an array of arrays. The computer stores all elements as contiguous bytes, with one complete subarray following another.

15. In a multidimensional array, the right-most subscript varies fastest.

16. The `sizeof` operator, applied to the name of a multidimensional array, gives us the number of bytes in the entire array.

17. In a two-dimensional array, initialization can be made with double sets of braces or just a single set. There is no difference in the methods, unless fewer than all elements are initialized.

Review Questions

1. Arrays are a series of data elements of the same type, such as `int` or `float` (True or False).

2. There is only one variable name for an array declaration regardless of how many array elements are involved (True or False).

3. Each array element can be referenced by an integer subscript, such as 0, 1, 2, and so on (True or False).

4. Each array element can be referenced by a character subscript, such as 'A', 'B', '+', and so forth, though this would not be commonly done (True or False).

5. Each array element can be referenced by a floating point subscript, such as 3.14, 2.0, 13.56, and so on (True or False).

6. Create an `int` array, `daysOfTheYear`, representing the number of customers who come into the store during the days of the year. Assume that there are 366 days per year.

7. Elements in an array are located contiguously in memory or storage (True or False).

8. The number of bytes per array element is dictated by data type (True or False).

9. The number of bytes per element is dictated by size of the array (True or False).

10. There is a special data type for strings in Standard C.

11. Strings exist as arrays of characters (True or False).

12. Declare an array, `customerName`, with room for 20 characters and a terminating NULL.

13. Strings are terminated by a NULL ('\0') character (True or False).

14. To have a proper C string, array size must be sufficient to accommodate the NULL character (True or False).

15. Array size is always automatically adjusted by the compiler to accommodate the NULL character (True or False).

16. A string constant is specified by double quotes (True or False).

17. "I" is a 2-byte character string (True or False).

18. No string-handling function requires a NULL character to signal termination of operation (True or False).

19. The name of an array is equivalent to the address of the first element of array (True or False).

20. Use a `for` loop to initialize the `daysOfTheYear` array to zero.

21. Use a `for` loop to initialize the `customerName` array to NULL ('\0') characters.

22. Assign 2345 to the 11th element of the `daysOfTheYear` array.

23. Assign 3452 to the 33rd element of the `daysOfTheYear` array.

Figure 6.11 *Two-Dimensional Spreadsheet Matrix with Values Diagonally from Northwest to Southeast*

3				
	3			
		3		
			3	
				3

24. Assign 3400 to the 233rd element of the `daysOfTheYear` array.
25. Write a complete program that prints out the nonzero values in the array using the following format:

    `daysOfTheYear[??] = the value`

    where ?? represents the location with the nonzero value.
26. Write a program that does the following:
    - Creates a two-dimensional minispreadsheet of `ints` with 5 rows and 5 columns
    - Initializes the entire spreadsheet to zeros
    - Prints the spreadsheet with zeros
    - Initializes the cells on the diagonal line in a northwest to southeast direction to 3, as shown in Figure 6.11
    - Initializes the cells located above the cells that make up the diagonal cells, excluding the diagonal line, of the spreadsheet to each have a value of 4, as shown in Figure 6.12
    - Prints the new spreadsheet
    - Initializes the cells located below the diagonal cells, excluding the diagonal line, to 7, as shown in Figure 6.13
    - Prints the new spreadsheet
27. Write a program that creates a three-dimensional spreadsheet with the first dimension representing the sheet, and the next two representing the row and column cells of the spreadsheet, respectively. Your program is to
    - perform the same operations as the previous problem for sheet 1, `sheet[0]`.
    - perform the same operations as the previous problem, except instead of top and bottom diagonal cells, we work with top and bottom cells. Instead of the diagonal line, we work with the middle line.

    Sheet 1 example: (see Figure 6.14)

    Sheet 2 example: (see Figure 6.15)

Figure 6.12 *Two-Dimensional Spreadsheet Matrix with Values Added to Northeast Triangle*

3	4	4	4	4
	3	4	4	4
		3	4	4
			3	4
				3

Figure 6.13 *Two-Dimensional Spreadsheet Matrix with Values Added to Southwest Triangle*

3	4	4	4	4
7	3	4	4	4
7	7	3	4	4
7	7	7	3	4
7	7	7	7	3

Figure 6.14 *Three-Dimensional Spreadsheet Matrix with Values in Middle and Upper Slices*

4	4	4	4	4
4	4	4	4	4
3	3	3	3	3

Figure 6.15 *Three-Dimensional Spreadsheet Matrix with Values Added in Lower Slice*

4	4	4	4	4
4	4	4	4	4
3	3	3	3	3
7	7	7	7	7
7	7	7	7	7

Programming Exercises

The specifications of the programming assignments were introduced in Chapter 1, at which time you were to

- think through the solution to these problems.
- identify the modules that, once implemented, will solve the problem.
- prepare a hierarchy chart of all the modules.
- prepare pseudocode/flowchart for each module in the hierarchy chart.
- write the program stubs the same way we did with the ACE Billing system application.

This chapter has added coverage of arrays to our C knowledge. We urge you to continue developing what you started in Chapter 1. If you have not started, we recommend that you start by applying the methodology presented in that chapter. We have helped you get started with some of the programming assignments by specifying only what can be done by this time.

Programming Assignment 6.1.1: Billing (batch processing)

Program Description

Modify Programming Assignment 5.1 so that the Product Number and Product Description can be read as separate fields. Follow the example presented in acech06.c in Section 6.10.

Input: Use the input record layout given in Programming Assignment 1.1.

Output: Use the output report layout given in Programming Assignment 1.1.

Programming Assignment 6.1.2: Billing (batch processing)

Program Description

Modify Programming Assignment 6.1.1 to set up parallel arrays for Product Number, Product Description, Quantity, and Cost Per Item. By parallel, we mean arrays processed in tandem. For example, the first item in the Product Number array corresponds to the first item in the Product Description array. The first item in Product Description array in turn corresponds to the first item in the Quantity array, which corresponds to the first item in the Cost Per Item array. The first report is to be similar to the one you created in Programming Assignment 5.1. The second report is to be sorted by Product Number. You may use the bubble sort algorithm that we used in acech06.c in Section 6.10.

Input: Use the input record layout given in Programming Assignment 1.1.

Output: Use the output report layout given in Programming Assignment 1.1.

Programming Assignment 6.1.3: Billing (interactive processing)

Program Description

Modify Programming Assignment 6.1.2 so that all the data is entered interactively from the terminal. The program is to prompt the user to enter data for each field, and the data entered is to be stored in the array setup for that field. This process is to continue until no more data remains to be entered. Thereafter, your program is to produce the report in the same format as Programming Assignment 6.1.1.

Input: Use the input record layout given in Programming Assignment 1.1.

Output: Use the output report layout given in Programming Assignment 1.1.

Programming Assignment 6.2.1: Payroll Report (batch processing)

Program Description

Modify Programming Assignment 5.2.1 so that the Employee Name and Employee Title are read in as separate fields, not merely as a stream of characters. You may follow the example of acech06.c in Section 6.10.

Input: Use the input record layout given in Programming Assignment 1.2

Output: Use the output report layout given in Programming Assignment 1.2

Programming Assignment 6.2.2: Payroll Report (batch processing)

Program Description

Modify Programming Assignment 6.2.1 so that it produces a report sorted by Employee Name. You may use the same bubble sort algorithm used in acech06.c in Section 6.10.

Input: Use the input record layout given in Programming Assignment 1.2

Output: Use the output report layout given in Programming Assignment 1.2

Programming Assignment 6.2.3: Payroll Report (interactive)

Program Description

Now that we have discussed arrays, we want you to modify Programming Assignment 5.2.2 to prompt the user for all the data specified in Programming Assignment 1.2. This data is to be stored into a series of parallel arrays—one array for each field. Once all the data has been entered, the full report specified in Programming Assignment 1.2 is to be produced.

Input: Use the input record layout given in Programming Assignment 1.2

Output: Use the output report layout given in Programming Assignment 1.2

Programming Assignment 6.3.2: OCS Payroll (interactive)

Program Description

Modify Programming Assignment 5.3.2 so that all the data entered is stored in a series of parallel arrays. By parallel we mean arrays used in tandem or arrays whose respective values correspond. When the system is in data-entry mode, your program is to accept as many data-entry values as the end user desires. In the same fashion, when the end user asks to print the data on current employees, they will see as many reports as there are pieces of employee information in the array. Make sure that your program pauses for the end user to see information on the current employee before viewing information on the next employee. For extra credit, write the program so that the end user can browse the employee information forward and backward. See Figure P6.3 for a sample data-entry screen.

Figure P6.3 *Sample Data-Entry Screen for Programming Assignment 6.3.2*

```
OCS Payroll Systems


1. Enter Employee Data
2. Print Employee Reports
3. Exit the System
```

Design your own data-entry screen to prompt the user for all the data required by the problem. Once the user selects menu item 1, the user is prompted for the rest of the data needed to calculate the employee's net pay. After all the data for one employee has been entered, the program is to prompt the user for data on the next employee.

Output: Design your own output report

Input: Data entered in response to the program's prompt for each field. All the fields are identified in Programming Assignment 5.3.2.

Programming Assignment 6.5.1: UNIX System Administration (batch processing)

Program Description

Write a program that reads a file in which fields are delimited by ":" and that produces the report given below. The User Name cannot exceed 8 characters, the UID (User ID) and GID (Group ID) are both integers, the Full Name is limited to 25 characters, and the Shell is limited to 30 characters. Make sure that all the data items are read in as separate data fields. The resulting fields include User ID, UID, GID, User Name, and Shell. Make sure that the data is sorted by User ID.

Input: As below; also on disk as `pa6-5.dat`.

```
bawolfso:104:500:Barry Austell-Wolfson:/usr/bin/ksh
jawolfso:105:500:Jennifer Austell-Wolfson:/usr/bin/ksh
jmnotieno:103:510:Joseph Mac-Omaya Otieno:/usr/bin/ksh
jrotieno:106:510:Joshua Raymond Otieno:/usr/bin/Csh
bnotieno:107:510:Benjamin Norman Otieno:/usr/bin/ksh
ldotieno:108:510:Lillian Danae Otieno:/usr/bin/ksh
```

Output: (see Figure P6.5)

Figure P6.5 *Output for Programming Assignment 6.5.1*

Program Name: PA6-5				Page: 1
Author: Your Name				Run Date: 12/19/2000
UNIX System Administration Report				
User Name	User ID	Group ID	Full Name	Shell
bjohnson	203	15	Bill Johnson	/usr/bin/ksh

Programming Assignment 6.5.2: UNIX System Administration (interactive processing)

Program Description

Modify Programming Assignment 6.5.1 so that all the data is entered interactively until the end-user has finished all data entry. Then you are to produce the same report that you produced in Programming Assignment 6.5.1.

Input: Use the input record layout given in Programming Assignment 5.5

Output: Use the output report layout given in Programming Assignment 5.5

Programming Assignment 6.9: Science and Engineering (Compiler Construction)

Program Description

Modify Programming Assignment 5.9 to read all the Pascal assignment statements to be processed into an array. Apply the logic for the syntax, checking against each Pascal assignment statement now resident in the array in memory.

Input Data:

```
B := 100;
B = 100;
B := 100
A := B;
C := 200;
B := B * 10 - C;
Radius := 100;
Circumference := 2 * Pi * Radius;
Area Of Circle := 2 * Pi * Radius * Radius;
Area := 2 * Pi * Radius * Radius;
Programming := Data_Structures + Algorithms;
100 := 20 + Alpha;
Sum := Sum New_Data_Value;
Sum := Sum + New_Data_Value;
Sum := Sum + New_Data_Value
```

Output Report: Use the output report format specified in Programming Assignment 3.9.

Programming Assignment 6.10: Science and Engineering ("Mathematics—The Game of Life")

Program Description

Complete Programming Assignment 1.10 interactively.

Input Data:

```
Enter size of the grid (between 3 and 8, inclusive):
Enter the number of generations:
```

Output Report: Use the same report layout headings given for Programming Assignment 3.10. The report is to consist of the original universe and its populations followed by successive generations and their populations. This is to continue until the entire population dies off, or until the number of specified generations has been displayed.

Programming Assignment 6.11.2: Distribution/ Packaging/Shipping (interactive processing)

Program Description

Modify Programming Assignment 5.11.2 so that it will prompt the end user for all the data fields needed by the packing slip. It is to read these data fields and print them in their respective places in the packing slip. Figure P6.11 shows a sample initial data-entry screen.

Figure P6.11   *Sample Initial Data-Entry Screen for Programming Assignment 6.11.2*

```
OCS Publishing Distribution

1.    Enter data and accept specified defaults
2.    Print the Distribution Slips in the system
3.    Exit the system
```

Input: Prompt users for the following information when they select menu item 1.

```
Invoice Number (6-digit number):
Invoice Date (mm/dd/yy) format:
Customer Number (6-digit number):
Order Date (mm/dd/yy) format:
Sales Order Number (6-digit number):
```

Expand the list of fields the user is prompted for to include all the data fields in the report.

Output Report Layout: Use the packing slip.

Programming Assignment 6.12: Invoicing (batch processing)

Program Description

Write the program to read data specified according to the input record specifications of Programming Assignment 1.12.

Input: `pa6-12.dat` on disk.

Output: Produce the Invoice specified in Programming Assignment 1.12.

Programming Assignment 6.16.1: EDI Claims Report (batch processing)

Program Description

Write a program that requests the Claim Number, Provider Number, Patient Last Name, Patient First Name, Charge, and Status for an unlimited number of claims. A zero entered for the Claim Number should indicate that data entry is complete.

This time, use an integer for the Status, and have the user enter 1 for accepted and 0 for rejected. Your program should then be able to calculate the total accepted charges, the total rejected charges, and the overall total charges.

Use the data below to test your program; also test the program with data of your own. Make sure your program can handle an invalid charge entry. Have the user reenter the charge until a valid number is entered.

Also notice that even though you had the user enter 0 or 1 for the claim status, the report still shows the more user-friendly ACCEPT or REJECT.

Tables P6.16A and P6.16B show the input record layouts and figure P6.16 shows the output report layout for this programming assignment.

Programming Assignment 6.16.2: EDI Claims Report (interactive processing)

Program Description

Modify Programming Assignment 5.16.2 so that the user can be prompted for all the data items demanded by this assignment, since we have just covered arrays. The program is to determine whether the claim is accepted or

Table P6.16A   *Input Record Layout for Programming Assignment 6.16.1: Claims Submitter Record*

Claims Submitter Record Layout			
Field Name	*Size*	*Data Attribute*	*No. of Decimal Positions*
SubmitterId	7	char	
SubmitterLastName	20	char	
SubmitterFirstName	15	char	

Table P6.16B   *Input Record Layout for Programming Assignment 6.16.1: Claims Record*

Claims Record Layout			
Field Name	*Size*	*Attribute*	*No. of Decimal Positions*
Claim Number	2	Integer	
Provider Number	7	long	
Patient Last Name	20	char	
Patient First Name	15	char	
Charge	5	float	2
Status	1	char (0 or 1)	

Figure P6.16   *Output Report Layout for Programming Assignment 6.16.1*

```
****************************************************************
Submitter: AA12124 - Smith, Jack D

                      Claim Editing Notice


Claim      Provider   Patient Name          Charge    Status
No.        No.

1          3445433    Simmons    Paul        60.00    ACCEPT

2          3445433    Carr       Gene        45.00    ACCEPT

3          3445433    Criss      Vincent     80.00    REJECT

4          3334434    Kraizee    Guy        100.00    ACCEPT

              Total Accept Charges: xxx.xx

              Total Reject Charges: xxx.xx

                    Total Charges: xxx.xx

********************End of Report*************************
```

rejected and is to accumulate the total charges rejected, the total charges accepted, and the net of all the charges. The program is to continue prompting for data until the user signals the end of file (for example, press `Ctrl` `Z` or `F6` on the PC and `Ctrl` `D` in UNIX).

Input Data: Prompts for all the data fields as identified in Programming Assignment 5.16.2.

Output: The output report layout is to have all the fields identified in Programming Assignment 6.16.1.

Programming Assignment 6.20.1: Programa Pro Rata (batch processing)

Program Description

This is a continuation of Programming Assignment 1.20. Modify the program so that it reads data from all the branch offices according to the format given in Table P6.20, calculates the prorated cost for each tire for each customer, and prints the result for each customer.

Input Record Layout: The input record layout in Table P6.20 is to have the Customer Name added to it at the beginning.

Table P6.20 *Input Record Layout for Programming Assignment 6.20.1*

OCS Tire Services			
Field Name	**Size**	**Attribute**	**No. of Decimal Positions**
Tread depth now			
Tread depth when new			
Price of a new tire			
The mounting and balancing charge			
The state tax rate			

Input Data: pa6-20-1.dat on disk.

Output Report Layout: Use the output report layout specified in Programming Assignment 1.20

Programming Assignment 6.20.2: Programa Pro Rata (interactive processing)

Program Description

This is a continuation of Programming Assignment 1.20. Modify the program so that it reads data from all the branch offices according to the specified format and calculates the prorated cost for each tire for each customer and prints the result for each customer.

Figure P6.20 *Initial Data-Entry Screen for Programming Assignment 6.20.2.*

```
         OCS Tire Service Center
1.   Enter data about your tire
2.   Calculate and print the pro-rated cost
3.   Exit the system
```

Input: Prompt users for the following information when they select menu item 1. The initial data-entry screen is shown in Figure P6.20.

- Customer Name (25 characters)
- Tread depth now (e.g., 3 mm)
- Tread depth when the tire was new (e.g., 9 mm)
- Price of a new tire (e.g., $21.00)
- Mounting and balancing charge (e.g., $2.50)
- State tax rate (program useful in any state) (e.g., 4%)

Output: Use the same output report layout specified in Programming Assignment 1.20.

CHAPTER 7

Pointers and Strings

OBJECTIVES

- To be able to determine, assign, and alter values at memory locations indirectly through variables whose values are addresses
- To learn different methods of assigning address values
- To understand how to increment and decrement pointers and compare their address values
- To distinguish between incrementing and decrementing the address values stored in pointers and the values they point to
- To become familiar with pointers whose values can be the address of any data type and learn limitations of such pointers

- To appreciate the close relationship between pointers and arrays and also see how they differ
- To become familiar with pointers to pointers and with double indirection
- To learn what strings are and how to measure their length
- To understand different methods of string creation and storage
- To examine string arrays and to compare arrays of pointers to char with multidimensional char arrays

NEW TERMS

address operator
dereferencing
deferencing operator
double indirection operator

indirection
indirection operator
literal string
pointer

pointer to void
string constant

Probably the most powerful tool in C is the ***pointer***. A pointer is a variable whose value is an address in RAM. We can use pointers to examine and manipulate the values found at the various locations in memory. The term *pointer* is used because a pointer "points to" the value contained at the address that is the pointer's value:

```
int num = 5;
int *ptr = &num;
```

Figure 7.1 shows what these two variables look like in memory.

Here, the pointer variable `ptr` points to the variable `num`; that is, `ptr`'s value is the address of `num`.

Figure 7.1 *A Pointer and Its Pointed-to Variable in Memory*

num	Variable	ptr
5	Value	*65524*
65524	Address	65522

Let's expand on our real estate development analogy from Section 2.3. Imagine that your computer's primary memory is an extremely long one-sided street with buildings along its length. The buildings can be given names by people ("the Greens' House," "Old Mansion," and the like), but the computers at the post office just know the buildings by address. They keep a chart to match names with addresses. Now imagine that the building at address 100 has four people. It's called "the Greens' House." The building at address 120 has no people. All there is inside the building is a sign with the number 100 on it—the address of the Greens' House. This building has been called "Reference Point for the Greens' House" for as long as people can remember, or "the Point" for short.

Now the census takers can either go directly to address 100 to find out how many people live there, or they can look at a camera installed at the Point, which is pointed right at the Greens' House, and find out that way. If any of the four occupants want to leave the Greens' House to see a movie or whatever, they can either leave the house directly, or they can go along a catwalk that runs from the Point to the Greens' House and leave from there. They have the same choice of direct or indirect access on the way back. We call peeking at or changing the number of people at the Greens' House through the Point *indirection* or *dereferencing.* And believe it or not, there is another building at address 140 called "Directions to the Reference Point for the Greens' House." Inside is a sign with the number 120, and a camera aimed at the camera inside the Point, so that the census takers now have a third choice of looking at the camera there to find out how many Greens are home. This is called *double indirection.*

You can now see why pointers in C are rightly said to be difficult to understand. Perhaps a historical perspective would be a good way to point us in the right direction, so to speak.

One of history's little known facts is that Lewis Carroll (1832–1898), noted Victorian writer and mathematician, created the first computer long before it was supposed by nearly everyone to have been invented, and gave it to Queen Victoria in an unsuccessful bid at knighthood. The following excerpt from *Through the Looking Glass* was really a means by which Lewis Carroll sent secret computer code to the Queen. (Also, "Off with her head!" is the origin of the term *executable code* and Lewis Carroll's real name *was* Charles Lutwidge Dodgson. We don't know what his real name was *called*, or even whether it was called anything at all. Some say it was Often Anonymous; others say it was Just A Nom de Plume.)

> "You are sad," the Knight said in an anxious tone: "let me sing you a song to comfort you."
>
> "Is it very long?" Alice asked, for she had heard a good deal of poetry that day.
>
> "It's long," said the Knight, "but very, very beautiful. Everybody that hears me sing it—either it brings the tears into their eyes, or else—"
>
> "Or else what?" said Alice, for the Knight had made a sudden pause.
>
> "Or else it doesn't, you know. The name of the song is called '*Haddocks' Eyes.*'"
>
> "Oh, that's the name of the song, is it?" Alice said, trying to feel interested.
>
> "No, you don't understand," the Knight said, looking a little vexed. "That's what the name is *called.* The name really *is* '*The Aged Aged Man.*'"
>
> "Then I ought to have said 'That's what the *song* is called'?" Alice corrected herself.
>
> "No, you oughtn't: that's quite another thing! The *song* is called '*Ways and Means*': but that's only what it's *called*, you know!"
>
> "Well, what *is* the song, then?" said Alice, who was by this time completely bewildered.
>
> "I was coming to that," the Knight said. "The song really *is* '*A-sitting On A Gate*': and the tune's my own invention."
>
> So saying, he stopped his horse and let the reins fall on its neck: then, slowly beating time with one hand, and with a faint smile lighting up his gentle foolish face, as if he enjoyed the music of his song, he began. . . .
>
> "But the tune *isn't* his own invention," she said to herself: "it's '*I give thee all, I can no more.*'" She stood and listened very attentively, but no tears came into her eyes.

Figure 7.2 shows what this little excerpt does. If you understand this, you will have little or no trouble with pointers, or else—

Figure 7.2   *A View Through the Looking Glass of Pointers and Variables*

Song Called = Variable's Name	Song is = Variable's Address
Song's Name Called = Pointer to Variable	Song's Name is = Address of Pointer to Variable

7.1   DECLARING POINTERS

To declare a pointer, you need three things: a type, the *indirection operator* (also called the *dereferencing operator*), and a variable name. For example:

```
int *iptr;
char *p1, *p2;
float *fptr;
```

Do not confuse the asterisk character used for the indirection operator with the same character used for the multiplication operator.

The asterisk is part of the declaration for each individual variable, not part of the type label. Contrast the following examples:

```
int *p1, *p2; /* two pointers to int */
char *ptr1, ptr2; /* pointer to char and a char, not two pointers to char */
```

You can also declare an array of pointers:

```
int *iptr[10]; /* an array of 10 pointers to int */
```

7.2   POINTER ASSIGNMENT

One means of assigning a value to a pointer is through the *address operator,* &. If num is an int variable, &num is the address of that int variable. We can assign values to pointers like this:

```
int num, val;
int *ptr;
ptr = &num; /* ptr points to num */
ptr = &val; /* now ptr points to val */
```

After the first assignment statement, ptr contains as its value whatever num's address is. After the second, it holds val's address as its value.

As is the case in this example, you generally will not need to know the address of the variable the pointer points to in order to assign its address to the pointer. You can, if you wish, however, determine the address and print it. On a system that uses linear addressing, this address value held by the pointer will be the absolute memory address; on a system with a segmented addressing architecture, such as the PC, this address would be only the offset in small-memory models but both the segment and offset in large-memory models. Appendix B discusses segmented memory models. On the PC, pointers that hold the address offset only are called near pointers and are 2 bytes in size; those that hold both the segment in 2 bytes and the offset in 2 bytes are called far pointers.

The pointers we discuss in this chapter are either the linear addressing system type or the offset portion of the segmented addressing system address. Since on a PC, these are 2-byte data objects, we could use %u, the unsigned int specifier, to print the address a pointer holds as a value (or, for that matter, the pointer's address itself):

```
int num = 5;
int *ptr = &num;
printf("num is located at %u; its value is %d\n", &num, num);
printf("ptr is located at %u; its value is %u, the address of num\n", &ptr, ptr);
```

The output looks like this:

```
num is located at 65524; its value is 5
ptr is located at 65522; its value is 65524, the address of num
```

Note the difference between ptr's address (that is, where ptr is located in memory) and the address its 2 bytes hold as its value.

You would normally use the %p specifier—a specifier designed specifically for pointers, to print out an address. Standard C guarantees that the %p specifier will correctly print an address value for a pointer on any system; however the format for the printout is implementation defined:

```
int num = 5;
int *ptr = &num;
```

```
printf("num is located at %p; its value is %d\n", &num, num);
printf("ptr is located at %p; its value is %p\n", &ptr, ptr);
```

The %p specifier prints the addresses out in hexadecimal notation on most systems:

```
num is located at FFF4; its value is 5
ptr is located at FFF2; its value is FFF4
```

7.2.1   Assigning One Pointer Value to Another

You can also assign the value of one pointer to another (that is, make both pointers point to the same variable):

```
int num = 5, val = 3;
int *p1, *p2;
p1 = &num; /* p1 points to num */
p2 = &val; /* p2 points to val */
p1 = p2; /* p1 now points to val */
```

When you assign the value of one pointer to another, you must make sure the first pointer has been initialized beforehand:

```
int num = 5;
int *p1, *p2;
p1 = &num;
p1 = p2; /* whoops! */
```

Both variables would initially just contain whatever garbage values found in the memory location the computer chose to allocate for them. In the final line of this code fragment, p1 is assigned whatever garbage value p2 had. You won't get an error message, but you won't get what you expected either.

7.2.2   Direct Address Assignment *(Optional)*

You can assign a particular memory address to a pointer with a type cast:

```
int *ptr = (int *) FFD8;
printf("ptr is located at %p; its value is %p\n", &ptr, ptr);
```

Apart from direct memory access, discussed in Appendix D, however, this usage is not common and is *highly* unportable. Be *very* careful if you do use it, particularly if you subsequently use the dereferencing operator to alter the value at the pointed-to location.

Thus, we now have three ways to assign values to pointers:

```
int num = 5, val = 3;
int *p1, *p2;
p1 = &num; /* 1: with & operator */
p2 = p1; /* 2: by assigning another pointer's value */
p1 = (int *) 65522; /* 3: by assigning a memory location */
```

You can initialize a pointer, just as you can ordinary variables:

```
int num = 5;
int *ptr = &num;
```

7.3   ALTERING AND USING POINTED-TO VALUES

So far, we've spoken of assigning values to pointers. You can also reach down a level to the variable pointed to and alter or use the value found there. This we do with the indirection or dereferencing operator, *, placed in front of the pointer variable name.

Whether we're using or altering the value found at the pointed-to location depends on which side of the assignment operator we're on. First, an example of altering the value of the variable a pointer points to:

```
int num = 5, val = 35;
int *ptr = &num;
*ptr = 3; /* num now equals 3 */
*ptr = val; /* num now equals 35, the value of val */
```

Now an example of employing the dereferencing operator to use the value a pointer points to, in this case assigning that value to another nonpointer variable:

```
int num = 5;
int val;
int *ptr = &num;
val = *ptr * 3; /* val now equals 15 */
```

The expression `*ptr` in the last statement of this second example is equivalent to 5, since that is the value found at that time in num, the variable at the pointed-to address. Note that, unlike the situation in the first example, the value of the variable the pointer points to is not changed.

7.3.1 Assigning a Value to a Memory Location without a Pointer *(Optional)*

Although the practice is not common and is highly unportable, you can assign a value to a specific memory location without the use of a pointer variable. For example,

```
*((int far *)0xB8000000) = 'A' ¦ (0117 << 8);
```

writes the letter 'A' in white foreground on red background at the top-left corner of the screen of a PC (see Appendix C for an explanation). What we've done here is to use a type cast to establish an unnamed pointer to a specific memory location and at the same time dereferenced with the dereferencing operator to assign a value at that memory location.

7.3.2 Uninitialized Pointers

With nonpointer variables, we have to take care not to use the values of uninitialized variables:

```
int num;
int val = num + 2; /* whoops! */
```

Since num was not initialized to any value and since there was no intervening postdeclaration assignment of a value to num, val will be assigned a value 2 greater than whatever garbage value num happens to hold.

The same sort of carelessness can get us into trouble with pointer variables:

```
char *p1;
char *p2 = p1;
```

Again, since p1 has not been set to any value, p2 has whatever garbage value p1 had. This oversight can have serious consequences if we try to reach down a level and make an assignment at the pointed-to location:

```
*p2 = 3;
```

The undefined value of p2 is used and interpreted as an address; then the contents of the byte at that address are overstored with the value of 3. This may destroy some important data in memory, or even a portion of the compiled program code.

7.4 RECAP: THREE DIFFERENT USES OF THE INDIRECTION OPERATOR

Focus on the three different uses of the indirection operator:

```
int num = 5, val = 3;
int number;
int *ptr; /* 1: declaration of a pointer */
ptr = &num;
*ptr = val; /* 2: left side of assignment operator: variable pointer points to (num)
                is changed; pointer still points to same place (num) */
number = *ptr; /* 3: right side of assignment operator: value of variable pointer
                  points to is assigned to a variable; no change in value of variable
                  pointer points to or where pointer points */
```

Take care to use the correct level:

```
float num, *ptr = &num;
scanf("%f", ptr);
printf("Value of num: %f\n", *ptr);
```

As we have seen, the scanf() function uses an address to store a value. We don't use the & address operator here because ptr already represents an address value. Conversely, the printf() statement calls for a float value, not the address of a float variable. We need the indirection operator to reach down to that level.

7.5   POINTER ARITHMETIC

We've seen that one way to change the address a pointer stores is to assign the pointer a new value, either by setting it to the address of another variable (ptr = &num) or by setting it to another pointer (ptr = iptr) (or, much less commonly, by directly assigning it a memory address as such). Another way is by pointer arithmetic.

 Each time we add or subtract 1 from a pointer, we increment or decrement the address stored in the pointer by the same number of bytes it takes to store a variable of the type the pointer points to.

```
float salary;
float *fptr = &salary;
int num;
int *iptr = &num;
char ch;
char *cptr = &ch;
printf("fptr points to %p\n", fptr);
fptr++;
printf("after incrementing by 1, fptr now points to %p\n", fptr);
printf("iptr points to %p\n", iptr);
iptr -= 3;
printf("after decrementing by 3, iptr now points to %p\n", iptr);
printf("cptr points to %p\n", cptr);
cptr += 7;
printf("after incrementing by 7, cptr now points to %p\n", cptr);
```

We get the following output on a PC:

```
fptr points to FFF2
after incrementing by 1, fptr now points to FFF6
iptr points to FFF0
after decrementing by 3, iptr now points to FFEA
cptr points to FFEF
after incrementing by 7, cptr now points to FFF6
```

Since a float contains 4 bytes, adding 1 to the pointer to float increments the pointed-to address by 4. Since an int contains 2 bytes, subtracting 3 from the pointer to int decrements the pointed-to address by 6. Since a char contains 1 byte, adding 7 to the pointer to char increments the pointed-to address by 7.

These operations have a more practical application with arrays:

```
int num[10], *ptr = &num[0];
ptr += 5;
```

Now we have ptr pointing to num[5]. What num[0]'s or num[5]'s address is, or how many bytes we have moved, is generally of little importance to us as programmers beyond an academic interest.

7.5.1   Pointers to Nonscalar Variables

 If we declare a pointer to a nonscalar variable, incrementing the pointer by 1 increases the address value stored in the pointer by the size of the entire data object pointed to.

For example:

```
int num[5][10];
int (*ptr)[10] = num; /* pointer to 10-int array */
printf("ptr: %p, &num[0][0]: %p\n", ptr, num[0]);
ptr++;
printf("ptr: %p, &num[1][0]: %p\n", ptr, num[1]);
```

Here, `ptr` is a pointer to an array of 10 `int`s. Incrementing by 1 should increment the address stored in `ptr` by 20, assuming each `int` is 2 bytes.

```
ptr: FF92, &num[0][0]: FF92
ptr: FFA6, &num[1][0]: FFA6
```

Incidentally, notice the difference in declaration format:

```
int (*ptr)[10]; /* pointer to array of 10 ints */
int *ptr[10]; /* 10-element array of pointers to int */
```

7.5.2   Pointer Arithmetic in Assigning and Using Values

All the examples in this section so far involve altering the pointer's value and determining the new pointed-to address. Pointer arithmetic is also helpful in using values found at pointed-to locations and in assigning new values to pointed-to memory areas:

```
char name[20];
char *ptr = &name[0];
char ch;
*(ptr + 5) = *(ptr + 6) = 'B';
ch = *(ptr + 5);
```

In the second to last statement, we assign the letter B (the value 66 on a PC or other platform that uses ASCII) to `name[5]` and `name[6]`; in the last statement, we use the value at the pointed-to location to store a B into `ch`.

7.5.3   Pointer and Array Notation Interchangeability

For either of these last two uses of pointer arithmetic (using a value at a pointed-to location or storing a value there), pointer and array notation are interchangeable. The computer uses pointers internally in either case, and apart from memory reservation considerations, there is no difference.

Thus, we could have written the preceding example's last two statements this way

```
ptr[5] = ptr[6] = 'B';
ch = ptr[5];
```

even though `ptr` is not formally an array. Similarly,

```
int slot = 5;
ptr = &name[slot];
ptr[-slot] = 'A';
```

would be a permissible way of storing an A into the first element of the array (as well as an illustration of the legitimate use of negative subscripts).

Conversely, for an array:

- You can use pointer notation rather than array notation.

- **The name of an array is equivalent to a pointer to its first element**

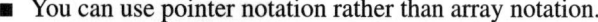

(for example, given `char name[20]`, it follows that `name` and `&name[0]` are the same).

Thus with the declaration

```
char name[20];
```

the following statements would not only have the same effect; they would compile to precisely the same executable code:

```
name[5] = 'B';
*(name + 5) = 'B';
```

Utilizing a pointer as, in effect, an array is useful only after we have assigned it a suitable value:

```
int num[20];
int *ptr = &num[0];
ptr[5] = 37;
```

Here, the declaration of num allocates 40 bytes to that array, assuming int has 2 bytes. By contrast, only a single block of 2 bytes is allocated by declaring ptr. After assigning the address of the start of num to ptr, we can use ptr[0], ptr[1], and so on to denote the same memory location as num[0], num[1], and so forth (at least until we alter ptr's value). If we had omitted the statement assigning the address of num[0] to ptr, the following statement would not be considered an error by the compiler. However, it is unlikely that the statement's result would have been intended by its originator. Assigning 37 to ptr[5] would store the value 37 at the 2 bytes found 10 bytes after whatever address the garbage value stored at the uninitialized ptr would be, interpreted as an address.

7.5.4   Simultaneous Dereferencing and Incrementing or Decrementing (Optional)

When you dereference and either increment or decrement in the same statement, you need to consider which is done first. That is, are we incrementing or decrementing the address pointed to (altering the pointer's value) or the value at the pointed-to address (leaving the pointer's value alone)? Take the following examples. But first, let us point out that while a very small amount of this may arise in linked- list programming, most of the more complicated stuff can be avoided by thoughtful programming, as we show later on.

```
int val[3] = {10, 20, 30};
int *ptr;
int num;
ptr = &val[0];
```

Figure 7.3 shows what we now have in memory.

```
num = *ptr++;
```

The indirection operator and the increment operator have the same precedence but associate from right to left. (See Appendix J.) Therefore, the increment operator operates on the pointer ptr, not the value it points to, *ptr. Since we used a postfix increment operator, num first gets its value (step 1; see Figure 7.4) and then ptr is incremented (step 2; see Figure 7.5). That is, first num is given the value val[0] has, ptr having pointed to val[0]; then ptr is made to point to val[1]. Figures 7.4 and 7.5 show the two steps and what variables and values look like in memory. The shaded bytes show the changes made by the statement.

Figure 7.3   *An Initialized Pointer and Its Unintialized Variable in Memory*

val[0]	val[1]	val[2]		ptr		*ptr		num
10	20	30		65520		10		?
65520	65522	65524		65518		65520		65516

Figure 7.4   *Step 1 in* num=*ptr++

val[0]	val[1]	val[2]		ptr		*ptr		num
10	20	30		65520		10		**10**
65520	65522	65524		65518		65520		65516

Figure 7.5   *Step 2 in* num=*ptr++

val[0]	val[1]	val[2]		ptr		*ptr		num
10	20	30		**65522**		20		10
65520	65522	65524		65518		65522		65516

Figure 7.6   *Step 1 in* num=*++ptr

val[0]	val[1]	val[2]		ptr		*ptr		num
10	20	30		**65524**		30		10
65520	65522	65524		65518		65524		65516

Figure 7.7   *Step 2 in* num=*++ptr

val[0]	val[1]	val[2]		ptr		*ptr		num
10	20	30		65524		30		**30**
65520	65522	65524		65518		65524		65516

Figure 7.8   (*ptr)--

val[0]	val[1]	val[2]		ptr		*ptr		num
10	20	**29**		65524		29		30
65520	65522	65524		65518		65524		65516

Using *(ptr++) instead of *ptr++ would have removed any doubt and is the recommended form. Indeed, the clearest formulation is to split the statement into two statements:

```
num = *ptr;
ptr++;
```

As usual, we give you all the possibilities so you can recognize them if you encounter them.

Now, a different configuration:

```
num = *++ptr;
```

Here, with a prefix increment operator, ptr is first advanced to point to ptr[2] (step 1; see Figure 7.6) and then num is assigned the dereferenced value (step 2; see Figure 7.7). (Again, we could have used num = *(++ptr) for clarity or used two statements.) But still, we are incrementing the address pointed to, not the value at that address.

Finally:

```
(*ptr)--;
```

This time, we have used parentheses to cause the alteration of the value found at the pointed-to location rather than altering the address pointed to. Here, the value of the variable where ptr now points, val[2], is decremented. The address ptr points to is unchanged. Figure 7.8 shows how this looks in memory.

7.5.5   Distance between Pointers

You can also subtract one pointer from another pointer that points to the same type to determine how far apart are the respective addresses they point to.

 When you subtract one pointer from another, the result is in number of units of the data type pointed to, not in number of bytes.

```
int val[11];
int *ptr1 = &val[0], *ptr2 = &val[2];
printf("ptr2 is %d ints from ptr1\n", ptr2 - ptr1);
printf("ptr2 is %d bytes from ptr1\n", (ptr2 - ptr1) * sizeof(int));
```

The output:

```
ptr2 is 2 ints from ptr1
ptr2 is 4 bytes from ptr1
```

The difference between two addresses is a signed integer. Therefore, an operation where you subtract a pointer with a higher address value from one with a lower address value, is valid. In the preceding example:

```
printf("ptr1 - ptr2: %d\n", ptr1 - ptr2);
```

If you want to store the result of a pointer subtraction, you could use `ptrdiff_t`, a `typedef` defined in `stddef.h`, for the type:

```
ptrdiff_t delta = ptr1 - ptr2, elements_moved = &val[current] - &val[previous];
```

(A `typedef` is a nickname for a defined Standard C type; see Chapter 13.)

7.5.6   Other Pointer Operations

Other arithmetic operations on addresses are not allowed. For instance, we cannot compute the sum of two addresses. If, in the example above, `ptr1` and `ptr2` were each set to some element of `val` that might vary depending on program results to that point, and we wanted to assign a value at the address located in the middle of the two, we could not do this:

```
*((ptr2 + ptr1) / 2) = 37; /* error! */
```

This formulation involves two illegal address operations, addition and division. Instead, we would have to do this:

```
*(ptr1 + (ptr2 - ptr1) / 2) = 37;
```

On the other hand, just about anything in C is possible with type casting (we do not recommend this construction; it's just for illustration):

```
*(int *)((unsigned) ptr2 + (unsigned) ptr1) / 2)) = 37;
```

You can use relational operators with pointers. For example, we can traverse an array by setting pointers to the first and last array elements and incrementing the first pointer until it equals the second:

```
#define SIZE 100
int num[SIZE] = {some assignment here};
int *p1 = &num[0], *p2 = &num[SIZE - 1];
int minimum = num[0];
while (++p1 < p2 - 1)
   if (*p1 < minimum)
      minimum = *p1;
```

You may likewise use the relational operators `<=`, `>=`, `==`, and `!=` with address comparisons.

One word of caution: You may not use relational operator comparisons of `far` pointers unless you are sure the pointers are in the same segment. You must use `huge` pointers instead. (See Appendix B for an explanation of `far` and `huge` pointers.)

You will make greatest use of pointer arithmetic once you begin to use string-handling functions, discussed in Chapter 9.

In summary, we can do the following arithmetic operations with pointers:

- Add an integer to a pointer: `p1 + 2` or `p1++`
- Subtract an integer from a pointer: `p1 - 3` or `p--`
- Subtract one pointer from another of the same type: `p2 - p1`
- Compare one pointer's value to another: `p1 > p2` or `p2 <= p1`

7.5.7   *Optional Reading*

No other operations are permitted, including adding one pointer to another, multiplying a pointer by a value or by another pointer, or dividing a pointer by a value or by another pointer.

Furthermore, all the pointer arithmetic operations that involve two pointers assume both pointers are of the same type (unless one is a pointer to `void`, discussed in the next section). If not, you would have to type cast one of the pointers:

```
int num, *iptr = &num;
double peachy, *dptr = &peachy;
int distance = iptr - (int *)dptr;
```

The same holds true for assignment. You cannot assign to a pointer that points to one type the address of a variable of another type or the value of a pointer that points to another type unless you type cast:

```
double doom = 3.14159, *lookingAtDoom;
char *charLook = (char *)&doom;
lookingAtDoom = (double *)charLook; /* *lookingAtDoom now = 3.14159 */
```

(By incrementing the char pointer, we could look at the individual bytes of this double.)

Actually, Standard C's requirements are somewhat more technical. Arithmetic operations and assignments are permitted for pointers where the pointer types are "compatible." For arithmetic types, compatibility means being considered by the compiler as the same type: int is compatible with signed int but not unsigned int. Qualifying otherwise compatible types in different ways (for example, one is const and the other is not) makes them incompatible. For nonscalar objects, the rules are more complex. (All rules on compatibility are spelled out in Chapter 13.)

To assign one pointer's value to another, in addition, both pointers have to point to compatible types and be similarly qualified. (Again, this is all spelled out in Chapter 13.)

One exception to these compatibility rules for pointers, in addition to the pointer to void case, discussed in the next section, is assigning NULL to a pointer, or comparing it to NULL, both of which are always allowed. This usage permits a function (our own or a Standard C library function) to return a NULL pointer in case of error. We can then test whether a pointer, to which we assign the return value of a function that returns a pointer, is equal to NULL to see whether the function was successfully called. (See Chapter 8.)

7.6 POINTERS TO void

Given this declaration

```
float num;
char *p_char;
```

you will get a warning if you attempt the following

```
p_char = &num;
```

though you could eliminate the warning with a type cast:

```
p_char = (char *)&num;
```

(Note that in this situation, incrementing or decrementing p_char would alter its address value by 1, not 4. Dereferencing in this situation would be one method of altering the value of 1 byte of a multibyte variable. See Chapter 13 for another way with unions.)

A *pointer to void* is a pointer whose value can be the address of any data object regardless of its type. In effect, a pointer to void is a "generic pointer." We do not need to type cast with pointers to void, so either of the following assignments is proper as is:

```
int num;
char *p_char;
void *p_void;
p_void = &num;
p_void = p_char; /* sensible only if p_char has been initialized, however */
```

We can use pointers to void in address comparisons:

```
if (p_void == p_char)
. . .
```

Since a pointer to void can have as its value the address of any type, however,

 You cannot apply pointer arithmetic to pointers to void.

```
*(p_void + 1) = 37; /* error! */
```

The compiler would not know how many bytes from the address stored in p_void the expression p_void + 1 would represent. Likewise,

 You cannot dereference a pointer to void with the * operator or by subscripting.

The most common use for pointers to void is as formal arguments to functions. Having a pointer to void as a formal argument allows us to pass the address of any type or a pointer of any type as an argument. (See Chapter 8 for an explanation of function arguments.) Standard C functions that handle string operations (see the next section for a discussion of strings) take pointers to char as arguments. However, Standard C functions that merely use addresses for a starting point for reading or writing—such as fread() and fwrite()—or copying a specified number of bytes or placing values into a specified number of bytes use pointers to void as arguments. Contrast these two:

```
char *strstr(const char *string, const char *substring);
   /* returns starting address of a substring inside another string */

void *memmove(void *destination, const void *source, unsigned num_bytes);
   /* copy byte values from one memory location to another */
```

When you make your own function that can take a pointer of any type as an argument, you should declare the formal parameter for that pointer as type void*. See the discussion in Chapter 9 of buffer manipulation functions for more extensive coverage of pointers to void and their use. See also Chapter 14 regarding the first arguments of the functions fread() and fwrite().

7.7   STRINGS

In some other computer languages, a separate type is created for strings. Not in C. In C, a string is simply a series of characters in memory, terminated by a NULL character—a nonprinting character represented as '\0', having a value of 0, and depicted visually on screen as a blank. (Actually, a string is a series of bytes whose values we choose to consider as characters and that is terminated by a byte with a value of zero.) All the functions that handle strings—printing, copying, comparing, and so on—are coded to look for the terminating NULL character.

In C, there are three ways to create strings: with literal strings, with char pointers, and with char arrays:

```
char name[20] = "Eustacia Vye";
char *ptr = "Adam Beede";
printf("%s\n", name); /* char array */
printf("%s\n", ptr); /* pointer to char */
printf("Angel Clare\n"); /* literal string */
```

Once we get to functions in Chapter 8, bear one rule in mind:

 Where a function argument is of type pointer to char, **you may pass a literal string, the name of a** char **array, or a pointer to** char.

7.8   STRINGS—LITERAL STRINGS

Literal strings, also called ***string constants,*** are created when we use a series of characters surrounded by double quotation marks as an argument within a function call. For example:

```
puts("I am a string constant");
```

On most systems, literal strings are placed in an area of memory known as *static memory* (see Chapter 10 and Appendix B). They last for the duration of the program. In most cases, you will have no reason to keep track of the location of the literal strings your program creates. If you do need to use the address of a literal string later in the program, you must determine the address on string creation and preserve the address in a variable.

 **Listing 7.1 constant.c**

```
/* constant.c */

/* string constants are stored in static memory & remain for program life */
```

```
#include <stdio.h>
#include <stdlib.h> /* atoi */

int main(void)
{
   char *ptr;
   char address[5];

   /* create a string out of the address of a literal string */
   sprintf(address, "%u", "guess what my address is");

   /* print that address string */
   printf("string 1 address: %s\n", address);

   /* create and print address of an identical but new literal string */
   printf("string 2 address: %u\n", "guess what my address is");

   /* point to start of first literal string */
   ptr = (char *)atoi(address);

   /* alter its first letter */
   *ptr = 'G';

   /* print out the altered string */
   puts(ptr);
}
```

The listing produces this output:

```
string 1 address: 173
string 2 address: 242
Guess what my address is
```

Each literal string is given its own memory location. The fact that the strings happen to be the same means nothing to the computer; each is given its separate spot. That is why we get two different addresses for the two identical strings here. Note that we used a %u specifier rather than %p here for convenience. We later use atoi() to convert the address string; atoi() recognizes only decimal notation, not the octal or hexadecimal notation we get with %p on most systems.

We have preserved the address of the first string with the aid of the sprintf() function, a function we will cover in Chapter 9. Briefly, that function writes starting at the address pointed to by the char pointer passed as the first argument instead of writing to the screen as printf() would, in the absence of redirection. Here, it stores the address of the first literal string as a string rather than as a numerical value ("173", rather than 173). After the printf() statement, we have two strings: the literal string, "guess what my address is", and that string's address in string form. Later in this code fragment, we use the atoi() function, also covered in Chapter 9 to assign the integer that the string spells out to ptr. We then use the dereferencing operator to change the first letter of the literal string ptr points to before printing the string out.

Actually, you should not count on each string having a separate memory location. Standard C permits compilers to store identical strings at the same address. Borland C, for example, has a programmer option "merge duplicate strings." A simple test for your implementation:

```
char *day = "ditto", *night = "ditto";
if (day == night)
   puts("Duplicate strings merged");
else puts("Duplicate strings are stored separately");
```

Furthermore, altering a literal string is not Standard C. Standard C says that if a program attempts to modify a literal string the behavior is "undefined," which could mean anything from ignoring the situation with unpredictable results to behaving differently in different environments—hence not portable. You are free to alter strings created with char arrays, however.

7.9   STRINGS—ARRAYS; THE `strlen()` FUNCTION

In terms of internal storage, there is no difference between a `char` array used to house a string and one used to house a series of `char`s without a terminating `NULL` character. You can, if you wish, even initialize a string in the same way as any other `char` array:

```
char string[] = {'I', ' ', 'a', 'm', ' ', 'a', ' ', 's',
  't', 'r', 'i', 'n', 'g', '\0'};
```

You have to remember to place a `NULL` character at the end so that the various string-handling functions treat this array as a string. Note how to write the `NULL` character's character representation.

The `printf()` function with a `%s` specifier and all the string-handling functions we will cover in Chapter 9 depend on the `NULL` character. They all start at the address passed to the function and do whatever it is they do until they first encounter a `NULL` character.

You could also have written the declaration for the "I am a string" string using the ASCII values of each letter (assuming you have a PC or other platform that uses ASCII—otherwise the values corresponding to EBCDIC or whatever other encoding system the computer uses) rather than character representations of the numbers stored in memory:

```
char string[] = {73, 32, 97, 109, 32, 97, 32, 115, 116, 114, 105, 110, 103, 0};
printf("%s\n", string);
```

giving us the output:

```
I am a string
```

This alternative method of assignment is merely an extension of the method available in assigning a single value to a `char`: you may assign a value or the character representation of the value. (Of course, in all cases, it is really only the value that gets stored in the computer.)

Standard C allows you to use a shortcut form of initializing strings, in which the braces are replaced by double quotation marks and the separating single quotes and commas are omitted. This is nearly always the method used to initialize strings:

```
char string[] = "I am a string";
```

As with other arrays, if you do not place a number within the array braces, the computer will size the array for you. For `char` arrays, however, there is a slight twist. Where you initialize a `char` array with the double-quote method, the compiler adds a `NULL` character and sizes the array to include the terminating `NULL` character. Therefore, this short-form assignment gives us the same result as both of our longer earlier assignments.

We can verify this conclusion.

```
printf("strlen: %d; sizeof: %d\n", strlen(string), sizeof(string));
```

gives us output of

```
strlen: 13; sizeof: 14
```

In other words, the array is 14 bytes long, including the `NULL` character plus the 13 characters counted by `strlen()`.

The `strlen()` function returns the number of bytes from the address passed to it (remember, `string` here is equivalent to the address of its first element) until the first `NULL` byte. This includes spaces and other punctuation characters and also the newline and formfeed characters—these characters are representations of values, just as letters and other characters are. The `sizeof` operator, as we have seen, gives us the number of bytes in the entire array, regardless of whether and where a `NULL` is found somewhere in there.

You can, of course, explicitly size the array:

```
char name[40] = "Dan Duryea";
```

 If you explicitly size a `char` array you use to store a string rather than letting the computer size it for you, be sure to include enough space for the terminating `NULL`. Otherwise, you can end up with a `char` array that is not a string.

```
char array[6] = "string";
char string[7] = "string";
```

Figure 7.9   *A Nonstring* char *Array*

array

s	t	r	i	n	g

Figure 7.9 and 7.10 show the difference between the two arrays.

It's not that the first example produces an error; on the contrary, the compiler is perfectly happy storing the six characters in array's six elements—even though doing so does not allow enough room to add the NULL character. It's just that when you try to use the array as string, you will not get the results you expect. For example,

```c
char array[6] = "string";
printf("%s\n", array);
```

might produce this output:

```
string0dieka= ♣oe9a98<34dioaYlHowdyDoody!@
```

The printf() function's %s specifier prints byte by byte, sending to the screen the character representation of each byte, starting with the address contained in the argument list corresponding to this specifier and continuing until a byte with a value of zero is reached. (As we have pointed out and as we will discuss more fully in later chapters, the name of an array is equivalent to the address of its first element, so array is an address.) What happens in this example is that the computer starts at the first element of array and keeps going until it just happens to find a NULL character in memory. It might have gone on for pages.

Likewise, assuming the following arrays are created in contiguous memory locations, Listing 7.2

 **Listing** **7.2 run_on.c**

```c
/* run_on.c */

/* what happens if you forget to leave room for NULL character */

#include <stdio.h>

int main(void)
{
    char string[] = " than I thought.";

    /* no room for NULL */
    char array[30] = "This string is a little longer";

    printf("%s\n", array);
}
```

produces

```
This string is a little longer than I thought.
```

The last character of array, the r, is stored right next to the first character of string, the space character. The printf() %s specifier runs on past the end of array, not finding any NULL there, until it encounters the NULL just after the period in string.

Figure 7.10   *A String* char *Array*

string

s	t	r	i	n	g	\0

Figure 7.11 *String Trucated by Inappropriate Input*

last_name

"	W	o	r	d	s	w	o	r	t

A similar problem can arise with inappropriate input where user response is to be handled by `scanf()` or `gets()` (see Chapter 9 for a discussion of `gets()`). Let's say user response is to be placed into this array with one of those functions:

```
char last_name[10];
```

Assume further that the user types in the following (mistakenly including the double quotes as part of the input despite your best instructions as a programmer not to):

```
"Wordsworth"
```

Figure 7.11 shows what you get in `last_name`.

See Listing 9.21, `truncate.c`, for a method of guarding against such invalid input.

7.10   STRINGS—POINTERS

You can use `char` pointers to create strings:

```
char *dictum = "\tCandy is dandy, \n"
    "\tbut liquor is quicker.\n";
printf("%s", dictum);
```

The compiler adds a terminating NULL character, reserves space for the string, stores it character by character, and then assigns the address of the first character to the `char` pointer.

Incidentally, note that the newline character or the tab character or similar nonprinting characters can be part of a string just as ordinary printing characters are. When you print the string to the screen or printer, it would first tab over before printing the rest of the string. In the middle, it would advance to the next line and tab in. At the end, it would advance to the next line:

```
    Candy is dandy,
    but liquor is quicker.
```

7.11   ARRAY VS. POINTER

Creating a string with a `char` array is similar in many ways to creating one with a `char` pointer. But the two methods are not identical. Arrays can waste memory. Pointers can be more flexible and use less memory, but they can be trickier to use. Take these flowery examples:

```
char *pointer = "You can lead a bore to culture, but you can't make him think";
char array[] = "A rose is a rose is a rose";
```

In each case, a string is created. In each case, a NULL character is added and the proper amount of memory is reserved for the string. But the similarity ends there.

In the first example, `pointer` is a pointer variable. On the other hand, while the name `array` can *serve* as a pointer to its first element for some purposes, it is *not* a pointer variable; it is a constant. The difference is more than abstract theory.

You can use pointer *notation* to identify an address within the `array` string other than the starting address. Thus,

```
char array[] = "I want to be alone";
printf("%s\n", array + 10);
```

will print

```
be alone
```

as would

```
printf("%s\n", array[10]);
```

However,

```
array++; /* error */
```

would not be permitted. You can increment variables, not constants. Though C *treats* the name of an array as a pointer to its first element, an array name is a constant without any explicit storage necessary to hold the address of the array's first element, whereas a pointer is an actual storage location capable of holding an address.

On the other hand, you can increment `pointer`, as the following minilisting shows.

 **Listing 7.3 point_up.c**

```
/* point_up */

/* incrementing pointers to char */

#include <stdio.h>
#include <string.h> /*strlen */

int main(void)
{
   char *pointer = "You can lead a bore to culture, but you can't \
      make him think";

   printf("pointer has a value of %p\n", pointer);
   pointer += strlen("You can lead a bore to culture, ");
   printf("Now pointer has a value of %p and points to \"%s\"", pointer, pointer);
}
```

We get the following output:

```
pointer has a value of 00AA
Now pointer has a value of 00CA and points to "but you can't make him think"
```

The pointer variable `pointer`, which initially pointed to the beginning of the string, now points to an intermediate location.

And you can even assign a char pointer a completely different value,

 **Listing 7.4 newpoint.c**

```
/* newpoint.c */

/* reassigning a char pointer pointing to a string,
   to another string */

#include <stdio.h>

int main(void)
{
   char *dream = "I want to be a rock singer";
   char drudge[] = "I plan to be an accountant";

   printf("dream has a value of %p\n", dream);
   printf("and points to \"%s\", starting at that address\n", dream);
   dream = drudge;
   printf("Now dream has a value of %p\n", dream);
   printf("and points to \"%s\"\n", dream);
}
```

giving this output:

```
dream has a value of 00C5
    and points to "I want to be a rock singer", starting at that address
Now dream has a value of FFDA
    and points to "I plan to be an accountant"
```

However, you could not do this:

```
char *dream = "I want to be a rock singer";
char reality[] = "I plan to be an accountant";
reality = dream; /* error */
```

You would get the error message, "Lvalue required". You cannot place a constant on the left side of an assignment statement. Also note that in the preceding example, if you neglect to do something (such as declaring another pointer and assigning it to dream's value) to store the address of the first character of "I want to be a rock singer", you will no longer be able to access it when you assign dream the address of the first element of reality.

7.11.1 Memory Differences

When you use pointers to create strings, you have to pay a little more attention to memory storage considerations than if you had used arrays. Contrast

```
char word[20];
scanf("%s", word);
```

with

```
char *word;
scanf("%s", word);
```

In the first case, you end up with just what you expect, assuming the user inputs no more than 19 letters. (In practice, you would test the length of the input before storing it into word and give the user an error message and ask for new input if the input is too long for the array.) In the second case, whatever is input is written over wherever word happens to point. "Wherever" might be unused memory, or it could be important data in your program.

You mainly run into this problem where you make a char pointer declaration without a simultaneous assignment. If you make a declaration and assignment at the same time, there is less chance of mishap:

```
char *names = "Moe, Larry and Curly";
```

The initial declaration sets aside an unused block of memory 21 bytes long and points names to the start of that block. There is a problem only where what's input to replace the initial string exceeds the initial string's length. That's a problem we could have with an array as well

```
char city[21];
```

but using the subscript probably leads us to focus more on the potential problem. In any case, we generally declare the array with a larger size than we expect to use. With the pointer assignment declaration, we don't usually have the same luxury. (At run time, however, we can allocate as much memory as we need for a pointed-to location by the use of the malloc() function. See Chapter 15).

Conversely, contrast these two declarations:

```
char name[4] = "Joe";
char *ptr = "Joe";
```

During initialization of the array, the 4 characters, including the NULL, are placed starting at &name[0]. We can later place other characters into this array, but its physical location and size will always remain the 4 bytes.

With the pointer variable ptr, the address of "Joe," not the characters themselves, is copied to ptr. That being so, we can make the following subsequent assignment of a longer string:

```
ptr = "Joe Cocomo";
```

(Note that the subsequent assignment does not cause any memory overstorage, as would have been potentially the case with a subsequent `scanf()` call. In the literal string assignment, we merely assign to `ptr` the address of a string the creation of which simultaneously reserves space in an unnamed memory location. With `scanf()`—or much more commonly the `gets()` or `strcpy()` functions we will learn about in Chapter 9—we copy a string to a location already pointed to by `ptr`. There may or may not be enough unused space there to accommodate the string to be placed at that location.)

We cannot make a subsequent assignment of a literal string to `name`, because we cannot assign an address value to a constant. We can copy a further literal string to `name` with `strcpy()` or similar functions, but that operation amounts to creating a separate literal string in a separate memory location and then placing a copy starting at `name`.

The most significant memory allocation difference between `char` arrays and `char` pointers comes when we need to use an array of strings, discussed below.

7.11.2 The `sizeof` operator vs. the `strlen()` Function

As with arrays, for `char` pointer-created strings, the `strlen()` function gives the number of bytes from the address passed, to the first NULL byte. So with

```
char *dictum = "\tCandy is dandy, \n"
    "\tbut liquor is quicker.\n";
```

the statement

```
printf("%d\n", strlen(dictum));
```

gives us 42.

Using the `sizeof()` operator would not be useful here; `sizeof(dictum)` would have a value of 2—the number of bytes in the `char` pointer variable, `dictum`. Nor would `sizeof(*dictum)`. The `sizeof` operator works on the basis of the memory space reserved for what we pass to it.

7.11.3 Array to Pointer Automatic Conversion; Differences

When an array identifier is part of an expression or is an argument to a function, the type of the identifier is automatically converted to a pointer to the first element of the array. As we've just seen, there is an exception to this automatic conversion for the `sizeof` operator. The `sizeof` operator returns the size in bytes of the entire array, not the size of its first element or the size of a pointer to its first element.

Furthermore, even though the array identifier is converted to a pointer in an expression, the array declaration itself reserves a specific block of memory, and we are not able to decouple the array name from the start of that memory.

7.12 STRING ARRAYS: ARRAY OF ARRAYS OR ARRAY OF POINTERS

A common use of two-dimensional arrays is an array of strings. For example, the following array might be used in a menu-driven interactive program, where users press a number or letter to signal which branch of the program they want to take:

```
char menu_heads[5][25] =
{
    "1. Create a report",
    "2. Edit existing report",
    "3. Print a report",
    "4. See list of reports",
    "5. Exit to DOS"
};
```

This declaration creates a two-dimensional `char` array. The first dimension consists of 5 `char` arrays, each with 25 bytes. The assignment puts a NULL character at the end of each subarray string. Beyond each NULL and before the start of the next subarray are unused bytes that just store whatever happens to be there at the time, or if the array is declared to be `static` or is external (see Chapter 10), NULL characters.

Figure 7.12 *Two-dimensional* `char` *Array*

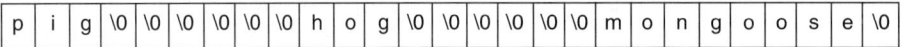

Figure 7.13 *Array of Pointers to* `char`

| p | i | g | \0 | h | o | g | \0 | m | o | n | g | o | o | s | e | \0 |

We could achieve a similar result by declaring an array of `char` pointers:

```
char *menu_heads[5] =
{
    "1. Create a report",
    "2. Edit existing report",
    "3. Print a report",
    "4. See list of reports",
    "5. Exit to DOS"
};
```

In the latter case, we have an array of 5 pointers to `char`, each of which, by virtue of the simultaneous assignment, points to a string allocated just enough memory to house the characters and terminating `NULL` character.

A shorter example, depicted in Figures 7.12 and 7.13, will illustrate the difference more graphically:

```
static char beasts[3][9] = {"pig", "hog", "mongoose"};
```

```
char *animals[3] = {"pig", "hog", "mongoose"};
```

 As you can see, *the* `char` *pointer array approach takes up significantly less memory and is generally to be preferred to the two-dimensional* `char` *array. On the other hand, if some or all of the original strings may later be replaced by others and we need to ensure a certain size space to accommodate the new strings, we must use the array of* `char` *arrays approach.*

In either case, but especially with an array of strings, where a very long string will not be flagged as an oversized initializer, be *very* careful not to omit any commas between strings:

```
char *menu_heads[5] =
{
    "1. Create a report",
    "2. Edit existing report" /* Oops! */
    "3. Print a report",
    "4. See list of reports",
    "5. Exit to DOS"
};
printf("menu_heads[1]: %s\n", menu_heads[1]);
```

See what happens:

```
2. Edit existing report3. Print a report
```

Thanks to the miracle of string concatenation, this missing comma does not trigger any error. Worse still would be making the declaration self-sizing

```
char *menu_heads[ ] =
```

and then writing to what you assume to be the last element

```
strcpy(menu_heads[4], "Some new heading");
```

where the result will be overwriting some memory area reserved for something else.

Other than with arrays of pointers to `char`, there is no automatic way to create a ragged set of nonuniform size arrays and initialize it at the same time. The route is a little more circuitous:

```
static double celsius[] = {-273.15, 0.0, 100.0};
static double fahrenheit[] = {0.0, 32.0, 212.0, 400.0};
static double kelvin[] = {-40.0, 512.0};
double *scales[] = {celsius, fahrenheit, kelvin};
```

We made the arrays static for a reason. If we had not done so, or declared them outside any function so that they were global variables, the initialization of the array of pointers would have been illegal. (See Chapter 10.)

7.12.1   A Pointer Array Example

We can also use an array of pointers to char to keep track of the starting locations of interactively entered strings. In word_ptr.c, we use an array of pointers to char to allow us to repeat an input line word by word.

 **Listing** 7.5 word_ptr.c

```
/* word_ptr.c */

/* use array of pointers to repeat input line word by word */

#include <stdio.h>
#define MAX 81

int main(void)
{
   char *word_ptr[25]; /* array of pointers to char  */
   char input_line[MAX];
   char *ltr_ptr;
   char ch;
   int words = 0, letters = 0;
   int i;

   /* point first element to start of input_line */

   word_ptr[0] = ltr_ptr = input_line;

   /* get user input of a line of text */

   while(letters++ < MAX &&
      (ch = getchar()) != '\n') /* stop on enter key or 80 ltrs */
   {
      /* fill word_ptr array with address in input_line if encounter space */
      if (ch == ' ') /* new word comes next */
      {
         /* mark end of word in input_line with NULL */
         *ltr_ptr = 0;
         ltr_ptr++;
         word_ptr[++words] = ltr_ptr;
      }

      /* otherwise, store letter in input_line */
      else
      {
         *ltr_ptr = ch;
         ltr_ptr++;
      }
   }

   /* close off last word */
   *ltr_ptr = 0;
   words++;

   /* print the line word-by-word in reverse */
   for (i = words - 1; i >= 0; i--)
      printf("%s ", word_ptr[i]);
}
```

Figure 7.14 `char` *Array* `input_line` *in Memory*

input_line

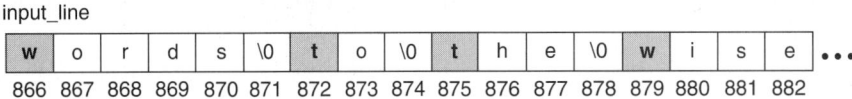

| w | o | r | d | s | \0 | t | o | \0 | t | h | e | \0 | w | i | s | e | •••|

866 867 868 869 870 871 872 873 874 875 876 877 878 879 880 881 882

Figure 7.15 *Array of Pointers to* `char` `word_ptr` *in Memory*

word_ptr

| 866 | 872 | 875 | 879 | 0 | ••• |

65466 65468 65470 65472 65474

We use the array of pointers to `char`, `word_ptr`, to keep track of the starting address of each word in the input line. We initialize `word_ptr`'s first element to the start of the input line array `input_line`.

We also utilize a pointer to `char`, `ltr_ptr`, to store letters into `input_line` as they are input. We likewise initialize `ltr_ptr` to point to the start of `input_line`.

We process the input letters in a `while` loop, stopping at the newline (generated when the user presses the [Enter] key), or sooner if the user has typed in 80 letters without pressing [Enter] . This latter is used to prevent array overflow.

On each keypress, we increment `ltr_ptr`, so that it points to the next byte of `input_line`. Along the way, we assign the input character to the decremented `ltr_ptr`, thus storing the character into `input_line`.

An exception to this process occurs if the letter is a space character, denoting the end of a word. We still increment `ltr_ptr`, moving it along to the next byte in `input_ptr`. However, instead of storing the space character in `input_line`, we take the opportunity of assigning the address `ltr_ptr` points to in `input_line` to the next element of `word_ptr`, and we mark the end of the word with a `NULL` character.

If the user inputs

```
words to the wise
```

the way things look in memory is shown in Figures 7.14 and 7.15.

We then print the words in reverse order.

7.13   DOUBLE INDIRECTION: POINTERS TO POINTERS

In `word_ptr.c`, we used a pointer to point to various elements of a `char` array. By incrementing the pointer and dereferencing, we were able to store characters into the array one by one. We did so as an alternative to using array notation for `input_line` and a counter:

```
input_line[count++] = ch;
```

This array-counter framework is what we did use, however, for `word_ptr`, the array of pointers each element of which held an address in `input_line` of the start of a word. Can we indirectly manipulate the array of pointers to `char` just as we did with the simple `char` array?

The answer is yes. We can declare a pointer to point to the various pointers to `char` contained in `word_ptr`. We declare a pointer to pointer with a ***double indirection operator:***

```
char **ptr_ptr;
```

The pointer to pointer to `char` variable `ptr_ptr` would contain an address—the address of a pointer to `char`, which would in turn contain the address of a `char` variable.

The following program, `word2ptr.c`, illustrates the use of the pointer to pointer technique to perform the same line-parsing operation we did in `word_ptr.c`.

 **Listing 7.6 word2ptr.c**

```c
/* word2ptr.c */

/* does the same thing word_ptr does with pointer to pointer
   to char */

#include <stdio.h>
#define MAX 81

int main(void)
{
   char *word_ptr[10]; /* array of pointers to char */
   char input_line[MAX];
   char *ltr_ptr;
   char **ptr_ptr;
   char ch;
   int letters = 0; /* limit input to 80 characters */

   ltr_ptr = input_line;
   ptr_ptr = word_ptr; /* point to first element of array of char pointers */

   /* store starting address of first word in word_ptr array */
   /* ltr_ptr points to start of input_line */
   *ptr_ptr++ = ltr_ptr;

   while(letters++ < MAX &&
       (ch = getchar()) != '\n') /* stop on enter key or 80 ltrs */
   {
      /* fill word_ptr array with address in input_line if encounter space */
      if (ch == ' ')
      {
         *ltr_ptr = 0; /* mark end of word with NULL */
         *ptr_ptr++ = ++ltr_ptr;
      }

      /* otherwise, store letters in input_line */
      else *ltr_ptr++ = ch;
   }

   /* close off last word */
   *ltr_ptr = 0; /* mark end of word with NULL */

   /* store sentinel value in word_ptr as stopping point for while loop below */
   *ptr_ptr = 0;

   ptr_ptr = word_ptr; /* reset from last element to first */
   while (*ptr_ptr) /* print word at a time; last address is NULL */
     printf("%s ", *ptr_ptr++);

#if 0
   {
      while(**ptr_ptr)
      {
         putchar(**ptr_ptr);
         (*ptr_ptr)++;  /* advance where word_ptr element points in input_line */

      }
      putchar(' ');
      ptr_ptr++; /* advance to next element of word_ptr */
   }
#endif
}
```

We initialize `ptr_ptr` to point to the first element of `word_ptr` just as we initialize `ltr_ptr` to point to the first element of `input_line`. We indirectly store values in `word_ptr` by using a single decrement operator

```
*ptr_ptr++ = ltr_ptr;
```

at the same time moving where `ptr_ptr` points to the next element of `word_ptr`.

At the end of input, we store a NULL in `word_ptr`'s next element:

```
*ptr_ptr = 0;
```

This gives us a sentinel value for the `while` loop that prints out the words. A sentinel value is an artificial value that has no independent significance apart from allowing us to terminate or take some action when we find it once again.

The `while` expression

```
while(*ptr_ptr)
```

continues until an element in `word_ptr` is found to contain a NULL. The resulting print operation

```
printf("%s ", *ptr_ptr++);
```

prints out the word this particular element of `word_ptr` points to by virtue of the indirection operator (`ptr_ptr` points to an element of `word_ptr`; `*ptr_ptr` points to the word itself pointed to by that element), and then increments the element in `word_ptr` that `ptr_ptr` points to by virtue of the increment operator. The question of precedence here is the same as we encountered earlier for pointer variables.

7.13.1   Reaching Down Two Levels

Using a single indirection operator brought us from the pointer to pointer level to the pointer level. We can reach down another level with a double indirection operator.

For example, instead of printing a word at a time

```
while(*ptr_ptr)
   printf("%s ", *ptr_ptr++);
```

we could proceed a letter at a time:

```
while (*ptr_ptr) /* print word at a time; last address is NULL */
{
   while(**ptr_ptr)
   {
      putchar(**ptr_ptr);
      (*ptr_ptr)++; /* advance where word_ptr element points in input_line */
   }
   putchar(' ');
   ptr_ptr++; /* advance to next element of word_ptr */
}
```

The expression

```
while(**ptr_ptr)
```

asks whether the letter pointed to by the element in `word_ptr` that `ptr_ptr` points to is a NULL. Thus we go from the starting letter of a word to its terminating NULL.

Meanwhile, we print each character in the word and then move to where in `input_line` the currently pointed-to element of `word_ptr` points. The statement that effects this advance is

```
(*ptr_ptr)++;
```

To overcome the rules of precedence, we use parentheses to first dereference the pointer and then increment. Here, by using a single indirection operator, we have dereferenced to the next level, that of the pointer to `char`.

Chapter Summary

1. A pointer is a variable whose value is an address in primary memory.
2. Pointers can be used to examine and manipulate the values found at the various locations in memory.
3. A pointer is declared with a type, the indirection operator, and a variable name.
4. The most common way to assign a value to a pointer is through the address operator, &. The value of one pointer can also be assigned to another of the same type.
5. An array of array of pointers can be declared.
6. Pointers can be initialized.
7. It is possible to reach down a level through the pointer to the variable pointed to and alter or use the value found there with the indirection or dereferencing operator, *, placed in front of the pointer variable name.
8. An array is a constant; a pointer is a variable. However, pointer and array *notation* are interchangeable in most situations.
9. Each time 1 is added or subtracted from a pointer, the address stored in the pointer is incremented or decremented by the same number of bytes it takes to store a variable of the type the pointer points to. With a pointer to a non-scalar variable, incrementing the pointer by 1 increases the address value stored in the pointer by the size of the entire data object pointed to.
10. Care must be taken to distinguish between incrementing or decrementing the address value housed by the pointer and incrementing or decrementing the value at the pointed-to location.
11. You can subtract one pointer from another pointer that points to the same type to determine how far apart are the respective addresses they point to. The result is in number of units of the data type pointed to, not in number of bytes.
12. You can use relational operators with pointers.
13. Apart from adding or subtracting an integer number to or from a pointer, subtracting one pointer from another, and comparing addresses, arithmetic operations on addresses are not allowed.
14. All pointer arithmetic operations that involve two pointers assume both pointers are of the same type.
15. A pointer to void is a pointer whose value can be the address of any data object regardless of its type.

16. You cannot apply pointer arithmetic to pointers to void. Nor can you dereference a pointer to void with the * operator or by subscripting.
17. A string is a series of characters in memory, terminated by a NULL character. There are three ways to create strings: literal strings, char pointers, and char arrays. Where a function argument is of type pointer to char, you may pass any of the three.
18. Literal strings are created when we use a series of characters surrounded by double quotation marks as an argument within a function call.
19. When char pointers are used to create strings, the compiler adds a terminating NULL character, reserves space for the string, stores it character by character, and then assigns the address of the first character to the char pointer. Just as much memory as is required to create the string is used.
20. A shortcut form of initializing strings in array form is available: braces are replaced by double quotation marks and the separating single quotes and commas are omitted. The compiler adds a NULL character and sizes the array to include the terminating NULL character.
21. The printf() function with a %s specifier and all Standard C string-handling functions start at the address passed to the function and do whatever it is they do until they first encounter a NULL character.
22. The strlen() function returns the number of bytes from the address passed to it until the first NULL byte.
23. A common use of two-dimensional arrays is an array of strings. A similar result can be achieved by declaring an array of char pointers.
24. Each element of an array of char pointers points to a string allocated just enough memory to house the characters and terminating NULL character, and so uses less memory than the two-dimensional char array approach. However, if the original strings may later be replaced by others and a certain size space must be guaranteed to accommodate the new strings, the array of char arrays approach is preferred.
25. A pointer to pointer holds the address of a pointer variable that in turn holds the address of a nonpointer variable. A pointer to pointer is declared with a double indirection operator.

Review Questions

1. Define a pointer.
2. Give a generic declaration of a pointer, and give two examples.
3. Which operator symbol gives the address of a variable?
4. Declare an integer variable, x, a pointer to an integer variable, xptr, and store the address of the integer variable to the pointer.
5. What does the unary operator & do?

6. What does the unary operator * do relative to pointers?
7. Explain the following statements; be sure to specify the values of all the variables:

```
int x = 100;
int y = 200;
int z[5] = {300, 400, 500, 600, 700};
int *xptr;
```

```
xptr = &x;
y = *xptr;
*xptr = -100;
xptr = &z[0];
```

8. List at least four reasons we use pointers.
9. An array name without [] is the address of the array (True or False).
10. Consider the following declaration:

```
int xyz[100];
```

To what does xyz[5] refer? To what does xyz refer?

11. What does *(xyz + k) equate to when subscripts are used?
12. What does xyz + k equate to when subscripts are used?
13. Declare a 5-element array, z, and initialize it. Write a program to sum up the values in the z array using subscripts.
14. Write a program to sum up the z array using pointer notation.
15. Execute the program in Figure 7.16 and show the results of doing so.

Figure 7.16

```
/*
  +---------------------------------------------------------------+
  +   Program Name:  7-15a.c
  +          Author:  Austell-Wolfson and Otieno
  +            Date:  12/19/2000
  +   Purpose:
  +      For students to review pointers and add their comments.
  +      For the sake of this exercise, let us assume the following
  +      addresses:
  +      name == address of 1000
  +      ptr  == address of 2000
  +      ch   == address of 3000
  +      Change this program by adding your own comments once
  +      you have gone over it.
  +---------------------------------------------------------------+
*/

#include <stdio.h>
int main(void)
{
    char name [] = "Marry";
    char * ptr;
    char ch;

    ptr = name;
    ch = *ptr;
    printf("1: ch = %c; *ptr = %c; ptr = %u; &ptr = %u; name = %s\n",
        ch, *ptr, ptr, &ptr, name);
    ch = *ptr + 3;
    printf("2: ch = %c; *ptr = %c; ptr = %u; &ptr = %u; name = %s\n",
        ch, *ptr, ptr, &ptr, name);
    ch = *(ptr + 3);
    printf("3: ch = %c; *ptr = %c; ptr = %u; &ptr = %u; name = %s\n",
        ch, *ptr, ptr, &ptr, name);
    *ptr += 3;
    ch = *ptr;
    name[1] += 4;
    printf("4: ch = %c; *ptr = %c; ptr = %u; &ptr = %u; name = %s\n",
        ch, *ptr, ptr, &ptr, name);
    (*ptr)++;
    ch = *ptr;
    printf("5: ch = %c; *ptr = %c; ptr = %u; &ptr = %u; name = %s\n",
        ch, *ptr, ptr, &ptr, name);
    ch = *ptr++;
    printf("6: ch = %c; *ptr = %c; ptr = %u; &ptr = %u; name = %s\n",
        ch, *ptr, ptr, &ptr, name);
    ch = *ptr = '\0';
```

Figure 7.16 *Continued*

```
    printf("7: ch = %c; *ptr = %c; ptr = %u; &ptr = %u; name = %s\n",
        ch, *ptr, ptr, &ptr, name);
    return 0;
}




/*
  +----------------------------------------------------------------+
  +    Program Name:  7-15b.c
  +          Author:  Austell-Wolfson and Otieno
  +            Date:  12/19/2000
  +    Purpose:
  +       For students to review pointers and add their comments.
  +       For the sake of this exercise, let us assume the following
  +       addresses:
  +       line == address of 1000
  +       ptr  == address of 2000
  +       ch   == address of 3000
  +       Assume the input entered was: This is the best C book.
  +       Change this program by adding your own comments once
  +       you have gone over it.
  +----------------------------------------------------------------+
*/
#include <stdio.h>

int main(void)
{
    char line[81];
    char * ptr;
    char ch;

    ptr = line;
    while ((ch = getchar()) != '\n')
    {
        *ptr++ = ch;
    }
    *ptr = '\0';
    ptr = line;
    while (*ptr)
    {
        putchar(*ptr++);
    }
    return 0;
}




/*
  +----------------------------------------------------------------+
  +    Program Name:  7-15c.c
  +          Author:  Austell-Wolfson and Otieno
  +            Date:  12/19/2000
  +    Purpose:
  +       For students to review pointers and add their comments.
  +       Change this program by adding your own comments once
  +       you have gone over it.
  +----------------------------------------------------------------+
*/
#include <stdio.h>
```

(continued on the next page)

Figure 7.16   *Continued*

```
int main(void)
{
    char *wordptr[10];
    char input_line[80];
    char * ptr;
    char ch;
    char words = 0;
    char letters = 80;
    char i;

    wordptr[0] = ptr = input_line;
    while(letters-- && (ch = getchar()) != '\n')
    {
        if (ch == ' ')
        {
            *ptr++ = NULL;
            wordptr[++words] = ptr;
        }
        else
        {
            *ptr++ = ch;
        }
    } /* end while */
    *ptr = NULL;
    putchar('\n');
    for (i = 0; i <= words; i++)
    {
        printf("%s ", wordptr[i]);
    }
    return 0;
}



/*
+----------------------------------------------------------------------+
+    Program Name:  7-15d.c
+          Author:  Austell-Wolfson and Otieno
+            Date:  12/19/2000
+    Purpose:
+       For students to review pointers and add their comments.
+       For the sake of this exercise, let us assume the following
+       addresses:
+              wordptr   == 1000
+              inputLine == 2000
+              ptr       == 3000
+              ptrptr    == 4000
+              ch        == 5000
+       Change this program by adding your own comments once
+       you have gone over it.
+----------------------------------------------------------------------+
*/

#include <stdio.h>
int main(void)
{
    char *wordptr[10];
    char inputLine[80];
    char *ptr;
    char **ptrptr;
    char ch;
```

Figure 7.16   *Continued*

```
    char letters = 80;
    char i;

    for (i = 0; i < 80; i++)
    {
        inputLine[i] = '\0';
    }

    for (i = 0; i < 10; i++)
    {
        wordptr[i] = 0;
    }

    ptr = inputLine + 1;
    ptrptr = wordptr + 1;
    *ptrptr++ = ptr;
    while(letters-- && (ch = getchar()) != '\n')
    {
        if (ch == ' ')
        {
            *ptr++ = NULL;
            *ptrptr++ = ptr;
        }
        else
        {
            *ptr++ = ch; /* store letters in inputLine */
        }
    } /* end while */
    *ptrptr = NULL;
    *ptr = NULL;
    ptrptr = wordptr + 1;
    putchar('\n');
    while (*ptrptr)
    {
        printf("%s ", *ptrptr++);
    }
    putchar('\n');
    ptrptr--;
    while (*ptrptr)
    {
        printf("%s ", *ptrptr--);
    }
    putchar('\n');
    ptrptr++;
    do
    {
        ptr = *ptrptr;
        while (*ptr)
        {
            ptr++;
        }
        ptr--;
        while (*ptr)
        {
            putchar(*ptr--);
        }
        putchar(' ');
    } while(*ptrptr++);
    return 0;
}
```

(continued on the next page)

Figure 7.16 *Continued*

```
/*
   +-------------------------------------------------------------------+
   +    Program Name:   7-15e.c
   +         Author:   Austell-Wolfson and Otieno
   +           Date:   12/19/2000
   +    Purpose:
   +       For students to review pointers and add their comments.
   +       Change this program by adding your own comments once
   +       you have gone over it.
   +-------------------------------------------------------------------+
*/
#include <stdio.h>
int main(void)
{
   char *words[20];
   char line[100];
   char **z;
   char *p;
   int c;

   z = words;
   *z = p = line;
   z++;
   while (1)
   {
      while ( (c = getchar()) > ' ' )
      {
         *p++ = c;
      }
      *p = '\0';
      if (c == '\n')
      {
         break;
      }
      *z++ = ++p;
   }
   for (z -= 1; z >= words; z--)
   {
      printf("%s ", *z);
   }
   return 0;
}
```

Programming Exercises

The specifications of the programming assignments were introduced in Chapter 1, at which time you were to

- think through the solution to these problems.
- identify the modules that, once implemented, will solve the problem.
- prepare a hierarchy chart of all the modules.
- prepare pseudocode/flowchart for each module in the hierarchy chart.
- write the program stubs the same way we did with the ACE Billing system application.

This chapter has added coverage of pointers and strings to our C knowledge. We urge you to continue developing what you started in Chapter 1. If you have not started, we encourage you to start by applying the methodology presented in that chapter. We have helped you get started with some of the programming assignments by specifying only what can be done by this time.

Some of the problems presented in Chapter 1 may have been completely solved by now. You may revise any of the programming assignments we have done up to this point so that your programs can benefit from new features afforded you by pointers.

Programming Assignment 7.27.1: Electronics

Program Description

This problem is a continuation of Programming Assignment 1.27. Be sure to have accurately determined which variables you will need to create from the problem statement in Chapter 1. Declare some of the variables the test program will require. Remember that you want to make the most efficient use of storage space possible, so consider what type of variable is required for each value to be stored. Some possible variables include ones that will store

- Address assigned to the microprocessor. The address in question here can be stored into a variable of the type char. This is possible because we are attempting to emulate an 8-bit processor. The possible address values, as presented in the first table in Programming Assignment 1.27, ranged from 0 to F, the full range of hexadecimal numbers.
- LED status (or equivalent value). This can also be stored in a char type variable.
- Data stored in micro (just 1 byte for now). A char variable is all that is needed to store such data.
- User's command input. This may be stored in a char variable as well. The possible values include
    - h to indicate that a hexadecimal value is about to be entered.
    - b to indicate that a binary variable is about to be entered.
    - q to indicate that you are terminating data entry.

Programming Assignment 7.27.2: Electronics

Program Description

Modify Programming Assignment 7.27.1 so that you write a test program for a PC that will allow users to manually type in the codes of the commands they wish to issue. For the test program, the computer will be the only processor running, but it still needs to store and update its address as commanded. Users should be able to select binary or hex. The transactions shown below provide an example of a test session.

```
ZEI processor testing software
bxxxxxxxxxxxxxxxx (16 bits) for binary input
hxxxx (4 nibbles) for hexadecimal input
spaces are ignored

Enter your command >h 00 20
                    response: h0000
```

In this example, the first character—h—indicates that what follows is a hexadecimal number. Notice that the blanks are ignored, as previously stated. The 00 that follow indicates that the processor we are emulating is at address 00. The last entry—20—is to be interpreted according to the first table in Programming Assignment 1.27. The 2 in the 20 is the command that tells the processor to reply with the processor address followed by values currently stored in the LED status. In the response, you see the h, which signals a hexadecimal number; the next 00 is the address of the processor; and the last 00 is the value of the LED status. This is appropriately 00 because we are just starting out.

```
Enter your command >b 00000000 00100000
                    response: b0000000000000000
```

In this example, the first character—b—indicates that what follows is a binary number. You are to read that number into a string and convert it into a hexadecimal number so that you can work with the tables presented in Programming Assignment 1.27. The rest of the examples can be afforded similar explanation as you refer to the details offered in Programming Assignment 1.27.

```
Enter your command >h 00 E5
                    response:
Enter your command >h 00 20
                    response:
Enter your command >h 05 20
                    response: h0500
```

```
Enter your command >h 05 54
                        response:
Enter your command >h 05 20
                        response: h0504
Enter your command >h 05 93
                        response:
Enter your command >h 05 A2
                        response:
Enter your command >h 05 30
                        response: h0523
Enter your command >Q
  ----PROGRAM TERMINATED----
```

Programming Assignment 7.27.3: Electronics

Program Description

Modify the Programming Assignment 7.27.2 program so that it can store 10 unsigned char values. Remember that for an 8-bit processor, an unsigned char is sufficient to hold an address. Implement the commands 0x08 Clear data element X, and 0x0B Locate Value. Create an array of 10 unsigned chars. Be sure to refer to Programming Assignment 1.27 for details.

Programming Assignment 7.27.4: Electronics

Program Description

This problem is an enhancement of Programming Assignment 7.27.3. When working with a real microprocessor, you will find that many special variables are actually pointers to specific memory locations. This is especially true when dealing with special function registers or the actual IO ports (that is, the pins) of the chip. If the address of the port we wanted to use to control our LEDs were 0xF1, the "variable" would be declared like this:

```
#define LED_PORT (* unsigned char (unsigned char ) (0xF1))
```

Manipulating LED_PORT would be exactly the same as manipulating any other variable—it can be assigned a value, tested, and modified. To simulate this function, make pointers to all of the variables you have used in your program thus far. Then manipulate only the pointers within your program.

Since we do not present bit manipulations until Chapter 12, your simulation is limited to performing the following operations: converting the input values from decimal to hexadecimal and looking up the tables provided in Programming Assignment 1.27. The rest of the operations will be performed after we have covered the chapter on bit manipulations.

CHAPTER **8**

Functions

OBJECTIVES

- To appreciate the need to divide the program into modules that perform discrete tasks
- To see the importance of function prototypes
- To become familiar with the proper syntax for function declarations, definitions, and calls
- To examine argument assignment and evaluation
- To learn the nature of variables declared inside function prototypes and inside functions
- To learn how to create functions that take arguments and return values
- To see how values are passed to and from functions and understand the difference between call by value and call by reference

- To understand how to use pass addresses to functions so as to alter values in the calling function and access array elements
- To learn how to create functions that call themselves or that have a variable number of arguments
- To see the differences in prototype checking and type conversion between functions with fixed and variable numbers of arguments
- To learn how to use function pointers and arrays of function pointers to make a dynamic selection from a group of functions and call the selected function indirectly

NEW TERMS

actual argument
argument
call by value
call by reference

dangling pointer
formal argument
function definition
function declaration

function call
prototype
recursion

Each C program starts executing statements at the beginning of a function called `main()`. You could theoretically write a program that lumps all statements into `main()`, without employing any other functions, but no one ever does. In practice, each program contains quite a number of functions.

The operative component of a function, called the *function definition,* is a series of statements that collectively perform a discrete task. A function is called into play to perform its designated task by a statement or part of a statement written in a special format. When you invoke a function in this way, it is said that you *call* it; the statement that invokes the function is referred to as a *function call.*

8.1   PROGRAM EXECUTION AND FUNCTION CALLS

Program execution starts and ends with `main()`. After digesting any preprocessor directives (see Chapter 11) and certain declarations of variables and functions, the program then moves to the statements of `main()`. Those statements are executed one by one, in the order in which they are written, diverting along the way when a function call is made. At those points, the function statements are likewise executed one by one (until, again, further function calls are encountered).

When the function call is completed, the program picks up in `main()` (or other calling function) at the statement following the function call. Once all statements in `main()` are executed, the program stops and the user is returned to whatever environment the user was in when the program started—DOS, the C editor, or some other environment. The program may terminate earlier if it encounters a call to a function such as `exit()` or `abort()`, whose job it is precisely to cause such early termination.

8.2   WHY USE FUNCTIONS?

What is the reason for this complex approach to programming? Why not just stick to a single function, `main()`, and put all our statements there?

The most obvious, though not the most important, reason is to avoid repetition of lengthy blocks of code statements. Suppose that at 20 places in your code, you take a series of numbers and do a statistical analysis of them—for instance, their arithmetic average, the average of the sum of the squares of the numbers minus the square of their average, and the square root of that last result (the mean, variance, and standard deviation, respectively). And suppose it takes a dozen lines of code to accomplish the analysis and print out its results. If you didn't use functions, you would have to write the dozen statements at each of those 20 points in the code where the analysis is required. That is clumsy at best. Every time you altered the block of code, you would have to make changes 20 separate times. Even if no changes were required, the executable program would be needlessly bloated in size. Instead, with functions, you can write the statements once, add a little minor housekeeping, and insert 20 function call statements at the appropriate spots.

But the key reason for using functions is efficiency. Breaking the program up into functions makes it easier to design, write, understand, and debug. Allocating discrete tasks to separate functions parallels the logical design process programmers use—first do this task, next do this task, then do this task, and so on.

Using functions also lets you write a particular block of code, test it with a sample miniprogram, and keep revising it until it works and is ready for incorporation into the real program. This approach is imperative where more than one programmer is working on the same program. Each team member is assigned a function or group of functions, to be written for incorporation with the other team members' functions.

Another advantage of functions is the ability to localize the effect of the intermediate programming steps in completing a certain task. With some exceptions, the variables used within one function are not communicated with other functions or even known to other functions. The variable of one function cannot inadvertently affect the variables of another function. Consequently, the programmer is not required to keep track of every spot in a program many hundreds or thousands of lines long that could conceivably change a particular variable.

8.3   STRUCTURE OF A FUNCTION

A function has three components: a declaration (also called a prototype), a definition, and calls. The *function declaration* is a single statement that advises the compiler of the number and types of values that are to be passed to, and the type of value to be returned from, the function, if any. The *function definition* contains the operative statements that carry out the function's task. The *function call* invokes the function.

Let's take a look at a very simple example, a program that contains a function that calculates the absolute value of the difference between two numbers.

 **Listing 8.1 absolute.c**

```
/* absolute.c */

/* simple function example: absolute value of difference between 2 numbers */

#include <stdio.h>
```

```
int absolute(int num, int val); /* function declaration */

int main(void)
{
    int number = 100, value = 50;
    int difference;

    /* call: variables as arguments */
    difference = absolute(number, value);
    printf("difference is %d\n", difference);

    /* call: constants as arguments */
    difference = absolute(187, 222);
    printf("difference is %d\n", difference);

    /* call: mixed expression as arguments */
    difference = absolute((number * 2) - 100, value + 50);
    printf("difference is %d\n", difference);
}

int absolute(int num, int val) /* function definition */
{
    int result = num - val;

    if (result < 0)
        result *= -1;
    return result;
}
```

The program contains two functions: `main()` and `absolute()`. The `main()` function calls `absolute()` and in so doing passes two values to `absolute()`; `absolute()` in turn returns the absolute value of the difference between the two numbers to `main()`. Here's the output we get:

```
difference is 50
difference is 35
difference is 0
```

Let's examine the various components and mechanics of this program.

8.4 FUNCTION DECLARATION (PROTOTYPE)

We can pass one or more values (called **arguments**) to a function for the function to use in performing its task, or we can pass it none. We can have the function return a single value to the function that called it or have it return none. The function declaration (also called a **prototype**) tells the compiler the name of the function, how many values are to be passed to the function and what their type is, and whether a value is returned and if so what its type is.

The function declaration in `absolute.c` is

```
int add(int num, int val);
```

This prototype indicates that the function `add()` takes two arguments, both `int`, and returns a value, also an `int`.

As we have seen, you cannot use variables before you declare them. Likewise:

 In C, you should not call a function before having declared it.

The declaration should be on an earlier line in the code than any statement that calls the function. By earlier, we mean physically on a higher line rather than conceptually prior to the program's flow of execution. The compiler works on a line-by-line basis. So if the compiler processes a function call before it has seen the prototype, it has no way to check the number and type of parameters. In the following faulty program, all you get is a warning that there is a call without a prototype.

 **Listing 8.2 no_dec.c**

```c
/* no_dec.c */

/* omitting declaration before function call prevents prototype checking */

#include <stdio.h>

int main(void)
{
    printf("%d\n", sum (1.1, 2.2, 3.3, 4.4));
    printf("%d\n", sum (1.1, 2.2));
}

int sum(int a, int b)
{
    return a + b;
}
```

Assuming that the implementation even links without error, the program compiles and runs and gives completely erroneous results. The compiler does not know to issue an error message for the first function call, to the effect that the number of parameters is incorrect. Nor does it know for either call that it is supposed to convert the floating point constant arguments to type int. If, however, you placed a declaration for sum() either above or inside and at the top of main(), you would get the appropriate error message.

If a declaration precedes a function call, the compiler will check to make sure the number of arguments match (and issue an error if they do not). It will also, if possible, convert each argument to the corresponding formal argument type if the type is different. (See Chapter 13 for permissible conversions.) Without a preceding prototype, the compiler will perform only the usual automatic conversions on the actual arguments (Chapter 13 provides a description of automatic conversions).

With few exceptions, you will generally place all your function declarations above main()—including those placed there by virtue of being included through a header file (see Chapter 11), so this declaration placement requirement rarely poses a problem. There is no reason to place a prototype inside a function. If you do, as with a variable, the function declaration must precede any nondeclaration statements in the function. There is no requirement for placing prototypes before or after variable declarations. You can mix them at will:

```c
int absolute(int num, int val), difference, *iptr;
```

(This last example is permitted because a function is considered to have whatever type it returns.)

Arguments are separated by commas, if there are more than one. A function declaration is a normal C statement, terminated by a semicolon. It is not necessary for the arguments in the prototype to have variable names; the types are all you need:

```c
int add(int, int);
```

 But it doesn't hurt to include variable names as well; indeed, the practice is highly recommended. *Using variable names in function prototypes tends to make the program easier to follow.* This is particularly so where the function definition (which *must*, as you will see, contain variable names as well as types) is in a different file from the function declaration, or only the object code version of the function definition rather than its text is part of your program (that is, where it is part of a library; see Chapter 17).

The only storage class specifier you may use for the type of a formal argument is register, and even then the compiler may ignore your hint. (See Chapter 10 on register and other storage class specifiers.)

8.4.1   Function Types

If the function does not return any value, you must indicate that by placing the word void in front of the function name in place of a type:

```c
void add(int num, int val); /* no return value */
```

This is done in both the function declaration and definition.

If your function has no explicit return type at all, even `void`, Standard C requires the compiler to assume a default of `int`. That assumption would be unfortunate if you simply omitted another return keyword inadvertently. (The default is the same as it is for variables where you use a storage class specifier or a type qualifier without any type specification; see Chapter 10.)

If the function also takes no arguments—that is, no values are passed to it—you indicate that by placing the word `void` between the parentheses, again in both the declaration and definition:

```
void prompt(void); /* no arguments or return value */
```

To this point, we have seen each of our programs commence with

```
int main(void)
```

That is, `main()` takes no arguments. Later, we will see how arguments can be passed to `main()` by typing the program name from an operating system prompt and following it by the arguments (see Chapter 16). The formulation

```
void main(void)
```

although not uncommon, is not Standard C and is therefore not guaranteed to work on all implementations.

You could have a function that takes no arguments but returns a value, although this combination would not be common:

```
int add(void);
```

In Standard C, the function itself is deemed to have the type of the value it returns. Thus a function that returns an `int` is referred to as a function of type `int`; a function returning no value is called a `void` function.

Functions may take or return any type other than arrays or functions (though in both cases they may, as we will see later in this chapter, take or return pointers to arrays or functions).

8.4.2   Prototype Type Checking

The compiler checks to see that the number and type of arguments in the prototype and the type of value returned match those of the function definition, and the *number* of arguments in any function call must match the number in the prototype. If not, you will get an error message.

You can place function prototypes directly in your source code. These nearly always are placed above `main()`. Function prototypes are instead often included in the source code by way of a header file, added through an `include` directive. Header files generally contain only function prototypes, `define` directives, and structure templates. (See Chapter 11 for a complete discussion of `include` and `define` directives.)

You include header files for the C library functions your source code uses. For example, when you include `stdio.h`, you thereby insert into your code the prototypes for `printf()` and `scanf()`, for `getchar()` and `putchar()`, for various file opening, closing, reading and writing, and manipulating functions, and for quite a number of other functions relating to input and output. Of these many functions, the compiler brings in function definitions only for functions actually used by your source code.

You can also include in a source code file header files for your own functions, the definitions of which are found either within that source code or in another source code file in the same program (see Chapter 17 on linking more than one source code together in a project file).

You can get away with not including the prototype for your own functions or C library functions that return an `int`; as we said earlier, by default, the compiler assumes that functions for which no prototypes are included return an `int`. But doing so is sloppy programming practice. For one thing, it prevents the compiler from checking for argument and type mismatches. In any case, you may not omit function prototypes for functions of any other type, including `void` functions. That includes most of the math functions, which generally return a `double`, and the string-handling functions, which typically return a `char` pointer.

From what we've just said, you would probably expect that omitting the prototype for one of the C library functions (other than one that returns an `int`) would be met with an error message. With your own functions, that is the case, but with the C library functions, no such luck. What will happen in all likelihood is that your program would generate incorrect results.

After a while, you'll come to remember which commonly used functions are found in which C library header file. If you're in doubt about whether you need to include a header file, include it. Including a header file in cases where you do not use a single one of the file's functions adds only a few bytes to the executable file. On our system, with Borland C, a blank source code with `main()` and no statements or headers produced an executable file of 6128 bytes; adding `stdio.h`, `stdlib.h`, `string.h`, `math.h`, and `alloc.h` added only 68 bytes. If you want to know what header file contains a particular C library function prototype, you can place the cursor on the function name and then press `Ctrl` `F1` if you're in the Borland C editor or `F1` if you're in the Microsoft C editor. See also the list of functions in Appendix I.

8.5   FUNCTION DEFINITION

The function definition includes its header and body. The header's format is similar to that of the prototype:

```
int add(int num, int val)
```

However, there is no semicolon following the closing parenthesis. Unlike the prototype, where inclusion of variable names is optional,

 In the function definition, you must include both types and variable names for each argument.

The variable names that make up the function definition header are referred to as *formal arguments.* The values passed to them in the function call are called the *actual arguments.*

The function header is followed by the function body—the function's declarations and other statements.

 Between the function header and the function body and then again after the function body, you must put braces—even if the function body is a single statement.

```
int square(int num)
{
    return num * num;
}
```

The brace instead of a semicolon after the parenthesis closing the header tells the compiler that what we have here is the function's definition, not its prototype. This is an exception to normal C syntax, where a construct requiring braces for multiple statements may be omitted if there is only a single statement (as with `if` statements or `for` or `while` loops).

8.5.1   Variable Declaration

As you already know, variables must be declared prior to being used.

 The argument portion of the function definition operates as a declaration of the variables in the definition.

That's why we told you earlier that you have to include both the type and variable name for each formal argument in the function definition header.

 Any other variables you use in the function must be declared in the usual fashion.

The compiler considers the variables in the header to be declared first; then come the explicitly declared variables. Therefore, you can initialize an explicitly declared variable in terms of one of the formal arguments:

```
int box(int height, int width, int top, int bottom, int left, int right)
{
    int left_col = left + 3;
    . . .
}
```

For the same reason, you cannot redeclare another variable inside the function definition with the same name as one of the formal argument names, as you can do with global variables (see Chapter 10).

 As a matter of clear style, *you should separate your variable declarations from the following operative statements in the function.*

```
void func_name(int variable)
{
    int some;
    float many;

    some = 1;
}
```

 In a long, complex function with many variable declarations and other statements, some programmers even insert a comment to indicate the end of declarations and the end of the function itself.

```
void func_name(int variable)
{
    int some;
    float many;

    /* end of declarations in func_name() */

    some = 1;

} /* end of function func_name() */
```

Standard C does not require the compiler to evaluate the function's formal arguments in any particular order; code that depends on a particular order—right to left as Borland C does, or left to right or some other way—is not portable:

```
num = add(++a, a + 1); /* dangerous */
```

All Standard C requires is that the actual argument be evaluated before being passed. The order of evaluation is up to the compiler.

With variables separately declared inside the function, you can use the shortcut of employing a variable type name followed by a series of variable names separated by commas. With the formal arguments in the function definition, you may not use that shortcut, even if all the variables are of the same type.

 The type has to be separately stated for each formal argument variable in the function declaration and definition header.

```
int width, length, number; /* nonfunction declaration: OK */

int calibrate(int degrees, int seconds, int minutes); /* OK */

int calibrate(int degrees, seconds, minutes) /* error! */
{
    . . .
}
```

Since the compiler effectively ignores the variable names in the prototype, you *could* have different variable names there from the corresponding ones in the function definition header, but that would be sloppy practice. (Actually, the prototype variable names are not ignored. The variable names in the prototype have what is called *function prototype scope*, which terminates at the end of the prototype. The effect is as though the surrounding parentheses constituted a miniblock inside a function insofar as scope is concerned. Thus, the following

```
int add(int a, int a);
```

would be flagged by the compiler as an error. By the same token, you could use variable names that are the same as global variables without error.)

The number of arguments in the prototype, function definition, and function call must all match. Otherwise, you will get an error message on compiling. In general, the argument types of the actual arguments in a function call and the formal arguments in the function definition need not match. Assuming you have properly used and placed a function prototype above the function call, the type of the actual argument is automatically converted to the type of the formal argument, if conversion is permitted. (On which conversions are permissible and which are not, see Chapter 13.)

```
float add(float one, float two);
int num = 7;
float val = 6.35;
float sum = add(num, val); /* OK */
```

 However, *where the type of an actual argument differs from the corresponding formal argument, it is good practice to use a type cast to signify that you are not unaware of the conversion and to make sure the conversion you expect takes place.*

```
float sum = add((float)num + val);
```

Be careful to avoid inadvertent data loss through type demotion on the automatic conversion.

If your actual type is of a different global category from that of the formal argument (for instance, ordinary variable versus pointer), you will get either an error message if conversion from one type to the other is not permitted in Standard C, or else a warning. (See Chapter 13 for type categories and permissible conversions.) In those rare instances in which you desire such an unusual result (for example, you want to pass the value of a pointer to an `unsigned` variable for use in a `movedata()` call; see Appendix C), it is highly recommended that you type cast and comment.

8.5.2   Placement of Function Definitions

 You may not put a function definition inside any other function body.

The order of function definitions is generally immaterial. The `main()` function is always called first and the order of statements within `main()` determines when functions are called no matter where they are in the source code. The common practice is to place `main()` first and the other function definitions alphabetically after `main()`.

The most significant exception relates to placement of function definitions vis-à-vis external variables. That question is discussed in Chapter 10.

Another exception relates to function declarations. Technically, a function definition is treated by the compiler as a declaration as well. Thus, you could place a function definition before `main()`, in lieu of the function declaration that normally would be placed there, without violating the rule that a function be declared before it is called. A simplified version of the `absolute.c` program we listed at the outset of this chapter could be written as follows instead.

 **Listing** 8.3 **define.c**

```
/* define.c */

/* using function definition above main instead of prototype */

#include <stdio.h>

int absolute(int num, int val)
{
    int result = num - val;

    if (result < 0)
        result *= -1;
    return result;
}

int main(void)
{
    int number = 100, value = 50;
    printf("difference is %d\n", absolute(number, value));
}
```

Some programmers cut corners by placing all function definitions above `main()`, so as to avoid having to include both a function definition and a function declaration for each function. Apart from the nondeclaration of `main()`, which is fairly universal, this practice is not recommended. To begin with, it is easier to read the program if its starting point, `main()`, comes first. In addition, where some functions in turn call other functions, it would become difficult to ensure that each function definition is on an earlier line in the source code than any line on which the function is called. In fact, this may be impossible in some cases, particularly in the case where functions call one another.

If you do omit the function declarations, you must take care not to place a function definition above the definition of any function it calls. Otherwise you may get a warning when the compiler encounters the function call without having found any prototype for the function, and an error when the compiler gets to the definition of the function called.

8.6   OLD STYLE DECLARATIONS AND DEFINITION HEADERS *(OPTIONAL)*

Before Standard C's adoption, there was another form of prototype and function definition header. Though you should definitely not use this old form, you should be able to recognize it: to avoid super-annuating zillions of lines of pre–Standard C code at one fell swoop, Standard C allows this old form. The only exception to this generous allowance is that variable-argument functions (see later in the chapter for an explanation of these) must have Standard C prototypes.

Table 8.1 depicts the old and the new side by side.

Table 8.1   *Standard C and Old Declaration/Definition Header*

Standard C	*Pre-Standard C*
Declaration:	*Declaration:*
`int multiply (int num, int val);`	`int multiply();`
or	
`int multiply (int, int);`	
Definition Header:	*Definition Header:*
`int multiply (int num, int val)`	`int multiply (num, val)`
`{`	`int num;`
`    . . .`	`int val;`
`}`	`{`
	`    . . .`
	`}`

 Whatever you do, do not mix Standard C prototypes with pre–Standard C definition headers or vice versa. You are likely to get very strange results.

8.7   FUNCTION CALLS

A function call statement causes the named function to be executed. When the called function is done, the program returns to the next statement after the function call.

8.7.1   Syntax

You make a function call with the name of the function followed by the actual arguments to be passed, separated by commas if there is more than one, and enclosed by parentheses:

```
add(num, val);
```

Note that where a variable is an argument, you include only the variable's name, not its type:

```
add(int num, int val); /* error! */
```

Nor do you include the function's return type:

```
int add(num, val); /* error! */
```

If the function does not take any arguments, you call the function with the name followed by parentheses alone:

```
void print_head(void); /* prototype */
. . .
print_head(); /* function call */
```

8.7.2   Values Passed = Variables in Function

For arguments, you can pass constants,

```
add(1, 3);
```

variables,

```
int num = 1, val = 3;
add(num, val);
```

or mixed constant-variable expressions,

```
add(num * 3, 17);
```

In any event, whatever is passed:

 Each function call argument is evaluated and passed as a single value.

You are even permitted to pass comma operator-separated expressions as a single argument. This permitted usage would nearly always be extremely poor coding style, but as usual we present an example so you can understand the usage if you happen to encounter it. The comma expressions must be enclosed in parentheses so that the compiler does not mistake the separate comma expressions for separate arguments:

```
int add(int num, int val); /* code omitted: just returns num + val */
int a, b;
b = add ((a = 3, b = 5), 4);
```

As we have learned, expressions separated by comma operators have the value of the right-most expression. Therefore, b is passed as the first argument, resulting in a final value for b of 9.

Where an actual argument in your function call represents a single variable,

```
int side1, side2, hypotenuse;
. . .
hypotenuse = root_sum(side1, side2);
```

it is tempting to use the same variable names in the formal argument of the function definition (and the prototype if you wish to include variable names there) as you use in the calling function. Resist this temptation. *To use the same variable names in the actual and formal argument obscures the fact that the variables in the calling function are altogether different from the variables in the called function.* They have different memory addresses and accordingly are different to the computer even if their names are the same to you.

Apart from a category of variables know as *external*, which we discuss in Chapter 10, all variables within a function are local variables. They come into being when the function is called (memory is reserved for them) and they die when the function is finished executing (memory is released); neither the variables nor their values are known to the other functions in the source code. As we said, you pass values to a function, not variables.

 Changes to the variables declared in the function to house those values do not change the values of the variables with the same names in the calling function.

 Where the value of a single variable is passed as one of the arguments, you should use names for the variable and the formal argument that convey the same meaning but are slightly different:

```c
int main(void)
{
    float root_sum(float adjacent1, float adjacent2);
    float side1, side2, hypotenuse;

    hypotenuse = root_sum(side1, side2);
    . . .
}

float root_sum(float adjacent1, float adjacent2)
{
    float root(float square_sum); /* code not included here */

    return root(adjacent1 * adjacent1 + adjacent2 * adjacent2);
}
```

We strongly recommend this practice. It emphasizes that only a copy of the variable's value is passed to the function, not the variable itself.

C's method of passing values to functions is called *call by value.* This is the only method C supports. When arguments are passed by value, a copy of the argument's value is sent to the function to do with it as it will. The other method, used by some other programming languages, is called *call by reference.* When an argument is passed by reference, the called function receives a reference to the argument, allowing it to modify the argument's value *within the calling function.* As we will see later in this chapter, C does simulate call by reference in the case of arrays (actually, pointers to arrays) as parameters.

8.7.3   Order of Argument Assignment and Evaluation

The values of what you pass as actual arguments are assigned to the formal arguments in the same order in which they appear in the formal argument list. It is critical that the order of the actual and formal arguments be the same, therefore. However, as noted earlier, implementations are not required by Standard C to evaluate function arguments in any particular order.

8.7.4   Using Function Calls

The function call can be an entire self-contained C statement:

```c
int main(void)
{
    void print_head(char *name, int pagenum);
    . . .
    print_head("SimpleSoft Database List", page++);
. . .
}

void print_head(char *name, int pagenum)
{
    printf("\t %-55s Page %d", name, pagenum);
}
```

In fact, where a function does not return a value, all you can do is make the call a self-contained C statement.

You can likewise make a call a self-contained statement where the function does return a value. In such a call, you effectively ignore the return value. That is generally what we do with `printf()`, for example (the `printf()` function returns the number of characters printed):

```
printf("I really don't care how many characters you print; just print them");
```

Where the function returns a value, however, you will generally make some use of the value it returns:

```
sum = add(1, 3);
```

 If not, *as a matter of style, some programmers expressly show that they are ignoring the return value of a function by type casting the function call to* void, *so their intention is clear to other programmers (or to themselves months later).* One common instance of this practice is the type of function coded to return one value if an error is encountered (often zero) or another value if everything works as expected (say, some nonzero value). In some cases, the non-error-checking components of the function are all that are of interest:

```
(void) open_database(filename); /* error-checking is irrelevant here */
```

8.8   RETURN STATEMENTS

We've taken a look at passing values from the calling function to the called function at the outset of the call. Now let's examine the reverse process—passing back a single value to the calling function on the termination of the called function.

You return a value with the keyword `return`:

```
int sum(int num1, int num2, int num3)
{
    return num1 + num2 + num3;
}
```

You saw earlier that an actual argument can be a variable, constant, or expression containing variables and constants. Prior to being passed, the actual argument is evaluated and a single value per argument is passed. The same is true for the value returned:

```
float area(float diameter)
{
    float radius = diameter / 2.;
    return (3.14159 * radius * radius);
}
```

The return value, or as in this last example, the entire expression, as evaluated, is converted to the function's return type, just as though the value were being assigned to a variable of that type, if it is not already that type (see Chapter 13 for permissible conversions and the conversion mechanism in general).

You can declare a separate variable in the function body to house the value to be returned, but it is not necessary to do so. The following function definitions produce the same result as one another:

```
int max(int num, int val)
{
    int maximum;

    if (num > val)
        maximum = num;
    else
        maximum = val;
    return maximum;
}

int max(int num, int val)
{
    if (num > val)
        return num;
```

```
    else
        return val;
}
```

Which formulation to use is a question of clarity, context, and personal preference. The example here is simple, so it may not be necessary to create a separate variable. If the intention of a lengthier code segment is not self-evident, having a separate variable to return may help document what is going on.

If we do use a separate variable for the return value, we must declare it in the function, just as we must declare any other variable we use. An exception is where we return a variable that is one of those in the formal argument list.

Along the same lines, the variable we use to house the return value, if any, is not known to the calling function; only a value is passed back. Hence, the following code would give an error message in the function call statement to the effect that maximum is not defined:

```
int main(void)
{
    int max(int num, int val);
    maximum = max(11, 17);
}

int max(int num, int val)
{
    int maximum;

    if (num > val)
        maximum = num;
    else
        maximum = val;
    return maximum;
}
```

The return statement can be the only statement in the function body:

```
int max(int num, int val)
{
    return num > val ? num : val;
}
```

 You can return only a single value from a function.

The following function produces a warning that the second return statement will be ignored by the compiler:

```
int two_timer(int willing, int able)
{
    willing += able;
    return willing;
    return able * 2;
}
```

Later in this chapter, you will learn how to affect variables in the calling function by passing the variables' addresses to the called function and using a dereferencing operator to manipulate the variables' values through their addresses. Short of that often-used device, and apart from external variables, the only communication between calling and called functions is passing values to the called function and returning a single value to the called function.

8.8.1   Another Effect of a Return Statement

If we can return only a single value, how is the following usage permitted?

```
double up(double good)
{
    if (good < 17.5)
        return 99.99;
    return 49.95;
}
```

If good is less than 17.5, won't this result in returning two values? No. The reason is as follows:

 A return statement has two effects. One effect is to pass a value back to the calling function. The other is to stop execution of the called function and pass control back to the calling function.

In the example above, if good is less than 17.5, the program never reaches the following statement. You should, incidentally, note from this example that the return statement may be part of a conditional statement.

You can use a blank return statement to cause an exit from a function even where the function returns no value:

```c
void print_head(char *name, int pagenum)
{
    if (strlen(name) > 55)
    {
        printf("Error in print_head: name too long\n");
        return;
    }
    printf("\t %-55s Page %d", name, pagenum);
}
```

You can also use one or more blank return statements in a function that returns a value:

```c
int add(int num, int val)
{
    if (num > 999 || val > 999)
    {
        printf("Value too large\n");
        return;
    }
    if (num < 0 || val < 0)
    {
        printf("Values passed must be positive\n");
        return;
    }
    return num + val;
}
```

However, on compiling, you will receive a warning message, "Both return and return with a value used." A better practice would be to have the function return a 0 or a –1 or some other out-of-range value on error. Here, for instance, instead of the blank return statement, you could have had

```c
return -1;
```

Nevertheless, Standard C allows a blank return statement even in a function defined to return a value of some type. However, if you call in a function in a statement that requires a return value, such as

```c
num = square(val);
```

the effect of a blank return statement is undefined. Watch out. Furthermore, if you fail to include a non-blank return statement in a function that is not void, you will receive a warning that the function should return a value.

 A common practice with a function where all the work is done inside the function so that it does not need to return a value, is to have the function return a 1 if the operation the function performs is successful and a 0 if it is unsuccessful. For instance, expanding on the example above:

```c
int print_head(char *name, int pagenum)
{
    if (strlen(name) > 55)
    {
        printf("Error in print_head: name too long\n");
        return 0;
    }
    printf("\t %-55s Page %d", name, pagenum);
    return 1;
}
```

This is the way many of the Standard C functions are set up. The advantage is that you can then test for whatever return value indicates an error and take appropriate action if there is an error:

```
if (print_head(name, pagenum++) == 0)
    exit(3);
```

If you have a `void` function (one not meant to return a value), you may include a blank return statement after the last function definition statement, or not as you choose:

```
int add_print(int a, int b)
{
    printf("%d + %d = %d\n", a, b, a + b);
    return; /* optional */
}
```

If you do not include one, the function's reaching its final statement will have the same effect as though you had included a blank `return` statement.

8.9   MAKING USE OF THE RETURN VALUE

You have several choices of what to do with the return value. You can

■ ignore the function's return value altogether, as we saw with `printf()` or our example of deliberately ignoring a function's error-checking return value.
■ use the return value as part of an assignment statement or function call without storing the value for later use in the program.
■ store the return value in a variable for later use.

You can do anything with the return value that you could do with any other value of that type. The value returned is, in effect, substituted for the text of the entire function call, just as though you had omitted the function call and typed in the return value in the first place. Thus, the last two lines of `main()` in the following example produce identical results:

```
int main(void)
{
    int add(int number, int value);
    int num = 5, val = 10;
    int quantity;

    quantity = 17 + add(num, val);
    quantity = 17 + 15; /* same as last line */
}

int add(int number, int value)
{
    return number + value;
}
```

If a function has a return value, C permits you to use that return value as an argument to another function without creating a separate variable to store the return value. You do this by including the entire function call as the argument. Contrast the following two approaches.

 Listing **8.4 two_cube.c**

```
/* two_cube.c */

/* shows you can create separate variable to house return value or not */

#include <stdio.h>

int cube(int number);

int main(void)
```

```
{
    int num = 5, val = 6;
    int cubed;

    cubed = cube(num);
    printf("num cubed is %d\n", cubed);
    printf("val cubed is %d\n", cube(val));
}

int cube(int number)
{
    return number * number * number;
}
```

In the first case, we declared a separate `int` variable and then used it to store the return value of `cube()`. In the second case, the return value of `cube()` is placed directly as an argument to the `printf()` function call. This shortcut would not be appropriate in a situation where you need to use the function's return value later in the program as well.

This shortcut can be used in nested fashion.

 **Listing** **8.5 nest.c**

```
/* nest.c */

/* nest function calls in a single statement */

#include <stdio.h>

int cube(int number);
int add(int number, int value);

int main(void)
{
    int num = 2;
    printf("Result: %d\n", cube(add(2, cube(num))));
}

int add(int number, int value)
{
    return number + value;
}

int cube(int number)
{
    return number * number * number;
}
```

giving the output

```
Result: 1000
```

The value of `num` is passed to `cube()`; `cube()`'s return value of 8 is passed, along with a 2 to `add()`; the return value of 10 is passed to `cube()`; the final return value of 1000 is passed as an argument to the `printf()` call, corresponding to its `%d` specifier.

Be careful to check what the function returns before using this device. For instance, the following fragment would not produce correct results:

```
printf("The number input is %d", scanf("%d", &num));
```

The `scanf()` function does not return the value of the variable or variables input; it returns the number of items correctly read in.

8.9.1 Assignment Operator Inside Conditional Expression of an `if` Statement—Revisited

As we briefly mentioned in Chapter 5 just because you see an assignment operator inside the conditional expression of an `if` statement, it does not mean there is an error. A frequent application of the assignment operator in the conditional expression of an `if` statement is its use in combining (1) a test of whether a call to a function that returns zero if unsuccessful met with success, with (2) an assignment of the function's return value to a variable

```
if ((file_ptr = fopen("c:\\autoexec.bat", "r")) == 0)
    printf("Error opening file\n");
```

or even more compactly, using a logical operator discussed in the next section,

```
if (!(file_ptr = fopen("c:\\autoexec.bat", "r")))
    printf("Error opening file\n");
```

Nevertheless, in *most* cases, use of the = inside the parentheses of an `if` statement indicates inadvertent use of the assignment operator in place of the == relational operator. Hence the warning. If you really mean to use the assignment operator, just ignore the warning (with a comment in the code to that effect) or, better, rewrite the code in a less compact way, if possible.

Say you are testing to see whether the value of an expression is not equal to zero. You could do something like this:

```
if (bytes_read = readfile(filename))
    <do something>
```

If any nonzero value is assigned, the expression will evaluate to true since the value of an assignment expression as a whole is the value assigned. And this is the intent of the code fragment here. However, to make it clear that the above statement was not just a mistaken way of writing

```
if (bytes_read == readfile(filename))
```

it is considered better style to make the testing against nonzero explicit:

```
if ((bytes_read = readfile(filename)) != 0)
```

8.10 RECURSION

Given the broad latitude and compactness C affords, it probably won't surprise you when we tell you that C allows a function to call itself. The process is called ***recursion***.

One of the statements in a recursive function contains a call to the function itself. To avoid infinite recursion, the argument passed on each successive call must change from call to call. There must also be some mechanism based on the passed argument to test whether yet another recursive call is to be made or whether the process is to end.

8.10.1 A Classic Recursion Example: Factorials

The classic simple example of recursion is the calculation of factorials. The factorial of a positive nonzero integer is the product of all integers from the number down to 1. (In addition, 0 factorial and 1 factorial are both defined to be equal to 1.) For example, 5 factorial (written 5!) is 5 * 4 * 3 * 2 * 1. If we parse this example, we can see that 5! is equal to 5 times 4! And 4! is equal to 4 times 3! . . . and so on. What this suggests is a function—that for some odd reason we will call *factorial*—to which we initially pass a number, num, and that has a statement that calls factorial(num - 1). Here's what it looks like:

 Listing **8.6 factor.c**

```
/* factor.c */

/* do factorials with recursion */

#include <stdio.h>
```

```c
#include <limits.h> /* ULONG_MAX */

#define TESTING 0
#define NOT_TESTING 1

int main(void)
{
    unsigned long factorial(int num, int mode);
    void prompt(void);
    int i = 1;
    int max, input;

    /* calculate largest integer OK as input without overflow & store in max */
    while (1)
    {
        /* ULONG_MAX is the largest value an unsigned long can take */
        if (ULONG_MAX / (unsigned long)(i + 1) < factorial(i, TESTING))
        {
            max = i;
            break;
        }
        i++;
    }

    prompt();
    while(scanf("%d", &input))
    {
        if (input < 0)
            printf("Does %d look like a NONZERO POSITIVE INTEGER to you?\n", input);

        /* weed out input too large */
        else if (input > max)
            printf("\n%d?\nI can't count that high\n" "%d is about my limit\n", input, max);

        /* input range OK: calculate factorial */
        else printf("%d! = %lu\n", input, factorial(input, NOT_TESTING));
        prompt();
    }
}

void prompt(void)
{
    printf("Input a positive integer\n" "Input a letter or noninteger to quit\n");
}

unsigned long factorial(int num, int mode)
{
    unsigned long result;

    if (mode == NOT_TESTING)
        printf("num is %d\n", num); /* just for illustration */
    if (num > 0)
        result = (unsigned long)num * factorial(num - 1, mode);
    else result = 1LU;

    if (mode == NOT_TESTING)
        printf("num is %d; result is %lu\n", num, result); /* just for illustration */
    return result;
}
```

To avoid having to repeat the two input instructions, we created a function, prompt(), that takes no arguments and returns nothing.

Next, we calculate the largest integer we can accept as input without causing an overflow (ULONG_MAX, a manifest constant defined in limits.h, being the largest value an unsigned long can accept: $(2 \wedge 32) - 1$):

```
if (ULONG_MAX / (unsigned long)(i + 1) < factorial(i))
    max = i;
```

Why can't we just say

```
if (factorial (i) > ULONG_MAX)
    max = i;
```

That's because we can't store a value large enough to ever make the conditional expression evaluate to false. Once we exceed the maximum number, we would cycle back in odometer-like fashion to zero and so on ad infinitum. (But then, you probably already saw that.)

We set our test so that we stop when the maximum value we can store in an unsigned long divided by the number we'd get on the next loop (i + 1) is less than the factorial of the number. Moving to the next loop would have the effect of multiplying the factorial of the current loop number by the number of the next loop (for example, moving from 16! to 17! merely involves multiplying 16! by 17). Therefore, if we went one more loop, we would exceed the maximum value; otherwise, the maximum value divided by that greater number would not have exceeded the factorial of the current loop number. (If you cannot follow this logic in the abstract, try a far smaller overflow value—say 50—and see how you can determine 4 in this example to be the maximum input factorial value with this divisor method.)

Now let's take a look at the recursive function itself. A good way to do that is by a simple example: assume we typed in the number 5. Here's the output we get:

```
num is 5
num is 4
num is 3
num is 2
num is 2; result is 2
num is 3; result is 6
num is 4; result is 24
num is 5; result is 120
5! = 120
```

Note that we didn't really need the printf() statements inside the function. In your actual working version, you would remove them. We've just included them here to show you some of the mechanics of recursive functions. We have eliminated them during the maximum number-testing portion of the program by including a second argument to the function. (The define directive mechanism we use to alter the value of the mode argument is explained in Chapter 11.)

Remember that whenever a function is called, the function creates local variables for each variable declared in the function, including those declared as arguments. Those variables last for the duration of the function call. If the function called in turn calls another function, the variables created by the calling function still remain until the calling function terminates. Even if the calling function and the called function have a variable with the same name—as will be the case with recursive functions—separate and distinct variables are created for each call. They may be the same names to you, but to the computer, each of the variable names is just an address and the two addresses are different.

The first time through, we first print out num's value and then call the function with a value of 5 as the first argument. That call again prints out num's value and then calls the function with a value of 4 as the first argument, and so on until num is 3 and we make a call with a value of 2 as the first argument. Then the conditional statement evaluates to false and we print the values of result and num, 2 and 2. The value of result is returned to the call where num was 3, giving a result of 6. That value is returned to the call where num was 4, giving a result of 24. Finally, that value is returned to the call in main(), where a result of 120 is returned.

The order of the printf() statements in the output tells us a little about recursive function calls. The statements in the function body before the recursive function call are executed in order of the function calls. Those after the recursive function call are executed in reverse order.

We can use the knowledge that statements within a recursive function following the recursive call are executed in reverse order, to write a function that prints the letters of a string passed to it in reverse order.

 Listing **8.7 reverse.c**

```
/* reverse.c */

/* use recursion to print letters of a string in reverse order */

#include <stdio.h>

void reverse(char *str);

int main(void)
{
    reverse("backward thinking");
}

void reverse(char *str)
{
    if (*str) /* stop when reach NULL */
        reverse(str + 1);
    putchar(*str);
}
```

What is passed from `main()` is the address of the start of the string in memory. The expression `*str` has the value stored at `str`'s address. Calling with `str + 1` as the argument passes the address of the next byte (see Chapter 7 on pointers).

It would be easy to code a simpler, nonrecursive version of this function (see Listing 8.19, `flipper.c`). So this function may be of little help apart from its educational value. A function that would be useful, however, is one that prints the digits of a decimal number in whatever other base the user chooses. (Only decimal, octal, hexadecimal, or binary notations are common. For a discussion of these and other theoretically possible bases, see Chapters 2, 9, and 12.)

 Listing **8.8 digits.c**

```
/* digits.c */
/* recursive transmuting of decimal integers to other bases */

#include <stdio.h>
int main(void)
{
    void prompt(void);
    void get_digits(int number, int base);
    int num, root;

    prompt();
    while (scanf("%d%d", &num, &root) == 2)
    {
        if(root > 36)
        {
            printf("base too high\n");
            prompt();
            continue;
        }
        printf("\n%d is ", num);
        get_digits(num, root);
        printf(" in base %d\n", root);
        prompt();
```

```
      }
  }

  void prompt(void)
  {
      printf("\n\nInput an integer\n"
          "and a base to print it in\n\n"
          "(Keep base under 37)\n\n"
          "Type a letter to quit\n\n");
  }

  void get_digits(int number, int base)
  {
      int digit = number % base;
      if (number >= base)
          get_digits(number/base, base);
      if (digit < 10)
          putchar('0' + digit);
      else putchar('A' + digit - 10);
  }
```

The second to right-most digit of a number in any base represents an integer times that base to the first power. If we divide the entire number by the base, what we're left with is the number of the right-most digit:

```
digit = number % base;
```

We lop off that remainder and call the function with the balance, in effect shifting the digits one to the right:

```
get_digits(number / base, base);
```

We stop when what's left is less than the base:

```
if(number >= base)
   get_digits(number / base, base);
```

At that point, we drop down to the two next statements and print the previously discarded digit in character form. For bases of 10 and under, or for larger bases where the particular digit is less than 10, the following statement does the trick:

```
putchar('0' + digit);
```

If the digit is 0, this statement gives us the character 0; if it is 1, this statement gives us the character 1, and so on. Past 10, capital letters are used—A for 10, B for 11, and so on. We accomplish this with

```
putchar('A' + digit - 10);
```

(The numeric conversion works in both ASCII and EBCDIC. The letter conversion does not work for all bases in EBCDIC.)

As we've seen earlier in C, if we value compactness over clarity and consideration for other programmers who might work with our code, we could have written the function in a somewhat more compact way:

```
void get_digits(int number, int base)
{
   int digit;
   if (number >= base)
      get_digits(number / base, base);
   putchar((digit = number % base) +
      ((digit < 10) ? '0' : 'A' - 10));
}
```

In C each expression has a value; the value of an assignment expression is the value assigned. We can take the expression

```
digit = number % base
```

and use it just as though we had that expression as a separate statement before the `putchar()` statement and used `digit` alone in its place in the `putchar` statement. The conditional operator lets us write the `if-else` statements in a more compact way.

8.10.2   Recursive vs. Nonrecursive Functions

It is generally possible to accomplish the task addressed by a recursive function with a nonrecursive function. We could, for instance, have written the factorial function like this:

```
unsigned long factorial(int num)
{
    unsigned long result;

    for (result = 1LU; num > 1; num--)
        result *= (unsigned long)num;
    return result;
}
```

But then, that wouldn't have been quite as much fun.

In general, if a task that could be programmed as a recursive function can also be programmed non-recursively without great difficulty, the nonrecursive version is preferable. One consideration is speed. The recursive version of factorial calculation will run more slowly than its nonrecursive version: function calls take more time than looping. Memory space is another consideration. Since additional local variables are declared with every successive recursive call, a deeply nested recursive function with large amounts of data can result in memory overflow.

Still, while some of the simple recursive functions can be rewritten nonrecursively, some of the complex ones are extremely difficult to accomplish nonrecursively. If you doubt that, try your hand at the recursive binary tree functions in Chapter 15. *Recursion is sometimes the most straightforward, logical, or natural way to approach certain types of tasks. In such cases, you might* *want to start with a recursive solution for testing or verification purposes even if you end up with a nonrecursive one.*

It can be shown that all recursive algorithms can be replaced by suitable program loop constructs. Essentially there exist two different loop types, the `for` loop and the `while` loop, both discussed in Chapter 5. The `for` loop iterates x times, where the bound x is to be fixed at the loop's entry. It is not possible to replace the recursion in some programming tasks with `for` loops: the number of iterations cannot be determined in advance. Such tasks are referred to as nonprimitive recursive. For instance, the so-called *Ackermann's Function*, discussed in Programming Assignment 1.25, can be computed only with `while` loops (and for all but trivial examples, a huge amount of memory and time).

Ackermann's Function was developed by Wilhelm Ackermann (1896–1962), a German mathemetician in the fields of mathematical logic, decidability, and set theory. Together with mathematician David Hilbert, he published the first modern textbook on mathematical logic.

8.10.3   Recursive Functions for Iterative Calculations

Recursive functions are particularly suited to tasks requiring iterative calculations—problems where there is no ready formula and we reach the result by a series of increasingly educated guesses. We will look at two programming examples. The first is a function that calculates square roots of numbers. The second is a refinement of the interest rate calculation program we solved earlier in Chapter 5 with a long series of `for` loops.

In `variance.c`, we read input from the keyboard and print out the highest and lowest numbers input, the average of the numbers, and the variance and standard deviation. The variance is the square of the average of the numbers subtracted from the average of the sum of the squares of the numbers. The standard deviation is the square root of the variance, and there's where we use our iterative recursive function.

 **Listing** `8.9 variance.c`

```
/* variance.c */

/*
    read numerical input from the keyboard and print out the highest and
    lowest numbers input; the average of the numbers input; variance
    (the square of the average subtracted from the average of sum of
    squares of the numbers); and the standard deviation (square root
    of the variance)
    includes recursive square root function
*/

#include <stdio.h>
#include <stdlib.h> /* exit */
#define PRECISION 1.0e-6

double square_root(double num, double root);

int main(void)
{
    double num, min, max, sum, square_sum, variance;
    int numbers_input = 0;

    printf("Type in a series of numbers\n"
        "Press Enter key after each\n"
        "Type in a letter to quit\n");
    while (scanf("%lf", &num))
    {
        if (numbers_input == 0) /* first time through */
        {
            sum = max = min = num;
            square_sum = num * num;
        }

        else
        {
            /* see whether current number is new min or max */
            if (num > max)
                max = num;
            if (num < min)
                min = num;

            /* accumulate current number in sum and in sum of squares */
            sum += num;
            square_sum += num * num;
        }
        numbers_input++;
        printf("Type in another number\n"
            "Type in a letter to quit\n");
    }

    /* exit if no numbers input */
    if (numbers_input == 0)
        exit(0);

    variance = (square_sum / numbers_input) -
        ((sum / numbers_input) * (sum / numbers_input));
    printf("\nNumber of entries: %d\n", numbers_input);
    printf(" %*s\n %*s %*s %*s %*s %*s\n", 50, "Standard", 8, "Minimum", 8, "Maximum", 10,
        "Average", 10, "Variance", 10, "Deviation");
```

```
    printf("%8.2f %8.2f %10.4f %10.4f %10.4f\n", min, max, sum / numbers_input, variance,
        square_root(variance, variance / 2.));
}

/* recursive function to calculate square root */
double square_root(double num, double root)
{
    if ((root * root) - num > PRECISION || num - (root * root) > PRECISION)
        root = square_root(num, (num/root + root)/2.);
    return root;
}
```

The square root function, `square_root()` uses what is known as *Newton's method* to arrive at a solution. Sir Isaac Newton (1642–1727) formulated a method of calculating the square root of any positive number by engaging in an iterative technique. This iterative technique is as follows:

Take a number whose square root is to be calculated, any positive number.
Take a guess at the number's square root.
Calculate the square root by improving on the current guess as indicated:
  Next guess = (number / current guess + current guess) / 2
Repeat this process until the difference between the next guess and the current is within the accepted level of accuracy. The better your guess, the fewer the number of iterations needed to get the square root. A good first guess is typically half the number whose square root is to be calculated. The process is then repeated until the desired accuracy is achieved.

Here is the algorithm:

Get a positive number whose square root is to be calculated from the user
Get the desired precision
While more numbers remain
  Calculate first guess, X_0
  Repeat

  $$X_n = 0.5 * (X_{(n-1)} + \text{Number} / X_{(n-1)})$$

  Until $\text{abs}(X_n - X_{(n-1)}) <= $ Desired precision
  Get a positive number whose square root is to be calculated from the user
  Get the desired precision
End while

Suppose the number whose square root is to be calculated is $A > 1$. Let X_0 be our first guess. If $A / X_0 = X_0$ then we are finished. If, on the other hand, $A / X_0 < X_0$, then $A < X_0^2$, and our initial guess was too large. If the first guess is too large, then $A / X_0 <$ square root of A. This means that the square root is between A / X_0 and X_0. The same argument will hold if the initial guess was too small. This is a necessary condition for iteration because it ensures convergence. In other words, you will ultimately get a square root.

We can write the same square root function nonrecursively.

 **Listing** **8.10 newton.c**

```
/*
    +-------------------------------------------------------------------+
    + Program Name: newton.c
    +        Author: Otieno and Austell-Wolfson
    +   Date: 04/01/00
    +   Purpose:
    +       To write a series of functions that calculate
    +       the square root of a number using Newton's iterative
    +       technique. The following function, newtonsMethod(),
    +       implements this technique.
    +-------------------------------------------------------------------+
```

```c
*/
#include <stdio.h>
#include <stdlib.h>
#include <math.h>
#define DESIRED_ACCURACY 1.0E-6

double newtonsSquareRoot(double number, int *numOfIterations, double randomGuess);

int main(void)
{
   int howManyNumbers;
   int numberOfIterations;
   double squareRoot;
   double standardSqrt;
   double number;
   int k;

   howManyNumbers = rand() % 20; /* Generate 0 to 19 numbers */
   if (howManyNumbers < 5)
   {
      howManyNumbers += 5;  /* just to have enough numbers */
   }

   for (k = 0; k < howManyNumbers; k++)
   {
      number = rand() % 100;
      standardSqrt = sqrt(number);
      squareRoot = newtonsSquareRoot(number, &numberOfIterations, 0.);
      printf("================================\n");
      printf("          number: %.f iterations: %d\n", number, numberOfIterations);
      printf("Newton\'s Square Root: %13.10f\n", squareRoot);
      printf("     Standard sqrt(): %13.10f\n", standardSqrt);
   }
}

/*
   +-------------------------------------------------------------+
   +  FUNCTION newtonsSquareRoot
   +-------------------------------------------------------------+
*/

double newtonsSquareRoot(double num, int * numOfIterations,
   double randomGuess)
{
   double nextGuess;
   double currentGuess;
   double precision;
   double standardSqrt;

   int numberOfTimes = 0;

   if (randomGuess)
   {
      nextGuess = (double) (rand() % 1000); /* # between 0 and 999 */
   }
   else
   {
      nextGuess = num / 2.0; /* Normal first guess by this method */
   }

   standardSqrt = sqrt(num);

   printf("\nCurrent Guess   Next Guess   Standard sqrt()\n");
```

```
    do
    {
        currentGuess = nextGuess;
        nextGuess = ((num / currentGuess) + currentGuess) / 2;
        numberOfTimes++;

        /* fabs: absolute value */
        precision = fabs(nextGuess - currentGuess);
        printf("%13.10f  %13.10f  %13.10f\n", currentGuess, nextGuess, standardSqrt);
    }
    while (precision > DESIRED_ACCURACY);

    *numOfIterations = numberOfTimes;
    return nextGuess;
}
```

8.10.4   Another Iterative Example

The interest rate program, get_rate.c, is a far more efficient version of Listing 5.16, rate.c. The rate.c program uses a series of for loops; get_rate.c uses recursion instead. In rate.c, we used the library function, pow() for calculating powers of numbers. Here, we roll our own power() function.

 **Listing** 8.11 get_rate.c

```
/* get_rate.c */

/* calculate interest rate (recursive version of rate.c) */

#include <stdio.h>

double power(double number, int pow);

int main(void)
{
    double get_rate(double rate, double increment, double loan, double pmt, int term);
    double principal, payment;
    int years, months;

    printf("Input the following, pressing [Enter] after each:\n");
    printf("Principal amount: ");
    scanf("%lf", &principal);
    printf("Monthly payment: ");
    scanf("%lf", &payment);
    printf("Term in years: ");
    scanf("%d", &years);
    months = years * 12;

    if (principal / (double) months > payment)
        printf("payment cannot be that low even if no interest\n");
    else
        printf("Annual interest rate is %.3f%%\n",
            100. * get_rate(.1, .1, principal, payment, months));
}

double get_rate(double rate, double increment, double loan, double pmt, int term)
{
    double payment, monthly_rate;

    while(1)
    {
```

```
          /* increase rate until too high (i.e., calculated pmt exceeds specified) */
          rate += increment / 10.;
          monthly_rate = rate / 12.;

      /* pmt: (p * i) / (1 - (1 + i) ^ -n)) */
          payment = ((loan * monthly_rate) / (1. - (1./power(1. + monthly_rate, term))));
          if (payment > pmt)
              break;
      }

   /* if calculated pmt is within a penny of specified pmt, quit */
      if (payment - pmt > .01 || payment - pmt < -.01)
      /* otherwise call with lower rate and smaller increment */
          rate = get_rate(rate - increment/10., increment/10., loan, pmt, term);
      return rate;
}

double power(double number, int exponent)
{
    double result = 1.;
    int i;

    for (i = 0; i < exponent; i++)
        result *= number;
    return result;
}
```

Standard C functions are highly optimized, so generally you will want to use them. However, in some cases, you may find that the standard function does not do precisely what you want it to do. In those cases, your own function may be required. Also, standard functions must take into account many unusual and infrequent exception cases. If your application has only simple run-of-the-mill cases, you may find your own simpler function more efficient.

8.11   ADDRESSES AND FUNCTIONS

In this section and the next, we will examine and apply three fundamental concepts:

- **If we pass an address to a function, we can, in the called function, use the dereferencing operator to alter the value stored at that address and thereby change the value of the variable at that address in the calling function.**
- **To the computer, the name of an array is the address of its first element.**
- **Given the preceding concept, when you use an array name as a function argument, you pass the address of the first element of the array. The called function then uses a pointer set to that address to access the array in the calling function.**

When you pass a nonpointer variable as an argument to a function call, a local variable is created in the called function with a value equal to that of the argument. Even though the values of the two variables are the same, they have different addresses. When the function call is finished, the local variable expires in the called function. Anything you do to the newly created variable inside the called function in no way affects the value of the variable passed as an argument.

 Listing **8.12 bad_swap.c**

```
/* bad_swap.c */
/* intro to pointers: shows function variables are local */

#include <stdio.h>
int main(void)
```

```
{
    void swap(int num, int val);
    int num = 10, val = 20;
    swap(num, val);
    printf("main(): num at %p is still %d; val at %p is still %d\n", &num, num, &val, val);
}

void swap(int num, int val)
{
    int temp;
    temp = num;
    num = val;
    val = temp;
    printf("swap(): num at %p is %d; val at %p is %d\n", &num, num, &val, val);
}
```

Here's the output on our system:

```
swap(): num at FFEE is 20; val at FFF0 is 10
main(): num at FFF4 is still 10; val at FFF2 is still 20
```

As advertised, altering the values of the local variables num and val does not change the values of num and val in the calling function. Since variables in these two sets are different variables, programmers, as we have said, generally give them different names to highlight the fact that a change in the called function will not affect the variables being passed:

```
swap(int number, int value);
```

However, if you pass the address of a variable, you can change the variable's value inside the calling function by using the dereferencing operator.

Listing 8.13 goodswap.c

```
/* goodswap.c */

/* working version of bad_swap.c */

#include <stdio.h>

void swap(int *num_ptr, int *val_ptr);
int main(void)
{
    int num = 10, val = 20;
    printf("main(): num at %p is %d; val at %p is %d\n", &num, num, &val, val);
    swap(&num, &val);
    printf("main(): num at %p is now %d; val at %p is now %d\n", &num, num, &val, val);
}

void swap(int *num_ptr, int *val_ptr)
{
    int temp;

    temp = *num_ptr;
    *num_ptr = *val_ptr;
    *val_ptr = temp;
    printf("swap(): num_ptr at %p has a value of %p\n"
        "\tand points to the value of %d stored there\n", &num_ptr, num_ptr, *num_ptr);
}
```

This program gives us the following output on our system:

```
main(): num at FFF4 is 10; val at FFF2 is 20
swap(): num_ptr at FFEE has a value of FFF4
    and points to the value of 20 stored there
main(): num at FFF4 is now 20; val at FFF2 is now 10
```

What accounts for declaring the function in the following way?

```
void swap(int *num_ptr, int *val_ptr);
```

Why are the arguments declared as pointers? Well, we want to pass addresses of `int`s. And we know that when we pass a variable as an argument, what gets passed is its value. So, what sort of variable has an address as a value? A pointer.

The statement

```
temp = *num_ptr;
```

assigns to `temp` the value located where `num_ptr` points to—that is, `num`'s value in `main()`. In

```
*num_ptr = *val_ptr;
```

the right side of the statement gets us the value located where `val_ptr` points, `val` in `main()`. The left side not only gets us to the location where `num_ptr` points, `num` in `main()`, but also assigns `val`'s value to `num`.

The final statement in the function

```
*val_ptr = temp;
```

completes the process by taking `num`'s former value, as preserved in `temp`, and assigning it to where `val_ptr` points, `val`. Notice that since we need to preserve `num`'s *value*, we declare `temp` as an `int`, not a pointer to `int`. Notice too that, by using the dereferencing operator, we are able to work with `num` and `val` as `int`s without having to declare any separate `int` variables in the called function.

Earlier we learned that you can return only a single value to a calling function. Here you've seen essentially how to circumvent that rule.

8.11.1   Caution: Pointer Is a Variable

By dereferencing a pointer passed to a function, we alter the value in the pointed-to location insofar as the calling function is concerned. But it does not follow that *any* changes to pointers passed to functions have similar nonlocal effect. Take the following example.

 **Listing** **8.14** `local.c`

```
/* local.c */

/* shows altering pointers inside function can have only
   local effects */

#include <stdio.h>

void local(int *ptr);

int main(void)
{
    int num;
    int *ptr = &num;

    printf("main before calling local: ptr points to %p\n", ptr);
    local(ptr);
    printf("main after calling local: ptr still points to %p\n", ptr);
}

void local(int *ptr)
{
    int val = 1;

    printf("local before assignment of local variable's address:\n"
        "\tptr points to %p\n", ptr);
    ptr = &val;
```

```
    printf("local after assignment of local variable's address:\n"
        "\tptr points to %p\n", ptr);
}
```

```
main before calling local: ptr points to FFF4
local before assignment of local variable's address:
   ptr points to FFF4
local after assignment of local variable's address:
   ptr points to FFEA
   main after calling local: ptr still points to FFF4
```

A pointer is a variable like any other variable for this purpose. Any changes to its value (here an address) are local only. Only by dereferencing an address value can you cause nonlocal changes.

8.12   ARRAYS AND FUNCTIONS

The task of using arrays in function calls is a tricky one. To tackle it, we must have a more sophisticated appreciation of the connection between pointers and arrays.

8.12.1   Using Pointer Notation for Arrays

To the computer, an array name is a shorthand way of expressing the address of the first element of the array. Expressed another way:

 An array name is equivalent to a pointer to its first element.

This rule is an extension of the concept that to the computer a variable is just an address. Thus, given

```
int data[3];
```

data is the same as &data[0]. We could, for instance, set a pointer to that first element this way:

```
int *ptr = data;
```

or this way:

```
ptr = &data[0];
```

We can build on this rule with other concepts we've learned earlier. Remember that when we increment or decrement a pointer by 1, we jump the address value stored in the pointer by the number of bytes the computer uses to store variables of the type pointed to. If we set a pointer to the first element of

```
int data[3];
```

and increment the pointer by 1, we increment the address value stored in the pointer by 2 if an int has 2 bytes, thus making it point to the second element of data.

In fact, given the declaration

```
int data[3];
```

and treating data as a pointer to its first element, we find that the pairs shown in Table 8.2 are equivalent.

For example:

```
int data[3];
int *ptr = data + 2;
*(data + 2) = 17;
```

The two assignment statements are the same as

```
int *ptr = &data[2];
data[2] = 17;
```

In fact, since data[2] is equivalent to *(data + 2) and since data + 2 is the same as 2 + data, the following will also work, despite its absurd appearance:

```
2[data] = 17;
```

Table 8.2 *Pointer-Array Notation Equivalency for* `int data[3]`

Pointer Notation	Array Notation
`data`	`&data[0]`
`*data`	`data[0]`
`data + 1`	`&data[1]`
`*(data + 1)`	`data[1]`
`data + 2`	`&data[2]`
`*(data + 2)`	`data[2]`

There is no reason for using this bizarre syntax other than to win bets with experienced programmers, who will swear even after the code compiles without error that it just ain't so. There are limits to this business, however. Even though an array name is treated as a pointer to its starting address, it is not a pointer. Even though we can do this

```
ptr = data;
```

`ptr` and `data` are not identical. The former is a variable and the latter is a constant.

```
ptr++; /* OK */
data++; /* error! */
data = ptr; /* error! */
```

C allows us to *use* pointer notation in place of array notation even though we are dealing with an array. In fact, if the truth be known, there is really no such thing as an array. The computer converts all our array usage to pointers. The only real effect of declaring an array instead of a pointer is to prevent the computer from assigning another variable to the memory space allotted to the array when it is declared. There really is a Santa Claus, however.

8.12.2   Using Arrays in Functions

 When we pass the name of an array as an argument to a function call, we have passed the address of the first element of the array.

We said earlier that the *name* of an array is equivalent to a pointer to its first element. In fact, when we pass an array name as an argument, the "equivalent" becomes "identical." Section 6.7.1 of the ISO C Standard (see the Preface for a discussion of the Standard) mandates as follows:

> On entry to the function, the value of each argument expression shall be converted to the type of its corresponding parameter, as if by assignment to the parameter. Array expressions and function designators as arguments are converted to pointers before the call. A declaration of a parameter as "array of *type*" shall be adjusted to "pointer to *type*," . . . as in 6.2.2.1 [which says that the pointer so converted shall point to the initial element of the array].

Remember that we declare as pointers arguments to which we want to pass addresses. Accordingly, even though the array name is a constant, in the function its address is assigned to a locally declared pointer. We can use that pointer to access and alter the array contents. And we can increment or decrement the pointer.

We often need to give functions access to an array's values. The most common case is passing NULL-terminated char arrays, or strings. However, passing a whole flock of values could create serious performance problems if we pass large arrays and pass them often. We could eat up a lot of time and memory passing copies of each and every element of the arrays.

C's compromise is to pass the address of the array's first element and allow the function to access the array through the dereferenced address. In effect, C simulates passing variables by reference in this way. If we want to allow the function to look at but not change the variables in the calling function, we can qualify the passed pointer value by making it const (see Chapter 10). To illustrate, we take the following listing, which contains a function that doubles each element of an array.

 **Listing 8.15 `twice.c`**

```
/* twice.c */

/* pass name of one-dimensional array to function to double each array member */

#include <stdio.h>

void twice(int *ptr, int size); /* pointer notation */

int main(void)
{
    int data[] = {17, 32, 5};
    int i;
    int elements = sizeof(data)/sizeof(int);

    twice(data, elements);
    for (i = 0; i < elements; i++)
      printf("data[%d] is %d\n", i, data[i]);
}

void twice(int *ptr, int size)
{
    int i;
    for (i = 0; i < size; i++)
       *(ptr + i) *= 2;
}
```

We get output of

```
data[0] is 34
data[1] is 64
data[2] is 10
```

The local variable `ptr` is a pointer to `int`. Therefore, if `ptr` points to `data[0]`, then `ptr + 1` points to `data[1]` and `ptr + 2` points to `data[2]`.

As we have seen, C allows us to use pointer notation in place of array notation even though we are dealing with an array. The converse is also true. We can use array *notation* even though we are formally dealing with pointers. Thus, though `ptr` is a pointer variable, C allows us to fudge and use array notation anyway. In place of

```
*(ptr + i) *= 2;
```

we can use

```
ptr[i] *= 2;
```

And in place of

```
void twice(int *ptr, int size);
```

we can use the declaration

```
void twice(int ptr[], int size);
```

Thus, we could rewrite the function this way:

```
void twice(int ptr[], int size)
{
    int i;
```

```
    for (i = 0; i < size; i++)
        ptr[i] *= 2;
}
```

Allowing us to use array notation within the function where we really have a pointer serves two purposes. First, many people find it easier to use and understand array notation than pointer notation. This is especially so for two-dimensional arrays, as you will see. Second, we can use the dereferencing operator to affect the members of the array, a pointer to the array has been passed to the function. Array notation may give us a better mental picture of what is happening in the *calling* function by such changes.

The computer allows us to indulge ourselves further with this array fiction and fill in the subscript number in the function declaration if we wish:

```
void twice(int ptr[3], int size);
```

But the compiler would ignore it; we are passing a single address, not an array—no matter how we write it. Though we can pass the value of a variable to a function,

 C does not allow us to pass the values of an entire array.

(As we will see in Chapter 13, however, we can pass the values of an entire *structure* to a function as an alternative to passing a pointer to the structure. This includes passing the values of a structure whose only member is an array!)

If we wish to use array notation and don't feel like including the variable name in the prototype (it must be in the function definition header, though), we would write it as follows:

```
void twice(int [], int);
```

We do not omit the brackets, just as we must include the indirection operator in the equivalent pointer notation declaration:

```
void twice(int *, int);
```

Since the computer really uses pointers no matter what we do, you can mix pointer notation for the declaration with array notation inside the function and vice versa, though we don't recommend such a confusing format:

```
void twice(int ptr[], int size)
{
    int i;

    for (i = 0; i < size; i++)
        *(ptr + i) *= 2;
}
```

But remember that although we can pretend we have an array if we find that using array notation is simpler or clearer, we really just have a pointer dressed up to look like an array. The array does not exist inside the function. Hence we had to pass the array's size rather than simply using the `sizeof` operator within the function to determine array size. The expression

```
sizeof(ptr)
```

would have a value of 2 on a PC (4 in a large data memory model; see Appendix B), no matter what the size of the array `ptr` points to.

In C, unlike some other languages, there is no automatic way to find a stopping point in traversing an array. When we use a `for` or `while` loop to traverse an array, for instance, we either have to hard-code the number of iterations, or depend on the `sizeof` operator to help us out (`while (i++ < sizeof(numArray) / sizeof(int))`), or else use a sentinel value in an array element—some value our data could not possibly contain inserted merely to tell us where to stop (`while (num[i++] != -999)`). (As you will see in the next chapter, C uses a zero byte in `char` arrays to act as the sentinel terminator for strings. The entire Standard C string library is constructed on that concept.) Inside functions to which pointers to arrays are passed, we lose the ability for the `sizeof` operator to be of assistance, unless we pass the result of the `sizeof` operator on the entire array as a separate parameter.

Conversely, because we are really dealing with a pointer, we can increment the pointer, even though we could not increment the array name it derives from:

```
void twice(int *ptr, int size)
{
    while (size--)
        *(ptr++) *= 2;
}
```

And, given the following:

```
void whereAmI(char *ptr);
int main(void)
{
    char string[] = "I am literal-minded";
    whereAmI(string);
    printf("&string and &string[0]: %p and %p\n", string, &string[0]);
}
void whereAmI(char *ptr)
{
    printf("&ptr and &ptr[0]: %p and %p\n", &ptr, &ptr[0]);
}
```

are you surprised by the first pair of addresses printed?

```
&ptr and &ptr[0]: FFE0 and FFE2
&string and &string[0]: FFE2 and FFE2
```

Remember, even though you can use array notation here, you are only dealing with a pointer to an array. The `ptr` variable is a separate variable; it just happens to point to the first element of the `string` array, which you happen to be able to refer to in dereferencing as `ptr[0]`.

Though we generally will pass a pointer to the array's first element to a function by simply using its name as the argument, there is nothing to prevent us from passing the address of an intermediate element:

```
int index = 3
num[5] = {1, 2, 3, 4, 5};
twice(&num[index], 5 - index);
```

Notice how careful you must be when using intermediate points of an array. C has an automatic mechanism at the end of strings (see Chapter 9), but there is no such mechanism for an array of numbers as such. You must create your own stopping mechanism—whether by sentinel or otherwise—to avoid overstepping array boundaries.

8.12.3   Multidimensional Arrays and Functions

We can extend the concepts we've learned to cover multidimensional arrays:

```
int data[3][3];
```

Start with the concept that the name of an array is equivalent to the address of its first element. The first element of the array is itself an array, `data[0]`. Thus,

```
data
```

is equivalent to

```
&data[0];
```

By extension, the same is true of the individual arrays of 3 `int`s each that comprise the array `data`. Thus, the following are equivalent:

```
data[0]    &data[0][0];
data[1]    &data[1][0];
data[2]    &data[2][0];
```

When we pass data to a function, we are passing the value of a pointer to an array of 3 ints, data[0]. How do we declare a pointer we want to set to data[0]?

```
int data[3][3];
int (*ptr)[3] = &data[0]; /* or simply, in place of &data[0], data */
```

The object pointed to is an array of 3 ints. This declaration of a pointer to an array should be distinguished from an array of pointers:

```
int *ptr[3]; /* an array of pointers to int, not a pointer to an array */
```

Since incrementing or decrementing a pointer jumps the address stored by the pointer by the size in bytes of the data object pointed to, incrementing or decrementing a pointer to an array of 3 ints by 1 jumps the address by 6 bytes if an int is 2 bytes. Let's see how this works—first in a nonfunction context.

 **Listing** **8.16 jump_two.c**

```
/* jump_two.c */

/*
    in two-dimensional array with subarrays of 3 ints each,
    incrementing pointer moves 6 bytes
*/

#include <stdio.h>

int main(void)
{
    int data[5][3] =
    {
        {0, 1, 2},
        {3, 4, 5},
        {6, 7, 8},
        {9, 10, 11},
        {12, 13, 14}
    };
    int (*ptr)[3] = &data[0];
    int i;

    for (i = 0; i < 5; i++, ptr++)
        printf("&data[%d]: %p; ptr: %p, **ptr: %d\n", i, &data[i], ptr, **ptr);
}
```

We get the following output:

```
&data[0]: FFD8; ptr: FFD8, **ptr: 0
&data[1]: FFDE; ptr: FFDE, **ptr: 3
&data[2]: FFE4; ptr: FFE4, **ptr: 6
&data[3]: FFEA; ptr: FFEA, **ptr: 9
&data[4]: FFF0; ptr: FFF0, **ptr: 12
```

Thus, we see that incrementing ptr moves us from &data[0] to &data[1] to &data[2] and so on. Each time ptr is incremented, we move 3 ints, or 6 bytes.

To get from ptr, which points to an array, to the value of an element of the array it points to, we use a double dereferencing operator. Incrementing the pointer moves where the pointer points from "row" to "row." To move from "column" to "column" within a "row," we need to dereference the already-dereferenced value. We've seen that

```
*(ptr + row)
```

gets us to data[row]. Since the array name data[row] is equivalent to a pointer to &data[row][0],

```
*(*(ptr + row))
```

gives us the *value* of data[row][0]. By adding 1 to *(ptr + row), we jump the pointed-to address an int at a time. In other words,

```
*(*ptr + row) + 1)
```

is equivalent to

```
data[row][1];
```

Where ptr is declared as a pointer to an array and assigned the starting address of a two-dimensional array arrayname, we can generalize by stating that

```
*(*ptr + row) + col)
```

is equivalent to

```
arrayname[row][col];
```

 Commit this formulation to memory; it will come in handy.
Now, let's see how this works in a function.

 **Listing   8.17 two_time.c**

```c
/* two_time.c */

/*
    pass a pointer to an array to a function by passing the array name
    and double each element by incrementing the pointer
*/

#include <stdio.h>
#define ROWS 3
#define COLS 3

/* void twice(int(*ptr)[COLS]); // version 1: pointer notation */
void twice(int ptr[][COLS]); /* version 2: array notation */

int main(void)
{
    int data[ROWS][COLS] =
    {
        {0, 1, 2},
        {3, 4, 5},
        {6, 7, 8},
    };
    int row, col;

    twice(data);

    /* show this worked */
    for (row = 0; row < ROWS; row++)
    {
        for (col = 0; col < COLS; col++)
            printf("%6d", data[row][col]);
        putchar('\n');
    }
}

/* version 1: pointer notation */
/*
    void twice(int(*ptr)[COLS])
    {
        int row, col;

        for (row = 0; row < ROWS; row++)
```

```
            for (col = 0; col < COLS; col++)
                *(*(ptr + row) + col) *= 2;
        }
    */

    /* version 2: array notation */
    void twice(int ptr[][COLS])
    {
        int row, col;

        for (row = 0; row < ROWS; row++)
            for (col = 0; col < COLS; col++)
                ptr[row][col] *= 2;
    }
```

We get the following output:

```
 0   2   4
 6   8  10
12  14  16
```

8.12.4   Array Notation for Pointers

Just as we saw with one-dimensional arrays, you can use array notation instead of pointer notation inside a function to which you have passed a pointer representing the name of a two-dimensional array:

```
void twice(int ptr[][COLS])
{
    int row, col;

    for (row = 0; row < ROWS; row++)
        for (col = 0; col < COLS; col++)
            ptr[row][col] *= 2;
}
```

This does not mean ptr *is* an array; it is not. It is just that the compiler lets you pretend ptr is an array and use array notation if you find it would be easier to follow.

Insofar as the function declaration is concerned, note that the following would *not* suffice:

```
void twice(int ptr[][]);
```

The compiler takes array notation and converts it to pointer notation. To know how many bytes each pointer increment or decrement translates to, the compiler must know the size of the object pointed to. The [3], in conjunction with the type int, furnishes the needed information.

Conversely, the function declaration need not contain the size of the first dimension:

```
void twice (int ptr[3][3]);
```

That declaration would not generate an error message. However, the first subscript number would be ignored by the compiler. The compiler needs to know how far to move the pointed-to address with each pointer increment or decrement; it does not need to know how many such moves are required to traverse the entire multidimensional array. Here, the compiler must be told that each increment or decrement jumps the address pointed to by 6 bytes if int has 2 bytes (3 ints times 2 bytes for each). The fact that three such moves will traverse the array is of no consequence to the compiler. Indeed, it is perfectly permissible to increment the pointer beyond the boundaries of the array—though in most (but not all) cases, such leaps are the result of inadvertent programming error; if they extend more than one element beyond the array's end, we have undefined behavior under Standard C.

The same logic holds for arrays of more than two dimensions:

```
int data[3][3][4];
void twice int (ptr[][3][4]); /* or void twice int (*ptr)[3][4] */
```

By contrast, when you declare the array itself, the compiler is concerned with reserving the proper amount of memory for the array. You may not leave out any dimension's size:

```
int data[][3]; /* error! */
```

8.13   POINTERS TO FUNCTIONS *(OPTIONAL)*

Recall that the compiler considers the name of an array equivalent to the address of its first element. Similarly, the name of a function is considered equivalent to the starting address of the code for the function in memory. (See Appendix B for where the code resides in memory.) Both the array name and the function name are constants.

Carrying the analogy farther, you can declare a pointer to a function just as you may declare a pointer to an array. Actually, on some computers, a pointer to a function houses the address of a block of information (including the address of the function definition's code) required to call the function rather than the address of the function's code in memory. However, the effect of declaring a function pointer is the same, and any difference is immaterial to the programmer.

The following statement declares a pointer to a function that returns an `int` and takes an `int` as an argument:

```
int (*fptr) (int);
```

Note the similarity in format to a declaration for a pointer to an array of `int`s:

```
int (*ptr)[3];
```

and compare the declaration to one for an array of three pointers to functions that take and return an `int` as arguments:

```
int (*fptr[3]) (int);
```

The declaration is also similar to a function declaration, except that in place of the function name, you have the pointer variable name (preceded by the dereferencing operator, as is usual for declarations of pointer variables) enclosed in parentheses. Once you have made this declaration, you can assign `fptr` the address of any function that takes an `int` and returns an `int`. There is no "generic" function pointer that takes the address of a function returning any type, as there is for object pointers (`void *`).

You must enclose both the asterisk and the function pointer name in parentheses, as in the first example above. If instead we wrote

```
int *fptr(int);
```

all we have is a function that takes an `int` and returns a pointer to `int`. If you look at Appendix J, you will note that the parentheses have the very highest precedence, one level higher than the dereferencing operator.

Once you have made this declaration, you can set a pointer to a function that takes and returns an `int` and call the function through the dereferenced pointer:

```
int factorial(int num), factor;
int is_prime(int val), prime;
fptr = factorial; /* name of function is equivalent to pointer to function */
factor = (*fptr)(7); /* same as factor = factorial(7); */
fptr = is_prime;
prime = (*fptr)(123);
```

You may also use the un-dereferenced format for the function call:

```
factor = fptr(7);
```

One use of the ability to assign a function address to a function pointer is making a conditional assignment of one of several different functions, depending on the results of earlier steps in the program. The following program does just that.

 **Listing**   **8.18 fun_ptr.c**

```
/* fun_ptr.c */

/* pointer to function illustration */

#include <stdio.h>
```

```
#include <ctype.h> /* toupper() */

int main(void)
{
    int doubled(int num), trebled(int num), squared(int num), cubed(int num);
    int (*fptr)(int num); /* ptr to function taking & returning int */
    int number;
    char function[15];

    printf("Type an integer and either \"double\", \"triple\", \"square\", or \"cube\"\n");
    while (scanf("%d%s", &number, function) == 2)
    {
        /* turn first letter of function array into caps */
        *function = toupper(*function);

        switch(*function)
        {
            case 'D': fptr = doubled; break;
            case 'T': fptr = trebled; break;
            case 'S': fptr = squared; break;
            case 'C': fptr = cubed; break;
            default:
                printf("Incorrect choice; try again\n");

                /* OK from switch for while loop; break not OK */
                continue;
        } /* end switch */

        printf("%d %s%c is %d\n", number, function, 'd', fptr(number));
        printf("Type an integer and either \"double\", \"triple\", \"square\", or \"cube\"\n");
        printf("Type Q to quit\n");
    } /* end while */
}


int doubled(int num)
{
    return num * 2;
}

int trebled(int num)
{
    return num * 3;
}

int squared(int num)
{
    return num * num;
}

int cubed(int num)
{
    return num * num *num;
}
```

First the user types in an integer and an operation to be performed. The operation name is stored in a char array, function. If the first letter of function is lowercase, we change it to uppercase so as to minimize the case labels in the switch statement. (The function we use to do that, toupper(), is covered in Chapter 9.) Alternatively, for an ASCII character-encoding system only, the following would achieve the same purpose:

```
if (*function >= 'a' && *function <= 'z')
    *function -= 'a' - 'A';
```

We set `fptr` to the starting address of the functions `doubled`, `trebled`, `squared`, or `cubed`, depending on the result of the `switch`. For example, if the user typed "double":

```
case 'D': fptr = doubled; break;
```

With this choice, when we call `fptr(number)` by including the call as an argument to `printf()`, it is just as if we had called `doubled(number)`. The call gives the computer the starting address of the code for `doubled` because, in this example, we have set `fptr` to that address.

8.13.1   Pointers to Functions as Arguments

Another use of pointers to functions is to pass a function name as an argument to another function. Again, the usage is similar to array names being passed to functions. If, for example, we have a function `reverse()` that returns a pointer to `char` and has as its sole parameter a pointer to a function that takes and returns a pointer to `char`, we would declare it this way:

```
char *reverse (char *(*fptr)(char *));
```

Let's take a look at a simple array example before we tackle functions. The following program uses a function that reverses characters in a string and returns a pointer to the string so it can be printed. (The `gets()` function utilized here allows the user to input an entire line of text, even one containing whitespace. See Chapter 9 for a description of the `gets()` function.)

 **Listing** **8.19 flipper.c**

```c
/* flipper.c */

/* reverse characters in string; return pointer to the string for printing */

#include <stdio.h>
#include <string.h> /* strlen */

char *flipperoo(char *str);

int main(void)
{
    char string[81];

    printf("Input a string\n");
    printf("\"%s\" backward is \"%s\"\n", string, flipperoo(gets(string)));
}

char *flipperoo(char *str)
{
    int len = strlen(str);
    static char flip[81]; /* must be static since address is returned */

    flip[len] = '\0'; /* close off new reverse string */
    while(*str) /* continue until get to NULL in str */
    /* start at end of flip & go backward */
        flip[--len] = *str++;
    return flip;
}
```

We pass to the function `flipperoo()` the name of an array as the argument that calls for a pointer to `char`. The compiler treats the array name as the address of its first element. The function takes whatever address is passed and uses it. The mechanics of `flipperoo()` will be discussed below.

We can do the same thing with a function name, as the next listing shows.

Listing 8.20 tri_flip.c

```c
/* tri_flip.c */

/* function pointer passed as argument to another function: reverse string */

#include <stdio.h>
#include <string.h>

char *flipperoo(char *), *bitflip(char *);
void choice(char *string[], char *(*fptr)(char *));

int main(void)
{
   char *string[3] = {"provincial", "boomerang", "reverse"};

   choice(string, flipperoo);
   choice(string, bitflip);
   choice(string, strrev); /* DOS-specific library function: char *strrev(char *) */
   return 0;
}

void choice(char *string[], char *(*fptr)(char *))
{
   int i;

   for (i = 0; i < 3; i++)
      printf("%s\n", fptr(string[i]));
}


char *flipperoo(char *str)
{
   int len = strlen(str);
   static char flip[81]; /* must be static since address returned */

   flip[len] = '\0'; /* close off new reverse string */
   while(*str) /* go until NULL in str */
   /* start at end of flip & go backwards */
      flip[--len] = *str++;
   return flip;
}


char *bitflip(char *str)
{
   int len = strlen(str);
   char *ptr = str + len - 1; /* point to character before NULL */

   while (str < ptr)
      *str ^= *ptr, *ptr ^= *str, *str++ ^= *ptr--;
   return (str - len / 2);
}
```

The choice() function has two arguments: a pointer to an array of char pointers and a pointer to a function that takes a pointer to char as its argument and returns a pointer to char. Note the syntax of the function pointer argument, taking particular note of its middle component in parentheses:

```c
char *(*fptr)(char*)
```

We have included three functions that take and return a pointer to char, namely, bitflip(), flipperoo(), and a DOS-specific library function, strrev(). We included the latter to show that the function pointers work with library functions as well as your own. There are no Standard C library functions that take and return a char * other than gets(), which is not suitable here because of its interactive nature (see Chapter 9).

Just as we pass simply the name of the array of pointers—string—to the argument that requires a pointer to a char pointer array, so we simply pass the name of the function to the argument that requires a pointer to a function, flipperoo, bitflip, or strrev. The name of the array is equivalent to a pointer to the array, and the name of the function is equivalent to a pointer to the function.

Note, too, the format of the call

```
fptr(string[i])
```

which is in lieu of any of the following:

```
flipperoo(string[i])
bitflip(string[i])
strrev(string[i])
```

The logic, once again, is the same as with strings:

```
char str1[] = "number one son";
char str2[] = "number two son";
char *ptr = str1;
printf("%s\n", ptr);
ptr = str2;
printf("%s\n" ptr);
```

In place of using str1 or str2 as an argument to printf(), we can use the name of a pointer that points to those strings. We do the same in two_flip.c with function pointers. Instead of using a function name—which is a pointer to its code—in a call, we use a pointer to that same code.

Note, however, that Standard C expressly allows, and some older compilers require, the dereferenced format for the call:

```
printf("%s\n", (*fptr)(string[i]));
```

instead of

```
printf("%s\n", fptr(string[i]));
```

In tri_flip.c, the functions we pass to choice() are just different methods of accomplishing the same task. In flipperoo(), we first use strlen() to find where to place the NULL character in a char array, flip, which we use to store the letters in reverse. The function's work is all done with the following statement:

```
while(*str)
    flip[--len] = *str++;
```

The assignment statement moves str 1 byte with each loop and moves where we store what str points to in flip with each loop. This is done with the increment and decrement operators. The conditional expression in the while loop stops us when str reaches the NULL character in string. At that time, *str is equal to 0 and the condition (which is the same as saying while(*str != 0)) evaluates to false. Meanwhile, the characters in string are placed one by one in flip, from the byte just before the NULL character we placed, backward to the starting address of flip. (Incidentally, there is no problem with incrementing str: as we have seen, even though string is a constant, the pointer passed by using string as an argument is not.)

Notice that we have declared the array, the starting address to which we return, as static. As you will see in Chapter 10, this reserves the entire memory area allocated to that variable for the life of the program. Otherwise, we would return the address of a memory area that would no longer be reserved; the nice reverse string we built could be overstored at the instant we return from the function. Pointers that refer to memory locations no longer allocated are referred to as ***dangling pointers.*** The error is common.

The bitflip() function uses bit manipulation to achieve the same effect without having to resort to creating a separate storage array like flip. We first place ptr at the last character in string. Then one by one, we switch characters between where str points and ptr points, using a bit manipulation device we cover in Chapter 12. Following each switch, we increment where str points and decrement where ptr points. We stop when the locations the two pointers point to cross. We then return a pointer to where str started pointing to before we moved it.

Note that both bitflip() and strrev() alter the passed string, whereas flipperoo() does not. Therefore, we can use bitflip() and strrev() to reverse a string or to print out the reverse of a string, or both. The flipperoo() function serves the latter purpose only. But for wanting to keep the arguments the same type in this example, we probably would have made the flipperoo() argument const char *.

In tri_flip.c, we have three functions, each of which takes a single argument and performs the same task. Of course, in an appropriate programming context, we could have included far more than three functions and they could have performed completely different tasks.

```
double add(double num, double val, double fig, int significance);
double mortgage(double principal, double rate, double term, int cap);
double volume(double height, double length, double width, int sides);
double(*fptr)(double, double, double, int) = add;
```

The only requirement is that they all return the same type and take the same number and type of arguments.

8.13.2   Array of Pointers to Functions

We can also create an array of pointers to functions, and if we wish, initialize them at the time of declaration. We can illustrate with a simplified version of triflip.c, fun_arry.c. We have omitted the reversing function definitions already contained in triflip.c to save space.

 **Listing 8.21 fun_arry.c**

```
/* fun_arry.c */

/* array of function pointers */

#include <stdio.h>
#include <string.h>

char *flipperoo(char *), *bitflip(char *);

int main(void)
{
    char *string = "A man a plan a canal Panama"; /* a Palindrome */
    char *(*reverseFunctions[])(char *) = {flipperoo, bitflip, NULL};
    int i = 0;

    while(*reverseFunctions[i])
        puts(reverseFunctions[i++](string));
}
```

We could have used this same function pointer formulation in fun_ptr.c and avoided the switch statement structure.

```
unsigned long (*fptr[])(unsigned long num) = {doubled, trebled, squared, cubed};
printf("Press a number to select: \n"
  "1. double\n2. treble\n3. square\n4. cube\n5. quit\n");
scanf("%d", &choice);
printf("%d %lu\n", number, fptr[choice - 1](number));
```

8.13.3   Returning a Function Pointer

We can create a lookup table of functions of the same type. We can get user input and return a pointer to one of these functions selected by the user or use the lookup table noninteractively, depending on program results to the point of using the table. The following program, fun_look.c, uses the interactive approach. The mechanism for soliciting user input is a command line argument following the program name. This mechanism is covered in Chapter 16 (code for flipperoo() and bitflip(), included above, not included in fun_look.c).

 **Listing** **8.22**   **fun_look.c**

```
/* fun_look.c */

/* create lookup table of functions & return pointer to function */

#include <stdio.h>
#include <string.h>
#include <stdlib.h> /* atoi() */

/* function that takes an int and returns a pointer to a function
   that takes and returns a pointer to char */
char *(*startUp(int choice))(char *string);

char *flipperoo(char *), *bitflip(char *);
char *(*reverseFunctions[])(char *) = {flipperoo, bitflip};

int main(int argc, char **argv)
{
    int selection;
    char string[] = "A man a plan a canal Panama"; /* a Palindrome */
    if (argc == 2 && (selection = atoi(argv[1])) > 0 && selection
        <= sizeof(reverseFunctions) / sizeof(char *(*)(char *)))
        puts(startUp(selection - 1)(string));
    else return -1;
}

char *(*startUp(int choice))(char *string)
{
    return reverseFunctions[choice];
}
```

8.14   VARIABLE NUMBER OF ARGUMENTS *(OPTIONAL)*

In some cases, it would be useful to have a function that could accept a variable number of arguments. For instance, assume we had a function whose job it is to return the sum of a series of numbers. If we knew in advance how many numbers are in the series—say, three—the problem would be trivial:

```
int sum(int one, int two, int three)
{
    return one + two + three;
}
```

But what if we want the ability to add up any number of values? The following function would handle that job:

```
int sum(int var_num, . . .)
{
    int total = 0;
    va_list arg_ptr;
    char i;

/* point to 1st variable argument by passing
last fixed argument to va_start macro */

    va_start(arg_ptr, var_num);
    for (i = 0; i < var_num; i++)

    * point to 1st variable argument first time;
      next variable argument subsequent times */

        total += va_arg(arg_ptr, int);
```

```
    va_end(arg_ptr); /* clean up */
    return total;
}
```

Examples of calls to this function:

```
printf("sum: %d\n", sum(10, 1, 2, 3, 4, 5, 6, 7, 8, 9, 10));
printf("sum: %d\n", sum(2, 25, 50));
```

The variable-argument function's operation is a task shared between the compiler and the programmer. The compiler, as directed by Standard C, gives the programmer a few macros to use. Armed only with those macros, the programmer is responsible, in coding the function definition, for indicating the type of each argument and for showing when the last variable argument has been reached—either by indicating how many variable arguments there are or by including some automatic stopping mechanism.

You many not realize it, but you have already seen variable-argument functions. Both `printf()` and `scanf()` are variable-argument functions. They use a format string in the function call to tell the function how many arguments there are (each conversion specifier corresponds to one argument) and what the type of each is (each specifier indicates a certain type: `%i` indicates an `int`, `%f` indicates a `double`, and so on).

8.14.1   Variable-Argument Function Prototype

Let's take another look at the prototype for the variable-length argument list function (which we will call *variable-argument function* for short) in the last example:

```
int sum(int var_num, . . .);
```

 The variable-argument function prototype must have at least one fixed parameter.

That is, there must be one parameter that will always appear in the function call. In the preceding example, the fixed parameter is a variable that happens to give the number of variable arguments that follow.

 The variable arguments must come immediately after the last fixed parameter. You must pass at least one variable argument in a call to the variable-argument function.

In a variable-argument function call, the fixed and variable arguments are separated by commas, as in a nonvariable-argument function call. The variable parameters are represented *in the prototype* by an ellipsis—three periods *with no spaces between them* ("...")—following the last fixed argument:

```
int convert(int val, int arg_num,...);
```

(Note that the three dots, or ellipsis, is to be written literally. At other points in this book, we have used an ellipsis to mean "something or other goes here," as for instance with the `[. . .]` and `[^. . .]` `scanf()` conversion specifiers; that is not the meaning here.)

When we say "fixed parameter," we don't mean to imply that the argument must be a constant, or that it always must have the same value, or that it must be of some `const` type. All we mean is that this argument must always be in the function call. For example, the prototype for a function that always takes three `int`s as arguments and one or more strings might look like this:

```
int add(int size, int mode, int arg_num, . . .);
```

In this example, we have three fixed arguments. That is, there will always be three `int` arguments in every call of this function. These fixed arguments are handled in the function in exactly the same way parameters normally are.

We may pass this function one string argument

```
add(4, mode, 1, "Joe");
```

or a dozen

```
add(num * 2, 5, 12, "John", "Mary", "Sue", "Hiroshi", "Pete",
    "Sam", "Fred", "Juanita", "Ted", "Jake", "Tim", "Fran");
```

Special handling is required in the function for these variable arguments.

8.14.2   Prototype Checking and Type Conversion

With nonvariable-argument functions, the compiler does both type checking and, where appropriate, type conversion from actual to formal argument type. If we use the wrong number of arguments in a function call, for example, the compiler will not allow this to get by (assuming, of course, the call has been properly preceded in the file by a prototype). If we use an inappropriate data type as an argument—we attempt to pass an int where the corresponding parameter is a pointer to a structure, for instance—we will get an error message on compiling. On the other hand, if the actual argument and formal argument are different types, but those that Standard C allows to be converted from one to the other (for example, we pass an int variable to a float argument), the compiler processes the statement without complaint; the actual argument's type is converted to that of the formal argument. (See Chapter 13 for a discussion of which types may be converted to which other types.)

With variable-argument functions, the compiler has nothing to check the types of the nonfixed arguments against. Nor, for the same reason, does automatic type conversion apply to the nonfixed arguments. There can be no conversion of the variable arguments to the types of the formal arguments: there *are* no corresponding formal arguments.

With this function definition,

```
long double sum (int num, . . .)
{
    va_list argp;
    long double total = 0;
    va_start(argp, num);
    while (num--)
        total += va_arg(argp, long double); /* long double
            variable argument expected */
    va_end(argp);
    return total;
}
```

the compiler would not detect the havoc that would be caused by the following call:

```
sum (6, 1, 2, 3, 4, 5, 6);
```

Or let's examine what happens on the following call to printf(), assuming a long is 4 bytes and a double is 8:

```
double payment = 4025.5, rate = 0.07875;
long days = 100000L, hours = 2000000L;
printf("%ld %ld %ld %ld\n", payment, rate, days, hours);
```

The computer places 8 bytes on the stack for payment and rate and 4 each for days and hours. When a long is 4 bytes, the %ld conversion specifier pulls four bytes from the stack. Thus, the first two conversion specifiers each take half the bytes of payment, figure out what value those bytes have if they were a long, and print out some very strange result. The same thing happens for the next two conversion specifiers and rate's 8 bytes. Even though those two conversion specifiers were the correct ones for days and hours, they never get that far; they read the wrong bytes. The last two variables are ignored completely. You can see that a variable-argument function places a great deal of responsibility on the programmer.

Each variable argument is automatically converted according to the accompanying chart (Table 8.3).

8.14.3   Mechanics of Variable-Argument Functions: Macros

The variable-argument function works with the aid of three macros and one typedef found in stdarg.h. (A typedef is a nickname for a Standard C type. See Chapter 13.) In the declaration we saw in sum() above,

```
va_list arg_ptr;
```

va_list is an implementation-defined typedef of a type suitable for holding information required by the three implementation-defined macros discussed below.

Table 8.3 *Variable Argument Type Conversions*

Type	Converted to
char	int
unsigned char	int
short	int
unsigned short	unsigned int (signed int if int has more bytes than unsigned short)
float	double
array	pointer to first element of array

Once inside the variable-argument function, we will proceed as follows:

1. We will declare a pointer variable of type va_list.
2. We point this va_list variable to the first variable argument. This we do with the aid of the va_start macro.
3. We will move from variable argument to variable argument with the aid of the va_arg macro.
4. We invoke the va_end macro for cleanup.

8.14.4   The va_start Macro

By passing our va_list variable, arg_ptr, and the last *fixed* argument to the macro va_start, we point arg_ptr to the first variable argument:

```
va_start(arg_ptr, var_num);
```

The va_start macro first sets our va_list pointer to the last fixed argument. Then it jumps over the fixed argument. Since, by hypothesis, we know the type of this argument, the computer knows how many bytes to jump over. Borland C's implementation of va_start is this:

```
#define __size(x) ((sizeof(x)+sizeof(int)-1) & \
    ~(sizeof(int)-1))
#define va_start(ap, parmN) \
    ((void)((ap) = (va_list) \
    ((char _FAR *)(&parmN)+__size(parmN))))
```

Apart from the missing semicolon, which we dutifully add when we invoke va_start, this is just an assignment statement where we assign the address of the fixed argument to the va_list pointer variable and then increment the pointer by the fixed argument's number of bytes.

8.14.5   The va_arg Macro

To move from one variable argument to another, in the order passed, we use the va_arg macro. The call to va_arg is similar to the call to va_start. The first argument is the va_list variable we have declared, arg_ptr. This time, the computer doesn't know the type of the argument. The second argument to the macro this time is the *type* of the variable argument. For instance:

```
va_arg(arg_ptr, int);
```

This will enable the compiler to move from argument to argument, moving the correct number of bytes each time.

Here's how Borland C defines va_arg:

```
#define __size(x) \
    ((sizeof(x)+sizeof(int)-1) & ~(sizeof(int)-1))
```

```
#define va_arg(ap,type) \
    (*(type _FAR *)(((*(char _FAR *_FAR *)&(ap)) \
    +=__size(type))-(__size(type))))
```

Why does this macro add the size of the current argument (+= __size(type)) and then subtract it (-__size(type))? Here's what it is doing. First, the macro increments the va_list variable to point to the *next* argument. It does this by adding the number of bytes that comprise the *current* argument. Then it returns the *value* of the *next* argument by taking this new value of the va_list pointer variable, as just assigned, subtracting the size of the current argument, and dereferencing that address and type casting to the type of the next argument. Since this time the subtraction is not done by way of assignment, as the addition was, the value of the va_list pointer is not changed; it still points to the next argument.

Consequently, the first time va_arg is invoked, it "returns" the first variable argument in the list. Each subsequent invocation "returns" the next variable argument in the list. By "returns," we mean that the va_arg macro expression has a value equal to the variable and thus can be used in the same fashion that we can use a function call: to assign a value, to act as an argument to another function, and so on. Hence the statement from the sum() example above:

```
total += va_arg(arg_ptr, int);
```

Here, invoking va_arg returns the *next* variable argument and assigns that argument's value to total. However, va_arg points to the *current* variable argument.

8.14.6   A Stopping Mechanism

The variable-argument macro-driven structure has no inherent mechanism for stopping at the last argument. You must provide that mechanism yourself.

There are two common methods for accomplishing this. The first is passing the number of variable arguments as one of the fixed arguments. You saw the first method in sum().

The other common method is the use of a sentinel—some artificial value that, when reached, announces that there are no more arguments. You could use 0 or its macro representation, NULL, or some value beyond the range that your actual arguments could possibly have (–1 or –99, and so on).

If your arguments are strings, and you want to use a NULL sentinel, be sure to use NULL rather than 0 if you use the large memory model on the PC (see Appendix B). In the large-memory model, the NULL macro is defined as 0L rather than 0; use of 0 for NULL pointers will almost certainly cause a serious run-time error (as you can verify by compiling var_msg.c below in the large memory model and replacing the NULL in the call with 0).

We can rewrite sum() using this second approach. Instead of using a for loop to traverse the argument list, we could use a while loop, stopping when the value returned by va_arg is our sentinel value:

```
void sum2(char *control_str, . . .)
{
    int total = 0;
    int value;
    va_list arg_ptr;

    /* point to 1st variable argument by passing last fixed argument */

    va_start(arg_ptr, control_str);

    /* stop at sentinel value, -99 */

    while((value = va_arg(arg_ptr, int)) != -99)
        total += value;
    va_end(arg_ptr); /* clean up */
    printf(control_str, total);
}
```

A sample call would be

```
sum2("Sum is %d\n", 1, 2, 3, 4, 5, 6, 7, 8, 9, 10, -99);
```

Still another approach to variable-argument traversal would be to use a format string, as the printf() or scanf() functions do, employing some special character to mark an argument and the number of such characters to tell the function how many arguments to expect. (See Listing 8.25, mix_type.c, for an example.)

8.14.7 Permitted Types

As we saw above, char, short, and float variable arguments are automatically converted to other types. Therefore, it would make no sense to pass one of these types to va_arg:

 You may not use char, short, **or** float **as the type you pass to** va_arg **as its second argument.**

If, for example, the variable argument were char, it would have been converted to int. If you pass char to va_arg, it would skip only a single byte to what it assumes is the next argument. But it would now point only to the second byte of the int to which the char had been converted.

However, a pointer to char or these other types will work. Furthermore, this prohibition does not mean that you cannot have one of these three types as the type of the actual variable argument. You must treat such types as converted in the variable-argument function you code to deal with them, though. This is why the printf() function, for example, treats the %c specifier as an int specifier, not char.

8.14.8 Pointers to char as Variable Arguments

Although, as we have seen above, you cannot sensibly pass char to va_arg, you can use pointers to char. The following function, var_puts(), for example, prints to stdout (the screen in the absence of redirection) a variable number of strings, each on its own separate line:

```
void var_puts(char *str, . . .)
{
   va_list arg_ptr;
   char *ptr;

   printf("%s\n", str);
   va_start(arg_ptr, str);
   while((ptr = va_arg(arg_ptr, char *)) != NULL)
      printf("%s\n", ptr);
   va_end(arg_ptr);
}
```

Here, we use NULL as a sentinel. A sample call:

```
var_puts("string1", "string2", "string 3", NULL);
```

Once we cover file operations (Chapter 14), you will be able to expand this function to write a variable number of strings to whatever file or stream you specify as its first argument:

```
void var_fputs(FILE *fp, . . .)
{
   va_list arg_ptr;
   char *ptr;

   va_start(arg_ptr, fp);
   while((ptr = va_arg(arg_ptr, char *)) != NULL)
      printf(fp, "%s\n", ptr);

   va_end(arg_ptr);
}
```

The following program, var_msg.c, takes a more sophisticated approach. It clears the screen and writes a series of message lines enclosed by a double-lined box. The function automatically sizes the box according to the length of the longest message string passed and the number of strings. It leaves a blank line space after the top double line, before the last string, and before the bottom double line. You can see an even more sophisticated, full-color example of the messagebox() function created here in the function by the same name on disk. There, we have a different color for the last message line.

 **Listing** **8.23 var_msg.c**

```c
/* var_msg.c */

/* print a messagebox using a variable argument list */

#include <stdio.h>
#include <stdarg.h> /* va_ */
#include <string.h> /* strlen, memset */
#include "c:\tc\binclude\box_char.h" /* Appendix H */

#define TOP 1
#define BOTTOM 2
#define BLANK 3

void messagebox(char *str, ...);
void print_line(char *margin, int length, int mode);

int main(void)
{
   int i;
   for (i = 0; i < 25; i++, putchar('\n')); /* clear screen */
   messagebox("Error!", "Unable to open file", "Press ENTER key to continue", NULL);
}


void messagebox(char *str, ...)
{
   va_list arg_ptr;
   char *ptr;
   int maxlen, numstrings, width, height, trow, lcol, spaces;
   int i;
   char tab[81];

   /* determine height and width of window: start with str */
   maxlen = strlen(str);
   numstrings = 1;

   /* point arg_ptr to first variable arg by passing last fixed arg */
   va_start(arg_ptr, str);
   /* return first var first time; next var arg each subsequent time */
   while((ptr = va_arg(arg_ptr, char *)) != NULL)
   {
      /* count string # & increase maxlen if encounter longer string */
      numstrings++;
      if (strlen(ptr) > maxlen)
         maxlen = strlen(ptr);
   }
   va_end(arg_ptr); /* cleanup */

   width = maxlen + 4; /* width of window inside box */

   /* height: box lines, space before 1st string & before & after last */
   height = numstrings + 5;

   /* center window in screen */
   trow = 12 - height / 2;
   lcol = 40 - width / 2;

   /* make spaces for tab to left of window */
```

```
      memset(tab, ' ', lcol);
      tab[lcol] = 0;

      /* get to top row */
      for (i = 0; i < trow; i++)
         putchar('\n');
      print_line(tab, width, TOP); /* top line of window */
      print_line(tab, width, BLANK); /* blank row */

      /* first message string */
      spaces = (width - strlen(str)) / 2;
      printf("%s%c%*s%s%*s%s%c\n", tab, V2, spaces, "", str, spaces, "",
         ((width - strlen(str)) % 2) ? " " : "", V2);

      va_start(arg_ptr, str); /* reset pointer to first variable arg */

      /* print rest of message strings */
      for (i = 1; i < numstrings; i++)
      {
         /* skip line before last string */
         if (i == numstrings - 1)
            print_line(tab, width, BLANK);

         /* point to next variable arg */
         ptr = va_arg(arg_ptr, char *);
         spaces = (width - strlen(ptr)) / 2;
         printf("%s%c%*s%s%*s%s%c\n", tab, V2, spaces, "", ptr, spaces, "",
            ((width - strlen(ptr)) % 2) ? " " : "", V2);

      }
      va_end(arg_ptr);
      print_line(tab, width, BLANK); /* blank row */
      print_line(tab, width, BOTTOM); /* bottom line of window */
      for (i = 0; i < (24 - numstrings) / 2 - 1; i++, putchar('\n'));
      getchar(); /* wait for user ENTER key press */
}

void print_line(char *margin, int length, int mode)
{
   char line_char = H2;
   int i;
   printf("%s", margin);
   if (mode == TOP)
      putchar(TL2);
   else
      if (mode == BOTTOM)
         putchar(BL2);
   else /* blank */
   {
      putchar(V2);
      line_char = ' ';
   }
   for (i = 0; i < length; i++)
      putchar(line_char);
   if (mode == TOP)
      putchar(TR2);
   else
      if (mode == BOTTOM)
         putchar(BR2);
   else
      putchar(V2);
   putchar('\n');
}
```

Note that calling `va_start` a second time resets our pointer to the start of the variable-argument list.

The `messagebox()` function uses the sentinel concept, stopping at a NULL. We could instead have passed the number of strings as one of the fixed arguments and dropped the final NULL sentinel. However, that would force the programmer to stop and count the number of strings correctly. Apart from the chance of a counting error, there is the likelihood of the programmer's later adding or deleting strings from a call and forgetting to change the string-number argument.

8.14.9   Variable-Argument Function for Multiple-String Concatenation

We could also use a variable-argument function to concatenate the various strings passed as arguments. The following function does that and returns a pointer to the resulting string:

```
char *merge_str(char *big_str, . . .)
{
    va_list arg_ptr;
    char *ptr;

    *big_str = NULL;
    va_start(arg_ptr, big_str);
    while((ptr = va_arg(arg_ptr, char *)) != NULL)
        strcat(big_str, ptr);
    va_end(arg_ptr);
    return big_str;
}
```

The `strcat()` function, covered in Chapter 9, tacks the second string onto the end of the first at the NULL. As you will also see in Chapter 9, you can accomplish the same thing with `sprintf()`:

```
sprintf(big_str, "Here are some names: %s %s %s", "Celia", "Rosamond", "Dorothea");
```

The chief advantage to the function we have created is that you can use the function call as an argument to another function that takes a pointer to char; with the `sprintf()` method, you would have to use a separate statement to make use of the resulting concatenated string.

8.14.10   Structures and Function Pointers as Variable Arguments

You can use more complex types as the variable arguments. The following simple example demonstrates structures and function pointers as variable arguments. (Structures are covered in Chapter 13.)

 **Listing** **8.24 var_type.c**

```
/* var_type.c */

/* show variable-argument function with structures and function
   pointers as variable arguments */

#include <stdio.h>
#include <stdarg.h>
#include <string.h> /* strchr */

int two_timer(int val);
int three_timer(int num);
int sum(int var_num, ...);
void whichever(char * string, ...);

struct record
{
    int salary;
    float hours;
};

int main(void)
{
```

```
         struct record rec[3] = {{300, 45.5}, {325, 46.}, {350, 50.}};

         whichever("11 12 13 14 oh_kindly_stop_here_please",
            two_timer, three_timer, two_timer, three_timer);

         printf("\nSum of salaries: %d\n", sum(3, rec[0], rec[1], rec[2]));
}

int sum(int var_num, ...)
{
    struct record current;
    int total = 0;
    va_list arg_ptr;
    int i;

    va_start(arg_ptr, var_num);
    for (i = 0; i < var_num; i++)
    {
        current = va_arg(arg_ptr, struct record);
        total += current.salary;
    }
    va_end(arg_ptr);
    return total;
}

void whichever(char * string, ...)
{
    va_list arg_ptr;
    int (*fp)(int);
    typedef int IntFunc();
    typedef IntFunc * IntFuncPtr;
    int num;
    char *ptr = string;

    va_start(arg_ptr, string);
    while (1)
    {
        if (sscanf(ptr, "%d", &num) == 0) /* read in next int  from string */
        /* stop when get to any nonnumeric part of string */ break;

        /* move to next argument and assign it to fp */
        fp = va_arg(arg_ptr, IntFuncPtr);
        printf("%d ", fp(num));
        ptr = strchr(ptr, ' ') + 1; /* move past space to next int in string */
    }

    va_end(arg_ptr);
}

int two_timer(int val)
{
    return val * 2;
}

int three_timer(int num)
{
    return num * 3;
}
```

The function pointer we used here was a pointer to functions returning int. The two functions used, two_timer() and three_timer(), are both simple int functions. (See Chapter 13 for an explanation for the typdef we used as a nickname for the type pointer to a function returning int. We could have used a pointer to a structure in lieu of a structure variable here, if we wished.)

8.14.11   Processing the Variable-Argument List in Another Function

It is sometimes useful to be able to have the variable-list function pass on the variable-argument list to one or more other functions for processing. To do this, you

1. Invoke va_start in the variable-argument function prior to calling the secondary function.
2. Pass the va_list variable to the secondary function as an argument.
3. Invoke va_end in the variable-argument function once the call to the secondary function is concluded.

To illustrate, we will replace the following statements from the messagebox() function of var_msg.c

```
maxlen = strlen(str);
numstrings = 1;
va_start(arg_ptr, str);
while((ptr = va_arg(arg_ptr, char *)) != NULL)
{
   numstrings++;
   if (strlen(ptr) > maxlen)
      maxlen = strlen(ptr);
}
va_end(arg_ptr);
```

with the following statements, function definition, and function call:

```
va_start(arg_ptr, str);
strings(arg_ptr, str, &maxlen, &numstrings);
va_end(arg_ptr);
. . .

void strings(va_list ap, char *fixed_str, char *max_len, char *num_strings)
{  /* determine number of strings and longest string */
   char *ptr;

   *max_len = strlen(fixed_str);
   *num_strings = 1;
   while((ptr = va_arg(ap, char *)) != NULL)
   {
      *num_strings = *num_strings + 1;
      if (strlen(ptr) > *max_len)
         *max_len = strlen(ptr);
   }
}
```

See response.c, on disk, for an example that goes three levels in: the variable-argument function messagebox() calls msg_box(), passing it an initialized va_list variable; then msg_box() calls strings() and msg_do_box(), passing them each the same va_list pointer passed in to it.

8.14.12   Mixing Types

Though all your variable arguments will generally be of the same type, this need not be so. If you do have different types, you need to give the variable-argument function not only some stopping mechanism, but also some mechanism for knowing the type and order of each argument.

In the following program, mix_type.c, we use three types: pointer to char, int, and double. The program contains a function capable of adding or averaging a series of numbers, which can be either integer or floating point numbers. Each series starts with a string: either "sum" or "avg." From that point until the next such string or the end of the argument list, the function adds up the series of numbers, and if the current string is "avg," it divides the sum by the number of entries in the series. Our fixed argument is a string containing a road map to the variable argument list. For each string argument, the fixed argument string contains an s; for every integer, a d; and for every floating point number, an f (borrowing characters from the print() specifiers).

 **Listing** **8.25 mix_type.c**

```c
/* mix_type.c */

/* variable arg list function with different types as arguments */

#include <stdio.h>
#include <stdarg.h> /* va_ */
#include <string.h> /* strlen */

void mix_types(char *type_str, ...);

int main(void)
{
    mix_types("sdffdsdffdsdddsfff", "avg", 2, 4.4, 6.6, 8, "sum", 2, 4.4, 6.6, 8,
        "sum", 1, 2, 3, "avg", 100.5, 200.5, 300.5);
}

void mix_types(char *type_str, ...)
{
    /* each ltr in format string = argument */
    char num_args = strlen(type_str);
    char adding = 0, averaging = 0;
    char i;
    int entries = 0;
    double total = 0.;
    va_list var_ptr;

    va_start(var_ptr, type_str);
    for (i = 0; i < num_args; i++)
    {
        switch(*type_str++)
        {
            case 's':
                if (averaging)
                    printf("average is %.2f\n", total / (double)entries);
                else if (adding)
                    printf("sum is %.2f\n", total);

                /* skip over "avg"/"sum" arg, reset accumulators
                   & set print flag */
                adding = averaging = 0;

                if (*va_arg(var_ptr, char *) == 'a') /* "avg" */
                    averaging = 1;
                else /* "sum" */
                    adding = 1;

                entries = 0;
                total = 0.;
                break;
            case 'd':
                total += (double)va_arg(var_ptr, int);
                entries++;
                break;
            case 'f':
                total += va_arg(var_ptr, double);
                entries++;
                break;
        }
    }
```

```
        va_end(var_ptr);
        if (averaging)
            printf("average is %.2f\n", total / (double)entries);
        if (adding)
            printf("sum is %.2f\n", total);
    }
```

As you can see, invoking va_arg not only returns the argument in the variable-argument list, but also it moves the pointer past the current argument to the next one. In doing so, it uses the size of the type we have passed it.

8.14.13   Creating Arrays on the Fly with Variable-Argument Functions

One interesting application for a variable-argument function is assembling the variable arguments and inserting them into an array. That way you can then conveniently use for loops to traverse this list of variables. Or you can have this variable-argument function pass the array name to another function.

For example, in the following function fragment, we create an array of strings:

```
#define MAX_STRINGS 20

void strings(int num_args, . . .)
{
    va_list arg_ptr;
    char str[MAX_STRINGS];
    int element = 0;

    if (num_args > MAX_STRINGS)
        num_args = MAX_STRINGS;
    va_start(arg_ptr, num_args);
    while(element < num_args)
        str[element++] = va_arg(arg_ptr, char *);
    va_end(arg_ptr);
    . . .
}
```

See if you can use this device to rewrite the first version of the messagebox() function we examined above. Rather than using va_start and va_arg twice—once to determine the length of the longest string and once to actually paint the strings inside the message box—use it to fill an array of strings. Then pass the array name to a function that returns the length of the longest string. Finally, use a simple for loop to traverse the array and paint the string to the screen.

You may find this array-filling device so useful that you end up using it to create a variable-argument function in a situation where the number of arguments is fixed rather than variable.

8.14.14   The vprintf() and vscanf() Family

The vprintf() function works basically the same way as printf(). The only difference is that instead of using an argument list as printf() does, vprintf() uses a va_arg variable after this variable has been initialized to point to the first variable argument in the argument list by invoking va_start.

For example, say that we have an error-printing statement:

```
char filename[45] = "c:\\data";
char mode[25] = "reading";
char reason[45] = "File does not exist";
printf("Unable to open file %s for %s\n%s\n", filename, mode, reason);
```

(Of course, in a real program these three strings would be filled in dynamically depending on current program results, instead of being hard-wired as they are here.) We can accomplish the same thing with a variable-list function that contains a call to vprintf():

```
err_print("Unable to open file %s for %s\n%s\n", filename, mode, reason);
. . .
void err_print(char *format, . . .)
```

```
{
    va_list arg_ptr;

    va_start(arg_ptr, format);
    vprintf(format, arg_ptr);
    va_end(arg_ptr);
}
```

But if the result is just the same, why use this more complex formulation? The answer is that it gives us more flexibility. We can take the argument list and manipulate it and use it more than once in the same function. For instance, we can expand the function to produce more extensive error reporting. The following version of err_print() prints out "Error!", beeps, writes the error message to the screen and to a file that acts as an error log, and if the error is of a specific type, halts the program:

```
void err_print(char *format, . . .)
{
    va_list arg_ptr;
    char err_msg[120];
    extern FILE *err_log; /* we assume this file has been opened */

    va_start(arg_ptr, format);
    printf("Error!\a ");
    vprintf(format, arg_ptr);
    vfprintf(err_log, format, arg_ptr);
    vsprintf(err_msg, format, arg_ptr);
    if (!strcmp(err_msg, "Unable to open c:\\primary for reading\nFatal Error\n"))
        exit(1);
    va_end(arg_ptr);
}
```

This version of the function uses vprintf(), vfprintf(), and vsprintf(). These functions work precisely the same way as their relatives without the v tacked on the front, with the exception we mentioned above.

The functions vscanf(), vfscanf(), and vsscanf() also exist. Again, they are the same as scanf(), fscanf(), and sscanf(), except for the substitution of the initialized va_list pointer as the final argument in lieu of an argument list. These three functions, however, are not part of Standard C.

The sprintf() and sscanf() functions are covered in Chapter 9; the fprintf() and fscanf() functions are covered in Chapter 14. The strcmp() function, treated in Chapter 9, compares two strings and returns zero if they match or some nonzero integer if they don't.

8.15 APPLICATION: ACE BILLING PROGRAM

Up to now, we have been using global variables so that we can share information between modules. Now that we have discussed functions and parameters, we wish to solve the same problem by declaring in main() all information to be shared by the various modules. We would then rely on passing the information back and forth among modules through parameters. The result is that we have a tremendous number of parameters to pass. We find ourselves in this situation primarily for pedagogical reasons. Typically this type of problem would be solved by using structures—data types treated in Chapter 13. We will find that this problem will then have far fewer parameters.

8.15.1 Input

Same input data as for acech06.exe in Chapter 6.

 **Listing 8.26 acech08.c**

```
/*
    +--------------------------------------------------------------+
    +  Program Name: acech08.c
    +     Author(s): Austell-Wolfson and Otieno
```

```
+          Date: 12/10/2000
+   Purpose:
+      This program processes a file of ACE Club member records, and
+      computes and prints the total amounts for all club members.
+
+   Process:
+     This program prints the prescribed headings for the report, and
+     processes each record by:
+        computing the individual member bill, equal to the sum of
+        member bill, membership fee, and activity fee, minus any
+        discount amount. Members are charged a special
+        membership fee of $2500 if they are special members,
+        indicated by a Y in the membership flag field. The
+        activity fees are based on the number of activities each
+        member requests. The more activities they request, the more
+        they are charged. A discount amount is applied if the member
+        has an average charge of over $8000 per bill.
+
+----------------------------------------------------------------+
*/
#include <stdio.h>
#include <string.h>

    int initialization(char * specialMembershipFlag, char customerName[100][16],
       char customerInitials[100][3], float * membershipFee, float * activityFee,
       float * discountAmount, float * chargeAmount, float * totalIndividualBill,
       float * aceClubTotals, float * charges,int * discount, int * averageCharges,
       int * numberOfCharges, int * clubMember);

    int processMemberRecord(char * specialMembershipFlag, char customerName[100][16],
       char customerInitials[100][3], float * membershipFee, float * activityFee,
       float * discountAmount, float * totalIndividualBill, float * aceClubTotals,
       float * charges,int * discount, int * averageCharges, int * numberOfCharges,
       int * clubMember);

    void termination(void);

    void printGrandTotals(float * membershipFee, float * activityFee, float * discountAmount,
       float * totalIndividualBill, float * charges, int * numberOfCharges);

    void initializeVariables(char * specialMembershipFlag, char customerName[100][16],
       char customerInitials[100][3], float * membershipFee, float * activityFee,
       float * discountAmount, float * chargeAmount, float * totalIndividualBill,
       float * aceClubTotals, float * charges,int * discount, int * averageCharges,
       int * numberOfCharges);

    void printHeadings(void);

    int readMemberRecord(char customerName[100][16], char customerInitials[100][3],
       int * numberOfCharges, char * specialMembershipFlag, int * discount,
       int * averageCharges, int * clubMember);

    void computeIndividualBill(char * specialMembershipFlag, float * membershipFee,
       float * activityFee, float * discountAmount, float * totalIndividualBill,
       float * aceClubTotals, float * charges, int * discount, int * averageCharges,
       int * numberOfCharges, int * clubMember);

    void writeDetailLine(char customerName[100][16], char customerInitials[100][3],
       float * membershipFee, float * activityFee, float * discountAmount,
       float * totalIndividualBill, float * charges, int * numberOfCharges, int * clubMember);

    void determineSpecialFee(char * specialMembershipFlag, float * membershipFee,
       int * clubMember);
```

```
void determineActivityFee(float * activityFee, int * numberOfCharges,
    int * clubMember);

void determineDiscountAmt(int * averageCharges, int * discount,
    float * discountAmount, int * clubMember);

void sortByClubMemberNames(char * specialMembershipFlag, char customerName[100][16],
    char customerInitials[100][3], float * membershipFee, float * activityFee,
    float * discountAmount, float * chargeAmount, float * totalIndividualBill,
    float * aceClubTotals, float * charges, int * discount, int * averageCharges,
    int * numberOfCharges, int * clubMember);

void printSortedReport(char customerName[100][16], char customerInitials[100][3],
    float * membershipFee, float * activityFee, float * discountAmount,
    float * totalIndividualBill, float * charges, int * numberOfCharges, int * clubMember);

void swapValues(char * specialMembershipFlag, char customerName[100][16],
    char customerInitials[100][3], float * membershipFee, float * activityFee,
    float * discountAmount, float * chargeAmount, float * totalIndividualBill,
    float * aceClubTotals, float * charges,int * discount, int * averageCharges,
    int * numberOfCharges, int currentPos);

int main(void)
{
    char    specialMembershipFlag[100];
    char    customerName[100][16];
    char    customerInitials[100][3];
    float   membershipFee[100];
    float   activityFee[100];
    float   discountAmount[100];
    float   chargeAmount[100];
    float   totalIndividualBill[100];
    float   aceClubTotals[100];
    float   charges[100];
    int     discount[100];
    int     averageCharges[100];
    int     numberOfCharges[100];
    int     readStatus = 0;
    int     clubMember = 0; /* Holds the count of all club members. It is also used to index
                               the array of club members; therefore its value starts at 0 */

/* see comment in acech05.c re input procedure below */
readStatus = initialization(specialMembershipFlag, customerName, customerInitials,
    membershipFee, activityFee, discountAmount, chargeAmount, totalIndividualBill,
    aceClubTotals, charges, discount, averageCharges, numberOfCharges, &clubMember);

while (6 == readStatus)
{
    readStatus = processMemberRecord(specialMembershipFlag, customerName, customerInitials,
        membershipFee, activityFee, discountAmount, totalIndividualBill, aceClubTotals,
        charges, discount, averageCharges, numberOfCharges, &clubMember);
}
printGrandTotals(membershipFee, activityFee, discountAmount, totalIndividualBill, charges,
    numberOfCharges);

sortByClubMemberNames(specialMembershipFlag, customerName, customerInitials, membershipFee,
    activityFee, discountAmount, chargeAmount, totalIndividualBill, aceClubTotals, charges,
    discount, averageCharges, numberOfCharges, &clubMember);

printSortedReport(customerName, customerInitials, membershipFee, activityFee,
    discountAmount, totalIndividualBill, charges, numberOfCharges, &clubMember);

printGrandTotals(membershipFee, activityFee, discountAmount, totalIndividualBill, charges,
    numberOfCharges);
```

```
      termination();
      return 0;
}

int initialization(char * specialMembershipFlag, char customerName[][16],
    char customerInitials[][3], float * membershipFee, float * activityFee,
    float * discountAmount, float * chargeAmount, float * totalIndividualBill,
    float * aceClubTotals, float * charges, int * discount, int * averageCharges,
    int * numberOfCharges, int * clubMember)
{
   int status;

   initializeVariables(specialMembershipFlag, customerName, customerInitials,
      membershipFee, activityFee, discountAmount, chargeAmount, totalIndividualBill,
      aceClubTotals, charges, discount, averageCharges, numberOfCharges);

   printHeadings();

   status = readMemberRecord(customerName, customerInitials, numberOfCharges,
      specialMembershipFlag, discount, averageCharges, clubMember);

   return status;
}

int processMemberRecord(char * specialMembershipFlag, char customerName[][16],
    char customerInitials[][3], float * membershipFee, float * activityFee,
    float * discountAmount, float * totalIndividualBill, float * aceClubTotals,
    float * charges, int * discount, int * averageCharges, int * numberOfCharges,
    int * clubMember)
{
   int status;

   computeIndividualBill(specialMembershipFlag, membershipFee, activityFee,
      discountAmount, totalIndividualBill, aceClubTotals, charges, discount,
      averageCharges, numberOfCharges, clubMember);

   writeDetailLine(customerName, customerInitials, membershipFee, activityFee, discountAmount,
      totalIndividualBill, charges, numberOfCharges, clubMember);

   status = readMemberRecord(customerName, customerInitials, numberOfCharges,
      specialMembershipFlag, discount, averageCharges, clubMember);

   return status;
}

/* see comment in acech06.c re termination function */
void termination(void)
{
   /* not implemented */
}

void initializeVariables(char * specialMembershipFlag, char customerName[][16],
    char customerInitials[][3], float * membershipFee, float * activityFee,
    float * discountAmount, float * chargeAmount, float * totalIndividualBill,
    float * aceClubTotals, float * charges, int * discount, int * averageCharges,
    int * numberOfCharges)
{
   int k;   /* This variable is used as an index to our customerName array */
   int rowCount;
   /* end of declarations */

   for (k = 0; k < 100; k++)
   {
```

```
            specialMembershipFlag[k] = 'Y';
            discount[k] = 0;
            averageCharges[k] = 0;
            membershipFee[k] = 0.0;
            activityFee[k] = 0.0;
            discountAmount[k] = 0.0;
            chargeAmount[k] = 0.0;
            numberOfCharges[k] = 0;
            totalIndividualBill[k] = 0.0;
            aceClubTotals[k] = 0.0;
            charges[k] = 0.0;
        }

    /* see comment in acech06.c re following initialization */
    for (rowCount = 0; rowCount < 100; rowCount++)
    {
        for (k = 0; k < 16; k++)
        {
            customerName[rowCount][k] = '\0';
        }
    }

    for (rowCount = 0; rowCount < 100; rowCount++)
    {
        for (k = 0; k < 3; k++)
        {
            customerInitials[rowCount][k] = '\0';
        }
    }
}

void printHeadings(void)
{
    printf("┌────────────────────────────────────────────────────────────────────┐\n");
    printf("│                                                                      │\n");
    printf("│    Program Name: ACECH08.EXE                              Page:   1  │\n");
    printf("│       Run Date: 12/10/2000                Ace Billing                │\n");
    printf("├──────────────────────────────────────────────────────────────────────┤\n");
    printf("│                                                                      │\n");
    printf("├──────────────────────────────────────────────────────────────────────┤\n");
    printf("│                                                                      │\n");
    printf("│ Customer Name   Charges      Bill     Mbr Fee    Act Fee   Disc  Total Bill │\n");
    printf("├──────────────────────────────────────────────────────────────────────┤\n");
    printf("│                                                                      │\n");
}

int readMemberRecord(char customerName[100][16], char customerInitials[100][3],
    int * numberOfCharges, char * specialMembershipFlag, int * discount, int * averageCharges,
    int * clubMember)
{
    int status;

    /* see comment in acech06.c re following scanf procedure */
    status = scanf("%15c%2c%2d%c%4d%4d\n", customerName[*clubMember],
        customerInitials[*clubMember], &numberOfCharges[*clubMember],
        &specialMembershipFlag[*clubMember], &discount[*clubMember],
        &averageCharges[*clubMember]);

    return status;
}

void computeIndividualBill(char * specialMembershipFlag, loat * membershipFee,
    float * activityFee, float * discountAmount, float * totalIndividualBill,
```

```
      float * aceClubTotals, float * charges, int * discount, int * averageCharges,
      int * numberOfCharges, int * clubMember)
{
   charges[*clubMember] = 200 * numberOfCharges[*clubMember];
   charges[99] += charges[*clubMember];
   numberOfCharges[99] += numberOfCharges[*clubMember];
   determineSpecialFee(specialMembershipFlag, membershipFee, clubMember);
   determineActivityFee(activityFee, numberOfCharges, clubMember);
   determineDiscountAmt(averageCharges, discount, discountAmount, clubMember);

   totalIndividualBill[*clubMember] = charges[*clubMember] + membershipFee[*clubMember] +
      activityFee[*clubMember] - discountAmount[*clubMember];
   totalIndividualBill[99] += totalIndividualBill[*clubMember];
   aceClubTotals[99] += totalIndividualBill[*clubMember];
}

void writeDetailLine(char customerName[][16], char customerInitials[][3],
   float * membershipFee, float * activityFee, float * discountAmount,
   float * totalIndividualBill, float * charges, int * numberOfCharges, int * clubMember)
{
   printf("| %15.15s  %s %2d  $%9.2f  $%8.2f  $%8.2f  $%5.f  $%9.2f",
      customerName[*clubMember], customerInitials[*clubMember], numberOfCharges[*clubMember],
      charges[*clubMember], membershipFee[*clubMember], activityFee[*clubMember],
      discountAmount[*clubMember], totalIndividualBill[*clubMember]);
   printf(" |\n");

   *clubMember = *clubMember + 1; /* Increase the number of club members */
}

void determineSpecialFee(char * specialMembershipFlag,
   float * membershipFee, int * clubMember)
{
   /* see comment in acech05.c re advantage of construct below */
   if ('Y' == specialMembershipFlag[*clubMember])
   {
      membershipFee[*clubMember] = 2500.0;
   }
   else
   {
      membershipFee[*clubMember] = 0.0;
   }

   membershipFee[99] += membershipFee[*clubMember];
}

void determineActivityFee(float * activityFee, int * numberOfCharges, int * clubMember)
{
   if (numberOfCharges[*clubMember] <= 6)
   {
      activityFee[*clubMember] = 250.0;
   }

   if ((numberOfCharges[*clubMember] > 6) && (numberOfCharges[*clubMember] <= 12))
   {
      activityFee[*clubMember] = 500.0;
   }

   if (numberOfCharges[*clubMember] > 12)
   {
      activityFee[*clubMember] = 750.0;
   }
```

```
      activityFee[99] += activityFee[*clubMember];
}

void determineDiscountAmt(int * averageCharges, int * discount,
    float * discountAmount, int * clubMember)
{
    if (averageCharges[*clubMember] > 8500)
    {
        discountAmount[*clubMember] = discount[*clubMember];
    }
    else
    {
        discountAmount[*clubMember] = 0;
    }

    discountAmount[99] += discountAmount[*clubMember];
}

void sortByClubMemberNames(char * specialMembershipFlag, char customerName[][16],
    char customerInitials[][3], float * membershipFee, float * activityFee,
    float * discountAmount, float * chargeAmount, float * totalIndividualBill,
    float * aceClubTotals, float * charges, int * discount, int * averageCharges,
    int * numberOfCharges, int * clubMember)
{
    int currentPos; /* Holds current array position being processed */
    int k; /* Loop index variable  */

    /* Determines whether to make more passes during the bubble sort algorithm */
    int morePasses = 1;
/*
    +----------------------------------------------------------------+
    +  Start the loop that makes as many passes through array of club
    +  member names as needed for the entire list to be sorted.
    +
    +----------------------------------------------------------------+
*/
    while (1 == morePasses)
    {
/*
    +----------------------------------------------------------------+
    +  Turn it off so that if the data is sorted, no
    +  passes will be necessary. If, however, there was
    +  a single swap, morePasses will be set to 1
    +  and the while loop repeats as it should.
    +
    +----------------------------------------------------------------+
*/
        morePasses = 0;
        for (k = 0; k < *clubMember - 1; k++)
        {
            if (strcmp(customerName[k], customerName[k + 1]) > 0)
            {
                currentPos = k;

                /* swap all the values in the parallel arrays */
                swapValues(specialMembershipFlag, customerName, customerInitials, membershipFee,
                    activityFee, discountAmount, chargeAmount, totalIndividualBill, aceClubTotals,
                    charges, discount, averageCharges, numberOfCharges, currentPos);
                morePasses = 1;
            }
        }  /*   end of for loop   */
```

```
    }   /*   end of while loop   */
}

void printSortedReport(char customerName[100][16], char customerInitials[100][3],
    float * membershipFee, float * activityFee, float * discountAmount,
    float * totalIndividualBill, float * charges, int * numberOfCharges, int * clubMember)
{
    int k; /* Loop index variable */

    /* print column headings for the sorted list of club members */
    printHeadings();

    for (k = 0; k < *clubMember; k++)
    {
        printf("| %15.15s  %s %2d  $%9.2f  $8.2f  $8.2f  $%5.f  $%9.2f", customerName[k],
            customerInitials[k], numberOfCharges[k], charges[k], membershipFee[k],
            activityFee[k], discountAmount[k], totalIndividualBill[k]);
        printf(" |\n");
    }
}

void swapValues (char * specialMembershipFlag, char customerName[][16],
    char customerInitials[][3], float * membershipFee, float * activityFee,
    float * discountAmount, float * chargeAmount, float * totalIndividualBill,
    float * aceClubTotals, float * charges, int * discount, int * averageCharges,
    int * numberOfCharges, int currentPos)
{
    /* see comment in acech06.c re array size in swap situation */
    int  tempPos;
    tempPos = 98;

    /* Swap the last name of club member */
    strcpy(customerName[tempPos], customerName[currentPos]);
    strcpy(customerName[currentPos], customerName[currentPos + 1]);
    strcpy(customerName[currentPos + 1], customerName[tempPos]);

    /* Swap the customer initials */
    strcpy(customerInitials[tempPos], customerInitials[currentPos]);
    strcpy(customerInitials[currentPos], customerInitials[currentPos + 1]);
    strcpy(customerInitials[currentPos + 1], customerInitials[tempPos]);

    /* swap the specialMembershipFlag */
    specialMembershipFlag[tempPos] = specialMembershipFlag[currentPos];
    specialMembershipFlag[currentPos] = specialMembershipFlag[currentPos + 1];
    specialMembershipFlag[currentPos + 1] = specialMembershipFlag[tempPos];

    /* swap the total membership fee */
    membershipFee[tempPos] = membershipFee[currentPos];
    membershipFee[currentPos] = membershipFee[currentPos + 1];
    membershipFee[currentPos + 1] = membershipFee[tempPos];

    /* swap the total activity fee */
    activityFee[tempPos] = activityFee[currentPos];
    activityFee[currentPos] = activityFee[currentPos + 1];
    activityFee[currentPos + 1] = activityFee[tempPos];

    /* swap the total discount amount */
    discountAmount[tempPos] = discountAmount[currentPos];
    discountAmount[currentPos] = discountAmount[currentPos + 1];
    discountAmount[currentPos + 1] = discountAmount[tempPos];

    /* swap the total charge amount */
    chargeAmount[tempPos] = chargeAmount[currentPos];
```

```
        chargeAmount[currentPos] = chargeAmount[currentPos + 1];
        chargeAmount[currentPos + 1] = chargeAmount[tempPos];

        /* swap the total individual bill */
        totalIndividualBill[tempPos] = totalIndividualBill[currentPos];
        totalIndividualBill[currentPos] = totalIndividualBill[currentPos + 1];
        totalIndividualBill[currentPos + 1] = totalIndividualBill[tempPos];

        /* swap the total ace club totals */
        aceClubTotals[tempPos] = aceClubTotals[currentPos];
        aceClubTotals[currentPos] = aceClubTotals[currentPos + 1];
        aceClubTotals[currentPos + 1] = aceClubTotals[tempPos];

        /* swap the total charges */
        charges[tempPos] = charges[currentPos];
        charges[currentPos] = charges[currentPos + 1];
        charges[currentPos + 1] = charges[tempPos];

        /* swap the total discount */
        discount[tempPos] = discount[currentPos];
        discount[currentPos] = discount[currentPos + 1];
        discount[currentPos + 1] = discount[tempPos];

        /* swap the total average charges */
        averageCharges[tempPos] = averageCharges[currentPos];
        averageCharges[currentPos] = averageCharges[currentPos + 1];
        averageCharges[currentPos + 1] = averageCharges[tempPos];
        /* swap the total number of charges bill */
        numberOfCharges[tempPos] = numberOfCharges[currentPos];
        numberOfCharges[currentPos] = numberOfCharges[currentPos + 1];
        numberOfCharges[currentPos + 1] = numberOfCharges[tempPos];
    }

void printGrandTotals(float * membershipFee, float * activityFee, float * discountAmount,
    float * totalIndividualBill, float * charges, int * numberOfCharges)
{
    printf("| %*s────────────────────────────────────────────┤\n",
        19, " ");
    printf("| ACE Club Totals    %3d  $%9.2f  $%8.2f  $%8.2f  $%5.f"
        " $%9.2f |\n",
        numberOfCharges[99], charges[99], membershipFee[99],
        activityFee[99], discountAmount[99], totalIndividualBill[99]);
    printf("|_____|\n\n");
}
```

8.15.2   Output

Same output report as for `acech06.exe` in Chapter 6.

Chapter Summary

1. A function declaration is a single statement that advises the compiler of the number and types of values that are to be passed to, and the type of value to be returned from, the function.

2. A function definition contains the operative statements that carry out the function's task.

3. Between the definition's header and body, and after the body, you must put braces—even if the function body is a single statement.

4. You may not put a function definition inside any other function body.

5. A function call invokes the function. You make a function call with the name of the function followed by the actual arguments to be passed, separated by commas if there is more than one, and enclosed by parentheses. If the function does not take any arguments, you call the function with the name followed by parentheses alone.

6. A function can take one or more arguments, or none at all.

7. Each function call argument is evaluated and passed as a single value.

8. C's method of passing values to functions is called call by value: only a copy of the argument's value is sent to the function.

9. If a declaration precedes a function call, the compiler will check to make sure the number of arguments match and will, if possible, convert each argument to the corresponding formal argument type if the type is different.

10. Type demotion on the automatic conversion can result in inadvertent data loss.

11. If the actual argument type is of a different global category from that of the formal argument, you will get either an error message if conversion from one type to the other is not permitted, or a warning.

12. Arguments are separated by commas, if there are more than one.

13. Normally the arguments in the prototype have variable names, but only the types are required. In the function definition, you must include both types and variable names for each argument. The type has to be separately stated for each formal argument variable in the function declaration and definition header.

14. The argument portion of the function definition operates as a declaration of the variables in the definition.

15. The variable names that make up the function definition header are referred to as formal arguments. The values passed to them in the function call are called the actual arguments.

16. The values of what you pass as actual arguments are assigned to the formal arguments in the same order in which they appear in the formal argument list.

17. Standard C does not require the compiler to evaluate the function's formal arguments in any particular order.

18. Since variables in the header are considered to be declared before explicitly declared variables, you can initialize an explicitly declared variable in terms of one of the formal arguments.

19. Apart from external variables, all variables within a function are local variables; they come into being when the function is called and die when the function is finished executing; neither the variables nor their values are known to the other functions.

20. When you pass a nonpointer variable as an argument to a function call, a local variable is created in the called function with a value equal to that of the argument. Anything you do to the newly created variable inside the called function in no way affects the value of the variable passed as an argument.

21. If you pass the address of a variable, you can change the variable's value inside the calling function by using the dereferencing operator.

22. The only storage class specifier you may use for the type of a formal argument is `register`.

23. Standard C guarantees that the following formulation will work on all systems:

```
int main(void)
```

24. You must include header files for the C library functions your source code uses. The compiler brings in function definitions only for those library functions actually used by the source code.

25. Pre-Standard C-form prototypes and function definition headers are permitted, but not for variable argument list functions.

26. When the called function is done, the program returns to the next statement after the function call.

27. A function can return a single value to the function that called it or return none. The function itself is deemed to have the type of the value it returns.

28. You can do anything with the return value that you could do with any other value of that type. You may use that return value as an argument to another function without creating a separate variable to store the return value.

29. You return a value with the keyword `return`. The return value is converted to the function's return type.

30. The `return` keyword also stops execution of the called function and passes control back to the calling function.

31. If you do not include a blank `return` statement in a `void` function, the function's reaching its final statement will have the same effect as if you had.

32. Functions may take or return any type other than arrays or functions.

33. If the function does not return any value, you must indicate that by placing the word `void` in front of the function name in place of a type in both the declaration and definition.

34. If a function has no explicit return type at all, not even `void`, Standard C requires the compiler to assume a default of `int`.

35. A function may call itself. The process is called recursion.

36. Statements in the function body before the recursive function call are executed in order of the function calls. Those after the recursive function call are executed in reverse order.

37. When you use an array name as a function argument, you pass the address of the first element of the array. The called function then uses a pointer set to that address to access the array in the calling function.

38. Even though the array name is a constant, in the function, its address is assigned to a locally declared pointer. We can use that pointer to access and alter the array contents. And we can increment or decrement the pointer.

39. We can use array *notation* inside a function even though we are formally dealing with pointers. However, the array does not exist inside the function, so `sizeof(array_name)` will give us the number of bytes of the pointer only.

40. C does not allow us to pass the values of an entire array.

41. You must declare an array, the starting address of which is returned, as `static`. Otherwise, you would return the address of a memory area that is no longer reserved.

42. There is no automatic way in C to find a stopping point in traversing an array.

43. Though we generally will pass a pointer to the array's first element to a function by simply using its name as the argument, there is nothing to prevent us from passing the address of an intermediate element.

44. Where `ptr` is declared as a pointer to an array and assigned the starting address of a two-dimensional array `arrayname`,

    `*(*ptr + row) + col)`

    is equivalent to

    `arrayname[row][col];`

45. With multidimensional arrays as function arguments, the size of the first dimension need not be given in the function declaration or definition, for example, `void twice(int ptr[][4]);`

46. You can declare a pointer to a function (or an array of such pointers) and call a function through the dereferenced pointer. The declaration is also similar to a function declaration, except that in place of the function name, you have the pointer variable name, preceded by the dereferencing operator, both enclosed in parentheses.

47. A function can accept a variable number of arguments.

48. The variable-argument function prototype must have at least one fixed parameter.

49. The variable arguments are indicated in the prototype by an ellipsis following the last fixed argument. The variable arguments must come immediately after the last fixed parameter. You must pass at least one variable argument in a call to the variable-argument function.

50. Automatic type conversion of actual to formal argument type is not applied to nonfixed arguments. Instead, each variable argument is automatically converted to a predetermined type: `char`, `unsigned char`, and `short` are converted to `int`; `unsigned short` to `unsigned int` or `signed`; `float` to `double`; and an array to a pointer to the first element of the array.

51. The variable-argument function works with the aid of three macros and one `typedef` found in `stdarg.h`: we declare a pointer variable of type `va_list`; we point this va_list variable to the first variable argument with the `va_start` macro; we move from variable argument to variable argument with the aid of the `va_arg` macro; we invoke the `va_end` macro for cleanup.

52. The first argument to `va_arg` is the `va_list` variable we have declared; the second argument is the *type* of the variable argument. In light of the automatic type conversions in variable argument-list functions, you may not use `char`, `short`, or `float` as the type you pass to `va_arg` as its second argument.

53. The variable argument structure has no inherent mechanism for stopping at the last argument. There are two common methods for accomplishing this: passing the number of variable arguments as one of the fixed arguments, and using a sentinel.

54. It is possible to have the variable-list function pass on the variable argument list to one or more other functions for processing.

55. The `vprintf()` function works basically the same as `printf()`. However, instead of using an argument list, `vprintf()` uses a va_arg variable after this variable has been initialized to point to the first variable argument in the argument list by invoking `va_start`. The `vfprintf()`, `vsprintf()`, `vscanf()`, `vfscanf()`, and `vsscanf()` functions work precisely the same way as their relatives without the v tacked on the front, with the same exception.

Review Questions

1. What is a function?
2. Provide a generic syntax for defining functions, and give an example.
3. Execute the following function, and show the results of doing so:

```
#include <stdio.h>
/* Function prototype */
float average(int, int);
int main(void)
{
    int num1;
    int num2;
    float avg;

    num1 = 101;
    num2 = 200;

    /* Function call */
    avg = average(num1, num2);
```

```
    printf("The average of %d and %d is /
    %6.2f\n", num1, num2, avg);
}

/* Function definition */
float average (int a, int b)
{
    int c;
    c = a + b;
    return c / 2;
}
```

4. List the two ways that parameters or data objects may be passed to functions generally.
5. How many data values can be transmitted to the calling function?
6. How many values can one return from a function through the return statement?
7. Distinguish between actual parameters or actual arguments and formal parameters or formal arguments.

8. Write a program to do the following tasks, with separate functions for each task (printing the result with a print function after each task):
   a. Initialize a two-dimensional 5-by-5 matrix to zeros.
   b. Fill the diagonal entries from northwest to southeast (or vice versa) to some specified value, as shown in Figure P8.1.
   c. Fill the matrix with sequential numbers starting with 1, row by row (Figure P8.2).
   d. Fill the top-right triangle of the matrix with a specified number (Figure P8.3).
   e. Do the same for the lower left triangle.
   f. Fill in the diagonal entries from northeast to southwest, or vice versa (Figure P8.4).
9. Write a recursive function to calculate factorials of a number.
10. Write a function to calculate factorials of a number nonrecursively.
11. The variable-argument function prototype must have at least one fixed parameter (True or False).
12. The variable arguments in the variable-argument function must come immediately after the last fixed parameter (True or False).
13. You must pass at least one variable argument in a call to the variable-argument function (True or False).
14. The function declaration (also called a prototype) tells the compiler the name of the function (True or False).
15. The function prototype tells the compiler how many values are to be passed to the function and what their type is (True or False).
16. The function prototype tells the compiler whether a value is returned and if so what its type is (True or False).
17. In C, you should not call a function before having declared it (True or False).
18. Using variable names in function prototypes, rather than just the types, tends to make the program easier to follow (True or False).
19. Since the `register` storage class specifier may be ignored by the compiler, you may not use this storage class specifier for the type of a formal argument (True or False).
20. If your function has no explicit return type at all, Standard C requires the compiler to assume a default of `void` (True or False).
21. Since the function prototype matches the function definition and since you do not need to include variable names in the prototype, in the function definition you need not include variable names for each argument (True or False).
22. The argument portion of the function definition operates as a declaration of the variables in the definition (True or False).
23. The type has to be separately stated for each formal argument variable in the function declaration and definition header (True or False).
24. You may put a function definition inside another function body if it is called only by the other function (True or False).
25. Each function call argument is evaluated and passed as a single value (True or False).

Figure P8.1 *Matrix: Diagonal Entries, Northwest to Southeast*

2				
	2			
		2		
			2	
				2

Figure P8.2 *Matrix: Sequential Entries*

1	2	3	4	5
6	7	8	9	10
11	12	13	14	15
16	17	18	19	20
21	22	23	24	25

Figure P8.3 *Matrix: Top–Right Triangle Entries*

2	2	2	2	2
	2	2	2	2
		2	2	2
			2	2
				2

Figure P8.4 *Matrix: Diagonal Entries, Northeast to Southwest*

				3
			3	
		3		
	3			
3				

26. Changes to the variables declared in the function to house those values do not change the values of the variables with the same names in the calling function (True or False).
27. You may not use `char`, `short`, or `float` as the type you pass to `va_arg` as its second argument (True or False).
28. When we pass the name of an array as an argument to a function call, we have passed the address of the first element of the array (True or False).
29. It is sometimes useful to be able to have the variable-list function pass on the variable-argument list to one or more other functions for processing. List the three things that you need to achieve this objective.
30. C allows us to pass the values of an entire array at once (True or False).

Programming Exercises

The specifications of the programming assignments were introduced in Chapter 1, at which time you were to

- think through the solution to these problems.
- identify the modules that, once implemented, will solve the problem.
- prepare a hierarchy chart of all the modules.
- prepare pseudocode/flowchart for each module in the hierarchy chart.
- write the program stubs the same way we did with the ACE Billing system application.

This chapter has added coverage of functions and parameters to our C knowledge. We urge you to continue developing what you started in Chapter 1. If you have not started, we recommend that you start by applying the methodology presented in that chapter. We have helped you get started with some of the programming assignments by specifying only what can be done by this time.

Modify all the programming assignments in Chapter 6 to use local variables and pass parameters instead of using global or external variables. See Section 8.15 for the `acech08.c` program.

Programming Assignment 8.28—Special Category

Program Description

Your counterpart is a spy in the government of Sri Lanka, formerly known as Ceylon and more formerly still as Serendib. The spy needs to relay a coded message to warn of any missile launch. Here is the code's "Rosetta Stone":

~ = conversion specifier; ^ = field width modifier placeholder;
letter = field width modifier, with 'a' as 1 and max of 'z' width;
1 = unsigned; 2 = character; 3 = string;

Write a variable-argument list function `decode()` to decode and print the message contained in this call:

```
decode("~^1 ~3 at ~b1 ~2.m. ~3 time",
   3, 11, "missiles launched", 3, 'a', "New Serendipity");
```

CHAPTER 9

String-Handling and Buffer Functions

OBJECTIVES

- To learn how to copy, combine, compare, search for, and parse strings
- To be familiar with Standard C character searching, set-matching, categorizing, and case-converting functions
- To learn how to read and write strings from and to standard input and output
- To write formatted output and read formatted input from or to a string in memory
- To see how various Standard C functions work from the same input stream
- To learn potential overstorage dangers with some of the Standard C string functions
- To learn advanced string manipulation techniques with pointer arithmetic and field-width and precision modifiers

- To learn different multiple-string concatenation methods
- To be familiar with Standard C string-to-number converting functions
- To learn how to write string and character processing functions of your own
- To learn how to copy and compare bytes between buffers and set bytes in a buffer to an arbitrary value
- To see how to deal with commas in string-number and number-string conversions
- To understand case sensitivity in string comparisons and learn how to deal with it

NEW TERMS

buffer
token

The Standard C library contains a number of useful string-handling functions. You will in all probability make heavy use of them. We will take a look at a number of the most commonly used ones. These functions all work on the principle of doing something from a certain address in RAM until a terminating NULL is found. Included in our perusal are functions that convert strings into numerical values and vice versa.

We will also look at functions that manipulate blocks of bytes irrespective of whether those bytes house a string.

9.1   SUMMARY OF STRING AND BUFFER FUNCTIONS

Here are summaries of string and buffer functions, categorized according to the type of job they do.

9.1.1   The Basics: String Copying/Combining/Comparing

```
char *strcpy(char *string1, const char *string2);
  /* places a copy of string2 starting at string1 */

char *strcat(char *string1, const char *string2);
   /* places copy of string2 starting at NULL
      character in string1, thus combining the strings */

int strcmp(const char *string1, const char *string2);
   /* checks whether strings are identical */
```

Each of these takes two char pointers (or array names or literal strings) as arguments. The prototype for each is found in string.h., as it is for their cousins:

```
char *strncpy(char *string1, const char *string2, unsigned num_bytes);

char *strncat(char *string1, const char *string2, unsigned num_bytes);

int strncmp(const char *string1, const char *string2, unsigned num_bytes);
```

These functions do essentially the same thing as strcpy(), strcat(), and strcmp(), but for only a specified number of characters in the second string. This number is added as the third argument.

9.1.2   Character and Substring Locators and Parsers

```
char *strchr(const char *string, int character);
   /* returns address of first occurrence of specified character in string */

char *strrchr(const char *string, int character);
   /* same as strchr(), except last occurrence */

char *strstr(const char *string, const char *substring);
   /* returns starting address of a substring inside another string */
```

Each of these functions returns a NULL if the specified character or substring, as the case may be, is not found within the string. Their prototypes are found in string.h:

```
char *strtok(char *string, char *delimiters); /* parse
        string into substrings at delimiting characters */
```

This function's prototype is also found in string.h, as are those in the next section.

9.1.3   Character Set Matching

```
size_t strcspn(const char *string1,
   const char *string2); /* position # of first occurrence in
        string1 of any character in string2 */

size_t strspn(const char *string1,
   const char *string2); /* position # of first occurrence in
        string1 of any character not in string2 */

char *strpbrk(const char *string1,
   const char *string2); /* address of first occurrence in
        string1 of any character in string2 */
```

9.1.4   Reading and Writing

```
char *gets(char *string); /* read a string from standard input */

int puts(const char *string); /* write a string to standard output */
```

```
int sprintf(char *string, const char *format_string, . . .);
   /* like printf(), except writes to a
      string in memory instead of standard output */

int sscanf(const char *string,
   const char *format_string, . . .);
   /* like scanf(), except reads from a string
      in memory instead from standard input */
```

The prototypes for these functions are found in stdio.h. You will find that you will make particularly heavy use of sprintf()—or at least you should.

9.1.5   String-Number Converters

```
double strtod(const char *number_string,
   char **stop); /* converts string to a double */

long strtol(const char *number_string,
   char **stop, int base); /* converts string to a long */

unsigned long strtoul(const char *number_string,
   char **stop, int base); /* converts a string to an unsigned long */

int atoi(const char *number_string); /* converts string to an int */

long atol(const char *number_string); /* converts string to a long */

double atof(const char *number_string); /* converts string to a double */
```

The prototypes for these functions are found in stdlib.h.

9.1.6   Character Classification Checking and Case Conversion

The following functions test whether the character representation of an integer value, according to the implementation's character-encoding system, is of a certain classification specified by the function. If it is that type, the function returns a nonzero value; otherwise it returns zero:

```
int isdigit (int character) /* is character a digit? */

int isalpha (int character) /* is character a letter? */

int isalnum (int character) /* is character a digit or a letter? */

int isxdigit (int character) /* is character a hexadecimal-digit character? */

int islower (int character) /* is character a lowercase letter? */

int isupper (int character) /* is character an uppercase letter? */

int isspace (int character) /* is character a whitespace character? */

int iscntrl (int character) /* is character a control character? */

int ispunct (int character) /* is character a printing
   character other than a space, a digit, or a letter? */

int isprint (int character) /* is character a printing
   character, including space? */

int isgraph (int character) /* is character a printing
   character other than space? */
```

The following functions handle case conversion:

```
int tolower (int character) /* if character is an uppercase
   letter, returns character as a lowercase letter;
      otherwise, returns the argument unchanged */

int toupper (int character) /* if character is a lowercase
   letter, returns character as an uppercase letter;
      otherwise, returns the argument unchanged */
```

Prototypes for all these character classification testing as well as case-conversion functions are found in `ctype.h`.

9.1.7   Buffer Manipulation

```
void *memset(void *buffer, int value, size_t num_bytes);
   /* set each byte in block of memory to same specified value */

void *memmove(void *destination, const void *source,
   size_t num_bytes); /* copy byte values from one memory location to another */

void *memcpy(void *destination, const void *source,
   size_t num_bytes); /* same as memmove, except no overlapping buffers allowed */

int memcmp(const void *buffer1, const void *buffer2,
   size_t num_bytes); /* same as strcmp, except comparison for
                          specified # of bytes rather than until NULL */

void *memchr(const void *buffer, int character,
   size_t num_bytes); /* same as strchr, but searches
                          specified # of bytes instead of stopping at NULL */
```

The prototypes for these functions are found in `string.h`.

9.2   THE gets() FUNCTION

Because we will be using `gets()` and `puts()` to illustrate the workings of many of the functions discussed in this chapter, we will turn to those two functions first. The `gets()` function is used to get a string from standard input—the keyboard, unless the standard input stream has been redirected (see Chapters 14 and 16).

The `gets()` function works as follows: It reads from standard input until it encounters a newline character (the newline character is generated when the user presses the ⏎Enter key). It copies all characters up to but not including the newline character and places them starting at the address passed to the function. It adds a terminating NULL, to make a string, and discards the newline character rather than placing it back into the input stream. A simple example:

```
char name[81];
printf("Type a name\n");
gets(name);
printf("You typed %s\n", name);
```

The `gets()` function takes a pointer to char as its argument. Here, we passed an array name (remember that the name of an array is treated as equivalent to a pointer to its first element). You can also use a pointer to make the assignment:

```
char name[81];
char *ptr = name;
printf("Type a name\n");
gets(ptr);
printf("You typed %s\n", ptr);
```

Though you will typically pass the starting address of an array, you need not do so. For instance:

```
char name[81];
int len;
printf("Type a last name\n");
gets(name);
len = strlen(name);
name[len] = ','; /* overstore terminating NULL */
name[len + 1] = ' ';
printf("Type a first name\n");
gets(name + len + 2);
printf("%s\n", name);
```

If we type in

```
Joshua
Rigg
```

we get back

```
Rigg, Joshua
```

9.2.1   Return Value of `gets()`

If the call to `gets()` is successful, the function returns the address passed to it (that is, it returns the value of the pointer passed as its argument, this value being an address). Thus, instead of ignoring the return value as we did in the last example, you can do the following:

```
char name[81];
char *ptr;
printf("Enter name\n");
ptr = gets(name);
printf("You entered %s\n", ptr);
printf("Enter another\n");
printf("You entered %s\n", gets(name));
```

In one case, we pointed a pointer to the address passed. In another case, we made the return address an argument to another function call.

If, however, the end of the file has been encountered, or something goes awry, `gets()` returns a NULL as an address. Thus, you could use the following formulation to test for the end of the file. This could occur if you have redirected standard input to a file. (See Chapters 14 and 16.)

```
char line[81];
while(gets(line) != NULL)
    continue;
```

This statement would have the effect, at each loop iteration, of both testing for the end of the file and storing any line found before the end of the file in input at the same time.

As we indicated, this construction would not have much practical use unless you are reading input from a file by redirecting the file to standard input. We have an example of this usage below. You will also use a similar construction with `fgets()` for direct reading from a file. See Listing 14.3, `f_copy_t.c`.

 Note that having `gets()` return a NULL upon reaching the end of the file is not the same as what happens if the user presses Enter without having entered any characters. *You cannot check whether the user has entered anything through a* `gets()` *call by comparing the call's return value against* NULL. Thus, you could not test to make sure the user has input anything this way:

```
char name[45];
printf("Enter a name\n");
if (gets(name) == NULL)
    printf("You did not enter a name");
else
    printf("Name is %s\n", name);
```

If the user presses ⌜Enter⌝ without having entered any data, the output will be

```
Name is
```

The gets() function does just what it is supposed to do. A blank string gets stored at name, followed by a terminating NULL. In other words, since there are no characters to store, all that happens is that name[0] is set to 0. The way to test for this possibility is

```
gets(name);
if (name[0] == 0)
    printf("You did not enter a name\n");
```

or

```
if (strlen(name) == 0)
    printf("You did not enter a name\n");
```

or, once we cover strcmp() below:

```
if (!strcmp("", gets(name)))
    printf("You did not enter a name\n");
```

We make use of blank string testing in the following program, letter.c. The program uses a series of gets() calls to read in a name, company name, street address, city, state, and zip code, and prints a letter and accompanying envelope.

 **Listing** 9.1 **letter.c**

```
/* letter.c */

/* read in record with gets & print letter */

#include <stdio.h>

void get_prompt(char *prompt, char *field);

int main(void)
{
    char first[25], last[25], title[10], company[50];
    char address[50], city[25], state[25], zip[12];

    get_prompt("first name", first);
    get_prompt("last name", last);
    get_prompt("title (e.g., Mr.", title);
    get_prompt("company name, if any (just press Enter key if none)", company);
    get_prompt("street address", address);
    get_prompt("city", city);
    get_prompt("state", state);
    get_prompt("zip code", zip);

    printf("\n%s %s\n%s%s%s\n%s, %s %s", first, last, company,
        company[0] == '\0' ? "": "\n", address, city, state, zip);
    printf("\n\nDear %s %s:\n\n", title, last);
    printf("\tYour bill is overdue. Pay up.\n\nThe Management\f");
}

void get_prompt(char *prompt, char *field)
{
    printf("Enter %s: ", prompt);
    gets (field);
}
```

Here, we use the conditional operator to allow us to print the company name if there is one, or to skip it if there is none:

```
printf("\n%s %s\n%s%s%s\n%s, %s %s", first, last, company,
    company[0] == '\0' ? "": "\n", address, city, state, zip);
```

If there is a company name, it would be printed for the third %s specifier. Otherwise, the specifier would correspond to a blank string (i.e., the specifier would start *and* end its task at the first element of company). If there is no company name (company[0] == '\0'), the next %s specifier takes on a blank string, "", thus printing nothing for that specifier. Otherwise, it takes on the newline character, to advance to the next line after the previous specifier has printed the company name.

9.2.2 The gets(), scanf(), and getchar() Functions and the Input Stream

The gets() function works from the same input stream as getchar() and scanf(). If there is nothing left to process in the input stream, calling any one of these functions causes the program to halt until the user enters data on the keyboard (or other standard input device if this stream has been redirected). All three functions are line-buffered: no user input is sent until the ⌜Enter⌝ key is pressed.

If, however, there is something left over in the input stream, any of these functions will process it without waiting for, or permitting, further user input. Sometimes having leftover input will not be unintentional. For instance, let's say we have redirected standard input to a file (see Chapters 14 and 16). The file contains inventory records, each of which has this format

```
060877240124191001748301 50CONDENSED MILK SEA SUPPLIES    76272260110039000024570L
```

with the various fields stored in one continuous line as shown above. Each record consists of the following fields:

field	characters
date	6
plant code	3
part code	5
quantity	3
lot number	6
rejects	3
item description	15
customer name	15
customer code	up to 24

Say we wanted to read in a series of records to prepare a report, but we were only interested in the first six fields of information for the purposes of this report. We could read in each record line with the following statements (note that we can use a %#c specifier to store data into a string, but, as we saw in Chapter 3, we have to add a NULL ourselves at the end of each field array. See Chapter 10 for a discussion of how the keyword static accomplishes that.)

```
static char date[7], plant[4], part[6], lot[7], junk[81];
int quantity, rejects;
scanf("%6c%3c%5c%3d%6c%3d", date, plant, part, &quantity, &lot, &rejects);
gets(junk);
```

The final statement just reads and discards the balance of the line, including the newline at the end, so the program can go on to the next record. We could have accomplished the same result somewhat less efficiently with the following as the last statement:

```
while(getchar() != '\n')
    continue;
```

Sometimes, having something left over in the input stream is an inadvertent programming error. Take care.

```
int id;
char name[45];
printf("Enter ID #\n");
```

```
scanf("%d", &id);
printf("Enter name\n");
gets(name);
printf("ID #: %d, Name: %s\n", id, name);
```

Once we type in a number, say 17, and press [Enter], we get this output without even being able to input a name:

```
ID #: 17, Name:
```

The scanf() function reads through the newline generated by pressing [Enter]. After storing 17 into id, it places the newline back into the input stream.

Since there is still something in the input stream, gets() operates on it without permitting any new input. It reads through the newline. Though it would generally store all characters up to the newline starting at name[0], here there is nothing to store. It then discards the newline, clearing the input stream. We need to replace the scanf() statement with

```
scanf("%d%*c", &id);
```

9.2.3   Danger! Overstorage

There is no mechanism inherent in gets() for checking whether there is enough space starting at the address passed for the input to be stored there. Any excess input will simply overflow into adjacent memory, potentially wreaking havoc without warning.

 With gets(), *you should test the length of the input against that of its intended resting place.* You can do that with a function such as that contained in get_chkr.c:

 **9.2 get_chkr.c**

```c
/* get_chkr.c */

/* input sentence with gets() and test length before copy into array */

#include <stdio.h>
#include <string.h> /* strlen, strcpy */

#define BIG 129 /* long enough to hold max DOS input line */
#define MAX 81

int gets_checker(char *test, char *str);

int main(void)
{
   char test_string[BIG];
   char string[MAX];

   printf("\nType in a sentence and press [Enter]\n");
   gets(test_string);
   if (gets_checker(test_string, string))
      puts(string);
}

int gets_checker(char *test, char *str)
{
   if (strlen(test) > MAX - 1)
   {
      printf("String entered with %d characters is too long\n",
         strlen(test));
      return 0;
   }
   strcpy(str, test);
   return 1;
}
```

Here, we have the input stored in a large temporary buffer, test_string. Only if we find that the input is small enough to fit into string do we then copy it from test_string to string, using the strcpy() function covered below.

You will see in the files chapter, Chapter 14, that the fgets() function makes an improvement on gets() in that it adds an argument that specifies the maximum number of characters to be read. This creates the potential problem, albeit less serious, of any unread input being left over in the input stream, however.

9.3   THE puts() FUNCTION

As with gets(), the puts() function takes a single address argument—a pointer to char, whether it be the name of an array, a pointer to char, or a literal string. It prints the string that starts at that address to standard output (the screen in the absence of redirection to the printer, a file, or another device) character by character until it encounters a NULL character byte:

```
char name[] = "Sir Tristram";
char *ptr = "Queen Iseult";
puts(name); /* array */
puts(ptr); /* char pointer */
puts("Sir Palomedes"); /* literal string */
```

giving us

```
Sir Tristram
Queen Iseult
Sir Palomedes
```

Insofar as the newline character is concerned, puts() works nicely in tandem with gets(). The gets() function discards the terminating newline in the input stream and adds a NULL character in its place; puts() stops at the NULL and adds a newline to the output string. Thus,

```
puts("Morgan Le Fay\n");
```

would print out two newline characters, thus causing a double space before the next printout.

As with gets(), you generally will, but need not always, pass the starting address of a string to puts():

```
char name[] = "Sir Thomas Malory";
puts(name + 4);
```

would give us:

```
Thomas Malory
```

Unlike many of the other string-handling functions, puts() returns a positive integer number as an int in the event of a successful call (often the value according to the computer's character-encoding system, of the last character successfully printed, generally the newline character) rather than returning the address passed to it as a pointer to char. In the event of error, puts() returns EOF (defined in stdio.h as an implementation designated negative constant: –1 in most PC implementations).

9.4   THE strcpy() FUNCTION

The strcpy() function takes two char pointers as arguments. It places a copy of the second string beginning at the address pointed to by the first:

```
char s1[] = "Go take a hike";
char s2[] = "Do";
strcpy(s1, s2);
printf("s1: %s; s2: %s\n", s1, s2);
```

This example produces

```
s1: Do; s2: Do
```

Figure 9.1 *"Go take a hike" and "Do" in Memory*

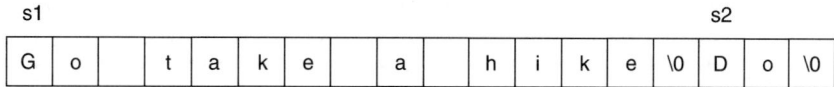

Figure 9.2 *String Copying Gives "Do Do" Results*

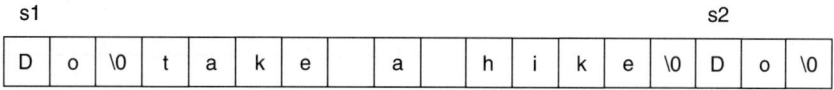

Figures 9.1 and 9.2 illustrate what happens in memory.

The second string is not *moved* to the first. Rather, a copy is placed byte by byte from its first byte *through* its NULL character, starting at the address pointed to by the first string.

Nor are the original string's bytes totally obliterated. The new first string prints out "Do" only because `printf()` gets to the NULL character before it gets to the balance of what used to be the string s1. We could, if we chose, print out the balance of the string:

```
char s1[] = "Go take a hike";
char s2[] = "Do";
strcpy(s1, s2);
printf("%s %s\n", s1, s1 + 3);
```

which prints out

```
Do take a hike
```

The `strcpy()` function not only copies s1 to s2 but also returns a pointer to s1. Consequently, the following would not only copy the literal string to the array but also print it out:

```
char name[40];
puts(strcpy(name, "Peter Featherstone"));
```

9.4.1 Danger! Overstorage

As is the case with `gets()`, the `strcpy()` function does not contain any error-checking mechanism to see whether there is enough room within s1's bounds to accommodate the input. Let's see what happens when we do a `strcpy()` with a second string longer than the first:

```
char s1[] = "Happy";
char s2[] = "Birthday!";
strcpy(s1, s2);
printf("s1: %s; s2: %s\n", s1, s2);
```

The output is

```
s1: Birthday!; s2: ay!
```

Oops! "Birthday" wrote over itself. Figures 9.3 and 9.4 show what happened in memory.

Figure 9.3 *"Happy" and "Birthday!" in Memory at s1 and s2*

Figure 9.4 *Stepping on Oneself: "Birthday!" and "Ay!" in Memory at s1 and s2*

The first %s specifier starts at s1 and reads to the NULL character; likewise, the second %s specifier starts at s2 and reads until the NULL character. In this case, they both read to the same NULL character.

When variables are declared, they are assigned memory locations one after another, just as you've seen in the preceding two examples (see Appendix B). We've used an example of memory overwriting for two directly adjacent variables so you could more easily see what is going on. In practice, the two strings you use in a strcpy() may be far apart in memory. The result of using a longer string for the second argument than you have room for in the first is the overwriting of some unrelated data. And worse still, you aren't alerted to it. Be careful! This sort of inadvertent overstoring could produce disastrous results—obliterating data or causing the computer to lock up (if, for example, the memory overwritten happens to contain the address of where the program is to return to after a function call is terminated).

 To be safe, you could include error-checking in your code to make sure the location pointed to by strcpy()*'s first argument is large enough to accommodate the second argument's string before making the call:*

```
char employee[26], worker[36];
printf("Enter worker's name (up to 25 characters)\n");
gets(worker);
if (strlen(worker) < sizeof(employee))
    strcpy(employee, worker);
else
    printf("employee > worker len: this can't ever happen\n");
```

9.4.2   Pointer Arithmetic

You can get pretty fancy with pointer arithmetic:

```
char s1[] = "Happy Birthday";
char *s2 = "Rough Trails";
strcpy(s1 + strlen("Happy"), s2 + strlen("Rough"));
puts(s1);
```

gives output of

```
Happy Trails
```

The strcpy() function takes the characters from the address passed as the second argument until the next NULL character and copies them starting at whatever address is passed as the first argument. In this example, the first argument is the address 6 bytes past where s1 points and the second argument is the address 6 bytes past where s2 points.

All these string functions, including printf() where a %s specifier is used, operate on the basis of starting at whatever address you pass it and dutifully proceeding, doing whatever it is supposed to do until encountering the first NULL character after that address. Although you typically will pass to the functions an address that represents the beginning of a string, as you can see, it ain't necessarily so.

9.4.3   Arguments

Remember that since array names and literal strings are just addresses to the computer, you can use either in place of a char pointer in any of the string-handling functions. For example,

```
char name[] = "Purple Rose of Cairo";
char river[] = "Suwannee River, way, way down";
puts(strcpy("Yellow Rose of Texas", name)); /* literal string and char array */
strcpy(river + strlen("Suwannee"),
    " how I love you!"); /* char array and literal string */
puts(river);
```

which, on our system, produces

```
Purple Rose of Cairo
Suwannee how I love you!
```

In the first instance, an array is copied onto a literal string, and in the second, the converse. Be careful. The first case is just to illustrate the possibilities. It is a practice definitely to be avoided. *In Standard C, literal strings are read-only constants; altering one may work (assuming the string constant is long enough) but under Standard C results in "undefined behavior."*

9.4.4   String Assignments

One final point about `strcpy()`. You can make an assignment of a string to a `char` array on declaration:

```
char name[] = "Frankenstein";
```

Apart from declaration time, however, the only way to accomplish the same thing is by using `strcpy()`. A simple assignment statement will not work, even if you try to use a pointer to `char` to a assist you:

```
char name[20];
char title[20] = "Phantom of the Opera";
char *ptr = title;
printf("ptr: %s at %p\n", ptr, ptr);
name = "Frankenstein"; /* try to copy new string into array: error! */
ptr = "Nosferatu"; /* try to copy new string with pointer:
                          no error, but incorrect result */
printf("ptr: %s at %p; title: %s at %p\n", ptr, ptr, title, title);
```

On our system, we got this output, after commenting out the third-to-last line:

```
ptr: Phantom of the Opera at FFE2
ptr: Nosferatu at 00CD; title: Phantom of the Opera at FFE2
```

The third-to-last statement generates an error message. The literal string, "Frankenstein," is equivalent to a pointer to the starting address of where the string is stored. The statement purports to assign a constant, `name`, to that address. But of course you can't assign a constant a different value from the one initially assigned it. That's why we call it a constant.

The second-to-last statement gets by the compiler, but it doesn't achieve the desired result of copying "Nosferatu" into the `title` array, where `ptr` points. Instead, it just moves where `ptr` points from the first element of `title` to some unknown location in static memory created to house the string "Nosferatu."

The following code fragment does the trick:

```
char name[20];
char title[20];
char *ptr = title;
strcpy(name, "Frankenstein"); /* OK */
strcpy(ptr, "Nosferatu"); /* OK */
```

"Frankenstein" is copied into `name`, and "Nosferatu" is copied into `title`. Also, `ptr` now points to "Nosferatu," the string that starts at `title`.

The inability to make assignments outside declarations is not a limitation unique to strings. Remember that assigning a string is really just filling in several of the elements of an array in one fell swoop. That sort of assignment is forbidden outside declaration for nonstrings as well.

9.5   THE `strcat()` FUNCTION

The `strcat()` function (short for *str*ing con*cat*enation) lets you tack one string onto the end of another. It copies characters starting from the address passed as its second argument up to and including the first NULL character it finds in the second string; it places them starting at the first NULL character after the address passed as the first argument. It thus disables that NULL byte as a stopping point for string evaluation:

```
char s1[25] = "O Wutta Goo";
char s2[] = "Cy is";
strcat(s1, s2);
printf("s1: %s; s2: %s\n", s1, s2);
```

The output is

```
s1: O Wutta GooCy is; s2: Cy is
```

 Assuming there is enough room in the location pointed to by the first pointer, the contents of the second string, as well as any other reserved memory, are left untouched. *Take care that there is enough room in the first string before you perform a* `strcat()` *call.*

Had we wanted to leave a space between the two concatenated strings, we could have done this:

```
char s1[25] = "O Wutta Goo";
char s2[] = "Cy is";
strcat(s1, " ");
strcat(s1, s2);
puts(s1);
```

The first statement places a space where the NULL character was and places a new NULL character after the space, thus making s1 "O Wutta Goo." We also could have written the last two statements more compactly:

```
char s1[25] = "O Wutta Goo";
char s2[] = "Cy is";
puts(strcat(strcat(s1, " "), s2));
```

This latter works because `strcat()` returns a pointer to the concatenated string and because C allows you to use the return value of a function as an argument to another function. (See Chapter 8.)

    On the other hand, *multiple concatenation with nested or successive* `strcat()` *calls is fine for a few relatively short strings. If you have an application that repeatedly concatenates long strings, you will find a* `strcpy()` *formulation with a moving pointer to be faster, since it prevents the computer from having to reread from the very first part of an ever-lengthening string.*

```
static char str_big[509]= "", *strings[] =
{
   str_big,
   "This starts out as a long string",
   " and it gets even",
   " bigger and bigger",
   " as it goes along",
   NULL
};
int i;

/* first alternative */
for (i = 1; strings[i]; i++)
   strcat(strings[0], strings[i]);
puts(str_big);

/* second alternative: these would not both be in the same program */
for (i = 1; strings[i]; i++)
   strcpy(*strings += strlen(strings[0]), strings[i]);
puts(str_big);
```

In the second alternative, we keep copying to an ever-advancing pointed-to address. After each `strcpy()`, we advance the pointer to the NULL at the new end of the string.

9.5.1   Pointer Arithmetic

As with `strcpy()`, you can use pointer arithmetic profitably with `strcat()` calls:

```
char ddmm[10] = "11/17", ddmmyy[10] = "12/03/93";
strcat(ddmm, ddmmyy + 5);
puts(ddmm);
```

We get:

```
11/17/93
```

9.6   THE `strcmp()` FUNCTION

Let's take a look at a program that purports to test whether one string matches another.

 **Listing** **9.3 `no_cigar.c`**

```
/* no_cigar.c */

/* erroneous program to test strcmp */

#include <stdio.h>

int main(void)
{
    char answer[81];
    puts("Why did the chicken cross the road?");
    gets(answer);
    if (answer == "To get to the other side")
        printf("How did you know?");
    else printf("No cigar!");
}
```

No matter what answer you type in, you get the "No cigar!" message. What gives?

We cannot use the equality operator to see whether one string is identical to another string any more than we could use the equality operator to test en masse whether one array of `int`s is identical element by element to another `int` array. Given this code fragment (and assuming the compiler does not merge duplicate strings)

```
int num[5] = {3, 5, 7, 9, 11};
int val[5] = {3, 5, 7, 9, 11};
char *s1 = "What's my line?";
char *s2 = "What's my line?";
if (num != val)
    puts("int arrays differ");
if (s1 != s2)
    puts("strings differ");
```

we get output of

```
int arrays differ
strings differ
```

In each case, all the conditional statement tests for is whether the addresses of the two items are the same. Of course, `num` (that is, `&num[0]`) is not the same as `val` (that is, `&val[0]`) any more than the address housed as `s1`'s value is the same as that of `s2`. They represent the starting addresses of separate memory locations.

The `strcmp()` function is what we need for this job. It compares two strings, character by character, and returns zero if the strings are identical. If not, it stops at the first character that differs; it returns a positive integer if the character in the second-string argument at that point comes lexicographically after (that is, has a higher encoded numerical value than) the character in the first-string argument in the computer's encoding system, or a negative integer if it comes before. (If the computer uses ASCII, the letter a comes after A, whereas the opposite is true for EBCDIC. See Appendix F.) Generally the implementation will return the difference in encoded values between the two characters at that point: the function subtracts the encoded value of the character in the string pointed to by `strcmp()`'s second argument from the encoded value of the corresponding character in the string pointed to by the first argument. Consider the following program.

 **Listing** **9.4 `how_far.c`**

```
/* how_far.c */

/* test strcmp(): show how far apart differing letter is */
```

```
#include <stdio.h>
#include <string.h>

int main(void)
{
    char * s1[4] =
    {
        "What a pain!",
            "Looks the same to me",
            "galoshes",
            "strings"
    };
    char * s2[4] =
    {
        "What a rain?",
            "looks the same to me",
            "galoshes",
            "string"
    };
    int i;

    for (i = 0; i < 4; i++)
        printf("%d\n", strcmp(s1[i], s2[i]));
}
```

We get this output

```
-2
-32
0
115
```

on a PC or other system that uses ASCII for its character encoding. The second set of strings, "Looks the same to me" and "looks the same to me," does not return a zero. Since strcmp() checks character by character for character-encoding values, a lowercase letter will not test as identical to an uppercase letter. The strcmp() test is case sensitive. On "strings" versus "string," the strings differ in the seventh character, where strcmp() subtracts 0 (the NULL character at the end of "string" in the seventh position) from 115, the ASCII value of s.

One common use for strcmp() is to test to see whether the user has input data into a string:

```
char path[45] = "";
printf("enter path: ");
gets(path);
if (!strcmp("", path))
    puts("Error! Path has not been set");
```

Note that comparing path to NULL would not be a correct test:

```
if (!path)
    puts("Error! Path has not been set"); /* incorrect test */
```

The declaration in the first line,

```
char path[45] = "";
```

does assign an address to path so that path's value is not zero; it's just that path's first element is a NULL character both at the time of the initialization to a blank string and later if the user presses Enter without anything having been input.

9.6.1   Mechanics of strcmp()

What happens if we try to use strcmp() on an array of ints?

 **Listing 9.5 intcmp.c**

```
/* intcmp.c */

/* use strcmp to compare two arrays of ints */

#include <stdio.h>
#include <string.h> /* strcmp */

int main(void)
{
    int i1[5] = {2237, 2383, 3293, 393, 0};
    int i2[5] = {2237, 2383, 3293, 393, 0};
    int i3[5] = {2237, 2383, 3293, 1, 0};
    int i4[3] = {3, 2, 0};
    int i5[3] = {3, 1, 0};

    printf("i1 and i2 %s match\n", strcmp((char *)i1, (char *)i2) ? "do not" : "");
    printf("i1 and i3 %s match\n", strcmp((char *)i1, (char *)i3) ? "do not" : "");
    printf("i4 and i5 %s match\n", strcmp((char *)i4, (char *)i5) ? "do not" : "");
}
```

Remember, all `strcmp()` does is to start at two addresses and move byte by byte from those points, comparing byte values along the way, until a NULL or mismatch is found. The arguments here are array names, so we have addresses; we make `strcmp()` happy by type casting the pointed-to objects as char.

Here's the program output:

```
i1 and i2 match
i1 and i3 do not match
i4 and i5 match
```

The first two tests work properly. But what about the third? Here, the function finds a 0 byte in the second element and stops before getting to the mismatch in the less significant byte of the int. Oh well, perhaps this unorthodox program has little practical value. But it shows just how `strcmp()` works.

As you see, `strcmp()` and all other string-handling functions do whatever they do until they find a terminating NULL. If you want to copy from one array or other memory area to another, or compare one to the other, or look for a specific character there, and so on, you may not use the string-handling functions unless those memory areas contain strings. Otherwise, you must use the buffer manipulation functions discussed near the end of this chapter: `memcpy()`, `memcmp()`, `memchr()`, `memset()`, and `memmove()`.

9.6.2 Case Insensitivity and `strcmp()`

Now that we understand how `strcmp()` works, let's try our riddle program example again.

 **Listing 9.6 chicken.c**

```
/* chicken.c */

/* primitive test of strcmp */

#include <stdio.h>
#include <string.h> /* strcmp */

int main(void)
{
    char answer[81];

    puts("Why did the chicken cross the road?");
```

```
     gets(answer);
     if (!strcmp(answer, "To get to the other side")
          || !strcmp(answer, "TO GET TO THE OTHER SIDE")
          || !strcmp(answer, "to get to the other side"))
         printf("How did you know?");
     else printf("No cigar!");
 }
```

We've used the more compact if (!strcmp(s1, s2)) in place of if (strcmp(s1, s2) == 0). Even with the less compact formulation, it may take you a while to get used to the notion that a successful match yields a zero or "false" value and failure yields a "true" value, instead of the other way around.

Since you'll probably have to deal with this quirk of strcmp() in someone else's code if not in your own, you'd better get used to it. On the other hand, if you'd rather fight than switch, you can try this approach:

```
int string_compare(const char *string1, const char *string2)
{
   return (strcmp(string1, string2) == 0);
}
```

Or in macro form (see Chapter 11):

```
#define string_compare(s1,s2) (strcmp(s1,s2)==0)
```

Bearing in mind strcmp()'s case-sensitive nature, we tried to anticipate three different possible responses in chicken.c. This approach works better than our first programming attempt, no_cigar.c, but we still run into trouble with answers like "To Get to the Other Side". What we probably need for this job is either an input function that turns the input to all uppercase or lowercase, or a string-comparison function that is not case-sensitive. We will defer construction of such a function until we have reviewed the toupper() and tolower() functions later in the chapter.

As far as canned functions are concerned, there are no Standard C functions that do the job we're looking for here. But there are three functions normally found in DOS-specific compilers that convert a string to uppercase, convert a string to lowercase, and reverse the characters of a string (other than the terminating NULL): strupr(), strlwr(), and strrev(), respectively. They all take a string as an argument, alter the string passed, and return a pointer to the altered string. A DOS-specific function, stricmp(), does the same thing as the Standard C function, strcmp(), on a case-insensitive basis.

9.7   LIMITING THE NUMBER OF CHARACTERS

Sometimes it is useful to compare, copy, or concatenate fewer than all the characters in a string. We've seen how you can use pointer arithmetic to start from a point other than the *beginning* of either or both strings. Pointer arithmetic won't help us stop short of the *end* of either string, however. To do that, we need to use strncpy(), strncat(), and strncmp(), rather than strcpy(), strcat(), and strcmp().

Each of these functions takes a third argument—an integer representing the number of characters you wish to copy, concatenate, or compare. They stop at the earlier of a NULL or the designated number of bytes.

9.7.1   The strncpy() Function

The strncpy() function copies a specified number of characters from the second-string argument to the first string:

```
char s1[35] = "no time like the present", s2[35] = "it's easy to lose your way";
strncpy(s1 + 7, s2 + 9, 8);
s1[13] = '\0';
puts(s1);
```

We get:

```
no time to lose
```

Figure 9.5   *"Oh" and "No" Assigned to* char *Arrays*

O	h	\0	g	a	r	b	a	g	e		h	e	r	e

N	o	\0	g	a	r	b	a	g	e		h	e	r	e

We'll see shortly why we had to close s1 with a terminating NULL character by ourselves.

If the string pointed to by strncpy()'s second argument is *shorter* than the number of characters specified, the function copies NULL characters to make up the difference. It does not go past the NULL character in the second string and copy characters there to the first string:

```
char s1[15] = "Oh";
char s2[15] = "No";
strncpy(s1, s2, 15);
```

Figures 9.5 and 9.6 show the results of the assignments and copying operation for each string.

More often, however, the converse will be true: you will specify a number of characters that is less than the second string's length. Be careful here! *When less than all of the second string is copied to the first string with* strncpy()*, a terminating* NULL *character is not added to close off the first string. If you don't add a* NULL *yourself by a separate statement, you may not get what you expect.* In the first example, if we omit the statement

```
s1[13] = '\0';
```

we get the following output:

```
no time to losee present
```

9.7.2   The strncat() Function

Just like strcat(), the strncat() function copies characters from the second string to the first, overwriting the first string's terminating NULL with the second string's first character in the process. However, strncat() stops copying at the earlier of encountering a NULL in the second string or on copying the number of characters specified by the third argument:

```
char s1[81] = "Time waits for ", s2[81] = "no man or woman";
strncat(s1, s2, 6);
puts(s1);
```

Our output:

```
Time waits for no man
```

If the string pointed to by the second argument is shorter than the number of characters specified, the extra characters are ignored, as though the third argument had been equal to the second string's length. This is different from strncpy()'s short-second-string case, where NULL characters are written for the balance. Also, whereas strncpy() does not add a terminating NULL character, strncat() does.

As with strcpy(), strncpy(), and strcat(), the strncat() function returns a pointer to its first string, as altered. Thus, in place of the last two statements in the previous example, we could substitute

```
puts(strncpy(s1, s2, 6));
```

Figure 9.6   *"No" Copied to "Oh"*

N	o	\0	\0	\0	\0	\0	\0	\0	\0	\0	\0	\0	r	e

N	o	\0	g	a	r	b	a	g	e		h	e	r	e

9.7.3   The `strncmp()` Function

The `strncmp()` function makes the same comparison as `strcmp()`. However, it stops comparing when it reaches the number of characters specified in its third argument. Thus

```
if (!strncmp("That's terrible! You brute!", "That's terribly nice of you", 14))
   printf("strings match");
else printf("no match");
```

prints out

```
strings match
```

As with `strcmp()`, `strncmp()` stops as soon as it hits a NULL in either string. This is so even if the number of characters compared to that point is less than the number specified in the third argument.

9.8   CHARACTER AND STRING LOCATORS AND PARSERS

Now that we've covered the basics of string copying, combining, and comparing, it's time to learn about more precise tasks: finding and dividing strings, substrings, and characters.

9.8.1   The `strchr()` and `strrchr()` Functions

The `strchr()` function returns the address of the first occurrence of a specified character in a string; `strrchr()` returns the address of the last occurrence. Each of these returns NULL instead, if the specified character is not found within the string. The search is case sensitive. Thus

```
strchr("little or nothing", 'N')
```

would have a value of NULL.

The following function uses `strchr()` to return the number of times a specified character is found within a string:

```
int char_count(const char *string, int ch)
{
   int num = 0;
   for (; (string = strchr(string, ch)) != NULL;
      string++, num++)
         continue;
   return num;
}
```

Say we had a date-validity checking function, where the date passed might be in either MM/DD/YY format or MMDDYY. Before conducting our date-checking, we might first want to determine which format we have. Assume the string pointer `date` has been passed as an argument:

```
if (strchr(date, '/')
   strcpy(year[i], atoi(date + 6));
else strcpy(year[i], atoi(date + 4));
```

(See below for the `atoi()` function, which converts numeric strings into integer values.)

 We can search for the NULL character with `strchr()` or `strrchr()`. This gives us a convenient method of setting a pointer to the last character in a string:

```
char string[] = "The End";
char *ptr = strchr(string, 0) - 1;
```

One alternative formulation would be

```
ptr = string + strlen[string] - 1;
```

This formulation is not only slightly longer, but we also may have to pause for a moment to reflect on whether

```
string + strlen[string]
```

gets us to the NULL or to the character before the NULL.

9.8.2 Avoiding NULL Pointer Assignment

 If you are using `strchr()` *or* `strrchr()` *not only to find the address of a certain character, but also to alter the value at that location, be careful to avoid a* NULL *pointer assignment.* Say, for example, you wanted to eliminate the newline character at the end of a string. An example of when you might do this: when you have derived string input from a file with `fgets()`, and you want to print the string out later with `puts()`. Unlike `gets()`, `fgets()` retains the final newline character. Unlike `fputs()`, `puts()` adds a newline. (See Chapter 14.)

```c
char name[] = "Dizzy Gillespie\n";
*strchr(name, '\n') = 0;
```

Here, the example has a newline at the end. However, if the string does not contain a newline, the function call will return a NULL and at the termination of your program, you may see "NULL pointer assignment" flash across the screen—if your program doesn't crash before then. A better method would be to make the assignment conditional only:

```c
if (strchr(name, '\n'))
   *strchr(name, '\n') = 0;
```

9.8.3 The `strstr()` Function

The `strstr()` function returns the starting address of a substring inside another string. As with `strchr()` and `strrchr()` for characters, if the substring `strstr()` looks for is not found within the main string, the function returns NULL:

```c
char *ptr;
char *substring = "side";
char *string = "insider";
ptr = strstr(string, substring);
ptr = strstr(string, "INSIDER");
```

After the first assignment, `ptr` contains the address of the third element of `string`—that is, it points to `string + 2`. After the second assignment, `ptr` has a value of NULL.

The following listing, `suffix.c`, assumes that the user has input a first and a last name as separate fields of a record, and that both first and last names have been converted to all uppercase. The function `switch_suffix()` checks to see whether a suffix has been input as part of the last name. If so, it cuts it off the last name and pastes it onto the first name. This cutting and pasting would be in order if the first and last names are index items in a database.

 **Listing 9.7 suffix.c**

```c
/* suffix.c */

/* use strstr to determine whether name has suffix */

#include <stdio.h>
#include <string.h> /* strstr, strrchr, strcat */

void suffix_switch(char *first, char *last);

int main(void)
{
   char first[35] = "MEMPHIS", last[35] = "SLIM, JR.";
   suffix_switch(first, last);
   printf("%s, %s\n", last, first);
}

void suffix_switch(char *first, char *last)
{
   char i;
   char *suf[6] = {"JR.", "JR", "SR.", "SR", "II", "III"};
```

```
        for (i = 0; i < 6; i++) /* check for each suffix 1 by 1 */
            if(strstr(last, suf[i]))
            {
            if (strrchr(last, ','))
            /* close off last name at comma */
                *strrchr(last, ',') = 0;
            else if (strrchr(last, ' '))

            /* in case there's no comma: to last space */
                *strrchr(last, ' ') = 0;
            strcat(first, " ");
            strcat(first, suf[i]); /* add suffix to first name */
            return;
        }
    }
```

The output:

```
SLIM, MEMPHIS JR.
```

9.8.4   Character Set Matching: `strcspn()`, `strpbrk()`, `strspn()` *(Optional)*

```
size_t strcspn(const char *string1, const char *string2);
```

Use `strcspn()` to locate the first occurrence in `string1` of any character in `string2`. The function returns the position number (zero for the very first character in `string1`) in `string1` if a character is found, or the length of `string1` if no characters are found. Or, if you prefer, you could think of this as a function that returns the length of the maximum initial segment of `string1` that consists entirely of characters not from `string2`:

```
char rock[] = "Scylla", hard_place[] = "Charybdis";
printf("Match found in character #%d\n", strcspn(rock, hard_place));
```

The return type `size_t` is a `typedef` (a nickname or alias for a defined C type—see Chapter 13) for an unsigned integer type defined in `stddef.h` as the type of the value returned by the `sizeof` operator. *If* `strcspn()` *finds no match, it returns the position number of the terminating* `NULL` *in* `string1`. *Because of this property and the fact that* `strcspn()` *returns an index number rather than a pointer, in certain cases you will find it more useful to call* `strcspn(string, "c")` *with a single character-string than* `strchr(string, 'c')`.

A first cousin of `strcspn()`:

```
char *strpbrk(const char *string1, const char *string2);
```

 This function does the same job as `strcspn()`, except that it returns a pointer to the first matching character rather than its position number (or `NULL` if there is no match). *By setting the dereferenced returned address to zero after a call to* `strpbrk()`, *you can cut off a string at a particular character.*

A contrariwise first cousin once removed to `strcspn()`:

```
size_t strspn(const char *string1, const char *string2);
```

The `strspn()` function returns the position number (also zero-based) of the first character in `string1` that does *not* belong to the set of characters in `string2`. The function returns the length of `string1` if all its characters are found within `string2`. Or again, you can view it from the other end of the telescope as a function that returns the length of the maximum initial segment of `string1` that consists entirely of characters from `string2`.

If every character in `string1` is found in `string2`, the total length of `string1` (not counting the terminating `NULL`—that is, `strlen(string1)`) is returned by a call to `strspn()`. If `string2` is a blank string, the first character of `string1` will not be found in it, so the call will return zero.

In all three functions in this section, `strspn()`, `strcspn()`, and `strpbrk()`, the order of the characters in `string2` is irrelevant, nor does it matter whether there are duplicates: only the unique characters in `string2` are considered the set of characters for which `string1` will be searched.

9.8.5 String Parsing: `strtok()` *(Optional)*

```
char *strtok(char *string, char *delimiters);
```

Use `strtok()` to split (called *parsing*) a string into substrings (called ***tokens***) by placing NULL characters wherever in the string any of the delimiting characters in the second-string argument appear.

Completely parsing the string requires successive calls to `strtok()`. In the first call, the string and the delimiting string are passed as arguments. On each successive call, NULL is passed as the first argument and the delimiting string as the second argument.

 **Listing** 9.8 `strtok.c`

```c
/* strtok.c */

/* illustrate strtok function */

#include <stdio.h>
#include <string.h> /* strtok */

int main(void)
{
    char *delimiters = "\t -";
    char *arg[10];
    char input[81];
    int args = 0;
    int i;

    gets(input);
    arg[args++] = strtok(input, delimiters);

    /* every subsequent time, use NULL as first argument */
    while((arg[args++] = strtok(NULL, delimiters)) != NULL)
        continue;

    for (i = 0; i < args - 1; i++)
        printf("argument %d: %s\n", i + 1, arg[i]);

}
```

Each call to `strtok()` returns a pointer to the beginning of the token and places a NULL at the delimiting character at its end. Where no delimiting characters are found, `strtok()` returns NULL. For input of

123 [Tab] 456   789-10

we get output of

```
123
456
789
10
```

Note that while you generally will, as in this programming example, pass the same delimiting string on each successive call, you need not do so.

9.9   THE `sprintf()` FUNCTION

The `sprintf()` function does the same job as `printf()`, except it writes starting at an address in memory instead of to the screen and adds a NULL character. For instance:

```c
int month = 2, day = 5, year = 1993;
char date_string[12];
sprintf(date_string, "%02d/%02d/%02d", month, day, year % 100);
```

would cause `date_string` to contain the string, "02/05/93."

As with `strcpy()` *and* `strcat()`, *with* `sprintf()` *you have to be careful not to overflow the array or pointer area into which copying is taking place. Also, there is no guarantee the function will work correctly if there is an overlap between the destination string and one of the strings that go into making up the destination string.*

```
char name[40] = "Rainey", first[10] = "Ma";
sprintf(name, "%s %s", first, name); /* won't work properly! */
puts(name);
```

9.9.1   Cutting and Pasting with `sprintf()`

We can use `sprintf()` *with a string specifier and a minimum field width modifier to "cherry-pick" characters from the middle of a string.* Take the following program, `date_cmp.c`, which uses `sprintf()` to check whether a specified start date is prior to a specified end date. You could use the `compare_dates()` function contained in this program in a report-generating program, where the user interactively specifies a reporting period for the program data printout.

 **Listing** **9.9 `date_cmp.c`**

```
/* date_cmp.c */

/* use sprintf to compare dates to see whether start date after end date */

#include <stdio.h>
#include <stdlib.h> /* atol */

int compare_dates(char *start, char *end);

int main(void)
{
   char s_date[12], e_date[12];

   printf("Input start and end dates\nFormat MMDDYY\n");
   gets(s_date);
   gets(e_date);
   if (compare_dates(s_date, e_date))
      puts("Dates OK");
}

int compare_dates(char *start, char *end)
{
   char start_date[12], end_date[12];
   char error[81];

   /* convert to YYMMDD for easy mathematical comparison */
   sprintf(start_date, "%2.2s%2.2s%2.2s", start + 4, start, start + 2);
   sprintf(end_date, "%2.2s%2.2s%2.2s", end + 4, end, end + 2);
   if (atol(start_date) > atol(end_date))
   {
      sprintf(error,"Error! Start date, %2.2s/%2.2s/%2.2s, is later than end date,
         %2.2s/%2.2s/%2.2s\n", start, start + 2, start + 4, end, end + 2, end + 4);
      puts(error);
      return 0;
   }
   return 1;
}
```

The input would be in format MMDDYY; the date-checking strings would be in format YYMMDD to allow ready numerical comparison; the error-message printout is in format MM/DD/YY. Of course, we could have used `printf()` instead of `sprintf()` and `puts()` in the final two statements. However, you will find yourself using `sprintf()` in this manner quite a bit once you develop your own more complex error-message printing functions that require several completed strings at once. (See, for example, the `messagebox()` example in on disk.)

We will get to the `atol()` function we used to convert the strings to `longs` shortly. *Note that to make a proper numerical comparison, the format of a date must be year-month-day in that order.*

9.9.2   Advanced Manipulation

Suppose that we have an invoice form for which the program is to create a 12-digit invoice number consisting of the date (here stored in format MM/DD/YY in a string, `date`) in the first six digits and, in the last six digits, the first six letters of a vendor name (stored in `vendor`) if the name is a single word or the first three letters of the first two words if the vendor name is more than one word. The `invoice_num()` function in `inv_num.c` would do the job.

 **Listing 9.10 `inv_num.c`**

```
/* inv_num.c */

/* use sprintf to create an invoice number */

#include <stdio.h>
#include <string.h> /* strchr */

char *invoice_num(char *vendor, char *date);

int main(void)
{
    puts(invoice_num("Pencils Galore!", "09/01/00"));
}

char *invoice_num(char *vendor, char *date)
{
    char *space_ptr;
    char vend_name[7];
    static char invoice_num[13];

/* use first 6 letters unless 2 words, in which case use first 3 of each */
    space_ptr = strchr(vendor, ' ');

    if (!space_ptr) /* only 1 word in vendor name, so no space */
        sprintf(vend_name, "%-6.6s", vendor);
    else
        sprintf(vend_name, "%-.3s%-.3s", vendor, space_ptr + 1);

    sprintf(invoice_num, "%02.2s%02.2s%02s%s", date, date + 3, date + 6, vend_name);
    return invoice_num;
}
```

The output:

```
090100PenGal
```

The `.6` in the `%-6.6s` specifier truncates the vendor name at six characters; the `–` portion left-justifies the name if it is fewer than six characters. If there is more than one word in the name, `space_ptr` will point to the space between the first and second words. Thus, `space_ptr + 1` will point to the first letter of the second word.

Note that we have made the string to be returned `static`. Otherwise its value will be lost when the function terminates. (See Chapter 10 for an explanation of `static` and external variables.)

The `sprintf()` function is flexible. Assume we have a function where a field length `len`, a string `string`, and a value `spaces`—which will either be 1 or 0—will be passed as arguments. The following statements give us the string left-justified within a series of spaces longer than the field length by two spaces (the spaces before and after the field being for appearances) if spaces is 1 and equal to the field length if spaces is 0:

```
char format[10];
char buffer[81];
if (spaces)
    strcpy(format, " %-*s ");
else
    strcpy(format, "%-*s");
sprintf(buffer, format, len, string);
```

Using the string-writing functions in Appendix C, this example would allow you to write a field to the screen in a highlighted color, either with or without a space before and after the text, depending on the function call parameter.

9.9.3   Multiple Concatenation

 The sprintf() *function is handy where you need to concatenate several strings onto one another.* For instance:

```
char *first = "John", *middle = "Orestes", *last = "Peters";
char name[45];
sprintf(name, "%s %s %s", first, middle, last);
```

See Listing 16.5, sys_copy.c, for another example.

9.10   THE sscanf() FUNCTION

The sscanf() function does the same job as scanf(); it reads starting at an address in memory instead of from the keyboard. The following program, frac_dec.c, uses sprintf() and sscanf() to convert fractional string input in a particular format to a decimal string.

 **Listing 9.11 frac_dec.c**

```
/* frac_dec.c */

/* use sprintf() and sscanf() to convert fractional input string to decimal */

#include <stdio.h>
#include <string.h>

char *convert(char *str);

int main(void)
{
    puts(convert("12 3/4"));
}

char *convert(char *str)
{
    int numerator, denominator;
    char frac_str[10];

    /* point to digit after space */
    char *ptr = strrchr(str, ' ') + 1;

    /* read in numerator & denominator from last part of string */
    sscanf(ptr, "%d/%d", &numerator, &denominator);

    /* store fractional decimal component in string */
    sprintf(frac_str, "%.3f", (double)numerator/(double)denominator);
```

```
/* tack decimal str onto integer portion of passed str, wiping out fraction */
/* ptr - 1 is space between integer and fraction */
strcpy(ptr - 1, frac_str + 1); /* skip over 0 in 0.xxx format from %.3f specifier above */
return str;
}
```

We start by setting a pointer to the first character of the fraction, being one character following the space after the integer portion of the string. We use sscanf() to split the fraction into a numerator and denominator, which we then turn into a floating point value. That floating point value is converted to a string by sprintf().

Copying from temp + 1 allows us to skip over the leading 0 in the floating point format stored in the sprintf()-created string. Likewise, ptr - 1 puts us back to the space after the integer portion of the passed string.

9.10.1 An sscanf() Financial Example

In ss_date.c, we determine the interest accrued on a corporate bond. When bonds are sold, the buyer pays not only principal but also the amount of interest that has accrued from the most recent interest payment date to the sale date. Bond interest is paid semiannually based on what is called a 360-day year. Each month is deemed to be 30 days, regardless of its actual length. Once we determine the number of months from the interest payment date, we apply the formula

$$interest = principal * semiannual\ interest\ rate^{number\ of\ 6\text{-month periods}}$$

Between interest payment dates, the exponent will be a noninteger.

 **Listing** 9.12 ss_date.c

```c
/* ss_date.c */

/* use sscanf to calculate accrued interest on bonds */

#include <stdio.h> /* */
#include <math.h> /* pow */

int main(void)
{
    char start_date[15], end_date[15];
    char *format = "(Format: MM/DD/YY)\n\t";
    int start_month, end_month, start_day, end_day, start_year, end_year;
    float periods, principal, rate;

    printf("Last interest payment date:\n%s", format);
    gets(start_date);
    printf("Bond sale date:\n%s", format);
    gets(end_date);
    printf("Bond principal amount:\n\t");
    scanf("%f", &principal);
    printf("Annual interest rate as a percent:\n\t");
    scanf("%f", &rate);

    /* turn annual percent to semiannual decimal */
    rate /= 200;

    /* split date into day, month & year components */
    sscanf(start_date, "%2d%*c%2d%*c%2d", &start_month, &start_day, &start_year);
    sscanf(end_date, "%2d%*c%2d%*c%2d", &end_month, &end_day, &end_year);

    /* apply 30-day investment banking conventions: */
    if (start_day == 31)
```

```
    start_day = 30;
if (end_day == 31)
    if (start_day == 30 ¦¦ start_day == 31)
    end_day = 30;

/* calculate # of 6-month periods or fraction */
periods = ((float)(end_month - start_month) + 12. * (float)(end_year - start_year)
    + (float)(end_day - start_day) / 30.) / 6.;
printf("The bond sale price is $%.2f", principal * pow(1. + rate, periods));
}
```

Here's a sample run:

```
Last interest payment date:
(Format: mm/dd/yy)
    06/15/93
Bond sale date:
(Format: mm/dd/yy)
    09/17/93
Bond principal amount:
    5000
Annual interest rate as a percent:
    8.25
The bond sale price is $5104.37
```

Let's look at the sscanf() statement:

```
sscanf(start_date, "%2d%*c%2d%*c%2d", &start_month, &start_day, &start_year);
```

The call takes the string stored at start_date, "06/15/93," and applies five conversion specifiers to it. The %2d specifier takes the first two characters of the string, converts them to an int, and stores the resulting value in start_month. Remember, for scanf() a digit modifier means that the function stops at the *earlier* of encountering whitespace or reading in the specified number of characters. The %*c specifier causes sscanf() to skip over the next character, the slash. The rest of the string is handled the same way.

Of course, we could have used scanf() in the first place, instead of inputting the string with gets() and then converting with sscanf():

```
printf("Last interest payment date:\n%s", format);
scanf(start_date, "%2d%*c%2d%*c%2d", &start_month,
    &start_day, &start_year);
```

However, in a real-world application, you probably would have read in the date with a fancier screen-reading function (such as we create in Appendix C) rather than the cruder scanf() or gets() functions. You would then have had the date in a string for sscanf() to work its magic on.

9.10.2   The scanf() Function's Input Stream Treatment

One thing to note about sscanf(): unlike scanf() or fscanf(), the sscanf() function does not keep track of what it has been read in by prior calls to sscanf(). Thus

```
int one, two, three;
char *ptr = "1  2  3";
sscanf(ptr, "%d%d%d", &one, &two, &three);
```

would correctly read in all three values, whereas the following three separate calls to sscanf()

```
sscanf(ptr, "%d", &one);
sscanf(ptr, "%d", &two);
sscanf(ptr, "%d", &three);
```

would read in the value 1 into all three variables. There is no concept of "string stream" for sscanf(). The second call here to sscanf() starts at ptr, not at the address in ptr where the first call left off.

9.11   STRING-NUMBER CONVERSION

Functions that convert numerical strings to numerical values are important in business-world applications, particularly in accounting work.

9.11.1   The `atoi()`, `atol()`, and `atof()` Functions

The `atoi()`, `atol()`, and `atof()` functions allow you to take a string representing a numerical value and assign the corresponding numerical value to an `int`, `long`, or `float`, respectively:

```
int days;
long miles;
float salary;
char *ptr = "90340000";
char comp[10] = "320.45";
days = atoi("30"); /* literal string */
miles = atol(ptr); /* pointer */
salary = atof(comp); /* array name */
```

The first inappropriate character ends the conversion:

```
int num;
char string[10] = "10AZ";
printf("%d\n", num = atoi(string) + 7);
```

The output:

```
17
```

The `atoi()`, `atol()`, and `atof()` functions will skip over leading tabs, spaces, and other whitespace (as defined by `isspace()`, discussed below). They will also recognize a leading sign (including where the leading sign follows leading whitespace, but not vice versa):

```
printf("%.2f\n", atof("\t17.3") * atof("   -2.52"));
```

The output:

```
-43.60
```

As you might expect, the `atof()` function also recognizes the decimal point and the characters appropriate for exponential notation: the upper or lowercase 'e' and a sign for the integer exponent. The character recognition rules differ slightly from Standard C's normal floating point syntax: no decimal point is required (omission of a decimal point will generally, but not always, slip by without disastrous consequences in assigning whole-number constants to floating point variables), and no suffix (`f`, `F`, `l`, or `L`) is recognized by `atof()`. Nor are any of the suffixes `L`, `l`, `U`, or `u` or any combination recognized by `atoi()` or `atol()`.

The functions return zero if no appropriate characters are encountered or if there is any other error.

These three functions have a simple format. However, they have several shortcomings. Most important, if they are unable to convert the input string, their behavior is undefined. Furthermore, neither the `atoi()` nor `atol()` function recognizes integer strings written in octal or hexadecimal notation. Thus,

```
printf("%d\n", atoi("0x10"));
```

will print 0, not 16. The function would halt at the x. Nor will they work on other base (though, possibly apart from binary, the occasions you will have for using a base other than decimal, octal, or hexadecimal are few).

9.11.2   The `strtod()`, `strtol()`, and `strtoul()` Functions

The `strtod()`, `strtol()`, and `strtoul()` functions allow you to take a string representing a numerical value and assign the corresponding numerical value to a `double`, `long`, or `unsigned long`, respectively. The prototype for these functions is found in `stdlib.h`. Their syntax is more complex:

```
double strtod(const char *number_string,
   char **stop); /* converts string to a double */
```

```
long strtol(const char *number_string,
   char **stop, int base); /* converts string to a long */

unsigned long strtoul(const char *number_string,
   char **stop, int base); /* converts a string to an unsigned long */
```

The base argument is 10, 8, or 16, for decimal, octal, or hexadecimal respectively. The stop argument is a pointer to a character in string where the conversion stopped during the function call (which would be the terminating NULL if no inappropriate characters are encountered in the string).

The strtol() and strtoul() functions work with any base from 2 through 36 (past 36, we run out of letters to represent high numerical values in a digit). The following

```
printf("%ld %ld", strtol("01111111", &end, 2), strtol("10J", &end, 20));
```

prints

```
127 419
```

These functions recognize all the characters the atoi(), atol(), and atof() functions respectively do. In addition, the strtol() and strtoul() functions recognize characters appropriate to the base specified. For example, with a base of 16, the characters a to f and A to F are recognized. As a special case, if the base is 16 (hexadecimal), the number may begin with 0x or 0X, which are recognized and then ignored.

If you use a base of zero, the number will be read as hexadecimal with 0x or 0X prefix, octal with a 0 prefix, or decimal if neither. Therefore, if you are reading in a series of number strings representing variously decimal, octal, and hex values, and they are in the normal C format, you are best off using a zero base.

If no conversion is possible because of inappropriate or no characters, the functions return zero. Since they stop at the very beginning of number_string in such cases, stop is set to number_string. If the converted number would cause overflow, strtod() returns HUGE_VAL (the macro defined in errno.h and math.h as the largest representable floating point value) with the appropriate sign; strtol() returns LONG_MAX or LONG_MIN; and strtoul() returns ULONG_MAX or ULONG_MIN. In all cases of inability to convert, errno is set to ERANGE. (See Chapter 16 for a discussion of errno and ERANGE.)

The strtol.c program demonstrates strtol().

 **Listing 9.13 strtol.c**

```
/* strtol.c */

   /* illustrate strtol (string to long) conversion function for hex
      and octal numbers, and with numerical strings containing commas */

   #include <stdio.h>
   #include <stdlib.h>

   long strtol_with_commas(char *str);

   int main(void)
   {
      int num;
      char *stop;
      char *string = "037790";

      printf("%d\n", (int)strtol("0xFF", &stop, 16)); /* hex example */
      printf("%d\n", (int)strtol("0377", &stop, 8)); /* octal example */

      /* stop at nonoctal digit "9" */

      num = (int)strtol("03779", &stop, 8);
      printf("conversion of string %s to num %d stopped at %s\n", string, num, stop);
```

```
        printf("%ld ", strtol_with_commas("123,456,789"));
        printf("%ld ", strtol_with_commas("56,789"));
        printf("%ld ", strtol_with_commas("89"));
        printf("%ld\n", strtol_with_commas("2,123,456,789"));
    }

    /* convert number string with commas to numerical value */

    long strtol_with_commas(char *str)
    {
        long num[4];
        long total = 0L;
        long factor = 1L;
        int i = 0;
        char *local_stop;

        /* keep on until whole number is converted
           (stop points to NULL) */
        do
        {
            num[i++] = strtol(str, &local_stop, 10);


            /* stop will have stopped at comma: move str to digit past comma */
            str = local_stop + 1;
        }
        while(*local_stop);

        /* multiply last element by 1, 2nd to last by 1000, 3rd to last by million */
        while(--i > -1)
        {
            total += num[i] * factor;
            factor *= 1000L;
        }

        return total;
    }
```

The output:

```
255
255
conversion of string 037790 to num 255 stopped at 9
123456789 56789 89 2123456789
```

Note that we pass &stop to the function for the pointer-to-pointer to char argument, stop being declared as a pointer to char.

The stopping point feature of strtod(), strtol(), and strtoul() allows you to handle the rest of the string however you want. In strtol.c, we used this behavior to create a function that converts a string containing commas to a numerical value. In strtol_with_commas(), we loop through the string piece by piece, calling strtol() each iteration. The strtol() function will stop at each comma. At each stopping point, we reset our pointer to the digit after the comma and store what we successfully read into an array, num.

After we've read the string entirely (at which point stop would point to the NULL and the while loop would halt), we multiply each element of num by an appropriate factor. For example, with the string "123,456,789," i would be 3 at the end of the first while loop. We start out the next loop by decrementing i to 2. This would be the index number of the last element of num with a value. This we multiply by 1. The second element of num, containing the thousands digits, gets multiplied by 1000, and the first element, num[0], containing the millions digits first read in, gets multiplied by 1,000,000.

9.11.3   Commas in String-Number Conversions

The `ato_()` and `strto_()` functions stop at a comma. So

```
printf("%d\n", atoi("35,535"));
```

will print

```
35
```

If you want to use one of these functions to convert a string containing commas to a number, you first have to remove the commas, as we do in `no_comma.c`, below. As you will see, this is simpler than the function we created in `strtol.c`.

 **Listing** **9.14 no_comma.c**

```c
/* no_comma.c */

/* remove commas in negative/positive integer or floating point number string */

#include <stdio.h>
#include <stdlib.h> /* atof */

char *comma_out(char *money_str);

int main(void)
{
   puts(comma_out("123,456,789"));
   puts(comma_out("12,345,678.90"));
   puts(comma_out("-123,456,789"));
   puts(comma_out("-12,345,678.90"));

   printf("%.2f\n", atof(comma_out("-12,345,678.90")) - 1.);
}

char *comma_out(char *comma_str)
{
   /* remove commas from number string & return comma-less string */
   char i = 0;
   static char plain_str[22]; /* static because is returned */

   /*   set ptr to string & go from 1st to last char, copying into plain_str */
   while(*comma_str)
   {
      /* only copy the pointed to character if it's not a comma */
      if (*comma_str != ',')
         plain_str[i++] = *comma_str;
      comma_str++;
   }
   plain_str[i] = 0; /* // close off the copy string */
   return plain_str;
}
```

9.12   NUMBER-STRING CONVERSION

There are no Standard C facilities specifically designed for converting numerical values to strings. For this purpose, use `sprintf()`:

```
sprintf(num_str, "%d", num);
```

The `sprintf()` function offers the added flexibility of allowing you to incorporate the converted number into a text string:

```
sprintf(num_str, "There are %d beans in this jar\n", num);
```

9.12.1 Commas in Number-String Conversions

There is no standard C function that inserts commas in appropriate spots as it converts from a numerical value to a string. You have to create your own function to insert commas, as we do in comma_in.c.

 **Listing 9.15 comma_in.c**

```
/* comma_in.c */

/* insert commas in negative/positive integer or floating pt # string */

#include <stdio.h>
#include <string.h> /* strchr, memset */

char *comma_in(char *num_str);

int main(void)
{
    char temp[12];

    puts(comma_in("123456789      "));
    puts(comma_in("      12345678.90"));
    puts(comma_in("-12345678"));
    puts(comma_in("-123456789"));
    puts(comma_in("-12345678.90"));
    return 0;
}

char *comma_in(char *num_str)
{
    /* add commas to neg or pos integer or floating point number string */
    int position = 18;
    int digits = 0; /* digit counter (at 3, insert comma) */
    int checking_trailing_spaces = 1;
    char *ptr;
    static char comma_string[22]; /* static because is returned */

    /* point to NULL in num_str */
    ptr = strchr(num_str, 0);

    /* create string with 19 blank spaces */
    memset(comma_string, ' ', sizeof(comma_string));
    comma_string[19] = 0;

    /* move ptr backward from last digit of num_str until get to 1st digit */
    while(--ptr >= num_str)
    {
        /* skip over trailing spaces & stop at first leading space */

        if (*ptr == ' ')
        {
            if(checking_trailing_spaces)
                continue;
            else /* stop at leading space */
                break;
        }

        /* to be able to get to this point, must be no more trailing spaces */
        checking_trailing_spaces = 0;

        /*
            place digit in num_str that ptr points to, in
            comma_string, starting at end of comma_string
        */
```

```
    comma_string[position--] = *ptr;

    /* keep track of # of digits so far, for purposes of comma insertion */
    digits++;

    /* if we get to the decimal point, reset the digits counter */
    if (*ptr == '.')
        digits = 0;

    /* when we get to 3 digits, insert comma into comma_string */

    else if (!(digits % 3)
    /* don't do this if we're on the left-most digit */
        && ptr > num_str
    /* or if the next digit is a minus sign */
        && *(ptr - 1) != '-')
        comma_string[position--] = ',';
    }

    return comma_string + position + 1;
}
```

We set a pointer to the last digit in num_str and work our way digit by digit to the first digit, copying them into comma_string and inserting commas at appropriate places. We have placed 19 blank spaces in comma_string. (See the description in Section 9.15.3 of the memset() function used for that purpose.) We insert digits into comma_string starting at comma_string[18] and work backward.

Every time we have placed three digits into comma_string, we insert a comma. We don't do this, however, if we are now on the first digit in num_str, or if we are on the second digit and the first digit is a minus sign. Otherwise we would end up with a result such as ",123,456" if the number of digits is evenly divisible by 3.

Note that we have not accommodated exponential notation in this function, nor have we included any error-checking for nonnumeric input.

9.13   APPLICATION: NAME AND DATE SHUFFLING

You are given the following assignment. Write a program that will accept input from the keyboard for several records, representing employee names and hire dates, in the following format:

```
Conrad L. Veidt, III              92/12/23
Sidney John Greenstreet, Jr.   91/01/25
```

Just prior to the record input, the very first input would be a number of days, either negative or positive. For instance:

```
38
Conrad Veidt, III                 92/12/23
Sidney John Greenstreet, Jr.   91/01/25
```

That number of days would be added to or, if negative, subtracted from the input dates for each record and the output printed in format "last name/first name/original date/adjusted date," as in the following example (assuming an initial input of 3):

```
Veidt          Conrad L. III    92/12/23  92/12/26
Greenstreet    Sidney John Jr.  91/01/25  91/01/28
```

This might be an employee list with hire dates and a date 90 days later for the start of health insurance eligibility or 180 days later for a salary reevaluation.

The program should contain two functions, one for adding the input number of days and one for splitting up the name. The date function should take the following arguments:

Argument	Type	Description
in_date	pointer to char	The input date in yy/dd/mm format. Test for valid date (month <= 12, day < max number of days in month). If the date is not valid, the function is to return a NULL; otherwise it should return the adjusted date as a string.
days	int	number of days to add or subtract

The name function should take the name string as an argument and return a string in the corrected format. Make the function flexible enough to recognize suffixes such as II, III, Jr., and Sr. (assume the suffixes are separated from the name by a comma). Make sure the new strings will line up the first names when printed out. Convert the entire name to uppercase.

Test your program by subtracting 35 days and, in another run, adding 180 days, to the following input:

```
Conrad L. Veidt, III          92/01/01
Leni Riefenstahl              91/01/25
Lina Wertmuller               89/01/18
Toshiro Mifune                93/12/23
Dooley Wilson                 89/04/09
Mary Astor                    87/09/01
Maria Ouspenskaya             89/07/09
Ingrid Bergman                87/02/27
Luis Bunuel                   89/05/28
Fernando Rey                  88/04/31
```

Assume all years are non-leap years. You can use the C editor to create data files for the two programs. Read the files into the respective programs with redirection from a system prompt (for example, `namedate < namedate.dat > prn`, to print out, or `namedate < namedate.dat > namedate.out`, to send output to a file; see Chapter 16 regarding redirection).

Here's a program that handles this assignment:

 **Listing** 9.16 `namedate.c`

```c
/* namedate.c */

/*
   splits and reverses names and adds or subtracts designated
   number of days from input date

   no prompts here: intended to get input from a file with format

   [input contained in c:\qc2\input\pa1a.dat:
   namedate < c:\qc2\input\pa1a.dat > c:\qc2\output\pa1a.out]

   -35
   Conrad L. Veidt, III              92/01/01

*/

#include <stdio.h>
#include <string.h>
#include <ctype.h> /* toupper */

char *strUpr(char *string);
char *chg_date(char *in_date, int days),
   *split_name(char *name);
```

```
int main(void)
{
    int days;
    char record[81], in_date[10], name[35];

    scanf("%d%*c", &days);
    while(gets(record) && record[0])
    {
        /* copy last 8 characters (date) in line into in_date */
        strcpy(in_date, record + (strlen(record) - 8));

        /* copy all but last 8 characters into name */
        strncpy(name, record, strlen(record) - 8);

        /* close off name string */
        name[strlen(record) - 8] = 0;
        printf("\t%35s%10s%10s\n", split_name(strUpr(name)), in_date, chg_date(in_date, days));
    }
}

char *chg_date(char *in_date, int days)
{
    int year, month, day, days_into_yr;
    int i;
    int days_per[12] = {31, 28, 31, 30, 31, 30, 31, 31, 30, 31,
        30, 31};
    static char temp[10]; /* must be static since it gets returned */

    sscanf(in_date, "%2d/%2d/%2d", &year, &month, &day);
    if (month > 12 || day > days_per[month - 1])
        return NULL;

    /* determine days from Jan 1 to 1st of string month */
    for (i = 0, days_into_yr = 0; i < month - 1; i++)
        days_into_yr += days_per[i];

    /* add days in string month & passed # of days */
    days_into_yr += day + days;

    /* make adjustment if goes beyond this year */
    if (days_into_yr > 365)
    {
        days_into_yr -= 365;
        year++;
    }
    if (days_into_yr < 0)
    {
        days_into_yr += 365;
        year--;
    }

    /* starting from Jan 1, see what date the new # of days_into_yr gets us */

    /* first determine the month (1st of month) */
    for (i = 0; days_into_yr > days_per[i] && i < 11; i++)
        days_into_yr -= days_per[i];

    /* the loop stops when < a full month's worth remains */
    month = i + 1;

    /* what's left is the day of that month */
    day = days_into_yr;
```

```
  sprintf(temp, "%02d/%02d/%02d", year, month, day);
     return temp;
}

char *split_name(char *str)
{
     char *ptr = str + strlen(str) - 1; /* start at last letter in string */
     char suffix[5] = "";
     char last[15], first[15], temp[81];

     /* any trailing spaces/tabs? */
     while(*(--ptr) == ' ' || *ptr == '\t');

     /* if so, truncate them */
     *(ptr + 1) = 0;
     ptr = strchr(str, ',');
     if (ptr) /* suffix found */
     {
          /* include space character */
          strcpy(suffix, ptr + 1);

          /* close off last name */
          *ptr = 0;
     }

     /* point to space before last name */
     ptr = strrchr(str, ' ');
     strcpy(last, ptr + 1);

     /* close off first name */
     *ptr = 0;
     sprintf(first, "%s%s", str, suffix); /* if no suffix, this does nothing */
     sprintf(temp, "%-17s%-17s", last, first);
     return temp;
}

char *strUpr(char *string)
{
     char *ptr = string;
     while(*ptr)
     {
          *ptr = toupper(*ptr);
          ptr++;
     }
     return string;
}
```

Here's the output for the –35 run:

```
VEIDT         CONRAD L. III  92/01/01  91/11/27
RIEFENSTAHL   LENI           91/01/25  90/12/21
WERTMULLER    LINA           89/01/18  88/12/14
MIFUNE        TOSHIRO        93/12/23  93/11/18
WILSON        DOOLEY R.      89/04/09  89/03/05
ASTOR         MARY           87/09/01  87/07/28
OUSPENSKAYA   MARIA          89/07/09  89/06/04
BERGMAN       INGRID         87/02/27  87/01/23
BUNUEL        LUIS           89/05/28  89/04/23
REY           FERNANDO       88/04/31  (null)
```

We use scanf() to assign the first input to days. We use a %*c specifier after the %d to discard the newline. Otherwise, the next gets() call would get only the newline discarded by the scanf() call. Remember that both scanf() and gets() work from the same input stream.

Moving on to the records themselves, we first copy the last 8 characters into `in_date` and the balance into `name`. We accomplish the latter operation with `strncpy()`, adding a terminating `NULL` ourselves.

We use `sscanf()` to split the date string we pass to `chg_date()` into `year`, `month`, and `day` components. This is preferable to the more cumbersome

```
year = atoi(in_date);
month = atoi(in_date + 3);
day = atoi(in_date + 6);
```

To accomplish the job of adding or subtracting the specified number of days from `in_date`, we first see how many days into the year `in_date` represents. We loop through an array that contains the number of days in each month, keeping a running total of the number of days from January 1 as we go and stopping just before the month of `in_date`. We then add `day` to the total. For example, if `in_date` were 91/02/02, we would add 2 to 31, for a total of 33 days. We then add or subtract the specified number of days. We add 1 to the year and subtract 365 from the number of days if the total number of days exceeds 365; we subtract a year and add 365 days if the day total is less than 0.

To determine what date the adjusted number of days gives, we go through the opposite looping process, subtracting the number of days in each month as we go instead of adding. We write the completed date with `sprintf()` and return it.

On to the name. The string passed will contain spaces or tabs at the end. We cut those off by setting a pointer to the end of the string and looping backward through the string until we get to a non-whitespace character. At that point, we set the following character to `NULL`. We use the `strchr()` function to check for a comma in the string, the existence of which we assume to signal a suffix. If we find one, we copy it into `suffix`. Then we close off the last name portion of the string by assigning a `NULL` to the element containing the comma. We then perform a similar operation for the last name: we use `strrchr()` to point to the space before the last name, copy the remaining string from one element after that point to `last`, close off the first-name portion of the string, and copy the remaining string to `first`. We use `sprintf()` to align the first and last names and return the resulting string.

9.14   CHARACTER CLASSIFICATION CHECKING AND CASE CONVERSION

There are many instances in which you will want to test whether a character is a digit or a letter, uppercase or lowercase, and so on. For instance, if the user is entering a social security field in a record interactively, you might want to ignore and discard mistakenly entered characters that are not digits. Or, if you store text record fields in all uppercase, you might want to test whether a character is lowercase and if so convert it (or just call the `toupper()` function, discussed below, in all cases without testing).

The functions described in this section test and convert characters. They are designed to work no matter what character-encoding system is in use. All the functions may also be implemented as macros. If so, if portability is an issue, you should undefine them and use the function versions. (See Chapter 11 for a discussion of macros and undefining them.)

9.14.1   The `is_()` Functions

The following functions test whether the character representation of an integer value, according to the implementation's character encoding system, is of a certain classification specified by the function. If it is that type, the function returns a nonzero value as an `int`; otherwise it returns zero.

Table 9.1 provides the definitions of the categories these functions test for and the respective functions; Table 9.2 shows graphically how the characters are arranged in categories.

Each of the function names is in format `"is<category name>"`:

```
int isdigit (int character) /* digit? */
int isalpha (int character) /* letter? */
int isalnum (int character) /* digit or letter? */
int isxdigit (int character) /* hex digit/character? */
int islower (int character) /* lowercase letter? */
```

Table 9.1 *Character Classification Categories*

Category	Characters Included	Function
digit	decimal digits, '0' through '9'	isdigit
hexadecimal digit	a digit (as defined above) and 'a' through 'f' and 'A' through 'F'	isxdigit
lowercase letter	the letters 'a' through 'z'	islower
uppercase letter	the letters 'A' through 'Z'	isupper
letter	an uppercase or lowercase letter (as defined above)	isalpha
alphanumeric	a digit or letter (as defined above)	isalnum
whitespace	the space character, form feed ('\f'), newline ('\n'), carriage return ('\r'), horizontal tab ('\t') and vertical tab ('\v')	isspace
control	control characters (see discussion below)	iscntrl
printing	any character that is *not* a control character (as defined above), plus the space character	isprint
graphic	a printing character (as defined above) *other than* the space character (and hence a character visible on a display device)	isgraph
punctuation	any printing character *other than* one that is alphanumeric	ispunct

Table 9.2 *Character Classification Chart*

		hexidigit	alphanum	graphic	printable
'0' – 9'	digit				
'a' – 'f'	lowercase				
'A' – 'F'	uppercase				
'g' – 'z'	lowercase				
'G' – 'Z'	uppercase				
!"#$%&'()*+,-./:;<=>?@[\]^_`{¦}~	punctuation				
[space]	whitespace				
'\t', '\n', '\v', '\f', '\r'					
decimal 0–8, 14–31, 127					control

```
int isupper (int character) /* uppercase letter? */
int isspace (int character) /* whitespace character? */
int iscntrl (int character) /* control character? */
int ispunct (int character) /* nonalphanumeric printing character? */
int isprint (int character) /* printing/space character? */
int isgraph (int character) /* printing character other than space? */
```

The following function, which illustrates `isalpha()` and `isalnum()`, would test for a valid C identifier:

```
int is_valid_id(const char *id)
{
   if (isalpha(*id) == 0 && *id != '_')
      return 0; /* letter or underscore */
   while(*(++id) != 0)
```

```
    if (isalnum(*id) == 0 && *id != '_')
        return 0; /* ltr, digit or underscore */
  return 1;
}
```

If the standard 128-character ASCII character set is in use, the punctuation characters are the space character plus the characters shown in Figure 9.7.

 However, *for maximum portability across all locales, you can count on only the characters in Figure 9.8 being the punctuation characters:*

Likewise, if the 128-character ASCII character set is in use, the control characters are those with numeric values of 0 to 31 (up to, but not including, the space character), plus 127. However, *if your program will be run in a non–English-speaking contexts, it is best to count on only the following being control characters: the whitespace characters (other than the space character), plus* *the backspace (\b) and alert (\a).*

If the character-encoding system is neither ASCII nor EBCDIC, you cannot necessarily assume that if a character is not a control character, it is printable, and vice versa. With ASCII character encoding, uppercase letters come before lowercase, and each set is sequential. So you can assume the following prints "Works!" if ch is a lowercase letter:

```
if (islower(ch) && isupper(ch - ('a' - 'A')))
  puts("Works!");
```

But the test will not work for EBCDIC, where lowercase comes before uppercase and the letters are not perfectly sequential. (Despite breaks between I and J and R and S in both lowercase and uppercase in EBCDIC, all uppercase letters have values 64 greater than the corresponding lowercase characters—that is, by 2^6. In ASCII, lowercase letters are 32 greater than uppercase letters, or 2^5. Ignoring portability problems, these uniform differences leave open the possibility of bit manipulation for even faster conversion. (See Chapter 12.) Nor is the test guaranteed to work on any other character-encoding system.

However, in any character-encoding system, you can assume that the digits include at least 0 to 9 and that they are sequential. Therefore, for fast conversion without a lot of overhead, to convert from a digit letter ltr to its numerical equivalent num, or vice versa:

```
num = ltr - '0';
ltr = num + '0';
```

Or, on a numeric string:

```
int num;
char *string = "12345";
for (num = 0; isdigit(*string); string++)
  num = num * 10 + (*string - '0');
printf("num: %d\n", num);
```

Many compilers implement the is_() functions as macros. To use the function version with those compilers, you must undefine the macro version. (See Chapter 11 for an explanation of macros and un-define, and the relative advantages and disadvantages of function versus macros.)

Figure 9.7 *Punctuation Characters (ASCII Set)*

!	"	#	$	%	&	'	(	)	*	+	,	-	.	/	:
;	<	=	>	?	@	[	\	]	^	_	'	{			}	~

Figure 9.8 *Punctuation Characters (Portable Set)*

!	"	#		%	&	'	(	)	*	+	,	-	.	/	:
;	<	=	>	?		[	\	]	^						

Here's a simple program that will show you which characters are within the various classifications on your system. We undefine all the macro versions of the functions and declare an array of pointers to all the various is_() functions to allow us to use a simple for loop. (We undefine out of an abundance of caution. The undefinition should not be required. The is_() macros are parameterized macros. In the function pointer array below, we use nonparameterized versions. These will not be operated on by the preprocessor. See Chapter 11.)

 Listing 9.17 is.c

```c
/* is.c */

/* show which characters are included in is_ classifications */

#include <stdio.h>
#include <ctype.h>

#undef isdigit
#undef isxdigit
#undef islower
#undef isupper
#undef isalpha
#undef isalnum
#undef isspace
#undef iscntrl
#undef isprint
#undef isgraph
#undef ispunct

int main(void)
{
    int (*fptr[11]) (int) = {isdigit, isxdigit, islower, isupper,
        isalpha, isalnum, isspace, iscntrl, isprint, isgraph, ispunct};
    char *name[11] = {"digit", "xdigit", "lower", "upper", "alpha",
        "alnum", "space", "cntrl", "print", "graph", "punct"};
    int f, i, j;

    /* to split up printing into 2 tables */
    int boundary[3] = {0, 65, 128};

    for (j = 0; j < 2; j++) /* 2 tables: from 0-64 and 65-127 */
    {
        putchar('\n');
        for (f = 0; f < 11; f++) /* for each of 11 is_ functions */
        {
            printf("\n%6s ", name[f]);

            /* 0-64 & 65-127 */
            for (i = boundary[j]; i < boundary[j + 1]; i++)
            {
                if (fptr[f](i)) /* within the classification */
                {
                    if (isprint(i))
                    {
                        if(isspace(i))
                            putchar('s');
                        else putchar(i);
                    }

                    /* x if within class but nonprintable */
                    else putchar('x');
                }
```

```
              else putchar(' '); /* not within the classification */
          }
      }
   }
}
```

Here's the output on our system:

```
digit                                           0123456789
xdigit                                          0123456789
lower
upper
alpha
alnum                                           0123456789
space           xxxxx               s
cntrl xxxxxxxxxxxxxxxxxxxxxxxxxxxxxxxxx
print                             s!"#$%&'()*+,-./0123456789:;<=>?@
graph                              !"#$%&'()*+,-./0123456789:;<=>?@
punct                              !"#$%&'()*+,-./          :;<=>?@


digit
xdigit ABCDEF                     abcdef
lower                             abcdefghijklmnopqrstuvwxyz
upper ABCDEFGHIJKLMNOPQRSTUVWXYZ
alpha ABCDEFGHIJKLMNOPQRSTUVWXYZ  abcdefghijklmnopqrstuvwxyz
alnum ABCDEFGHIJKLMNOPQRSTUVWXYZ  abcdefghijklmnopqrstuvwxyz
space
cntrl                                                     x
print ABCDEFGHIJKLMNOPQRSTUVWXYZ[\]^_`abcdefghijklmnopqrstuvwxyz{¦}~
graph ABCDEFGHIJKLMNOPQRSTUVWXYZ[\]^_`abcdefghijklmnopqrstuvwxyz{¦}~
punct                           [\]^_`                    {¦}~
```

9.14.2   The `toupper()` and `tolower()` Functions

The following functions handle case conversion:

```
int tolower (int character) /* if character is an uppercase letter, returns
    character as a lowercase letter; otherwise, returns the argument unchanged */

int toupper (int character) /* if character is a lowercase letter, returns
    character as an uppercase letter; otherwise, returns the argument unchanged */
```

Prototypes for all these case-conversion functions, as well as the character classification testing functions just discussed, are found in `ctype.h`. A simple example:

```
puts("Type O to print old records\n"
    "N to print new records, or\n"
    "B to print both old and new records");
ch = toupper(getchar());
switch (ch)
{
    case 'O':
. . .
```

The `toupper()` and `tolower()` functions are also useful in constructing a function for converting an entire string to uppercase or lowercase. You will likely often have occasion to use such a function. Frequently, we will get input interactively and store the input in a database; or we will use input in a database search—for instance, the user types in a last name and first name and your program looks through a database and retrieves a record if it finds a match. The most common technique for avoiding a case mismatch would be to store all such data in all capital letters and convert any user input to all uppercase. The next simple program, `caps.c`, implements such a function.

 **Listing** **9.18 caps.c**

```
/* caps.c */

/* capitalize strings for reliable strcmp */

#include <stdio.h>
#include <string.h>
#include <ctype.h>

int main(void)
{
   char *caps(char *string);
   char six_of_one[81], half_a_dozen[81];
   printf("Input two strings, pressing [Enter] after each\n");
   gets(six_of_one);
   gets(half_a_dozen);
   if (!strcmp((caps(six_of_one)), caps(half_a_dozen)))
      printf("Strings match");
   else printf("Strings differ");
   return 0;
}

char *caps(char *string)
{
   char *ptr = string;
   while(*ptr)
   {
      *ptr = toupper(*ptr);
      ptr++;
   }
   return string;
}
```

We change each letter in the input string to a capital letter with caps(). Then we can safely use strcmp() for a comparison. Since we passed an address to caps(), and used the dereferencing operator inside the function to assign values, we actually alter the string. That being the case, it was not really necessary to have the function return the passed string's address. However, doing so allowed us to shorten the code. Otherwise, we would have had to do the following:

```
gets(six_of_one);
gets(half_a_dozen);
caps(six_of_one);
caps(half_a_dozen);
if (!strcmp(six_of_one, half_a_dozen))
   printf("Strings match");
```

At the other extreme, if you are really bent on writing compact, hard-to-read code:

```
if (!strcmp((caps(gets(six_of_one))), caps(gets(half_a_dozen))))
   printf("Strings match");
```

If you want a function that returns a pointer to an address of a converted string but that does *not* convert the passed string, you can do so this way.

 **Listing** **9.19 caps_ltd.c**

```
/* caps_ltd.c */

/* return capitalized string without changing passed string */

#include <stdio.h>
#include <string.h>
```

```
#include <ctype.h>

char *caps(const char *string);

int main(void)
{
   char name[] = "Margot Fontaine";
   puts(caps(name));
   printf("Name is still %s\n", name);
   return 0;
}

char *caps(const char *string)
{
   static char big_string[81];
   char *ptr = big_string;

   strcpy(big_string, string);
   while(*ptr)
   {
      *ptr = toupper(*ptr);
      ptr++;
   }
   return big_string;
}
```

The output:

```
MARGOT FONTAINE
name is still Margot Fontaine
```

Once again, we have made the string to be returned static to avoid having the returning pointer to char pointing to a memory area no longer reserved. Notice also that we have made the parameter const char *, to avoid inadvertently altering the passed string. You may have noted that many of the Standard C functions described in this chapter use the same device. (See Chapter 10 for a discussion of the type qualifier, const.)

Now for a case-*insensitive* string-comparison function.

 **Listing 9.20 insense.c**

```
/* insense.c */

/* case-insensitive strcmp */

#include <stdio.h>
#include <ctype.h>

int main(void)
{
   char my_strcmp(char *s1, char *s2);
   char miney[81], moe[81];

   printf("\nInput two strings, pressing [Enter] after each\n");
   gets(miney);
   gets(moe);

   if (!my_strcmp(miney, moe))
      puts("Strings match");
   else puts("Strings differ");
}
```

```
char my_strcmp(char *s1, char *s2)
{
    while((*s1 == *s2 ¦¦ *s1 == toupper(*s2) ¦¦ *s1 == tolower(*s2)) && *s1)
    {
        s1++;
        s2++;
    }
    return *s1 - *s2; /* returns 0 if strings equal */
}
```

In this approach, we pass both strings. We do not alter them inside the function. Rather, we check character by character to see whether there is a match or would be a match if we made the character in s1 a capital or lowercase letter. We do this for each letter, stopping when we reach the end of s1. The

```
while(. . . && *s1)
    . . .
```

test at the end does the job of stopping at the end of s1 if there is a match all along the way. Otherwise, we stop at the first mismatch.

The first approach—that of converting all input strings to capital letters—is the more widely used approach for handling string comparisons. String comparisons are particularly important in searching databases for particular records. *The simplest approach in database programs is to convert user input to all uppercase before storing records in the database and to use all uppercase strings for queries.*

9.15   BUFFER FUNCTIONS—MANIPULATING MEMORY BLOCKS WITH POINTERS TO void *(OPTIONAL)*

In addition to declaring a pointer to any recognized type (including types we create ourselves; see Chapter 13 regarding structure pointers), we can declare a pointer to void:

```
char buffer[81];
void *ptr = buffer;
```

A pointer to void is not limited to pointing to a specific type or data object. As we observed in Chapter 7 we cannot use the increment or decrement operator in connection with a pointer to void: the compiler does not know how many bytes to add. Pointer arithmetic on pointers to void is prohibited for the same reason.

What we *do* use pointers to void for is to serve as a generic, all-purpose way of pointing to the start of a memory area. We can then carry out certain operations on that area without having to worry about what variable types have reserved the area. These reserved blocks of memory that we manipulate or use for temporary or indefinite storage are often referred to as *buffers.* For example, we can say that the following declaration establishes a 81-byte buffer:

```
char name[81];
```

Many of the Standard C functions that manipulate buffers employ pointers to void to point to these buffers. There are several functions designed to allow us to copy bytes from one buffer to another or to set a designated number of bytes in a buffer all to the same designated value. (Actually, though we will nearly always use these functions to perform whatever it is they perform on reserved memory blocks, we could theoretically pass the functions any address, whether that address marks the beginning of a reserved block of memory or not. Although such an operation would likely work, technically under Standard C the results are undefined.) The prototypes for the functions are found in string.h.

These functions—memchr(), memcmp(), memset(), memcpy(), memmove(), and movedata()—do no checking for a terminating NULL character. Consequently, they work faster than their str country cousins.

Apart from better performance, these functions are also useful in cases where you are comparing, checking, or manipulating arrays or other data objects where storing is not done on a string basis. For instance, some of the commercial databases store fields in NULL-padded arrays and send them in that fashion to a file (and read them back the same way). To compare one field to another, it may not be sufficient to deal with the string portion only.

Many of these functions look for or copy or compare an int value as one of their arguments. However, Standard C requires that these be converted to unsigned char inside the function itself. We are looking for, copying, comparing, or setting a byte at a time in these functions with unsigned char values—not two or more bytes at a time with int values.

9.15.1   Searching Buffer for a Character: memchr()

The memchr() function performs the same task as strchr(), discussed earlier in the chapter, but searches a specified number of bytes from the passed address instead of stopping at a NULL character:

```
void *memchr(const void *buffer, int character, size_t num_bytes); /*
    same as strchr, but searches specified # of bytes instead of stopping at NULL */
```

Both character and num_bytes are interpreted as unsigned char for the purpose of this search.

 As with strchr(), *the* memchr() *function returns* NULL *if there is no match, so be sure to test the return value before using it to access and attempt to place values in memory areas. Also, since the return type is* void*, *you can assign the value to a* char *pointer, but you must type cast before using the pointer to access pointed-to memory.*

```
char buffer[] = "aa\377WPCaa"; /* file fragment */
char *ptr;
if ((ptr = (char *)memchr(buffer, '\377', sizeof(buffer))) != 0)
{
    if (memcmp(ptr + 1, "WPC", strlen("WPC")) == 0)
        puts("WordPerfect graphic found"); /* should print */
}
```

And that brings us to our next function, memcmp().

9.15.2   The memcmp() Function—Comparing Values of Memory Blocks

```
int memcmp(const void *buffer1, const void *buffer2, size_t num_bytes);
    /* same as strcmp, except comparison for specified # of bytes rather
       than until NULL */
```

The memcmp() function begins at two starting addresses passed to it and compares byte by byte for a designated number of bytes. As with strcmp(), the function stops as soon as it finds a mismatch and returns the difference between the value of the two bytes (the first minus the second). If the buffers are the same, the call returns 0. Unlike strcmp(), memcmp() does not stop simply because it encounters a 0 byte.

Because strcmp() stops only at a NULL, that function is not suitable for comparing portions of two strings. If you want to halt comparison at the sooner of a NULL or a specified number of characters, use strncmp(). If you do not want comparison to stop at a NULL, use the memcmp() function instead.

The memcmp() prototype indicates that the two address arguments are pointers to void. That means that the values at the pointed-to locations may be of any type—char, int, long, or floating point.

In the chapter on arrays, Chapter 6, we noted that you cannot make a simple en masse comparison of two arrays with the relational operators.

```
int num[] = {1, 2, 3, 4, 5}, val[] = {1, 2, 3, 4, 5};
printf("Arrays are %s\n", num == val ? "equal" : "not equal"); /* invalid! */
```

You can make such comparisons with memcmp():

```
printf("Arrays are %s\n", !memcmp(num, val, sizeof(num)) ? "equal" : "not equal");
```

Since both num and val, being array names, are pointers to the first elements of the arrays, there is no need to use the & operator.

You could even use `memcmp()` to compare arrays consisting of different types. Be careful here, however. Because of the different storage and interpretation methods for integer and floating point numbers (see Chapter 12), the following sort of comparison will not give meaningful results:

```
long num = 5L;
float val = 5.;
printf("%d\n", memcmp(&num, &val, sizeof(long)));
```

Likewise, `memcmp()` would seem to be the ticket to compare variables of two identically composed but different structure types. However, the contents of any padding bytes use for alignment purposes (see Chapter 13) are indeterminate and may pose problems for such a comparison. The same potential difficulty would lie with unions.

9.15.3 The `memset()` Function—Setting Memory Blocks to a Uniform Value

The `memset()` function takes a designated number of bytes, starting at a specified address, and sets them each to a specified byte value. The prototype is this:

```
void *memset(void *buffer, int value, size_t num_bytes);
/* set each byte in block of memory to same specified value */
```

The fact that the first argument is a pointer to `void` means that you can pass a pointer to any type. The `memset()` function returns a pointer to the address passed to it.

A common application for `memset()` is zeroing out an entire array:

```
char name[20] = "Pablo Casals";
puts(name);
memset(name, 0, sizeof(name));
```

One instance where `memset()` is useful is a database function that compares a user-inputted string with a series of bytes stored in memory to locate and retrieve a record based on a key field, and doing so byte by byte instead of using a string-handling function (which stops at the first NULL character). When you create a new record, you would zero out the buffer whose starting address is passed to a database record-creation function prior to first copying the user-inputted data to that buffer and then passing the buffer to the database function. You would again do the same just prior to retrieving the record. The user would request a record by inputting a key field. That data would be copied into a zeroed-out buffer. That buffer's data would be passed to the database record-retrieval function for comparison with an index of the key field.

9.15.4 The `memmove()`, `movedata()`, and `memcpy()` Functions—Copying Memory Blocks

The `memmove()` function allows us to copy the values of the bytes in one location to another location:

```
void *memmove(void *destination, const void *source, size_t num_bytes);
    /* copy byte values from one memory location to another */
```

As with `memset()`, the addresses passed can hold any type. Thus, you could use `memmove()` to circumvent the rule that you cannot copy the elements of an array en masse to another array:

```
float val[4] = {2343.33, -34343., 399.25, 1234.56};
float copy[4];
memmove(copy, val, sizeof(val));
for (i = 0; i < 4; i++)
   printf("copy[%d]: %.2f  ", i, copy[i]);
```

Output:

```
copy[0]: 2343.33  copy[1]: -34343.00  copy[2]: 399.25  copy[4]: 1234.56
```

The `memmove()` function returns the address of the start of the destination buffer.

We can use `memmove()` to help us in a function designed to cut out leading and trailing spaces in a string and return a pointer to the truncated string. This is often necessary in cases where we are reading a string representing a field of a record from a specific location on the screen (see Appendix C). For more pedestrian user input utilizing scanf() or gets(), this function would deal with the user's mistakenly enclosing the input in double quotes.

 **Listing** **9.21 truncate.c**

```c
/* truncate.c */

/* cut out leading & trailing spaces & double quotes in string
   and return pointer to the truncated string */

#include <stdio.h>
#include <stdarg.h>
#include <string.h>

char *truncate(char *string);

int main(void)
{
    puts(truncate("  \"  John Doe   \"  "));
}


/* +-------------------------------------------------------------------+
   +  TRUNCATE
   +
   +  Cuts out leading and trailing spaces in string and returns a
   +  pointer to the truncated string.
   +
   +  Does not actually change the passed string. The passed string
   +  gets copied to another location and the other location gets
   +  returned.
   +
   +  Argument:
   +
   +  - string: the string to be truncated
   +
   +-------------------------------------------------------------------+
*/
char *truncate(char *string)
{
    int start = 0, /* number of first nonspace character in string */
        end = strlen(string) - 1; /* number of last nonspace char */

    char *ptr;

    static char short_string[81]; /* copy buffer */

    /* blank out copy buffer */
    memset(short_string, 0, sizeof(short_string));

    /* set pointer to start of passed string */
    ptr = string;

    /* move pointer to first letter after last leading space */
    while(*ptr == ' ' || *ptr == '"')
    {
        /* record # of that spot in start */
        start++;
        /* at the last space, this will point us to the next letter */
        ptr++;
    }
```

```
    /* point to last character in string, including trailing spaces */
    ptr = string + end;

    /* move pointer to letter before first trailing space */
    while(*ptr == ' ' || *ptr == '"')
    {
        /* record # of that spot in end (end starts at last character in string) */
        end--;

        /* at the last space, this will point us to the preceding ltr */
        ptr--;
    }

    /*
        copy from first nonspace character to copy buffer

        end - start + 1 gives us # of nonspace characters in string

        end >= start test lets us ignore case where a blank string was passed in.
    */
    if (end >= start)
        memmove(short_string, string + start, end - start + 1);

    return short_string;
}
```

We use a pointer to locate the start and end of the non-whitespace/quotation mark string. Then we use memmove() to extract the target string and place it gently into a separate buffer.

The memcpy() function performs the same job as memmove(). However, memmove() is guaranteed to work where the source and destination buffers overlap; with memcpy(), there is no such guarantee. Therefore, it is always safer to use memmove(). The memcpy() function has a simpler syntax, works somewhat more quickly, and makes for a smaller executable code than memmove(), however. If you are certain the destination and source buffers do not overlap, use memcpy(); otherwise use memmove():

```
void *memcpy(void *destination, const void *source, size_t num_bytes);
    /* same as memmove, except no overlapping buffers allowed */
```

When we discuss video memory in DOS applications in the appendixes, we will use movedata(). This is *not* a Standard C function. The memmove() function is used in the normal case where the two buffers are in the same DOS memory segment (see Appendix B). If they are not, we will use movedata() instead:

```
void movedata(unsigned source_segment, unsigned source_offset,
    unsigned destination_segment, unsigned destination_offset, size_t num_bytes);
```

Note that the source comes first, just the opposite of memmove(). Since the most common use of movedata() involves video memory, located in a different memory segment from our program data, and since we have not yet learned about memory segments, we will defer discussion of the movedata() function until Appendix B.

9.16   APPLICATION: ACE BILLING PROGRAM

In our latest refinement to the ACE Billing system program, we make heavy use of the scanf() function to parse input.

9.16.1   Input

Same input data as for acech06.exe in Chapter 6.

Listing **9.22 acech09.c**

```
/*
+----------------------------------------------------------------+
+  Program Name: acech09.c
+  Author(s): Austell-Wolfson and Otieno
+     Date: 12/10/2000
+  Purpose:
+    This program processes a file of ACE Club member records and
+    computes and prints the total amounts for all club members.
+
+  Process:
+    This program prints the prescribed headings for the report and
+    processes each record by:
+    computing the individual member bill, equal to the sum of
+    member bill, membership fee, and activity fee, minus the
+    discount amount (if any). Members are charged a special
+    membership fee of $2500 if they are special
+    members, indicated by a Y in the membership flag field. The
+    activity fees are based on the number of activities each
+    member requests. The more activities they request, the more
+    they are charged. A discount amount is applied if the member
+    has an average charge of over $8000 per bill.
+----------------------------------------------------------------+
*/
#include <stdio.h>
#include <string.h>
#include <stdlib.h>

/* see caveat re structures in acech08.c */
void initialization(char * specialMembershipFlag, char customerName[100][16],
   char customerInitials[100][3], float * membershipFee, float * activityFee,
   float * discountAmount, float * chargeAmount, float * totalIndividualBill,
   float * aceClubTotals, float * charges,int * discount, int * averageCharges,
   int * numberOfCharges);

void processMemberRecord(char * inputBuffer, char * specialMembershipFlag,
   char customerName[100][16], char customerInitials[100][3], float * membershipFee,
   float * activityFee, float * discountAmount, float * totalIndividualBill,
   float * aceClubTotals, float * charges, int * discount, int * averageCharges,
   int * numberOfCharges, int * clubMember);

void termination(void);

void printGrandTotals(float * membershipFee, float * activityFee, float * discountAmount,
   float * totalIndividualBill, float * charges, int * numberOfCharges);

void initializeVariables(char * specialMembershipFlag, char customerName[100][16],
   char customerInitials[100][3], float * membershipFee, float * activityFee,
   float * discountAmount, float * chargeAmount, float * totalIndividualBill,
   float * aceClubTotals, float * charges,int * discount, int * averageCharges,
   int * numberOfCharges);

void printHeadings(void);

void computeIndividualBill(char * specialMembershipFlag, float * membershipFee,
   float * activityFee, float * discountAmount, float * totalIndividualBill,
   float * aceClubTotals, float * charges, int * discount, int * averageCharges,
   int * numberOfCharges, int * clubMember);

void writeDetailLine(char customerName[100][16], char customerInitials[100][3],
   float * membershipFee, float * activityFee, float * discountAmount,
   float * totalIndividualBill, float * charges, int * numberOfCharges, int * clubMember);
```

```
void determineSpecialFee(char * specialMembershipFlag, float * membershipFee,
   int * clubMember);

void determineActivityFee(float * activityFee, int * numberOfCharges, int * clubMember);

void determineDiscountAmt(int * averageCharges, int * discount, float * discountAmount,
   int * clubMember);

void sortByClubMemberNames(char * specialMembershipFlag, char customerName[100][16],
   char customerInitials[100][3], float * membershipFee, float * activityFee,
   float * discountAmount, float * chargeAmount, float * totalIndividualBill,
   float * aceClubTotals, float * charges, int * discount, int * averageCharges,
   int * numberOfCharges, int * clubMember);

void printSortedReport(char customerName[100][16], char customerInitials[100][3],
   float * membershipFee, float * activityFee, float * discountAmount,
   float * totalIndividualBill, float * charges, int * numberOfCharges, int * clubMember);

void swapValues(char * specialMembershipFlag, char customerName[100][16],
   char customerInitials[100][3], float * membershipFee, float * activityFee,
   float * discountAmount, float * chargeAmount, float * totalIndividualBill,
   float * aceClubTotals, float * charges, int * discount, int * averageCharges,
   int * numberOfCharges, int currentPos);

int main(void)
{
   char   inputBuffer[1024]; /* Holds an incoming input record*/
   char   specialMembershipFlag[100];
   char   customerName[100][16];
   char   customerInitials[100][3];
   float  membershipFee[100];
   float  activityFee[100];
   float  discountAmount[100];
   float  chargeAmount[100];
   float  totalIndividualBill[100];
   float  aceClubTotals[100];
   float  charges[100];
   int    discount[100];
   int    averageCharges[100];
   int    numberOfCharges[100];
   int    clubMember = 0; /* Holds the count of all club members.
                             It is also used to index the array of club members; therefore
                             its value starts at 0. */

   initialization(specialMembershipFlag, customerName, customerInitials, membershipFee,
      activityFee, discountAmount, chargeAmount, totalIndividualBill, aceClubTotals, charges,
      discount, averageCharges, numberOfCharges);

   while (gets(inputBuffer) != NULL)
   {
      processMemberRecord(inputBuffer, specialMembershipFlag, customerName, customerInitials,
         membershipFee, activityFee, discountAmount, totalIndividualBill, aceClubTotals,
         charges, discount, averageCharges, numberOfCharges, &clubMember);
   }
   printGrandTotals(membershipFee, activityFee, discountAmount, totalIndividualBill,
      charges, numberOfCharges);

   sortByClubMemberNames(specialMembershipFlag, customerName, customerInitials, membershipFee,
      activityFee, discountAmount, chargeAmount, totalIndividualBill, aceClubTotals, charges,
      discount, averageCharges, numberOfCharges, &clubMember);

   printSortedReport(customerName, customerInitials, membershipFee, activityFee,
      discountAmount, totalIndividualBill, charges, numberOfCharges, &clubMember);
```

```
      printGrandTotals(membershipFee, activityFee, discountAmount, totalIndividualBill, charges,
         numberOfCharges);

      termination();
      return 0;
}

void initialization(char * specialMembershipFlag, char customerName[][16],
   char customerInitials[][3], float * membershipFee, float * activityFee,
   float * discountAmount, float * chargeAmount, float * totalIndividualBill,
   float * aceClubTotals, float * charges, int * discount, int * averageCharges,
   int * numberOfCharges)
{

   initializeVariables(specialMembershipFlag, customerName, customerInitials, membershipFee,
      activityFee, discountAmount, chargeAmount, totalIndividualBill, aceClubTotals,
      charges, discount, averageCharges, numberOfCharges);

   printHeadings();
   return;
}

void processMemberRecord(char * inputBuffer, char * specialMembershipFlag,
   char customerName[][16], char customerInitials[][3], float * membershipFee,
   float * activityFee, float * discountAmount, float * totalIndividualBill,
   float * aceClubTotals, float * charges, int * discount, int * averageCharges,
   int * numberOfCharges, int * clubMember)
{
   int status;

   /*
      +------------------------------------------------------------+
      + Parse the input record by extracting the fields of interest.
      + Read the rest of the data items/fields from the input data
      + stream. The input data stream is assumed to be a file of a
      + particular record layout. This file is read through the
      + mechanism that your operating system has provided to handle
      + standard input from a file instead of a keyboard.
      +------------------------------------------------------------+
   */
   status = sscanf(inputBuffer, "%15c%2c%2d%c%4d%4d", customerName[*clubMember],
      customerInitials[*clubMember], &numberOfCharges[*clubMember],
      &specialMembershipFlag[*clubMember], &discount[*clubMember],
      &averageCharges[*clubMember]);

   if (status != 6)
   {
      printf("There is a problem with the file format.\n");
      printf("The program is terminated midstream\n");
      exit(1);
   }

   computeIndividualBill(specialMembershipFlag, membershipFee, activityFee, discountAmount,
      totalIndividualBill, aceClubTotals, charges, discount, averageCharges, numberOfCharges,
      clubMember);

   writeDetailLine(customerName, customerInitials, membershipFee, activityFee, discountAmount,
      totalIndividualBill, charges, numberOfCharges, clubMember);
   return;
}

/* see comment in acech06.c re termination function */
void termination(void)
{
```

```
        /* not implemented */
}

void initializeVariables(char * specialMembershipFlag, char customerName[][16],
    char customerInitials[][3], float * membershipFee, float * activityFee,
    float * discountAmount, float * chargeAmount, float * totalIndividualBill,
    float * aceClubTotals, float * charges,int * discount, int * averageCharges,
    int * numberOfCharges)
{
    /*
      +-----------------------------------------------------------------+
      + void *memset (void *s, int c, size_t n);
      + memset sets the first n bytes of the array s to the character c.
      + in our case, we set the first 100 bytes to 0 or NULL or '\0' in
      + the case of characters, or 100 * sizeof(int), or
      + 100 * sizeof (float) to 0.
      +-----------------------------------------------------------------+
    */
    memset(specialMembershipFlag,'\0',100);
    memset(discount, 0, 100 * sizeof (int));
    memset(averageCharges, 0, 100 * sizeof (int));
    memset(membershipFee, 0, 100 * sizeof (float));
    memset(activityFee, 0, 100 * sizeof (float));
    memset(discountAmount, 0, 100 * sizeof (float));
    memset(chargeAmount, 0, 100 * sizeof (float));
    memset(numberOfCharges, 0, 100 * sizeof (int));
    memset(totalIndividualBill, 0, 100 * sizeof (float));
    memset(aceClubTotals, 0, 100 * sizeof (float));
    memset(charges, 0, 100 * sizeof (float));
    memset(customerName, 0, 100 * 16);
    memset(customerInitials, 0, 100 * 3);
}

void printHeadings(void)
{
    printf("┌─────────────────────────────────────────────────────────┐\n");
    printf("│                                                         │\n");
    printf("│   Program Name: ACECH09.EXE                   Page:  1  │\n");
    printf("│      Run Date: 12/10/2000          Ace Billing          │\n");
    printf("│                                                         │\n");
    printf("│                                                         │\n");
    printf("├─────────────────────────────────────────────────────────┤\n");
    printf("│                                                         │\n");
    printf("│ Customer Name  Charges     Bill   Mbr Fee   Act Fee   Disc  Total Bill │\n");
    printf("├─────────────────────────────────────────────────────────┤\n");
    printf("│                                                         │\n");
}

void computeIndividualBill(char * specialMembershipFlag, float * membershipFee,
    float * activityFee, float * discountAmount, float * totalIndividualBill,
    float * aceClubTotals, float * charges, int * discount, int * averageCharges,
    int * numberOfCharges, int * clubMember)
{
    charges[*clubMember] = 200 * numberOfCharges[*clubMember];
    charges[99] += charges[*clubMember];
    numberOfCharges[99] += numberOfCharges[*clubMember];
    determineSpecialFee(specialMembershipFlag, membershipFee, clubMember);
    determineActivityFee(activityFee, numberOfCharges, clubMember);
    determineDiscountAmt(averageCharges, discount, discountAmount, clubMember);

    totalIndividualBill[*clubMember] = charges[*clubMember] + membershipFee[*clubMember] +
        activityFee[*clubMember] - discountAmount[*clubMember];
    totalIndividualBill[99] += totalIndividualBill[*clubMember];
```

```c
      aceClubTotals[99] += totalIndividualBill[*clubMember];
}

void writeDetailLine(char customerName[][16], char customerInitials[][3],
    float * membershipFee, float * activityFee, float * discountAmount,
    float * totalIndividualBill, float * charges, int * numberOfCharges, int * clubMember)
{
    printf("| %15.15s  %s %2d  $%9.2f  $%8.2f  $%8.2f  $%5.f  $%9.2f",
        customerName[*clubMember], customerInitials[*clubMember], numberOfCharges[*clubMember],
        charges[*clubMember], membershipFee[*clubMember], activityFee[*clubMember],
        discountAmount[*clubMember], totalIndividualBill[*clubMember]); printf(" |\n");

    *clubMember = *clubMember + 1; /* Increase the number of club members */
}

void determineSpecialFee(char * specialMembershipFlag, float * membershipFee,
    int * clubMember)
{
    /* see comment to acech05.c re following construction */
    if ('Y' == specialMembershipFlag[*clubMember])
    {
        membershipFee[*clubMember] = 2500.0;
    }
    else
    {
        membershipFee[*clubMember] = 0.0;
    }

    membershipFee[99] += membershipFee[*clubMember];
}

void determineActivityFee(float * activityFee, int * numberOfCharges, int * clubMember)
{
    if (numberOfCharges[*clubMember] <= 6)
    {
        activityFee[*clubMember] = 250.0;
    }

    if ((numberOfCharges[*clubMember] > 6) && (numberOfCharges[*clubMember] <= 12))
    {
        activityFee[*clubMember] = 500.0;
    }

    if (numberOfCharges[*clubMember] > 12)
    {
        activityFee[*clubMember] = 750.0;
    }

    activityFee[99] += activityFee[*clubMember];
}

void determineDiscountAmt(int * averageCharges, int * discount, float * discountAmount,
    int * clubMember)
{
    if (averageCharges[*clubMember] > 8500)
    {
        discountAmount[*clubMember] = discount[*clubMember];
    }
    else
    {
        discountAmount[*clubMember] = 0;
    }
```

```
      discountAmount[99] += discountAmount[*clubMember];
}

void sortByClubMemberNames(char * specialMembershipFlag, char customerName[][16],
   char customerInitials[][3], float * membershipFee, float * activityFee,
   float * discountAmount, float * chargeAmount, float * totalIndividualBill,
   float * aceClubTotals, float * charges, int * discount, int * averageCharges,
   int * numberOfCharges, int * clubMember)
{
   int currentPos; /* Holds current array position being processed */
   int k; /* Loop index variable  */

   /* Determines whether to make more passes during the bubble sort algorithm */
   int morePasses = 1;
/*
   +--------------------------------------------------------------+
   +  Start the loop that makes as many passes through array of club
   +  member names as needed for the entire list to be sorted.
   +
   +--------------------------------------------------------------+
*/
   while (1 == morePasses)
   {
/*
   +--------------------------------------------------------------+
   +  Turn it off so that if the data is sorted, no
   +  passes will be necessary. If, however, there was
   +  a single swap, morePasses will be set to 1
   +  and the while loop repeats as it should.
   +
   +--------------------------------------------------------------+
*/
      morePasses = 0;
      for (k = 0; k < *clubMember - 1; k++)
      {
         if (strcmp(customerName[k], customerName[k + 1]) > 0)
         {
            currentPos = k;

            /* swap all the values in the parallel arrays.  */

            swapValues(specialMembershipFlag, customerName, customerInitials, membershipFee,
               activityFee, discountAmount, chargeAmount, totalIndividualBill, aceClubTotals,
               charges, discount, averageCharges, numberOfCharges, currentPos);
            morePasses = 1;
         }
      }   /*   end of for loop   */
   }   /*   end of while loop   */
}

void printSortedReport(char customerName[100][16], char customerInitials[100][3],
   float * membershipFee, float * activityFee, float * discountAmount,
   float * totalIndividualBill, float * charges, int * numberOfCharges, int * clubMember)
{
   int k; /* Loop index variable */

   /* print column headings for the sorted list of club members */
   printHeadings();

   for (k = 0; k < *clubMember; k++)
   {
      printf("| %15.15s  %s %2d  $%9.2f  $%8.2f  $%8.2f  $%5.f  $%9.2f", customerName[k],
```

```
            customerInitials[k], numberOfCharges[k], charges[k], membershipFee[k],
            activityFee[k], discountAmount[k], totalIndividualBill[k]);
        printf(" |\n");
    }
}

void swapValues (char * specialMembershipFlag, char customerName[][16],
    char customerInitials[][3], float * membershipFee, float * activityFee,
    float * discountAmount, float * chargeAmount, float * totalIndividualBill,
    float * aceClubTotals, float * charges, int * discount, int * averageCharges,
    int * numberOfCharges, int currentPos)
{

    /* see comment to acech06.c re larger than required array and number of swap slots used */
    int  tempPos;
    tempPos = 98;

    /* Swap the last name of club member */
    strcpy(customerName[tempPos], customerName[currentPos]);
    strcpy(customerName[currentPos], customerName[currentPos + 1]);
    strcpy(customerName[currentPos + 1], customerName[tempPos]);

    /* Swap the customer initials */
    strcpy(customerInitials[tempPos], customerInitials[currentPos]);
    strcpy(customerInitials[currentPos], customerInitials[currentPos + 1]);
    strcpy(customerInitials[currentPos + 1], customerInitials[tempPos]);

    /* swap the specialMembershipFlag */
    specialMembershipFlag[tempPos] = specialMembershipFlag[currentPos];
    specialMembershipFlag[currentPos] = specialMembershipFlag[currentPos + 1];
    specialMembershipFlag[currentPos + 1] = specialMembershipFlag[tempPos];

    /* swap the total membership fee */
    membershipFee[tempPos] = membershipFee[currentPos];
    membershipFee[currentPos] = membershipFee[currentPos + 1];
    membershipFee[currentPos + 1] = membershipFee[tempPos];

    /* swap the total activity fee */
    activityFee[tempPos] = activityFee[currentPos];
    activityFee[currentPos] = activityFee[currentPos + 1];
    activityFee[currentPos + 1] = activityFee[tempPos];

    /* swap the total discount amount */
    discountAmount[tempPos] = discountAmount[currentPos];
    discountAmount[currentPos] = discountAmount[currentPos + 1];
    discountAmount[currentPos + 1] = discountAmount[tempPos];

    /* swap the total charge amount */
    chargeAmount[tempPos] = chargeAmount[currentPos];
    chargeAmount[currentPos] = chargeAmount[currentPos + 1];
    chargeAmount[currentPos + 1] = chargeAmount[tempPos];

    /* swap the total individual bill */
    totalIndividualBill[tempPos] = totalIndividualBill[currentPos];
    totalIndividualBill[currentPos] = totalIndividualBill[currentPos + 1];
    totalIndividualBill[currentPos + 1] = totalIndividualBill[tempPos];

    /* swap the total ace club totals */
    aceClubTotals[tempPos] = aceClubTotals[currentPos];
    aceClubTotals[currentPos] = aceClubTotals[currentPos + 1];
    aceClubTotals[currentPos + 1] = aceClubTotals[tempPos];
    /* swap the total charges */
    charges[tempPos] = charges[currentPos];
```

```
          charges[currentPos] = charges[currentPos + 1];
          charges[currentPos + 1] = charges[tempPos];

          /* swap the total discount */
          discount[tempPos] = discount[currentPos];
          discount[currentPos] = discount[currentPos + 1];
          discount[currentPos + 1] = discount[tempPos];

          /* swap the total average charges */
          averageCharges[tempPos] = averageCharges[currentPos];
          averageCharges[currentPos] = averageCharges[currentPos + 1];
          averageCharges[currentPos + 1] = averageCharges[tempPos];

          /* swap the total number of charges bill */
          numberOfCharges[tempPos] = numberOfCharges[currentPos];
          numberOfCharges[currentPos] = numberOfCharges[currentPos + 1];
          numberOfCharges[currentPos + 1] = numberOfCharges[tempPos];
     }
     void printGrandTotals(float * membershipFee, float * activityFee,
          float * discountAmount, float * totalIndividualBill,
          float * charges, int * numberOfCharges)
     {
          printf("| %*s———————————————————————————————————|\n",
             19, " ");
          printf("| ACE Club Totals    %3d  $%9.2f  $%8.2f  $%8.2f  $%5.f"
             " $%9.2f |\n",
             numberOfCharges[99], charges[99], membershipFee[99],
             activityFee[99], discountAmount[99], totalIndividualBill[99]);
          printf("|_____|\n\n");
     }
```

9.16.2   Output

Same output report as for `acech06.exe` in Chapter 6.

Chapter Summary

1. Standard C's string-handling functions all work on the principle of doing something from a certain address in RAM until a terminating NULL is found.
2. You can use array names or literal strings in place of a `char` pointer in any of the string-handling functions.
3. The `gets()` function is used to get a string from standard input. It reads from standard input until it encounters a newline character, copies all characters up to but not including the newline and places them starting at the address passed to the function, adds a terminating NULL to make a string, and discards the newline.
4. If the call to `gets()` is successful, the function returns the address passed to it; otherwise, it returns NULL. Having `gets()` return a NULL on reaching the end of the file is not the same as what happens if the user presses ‚Enter‚ without having entered any characters.
5. The `gets()` function works from the same input stream as `getchar()` and `scanf()`. If there is nothing left to process in the input stream, calling any one of these functions causes the program to halt until the user enters data on the standard input device. All three functions are line-buffered.

6. If there is something left over in the input stream, any of these functions will process it without waiting for, or permitting, further user input.
7. There is no mechanism inherent in `gets()`, `strcpy()`, or `strcat()` for checking whether there is enough space starting at the address passed for the input to be stored there.
8. The `puts()` function takes a pointer to `char` as its argument. It prints the string that starts at that address to standard output character by character until it encounters a NULL character byte. The function adds a newline to the output string.
9. Unlike many of the other string-handling functions, `puts()` returns a positive integer number as an `int` in the event of a successful call.
10. The `strcpy()` function takes two `char` pointers as arguments. It places a copy of the second string beginning at the address pointed to by the first. The `strcpy()` function returns its first argument.
11. The `strcat()` function copies characters starting from the address passed as its second argument up to and including the first NULL character it finds in the second

string; it places them starting at the first NULL character after the address passed as the first argument.

12. The strcmp() function compares two strings, character by character, and returns zero if the strings are identical. If not, it stops at the first character that differs and returns a positive integer if the character in the second-string argument at that point comes lexicographically after the character in the first-string argument in the computer's encoding system, and negative if it comes before.

13. The strncpy(), strncat(), and strncmp() functions do essentially the same thing as strcpy(), strcat(), and strcmp(), but for only a specified number of characters in the second string.

14. If the string pointed to by strncpy()'s second argument is shorter than the number of characters specified, the function copies NULL characters to make up the difference. When less than all of the second string is copied to the first string, a terminating NULL is not added to close off the first string.

15. If the string pointed to by the second argument to strncat() is shorter than the number of characters specified, the extra characters are ignored. The strncat() function adds a NULL character.

16. The strchr() function returns the address of the first occurrence of a specified character in a string; strrchr() returns the address of the last occurrence. Each of these returns NULL instead, if the specified character is not found within the string. The search is case sensitive.

17. Searching for the NULL character with strchr() or strrchr() gives us a convenient method of setting a pointer to the last character in a string.

18. The strstr() function returns the starting address of a substring inside another string; if the substring is not found, the function returns NULL.

19. The strcspn() function locates the first occurrence in string1 of any character in string2. If strcspn() finds no match, it returns the position number of the terminating NULL in string1.

20. The strpbrk() function does the same job as strcspn(), except that it returns a pointer to the first matching character rather than its position number (or NULL if there is no match).

21. The strspn() function returns the zero-based position number of the first character in string1 that does *not* belong to the set of characters in string2. The function returns the length of string1 if all its characters are found within string2.

22. The strtok() function parses a string into substrings or tokens by placing NULL characters wherever in the string any of the delimiting characters in the second string argument appear. Completely parsing the string requires successive calls to strtok(). In the first call, the string and the delimiting string are passed as arguments. On each successive call, NULL is passed as the first argument and the delimiting string as the second argument.

23. The sprintf() function does the same job as printf(), except it writes starting at an address in memory instead of to the screen and adds a NULL character.

24. The sscanf() function does the same job as scanf(); it reads starting at an address in memory instead of from standard input.

25. Unlike scanf() or fscanf(), the sscanf() function does not keep track of what it has been read in by prior calls to sscanf().

26. The atoi(), atol(), and atof() functions take a string representing a numerical value and assign the corresponding numerical value to an int, long, or float, respectively.

27. The three functions skip over leading tabs, spaces, and other whitespace. They recognize a leading sign; the atof() function recognizes the decimal point and the characters appropriate for exponential notation. The first inappropriate character ends the conversion.

28. None of the functions recognize any type suffix. Neither the atoi() nor atol() functions recognize integer strings written in octal or hexadecimal notation.

29. The strtod(), strtol(), and strtoul() functions take a string representing a numerical value and assign the corresponding numerical value to a double, long, or unsigned long, respectively.

30. These functions recognize all the characters the atoi(), atol(), and atof() functions respectively do. In addition, the strtol() and strtoul() functions recognize characters appropriate to the base specified; they work with any base from 2 to 36.

31. The ato_() and strto_() functions stop at a comma. If you want to use one of these functions to convert a string containing commas to a number, you first have to remove the commas manually. There is no Standard C function that inserts commas in appropriate spots as it converts from a numerical value to a string. You have to create your own function to insert commas.

32. There are no Standard C facilities specifically designed for converting numerical values to strings. For this purpose, use sprintf().

33. The is_() functions test whether the character representation of an integer value, according to the implementation's character-encoding system, is of a certain classification specified by the function: a digit, a letter, a digit or letter, a hex digit, a lowercase letter, an uppercase letter, a whitespace character, a control character, or a printing character.

34. The tolower() function returns the lowercase version of an uppercase character; if the argument is not an uppercase character, it returns the argument unchanged. The toupper() function does the same for the opposite case.

35. In addition to declaring a pointer to any recognized type, we can declare a pointer to void. A pointer to void is not limited to pointing to a specific type of data object.

36. Many of the Standard C functions that manipulate buffers employ pointers to void to point to these buffers.

37. These buffer manipulation functions do no checking for a terminating NULL character.

38. The memchr() function performs the same task as strchr() but searches a specified number of bytes from the passed address instead of stopping at a NULL character.

39. The memcmp() function begins at two starting addresses passed to it and compares byte by byte for a designated number of bytes.

40. The memset() function takes a designated number of bytes, starting at a specified address, and sets them each to a specified byte value.

41. The `memmove()` function copies the values of the bytes in one location to another location.
42. The `memcpy()` function performs the same job as `mem‑move()`. However, `memmove()` is guaranteed to work where the source and destination buffers overlap; `memcpy()` comes with no such guarantee.

Review Questions

1. State the purpose of each of the following functions.
   a. `memchr()`
   b. `memcmp()`
   c. `memcpy()`
   d. `memmove()`
   e. `memset()`
   f. `strcspn()`
   g. `strpbrk()`
   h. `strrchr()`
   i. `strspn()`
   j. `strtok()`

2. Execute the following segment of code and show the results:

```
char source[30] = "Our first book has no /
errors";
char destination[35] = "actually 10 errors.";
memmove(destination +  16, source, 19);
printf("%s has a length of %d\n", destination,
   strlen(destination));
```

3. Execute the following segment of code and show the results:

```
char source[30] = "Our first book has no /
errors";
char destination[35] = "actually 10 errors."
memcpy(source +  4, source + 3, 10);
printf("%s has a length of %d\n", source,
   strlen(destination));
```

4. Execute the following segment of code and show the results:

```
int result;
char source[30] = "Our first book has no /
errors";
char destination[35] = "actually 10 errors."
result = memcmp(source, destination, 10);
printf("Result is %d\n", result);
```

5. Execute the following segment of code and show the results:

```
char source[30] = "Our first book has no /
errors";
char destination[35] = "actually ten errors."
result = strlen(destination);
printf("Result is %d, but the size is %d\n",
   result, sizeof (destination));
```

6. Execute the following segment of code and show the results:

```
char publicationDates[] = "The first date /
was 4/15/00 the second 5/15/00 and";
char scanset[] = "0123456789";
char * substring;

substring = strpbrk(publicationDates,
   scanset);
printf("%s\n", substring);
substring = strpbrk(substring + 8, scanset);
printf("%s\n", substring);
```

7. Execute the following segment of code and show the results:

```
char source[30] = "Our first book has no /
errors";
char destination[35] = "actually 10 errors."
char outputBuffer[128];
int messageLength;

messageLength = sprintf(outputBuffer, "%s",
   source);
messageLength += sprintf(outputBuffer +
   messageLength, " is %d bytes before %s",
   messageLength, destination);
printf("The entire message is %s.\n"
   " The entire message length is %d\n",
   outputBuffer, messageLength);
```

Programming Exercises

The specifications of the programming assignments were introduced in Chapter 1, at which time you were to

- think through the solution to these problems.
- identify the modules that, once implemented, will solve the problem.
- prepare a hierarchy chart of all the modules.
- prepare pseudocode/flowchart for each module in the hierarchy chart.
- write the program stubs the same way we did with the ACE Billing system application.

This chapter has added coverage of strings our C knowledge. We urge you to continue developing what you started in Chapter 1. If you have not started, we recommend that you start by applying the methodology presented in that chapter. We have helped you get started with some of the programming assignments by specifying only what can be done by this time.

Modify all the programming assignments you did in Chapter 8 to use the following functions where applicable and where it would lead to a simplification or streamlining of your programs: `memset()`, `memcpy()`, `sscanf()`, and `sprintf()`. (See Section 9.16 for the `acech09.c` program.)

Additional enhancements and modifications for each programming assignment are specified accordingly.

The original programming assignments have been modified to include date fields. In addition, the data is unclean in that the numeric fields may contain commas and dollar signs, since some of these files were produced from spreadsheets. You are to modify your program to validate the date field for each record that you read and remove the commas and dollar signs if present in the respective numeric fields. Each record with an invalid date is to be excluded from the calculations and the output report and is to be counted as an invalid record. In addition to the current report being produced by each programming assignment, you are also required to produce a control report before terminating your program. The control report is to have the following information:

- Total number of valid records
- Total number of invalid records
- Total number of all records read

Finally, your output report is to be edited so that the numeric output fields will have commas and dollar signs as applicable. For example one thousand dollars should be printed as $10,000.00, while a quantity ten thousand items is to be printed as 10,000 in your report. It is not necessary for you to include the date in your report.

Programming Assignment 9.1: Billing

Program Description

Table P9.1 gives the new input record layout.

Table P9.1   *Input Record Layout for Programming Assignment 9.1*

Customer Order File			
Field Name	*Size*	*Type*	*No. of Decimal Positions*
Order Date	8	Alphanumeric (MM/DD/YY)	
Product Number	6	Alphanumeric	
Product Description	25	Alphanumeric	
Quantity	5	Alphanumeric (up to 32,000)	
Cost per item	8	Alphanumeric (up to 999,999.99)	2

Programming Assignment 9.2: Payroll

Program Description

Table P9.2 shows the new input record layout.

Table P9.2   *Input Record Layout for Programming Assignment 9.2*

Payroll File Record Layout			
Field Name	*Size*	*Type*	*No. of Decimal Positions*
Payroll Date	8	Alphanumeric (MM/DD/YY)	
Employee Name	25	Alphanumeric	
Social Security No.	9	Alphanumeric	
Employee Title	15	Alphanumeric (up to 32,000)	
Employee Salary	6	Alphanumeric (up to 999,999.99)	2

Programming Assignment 9.3: Payroll Processing

Program Description

The new input record layout is in Table P9.3.

Table P9.3 *Input Record Layout for Programming Assignment 9.3*

Payroll File Record Layout			
Field Name	*Size*	*Type*	*No. of Decimal Positions*
Payroll Date	8	Alphanumeric (MM/DD/YY)	
Social Security Number	9	Alphanumeric	
Hourly Pay Rate	5	Alphanumeric	
Number of Exemptions	2	Alphanumeric (0–19)	
Hours Worked	5	Alphanumeric (999.99)	2

Programming Assignment 9.8: Science and Engineering (Chemical Engineering)

Program Description

Each set of numbers for the steam tables is now preceded by the date when these numbers were generated. The input file now has the following pattern to it:

[Date Tables were generated]
{steam table values}
[Date Tables were generated]
{steam table values}

This pattern continues until the end of file is reached.

Programming Assignment 9.11: Distribution/Packaging/Shipping

Program Description

There are no new fields for this programming assignment. However, date validation is needed for these fields: Invoice Date and Order Date. It is not necessary to strip the numeric fields of any embedded commas because none are used for calculations.

Programming Assignment 9.12: Invoicing

Program Description

There are no new date fields added. However, date validation is needed for these fields: Invoice Date and Order Date. Any commas must be extracted from the numeric fields being read. The Unit Price and the Extended Price fields must be written out to include the dollar sign as well as any commas if the amounts should exceed 10,000.

Programming Assignment 9.19: Inventory

Program Description

This problem is a modification of Programming Assignment 1.19. No new date fields are needed. However, the existing ones need to be validated.

Programming Assignment 9.20: Programa Pro Rata

Program Description

Add the Adjustment Date at the beginning of the input file. Validate the date field. Also add dollar signs and commas to the numeric fields of the output as applicable.

Programming Assignment 9.22: Police Department

Program Description
Add the date for the speeding violation at the beginning of each record. Validate this date field. Also add dollar signs and commas to the numeric fields of the output as applicable.

CHAPTER 10

Scope and Duration

OBJECTIVES

- To understand the extent to which a variable is known in various parts of a program and how long it remains in existence
- To see how scope and duration apply to nonscalar data types
- To examine the scope of functions
- To understand the difference in default initialization of local versus global variables
- To learn the extent to which variables' values are preserved between function calls
- To see how to make a function or variable the private property of one source code

- To understand the concept of hiding a global variable
- To see how declaring variables as static can improve performance
- To examine the process of storing variables' values in registers
- To see how to prevent postinitialization variable value alteration and how to warn the compiler that an instrumentality outside the program can alter program values
- To learn the proper syntax for combining variable types, storage class specifiers, and type qualifiers

NEW TERMS

automatic variable
block scope
duration

external variable
global variable
local variable

scope
storage class specifier

A *global variable* is one that is available programwide. Each time the value of the variable is changed, the change is reflected in all subsequent occurrences of that variable elsewhere in the program. In contrast, the effect of a *local variable* is confined to a specific function or block of code. Changing the value of a local variable in one part of the program will not affect an identically named variable in another part of the same program.

10.1   GENERAL SCOPE AND DURATION RULES

The extent to which a variable is known or accessible from various locations in a program is referred to as its *scope.* How long the variable remains in existence—during the entire life of the program or for a shorter period—is known as its *duration.* In this chapter, we will examine what are referred to as *storage class specifiers:* static, extern, register, and auto. These specifiers determine the extent of a variable; the first two can modify a function.

With regard to scope, variables are normally known only to the function in which they are declared. We call such variables local rather than global. If you declare a variable num within a function and attempt to use num in another function without declaring a different variable num there, the compiler will scream error, "undefined symbol 'num'."

With regard to duration, variables usually come into existence (memory space is reserved for them) when the function in which they are declared is called. They die (the memory space is freed) when the function's statements have been executed and program control returns to the calling function.

There are several advantages to this general scheme of scope and duration:

- It minimizes memory usage. Storage space for variables is allocated only when you need to use them.
- It promotes modularity, making for better-organized, easier-to-read programs.
- It prevents activities in one part of the program from inadvertently affecting the variables in another part.

10.2   USING GLOBAL VARIABLES

The general bias toward using local variables notwithstanding, there are instances where a variable is used so pervasively throughout a program that stubbornly insisting on preserving the local nature of variables may be more trouble than it's worth. Say, for example, that your program writes text to the screen in a particular color at different points in the program. You store the particular background and foreground color combination in a variable called `color`. You *could* make a declaration assignment of a color in each and every function that uses this same color for screen printing. Or you could declare and assign `color` in `main()` and then add `color` as an additional argument to every function that uses `color`. So, `main()` would pass `color` to `print_string()`, which would in turn pass `color` to `print_chars()`, and so on. Either way, it's a messy business.

The alternative would be to make `color` a global variable, available to more than one function. (Still another solution would be to use a macro. See Chapter 11.)

 If you have a variable whose declaration is not found inside *any* function, the variable is known to every function in the source code whose definition follows it in the source code.

Because of the way global variables are declared, we also call such variables ***external variables*** or "top-level" variables. Some programmers follow the convention of making the initial letter of global variables uppercase:

```
int Color;

int main(void)
. . .
```

Not only would making `color` an external variable simplify the coding, but it would also speed the program up somewhat. If we keep `color` local, it takes time for the computer to allocate and fill memory space for `color` each time a function containing it is called and free the memory space when the call is concluded.

The following program, `ext.c`, illustrates the declaration and use of a global variable.

 **10.1 ext.c**

```
/* ext.c */

/* shows scope of external variables */
#include <stdio.h>

void increase(void);
void decrease(void);

int ubiquitous = 3;

int main(void)
```

```
{
    ubiquitous++;
    printf("ubiquitous before increase(): %d\n", ubiquitous);
    increase();
    printf("ubiquitous after increase(): %d\n", ubiquitous);
    decrease();
    printf("ubiquitous after decrease(): %d\n", ubiquitous);
}

void increase(void)
{
    ubiquitous++;
}


void decrease(void)
{
    ubiquitous--;
}
```

The output:

```
ubiquitous before increase(): 4
ubiquitous after increase(): 5
ubiquitous after decrease(): 4
```

The variable ubiquitous is not declared within any of the program's three functions. Consequently, it is external. Each of the functions in ext.c access and alter its value. Each change affects ubiquitous's value for the rest of the functions. The variable starts out with a value of 3, is incremented to 4 in main(), is incremented further to 5 in increase(), and is decremented back to 4 in decrease().

10.2.1 Limiting Scope of Global Variables by Placement

There are three ways of limiting the scope of a global variable. One is through the use of the keyword static. This use, which relates to limiting the scope of a global variable to a single source code within a multi-source code program, will be discussed in a later section in this chapter.

The second way is through placement of the variable declaration within the code. As a general matter, a global variable is known only to functions defined below it in the source code.

Thus, if we were to move ext.c's ubiquitous declaration statement from its position before main() to between main() and increase(), then ubiquitous would be known only to increase() and decrease(). Our attempt to use ubiquitous in main() would now only generate the error message, "undefined symbol 'ubiquitous'."

 **Listing** **10.2 bad_ext.c**

```
/* bad_ext.c */

/* limit scope of global variables by placement in code: nonworking program */

#include <stdio.h>

void increase(void);
void decrease(void);

int main(void)
{
    ubiquitous++;
    printf("ubiquitous before increase(): %d\n", ubiquitous);
```

```
   increase();
   printf("ubiquitous after increase(): %d\n", ubiquitous);
   decrease();
   printf("ubiquitous after decrease(): %d\n", ubiquitous);
}

int ubiquitous = 3; /* not available to main */

void increase(void)
{
   ubiquitous++;
}

void decrease(void)
{
   ubiquitous--;
}
```

Note that when we say the general rule is that an external variable is known only to functions defined below its declaration in the source code, we mean *defined*, not declared. In bad_ext.c, *declaring* increase() before the ubiquitous declaration doesn't make ubiquitous available to the increase() function.

Also, "defined below" has reference to the line number in the source code—the declaration's physical or geographic location in the code, not its logical placement. By placing the ubiquitous declaration in bad_ext.c where we have, all functions whose definitions are found starting on a line below that have ubiquitous available to them. Those above it do not, even if they are called at an earlier point in the program or if in some other conceptual sense they can be thought of as having precedence over the variable declaration.

10.2.2   Using extern to Extend Scope

There is an exception to this just-stated general rule. If we use the keyword extern in declaring a variable in a function whose definition precedes the external variable's declaration, the variable becomes known to that function as well. The effect is just as though we had declared the variable above that function's definition.

 **Listing** 10.3 extern.c

```
/* extern.c */

/* how to make external variable available to function above declaration */

#include <stdio.h>

void increase(void);
void decrease(void);

int main(void)
{
   extern int ubiquitous; /* make variable available to main */
   ubiquitous++;
   printf("ubiquitous before increase(): %d\n", ubiquitous);
   increase();
   printf("ubiquitous after increase(): %d\n", ubiquitous);
   decrease();
   printf("ubiquitous after decrease(): %d\n", ubiquitous);
}
```

```
int ubiquitous = 3;

void increase(void)
{
    ubiquitous++;
}

void decrease(void)
{
    ubiquitous--;
}
```

The output is now the same as that from ext.c.

Also, to make a global variable in one source code available to functions in another source code in the same program, (1) you must declare the variable in that other source code above any functions in which you want to use that variable, and (2) such declaration must be preceded by the keyword extern. (See Chapter 17 for examples and a further explanation.)

By using the keyword extern in both these situations (same source code above declaration or other source code), the declaration is generally treated by the compiler as a referencing declaration only, one that does not reserve memory. (Again see Chapter 17.)

You can also use the keyword extern to access global system variables such as _stklen, _heaplen, and errno. See, for example, Listing 16.3, err_list.c.

10.2.3 Incomplete Declarations

In Chapter 8, we found that we may omit the subscript number of a one-dimensional array that serves as a parameter to a function, or the subscript number of the first dimension of a multidimensional array:

```
void twice(int array[], int size);
```

Likewise, where we declare an array as extern in order to access it in another file or in a function within the same file, we may make the same omission if we wish. In fact, in both cases, the compiler ignores the number if we include it:

```
extern int array[];
```

As you will see later with the other storage specifiers, you may omit the type specifer

```
extern ubiquitous;
```

and the compiler will assume a default type of int, but this is sloppy practice, definitely not recommended.

10.2.4 Limiting the Scope of Global Variables by Declaring Local Variables of the Same Name

A third way the scope of global variables can be limited is by declaring a variable of the same name within a function without using the keyword extern. (This is not a practice we recommend, by the way.) The locally declared variable is considered by the computer to be a separate variable altogether. See Listing 10.4, for example.

 **Listing 10.4 semi_ext.c**

```
/* semi_ext.c */

/* declaring local variable with same name as global creates new variable */

#include <stdio.h>

void increase(void);
```

```
void decrease(void);

int ubiquitous = 3;

int main(void)
{
   ubiquitous++;
   printf("ubiquitous in main before increase(): %d at %p\n", ubiquitous, &ubiquitous);
   increase();
   printf("ubiquitous in main after increase(): %d\n", ubiquitous);
   decrease();
   printf("ubiquitous in main after decrease(): %d\n", ubiquitous);
}

void increase(void)
{
   int ubiquitous = 99;
   ubiquitous++;
   printf("ubiquitous in increase: %d at %p\n", ubiquitous, &ubiquitous);
}

void decrease(void)
{
   ubiquitous--;
}
```

The output shows the locally declared variable is a separate variable, with a different memory location from the global variable by the same name:

```
ubiquitous in main before increase(): 4 at 00AA
ubiquitous in increase(): 99 at FFF0
ubiquitous in main after increase(): 4
ubiquitous in main after decrease(): 3
```

The variable `ubiquitous` in `increase()` may have the same name as the external variable, but it has a separate memory address. To the computer, it's not the same at all. Since the global variable `ubiquitous` is not accessible to `main()`, it is often said that the declaration of a local variable with the same name as a global variable "hides" the global variable inside the function.

You cannot use the same double declaration device with a second *global* variable of the same name to "hide" the first. You could not, for example, declare `ubiquitous` both above `main()` and between `increase()` and `decrease()`. This will result in an error message.

10.3   BLOCK SCOPE

At the other extreme from global variables are local variables declared inside a block within a function. Such variables have a **block scope**—scope limited to the block in which they are declared. Separate declarations of variables with a block of code is not common, but the possibility is available. Listing 10.5 provides an example.

 Listing **10.5 `block.c`**

```
/* block.c */

/* declaration of variable within block with same name as one outside block */

#include <stdio.h>
```

```
int main(void)
{
   int i = 10, doppelganger = 20;

   printf("doppelganger outside block is %d\n", doppelganger);
   while (i > 4)
   {
      int doppelganger = 0;
      while (doppelganger++ < i--)
         printf("doppelganger within block is %d\n", doppelganger);
   }
   printf("doppelganger outside block is still %d\n", doppelganger);
}
```

Here's the output:

```
doppelganger outside block is 20
doppelganger within block is 1
doppelganger within block is 2
doppelganger within block is 3
doppelganger within block is 4
doppelganger within block is 5
doppelganger outside block is still 20
```

The variable doppelganger outside the block is a different variable altogether from the one declared within it. That latter variable has a scope limited to the outside while loop block. Any change to the doppelganger outside the block does not affect the doppelganger within the block and vice versa. (Incidentally, make sure you understand why the last printf() statement within the loop shows doppelganger to have a value of 5. Also, the a in doppelganger should have an umlaut. But since the ä character [ASCII 132; see Appendix F] is not a permissible character for variable names [see Section 2.1], we will let the solecism slide.)

You cannot narrow this hyperlocalization to a single statement. Variables cannot be declared willynilly throughout the code. As with variables declared within the entire function, variables declared within a block must follow the opening braces prior to any nondeclaration statements. The following will not do.

 **Listing** **10.6 bad_blk.c**

```
/* bad_blk.c   */

/* must declare variable in block before nondeclaration statements in block */

#include <stdio.h>

int main(void)
{
   int num;

   scanf("%d", &num);
   if (num < 10)
   {
      for (int tot = 0, int i = 0; i < num; i++) /* many errors! */
         tot += i;
      printf("total is %d\n", tot);
   }
   printf("num is %d\n", num);
}
```

10.3.1   Extent of Local Scope

As you have undoubtedly gathered by now, absent declaring a variable of the same name within a block inside a function, a variable declared within a function is available to every statement within the function from the point of its declaration. That is so whether the statements are within blocks of code or not.

Likewise, a variable declared within a block is available to all statements within the block from the point of its declaration, including statements within interior blocks. Again, the sole exception is where you declare within an interior block a variable of the same name, as the following example shows.

 **Listing   10.7 block_in.c**

```c
/* block_in.c */

/* declare variable in interior block of same name as 1 in exterior block */

#include <stdio.h>

int main(void)
{
   int height = 10, width = 10;
   int market;

   printf("input market number\n");
   scanf("%d", &market);
   if (market > 5)
   {
      int height, width; /* local to this if block */
      printf("input height and width\n");
      scanf("%d%d", &height, &width);
      if (market > 10)
      {
         if (width < 50)
         {
            int width = 50; /* local to this if block */
            printf("Submarket A of Market %d: make 15 widgits %d by %d\n", market,
               height, width);
         }
         else printf("Submarket B of Market %d: make 20 widgits %d by %d\n", market,
            height, width * 2);
      }
      printf("Make 100 widgits %d by %d\n", height + 10, width + 10);
   }
   printf("Make 200 widgits %d by %d\n", height, width);
}
```

Here's some sample input and output:

```
input market number:
   20
input height and width:
   20 30
Submarket A of Market 20: make 15 widgets 20 by 50
Make 100 widgets 30 by 40
Make 200 widgets 10 by 10
```

The variables `height` and `width` are declared both outside and inside the first `if` statement block. The variables of those names outside the block are different from those inside. The `width` variable is even further redeclared within an interior block. Accordingly, `width` outside the interior block is not known within the interior block, but `height` is. The variable `market`, being declared outside any of the blocks and not being redeclared inside any, is known even to the interior block.

Limiting the scope of a variable to a block of code smaller than a function is not a common practice, but it is available. In the last example, it probably would have been simpler and easier to follow to have used variables of different names but similar import (wide and high instead of width and height, for instance) rather than to have used variables of the same name but different memory locations. In fact, *the practice of using different variables with the same name is strongly discouraged.*

10.4 DURATION

An external variable lasts for the life of the program.

Go back and look at ext.c. The declaration assignment for ubiquitous has been accomplished even before the program starts executing statements in main(). By contrast,

a local variable generally lasts only from the time of the calling of the function (or start of execution of the block in which it is declared) until completion of the function (or block).

If one function calls another, the local variables in the calling function remain in memory throughout the call even though those local variables are not known to the called function. (If the variables are passed as arguments, the variables are not known to the called function; only their values are passed to variables local to the called function.) The exception, static local variables, will be covered below.

Since a local variable has a duration limited to its function or block, whatever value it has is not preserved from one function call (or block execution) to the next.

See the next section for an exception.

10.4.1 Static Local Variables

If, however, we prepend the keyword static to the declaration of a local variable, the variable still has local scope—it is available only within the function—but its value is preserved throughout all calls of the function in which it is declared. (We will see in Appendix B that local variables are stored in an area of memory called the *stack*. They are placed "on the stack" as the function in which they are declared is called, and taken "off the stack" on a last-in, first-out basis when the function terminates. To avoid interfering with this scheme, static variables are stored in a completely different area of memory.)

Local variables that are not static are called ***automatic variables.*** In a sense, a static local variable is conceptually midway between an external variable, which retains its value throughout the program and is known to all functions below it, and an automatic variable, which is local to its function (or, far less commonly, block) and loses its value from function call to function call (or block execution to block execution).

Local variables declared without the keyword static are automatic without your having to say so. If you wish, you can prepend the keyword auto

```
auto int tuition;
```

but this generally only serves a comment-like purpose—where there is an external variable of the same name, using auto can highlight that this is a different variable. In a rare case where you want to prevent the compiler from making a variable a register variable (discussed later in this chapter) on its own, using auto may do the trick.

Though we do not recommend the practice, you may use the keyword static before a variable name without a type declared; int is assumed

```
static num = 40000; /* an int is created */
```

(which would be a major problem here, since 40,000 is outside the integer range for many implementations of C).

The following miniprogram shows the difference between an automatic variable and a static variable.

 **Listing 10.8 autostat.c**

```
/* autostat.c */

/* difference between automatic and static variables */

#include <stdio.h>

void diff(void);
int eternal;

int main(void)
{
   for (eternal = 0; eternal < 4; eternal++)
   {
      printf("eternal in main: %d; ", eternal);
      diff();
   }
}

void diff(void)
{
   static int eternal = 10;
   int ephemeral = 20;

   printf("eternal in diff: %d; ephemeral in diff: %d\n", eternal += 20, ephemeral += 20);
}
```

```
eternal in main: 0; eternal in diff: 30; ephemeral in diff: 40
eternal in main: 1; eternal in diff: 50; ephemeral in diff: 40
eternal in main: 2; eternal in diff: 70; ephemeral in diff: 40
eternal in main: 3; eternal in diff: 90; ephemeral in diff: 40
```

The program shows two differences between automatic and `static` local variables. First:

 The value of `static` variables is preserved from function call to function call.

That of the automatic variable `ephemeral` is not. Note that the value of the `static` local variable `eternal` is not affected by intervening changes in value of the global variable by the same name.
Second:

 If automatic variables are assigned a value on declaration (initialized), this assignment occurs at each call; `static` local variables are assigned a value on declaration only once, not each time the function is called.

Thus, the declaration assignment

```
static int i = 10;
```

is *not* reexecuted each time the function is called. The `static` local variable `eternal` is initialized just once to 10 and increases by 10 on each successive call. The assignment declaration of the automatic local variable `ephemeral`, by contrast, is made on each successive call of `diff()`.

In fact, as the following program shows, a `static` local variable is initialized before its function or even `main()` is called, just as external variables are.

 **Listing 10.9 when.c**

```
/* when.c */

/* verify that static local variable initialized pre-main */

#include <stdio.h>
```

```
void do_nothing(void);

int main(void)
{
    printf("Value in address 00AA prior to function call: %d\n",
        *(int *)0x00AA);
    do_nothing();
}


void do_nothing(void)
{
    static int precocious = 5;

    printf("precocious is located at %p & has a value of %d\n", &precocious, precocious);
}
```

The output:

```
Value in address 0X00AA prior to function call: 5
precocious is located at 00AA and has a value of 5
```

We derived the address in main()'s first line by running the program first with a dummy value there, and taking the address printed out by do_nothing() and substituting that address for the dummy value.

10.4.2 Performance and Other Nonpreservation Considerations for `static` Local Variables

Even if it is not important in a particular program application to preserve the value of a variable from call to call, declaring a local variable as static can serve a purpose. In the following function

```
int mod_num(int num)
{
    static int val;

    if (num % 2)
        val = 7;
    else val = 8;
    return num % val;
}
```

a value is assigned to val at each call. Preserving val's value accomplishes nothing. But declaring val as static does save some time. It avoids having to spend time reallocating and deallocating memory for val with each call of the function. *Declaring as* static *a limited number of local variables in often-called functions can speed up program execution.* [The following program ran some 20 percent slower on our system when we omitted the keyword static.]

 **Listing** **10.10 how_fast.c**

```
/* how_fast.c */

/* shows that using static keyword speeds up program */

#include <stdio.h>

int do_nothing(int);

int main(void)
{
    int i, j;
```

```
      for (j = 0; j < 20000; j++)
         for (i = 0; i < 20000; i++)
            do_nothing(i);
   }

   int do_nothing(int num)
   {
      static int how_fast = 4;
      return num + how_fast;
   }
```

 You can also use a static local variable as a "flag" to cause a function to execute certain ini-tializing statements only the first time the function is called.

```
void example(void)
{
   static int first_time = 1;

   if (first_time)
   {
      statements;
      first_time = 0;
   }
   else
   {
      other statements;
   }
}
```

Still another occasion to use `static` is whenever you return the address of a locally declared `char` array used as a string. If you fail to declare the local array as `static`, the string bytes' values will be lost when the function terminates. See Listing 9.10, `inv_num.c`, and Listing 8.20, `tri_flip.c`, for examples.

However, if you have quite a number of functions that return strings and you make them all `static` local variables, you will eat up memory in the process. One alternative is to repeatedly make use of one scratch global string for all such functions. This has its own dangers, however. *If you use a global array as a scratch pad, make very sure no function that uses this global scratch string calls another function that also uses it.*

10.5   STATIC EXTERNAL VARIABLES

In our discussion above, we were careful to speak of `static` *local* variables. If you suspected we did that because there are also `static` *external* variables, you were right. The keyword `static`, as applied to local variables, does not affect scope, only duration. As applied to external variables, the opposite is true.

 External `static` variables remain in existence for the life of the program, just as external non`static` ones do. However, they are limited in scope to the source code in which they are declared.

A `static` external variable serves a purpose only in a multi–source code program.

Say we had a team of several programmers, each working on separate source codes to be combined into the same program. (See Chapter 17 on projects, for the mechanics of such an operation.) One programmer declares as an external variable `int num`, above all the functions in the source code, whose value can be potentially changed by any of several functions in the source code. If a second programmer does the same thing in another source code, with a variable of the same name, the result will be a linker error.

The error can be resolved by the first programmer's declaring the variable as `static`:

```
static int num;
```

The second programmer can also do the same thing, unless the variable declared in this second source code is to be available to source codes other than the first.

10.6   COMPLEX DATA TYPES

The same rules for external, automatic, and `static` variables apply to each element of an array or structure.

 Each element of an array, and each member of a structure or union variable, is global, automatic, or `static` according to how the array or structure or union variable is declared.

You could, in the same source code, for example, declare both an external array by placing the declaration outside all functions, and a local array of the same name by placing the declaration within a function (again, this is not a recommended practice). If you declare an array or structure variable as `static`, each of its elements or members is `static`.

 **10.11 stat_ray.c**

```
* stat_ray.c */

/* entire array can be declared static */

#include <stdio.h>

void stat_array(int loop);

int main(void)
{
    int i;

    for (i = 0; i < 3; i++)
        stat_array(i);
}

void stat_array(int loop)
{
    static int perpetual[] = {1, 2, 3};
    int i;

    for (i = 0; i < sizeof(perpetual) / sizeof(int); i++)
    {
        perpetual[i] *= 2;

        /* print out values on the final call from main only */
        if (loop == 2)
            printf("element %d: %d\n", i, perpetual[i]);
    }
}
```

Let's see what prints:

```
element 0: 8
element 1: 16
element 2: 24
```

The values of each element of the array have been preserved from one function call to the next, demonstrating that each is `static`. Furthermore, notice that each element of the static array is initialized only once, just as any nonscalar `static` variable would be.

Structures are covered in Chapter 13. Briefly, structures are akin to arrays, except that, among other differences, the members of a structure do not have to be of the same data type. Declaring a structure variable involves first establishing a new type of your own making through what is called a *structure template*, and then declaring a variable of that type.

```
struct worker
{
    char name[40];
    int salary;
}; /* structure template: make type struct worker */

struct worker office; /* declare variable of type struct worker */
```

Since the template itself reserves no memory, it is the structure variable that can be declared as static or whose position in the source code determines whether the members of the structure are external or local, not the template.

```
static struct worker /* template only: keyword static incorrect here! Ignored */
{
    char name[40];
    int salary
};

static struct worker office; /* structure variable
                                declaration: correct */

static struct worker warehouse =
{
    "Joseph Stalin",
    750
}; /* simultaneous structure template and variable declaration: correct */
```

For the same reason, it is not possible for a some of a structure's members to be static and others automatic.

The rule set forth at the beginning of this section applies recursively to submembers and subelements and also includes type qualifiers, discussed later in this chapter. Thus, declaring as static a variable of a structure type that has another structure and an array as members makes all the inner structure's members and all array elements static.

10.7   SCALAR AND COMPLEX VARIABLE DEFAULT VALUES

In the absence of express initialization, what values do variables have? The answer depends on whether the variable is automatic.

 External variables and static local variables are set to zero in the absence of express initialization. Automatic variables have whatever garbage value happens to be in memory at the allocated address.

If the variables are pointers, they are set to NULL. If they are floating point variables, they are set to a value of 0.0. On nearly all systems (including the PC and all others that use the IEEE Standard for Binary Floating-Point Arithmetic; see Chapter 12), this latter operation will zero out all bits. But on other systems, it may not. On such systems, the following

```
union number_tag
{
    int num;
    float val;
} static number;
if (number.val == 0)
    . . .
```

may evaluate to false. (See Chapter 13 for a discussion of unions: the first member is the one initialized.)

The same rule applies to all the elements of an array (or members of a structure variable). Elements that are not initialized explicitly by assignment at the time of declaration are automatically initialized to 0 if the array is external or `static`.

 **Listing** **10.12 init.c**

```
/* init.c */

/* shows external array elements are initialized to 0 by default */

#include <stdio.h>

int numbers[5] = {3, 4, 5}; /* external array */

int main(void)
{
    int i;

    for (i = 0; i < sizeof(numbers)/sizeof(int); i++)
        printf("element %d: %d\n", i, numbers[i]);
}
```

Notice the zeros in the last two output lines:

```
element 0: 3
element 1: 4
element 2: 5
element 3: 0
element 4: 0
```

Some texts distinguish between `char` arrays and other arrays, saying that external and `static` non-char arrays' elements are initialized by default to 0 and those of `char` to `NULL` characters. However, a `NULL` character *is* 0; its character representation is a `NULL` character (that is, assigning either a 0 or \0 to an element of a `char` array is the same thing and will have precisely the same effect of closing off a string).

10.7.1   Array Initialization

 Express array initialization must either be with (1) constants or constant expressions or (2), for an array of pointers, the addresses of global or `static` variables (plus or minus a constant).

Contrast the following:

```
char name[20], address[20], city[20], state[3], zip[6];
int main(void)
{
   static char level[20], location[20];
   char phone[13], ssn[12];
   char *p1[5] = {name, address, city, state, zip}; /* external: OK */
   char *p2[2] = {level, location}; /* static: OK */
   char *p3[2] = {phone, ssn}; /* local nonstatic: error!
                                  "Illegal initialization" */
}
```

Nonpointer arrays may not be initialized with variables' values even if the variables are global or `static`:

```
int val = 3, num = 5;
int main(void)
{
    int data[2] = {val, num}; /* error! "Illegal initialization" */
    . . .
}
```

10.8   REGISTER VARIABLES *(OPTIONAL)*

Normally, variables' values are stored in RAM. In a very limited number of cases, a variable's value can be stored in the computer's registers instead. The computer can access its registers faster than it can access RAM. (See Chapter 1.)

The number of registers in the computer may be quite limited. As Appendix B discusses in much greater detail, on a lowest-common-denominator basis, the PC has only 14 of them, and most are dedicated to specific tasks and thus not available to store the value of a garden-variety variable in your program.

You can *request* that the computer store a variable in a register by using the keyword `register`:

```
register char ch;
```

If the computer has a register available, this declaration will cause the register to be allocated to `ch` during `ch`'s life. Otherwise, `ch` is simply allocated memory on the stack (see Appendix B) as an ordinary automatic variable.

10.8.1   Register Variable Restrictions

Certain restrictions apply to `register` variables. Since the register is not located in RAM, there is no address you can access. Thus, both the following are illegal:

```
register int num;
int *ptr;

ptr = &num; /* illegal! "Must take address of a memory location" */
scanf("%d", &num); /* illegal! "Must take address of a memory location" */
```

You may apply the keyword `register` only to automatic variables, not to variables that have a program-long duration. Automatic variables in this context include parameter declarations in functions:

```
int convert (register int counter, int value);
```

 You would generally use the `register` keyword for repeatedly used variables, such as a loop counter or certain variables in recursive functions such as binary tree functions (see Chapter 15) or those that do sorting. However, even if you do not use the keyword `register`, most compilers will assign certain variables to registers to speed up program operation. In fact, most compilers today do a far more efficient job of assigning registers than you would. *In nearly all cases, you are better off forgetting about using the keyword* `register` *and letting the computer decide how to utilize* `registers` *in your program.*

10.9   TYPE QUALIFIERS *(OPTIONAL)*

There are two type qualifiers, `const` and `volatile`.

10.9.1   The `const` Type Qualifier

The `const` type qualifier prevents any postinitialization assignments or other modifications such as incrementing or decrementing. Thus, the last two statements below would both generate error messages:

```
const double pi = 3.1415926;
const char first = 'A';

pi = 3.2;
first++;
```

The `const` type qualifier used by itself is equivalent to `const int`, but it is not good practice to use that construction:

```
const value = 100;
```

As you can see from the preceding examples, you can initialize a const variable. In fact, if you don't assign a value on declaration, you are stuck with whatever garbage value the variable has on declaration:

```
const int num;
num = 5; /* "Error cannot modify a const object" */
```

Initialization of a const object is not limited to a constant or constant expression:

```
double radius = 2.;
const double area = 3.1415926 * radius * radius;
```

You can use the const keyword to create an array of data the program cannot later alter:

```
const int days_per_month[12] = {31, 28, 31, 30, 31, 30, 31, 31, 30, 31, 30, 31};
```

After this declaration, each element of the array is a const int.

The most common use of the const type qualifier is for pointer arguments to functions. We now turn to pointers. (See also Chapter 8 for more examples and Chapter 11 for a comparison of const variables to define preprocessor macros.)

10.9.2   Pointers and Type Qualifiers

The most common application for the const qualifier is passing a pointer to an array as a function argument. When we pass a pointer's value to a function, we make the memory area pointed to by the pointer available for tinkering by the function, thus simulating call by reference (which C does not support—only call by value). With the const qualifier, the values pointed to are made available but cannot be altered by the function. In effect we say to the function: "Here are some values you examine and use, but do not even think about changing them: look but don't touch."

```
char *flipper(const char *str) /* return string reversed */
{
    int len = strlen(str);
    static char flip[81]; /* static: address is returned */

    flip[len] = '\0'; /* close off new reverse string */
    while(*str) /* go until NULL in str */
        flip[--len] = *str++; /* start at end & go backward */
    return flip;
}
```

Many of the Standard C string-handling functions have const char * arguments, at least those not designed to alter the string or strings passed. (See Chapter 9.)

Pointers are more complicated because you have to distinguish between making the pointer itself const or volatile or both on the one hand, and making the value pointed to const or volatile or both on the other. Or you can qualify both the pointer and the object it points to.

Let's examine the following code fragment for the examples in this section.

```
const int cement = 100, concrete = 200;
const int *ptc = &cement;
int jello = 99, putty = 199;
int *ptv = &jello;
int *const cptr = &jello;
const int *const cptrc = &concrete;
const char name[40] = "Stiva Oblonsky";
```

The declaration

```
const int *ptc; /* ptc points to a const int variable */
```

establishes that ptc points to a variable that must remain constant. We cannot point a pointer-to-const to a variable and then attempt to alter the value at the pointed-to location through dereferencing, any more than we could change the value of the variable itself by direct assignment:

```
*ptc = 13; /* error! "cannot modify a const object" */
```

The value of `ptc` itself can be changed, however. For example, it can be set to point to another `const` value:

```
ptc = &concrete;
```

Perhaps surprisingly, many compilers allow a pointer-to-const to point to a nonconst variable:

```
ptc = &jello; /* pointing pointer-to-const to non-const variable OK */
```

So watch out for inadvertent error. If you do this sort of thing intentionally, you should use a type cast and a comment to clarify your intentions:

```
(int *)ptc = &jello; /* we do this for the following reason: */
```

After the statement in the last example, we could use or print the dereferenced value with `*ptc`:

```
jello += *ptc;
```

However, we cannot now alter the value of the pointed-to variable with the dereferencing operator, even though the variable pointed to is not a `const` variable:

```
*ptc = 13; /* error: "cannot modify a const object" */
```

The compiler is not that smart. Not surprisingly, it assumes you have set this pointer-to-const to point to a `const` variable even if you haven't.

In other words, the purpose of a pointer-to-const would appear to be to prevent you from indirectly altering anything that pointer might point to, rather than to prevent you from pointing the pointer to a non-const variable.

In contrast to the very first declaration in this section,

```
const int *ptc; /* ptc points to a const int variable */
```

the declaration

```
int *const cptr = &jello; /* cptr: const pointer to int */
```

says that the pointer `cptr` itself cannot have its value changed. It must always point to the same (`int`) address, and unless you assign an address on declaration, you will not be able to use `cptr` any more than you could use a `const` variable that you forget to initialize on declaration (at least, in each case, without type casting or some other fancy footwork later):

```
cptr = &putty; /* error: "cannot modify a const object" */
```

But the pointed-to value can change through the dereferenced `const` pointer:

```
*cptr = -1; /* OK */
```

Finally, the declaration

```
const int *const cptc = &concrete;
```

means *both* that `cptc` must always point to the same address and that the value stored at that address may not change.

```
const int *const cptc = &concrete;
*cptc = -1; /* error! "cannot modify a const object" */
cptc = &cement; /* error! "cannot modify a const object" */
```

You cannot, of course, alter the value of a `const` variable directly by assignment. And, as we have seen, you cannot do so indirectly by dereferencing a pointer-to-const that is pointed to it. However, again perhaps surprisingly, you can alter the value of a `const` variable indirectly by pointing an ordinary pointer to it (with a type cast to avoid any warning) and dereferencing. This is the flip side of our determination that we cannot indirectly alter a non-const variable by dereferencing a pointer-to-const that points to it. Again, you should note that the compiler assumes that if we point an ordinary pointer to some variable, that variable is not a `const` variable:

```
ptv = (int *)&concrete;
*ptv = 155;
```

And although, given the declaration

```
const char name[40] = "Stiva Oblonsky";
```

the following statement will result in an error

```
name[0] = 'A';
```

on most compilers, the following will give only a warning ("suspicious pointer conversion"):

```
strcpy(name, "Dolly Oblonsky");
```

We can easily get rid of this warning by type casting

```
strcpy((char *) name, "Dolly Oblonsky");
```

to conform to the first of strcpy()'s prototype arguments:

```
strcpy(char *s1, const char *s2);
```

In short, the entire business of const pointers is not so tightly monitored in C that you cannot break the rules if you are bound and determined to do so. If you want to break the rules, type cast and comment. You do so at your peril! Even in those instances above where we were met with outright errors, we could cure the error by type cast:

```
const int cement = 100, concrete = 200;
const int *ptc = &cement;
int jello = 99, putty = 199;
int *ptv = &jello;
int *const cptr = &jello;
const int *const cptrc = &concrete;

*(int *)ptc = 155; /* dereference pointer to const */
(int)cement = 155; /* alter const variable by direct assignment */
(int *)cptr = &putty; /* alter const pointer */
*(int *)cptc = -1; /* dereference const pointer to const */
(int *)cptc = (int *)&cement; /* change where const pointer to const points */
```

If, on the other hand, you are on the straight and narrow, watch out for inadvertent errors in this fast-and-loose area.

Nearly all the above rules and considerations apply to the volatile type qualifier, discussed in the next section, and combined const and volatile type qualifiers. Pointers are common applications for the volatile type qualifier in a direct memory access situation. (See Appendix D.) You may assign the pointer an absolute address in RAM or an address of a port directly. The value found there may change not by anything your program does but by some hardware activity completely outside your program.

10.9.3   The volatile Type Qualifier

The volatile type qualifier warns the compiler that the variable may be modified by some mechanism outside the program, such as an interrupt routine or an input/output port. This alerts the compiler not to make assumptions about the variable's value while evaluating expressions containing the variable.

In the following code fragment, the program will execute the while statement over and over until ticks has a value less than that of interval:

```
int ticks, interval = 100;

ticks = 0;
while (ticks < interval)
    continue;
```

The compiler would see that ticks's value will not change with each iteration. That being the case, the compiler would in all likelihood make ticks a register variable or load it in some other memory area that prevents updating, and not even load its value after setting it initially to zero. The result would be an infinite loop.

However, if `ticks` is associated with a hardware clock interrupt and changes its value outside the program, the compiler would have outsmarted itself here. The following declaration

```
volatile int ticks;
```

would force the compiler to reload the value of `ticks` with each execution of the statement and would prevent the variable from being made a `register` variable.

A variable can be both `const` and `volatile`. At first, this may seem inconsistent. How can a variable you fully expect to change be unchangeable by hypothesis? But it makes perfect sense. All the combination means is that the variable's value cannot be changed *by the program's statements*; the change is anticipated to come from an outside instrumentality.

For example, a hardware clock setting should normally not be altered by the program, so a variable to house that setting should be a `const`. But it is anticipated to be changed by some mechanism outside the program, making it `volatile`. You use both modifiers in the same declaration. The order is not material:

```
volatile const int ticks;
const volatile long clocktime;
```

See the next section on combining type qualifiers with storage class specifiers.

10.10   ORDER OF SPECIFIERS AND QUALIFIERS

In this chapter, we discussed the storage class specifiers, `static`, `extern`, `auto`, and `register`, and the type qualifiers, `const` and `volatile`. Way back when, we examined type specifiers (which may consist of one or more than one keyword—for example, `int` or `unsigned long int`).

For each variable, you must have one type specifier (unless you have a storage class specifier or a type qualifier and you follow the sloppy practice of omitting the type and having the compiler assume `int` by default), you may have no more than one storage class specifier, and you may have either, both or no type qualifiers.

The preferred order, by convention, is storage class specifier, type qualifier, type specifier:

```
static const volatile unsigned long int compulsive;
```

However, any order is permitted. You may even split up the type name and reverse its normal order, as in the following horrid example:

```
long static const unsigned volatile int disarray;
```

10.11   SCOPE OF FUNCTIONS

Any data object's scope is determined by the placement of its definition. No function may be defined inside another, so all functions are external.

We saw earlier that to make a global variable in one source code available to functions in another source code in the same program, you must declare the variable, preceded by the keyword `extern`, in that other source code above any functions in which you want to use that variable. There is no such requirement for functions. With one exception, any function defined anywhere in a source code or in any other source codes that are part of the same program can be called from any other functions in the program.

As we have seen in Chapter 8, however, there is a good reason apart from scope for a referencing declaration for functions. To allow the compiler to check the number and (to a limited extent) type of actual arguments in a function call against those of the function's parameters, the compiler must have encountered the function definition or declaration on a line above the function call in the same source code file as the function call.

Now for the exception. As with global variables, we can limit the scope of a function to a single file. By prepending the keyword `static` to a function definition, you make that function the private property of the source code module in which the function is defined:

```
static int square_hypotenuse(int side_a, int side_b);
```

Functions in other source code modules may not call the function. Conversely, you may have a function by the same name in another source code module without any conflict. *Making functions* static *is useful to avoid name conflicts among different modules of the same program created by different programmers.*

Say you have source codes A, B, C, and D in the same program. If you define file_open() as a static function in source code A, and you have another completely different non-static function by the same name in file B, any calls in source codes B, C, or D to the function will be to the function in source code B; any calls to the function in source code A would be to the static function in source code A. If there were no such function in any other module but source code A, no function calls to the function in modules B, C, or D to the function would be permitted.

Often, you will have a block of code inside a function that could just as well have been left inside the function, but for clarity and modularity, you want to convert that code block into a separate function. You can, and generally should, do so. But there is no way to keep the smaller "helper" function the private property of the larger function, available for call only by that larger function. The best you can do is to limit availability to the source code in which it is defined.

Chapter Summary

1. The extent to which a variable is known or accessible from various locations in a program is its scope. How long it remains in existence is its duration.
2. A variable whose declaration is not found inside any function—a global variable—is known to every function in the source code whose definition follows it in the source code. Each time the value of a global variable is changed, the change is reflected in all subsequent occurrences of that variable elsewhere in the program.
3. The effect of a local variable is confined to a specific function or block of code. Local variables are known only to the function in which they are declared.
4. Local nonstatic variables come into existence when the function in which they are declared is called and die when the function's statements have been executed and program control returns to the calling function.
5. The scope of a global variable may be limited in three ways: with the keyword static, through placement of the variable declaration within the code, and by declaring a variable of the same name within a function without using the keyword extern.
6. A global variable is known only to functions defined below it in the source code unless we use the keyword extern.
7. You can use the keyword extern to access global system variables such as errno.
8. Local variables declared inside a block within a function have block scope, limited to the block in which they are declared.
9. An external variable lasts for the life of the program.
10. A local non-static variable (called an automatic variable) lasts only from the time of the calling of the function (or start of execution of the block in which it is declared) until completion of the function (or block). Whatever value it has is not preserved from one function call (or block execution) to the next.
11. Static local variables have local scope but, their value is preserved throughout all calls of the function in which they are declared.

12. Automatic variable initialization occurs at each call; static local variables are initialized only once, not each time the function is called.
13. Declaring as static a limited number of local variables in often-called functions can speed up program execution. You can also use a static local variable as a "flag" to cause a function to execute certain initializing statements only the first time the function is called and to preserve the value of an array the starting address of which is returned from a function.
14. External static variables remain in existence for the life of the program; however, they are limited in scope to the source code in which they are declared.
15. Each element of an array, and each member of a structure or union variable, is global, automatic, or static according to how the array or structure or union variable is declared. This rule applies recursively to submembers and subelements and also applies to type qualifiers.
16. External variables and static local variables are set to zero in the absence of express initialization. Automatic variables have whatever garbage value happens to be in memory at the allocated address. The same rule applies to all the elements of an array (or members of a structure variable).
17. Express array initialization must either be with (1) constants or constant expressions or (2), for an array of pointers, the addresses of global or static variables (plus or minus a constant).
18. You request that the computer store an automatic variable in a register with the keyword register. A register variable has no address for access.
19. The const type qualifier prevents any postinitialization assignment or other modification such as incrementing or decrementing.
20. You must initialize const variables.
21. With pointers, you have to distinguish between making the pointer itself const or volatile or both, and making the value pointed to const or volatile or both.

22. The `volatile` type qualifier warns the compiler that the variable may be modified by some mechanism outside the program.

23. A variable can be both `const` and `volatile`: the variable's value cannot be changed *by the program's statements*; the change is anticipated to come from an outside instrumentality.

24. For each variable, you must have one type specifier; you may have no more than one storage class specifier; and you may have either, both, or no type qualifiers. The preferred order is storage class specifier, type qualifier, type specifier, but any order is permitted.

25. All functions are external.

26. Unless a function is made `static`, any function defined anywhere in a source code or in any other source codes that are part of the same program can be called from any other functions in the program. A `static` function makes the function the private property of the source code module in which the function is defined.

Review Questions

1. Define the term *scope* as it relates to program variables.
2. Define the term *duration* as it relates to program variables.
3. List the four storage class specifiers.
4. What storage class specifier is the default for all variables defined inside functions?
5. Variables of what storage classes are allocated when a function or block is entered?
6. Variables of what two storage classes are deallocated when a function or block is exited?
7. Variables of what two storage classes are undefined when they are declared (or allocated)?
8. Variables of what two storage classes are limited in scope to the block that declares them?
9. Variables with what sort of storage are initialized to zeros of appropriate types when declared?
10. Variables of what storage class are freed only when the program ends?
11. What storage class specifier is the default for all variables defined outside functions?
12. What storage class specifier may be ignored by the compiler?
13. If you have a variable whose declaration is not found inside *any* function, the variable is known to every function in the source code whose definition follows it in the source code (True or False).
14. An external variable lasts for the life of the program (True or False).
15. A local variable generally lasts only from the time of the calling of the function (or start of execution of the block in which it is declared) until completion of the function (or block) (True or False).
16. The value of a local nonstatic variable is not preserved from one function call (or block execution) to the next (True or False).
17. The value of `static` variables is preserved from function call to function call (True or False).
18. The value of `static` variables is never preserved from function call to function call (True or False).

19. If automatic variables are assigned a value on declaration (initialized), this assignment occurs at each call (True or False).
20. If automatic variables are assigned values on declaration (initialized), this assignment occurs only at the first call (True or False).
21. `Static` local variables are assigned a value on declaration only once, not each time the function is called (True or False).
22. External `static` variables remain in existence for the life of the program, just as external non-`static` ones do (True or False).
23. External `static` variables are limited in scope to the source code in which they are declared (True or False).
24. Each element of an array, and each member of a structure or union variable, is global, automatic, or `static` according to how the array or structure or union variable is declared (True or False).
25. External variables and `static` local variables are set to zero in the absence of express initialization (True or False).
26. On uninitialized declaration, automatic variables have whatever garbage value happens to be in memory at the allocated address (True or False).
27. Express array initialization must either be with (1) constants or constant expressions or (2), for an array of pointers, the addresses of global or `static` variables (plus or minus a constant) (True or False).
28. Any data object's scope is determined by the placement of its definition (True or False).
29. No function may be defined inside another, so all functions are external (True or False).
30. Functions may be defined inside another (True or False).
31. All functions are external (True or False).
32. All functions are internal because function definitions permit nesting for as deep as needed (True or False).

Programming Exercises

The specifications of the programming assignments were introduced in Chapter 1, at which time you were to

- think through the solution to these problems.
- identify the modules that, once implemented, will solve the problem.

- prepare a hierarchy chart of all the modules.
- prepare pseudocode/flowchart for each module in the hierarchy chart.
- write the program stubs the same way we did with the ACE Billing system application.

This chapter has added coverage of scope and duration to our C knowledge. We urge you to continue developing what you started in that chapter. If you have not started, then we recommend that you start by applying the methodology presented in Chapter 1.

Modify all the programming assignments given in Chapter 9 to incorporate the most applicable features to the programs you have already done in Chapter 9. In maintenance programming, there is usually a compelling reason to make changes to an existing program. In the process of making the changes to respond to the latest request, it is not uncommon to identify areas of improvement that may not relate directly to the most recently requested change. In Chapter 10, we have given you additional background. We now challenge you to go back to the programs you have already written and make any major improvements based on your newly acquired knowledge. If you are using this book as a school textbook, your instructor may suggest changes you ought to make.

CHAPTER 11

The Preprocessor

OBJECTIVES

- To investigate the purpose and mechanics of the preprocessor
- To see the differences between preprocessor directive lines and C statements
- To see how to insert files containing function prototypes, symbolic constants, and aggregate data type templates into a source code file
- To learn how to create symbolic constants
- To learn how to create macros with and without parameters
- To learn how to splice identifiers or tokens together with macros and convert macro arguments to literal strings
- To investigate the relative advantages and drawbacks to using macros versus functions and macros versus typedef and const

- To learn about conditional compilation and its uses
- To see how to uncover and automatically report errors that occur during conditional compilation
- To examine the processing order and scope of preprocessing directives
- To learn how to pinpoint and automatically print out the source code name and line number in which errors occur
- To see how to use assertions to test and automatically report on the existence of conditions
- To learn about predefined system macros

NEW TERMS

header file
macro

manifest constant
preprocessor directive

The compiler processes a type of instruction, called ***preprocessor directives,*** in the source code before compiling. All these preprocessor directives start with # to signal the compiler that the line contains a preprocessor directive. Notice we say *directive*, not *statement*. Preprocessor directives are not terminated by semicolons, and unlike the situation with C statements, the presence or absence of spacing on a line is significant.

11.1   FORMAT

 The directive keywords themselves, like #define **and** #include, **must be in all lowercase.**

Preprocessor directives are generally placed at the very beginning of the source code, but they can legally appear at any point. In fact, for some uses discussed below, such as conditional compilation, the directives are often placed in the middle of the source code.

442

By convention, preprocessor directives start at the left-most column of a line, with no spaces between the # and the rest of the directive label:

```
#include <string.h>
#define E 2.718281828
```

However, on most compilers, spaces are allowed, both before and after the #; in fact, Standard C permits whitespace to precede and follow the #. All these approaches work fine on most compilers, despite their sloppiness:

```
#     include     <string.h>
#         define E         2.7178281828
```

Nevertheless, some older compilers require preprocessor directives to begin the line and to have no spaces between the # and the directive keyword, so you might want to follow those least common denominators.

Furthermore, for include directives, described in the next section, you may not have any space between the left angle bracket and the file name:

```
#include <  math.h> /* error! "Unable to include file '  math.h' */
```

Also, see special rules on spacing in macros and in long directive lines with literal strings, below.

Unlike C statements, a preprocessor directive must be completely within a single line. You may however, combine two or more physical lines into one logical line with backslashes. See Section 11.3.4.

11.2   THE include DIRECTIVE

The include directive directs the computer to insert another file verbatim just as though you had typed it letter for letter at that point. The include file generally contains function prototypes, define directives (and their distant cousins, typedefs, covered in Chapter 13), and structure and union templates, also covered in Chapter 13.

The file included is referred to as a ***header file.*** By convention, the extension portion of a header file name is .h—for example, colors.h. You are by no means required to follow this convention, just as you are not required to use .c as the extension for your source code files, though both conventions are almost universally adhered to by C programmers.

The include header files can be Standard C library files, those you make up yourself, or those from a third party's commercial software. Standard C library header files are generally found in the "\include" subdirectory of the directory that contains your C compiler's executable file.

11.2.1   When to Use include Directives

You must include in your source code Standard C library header files that contain prototypes for any Standard C functions called by the source code. The same holds true for any third-party libraries you include in your program (see Chapter 17).

Insofar as your own header files are concerned, there are chiefly two situations in which you will include them. One instance is inclusion of header files that contain define directives for groups of constants you have occasion to use in a number of your programs. These would typically be files that contain constants relating to a specific area of general application. See, for instance, the header files color.h (color byte values), keys.h (scan codes for user key presses), and box_char.h (values for single- and double-lined box characters), found in Appendix H.

The second instance is in connection with multi–source code programs (see Chapter 17 for a description of the mechanics of such programs). In this latter instance, you have program-specific constants you use in several source code modules in the same program.

11.2.2   Nested include Directives

It is perfectly proper for one header file to itself contain one or more include directives:

```
/* colors.h */
#include <fore.h>
```

```
#include <back.h>

. . .

/* fore.h */
#include <intense.h>

. . .

/* intense.h */

. . .
```

Standard C requires that a compiler support at least eight levels of `include` file nesting.

In some cases, including a header file that contains one or more `include` directives will result in the same file being included twice in a single source code. A common example of nested header files is the situation where nonlibrary header files with `include` directives for `stdio.h`, `string.h`, or other often-used Standard C library headers are themselves included in a source code file that also has these Standard C header files.

Generally, this double inclusion will not cause a problem. In some cases, however, duplicate file inclusion can lead to difficulties. For example, you can include a function prototype more than once within a source code, but you cannot do the same for a structure template (see Chapter 13). Later in this chapter, we show you how to guard against inadvertent double-header inclusion.

 If your program contains more than one source code (see Chapter 17), you have to be careful where the same header file is included in more than one source code, as it often will be. *If you recompile after altering a header file, you must recompile all source codes that contain the same header file. Otherwise, the unrecompiled source codes' object modules have the old version of the functions and templates and* `define` *directives and so on included in the header.*

11.2.3   Standard C Header Files

You may include a Standard C header file any number of times, in any order. Standard C requires that the effect be as though you included it only once. Implementations often use the same devices we just alluded to so as to prevent including certain portions of the header files twice even if you include the file itself more than once. For instance, Borland C begins every header file the following way, using a conditional compilation concept discussed later in this chapter:

```
/*  time.h
    Struct and function declarations for dealing with time. */
#ifndef __TIME_H
#define __TIME_H
<entire text of header file>
#endif
```

No Standard C header file may require that another Standard C header file also be included for the first header file to work as advertised. Standard C prohibits any Standard C header file from including another Standard C header file. However, implementations may include non–Standard C header files of their own—for example, in Borland C's version of the Standard C header file, `time.h`:

```
#if !defined(__DEFS_H)
#include <_defs.h>
#endif
```

11.2.4   The `include` Directive Format

There are two formats for `include` directives, paired angle brackets and paired double quotes:

```
#include <filename.h>
#include "filename.h"
```

As a general matter, the angle bracket format is meant to be used for Standard C header files, and the double-quote method, for your own header files or those of a third-party toolkit vendor's.

Thus, an include directive for a Standard C library header file is normally written like the following example:

```
#include <stdio.h>
```

Note the absence of spaces inside the angle brackets. The angle brackets tell the computer to look in a specific directory or directories for the header file. Just which directory or directories are searched is implementation specific. Normally, the places searched include wherever the compiler's Standard C header files are found.

Nonlibrary header files (ones you write yourself or those of third-party vendors) are generally included in the following manner:

```
#include "notes.h"
```

Here again, the directories searched are implementation specific. Generally, the compiler will first look in the current directory and, if it does not find the file there, then in the same spot or spots it would look in had you used angle brackets instead.

With both Borland C and Microsoft C, you can designate one or more directories in addition to the default directory. For instance, if you create a separate subdirectory for your personal header files (a practice we recommend, just as we would recommend keeping all your batch, .exe, and .com files in a separate subdirectory and following a similar practice for any other group of related files), you could add that directory. Then you could use the same angle bracket format for the standard library header files and your own personal header files, though by convention this usage is reserved for Standard C library header files.

Finally, if you find all this too confusing or not worth the trouble, you may simply use quotation marks with the entire pathname:

```
#include "c:\bc\header\colors.h"
```

However, this practice can lead to problems if other programmers use your source code and place your header files in a location different from yours. Furthermore, the usage is nonportable. Standard C specifically provides that the practice of having an apostrophe or backslash (characters that could be misinterpreted as the start of a character constant or escape sequence) between the delimiting angle braces or double quotes of the include formats is undefined. In any event, note that, in contrast to the practice with the normal C string, we do *not* put backslashes before each backslash within the quotes.

11.3 THE define DIRECTIVE—MANIFEST CONSTANTS

There are two types of define directives—those without arguments and those with arguments. In either case, Standard C requires that compilers recognize at least the first 31 characters of a define identifier as significant in distinguishing one from another, as with variable names. The compiler must also support at least 1024 simultaneously active define identifiers of either type. These identifiers are also referred to as *macros*.

The simplest use of define directives, the no-argument type, is to employ them as simple word processing search-and-replace devices. If, for example, we have the following define directives

```
#define WAGERATE1  4.75
#define WAGERATE2  5.5
#define WAGERAGE3  6.0
#define WAGERATE4  7.5
```

each time the preprocessor encounters WAGERATE1 in the source code, it simply replaces it with 4.75, as though you had typed 4.75 at that point in the source code; it likewise replaces every occurrence of WAGERATE2 with 5.5, and so on.

The general format for no-argument define directives is

```
#define identifier replacement_item
```

The replacement item can be any sequence of C tokens, including variable names, keywords, numbers, character constants, literal strings, operators, and punctuation. For instance:

```
#define OOPS puts("Fatal error"); closeall(); exit(3)
```

We often refer to identifiers that represent a constant numerical value as ***manifest constants***. It is the usual practice to use all capital letters for manifest constants, just as it is to use all lowercase letters for C variables. In any case, for `define` directive identifiers, you must adhere to the C rules for permissible letters in variable names: only letters, digits, or the underscore character, with the first character being a letter or the underscore character. If you use any other characters, the compiler will stop the identifier at the unauthorized character, so that with

```
#define NUM? 11
. . .
int num = NUM?;
```

`NUM` is replaced by `?` `11` and a second `?` is tacked on, so you get

```
int num = ? 11?;
```

11.3.1   General Properties

 The preprocessor considers what is between the first and second space after the word `define` **to be the identifier that is to be replaced. For this purpose, "space" includes an entire block of spaces or tabs, not only a single space.**

For example, with

```
#define     MIN         (a          -          b)
```

`MIN` is the identifier, not `"     MIN     "`.

 What's between the second and last space on the `define` **directive line (or the end of the line if there are no spaces at the end) is the replacement item.**

Any internal spaces in the replacement item are part of the replacement item itself. Thus,

```
(a          -          b)
```

is the replacement item in the preceding example. Generally, inclusion of spaces in the source code has no effect, of course. However, see Section 11.3.4 for an exception in the case of literal strings.

 Be careful not to insert any extraneous symbols; they will become part of the replacement item. Two common mistakes are inserting = between the identifier and the replacement item, and placing a semicolon after the replacement item as though the line were a normal C statement.

```
#define N=100
. . .
int a[N]; /* becomes a[=100] */

#define N 100;
. . .
int a[N]; /* becomes int a[100;] */
```

One identifier may be defined in terms of another:

```
#define PI 3.14159
#define TWO_PI (2 * PI)
```

When the preprocessor encounters the symbol `TWO_PI` later in the program, it replaces it by `(2 * PI)`. The preprocessor then rescans the replacement items to see whether they contain invocations of other macros (`PI` in this case). The preprocessor will rescan the replacement items as many times as is necessary to eliminate all macro identifiers.

The preprocessor ignores identifiers embedded in replacement items, character constants, and literal strings.

```
#define SIZE 256
char error_msg[] = "Error! SIZE elements exceeded";
    /* literal string: not replaced */
if (BUFFER_SIZE > SIZE) /* only second SIZE is replaced; first is embedded */
    printf("%s\n", error_msg);
```

 Identifiers appearing in their own replacement items will not be replaced.

In effect, you cannot have recursive macros. Consider the effect of "infinite" macro expansion. Thus, the following—a risky attempt at creating portable code—works

```
#define int unsigned int
```

though such a substitution has great potential to cause unexpected results in your code. See Chapter 13 for how to use typedefs to create a portable type definition without the same risk.

Likewise, you can alter function calls to work in non-normal ways. For example, you can hardwire fputc(), described in Chapter 14 to always print in uppercase and always to stdout

```
#define fputc(ch) fputc(toupper(ch), stdout)
```

since fputc() in the replacement item will not itself be replaced. Again, this sort of nonstandard substitution can cause unexpected problems, and it can be especially tricky if you are not the only one coding your program or if you inserted this little gem months ago and return to work on the program much later. (See Section 11.5 for an explanation of this parameterized define directive.)

You cannot use define directives to substitute for other preprocessor directives:

```
#define IO #include <stdio.h>
IO /* error! */
```

All that results is the line

```
#include <stdio.h>
```

showing up in the source code file after preprocessing, which results in an error message on compiling, "Illegal character '#'". The reason is that include directives are processed before define directives. (See Section 11.5.5.)

The following is permitted, however:

```
#define IO <stdio.h>
#include IO
```

The only requirement is that when expanded, the resulting include directive is in one of the two acceptable formats (angle brackets or double quotes).

Since preprocessing occurs before program compilation, preprocessor identifiers may have the same names as variable names without causing conflict:

```
#define remainder(a,b) ((a)%(b))
. . .
int remainder;
```

The same holds true for preprocessor identifiers and those in other name spaces. See Chapter 13 on the three separate nonpreprocessor name spaces.

11.3.2   Uses for define Directives

One advantage to using define directives rather than variables is to isolate and place in a noticeable, easily accessible location values we suspect might change in the future. Taking the WAGERATE examples, if the wage rates change in the future, we can look at one spot to make changes rather than scan the entire program.

Isolation of values is particularly useful in the situation where we have a number of arrays in our program with the same number of elements but where that number might change in the future or in an application for another user. Since we cannot use a global variable at the outset of the program to specify array size (the size of an array must be a constant, determinable at compile time, not at run time), using a `define` directive to specify the size lets us make one change rather than several if the size changes in the future.

Using `define` directives can also improve program readability. Seeing RED or PGUP in code is more easily understood than the 4 or 73 they respectively represent as color and key press values (see Appendixes C and A, respectively).

You can also use `define` directives for reasons of portability. (See Section 11.4.4 for examples.) In this connection, we point out that it is legal, but generally ill-advised, to use C keywords in `define` directives. Remember, these are not C statements; the preprocessor does not distinguish C keywords from other text.

```
#define int short
```

The problem with this usage is twofold. First, you have inadvertently made this replacement in all prototypes in header files you include that have `int` arguments or that return `int` values. Second, it is unlikely that you want to cause this substitution for *all* your ints. Keeping track of which ones you do not want to replace is difficult. The preferred technique is a selective approach:

```
#define INT short
```

11.3.3   Manifest Constants versus `typedef` and `const`

Since the preprocessor makes its substitutions before compilation, you cannot use any debugging features of your implementation with macros. You can do so with `const` variables. Nevertheless, manifest constants can be used in places where a true constant is required, not just one masquerading as a constant: in sizing an array; in initializing global variables, arrays, unions, or structures; for case statements; and for sizing bit fields.

```
const int cement = 3;
int global = cement; /* error */

int main(void)
{
   int val[cement]; /* error */
   int array[2] = {1, cement}; /* error */
   enum stone {granite = 5, aggregate = cement}; /* error */
   struct record
   {
      int salary;
      unsigned field_a : 2;
      unsigned field_b : cement; /* error */
   } record = {cement}; /* error */
   union save_space
   {
      int salary;
      float hours;
   } mini_mart = {cement}; /* error */

   switch(num)
   {
      case cement: global--; break; /* error */
      case 2: global++;
   }
   return 0;
}
```

If you commented out the `cement` declaration statement and substituted

```
#define cement 3
```

above `main()`, everything would work fine.

See Chapter 13 for a comparison between macros and `typedef` and see later in this chapter for a comparison between macros and functions.

11.3.4   Long Directive Lines

If a source code line—preprocessor or C statement—ends with a \, the "line" is considered to extend to the following line, as though that second line were moved up to exactly the position of the \. Both the \ and the newline are discarded when this cut-and-paste is done. Accordingly, a replacement item can be considerably lengthier than our first examples. For instance, if the same error message can occur in several places in your program, you can cut down your typing job and the length of your hard-copy code by a `define` directive:

```
#define ERR_MSG "Record access error.\n\
The name you have specified is not in the \
customer database.\n\
Press any key to choose from sorted customer \
database."
```

If the `define` directive extends over more than one line and the replacement item, as in this example, is a literal string, you have to be careful to place all lines after the first at the very left-most column as we have done here. Given this example and the following code fragment

```
if (fill_record(name) == 0)
    puts(ERR_MSG);
```

we would get the following output in case of error:

```
Record access error.
The name you have specified is not in the customer database.
Press any key to choose from sorted customer database.
```

However, if our `define` directive is

```
#define ERR_MSG "Record access error.\n\
    Name you have specified is not in \
    customer database.\nPress any key to make a \
    selection from customer database."
```

the resulting message is

```
Record access error.
Name you have specified is not in       customer database.
Press any key to make a       selection from customer database.
```

The space between the left-most column and the first letter becomes part of the replacement item.

Since the compiler removes all comments before preprocessing, line breaks with comments embedded in the middle of a preprocessor directive will not terminate the preprocessor line prematurely. Thus,

```
#define SIZEOF_INT /* We assume that we have a 2-byte int on this machine
               */ 2
```

becomes

```
#define SIZEOF_INT 2
```

11.3.5   Literal Strings

As indicated above, the preprocessor does not look within literal strings in the code for possible replacements. Thus,

```
#define T3 \t\t\t
#define D7 \n\n\n\n\n\n\n

. . .

printf("T3Total Sales in AprilD7");
```

will print

```
T3Total Sales in AprilD7
```

The correct way to implement a replacement within a literal string is through %s conversion specifiers:

```
printf("%sTotal Sales in April%s", T3, D7);
```

This line would tab over three tab stops, print "Total Sales in April", and then drop down seven lines.

The following example contains a function that prints a heading at the top of each page of a report and then skips four lines. (The line characters used here are ASCII 205 for the horizontal character; 186 for the vertical character; and 201, 187, 200, and 188 for the corner characters, respectively; see Appendix F.)

```
#define TOP \
"╔════════════════════════════════════════════╗"
#define BOT \
"╚════════════════════════════════════════════╝"
    #define BLANK \
"║                                            ║"
    #define D4 "\n\n\n\n"
    . . .
    prthd(1, "Timothy Green", "12/22/00");
    . . .
    void prthd(int pagenum, char *client, char *date)
    {
        int i;

        printf("\t%s\n\t%s\n", TOP, BLANK);
        printf("\t* Neuropsychological Deficit Scale for Children"
           "\t\t    Page %d *\n", pagenum);
        printf("\t%s\n", BLANK);
        printf("\t*  Client: %s", client);
        for (i = 30 - strlen(client); i > 0; i -= 8)
            putchar('\t'); /* calculate tab stops */
        printf("\t    Date: %s *\n", date);
        printf("\t%s\n\t%s%s", BLANK, BOT, D4);
    }
```

Figure 11.1 provides the output.

It may be preferable in some cases to define the multiple tab or newline as self-contained printf() statements:

```
#define T3 printf("\t\t\t")
#define D7 printf("\n\n\n\n\n\n\n")
```

Note the absence of a semicolon at the end of each line, so that we can use

```
T3;
```

as a statement rather than the weird-looking

```
T3
```

Figure 11.1 *Using* define *Directives to Rationalize Print Output*

```
╔════════════════════════════════════════════╗
║ Neuropsychological Deficit Scale for Children    Page 1 ║
║                                            ║
║ Client: Timothy Green          Date: 12/22/00 ║
╚════════════════════════════════════════════╝
```

Even if you included the semicolons in both the directives and the statements, you would not likely
have a problem, however. All that would result in most cases is a null statement:

```
printf("\t\t\t");;
```

11.3.6   Redefinition and #undef

Generally, a `define` identifier remains in effect from the point at which it appears, to the end of the file.
However, it may be undefined by the directive

```
#undef identifier
```

and is no longer effective from that point in the code down.

An error message will be generated if you define the same constant twice without an intervening undefinition and the definitions are not identical. Thus

```
#define COLS 80
. . .
#define COLS 79
```

will generate an error, but

```
#define COLS 80
. . .
#define COLS 80
```

will not. In this context, "identical" means just that. The following will give you an error message:

```
#define ABCD   a  +  b  +  c +  d
. . .
#define ABCD   a+b+c+d
```

 **Any redefinition without intervening undefinition must include whitespace in the same
places as in the earlier definition**

although the type (for example, tab versus space character) and number of whitespace characters can
differ. So none of the following are identical:

```
#define ADD (4+5)
#define ADD (4    +   5)
#define ADD (4    +   5   )
```

But the following two, with three spaces versus two tabs, respectively, are:

```
#define ADD (4    +   5)
#define ADD (4              +              5)
```

Apart from special cases, it is generally a good practice to put all your `define` directives in one
place in your program, usually above `main()` (either directly or by way of a header file or files placed
there). If you follow that practice, you will minimize any possible redefinition conflicts. Conflicts will
normally arise between `define` directives in different header files or between your own definitions and
those in a Standard C header file.

To accomplish a permissible nonidentical redefinition, you need to issue an `undef` directive somewhere between the two `define` directives:

```
#define COLS 80
. . .
#undef COLS
#define COLS 79
```

It is not an error to use an `undef` for an identifier that has not in fact been defined at all. We may use
it to cancel any previous definition of an identifier without being sure there is one already:

```
#undef BYTES_PER_PAGE
#define BYTES_PER_PAGE 4096
```

Say you want to use a `define` directive, but only if it is not already defined in another header file your source code includes. Assume you are not sure whether the definition already exists in another header file your program includes. The following technique will avoid any potential conflict and give precedence to any existing definition:

```
#if !defined BYTES_PER_PAGE
   #define BYTES_PER_PAGE 4096
#endif
```

And that leads us to our next topic: conditional directives.

11.4   CONDITIONAL DIRECTIVES

The preprocessor provides a conditional test construction to control whether statements or other lines of text are included in the compiled version of the source code. If the test condition is true, the text is included; if it is false, the text is omitted, just as though you had commented it out.

The syntax is `#if . . . #elif . . . #elif . . . #else . . . #endif`. Of course, as you may expect, you can have as many `#elif`s as you wish or none at all, and you need not necessarily have an `#else`—all depending on the logic of the situation, just as with analogous C conditional statements:

```
#if constant expression
   line(s) of text
#elif constant expression
   line(s) of text
#elif constant expression
   line(s) of text
#else constant expression
   line(s) of text
#endif
```

"Line(s) of text" will generally include C statements or preprocessor directives. However, any text (or even none at all) will do, subject to the requirement that the resulting text, if included as part of the source code, makes sense there:

```
int sum =
#if defined LARGE
a+b+
#endif
c+d;
```

Although the `elif` directive is Standard C, some older compilers do not recognize it. You can achieve the same result—albeit a little more awkwardly—with combinations of `if` and `else` directives:

```
#if constant expression
line(s) of text
#else
#if constant expression
line(s) of text
#else
line(s) of text
#endif
#endif
```

11.4.1   Preprocessor Directives versus C Statements

Note that

 you *must* have an `#endif` **for each** `#if`

whichever construction you use, so that with the `if - else` combination in lieu of `elif`, you will have multiple `endif` directives, as you can see from the last example. There is no similar command for ordinary C conditional statements; you use braces to achieve the same effect.

The requirement for an `#endif` with every `#if` includes the `#if defined` or its alternative formulation `#ifdef` and `#if !defined` or its alternative formulation `#ifndef` combination directives, discussed below. Likewise, you may use `#else` to indicate alternative action if an `#if` or any of those combination directives just named evaluates to false.

Also note that

 `#else` **and the** `#if` **that follows it immediately must be on separate lines. Any lines of text for an** `else` **case must start at the line** *following* **the** `#else`.

Contrast the following two comparison preprocessor examples:

```
#if SYSTEM
#define NUM 1
#else
#define NUM 2
```

```
#if SYSTEM
#define NUM 1
#else #define NUM 2
```

In the second case, `#define NUM 2` will be completely ignored and `NUM` will not, in consequence, be defined.

With ordinary C code, the compiler depends on the semicolon to separate distinct statements. There is no such device with preprocessor directives, which depend on line termination for separation.

On the other hand, since the preprocessor works on a single-line basis, you need not use parentheses to encompass the conditional test, unlike a C conditional statement, though you can, for clarity, if you wish:

```
#if constant expression
```

or

```
#if (constant expression)
```

11.4.2   Permissible Constant Expressions in Conditional Directives

More important than the above format differences, unlike C conditional statements, the conditional directive test is evaluated at compile time, not run time, since its whole purpose is to determine whether the code is in the compiled source code in the first place. For this reason,

 In conditional compilation directives, the test conditions may not contain any variables—only constants or constant expressions that evaluate to a constant.

For example:

```
#define MAX 40
#define ARRAY_SIZE 20
#define SIZEOF_INT 2
int main(void)
{
   int num[ARRAY_SIZE];
#if (ARRAY_SIZE * SIZEOF_INT) - 1 <= MAX
   num[ARRAY_SIZE - 1] = 0;
#else
   num[ARRAY_SIZE - 1] = B1;
#endif
}
```

On a PC, this compiles to

```
int main(void)
{
   int num[20];
   num[20 - 1] = 0;
}
```

If `MAX` were changed to 30, or if `int` contained 4 bytes on a particular system, the second statement would instead be

```
num[20 - 1] = -1;
```

Since in C++, the `sizeof` operator is evaluated at compile time, with C++ and combination C/C++ compilers, the following will work in place of the `#if` line above:

```
#if (ARRAY_SIZE * sizeof(int)) - 1 <= MAX
```

You should avoid this usage since it is not portable.

In addition to the `sizeof` operator prohibition, you may not use type casts in conditional directive lines. Neither of these prohibitions applies, of course, to the text that is to be conditionally included.

In the conditional compilation directive line, you may not generally use any floating point constants. Many compilers ignore this prohibition, however.

In addition to the `defined` directive (see next section), in conditional compilation directives, you may use integer constants (including character constants, in turn including escape sequences), relational operators, arithmetic operators, logical operators, and even bitwise operators:

```
#if defined VALUATION && \
   (MAX + ((SUM % 8) << 2) > (MIN < 2 ? 5 : 10))
. . .
```

11.4.3   Conditional Code Block Inclusion; Portability

 You can use conditional directives as a convenient way to insert or remove one or more blocks of code. For example:

```
#define A 0
#define B 1
#define C 0
#if A
   line(s) of text
#endif
#if B
   line(s) of text
#endif
#if C
   line(s) of text
#endif
```

If you want to make the `A` block active, you need only alter the `define` directive replacement item to 1. If only one of these three blocks should be operative in your program, you can guard against inadvertently setting more than one (or none) to 1 with the `#error` directive, covered below.

 Conditional directives are also often used for reasons of portability. For instance, if you are not sure whether the program will be run on a computer that uses ASCII or EBCDIC character encoding:

```
#if 'B' > 'A' /* ASCII */
#define ASCII
#define EOT '\4' /* end of transmission */
#define ENQ '\5' /* inquiry */
#define NAK '\25' /* negative acknowledge */
#else
#define EBCDIC
#define EOT '\67'
#define ENQ '\55'
#define NAK '\75'
#endif
```

11.4.4   Conditional Define Directives—Debugging and Commenting Out Code

One common use of the conditional compilation directive is in connection with a `define` directive as the conditional test, using the preprocessor `defined` operator. The directive

```
#if defined TESTING
```

evaluates to true if TESTING has been defined (even with a 0 value or blank replacement item), and false if it has not been defined. You may use the defined operator only in conjunction with an if or elif directive.

Say that, in the course of building and debugging a program, you had so many variables to look at that the editor's normal debug/watch-and-inspect devices would be cumbersome (or you are in an environment that does not have tracing or debugging facilities). You could insert, at appropriate places in your source code, statements that would print results at those points to a file that you could later look at. One define directive could cause all these print statements to take or cease to take effect:

```
#define TESTING
. . .
#if defined TESTING
   fp = fopen("a:\\test", "w");
#endif
. . .
#if defined TESTING
   fprintf(fp, "main: name = %s\n", name);
   fprintf(fp, "main: value = %d\n", value);
#endif
. . .
#if defined TESTING
   fclose(fp);
#endif
```

Notice that you need not have any replacement item for TESTING in the #define TESTING directive in order that the preprocessor considers it defined. To turn off the file creating, printing, and closing, all you need do is comment out the first define directive. You could also undefine TESTING before a particular block of code and redefine it after the block to omit printing in that block of code only. Notice too, that, as we indicated earlier, the preprocessor directives can appear anywhere in the source code, not just at the very beginning.

You generally will use the #if defined formulation where you are really not certain whether the identifier will be defined. Otherwise, you can use a simpler formulation for the TESTING example above:

```
#define TESTING 0
   . . .
if TESTING
   . . .
```

Here, you can turn printing on or off by setting TESTING to 1 (or some other nonzero value) or 0.

 Note, however, that *you must take care to distinguish between the usage of blank replacement item* if defined *identifiers and zero or nonzero replacement item* if *identifiers. Mixing them is a common mistake:*

```
#define TESTING
. . .
if TESTING
. . .
```

If you are using a compiler that does not afford you the option of nesting comments, or if you wish to improve portability even if yours does (other programmers are compiling your code on other platforms), you could "comment out" a block of code that itself contains one or more comments as follows:

```
#define COMMENT_OUT
#if defined  COMMENT_OUT
   <lots of code with comments>
#endif
```

You could then quickly put the block back in by commenting out the define directive line itself—or, even simpler, by using a conditional directive without if defined:

```
#if 0
   <code with comments>
#endif
```

To reinsert the code, you could just change the 0 to 1.

11.4.5   Machine-Dependent or Global Situation–Specific Code Blocks

You can also use this `if defined` device to prevent portability problems that arise when one system uses a different function for a task from another, or requires different code. There are two basic approaches to this problem. The more customary method is to define a single identifier that activates one of several conditional directives. For example:

```
#define PC
#if defined PC
    PC-specific code
#elif define VAX
    VAX-specific code
#elif defined SUN
    SUN-specific code
#endif
```

For later convenient switching, you might also place the other choices at the top of the block and comment all but one out:

```
#define PC
/* #define VAX */
/* #define SUN */
```

The other approach is to define all identifiers with replacement item values, only one of which is nonzero, and use simple `if` directives rather than `if defined`:

```
#define PC 1
#define VAX 0
#define SUN 0
#if PC
    PC-specific code
#elif VAX
    VAX-specific code
#elif SUN
    SUN-specific code
#endif
```

You may use your own definition identifiers to achieve conditional compilation, as in the last example, or implementation-defined identifiers that are built in without your having to define them:

```
#if defined __BORLANDC__
#define CLEAR_SCREEN clrscr
#else
#define CLEAR_SCREEN clearscreen
#endif
```

11.4.6   Conditional Compilation of Preprocessor Directives

Preprocessor directives as well as C statements can be the subject of conditional compilation directives. Say you have written a toolkit meant to be incorporated in other programmers' source codes. You know that one of the compilers, say Lattice C, has some functions that are inconsistent with certain of the prototypes from the headers of some other compilers. You could conditionally include those headers like this:

```
#if !defined LATTICE
#include <io.h>
#include <process.h>
#endif
```

11.4.7   Preventing Multiple File Inclusion

As you have seen, it is permissible to include the same header file more than once in a source code. In some cases, however, if a source file includes the same header file twice, compilation errors may result.

This double inclusion is common when header files include other header files. You can use conditional directives to protect against multiple inclusion:

```
/* junk.h */
#define JUNK_H
. . .

/* trash.h */
. . .
#if !defined JUNK_H
#include <junk.h>
#endif
. . .
```

Notice that JUNK_H will be defined if junk.h is already included. If so, it will not be included through the trash.h file.

You can use a similar device to prevent multiple inclusion of a portion of a header file among different source-code modules of the same program. For example, say you—contrary to normal usage—include variable declarations in a header file. (You might do this for consistency in different programs of large multiprogram jobs.) You can do the following to prevent a duplicate variable declaration error:

```
/* master.h */
struct record
{
    . . .
};
struct vendor
{
    . . .
};
#if !defined TEMPLATE_ONLY
    struct record employee;
    struct vendor buyer;
#endif
. . .

/* job.h */
#include <master.h>
. . .

/* data.h */
#define TEMPLATE_ONLY
#include <master.h>
. . .
```

11.4.8   Alternative Forms and Formats

Except as described in Section 11.4.9, the following older forms of the conditional directives can be substituted for those shown above as alternative forms:

```
#if defined    or    #ifdef
#if !defined   or    #ifndef
```

You may use parentheses following the conditional directives, or not, as you choose:

```
#if defined (HORSE)       or    #if defined HORSE
#if !defined (SCHEDULE) or    #if !defined SCHEDULE
#if (TESTING)             or    #if TESTING
```

Thus, #if defined (HORSE) checks for a definition of HORSE, not (HORSE).

11.4.9   Combining and Nesting Conditional Directives

In addition to the ! operator, you can use the logical operators ¦¦ and && to combine conditional directives:

```
#if defined (SYSTEM) && !defined (PRINTER)
```

You do not repeat the # or the `if` for the second portion of the directive.

Note that it would not be possible to substitute `#ifdef` for `#if defined` here. The older alternative forms `#ifdef` and `#ifndef` may not be used where there is a combination with logical operators.

It is perfectly permissible to mix constant expressions with `defined` identifiers:

```
#if defined SYSTEM && !defined PRINTER && TESTING
```

Comparing this example with the preceding one, you can see, as we pointed out in the previous section, using parentheses to close off the conditional define is permitted but not required. However, as with `if` statements, where you have a complex combination of conditions, you must use parentheses to clarify your intentions. (See the PC/VAX/SUN example in the `#error` section—Section 11.6.)

You can also nest conditional directives; be careful that each `#if` is closed off by an `#endif`:

```
#define DOS 1
#define UNIX 2
#define SYSTEM DOS
#define MONO 7
#define CGA 1
#define VGA 9
#define MONITOR VGA
#if SYSTEM == DOS
#if MONITOR == VGA
#define HEADER "vga.h"
#elif MONITOR == CGA
#define HEADER "cga.h"
#else
#define HEADER "mono.h"
#endif
#include HEADER
#endif
```

Standard C requires that a compiler support at least eight levels of nesting of conditional directives.

11.5   MACROS WITH ARGUMENTS

Function-like `define` directives allow you to use parameters. Not only is the identifier replaced by the replacement item, but the parameters within the replacement item are replaced by the actual arguments you use. For example,

```
#define NOTE_INTERVAL(a,b) \
   interval = (log(b) - log(a)) / 12;
NOTE_INTERVAL(261.63, 261.63 * 2)
```

will produce

```
interval = (log(261.63 * 2) - log(261.63)) / 12;
```

Likewise, take the following useful loop example:

```
#define for_loop(counter,start,stop,step) for ((counter) = (start); \
   (counter) * ((start) > (stop) ? -1: 1) \
   <= (stop) * ((start) > (stop) ? -1: 1); \
   (counter) += (step))
#define for_one(counter,start,stop)\
   for ((counter) = (start); (counter) <= (stop); (counter)++)

. . .

int i;
for_loop(i, 4, -8, -2)
   printf("i: %d\n", i);
for_one(i, 0, 10)
   printf("i: %d\n", i);
```

(The conditional expression's working for both incrementing and decrementing counters depends on the algebraic notion that $a <= b$ is equivalent to $-a >= -b$.) We could substitute the following for the three-parameter version above:

```
#define for_one(counter,start,stop) for_loop(counter,start,stop,1)
```

You can place one parameter—or two or more parameters—within the parentheses, as long as multiple parameters are separated by commas. (Standard C requires that a compiler allow at least 31 parameters in a macro definition, as with a function.) In fact, if you want to mimic a function without arguments, you can omit any parameters within the parentheses. For example:

```
#define FILE_ERROR() \
   {puts("Error opening file"); \
   if (strcmp(mode, "r") == 0) \
      puts("Please see administrator"); \
   exit (1);}
. . .
if (fp = fopen(filename, mode) == NULL)
   FILE_ERROR();
```

The preprocessor treats the macro with blank parentheses as a macro with arguments; thus

```
#define errfile(     ) printf("error opening file"); exit(1)
```

will work just as well as

```
#define errfile() printf("error opening file"); exit(1)
```

The preprocessor will consider the identifier to be `errfile()`, not `errfile(`. However,

 You must not allow a space between the macro identifier and the open parentheses.

If a left parenthesis does not immediately follow the name to be defined, the supposed macro is taken as an ordinary `define` directive without parameters. If we inadvertently placed a space in the example above,

```
#define NOTE_INTERVAL (a,b) interval = (log(b) - log(a)) / 12;
NOTE_INTERVAL(261.63, 261.63 * 2)
```

the result would be a literal substitution of everything on the line after the space for `NOTE_INTERVAL`:

```
(a,b) interval = (log(b) - log(a)) / 12;(261.63, 261.63 * 2)
```

Spaces within the parentheses are not material. Either of the following would work equally well:

```
#define ADD(a,b) ((a) + (b))
#define ADD(a,  b) ((a) + (b))
```

We have seen that after each `define` directive search and replacement, the preprocessor reviews the expanded text for further substitutions. This process holds true for macros. For example, given the following preprocessor directive taken from a listing on disk, `scale.c`,

```
#define CLOCK_CYCLE 1193180.
#define C4 261.63
#define NOTE(freq) CLOCK_CYCLE / freq
#define Q(t) play(NOTE(t), .25)
```

the C statement

```
Q(C4);
```

expands first to

```
play(NOTE(261.63), .25)
```

which in turn expands to

```
play(1193180. / 261.63, .25)
```

However, as we have already seen for no-argument `define` directives, identifiers appearing in their own replacement items are not replaced. Thus the following usage is permitted, thereby allowing special-case function handling:

```
#define divisor(n)   ((n) != 0 ? divisor(n) : divisor(-99))
```

11.5.1   Liberal Use of Parentheses with Macros

The literal way the `define` directive macro replaces can trip up the unwary. Take the following code fragment:

```
#define CUBE (X) X*X*X
. . .
int num = 1;
int val = CUBE(num + 2);
```

The result is not the 27 you might expect. The second statement expands to

```
int val = num + 2 * num + 2 * num + 2;
```

Given the rules of precedence, the result is 7. To get the correct result, we must add parentheses to the macro definition:

```
#define CUBE (X)   (X)*(X)*(X)
```

But even this safeguard won't work in all cases:

```
num = 4 / CUBE(value);
```

is expanded to

```
num = 4 / (value) * (value) * (value);
```

thereby setting `num` to : $(4 / value) + value^2$. To cure this defect, we must refine the macro:

```
#define CUBE(X) ((X)*(X)*(X))
```

 To be safe, observe the following rule of thumb: Put parentheses around each argument in the replacement item and around the entire replacement item.

11.5.2   Macros—Merging and String Conversion (# and ##)

If you want to include the macro argument as a literal string in the replacement item, you can put a # in front of the corresponding argument in the replacement item. That portion of the replacement item is replaced by the macro argument enclosed in double quotes. For instance, given the following macro and variable declaration assignments,

```
#define PRINT(SPECIFIER,WORD_NUM) \
printf(#WORD_NUM " = %" #SPECIFIER\
 "\n", WORD_NUM)
int number = 2;
char character = '2';
char string[] = "2";
```

the following statements

```
PRINT(d,number);
PRINT(c,character);
PRINT(s,string);
```

expand to

```
printf("number" " = %" "d" "\n", number);
printf("character" " = %" "c" "\n", character);
printf("string" " = %" "s" "\n", string);
```

which concatenate to

```
printf("number = %d\n", number);
printf("character = %c\n", character);
printf("string = %s\n", string);
```

which produce the following output:

```
number = 2
character = 2
string = 2
```

 Notice from this example that *you can use the same parameter more than once in the same macro, both with and without* #. We can use this example to rewrite the value-testing macro described earlier:

```
#define TESTING
#define TRACE(file, function, variable, conversion_spec) \
    fprintf(file, #function": " #variable " = %"\ #conversion_spec"\n", variable)
. . .
#if defined TESTING
    fp = fopen("a:\\test", "w");
#endif
. . .
#if defined TESTING
    TRACE(fp, main, name, s);
    . . .
    TRACE(fp, main, value, d);
#endif
. . .
#if defined TESTING
    fclose(fp);
#endif
```

You can merge two macro arguments by using ## between them in the replacement item. For example, given the define directive

```
#define M(X,Y) (X##Y)
```

the statement

```
number = M(X,6);
```

expands to

```
number = x6;
```

An example of this device is found in Listing 13.12, bit_look.c.

You may connect more than two arguments. For example. given

```
#define WRITE(ptr,token,field) fwrite(ptr##token##field, 1,\
    strlen(ptr##token##field), fp)
```

the following

```
WRITE(current,->,name);
```

expands to

```
fwrite(current->name, 1, strlen(current->name), fp);
```

You need not use all arguments in each portion of the replacement item, nor must they be in the same order as in the argument list. For instance,

```
#define M(a,b,c,d) ((a##b##c) + (a##d))
total = M(x,1,2,3);
```

produces

```
total = x21 + x3;
```

You can also concatenate arguments with nonargument text. Thus,

```
#define SUBZERO(x) x##[0]
SUBZERO(num) = 2;
```

produces

```
num[0] = 2;
```

You can use ## to create "generic" functions.

```
#define generic_max(type)          \
type type##_max(type x, type y)  \
{                                \
   return x > y ? x : y;         \
}
```

The generic_max macro could be used in the following way:

```
generic_max(float)
```

The preprocessor expands this line into the following code:

```
float float_max(float x, float y)
{
   return x > y ? x : y;
}
```

11.5.3   Macro vs. Function

You may have remarked to yourself as you read the CUBE macro example above that this task could have been accomplished by a simple function:

```
int cube(int num)
{
   return num * num * num;
}
```

Some other examples of macros that serve as alternatives to functions (see Chapter 12, on bit manipulation, for an explanation of the second example's effect):

```
#define max(x,y) ((x) > (y) ? (x) : (y))
#define swap_bytes(i) ((i) << 8 ¦ (i) >> 8)
#define even(n) ((n) % 2 == 0)
#define odd(n) ((n) % 2 != 0)
#define toupper(ch) ('a' <= (ch) && (ch) <= 'z' ?\
   (ch) - 'a' + 'A' : (ch))
```

There are several considerations in deciding which form to use—macro or function. To begin with, macros, as the CUBE example shows, can have some untoward side effects that are not apparent at first blush. Functions also afford greater insulation, since they use their own local variables.

You can create and use pointers to functions. That device is not available with macros.

If you have compiled all your repeatedly used functions into a library (see Chapter 17), using the function version rather than the macro version will be more convenient. If you use the function version, you don't need to do anything more than just use the function whenever you need it. If you use the macro version, you have to remember to define it in whatever source code module you use it in (or define the macro in a header file that you then include in that module).

On the other hand, macros in some situations are somewhat more flexible, since they use no data types. The CUBE macro example can be used just as easily with float, double, or long variables as with ints, for instance. We could modify the cube() function to take and return a double so as to accommodate all these possibilities, but then when we pass an int, we not only have the overhead of a function call and type conversion, but also the slower process of floating point computation.

But sometimes this flexibility comes with a price. The absence of type-checking in these generic macros can lead to undetected errors that would have been flagged easily by the compiler in a function call. Consider the two different approaches to a simple task—producing the absolute value of the difference between two values. Consider this version

```
int abs_diff(int num, int val);
int main(void)
{
   char *str = "what day is it?";
   printf("%d\n", abs_diff(str, -9));
}

int abs_diff(int num, int val)
{
   return num - val >= 0? num - val: val - num;
}
```

versus the following in place of the prototype and function definition:

```
#define abs_diff(a,b) ((a) - (b)) > 0? ((a) - (b)): ((a) - (b))
```

The first version screams at us that we have incompatible types in the first argument. The second version happily returns a value of 179 on our system. Presumably the string str was stored at an offset of 170 in the data segment of our program, so the computer, doing the best it could, converted that address to an int.

Along the same lines, we've seen how macros' side effects can trip us up. Sometimes it is not possible to eliminate the damage with liberal use of parentheses. Consider the following

```
#define treble(a) ((a) * (a) * (a))
. . .
int num = 3, val = treble (num++);
printf("val = %d, num = %d\n", val, num);
```

versus the following in lieu of the define directive:

```
int treble(int quantity)
{
   return quantity * quantity * quantity;
}
```

In the first case, we get values of 60 (that is, 3 * 4 * 5) and 6 on our system; on other systems, you might get a correct value of 9 for val but an incorrect value of 6 for num. The function version always produces the anticipated values of 27 and 4. (Of course, neither is good programming style: the better practice would be to make num++ a separate statement following the trebling business.)

Beyond that, the considerations are essentially the same as the ones you weigh when you try to decide whether to create a simple function to replace one or more lines of code that recur in your program. A function shortens the code and makes it more efficient and modular; on the other hand, a macro and the code it generates are slightly faster to run than a function since jumping from the calling code to the function and back, and passing arguments, takes some time.

Generally, you should opt for functions unless the task is a very simple one and one that occurs frequently in the program, as for instance:

```
#define MAX(X,Y) ((X) > (Y) ? (X) : (Y))
. . .
for (i = 0; i < 100, i++)
   for (j = 0; j < 100; j++)
      price[i][j] = MAX(cost[i][j] * 2, gross[i][j]);
```

or

```
#define AREA(X) (3.1415926536*(X)*(X))
. . .
area = AREA(radius);
```

Again, notice the abundance of parentheses to prevent untoward side effects on macro expansion.

You can use macros in lieu of, or as supplements to, functions if you find the "reverse logic" of some functions confusing:

```
#define same_string(s1,s2) (strcmp(s1, s2) == 0)
```

(Of course, this macro doesn't serve precisely the same purpose as strcmp(), but instances in which you need to know the difference between the character-encoded values at the point that the strings differ are rare.)

Then again, you could have accomplished the same result through a function:

```
char same_string(char *s1, char *s2)
{
    if (strcmp(s1, s2))
        return 0;
    return 1;
}
```

11.5.4   Macros Masquerading as Functions

Many of what look to the novice programmer like Standard C functions are really macros. For example, in Borland C's version of stdio.h:

```
#define getc(f) \
    ((--((f)->level) >= 0) ? (unsigned char)(*(f)->curp++) : fgetc (f))

#define putc(c,f) \
    ((++((f)->level) < 0) ? (unsigned char)(*(f)->curp++=(c)) : fputc ((c),f))

#define getchar()  getc(stdin)
#define putchar(c) putc((c), stdout)
```

The #undef directive will undefine macros—including macros passing for functions—as well as constant definitions. For example, toupper exists in both function form, toupper( ), and macro form, _toupper( ) (the same goes for tolower). Both are found in ctype.h. The function form checks to see whether what has been passed is a lowercase letter; if not, it just returns what was passed. The macro form does no such checking and is guaranteed to work properly only on platforms that use ASCII rather than EBCDIC in any case. (In ASCII, uppercase letters have lower values than lowercase, and both run in uninterrupted sequence from a to z and A to Z; in EBCDIC, lowercase letters precede uppercase, and there are gaps between certain characters, namely, gaps of 8 and 9, respectively, between i and j and between r and s in both uppercase and lowercase letter sets.)

```
#define _toupper(c) ((c) + 'A' - 'a')
```

If you want to include ctype.h for some other purpose but wish to use a redefined version of the macro form of toupper, you can do so this way:

```
#include <ctype.h>
#undef _toupper
#if 'a' >  'A' /* ASCII: upper before lower; both in sequence */
#define _toupper(c)           \
    ((c) >= 'a' && (c) <= 'z' ? (c) - ('a' - 'A') : (c))
#elif 'A' - 'a' == 64 && 'J' - 'I' == 8 /* EBCDIC */
#define _toupper(c)           \
    (((((c) >= 'a' && (c) <= 'i') || ((c) >= 'j' && (c) <= 'r') || \
    ((c) >= 's' && (c) <= 'z')) ? ((c) + 64): (c))
#else
#error Not ASCII or EBCDIC. Famous last words: "This line can never print"
#endif
```

Standard C requires that compilers have function versions of the various Standard C library facilities that handle function-like tasks, even if they also have an overriding macro version of the same thing. If you want to use the function version instead—say you want to create a pointer to that and other functions and use it as we suggested above—you would undefine the macro version, as shown in the last example.

11.5.5 Processing Order and Scope

Preprocessor directives are processed in the following order: conditional directives, `include` directives, `define` directives. However, `define` directives are processed if required to complete conditional directives or `include` directives, even if the processing involves more than one level of expansion of the `define` directive. For instance:

```
#define INCLUDE_STDIO 0
#define HEADERFILE(dir,file) <dir##file>
#if INCLUDE_STDIO
#define HEAD HEADERFILE(stdio,.h)
#else
#define HEAD HEADERFILE(stdlib,.h)
#endif
#include HEAD
```

To determine whether `#if INCLUDE_STDIO` evaluates to true or false, the `#define INCLUDE_STUDIO` directive must be evaluated. Likewise, the `#include HEAD` directive requires evaluation of not only whichever of the two `#define HEAD` directives is conditionally included, but also the `HEADERFILE` macro. The final result is

```
#include<stdio.h>
```

If the 0 in the first line were changed to a nonzero number, the result would be

```
#include <stdlib.h>
```

On the other hand, we have seen that the following does not work because of the processing order:

```
#define IO <stdio.h>
IO
```

Nor will the following fare any better:

```
#define NUM #define MAX 2
NUM
```

Although each level of preprocessing is carried out in full, including any required replacement-item expansions, no level is repeated.

The processing order described above makes sense. How can we tell what code (including `include` and `define` directives) is to be included at all unless the conditional directives are processed first? Likewise, since many files included by an `include` directive may contain `define` directives, how can we process all `define` directives, some of which may depend on others for further expansion, unless we process all `include` directives before the `define` directives?

Apart from other `define` directives' replacement items that are also above a particular replacement string, `define` directives operate only on replacement strings below them in the code. Thus, the first of the following two formulations works, while the second does not:

```
int main(void)
{
#define NUMBER 2
    int num = NUMBER; /* OK */
}

int main(void)
{

    int num = NUMBER; /* error! "undefined symbol NUMBER" */
#define NUMBER 2
}
```

The same is true for the following pair of formulations:

```
#define NUMBER TWO
int main(void)
{
#define TWO 2
   int num = NUMBER;  /* OK */
}

#define NUMBER TWO
int main(void)
{
   int num = NUMBER;  /* error! "undefined symbol TWO" */
#define TWO 2
}
```

Assuming that a `define` directive, as well as any other `define` directive required for full expansion, is located above a particular replacement string in the source code file, their order relative to one another is not material. Thus any of the following formulations works equally well:

```
#define TWO 2
#define NUMBER TWO
int main(void)
{
   int num = NUMBER;
}

#define NUMBER TWO
#define TWO 2
int main(void)
{
   int num = NUMBER;
}

#define NUMBER TWO
int main(void)
{
#define TWO 2
   int num = NUMBER;
}

int main(void)
{
#define NUMBER TWO
#define TWO 2
   int num = NUMBER;
}
```

11.6   THE #error DIRECTIVE (OPTIONAL)

You can use the `#error` directive to prevent an erroneous or undesirable compile-time error. The format is

```
#error <line of text>
```

Let's take an expanded version of our earlier machine-dependent example. We will have three different versions of our executable code, `acct_pc.exe`, `acct_vax.exe`, and `acct_sun.exe`. We plan to distribute the appropriate one to users with one of the three target machines. At various locations in the code, we want different blocks of statements compiled, depending on which version of the executable code we have. We do this by defining one of three manifest constants and then including conditional compilation directives:

```
#define PC
/* #define VAX */
/* #define SUN */
. . .
#if defined PC
   PC-specific code
#elif defined VAX
   VAX-specific code
#elif defined SUN
   SUN-specific code
#endif
. . .
#if defined PC
   PC-specific code
#endif
. . .
#if defined SUN
   SUN-specific code here
#endif
```

Two of these define directives must be commented out or omitted (or you could define two of them as zero and the other with a nonzero value and drop the defined from the conditional directives). We want to make sure we don't forget to define one of these three, and we also want to make sure we haven't defined more than one of them. The following set of directives will accomplish those tasks:

```
/* #define PC */
#define VAX
/* #define SUN */

/* prevent programmer from not defining SUN/VAX/SUN or defining > 1 */

#if (!defined PC && !defined VAX && !defined SUN)
   #error PC, VAX or SUN must be defined
#endif

#if (defined PC && (defined VAX || defined SUN)) || \
   (defined VAX && (defined PC || defined SUN)) || \
   (defined SUN && (defined PC || defined VAX))
      #error Only 1 of PC, VAX & SUN can be defined
#endif
```

If the directive that precedes the error directive is true, you will get an error message on compiling the program. The text of the error message will be what follows error on the same line. Note that this is a compile error, not a run-time error. Also note that what follows #error is a string, so there is no expansion of any replacement items there.

Another common example of the error directive would be to prevent programmers from using the wrong compiler for a compiler-dependent source code:

```
#if !defined __BORLANDC__
#error You must compile this code with Borland C
#endif
```

You can also guard against inadvertent violation of desired program constraints:

```
#define FILE_BUFFER <some value>
#if FILE_BUFFER % BUFSIZ /* defined in stdio.h */
#error FILE_BUFFER must be an integral multiple of BUFSIZ
#endif
```

11.7   USING __LINE__ AND __FILE__ *(OPTIONAL)*

There are any number of ways to identify where in your program a particular error message or other message emanates from. The simplest way is to include a precise message that leaves no doubt as to the origin:

```
if (!open_database(form_db))
    printf("Error calling open_database from form_handler()\n");
```

Another is to use unique error numbers:

```
if (strlen(name) > sizeof(testbuf))
    printf("Error #31\n");
```

You can home in on the very line that caused the message to be issued with __LINE__. The predefined __LINE__ macro is, by default, replaced with the line number of the source code in which the macro is found, expressed as a decimal integer constant:

```
if (!open_database(form_db))
    printf("Error calling open_database: line %d\n", __LINE__);
```

Assuming this particular printf() statement happened to be on line 198 of the source code file, the preprocessor would leave the following in its wake:

```
if (!open_database(form_db))
    printf("Error calling open_database: line %d\n", 198);
```

This line number refers to the post-preprocessed code and is generally the line number in your source code without counting any included files. If an error is encountered in an included file in the course of compiling a source code file, generally the line number would refer to a line number in the included file itself. For example, if you were to use Borland C's preprocessor utility (discussed below) to see what Listing 8.24, the var_type.c file, looks like after preprocessing, you might see something like the following (blank lines are omitted and lines are renumbered):

```
c:\bc\include\stdio.h 1: typedef unsigned size_t;
c:\bc\include\stdio.h 2: typedef long  fpos_t;
c:\bc\include\stdio.h 3: typedef struct {
c:\bc\include\stdio.h 4: int level;
c:\bc\include\stdio.h 5: unsigned flags;
c:\bc\include\stdio.h 6: char fd;
c:\bc\include\stdio.h 7: unsigned char hold;
c:\bc\include\stdio.h 8: int bsize;
c:\bc\include\stdio.h 9: unsigned char *buffer;
c:\bc\include\stdio.h 10: unsigned char *curp;
c:\bc\include\stdio.h 11: unsigned istemp;
c:\bc\include\stdio.h 12: short token;
c:\bc\include\stdio.h 13: } FILE;
. . .
c:\bc\include\stdarg.h 1: typedef void *va_list;
. . .
c:\bc\include\string.h 1: char *__cdecl strlwr(char *__s);
c:\bc\include\string.h 2: char *__cdecl strrev(char *__s)
c:\bc\include\string.h 3: char *__cdecl strupr(char *__s);
. . .
c:\bsource\var_type.c 1: int two_timer(int val);
c:\bsource\var_type.c 2: int three_timer(int num);
c:\bsource\var_type.c 3: int sum(int var_num, ...);
c:\bsource\var_type.c 4: void whichever(char * string, ...);
c:\bsource\var_type.c 5:
c:\bsource\var_type.c 6: struct record
c:\bsource\var_type.c 7: {
```

```
c:\bsource\var_type.c 8: int salary;
c:\bsource\var_type.c 9: float hours;
c:\bsource\var_type.c 10: };
c:\bsource\var_type.c 11:
c:\bsource\var_type.c 12: int main(void)
c:\bsource\var_type.c 13: {
. . .
```

However, some implementations count included files in numbering a source code, so that if the three headers included in var_type.c contained 322 lines and an error occurred in the line just after main(), the error line would be line 336—a reference that is not altogether enlightening without some head-scratching. To remedy this problem, you can use the line directive discussed in the next section.

If you also wish to include the file name, you can use __FILE__. The __FILE__ predefined macro is, by default, replaced by the name of the source code file in which the directive appears, expressed as a string constant.

Assuming the following were in a source code named db.c, the statements

```
if (!open_database(form_db)
    printf("Error calling open_database: line %d of %s\n", __LINE__, __FILE__);
```

would be transmuted on preprocessing into

```
if (!open_database(form_db)
    printf("Error calling open_database: line %d of %s\n", 198, "db.c");
```

As indicated, the __FILE__ macro is replaced by the file name enclosed in double quotes; the __LINE__ macro is replaced by an integer constant.

11.7.1   The #line directive

You can manipulate the values substituted for __LINE__ and __FILE__ with the #line directive. The syntax is

```
#line <line number> "<file name or other identifier>"
```

From the point in the file at which this directive appears until another such directive is found, the preprocessor will replace __FILE__ with the quote-enclosed part of the directive and will replace __LINE__ with the number of lines from the directive to the statement in which __LINE__ appears plus the line number specified in the directive.

Though __FILE__ would seem to imply a file name (and indeed it yields the source code file name if there is no #line directive), you can use the #line directive in conjunction with function names or anything else you like:

```
int some_function(int value)
{
   int some_number;
#line 1 "some_function"
   if (value < 0)
      printf("Invalid value in line %d of %s", __LINE__, __FILE__);
   . . .
}
```

The result of passing –1:

```
Invalid value in line 2 of some_function.
```

This non-filename usage may slightly confuse the compiler; if the function containing the directive generates a compile-time error or warning, the compiler may tell you the error or warning is in the "[whatever you have within the quotes after #line] file."

The line-number specification can be any integer constant or constant expression evaluating to between 0 and 32,767. If the directive would produce a number larger than 32,767 anywhere the directive or `__LINE__` appears, you will receive a compile error message. If you prefer not to start renumbering from 1 in each function, you can use `__LINE__` in the `#line` directive itself:

```
int some_function(int value)
{
#line __LINE__ "some_function"
   if (value < 0)
   printf("Invalid value in line %d of %s", __LINE__, __FILE__);
      . . .
}
```

The sole purpose here is to change the `__FILE__` designation.

Conversely, you can use the format

```
#line <line number>
```

without a double-quote-enclosed message following the `line` directive. That resets the value of `__LINE__` but leaves `__FILE__` unaltered. Thus, if `some_function( )` is found in file `math.c` and your directive there is `#line 901`, you would get the following after passing a negative number:

```
Invalid value in line 902 of math.c
```

You can use a replacement item of a `define` directive as part of a `#line` directive, as long as the expanded result is one of the two formats above:

```
#define LINENUM 3
. . .
#line LINENUM
```

11.8   MORE SOPHISTICATED DEBUGGING AND TESTING: assert MACRO (OPTIONAL)

Earlier in this chapter, we saw the following formulation for testing statements interspersed throughout the code:

```
#define TESTING
. . .
#if defined TESTING
   fp = fopen("a:\\test", "w");
#endif
. . .
#if defined TESTING
   if (!(num >= -999 && num <= 999))
      printf("Assertion failed: !(num >= -999 && num <= 999)");
#endif
. . .
#if defined TESTING
   fclose(fp);
#endif
```

Now we know how to make that a little more automated and informative:

```
#if defined TESTING
   if (!(num >= -999 && num <= 999))
   {
   /* num should be between -1000 and 1000 */
      printf("Assertion failed: !(num >= -999 && num <= 999)\n"
         "File: %s, Line: %d\n", __LINE__, __FILE__);
      abort();
   }
#endif
```

Assuming we are repeatedly testing for whether certain assumptions we make in the course of the program regarding values or the like are true (as opposed to just printing out values as we go), we can automate the process even further with the use of the `assert` macro. This macro is found in `assert.h`, which you must include if you wish to use it.

The argument to `assert` is any expression that could be true or false. If the expression evaluates to 1 (that is, it is true), nothing happens. If the expression evaluates to 0 (that is, it is false), the following are printed to the standard output device (see Chapter 14): the expression verbatim, the file name, and the line number; then the `abort()` function is called (see Chapter 16) to terminate the program.

In place of the lengthy example above, we can simply include a single statement with precisely the same effect:

```
assert(num >= -999 && num <= 999);
```

You don't even need the comment any longer.

To disable all the `assert` statements in the program, all you need to do is to insert the following toward the top of the code:

```
#define NDEBUG
```

Here's how an implementation might manage the whole process in `assert.h` (the `#p` prints the text of the expression passed verbatim):

```
#ifdef NDEBUG
#define assert(p) ((void)0)
#else
#define assert(p) ((p) ? (void)0 : (void) __assertfail( \
    "Assertion failed: %s, file %s, line %d\n", \
    #p, __FILE__, __LINE__ ))
#endif

void __assertfail(char *format_string, char *condition, char *filename, int line);
```

with `__assertfail()` being defined something along these lines:

```
void __assertfail(char *format_string, char *condition, char *filename, int line)
{
    printf(format_string, condition, filename, line);
    abort();
}
```

Therefore, if you have dozens of assert statements in the code and you no longer need them because the program is now operational, all you have to do is to define `NDEBUG`, and all these statements are replaced with something intentionally innocuous and without any run-time overhead like

```
(void)0;
```

Otherwise, our example gets replaced on preprocessing with something like

```
((num >= -999 && num <= 999) ? (void)0 :
    (void) __assertfail( "Assertion failed: %s, file %s,
    line %d\n", "num > 2 && num < 99", "c:\\junk.c", 22 ));
```

11.9   OTHER PREDEFINED MACROS *(OPTIONAL)*

You can use `__DATE__` and `__TIME__` to advise the programmer or user of the date and time of program compilation. That way, you can make sure the latest version is being run or tested. For instance:

```
printf("DataBlaster Version %s %s\n", __DATE__, __TIME__);
```

What these produce, respectively, are in the following formats:

```
Nov 24 2000 14:32:21
```

If the __STDC__ macro is defined, it has a value of 1 and indicates that the compiler conforms to the 1990 C Standard. If __STDC_VERSION__ is defined, it has the value 199409L, which indicates that the compiler conforms to Standard C, including Technical Corrigendum 1. (See the preface for a discussion of the Standard and its 1994 amendment.)

Any attempt to undefine or redefine __LINE__, __FILE__, __DATE__, __TIME__, __STDC__, __STDC_VERSION__, or any other predefined macros will give you an error that will prevent you from compiling.

11.10   DEBUGGING PREPROCESSOR DIRECTIVES *(OPTIONAL)*

Both Borland C and Microsoft C provide utilities that allow you to see the results of inserting files with include directives and carrying out define directive substitution or conditional compilation. The Borland C utility is cpp.exe. It is run from the command line. You simply type cpp and the name of the source code file (with the path if the source code is not located in the current directory). The result is stored in a file with the same base name as the source code and a .i extension. This file gets placed in whatever directory the cpp utility is executed from.

For example, the following source code, preptest.c,

```
#define CLOCK_CYCLE 1193180.
#define C4 261.63
#define NOTE(freq) CLOCK_CYCLE/freq
#define Q(t) play(NOTE(t), .25)
void play(double, double);
int main(void)
{
    Q(C4);
}
```

produces preptest.i:

```
preptest.c 1:
preptest.c 2:
preptest.c 3:
preptest.c 4:
preptest.c 5: void play(double, double);
preptest.c 6: int main(void)
preptest.c 7: {
preptest.c 8:
preptest.c 9: play(1193180./261.63, .25);
preptest.c 10: }
preptest.c 11:
```

This utility is particularly useful in trying to decipher error messages caused by a logical or syntax error in a define directive. For example, if we mistakenly add a semicolon to a define directive

```
#define ADD(a,b) ((a) + (b));
. . .
int c = ADD(17, 12) * ADD(19, 22);
```

we get the confusing message "Invalid indirection." If we view the processed code, we will see that the * appearing after the inadvertent semicolon is taken as an indirection operator rather than a multiplication operator.

11.11   PRAGMAS *(OPTIONAL)*

Although it is generally preferable to limit our code to what is acceptable on any C compiler, it may be necessary or desirable to deviate from this preference and to use facilities that depend on a particular compiler. Such system-dependent facilities are to be used by a particular compiler by means of a line in the following format

```
#pragma . . .
```

where the ellipsis denotes some compiler-defined text that causes the compiler, if it recognizes the text, to perform certain prescribed actions. If not, the line is simply ignored, after which compilation continues.

Nevertheless, if you are concerned that a particular pragma for a specific compiler will also be recognized by a different compiler but accorded different treatment, you can use the pragma conditionally, and in fact, to be safe, there is probably little reason for not doing so:

```
#if defined __BORLANDC__
#pragma startup initialize
#pragma exit cleanup
#pragma saveregs
#pragma inline
#endif
```

As with #line, what follows #pragma can include the replacement item of a define directive.

11.12   APPLICATION: ACE BILLING PROGRAM

We can improve the maintainability of the ACE Billing program by liberal use of manifest constants and macros.

11.12.1   Input

Same input data as for acech06.exe in Chapter 6.

 Listing 11.1 acech11.c

```
#ifndef acech11_H
#define acech11_H
/*
    +---------------------------------------------------------------+
    +    Program Name: acech11.h
    +        Author(s): Austell-Wolfson and Otieno
    +             Date: 12/10/2000
    +    Purpose:
    +        This file has all the manifest constants or macros needed by
    +        acech11.c program.
    +
    +---------------------------------------------------------------+
*/
#define CUSTOMER_NAME_SIZE        16
#define INPUT_BUFFER_SIZE         1024
#define NUMBER_OF_CUSTOMERS       100
#define CUSTOMER_INITIALS_SIZE    3
#define TOTALS_POSITION           NUMBER_OF_CUSTOMERS - 1
#define TEMPORARY_POSITION        TOTALS_POSITION - 1
#define NUMBER_OF_INPUT_FIELDS    6
#define CHARGE_RATE               200
#define SPECIAL_MEMBERSHIP_FEE    2500
#define MIN_ACTIVITY_CEILING      6
#define MID_ACTIVITY_CEILING      11
#define UPPER_ACTIVITY_FLOOR      12
#define MIN_ACTIVITY_RATE         250.00
#define MID_ACTIVITY_RATE         500.00
```

```
#define UPPER_ACTIVITY_RATE       750.00
#define MIN_CHARGE_DISCOUNT_LEVEL 8500.00
#define MEMBERSHIP_FLAG           'Y'

/* See comment to acech08.c: using structures once we reach Chapter 13 */
   char  specialMembershipFlag[NUMBER_OF_CUSTOMERS];
   char  customerName[NUMBER_OF_CUSTOMERS][CUSTOMER_NAME_SIZE];
   char  customerInitials[NUMBER_OF_CUSTOMERS][CUSTOMER_INITIALS_SIZE];
   float membershipFee[NUMBER_OF_CUSTOMERS];
   float activityFee[NUMBER_OF_CUSTOMERS];
   float discountAmount[NUMBER_OF_CUSTOMERS];
   float chargeAmount[NUMBER_OF_CUSTOMERS];
   float totalIndividualBill[NUMBER_OF_CUSTOMERS];
   float aceClubTotals[NUMBER_OF_CUSTOMERS];
   float charges[NUMBER_OF_CUSTOMERS];
   int   discount[NUMBER_OF_CUSTOMERS];
   int   averageCharges[NUMBER_OF_CUSTOMERS];
   int   numberOfCharges[NUMBER_OF_CUSTOMERS];

void initialization(char * specialMembershipFlag,
   char customerName[NUMBER_OF_CUSTOMERS][CUSTOMER_NAME_SIZE],
   char customerInitials[NUMBER_OF_CUSTOMERS][CUSTOMER_INITIALS_SIZE],
   float * membershipFee, float * activityFee, float * discountAmount,
   float * chargeAmount, float * totalIndividualBill, float * aceClubTotals,
   float * charges, int * discount, int * averageCharges, int * numberOfCharges);

void processMemberRecord(char * inputBuffer, char * specialMembershipFlag,
   char customerName[NUMBER_OF_CUSTOMERS][CUSTOMER_NAME_SIZE],
   char customerInitials[NUMBER_OF_CUSTOMERS][CUSTOMER_INITIALS_SIZE],
   float * membershipFee, float * activityFee, float * discountAmount,
   float * totalIndividualBill, float * aceClubTotals, float * charges, int * discount,
   int * averageCharges, int * numberOfCharges, int * clubMember);

void termination(void);

void printGrandTotals(float * membershipFee, float * activityFee, float * discountAmount,
   float * totalIndividualBill, float * charges, int * numberOfCharges);

void initializeVariables(char * specialMembershipFlag,
   char customerName[NUMBER_OF_CUSTOMERS][CUSTOMER_NAME_SIZE],
   char customerInitials[NUMBER_OF_CUSTOMERS][CUSTOMER_INITIALS_SIZE],
   float * membershipFee, float * activityFee, float * discountAmount, float * chargeAmount,
   float * totalIndividualBill, float * aceClubTotals, float * charges, int * discount,
   int * averageCharges, int * numberOfCharges);

void printHeadings(void);

void computeIndividualBill(char * specialMembershipFlag, float * membershipFee,
   float * activityFee, float * discountAmount, float * totalIndividualBill,
   float * aceClubTotals, float * charges, int * discount, int * averageCharges,
   int * numberOfCharges, int * clubMember);

void writeDetailLine(
   char customerName[NUMBER_OF_CUSTOMERS][CUSTOMER_NAME_SIZE],
   char customerInitials[NUMBER_OF_CUSTOMERS][CUSTOMER_INITIALS_SIZE], float * membershipFee,
   float * activityFee, float * discountAmount, float * totalIndividualBill,
   float * charges, int * numberOfCharges, int * clubMember);

void determineSpecialFee(char * specialMembershipFlag,
   float * membershipFee, int * clubMember);
```

```
void determineActivityFee(float * activityFee, int * numberOfCharges, int * clubMember);
void determineDiscountAmt(int * averageCharges, int * discount,
   float * discountAmount, int * clubMember);

void sortByClubMemberNames(char * specialMembershipFlag,
   char customerName[NUMBER_OF_CUSTOMERS][CUSTOMER_NAME_SIZE],
   char customerInitials[NUMBER_OF_CUSTOMERS][CUSTOMER_INITIALS_SIZE], float * membershipFee,
   float * activityFee, float * discountAmount, float * chargeAmount,
   float * totalIndividualBill, float * aceClubTotals, float * charges, int * discount,
   int * averageCharges, int * numberOfCharges,  int * clubMember);

void printSortedReport(
   char customerName[NUMBER_OF_CUSTOMERS][CUSTOMER_NAME_SIZE],
   char customerInitials[NUMBER_OF_CUSTOMERS][CUSTOMER_INITIALS_SIZE], float * membershipFee,
   float * activityFee, float * discountAmount, float * totalIndividualBill, float * charges,
   int * numberOfCharges, int * clubMember);

void swapValues(char * specialMembershipFlag,
   char customerName[NUMBER_OF_CUSTOMERS][CUSTOMER_NAME_SIZE],
   char customerInitials[NUMBER_OF_CUSTOMERS][CUSTOMER_INITIALS_SIZE], float * membershipFee,
   float * activityFee, float * discountAmount, float * chargeAmount,
   float * totalIndividualBill, float * aceClubTotals, float * charges, int * discount,
   int * averageCharges, int * numberOfCharges, int currentPos);

#endif

/*
   +-----------------------------------------------------------------+
   +    Program Name: acech11.c
   +       Author(s): Austell-Wolfson and Otieno
   +            Date: 04/10/2000
   +    Purpose:
   +       This program processes a file of ACE Club member records and
   +       computes and prints the total amounts for all club members.
   +
   +    Process:
   +      This program prints the prescribed headings for the report, and
   +      processes each record by:
   +         computing the individual member bill, equal to the sum of
   +         member bill, membership fee, and activity fee, minus any
   +         discount amount. The members are charged a special
   +         membership fee of $2500 if the person is a special
   +         member, indicated by a Y in the membership flag field. The
   +         activity fees are based on the number of activities each
   +         member requests. The more activities they request, the more
   +         they are charged. A discount amount is applied if the member
   +         has an average charge of over $8000 per bill.
   +-----------------------------------------------------------------+
*/
#include <stdio.h>
#include <string.h>
#include <stdlib.h>
#include "acech11.h"

int main(void)
{
   char  InputBuffer[INPUT_BUFFER_SIZE]; /* incoming input record */
   char  specialMembershipFlag[NUMBER_OF_CUSTOMERS];
   char  customerName[NUMBER_OF_CUSTOMERS][CUSTOMER_NAME_SIZE];
   char  customerInitials[NUMBER_OF_CUSTOMERS][CUSTOMER_INITIALS_SIZE];
```

```
    float membershipFee[NUMBER_OF_CUSTOMERS];
    float activityFee[NUMBER_OF_CUSTOMERS];
    float discountAmount[NUMBER_OF_CUSTOMERS];
    float chargeAmount[NUMBER_OF_CUSTOMERS];
    float totalIndividualBill[NUMBER_OF_CUSTOMERS];
    float aceClubTotals[NUMBER_OF_CUSTOMERS];
    float charges[NUMBER_OF_CUSTOMERS];
    int   discount[NUMBER_OF_CUSTOMERS];
    int   averageCharges[NUMBER_OF_CUSTOMERS];
    int   numberOfCharges[NUMBER_OF_CUSTOMERS];

    /*
    +----------------------------------------------------------------+
    + clubMember holds the count of all club members. It is also used
    + to index the array of club members; therefore its value starts
    + at 0.
    +----------------------------------------------------------------+
    */
    int clubMember = 0;

    initialization(specialMembershipFlag, customerName, customerInitials, membershipFee,
       activityFee, discountAmount, chargeAmount, totalIndividualBill, aceClubTotals, charges,
       discount, averageCharges, numberOfCharges);

    while (gets(InputBuffer) != NULL)
    {
       processMemberRecord(InputBuffer, specialMembershipFlag, customerName, customerInitials,
       membershipFee, activityFee, discountAmount, totalIndividualBill, aceClubTotals, charges,
       discount, averageCharges, numberOfCharges, &clubMember);
    }
    printGrandTotals(membershipFee, activityFee, discountAmount, totalIndividualBill,
       charges, numberOfCharges);

    sortByClubMemberNames(specialMembershipFlag, customerName, customerInitials, membershipFee,
       activityFee, discountAmount, chargeAmount, totalIndividualBill, aceClubTotals, charges,
       discount, averageCharges, numberOfCharges, &clubMember);

    printSortedReport(customerName, customerInitials, membershipFee, activityFee,
       discountAmount, totalIndividualBill, charges, numberOfCharges, &clubMember);

    printGrandTotals(membershipFee, activityFee, discountAmount, totalIndividualBill, charges,
       numberOfCharges);

    termination();
    return 0;
}

void initialization(char * specialMembershipFlag,
    char customerName[][CUSTOMER_NAME_SIZE], char customerInitials[][CUSTOMER_INITIALS_SIZE],
    float * membershipFee, float * activityFee, float * discountAmount, float * chargeAmount,
    float * totalIndividualBill, float * aceClubTotals, float * charges,
    int * discount, int * averageCharges, int * numberOfCharges)
{
    initializeVariables(specialMembershipFlag, customerName, customerInitials, membershipFee,
       activityFee, discountAmount, chargeAmount, totalIndividualBill, aceClubTotals, charges,
       discount, averageCharges, numberOfCharges);

    printHeadings();
    return;
}
```

```
void processMemberRecord(char * InputBuffer, char * specialMembershipFlag,
   char customerName[][CUSTOMER_NAME_SIZE], char customerInitials[][CUSTOMER_INITIALS_SIZE],
   float * membershipFee, float * activityFee, float * discountAmount,
   float * totalIndividualBill, float * aceClubTotals, float * charges, int * discount,
   int * averageCharges, int * numberOfCharges, int * clubMember)
{
   int status;

   /* see comment to acech09.c re input parsing process */
   status = sscanf(InputBuffer, "%15c%2c%2d%c%4d%4d",
   customerName[*clubMember], customerInitials[*clubMember],
   &numberOfCharges[*clubMember], &specialMembershipFlag[*clubMember],
   &discount[*clubMember], &averageCharges[*clubMember]);

   if (status != NUMBER_OF_INPUT_FIELDS)
   {
      printf("There is a problem with the file format.\n");
      printf("The program is terminated mid-stream\n");
      exit(1);
   }

   computeIndividualBill(specialMembershipFlag, membershipFee, activityFee, discountAmount,
   totalIndividualBill, aceClubTotals, charges, discount, averageCharges, numberOfCharges,
   clubMember);

   writeDetailLine(customerName, customerInitials, membershipFee, activityFee, discountAmount,
      totalIndividualBill, charges, numberOfCharges, clubMember);
   return;
}

/* see comment in acech06.c re termination function */
void termination(void)
{
   /* not implemented */
}

void initializeVariables(char * specialMembershipFlag,
   char customerName[][CUSTOMER_NAME_SIZE], char customerInitials[][CUSTOMER_INITIALS_SIZE],
   float * membershipFee, float * activityFee, float * discountAmount, float * chargeAmount,
   float * totalIndividualBill, float * aceClubTotals, float * charges,
   int * discount, int * averageCharges, int * numberOfCharges)
{
   /* see comment to acech09.c re series of memset calls here */
   memset(specialMembershipFlag,'\0',NUMBER_OF_CUSTOMERS);
   memset(discount, 0, NUMBER_OF_CUSTOMERS * sizeof (int));
   memset(averageCharges, 0, NUMBER_OF_CUSTOMERS * sizeof (int));
   memset(membershipFee, 0, NUMBER_OF_CUSTOMERS * sizeof (float));
   memset(activityFee, 0, NUMBER_OF_CUSTOMERS * sizeof (float));
   memset(discountAmount, 0, NUMBER_OF_CUSTOMERS * sizeof (float));
   memset(chargeAmount, 0, NUMBER_OF_CUSTOMERS * sizeof (float));
   memset(numberOfCharges, 0, NUMBER_OF_CUSTOMERS * sizeof (int));
   memset(totalIndividualBill, 0, NUMBER_OF_CUSTOMERS * sizeof (float));
   memset(aceClubTotals, 0, NUMBER_OF_CUSTOMERS * sizeof (float));
   memset(charges, 0, NUMBER_OF_CUSTOMERS * sizeof (float));
   memset(customerName, 0, NUMBER_OF_CUSTOMERS * CUSTOMER_NAME_SIZE);
   memset(customerInitials, 0,
      NUMBER_OF_CUSTOMERS * CUSTOMER_INITIALS_SIZE);
}

void printHeadings(void)
```

```
{
    printf("┌──────────────────────────────────────────────────────────────────────┐\n");
    printf("│                                                                        │\n");
    printf("│    Program Name: ACECH11.EXE                              Page:  1     │\n");
    printf("│       Run Date: 12/10/2000              Ace Billing                     │\n");
    printf("│                                                                        │\n");
    printf("│                                                                        │\n");
    printf("├────────────────────────────────────────────────────────────────────────┤\n");
    printf("│                                                                        │\n");
    printf("│ Customer Name   Charges     Bill    Mbr Fee     Act Fee    Disc  Total Bill │\n");
    printf("├────────────────────────────────────────────────────────────────────────┤\n");
    printf("│                                                                        │\n");
}

void computeIndividualBill(char * specialMembershipFlag, float * membershipFee,
    float * activityFee, float * discountAmount, float * totalIndividualBill,
    float * aceClubTotals, float * charges, int * discount, int * averageCharges,
    int * numberOfCharges, int * clubMember)
{

    charges[*clubMember] = CHARGE_RATE * numberOfCharges[*clubMember];
    charges[TOTALS_POSITION] += charges[*clubMember];
    numberOfCharges[TOTALS_POSITION] += numberOfCharges[*clubMember];
    determineSpecialFee(specialMembershipFlag, membershipFee, clubMember);
    determineActivityFee(activityFee, numberOfCharges, clubMember);
    determineDiscountAmt(averageCharges, discount, discountAmount, clubMember);

    totalIndividualBill[*clubMember] = charges[*clubMember] + membershipFee[*clubMember] +
    activityFee[*clubMember] - discountAmount[*clubMember];
    totalIndividualBill[TOTALS_POSITION] += totalIndividualBill[*clubMember];
    aceClubTotals[TOTALS_POSITION] += totalIndividualBill[*clubMember];
}

void writeDetailLine(char customerName[][CUSTOMER_NAME_SIZE],
    char customerInitials[][CUSTOMER_INITIALS_SIZE],
    float * membershipFee, float * activityFee, float * discountAmount,
      float * totalIndividualBill, float * charges, int * numberOfCharges, int * clubMember)
{
    printf("│ %15.15s  %s %2d  $%9.2f  $%8.2f  $%8.2f  $%5.f  $%9.2f",
      customerName[*clubMember], customerInitials[*clubMember], numberOfCharges[*clubMember],
      charges[*clubMember], membershipFee[*clubMember], activityFee[*clubMember],
      discountAmount[*clubMember], totalIndividualBill[*clubMember]);
    printf("  │\n");

    *clubMember = *clubMember + 1; /* Increment number of club members */
}

void determineSpecialFee(char * specialMembershipFlag,
    float * membershipFee, int * clubMember)
{
    if (MEMBERSHIP_FLAG == specialMembershipFlag[*clubMember])
    {
        membershipFee[*clubMember] = SPECIAL_MEMBERSHIP_FEE;
    }
    else
    {
        membershipFee[*clubMember] = 0.0;
    }

    membershipFee[TOTALS_POSITION] += membershipFee[*clubMember];
}
```

```
void determineActivityFee(float * activityFee, int * numberOfCharges, int * clubMember)
{
   if (numberOfCharges[*clubMember] <= MIN_ACTIVITY_CEILING)
   {
      activityFee[*clubMember] = MIN_ACTIVITY_RATE;
   }

   if ((numberOfCharges[*clubMember] > MIN_ACTIVITY_CEILING) &&
       (numberOfCharges[*clubMember] <= MID_ACTIVITY_CEILING + 1))
   {
      activityFee[*clubMember] = MID_ACTIVITY_RATE;
   }

   if (numberOfCharges[*clubMember] > UPPER_ACTIVITY_FLOOR)
   {
      activityFee[*clubMember] = UPPER_ACTIVITY_RATE;
   }

   activityFee[TOTALS_POSITION] += activityFee[*clubMember];
}

void determineDiscountAmt(int * averageCharges, int * discount, float * discountAmount,
   int * clubMember)
{
   if (averageCharges[*clubMember] > MIN_CHARGE_DISCOUNT_LEVEL)
   {
      discountAmount[*clubMember] = discount[*clubMember];
   }
   else
   {
      discountAmount[*clubMember] = 0;
   }

   discountAmount[*clubMember] = 0;
}

void sortByClubMemberNames(char * specialMembershipFlag,
   char customerName[][CUSTOMER_NAME_SIZE], char customerInitials[][CUSTOMER_INITIALS_SIZE],
   float * membershipFee, float * activityFee, float * discountAmount, float * chargeAmount,
   float * totalIndividualBill, float * aceClubTotals, float * charges, int * discount,
   int * averageCharges, int * numberOfCharges, int * clubMember)
{
   int currentPos; /* Holds current array position being processed */
   int k; /* Loop index variable  */

   /* Determines whether to make more passes during the bubble sort algorithm */
   int morePasses = 1;
/*
   +------------------------------------------------------------------+
   +  Start the loop that makes as many passes through array of club
   +  member names as needed for the entire list to be sorted.
   +
   +------------------------------------------------------------------+
*/
   while (1 == morePasses)
   {
/*
   +------------------------------------------------------------------+
   +  Turn it off so that if the data is sorted no
   +  passes will be necessary. If, however, there was
```

```
    +   a single swap, morePasses will be set to 1
    +   and the while loop repeats as it should.
    +
    +----------------------------------------------------------------+
*/
        morePasses = 0;
        for (k = 0; k < *clubMember - 1; k++)
        {
            if (strcmp(customerName[k], customerName[k + 1]) > 0)
            {
                currentPos = k;

                /* swap all the values in the parallel arrays */
                swapValues(specialMembershipFlag, customerName,
                customerInitials, membershipFee, activityFee,
                discountAmount, chargeAmount, totalIndividualBill,
                aceClubTotals, charges, discount, averageCharges,
                numberOfCharges, currentPos);
                morePasses = 1;
            }
        }   /* end of for loop */
    }   /* end of while loop */
}

void printSortedReport(char customerName[][CUSTOMER_NAME_SIZE],
    char customerInitials[][CUSTOMER_INITIALS_SIZE], float * membershipFee,
    float * activityFee, float * discountAmount, float * totalIndividualBill,
    float * charges, int * numberOfCharges, int * clubMember)
{
    int k; /* Loop index variable */

    /* print the column headings for the sorted list of club members */
    printHeadings();

    for (k = 0; k < *clubMember; k++)
    {
        printf("| %15.15s  %s %2d  $%9.2f  $%8.2f  $%8.2f  $%5.f  $%9.2f", customerName[k],
            customerInitials[k], numberOfCharges[k], charges[k], membershipFee[k],
            activityFee[k], discountAmount[k], totalIndividualBill[k]);
        printf(" |\n");
    }
}

void swapValues (char * specialMembershipFlag, char customerName[][CUSTOMER_NAME_SIZE],
    char customerInitials[][CUSTOMER_INITIALS_SIZE], float * membershipFee,
    float * activityFee, float * discountAmount, float * chargeAmount,
    float * totalIndividualBill, float * aceClubTotals, float * charges,int * discount,
    int * averageCharges, int * numberOfCharges, int currentPos)
{


    /* see comment to acech06.c re larger than required array and number of swap slots used */

    /* Swap the last name of club member */
    strcpy(customerName[TEMPORARY_POSITION], customerName[currentPos]);
    strcpy(customerName[currentPos], customerName[currentPos + 1]);
    strcpy(customerName[currentPos + 1], customerName[TEMPORARY_POSITION]);
```

```
/* Swap the customer initials */
strcpy(customerInitials[TEMPORARY_POSITION],customerInitials[currentPos]);
strcpy(customerInitials[currentPos], customerInitials[currentPos + 1]);
strcpy(customerInitials[currentPos + 1], customerInitials[TEMPORARY_POSITION]);

/* swap the specialMembershipFlag */
specialMembershipFlag[TEMPORARY_POSITION] = specialMembershipFlag[currentPos];
specialMembershipFlag[currentPos] = specialMembershipFlag[currentPos + 1];
specialMembershipFlag[currentPos + 1] = specialMembershipFlag[TEMPORARY_POSITION];

/* swap the total membership fee */
membershipFee[TEMPORARY_POSITION] = membershipFee[currentPos];
membershipFee[currentPos] = membershipFee[currentPos + 1];
membershipFee[currentPos + 1] = membershipFee[TEMPORARY_POSITION];

/* swap the total activity fee */
activityFee[TEMPORARY_POSITION] = activityFee[currentPos];
activityFee[currentPos] = activityFee[currentPos + 1];
activityFee[currentPos + 1] = activityFee[TEMPORARY_POSITION];

/* swap the total discount amount */
discountAmount[TEMPORARY_POSITION] = discountAmount[currentPos];
discountAmount[currentPos] = discountAmount[currentPos + 1];
discountAmount[currentPos+1] = discountAmount[TEMPORARY_POSITION];

/* swap the total charge amount */
chargeAmount[TEMPORARY_POSITION] = chargeAmount[currentPos];
chargeAmount[currentPos] = chargeAmount[currentPos + 1];
chargeAmount[currentPos + 1] = chargeAmount[TEMPORARY_POSITION];

/* swap the total individual bill */
totalIndividualBill[TEMPORARY_POSITION] = totalIndividualBill[currentPos];
totalIndividualBill[currentPos] = totalIndividualBill[currentPos + 1];
totalIndividualBill[currentPos + 1] = totalIndividualBill[TEMPORARY_POSITION];

/* swap the total ace club totals */
aceClubTotals[TEMPORARY_POSITION] = aceClubTotals[currentPos];
aceClubTotals[currentPos] = aceClubTotals[currentPos + 1];
aceClubTotals[currentPos + 1] = aceClubTotals[TEMPORARY_POSITION];

/* swap the total charges */
charges[TEMPORARY_POSITION] = charges[currentPos];
charges[currentPos] = charges[currentPos + 1];
charges[currentPos + 1] = charges[TEMPORARY_POSITION];

/* swap the total discount */
discount[TEMPORARY_POSITION] = discount[currentPos];
discount[currentPos] = discount[currentPos + 1];
discount[currentPos + 1] = discount[TEMPORARY_POSITION];

/* swap the total average charges */
averageCharges[TEMPORARY_POSITION] = averageCharges[currentPos];
averageCharges[currentPos] = averageCharges[currentPos + 1];
averageCharges[currentPos + 1] = averageCharges[TEMPORARY_POSITION];

/* swap the total number of charges bill */
numberOfCharges[TEMPORARY_POSITION] = numberOfCharges[currentPos];
```

```
        numberOfCharges[currentPos] = numberOfCharges[currentPos + 1];
        numberOfCharges[currentPos + 1] = numberOfCharges[TEMPORARY_POSITION];
}

void printGrandTotals(float * membershipFee, float * activityFee, float * discountAmount,
    float * totalIndividualBill, float * charges, int * numberOfCharges)
{
    printf("| %*s--- ---------- --------- --------- ------ ----------|\n",
        19, " ");
    printf("| ACE Club Totals     %3d  $%9.2f  $%8.2f  $%8.2f  $%5.f"
        " $%9.2f |\n",
        numberOfCharges[TOTALS_POSITION], charges[TOTALS_POSITION],
        membershipFee[TOTALS_POSITION], activityFee[TOTALS_POSITION],
        discountAmount[TOTALS_POSITION],
            totalIndividualBill[TOTALS_POSITION]);
    printf("+--------------------------------------------------------------------------+\n\n");
}
```

11.12.2   Output

Same output report as for acech06.exe in Chapter 6.

Chapter Summary

1. Preprocessor directives are processed before the source code is compiled.
2. All preprocessor directives start with #. Whitespace may precede and follow the #.
3. Preprocessor directives are not terminated by semicolons; the presence or absence of spacing on a line is generally significant. The directive keywords must be in all lowercase.
4. A preprocessor directive must be completely within a single line. Two or more physical lines may be combined into one logical line with backslashes.
5. The include directive directs the computer to insert another file—called a header file—verbatim. The include file generally contains function prototypes, define directives, typedefs, and structure and union templates.
6. An included header file may contain one or more include directives.
7. If you recompile after altering a header file, you must recompile all source codes that contain the same header file. Otherwise, the unrecompiled source codes' object modules have the old version of the functions and templates and define directives included in the header.
8. You may include a Standard C header file any number of times, in any order.
9. There are two formats for include directives: paired angle brackets and paired double quotes. The angle bracket format is meant to be used for Standard C header files; the double-quote method, for your own header files or those of a third-party toolkit vendor.
10. There are two types of define directives—those without arguments and those with arguments.

11. The simplest use of define directives, the no-argument type, is to employ them as simple word processing search-and-replace devices.

    ```
    #define identifier replacement_item
    ```

12. The replacement item can be any sequence of C tokens, including variable names, keywords, numbers, character constants, literal strings, operators, and punctuation. For define directive identifiers, you must adhere to the C rules for permissible letters in variable names.
13. Macro identifiers that represent a constant numerical value are called manifest constants.
14. The preprocessor considers what is between the first and second space after the word define to be the identifier that is to be replaced. For this purpose, "space" includes an entire block of spaces or tabs, not only a single space.
15. What's between the second and last space on the define directive line is the replacement item. Any internal spaces in the replacement item are part of the replacement item itself.
16. The preprocessor ignores identifiers embedded in replacement items, character constants, and literal strings; however, identifiers appearing in their own replacement items will not be replaced. The correct way to implement a replacement within a literal string is through %s conversion specifiers.
17. Since preprocessing occurs before program compilation, preprocessor identifiers may have the same names as variable names without causing conflict.
18. A define identifier normally remains in effect from the point at which it appears to the end of the file. However, it may be undefined by the undef directive.

19. An error message will be generated if you define the same constant twice without an intervening undefinition and the definitions are not identical. Any redefinition without intervening undefinition must include whitespace in the same places as in the earlier definition

20. It is not an error to use an `undef` for an identifier that has not been defined.

21. The preprocessor provides a conditional test construction to control whether statements or other lines of text are or are not included in the compiled version of the source code. The syntax is `#if . . . #elif . . . #elif . . . #else . . . #endif`.

22. There must be an `#endif` for each `#if`. This requirement includes the `#if defined` or `#ifdef` and `#if !defined` or `#ifndef` combination directives.

23. The `#else` and the `#if` that follows it immediately must be on separate lines. Any lines of text for an `else` case must start at the line following the `#else`.

24. It is not necessary to use parentheses to encompass the conditional test.

25. In conditional compilation directives, the test conditions may include only constants or constant expressions that evaluate to a constant.

26. Preprocessor directives as well as C statements can be the subject of conditional compilation directives.

27. In addition to the `defined` directive, in conditional compilation directives, you may use integer constants, relational operators, arithmetic operators, logical operators, and bitwise operators.

28. In addition to the `!` operator, you can use the logical operators `¦¦` and `&&` to combine conditional directives. Conditional directives can be nested.

29. Function-like `define` directives allow you to use parameters. Any multiple parameters must be separated by commas.

30. You must not allow a space between the macro identifier and the open parentheses. Spaces within the parentheses are not material.

31. Put parentheses around each argument in the replacement item and around the entire replacement item.

32. If you want to include the macro argument as a literal string in the replacement item, you can put a `#` in front of the corresponding argument in the replacement item. That portion of the replacement item is replaced by the macro argument enclosed in double quotes.

33. You can use the same parameter more than once in the same macro, both with and without `#`.

34. You can merge two macro arguments by using `##` between them in the replacement item. You may connect more than two arguments this way.

35. You need not use all arguments in each portion of the replacement item, nor must they be in the same order as in the argument list.

36. You can concatenate arguments with nonargument text using `##`.

37. Macros can have untoward side effects. Functions afford greater insulation, since they use their own local variables. You can create and use pointers to functions but not with macros. If you have compiled functions into a library, using the function version rather than the macro version will be more convenient. A function shortens the code and makes it more efficient and modular.

38. Macros can be more flexible than functions since they use no data types. A macro and the code it generates is faster to run than a function.

39. Many Standard C functions have macro versions as well. To use the function version, you may need to undefine the macro.

40. Preprocessor directives are processed in the following order: conditional directives, `include` directives, `define` directives. However, `define` directives are processed if required to complete conditional directives or `include` directives, even if the processing involves more than one level of expansion of the `define` directive.

41. If a directive that precedes the `error` directive is true, on compiling you will get as an error message whatever follows `error` on the same line.

42. The predefined `__LINE__` macro is, by default, replaced with the line number of the source code in which the macro is found, expressed as a decimal integer constant.

43. The `__FILE__` predefined macro is, by default, replaced by the name of the source code file in which the directive appears, expressed as a string constant.

44. You can manipulate the values substituted for `__LINE__` and `__FILE__` with the `#line` directive.

45. The line number specification can be any integer constant or constant expression evaluating to between 0 and 32,767.

46. The `assert` macro tests whether an expression is true. If it is true, nothing happens. If it is false, the following are printed to standard output: the expression verbatim, the file name, and the line number; then the `abort()` function is called to terminate the program.

47. To disable all the `assert` statements in the program, you insert toward the top of the code: `#define NDEBUG`

48. The `__DATE__` and `__TIME__` macros print the date and time of program compilation.

49. If the `__STDC__` macro is defined, it has a value of 1 and indicates that the compiler conforms to the 1990 C Standard.

50. Any attempt to undefine or redefine `__LINE__`, `__FILE__`, `__DATE__`, `__TIME__`, `__STDC__`, or any other predefined macros will give you an error that will prevent you from compiling.

51. System-dependent facilities are to be used by a particular compiler by

    `#pragma . . .`

    where the ellipsis denotes some compiler-defined text that causes the compiler, if it recognizes the text, to perform certain prescribed actions. If not, the line is simply ignored, after which compilation continues.

Review Questions

1. List four functions that the preprocessing directives enable the programmer to do.
2. Preprocessor directives must begin with # (True or False).
3. A preprocessor keyword must follow the # (True or False).
4. Directives end at the end of the line unless a \ character is used to continue it to the next physical line (True or False).
5. Preprocessor directives can generally be placed anywhere in the code (True or False).
6. #define causes all subsequent occurrences of the macro to be replaced with tokens defined (True or False).
7. Macros may not have parameters; otherwise the compiler will confuse them with functions (True or False).
8. The scope of a #define continues until the end of compilation or an #undef directive (True or False).
9. Macros can be redefined after an #undef (True or False).
10. Macros once defined can never be redefined because all macros are handled by the preprocessor, which cannot go back and undo what it has defined (True or False).
11. Show the code generated by the definition and use the following macro:

```
#define TUITION(credits) (225 * credits)
int creditsTaken;
int studentTuition = TUITION(creditsTaken);
```

12. Execute the following macro and show the respective results:

    a.
    ```
    #define PROBLEM_11_14(parm) #parm
    int questionNumber = 14;
    printf("The value of %s is %d\n",
        PROBLEM_11_14(questionNumber),
            questionNumber);
    ```

    b.
    ```
    #define JOIN(x,y) x##y
    #define TODAY  "May 26, 2000"
    printf("Today is %s\n", JOIN(TOD,AY) );
    ```

13. Conditional directives are used to include or exclude portions of code (True or False).
14. List six conditional directives.
15. Conditional directives can be nested (True or False).
16. Nesting is a feature of Standard C's decision and looping constructs but is not permitted for preprocessor directives (True or False).
17. The directive keywords themselves—for example, #define and #include—must be in all lowercase (True or False).
18. #pragma allows compiler-dependent directions (True or False).

Programming Exercises

The specifications of the programming assignments were introduced in Chapter 1, at which time you were to

- think through the solution to these problems.
- identify the modules that, once implemented, will solve the problem.
- prepare a hierarchy chart of all the modules.
- prepare pseudocode/flowchart for each module in the hierarchy chart.
- write the program stubs the same way we did with the ACE Billing system application.

We have added variable and function scope as well as preprocessor directives to our C knowledge. We urge you to continue developing what you started in Chapter 1. If you have not started, we recommend that you start by applying the methodology presented in that chapter. We have helped you get started with some of the programming assignments by specifying only what can be done by this time.

Modify all the programming assignments you did in Chapter 9 to

- implement the use of macros where applicable.
- create a header file of all the function prototypes and any macros you have deemed necessary. See the application programming example acech11.c.
- create a TESTING macro and assign a value of 1 to it to signal testing mode or a 0 to signal production. Incorporate portions of code that could be used during testing to display values for a variety of variables. Write the appropriate conditional macros so that the execution of these statements will be determined by the value of the manifest constant, TESTING.

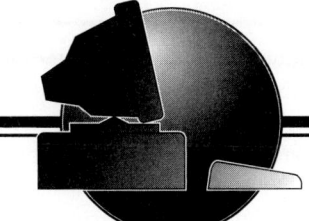

CHAPTER 12

Byte Structure and Bit Manipulation

OBJECTIVES

- To understand how integer and floating point numbers are represented and evaluated on a bit level
- To understand how negative numbers are represented in memory
- To learn Standard C's minimum ranges and precision for different types and see how to find out what a particular implementation's type ranges and precision are
- To understand binary, octal, and hexadecimal notation and the bit-level relationship among them

- To see how to manipulate data with bitwise operators
- To learn how to speed up code by using bit manipulation instead of simple mathematical operations
- To learn how to use bit masks to turn bits on or off or toggle them, or determine whether bits are on
- To examine portability concerns inherent in bit shifting and toggling

NEW TERMS

ANDing	complement operator	mask
AND operator	eXclusive OR operator	most significant bit
arithmetic shift	exponent	ORing
biasing	high-order bit	OR operator
binary number	least significant bit	precision
bitwise logical operator	logic shift	setting bit
bitwise shift operator	low-order bit	toggle
clearing bit	mantissa	XORing

Up to this point, we've looked at variables primarily as black-box entities. C, however, allows us to directly manipulate the bits of an integer value. In fact, some of the more sophisticated techniques for console control, sound production, and equipment status checking that we will be studying shortly require that we act directly on individual bits. In other instances, we will find that we can use bit manipulation to speed up multiplication or division operations slightly, though this use is not mandatory.

C offers two methods of manipulating bits and determining what the individual bits contain: bitwise operators and bit fields. Bit fields will be covered in the next chapter. We will examine bitwise operators shortly.

However, first we will take a look at the precise structure of a byte and see how bits are used to represent value. Then we can more intelligently use the bitwise operators. Before discussing bitwise operators, we will also examine bases of numbers other than decimal. Using octal or hexadecimal numbers will allow us to represent certain bit configurations more easily before attempting to manipulate the bits.

12.1   BITS AND BYTES

What do we know about variables so far? First, each variable has a unique name. The computer uses the names as aliases for memory addresses: to the computer each variable has a unique address. We also know how much memory space each takes up in memory in units called bytes that correspond to slots in the computer's addressing system. What is a byte? And how are variables' values stored in those bytes?

Let's take an imaginary trip back to really ancient times—insofar as computers are concerned. It's the early 20th century. We're about to build the first computer. What do we have to start with? Just electricity and some crude electrical components. And all we can do with them is introduce either a negative or positive charge to the components. Our components can accept and analyze bursts of eight charges at once. We'll call each of these electrical impulses a *bit*. A group of 8 bits will comprise a *byte*.

We decide that every time we want to express the number 1, we'll send a positive-charged bit; every time we want to express the number 0, we'll send a negative-charged bit. We'll refer to the negative-charged bit as being "off" and the positive-charged bit as being "on." We will refer to the first bit in a byte as bit 0, the second bit as bit 1, and so on through the eighth bit, bit 7.

Let's say we want to start off by inserting the number 27 into the computer. No problem. We just send 27 separate electrical impulses. That works fine for starters, but when someone asks us to store the size of the national debt or the distance to the sun, we start to wonder whether there isn't some faster way to do this. And there is.

12.1.1   Using Powers of 2—Binary Numbers

We can take advantage of the computer's ability to count quickly on its two electrical-impulse fingers. We can provide that for each successive bit within a byte, the size of our number will augment geometrically by a factor of 2 rather than just mathematically. In other words, starting with a value of 0: if bit 0 is on, our number will increase from 0 to 1; if bit 1 is on, our number will be larger by 2; if bit 2 is on, our number will be larger by 4; if bit 3 is on, our number will be larger by 8; if bit 4 is on, our number will be larger by 16; if bit 5 is on, our number will be larger by 32; if bit 6 is on, our number will be larger by 64; if bit 7 is on, our number will be larger by 128. Each bit from 0 (2, or any other number for that matter, to the zero power is 1) to 7 represents a successively greater power of 2.

To transmit the number 27 to the computer, we would send a byte consisting of a positive charge (2^0 = 1), a positive charge ($2^1 = 2$), a negative charge, a positive charge ($2^3 = 8$), a positive charge ($2^4 = 16$), and three negative charges. We could depict the transmitted byte bit by bit, from right to left, as in Figure 12.1.

The largest number we could fit into a single byte would be 255. With the same scheme of representation, that number would be depicted as in Figure 12.2.

Numbers expressed in this fashion are called ***binary numbers.*** (Actually, it is more correct to say "binary representation of numbers," but use of "binary numbers" has become as pervasive as "the proof's in the pudding" has for "the proof of the pudding's in the tasting." And so we'll often use the termi-

Figure 12.1   *A Bit Number Example: 27*

Bit #	7	6	5	4	3	2	1	0
	0	0	0	1	1	0	1	1
Value	0	0	0	16	8	0	2	1

Figure 12.2   *Another Bit Number Example: 255*

Bit #	7	6	5	4	3	2	1	0
	1	1	1	1	1	1	1	1
Value	128	64	32	16	8	4	2	1

nology "binary numbers" as well as "octal numbers" or "hexadecimal numbers" when referring to numbers represented in base 8 or base 16. We will also refer to binary notation or octal notation or hexadecimal notation.)

Binary numbers are said to be in base 2, just as the decimal numbers we've grown up with are in base 10. Decimal digits are, of course, from 0 to 9. Binary digits are 0 and 1. Each decimal digit from right to left represents a successively higher power of 10, starting with a power of 0. Each binary digit from right to left represents a successively higher power of 2.

Where the variable is of a type stored in more than one byte, the geometric progression continues from one byte to the next. For instance, the 0 bit of the second byte of an int has a value of 256 if turned on.

12.1.2 Value Ranges: Integers

All right then, we know how many bits there are in a byte (actually, PCs and nearly all other computer types have 8 bits per byte, but a small number of computers have 7 or 9 bits). And in Chapter 2 we learned how many bytes there are in each integer type. (To refresh your recollection: Standard C requires that char have a single byte. An int must be at least as many bytes as a short, and a long must be at least as many bytes as an int. On a PC, both a short and an int are 2 bytes, and a long is 4 bytes. This configuration is common on other computer types as well, except that int is 4 bytes on a number of them.)

For unsigned integer types, all bits are used to represent value. Therefore, assuming we have an 8-bit byte and char, short, int, and long are 1, 2, 2, and 4 bytes, respectively, we can determine the maximum value each type can accommodate. (See Table 12.1.)

These respective values are the result when all the bits in all the bytes are set to 1. Those values are equal to 2^n-1, where n is the total number of bits (for example, $2^8-1 = 255$).

How do we then accommodate negative numbers?

12.1.3 Signed Integers

The numbering system for *signed* integer types, rather than unsigned, is machine dependent. By far the most pervasive system—used by the PC and most other computer types—is the two's complement method. With that method, the most significant bit (that is, bit 7 for a char, bit 15 for an int, bit 31 for a long) is reserved for the sign: if it is 0, the number is positive; if it is 1, the number is negative. (The highest-value bit or bits in a variable are referred to as the ***high-order*** bits or the ***most significant*** bits; the lowest-value bit or bits are referred to as the ***low-order*** bits or the ***least significant*** bits. The same terminology is used for bytes. For example, the byte in a 2-byte int with bits 0 to 7 would be the low-order byte and the other byte, the high-order byte.)

However, the value determined by the remaining bits is different for negative numbers than for positive numbers. With positive numbers (that is, the most significant bit is 0), we just use the value of the remaining bits. Negative numbers are trickier. To determine the absolute value for a signed char with bit 7 on, you subtract the value bits 0 to 6 would have if the number were positive from 128. For a signed int, subtract the value bits 0 to 14 would have if the number were positive from 32,768. (These

Table 12.1 *Maximum Values for Unsigned Integer Types of Assumed Byte Sizes*

Type	Assumed Bytes	Maximum Value
unsigned char	1	255
unsigned short	2	65,535
unsigned int	2	65,535
unsigned long	4	4,294,967,295

Table 12.2 *Magnitude of Negative* char

Binary Number	Value of Right-Most 7 Bits	Result
11111111	127	−1
11111110	126	−2
10110111	55	−73
10000010	2	−126
10000001	1	−127
10000000	0	−128

two numbers represent the value the most significant bit would have if the variable were unsigned and the bit were on.) Table 12.2 provides a few examples.

Observe that the number with the highest absolute value has all the right-most 7 bits off and the lowest, all on—seemingly, just the opposite of positive numbers. However, when speaking of negative numbers, by convention we speak of a number with the larger absolute value as being the smaller number (for example, −3 is smaller than −2), and any negative number is said to be smaller than any positive number.

Now, let's determine the converse of the question just addressed, namely, what decimal value a particular binary representation with bit 7 on has. The simplest way to do this is to take the binary bit configuration of the number if it were positive (that is, the binary representation of the absolute value of the number), *toggle* each bit (all 1s become 0s and vice versa), and then add 1 to the result. The extra 1 gets added because the greatest negative number is −128, whereas the highest positive number is 127—the difference being that the positive side's 128 slots must accommodate 0. Table 12.3 offers some examples. We can confirm the final result in the right-most column against the corresponding results in the previous table. For instance, we find that 10000001—the result of representing decimal 127 in binary notation, toggling, and adding 1—is −127.

There is nothing magical about how we've constructed our computer system. As long as we observed the rule that the computer can only count on two fingers, we could have built a completely different structure. It just so happens that the computer world has gotten together and decided on this particular configuration. The same applies to our everyday number system. It just as well could have been decided to represent the number formed from 4 hundreds, 7 tens, and 3 ones as 374 instead of the 473 we see today; it just wasn't. The same reasoned arbitrariness, which pervades computers in general, and C language in particular, works because we all agree on the same conventions.

Table 12.3 *Binary Representation of Negative Integers*

Negative Number	Absolute Value	Absolute Value in Binary	Toggled	+ 1 = Binary Result
−1	1	00000001	11111110	11111111
−2	2	00000010	11111101	11111110
−73	73	01001001	10110110	10110111
−126	126	01111110	10000001	10000010
−127	127	01111111	10000000	10000001

Table 12.4 *Range for Integer Types: Two's Complement System*

Type	Assumed Bytes	Range
signed char	1	−128 to 127
unsigned char	1	0 to 255
signed short	2	−32,768 to 32,767
unsigned short	2	0 to 65,535
signed int	2	−32,768 to 32,767
unsigned int	2	0 to 65,535
signed long	4	−2,147,483,648 to 2,147,483,647
unsigned long	4	0 to 4,294,967,295

Assuming we have a PC or other computer that uses the two's complement system for negative numbers, and for char, short, int, and long has respectively 1, 2, 2, and 4 bytes, we can determine the range for the signed versions of each type—that is, the smallest negative number (remember, the negative number with the largest absolute value is by convention referred to as the "smallest") and the largest positive number. (See Table 12.4.)

Thus, with the two's complement system, the range for signed integer numbers can be expressed as -2^{n-1} through $2^{n-1}-1$. Since the most significant (highest-value) bit is used for the sign, it should not surprise you to find that the highest possible positive number for a signed variable is half that for its unsigned version.

The other methods for valuing negative numbers are the one's complement system and the sign magnitude method. In the one's complement system, negation merely complements all bits. In sign magnitude, negation merely toggles the sign bit. With either the two's complement system or the sign magnitude system, there is one less negative value and there are two representations of zero (positive and negative versions). The smallest negative number is equal to the absolute value of the largest positive number. In other words, the range for either of these two alternative systems can be expressed as $-(2^{n-1}-1)$ through $2^{n-1}-1$: that is, −127 through 127 for a char, −32,767 through 32,767 for a 2-byte type, and −2,147,483,648 through 2,147,483,648 for a 4-byte type.

Note that all three systems represent positive numbers the same way: all bits are used for value.

12.1.4   Standard C Minimums on Integer Values

As we saw earlier, Standard C requires that char have a single byte, that an int be at least as many bytes as a short, and that a long be at least as many bytes as an int. In addition, Standard C in effect requires that a short be at least 2 bytes (and hence, an int must also be at least 2 bytes) and a long be at least 4 bytes.

These byte minimums are not set forth directly in Standard C. Rather, we glean them from value ranges. Standard C imposes certain minimum numeric values for each integer type. Each of them has a macro name and minimum value. Those names and the corresponding actual values for a particular implementation are found in the Standard C file limits.h. To use any of these macros, just include that file in your source code. Table 12.5 lists the Standard C minimums and the values for a system (such as the PC) that uses the two's complement system and has a 2-byte short and int and a 4-byte long.

Focus on the meaning of "minimum" in the context of lowest and highest values. For example, an int must have a lowest possible value of at least −32,767. Its actual lowest value can be *lower* than that (for instance, on a two's complement system, it will be −32,768, or on a machine that uses two's complement and has a 4-byte int, it will be −2,147,483,648), but its lowest possible value has to be at least that low. Likewise, an int must have a highest possible value of at least 32,767. Its actual highest possible value can be *higher* value than that (for example, it will be 4,294,967,295 if it has 4 bytes), but its highest possible value has to be at least that high. You could also speak of minimum minimum values and minimum maximum values (as these names imply), but we found that too confusing.

Table 12.5 *Required Minimum Integer Values*

Name	Standard C Minimums	Values on a PC	Meaning
CHAR_BIT	8	8	Number of bits in a char
CHAR_MAX	If char is signed by default, SCHAR_MIN; otherwise 0		Highest char value
CHAR_MIN	If char is signed by default, SCHAR_MAX; otherwise UCHAR_MIN		Lowest char value
SCHAR_MIN	−127	−128	Lowest signed char value
SCHAR_MAX	127	127	Highest signed char value
UCHAR_MAX	255	255	Highest unsigned char value
SHRT_MIN	−32,767	−32,768	Lowest short value
SHRT_MAX	32,767	32,767	Highest short value
USHRT_MAX	65,535	65,535	Highest unsigned short value
INT_MIN	−32,767	−32,768	Lowest int value
INT_MAX	32,767	32,767	Highest int value
UINT_MAX	65,535	65,535	Highest unsigned int value
LONG_MIN	−2,147,483,647	−2,147,483,648	Lowest long value
LONG_MAX	2,147,483,647	2,147,483,647	Highest long value
ULONG_MAX	4,294,967,295	4,294,967,295	Highest unsigned long value

In an implementation that, like Borland C, permits the programmer to choose by option whether char is signed or unsigned by default, the selection of values for CHAR_MAX and CHAR_MIN is generally accomplished by conditional directive (see Chapter 11) in the implementation's `limits.h` file:

```
#if ('\x80' < 0)
#define CHAR_MAX   127
#define CHAR_MIN   (-128)
#else
#define CHAR_MAX   255
#define CHAR_MIN   0
#endif
```

If your implementation does not have a `limits.h` file, you can create your own. For maximum portability, you should not depend on an int having a range beyond Standard C's minimums (−32,767 to 32,767: one's complement, 2-byte). If your program may have values outside that range, use long instead.

12.2   OCTAL AND HEXADECIMAL NUMBERS

People normally use decimal notation to represent numerical values. It hardly takes an anthropological genius to conclude that the reason we "noncomputer units" count in base 10 has something to do with the number of fingers and toes we have. In base 10, each digit from right to left represents an increasingly higher power of 10. Thus, the number 35,276 represents $(3 \times 10^4) + (5 \times 10^3) + (2 \times 10^2) + (7 \times 10^4) + (6 \times 10^0)$ in base 10.

Computer programmers, however, commonly use hexadecimal notation, or to a lesser extent, octal notation to represent numerical values. With octal or hexadecimal notation, each digit from the right represents a successively higher power of 8 or 16, just as each digit represents a successively higher power of 10 in decimal notation and a successively higher power of 2 in binary notation.

In C, octal numbers are written with a 0 followed by the octal digits. For example, the number 0451 would represent $(4 \times 8^2) + (5 \times 8^1) + (1 \times 8^0)$, or 297 in decimal notation.

Hexadecimal numbers are written with a 0x (or 0X) followed by the hexadecimal digits. Hexadecimal digits 10 to 15 are represented by the letters A to F (or a to f). Thus, the number 0xD7 would represent $(13 \times 16^1) + (7 \times 16^0)$, or 215 in decimal notation.

12.2.1 Octal-Hexadecimal/Binary Conversion

Regardless of whether you use decimal, octal, or hexadecimal notation for assignment, the computer stores the number in binary notation—both integer and floating point numbers. And, since we're all much more familiar with decimal notation, why bother with octal or hexadecimal notation?

The answer is that in some cases, using hexadecimal or octal notation is actually easier and clearer than using decimal notation. At times, we are concerned not with the value a particular bit configuration yields when interpreted as one particular variable type or other. Rather, we are concerned with the particular configuration itself. We will see examples of this when we examine bit fields in the next chapter.

Since 16 represents 2 to the fourth power and 8 represents 2 to the third power, each hexadecimal digit corresponds to a 4-digit binary number and each octal digit corresponds to a 3-digit binary number. Tables 12.6 and 12.7 demonstrate the correspondence.

Table 12.6 *Octal-Binary Conversion Chart*

Octal Digit	Binary Digits
0	000
1	001
2	010
3	011
4	100
5	101
6	110
7	111

Table 12.7 *Hexadecimal-Binary Conversion Chart*

Hexadecimal Digit	Binary Digits	Hexadecimal Digit	Binary Digits	Hexadecimal Digit	Binary Digits
0	0000	6	0110	C	1100
1	0001	7	0111	D	1101
2	0010	8	1000	E	1110
3	0011	9	1001	F	1111
4	0100	A	1010		
5	0101	B	1011		

For instance, the value of an unsigned char with all bits but bit 7 off would be 0x80 in hexadecimal notation. The less significant 4 bits have a value of 0, giving us a 0 hex digit, and the value of the more significant 4 bits would be 8 (that is, 2^3), giving us a hex digit of 8. Likewise an int with all bits on would be 0xFFFF. It's probably easier and faster for most people to figure out that binary 10000000 is 0x80 than 128 in decimal representation.

12.3   FLOATING POINT NUMBERS

As we saw earlier, in C, one way to express floating point constants in the source code is exponential notation: as a floating point number in decimal format raised to an integral power of 10 (for example, 3.2e15 or 83.9994e-5). In fact, this exponential form is used by the computer to store floating point numbers in all cases, no matter what format the programmer uses. However, the computer stores both the integer-fractional portion and the exponential portion in binary, not in the decimal form you must use in making an assignment of a value to a floating point variable. The portions are stored separately after conversion to base 2 from base 10.

Floating point values are automatically represented internally as a number between 1 and 2 (called the **mantissa**) raised to a power of 2 (called the **exponent**). This power is a positive integer for values greater than 1 and negative for values less than 1:

$$(1 <= \text{mantissa} < 2) * 2^{\text{exponent}}$$

12.3.1   Floating Point Numbers on a Bit Level

On a bit level, the method of representing floating point values is implementation and machine specific. Both Microsoft and Borland C compilers and many others use the Institute for Electrical and Electronic Engineers (IEEE) Standard for Binary Floating-Point Arithmetic. Figure 12.3 shows the format for a float:

where s represents the sign bit
          x represents the exponent bits
          m represents the mantissa bits

Note how this scheme largely ignores byte boundaries—indicated by the double vertical lines. The mantissa bits, from left to right, represent successively greater *negative* powers of 2, starting with 2^{-1}. A number to a negative power is equal to 1 divided by the number to the absolute value of the power (for example, 2 to the –2 power = $^1/2^2$ = $^1/4$). This mantissa scheme then gives us successively smaller positive fractions from left to right. Or, looking at it from the other end of the telescope: as with integer variables, the values are successively greater by a power of 2 as we move from least to most significant significant bit.

So, for instance if the 23 mantissa bits were this

$$0001110\ 10011011\ 00111001$$

we would have

$$2^{-4} + 2^{-5} + 2^{-6} + 2^{-8} + 2^{-11} + 2^{-12} + 2^{-14} + 2^{-15} + 2^{-18} + 2^{-19} + 2^{-20} + 2^{-23} = 0.114112016$$

As you can see from the progression of *m*-bit values, we will never reach the value 1: if the first bit were on, we have a value of $^1/2$, leaving us $^1/2$ short of 1; adding $^1/4$ leaves us $^1/4$ short of 1; and so on. If all *m*-bits are on, we are short of 1 by the value of the last *m*-bit. So the sum of the *m*-bit values is always a positive fraction (or zero).

Figure 12.3 *Bit Allocation for a float (IEEE)*

	Byte 3								Byte 2								Byte 1								Byte 0							
S	X	X	X	X	X	X	X	X	M	M	M	M	M	M	M	M	M	M	M	M	M	M	M	M	M	M	M	M	M	M	M
31	30	29	28	27	26	25	24	23	22	21	20	19	18	17	16	15	14	13	12	11	10	9	8	7	6	5	4	3	2	1	0

The compiler then takes this fraction and adds it to 1 to get the mantissa:

$$1 + 0.114112016 = 1.114112016$$

The maximum possible value—all 23 bits set to 1—would be just less than 2. The effect is as though we had an extra mantissa bit to the left of the 2^{-1} bit and pretended this 2^0 bit were always set to 1 (that is, $2^0 = 1$). Indeed, many publications describe the 1 we add to the mantissa bits as "assumed" or "implicit." The fractional portion of the mantissa is stored; the integer portion is "implicit."

12.3.2   Exponent Bits: Biasing

The 8 exponent bits could give us a maximum value of 255. But we need to allow for negative numbers here as well as positive—a range of –128 to 127, just as we saw earlier for a `signed char`. With integer types, we saw that negative numbers generally are accommodated by the two's complement method, in which the most significant bit is used for sign rather than value. Here, a different method is used. Each bit, including the most significant one, is used for exponent value, so that the apparent range is from 0 to 255. However, this range is arbitrarily split into two by subtracting 127 (half the maximum range) from the value all 8 bits represent. Accordingly, a *stored* exponent value of 2 would have an *actual* exponent value of –125, and a value of 255 would be read as 127. This process is called **biasing**: we say that with a `float`, the exponent is "biased" by 127.

To take an example, with exponent bits of

$$01110000$$

we have a stored value of 112, which gives us an actual value of $112 - 127 = -15$. If these bits were the exponent bits for the mantissa bits in the example above

$$01110000 \quad 00111010011011100111001$$

we would have

$$1.114112016 * 2^{-15} = 0.000034$$

We can verify this result with Listing 13.11, `floating.c`, or Listing 13.12, `bit_look.c`—programs that use two different methods for directly looking at the bits of a floating point value.

There is one exception to this scheme. If the stored exponent value is zero, the actual value assigned by the compiler is –126; also, the normally implicit 1 value is not added to the mantissa in such a case.

12.3.3   Sign Bit

Under the IEEE Standard, if the most significant bit of byte 0 is 1, the number as a whole is negative; otherwise it is positive:

$$0 \quad 01110000 \quad 00111010011011100111001 = 0.000034$$
$$1 \quad 01110000 \quad 00111010011011100111001 = -0.000034$$

Thus, to recap for this example of .000034, for a `float`, the integer portion of the mantissa (the 1) is implicit; the fractional portion (the .114112016 in this example) is stored in bits 0 to 22; the exponent, representing a power of 2, is stored in bits 23 to 30; and the sign is stored in bit 31.

12.3.4   Larger Floating Point Types

The scheme for `double` and `long double` under the IEEE Standard is similar to that for `float` (see Figures 12.4A to 12.4C).

To split the exponent range in two, a `double` uses a bias of 1,023 ($2^{11} - 1$) and a `long double` uses a bias of 16,383 ($2^{15} - 1$). In other words, for the actual exponent of a `double`, we take the stored exponent and subtract 1023, and for the actual exponent of a `long double`, we take the stored exponent and subtract 16,383.

There generally is one difference between how the fractional part of a `float` and a `double` on the one hand, and a `long double` on the other, is stored. With a `float` or a `double`, the value derived from the mantissa bit is added to 1 and the result raised to a power. The most significant mantissa bit has a

Figure 12.4A *Bit Allocation in Floating Point Types (IEEE):* `float`

±	Exponent	Mantissa

bits   31   23–30   0–22

Figure 12.4B *Bit Allocation in Floating Point Types (IEEE):* `double`

±	Exponent	Mantissa

bits   63   52–62   0–51

Figure 12.4C *Bit Allocation in Floating Point Types (IEEE):* `long double`

±	Exponent	Mantissa

bits   79   64–78   0–63

value of 2^{-1}. With a `long double`, a 1 is actually stored in the left-most mantissa bit, bit 63, with a value of 2^0, rather than being implicit. The result is the same as the method for `float` and `double`; it's just that with those two types the mantissa bits are added to 1 before being raised to a power; with a `long double`, the 1 is already hard-wired in.

Furthermore, some implementations use the two's complement method for determining the value of the 15 exponent bits of a `long double` rather than biasing. (See the discussion of the two's complement method in Section 12.1.3.)

12.3.5   Range and Precision

Since a `float`'s 8 allocated exponent bits, as biased, produce a maximum value of 127, and since the maximum value of the mantissa is just under 2, the largest number a `float` can hold would be just under 2.0×2^{128}, or approximately $3.4e^{38}$ in decimal exponential notation (3.4 times 10 to the 38th power). Likewise, given the smallest exponent of –126, the minimum absolute value would be 1×2^{-127}, or approximately $1.18e^{-38}$ in decimal exponential notation. These are *extremely* large and *extremely* small values, as are often required in scientific or engineering applications.

We can't fit numbers larger than the equivalent of 6 decimal digits long into the 23 bits allocated in a `float` for the mantissa. If we try to store more than that, the computer essentially ignores the extra digits. For example, if we attempt to store the following two values into `float` variables

```
88888888.11111111111
8888.888811111111111
```

and then print the values the computer's memory holds for those values, we get

```
8888888.000000
8888.888672
```

So you can see that although a `float` has a large range of values, the ***precision*** afforded is quite limited. The extra bits generally allotted for both mantissa and exponent in `double` and `long double` offer greater precision as well as greater magnitudes.

As we saw above with integers, Standard C imposes certain minimums on the range, digits of precision, and mantissa bits for each floating point type. Each of the minimums has a macro name and a minimum value. Those names and the corresponding actual values for a particular implementation are found in the Standard C file `float.h`. Table 12.8 lists the Standard C minimums and the values for a typical system that follows the IEEE Standard.

Note that the C Standard does not guarantee that a `long double` will have greater precision than a `double` or that `double` or even `long double` will have a greater range than `float`.

The ranges for negative values are the same as for positive value. For example, a `float` has a range from $-1.17549e^{-38}$ to $-3.40282e^{38}$ and from $1.17549e^{-38}$ to $3.40282e^{38}$. In each case, e represents a power of 10.

Table 12.8   *Required Minimum and Typical Floating Point Values*

Name	Standard C Minimums	Typical IEEE Values	Meaning
FLT_DIG	6	6	Minimum number of decimal digits precision for a `float`
DBL_DIG	10	15	Minimum number of decimal digits precision for a `double`
LDBL_DIG	10	19	Minimum number of decimal digits precision for a `long double`
FLT_MANT_DIG	no min	24	Minimum number of bits in mantissa for a `float`
DBL_MANT_DIG	no min	53	Minimum number of bits in mantissa for a `double`
LDBL_MANT_DIG	no min	64	Minimum number of bits in mantissa for a `long double`
FLT_MIN	e^{-37}	$1.17549e^{-38}$	Smallest positive value for a `float`
DBL_MIN	e^{-37}	$2.22507e^{-308}$	Smallest positive value for a `double`
LDBL_MIN	e^{-37}	$3.36210e^{-4932}$	Smallest positive value for a `long double`
FLT_MAX	e^{37}	$3.40282e^{38}$	Largest positive value for a `float`
DBL_MAX	e^{37}	$1.79769e^{308}$	Largest positive value for a `double`
LDBL_MAX	e^{37}	$1.18973e^{4932}$	Largest positive value for a `long double`

The following program prints the respective actual macro values for your implementation for integer and floating point types, as well as the number of bytes for each type.

Listing   12.1 num_stat.c

```
/* num_stat.c */

/* number of bytes, ranges, & precision for integer and
   floating point numbers */

#include <stdio.h>
#include <float.h>
#include <limits.h>

#define S(a,b) a##pace, "unsigned", b##pace, "signed" /* sign */
#define T(t,a,b) a##pace, #t, b##pace, #t /* type */
#define B(t,a,b) a##pace, sizeof(t), b##pace, sizeof(t) /* bytes */

int main(void)
{
   int uspace = 8, space = 6, lspace = 10, fspace = 12;
   printf("\n s%*%s\n\n", (80 - sizeof("INTEGER TYPE BYTES AND RANGE"))/2,
      "", "INTEGER TYPE BYTES AND RANGE");
```

```
    printf("%*s %*s %*s %*s %*s %*s %*s %*s  %*s\n", 4, "", S(us,s), S(us,s), S(us,s),
        S(ls,ls));
    printf("%*s %*s %*s %*s %*s %*s %*s %*s  %*s\n", 4, "", T(char,us,s), T(short,us,s),
        T(int,us,s), T(long,ls,ls));
    printf("Bytes%*d %*d %*d %*d d %*d %*d  %*d\n", B(char,us,s), B(short,us,s), B(int,us,s),
        B(long,ls,ls));
    printf("  Max%*u %*i %*u %*i %*u %*i %*lu  %*ld\n", uspace, UCHAR_MAX, space, SCHAR_MAX,
        uspace, USHRT_MAX, space, SHRT_MAX, uspace, UINT_MAX, space, INT_MAX, lspace, ULONG_MAX,
        lspace, LONG_MAX);
    printf("  Min%*u %*i %*u %*i %*u %*i %*lu %*ld\n", uspace, 0, space, SCHAR_MIN, uspace, 0,
        space, SHRT_MIN, uspace, 0, space, INT_MIN, lspace, 0L, lspace, LONG_MIN);

    printf("\n%*s %s\n\n", (80 - sizeof("FLOATING POINT TYPE BYTES, RANGE, AND PRECISION"))/2,
        "", "FLOATING POINT TYPE BYTES, RANGE, AND PRECISION");
    printf("%*s\n", fspace * 5 + 1, "long");
    printf(" %*s %*s %*s %*s\n", fspace + 8, "", fspace, "float", fspace, "double", fspace + 1,
        "double");
    printf("Bytes %*d %*d %*d\n", fspace * 2 + 4, sizeof(float), fspace, sizeof(double),
      fspace + 1, sizeof(long double));

    printf("Min Positive: %*lg %*lg %*Lg\n", lspace * 2, FLT_MIN, fspace, DBL_MIN, fspace + 1,
        (long double)LDBL_MIN); printf("Max Positive:  lg  lg  Lg\n", lspace * 2, FLT_MAX,
        fspace, DBL_MAX, fspace + 1, (long double)LDBL_MAX);

    printf("Mantissa bits: %*d %*d %*d\n", lspace * 2 - 1, FLT_MANT_DIG, fspace, DBL_MANT_DIG,
        fspace + 1, LDBL_MANT_DIG);
    printf("Significant digits:  %*d %*d %*d\n", fspace + 1, FLT_DIG, fspace, DBL_DIG,
        fspace + 1, LDBL_DIG);
}
```

12.3.6   Floating Point Considerations

Because of the complicated method for storing floating point variables, calculations you make with them in your programs take considerably longer than do those with integer type variables. You'll notice this particularly when doing iterative calculations (calculations not amenable to specific formula, where you have to derive the result by a series of educated guesses), like determining the yield on an investment from a stream of repayments. Also, because of the difference in the way the integer portion of the mantissa is handled in `float` and `double` values (an implicit 1 is added to the fractional value in the mantissa bits) versus `long double` (the 1 is actually stored in the most significant mantissa bit), co-processors can load and automatically convert `float` and `double` values, but not `long double` values.

 If you are doing a lot of number crunching and can avoid floating point variables, do so to the extent possible. Try to avoid extensive use of `long double`*.*

The bifurcated method for storing floating point variables can also be a trap for the unwary. You can't assume that just because you have 7-digit precision, you won't get some unanticipated rounding errors with fewer digits. You know that some decimal floating point numbers are only approximations of fractions. Decimal 0.25 is a zero-terminated precise equivalent of the fraction one-quarter; decimal 0.3333333 is not the precise equivalent of the fraction one-third.

The same holds true for a decimal floating point number we ask the computer to store—even one that is zero-terminated. In its internal binary form, a floating point value often only approximates the real number it represents. The example after Listing 5.13, `tempconv.c`, gives an example of lurking traps in floating point numbers.

 Because of the potential round-off error is greatest with a `float`*, and since all the Standard C library math functions expect a* `double`*, you are generally best off sticking with* `double` *for floating point calculations, unless you need more precision, in which case, you should use* `long double`*.*

Table 12.9 *Bitwise Operators*

Logical Operators		
~	Complement	
&	AND	&=
¦	OR	¦=
^	eXclusive OR	^=
Shift Operators		
<<	Left shift	<<=
>>	Right shift	>>=

12.4   BITWISE OPERATORS *(OPTIONAL)*

C has four *bitwise logical operators* and two *bitwise shift operators.* Like the arithmetic operators +, -, *,), and %, the bitwise operators can, with the exception of the ~ operator, be used in combination with the = assignment operator as a shorthand designation (see Table 12.9).

The &, ¦, and ^ operators are conventionally written out in capital letters and spoken of in gerund form—*ANDing*, *ORing,* and *XORing* a number, respectively, is common terminology.

 You may use bitwise operators only with integer type variables or constants.

Careful—it is a common mistake to use the bitwise operator & or ¦ in place of the logical operator && or ¦¦, and vice versa.

12.5   ~ OPERATOR *(OPTIONAL)*

The *complement operator* ~ toggles all bits. It takes an integer and produces another integer that has a 1 in each bit that is a 0 in the first integer and vice versa. Figure 12.5 shows that if num has a value of 1, ~num is 0xFE.

Note that the ~ operator does not alter num's value any more than num + 2 would change it:

```
unsigned char num = 1;
unsigned char val = ~num;
printf("val is %#X; num is %#X\n", val, num);
```

This produces the following output:

```
val is 0XFE; num is 0X1
```

It is only when we combine the ~ operator with an = operator that we effect a change. The code statements

```
unsigned char num = 1;
unsigned char val = ~num;
printf("val is %#X; num is %#X\n", val, num);
num = ~num;
printf("num is now %#X\n", num);
```

produce

```
val is 0XFE; num is 0X1
num is now 0XFE
```

Figure 12.5 *Bit Toggling with the Complement Operator*

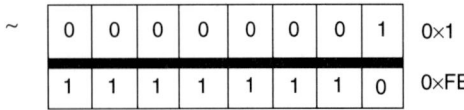

Nor does the complement operator convert, say, 99 into –99. It toggles all bits, not the sign of the number. On a two's complement system, ~99 is equal to –100. Make sure you understand why; if not, go back to the beginning of the chapter and review the two's complement method.

As we have seen, while positive integers are represented the same on all computer systems, regardless of type, different systems represent negative integers differently. Many computers, including the PC, use the two's complement method, but others use the one's complement method or other methods. Consequently, *applying the ~ to negative integers may not produce perfectly portable results.*

12.5.1   Distinguishing ~ from Other Bitwise Logical Operators

While the combination operators &=, |=, and ^= exist, there is no combination ~ and = operator. So

```
num ~= num; /* error! */
```

would give you a "Code has no effect" error message on compiling.

Unlike the binary &, |, and ^ operators, which compare two integer values and come up with a third based on the results of the comparison, the unary ~ operator simply takes one integer value and produces a second integer value that is the first integer value's bitwise flip side.

12.6 | OPERATOR *(OPTIONAL)*

The *OR operator* | makes a bit-by-bit comparison of two integer values (comparing bit 0 of one value with bit 0 of the second, bit 1 of the first value with bit 1 of the second, and so forth) and produces a value based on the comparison. For each bit position, the resulting bit is 1 if *either* bit of the compared numbers is a 1; otherwise, the result is 0. Thus, 0x75 | 0x23 produces 0x77 (see Figure 12.6):

```
unsigned char num = 0x75, val = 0x23;
unsigned char result = num | val;
printf("num: %#X, val: %#X; result of ORing: %#X\n", num, val, result);
```

The results of ORing:

```
num: 0X75, val: 0X23; result of ORing: 0X77
```

You can combine the | and = operators:

```
unsigned char num = 0x75, val = 0x23;
num |= val; /* same as num = num | val; */
printf("num: %#X, val: %#X\n", num, val);
```

The results:

```
num: 0X77, val: 0X23
```

Figure 12.6 *Bit-by-Bit Comparison of Two Values with the OR Operator*

Figure 12.7 *Bit-by-Bit Comparison of Two Values with the AND Operator*

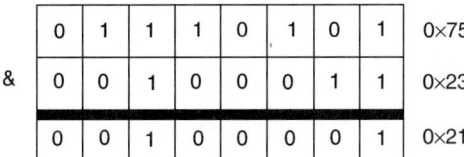

	0	1	1	1	0	1	0	1	0×75
&	0	0	1	0	0	0	1	1	0×23
	0	0	1	0	0	0	0	1	0×21

12.7 & OPERATOR *(OPTIONAL)*

The *AND operator* & makes a bit-by-bit comparison of two integer values and produces a value based on the comparison. For each bit position, the resulting bit is 1 only if *both* bits of the compared numbers are 1's; otherwise, the result is 0. Thus, 0x75 & 0x23 produces 0x21 (see Figure 12.7):

```
unsigned char num = 0x75, val = 0x23;
unsigned char result = num & val;
printf("num: %#X, val: %#X; result of ANDing: %#X\n", num, val, result);
```

The results of ANDing:

```
num: 0X75, val: 0X23; result of ANDing: 0X21
```

You can combine the & and = operators:

```
unsigned char num = 0x75, val = 0x23;
num &= val; /* same as num = num & val; */
printf("num: %#X, val: %#X\n", num, val);
```

The output:

```
num: 0X21, val: 0X23
```

Incidentally, though most of our examples will use chars for simplicity, all the bit examples in this chapter can be used with ints or longs. For instance, 0x051E & 0x8104 produces 0x0104 (see Figure 12.8).

12.8 BIT MASKS *(OPTIONAL)*

A value we use in conjunction with the bitwise operators to turn specific bits on, or turn them off, or toggle them from what they are currently to the opposite, or determine the value of specific bits is called a **mask.** Use of a mask is common in C programming, as indeed is bit manipulation in general.

The mask allows us to essentially ignore certain bits, whose values we may not know or even care about, while at the same time altering or ascertaining the values of target bits.

12.9 TURNING DESIGNATED BITS OFF: num &= MASK *(OPTIONAL)*

Suppose a particular application required that you take a byte and turn off one or more specific bits without altering the other bits. (That is, set them to 0, also referred to as *clearing bits.* Turning bits on, that is, setting them to 1, is also referred to as *setting bits*.)

Figure 12.8 *Bit Operation on Two ints*

	0	0	0	0	0	1	0	1	0	0	0	1	1	1	1	0	0×051E
&	1	0	0	0	0	0	0	1	0	0	0	0	0	1	0	0	0×8104
	0	0	0	0	0	0	0	1	0	0	0	0	0	1	0	0	0×0104

To clear one of more bits, we AND the byte's value with either (1) a second value that has 0s in the bit or bits we want to turn off and 1s in all other bits or, with what amounts to the same value, (2) the complement of a second value that has 1s in the bit we want to turn off and 0s in all other bits.

All bits ANDed with 0s will be 0s by hypothesis whether they are 0s or 1s. All bits ANDed with 1s will remain what they are: 0 AND 1 produces 0; 1 AND 1 produces 1.

12.9.1   Some Colorful Examples

In Appendix C, we'll see that the "attributes" (flashing or not, background color, intensity of foreground color, foreground color) of a character placed on the screen of a PC are determined by a single byte in the video memory area of RAM. If bit 7 is on, the character will flash on and off. Let's say the attribute byte had a value of 0xFC (blinking light-red foreground on gray background) and we wanted to turn the blink bit off.

We can AND the attribute byte with the complement of a value that has a 1 in bit 7 – the target bit we want to turn off—and 0s in all other bits:

```
attribute = 0xFC;  /* blinking light red on grey */
attribute &= ~0x80;
```

or we can AND with a number that has a 0 only in bit 7 and 1s in all other bits, since that value is the same as the complement of one that has 1 in the target bit and 0s in the rest (see Figure 12.9):

```
attribute &= 0x7F;
```

After we examine bit shifting and see how we can use bit shift operators to simplify bit masking and turning bits on or off, you will see why it is often preferable to use the complement method, even though at first blush, it may seem needlessly indirect.

Say we wanted to turn bits 7 and 3 off at the same time (blink off and change light red to dark red); we could AND with a value that has 0s only in bits 7 and 3 (see Figure 12.10):

```
attribute = 0xFC;
attribute &= 0x77;
```

While it just so happens that we know the value of the variable `attribute` in the preceding example, we needn't have in order to have used the `&= 0x77` to make sure bits 7 and 3 were set to 0 afterward. At the point where our code encountered the line

```
attribute &= 0x77;
```

we may not know what the background or foreground color is or whether the blink bit or foreground intensity bit is on or off—particularly if we let users pick their own colors interactively at run time or

Figure 12.9 *ANDing with Complement of Value with Target Bit On: Turn Bit Off*

1	1	1	1	1	1	0	0	0×FC
0	1	1	1	1	1	1	1	0×80
0	1	1	1	1	1	0	0	

(& at left of second row)

Figure 12.10 *Turning Off Two Bits at Once with ANDing*

1	1	1	1	1	1	0	0	0×FC
0	1	1	1	0	1	1	1	0×77
0	1	1	1	0	1	0	0	

(& at left of second row)

Figure 12.11 *Turning Off Bits with ANDing—
Nontarget Bits Unknown*

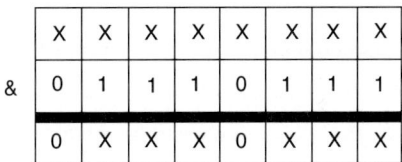

if we created a color selection utility for users (see `select.c` on disk) that allows users to make color selections and that stores the selections in a file to be read by the program on subsequent runs. Nevertheless, what we can be sure of is that after executing this statement, the background color would remain whatever it had been before the statement; whatever foreground color we had would be still be the same (except it would now be dark, whether it had been light or dark before); and the character would not flash, whether it did before or not. (See Figure 12.11.)

12.9.2 A Capital Example

You may have noticed that in the ASCII system, capital letters differ from the corresponding lowercase letters only in that bit 5 is off in the capital letter and on in the lowercase letter, with A and a being off in all other bits save bit 0 (see Figure 12.12). Likewise, the values 0 to 9 differ from the characters 0 through 9 only in that the former have bits 4 and 5 off and the latter have them on (see Figure 12.13).

Figure 12.12 *Case Difference on a Bit Level*

'A'	0	1	0	0	0	0	0	1
'a'	0	1	1	0	0	0	0	1

Figure 12.13 *Value and Character
Difference on a Bit Level*

0	0	0	0	0	0	0	0	0
'0'	0	1	1	1	0	0	0	0

Provided our computer uses ASCII, then, we can AND with a bit mask of 0xDF (all bits but bit 5 on) to turn letters in a string to all capital letters.

 **Listing** **12.2 bit_caps.c**

```
/* bit_caps.c */

/* turn string all uppercase by ANDing with mask to turn bit 5 off */

#include <stdio.h>

#define MASK 0xDF  /* bit 5 off and all others on */

char *bit_caps(char *string);

int main(void)
{
```

```
        puts(bit_caps("this is all uppercase now"));
    }

    char *bit_caps(char *string)
    {
        char *ptr = string;
        while(*ptr)
        {
            if (*ptr >= 'a' && *ptr <= 'z')
                *ptr &= MASK;
            ptr++;
        }
        return string;
    }
```

12.10   DETERMINING WHETHER ONE OR MORE BITS ARE ON: `if (num & MASK == MASK)` *(OPTIONAL)*

Sometimes we need to determine whether one or more bits in a variable or constant are on.

 To determine whether one or more bits in a variable or constant are on, we AND with a mask that contains 1s in the bits we want to look at and 0s in the other bits. Then we check to see whether the resulting value is equal to the mask.

Bits that are ANDed with 0s yield 0s, as in the mask. If the target bits in the number we're checking are 1s, so that ANDing with 1 yields 1s as in the mask, the result of

```
if (num & MASK == MASK)
```

will be true if the target bits all are on and false if one or more is off.

12.10.1   A Bit Mask Example: Checking the Equipment `int`

In Appendix B, we will see how to use interrupts in a PC to obtain an `int` value the bits of which indicate how many floppy disk drives are present, what kind of monitor is attached, whether a printer is attached, and other peripheral equipment status information. In the next chapter, we will use structures and bit fields within them to isolate and determine the various bits that give this information. We can do the same thing with bitwise operators. Let's take the number of floppy drives as an example.

Bit 0 in the equipment `int` indicates whether there are any disk drives present; if so bits 6 and 7 tell us the number of disk drives present (00 = 1 drive, 01 = 2 drives, 10 = 3 drives, 11 = 4 drives—that is, the binary value of the bits plus 1). Disregarding for right now the mechanics of deriving the `int` value to store in the variable we've called `equip`, here's how we determine the number of disk drives.

 **Listing   12.3 `d_drives.c`**

```
/* d_drives.c */

/* use bit mask to determine how many floppy drives computer has */

#include <stdio.h>
#include <dos.h>

int main(void)
{
    union REGS in, out;
    unsigned equipment_int, drives;
```

```
      int disk_mask = 1; /* 1 in bit 0; all other bits off */
      int drivenum_mask = 0xC0; /* bits 6 & 7 on; all others off */

      equipment_int = int86(0x11, &in, &out);
      if ((equipment_int & disk_mask) != disk_mask)
         puts("No floppy disk drives");
      else
      {
         drives =  1 +
         /* all bits off but 6&7 */
            ((equipment_int & drivenum_mask)
            >> 6); /* shift bits 6 & 7 to 0 & 1 */

         printf("%d floppy disk drive%s\n", drives,
            drives == 1 ? "": "s");
      }
   }
```

Since we are inquiring initially about bit 0, we first have ANDed the equipment byte value with a mask with 1 in bit 0 and 0 in the other bits—that is, the number 1. If the comparison is false, indicating that the target bit, bit 0, is off, we report that there are no disk drives. Otherwise, we look at bits 6 and 7 for the number of drives and add 1.

We determine the value the equipment int would have if we turned all bits but bits 6 and 7 off by ANDing with the mask 0xC0, a value with all bits but 6 and 7 off. See later in the chapter for a discussion of how we determine the value of the isolated contiguous bits by bit shifting all the way to the right, as we did here.

12.11 ASCERTAINING THE VALUE OF SEVERAL BITS AT ONCE: num & MASK *(OPTIONAL)*

 To ascertain the value of several specific contiguous bits, all of which are low-order bits, you AND with a mask that has 0s in the bits you are not interested in and 1s in those you are.

Thus, to ascertain the value of bits 0–2 of a number:

```
val = num & 0x7; /* 0x7 has bits 0-2 on and rest off */
```

This zeroes out bits 3–7 and leaves bits 0–2 with their original settings, thus isolating the value they contain.

You will see below under the discussion of bit shifting how we can determine the value of several contiguous bits where the bit field is not at the right-most end by moving the mask-isolated value to the right, as we did in d_drives.c above. Meanwhile, you can use a less straightforward but perhaps more commonsense method. We can divide the bit 6- and 7-isolated value from our d_drives.c example by a value that has bit 6 on only, 0x40:

```
drives = 1 + ((equipment_int & drivenum_mask) / 0x40);
```

We get something like the following before dividing (see Figure 12.14).

Dividing this value by a value that has bit 6 on only gives us the value in bits 6 and 7, just as dividing the following decimal value by decimal 100 would give us the value in the thousands and hundreds places (see Figure 12.15).

For example, 2100 / 100 = 21.

Figure 12.14 *Value to AND with a Mask that Has Bits 6 and 7 On*

0	0	0	0	0	0	0	0	x	x	0	0	0	0	0	0

Figure 12.15 *Dividing Decimal Value by 100*

X	X	0	0

12.12   TURNING DESIGNATED BITS ON: num ¦= MASK *(OPTIONAL)*

 To turn one or more designated bits in a value on and leave the rest unchanged, we OR the value with a mask that has a 1 in the target bits and 0s everywhere else.

Any bit ORed with 1 obviously produces a 1. ORing with 0 preserves the bit's value: a 0 bit ORed with a 0 remains 0; a 1 bit ORed with 0 remains 1.

In the sound production material on disk, we will learn how to turn the computer's speaker on by retrieving the speaker port's current value and then, without bothering to determine what that value is, turning bits 0 and 1 on. The second of the following statements shows how we turn the target bits on:

```
old_port = inp(0x61); /* get current bit setting value & store it in old_port */
new_port = old_port ¦ 0x3;
outp(0x61, new_port); /* change setting: turn on bits 0 and 1 */
```

12.13   ^ OPERATOR *(OPTIONAL)*

The *eXclusive OR operator* ^ makes a bit-by-bit comparison between two integer values and, for each bit position, yields a 1 if one of the bits is 1 and the other is 0; the result is 0 if both bits are 0s or both are 1s. So 0x99 ^ 0xDA yields 0x43. (See Figure 12.16.) You can turn all bits in a number off by XORing the number with itself:

```
num ^= num;
```

Of course, you could do the same thing by assigning 0 to the variable.

Figure 12.16 *Bit-by-Bit Comparison of Two Values with eXclusive OR Operator*

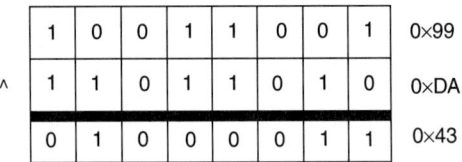

12.14   TOGGLING BITS: num ^= MASK *(OPTIONAL)*

 You can use the ^ XOR operator with the assignment operator and a mask to toggle one or more bits. Bits corresponding to 1s in the mask are toggled and those corresponding to 0s in the mask are left unchanged.

(By toggling a bit, we mean turning it off if it is on and vice versa.)

The ^= device is used for toggling individual bits. If you want to toggle all bits at once, just use the complement operator.

12.15   BITWISE SHIFT OPERATORS *(OPTIONAL)*

The bitwise shift operators move all the bits in an integer value to the right or left the number of bits indicated by an integer directly following the >> or << operator. For example, `0x1F << 3` produces 0xF8 (see Figure 12.17).

The number of bits to be shifted can be expressed as a constant, a variable, or a constant-variable expression, as long as only integers are involved in any case:

```
int num = 16, val = 4;
num >>= (val / 2) + 1;
printf("num: %d\n", num);
```

```
num: 2
```

Since each bit represents a successively higher power of 2, shifting bits to the right has the effect of dividing a value by 2 for each bit shift. (See, however, Section 12.15.1 for a possible exception in the case of negative unsigned values.) Shifting left has the effect of multiplying by 2 for each bit shift.

Any bits shifted past the last bit on the right side are lost, with the vacated bits replaced with 0s. (Again, see below for a potential exception.) Thus, `0x1F >> 4` produces 0x1 (see Figure 12.18). This lost-bit result reflects the effects of integer division:

```
unsigned char num = 0x1F;
unsigned char val = num >> 4;
printf("%#X >> 4: %#X\n", num, val);
val = num / 16;
printf("%u / 16: %u\n", num, val);
```

```
0X1F >> 4: 0X1
31 / 16: 1
```

The same holds for bits shifted beyond the left-most bit. Bits shifted past the left side are lost, with the vacated bits being replaced with 0s. Thus, `0x1F << 7` yields 0x80 (see Figure 12.19).

Here, the lost-bit result reflects the odometer-like effect of integer type overflow:

```
unsigned char val, num;
val = num << 7;
printf("%#X << 7: %#X\n", num, val);
val = num * 128;
printf("%u * 128: %u\n", num, val);
```

```
0X1F << 7: 0X80
31 * 128: 128
```

Figure 12.17   *Bit Shift Left*

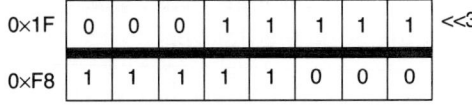

| 0×1F | 0 | 0 | 0 | 1 | 1 | 1 | 1 | 1 | <<3 |
| 0×F8 | 1 | 1 | 1 | 1 | 1 | 0 | 0 | 0 | |

Figure 12.18   *Bit Shift Right—Vacated Bits Replaced by Zeros*

| 0×1F | 0 | 0 | 0 | 1 | 1 | 1 | 1 | 1 | >>4 |
| 0×01 | 0 | 0 | 0 | 0 | 0 | 0 | 0 | 1 | |

Figure 12.19 *Bit Shift Left—Vacated Bits Replaced by Zeros*

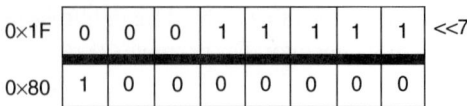

Figure 12.20 *Bit Shifting Left with an* int *Value*

0x001F	0	0	0	0	0	0	0	0	0	0	0	1	1	1	1	1	<<7
0x0F80	0	0	0	0	1	1	1	1	1	0	0	0	0	0	0	0	

Of course, with an int, shifting to the left past bit 7 only pushes the bits shifted into the high-order byte. So 0x1F << 7 produces 0xF80 without any bit loss if the value was stored as an int (see Figure 12.20):

```
unsigned int int_num = 0x1F;
unsigned int int_val = int_num << 7;
printf("%#X << 7: %#X\n", int_num, int_val);
int_val = int_num * 128;
printf("%u * 128: %u\n", int_num, int_val);


0X1F << 7: 0XF80
31 * 128: 3968
```

Also, see Listing 12.4, rotate.c, for a simple way to rotate the pushed-aside bits around to the vacated bits' slots on the other side.

As with the bitwise logical operators, the bitwise shift operators produce new values but do not affect any variables they operate on unless you do so expressly by using them in conjunction with the = assignment operator:

```
unsigned char val = 0x1F;
unsigned char num;
num = val << 3;
printf("val is %#X; num is %#X\n", val, num);
val <<= 3;
printf("val now is %#X\n", val);


val is 0X1F; num is 0XF8
now val is 0XF8
```

12.15.1   Negative Numbers

 For bits shifted to the left—regardless of sign—and for bits shifted to the right where the value is either unsigned or signed but positive, vacated bits are filled with 0s. However, for signed numbers that are negative, a right shift may cause vacated bits to be filled with all 0s or all 1s, depending on the implementation.

With most compilers, the vacated bits are replaced with 1s rather than 0s. This method of replacement preserves the negative sign of the value. Replacement with 1s also effectuates the notion that for negative numbers shifting right 1 is the same as dividing the number by 2. For instance, -126 >> 1 produces –63, as we would expect (see Figure 12.21). Remember, with a two's complement system, you can figure out the value of a negative signed char by figuring out what value the least significant 7 bits would have if the number were positive and then subtracting that result from 128 (for an int, figuring out what value the least significant 15 bits would have if the number were positive and then subtracting 32,768 from that result: $2^0 + 2^6 = 65; 128 - 65 = 63$).

Figure 12.21   *Right Bit Shift of a Negative Value*

−126	1	0	0	0	0	0	1	0

>>1

−63	1	1	0	0	0	0	0	1

Some compilers replace with 0s even for right-shifting of negative signed values. This is sometimes referred to as a *logic shift* rather than the 1-propagating *arithmetic shift.*

 If you have a negative signed number and you want to make sure the left-most bits are replaced with 0s, you can either AND with a mask containing 0s in the vacated bits and 1s in the other bits following the shift right,

```
signed char neg = -1; /* all bits on if two's complement */
neg = neg >> 4 & 0xF; /* 0xF: 0s in left 4 bits */
```

 or you can type cast the value as unsigned.

```
neg = ((unsigned) neg) >> 4;
```

12.15.2   Automatic Conversions

Another thing to take note of for bit shift operations is the automatic type conversion C makes in the course of a bit shift. As we will see in Chapter 13, Standard C requires compilers to automatically convert types in several situations. Two of these situations are automatic conversions for operands of unary operators and automatic conversions for operands of binary operators.

Even though bit shifts are binary operators, Standard C applies the automatic *unary* conversions to the two operands on either side of the bit shift operator. Briefly, if an operand is a char, unsigned char, or short, it is converted to an int; if it is an unsigned short it is converted to unsigned (int if int has more bytes than unsigned short); int, unsigned int, long, and unsigned long are left alone. In the following example,

```
unsigned char ch = 128;
unsigned val = ch << 2;
```

we get a value of 512. The constant 2 has type int (remember from Chapter 2 that a decimal integer constant without any suffix has the first of the following types that will fit its value: int, long, unsigned long), so it is left untouched. However, the char value is converted to int. That gives us the ability to shift values into a second byte that ch itself does not have. But for this conversion, the value after shifting would be zero. The single 1 in bit 7 that 128 is consists of would get shifted left into oblivion.

Incidentally, even if you are 100% certain of the conversion in this case, good programming practice and solicitousness for those of us less fortunate would dictate a type cast to int for ch and a comment explaining why it is probably not necessary.

12.15.3   Undefined Shifts

 Shift operations can produce undefined results if the number of bits to be shifted in either direction is a negative integer or if the number of bits to be shifted in either direction exceeds the total number of bits.

```
num <<= -2;
unsigned char num = 255;
num >>= 9;
```

In most cases, either of these situations will occur not as a result of express code instruction, as we have in the two examples above, but because the number of bits to be shifted is expressed as a variable.

In such cases, you should simply make sure that you have installed the appropriate safeguard against inadvertently attempting to shift a negative number of bits or to shift too many bits:

```
int num, val;
. . .
if (val > 0 && val < sizeof(num) * 8)
   num >>= val;
else . . .
```

Note that our test is for greater than 0, not greater than –1: if the variable number of bits happens to produce 0, there is no problem; shifting simply does not take place.

12.15.4   Multiple Shifts

As long as you are careful with your parentheses,

 You can use more than one bit operation in a single expression.

For example, the following

```
color = ((1 << 7) ¦ 7 ¦ (1 << 3) ¦ (4 << 4));
```

would set `color` on a PC to blinking white on red, where turning bit 7 on (1 << 7) produces blinking; a value of 7 is gray; turning bit 3 on (1 << 3) makes the color intense (intense gray is white); and shifting a 4 (red) left 4 bits (4 << 4) produces a red background (see Appendix C). And as you will understand in Appendix C, the following would print an A in blinking white on red at the top-left corner of the screen of a PC:

```
*((int far *)0xB8000000) =
   'A' ¦ (((((1 << 7) ¦ 7 ¦ (1 << 3)) ¦ (4 << 4)) << 8);
```

The following function will reverse the 2 bytes of an `int` (provided the value is positive):

```
int reverse_int(int num)
{
   return (num << 8) ¦ (num >> 8);
}
```

Assume `num` had a value of 0x0803 (see Figure 12.22). The result is 0x0308. Shifting 8 bits left or right moves the byte value left or right and leaves 0s in the vacated byte. ORing with the 0 byte on either side leaves the shifted byte value unaltered.

If you want to make sure the function will work even for negative values, you can use a mask for the right-shifted portion:

```
return (num << 8) ¦ ((num >> 8) & 0x00FF);
```

The ANDing here zeroes out the left byte of the right-shifted value (all 0s there: 0 AND anything is 0), without altering the value of the right byte (all 1s there: 0 AND 1 remains 0; 1 and 1 remains 1).

Or, as we noted above, even simpler—type cast the right-shifted portion to unsigned:

```
return (num << 8) ¦ ((unsigned) num >> 8);
```

Figure 12.22   *Byte Flipping by ORing Left- and Right-Shifted Value*

0	0	0	0	1	0	0	0	0	0	0	0	0	0	1	1	num
0	0	0	0	0	0	1	1	0	0	0	0	0	0	0	0	num << 8
0	0	0	0	0	0	0	0	0	0	0	0	1	0	0	0	num >> 8
0	0	0	0	0	0	1	1	0	0	0	0	1	0	0	0	num << 8 ¦ num >> 8

Thus, either of the last two of the following formulations produces the desired byte-reversed result; the first does not on a compiler that fills in with 1s for right-shifted negative values:

```
int num = 0xFF00;
printf("%#X\n", (num >> 8) ¦ (num << 8));
printf("%#X\n", (num >> 8) ¦ ((num << 8) & 0x00FF));
printf("%#X\n", (num >> 8) ¦ ((unsigned) num << 8));


0XFFFF
0XFF
0XFF
```

The following listing, rotate.c, generalizes the previous example. It shifts bits to the left a variable number of digits and, instead of wiping out the digits moved past the left byte boundary, reinserts those digits at the right side of the variable.

 **Listing** **12.4 rotate.c**

```
/* rotate.c */

/* rotate bits to the left a variable number of digits */

#include <stdio.h>
#define SIZE (8 * sizeof(unsigned))

unsigned rotate(unsigned number, int left);

int main(void)
{
   unsigned bits_left, num;

   while(1)
   {
      printf("\nType an integer from 1 to 65,535 \n"
         "and the number of bits to rotate to the left\n\n"
         "Type any letter instead to quit\n");
      if (scanf("%u%u", &num, &bits_left) != 2)
         break;
      printf("\n%u, with bits rotated to the left %u positions, is %u\n",
         num, bits_left, rotate(num, bits_left));
   }
}

unsigned rotate(unsigned number, int left)
{
   return ((number >> (SIZE - left)) ¦ (number << left));
}
```

Note that all this activity is accomplished in a single statement, without having to preserve the shifted-out bits in a separate variable for subsequent ORing. That being so, you can use a macro instead of a function if you prefer:

```
#define rotate(number,left) \
((number >> (SIZE - left)) ¦ (number << left))
```

12.15.5 Ascertaining the Value of Several Bits at Once

We saw earlier in the chapter that if you want to ascertain the value of several specific contiguous bits, all of which are low-order bits, you simply AND with a mask that has 0s in the bits you are not interested in and 1s in those you are.

You can combine a mask operation with a bit shift to ascertain the value of several contiguous bits at once where the bit field is not at the right-most end.

This is what is we accomplished in d_drives.c, earlier in this chapter:

```
drives =  1 + ((equipment_int & drivenum_mask) /* turn all bits off but 6&7 */
    >> 6); /* shift bits 6 & 7 to 0 & 1 */
```

12.15.6   Binary Conversion with Bit Shifting

In Listing 8.8, digits.c, we saw how to use recursion to convert numbers from one base to another. We can do the same thing for conversion specifically to binary notation with bit shifting. The next program, dec_bin.c, accomplishes this task.

 **Listing 12.5 dec_bin.c**

```c
/* dec_bin.c */

/* decimal to binary conversion with bit shifting */

#include <stdio.h>

void binary(unsigned number);

int main(void)
{
   unsigned num;

   while(1)
   {
      printf("\n\nType an integer from 1 to 65,535\n"
         "Type any letter instead to quit\n");
      if (!scanf("%u", &num))
         break;
      printf("\nDecimal number %u is this in binary notation:   ", num);
      binary(num);
   }
}

void binary(unsigned number)
{
   int i;
   int num_bits = sizeof(number);

   for (i = 0; i < num_bits; i++, number <<= 1)
   {
      /* for easier reading, separate bytes every 8 bits with space character */
      if(i && !(i % 8))
         putchar(' ');

      /* AND with 1 in high bit; then shift ANDed bit all way to right */
      putchar(((number & 0x8000) >> (num_bits - 1)) + '0');

      /* after print bit, update in for loop shifts it out so we can see next bit */
   }
}
```

We use a mask that has 0s in every bit except for bit 15, 0x8000. We use that mask to AND the user-specified unsigned int. The effect of ANDing with this mask is to produce an int that has 0s in the 15 least significant bits (0 AND either 1 or 0 is 0) and whatever our original number has in its most significant bit in bit 15 (1 AND 1 is 1; 1 AND 0 is 0). Next, we shift that bit all the way to the right—from the most significant bit to the least significant. We then print the character representation of that bit by adding the character 0 (note that this is the character representation of 0, with an ASCII value of 48 (or EBCDIC value of 240), not the NULL character, '\0', with an ASCII value of 0). If the bit is 0, adding it to the character 0 will produce the character 0; if the bit has a value of 1, adding it to the character 0 will produce the character 1. In this way we have printed the most significant bit first.

Since we did not combine the bit shift right operation with the assignment operator, the shift operation does not change the value of the input number. On the next loop, we shift the bits of the number to the left 1 bit. This time we do change the number's value. That moves what was in bit 15 into oblivion and what was in bit 14 into bit 15, where we can once again mask it, shift it 15 to the right, add the result to the character 0, and print. We do this until what started out in bit 0 ends up in bit 15 and gets printed.

To avoid having to stop and figure out that 0x8000 is the value that has 1 in bit 15 and 0s in all other bits, we could have instead used

```
(1 << 15)
```

12.15.7   Speeding Up Code with Bit Shifting

Since each bit from bit 0 represents an increasing power of 2,

 The effect of a bit shift to the left is to multiply the number by 2 for each shift. Likewise, a shift to the right has the effect of dividing the number by 2 for each shift.

 Bit shifting executes faster than multiplying or dividing. Therefore, it might be useful in an appropriate case to use the bitwise shift operators in lieu of simple division or multiplication operators. One place this might be useful is when we use direct memory access to place images on the screen rapidly (a process we cover in Appendix D), where we may need to place values in several thousand bytes in the video memory portion of RAM. Compare

```
scrptr = (unsigned char far *) ((row % 2) ? 0xBA000000L : 0xB8000000L);
byte = 80 * (row / 2) + (col / 4);
bit = 2 * (3 - (col % 4));
```

with

```
scrptr = (unsigned char far *) ((row & 1) ? 0xBA000000L : 0xB8000000L);
byte = 80 * (row >> 1) + (col >> 2);
bit = 2 * (3 - (col & 3));
```

Using bitwise operators instead of the division or multiplication or modulus operators makes the code somewhat more difficult to follow. So, unless you're doing quite a few of the same operations repeatedly, this trick may not be worth the trouble. If you do substitute bit shift operators for mathematical operators, be sure to comment the code.

12.16   SIMPLIFIED MASKING WITH BIT SHIFT OPERATIONS *(OPTIONAL)*

 If you need to turn a bit off or on, you can use bit shift operators in lieu of bitwise logical operators. Though the resulting formulation may be lengthier, it may also more clearly illustrate the operation.

12.16.1   Turning Bits Off

 You can use a bit shift operator to turn a bit off.

Say you wanted to turn off bit 3. (If this byte represented a screen color, the effect of turning this bit on would be to make the color dark; see Appendix C.) Earlier in this chapter, we saw how to do this with the & operator and a mask that has bit 3 off and the rest on:

```
color &= 0xF7;
```

An arguably clearer way is to use the << operator:

```
color &= (~(1 << 3));
```

The statement shows that we're simply placing a 0 in bit 3 of `color`.

This bit shift format is especially useful if the bit position is to be a variable:

```
color &= (~(1 << num_bits));
```

12.16.2   Turning Bits On

 You can use a bit shift operator to turn a bit on.

Earlier in the chapter, we saw how to use the ¦ operator to turn certain bits on without disturbing the other bits. For example, to turn bit 7 on (if this byte represented a color, the effect would be to turn blinking on; see Appendix C):

```
color ¦= 0x80; /* mask has bit 7 on only */
```

With the bit shift operator:

```
color ¦= (1 << 7);
```

or for a variable bit number:

```
color ¦= (1 << num_bits);
```

12.16.3   Determining the Bit Value

 You can use a bit-shift operator to assist in ascertaining the value of a bit.

Take this example:

```
if (num & 0x10 == 0x10) /* test bit 4 */
. . .
```

Instead of stopping to figure out that 0x10 is the appropriate mask value, you can use a bit shift:

```
if (num & (1 << 4) == (1 << 4))
    . . .
```

This alternative formulation is particularly valuable for testing a variable bit number:

```
if (num & (1 << num_bits) == (1 << num_bits)
    . . .
```

Chapter Summary

1. A bit can hold a 0 or 1. Each bit from bit 0 represents a successively greater power of 2 if set to 1. Where the variable is of a type that is stored in more than one byte, the geometric progression continues from one byte to the next.
2. On most computers, a byte has 8 bits.
3. For unsigned integer types, all bits are used to represent value.
4. The numbering system for signed integer types is machine dependent. The most common system is the two's complement method: if the most significant bit is 0, the number is positive; otherwise, it is negative. Absolute value is determined by subtracting the value the non-sign bits would have if the number were positive from the value the sign bit would have if the type were unsigned and set to 1.
5. Standard C imposes certain minimum numeric values for each integer type and a minimum numeric range and precision for floating point values. Each of them has a macro name and corresponding minimum value.
6. With octal or hexadecimal notation, each digit from least to most significant represents a successively higher power of 8 or 16.
7. Octal numbers are written with a 0 followed by the octal digits. Hexadecimal numbers are written with a 0x (or 0X) followed by the hexadecimal digits. Hexadecimal digits 10 to 15 are represented by the letters A to F (or a to f).
8. Regardless of whether you use decimal, octal, or hexadecimal notation for assignment, the computer stores the number in binary form.

9. Each hexadecimal digit corresponds to a 4-digit binary number, and each octal digit corresponds to a 3-digit binary number.

10. Floating point values are automatically represented internally as a number between 1 and 2 (called the mantissa) raised to a power of 2 (called the exponent).

11. On a bit level, the method of representing floating point values is implementation and machine specific. Generally the bits assigned to the exponent and mantissa cross byte boundaries, so the method of evaluating floating point numbers is different from that for integer values and is more complex and slower.

12. Although floating point variables have a large range of values, the precision afforded is limited.

13. There are four bitwise logical operators, ~ (complement), & (AND), ¦ (OR), and ^ (eXclusive OR) and two bitwise shift operators, << (left shift) and >> (right shift).

14. The bitwise operators can, with the exception of the ~ operator, be used in combination with the = assignment operator as a shorthand designation.

15. The bitwise logical operators and the bitwise shift operators produce new values but neither affect any variables they operate on unless you do so expressly by using them in conjunction with the = assignment operator.

16. You may use bitwise operators only with integer type variables or constants.

17. The ~ complement operator toggles all bits. It takes an integer and produces another integer that has a 1 in each bit that is a 0 in the first integer and vice versa.

18. Applying the ~ operator to negative integers may not produce portable results.

19. The ¦ OR operator makes a bit-by-bit comparison of two integer values and produces a value based on the comparison. For each bit position, the resulting bit is 1 if *either* bit of the compared numbers is a 1; otherwise, the result is 0.

20. The & AND operator makes a bit-by-bit comparison of two integer values and produces a value based on the comparison. For each bit position, the resulting bit is 1 only if *both* bits of the compared numbers are 1s; otherwise, the result is 0.

21. A value we use in conjunction with the bitwise operators to turn specific bits on, or turn them off, or toggle them from what they are currently to the opposite, or determine the value of specific bits is called a mask.

22. The mask allows us to ignore certain bits, whose values we may not know or even care about, while at the same time altering or ascertaining the values of target bits.

23. To clear one or more bits, we AND the byte's value with either (1) a second value that has 0s in the bit or bits we want to turn off and 1s in all other bits or (2) the complement of a second value that has 1s in the bit we want to turn off and 0s in all other bits.

24. To determine whether one or more bits in a variable or constant are on, we AND with a mask that contains 1s in the bits we want to look at and 0s in the other bits. Then we check to see whether the resulting value is equal to the mask.

25. To ascertain the value of several specific contiguous bits, all of which are low-order bits, you AND with a mask that has 0s in the bits you are not interested in and 1s in those you are.

26. To turn one or more designated bits in a value on and leave the rest unchanged, we OR the value with a mask that has a 1 in the target bits and 0s everywhere else.

27. The ^ eXclusive OR operator makes a bit-by-bit comparison between two integer values and, for each bit position, yields a 1 if one of the bits is 1 and the other is 0; the result is 0 if both bits are 0s or both are 1s.

28. You can use the ^ XOR operator with the assignment operator and a mask to toggle one or more bits. Bits corresponding to 1s in the mask are toggled and those corresponding to 0s in the mask are left unchanged.

29. The bitwise shift operators move all the bits in an integer value to the right or left the number of bits indicated by an integer directly following the >> or << operator.

30. The number of bits to be shifted can be expressed as a constant, a variable, or a constant-variable expression, as long as only integers are involved.

31. Shifting bits to the right has the effect of dividing a value by 2 for each bit shift, at least if the value is positive.

32. Any bits shifted past the last bit on the right side are lost, with the vacated bits replaced with 0s, assuming the value is positive. This lost-bit result reflects the effects of integer division.

33. For signed numbers that are negative, a right shift may cause vacated bits to be filled with all 0s or all 1s, depending on the implementation. With most compilers, the vacated bits are replaced with 1s.

34. If you have a negative signed number and you want to make sure the left-most bits are replaced with 0s, you can either AND with a mask containing 0s in the vacated bits and 1s in the other bits following the shift right or you can type cast the value as unsigned.

35. Shifting left has the effect of multiplying by 2 for each bit shift.

36. Bits shifted past the left side are lost, with the vacated bits being replaced with 0s. The lost-bit result reflects the odometer-like effect of integer type overflow.

37. Bit shifting executes faster than multiplying or dividing.

38. Standard C applies the automatic *unary* conversions to the two operands on either side of the bit shift operator. If an operand is a char, unsigned char, or short, it is converted to an int; if it is an unsigned short it is converted to unsigned or int.

39. Shift operations can produce undefined results if the number of bits to be shifted in either direction is a negative integer or if the number of bits to be shifted in either direction exceeds the total number of bits.

40. You can use more than one bit operation in a single expression.

41. You can combine a mask operation with a bit shift to ascertain the value of several contiguous bits at once where the bit field is not at the right-most end.

42. If you need to turn a bit off or on, you can use bit shift operators in lieu of bitwise logical operators. You can also use a bit shift operator to assist in ascertaining the value of a bit.

Review Questions

1. Define *high-order bits* or the *most significant bits* of any variable.
2. Define *low-order bits* or the *least significant bits* of any variable.
3. Define *mantissa*.
4. Define *exponent*.
5. List the three parts into which the bit allocation for a float (IEEE) is grouped.
6. List the four bitwise logical operators.
7. List the two bitwise shift operators.
8. You may use bitwise operators only with integer type variables or constants (True or False).
9. What does the ~ complement operator do?
10. The effect of a bit shift to the left is to multiply the number by 2 for each shift (True or False).
11. A shift to the right has the effect of dividing the number by 2 for each shift (True or False).
12. You can use a bit shift operator to turn a bit off (True or False).
13. You can use a bit shift operator to turn a bit on (True or False).
14. You can use a bit shift operator to assist in ascertaining the value of a bit (True or False).
15. Construct a table for bitwise & (AND).
16. Construct a table for bitwise ¦ (OR).
17. Construct a table for bitwise ^ (eXclusive OR).
18. Construct a table for bitwise ~ (negation).
19. Evaluate the following expressions and give their respective results:

```
printf("(a): ~3 = %d and %x\n", ~3, ~3);
printf("(b): ~9 = %d and %x\n", ~9, ~9);
```

```
printf("(c): ~110 = %d and %x\n",
    ~110, ~110);
printf("(d): ~(~3) = %d and %x\n",
    ~(~3), ~(~3));
printf("(e): 3 << 4 = %d and %x\n",
    3 << 4, 3 << 4);
printf("(f): 3 >> 4 = %d and %x\n",
    3 >> 4, 3 >> 4);
printf("(g): 8 << 4 = %d and %x\n",
    8 << 4, 8 << 4);
printf("(h): 2 & 1 = %d and %x\n", 2 & 1,
    2 & 1);
printf("(i): 2 ¦ 1 = %d and %x\n", 2 ¦ 1,
    2 ¦ 1);
printf("(j): 2 ^ 1 = %d and %x\n", 2 ^ 1,
    2 ^ 1);
```

20. What is decimal 106 expressed in binary notation?
21. What is decimal 106 expressed in hexadecimal notation?
22. What is binary 0101 1101 expressed in decimal notation?
23. What is binary 0101 1101 expressed in hexadecimal notation?
24. What is hexadecimal 8C expressed in decimal notation?
25. What is hexadecimal 8C expressed in binary notation?
26. The number 260 is a value expressed in base 20 (just as 31 is a value expressed in base 3—that is, the decimal number 10). What is this base-20 value expressed in base 30? (No one uses base 20 or base 30; this is just to test your understanding of how different bases work.)

Programming Exercises

Programming Assignment 12.27: Electronics

Programming Assignment 1.27 could not be effectively handled until this chapter. We will now look at the sample commands and responses to make sure you understand them. Before we do that we will slightly expand the command set by allowing the user to enter commands in hex, octal, decimal, or binary notation by typing h, o, d, or b as the first letter in the command followed by one or more spaces.

Remember that the set of digits between the whitespace after the initial base-determining letter and the following whitespace is the address of the processor. Since addressing is only 8-bit, the device we are working with has an addressing range of 0 to 255. This device sends commands to processors located in different physical locations. Since we have only 255 possible addresses, we can have no more than 255 processors. In practice, the device will use far fewer than that. However many processors the device is working with, it assigns them addresses arbitrarily to differentiate them. If, for instance, we had only one processor, and we assign it an address of 4, we must subsequently send commands to processor address 4; otherwise our only processor will ignore the command, assuming it is directed to another processor. *To simplify the program, we will assume that there is only one processor.* However, the program must be able to alter the address of this processor.

The final set of digits represents the command itself and its value, with the high-order nibble representing the command and the low-order nibble representing the value. With the unexpanded problem, where we used only hexadecimal or binary command-value numbers, breaking the last set of digits into command and value is simple: for hex, each digit represents the command and value respectively; for binary, the first four digits and the last four digits represent the command and value respectively. For decimal and octal values, your program must store the digits as a single numerical value and use bit operations to determine the respective values in the high- and low-order nibbles.

In other words, if all commands were to be in hexadecimal notation, all you would have to do is use `scanf()` (or later, after the chapter on files, `fscanf()`) to read in each of the two characters separately and go directly to the function description table. With binary, you could likewise read in four characters at a time and again use the function table. With the introduction of decimal and octal, this simple read-lookup is no longer available. The table is reproduced as Table P12.27A.

Table P12.27A   *Command Table*

MSN	Hex	Function Description	Auxiliary Data use (LSN)
0001	1	Replay	[None]
0010	2	Reply with Address + LED status	[None]
0011	3	Reply with data from specified element	Element number (0–9)
0100	4	Turn off certain LEDs	Which LEDs
0101	5	Turn off certain LEDs	Which LEDs
0110	6	Toggle certain LEDs	Which LEDs
0111	7	[invalid command; reserved]	
1000	8	Clear a specified element	Element number (0–9)
1001	9	Score low-order nibble	Low nibble value
1010	A	Store high-order nibble	High nibble value
1011	B	Locate value in low-order nibble	Value to find
1100	C	Locate value in high-order nibble	Value to find
1101	D	[invalid command; reserved]	
1110	E	Increment address by x	Specify value to add to address
1111	F	decrement address by x	Specify value to subtract from address

Each processor has storage for 10 byte values. However, it is possible to store only a nibble at a time. Storage of an element of the 10 bytes must take place by paired commands: one to store the low-order nibble first and a second command immediately following that command to store the high-order nibble. Likewise, to search for a byte value, we first send a low-order value to look for and then send a high-order value to look for.

It is not possible to specify the element number for storage of a value. Values are stored starting at element 0 and moving sequentially through 9. Once values are in all elements, the next value is stored in element 9, and all other elements' values move down to the next element (the value in element 9 is move to element 8; the value in element 8 is moved to element 7; and so on, with the value in element 0 being shifted into oblivion).

Each processor has an LED indicator with 4 bits. When a command is issued to turn on or turn off or toggle LEDs, the value passed carries out the issued command on whichever bits are represented by the value contained in the second nibble of the command. For instance, if we wish to turn on LEDs 0 and 3, we would issue a command value of 5 (or binary 0101). The command "turn on" affects the bits that are 1s in the command value. Be careful when you attempt to turn off or toggle LED bits. A command to turn off LED indicators 0 and 3 would require a second nibble command value of 5 (or binary 0101), just as would turning them on. Thus we specify a value of 1 to turn a bit off—a potentially confusing concept. The difference is that we use a different command to accomplish turning off as opposed to turning on.

What follows are the sample commands and an explanation for each:

```
ZEI processor testing software
bxxxxxxxxxxxxxxxx (16 bits) for binary input
hxxxx (4 nibbles) for hexadecimal input
spaces are ignored
```

Enter your command >h 00 20
                          response: h0000

Explanation: The first character, h, indicates that what follows is a hexadecimal number command. The 00 that follows indicates that the processor we are emulating is at address 0. The last entry, 20, is to be interpreted according to Table 12.27A. The 2 in the 20 is the command that tells the processor (processor 0 in this case) to reply with its address (only one processor can be "active," or addressed, at one time). It also solicits the value of the LEDs. The LEDs have only 4 bits, so they collectively can hold only values ranging from 0 through decimal 15 (0xF). At the outset of the program, all processors and LEDs are automatically initialized to 0. Since no other action is called for by this function, it makes no difference what value follows the 2.

In the response, you see the h, which signals a hexadecimal number; then, since the command we just issued calls for the processor address, 00; then another 00 for the value of the LED status, since we have not yet set any of them. This is appropriately 00 because we are just starting out:

Enter your command >b 00000000 00100000
                          response: b0000000000000000

In this example, the first character, b, indicates that what follows is a binary number. This command is the same as the last one, except that it is in binary form. We get the same response, but again, it's in binary notation:

Enter your command >h 00 E5
                          response:

We are still dealing with processor 0. The following command, E5, tells the unit to increment the address (the E does this) by 5. So now we are addressing processor 5. This command does not call for a response, so there is none:

Enter your command >h 00 20
                          response:

Since we are dealing now with processor 5, commands directed to processor 0, as is attempted here, are ignored:

Enter your command >h 05 20
                          response: h0500

Now we address the "active" processor with the same command, and this time we get a proper response. Processor 5 is asked by command 20 to reply with its address and the LED status. It responds accordingly. Again, the LEDs have not been altered from their 0 default value:

Enter your command >h 05 54
                          response:

Again, we properly address processor 5. Command 54 is to turn on LED 3. The 5 is the command to turn on LEDs; the 4 value (binary 0100) tells us this command is to be applied to LED 3:

Enter your command >h 05 20
                          response: h0504

Processor 5 is still addressed. Now we simply request the LED status after having just altered the LED value. We get back the processor's address and the new LED status:

Enter your command >h 05 93
                          response:

This time we issue a command to processor 5 to store a 3 in the four least significant bits (function 9 directs the processor to store low-order nibble):

```
Enter your command >h 05 A2
                      response:
```

Here we direct processor 5 to store a value of 2 in the high-order nibble (function A directs the processor to store high-order nibble):

```
Enter your command >h 05 30
                      response: h0523
```

Finally, we query processor 5 to verify that the data we directed to store in the high- and low-order nibble is in fact there: function 3 is reply with data; the 0 portion of the command asks for the value in element 0. Since we have stored only a single value and since, by hypothesis, this value is stored in element 0 (this is the first value we have stored), that's where the two-step value storage goes. The response tells us that we have a 2 in the high-order nibble and a 3 in the low-order nibble, as advertised:

```
Enter your command >h 05 B3
                      response:
```

```
Enter your command >h 05 C2
                      response: h0500
```

In the previous command, we asked the processor to look for a low-order value of 3; here we complete the two-part search command and ask it to look for a high-order value of 2. It responds as we expect, with element 0:

```
Enter your command >Q
  ----PROGRAM TERMINATED----
```

The following sample will store 10 values, then perform a few locates:

- The first value stored will go in index 0
- The last value stored will go in index 9

The address of the sample processor will be indicated by XX; any time you see XX, it would be replaced by the address of the processor. The h in the stored HEX column is just to indicate that the number is a hex number; it has no value (see Table P12.27B).

Table P12.27B   *Sample Commands and Responses*

Full command (Hex)	Stored Hex	Stored Decimal	Array Index
XX9B			
XXA1	1Bb	27	0
XX97			
XXA2	27b	39	1
XX92			
XXA5	52h	82	2
XX9D			
XXA6	6Dh	109	3

(continued on the next page)

Table P12.27B *(Continued)*

Full command (Hex)	Stored Hex	Stored Decimal	Array Index
XX95			
XXA0	05h	5	4
XX9C			
XXA4	4Ch	76	5
XX92			
XXA1	12h	18	6
XX92			
XXA5	52h	82	7
XX9F			
XXA2	2Fh	47	8
XX93			
XXA6	63	99	9

Now that we have a filled array, we will perform some locates. Again, XX is the address of the processor (see Table P12.27C).

Table P12.27C *Locates*

Command	Response (hex)	Explanation
XXB7	-none-	Note enough info to search yet
XXC2	XX01	Hex 27 is located in index 1
XXBD	-none-	Note enough info to search yet
XXC6	XX03	Hex 6D is located in index 3
XXBF	-none-	Note enough info to search yet
XXC7	-none-	Element not found
XXb2	-none-	Note enough info to search yet
XXC5	XX02	First occurence located in index 2

And two reply with data commands just for good measure (see Table P12.27D). Good luck. This is a real-life example, by the way.

Table P12.27D   *Data Commands*

Command	Response (hex)	Explanation
XX36	XX4C	Data located in element 6 = 4C
XX39	XX63	Data located in element 9 = 63

CHAPTER 13

Complex Data Types and Type Conversion

OBJECTIVES

- To create your own aggregate data types that can hold data of different types and to learn how to access and initialize structure members and assign them values
- To learn how to copy values from one structure variable's members to another's and to see how to access structure members indirectly with pointers
- To compare two different approaches to passing values of a structure variable's members to a function
- To examine bit- and byte-configuration and data alignment differences in different systems and to address the resulting portability concerns
- To investigate scope and storage considerations for structures

- To see how to use less-than-byte-size data objects: to store data compactly, to examine the values of individual bits, and to match hardware configurations
- To see how unions can be used to examine individual byte components of a variable
- To learn the basics of reading data into a structure and writing it out
- To see how to create more readable constants with enumerations and how to piece together easier-to-follow nicknames for complex data types
- To see when type conversion occurs automatically and when conversion is prohibited, as well as to examine the concept of type compatibility

NEW TERMS

automatic binary conversion	enumeration constant	structure template
automatic unary conversion	forward reference	typedef
bit field	structure	unions
byte alignment	structure member	word alignment
compatible type	structure pointer operator	
dot operator	structure tag	

We've seen how useful arrays can be. Yet they have a significant limitation—the type of all elements in an array must be the same. A structure is a complex data type that allows you to store data of different types. *Structures* are a perfect vehicle for record processing. All the fields in a single record can be stored in one structure variable, each of these fields being referred to as a ***structure member.*** If there is a large number of such records, they can be stored in an array of structure variables, giving us a convenient means of manipulating the record data.

In this chapter, we will discuss structures extensively. We will cover another new type, ***unions.*** Like structures, unions can have members of different types, but unlike structures, only one of them can occupy the union's memory location at one time.

Then we will cover another Standard C concept said to be simply a method of creating an alias or substitute or nickname for a Standard C type, `typedef`. We will also cover one last type, enumerations.

Technically, under Standard C, the enumeration is a programmer-created type, with each enumeration—even one identical to another enumeration—being considered a separate type, just as with structures and unions. But you will see that the relatively loose typing rules for enumerations make them really little more than easier-to-read constants and variables.

Finally, since we will now have discussed in detail all the various Standard C types, we will treat conversions among the various types—both those the programmer explicitly makes, and those stealth-like automatic conversions Standard C constrains compilers to make.

13.1   STRUCTURE TEMPLATE

The basic data types used in C, such as int and float, are predefined by the compiler. When you use a float on a PC, for instance, you know that it will consist of 4 bytes and that the compiler will evaluate the contents of those 4 bytes in certain defined ways.

Not so with structures. A structure is defined by the programmer. Each structure constitutes its own type.

Since a structure may contain any number of members of different types, the program must advise the compiler what a particular structure is going to look like before using variables of that type. The advice-giving mechanism is the *structure template.* Here's what a template looks like:

```
struct complex
{
    double real;
    double imaginary;
};
```

A template is a model or road map for the compiler.

 A structure template does *not* reserve any memory.

What it does is to create a new data type and let the compiler know how it is made up, so that when you declare a variable of this type, the compiler knows how much memory to set aside for the variable and how to evaluate the bytes within the reserved memory area.

First comes the keyword struct, followed by the *structure tag.* (The tag may be omitted in certain limited cases described below.) The type that is created is struct *tag name*—here, struct complex. Note that the tag name complex is not a variable name; it is part of the type name.

Following the tag are braces and a semicolon. Within the braces are the structure members (we refer to array components as *elements* and to structure components as *members*). When you declare a variable of type struct complex, for example, it would have two members: both double. Note that a semicolon follows the closing braces, even though the individual member declarations each are closed by semicolons. This rule is different from other instances of braces—for loops, while loops, if statements, function bodies—where no semicolon follows the closing braces.

Each member has both a type and name. The rules for declaring structure members are similar to those of ordinary variables: the declaration is terminated by a semicolon, and members of identical type may be aggregated with one type name if you separate them by commas:

```
struct worker
{
    char first[10], last[30];
    int salary, id_num;
    float taxrate, fica;
};
```

You may, however, list a type separately for each member or aggregate some and have separate types for others—just as you could with ordinary variable declarations. On the other hand, you may not initialize the members within the template any more than you could fit a horse inside the blueprint for a barn. Remember, the template itself reserves no memory.

This may seem a little strange. The template format may make it look as though we have reserved memory: the member statements surely look like variable declarations, but they are not. However, when we declare a variable of this structure type

```
struct worker clerical;
```

now we have memory reservation. On a PC, `clerical` would contain 52 bytes, the sum of its members' memory slots—a 10-byte and a 30-byte `char` array, two `int` members, and two `float` members.

13.2   DECLARING STRUCTURE VARIABLES

It is the template itself, without the tag, that tells the compiler what the structure looks like. The tag is for use in declaring variables of the type created by the template:

```
struct worker
{
    char name[40];
    int salary;
};

struct worker construction, office, maintenance, sales;
```

The template, including tag, creates a type `struct worker`, allowing us to declare four variables of that type.

The declaration of the structure variable or variables can be made in the same statement as the template declaration:

```
struct worker
{
    char name[40];
    int salary;
} advertising, marketing;
```

This declaration both establishes a type `struct worker` and reserves memory for two variables of that type. The variable names come after the closing brace and before the semicolon.

You can also make the variable declaration both in the same statement as the template declaration and later separately:

```
struct worker
{
    char name[40];
    int salary;
} advertising, marketing;

struct worker maintenance;
struct worker mill, trucking;
```

These declarations create five variables of type `struct worker`.

Generally, the template includes a tag, as all of our previous examples have. You may, however, omit the tag:

```
struct
{
    char name[40];
    int salary;
} advertising, marketing;
```

If you omit the tag, you may not create any variables of this structure type apart from the those declared simultaneously with the template declaration, as here. *Most programmers use tags in all cases, and we recommend the practice. Just because you don't need one now doesn't mean you won't need one later.*

13.3   NAME DUPLICATION

If you use a tag name,

 You may have a structure variable with the same name as the tag name.

```
struct worker
{
    char name[40];
    int salary;
} worker; /* same structure variable name as tag name: OK */
```

 This usage is not uncommon, though some counsel avoiding it. *We recommend a different tag name from any structure variable name. Any other practice may be confusing and hide potentially useful differentiating information. If you are at a loss for a different but similar name for the tag, try adding* _tag *or* _struct *to the name.*

And, though this usage would be unusual, you may have a structure variable with the same name as the tag name of another structure type:

```
struct employee
{
    char name[40];
    int salary;
} clerical;

struct worker
{
    char first[10], last[40];
    float salary;
} employee;
```

Here, we definitely counsel against such a practice.

Likewise:

 You can have a structure member with the same name as (1) a tag name for its own structure type or that of a different structure type or (2) a structure variable of the same or a different structure type,

but this may cause needless confusion. The following examples are theoretically permissible:

```
struct worker
{
    char worker[40]; /* same member name as tag name: OK */
    int salary;
} office;

struct employee
{
    char staff[40]; /* same member name as structure variable name: OK */
    int comp;
} staff;

struct laborer
{
    char office[40]; /* same member name as name of structure
                        variable of different type: */ OK
    int salary;
};
```

 You cannot have two different structure types with the same tag name.

```
struct worker
{
    char name[40];
```

```
    int salary;
};

struct worker /* illegal! */
{
    char first[15], last[25];
    int comp;
};
```

 Two members of the same structure type cannot have the same name.

```
struct employee
{
    char worker[40];
    int compensation;
    char worker[20]; /* illegal! */
};
```

However,

 members of different structure types can have the same name:

```
struct worker
{
    char name[40];
    int salary;
};

struct employee
{
    char name[40];
    int salary;
};
```

And in fact, this latter usage is not uncommon.

Members of a structure type may also have the same name as ordinary nonstructure/union variables:

```
struct worker
{
    char name[40];
    int salary;
};
int salary;
```

However,

 you cannot have a structure variable of the same name as an ordinary variable.

```
struct worker
{
    char name[40];
    int salary;
} office;

char office[20]; /* illegal! */
```

Essentially, there are three separate name spaces (see Figure 13.1). You cannot have duplication within any one category. Or, more precisely, you cannot have duplication within any one category by variables *with the same scope*. You are as free to declare an external and a local structure variable of the same structure type as you would be for ordinary variables. Then too, as with structure variables, simply because you *can* do it doesn't mean that it's a recommended practice.

Figure 13.1 *Separate Name Spaces*

```
Structure Tag Names
Union Tag Names
Enum Tag Names

Member Names within a Particular Structure or Union

Ordinary Scalar Variable Names
Array Variable Names
Structure Variable Names
Union Variable Names
Enumeration Constants and Variables
Typedef Names
Function Names
```

Actually, there is a fourth separate name space, if you consider the preprocessor:

```
#define remainder(a,b) (a%b)
. . .
int remainder;
```

13.4 PERMISSIBLE MEMBERS AND VARIABLE TYPES

You can have any type of variable as a structure member, including a variable of a union, an enumeration type, or *another* structure. (A union is essentially a structure where, instead of all members being in memory at the same time, only one member exists in memory at any given time. We will discuss unions later in this chapter. See Section 13.14 for a discussion of *enums*.) Where an enumeration, union, or structure variable is a member, you can declare the template for that member separately

```
union pension
{
    int self;
    int company;
};

struct vacation
{
    int sick_time;
    int accrued;
    int current;
};

struct worker
{
    char name[2][20];
    int salary;
    float taxrate;
    char *id;
    union pension corporate; /* union pension variable */
    struct vacation management; /* struct vacation variable */
} office;
```

or within the master structure itself:

```
struct worker
{
    char name[2][20];
```

```
    int salary;
    float taxrate;
    char *id;
    union pension
    {
        int self;
        int company;
    } corporate;
    struct vacation
    {
        int sick_time;
        int accrued;
        int current;
    } management;
} office;
```

(See Listing 13.9, `unionflg.c`, for an example of both a union and enumeration template and variable inside a structure template.) In either case, note that just as we have types and variable names for the nonstructure/union members (int `current`, not just int), so we have structure variable names as members, not simply structure templates or tag names; the structure template is just the type. You could no more declare a tag name alone as a structure member than you could just declare char or int without a variable name:

```
struct worker
{
    char; /* illegal! */
    struct vacation; /* illegal! */
};
```

The compiler doesn't need the variable name to size the structure or know how to evaluate its respective bytes. However, both you and the compiler will need the names once you later make assignments.

Also, note that the nested structure type must be declared either before the encompassing structure template that uses it or within the encompassing structure template, as we saw in the two examples above. The following will not work:

```
struct worker
{
    char name[2][20];
    char *id;
    struct vacation management; /* error! Undefined structure vacation */
} office;

struct vacation
{
    int sick_time;
    int current;
};
```

See Section 13.10.2 for a discussion of when a structure type *can* be used before it has been defined.

You may also declare an array of structures,

```
struct worker
{
    char name[40];
    int salary;
} office[5];
```

a pointer to a structure,

```
struct worker *sptr;
```

a pointer to an array of structures,

```
struct worker (*sptr)[5];
```

an array of pointers to a structure,

```
struct worker *sptr[3];
```

a pointer to an array of pointers to a structure,

```
struct worker office[5], *sptr[5], **sptr;
```

and so on. We will discuss structure pointers shortly.

A structure *cannot* contain a variable of the structure itself as one of its members: there would be no end to such a declaration:

```
struct worker
{
    char name[40];
    int salary;
    struct worker office; /* illegal! */
};
```

However, it can contain a pointer to a variable of the same (or another) structure type:

```
struct record
{
    char name[40];
    int salary;
    struct record *next;
};
```

See Chapter 15 for an important application of such internal structure pointers in connection with linked lists of dynamically allocated structure variables.

13.5   ACCESSING, INITIALIZING, AND ASSIGNMENT

You've seen that we access array elements with the name of the array followed by a subscript number in parentheses:

```
int num[10];
num[5] = 23;
```

Since structures generally consist of different data types, this sort of numbering system is not suitable for structure members. Instead, we access structure members through the name of the structure variable followed by the ***dot operator*** and the member name:

```
struct worker
{
    char name[100][40];
    int salary;
} office, plant[5];

office.salary = 275;
plant[3].salary = 500;
strcpy(office.name[10], "Brahman Motoley");
```

Of course, it is the variable name that appears before the dot operator, not the tag name.

Once you use the dot operator to access a structure member, the member can be used in the same manner as any ordinary variable of that same type. This is no different from saying that an element of an array of ints can be used in the same manner as any nonarray int:

```
struct worker
{
    float taxrate;
    int salary;
} boilerroom;
```

```
boilerroom.salary = 275;
boilerroom.taxrate = .15;
printf("Input salary for next year\n");
scanf("%d", &boilerroom.salary");
boilerroom.taxrate *= 1.05;
```

The same applies to structure members that are arrays; they can be used just like any other nonstructure arrays:

```
struct worker
{
   char name[50][40];
   int salary[50];
   char grade;
} office;


office.salary[3] = 330;
```

If you have an array of structures, you must take care where you put the subscript:

```
struct worker
{
   char name[50][40];
   int salary[50];
   char grade;
} office[3];


office[2].salary[3] = 330;

office[0].grade = 'E'; /* correct */
office.grade[0] = 'E'; /* incorrect! */
```

The subscript follows the structure variable name. Contrast this example with the following (which works only on machines that use ASCII):

```
struct worker
{
   char name[50][40];
   int salary[50];
   char grade;
} office[3];


gets(office[1].name[12]);
if (office[1].name[12][0] >= 'a'
   && office[1].name[12][0] <= 'z')
      office[1].name[12][0] -= ('a' - 'A');
```

The dot operator extends to a structure member that is itself a union or structure variable:

```
struct vacation
{
   int sick_days;
   int accrued;
};


struct worker
{
   char name[40];
   struct vacation salaried;
} truckers[50];


truckers[10].salaried.sick_days = 15;
```

The last statement assigns a value of 15 to the `sick_days` member of the `salaried` member of the 11th element of the `truckers` array of type `struct worker`.

13.5.1   Initialization of Structure Variable Members

As with elements of an array, we can initialize members of a structure variable at the time of declaration. The only restriction for structure initialization is that the initializers must all be constants or constant expressions—no variables. Allowable constants include floating point constants, integer constants, character constants, enumeration constants (see later in this chapter), string constants, and the `sizeof` operator with any operand, even a variable or type:

```
struct worker
{
    char name[40];
    int salary;
} office =
    {
        "John Peterson",
        500
    };
```

Notice the similarity to array initialization: we use braces to enclose the initialization; strings can be initialized with double quotes; the members are separated by commas; there need not be any comma after the final member.

The double-brace method of initializing two-dimensional arrays is also used for structure arrays. Within the inner braces, you may also use braces to enclose an array member:

```
struct menu_pages
{
    char title[25];
    char headings[3][45];
    int head_row[3];
} page[2] =
    {
        { /* page[0] */
          "Main Menu", /* title */
          { /* headings array */
            "Print a Report",
            "Edit a Report",
            "Create New Report"
          },
          {5, 7, 9}
        },
        { /* page 1 */
          "Print Menu",
          {
            "Print to File",
            "Print to Screen",
            "Print to Printer"
          },
          {5, 7, 9}
        }
    };
```

You need not initialize all members:

```
struct menu_pages
{
    char title[25];
    char headings[3][45];
```

```
    int head_row[3];
} page[3] =
   {
      {
         "Main Menu",
         {
            "Print a Report",
            "",
            "View List of Reports"
         },
         {5, 7, 9}
      }, /* page[0] */
      {
         "Print Menu",
         {
            "Print to Printer"
         },
         {5, 7, 9}
      }, /* page[1] */
      {
         "View List Menu",
         {
            ""
         },
         {0}
      } /* page[2] */
   };
```

Pay particular attention to the third element of this structure example. You cannot completely leave out a member without some placeholder.

As with arrays, you could omit some or all of the braces other than the two outside-most ones, though braces throughout makes the declaration clearer:

```
struct menu_pages
{
   char title[25];
   char headings[3][45];
   int head_row[3];
} page[2] =
   {
      "Main Menu", "Print a Report", "Edit a Report", "Create New Report", 5, 7, 9,
      "Print Menu", "Print to File", "Print to Screen", "Print to Printer",
      5, 7, 9
   };
```

To the extent that you do not initialize the structure members at the time of declaration, you may later assign values one by one, as with arrays.

13.5.2   Structure Variable Copying

In contrast to the prohibition against wholesale copying of arrays, we can copy all values of one structure's members into the members of another structure variable of the same structure type:

```
struct worker
{
   int salary;
   float taxrate;
} office, clerical;

office.salary = 500;
office.taxrate = .15;
```

```
clerical = office;
printf("clerical salary of %d, taxrate of %.f%%",
   clerical.salary, clerical.taxrate * 100.);
```

```
clerical salary of 500, taxrate of 15%
```

This copying technique will work even if a member is an array. If we wanted code that allowed us to copy the contents of one array into another, we could circumvent the prohibition against copying the values of one array wholesale into another by inserting the arrays into a structure.

 **Listing   13.1 coparray.c**

```
/* coparray.c */

/* can copy arrays when copy structure */

#include <stdio.h>

struct do_nothing
{
   int num[4];
};

int main(void)
{
   int i;

   struct do_nothing source = {{1, 2, 3, 4}};
   struct do_nothing target;

   target = source;
   for (i = 0; i < 4; i++)
      printf("%d  ", target.num[i]);
}
```

```
1, 2, 3
```

Structure copying does not move the memory location of either structure variable any more than assigning the value of one ordinary variable to another variable does. We can see this from the following example.

 **Listing   13.2 no_share.c**

```
/* no_share.c */

/* copying structures copies only values; no shared memory location */

#include <stdio.h>
#include <string.h> /* strcpy */

struct worker
{
   char name[30], id[3];
   int salary;
};

int main(void)
{
   struct worker actor = {"Conrad Veidt", "32", 4000};
```

```
    struct worker newWorker;

    printf("%s earns $%d a week.\n", actor.name, actor.salary);
    newWorker = actor;
    strcpy(newWorker.name, "Marcel Dalio");
    actor.salary += 1000;
    printf("%s now earns $%d a week.\n", actor.name, actor.salary);
    printf("%s still earns $%d a week.\n", newWorker.name, newWorker.salary);
}
```

```
Conrad Veidt earns $4000 a week.
Conrad Veidt now earns $5000 a week.
Marcel Dalio still earns $4000 a week.
```

Thus, even after we have set the values of the members of one structure variable to those of the values of the members of another structure variable, a change to the value of one variable's members does not change the value of the corresponding member of the other structure variable.

Each structure template creates a unique structure type. Therefore,

 You cannot copy the values of one structure variable to those of another if the variables are of different structure types.

That prohibition holds even if the members of the two structure types have identical configurations:

```
struct worker
{
    char name[30], id[3];
    int salary;
} actor = {"Jean-Louis Barrault", "32", 4000};

struct employee
{
    char name[30], id[3];
    int salary;
} mime;
```

```
mime = actor; /* error! */
```

This cannot be cured even by type cast:

```
mime = (struct worker)actor;
    /* error! incompatible type conversion */
```

However, you can point a pointer to a structure of one type to the address of a structure variable of another type with a suitable type cast. (Pointers to structures are discussed below.) The following will compile without even a warning:

```
struct one_struct{char a} one, *onePtr;
struct two_struct{char b} two, *twoPtr = (struct two_struct *)&one;
```

For the reasons for the difference in result, see Sections 13.17.1 and 13.17.2.

Of course, since an individual member of a structure is treated as any other variable, you can make assignments on a member-by-member basis. Taking the previous structure declarations as an example:

```
strcpy(mime.name, actor.name);
mime.salary = actor.salary;
```

You may not make a wholesale comparison of the values of one structure variable's members to those of another:

```
struct worker_struct
{
    char name[40];
    int salary;
```

```
} worker, employee;
if (worker == employee)
    /* error: illegal structure operation! */
    . . .
```

Of course, you could easily create a function that would compare the various members of the structure variables one by one.

Nor are arithmetic operations to a structure variable as such permitted:

```
struct tiny {char a;} minuscule = 2; /* error! */
minuscule /= 2; /* error! */
```

13.6   POINTERS TO STRUCTURES

Just as you can create a pointer to an array, so you can create a pointer to a structure. Structure pointers are useful in passing the address of a structure to functions, in order to access and manipulate the structure's members. Structure pointers are also invaluable in database management techniques such as linked lists and binary trees, covered in Chapter 15.

The syntax is just what you might expect. It is the same as for any other pointer:

```
struct worker
{
    char name[40];
    int salary;
} *sptr1;

struct worker *sptr2;
```

The syntax for assigning a structure variable's address to a pointer is likewise similar to that of pointers to nonstructure variables. The & operator is used:

```
struct worker
{
    char name[40];
    int salary;
} office, *ptr;

ptr = &office;
```

In contrast to the rule for array names,

 The compiler does not consider a structure variable name as equivalent to the address of its first member.

Note the following usage:

```
struct worker
{
    char name[40];
    int salary;
} office, garage, *sptr;

sptr = &office; /* OK */
sptr = garage; /* illegal! */
```

On the other hand, an array of structures is still an array, and the following is permitted:

```
struct worker
{
    char name[40];
    int salary;
} office[3], *ptr = office; /* OK */

ptr = &office[0]; /* OK: same as last */
```

As with scalar variables or with arrays, incrementing or decrementing a structure pointer moves the pointed to address by the size in bytes of the pointed to object. With an array of structures, this means that incrementing the pointer by 1 moves where the pointer points to by one element:

```
struct worker
{
   char name[40];
   int salary;
} office[5], *ptr = office; /* ptr points to office[0] */

ptr += 2; /* ptr now points to office[2] */
```

Remember that a structure template creates a unique type. When you declare a pointer to a structure, you may assign it only the address of a structure variable of that type, not just any structure variable. Just as we saw earlier with copying structure values, this pointer assignment limitation holds even if the configuration of another structure type is identical to that of the structure type the pointer is declared to point to:

```
struct worker
{
   char name[30], id[3];
   int salary;
} *ptr, actor = {"Pierre Brasseur", "32", 4000};

struct employee
{
   char name[30], id[3];
   int salary;
} mime = {"Marcel Marceau", "34", 2500};

ptr = &mime; /* error! */
```

However, this defect can be cured by type cast:

```
ptr = (struct employee *)&mime; /* OK */
```

13.7   ACCESSING STRUCTURE MEMBERS BY POINTER

Let's take a look at a simple non–structure pointer example:

```
int num = 8;
int *ptr = &num;
*ptr = 7;
```

The result is that 7 is assigned to num. To access the variable located where the pointer points, we use the dereferencing operator. In effect, the dereferencing operator plus the pointer name collectively stand in place of the name of the variable pointed to.

The same is true of structure pointers, except that for precedence reasons, the dereferencing operator–pointer name unit must be enclosed in parentheses:

```
struct worker
{
   char name[40];
   int salary;
} office, *ptr = &office;

(*ptr).salary = 200; /* office.salary now is 200 */
strcpy((*ptr).name, "Jason Talmadge"); /* office.name is now Jason Talmadge */
```

There is also a special operator to use for dereferencing structure pointers. Instead of the two last statements, we could write:

```
ptr->salary = 200; /* office.salary now is 200 */
strcpy(ptr->name, "Jason Talmadge");
```

These assignment statements are identical to the earlier two. The ***structure pointer operator*** consists of a hyphen and the greater-than sign, with no spaces between the two characters. Nearly all programmers use this operator in lieu of the dot operator–dereferencing operator combination.

13.8   STRUCTURES AND FUNCTIONS

As we've said earlier, an individual structure variable member is treated the same as any scalar variable of the member's type. Passing the value of a structure variable member to a function or, where you want to manipulate the member's value through the function, its address, presents nothing new.

 **Listing** **13.3 ordinary.c**

```
/* ordinary.c */

/* pass structure member's value & address of structure member as arguments */

#include <stdio.h>

void tax(float *salary, float rate);

struct worker
{
   float salary, taxrate;
};

int main(void)
{
   struct worker management = {425., .15};

   tax(&management.salary, management.taxrate);
   printf("salary is now $%.2f\n", management.salary);
   printf("tax rate is still %.f%%\n", management.taxrate * 100.);
}

void tax(float *salary, float rate)
{
   float tax;

   rate *= 1.07;
   tax = *salary * rate;
   printf("tax is $%.2f\n", tax);
   if (tax > 50.)
      *salary += 30.;
}
```

```
tax is $68.21
salary is now $455.00
tax rate is still 15%
```

We have passed a pointer to a structure variable as one argument and a structure variable's value as another. Inside the function, we first dereference the passed `float` member's address to obtain and use its value. We multiply that value by the `taxrate` member. This member itself has not been passed, just its value, which is assigned to a local variable. The change we make to this local variable's value has no effect on `taxrate` in `main( )`.

In the final statement in the function, however, we assign a value to the dereferenced address of the `salary` member. This does alter the member's value in `main( )`.

Often, it is useful to have a function access the entire structure at once or to pass all the structure members' values to a function. Here, you have two choices:

1. You can pass the values of the entire structure.
2. You can pass a pointer to the structure as an argument.

13.8.1   Passing an Entire Structure

You cannot pass an entire array's values, as such, to a function. You *can* do this with a structure.

 **Listing** **13.4 entire.c**

```
/* entire.c */

/* structure variable passed as argument */

#include <stdio.h>

struct worker
{
   char id[3];
   float salary;
};

void tax_calc(struct worker group);

int main(void)
{
   struct worker management = {"27", 395.};

   tax_calc(management); /* pass structure variable */
   printf("salary is $%.2f\n", management.salary);
}

void tax_calc(struct worker group)
{
   float tax = group.salary * .1;

   printf("tax is $%.2f\n", tax);
   if (tax > 30.)
      group.salary += 25.;
}
```

```
tax is $39.50
salary is $395.00
```

What happened to management's salary increase? It was an illusion. When you pass an entire structure, all you pass are the *values* of each of its members to a locally created structure variable, not the structure variable itself or its address. Any changes you make within the function are local only. Passing structure variables is no different in this regard from passing scalar variables.

13.8.2   Passing a Structure Pointer

If we want to manipulate any of the structure members themselves, we must pass a structure pointer rather than the entire structure variable's values. The following listing shows the difference between passing a structure variable and passing a pointer to the structure variable.

 **Listing** **13.5 two_pass.c**

```c
/* two_pass.c */

/* pass structure: only passes values; pass pointer: can change member values */

#include <stdio.h>
#include <string.h> /* strcpy */

struct worker
{
    char name[30], id[3];
    int salary;
};

void structure_pass(struct worker, char *who, int pay);
void pointer_pass(struct worker *sptr, char *who, int pay);

int main(void)
{
    struct worker actor = {"Leslie Howard", "23", 2000},
    *ptr = &actor;

    /* pass structure variable to function */
    structure_pass(actor, "Merle Oberon", 4500);
    printf("But still %s earning $%d a week.\n", actor.name, actor.salary);

    /* pass pointer to structure to function */
    pointer_pass(ptr, "Laurence Olivier", 3500);
    printf("Now %s earning $%d a week.\n", actor.name, actor.salary);
}

void structure_pass(struct worker group, char *who, int pay)
{
    group.salary = pay;
    strcpy(group.name, who);
    printf("New actor: %s; salary: $%d a week.\n", group.name, group.salary);
}

void pointer_pass(struct worker *sptr, char *who, int pay)
{
    sptr->salary = pay;
    strcpy(sptr->name, who);
}
```

```
New actor: Merle Oberon; salary $4500 a week.
But still Leslie Howard earning $2000 a week.
Now Laurence Olivier earning $3500 a week.
```

In the call to structure_pass(), we altered the value of the salary member and copied a different string into the name member. Yet when we return to main(), the value of the salary member of the structure variable passed is unchanged. To highlight the local nature of this function, we have used a different variable name in the formal argument from that passed.

This limitation should not surprise us. When we pass ordinary scalar variables as arguments, we pass only the value of the variable to a locally created variable. Passing a structure variable has the same effect as if we expanded the structure variable argument to include a separate argument for each of its members.

By contrast, the call to pass_pointer() changes the salary members' values in the calling function. By passing a structure pointer and dereferencing within the function called, we can alter the value of the structure's members in the calling function.

13.8.3   Mechanics of Passing Structure Pointers

Let's focus on the pointer passing portion of two_pass.c:

```
struct worker *ptr = &actor;
pointer_pass(ptr);
```

We could have substituted the following for the function call statement:

```
pointer_pass(&actor);
```

Where a pointer to an object is called for as a function argument, we can pass the address of such an object directly. The concept is in line with what we've already seen in a nonstructure context:

```
void multiply(int *num);
void reverse(char * str);
int num = 3;
int *iptr = &num;
char word[] = "Toothfairy";
char *sptr = word;

multiply(&num);
multiply(iptr); /* same as last */
reverse(word); /* or &word[0]: name of array = pointer to array */
reverse(sptr); /* same as last */
```

What you *cannot* do is to pass the name of a structure variable where the function calls for a pointer to that structure type:

```
struct worker actor, *ptr = &actor;
pointer_pass(ptr);
pointer_pass(&actor); /* OK */
pointer_pass(actor); /* incorrect! */
```

This prohibition is in contrast to the rule for arrays. As we have already noted, the name of a structure is not equivalent to a pointer to the address of its first member. Keep in mind that we cannot pass all values of an array en masse by simply passing the name of the array. We can do this with structures. Were the name of a structure equivalent to a pointer to its first member, it would be hopelessly confusing as to whether we were passing the structure members' values or passing the address of its first member when we passed the structure name as an argument.

On the other hand, with an array of structures, the following usage is permitted:

```
struct worker actor[3];
void pointer_pass(struct worker *thespian);
pointer_pass(actor);
pointer_pass(&actor[0]); /* same as last */
```

13.8.4   Returning a Structure Pointer

You can also return a structure pointer (that is, the address of a structure variable) from a function. The following short program shows the mechanics of passing a structure pointer to a function that returns a pointer to a structure.

 Listing **13.6 ret_sptr.c**

```
/* ret_sptr.c */

/* pass pointer to structure to function that returns pointer to structure */
```

```
#include <stdio.h>
#include <string.h>
#include <ctype.h> /* toupper */

struct err_msg
{
    char msg[40];
    int err_code;
};

struct err_msg *caps(struct err_msg *sptr);
int main(void)
{
    struct err_msg file;
    strcpy(file.msg, "Error reading file");
    puts(caps(&file)->msg);
}

struct err_msg *caps(struct err_msg *sptr)
{
    char *ptr = sptr->msg;
    while (*ptr)
    {
        *ptr = toupper (*ptr);
        ptr++;
    }
    return sptr;
}
```

Note that if we did not place the structure template declaration outside `main()` above the declaration of a function one of whose arguments is a pointer to the structure, the function declaration would not have "known" the structure, and we would have had an error. We had the same phenomenon earlier in Listing 13.4, `entire.c`, one of whose function's arguments was a structure variable.

13.8.5   Passing Structure Pointer versus Passing Structure

If we want to manipulate the structure members' values in the calling function, we must use a structure pointer. Passing a structure passes only its members' values; all changes in the called function are local.

Even if we have no wish to alter the structure members' values, we still might opt for the pointer form. *Passing the entire set of structure members' values takes more time than passing a pointer, and it takes up more memory as well during the time the called function is active.* It seems overkill to pass an entire structure if there are quite a few members and we only want to deal with one or two members in the function.

On the other hand, passing the structure variable name results in code that is somewhat easier to read. We would be wise to use a different name in the function's formal argument to emphasize the fact that we are only passing values, however.

Sometimes a weakness in one context is a strength in another. Passing the structure name prevents inadvertent alteration of values in the calling function. All changes are local.

On this latter point, there is a middle ground. *If you want to pass a structure pointer to save time and conserve memory and yet guard against accidentally affecting data in the original structure variable, you can use the keyword* `const` *in the formal argument.*

```
void pointer_pass(const struct worker *ptr);
```

With that argument, any attempt to alter the value of any member in the pointed-to structure variable would result in an error message. At the same time, you would be free to alter structure members' values while in the calling function.

Figure 13.2 *Structure Array Viewed on a Byte Level*

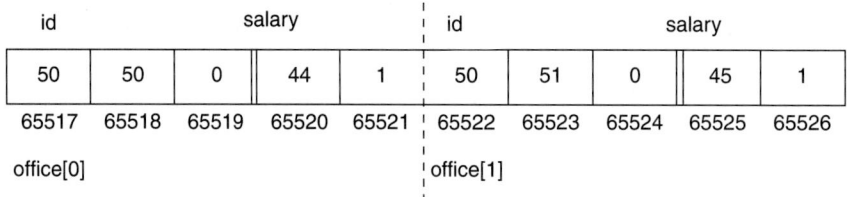

13.9   DATA ALIGNMENT AND THE `sizeof` OPERATOR

Except in the case of bit fields and except for any alignment requirements—both discussed below—the members in a structure variable are stored in contiguous memory locations. Standard C requires that the compiler allocate space in the order in which you list members in the template, in successively higher memory locations, with the first member starting at the address of the start of the structure variable itself. For instance, given the following declaration and assignment,

```
struct worker
{
    char id[3];
    int salary;
} office[2] =
    {
        {"22", 300},
        {"23", 301}
    };
```

Figure 13.2 shows what we might have in memory on a byte level.

Each element of `office` is allocated a total of 5 bytes, 3 for the 3-element `char` array and 2 for the `int`. (As to the byte values shown for `id`, remember that the character 2 is 50 in decimal; as to the byte values shown for `salary`, the 1 in the significant byte of `office[0].salary` (at 65521) and `office[1].salary` (at 65526) is equal to 256.) Here's a program that maps this memory configuration for us.

 **Listing** **13.7 bytesize.c**

```c
/* bytesize.c */

/* shows how structure variables are stored */

#include <stdio.h>

int main(void)
{
    struct worker
    {
        char id[3];
        int salary;
    } office[2] =
    {
        {"22", 300},
        {"23", 301}
    };

    char *ptr = (char *)office; /* type cast to see byte-by-byte values */
    int i;

    for (i = 0; i < sizeof(office); i++)
```

```
    printf("address: %p; value: %d\n", ptr, *ptr++); /* ptr++: move 1 byte */
  printf("the size of one office element is %d\n", sizeof(office[0]));
  printf("for that matter, the size of any worker variable is %d\n", sizeof(struct worker));
}
```

```
address: FFED; value: 50
address: FFEE; value: 50
address: FFEF; value: 0
address: FFF0; value: 44
address: FFF1; value: 1
address: FFF2; value: 50
address: FFF3; value: 51
address: FFF4; value: 0
address: FFF5; value: 45
address: FFF6; value: 1
the size of one office element is 5
for that matter, the size of any worker variable is 5
```

Notice the statement

```
char *ptr = (char *)office;
```

We can always move byte by byte with this device of declaring a pointer to char and using a type cast to make the pointer point at whatever byte we want, even if what's at that address is not simply a char. We could do the same thing for sets of 2 bytes with a pointer to int and a type cast. No matter how complex our data types or program, all we have in memory is a series of bytes containing values by what's in their respective 8 bits. It is only how our program and the compiler interpret and move among these bytes that give us concepts like arrays and structures. As you will see in Appendix D on direct memory access, this type-casting device is of more than academic interest.

On the other hand, we could have accomplished a byte-by-byte view more easily with a union:

```
union test
{
  struct worker
  {
    char id[3];
    int salary;
  } office[2];
  char char_view[10];
} test;
```

See Listing 13.13, union_vu.c, for another example, and see the discussion on unions below in general. See also Chapter 12 for another method of examining individual bits in a data object.

As you see from the bytesize.c listing and output, you can apply the sizeof operator either to the structure type itself or to a variable of that type. This is no different from

```
int num;
if (sizeof(int) != sizeof(num))
  puts("something strange is going on here");
```

Since office is a 2-element array of two structure variables, sizeof(office) gives us the number of bytes of office[0] and office[1] collectively, allowing us to loop through the entire structure byte by byte with a for loop.

(Actually, Standard C allows us to define a type within the sizeof operator:

```
int struct_size = sizeof(struct worker{char name[40];
  int salary;});
```

This would be horrible style, though.)

The storing of structure data in sequential bytes is known as *byte alignment*. On at least some processors, the speed with which data is retrieved and stored is somewhat increased if all structure members begin at an even number of bytes from the structure's starting address and if the structure as a whole contains an even number of bytes. Such a system is called *word alignment.*

With word alignment, the structure variable itself and all members that are larger than byte size must begin at an even memory address. Thus, the structure

```
struct byteword{char a; int b; char c; int d; char e};
```

would have 7 bytes with byte alignment and 10 bytes with word alignment, and

```
struct byteword{char a1; char a2; int b; char c; int d;
    char e};
```

would have 8 and 10 bytes, respectively.

The default for Borland C is byte alignment, but you can select an option to use word alignment instead. Microsoft C uses word alignment in all cases. The tradeoff for increased speed through word alignment is increased memory usage—no small consideration for large arrays of large structures. On the other hand, if the structures are large and many, you'd be better off using external storage/file I/O in many cases.

To generate the output from `bytesize.c` above, we selected byte alignment. Let's see how the output changes if we specify word alignment:

```
address: 65515; value: 50
address: 65516; value: 50
address: 65517; value: 0
address: 65518; value: 0
address: 65519; value: 44
address: 65520; value: 1
address: 65521; value: 50
address: 65522; value: 51
address: 65523; value: 0
address: 65524; value: 0
address: 65525; value: 45
address: 65526; value: 1
the size of one office element is 6
for that matter, the size of any worker variable is 6
```

The compiler skips a byte between the 3-element `char` array and the `int`. Since, with word alignment, the structure variable has an even number of bytes, the resulting size would be 6 even if the order of the `int` and the `char` array were reversed. The skipped byte would come at the end of the structure variable instead of in the middle.

Apart from memory considerations and academic interest, there are reasons for knowing just how many bytes from the start of a structure variable in memory the various members are located (it will rarely be useful to know the precise memory address). For instance, some commercial database toolkits require the program to establish a structure to store the various fields of a record. These toolkits use designated key fields for searching, inserting, deleting, and sorting records in the database. You designate whatever member you want (last name, city, state, and so on) as the key. You generally have to tell the database function how many bytes from the start of the structure that particular member is.

Of course, the safest way to determine how many bytes from the start a particular member is, is not to guess:

```
unsigned bytes_to_salary;
struct record_struct
{
    char id[3];
    int salary;
} record;
char *p1 = (char *)&record;
char *p2 = (char *)&record.salary;
bytes_to_salary = p2 - p1;
```

13.9.1 Other Platforms *(Optional)*

You may encounter differences in the structure composition and size on platforms other than the PC. To begin with, some computers store the most significant bytes first in memory rather than the other way around. Take our earlier example:

```
struct worker
{
    char id[3];
    int salary;
} office[2] = {"22", 300, "23", "301"};
```

Figures 13.3 and 13.4 show how the structure would look in memory on a PC and how it would look on a computer (such as one in the Motorola 68000 microprocessor family) that stores significant-byte first (the high-order bytes are shaded).

Nevertheless, the difference in byte ordering does not affect the alignment of the various structure members or overall structure size—only the relative byte configuration for a particular member. On all systems, the structure members will be found in order of declaration, starting at the lowest memory address and moving up in memory, as both figures show. (Nor does it affect the way constants are written: the first digit is the most significant. For instance, the constant 0x2F3A, has a value of 2 in the most significant byte and A in the least significant byte no matter which way the computer does byte ordering.)

There may, however, be internal padding to satisfy memory addressing concerns. In addition to word alignment, discussed above, some computers require that every structure variable start on an address that is a multiple of 4; some require that `float` or 4-byte `int` members start on an address that is a multiple of 4; some require that `double` members start on an address that is a multiple of 8; and so on. For example, on a computer that requires that `float` members have an address that is a multiple of four, the following declaration

```
struct worker
{
    char id;
    float salary;
} office;
```

would have a size of 8 bytes (padding bytes are shaded). (See Figure 13.5.)

Furthermore, these rules may produce padding at the end of the structure variable. The rule is as follows:

 a structure variable will be sized as though it is an element of an array of variables of that structure type, whether it is or not.

Figure 13.3 *PC Memory Map*

id			salary		id			salary	
50	50	0	44	1	50	51	0	45	1
65517	65518	65519	65520	65521	65522	65523	65524	65525	65526

office[0]   office[1]

Figure 13.4 *Significant Byte-First Memory Map*

id			salary		id			salary	
50	50	0	1	44	50	51	0	1	45
65517	65518	65519	65520	65521	65522	65523	65524	65525	65526

office[0]   office[1]

Figure 13.5 *Structure Byte Padding*

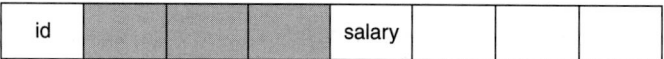

Figure 13.6 *Structure Byte Padding at End*

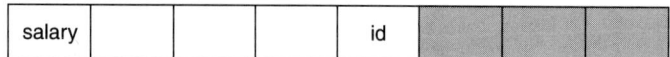

Thus, if the member declaration order in the previous example were reversed,

```
struct worker
{
    float salary;
    char id;
} office;
```

we would still have a size of 8 bytes, but the padding would move to the end (see Figure 13.6).

Some compilers impose certain alignment configurations in addition to those imposed by a particular computer. See also Section 13.11 for additional configuration and padding considerations.

13.10   SCOPE AND STORAGE CLASSES

The extension of the scope and storage-class concepts we learned in Chapter 10 to structures is a bit tricky.

13.10.1   Scope of Structure Type Definition and Tag Name

Notice that in Listing 13.4, `entire.c`, we defined the structure template outside `main()`. Such a declaration does not make `management` an external variable. (See Section 13.10.3.) Nonetheless, placing the template outside `main()` serves an important purpose. Had we not placed the template outside any function, the compiler would not have known what type `struct worker` was when it got to the `tax_calc()` definition.

The scope of a structure type definition and, if it has one, tag name is the same as that of a structure variable, or indeed, an ordinary scalar variable, at the same point: if it is defined outside any function, its scope is from that point in the file down; if it is defined inside a function (or block), its scope is from that point to the end of the function (or block). Likewise, as with variables, a definition inside a function (or block) can "hide" an external definition (or one outside the block). Thus, the following permitted usage would create two completely different structure types:

```
struct worker
{
    int hours;
} clerical;

int main(void)
{
    struct worker
    {
        char name[40];
        int salary;
    } clerical;
}
```

The variable `clerical` inside `main()` is of a completely different type from the global variable `clerical`. The `worker` structure defined externally is not visible within `main()`. Accordingly, if we add the two following assignment statements inside `main()`,

```
clerical.hours = 40; /* error */
clerical.salary = 500;
```

we find that the first statement produces an error "undefined symbol 'hours'," while the second statement is fine. The externally defined structure type has no scope within the function that defines a structure type with the same tag name, just as an externally declared scalar variable would have no scope within a function that declared a variable of the same name. (We do not recommend either practice.)

We have a similar problem with the following program, a rewritten version of Listing 13.4, en-tire.c, presented earlier in the chapter.

 **Listing** **13.8 no_go.c**

```
/* no_go.c */

/*
    nonworking program: structure template must be external if a
    function has the structure type or a pointer to it as an argument
*/

#include <stdio.h>

void tax_calc(struct worker group);

int main(void)
{
    struct worker
    {
        char id[3];
        float salary;
    } management ' {"27", 395};

    tax_calc(management);
}

void tax_calc(struct worker group)
{
    printf("tax is %.2f\n", group.salary * .1);
}
```

The struct worker type has only local scope, so it is not available to any other function but the one in which it is found.

With rare exceptions, you will place all structure templates above main(), either directly or by way of the header file included above main(). Furthermore, the relative placement of templates and function definitions or declarations that have structure variables or pointers to structure variables is significant. Let's take the example from entire.c and another from a program in the next chapter, Listing 14.13, structfl.c. In the first case, the function has a structure variable as an argument; in the second case, the function take structure pointers as arguments:

```
struct worker /* entire.c */
{
    char id[3];
    float salary;
};
void tax_calc(struct worker group);

struct worker /* structfl.c */
{
    char name[22];
    char address[22];
    char city[15];
    char state[3];
    char zip[6];
};
```

```
char enter_record(struct worker *ptr);
void print_rec(FILE *file, struct worker *wptr,
   int record, char *carriage_rtn);
```

If, in either case, we were to reverse the order of structure template and function prototype, we would have an error. The compiler would know how what the structure type was at the point of reaching the function declaration. We could, however, make a referencing declaration above the functions:

```
extern struct worker;
void tax_calc(struct worker group);
. . .
struct worker /* entire.c */
{
   char id[3];
   float salary;
};
```

13.10.2   Forward References

As long as the size of the structure type is not required, references to a not-yet completely defined structure type are allowed. Use of an incomplete structure type is called a *forward reference*. This forward reference ability is what allows us to include a pointer to the structure type inside the structure template, for instance—a use critical to creating linked lists of dynamically created structure variables (see Chapter 15):

```
struct record
{
   char name[40];
   int salary;
   struct record *next;
};
```

We can also create two structure types, each of which contains pointers to a variable of the other structure type:

```
struct accounting
{
   char address[40];
   struct customer *cptr;
};

struct customer
{
   char name[40];
   struct accounting *aptr;
};
```

You could also have created the same thing by defining one template within the other:

```
struct accounting
{
   char address[40];
   struct customer
   {
      char name[40];
      struct accounting *aptr;
   } *cptr;
};
```

Although you will rarely have occasion to make use of this ability, you can also use the forward reference ability to create a new local structure type where a global one of the same tag name exists, without at the same time fully defining the local structure type. Take the following example:

```
struct customer {char name[40];} current;
int main(void)
{
```

```
        struct customer;
        struct accounting
        {
            char client[40];
            struct customer *cptr;
        } past_due;

        struct customer
        {
            struct accounting *aptr;
            char address[80];
            char phone[12];
            float orders[12];
        } newCustomer;

        past_due.cptr = &newCustomer;
        past_due.cptr = &current;
}
```

Here, the forward reference `struct customer` at the top of `main()` "hides" the global `struct customer` before declaring a pointer to a local one inside the `struct accounting` template. With this forward reference, the last line merits a "suspicious pointer conversion" warning; the second to last works fine. The last line refers to a structure type not in scope in `main()`. On the other hand, if we deleted or commented out the forward reference, the roles are reversed: the first line gives rise to a warning; the second works fine.

The forward reference ability allows us to create a `typedef` name (discussed later in this chapter) as an alias for the structure type at the same time we define the structure type:

```
typedef struct record
{
    char name[40];
    int salary;
} RECORD;
```

Be careful with syntax. You can't make use of the forward reference ability where the reference is not truly "forward" but in arrears, so to speak. Contrast the following three examples, the first two of which are valid and the third of which is invalid:

```
struct worker
{
    char name[40];
    struct worker *next; /* OK */
};

typedef struct client
{
    char name[40];
    struct client *next; /* OK */
} CLIENT;

typedef struct
{
    char name[40];
    struct customer *next; /* invalid: customer not yet declared */
} customer;
```

The `pointer` case and the `typedef` case are the only two permitted uses of forward references for structures. We cannot extend our forward reference ability to include an entire structure variable:

```
struct worker
{
    char name[2][20];
    int salary;
    float taxrate;
```

```
   char *id;
   union pension corporate; /* error! */
   struct vacation management; /* error! */
} office;

union pension
{
   int self;
   int company;
};

struct vacation
{
   int sick_time;
   int accrued;
   int current;
};
```

At the point the compiler reaches the last two members of `struct worker`, the compiler does not know what `struct vacation` or `union pension` means and our forward reference ability exceeds its limits. You would have to place both the `struct vacation` and `union pension` templates above the `struct worker` template.

13.10.3   Storage Classes

We saw earlier that the location of the structure template is important for functions that use a structure variable or a pointer to a structure variable as an argument. Apart from that consideration, it is the location of the structure variable declaration that is significant, not the location of the template.

No matter where the template resides, the question of whether a structure variable is external, automatic, or `static` depends on where the variable is declared. A structure variable has whatever storage class a nonstructure variable would have if it were in the same spot as the structure *variable* declaration:

```
struct worker
{
   char name[40];
   int salary;
} static office;

struct employee
{
   char name[40];
   int salary;
};

struct worker management;
static struct worker truckers;

int main(void)
{
   static struct worker assembly;
   struct worker factory;
   extern struct employee drivers;
}

struct employee drivers;
```

This code declares the following variables of type `struct worker`: two global `static` variables, `office` and `truckers`; a global variable, `management`; a local variable, `factory`; and a `static` local variable, `assembly`. It also declares a global variable of type `struct employee`, which is made available to `main()` by use of the keyword `extern`.

There are several things to note here. The external variable `drivers` would not have been available to `main()` without the keyword `extern`, despite the placement of the template declaration. The template declaration for `struct employee` had to be above `main()` in order that the compiler recognized that type when it got to the line containing the `extern struct employee drivers` declaration. (You don't have this problem with, say, an `int` that is made available to a function by the keyword `extern`: the compiler knows what the type `int` is. It doesn't know what type `struct employee` is until you declare the template and the keyword `extern` does nothing for it in that regard.)

The keywords `static` and `extern` are only used in conjunction with a variable of a structure type, not with the template itself. Thus, in the following example,

```
static struct worker
{
    char name[40];
    int salary;
};
. . .
struct worker clerical;
```

the variable `clerical` will not be of `static` storage class. The `static` storage class specifier in the structure template will be simply ignored by the compiler.

 The storage class specifier and any type qualifier of a structure variable apply to each of its members (including recursively to members that are arrays, unions, or structure variables).

13.11 BIT FIELDS *(OPTIONAL)*

Structures are permitted to have members that are smaller than 1 byte. Appropriately enough, these members are called *bit fields*. Bit fields can be used to conserve memory. They also can be used to isolate the value of certain bits of a integer variable—just as we have done in a less direct way with bitwise operations and masking.

To establish a bit field member, you include in the structure template a bit field name followed by a colon and the number of bits to be covered:

```
struct bits
{
    signed field_a : 2;
    signed field_b : 2;
    signed field_c : 2;
} bitfields;
```

Though generally the declaration would be as above, with bit field members, you may aggregate declarations of the same type. The following syntax, though not the best style, is permitted:

```
struct bits {signed a : 2, b : 2, c : 2;} bitfields;
```

The bit field size must be an integer constant or constant expression:

```
int num = 2;
struct bits
{
    signed field_a : 2 + 4 / 2; /* OK */
    signed field_b : num; /* error! */
};
```

Allowable constants include integer constants, character constants, enumeration constants (see later in this chapter), and the `sizeof` operator with any operand, even a variable or type.

You may also make bit fields unsigned:

```
struct equip_bits
{
    unsigned mother_bd  : 2;
```

```
    unsigned video_mode : 2;
    unsigned drives     : 2;
} equipment_byte;
```

In this latter example, you could store values of between 0 and 3 in a member, given their two bits each. In the preceding example, you could only store values of –2, –1, 0, or 1 on a PC or other two's complement machine. (Remember, to derive the absolute value of a negative number on such a machine—one with the high-order bit on—toggle each bit, determine the resulting value if the number were positive, and add 1. See Chapter 12.)

More generally, a bit field of b bits can hold values of 0 through $2^b - 1$ if unsigned and -2^{b-1} through $2^{b-1} - 1$ if signed. As with chars or ints, an attempt to store a larger number just operates to store a number within the permissible range in odometer-like fashion.

You can mix signed and unsigned bit fields:

```
struct record
{
    signed storage     : 2
    unsigned data       : 2
    signed customer_id : 2
    signed end         : 2
};
```

Standard C permits bit fields to be int, signed int, or unsigned int. By default, without any type label, bit fields are of type int (as is the case with non-bit field variables declared only with a storage class specifier or a type qualifier). Unlike non-bit field ints, however, where an int by default is signed, int bit fields (expressly or by default without any type label) are treated the same way as a char that is not preceded by signed or unsigned. That is, the implementation may treat it as signed, unsigned, or mixed—"mixed" meaning it can hold only positive values, but for purposes of automatic conversions (see Section 13.17.4) it is signed. Of course, the bit fields cannot house values as large as an int can (unless you have a bit field of the maximum 16-bit size, or 32-bit, with a 4-byte int), but for purposes of, for instance, type conversion on assignment or adding of expressions, they are either signed int or unsigned int.

Assignment of a value to a bit field is made with the dot operator, as for any other structure member:

```
equipment_bytes.drives = 1;
```

Since several bit fields may access the same byte, we cannot uniquely identify them by address. Nor can we use the & operator in connection with bit fields.

Standard C permits compilers to dictate address boundaries that bit fields are not permitted to cross. If a bit field would otherwise cross such a boundary, it will be moved. Generally, the only limitation a compiler imposes is that a single bit field is not permitted to straddle two different ints. The compiler automatically shifts an overlapping bit field and pushes it into the start of the next int. For example:

```
struct client
{
    unsigned component : 3;
    unsigned process   : 3;
    unsigned sales     : 3;
    unsigned target    : 3;
    unsigned miss      : 2;
    unsigned connect   : 3;
    unsigned pvc       : 2;
} config;
```

The connect member will start at the second int. The last two bits in the first int will not be part of a bit field. The structure will have a size of 3 bytes, assuming there is no word alignment (shaded bits indicate padding); see Figure 13.7.

Note from this example, however, that most compilers will permit a bit field to straddle a *byte* boundary, as opposed to an int boundary.

Figure 13.7 *Bit Field Example: Shifting to Next* int

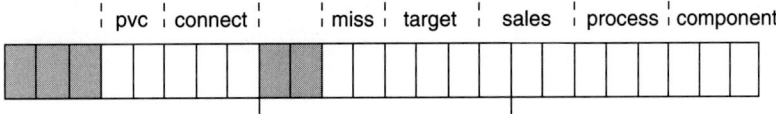

If the computer or compiler uses word alignment, sales will still straddle bytes 0 and 1. There will be an additional byte of padding at the end; the variable will have a total of 4 bytes; see Figure 13.8.

You can intentionally leave gaps between bit fields if you wish to look only at certain designated bits. This allows you, for example, to conveniently match the bit pattern of hardware registers, where some bits are unused. You leave gaps by making unnamed bit fields—by placing the colon and number of bits within the template but omitting the bit field name:

```
struct bits
{
    unsigned drive          : 1;
    unsigned coprocessor     : 1;
                             : 2;
    unsigned video_mode      : 2;
    unsigned drives          : 2;
                             : 1;
    unsigned serial_cards    : 3;
    unsigned game_port       : 1;
                             : 1;
    unsigned printers        : 2;
} bit_view;
```

Figure 13.9 what we have in memory.

You could achieve a similar result by naming but just not using some bit fields

```
struct bits
{
    unsigned drive          : 1;
    unsigned coprocessor     : 1;
    unused_1                 : 2;
    unsigned video_mode      : 2;
    unsigned drives          : 2;
    unused_2                 : 1;
    unsigned serial_cards   : 3;
    unsigned game_port       : 1;
    unused_3                 : 1;
    unsigned printers        : 2;
} bit_view;
```

Figure 13.8 *Bit Field Example: Word Alignment*

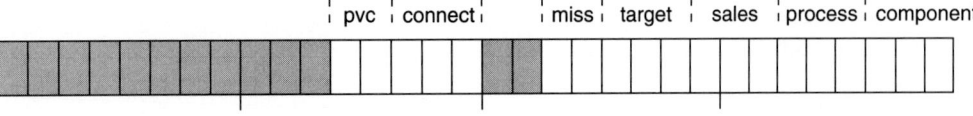

Figure 13.9 *Bit Field Example: Intentional Padding*

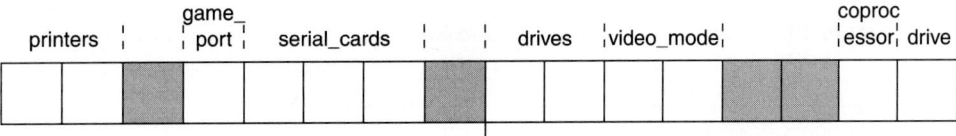

but there are some differences. There is no way to reference unnamed bit fields, and in any event their value at run time is unpredictable. They do not figure in any initialization of structure variables. Otherwise, bit fields can be initialized in the same fashion as other non–bit field members:

```
struct record
{
   unsigned storage   : 2;
   unsigned data      : 2;
                      : 2;
   unsigned end       : 2;
} customer = {1, 2, 3};
```

The three named bit fields would have values of 1, 2, and 3, respectively. If you tried to add a fourth value to the initializers here, you would get an error.

Putting a 0 as the bit field size causes the next bit field to start at the next int. On some compilers, a zero bit field will cause the next bit field to start at the next byte, particularly those that expand Standard C by allowing char bit fields—with Borland C, a zero bit field causes a jump to the next byte, even where the word alignment option is selected. (See Figure 13.10.)

```
struct client

   unsigned component : 3;
   unsigned process   : 3;
   unsigned sales     : 1;
                      : 0;
   unsigned miss      : 3;
   unsigned connect   : 2;
   unsigned pvc       : 2;
} config;
```

There is nothing wrong theoretically with mixing bit fields with ordinary variables in the same structure, although the combination would be unusual:

```
struct record
{
   unsigned id        : 2;
   unsigned hours     : 4;
   unsigned salary;    /* no bit field here */
   unsigned grade     : 2;
   unsigned taxlevel  : 4;
} employee;
```

The int member and the succeeding bit fields would be aligned on a byte boundary (or int boundary if word alignment is used). Furthermore, although bit fields are generally fewer than 8 bits, they can be as large as 16 bits where an int is 2 bytes and a byte is 8 bits, or 32 bits where an int is 4 and a byte is 8 bits:

```
struct record
{
   unsigned id        : 2;
   unsigned hours     : 4;
   unsigned salary    : 16;
   unsigned grade     : 2;
   unsigned taxlevel  : 4;
} employee;
```

Figure 13.10   *Bit Field Example: Forcing to Next Byte*

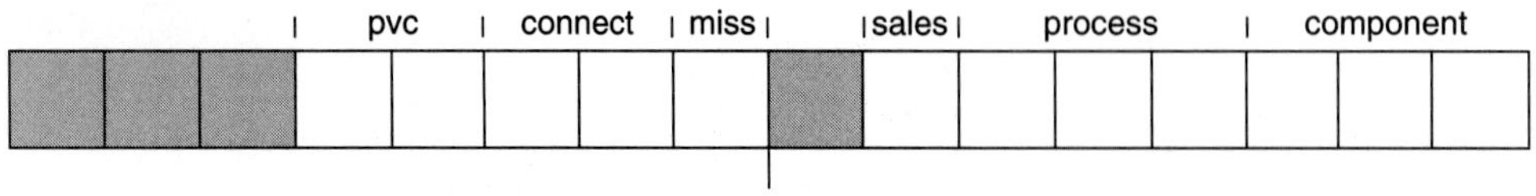

However, Standard C allows compilers to limit the maximum size of a bit field to fewer than the number of bits in an `int`. In any case,

 The width of a bit field cannot exceed the number of bits in an `int`.

13.11.1   Rationale for Bit Fields

There are quite a few instances where the computer places a number of separate values in one `int`. You will see examples in Appendix K, when we discuss file opening modes in low-level I/O, and the `stat()` function. The computer does this in order to conserve RAM.

You can use bit fields in your programs for the same purpose. Early on, in Chapter 2, we discussed the choice between `int` variables and `char` variables. We noted that although many of us think of `int`s as being used only for numbers and `char`s only for characters, in reality this distinction is artificial. You can, for instance, use `char`s for integer numerical data where you are certain the maximum values to be stored do not exceed the range for `char`.

If memory is really at a premium in one of your applications, you can carry this logic further and store data values in bit fields. This assumes you have quite a bit of data with values that would fit into a few bits only. When you store the data in a file, you would, of course, store the values of the bytes as a whole. When you later read the data back out of the file, you would read the byte values back into the bit field structure that generated the byte values in the first place.

Bit fields are also often used in machine-specific applications that demand a data configuration that matches a certain hardware structure. Once we cover unions, we will show you some other important uses for bit fields.

13.11.2   Portability Concerns

If you have been closely following the alignment and byte-ordering rules for structures, you can see that there may be considerable variation from one machine to another. Some computers use word alignment; others use byte alignment. Some computers require that every structure variable start on an address that is a multiple of 4; some require that `float` or 4-byte `int` members start on an address that is a multiple of 4; some require that `double` members start on an address that is a multiple of 8; and so on. Some computers store the most significant bytes first in memory; others do it the other way around. Some compilers impose certain alignment configurations in addition to those imposed by a particular computer.

There is even more variation possible with bit fields in particular. Some implementations allow only `int` types for bit fields; others allow any integer type, including `char`. Some computers have a maximum bit field size of 32 bits, while others have a maximum bit size of 16 since their `int` size differs; some implementations limit bit fields to fewer bits than the size of an `int`. On most implementations, a zero bit field size causes the next bit field to start at the next `int`; with others, it will start at the next byte. Standard C permits compilers to dictate address boundaries that bit fields are not permitted to cross. Standard C also permits implementations to treat plain `int` bit fields in one of three ways with respect to their signed or unsigned status.

 If you are using bit fields to achieve memory savings where the size of a data structure dictates packing data in as tightly as possible, you should not depend on a particular packing configuration unless your program will run only on a single platform. If you are using bit fields to match a particular hardware configuration, bear in mind that such a scheme is likely to be highly unportable. Generally, that latter concern is not great, since normally hardware-matching code is meant to be machine specific. In any case, if you have a coding task that requires a specific alignment and packing, you should be careful to do testing to verify that the results of your implementation and system are as you expect or as the documentation advertises.

If portability is a strong concern in a predefined configuration-matching situation, in some cases you may want to eschew bit fields altogether and use bit shifting and masking operations instead. For example, let's say that the current video page, row, and column were stored in 2 bytes at a certain absolute memory address in the configuration shown in Figure 13.11.

Figure 13.11 *Field Configuration Example*

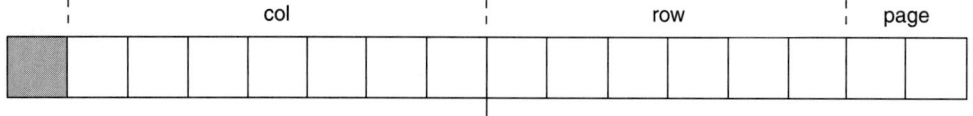

If the computer stores bits from right to left, as on a PC, the following structure would be appropriate for easy reading of the three components of the `int`:

```
struct video
{
    unsigned page   : 3;
    unsigned row    : 5;
    unsigned col    : 7;
} video_config;
```

But if the computer stores bits from left to right, the following would be the required configuration:

```
struct video
{
                    : 1;
    unsigned col    : 7;
    unsigned row    : 5;
    unsigned page   : 3;
} video_config;
```

If we created the first version of this structure and the target machine were in the Motorola 68000 family, which stores bits from left to right, we would get an incorrect value:

```
int page = video_config.page, col = video_config.col, row = video_config.row;
```

Our `bit_look.c` program later in this chapter, Listing 13.12, would suffer the same fate. However, if the three values were stored in an `int` named `video_locus`, we could get, say, the row component more reliably in the following manner:

```
int row = video_locus = (col >> 8)
    & 0x7F; /* 0x7F: 1's in 7 least significant bits, rest 0's */
```

(See Chapter 12 for an explanation.) There would generally be some overhead involved in this more portable version, however.

If you have a coding task that requires a specific alignment and bit packing, you should be careful to do some testing to verify the particular configuration of your implementation.

13.12   UNIONS *(OPTIONAL)*

A union is essentially a structure where, instead of all members being in memory simultaneously, only one member exists in memory at any given time. There are several situations in which unions are useful. If we have a very large record, with many fields, or a large number of records we need to examine at one time, but in either case, we need only deal with one field at a time, the memory savings between a structure or array of structures and a union or array of unions can be huge.

If we need a data object that can alternatively store either an integer value or a floating point value at different times depending on the situation, a union is perfect for the situation:

```
union record
{
    int whole;
    float fractional;
};
```

Unions are also a tool for examining only part of a data object. We will examine this last use in greater detail later in the chapter.

13.12.1   Union Sizing and Assignment

The union as a whole is given as much space in memory as its largest member requires. For example:

```
union employee
{
    char id;
    int salary;
    long sales;
    float hours;
} worker;
```

The largest member takes up 4 bytes, assuming float and long are both 4 bytes, and the union is therefore allotted 4 bytes. We can refer to worker.id, worker.salary, worker.sales, and worker.hours. However, only one of those variables is in memory at one time—the most recent member to which assignment was made.

If we assign a value to worker.id

```
worker.id = 'g';
```

one of the union's bytes holds a g. Whichever member is active at the time is stored starting at the union's first byte. If we assign a value to worker.salary

```
worker.salary = 350;
```

two of the union's bytes hold the value (assuming int has 2 bytes). Now, if we assign a value to worker.sales

```
worker.sales = 120500L;
```

all 4 bytes hold the value. Finally, if we assign a value to worker.hours

```
worker.hours = 40.5;
```

the value is stored in the union's 4 bytes, but, as you know from Chapter 12 the 4 bytes are used differently for this float variable than they were for the long variable that occupied the same space earlier.

Only one variable occupies the union memory space at one time. You could not store both id and salary at the same time even though there would be enough space to do so.

It is the programmer's job to keep track of which member is currently occupying the union's memory space, if that matters to the application. One way to accomplish this is to create a structure comprised of the union and a "flag" member. Every time you make an assignment, you also set the flag:

```
struct
{
    union employee_flag
    {
        char id[3];
        int salary;
        long sales;
    } worker;
    char flag;
} record;

record.worker.salary = 350;
record.flag = 'i';
switch (recordl.flag)
{
    case 's': printf("Id #: %s\n", record.id); break;
    case 'i': printf("Salary: %d\n", record.salary); break;
    case 'l': printf("Sales: %ld\n", record.sales); break;
    default: printf("Oops!");
}

Salary: 350
```

It might be more convenient to use manifest constants or enumerated constants (see below) for the flag values rather than character constants or other arbitrary values. For instance:

```
#define EMP_ID
#define EMP_SALARY
#define EMP_SALES
. . .
record.worker.salary = 350;
record.flag = EMP_SALARY;
```

The following simple program illustrates the use of enumeration constants (covered later in this chapter) as flag values. It contains a function that allows us to print the value of the active union member without knowing what type was last assigned.

 **Listing** 13.9 `unionflg.c`

```c
/* unionflg.c */
/* show use of enum flags for unions */

#include <stdio.h>

struct wrapper
{
   enum flag
   {
      flag_id, flag_salary, flag_sales
   } flag;
   union employee_tag
   {
      char id[3];
      unsigned salary;
      long sales;
   } employee;
};

void print_field(struct wrapper *rec);

int main(void)
{
   struct wrapper record;
   record.employee.salary = 30000;
   record.flag = flag_salary;
   print_field(&record);
}

void print_field(struct wrapper *rec)
{
   switch (rec->flag)
   {
      case flag_id: printf("Id: %s\n", rec->employee.id);
         break;
      case flag_salary: printf("Salary: %u\n", rec->employee.salary);
         break;
      case flag_sales: printf("Sales: %ld\n", rec->employee.sales);
         break;
      default: puts("print_field(): This can't ever happen");
   };
}
```

You can have different elements of an array of unions holding different types:

```
union record
{
   long sales;
   float revenues;
} books[2];

books[0].sales = 89292L;
books[1].revenues = 89292.;
```

The bit configurations for these two identical values will be different in each of the elements.

13.12.2   Union Rules

Apart from the significant memory difference between structures and unions, and apart from using the keyword `union` rather than `struct`, all the rules for structures apply to unions:

- The template declaration syntax is identical.
- Union variables can be declared simultaneously with the template, or separately.
- In addition to ordinary scalar variables, permissible union members include arrays, structure variables, structure pointers, variables of another union, union pointers, and bit fields. You may not include a variable of the union itself.
- Where a union or structure variable is a member, you can declare the template for the member separately (as long as the template declaration precedes the union declaration) or within the master union itself.
- You can have an array of unions.
- You can access union members with the dot operator, or indirectly with the -> operator. Where a member is another union or structure variable, you use two dot operators to access a submember (for example, `master.sub.variable`).
- You can copy the value of one union variable into another with an assignment statement (or `strcpy()` for a string) by using the union variable names alone. (However, with unions, only one value is copied.) Copying by assignment is not possible if the two union variables are not of identical type, even with type casting. You may not compare one union variable to another for equality even if it is of identical type.
- The name of a union variable is not a pointer to its starting address.
- You can use forward references in the same situations we covered earlier for structures.
- Whether a union is external, automatic, or `static` depends on where the union variable is declared, not where the template is declared.
- Initializers must all be constants or constant expressions: floating point constants, integer constants, character constants, enumeration constants (see later in this chapter), string constants, and the `sizeof` operator with any operand.

When you initialize a union variable, only one member is initialized, of course.

 Union variable initialization initializes the first member. You *must* enclose the initializers in braces, even if there is only one initializer.

```
union worker
{
   int id;
   float salary;
} clerical = {3};
```

(The same holds true for a structure with a single member, although as applied to structures, this rule is probably of academic interest only).

If the first member is a structure variable, you initialize with more than one initializer, just as you would for any structure variable:

```
union worker
{
   struct worker_name
```

```
   {
      char first[15], middle[2], last[45];
   } govt;
   int id;
   float salary;
} boss = {"Richard", "J", "Daley"};
```

Platform-specific rules (for example, a `double` starting at an address evenly divisible by 8) can produce padding at the end of a union. Padding will occur to the greatest extent required by any of its members.

Furthermore, as with a structure, a union variable will be sized as though it is an element of an array of variables of that union type, whether it is or not. For instance, on a computer that requires a `float` and a `double` to start on an address that is an even multiple of 4 or 8 respectively,

```
union worker
{
   char id[9];
   float salary;
   double comp_rate;
};
```

will have 16 bytes, even though its longest member is only 9 bytes, and

```
union worker
{
   char id[9];
   float salary;
};
```

would have 12 bytes.

Since only one member can be active at once, all padding occurs at the end of a union variable. Standard C requires that each union member be stored starting at the same memory address as that of the union variable itself. Accordingly, you can always be sure that the following test will evaluate to true no matter which member you happen to select for the test and which other member or members happen to precede or follow it in order of declaration:

```
union type_tag
{
   char a;
   int b;
   long c;
   float d;
   double e;
   long double f;
} types, *uptr = &types;
if ((union type_tag *)&(uptr->c) != &types || (union type_tag *)&(uptr->c) != uptr)
      puts("This can't possibly happen");
```

13.12.3   An Important Union Application: Seeing Values through the Eyes of Another

Possibly the most important attribute of unions is the ability to assign a value to one of its members and then look at that value through the eyes of another member of a different type. To take a simple example:

```
union views
{
   char ch;
   int num;
} two_view;

two_view.ch = 'a';
```

```
printf("two_view.num = %d\n", two_view.num);
```

```
two_view = 97
```

The `int` member `two_view.num` assumes the value that has been assigned to the `char` member `two_view.ch`, since this is the only value the union has. Since `int` and `char` variables' bits are evaluated in the same fashion, we get a sensible result here. However the output of the following is not so sensible:

```
union skipper
{
   unsigned long line;
   float my_boat;
} skew;
skew.my_boat = 255.;
printf("line: %lu\n", skew.line);
```

The output:

```
line: 113296544
```

The bits are not given the new values geared to produce the same 255 value. Absent *new assignment* to the `unsigned long` member, the bits remain the same. Thus if we have a union with a single `float` variable and a single `char` variable, we make an assignment to the `float` variable and then an assignment to the `char` variable, it is only byte 0 whose bits are given new values; the other 3 bytes are left untouched.

We spoke earlier of only one of a union's members being "active" at any one time. What does being "active" mean? And how do we make one particular member active?

Whenever we assign a value to a union member, the union's bits are given values in a manner appropriate for that member's type. It is only in this sense that this member is "active." It isn't that this member has any special future claim on the union's memory space, or that the memory space becomes the type of the active member.

We are free to look at the union's memory area as representing the value of a nonactive member if we wish, even though that area is guaranteed to make sense only if we look at it as representing the value of the active member. If a union's two members are a `long` and a `float`, as we saw in the last example, assigning a value to one of these members and looking at the union's 4 bytes as though it were the other member would make little sense because of the different way the bits are assigned as between a `long` and a `float`.

We have to be especially careful if we have nonscalar variables whose elements or members are of different types from one another. For example:

```
union worker
{
   float rate[6];
   unsigned hours[12];
} clerical;
int i;

for (i = 0; i < 6; i++)
   clerical.rate[i] = 1.;
for (i = 0; i < 12; i++)
   printf("%d ", clerical.hours[i]);
putchar('\n');
   clerical.hours[0] = 1;
for (i = 0; i < 12; i++)
   printf("%d ", clerical.hours[i]);
```

The output:

```
0 16256 0 16256 0 16256 0 16256 0 16256 0 16256
1 16256 0 16256 0 16256 0 16256 0 16256 0 16256
```

Table 13.1 *PC Equipment* int

Bits	Significance	Values
0	disk drives	1 if installed
1	math coprocessor	1 if installed
2–3	not used (in original IBM PC, motherboard memory: from 16K to 64K)	
4–5	initial video mode	1: 40 x 25 color 2: 80 x 25 color 3: 80 x 25 monochrome
6–7	disk drives	number of diskette drives – 1
8	not used	
9–11	serial cards	number of serial cards
12	game port	1 if installed
13	not used	
14–15	printers	number of printers

We first assigned values to each of the float array elements. Then we assigned a value to just one of the unsigned array elements. It does not follow that simply because we make an assignment of a single unsigned value in the union the entire union memory space will be reconfigured to store the same values previously assigned as float in a manner consistent on a bit level with unsigned. Only the bits of the element we specifically assigned a value to were altered.

Nevertheless, if our members are all ints and chars or ints and bit fields, this sort of "nonactive looking" can produce sensible results in a proper application. Let's see such an application.

13.12.4 An int Bit Field Example

We can use the nature of union value storage and assessment to make use of the bit field example we looked at earlier in the chapter. In RAM, the 2 bytes starting at address 0x00400010 contain information about the PC. The information is meaningful only on a bit level. The following bits convey the information shown in Table 13.1.

We can store the value of these 2 bytes in an int and then look at the bits of the 2 bytes with bit fields, as equip.c shows.

 Listing   **13.10 equip.c**

```
/* equip.c */

/* look at the bits in the equipment int with bit fields */

#include <stdio.h>

int main(void)
{
    int far *equipment_memory = (int far *)0x00400010;
    union see_equip
    {
        unsigned int int_view;
```

```
        struct bits
        {
            unsigned drive           : 1;
            unsigned coprocessor     : 1;
                                     : 2;
            unsigned video_mode      : 2;
            unsigned drives          : 2;

                                     : 1;
            unsigned serial_cards    : 3;
            unsigned game_port       : 1;
                                     : 1;
            unsigned printers        : 2;
        } bit_view;
    } equipment;

    /* assign value to int member */
    equipment.int_view = *equipment_memory;

    /* now view that value through bit field members perspective */
    printf("%scoprocessor installed\n", equipment.bit_view.coprocessor ?
        "" : "no ");
      printf("intial video mode: %s\n", equipment.bit_view.video_mode == 1 ?
          "40 x 25 color" : equipment.bit_view.video_mode == 2 ?
          "80 x 25 color" : "80 x 25 monochrome");
      printf("%d disk drive%s\n", !equipment.bit_view.drive ? 0 :
          equipment.bit_view.drives + 1, !equipment.bit_view.drives ?
          "" : "s");
      printf("%d serial card%s\n", equipment.bit_view.serial_cards,
          equipment.bit_view.serial_cards == 1 ? "" : "s");
      printf("%sgame port installed\n", equipment.bit_view.game_port ?
          "" : "no ");
      printf("%d printer%s\n", equipment.bit_view.printers,
          equipment.bit_view.printers == 1 ? "" : "s");
      return 0;
}
```

We get the following output on our system:

```
coprocessor installed
initial video mode: 80 x 25 color
1 disk drive
3 serial cards
no game port installed
3 printers
```

First we set an int pointer to the address where the equipment information is stored (we will explain far pointers, and direct memory access in general, in Appendix D). We declare a union that has two members: an int called int_view and a structure with bit field members. The value in the equipment int is stored in the union's int by dereferencing. We then simply look at the bits of this value by using the bit field members of the union, without changing the value the union now houses.

You will see how critical this see-through-the-eyes-of-another characteristic of unions is when we cover interrupts in Appendix B. We could, incidentally, have derived the value of the equipment int with an interrupt, rather than using a pointer (see Appendix B).

We can combine even integer variables and floating point variables in a union and look at one type through the eyes of the other to "look under the hood" and get a better picture of how our system works on a bit level. Compare the following three approaches to viewing floating point storage on a bit level.

 **Listing** **13.11 floating.c**

```
/* floating.c */

/* shows typecasting with char pointer to look at float bits;
   shows how floating point numbers are stored in bits */

#include <stdio.h>

void binary(char, int);

int main(void)
{
   float num;
   float sample[10] = {.000034F, .00025F, .00333333F, .0625F, .985F,
      1.F, 1.999999F, 27.256F, 128.88F, -128.88F};
   char *ptr;
   int i, j;

   putchar('\n');
   for (num = 2.F, i = 0; i < 10; i++, num *= 2.F)
   {
      printf("\n%15f: ", num);
      for (j = 0, ptr = (char *)&num + 3; j < 4; j++)
      {
         binary(*ptr--, j);
      }
   }
   putchar('\n');
   for (i = 0; i < 10; i++)
   {
      printf("\n%15f: ", sample[i]);
      for (j = 0, ptr = (char *)&sample[i] + 3; j < 4; j++)
      {
         binary(*ptr--, j);
      }
   }
}
void binary(char n, int count)
{
   int i;

   for (i = 0; i < 8; i++, n <<= 1)
   {
      putchar ( ((n & 128) >> 7) + '0'); /* 128: binary 10000000 */
      if (count == 0 && i == 0) putchar(' '); /* space after sign */
      if (count == 1 && i == 0) printf("  "); /* space after expt */
      if (count == 1 && i == 7) putchar(' ');
      if (count == 2 && i == 7) putchar(' ');
   }
}
```

 **Listing** **13.12 bit_look.c**

```
/* bit_look.c */

/* bit field version of floating.c (looks at float bit by bit) */

#include <stdio.h>
```

```
#define Q(P,N) \
printf("%d", float_or_bits.bit_structure_choice.bit_##N);

int main(void)
{
   struct bits
   {
      unsigned bit_0: 1; /* mantissa */
      unsigned bit_1: 1;
      unsigned bit_2: 1;
      unsigned bit_3: 1;
      unsigned bit_4: 1;
      unsigned bit_5: 1;
      unsigned bit_6: 1;
      unsigned bit_7: 1;

      unsigned bit_8: 1;
      unsigned bit_9: 1;
      unsigned bit_10: 1;
      unsigned bit_11: 1;
      unsigned bit_12: 1;
      unsigned bit_13: 1;
      unsigned bit_14: 1;
      unsigned bit_15: 1;

      unsigned bit_16: 1;
      unsigned bit_17: 1;
      unsigned bit_18: 1;
      unsigned bit_19: 1;
      unsigned bit_20: 1;
      unsigned bit_21: 1;
      unsigned bit_22: 1;

      unsigned bit_23: 1; /* exponent */
      unsigned bit_24: 1;
      unsigned bit_25: 1;
      unsigned bit_26: 1;
      unsigned bit_27: 1;
      unsigned bit_28: 1;
      unsigned bit_29: 1;
      unsigned bit_30: 1;

      unsigned bit_31: 1; /* sign */
   };
   union
   {
      struct bits bit_structure_choice;
      float float_choice;
   } float_or_bits;

   printf("type in floating point numbers; type a letter to quit\n");

   /* first use float member of union for input-storage */
   while (scanf("%f", &float_or_bits.float_choice))
   {
      /* print the decimal representation of the value */
      printf("%15.6f: ", float_or_bits.float_choice);

      /* print out the bits using the bit fields of the
         struct member of union */
```

```
        /* first, do the sign bit */
        Q(P,31) /* => printf("%d",
          float_or_bits.bit_structure_choice.bit_31); */
          putchar(' ');

        /* do the exponent bits */
        Q(P,30) Q(P,29) Q(P,28) Q(P,27) Q(P,26) Q(P,25)
          Q(P,24) Q(P,23)
          putchar(' ');

        /* do the mantissa bits, byte by byte */
        Q(P,22) Q(P,21) Q(P,20) Q(P,19) Q(P,18) Q(P,17) Q(P,16)
          putchar(' ');
        Q(P,15) Q(P,14) Q(P,13) Q(P,12) Q(P,11) Q(P,10) Q(P,9) Q(P,8)
          putchar(' ');
        Q(P,7) Q(P,6) Q(P,5) Q(P,4) Q(P,3) Q(P,2) Q(P,1) Q(P,0)
          printf("\n\n");
    }
}
```

 **Listing** 13.13 `union_vu.c`

```
/* union_vu.c */

/* use union to see how float stored */

#include <stdio.h>

int main(void)
{
    union float_store
    {
        float four;
        unsigned char one[4];
    } storage;
    int i;

    storage.four = .000034;
    putchar('\n');
    for (i = 0; i < 4; i++)
        printf("byte %d: %u\n", i, storage.one[i]);
}
```

The union method is by far the simplest of the three. Regrouping the output for the 0.000034 example in floating.c gives us

```
00111000 00001110 10011011 00111001
```

or 56, 14, 155, and 57, respectively, from high to low memory (on a most significant byte–first machine). The output for union_vu.c for the same value:

```
byte 0: 57
byte 1: 155
byte 2: 14
byte 3: 56
```

13.13   APPLICATIONS—STRUCTURES

The following program, instruct.c, creates a 50-element array of structures, each with an employee's name, salary, and ID number (two char arrays and an int). After the number of records to be entered is input with scanf(), the program provides the data through a function that is passed the address of the first structure array element and uses gets() and scanf() to fill each member of each element up to the specified number of records. The function increments the structure pointer from one element to the next. The program contains a print function that is passed the address of the first array element and that prints out the data for each employee just entered. It also contains a final function that totals salaries of all the inputted workers.

 Listing   **13.14 instruct.c**

```
/* instruct.c */

/* problem: create a 50-element array of structures, each with an
   employee's name, salary and id number (two char arrays and an int).

   After the number of records to be entered is input with scanf(),
   have the program provide the data through a function that is
   passed the address of the first structure array element and uses
   gets() and scanf() to fill each member of each element up to
   the specified number of records. Have the function increment
   the structure pointer from one element to the next.

   Make a print function that is passed the address of the first array
   element and that prints out the data for each employee just entered

   Make a final function that totals salaries of all the inputted workers
*/

#include <stdio.h>
#include <string.h> /* strlen, strcmp */

struct personnel
{
   char name[40];
   int salary;
   char id[3];
} employee[50];

int get_data(struct personnel *ptr, int max_recs);
void print_data(struct personnel *ptr, int max_recs),
   tot_salary(struct personnel *ptr, int max_recs);

int main(void)
{
   int records;

   printf("\nHow many records to be entered?  ");
   scanf("%d%*c", &records); /* gobble up input after number */
   /* employee is an address only because it is an array */
   records = get_data(employee, records);
   print_data(employee, records);
   tot_salary(employee, records);
}
```

```c
int get_data(struct personnel *ptr, int max_recs)
{
   int element = 0;

   while (element < max_recs)
   {
      printf("\nEntry number %d", element + 1);
      printf("\nPress Enter key without name to stop record input process");
      printf("\nName:   ");
      gets(ptr->name);
      if (strcmp(ptr->name,"") == 0)
      {
         element--;
         break;
      }
      printf("\nWeekly salary:   ");
      scanf("%d", &(ptr->salary)); /* note parentheses */
      printf("\n2 digit ID number:   ");

      /* avoid array overflow with %2s specifier */
      scanf("%2s", ptr->id);

      /* gobble up any excess portion of last one */
      while(getchar() != '\n');
      ptr++;
      element++;
   }
   return element + 1;
}

void print_data(struct personnel *ptr, int max_recs)
{
   int i, wide;

   printf("\nEmployee data:\n\n");

   /* determine width of longest name for lined-up printing */
   /* ptr++: point to next element */
   for (wide = i = 0; i < max_recs; i++, ptr++)
      if (strlen(ptr->name) > wide)
         wide = strlen(ptr->name);

   /* back up to point to first structure array element */
   ptr -= max_recs;
   for (i = 0; i < max_recs; i++, ptr++)
      printf("%-*s$%4d%4s\n", wide + 2, ptr->name, ptr->salary,
         ptr->id);
}

void tot_salary(struct personnel *ptr, int max_recs)
{
   int i;
   long salaries;

   for (salaries = i = 0; i < max_recs; i++, ptr++)
      salaries += ptr->salary;
   printf("\nTotal weekly salaries: $%ld\n", salaries);
}
```

Of course, this manual input process would be tedious. Normally, we would read in such data from a file. See Chapter 14.

13.14   ENUMERATED TYPES *(OPTIONAL)*

Sometimes we use manifest constants with names that tell us what purpose they serve, and with values that are irrelevant. For example, say we had a function that would print a report to the screen, to a file, or to the printer, depending on user choice made just before the function is called. We would pass this choice as an argument and take action accordingly. The choices and function call might look something like this:

```
#define PRINTS 1
#define PRINTP 2
#define PRINTF 3
  . .
char response;
char filename[45];
int print_mode;
struct record
{
  . . .
} data;
  . . .
puts("Print report to screen (S), printer (P) or file (F)?");
response = toupper(getchar());
if (response == 'S')
   print_mode = PRINTS;
else if (response == 'P')
   print_mode = PRINTP;
else
{
   print_mode = PRINTF;
   puts("Name of file");
   gets(filename);
}
print_report(&data, print_mode, filename);
```

Now, we really don't care whether the values of these three manifest constants are 1, 2, and 3, or 87, 2, and −17. All that matters is that they have unique values among themselves.

The enumerated type is another way to declare symbolic names to represent such integer constants. For example, the declaration

```
enum days
{
   sun, mon, tues, wed, thurs, fri, sat
} yesterday, today, tomorrow;
```

create:

- a unique integer type enum days.
- three variables of that type.
- seven constants with integer values from 0 through 6.

Note the similarity to the format for structures and unions. Like structures and unions, this declaration creates a unique type: enum days here. The enumerated type is an implementation-defined integer type (and is compatible with that type; see Section 13.17.1). Nevertheless, Standard C provides that an enumeration type can be used in an expression wherever an int or unsigned int may be used. As will be shown, because of the weak typing Standard C accords enumeration types, they amount to just arguably more readable ways of naming integer constants.

13.14.1   Values of Enumeration Constants

In the absence of explicit initializers, **enumeration constants** (the comma-separated objects inside the template, also called "enumerators") have values starting at 0 and increasing by 1 from left to right. Thus, in the preceding example sun has a value of 0, mon has a value of 1, tues has a value of 2, and so on. Note that the enumeration constants are separated by commas, not semicolons.

You can make explicit initializations with any integer value, negative or positive, that can be accommodated by a signed int (that is, –32,768 to 32,767 on a PC):

```
enum birds {robin = 10, eagle = 20, nightingale = 25};
```

Any value outside the signed int range will generate an error. There is no automatic odometer-like overflow effect here. Allowable constants include integer constants, character constants, other enumeration constants and the sizeof operator with any operand, even a variable or type.

You can initialize some enumeration constants and not others, in which case each uninitialized constant has a value 1 greater than the constant to its left:

```
enum workers {painter = 10, typist, clerk, driver = 92};
```

Here, typist and clerk have values of 11 and 12, respectively.

The values need not be unique, though they generally will be. You would commonly make nonunique assignments where you need unique values, but you want the ability to use one of two or more names for the same concept:

```
enum dayTimes {morning = 1, afternoon,
   twilight, dusk = 3, evening}; /* twilight & dusk = 3 */
```

As with variables, one constant can be initialized to the value of a previously initialized constant (not all compilers allow this, however). You can use a constant expression instead of a simple constant:

```
enum coins {penny = 1, twopence, nickel = penny * 5,
   dime = nickel * twopence, quarter = nickel * nickel};
```

However, no variables are permitted:

```
int num = 2;
enum coins {penny = 1; twopence = penny * num}; /* error! */
```

13.14.2   Use of Enumeration Constants

Once you've made a declaration, you can use any of the enumeration constants in the same manner you would use any integer constant. Enumeration constants (and variables, discussed in the next section) are of type int:

```
enum stockClasses {nonvoting, classA, classB, classC};
int votingShares = classA * 2 + classB * 4 + classC * 7;
int preferredShares = nonvoting * 10;
```

This usage would be relatively uncommon, however. Generally we use enumeration constants where we don't care about the values assigned and where we don't want to use those values as such. Let's say our program gives the user the choice of writing program results to the screen, to the printer, or to a file. (See Chapter 14 for the file operations covered in the following listing.)

 **Listing** **13.15 enum.c**

```
/* enum.c */

/* demonstrate use of enumeration constants: values irrelevant */

#include <stdio.h>
#include <string.h>
#include <ctype.h>
```

```c
int main(void)
{
    enum mode {screen, printer, file};
    int write_mode = screen;
    char name[81], file_name[45], temp[15];
    FILE *write_file;

    puts("Enter your name");
    gets(name);

    puts("\nResults to screen?\tS\n"
        "Results to printer?\tP\n"
        "Results to file?\tF\n");

    gets(temp);

    switch(toupper(*temp))
    {
        case 'S': write_mode = screen; break;
        case 'P': write_mode = printer; break;
        case 'F': write_mode = file; break;
    }

    if (write_mode == screen)
        printf("Name is %s\n", name);

    /* this printer line: DOS only */
    else if (write_mode == printer)
        fprintf(stdprn, "Name is %s\r\n", name);

    else
    {
        puts("Name of file?");
        gets(file_name);
        write_file = fopen(file_name, "w");
        fprintf(write_file, "Name is %s\n", name);
    }
}
```

Of course, in this simple example, we could have just brought the three separate print statements into the switch construction directly and avoided the enumeration constant concept. But in a more complex case, you might repeatedly have to differentiate among these three choices and the enum would be useful. See Listing 13.9, unionflg.c, for another example.

In the odd case where you do have occasion to mix enumeration constants with ordinary variables or constants, clear programming style would dictate a type cast:

```c
int preferredShares = (int)nonvoting * 10;
```

Of course, since we are dealing with constants, none of the following would be permitted:

```c
nonvoting = 7; /* error! */
classA++; /* error! */
classB = classC; /* error! */
```

The first statement, for instance, would be equivalent to

```c
0 = 7;
```

If we choose to assign specific nondefault values to an enumeration constant, we may do so only at the time of declaration.

13.14.3   Enumeration Variables

In theory, the purpose of declaring an enumeration variable is to define a discrete set of values that the variable can take on. Thus, in the declaration we have seen earlier,

```
enum days
{
    sun, mon, tues, wed, thurs, fri, sat
} yesterday, today, tomorrow;
```

`yesterday` should not be able to be assigned anything but one of the enumeration constants:

```
today = 23; /* should be error */
today = tues; /* OK */
```

The enumeration constant `tues` is a contemplated assignment; 23 is not. You might also suspect that the following would generate an error even though `mon` is equal to 1:

```
today = 1; /* should be an error even though mon has a value of 1 */
```

You might think that's why the constants are called enumerators—they enumerate the possible values for the enumeration variables.

All of these examples, however, are valid in Standard C. As we said earlier, despite a superficial resemblance to structures and unions, `enum`s in Standard C are hardly more than glorified constants. Nevertheless, despite the weak typing of the `enum`, and in spite of the absence of any real need to do so, as we saw above with enumeration constants, good programming style would dictate a type cast where you mix enumeration variables with non-enumeration constants or variables, as we did in the examples above:

```
today = (enum days)23;
```

In any event, there would seem to be really very little reason to use enumeration *variables*. (But see Listing 13.9, `unionflg.c`.) If you do use them, you may omit the tag name in the declaration:

```
enum
{
    sun, mon, tues, wed, thurs, fri, sat
} yesterday, today, tomorrow.
```

But, as with structure or union templates, you would not be able to make further declarations of enumeration variables of this type later in your code. If you use a tag name, you can make subsequent declarations of variables of this newly created type:

```
enum category
{
    management, research, clerical, sales
};

int main(void)
{
    enum category worker, employee;
}
```

In general, enumerations—even enumeration constants—are not widely used, though of course you need to recognize and understand them if you do run across them in someone else's code. One potential advantage to enumeration constants over manifest constants created by `define` directive is that—provided you eschew explicit initializations—you can, with enumerators, avoid inadvertently creating a nonunique pair of manifest constants where you have a long list of constants whose values are irrelevant but that must be unique. Another potential advantage is that with some compilers, the values of `enum` constants are shown in the debugger; manifest constants have disappeared by that point. But generally, if enumerations persist in the debugger at all, it's only the values of the far less often used enumeration variables, not constants, that show up.

13.15   USING `typedef`—ALIASES

A *typedef* lets you create your own name for a data type. The syntax is the keyword `typedef` followed by a C statement you would use if you were declaring a variable. What would normally be the variable name's in such a declaration then becomes the `typedef` for subsequent use. For example, consider the following `typedef` statements and their post-`typedef` declarations.

```
typedef int *INT_PTR;
INT_PTR p1, p2; /* two pointers to int named p1 and p2 */
typedef int[8] ARRAY_8_INT
ARRAY_8_INT values; /* 8-element of ints named values */
```

All the `typedef` statement does is to create an alias or nickname or substitute or synonym for a simple or complex valid C type, for later use in declaring variables of that type with the nickname instead of the actual type name it stands for. Using a `typedef` does *not* create a new type, as we do when we declare a structure template; it merely creates convenient labels.

Since the only purpose then of the `typedef` declaration is to create a type nickname for later use, you cannot combine such a declaration with anything that defines variables or allocates storage. The following is not permitted:

```
typedef char *STRING s1, s2, s3;
```

On the other hand, since you are just making up a nickname rather than creating a new type, after you make a `typedef`, you can use the `typedef` for that type exclusively, or you can continue to use the actual type name as well:

```
typedef struct client
{
   char name[40], address[80];
} CLIENT;
CLIENT newClient;
struct client oldClient;
```

The scope of a `typedef` is the same as for variables. If a `typedef` definition is made within a function, its scope is local. If the definition is outside any function, its scope is global. As with variables, a global `typedef` may be overridden within a function (or a local `typedef` may be overridden within an inner block inside a function):

```
typedef int Number;
int main(void)
{
   Number widget;
   int Number; /* OK: overrides typedef */
   Number wonk; /* invalid */
   . . .
```

You can nest `typedef`s:

```
typedef struct
{
   int x;
   int y;
} LOCUS;

typedef LOCUS *LOCUS_PTR;
```

Or again:

```
typedef char *STRING; /* pointer to char */
typedef STRING * STR_PTR; /* pointer to pointer to char */
```

In both these cases, you could have reached the final result in a single `typedef` statement. However, *sometimes it is easier to read and follow the logic if you break a complex type into two or more snippets with separate* `typedef` *declarations.* For example:

```
typedef char *(*ARRAY_PTR_FUNC[4]) (char *ptr);
   /* 4-element array of pointers to
       functions that take and return pointer to char */
```

versus

```
typedef char * FUNC (char *); /* function that takes
                               and returns a pointer to char */
typedef FUNC *PTR_FUNC; /* pointer to such a function */
typedef PTR_FUNC[4] ARRAY_PTR_FUNC; /* 4-element array of such pointers */
```

or again, contrast:

```
typedef int (*(*ARR_FUNC_PTR[5])())[10];

typedef int ARRAY[10]; /* array of 10 ints */
typedef ARRAY *PTR_A; /* pointer to array of 10 ints */
typedef PTR_A (*FPTR); /* pointer to function returning
                          pointer to array of 10 ints */
typedef PTR_A ARR_FPTR[5]; /* array of pointers to functions
                              returning pointers to arrays of 10 ints */
```

 In many cases, using `typedef` *provides programmers with a more intuitive syntax for complex declarations.* For instance, take the following declaration from Listing 8.22, `fun_look.c`, a function that takes an `int` and returns a pointer to a function that takes and returns a pointer to `char`:

```
char *(*startUp(int choice))(char *string);
```

See how much more obvious the `typedef` makes the declaration syntax:

```
typedef char *(*Fptr)(char *);
Fptr startUp (int choice);
```

The `typedef` allows us to put the entire return type in the position where normally the return type for an ordinary function would go, rather than splitting it up in the non-`typedef` declaration above.

13.15.1   Using `typedef` versus `define` Directive

A `typedef` is similar to a `define` directive (see Chapter 11) in its result but differs in several respects:

- You can use `typedef` to give symbolic names to data types only.
- Within that limitation, `typedef` is more flexible than `define`.
- Like enumeration constants, a `typedef` substitution is performed by the compiler, not the preprocessor. You need to terminate `typedef` statements with semicolons.
- As we've seen, the scope of a `typedef` is the same as for variables. If a `typedef` definition is made within a function, its scope is local. If the definition is outside any function, its scope is global. A `define` directive is effective from that point in the source code down.

Often, programmers use uppercase letters to remind us that the type name is really just a symbolic abbreviation, akin to a `define` macro.

```
typedef unsigned char BYTE;
```

This example could be duplicated with a `define` directive:

```
#define BYTE unsigned char
```

But this one couldn't be:

```
typedef char *STRING;
STRING s1, s2, s3;
```

Since a `typedef` is a true alias for a type, after the above `typedef` and declaration, we have three pointers to `char`. Contrast:

```
#define STRING char *
STRING s1, s2, s3;
```

All we have after macro expansion is one single `char` pointer and two nonpointer `char` variables.

On the other hand, Standard C expressly forbids extending a `typedef` with any other type specifiers, so in the following situation a `define` directive accomplishes what is not permitted with `typedef`:

```
#define WORD int
unsigned WORD number;  /* OK */
typedef int NUMBER
unsigned NUMBER value;  /* error */
```

13.15.2   Uses for `typedef`

Often a `typedef` is used to replace a lengthy, complex data type name with a simpler, shorthand version. For example, after the following declaration

```
typedef char (FUNC_STR ()) [81];
```

`FUNC_STR` can be used as an alias for a function that returns a pointer to an 81-element `char` array. You could then declare a pointer and an array of pointers to such a function this simple way:

```
FUNC_STR * fptr, *array_fptr[3];
```

Given the ability to nest `typedef`s, we are able to break a very complex, barely intelligible declaration into shorter more easily grasped bites, as in our `ARRAY_PTR_FUNC` example above. Try to see how easily you can code Listing 8.24, `var_type.c`, without the function pointer `typedef` there. You cannot, however, use a `typedef` to actually declare or define a function.

Perhaps the most common use of `typedef` is in connection with structures. For example, you could assign a new type name to a database control structure type in your program like this:

```
typedef struct
{
    int is_open;
    long offset;
    unsigned rec_num;
    int rec_mode;
    long date_mode;
    char *error_str;
} DB_CONTROL;
```

By placing this declaration in a header file, and including the header in a source code module, you could make the following declaration:

```
DB_CONTROL inventory_db, *db_handler;
```

Notice that with a `typedef`, we do not need to use a structure tag name to preserve the ability to make subsequent variable declarations, though we could have inserted one in the `typedef` declaration if we so chose. Of course, despite this widely employed `typedef` usage, you can see that all this accomplishes for structures is to allow you to omit the tag name in the template (and we recommend you include it anyway; why hide useful information) and omit the `struct` keyword in any declaration of a variable of this type. We believe the `typedef` device as a stand-in for structures is overused.

The `typedef` can be used to declare portable types. For example, let's say in one or more places in your program, you require an entity that is no more and no less than 4 bytes. If `int` is 4 bytes on one system on which this code may be run, you could use this `typedef`:

```
typedef int fourByte;
```

In each instance where you use this 4-byte entity, you would use `fourByte` instead of `int`.

```
fourByte equipment;
```

If you run the same code on a machine where an int is only 2 bytes and long is 4, you need only make a single alteration:

```
typedef long fourByte;
```

You can place this and other similar typedefs or conditional compilation lines in a header file called something like portable.h, and then include it in all source codes that need it.

13.16   COMPLEX DECLARATIONS *(OPTIONAL)*

We've already seen the distinction between the following two declarations:

```
char *str_ptr[12]; /* 12-element array of pointers to char */
char (*ptr_str)[12]; /* pointer to 12-element char array */
```

These declarations, respectively, illustrate two rules:

- The [ ], denoting an array and the ( ), denoting a function, have a higher precedence than the * operator. See Appendix J.
- Parentheses used for grouping overcome rules of precedence to create higher precedence.

In an appropriate programming situation, variable declarations can become tricky. Compare the following:

```
char *ptr_array[4][8]; /* 4 x 8 array of pointers to char */
char (*ptr_array[4])[8]; /* 4-element array of pointers to 8-element char arrays */
char (*array_ptr)[4][8]; /* pointer to 4 x 8 char array */

char *func(char *ptr); /* function taking and returning pointer to char */
char (*func(char *ptr))[] /* function taking a pointer to
      char and returning a pointer to an array of chars */
char *(*func_ptr)(char *ptr); /* pointer to function taking
      and returning pointer to char */
char *(*ptr_func[4])(char *ptr); /* 4-element array of pointers to functions that
      take and return pointer to char */
```

13.17   TYPE CONVERSION *(OPTIONAL)*

There are four situations (five if we count automatic conversion of function arguments and return values as separate cases) in which values of one C type may be converted to values of another type:

- A type cast is used by the programmer to convert a value from one type to another.
- An actual argument to a function is automatically converted to the type of the corresponding formal argument, and the type of the value to be returned is automatically converted to the function type (that is, the type the function is declared to return) if the types differ.
- An operand may in some cases be automatically converted to another type before it is assigned to a variable or before some arithmetic or logical operation is performed.
- A value of one type that is assigned to a variable will be automatically converted to the type of the variable if they are of different types (after applying any automatic conversion in the previous case).

However, only certain type categories can be converted from one to another. Even within categories where conversion is permitted, sometimes conversion will take place only between *compatible types*. Let's take a look first at what the type categories are, and second, at what constitute "compatible types."

The various C types can be broken down into the somewhat overlapping categories shown in Table 13.2.

Table 13.2 *Type Categories*

	Type	Major Type Category	
Arithmetic Types	char, unsigned char, signed char	Integer	Scalar Types
	short, int, long, unsigned short, unsigned int, unsigned long		
	enum		
	float, double, long double	Floating Point	
	* <any type>	Pointer	
	<any type> [ ]	Array	Aggregate Types
	struct	Structure	
	union	Union	
	<any type> (<any types>)	Function	
	void	Void	

13.17.1 Compatibility

The key relevance of compatibility is in determining which assignments are permitted without type cast, and which conversions are not permitted even with type cast. The set of permitted assignments and type casts is set forth in Table 13.3. The table shows, for example, why you cannot assign a structure variable's values en masse to a variable of another structure type even if both structure types have identical members, but you can assign to a pointer of one structure type the address of a variable of another structure type with an appropriate type cast. Before we can make use of the table, we must first understand which types are compatible.

The concept of compatibility is a very narrow one—far narrower than the permissible set of conversions. No type in one major category above is compatible with a type from another major category. Within the categories, the rules are strict.

Arithmetic Type Compatibility   Two arithmetic types are compatible only if they are the same type. In this connection, types treated by the compiler as identical are considered to be the same type. This includes not only the obvious ones that involve only alternative ways of writing the same type (for example, short and short int), but also short and signed short, int and signed int (except where they are used in bit fields, where an implementation is free to treat int in one of three ways, just as with plain char), and long and signed long.

Thus, while signed int is a compatible type with int, it is incompatible with unsigned int. The types char, signed char, and unsigned char are always incompatible with one another since, as we saw in Section 2.2, an implementation is free to treat plain char as signed or unsigned or "mixed."

Otherwise compatible arithmetic types become incompatible if either has a type qualifier the other does not have.

Pointer Compatibility   Two pointer types are compatible only if they point to compatible types. Otherwise compatible pointer types become incompatible if either has a type qualifier the other does not have.

Array Type Compatibility   Array types are compatible only if (1) the type of their elements is compatible (for instance, an array of signed int is compatible with an array of int, but not with an array

Table 13.3 *Permissible Conversions (P = permissible conversion with type cast; A = value can be assigned directly; Shaded = can't convert even with type cast)*

To → ↓ From	Integer/ enum	Floating Point	Pointer	Array	Structure	Union	Function
Integer/ enum	P A	P A	P				
Floating Point	P A	P A					
Pointer	P		P but obj-func only via integer. A if similarly qualified and point to compatible types				
Array			automatically converted to pointer to first element				
Structure					A if compatible		
Union						A if compatible	
Function			automatically converted to starting address of function code				

of const signed int or unsigned int, under the compatibility rules for arithmetic types above), and (2) if both types specify element numbers on declaration, the number of elements must be the same:

```
int num[4];
signed int val[4]; /* compatible: compatible arithmetic
        types; both specify array size */

int num[4];
const int val[4]; /* incompatible: incompatible arithmetic
        types because of qualifier */

int num[4];
int val[]; /* compatible: only one specifies size */

int num[4];
int val[3]; /* incompatible: different size */

int num[];
int val[]; /* compatible: neither specifies size */
```

Structure, Union, and Enumeration Compatibility   Each of these by hypothesis creates a new type. Therefore, no two different structure, union, or enumeration types are compatible:

```
struct employee
{
    char name[40], address[85];
};
struct worker
```

```
{
    char name[40], address[85];
};
```

Even though they contain identical members, declared in the same order, these two structure types are incompatible.

Function Type Compatibility   Functions are compatible only if (1) their return types are compatible, (2) the number of formal arguments is the same (including the number of fixed arguments if the function is has variable arguments), and (3) the corresponding formal arguments have compatible types.

13.17.2   Permitted Conversions

Table 13.3 shows all possible type conversions. Some of these conversions take place automatically. Others must be explicitly cast—in two cases by two type casts, with an intermediate step. The shaded boxes represent conversions that cannot take place even with type casts.

The P in the table indicates that conversion is permissible. In all those cases, the programmer can cast from the type in the vertical column to the type in the horizontal row. An A indicates that a value of one the type in the column can be assigned directly, with or without type cast. If a such an assignment is made, the conversion will take place automatically if there is no type cast:

```
int num = 5;
double payment = num;
```

In the second statement, the value of num will be converted automatically to double before it is assigned to payment.

For conversion from an object pointer to a function pointer, or vice versa, you must first convert the pointer to an integer type and then reconvert to the desired type.

In addition to the possible conversions listed in the chart, any type can be cast to type void.

13.17.3   Automatic Unary Conversions

To minimize the number of different types in an arithmetic expression, Standard C requires certain automatic conversions to operands (what is on either side of an operator) in certain cases. The conversions listed in Table 13.4 occur:

- For the operand of a unary !, –, ~, or * operator, and for both operands on either side of the binary bit shift operators, << and >>. All these conversions occur before application of the respective operator.
- As a preliminary step to the automatic binary conversions below, the automatic unary conversions are first applied to each operand.

These conversions are referred to as ***automatic unary conversions.***

The former automatic conversion from float to double is no longer required by Standard C.

Table 13.4   *Automatic Unary Conversions*

Type	Converted to
char	int
unsigned char	int
short	int
unsigned short	unsigned (int if int has more bytes than unsigned short)
array	pointer to first element of array
function	pointer to function

13.17.4   Automatic Binary Conversions

Other than for the bit shift operators, when the two operands of a binary operator (or the second and third operators of the conditional operator) are operated on (for example, before adding a to b in $a + b$, or before multiplying c by d in $c * d$), they are first each converted by the automatic unary conversions listed in the table in the last section. After that conversion, each is converted to the same type. That type is the first applicable conversion in Table 13.5. These latter conversions are referred to as ***automatic binary conversions.***

(As to the type of the last three, the ones shown for "type of other operand" are the only possibilities, since `char` or `short` would have been already converted by automatic unary conversion to `int` or `unsigned`.) As you can see, if you have a floating point type and an integer type, the integer type gets converted to floating point. Where both are either floating point types or integer types, the smaller type of the two gets converted to the larger (with the exception of an `unsigned` with a `long` being converted to `unsigned long` if `long` on the system has the same number of bytes as `unsigned`.)

13.17.5   Function Argument Conversion

The manner in which actual arguments in a function call are converted depends on whether the compiler has seen a Standard C–conforming prototype beforehand. If the call is not checked against a Standard C prototype (or for any of the nonfixed arguments in a variable argument function call even where the function call is governed by a Standard C prototype), the value of each argument is converted before being passed according to Table 13.6.

Table 13.5   *Automatic Binary Conversions*

Type of One Operand	Type of Other Operand	Converted to
`long double`	*any type*	`long double`
`double`	*any type*	`double`
`float`	*any type*	`float`
`unsigned long`	*any type*	`unsigned long`
`long`	`unsigned`	`long` (`unsigned long` if `long` has the same number of bytes as `unsigned`)
`long`	`int`	`long`
`unsigned`	`int or unsigned`	`unsigned`
`int`	`int`	`int`

Table 13.6   *Automatic Function Conversions (in Some Cases)*

Type	Converted to
`char`	`int`
`unsigned char`	`int`
`short`	`int`
`unsigned short`	`unsigned` (`int` if `int` has more bytes than `unsigned short`)
`float`	`double`
`array`	pointer to first element of array

The list in the table is essentially the same as the automatic unary conversions table above, with the addition of automatic conversion of `float` to `double`.

Once the arguments are then passed, they are all converted to the formal argument if the argument type, as possibly automatically converted, is not the same as that of the formal argument. For example, if a nonprototyped function has a `char` as its sole formal argument, and it is called with an argument of `char`, the `char` of the actual argument is converted to `int`, passed and then reconverted to `char`.

The fact that the variable arguments in a variable argument function call (see Chapter 8) get promoted automatically accounts for why you can pass a `char` or `short` argument just as well as an `int` to be read by a `%d` conversion specifier: both are converted to `int`.

Where the compiler has encountered a Standard C prototype, the arguments normally are each simply converted to the type of the corresponding formal parameter. Likewise, the value to be returned is automatically converted to the function's return type if it is not already that type. Standard C permits an implementation to perform the automatic function conversions listed above before passing the arguments if it wishes (it must do so on the nonfixed arguments in a variable argument function, as noted above).

It is important to note that the conversion of actual to formal argument types or return value to return type is, of course, only accomplished where the conversion is one of those allowed, according to Table 13.3. Otherwise, you will get an error on compiling.

13.17.6 Sequence of Conversion

It is important to note that the above conversion steps occur in the stated order. Evaluation takes place completely on the right side of the assignment operator, including any binary or unary conversions, and only the final result is converted to the type of the variable on the left side if the types are different. Thus, with

```
unsigned num = 256;
long sum = num * num;
```

the fact that `sum` is a `long` does not prevent the odometerlike overflow that occurs, resulting in sum having a value of 0 instead of 65536, one more than an `unsigned` can hold. On the other hand, if we do this

```
unsigned num = 256;
long sum = (long) num * num;
```

we get the correct result. We could have also type cast the other `num`, but the rules of binary conversion cause that conversion anyway.

Likewise, in the following, assuming `int` has 2 bytes,

```
unsigned long num = 66 << 24;
```

`num` has a value of 0: the constant 66 has type `int`, and shifting 24 to the left moves the value beyond its 2-byte boundary. The subsequent conversion to `unsigned long` comes too late. However, the following works fine:

```
unsigned long num = 66LU << 24;
```

Similarly, the fact that variables passed as arguments are converted to the corresponding formal parameter type (assuming a proper prototype and the argument's not being a variable argument in a variable argument function such as `printf()`) does not save the very same disaster from befalling this call:

```
void printLong(long val) {printf("%ld\n", val);}
int main(void)
{
    unsigned num = 256;
    printLong(num * num);
}
```

The damage is already done before the zeroed out result is converted to a `long`.

13.18   APPLICATION: ACE BILLING PROGRAM

The long-awaited addition of the structure concept to our ACE Billing program lends an important modularizing level of sophistication.

13.18.1   Input

Same input data as for `acech06.exe` in Chapter 6.

 **Listing**   **13.16 acech13.c**

```c
#ifndef acech13_H
#define acech13_H
/*
   +----------------------------------------------------------------+
   +    Program Name: acech13.h
   +       Author(s): Austell-Wolfson and Otieno
   +            Date: 12/10/2000
   +    Purpose:
   +       This file has all the manifest constants or macros needed by
   +       acech13.c program.
   +
   +----------------------------------------------------------------+
*/

#define CUSTOMER_NAME_SIZE       16
#define INPUT_BUFFER_SIZE        1024
#define NUMBER_OF_CUSTOMERS      100
#define CUSTOMER_INITIALS_SIZE   3
#define TOTALS_POSITION          NUMBER_OF_CUSTOMERS - 1
#define TEMPORARY_POSITION       TOTALS_POSITION - 1
#define NUMBER_OF_INPUT_FIELDS   6
#define CHARGE_RATE              200
#define SPECIAL_MEMBERSHIP_FEE    2500
#define MIN_ACTIVITY_CEILING     6
#define MID_ACTIVITY_CEILING     11
#define UPPER_ACTIVITY_FLOOR     12
#define MIN_ACTIVITY_RATE        250.00
#define MID_ACTIVITY_RATE        500.00
#define UPPER_ACTIVITY_RATE      750.00
#define MIN_CHARGE_DISCOUNT_LEVEL 8500.00
#define MEMBERSHIP_FLAG          'Y'

struct CustomerInfo
{
   char   specialMembershipFlag;
   char   customerName[CUSTOMER_NAME_SIZE];
   char   customerInitials[CUSTOMER_INITIALS_SIZE];
   float  membershipFee;
   float  activityFee;
   float  discountAmount;
   float  chargeAmount;
   float  totalIndividualBill;
   float  aceClubTotals;
   float  charges;
   int    discount;
   int    averageCharges;
   int    numberOfCharges;
};
```

```
void initialization(struct CustomerInfo * customerData);
void processMemberRecord(struct CustomerInfo * customerData, char * inputBuffer,
   int * clubMember);
void termination(void);
void printGrandTotals(struct CustomerInfo * customerData);
void initializeVariables(struct CustomerInfo * customerData);
void printHeadings(void);
void computeIndividualBill(struct CustomerInfo * customerData, int * clubMember);
void writeDetailLine(struct CustomerInfo * customerData, int * clubMember);
void determineSpecialFee(struct CustomerInfo * customerData, int * clubMember);
void determineActivityFee(struct CustomerInfo * customerData, int * clubMember);
void determineDiscountAmt(struct CustomerInfo * customerData, int * clubMember);
void sortByClubMemberNames(struct CustomerInfo * customerData, int * clubMember);
void printSortedReport(struct CustomerInfo * customerData, int * clubMember);
void swapValues(struct CustomerInfo * customerData, int currentPos);

#endif

/*
  +----------------------------------------------------------------+
  +    Program Name: acech13.c
  +        Author(s): Austell-Wolfson and Otieno
  +            Date: 04/10/2000
  +    Purpose:
  +       This program processes a file of ACE Club member records and
  +       computes and prints the total amounts for all club members.
  +
  +    Process:
  +      This program prints the prescribed headings for the report and
  +      processes each record by:
  +         computing the individual member bill, equal to the sum of
  +         member bill, membership fee, and activity fee, minus any
  +         discount amount. The members are charged a special
  +         membership fee of $2500 if the person is a special
  +         member, indicated by a Y in the membership flag field. The
  +         activity fees are based on the number of activities each
  +         member requests. The more activities they request, the more
  +         they are charged. A discount amount is applied if the member
  +         has an average charge of over $8000 per bill.
  +----------------------------------------------------------------+
*/
#include <stdio.h>
#include <string.h>
#include <stdlib.h>
#include "acech13.h"

int main(void)
{
   struct CustomerInfo customerData[NUMBER_OF_CUSTOMERS];
   char InputBuffer[INPUT_BUFFER_SIZE]; /* Incoming input record */

   /*
     +----------------------------------------------------------------+
     + clubMember holds the count of all club members. It is also used
     + to index the array of club members, therefore its value starts
     + at 0.
     +----------------------------------------------------------------+
   */
   int clubMember = 0;
```

```
   initialization(customerData);
   while (gets(InputBuffer) != NULL)
   {
      processMemberRecord(customerData, InputBuffer, &clubMember);
   }
   printGrandTotals(customerData);
   sortByClubMemberNames(customerData, &clubMember);
   printSortedReport(customerData, &clubMember);
   printGrandTotals(customerData);

   termination();
   return 0;
}

void initialization(struct CustomerInfo * customerData)
{
   /*
     +----------------------------------------------------------------+
     + void *memset (void *s, int c, size_t n);
     + memset sets the first n bytes of the array s to the character c.
     + in our case, we initialize the entire structure to 0.
     +----------------------------------------------------------------+
   */
   memset(customerData, 0, sizeof (struct CustomerInfo) * NUMBER_OF_CUSTOMERS);
   printHeadings();
   return;
}

void processMemberRecord(struct CustomerInfo * customerData, char * InputBuffer,
   int * clubMember)
{
   int status;
   /* see comment to acech09.c re input parsing process */
   status = sscanf(InputBuffer, "%15c%2c%2d%c%4d%4d", customerData[*clubMember].customerName,
      customerData[*clubMember].customerInitials, &customerData[*clubMember].numberOfCharges,
      &customerData[*clubMember].specialMembershipFlag, &customerData[*clubMember].discount,
      &customerData[*clubMember].averageCharges);

   if (status != NUMBER_OF_INPUT_FIELDS)
   {
      printf("There is a problem with the file format.\n");
      printf("The program is terminated mid-stream\n");
      exit(1);
   }

   computeIndividualBill(customerData, clubMember);
   writeDetailLine(customerData, clubMember);

   return;
}

/* see comment in acech06.c re termination function */
void termination(void)
{
   /* not implemented */
}

void printHeadings(void)
{
```

```
    printf("┌──────────────────────────────────────────────────────────┐\n");
    printf("│                                                          │\n");
    printf("│    Program Name: ACECH13.EXE                    Page:  1 │\n");
    printf("│        Run Date: 12/10/2000          Ace Billing         │\n");
    printf("│                                                          │\n");
    printf("│                                                          │\n");
    printf("├──────────────────────────────────────────────────────────┤\n");
    printf("│                                                          │\n");
    printf("│ Customer Name  Charges      Bill  Mbr Fee  Act Fee  Disc  Total Bill │\n"));
    printf("├──────────────────────────────────────────────────────────┤\n");
    printf("│                                                          │\n");
}

void computeIndividualBill(struct CustomerInfo * customerData,
   int * clubMember)
{
   customerData[*clubMember].charges = CHARGE_RATE *
      customerData[*clubMember].numberOfCharges;
   customerData[TOTALS_POSITION].charges += customerData[*clubMember].charges;
   customerData[TOTALS_POSITION].numberOfCharges += customerData[*clubMember].numberOfCharges;
   determineSpecialFee(customerData, clubMember);
   determineActivityFee(customerData, clubMember);
   determineDiscountAmt(customerData, clubMember);

   customerData[*clubMember].totalIndividualBill = customerData[*clubMember].charges +
      customerData[*clubMember].membershipFee + customerData[*clubMember].activityFee -
   customerData[*clubMember].discountAmount;

   customerData[TOTALS_POSITION].totalIndividualBill +=
      customerData[*clubMember].totalIndividualBill;
   customerData[TOTALS_POSITION].aceClubTotals +=
      customerData[*clubMember].totalIndividualBill;
}

void writeDetailLine(struct CustomerInfo * customerData,
   int * clubMember)
{
   printf("│ %15.15s  %s %2d  $%9.2f  $%8.2f  $%8.2f  $%5.f  $%9.2f",
      customerData[*clubMember].customerName, customerData[*clubMember].customerInitials,
      customerData[*clubMember].numberOfCharges, customerData[*clubMember].charges,
      customerData[*clubMember].membershipFee, customerData[*clubMember].activityFee,
      customerData[*clubMember].discountAmount,
      customerData[*clubMember].totalIndividualBill);
   printf(" │\n");

   *clubMember = *clubMember + 1; /* Increment number of club members */
}

void determineSpecialFee(struct CustomerInfo * customerData, int * clubMember)
{
   if (MEMBERSHIP_FLAG == customerData[*clubMember].specialMembershipFlag)
   {
      customerData[*clubMember].membershipFee = SPECIAL_MEMBERSHIP_FEE;
   }
   else
   {
      customerData[*clubMember].membershipFee = 0.0;
   }
```

```
      customerData[TOTALS_POSITION].membershipFee += customerData[*clubMember].membershipFee;
}

void determineActivityFee(struct CustomerInfo * customerData, int * clubMember)
{
   if (customerData[*clubMember].numberOfCharges <= MIN_ACTIVITY_CEILING)
   {
      customerData[*clubMember].activityFee = MIN_ACTIVITY_RATE;
   }

   if ((customerData[*clubMember].numberOfCharges > MIN_ACTIVITY_CEILING) &&
      (customerData[*clubMember].numberOfCharges <
      MID_ACTIVITY_CEILING + 1))
   {
      customerData[*clubMember].activityFee = MID_ACTIVITY_RATE;
   }

   if (customerData[*clubMember].numberOfCharges > UPPER_ACTIVITY_FLOOR)
   {
      customerData[*clubMember].activityFee = UPPER_ACTIVITY_RATE;
   }

   customerData[TOTALS_POSITION].activityFee += customerData[*clubMember].activityFee;
}

void determineDiscountAmt(struct CustomerInfo * customerData, int * clubMember)
{
   if (customerData[*clubMember].averageCharges > MIN_CHARGE_DISCOUNT_LEVEL)
   {
      customerData[*clubMember].discountAmount = customerData[*clubMember].discount;
   }
   else
   {
      customerData[*clubMember].discountAmount = 0;
   }

   customerData[TOTALS_POSITION].discountAmount += customerData[*clubMember].discountAmount;
}

void sortByClubMemberNames(struct CustomerInfo * customerData, int * clubMember)
{
   int k; /* Loop index variable  */

   /* Determines whether to make more passes during the bubble sort algorithm */
   int morePasses = 1;
/*
   +----------------------------------------------------------------+
   + Start the loop that makes as many passes through array of club
   + member names as needed for the entire list to be sorted.
   +
   +----------------------------------------------------------------+
*/
   while (1 == morePasses)
   {
/*
   +----------------------------------------------------------------+
   + Turn it off so that if the data is sorted, no
   + passes will be necessary. If, however, there was
   + a single swap, morePasses will be set to 1
```

```
    +   and the while loop repeats as it should.
    +
    +---------------------------------------------------------------+
*/
      morePasses = 0;
      for (k = 0; k < *clubMember - 1; k++)
      {
         if (strcmp(customerData[k].customerName, customerData[k + 1].customerName) > 0)
         {
            /* swap all the values in the parallel arrays */
            swapValues(customerData, k);
            morePasses = 1;
         }
      }   /* end of for loop */
   }   /* end of while loop */
}

void printSortedReport(struct CustomerInfo * customerData,
   int * clubMember)
{
   int k;  /* Loop index variable */

   /* print the column headings for the sorted list of club members */
   printHeadings();

   for (k = 0; k < *clubMember; k++)
   {
      printf("| %15.15s  %s %2d  $%9.2f  $%8.2f  $%8.2f  $%5.f  $%9.2f",
         customerData[k].customerName, customerData[k].customerInitials,
         customerData[k].numberOfCharges, customerData[k].charges,
         customerData[k].membershipFee, customerData[k].activityFee,
         customerData[k].discountAmount, customerData[k].totalIndividualBill);
      printf("  |\n");
   }
}

void swapValues (struct CustomerInfo * customerData, int currentPos)
{
   customerData[TEMPORARY_POSITION] = customerData[currentPos];
   customerData[currentPos] = customerData[currentPos + 1];
   customerData[currentPos + 1] = customerData[TEMPORARY_POSITION];
}

void printGrandTotals(struct CustomerInfo * customerData)
{
   printf("| %*s("|_____|\n",
      19, " ");
   printf("| ACE Club Totals    %3d  $%9.2f  $%8.2f  $%8.2f  $%5.f  $%9.2f  |\n",
      customerData[TOTALS_POSITION].numberOfCharges, customerData[TOTALS_POSITION].charges,
      customerData[TOTALS_POSITION].membershipFee, customerData[TOTALS_POSITION].activityFee,
      customerData[TOTALS_POSITION].discountAmount,
      customerData[TOTALS_POSITION].totalIndividualBill);
   printf("|_____|\n\n");
}
```

13.18.2   Output

Same output report as for `acech06.exe` in Chapter 6.

Chapter Summary

1. A structure is a complex data type, defined by the programmer, that allows storing different type data into structure members.
2. Each member has both a type and name.
3. Each structure constitutes its own type.
4. The structure tag name is part of the type name. The tag is also used in declaring variables of the type created by the template.
5. You can omit the tag name, but then you cannot create any structure variables apart from those declared simultaneously with the template definition.
6. The structure template advises the compiler how much memory to set aside for a structure variable and how to evaluate the bytes within the reserved memory area.
7. A structure template does not reserve any memory; you may not initialize the members within the template.
8. Structure variable declaration can be made in the same statement as the template declaration or separately.
9. There are four separate name spaces: structure, union, and enum tag names; member names within a particular structure or union; preprocessor identifiers; and everything else. You cannot have duplication within any one space category with the same scope.
10. You can have any type of variable as a structure member, including a variable of a union or another structure or a pointer to the structure itself, but not a variable of the structure itself.
11. Where a union or structure variable is a structure member, you can declare the template for that member separately (prior to the master structure template declaration) or within the master structure itself. The variables are the members, not the templates.
12. Structure members are accessed through the name of the structure variable followed by the dot operator and the member name, not with subscripting; the dot operator extends recursively to a structure member that is itself a union or structure variable.
13. Members of a structure variable can be initialized, provided the initializers are constants or constant expressions.
14. We use braces to enclose the initialization; strings can be initialized with double quotes; the members are separated by commas.
15. We can copy all values of one structure's members into the members of another structure variable of the same structure type by simple assignment statement—but not if the structure types of the variables are not the same, even if they have identical members.
16. You may not make a wholesale comparison of the values of one structure variable's members to those of another with a relational operator, however.
17. With structure pointers, for precedence reasons, the dereferencing operator–pointer name unit must be enclosed in parentheses: (*ptr).salary = 200;
18. There is also a special structure pointer operator to use for dereferencing structure pointers. ptr->salary = 200;
19. You have the choice of passing a structure variable to a function or a pointer to a structure variable. In the former case, copies of each member are passed and all changes are local; in the latter case, by dereferencing, changes can be made to members' values in the calling function.
20. Except in the case of bit fields and except for any alignment requirements, the members in a structure variable are stored in contiguous memory locations. The compiler allocates space in the order you list members in the template, in successively higher memory locations, with the first member starting at the address of the start of the structure variable itself.
21. The compiler does not consider a structure variable name as equivalent to the address of its first member despite the identity of addresses.
22. The storing of structure data in sequential bytes is known as byte alignment. Some computers use word alignment—all structure members begin at an even number of bytes from the structure's starting address and the structure as a whole contains an even number of bytes.
23. There may also be internal padding to satisfy other memory addressing concerns on certain computers or with certain compilers (for example, 4-byte members must start on an address that is an even multiple of 4).
24. A structure or union variable will be sized as though it is an element of an array of variables of that structure type, whether it is or not.
25. Some computers store the most significant bytes of variables first in memory; others do the opposite. The difference in byte ordering does not affect the alignment of the various structure members or overall structure size, only the relative byte configuration for a particular member.
26. The scope of a structure type definition tag name is the same as that of any variable at the same point.
27. Whether a structure variable is external, automatic, or static depends on where the variable is declared, not the template. The storage class specifier and any type qualifier of a structure variable apply to each of its members (including recursively to members that are arrays, unions or structure variables).
28. As long as the size of the structure type is not required, forward references to an incomplete structure type are allowed; this allows us to create a structure template where one of the members is a pointer to the not-yet-created structure type or a typedef name as an alias for the structure type at the same time we define the structure type.
29. Structures are permitted to have members that are smaller than one byte, called bit fields.
30. To establish a bit field member, you include in the structure template a bit field name followed by a colon and the number of bits to be covered.
31. The bit field size must be an integer constant or constant expression. The field size may not exceed the number of bits in an int.
32. Bit fields can be signed or unsigned; by default bit fields are of type int.

33. A bit field of b bits can hold values of 0 through $2^b - 1$ if unsigned and -2^{b-1} through $2^{b-1} - 1$ if signed.

34. Assignment of a value to a bit field is made with the dot operator, as for any other structure member.

35. We cannot uniquely identify bit fields by address. Nor can we use the & operator in connection with bit fields.

36. By making unnamed bit fields, you can intentionally leave gaps between bit fields.

37. There is no way to reference unnamed bit fields; their value at run time is unpredictable; they do not figure in any initialization of structure variables.

38. Apart from unnamed bit fields, bit fields can be initialized in the same fashion as other nonbit field members.

39. Alignment and byte and bit configuration differences among computers and implementations make bit fields relatively unportable. If portability is a strong concern, you may want to use bit shifting and masking operations instead of bit fields.

40. A union is essentially a structure where, instead of all members being in memory simultaneously, only one member exists in memory at any given time.

41. The union as a whole is given as much space in memory as its largest member requires.

42. Only one variable occupies the union memory space at one time.

43. It is the programmer's job to keep track of which member is currently occupying the union's memory space. This is often done by adding a separate flag member.

44. Most rules for structures apply to unions, including template declaration syntax, scope rules, permissible members, access with dot operator, alignment padding rules, and forward reference ability.

45. Union variable initialization initializes the first member. You must enclose the initializers in braces, even if there is only one initializer. If the first member is a nonscalar, you initialize with more than one initializer.

46. Each union member be stored starting at the same memory address as that of the union variable itself.

47. The enumerated type allows us to declare symbolic names to represent integer constants.

48. An enumeration template declaration creates a unique type, but because of the weak typing Standard C accords enumeration types, they amount to no more than more readable ways of naming integer constants.

49. In the absence of explicit initializers, enumeration constants have values starting at 0 and increasing by 1 from left to right.

50. You can make explicit initializations with any integer value that can be accommodated by a `signed int`.

51. If you initialize some enumeration constants and not others, each uninitialized constant has a value 1 greater than the constant to its left; the values need not be unique.

52. A `typedef` lets you create your own nickname for a data type; it does not create any new type.

53. You cannot combine a `typedef` declaration with anything that defines variables or allocates storage.

54. The scope of a `typedef` is the same as for variables.

55. We can nest `typedef`s, giving us the ability to break a complex declaration into shorter, more easily grasped fragments.

56. In addition to explicit type conversion with type casting, C converts types automatically when the formal argument type is different from the argument type passed, when the type of the value to be returned from a function differs from the function's type, when a value of one type is assigned to a variable of another type, and with operands of unary and binary operators.

57. Evaluation takes place completely on the right side of the assignment operator, including any binary or unary conversions, and only the final result is converted to the type of the variable on the left side if the types are different.

58. The integer types and floating point types are collectively referred to as arithmetic types; those and pointers are collectively called scalar types. Arrays and structures are aggregate types. Unions and functions make up their own types.

59. Only certain type categories can converted from one to another, as shown in Table 13.3.

60. The key relevance of compatibility is in determining which assignments are permitted without type cast and which conversions are not permitted even with type cast.

- Two arithmetic types are compatible only if they are the same type.
- Two pointer types are compatible only if they point to compatible types and are similarly qualified.
- No two different structure or union types are compatible.
- Array types are compatible if the type of their elements is compatible and, if both types specify element numbers on declaration, the number of elements is the same.

61. To minimize the number of different types in an arithmetic expression, Standard C requires certain automatic conversions to operands in certain cases.

- Automatic unary conversion: char, unsigned char, and short to int; unsigned short to unsigned or int; array to pointer to first array element; and function to function pointer occur:
- For the operand of a unary !, -, ~, or * operator, and for operands on either side of the binary bit shift operators.
- As a preliminary step to the automatic binary conversions, the automatic unary conversions are first applied to each operand.

62. Automatic binary conversion: Other than for the bit shift operators, when the two operands of a binary operator (or the second and third operators of the conditional operator) are operated on, they are first each converted by the automatic unary conversions. Then, each is converted to the same type (essentially any integer type is converted to floating point type if there are both types, and the shorter type is converted to the longer type).

63. Absent prototyping (or for any of the non-fixed arguments in a variable argument function call even with prototyping), each argument is converted before being passed, according to Table 13.6 (essentially the same as the automatic unary conversions, with the addition of automatic conversion of float to double).

64. As function arguments are passed, they are all converted to the formal argument if the actual argument type, as possibly automatically converted, is not the same as that of the formal argument.

65. The value to be returned from a function is converted to the function's return type if it is not already that type.

Review Questions

1. Since a structure template reserves no memory, there is no requirement that the members in the template have variable names (True or False).
2. Without a structure tag name, you can never have variables of that structure type (True or False).
3. As with a function definition, in a structure template, if you have more than one variable of the same type, you cannot aggregate the variable names with one type (for example, `int a, b, c` is not permitted) (True or False).
4. The following name usage is permitted despite the duplication of names (True or False):

```
struct triplet {int triplet, diapers;}
   triplet;
```

5. Since structure member names are in the same name space, the following is not permitted (True or False):

```
struct decimal {int copycat, kilometers;}
   system;
struct english {int copycat, miles;}
   methodology;
```

6. Since structures can be declared within other structures, the following is permitted (True or False):

```
struct celsius {float freezing, boiling};
struct fahrenheit {float freezing,
   boiling};
struct temperature {struct celsius; struct
   fahrenheit;};
```

7. Although a structure may contain a variable of another structure type or pointer to such a variable, a structure may contain neither a variable of its own structure type nor a pointer to a variable of its own type.
8. Given the following declarations

```
struct factory {int id; char
   product[20][10];} steel;
struct plant
{
   int id;
   struct factory steel[5];
} rebar[3];
```

How do you assign "structural" to the first element of the two-dimensional `product` array of the first element of the `steel` array of the second element of the `rebar` array?

9. The following will compile without error (True or False):

```
struct top {int page[3], row[3]; char
   title[3][8];} heads =
{{0}, {0}, {"Data", "", "Info"},};
```

10. Since what is to the left of the assignment operator must be a single variable, the following is not permitted (True or False):

```
struct atom {int protons; float
   atomic_weight;} lead, gold =
   {79, 196.9665};
struct nuclear {int protons; float
   atomic_weight;} uranium;
lead = gold;
```

11. Given the declarations in the last question, none of the following is permitted (True or False):

```
gold *= 2;
if (lead == gold)
   puts("whoppee");
uranium = gold;
```

12. Given the following code fragment, what prints?

```
struct tight {int squeeze_in;} cramp;
if (&cramp == &cramp.squeeze_in)
   puts("you're in my space");
else puts("I'm right behind you");
```

13. Given the following declaration:

```
struct tight {unsigned squeeze_in;}
   cramp[3], *ptr;
```

a. Will the following compile and if so, what prints?

```
if (cramp == &cramp].squeeze_in)
   puts("you're in my space");
else puts("room for all");
```

b. Is the following valid:

```
ptr = cramp;
```

c. Is the following valid, and if so what value does `squeeze_in` have?

```
ptr = cramp;
*ptr.squeeze_in = 65535;
```

14. No matter how the `copy()` or `doubled()` prototypes are declared, neither of the following calls is permitted (True or False):

```
struct sheep {int array[500];}
   wolfs_clothing;
copy(wolfs_clothing);
doubled(&wolfs_clothing);
```

15. How would you declare the two function prototypes in the last question (assuming they were both void functions and took only one argument)?

16. Will the following compile properly (assuming the function to have been properly and appropriately prototyped and defined)?

```
struct sheep {int array[500];}
    wolfs_clothing[3];
doubled(wolfs_clothing);
```

17. Given the code fragment in the last question, and ignoring any alignment or other padding and assuming int has 2 bytes, what would the following print?

```
printf("%d\", sizeof(wolfs_clothing));
```

18. Assuming the following are made outside main():

```
struct sheep {int array[500];}
    wolfs_clothing[3], *sptr[2] =
    {&wolfs_clothing[0],
     &wolfs_clothing[1]};
char *ptr[2] = {(char *)
    &wolfs_clothing[0],
    (char *)&wolfs_clothing[1]};
```

What would print here (ignoring any alignment or other padding and assuming int has 2 bytes)?

```
printf("%d\ %d\n", sptr[0] - sptr[1],
    ptr[0] - ptr[1]);
```

19. Since there is no extra pointer variable to declare, simply passing a structure variable to a function generally has less overhead (works faster, consumes less memory) than declaring a pointer to the structure variable and passing the pointer (True or False).

20. No matter what sort of memory configuration a computer or implementation has, given the following code fragment and assuming unsigned has 2 bytes:

```
struct t {unsigned a; unsigned b;} twin =
    {1 << 8, 1 << 8};
unsigned char *ptr = (unsigned char *)
    &twin.a + 1;
printf("%d\n", *ptr);
```

a. the print results can never be 1 (True or False).
b. the print results will always be 1 (True or False).

21. Assuming a float has 4 bytes, on a computer that requires float structure members to have an address that is an even multiple of 4, given the following declaration:

```
struct tramp {float steamer; char id;}
    tug;
```

a. both steamer and tug will have a starting address that is an even multiple of 4 on all such systems (True or False).
b. on all such systems, sizeof(tug) will be equal to 8.

22. The following will compile properly (True or False):

```
struct worker {int id;} post;
int main(void)
{
    struct worker {float salary;} post;
    return 0;
}
```

23. The following, declared inside a function, will always print 0 (True or False):

```
struct office {int id[3];} clerical;
struct worker
{
    struct office clerical;
    int salary;
} static post;
printf("%d\n", post.clerical.id[2]);
```

24. The following, declared inside a function, will always print 0 (True or False):

```
struct office {int id[3];} clerical;
static struct worker
{
    struct office clerical;
    int salary;
};
struct worker post;
printf("%d\n", post.clerical.id[2]);
```

25. The following, declared inside a function, will always print 0 (True or False):

```
struct office {int id[3];} clerical;
static struct worker
{
    struct office clerical;
    int salary;
} post;
printf("%d\n", post.clerical.id[2]);
```

26. Since struct record has not been defined at the point of the keyword typedef, the following is illegal (True or False):

```
typedef struct illegal {int num;} ILLEGAL;
```

27. Given the following declaration:

```
struct hardware {unsigned wonk: 2;
    unsigned or: 2;} config;
```

the largest value wonk can hold:
a. Depends on whether the platform uses two's complement or one's complement (True or False).
b. Will always be 3 (True or False).

28. Bit field members can be accessed with the & operator provided they are at least 1 byte in size (True or False).

29. The following will compile properly:

```
struct record {unsigned a: 2, b: 2, c: 2,
    : 2;}
    rec = {1, 2, 3, 3};
```

30. In the following, rec.a will necessarily be equal to 0 (True or False).

```
struct record {unsigned a: 2, b: 2, c: 2,
    : 2;} static rec;
```

31. Since the compiler does not know which member to initialize, you cannot initialize a union variable (True or False).

32. Given the following code fragment, is it certain what will print, or will the results be uncertain since a is the active member; if the results are certain, what prints:

```
union un {unsigned a; unsigned char b[2];}
   ion = {1 + (1 << 8)};
printf("%u %u\n", ion.b[0], ion.b[1]);
```

33. What value does summer have:

```
enum seasons {winter, spring, summer,
   autumn};
```

34. Since a typedef stands in place of a Standard C type, it is not possible to nest typedefs (True or False).

35. The results of the following pairs are identical (True or False):

```
typedef int *INT_PTR;
INT_PTR a, b;

#define INT_PTR int *
INT_PTR a, b;
```

36. Assuming that float and long have 4 bytes and int has 2, the results of automatic conversion should result in both num and val having values of 35,000 (True or False).

```
float var = 35000.4;
int num = var;
long val = var;
```

37. Given the statements in the last question, in the following statement, two automatic type conversions will take place (True or False):

```
var = val + num;
```

38. Automatic binary conversion will occur on the right side of the assignment operator in the following case:

```
int num = 3 << 3;
```

39. If there is no function prototype, an actual argument is converted according to the automatic function conversions, but the resulting type is not reconverted to the type of the corresponding formal argument, since the compiler does not know what type the formal argument is (True or False).

40. A variable argument in a prototyped function does not get automatically converted according to the automatic function conversions (True or False).

41. The return statement in the following definition engenders two automatic conversions (True or False):

```
int mix_add(int num, float val) {return
   num + val);}
```

Programming Exercises

The specifications of the programming assignments were introduced in Chapter 1, at which time you were to

- think through the solution to these problems.
- identify the modules, that, once implemented, will solve the problem.
- prepare a hierarchy chart of all the modules.
- prepare pseudocode/flowchart for each module in the hierarchy chart.
- write the program stubs the same way we did with the ACE Billing system application.

We have added structures to our C knowledge. We urge you to continue developing what you started in Chapter 1. If you have not started, then we recommend that you start by applying the methodology presented in that chapter. We have helped you get started with some of the programming assignments by specifying only what can be done by this time.

Modify all the programming assignments you did in Chapter 11 to implement the use of structures where applicable. See the application programming example acech13.c.

CHAPTER 14

Files

OBJECTIVES

- To understand how file contents relate to values in primary memory
- To learn how to open and close files, create, rename, and delete files, and understand the different file-opening modes
- To see how to redirect file streams from their default device or file
- To see how to read from and write to files as text or as binary values and to determine in what situations text or binary mode should be favored
- To learn how to test for and clear end-of-file condition and read-write errors and determine how to distinguish one from the other

- To learn what buffering is, how to alter default file buffers, and how to avoid inadvertently reading from or writing to a buffer in update file modes
- To understand how to access files both sequentially and randomly
- To learn how to write records to files and read them back as the same aggregate data types, as well as edit and add records
- To examine differences in how implementations treat text and binary files and appreciate portability problems with each and see how to minimize the problems

NEW TERMS

appending
binary function
binary mode
random access

reading
sequential access
stream
text function

text mode
update mode
writing

The programs we have looked at so far derive their input from the keyboard and direct their output to the screen. Of course, in real-life applications, it is more common for input to emanate from a file or from a file and the keyboard, and for data to be stored in a file or to be partly stored in a file and partly directed to the screen.

When we speak of the processes of data input and output (or I/O for short), we say that we are, respectively, "reading" from a file or "writing" to a file—or more properly, reading from or writing to a *stream*, including, for this purpose, devices such as the screen or the keyboard or the printer or a tape drive, as well as disk files. By *reading*, we mean taking data from a file and placing a copy of it in the computer's primary memory. In so doing, we overstore the data already there, assigning new values to any variables that have a claim to that memory space. By *writing*, we mean the converse process: taking data from the computer's RAM and placing a copy of it into a file. We can write over existing data in the file, just as we do with RAM when we read from a file. Or we can place the data just after the end of the existing data in the file, thereby enlarging the file. The latter process can be variously referred to as writing or as *appending*.

14.1   FILES VERSUS RAM

In many ways, then, a file is like RAM. But there are also significant differences. One key difference is storage locations. When we store a value in RAM, we generally do so by declaring a variable and making an assignment of the value to the variable. We can, but generally do not, specify a particular address, as such, for storage of the value (even though that is what we effectively do by specifying a particular variable). Likewise, when we want to take the value stored in one RAM location and copy it or a value in which it plays a part to another RAM location, we do so by a simple assignment statement:

```
num = val + 2;
```

We need not trouble ourselves about num's or val's precise location in memory, although we already have the tools to determine those locations if we wish. The computer takes care of that for us. In fact, by using variable names in this example, we have given the computer the variables' addresses, for that is all a variable name is to the computer. With a file, there is no such concept as variable names. There are locations in a file, being the number of bytes from the start of the file, but it is your job as programmer to keep track of what data is stored at what location.

On the other hand, when dealing with RAM, we can, if we wish, specify addresses as such for storage of values. We do so, for instance, with the direct memory access techniques discussed in Appendix D. With certain limitations (such as not writing over our own program code), we can choose pretty much any address in RAM to store data.

With a file, we are much more limited. The file expands as data is added to it. If we start with a file of 0 bytes and add 1 byte of data, the file now has a size of 1 byte. If we add a second byte, we have only two choices of location: we can place the new byte over the first one, destroying the first byte and leaving the file with a size of 1, or we can add the second byte immediately after the first one. We cannot generally jump wildly somewhere further into the file.

14.1.1   Storage Differences

The second key difference between RAM and a file is the way values are stored. In RAM, each location, representing a byte in memory, is actually stored bit by bit. Though C generally interprets the bytes as integral wholes, this is not always so. We have already seen two examples—storage and interpretation of floating point numbers, and bit fields in structures—where the individual bits take on a significance independent of byte boundaries. We will be seeing other examples, both in this chapter and in later chapters.

In a file, data is always stored on a byte level only.

 What is stored in the file are the character representation of values 0 to decimal 255, according to ASCII, EBCDIC, or whatever other character-encoding system the computer uses.

14.1.2   Buffering

A third difference is the immediacy with which orders are carried out. When you copy a value from one RAM address to another, the value is stored immediately on execution of the assignment statement designed to accomplish this job. When we copy data from a file to RAM (that is, we read data) or from RAM to a file (that is, we write data), the transfer is not typically immediately accomplished. Generally, what happens instead is that the computer saves up a few of these RAM-file transfer requests and does them all at once.

The reason for this delayed batch processing is speed. Disk operations are far and away the slowest part of the computer process. If we batch operations that require CPU-disk interface, we minimize the delay. The way this is done is to establish an area of RAM to serve as a buffer. Let's say we establish a buffer of 512 bytes, to pick a number, either by declaring a 512-element char array, or by assigning a 512-byte memory area to a char pointer with the dynamic memory allocation techniques discussed in Chapter 15. If we start writing 50-byte blocks of data, we can write 10 blocks before the buffer gets close to filling up. On the 11th write, the computer can then copy data from the buffer to the file.

We can do something similar for reading 10 bytes of data at a time. On the first read-10-bytes command, the computer can place the first 512 bytes of the file (assuming the file is that large) into the buffer and transfer 10 of those bytes to RAM. On each successive 10-byte read request, the computer can transfer the next bytes out of the buffer until the buffer is empty. At that point, the computer can just dump another 512 bytes in from the file to the buffer.

Of course, all this assumes that we want to read out the 10-byte increments in the same order as they are stored in the file. If, on the other hand, we want to read the first 10 bytes and then 10 bytes starting 30 bytes from the beginning of the file, and then 10 bytes from a point 45 bytes away from where we ended up reading from the second time, and so forth, this whole business of trying to use a buffer doesn't help us much. Or at the very least, we will have to create some specialized sort of buffering system.

14.1.3   Standard versus Low-Level I/O

We will cover two different types of file I/O: standard I/O and, much more briefly in Appendix K, low-level I/O. With low-level I/O, reading and writing takes place directly with a file. If you want to use any sort of buffer, you must create and maintain your own, and you must monitor transfers of data into and out of it. With standard I/O, the C functions read data from and write data to a buffer. The buffer is created automatically on file opening, and the computer takes care of the data transfers into and out of it.

Each file you open in standard I/O has its own separate buffer associated with it. This buffer is located in the heap on a PC (see Appendix B for a discussion of the heap and other program data memory areas). There is also a separate buffer for the files, discussed below, that C opens automatically at the outset of a program. By default, each buffer is the number of bytes defined in `stdio.h` as BUFSIZ (512 on a PC—the number of bytes in a disk sector). Standard C requires that BUFSIZ be defined to have a value of at least 256.

Since Standard I/O is far more commonly used, we will start there. Low-level I/O is essentially limited to those writing code for very small systems, such as computerized medical devices. None of the low-level I/O functions are part of Standard C.

14.2   STANDARD I/O—TEXT VERSUS BINARY FUNCTIONS

We indicated above that what is stored in a file is character representations of ASCII (or EBCDIC or whatever other character-encoding system the computer uses) values from 0 to 255. Whether the program that writes those characters to the file or reads them back out at some later time treats those characters as literal characters or as representative of the values they represent is not a function of the file. Rather, it is a question of the type of function that writes or reads the characters.

There are two different types of functions for writing and reading data to and from a file. We will refer to them as **_text functions_** and **_binary functions_**. The text functions read and write characters as characters. The binary functions treat the characters written to or read from a file as only a graphic way of expressing the byte values the characters represent.

 With text reading and writing functions, we essentially treat a file as though it were the screen.

Table 14.1 shows the text functions.

Table 14.1   _Text Functions_

Type	Writing	Reading
formatted	fprintf()	fscanf()
string	fputs()	fgets()
character	fgetc()	fputc()

Table 14.2 *Binary Functions*

Writing	Reading
fwrite()	fread()

We can place numerical data as well as text into the file with these text functions, but the numerical data is simply stored in character form, just as it would appear on the screen as a result of a `printf()` statement. Standard C refers to both the string functions and the character functions as "character input/output" functions.

Table 14.2 shows the binary functions. The C Standard refers to them as "direct input/output" functions.

 With binary reading and writing functions, we essentially treat the file as an extension of the computer's random access memory.

All data, text and numerical, is stored in the file byte by byte. What is stored is the character representation of the numerical value derived from the 8 bits that make up the byte in RAM.

We will give you examples of reading and writing with text functions and with binary functions in a later section, once we have covered the syntax of the various functions in detail. We gave you a brief overview first, however, because we wanted to emphasize the importance of the difference in purpose between the two types of functions. Shortly, we will cover the two basic mode types for opening files, also called text and binary. In discussing files, some C books focus chiefly on the choice of file-opening mode and only incidentally on the choice of function type. We believe this focus has the cart pulling the horse.

14.3   OPENING A FILE

Before we can write to or read from a file, we must open it. We open a file by calling `fopen()` and setting a pointer to `fopen()`'s return value.

The pointer is of type pointer to `FILE`. `FILE` is a derived type known as a *structure*, a topic covered in the last chapter. The `FILE` structure, found in `stdio.h`, contains various bits of information about the file we have opened, used by C to process the file.

The `FILE` structure contains, among other things,

- a file position indicator that notes the next byte to be read from or written to the file. (This information is meaningful only for files, not for interactive devices such as the monitor or printer.)
- an error indicator that notes whether a read or write resulted in a data transfer error.
- an end-of-file indicator that notes whether you have tried to read past the end of the file.
- read-write buffer information, such as the presence, size, and starting address of the buffer, as well as the address of the most recently read or written character in the buffer.
- the file handle number.

If you are curious, and your implementation does not wisely hide the details, you can look at your implementation's version of the `FILE` data object in `stdio.h`. However, if you attempt to alter any of the `FILE`'s fields or copy them elsewhere, Standard C warns you that this may lead to undefined behavior. The `FILE` data object is meant to be a black-box magic cookie, the details of which are hidden from the programmer. Certainly, the `FILE` structure for one implementation will be different from that of another. For example, compare that of Borland C with that of Microsoft.

The Borland C version of `FILE`:

```
typedef struct
{
    short level; /* bytes left in buffer */
    unsigned flags; /* assorted file information */
    char fd; /* file handle */
    unsigned char hold; /* ungetc() char if no buffer */
```

```
    short bsize; /* buffer size */
    unsigned char *buffer; /* address of start of buffer */
    unsigned char *curp; /* address of current char in buffer */
    unsigned istemp; /* temporary file indicator */
    short token; /* used for validity checking */
} FILE;
```

The Microsoft C approach:

```
struct _iobuf
{
    char *_ptr; /* address of current char in buffer */
    int _cnt; /* bytes left in buffer */
    char *_base; /* address of start of buffer */
    char _flag; /* assorted file information */
    char _file; /* file handle */
};
typedef struct _iobuf FILE;
```

You must use the FILE pointer returned by fopen() as an argument in all operations relating to the file, not the filename. This would include closing the file, moving within the file, and reading from or writing to the file.

14.3.1   The fopen() Function: Arguments and Return Value

The fopen() function takes two arguments, both pointers to char. The first argument is the name of the file to be opened; the second is the mode in which the file is to be opened:

```
FILE *fopen(const char *filename, const char *mode);
```

If the file is opened successfully, fopen() returns a pointer to the FILE structure established for the file. In the case of error, the function returns NULL and stores an error code into the global variable errno (discussed in Chapter 16):

```
char filename[FILENAME_MAX] = "c:\\data\\record.dat";
if ((rfile = fopen(filename, "r")) == NULL)
    printf("Error opening file %s\n", filename);
```

The filename argument can be a literal string or a pointer to an address containing a filename:

```
FILE *rfile, *wfile;
char writefile[FILENAME_MAX];
rfile = fopen("c:\\data", "r"); /* literal string */
printf("Specify file name to write to");
gets(writefile);
wfile = fopen(writefile, "w"); /* pointer/array */
```

Note the double backslash in the literal string example.

14.3.2   Error-Checking with fopen()

Throughout the sample programs and examples illustrating the various file operations in this chapter, we will often omit error-checking mechanisms for reasons of space and clarity. We did so in the last example. However, in your programs, you should include error-checking on most of the file operation functions. Also, in the instances where we do illustrate error-checking, it generally is only to print an error message on error. Depending on your particular program and the function you are checking, you may want instead to terminate the program, cause a premature return from a function, or, after ascertaining the particular cause for error (for example, a file can't be opened because the floppy drive is not closed), ask the user to correct the error and try again.

Insofar as file opening is concerned, error-checking is particularly important for opening a file in a read mode, where a common cause for error is specifying a nonexistent file. Even with opening a file for writing, an error could be caused by a mechanical problem, such as a floppy drive not being closed,

Table 14.3 *Automatically Created File Structures*

File	FILE Pointer	Device
standard input	stdin	keyboard-screen
standard output	stdout	screen
standard error	stderr	screen
Additional DOS Streams		
standard auxiliary	stdaux	port
standard printer	stdprn	printer

or a disk being full, or the filename being illegal, or because access is restricted. Or perhaps you have already opened the maximum number of files your implementation allows to be opened at once, or possibly the operating system permits only a certain number of files to be created in one location and you are already at that number. This latter is specified in the macro FOPEN_MAX, defined in stdio.h. Standard C requires that FOPEN_MAX must have a value of at least eight (including the three standard text streams discussed in the next section).

An error can also be caused by attempting to open a read-only file (a concept we cover in a later section) for writing. We will cover error handling for file opening in more detail later.

14.3.3 Automatically Opened Streams

Standard C requires that when your C program starts, three text-stream FILE structures be automatically opened: standard output, standard input, and standard error. (Most DOS implementations add two more. These are actually input or output devices, treated by DOS as files.) In an interactive environment, these are all generally associated with the computer screen and, except for standard error, are buffered.

What the user types on the keyboard and then shows up on the screen becomes part of standard input when the user presses the Enter key. It can then be processed by the functions that handle standard input, such as scanf() or gets() or getchar(). Conversely, when your programs use functions that write to standard output, such as printf() or puts() or putchar(), their output shows up on the screen.

When an error is signaled in certain library functions, a message is sent to standard error. For example, if you pass a negative number to the square root function, sqrt(), a message something like "sqrt: DOMAIN error" may be sent to the screen even if you do not test for an error return value. You can also send your own error messages to standard error. We will show you how to do so in this chapter.

As we discuss in Chapter 16 and later in this chapter, standard input can be redirected to obtain data from a file rather than the screen, and standard output or standard error can be redirected to write to a file or a device other than the screen (such as the printer). It is a common practice to redirect normal data output statements to a disk file or some location other than the screen and to print error messages to standard error so that the user sees them immediately and can take any appropriate action.

The stdio.h header file assigns these files FILE pointer names that you can then use to access these devices. Table 14.3 lists these automatically created streams.

These streams are opened even if your program has nothing to do with files.

14.4 TEXT FILE MODES

The file mode dictates whether the file is opened for reading, writing, or appending (writing new data at the end of an existing file). Table 14.4 lists the possible modes and indicates what occurs if the file does or does not already exist.

The w mode opens the file for writing. If the file already exists, it is truncated to zero length, discarding the existing data in the file. If you open an existing file unintentionally, there is no way to recover the lost

Table 14.4 *Text File-Opening Modes*

Mode	Operation	Result if File *Does Not Exist*	Result if File *Already Exists*
r	read	*error!*	normal case
w	write	creates file	destroys existing file data
a	append (write at end of file)	creates file	normal case
r+	read and write	*error!*	normal case
w+	read and write	creates file	destroys existing file data
a+	read and append	creates file	normal case

data. Closing the file immediately leaves the file with no data. (Whether a file of zero length—in which no characters have been written by an output stream—actually exists is implementation defined. Such a file does exist on a PC.) Nor can any commercial unerase utilities restore the data.

Use of either the a or a+ mode will prevent the overwriting of existing file data—accidental or intentional. Later in this chapter, you will learn how to move from position to position in the file. However, if you open a file in either append mode, any attempt to write will automatically cause a jump to wherever the end of the file is as of the attempted writing. *If you want to append records at the end of a file and overwrite data earlier in the file, you should open the file in the r+ mode and manually move to the end of the file whenever you want to add records.*

When you open a file in the r+ mode, you start out at the beginning of the file. With some compilers, when you open a file in an append mode, you start out at the end of the file. In that case, if you open a file in a+ mode, you cannot begin with an fread() statement without first moving elsewhere in the file. With others, such as Borland C, the file position indicator for files opened in an append mode will start at the beginning of the file and be automatically reset to the end of the file before a write.

For append mode, Standard C allows implementations to initially place the file position indicator either at the beginning or end of the file.

14.5 CLOSING THE FILE: fclose() AND freopen()

We've seen how to open files. Now let's find out how to close them. We'll also see how to close a file and open another at the same time.

14.5.1 The fclose() Function

You close the file with fclose():

```
int fclose(FILE *stream);
```

The fclose() function takes a single argument, the FILE pointer:

```
FILE *fp;
fp = fopen("data", "r");
fclose(fp);
```

This does not destroy the FILE pointer, so you can use it again in the same program to open another file:

```
FILE *fp;
fp = fopen("data", "r");
fclose(fp);
fp = fopen("moredata", "r");
fclose(fp);
```

Closing the file flushes the buffer of any output stream, ensuring that all data you've written actually makes its way to the file. Closing the file also releases the buffer that opening the file creates in the heap on a PC, as the following simple program demonstrates.

 **Listing 14.1 buf_heap.c**

```
/* buf_heap.c */

/* shows how file buffer is created in heap and released */

#include <stdio.h>
#include <alloc.h> /* coreleft(): DOS only */

int main(void)
{
  FILE *fp;

  printf("heap before opening file: %ld\n", coreleft());
  fp = fopen("c:\\junk\\junk", "w");
  printf("heap after opening file: %ld\n", coreleft());
  fclose(fp);
  printf("heap after closing file: %ld\n", coreleft());
  return 0;
}
```

```
heap before opening file: 63504
heap after opening file: 62992
heap after closing file: 63504
```

The unused heap gets 512 bytes smaller when the file is opened and 512 bytes larger when it is closed. (See Appendix B for a discussion of the heap and other program data memory areas on a PC.)

Likewise, if the program reaches the end of main() or upon the calling of exit() to terminate the program prematurely, all open files are closed, and thus all output streams flushed, before program termination. With other paths to program termination, such as calling abort(), an implementation need not, and generally will not, close all files properly. See Chapter 16 for further discussion of exit() and abort().

The fclose() function returns a zero if the file is closed successfully; otherwise, it returns EOF (defined in most compilers' stdio.h file as –1; however, C permits EOF to be defined as any negative integer value). A file-closing error might arise from a disk being full or a floppy drive not being closed. Ignoring the results of fclose() might result in loss of data. For files opened for writing or appending, you might consider something along these lines:

```
if (fclose(fp))
   printf("Error closing %s", filename);
```

14.5.2   The freopen() Function and Redirection *(Optional)*

You could think of freopen() as an environmentally sound FILE pointer-recycling facility:

```
FILE *freopen(const char *new_filename, const char *mode,
   FILE *existing_stream)
```

It attempts to close the file currently associated with existing_stream (this is not new_filename; it would be whatever filename was used to open the stream now pointed to by existing_stream). However, any errors in closing the file are ignored. Then, it attempts to open another file, pointing the same FILE pointer now to that latter file, so that the FILE stream and its buffering and file-positioning and file status indicator mechanism, and so on, now handle the second file:

```
FILE *fp = fopen("first_file", "r");
char ch = fgetc(fp);
putchar(ch);
freopen("second_file", "w", fp);
```

Apart from the absence of the ability to check for a valid call to `fclose()` before bothering to call `fopen()`, the following would be identical to the code fragment above:

```
FILE *fp = fopen("first_file", "r");
char ch = fgetc(fp);
putchar(ch);
fclose(fp);
fp = fopen("second_file", "w");
```

The `freopen()` function returns the reused `FILE` pointer if it is successfully called; otherwise a `NULL` pointer is returned.

One of the most common uses for `freopen()` *is to redirect a file to* `stdin` *or redirect* `stdout` *to a file.* That way, for example, you can use the simple standard output and input functions such as `getchar()`, `scanf()`, and `gets()` to read input from a file and `putchar()`, `printf()`, and `puts()` to send output to a file. Since these streams are automatically opened at the start of program execution, you can, in this situation, call `freopen()` without having made any calls to `fopen()` and without declaring any `FILE` pointer:

```
char ch;
freopen("c:\\temp\\junk", "w", stdout);
/* now I/O writing functions hard-wired to stdout will write to the file */
puts("This will go into the file, not on the screen");
freopen("c:\\temp\\trash", "r", stdin);
/* now all I/O reading functions that are hard-wired to stdin
   will read from trash; assumes trash file exists */
ch = getchar();
```

See Chapter 16 for how to redirect `stdin` or `stdout` through operating system commands rather than through `freopen()`. (In DOS and in many other operating systems, `stderr` cannot be redirected with system commands.)

Another common use for `freopen()` *is to redirect* `stderr` *to an error log file for future review.*

```
double root;
freopen("errorlog", "w", stderr);
root = sqrt(-1); /* error calling sqrt with negative # */
if(errno)
   fprintf(stderr, strerror(errno));
```

After those statements, the following shows up in the `errorlog` file, the first written by `sqrt()` itself to `stderr`, as redirected, and the second from your `fprintf()` statement explicitly to `stderr`, as likewise redirected:

```
sqrt: DOMAIN error
Math argument
```

Conversely, *in interactive, nonbatch applications, good programming practice may dictate not redirecting* `stderr` *to a file, but rather making sure all your error messages are explicitly directed to* `stderr`, as in the `fprintf()` example above. That way if standard output is redirected in the program or through the operating environment (see Chapter 16 for system redirection), error messages will still show up on the screen.

In any case, `stderr` and `stdout` are different streams, even though by default they are normally associated with the same computer monitor. Since `stderr` is normally unbuffered and `stdout` is normally buffered, writing to one and then the other alternately, without having redirected one or the other, may in some cases produce unanticipated results—for example, a later-executed statement may show up before an earlier-executed one.

14.6   TEXT VERSUS BINARY MODE

Each of the modes listed in Table 14.4 is a so-called ***text mode***. For each text mode there is a ***binary mode*** counterpart. In terms of the mode string, the only difference between the two is the addition of a b at the end of each string (see Table 14.5).

Table 14.5 *Text and Binary File-Opening Modes*

Operation	Text Mode	Binary Mode	Alternative Form
read	r	rb	
write	w	wb	
append (write at end of file)	a	ab	
read and write	r+	rb+	r+b
read and write	w+	wb+	w+b
read and append	a+	ab+	a+b

Standard C allows implementations to add additional characters after any of these mode forms. For instance, Borland C allows you to add a t at the end of any of the text modes to more clearly distinguish text modes from binary modes. Other implementations may allow you to effectively add additional arguments by inserting comma-separated designations within the mode string for creating field-length records of a specified size, and so on. If portability is a concern, you should avoid any file mode additions.

In general, you will use a text mode when the storage and retrieval needs of a programming task are best served by the text functions and a binary mode when those needs are best served by the binary functions. (We will discuss later in this chapter when one or the other function set serves best.) However, there is no prohibition against using text functions to read from or write to a file opened in binary mode or using binary functions to read from or write to a file opened in text mode, and you will occasionally find it useful to do so.

14.6.1 Implementation-Specific Treatment in Text Mode

Whether a file has been written in binary or in text mode, the file contains a series of characters having an ASCII (or EBCDIC) value of between 0 and 255. However, some of these characters have special reserved meanings in text mode on different systems. Standard C permits implementations to add, alter, or delete characters on reading or writing to conform to system conventions and requirements for representing text. In the next section, we will take DOS as an example—specifically, the way DOS recognizes how the end of a line is signaled and how the end of a file is signaled. Toward the end of the chapter, as part of a general discussion of portability in file operations, we will see what characters can be depended on to be uniformly treated across systems.

14.6.2 Ends of Lines and Files in DOS *(Optional)*

In C, the end of a line is signified by a newline character (\n, ASCII 10). In DOS, the end of a line is signified by the combination of a carriage return character (\r, ASCII 13) and a newline character. If, in DOS, you use the text functions to write to a file opened in text mode, the newline character will be stored in the file as two characters: the carriage return character and a newline character. Conversely, when, in DOS, you open a file in text mode and use the text functions to read from it, the combination carriage return–newline is read as a newline only.

Generally there is no character at the end of a file to signify that the end of the file has been reached. If, for instance, you happen to be reading a character at a time with fgetc(), discussed below, when the end of the file is reached, C arbitrarily causes the next fgetc() call to return EOF. It is not that there is a character there with an ASCII value of whatever negative integer your implementation defines EOF to be; rather, C simply takes advantage of the fact that character encoding runs from 0 to 255 and picks a return value outside that range. (We can then put this arbitrariness to use in our coding by testing whether an fgetc() call returns EOF.)

However, in addition to the actual end of file, DOS treats the [Ctrl] [Z] character (decimal 26 in ASCII) as the end of file. Conversely, in DOS, if you are reading a file opened in text mode and come to a byte with a decimal value of 26, reading will stop.

The text mode writing of the newline as a combination carriage return–newline, and reading of a carriage return–newline as a newline and [Ctrl] [Z] as end-of-file, applies even if reading and writing are accomplished by the binary functions `fread()` and `fwrite()`.

A problem can occur when a file previously opened in binary mode is read in text mode. Let's take an example. If we store an `int` having a value of 228 in binary mode, it will be represented like this in the file:

→ (

That is, it will have a first byte of 26 and a second byte of 1 (on a significant byte-last system). If we read the file in text mode, reading will stop with this `int` even if there is more data in the file. Termination occurs even if reading is done with the binary function `fread()`.

We can verify this with a simple program run on a PC. We will open a file in binary write mode and then write first a sentence of text, then a value that contains a byte with a value of 26, and, finally, another sentence of text. Then we will close the file and reopen it in text read mode and attempt to read the entire file into an array. The value returned by `fread()` will tell us how many bytes were read.

 **Listing** **14.2 text_bin.c**

```c
/* text_bin.c */

/* even binary functions stop at CTRL-Z in text mode on a PC */

#include <stdio.h>
#include <string.h> /* strlen */

int main(void)
{
   char temp[BUFSIZ];
   int balance = 26;
   int bytes;
   FILE *fp;


   fp = fopen("c:\\junk\\junk", "wb");
   fwrite("This is a test", strlen("This is a test"), 1, fp);
   fwrite(&balance, sizeof(int), 1, fp); /* value with 26 in 1 byte */
   fwrite("This is a test", strlen("This is a test"), 1, fp);
   fclose(fp);

   fp = fopen("c:\\junk\\junk", "r");
   bytes = fread(temp, 1, BUFSIZ, fp);
   fclose(fp);
   printf("bytes read: %d\n", bytes);
}
```

We get the following output:

```
bytes read: 14
```

Thus reading stops after the first test sentence written to the file, just as we expected. (Note that since a literal string is given its own address, we can use a literal string as the first argument to `fwrite()`. We will cover the mechanism of `fread()` and `fwrite()` later in this chapter.)

If we change the second file-opening mode from `r` to `rb`, the entire file is read:

```
bytes read: 30
```

The lesson we should draw from all this is that *if we open a file in one mode (binary versus text) originally, we had better open it again in the same mode or pay careful attention to the differences.* On most systems, there is no inherent difference between the files created in either mode. Nor does the file have any sort of label or designator associated with it to say it is a binary or text file. It is only the way our program or the operating system interprets the character representation of the bytes in each that differs. It is your responsibility as a programmer to keep track of what mode a file is created in. Nothing in C will yell at you if you attempt to read in text mode a file created in binary mode. You will just get nonsense results. As one of our reviewers aptly noted, C always lets you shoot yourself in the (virtual) foot.

The above caution relates to files read and written on the same system. There are a number of similar concerns when the possibility of cross-system reading and writing is involved. We address these portability concerns toward the end of the chapter.

14.7   TEXT FUNCTIONS—fprintf() AND fscanf()

The fprintf() and fscanf() functions work the same way as printf() and scanf(), with the addition of specifying a FILE pointer as an additional first argument:

```
int fprintf(FILE *stream, const char *format, . . .);
int fscanf(FILE *stream, const char *format, . . .);
```

For example:

```
fprintf(fp, "There are %d customers in the region\n", customers);
fscanf(pfile, "%d", &num);
```

Calling fprintf() or fscanf() with stdout as the FILE pointer would be identical to calls to printf() and scanf(). *You can use that fact in a conditional statement that allows the user to specify whether printing of data is to be made to the screen or to a file. This would allow the user to review and approve data before sending it to a file.*

```
char mode;
FILE *fp = fopen("data", "w");
printf("Type \"S\" to print to screen or"
   " \"F\" to print to file\n");
mode = toupper(getchar());
fprintf(mode == 'S' ? stdout : fp, "%-20s %-20s %-15s %-10s %-5s\n",
   name, address, city, state, zip);
```

See Listing 16.12, pick_cl.c, for an interesting example of this concept. That program allows the user to print a file to the screen, the printer, or a designated file, as well as specify the number of copies, the number of lines space between each text line, and the number of spaces to indent each line from the left margin.

Like scanf(), fscanf() returns the number of items successfully read. Therefore, you can use a loop like this to move through a file:

```
while (fscanf(fp, "%d", &num) == 1)
   sum += num;
```

The fscanf() function returns EOF (defined in stdio.h to be an implementation-specified negative integer) if you attempt to read past the end of the file, so it would not be correct to omit the == 1 in this code fragment, as you could with scanf() (unless you use scanf() to read a file through redirection). The return value of a negative integer would be evaluated as true if used as a logical value.

In fact, you might want to move in the other direction and expand the code to make use of the difference in return value on failure, to distinguish between failure due to invalid characters and due to end of file:

```
int sum = 0;
int num, result;
while ((result = fscanf(fp, "%d", &num)) == 1)
   sum += num;
if (result != EOF)
   puts("Invalid character encountered");
```

The conditional device used above should be portable. Standard C allows implementations to treat the address of the FILE object used to control a stream as significant; a copy of the FILE object need not serve in place of the original with precisely the same effect. However, here we have merely created another pointer to the same FILE object. Similarly any of the three following devices for cross-function file operations will work fine:

```c
#include <stdio.h>
#define A 1
/* #define B 1 */
/* #define C 1 */

void filePointerPass(FILE *file);
FILE *filePointerReturn(void);
void passPointerToFilePointer(FILE **file);

int main(void)
{
#if A
   FILE *fp = fopen("c:\\bonds\\junk", "w");
   filePointerPass(fp);
#endif

#if B
   FILE *fp = filePointerReturn();
   fprintf(fp, "this works");
#endif

#if C
   FILE *fp;
   passPointerToFilePointer(&fp);
   fprintf(fp, "this works");
#endif
return 0;
}

void filePointerPass(FILE *file)
{
   fprintf(file, "this works");
   fclose(file);
}

FILE *filePointerReturn(void)
{
   static FILE *file;
   file = fopen("c:\\bonds\\junk", "w");
   return file;
}

void passPointerToFilePointer(FILE **file)
{
   *file = fopen("c:\\bonds\\junk", "w");
}
```

14.7.1   The `fgets()` and `fputs()` Functions

The `fputs()` and `fgets()` functions add a FILE pointer argument to the char pointer argument that `puts()` and `gets()` each has. Unlike the case with `fprintf()` and `fscanf()`, with `fputs()` and `fgets()`, the FILE pointer argument comes last, not first. (Since `fprintf()` and `fscanf()` are variable-argument list functions—see Chapter 8—the variable arguments rather than the FILE pointer argument must come last. Why the FILE pointer argument wasn't also placed first in the fgets(), fputs(), and fputc() functions for consistency, we can't guess.)

```
int fputs(const char *string, FILE *stream);
char *fgets(char *string, int max_characters, FILE *stream);
```

The prototype indicates that the fgets() function adds still another argument as the second argument, the maximum number of characters to be read:

```
gets(address);
puts(address);


fgets(address, 81, pfile);
fputs(address, fp);
```

 Hence, fgets() *is safer to use than* gets() *if you do not include your own function to ensure that before* gets() *reads input, the input is truncated or otherwise made to fit within the area pointed to by the argument to* gets().

As you have already seen, the gets() and puts() functions work in tandem insofar as the newline character is concerned. The gets() function discards the newline and the puts() function adds one. The fgets()-fputs() pair do the reverse. The fgets() function retains the newline and the fputs() function does not add one. Nor does fputs() write the terminating NULL character.

Like gets(), fgets() generally reads to the newline. However, fgets() stops when it has read one character less than the maximum number of characters specified as its second argument (that is, this argument reflects the maximum string size, including the terminating NULL, rather than the strlen()). This allows it always to store the NULL character at the end of the string but leaves no room for the newline if this point is reached.

 If you use fgets() *in conjunction with* puts() *or you want to store the data obtained by* fgets() *for future use without the newline, you may have to manually eliminate the newline automatically stored by* fgets().

```
fgets(address, sizeof(address), fp);
if (strrchr(address, '\n') != NULL);
    *strrchr(address, '\n') = 0;
puts(address);
```

On the other hand, if storing a newline doesn't interfere with your plans, you can use fputs() with stdout as the stream to avoid doubling up on the newline with a string that had been previously read in by fgets().

 By the same token, *if you obtain your data interactively with* gets() *and then store the data with* fputs(), *you may in some situations want to add a newline before using* fputs().

```
gets(name);
strcat(name, "\n");
fputs(name, fp);
```

Like gets(), fgets() returns a pointer to the string into which the data read has been copied, or NULL if there has been a failure. Both will stop reading when the end of file is reached and return a NULL. Similarly, fputs(), like puts(), returns a nonnegative integer value, or EOF on failure.

14.7.2   A Text File-Copying Example

You can make use of fgets()'s end-of-file behavior to make a simple, effective program for copying a file containing text.

 **Listing** **14.3 f_copy_t.c**

```
/* f_copy_t.c */

/* simple file-copying program with text functions */

#include <stdio.h>
```

```
int main(void)
{
    FILE *original, *copy;
    char temp[81];

    /* error-checking omitted */
    original = fopen("c:\\config.sys", "r");
    copy = fopen("c:\\junk\\junk", "w");
    while(fgets(temp, 81, original))
        fputs(temp, copy);
}
```

This program would work on a file created with a text editor or with a C program that used the text functions `fputs()` or `fprintf()`. Such a file would not generally have more than 80 characters between newline characters. If, however, you thought the lines might be longer and you had used `fputs()` or `fprintf()` in the first instance, you would have to alter f_copy_t.c's `fgets()` call and the size of the `char` array.

The program would not work properly on a word processing program-created file, even though you might think of such a file as containing "text." Those programs add control characters and characters representing ASCII values beyond 127 for formatting purposes. Some of those characters would cause the text reading and writing functions to stop reading the file or do funny things like beep. Also, word processing programs are paragraph oriented, not line oriented—a phenomenon referred to as *word wrap*. Newline characters appear at the end of each paragraph, not at the end of each screen line.

14.7.3   The `fgetc()` and `fputc()` Functions; `ungetc()`

The `fgetc()` and `fputc()` functions operate precisely the same as `getchar()` and `putchar()` do for the standard input stream. Each takes a `FILE` pointer as an additional argument:

```
int fgetc(FILE *stream);
int fputc(int character, FILE *stream);
```

The `fgetc()` function takes the next character as an `unsigned char` converted to an `int` from the input stream pointed to by `stream`. The `fputc()` function writes the character specified as its first argument (converted to an `unsigned char`) to the output stream pointed to by `stream`.

An example:

```
ch = fgetc(fp);
fputc(ch, pfile);
```

Note that as with `fputs()` and `fputs()`, and *unlike* `fprintf()` and `fscanf()`, the `FILE` pointer argument is last. To remember the order, try to recall that the `FILE` pointer argument is last except when used in variable-argument list functions, where it is first instead.

The `fgetc()` and `fputc()` functions return the character read or written. If the stream is at the end of the file, a call to `fgetc()` sets the end-of-file indicator for the stream and returns `EOF`. If a read error occurs through a call to `fgetc()` or a write error occurs with a call to `fputc()`, `EOF` is likewise returned and the stream's error indicator is set.

Using a `FILE` pointer of `stdin` for `fgetc()` and `stdout` for `fputc()` would make them identical to `getchar()` and `putchar()`. In fact, unless you undefine `getchar()` and `putchar()`, many implementations give you the macro rather than the function versions of `getchar()` and `putchar()`, generally defined by an implementation like this:

```
#define getchar() getc(stdin)
#define putchar(c) putc((c),stdout)
```

In any case, the call `getchar()` is equivalent to one to `getc(stdin)`, and the call `putchar(ch)` is equivalent to one to `putc(ch, stdout)`.

You can use `ungetc()` to place a character into the associated input stream ahead of what is already there:

```
int ungetc(int character, FILE *stream);
```

You can be guaranteed of placing only a single character into an input stream without an intervening read function call. Depending on the implementation, a second call to ungetc() without an intervening read call from the same stream may be ignored. If multiple calls to ungetc() are supported by the implementation, subsequent reads are to the characters on a last-in, first-out basis.

The ungetc() function returns the character sought to be pushed into the input stream if the call is successful and EOF if it is not. An attempt to push an EOF into the stream will fail.

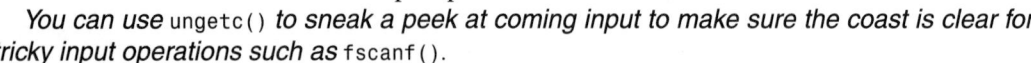

You can use ungetc() *to sneak a peek at coming input to make sure the coast is clear for tricky input operations such as* fscanf().

 **14.4 ungetc.c**

```
/* ungetc.c */

/* illustrate ungetc() function */

#include <stdio.h>
#include <ctype.h> /* isdigit */
#define MAX_NUMS 5

int main(void)
{
   int ch, i;
   static num[MAX_NUMS];

   FILE *fp = fopen("c:\\temp\\junk", "w+");

   fprintf(fp, "ab104ab105");
   rewind(fp);
   for (i = 0; i < MAX_NUMS; /* nothing here; updated below */)
   {
     if((ch = fgetc(fp)) == EOF)
        break;

     /* if next character is not a digit or minus sign, continue;
        otherwise, put it back for the next scanf read */
     if (isdigit(ch) || ch == '-')
        ungetc(ch, fp);
     else continue;

     if (fscanf(fp, "%d", &num[i++]) != 1)
        break;
   }
}
```

We look at the next character in the input stream. If it is a digit or the unary sign operator '–', we place the character back into the input stream with ungetc(), ready for rereading by fscanf() now. Otherwise, we just let it be gobbled up and continue the next iteration and another character reading. Without this clearing operation, fscanf() would have been perpetually stuck on the letter input, since it would have persisted in throwing it back into the input stream after finding it unsuitable for its %d conversion specifier.

Typically, ungetc() is used to place back a character just read in by fgetc(), but this need not be so. The character will be read on the next call to fgetc() or any other read operation function on the same stream (getc(), getchar() if fp points to stdin, fgets(), fscanf(), or fread()).

Standard C speaks of pushing characters back into an input stream, and the name of the ungetc() function implies undoing a previous read. But you need not replace characters that have been previously read. If that were so, there would have been no need for the first argument; we would need only a pointer to the stream. Any character you specify will do.

Yet, the `ungetc()` function undoes a previous read in the sense that, at least for a binary stream, the file position gets backed up one (for each successful call, if the implementation supports more than one unread-interrupted call to `ungetc()`). Let's say we have a file that has 12345 as its contents; we open the file in binary mode and point the stream to `fp`; and read two characters, 1 and 2. The file position would now be 2. If we then called

```
ungetc('!', fp);
```

the file position would now be 1, not 2. It is as though we replaced the 2 in the file with a ! and backed up to where the 2 used to be. The next two character reads would produce ! and 3 and the file position would now be 3, just as it would be if we had just read three characters from the file from the outset.

Actually, the `ungetc()` function does not really write to the file, even if the stream is a disk file. Rather, it simply places the specified character in the buffer, as though it came from the file. Consequently, any successful call by a function that flushes the buffer for a particular stream discards all characters previously pushed into that stream by `ungetc()`. Flushing would take place with `fflush()`. Any of the file-positioning functions will also clear any characters inserted into the input stream by `ungetc()`: `fsetpos()`, `fseek()`, or `rewind()`. We provide a description of these flushing and file-positioning functions later.

For a text stream, the file position is undefined until all characters pushed back onto the stream by `ungetc()` calls have been read or cleared. See below for a discussion of random access and file positioning.

14.7.4   Text Functions and the Printer *(Optional)*

As you can imagine, there is little uniformity when it comes to using hardware such as printers or modems on different platforms. Although Standard C requires implementations to establish automatic streams for standard output, input, and error, there is no such requirement for the printer. Most DOS implementations open two more streams automatically at the beginning of each program: `stdprn` for the printer and `stdaux` for a serial port device. These are not part of Standard C.

In a DOS application, you can write to the printer simply by using `stdprn` as the stream:

```
fputs("This goes to the printer\n", stdprn);
```

One quirk here. If you send a newline character to `stdout` or `stderr`, the text moves to the left-most part of the following line. However, with many implementations and printers, if you send a newline character to `stdprn` directly, the next character will print on the next line, but just to the right of the character before the newline. If you get to the edge of the page, the text goes off east into the sunset, on the next line but out of sight:

```
fputs("This goes to the printer\n", stdprn);
fputs("This too: on the next line\f", stdprn);
```

We get this on the printed page:

```
This goes to the printer
                        This too: on the next line
```

To remedy this problem, you should pass a combination newline–carriage return (`\n\r` or `\r\n`):

```
fputs("This goes to the printer\n\r", stdprn);
```

If, however, you either use `puts()` and redirect output from the operating system to the printer, or you print to a file and then redirect the file from the operating system to the printer, you do not need the carriage return. But including it doesn't hurt. So if we are in the DOS environment, we can now expand the earlier conditional printing example from

```
printf("Type \"S\" to print to screen or"
    " \"F\" to print to file\n");
mode = toupper(getchar());
fprintf(mode == 'S' ? stdout : fp, "%-20s %-20s %-15s %-10s %-5s\n",
    name, address, city, state, zip);
```

to

```
printf("Type \"P\" to print to printer, \"S\" "
    "to print to screen or \"F\" to print to file\n");
mode = toupper(getchar());
fprintf(mode == 'P' ? stdprn : mode == 'S' ? stdout : fp,
    "%-20s %-20s %-15s %-10s %-5s\n\r", name, address, city, state, zip);
```

On some non-DOS operating systems, there may be an automatically available analog to stdprn, such as lp in UNIX. On others, you will have to explicitly open the printer stream in the fashion dictated by the system and implementation just as you would a disk file. However you do it, you could then make use of conditional write statements in the fashion illustrated above for a DOS system. As with the carriage return character on a DOS-based system for moving to the left of the next line, certain system-dependent control characters may be required for various purposes. This obviously is a highly nonportable matter.

 You should also be aware of the printing parameters of your system and printer for purposes of creating reports from your program data. On a typical PC operation, a text line is 80 characters long (just as on the screen), with 10 characters per inch horizontally and 6 lines per inch vertically. On a typical mainframe application, a text line is 132 characters with 10, 12, or 16.5 characters per inch, with 6 or 8 lines per inch.

14.8   BINARY FUNCTIONS—fwrite() AND fread()

The formats for fwrite() and fread() are identical:

```
size_t fwrite(void *ptr, size_t bytes_per_block,
    size_t number_of_blocks, FILE *fp);
size_t fread(void *ptr, size_t bytes_per_block,
    size_t number_of_blocks, FILE *fp);
```

For fwrite(), the first argument is the starting address in RAM of where we are copying from. For fread(), the first argument is the starting address in RAM of where we are copying to. In each case the pointer is of type pointer to void, so that we may use the address of any type of variable to copy from or assign to without having to use a type cast for the first argument.

These two functions write or read in blocks of bytes at a time. We specify both the number of bytes in each block and the number of such sized blocks to write or read with one call. (The type of each of these arguments, as well as that of the function's return value, is size_t, a typedef—a nickname or alias for a defined C type; see Chapter 13 for an unsigned integer type defined in stddef.h as the type of the value returned by the sizeof operator.)

For instance, if we have an array of floats, we can copy their values to a file this way:

```
float salary[5] = {437.5, 325.25, 300., 395.5, 390.};
fwrite(salary, sizeof(float), 5, fp);
```

Since salary is an array, its name is treated as equivalent to the address of its first element, &float[0]. Hence, the first argument conforms to the requirement that we pass an address. The second argument specifies 4-byte blocks (assuming float is 4 bytes) and the third argument dictates that five such 4-byte blocks be written. If we wanted to copy only element 1 to the file instead of the whole array, we would write either

```
fwrite(&salary[1], sizeof(float), 1, fp);
```

or

```
fwrite(&salary[1], 4, 1, fp);
```

The first formulation is more portable. To write the entire array, we could also have written as an alternative to the first formulation:

```
fwrite(salary, sizeof(salary), 1, fp);
```

All we are doing with an `fwrite()` call is to pass as the first argument a starting address in RAM to copy from and a number of bytes to copy—the product of the next two arguments. This process is similar to a `memcpy()` call (see Chapter 9), except here we copy to a file instead of to another RAM location.

In this process, we typically use devices such as `sizeof()` or `strlen()` to help us copy the correct number of bytes we want to copy. For example, with strings:

```
char name[25] = "Tom Peters";
char *address = "35 Park Avenue";
fwrite(name, strlen(name), 1, fp);
fwrite(address, strlen(address), 1, fp);
```

The `sizeof` operator is particularly useful in conjunction with `fwrite()` and `fread()` operations involving structures. (See Section 14.16.)

Of course, we don't have to pass the starting address of a data object. For instance,

```
fwrite(strrchr(name, ' ') + 1,
    strlen(strrchr(name, ' ') + 1), 1, fp);
```

would have the result of copying Mr. Peters's last name alone into the file. Also, since literal strings are assigned addresses, the following is permissible:

```
fwrite("Tom Peters", strlen("Tom Peters"), 1, fp);
```

Remember when we dealt with pointers in Chapter 7, we discussed how at times there are legitimate reasons in a particular application for going past the boundaries of an array but warned that this additional freedom implies added responsibility for the programmer. The same caution applies with `fwrite()` and `fread()`. Thus, the computer would be perfectly happy with

```
float salary[5] = {437.5, 325.25, 300., 395.5, 390.};
fwrite(salary, 27, 1, fp);
```

even though the likely result would be to store in the file 7 meaningless bytes from whatever happened at the time to be in memory immediately after the `salary` array.

If we later wanted to read into another array the salaries we earlier wrote to the file, we could do the following:

```
float wages[5];
fread(wages, sizeof(salary), 1, fp);
```

The process is the exact reverse of writing with `fwrite()`. We copy bytes from the file to RAM, starting at the address we pass at the first argument and proceeding byte by byte sequentially in RAM from that point for the number of bytes equal to the product of the second and third arguments.

The thing to keep in mind is that

 Whether you are writing or reading, the address argument is an address in RAM.

It has nothing to do with where in the file you read from or write to. Unless you use one of the file-positioning functions discussed below, you write or read starting at whatever position you currently are at in the file. The salary-writing and salary-reading example above assumes you repositioned between write and read calls to the same point in the file.

14.8.1 Return Value of `fread()` and `fwrite()`

The `fwrite()` and `fread()` functions return the number of blocks of designated size written or read (not the number of bytes read). However, assuming we are reading from or writing to a disk file or other device where a file position has meaning, calls to `fread()` or `fwrite()` advance the file-position indicator by the number of characters read or written, respectively.

Simply because the return value is less than the number of blocks in the call, it does not follow that a read or write error has occurred. For example, take the following simplified file-copying program.

 **Listing** **14.5 f_copy_b.c**

```
/* f_copy_b.c */

/* simple file-copying program with binary functions */

#include <stdio.h>

int main(void)
{
    FILE *original, *copy;
    int blocks;
    char temp[BUFSIZ];

    /* error-checking omitted */
    original = fopen("c:\\config.sys", "rb");
    copy = fopen("c:\\junk\\junk", "wb+");
    while((blocks = fread(temp, 1, BUFSIZ, original)) > 0)
        fwrite(temp, 1, blocks, copy);
}
```

We keep reading BUFSIZ-byte blocks at a time until we finally get to a point where there are fewer than BUFSIZ bytes remaining in the file. On that final call, fread() returns the number of bytes read, being the number of unread bytes remaining in the file. The following fwrite() statement uses this return value to write just that number of bytes in our duplicate file.

Note that we have read and written BUFSIZ "blocks" of 1 byte each with each fwrite() and fread() statement. We needed this formulation rather than one block of BUFSIZ bytes each time in order to coordinate the final pair of fread() and fwrite() statements. In other contexts, the converse formulation, with the bytes per block being greater than 1 and the number of blocks being 1 or a number greater than 1, is probably more common. This gives rise to two questions. First, you might be inclined to guess that reading or writing BUFSIZ blocks of 1 byte would be slower than reading or writing 1 block of BUFSIZ bytes. In fact, in most implementations, both functions just use the product of these two arguments in actually reading or writing. There is no difference in speed at all between the two formulations on such implementations.

Second, a question arises: What if we called fread() with 1 block of BUFSIZ bytes each call? Assuming the total number of bytes in the file is not evenly divisible by BUFSIZ, what happens on the final fread() call, where zero (for the number of blocks, not bytes, read) is returned? Have we read the final bytes in the file or not? The answer is yes.

Unfortunately, you cannot rely on the return value of fwrite() to indicate an error to the same extent as fread(). If you try to use fwrite() to write to a file that has not been opened, the call will return zero. However, if you attempt to write to a file that has been opened and closed, or write to a file opened in read mode, the call may return the number of bytes you attempted to write. A check of the file will reveal that nothing has been actually written by the call.

If either the bytes_per_block or number_of_blocks argument to fread() or fwrite() is zero (of course, this would happen as a result of passing a variable as an argument and the value of the variable at that point just happening to be zero), no characters are read or written, and zero is returned.

14.9   TEXT OR BINARY FUNCTIONS?

Now that we have covered the mechanics of both text and binary functions, we will take simple examples of reading and writing text and numerical values with each in order to determine which set of functions best suit particular applications.

Numbers first. Let's assume that your checking account balance looks like this:

```
float balance = 125829.17;
```

We could write that amount to a file in one of two ways:

```
fprintf(fp, "%.2f", balance);
```

or

```
fwrite(&balance, sizeof(float), 1, fp);
```

In the first case, with a text function, the file looks just like it would if we printed to the screen:

```
125829.17
```

The `float` value in this example takes 9 bytes to store. The output is formatted, which means the computer has to take the time to translate the numerical value into these 9 characters before writing to the file.

In the second case, writing with a binary function on a system that uses ASCII character encoding and stores most significant byte last, the file looks like this:

û$_T$⌡G

Here, `balance`, takes 4 bytes to store, assuming a `float` has 4 bytes.

Let's examine the 4 characters used to represent balance. Using Listing 13.11, `floating.c`, we can determine that the bit representation of 125829.17 in RAM is this:

```
01000111  11110101110000101001010110
```

On a byte-by-byte level, from least to most significant, we have the following values:

```
150   194   245   71
```

These decimal values correspond to the ASCII characters we showed you above:

û$_T$⌡G

Note that this method of file storage ignores how C actually treats the bit configuration in deriving a value. As we saw in Chapter 12, the division of bits in a `float` into mantissa, exponent, and sign crosses byte boundaries. But, provided we are careful to direct the placement of those 4 bytes to the address of a `float`, when we read the generated characters back with `fread()`, C will then again be able to interpret across byte boundaries and give us the correct value, 125829.17. (Note: This assumes the same character-encoding system, significant byte-first or significant byte-last order, and variable type size on both the reading and writing end. See Section 14.17.)

```
fread(&balance, sizeof(float), 1, fp);
```

Now let's take a look at a simple text example. First, we use a text function:

```
char name[15] = "Ronald Coleman";
strcpy(name, "Joe Fin");
fputs(name, fp);
```

Using `fputs()`, a text function, Figure 14.1 depicts the file.

We can read the data back this way:

```
fgets(name, fp);
```

Instead of initially writing with a text function, we could have used a binary function:

```
fwrite(name, sizeof(name), 1, fp);
```

The file would look like the one in Figure 14.2 instead of what we saw earlier.

Even though it looks to us like there are three blanks, the first blank is the space character; the second and final ones are NULL characters.

Figure 14.1 *File Contents After Writing with Text Function*

J	o	e		F	i	n

Figure 14.2 *File Contents After Writing with Binary Function*

| J | o | e | | F | i | n | | o | l | e | m | a | n | |

Why this extra garbage after Joe's name? Have we made a mistake? Not at all. We do the same thing in RAM all the time. When we first used `strcpy()` to copy "Joe Fin" into the `name` array, that array looked just like our file looks now. When we use a string-handling function like `strcpy()` or `strcat()` to copy name elsewhere, all that goes is "Joe Fin" and a terminating `NULL`.

The same thing happens when we read back the name to `name` or to another array:

```
fread(name, sizeof(name), 1, fp);
```

The `fread()` function takes the 15 bytes from the file and copies them starting at `name` (that is, `&name[0]`). The garbage after the `NULL` comes along, but the garbage is irrelevant because we use string-handling functions to ignore it after we recopy it to RAM. As we indicated before, with the binary functions, we use the file essentially as an extension of RAM.

14.9.1   Choosing a Method

 Use the text functions when you want to write text to the file, including numerical data you find more convenient to store as text.

Say that we have a series of bank customer records. Each contains a name, street address, city, state, zip code, social security number, account number, and account balance. Examine these various bits of data. Even though the zip code, social security number, and account number may consist of only numbers, the numbers have no meaning as numerical values. It makes more sense to input and store them as strings.

The account balance is different. Here, the numbers have a significance as a numerical value. However, it may prove more convenient to input and store the balance as a string too. That way we can use a single loop to input all the data fields in an entire record interactively or from a file. If we do ever need to use the account balance figure in a mathematical calculation, we can simply convert it back to a numerical value with `atof()`.

Also:

 Use text functions when portability is paramount.

The reasons are detailed in Section 14.17.

 Use the binary functions:

1. *when you want to write numerical data, as such, to a file. Here you <u>must</u> use the binary functions.*
2. *when you want to store text or text and numerical data en masse, as large data objects.*

Say you had an array of names:

```
char name[100][35];
```

Writing this array of names to a file with `fputs()` or `fprintf()` would take 100 separate computer operations—though as a programming matter accomplished in a single loop:

```
for (i = 0; i < 100; i++)
fputs(name[i], fp);
```

With `fwrite()`, the entire job can be accomplished in a single step. This speeds the program up:

```
fwrite(name, sizeof(name), 1, fp);
```

Apart from saving steps, the binary functions are quicker because they avoid character conversion of numerical values into their character equivalents. The tradeoff for enhanced speed and efficiency is squandered disk storage space and potential portability problems. Taking the `name` array example, with the text functions, each name takes up only as many bytes in the file as it has characters. With `fwrite()`, each name takes up 35 bytes. This size consideration may be partly offset by the extra number of bytes it takes to represent a number as a series of characters, particularly with floating point numbers where accuracy to the sixth or seventh decimal is important to your application. On the other hand, if the strings are subject to change, with their lengths growing and shrinking, this may be a clue that the binary function method is better in such a case.

The binary functions are particularly useful for reading and writing structures of data to and from a file. See, for example, Listing 14.13, `structfl.c`.

14.10 RANDOM ACCESS

Generally, you will write to the file successively without moving the file position, one write simply following another. When you read the data back, you will do so in the same order. This is known as *sequential access*.

In some instances, however, it will be necessary to jump about in the file, either during writing or reading or both. This is known as *random access* or direct access. In Chapter 15, we will examine in detail whether sequential access or random access is better suited to particular applications.

C has functions to facilitate file movement: `ftell()` to let you know how many bytes from the beginning of the file you happen to be and `fseek()` to let you move a specified number of bytes after the beginning, before the end, or before or after the current position in the file.

The `ftell()` and `fseek()` functions, and other file positioning functions we will cover in this chapter, such as `fgetpos()` and `fsetpos()`, are meaningful only when the file is a disk file rather than some interactive device such as a printer or monitor.

14.10.1 The `ftell()` Function

The `ftell()` function takes a single argument—the `FILE` pointer. It returns the number of bytes from the beginning of the file to the current file position, with the first byte being zero. The value returned is a `long`:

```
long ftell(FILE *stream);
```

We can use `ftell()` to demonstrate how reading or writing moves the file position.

 **Listing 14.6 position.c**

```
/* position.c */

/* writing or reading moves file position */

#include <stdio.h>

int main(void)
{
    FILE *fp;
    char address[35];

    fp = fopen("c:\\temp\\junk", "wb+");
    printf("\nfile opened wb+. Position: %ld\n", ftell(fp));
    fputc('2', fp);
    printf("fputc. Position: %ld\n", ftell(fp));
    fputs("222 North Riverside\n", fp);

    /* 21 if w+ mode */
    printf("fputs 20 chars. Position: %ld\n", ftell(fp));

    rewind(fp);
    printf("rewind. Position: %ld\n", ftell(fp));
    fgetc(fp);
```

```
        printf("fgetc. Position: %ld\n", ftell(fp));
        fgets(address, 10, fp);
        printf("fgets 10 max. Position: %ld\n", ftell(fp));
        fseek(fp, 5L, SEEK_SET);
        fputs("South", fp);

        rewind(fp);
        fgets(address, 81, fp);

        /* also note fputs does not write terminating NULL to file */
        puts(address);
        fclose(fp);
    }
```

Here is the output:

```
file opened wb+. Position: 0
fputc. Position: 1
fputs 20 chars. Position: 21
rewind. Position: 0
fgetc. Position: 1
fgets 10 max. Position: 10
2222 South Riverside
```

When the file is opened, the file position is 0. Using `fputc()` advances us to 1. Calling `fputs()` to write a 20-character string advances us to 21. Note that, as we indicated earlier, `fputs()` does not print the terminating NULL character to the file.

Rewinding the file puts us back to byte 0 (see `rewind()` discussion at the end of this section). Calling `fgetc()` advances the file position 1 just as `fputc()` does. We then use `fseek()` to move us 5 bytes from the beginning of the file, to the N in "North." We then use `fputs()` to change the address from "North" to "South," rewind the file, and use `fgets()` to copy the address into the address array and `puts()` to print it out. Observe that writing "South" to the file causes the 5 bytes at the file position to be overwritten rather than pushing the bytes aside and inserting the new bytes.

We opened the file in binary mode. The text functions we use here have no trouble working in binary mode. Typically, you will use a text mode with text functions. However, as you will see in Section 14.17, implementations are free to add, delete, or modify characters in text mode. (For example, had we opened the file in text mode on a PC, the `fputs()` call would have written 22 characters to the file, not 21: the newline would have been written as a newline-carriage return.) Therefore, the file positioning functions are not reliable in text mode—with three exceptions, discussed under Section 14.11.

While, as we indicated above, for binary files, the value returned by `ftell()` will be the number of characters preceding the current file position, for text files, the result is implementation defined.

The `ftell()` function returns –1L on error and sets the global variable `errno` to an implementation-specific positive integer value. Some possible problems in the call would be an attempt to call the function where the stream is associated with an interactive device such as the printer or screen instead of a disk file, or an attempt to report a file position that cannot be represented as a `long` (because of the file configuration or because the file is too big).

14.10.2   The `fseek()` Function

The `fseek()` function we just used has three arguments:

```
int fseek(FILE *ptr, long offset, int mode);
```

Its first argument is a FILE pointer. In the third argument, called the mode, you specify whether you want to move with reference to the beginning, end or current file position. You use a symbolic constant defined in `stdio.h` for this purpose (see Table 14.6).

The second argument, called the offset, is the number of bytes from the point specified by the mode argument to move. This argument must be a `long`. *If you use a constant instead of a variable for*

Table 14.6 `fseek()` *File Position Symbolic Constants*

Mode Symbolic Constant	Meaning
SEEK_SET	beginning of file
SEEK_CUR	current file position
SEEK_END	end of file

the offset argument, be sure to place the letter L after the integer. The offset can be zero (go to the place indicated by the mode), positive (go that number of bytes past the place indicated by the mode), or negative (go that number of bytes before the place indicated by the mode). For example:

```
fseek(fp, 0L, SEEK_END); /* go to the end of the file */
fseek(fp, -10L, SEEK_CUR); /* go 10 bytes prior to the current file position */
fseek(fp, -15L, SEEK_END); /* go to 15 bytes before the end of the file */
```

The `fseek()` function returns zero if the move was successful and a nonzero value if there is an error. The value of `errno` is not set on an unsuccessful call. You might assume that the following calls would result in errors:

```
fseek(fp, -100L, SEEK_SET); /* move before file beginning */
fseek(fp, 100L, SEEK_END); /* move past end of file */
```

But nothing prevents you from making such calls—which means you could do so inadvertently without being warned. If you attempt to write or read at those points, the behavior is undefined. For example, if you open a file, move to position 100L, write a single character, and then close the file, you might get the character you wrote plus 99 garbage characters, or equally bizarre and unpredictable behavior. Before actually reading or writing after a file-positioning call, you might consider a check of the file position.

A successful call to `fseek()` clears the end-of-file indicator and wipes out any pending `ungetc()` characters waiting in the buffer, but it does not clear any file error indicator.

The following program, `file_len.c`, uses the `ftell()` function to show us that 0L as an argument to an `fseek()` call with a final argument of SEEK_END gets us to the position immediately *after* the final byte of the file.

 Listing **14.7 file_len.c**

```
/* file_len.c */

/* illustrate file position with fseek(__, 0L, SEEK_END) */
#include <stdio.h>

int main(void)
{
    FILE *fp = fopen("c:\\temp\\junk", "wb");

    printf("file position: %ld\n", ftell(fp));
    fputs("len", fp);
    fseek(fp, 0L, SEEK_END);
    printf("file position: %ld\n", ftell(fp));
    fclose(fp);
}
```

The output:

```
file position: 0
file position: 3
```

Figure 14.3 SEEK_END's *Position in a File*

```
0        1        2        3
┌────────┬────────┬────────┐
│        │        │        │   x
└────────┴────────┴────────┘
```

Since we count from 0, the value here indicates the first position after the end of the file (see Figure 14.3).

For reasons discussed in Section 14.17, a binary stream need not meaningfully support fseek() calls with a mode of SEEK_END.

14.10.3   The rewind() Function

We can close a file and open it again in the same program. This would enable us, after having written data to the file, to go back to the beginning of the file and read the data just written. This method has the effect of switching from an output to an input mode and moving to the beginning of the file.

If the mode is to remain the same, we can go back to the beginning more quickly like this:

```
rewind(fp);
```

The rewind() function takes the FILE pointer as its only argument:

```
void rewind(FILE *stream);
```

If you have any file reading or writing error, further calls of fseek() may be ignored. The rewind() function not only moves the file position to the beginning of the file, just as fseek(fp, 0L, SEEK_SET) would, but it also clears the error indicator (fseek() clears only the end-of-file indicator). With that one difference,

```
rewind(fp);
```

is equivalent to

```
(void) fseek(fp, 0L, SEEK_SET);
```

Since such a call is guaranteed to work even for text files, the rewind() function works equally well for binary and text streams.

 Use rewind() *whenever you need to get back to the beginning of the file unless you also need to change modes. In that latter case, close the file and open it in the new mode.*

The clearerr() function also clears both the end-of-file indicator and error indicator for the stream. See Section 14.13.

14.10.4   The fgetpos() and fsetpos() Functions

One convenient way to mark your place between write or read statements so that you can return there is the combination of fgetpos() and fsetpos():

```
int fgetpos(FILE *stream, fpos_t *position);
int fsetpos(FILE *stream, const fpos_t *position);
```

Each function takes two arguments. The first is the FILE pointer. The second is the address of an object of type fpos_t to house the position in the file. The type fpos_t is a typedef defined in stdio.h. It is meant to be an object capable of recording all the information needed to specify uniquely every position in a file.

These two functions were added to Standard C to handle two situations—files too large for their positions to be representable by a long (the way ftell() and fseek() represent file position), and system file structures where file position is more complex than simply a matter of a fixed number of bytes from the beginning (for example, an offset from a record within a block).

Calling fgetpos() causes the current file position to be assigned to the location the second argument points to. The value stored there contains unspecified information usable only by fsetpos() for repositioning the file position to the same spot it was when fgetpos() was last called.

A common use of the functions would be something like this:

```
fpos_t position;
fgetpos(fp, &position); /* mark position */
fread(&record, sizeof(record), 1, fp);
fsetpos(fp, &position); /* return to position marked */
```

You could accomplish the same thing with `ftell()` and `fseek()`

```
long position;
position = ftell(fp);
fread(&record, sizeof(record), 1, fp);
fseek(fp, position, SEEK_SET);
```

but only in situations where a `long` is perfectly adequate to specify file position in all cases.

The `fgetpos()` and `fsetpos()` functions each return zero if successful; on error they return a nonzero value and set `errno` to an implementation-defined positive integer value.

As with `fseek()`, a successful call to `fsetpos()` clears the end-of-file indicator for the stream and undoes any lingering effects of previous calls to `ungetc()` for the stream; after the call, the next operation on an update stream may be either reading or writing. Likewise, the `fgetpos()`–`fsetpos()` combination works for both text and binary streams, just as the `ftell()`–`fseek()` combination does. Because of their broader nature, the `fgetpos()`–`fsetpos()` combination is more portable. However, for binary streams, as we have seen, `ftell()` and `fseek()` are usable independently from one another in certain cases to determine such things as number of characters written or read, and so on.

14.11 RANDOM ACCESS WITH TEXT MODE *(OPTIONAL)*

Generally, random access is used with binary modes. Theoretically, the random access functions are available for text modes as well. Working with random access in text mode is tricky, however. Take the following programming example.

 Listing **14.8 txt_wind.c**

```
/* txt_wind.c */

/* shows difficulty with random access in text mode */

#include <stdio.h>
#include <string.h>

int main(void)
{
    char address[35];
    FILE *fp;

    /* change next line to wb+ for different result */
    fp = fopen("c:\\temp\\junk", "w+");
    fputs("2222 South Riverside\n", fp);
    printf("file position: %ld\n", ftell(fp));
    fseek(fp, -1L * (long)strlen("South Riverside\n"), SEEK_END);
    fputs("North", fp);
    rewind(fp);
    puts(fgets(address, sizeof(address), fp));
    fclose(fp);
}
```

Here's the output we get on a PC:

```
file position: 22
2222 SNorthRiverside
```

On the other hand, if we open the same file in wb+ mode, we get this output:

```
file position: 21
2222 North Riverside
```

Running the program in the DOS environment causes transformation of the newline into a combination carriage return–newline when we open the file in text mode and use a text function to write to the file. We neglected to take that into account when we moved the file position. This concern did not arise when we opened the file in binary mode. (See Section 14.17 for a more complete discussion of problems with both text and binary files.)

The latitude given implementations to add and delete characters in a text stream (again, see Section 14.17) makes using file-position placement and reading functions unreliable—if you need an accurate byte count of where you are in the file or how many characters have been read or written between calls to file-positioning functions. Furthermore, a position within a text file may not correspond directly to the file's internal representation. For instance, a text file on a particular system may be structured into blocks and records within the blocks; getting to a particular point may require the block and record number, as well as an offset from the record start. Packing all that information into a long may not be possible. Likewise, on some systems, a file may be larger than the largest possible value representable by a long.

There are some uses for ftell() and fseek() in text mode, however. For one thing, the file-position indicator returned by a call to ftell() would later be usable by fseek() for returning the file-position indicator to its position at the time of an earlier call to ftell() (even though you could not depend on the difference between the return values of two calls to ftell() to indicate how many characters were written, for instance). Also, a call to fseek() with an offset of 0L will work if the mode argument is SEEK_SET or SEEK_END—that is, you can get to the beginning or end of the file (the latter is not guaranteed with binary mode; see Section 14.17).

The first exception above is fairly narrow. You cannot depend on the value of ftell() being usable for calls to fseek() beyond the current execution of the program or even from one file opening to another during the same program execution. You cannot save the value returned by ftell(), close the file, go on about some other business in the program, and then reopen the file and be sure that fseek() will get you to the same spot earlier reported by ftell().

14.12 BUFFER FLUSHING IN UPDATE MODES

The r+, w+, and a+ modes are sometimes referred to as ***update modes***. They allow for both reading and writing to a file. Writing data when there is already data at the file position overwrites data to the extent of the data written rather than pushing the existing data aside and inserting the new data.

Care must be taken when switching from reading to writing or vice versa, for a particular file.

 The buffer for the file must be flushed between read and write calls to the same file.

This is so whether you use the binary functions or the text functions.

As we indicated above, reading and writing take place between the reading and writing functions and a buffer associated with each file. Data transfer between the file and its buffer takes place only when the buffer is flushed. A file's buffer is flushed only when it is full, when a file is closed, when you change position in the file, or when you call a special buffer-flushing function.

If we make successive data reads with a file, we will read from the buffer until there is no more data in the buffer. At that point, another BUFSIZ bytes' worth of data will be transmitted from the file into the file's buffer, even if we read only a single byte, as the following program shows.

 **Listing 14.9 buf_fill.c**

```
/* buf_fill.c */

/* shows how buffer can be filled completely by reading
   a single character */
```

```
   #include <stdio.h>
   #include <string.h> /* memset() */

   int main(void)
   {
      FILE *fp;

      fp = fopen("c:\\config.sys", "r");
      memset(fp->buffer, 1, BUFSIZ); /* fill buffer with happy faces */
      fp->buffer[BUFSIZ] = 0; /* close off "string" */
      printf("%s\n", fp->buffer);
      fgetc(fp);
      printf("%s\n", fp->buffer);
      fclose(fp);
   }
```

We first open the config.sys file. We replace any garbage in the file's buffer (BUFSIZ is defined in stdio.h—512 on the PC) with the happy-face character by calling memset(). (We do this for illustration purposes only. The FILE pointer variable members are implementation specific. We used Borland C's. Also, using the members directly in any way is considered undefined behavior in Standard C.) Then we read a single character. By comparing the output of the buffer printing just after the memset() call with output after reading a single character, you will see that the entire file is read in even though we have asked for only a single character to be read from the file. First printf():

```
☺☺☺☺☺☺☺☺☺☺☺☺☺☺☺☺☺☺☺☺☺☺☺☺☺☺☺☺☺☺☺☺☺☺☺☺
☺☺☺☺☺☺☺☺☺☺☺☺☺☺☺☺☺☺☺☺☺☺☺☺☺☺☺☺☺☺☺☺☺☺☺☺
☺☺☺☺☺☺☺☺☺☺☺☺☺☺☺☺☺☺☺☺☺☺☺☺☺☺☺☺☺☺☺☺☺☺☺☺
☺☺☺☺☺☺☺☺☺☺☺☺☺☺☺☺☺☺☺☺☺☺☺☺☺☺☺☺☺☺☺☺☺☺☺☺
☺☺☺☺☺☺☺☺☺☺☺☺☺☺☺☺☺☺☺☺☺☺☺☺☺☺☺☺☺☺☺☺☺☺☺☺
☺☺☺☺☺☺☺☺☺☺☺☺☺☺☺☺☺☺☺☺☺☺☺☺☺☺☺☺☺☺☺☺☺☺☺☺
☺☺☺☺☺☺☺☺☺☺☺☺☺☺☺☺☺☺☺☺☺☺☺☺☺☺☺☺☺☺☺☺☺☺☺☺
☺☺☺☺☺☺☺☺☺☺☺☺☺☺☺☺☺☺☺☺☺☺☺☺☺☺☺☺☺☺☺☺☺☺☺☺
☺☺☺☺☺☺☺☺☺☺☺☺☺☺☺☺☺☺☺☺☺☺☺☺☺☺☺☺☺☺☺☺☺☺☺☺
☺☺☺☺☺☺☺☺☺☺☺☺☺☺☺☺☺☺☺☺☺☺☺☺☺☺☺☺☺☺☺☺☺☺☺☺
☺☺☺☺☺☺☺☺☺☺☺☺☺☺☺☺☺☺☺☺☺☺☺☺☺☺☺☺☺☺☺☺☺☺☺☺
☺☺☺☺☺☺☺☺☺☺☺☺☺☺☺☺☺☺☺☺☺☺☺☺☺☺☺☺☺☺☺☺☺☺☺☺
☺☺☺☺☺☺☺☺☺☺☺☺☺☺☺☺☺☺☺☺☺☺☺☺☺☺☺☺☺☺☺☺☺☺☺☺
☺☺☺☺☺☺
```

Second printf():

```
DEVICE=C:\DOS\HIMEM.SYS
DEVICE=C:\DOS\EMM386.EXE 2880 RAM
DOS=HIGH,UMB
DEVICEHIGH=C:\DOS\ANSI.SYS /x /l
DEVICEHIGH=C:\DOS\SETVER.EXE
BUFFERS=30
FILES=20
SHELL=C:\DOS\COMMAND.COM C:\DOS\  /p
☺☺☺☺☺☺☺☺☺☺☺☺☺☺☺☺☺☺☺☺☺☺☺☺☺☺☺☺☺☺☺☺☺☺
☺☺☺☺☺☺☺☺☺☺☺☺☺☺☺☺☺☺☺☺☺☺☺☺☺☺☺☺☺☺☺☺☺☺
☺☺☺☺☺☺☺☺☺☺☺☺☺☺☺☺☺☺☺☺☺☺☺☺☺☺☺☺☺☺☺☺☺☺
☺☺☺☺☺☺☺☺☺☺☺☺☺☺☺☺☺☺☺☺☺☺☺☺☺☺☺☺☺☺☺☺☺☺
☺☺☺☺☺☺☺☺☺☺☺☺☺☺☺☺☺☺☺☺☺☺☺☺☺☺☺☺☺☺☺☺☺☺
☺☺☺☺☺☺☺☺☺☺☺☺☺☺☺☺☺☺☺☺☺☺☺☺☺☺☺☺☺☺☺☺☺☺
☺☺☺☺☺☺☺☺☺☺☺☺☺☺☺☺☺☺☺☺☺☺☺☺☺☺☺☺☺☺☺☺☺☺
☺☺☺☺☺☺☺☺☺☺☺☺☺☺☺☺☺☺☺☺☺☺☺☺☺☺☺☺☺☺☺☺☺☺
☺☺☺☺☺☺☺☺☺☺☺☺☺☺☺☺☺☺☺☺☺☺☺☺☺☺
```

If we write data and then read, we may read not from the file but from the data just written into the buffer. The result is that the written data is lost and the data read is incorrect. Flushing the file's buffer avoids any such problem. (On the other hand, since each file has its own buffer, no flushing need be done between read calls from one file and write calls to another.)

One way to flush the buffer expressly is to call `fflush()` with the name of the `FILE` pointer as the argument:

```
fflush(fp);
```

The `fflush()` function returns zero on success and `EOF` on error:

```
int fflush(FILE *stream);
```

To flush the buffers for all files, call

```
fflush(NULL);
```

The flushing of all buffered files includes the standard files automatically established at the commencement of the program.

 Another way to flush the buffers is to call one of the file positioning functions, `fsetpos()`, `fseek()`, *or* `rewind()`. *After calls to any of these functions for a stream, the next data transfer operation for the stream can be either read or write.*

14.13   DEALING WITH I/O ERRORS:
`clearerr()`, `feof()`, `ferror()`

Once you have an error in calling an I/O function for a particular stream, and as a consequence, the error indicator for the stream is set, further stream operations will continue to fail and return their appropriate error status value until the error indicator is cleared. That is so even if the cause of the error has been cured. For instance, if a read error is caused by an open floppy disk drive, a subsequent attempt to read from the file without clearing the error indicator for the file will not work even if the drive has been properly closed in the interim.

We have already seen one way to clear the error indicator—with a call to `rewind()`. Closing a file will also clear the error indicator, so if you open it again, you start with a clean slate.

You can explicitly clear the error indicator with `clearerr()`:

```
void clearerr(FILE *stream);
```

This function clears both the error indicator for a stream and its end-of-file indicator.

Attempting to read at the end of the file, and consequently having the end-of-file indicator for the file set, will prevent further read operations but not further write operations. You can clear the end-of-file indicator with a call to `fseek()` or `fsetpos()`, as well as `clearerr()`.

In many cases, it will not be clear whether an abnormal return value indicates the end of the file has been reached or whether some other error has occurred. For instance, an unsuccessful call to `fgetc()` or `fputc()` will return `EOF` whether the stream is at its end or there is some other cause for the error. Likewise, `fread()` returns a zero and `fgets()` returns `NULL` if an error occurs, whether the cause of the error is having reached the end of the file already, attempting to read from a file opened for writing only, or some other error.

In other cases, the error status return value will also be a legitimate return value for a successful call (albeit in an unusual case). For example, `ftell()` returns a –1L if an error has occurred in the call. However, a return value of –1L could be a legitimate return value for `ftell()`, since a –1L position in a file is a valid (though unusual) file position.

If you are interested in ascertaining the precise cause for an error in calling a library function, the simplest method is to use `perror()`. The `perror()` function allows us to automatically print to `stderr` (generally, the screen) the implementation-defined `sys_errlist` string corresponding to the current value of `errno`. The `perror()` function takes a single argument, a pointer to `char`. What gets printed to the screen is the string we pass as an argument (which can be a blank string), a colon, a space, the `sys_errlist` string corresponding to the current value of `errno`, and finally, a newline. See Chapter 16 for a more complete explanation and examples.

There are two functions specifically designed to test for end of the file and other errors in file operations. Each takes as its only argument the FILE pointer for the stream:

```
int feof(FILE *stream);
int ferror(FILE *stream);
```

Headers for these functions are found in stdio.h.

The feof() function tests whether the end-of-file indicator for the stream is on, returning an nonzero integer if it is and zero if it is not. The end-of-file indicator will not be set simply because the end of the file has been reached and no characters remain to be read, unless there is an attempt to read at that point. For instance, if you open a 10-byte file and read 10 bytes, the end-of-file indicator will not be set. If you now attempt to read another, it will be.

The ferror() function tests whether the error indicator is set, also returning a nonzero integer if it is and zero if it not:

```
while(fgets(line, 81, readfile) != NULL)
    fputs(line, readfile);
if (feof(readfile) != 0)
    puts("End of the file reached");
else if (ferror(readfile) != 0)
{
    perror("Error reading file");
    clearerr(readfile);
}
```

These two functions are also sometimes defined as macros in stdio.h as well—something along these lines:

```
#define ferror(fp) ((fp)->flags & _F_ERR)
#define feof(fp) ((fp)->flags & _F_EOF)
```

14.14 AN UPDATE TRICK (OPTIONAL)

Say a particular file contains a series of records. We want to read each record and, depending on the record's contents, possibly alter the record.

The usual way of accomplishing this task would be to open the file in a r+ or rb+ mode. After each read, we would examine the relevant portion of the record and, if necessary, back up in the file to where we recently started reading and writing.

We can do the same job faster by opening the file twice at the same time—once in r or rb mode and once in r+ or rb+ mode. We can use the FILE pointer associated with the read mode-opened file to read and the FILE pointer associated with the read and write mode–opened file to write.

As long as we alternate reading and writing, we don't have to worry about repositioning the file position. Each of the FILE pointers would have its own separate file position. Also, each would have its own buffer. That being so, we would not have to worry about buffer flushing between reading and writing: one buffer is used only for reading and the other only for writing.

Here's a program that compares the two methods, fopen_2.c. The program is designed to convert every lowercase character in the file to uppercase.

Note that this simultaneous file-opening application is not necessarily portable. A file can be opened in one mode and closed and then opened again in a different mode during the same program. However, Standard C specifically provides that "whether the same file can be simultaneously opened multiple times is also implementation-defined."

 **Listing**   **14.10 fopen_2.c**

```
/* fopen_2.c */

/* opening file already opened */

#include <stdio.h>
```

```
#include <ctype.h> /* toupper */

int main(void)
{
   FILE *one, *two;
   long size;
   unsigned char ch;

   if (!(one = fopen("c:\\temp\\junk.txt", "rb+")))
      printf("error opening file with one");;

   /* no error opening file twice in different modes */
   if (!(two = fopen("c:\\temp\\junk.txt", "rb")))
      printf("error opening file with two");

   /* determine number of bytes in file:
      move to end and call ftell */
   fseek(one, 0L, SEEK_END);
   size = ftell(one);
   rewind(one);
   while(size--)
   {
      /* read in one stream and write in the other */
      fread(&ch, 1, 1, two);
      if (ch >= 'a' && ch <= 'z')
      ch = toupper(ch);
      fwrite(&ch, 1, 1, one);
   }

   /* compare to normal method */
   one = fopen("c:\\temp\\trash.txt", "rb+");
   fseek(one, 0L, SEEK_END);
   size = ftell(one);
   rewind(one);
   while(size--)
   {
      fread(&ch, 1, 1, one);
      if (ch >= 'a' && ch <= 'z')
      {
         ch = toupper(ch);

         /* back up one byte and write */
         fseek(one, -1L, SEEK_CUR);
         fwrite(&ch, 1, 1, one);

         /* call fseek to clear buffer */
         fseek(one, 0L, SEEK_CUR);
      }
   }
}
```

We copied a text file containing 1,522,252 bytes to our two test files. In each case, we ascertained the file length by calling fseek() with a 0L offset from SEEK_END and then calling ftell(). The double file-opening method took 3.68 seconds on our machine; the traditional method took 56.57 seconds—more than 15 times longer. There were 770,239 characters converted to uppercase.

   This double file-opening method is nonstandard usage. Check it carefully on your particular implementation before using it.

Table 14.7 `setvbuf()` *Buffering Modes*

Mode Symbolic Constant	Meaning
`_IOFBF`	fully buffered
`_IOLBF`	line buffered
`_IONBF`	no buffering

14.15   MANIPULATING FILE BUFFERS—`setvbuf()` *(OPTIONAL)*

Clearly the biggest bottleneck in your computer system is disk I/O. Disk I/O is many times slower than CPU processing. It is, therefore, important in many cases to make every effort to minimize the time spent transferring data to and from the disk.

By default, when you open a file with `fopen()`, a `BUFSIZ`-byte buffer is established for data transfers to and from the file. If your program deals with large data objects, you can profitably decrease the time spent on disk I/O by increasing the buffer size. If, for instance, you have records consisting of 1000 bytes each, stored in a structure, you might increase the buffer size to 1000, or even some multiple of 1000.

You increase (or, if you prefer instead, decrease) buffer size for a particular file by calling `setvbuf()`. The prototype for `setvbuf()` is as follows:

```
int setvbuf(FILE *file_pointer, char *buffer,
  int mode, size_t size);
```

The first argument is the typical `FILE` pointer. The second argument can cause some confusion. If you call `setvbuf()` with a second argument of `NULL`, the function assigns the file a buffer on its own through `malloc()`. (See Chapter 15 for a discussion of `malloc()`. As with the standard default file buffer, this buffer is automatically freed on closing the file; you do not have to make an explicit call to `free()`.) Otherwise, you pass the address of a buffer you establish yourself—by, for example, declaring a local or global `char` array or with a `char` pointer and `malloc()`. (See Chapter 15 for this latter method.)

The third argument establishes the type of buffering you want, either fully buffered, line-buffered, or no buffering at all. As with `fseek()`, you use a symbolic constant defined in `stdio.h` for this purpose (see Table 14.7).

Line buffering works the same way as full buffering on input: when the buffer is empty, the next input operation will cause the buffer to be completely filled to the extent data remains in the file. However, on output, a line-buffered buffer will be flushed whenever a newline character is written to the file.

As to the implicitly opened streams, the standard error stream is not fully buffered, and the standard input and output streams are fully buffered if and only if the stream can be determined to refer to a true file rather than, as it generally would be, an interactive device such as a keyboard or screen.

The final argument is the buffer size. The size may not exceed `size_t`, the unsigned integer type that is the result of the `sizeof` operator and that is defined in `stddef.h`.

 You must call `setvbuf()` **immediately after opening the file.**

To test the effect of `setvbuf()` on performance, we revised the file-copying program shown earlier in Listing 14.5, `f_copy_b.c`, to include `setvbuf()` calls for both original and copy files. Here was our basic test program.

 **14.11 f_speed.c**

```
/* f_speed.c */

/* increase speed of file copying with setvbuf */

#include <stdio.h>
```

```
#define MULT 48 /* 2 then 10, then 40 then 48 */

int main(void)
{
    FILE *original, *copy;
    int blocks;
    char temp[BUFSIZ * MULT];
    unsigned big_buf = BUFSIZ * MULT;

    original = fopen("c:\\atlas5\\nameshap.dat", "rb");
    setvbuf(original, NULL, _IOFBF, big_buf);
    copy = fopen("c:\\temp\\trash", "wb+");
    setvbuf(copy, NULL, _IOFBF, big_buf);
    while((blocks = fread(temp, 1, big_buf, original)) > 0)
        fwrite(temp, 1, blocks, copy);
}
```

We ran each program with a 11,261,553-byte file. The f_copy_b.exe program, with the default buffers of 512 bytes, took 2.97 seconds.

Doubling the buffer size in f_speed.c cut the time almost in half: 1.65 seconds. We then increased MULT to increase the buffer size and reran the program. Buffer sizes of 5K took 1.10 seconds and buffer sizes of 24K took 0.82 seconds—less than a third the default buffer size run time. On a PC, to increase the buffers much more, we might have to switch to a larger memory model, and that would cost us more time than we would save. (See Appendix B.)

14.15.1   The setbuf() Function

A function somewhat related to setvbuf() is setbuf(). As you have seen, setvbuf() allows you to customize the buffer allocated automatically to files you open by altering its size or its type. The setbuf() function is more limited. It allows you to set up your own buffer of BUFSIZ bytes and have the file you open use that buffer instead of the one created automatically by opening the file.

The setbuf() function takes two arguments: the FILE pointer and a pointer to the buffer you have set up:

```
void setbuf(FILE *file_pointer, char *buffer);
```

The call to setbuf() must take place immediately after opening the file or after a call to fseek(). You may not alter the size of the buffer, nor may you alter its type, as you can with setvbuf().

Except that it returns no value, a call to setbuf() is equivalent to invoking setvbuf() with _IOFBF for the mode argument (or if the buffer argument to setvbuf() is NULL, with _IONBF) and BUFSIZ for the size argument.

You can use setbuf() to make buffered a file that is normally unbuffered. For example, you can use setbuf() to make stdout, which is otherwise unbuffered, buffered. If you step through the following program, you will see that nothing gets to the screen until the buffer is explicitly flushed.

 **Listing   14.12 setbuf.c**

```
/* setbuf.c */

/* change stdout from unbuffered to buffered */

#include <stdio.h>

int main(void)
{
    static char my_buffer[BUFSIZ];
    char name[35] = "Joe Jones";
    char address[35] = "111 Main Street";
    char city[20] = "Chicago";
```

```
        char state[3] = "IL";
        char zip[6] = "60611";

        setbuf(stdout, my_buffer);
        puts(name);
        puts(address);
        puts(city);
        puts(state);
        puts(zip);
        fflush(stdout);
    }
```

Any intervening use of `stdin` will flush the buffer also.

Conversely, you can use `setbuf()` to turn off the buffering for a file. You call `setbuf()` with `NULL` as the second argument:

```
setbuf(fp, NULL);
```

14.16   APPLICATION: READING AND WRITING RECORDS

The following listing, `structfl.c`, allows the user to add, retrieve, and edit records stored in a database file. The user can also print out the records, either to the screen, to the printer, or to a user-specified file.

 **Listing   14.13 structfl.c**

```
/* structfl.c */

/* save/retrieve/add/edit recs from file with
   structures & binary functions */

#include <stdio.h>
#include <stdlib.h> /* exit */
#include <conio.h> /* getch */
#include <string.h> /* strcmp */
#include <ctype.h> /* toupper */

#define MAXRECS 100

struct worker
{
    char name[22];
    char address[22];
    char city[15];
    char state[3];
    char zip[6];
};

char *ltd_gets(char *str, int length);
char menu(void);
char select_mode(void);
void suspend(void);
char enter_record(struct worker *ptr);
void print_rec(FILE *file, struct worker *wptr, int record, char *carriage_rtn);

int main(void)
{
    static struct worker employee[MAXRECS];
    struct worker *sptr, temp;
    int recnum = 0, oldrecs = 0;
```

```
   int rec_selected;
   int rec_count; /* counter for record printing purposes */
   int size = sizeof(struct worker);
   int print_it = 0;
   char record_choice; /* print old, new or all recs; add or edit rec; quit */
   char print_mode; /* print to screen, printer or file */
   char db_file[] = "c:\\temp\\junk";
   char filename[FILENAME_MAX];
   char junk[10];
   char newline[3] = "\n"; /* \r\n for printer */
   FILE *fp, *copyfile;

   /* see whether there already is a database file; if so, open it,
      and print current database to screen
   */

   if ((fp = fopen(db_file, "rb+")) != 0)
   {
      puts("Current database list\n");
      printf("#   %22s %22s %15s %5s %6s\n\n", "Name", "Address", "City", "State", "Zip");
      while((recnum < MAXRECS) &&
          (fread(&employee[recnum], size, 1, fp) == 1))
      {
         print_rec(stdout, &employee[recnum], recnum, "\n");


         /* print a screen's worth at a time */
         if (++recnum % 20 == 0)
            suspend(); /* halt every 20 lines so user can view */
      }

      suspend();

      /* record original # of records: recnum is now actual #,
         not 0-based */
      oldrecs = recnum;
   }

   /* if no database file already exists, create one */
   else if (!(fp = fopen(db_file, "wb+")))
   {
      printf("Error: unable to open %s\n", db_file);
      exit(2);
   }

   /* print, add, edit or quit */
   while((record_choice = menu()) != 'Q') /* get user menu choice */
   {
      switch(record_choice)
      {
         case 0: /* invalid selection */
            puts("You must type O or N or B or A or E or Q");
            break;

         case 'A': /* add selected */
            if (++recnum == MAXRECS)
            {
               puts("\n\n\t\tDatabase file is full\n\n\n");
               recnum--;
               break;
            }
            if (enter_record(&employee[recnum]) == 0)
```

```
            {
                puts("\nNo record entered");
                recnum--;
                break;
            }

            /* to end of file to add records */
            fseek(fp, 0L, SEEK_END);
            fwrite(&employee[recnum], size, 1, fp);
            break;

    case 'E': /* edit selected */
        if (!recnum)
        {
            puts("\n\n\t\tNo records in database\n\n\n");
            break;
        }
        puts("Specify record number");
        rec_selected = atoi(ltd_gets(junk, sizeof(junk)));
        if (rec_selected < 1 || rec_selected > recnum)
        {
            puts("\n\n\tIncorrect record number\n\n\n");
            break;
        }
        rec_selected--; /* turn into 0-based number */
        sptr = &employee[rec_selected];

        /* show current contents of record before ask to edit */
        print_rec(stdout, sptr, rec_selected, "\n");
        puts("Edit record");

        /* overstore new record in RAM */
        if (enter_record(sptr) == 0)
            break;

        /* get to file position where this record is */
        fseek(fp, (long)(size * rec_selected), SEEK_SET);
        fwrite(sptr, size, 1, fp); /* write new rec over old */
        print_rec(stdout, sptr,
            rec_selected, "\n"); /* new rec to screen */
        break;

        /* print to screen, printer or file selected */
    case 'O': /* old only */
    case 'N': /* new only */
    case 'B': /* both old and new */

        print_it = 1;

        /* if new records only, get to file position
           where they start */
        if (record_choice == 'N' && oldrecs == recnum)
        {
            puts("\n\n\t\tNo new records entered\n\n\n");
            break;
        }

        if (record_choice == 'O' && !oldrecs)
        {
            puts("\n\n\t\tNo old records\n\n\n");
            break;
        }
```

```
      if (!recnum)
      {
         puts("\n\n\t\tNo records in database\n\n\n");
         break;
      }

      /* select where to print */
      switch (print_mode = select_mode())
      {  /* if file selected, specify and open file */
         case 'F': /* print to file */
            puts("\nSpecify filename, using full path");
            ltd_gets(filename, sizeof(filename));
            if (!(copyfile = fopen(filename, "wb")))
            {
               printf("Error: unable to open %s\n", filename);
               exit(3);
            }
            break;
         case 'S': /* print to screen */
            copyfile = stdout;
            strcpy(newline, "\n");
            break;
         case 'P': /* print to printer */
            copyfile = stdprn;
            strcpy(newline, "\r\n");
            break;
         default:
            puts("\n\n\tYou must type S or P or F\n\n\n");
            print_it = 0;
            break;
      }

      if (print_it == 0)
         break;

      /* new records selected: locate first new record */
      if (record_choice == 'N')
      {
         fseek(fp, (long)(size * oldrecs), SEEK_SET);
         rec_count = oldrecs;
      }
      else /* all or old recs selected: */
      {        /*go to file/record beginning */
         rewind(fp);
         rec_count = 0;
      }

      /* unless printing to file, say what's about to print */
      if (print_mode != 'F')
         fprintf(copyfile, "%sDatabase list: %s records%s%s", newline,
         record_choice == 'B' ? "all" : record_choice == 'N' ? "new" : "old", newline,
         newline);

      /* now print a record at a time */
      while(fread(&temp, size,
         1, fp)) /* each read moves file location */
      {
         sptr = &temp;

         switch (print_mode)
         {
            case 'F': /* to file */
               fwrite(&temp, size, 1, copyfile);
```

```
                                    break;
                                case 'S': /* to screen */
                                    if (print_mode == 'S' && (rec_count % 20 == 0))
                                        suspend(); /* note: no break here */
                                case 'P': /* to printer */
                                    print_rec(copyfile, sptr, rec_count++,
                                    newline);
                                    break;
                        }

                        /* if just old records selected, stop when get to end of them */
                        if (record_choice == 'O' && rec_count > oldrecs)
                            break;
                }

                /* eject page if to printer; pause for viewing if to screen */
                if (print_mode == 'P')
                    fputc('\f', stdprn);
                else if (print_mode == 'S')
                    suspend();

                break; /* end print to screen/file/printer menu choice */
        } /* end switch record_choice*/
    } /* end while loop for menu choices */
    return 0;
}

char enter_record(struct worker *ptr)
{
    puts("Enter name");

    /* return 0 if no name entered */
    if (!(strcmp(ltd_gets(ptr->name, sizeof(ptr->name)), "")))
        return 0;
    puts("Enter address");
    ltd_gets(ptr->address, sizeof(ptr->address));
    puts("Enter city");
    ltd_gets(ptr->city, sizeof(ptr->city));
    puts("Enter state (2-letter code)");
    ltd_gets(ptr->state, sizeof(ptr->state));
    puts("Enter zip (5-digit code)");
    ltd_gets(ptr->zip, sizeof(ptr->zip));
    return 1;
}

char *ltd_gets(char *str, int length)
{
    /* get input, cut off excess & capitalize string */
    char big_str[128];
    char *ptr = big_str;

    gets(big_str);
    big_str[length - 1] = 0; /* cut off excess input, if any */
    while (*ptr)
    {
        *ptr = toupper(*ptr);
        ptr++;
    }
    strcpy(str, big_str);
    return str;
}

char menu(void)
```

```
{
   /* choose which records to print or add or edit or quit */
   static char choice[15];

   puts("\nPrint old records only (O)");
   puts("Print new records only (N)");
   puts("Print all records (B)");
   puts("Add a record (A)");
   puts("Edit a record (E)");
   puts("Quit (Q)");
   printf("\n\tSelection: ");
   ltd_gets(choice, sizeof(choice));
   *choice = toupper(*choice);
   if (*choice != 'O' && *choice != 'N' && *choice != 'B' &&
      *choice != 'A' && *choice != 'E' && *choice != 'Q')
      return 0;
   return *choice;
}


void print_rec(FILE *file, struct worker *wptr, int record,
   char *carriage_rtn)
{
   fprintf(file, "%3d%22s%22s%15s%3s%6s%s", record + 1, wptr->name, wptr->address, wptr->city,
      wptr->state, wptr->zip, carriage_rtn);
}


char select_mode(void)
{
   /* select printing to printer, screen or file */
   static char choice[15];

   puts("\nPrint to screen (S)");
   puts("Print to printer (P)");
   puts("Print to file (F)");
   ltd_gets(choice, sizeof(choice));
   *choice = toupper(*choice);
   if (*choice != 'S' && *choice != 'P' && *choice != 'F')
      return 0;
   return *choice;
}


void suspend(void)
{
   /* give user message and halt program until user presses key */
   puts("Press any key to continue");
   if (!getch())
      getch();

   /* Non-DOS version:

      puts("Press Enter key to continue");
      getchar();

   */
}
```

The first step is to print the current database records to the screen. If the file exists, we read the records one by one and print them to the screen. We read the records from the file into an array of structures, `struct worker employee[MAXRECS]`. As you will see, when the records were originally added to the file, they were written a structure at a time. We read them back a structure at a time:

```
fread(&employee[recnum], size, 1, fp)
```

We have made `size` equal to `sizeof(struct worker)` so that we can use this shorter formulation throughout the code. Thus, here we read one structure array element at a time. Since `fread()` returns the number of byte blocks read, the `while` loop that incorporates this `fread()` call will automatically stop when the end of the file is reached and there are no more records to read.

As we read the records into our structure array, we also write to the screen. We set a structure pointer to the current structure array element to simplify the `printf()` statement that writes to the screen.

So that the user can view a screen's worth of records at a time, we pause the program after each set of 20 records has been written to the screen:

```
if (++recnum % 20 == 0)
suspend();
```

The `suspend()` function asks the user to press a key and then waits until a key is pressed by calling `getch()`. The formulation

```
if(!getch())
getch();
```

is written to gobble up the second byte in case the user presses one of the special keys (such as a function key or an arrow key) that generate two bytes, the first of which is a zero byte (see Appendix A). On a non-PC system, use `getchar()` and ask the user to press Enter instead.

When the file is opened, the file position is set to the start of the file. Thus, there is no need to call `rewind()` to make sure we are starting our reading with the first record.

If, on the other hand, the database file doesn't exist, we create it by opening the file in `wb+` mode rather than `rb+` mode.

The balance of `main()` consists of a `while` loop where the user is repeatedly given a menu of choices: print records (old, new, or all records), edit a record, add a record, or quit. Selecting the quit option terminates the loop and the program. If the user fails to select one of the given choices, the `menu()` function, where the choices are presented and processed, returns a zero and `menu()` is called again.

14.16.1 Adding a Record

If the user wishes to add a record, we must position ourselves in the file after the last record. Rather than worrying about how many records there now are, we simply call

```
fseek(fp, 0L, SEEK_END);
```

and place ourselves at the very end of the file.

We then call `enter_record()`. We pass the address of the next structure array element, having kept track of the number of records initially in the file as we read them on entering the program, and having incremented each time a record is added. For each structure member, we issue the appropriate prompt and then call `ltd_gets()` to fill the structure member.

14.16.2 Avoiding String Input Overflow

We use our own function rather than simply using `gets()` to avoid overflowing the structure member with input greater than its array size will allow. Only after we have called `gets()`, stored the user response in a large buffer area, and cut off any excess input with an appropriately placed `NULL` character do we copy the response into the structure member.

We could have tried to tackle this problem instead with `fgets()`, using the size of the structure member array as the second argument and `stdin` as the `FILE` pointer. There would be two problems with that approach, however. In the first place, we would have to eliminate the newline character `fgets()` retains if it has room. That would not be difficult to accomplish. But the thornier problem is that if there is input that would exceed the structure member's array boundaries and we stop short by virtue of `fgets()` stopping at the earlier of the newline or one character less than the maximum specified in the second argument, the excess is still in the input stream. Thus, for instance, the last part of an overly long name input would be read into the address member.

Once the structure member is filled, we write it to the file:

```
fwrite(&employee[recnum], size, 1, fp);
```

14.16.3   Editing a Record

The edit-a-record choice works much like adding a record. The user designates a record number. We use this record number to print the record to the screen with `printf()`, having first set a pointer to the structure in memory. We call the same `enter_record()` function, this time passing a pointer to a previously filled structure array element for overstorage.

When we were adding a record, we just moved to the end of the file. Here, before we write to the file, we need to move to the beginning of the relevant record's location in the file:

```
fseek(fp, (long)(size * rec_selected), SEEK_SET);
```

Since `rec_selected` is the record number and `size` is the size in bytes of each record, this call positions us just where we want to be.

14.16.4   Printing Records

After we ask the user to indicate whether old, newly added, or all records are to be printed out, and we have verified that the designated choice makes sense (for example, if the newly added records choice is selected, there actually are such records), we position ourselves at the appropriate place in the file, preparatory to reading.

We then ask the user to select the print mode: to the screen, to the printer, or to a file. If the user wants print done to a file, the user then specifies the filename and we open that file for writing. If printing is to be to the screen or to the printer, we set our `FILE` pointer to the appropriate stream, `stdin` or `stdprn`, by simple assignment statement. For example:

```
case 'P':
   copyfile = stdprn;
   strcpy(newline, "\r\n");
```

The newline concept, with combination carriage return–newline character (\r\n or \n\r), may be necessary for printing to the printer. Otherwise, some printers, when encountering a newline alone, will move to the next line without also returning to the left margin, thus printing off the page in Never-Never Land (albeit one line down).

If printing to a file is specified, the user enters the filename interactively. The array that holds the filename is sized to `FILENAME_MAX`, required by Standard C to be defined in `stdio.h` to be whatever size is needed for an array of `char` large enough to hold the longest filename string that the implementation guarantees to be opened.

14.17   PORTABILITY ISSUES

Nearly every operating system distinguishes between binary and text files and treats them differently. As we have taken pains to point out earlier in this chapter, for example, on the PC, we can use the same functions to write to either binary or text files. But for text files, DOS converts the newline that terminates each line to a combination carriage return–newline. When DOS reads back in a text file, it must drop the carriage return portion of these combinations. Conventions for handling line terminations in text files vary widely among different operating systems.

Furthermore, different systems treat certain characters differently in a text file. Standard C permits implementations to add, alter, or delete characters on input and output to conform to system conventions for representing text. As with DOS's combination carriage return–newline, there need not be a one-to-one correspondence between the characters in a text stream and an external representation of them. A [Ctrl] [X] may be interpreted as the end of the file; a formfeed character or a vertical tab character may get gobbled up or converted to something weird; and so on.

Standard C guarantees that data read in from a text stream will be the same as data earlier written out to that stream only if the data consists of the printable characters

```
! " # $ % & ' ( ) * + , - . / 0 1 2 3 4 5 6 7 8 9 : ; < = > ? @ A B C D
E F G H I J K L M N O P Q R S T U V W X Y Z [ \ ] ^ _ ` a b c d e f g h
i j k l m n o p q r s t u v w x y z { ¦ } ~
```

horizontal tab character, and newline character. That eliminates the formfeed character and all other control characters but the two just named, as well as anything with a numerical encoding value beyond 127.

Some systems have trouble with a last line in a file that does not terminate in a newline character. These systems may drop anything after the last newline character, or they may gratuitously add a newline at the end of the file or act up at run time.

Some systems limit lines to a specific length. If you exceed the limit, the excess may be discarded, or the system may parse the line and stick newlines at the end of the fragments, or the system may complain at run time. Standard C guarantees that any length up to and including 254 characters per line will work fine (including the terminating newline).

 To make sure what you write to a text file comes back the same when you read it in later: you should write to a text file only the printing characters (those for which a call to isprint() *returns a positive nonzero value), the space character, the newline character, and the horizontal tab character; you should make sure the last line in the file ends with a newline character; you should eliminate trailing spaces on any text line before the newline; and you should limit your lines to 254 characters (including the terminating newline).*

Apart from the question of reading and writing, the latitude given implementations to add and delete characters in a text stream makes using file-position placement and reading functions fairly unreliable. The file-position indicator would be usable by fseek() for returning the file-position indicator to its position at the time of an earlier call to ftell(), but you cannot depend on the difference between the return values of two calls to ftell() to indicate how many characters were written, for instance.

DOS, like many operating systems, has no trouble representing a file of zero bytes. Such files show up in a directory listing command, with a 0 where the number of bytes goes. Other systems cannot distinguish between blank files and ones that do not exist, so they just delete such files. Standard C permits them to do that. *For maximum portability, do not depend on the existence of files that by design or happenstance end up with zero bytes.*

UNIX and just a few other systems make no distinction between binary and text files. Standard C permits implementations to ignore the b modes as having any significance.

For binary files, Standard C requires that data read in match data written earlier, but this is only guaranteed for the same implementation on both the writing and reading end of the process. Otherwise, there are a whole host of reasons why depending on complete portability across systems for binary files is dicey at best.

The most obvious potential problem is differences in the character-encoding system. A value of 65 will be written to the file as A on a system that uses ASCII character encoding. If the same character is read back in on a system that uses EBCDIC, it will be translated to a value of 193—not very good, even for horseshoes. If this sort of cross-system reading is a potential, you might have to write a sentinel first byte to the file, and then depending on the result on reading, leave all byte values read in as is, or convert them from one character encoding to the other based on a lookup table you code.

Some systems add lots of NULL characters at the end of a file for padding purposes. Standard C permits them to do so, but only at the end of the file, after the last byte of data. If portability is an issue, you may need to consider writing some sort of byte combination sentinel values to mark the end of the file (this is trickier in binary files, where just about any byte value could show up in legitimate data—perhaps an unlikely series of unlikely characters would work), or code so that trailing NULL bytes will not play havoc with whatever program reads back the surplus trailing zero bytes. Because of this padding liberty, binary streams need not meaningfully support calls to fseek() where the mode is SEEK_END.

Reading and writing an array of structure variables, representing a number of records, is conveniently done with binary functions. You can write a large number of records this way with a single fwrite() call. But the alignment and padding problems we discussed at length in Chapter 13 make reading and writing across systems a risky business.

Even for scalar variables, we have the difference between those systems, such as UNIX, that store the most significant bytes first and those, such as DOS, that do it the other way around. Again, perhaps some sentinel 2-byte value you store at the beginning of the file would cause you to accept or reverse the order of bytes for each variable, in the latter case passing a pointer to the variable to a switching function you create.

And then there is the possibility that the same variable type has a different size on two different systems. Writing a 4-byte int on system A and reading back on a 2-byte int system will not produce good results. Again, you could write the respective sizes of all the arithmetic types at the beginning of the file (being careful to do this *after* deciding whether the writing system was ASCII or EBCDIC), but you can see that this is getting to be a messy business.

There is also the problem of different methods for handing negative integer values (two's complement, one's complement, sign magnitude, and so on) and different methods for storing floating point values even where the number of bytes of the respective types is the same from system to system (allocation of bits to mantissa and exponent, implicit or explicit $2^{\wedge 0}$, biasing or two's complement method of valuing exponent, special treatment for 0 exponent case, and so on).

If portability is an issue, you may have to decide either to stick to text files, despite the massive pain this would be for very large financial records with lots of floating point values, or else be very careful about potential conflicts.

Unless you are working with only a single system, it is best not to try to tinker with such things as buffer sizes (one implementation's meat is another's poison), double file-opening tricks, or reading and writing without the proper intervening buffer-clearing/file-positioning function calls in between.

With respect to naming files, as opposed to reading already-existing files, there are several things you can do to maximize portability, if that is a concern. You should keep filenames to six characters (letters only), a dot, and a single letter for an extension. That meager fare will work on nearly all systems. You should assume case may not be significant: don't create a file "notes.h" and another named "Notes.h".

It is best to avoid hard-wiring filenames into your code. You should use a `char` array to create or store a filename obtained interactively. The array that holds the filename should be sized to FILE-NAME_MAX. You can use some sort of screening function to temporarily read any file name to avoid overrunning even this generous size, either interactively or as a result of some glitch in your code.

When reading files, you should allow for case being significant: trying to read "notes.h" may miss "Notes.h". In naming files in the first instance, you should take this latter possibility into account. You should not rule out any characters in reading filenames.

14.18   MISCELLANEOUS FILE-HOUSEKEEPING FUNCTIONS (OPTIONAL)

14.18.1   Deleting a File with `remove()`

You can delete a file with the `remove()` Standard C library function:

```
int remove (const char *filename);
```

You pass the function a string containing the filename. On successful deletion, the function returns zero; otherwise it returns a nonzero integer (generally –1) and sets the global variable `errno` to either ENOENT if the filename is not found, or to EACESS if the filename is that of a directory of a read-only file. (See Chapter 16 for a description of `errno` and related functions.)

If the file you attempt to remove is open, the results of a call are implementation defined.

14.18.2   Renaming a File with `rename()`

You can rename a file with another library facility, `rename()`:

```
int rename(const char *oldname, const char *newname);
```

The return values are the same as for successful or unsuccessful calls to `remove()`, described above. Among the reasons that a function call could fail is that the file is open or that it is necessary to copy its contents to effectuate its renaming, or you have violated some rule of the operating system (for example, in DOS, you cannot rename a directory and you cannot specify a new drive or path for the file; only the name may change).

14.18.3   Scratch-Pad Temporary File with `tmpfile()`

The `tmpfile()` function is a useful tool if you need to create a temporary file, to be used during the life of the program only. This function opens a temporary binary file in the current working directory in `wb+` mode. The `tmpfile()` function returns a FILE pointer to the temporary file, which will be NULL in case of error:

```
FILE *tmpfile(void);
```

You have no access to the name of the file during its existence. At normal termination of the program or explicit closing of the file, the file is automatically deleted, just as though you explicitly called `remove()`. If the program terminates abnormally, whether the file is deleted is implementation defined.

14.19   APPLICATION: ACE BILLING PROGRAM

Now that we have covered files, we can move to a much higher level of sophistication in our ACE Billing program. We are now firmly at the point of real-life business applications and problems.

14.19.1   The ACE Club Problem

The ACE club is an international organization that caters to the tastes of the wealthy elite. Each ACE club contains within its walls a restaurant, bar, barbershop, health spa, and tobacconist. It is an exclusive organization with a limited number of members. There are just over 100 cities in the world that have ACE clubs. Catering to the rich is not easy. They demand the best services and are willing to pay for them. The owners of ACE Clubs International, Inc., know that the slightest delay of service could cost them a valuable customer. Fortunately, ACE is doing quite well in the industry. In fact, they've been growing at a rapid rate.

The IT department has a problem. The company is growing so rapidly that its current billing system is unable to keep up with the growth. Some changes will be necessary in order to maintain the current member database while allowing for the current trend in growth. There are several reasons to make changes to the current system. The current information system is located on a mainframe in Paris. This mainframe has been functioning for many years. The system is in good working order and is still inexpensive to maintain. However, there are a few problems with the interface to the mainframe. Every time a club member makes a transaction with ACE, an entry is made in the transaction file. This file is located on the mainframe and becomes extremely large. The batch job, which updates the master file with these transactions, is beginning to take longer than the allotted time. This situation is increasingly apparent as ACE clubs become more popular.

Other problems with the current system include the fact that the terminals, which are located at each ACE club, are starting to show their age. Repair costs for these terminals are high. It is difficult to find replacements and almost impossible to find new units to place in ACE clubs now opening. These terminals require constant connection to the host, since all updates are made to the transaction file that resides on the host. The mainframe is also low on resources required to add new terminals. The owners of ACE Clubs International, Inc., also believe that they can improve customer service by having attendants carry around handheld computers (PDAs) into which they can enter orders and customer information. The current system does not allow this functionality.

14.19.2   New System

Three separate sets of files are maintained: one for transactions, one for customer records and one for billing. Their record layouts and sample data are shown in Tables 14.8 to 14.10; sample data for each is shown after each table.

Table 14.8   *Billing Record Layout*

BILLING RECORD LAYOUT			
Field Name	*Size*	*Type*	*No. of Decimal Positions if Numeric*
numberOfCharges	2	Alphanumeric (digits)	
discounts	4	Alphanumeric (digits)	2
bill	5	Alphanumeric (digits)	2
memberId	4	Alphanumeric (char)	

```
10019991201100003215400
40019991201025003228350
25019991201020253323100
10019991201015003432300
10019991201200003432300
10019991201025003853325
10019991201015503939200
20019991201012255233200
20019991201102005233200
50019991201235755235325
25019991201100005283200
30019991200010005333200
30019991200050005333200
10019991201100005532200
25019991201050005633500
30019991201050006532300
```

Table 14.9 *Customer Record Layout*

CUSTOMER RECORD LAYOUT			
Field Name	Size	Type	No. of Decimal Positions if Numeric
memberLastName	20	Alphanumeric (char)	
memberFirstName	15	Alphanumeric (char)	
memberInitials	1	Alphanumeric (char)	
gender	1	Alphanumeric (char)	
specialMemberFeeFlag	1	Alphanumeric (char)	
streetAddress	26	Alphanumeric (char)	
city	18	Alphanumeric (char)	
state	2	Alphanumeric (char)	
zipCode	5	Alphanumeric (digits)	
phoneNumber	10	Alphanumeric (digits)	
country	3	Alphanumeric (char)	
memberId	4	Alphanumeric (char)	
clubID	3	Alphanumeric (char)	

```
Adenauer      Konrad          M  999 N Crawford    Ave   Globe     AZ852336029832777USA321540021200019000
Addison       Joseph          HM 933 N Tullman Lane       Globe     AZ852336029832777USA321540021200019000
Goodall       Jane            HF 994 N Billingsly Ave     Globe     AZ852336029832777USA321540021200019000
Tubman        Harriet         F  94 Boulder Cliff Ave     Globe     AZ852346029832777USA321540021200019000
Daimler       Gottlieb        HM 999 N Billingsly Ave     Globe     AZ852346029832777USA321540021200019000
Daubigny      CharlesFrancois M  3399 Beaumont Ln         Phoenix   AZ852836029832777USA321540021200019000
Earhart       Amelia          HF 99 SE Marsh Ave          Phoenix   AZ852836029832777USA321540021200019000
Milaud        Darius          M  994 N Billingsly Ave     Phoenix   AZ852836029832777USA321540021200019000
Darwin        Charles         HM 929 N Clairn Way         Phoenix   AZ852846029832777USA321540021200019000
Delacroix     Eugene          HM 994 N Everson Dr         Phoenix   AZ852846029832777USA321540021200019000
Planck        Max             HM 93 O'Toole Court         Phoenix   AZ852846029832777USA321540021200019000
Forssmann     Werner          TM 993 N Billingsly Ave     Phoenix   AZ852846029832777USA321540021200019000
Franco        Francisco       SM 2339 Kent Cir            Atlanta   GA303304042322382USA653230017700008000
Longfellow    Henry           M  2359 Kent Cir            Atlanta   GA303304042322382USA653230017700008000
Ledbetter     Huddie          M  2399 Randy Ave           Atlanta   GA303304042322382USA653230017700008000
Schick        Bela            SM 239 Hampton Ct           Atlanta   GA303304042322382USA653230017700008000
Scarlatti     Alessandro      GM 2333 Kent Cir            Atlanta   GA303404042322382USA653230017700008000
```

Santa Anna	AntonioLopez de	SM 2339 Pierpont Cir	Atlanta	GA303404042322382USA653230017700008000
Schiller	Friedrich von	SM 2399 Brent Dr	Atlanta	GA303404042322382USA653230017700008000
Sandburg	Carl	SM 2339 Kent Cir	Atlanta	GA303404042322382USA653230017700008000
Rommel	Erwin Johannes	EM 2393 Kent Cir	Atlanta	GA303504042322382USA653230017700008000
Roosevelt	Eleanor	SF 2499 Camden Way	Atlanta	GA303504042322382USA653230017700008000
Rickover	Hyman	GM 2344 Kent Cir	Atlanta	GA303504042322382USA653230017700008000
Richter	Jean Paul	FM 2394 Kent Cir	Atlanta	GA303504042322382USA653230017700008000
Romanov	Michael	MMY9393 Concord Ave	Augusta	GA349937062322832USA322835020100005000
Schelling	Friedrich Wm	JMY9393 Concord Ave	Augusta	GA349937062322832USA322835020100005000
Sardou	Victorien	MMY9393 May Ave	Augusta	GA349937062322832USA322835020100005000
Samuelson	Paul	AMY9393 Concord Ave	Augusta	GA349937062322832USA322835020100005000
Schonberg	Arnold	MMY9393 State St	Augusta	GA349947062322832USA322835020100005000
Segovia	Andres	MMY9393 Camgord Ave	Augusta	GA349947062322832USA322835020100005000
Selden	John	MMY9393 Camden Way	Augusta	GA349947062322832USA322835020100005000
Steinbeck	John	EMY9393 Concord Ave	Augusta	GA349947062322832USA322835020100005000
Stanton	Elizabeth	MFY9393 Ridgeway Blvd	Augusta	GA349947062322832USA322835020100005000
Beyle	Marie Henri	MMY9393 Concord Ave	Augusta	GA349957062322832USA322835020100005000
Stevenson	Robert Louis	BMY9393 Main St	Augusta	GA349957062322832USA322835020100005000
Truman	Harry	SMY9393 Concord Ave	Augusta	GA349957062322832USA322835020100005000
Thatcher	Margaret	FY2893 N Elm Ave	Savannah	GA300014043338989USA343230011100002000
Gorbachev	Raisa	RFY289 Avenue A	Savannah	GA300014043338989USA343230011100002000
Ghandi	Indira	RFY2893 N Elm Ave	Savannah	GA300014043338989USA343230011100002000
Maimonides	Moses	RMY2893 Hunely Dr	Savannah	GA300024043338989USA343230011100002000
Mayo	Charles	HMY2893 N Elm Ave	Savannah	GA300024043338989USA343230011100002000
Mazarin	Jules	RMY289 La Vista Ave	Savannah	GA300024043338989USA343230011100002000
McCarthy	Eugene	JMY28 King Arthurs Court	Savannah	GA300024043338989USA343230011100002000
Mulroney	Brian	RMY2893 N Elm Ave	Savannah	GA300034043338989USA343230011100002000
Metternich	Clemens	WMY283 Beauregard Ave	Savannah	GA300034043338989USA343230011100002000
Messerschmitt	Willy	RMY28 Jefferson Ave	Savannah	GA300034043338989USA343230011100002000
Muhammad	Elijah	MY289 Marshall Cir	Savannah	GA300034043338989USA343230011100002000
Magellan	Ferdinand	RMY2893 N Elm Ave	Savannah	GA300034043338989USA343230011100002000
Maginot	Andre	JMY909 S Eudora Ave	Rome	GA339557068382887USA523532522300020000
Whistler	James Abbott	MMY909 S Euclid Ave	Rome	GA339557068382887USA523532522300020000
Douglass	Frederick	JMY909 N Eudora Ave	Rome	GA339557068382887USA523532522300020000
Daumier	Honore	JMY909 S Eudora Ave	Rome	GA339517068382887USA523532522300020000
Copernicus	Nicolaus	JMY909 E Lawn Dr	Rome	GA339517068382887USA523532522300020000
Davis	Jefferson	JMY909 S Clement Cir	Rome	GA339518068382887USA523532522300020000
X	Malcolm	JMY909 Downs Way	Rome	GA339518068382887USA523532522300020000
Zwingli	Huldrych	JMY3033 Peters Court	Rome	GA339518068382887USA523532522300020000
Zola	Emile	JMY909 Gayton Dr	Rome	GA339528068382887USA523532522300020000
Zigfeld	Florenz	JMY909 S Eudora Ave	Rome	GA339528068382887USA523532522300020000
Xavier	Francis	JMY909 S Eudora Ave	Rome	GA339528068382887USA523532522300020000
Bacon	Francis	JMY909 S Eudora Ave	Rome	GA339528068382887USA523532522300020000
Wodehouse	Pelham	GM 3939 Devon Ave	Snyder	GA339647730283898USA385332518800009000
Wilson	Woodrow	LM 3939 Devon Ave	Snyder	GA339647730283898USA385332518800009000
Westinghouse	George	LM 3939 Devon Ave	Snyder	GA339647730283898USA385332518800009000
Wellington	Arthur	WM 3939 Breach Dr	Snyder	GA339648730283898USA385332518800009000
Weber	Max	LM 399 Devon Ave	Snyder	GA339748730283898USA385332518800009000
Marx	Karl	LM 3939 Devon Ave	Snyder	GA339748730283898USA385332518800009000
Watt	James	LM 39 N Altoona Rd	Snyder	GA339849730283898USA385332518800009000
Voltaire	Francois-Marie	AM 393 Beacon Dr	Snyder	GA339849730283898USA385332518800009000
Volstead	Andrew	LM 393 Knucles Cir	Snyder	GA339849730283898USA385332518800009000
Vinci	Leonardo da	LM 393 Crawford-Long Dr	Snyder	GA339849730283898USA385332518800009000
Velazquez	Diego Rodriguez	SM 39 Pontiac Blvd	Snyder	GA339949730283898USA385332518800009000
Vanderbilt	Cornilius	LM 3939 Devon Ave	Snyder	GA339949730283898USA385332518800009000
Turgenev	Ivan	SMY1023 Harbor Ferry Rd	Chicago	IL606068744583888USA393920010100001000
Trudeau	Pierre	JMY10 N Elm St	Chicago	IL606068744583888USA393920010100001000
Trotsky	Leon	DMY10232 S Windward Pkwy	Chicago	IL606068744583888USA393920010100001000
Tolstoy	Lev	JMY10232 Alsip Way	Chicago	IL606068744583888USA393920010100001000
Tito	Josef	JMY102 Mason Dixon Line Rd	Chicago	IL606068744583888USA393920010100001000
Truth	Sojourner	BFY132 Court Park	Chicago	IL606078744583888USA393920010100001000
Flavius	Titus	JMY1033 Royal Way	Chicago	IL606078744583888USA393920010100001000
Tintoretto	Jacobo	JMY133 Indigo Girls Pkwy	Chicago	IL606078744583888USA393920010100001000
Tildy	Zoltan	JMY1033 NE Windward Pkwy	Chicago	IL606078744583888USA393920010100001000
Tiffany	Charles	JMY10332 S Windward Pkwy	Chicago	IL606098744583888USA393920010100001000
Thurber	James	JMY102 Clark St	Chicago	IL606098744583888USA393920010100001000
Thoreau	Henry	DMY1033 Ridgeway Dr	Chicago	IL606098744583888USA393920010100001000
Thomas	Dylan	JMY15443 Freemanville Rd	Downers Grove	IL610457083888832USA533320013300004000
Thant	U	MY155 Clement Dr	Downers Grove	IL610457083888832USA533320013300004000
Teresa	Mother	JFY1548 Oklahoma Ave	Downers Grove	IL610457083888832USA533320013300004000
Terbrugghen	Hendrick	JMY154 Beverly Dr	Downers Grove	IL610457083888832USA533320013300004000
Tennyson	Alfred	JMY15489 Freemanville Rd	Downers Grove	IL610457083888832USA533320013300004000
Telemann	Georg	JMY1554 Hollywood Ave	Downers Grove	IL610457083888832USA533320013300004000

```
Taylor              Zachary          JMY15433 Freemanville Rd      Downers Grove    IL610467083888832USA533320013300004000
Tamerlane           Timur            JMY1538 Park Lawn Dr          Downers Grove    IL610467083888832USA533320013300004000
Talleyrand-Perigord Charles-MauriceJMY954 Lincoln Center           Downers Grove    IL610467083888832USA533320013300004000
Symington           Stuart           JMY15389 Freemanville Rd      Downers Grove    IL610467083888832USA533320013300004000
Svedberg            Theodor          JMY1538 Tremont Ave           Downers Grove    IL610467083888832USA533320013300004000
Sutherland          Joan             JFY15443 Freemanville Rd      Downers Grove    IL610467083888832USA533320013300004000
Sun                 Yat-sen          JMY1382 Avenue D              Cairo            IL604307089939939USA523320012200003000
Sully               Thomas           JMY13892 Park Lane            Cairo            IL604307089939939USA523320012200003000
Stubbs              William          JMY1382 23rd St               Cairo            IL604307089939939USA523320012200003000
Strauss             Johann           JMY13892 23rd St              Cairo            IL604317089939939USA523320012200003000
Strauss             Richard          JMY132 Ogglethorpe Ave        Cairo            IL604317089939939USA523320012200003000
Stradiveri          Antonio          JMY13892 23rd St              Cairo            IL604317089939939USA523320012200003000
Stravinsky          Fyodorovich      JMY132 23rd St                Cairo            IL604317089939939USA523320012200003000
Stuben              Friedrich        JMY13892 Wendell Day Rd       Cairo            IL604337089939939USA523320012200003000
Stern               Otto             JMY132 Ohaha Ave              Cairo            IL604337089939939USA523320012200003000
Steinmetz           Charles          JMY13892 23rd St              Cairo            IL604337089939939USA523320012200003000
Steffans            Lincoln          JMY192 Clark St               Cairo            IL604337089939939USA523320012200003000
Standish            Myles            JMY192 23rd St                Cairo            IL604347089939939USA523320012200003000
Stalin              Joseph           JMY15443 Freemanville Rd      Glen Ellyn       IL600487083894223USA528320016600007000
Spinoza             Benedict         KMY9007 S. Jeffrey Blvd       Glen Ellyn       IL600487083894223USA528320016600007000
Speilberg           Steven           KMY29823 Claire Ln            Glen Ellyn       IL600487083894223USA528320016600007000
Bogart              Humphrey         KMY9007 S. Jeffrey Blvd       Glen Ellyn       IL605487083894223USA528320016600007000
Falk                Peter            KMY900 Ozzie Harriet Way      Glen Ellyn       IL605587083894223USA528320016600007000
Davis               Bette            KFY90 NE Dravelyn Ct          Glen Ellyn       IL605687083894223USA528320016600007000
Crawford            Joan             KFY9007 S. Jeffrey Blvd       Glen Ellyn       IL605787083894223USA528320016600007000
```

Table 14.10 *Transaction Record Layout*

TRANSACTION RECORD LAYOUT			
Field Name	**Size**	**Type**	**No. of Decimal Positions if Numeric**
itemNumber	3	Alphanumeric (digits)	
transactionDate	8	Alphanumeric (digits)	
charge	5	Alphanumeric (digits)	2
memberId	4	Alphanumeric (char)	
storeID	3	Alphanumeric (char)	

```
100199991201393920 0
100199991201343230 0
200199991201523320 0
300199991201533320 0
100199991201553220 0
250199991201563350 0
250199991201528320 0
300199991201653230 0
100199991201385332 5
250199991201332310 0
400199991201322835 0
100199991201321540 0
500199991201523532 5
```

Each day the sorted transaction files from each location are transmitted electronically to central headquarters. The member ID is the key field on which sorting is based. The transmitted transaction files are consolidated into a single sorted transaction file. During the consolidation process, multiple transactions for a member are merged into a single transaction record.

The consolidated transaction file is then used to update the billing file. The billing file contains an entire month's records for all locations. The updating process brings current for each member the number of charges, discounts, and amount owed.

At least once a week, a report summarizing club and member activities is generated and analyzed by management. Once a month, customer bills are generated and sent. The billing process pulls in details from the transaction files and the customer record files. Graphically, Figures 14.4 to 14.7 show what the process looks like.

Figure 14.4 *ACE Billing Process—Flowchart*

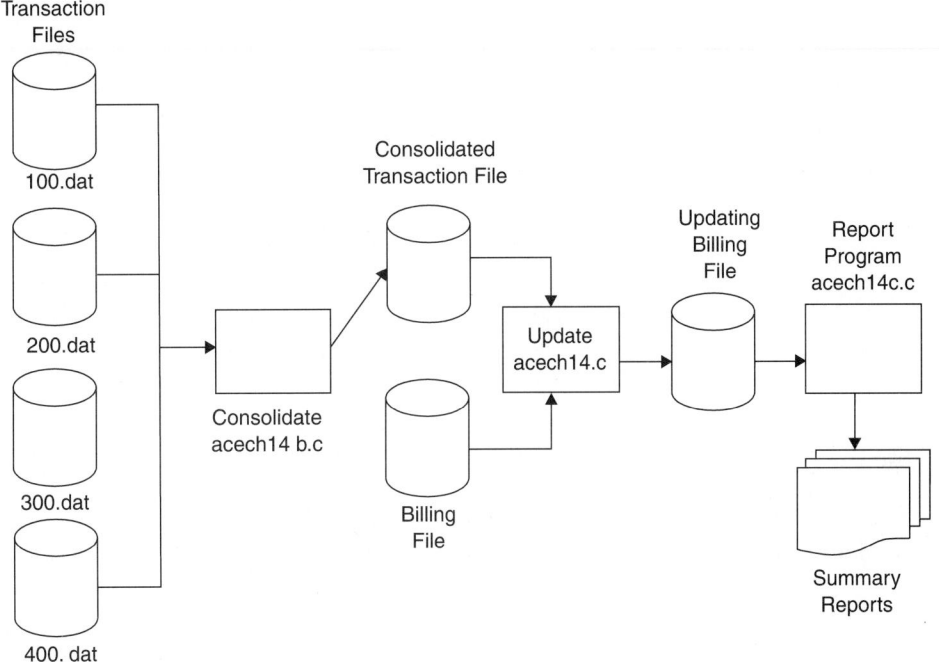

Figure 14.5 *ACE Billing Process—Update* (`acech14.c`)

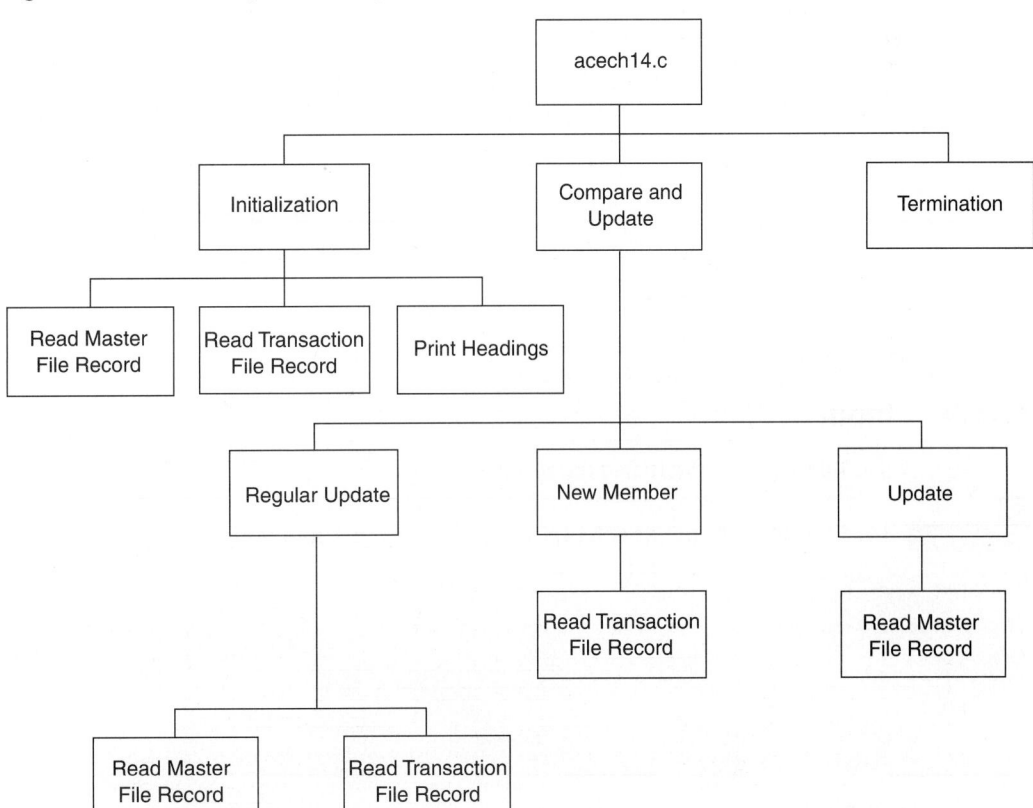

Figure 14.6 *ACE Billing Process—Consolidation (*`acech14b.c`*)*

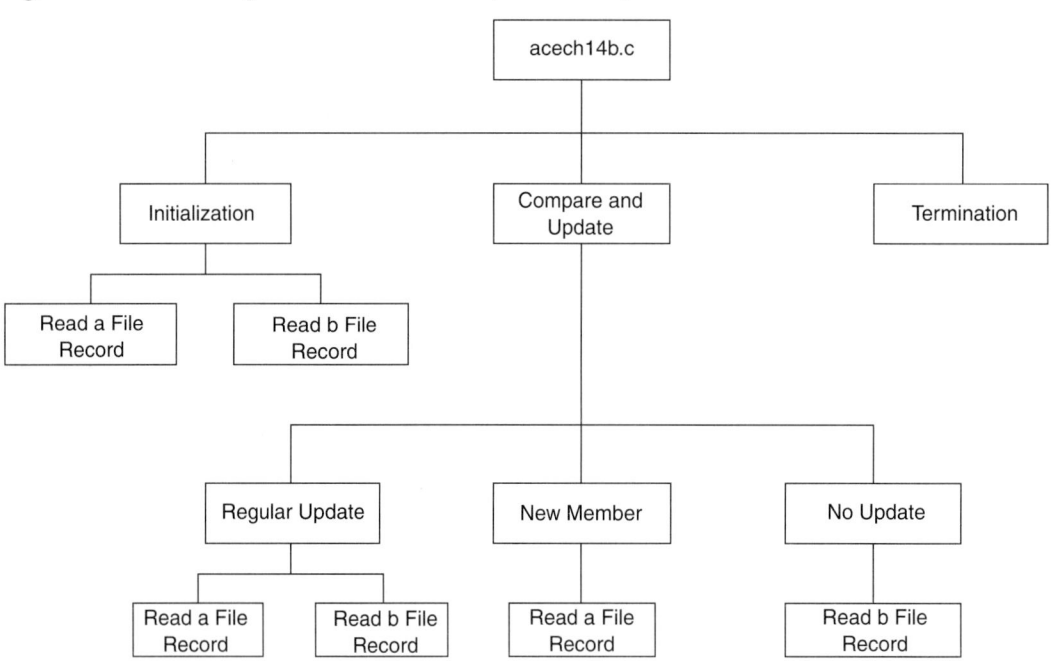

Figure 14.7 *ACE Billing Process—Report (*`acech14c.c`*)*

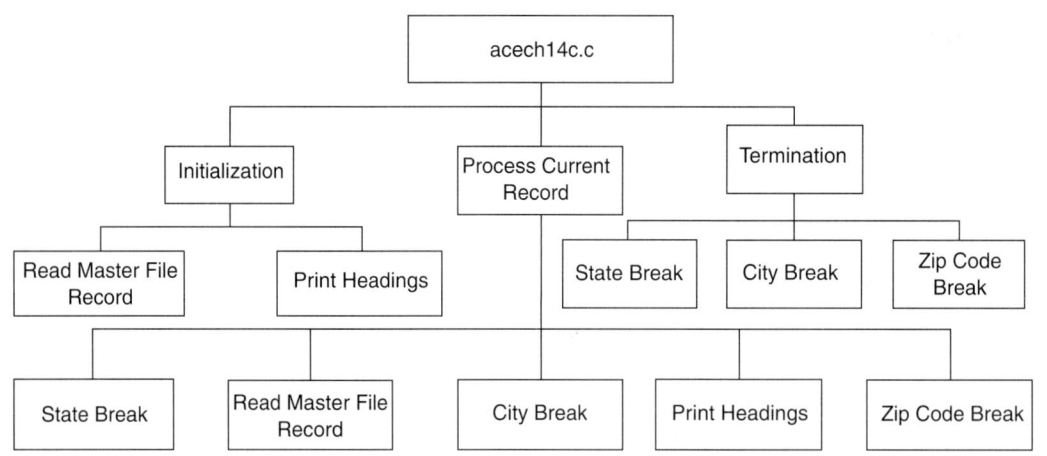

14.19.3   Input

See Tables 14.8 to 14.10 and the accompanying data.

 **Listing 14.14 acech14.c, acech14a.c, acech14b.c, and acech14c.c**

```
#ifndef acech14_H
#define acech14_H
/*
+----------------------------------------------------------------+
+    Program Name: acech14.h
+       Author(s): Austell-Wolfson and Otieno
+            Date: 12/10/2000
```

```
+   Purpose:
+       This file has all the manifest constants or macros needed
+       by the acech14.c program.
+
+-------------------------------------------------------------------+
*/

#define MEMBER_ID_SIZE          4
#define STORE_ID_SIZE           3
#define INPUT_BUFFER_SIZE       256
#define DATE_SIZE               8

struct ControlListingStatistics
{
    int currentMasterFileRecordCount;
    int transactionFileRecordCount;
    int newMasterFileRecordCount;
    int memberIdCountInBothFiles;
};

struct TransactionRecordLayout
{
    int     itemNumber;
    char    transactionDate[DATE_SIZE + 1];
    float   charge;
    char    memberId[MEMBER_ID_SIZE + 1];
    char    storeId[STORE_ID_SIZE + 1];
};
void Initialization(struct TransactionRecordLayout * masterRecord,
    struct TransactionRecordLayout * transRecord, struct ControlListingStatistics * stats);

void ReadMasterFileRecord(struct TransactionRecordLayout * masterRecord);

void ReadTransactionFileRecord (struct TransactionRecordLayout * transRecord);

void CompareAndUpdate (struct TransactionRecordLayout * masterRecord,
    struct TransactionRecordLayout * transRecord, struct ControlListingStatistics * stats);

void RegularUpdate (struct TransactionRecordLayout * masterRecord,
    struct TransactionRecordLayout * transRecord);
void NoUpdate (struct TransactionRecordLayout * masterRecord);
void NewMember(struct TransactionRecordLayout * masterRecord);
void Termination(struct ControlListingStatistics * stats);
#endif
```

```
/*
    +-------------------------------------------------------------------+
    +   Program Name: acech14.c
    +       Author(s): Austell-Wolfson and Otieno
    +           Date: 12/10/2000
    +   Purpose:
    +   This program performs an update of the master file by the data
    +   from the transaction file. It is assumed that both the master
    +   file and the transaction file are sorted by the memberID which
    +   is the primary key. This solution also assumes that there are
    +   unique records in the transaction file and unique records in
    +   the master file.
    +
```

```
+   Process:
+
+   Here is a summary of the mechanics of processing transaction records
+   where there are not multiple records with the same key
+   field value. (In other words, member 2223 cannot have more than
+   one charge to be added to the master record file.)
+   The second case, where there may be multiple records for a single
+   key field value, is handled in acech14a.c. A solid
+   understanding of this first program will help you understand the
+   next one, since you would only need to focus on the portion that
+   has been added to handle duplicate transaction records.
+
+   We read from both the transaction and master file simultaneously:
+
+      Case A: Transaction-Key = Master-Key, do the following:
+         A.1 Update the old master file record and write the
+                updated record to the new master file
+         A.2 Read from both files
+      Case B: Transaction-Key < Master-Key, do the following:
+         B.1 Write New a Master Record from a Transaction Record
+         B.2 Read from Transaction File Only
+      Case C: All other conditions, do the following:
+         C.1 Write a new Master Record from the old master Record
+         C.2 Read from the Master file
+
+      What follows is the pseudocode that is implemented:
+
+      Initialization
+      while (not EOF on either file)
+         CompareAndUpdate
+      end while
+      Termination
+
+    Initialization Function
+         Open the master and transaction files
+         ReadMasterFileRecord
+         ReadTransactionFileRecord
+
+      ReadMasterFileRecord Function
+         Read a record from MasterFile and parse it into its
+            respective fields
+
+      ReadTransactionFileRecord Function
+         Read a record from TransactionFile and parse it into its
+            respective fields
+
+      CompareAndUpdate Function
+         If TransactionMemberId = MasterMemberId
+            RegularUpdate
+         else
+            If  TransactionMemberId < MasterMemberId
+               NewMember
+            else
+               NoUpdate
+            end if
+         end if
+
+    RegularUpdate Function
+         Update and Write the master record
+         ReadmasterFileRecord
+         ReadTransactionFileRecord
```

```
    +
    +       NewMember Function
    +           Write a new Master Record from the Transaction Record
    +           ReadTransactionFileRecord
    +
    +       NoUpdate Function
    +           Write a New master Record from an Old Master Record
    +           ReadMasterFileRecord
    +
    +     Termination Function
    +           Close files
    +--------------------------------------------------------------+
*/
#include <stdio.h>
#include <string.h>
#include <stdlib.h>
#include "acech14.h"

/*
    +--------------------------------------------------------------+
    +   We have employed external variables for file pointers because these
    +   file pointers are used by several files. These functions depend
    +   on the pointers pointing to the next record to be read remaining
    +   unchanged. Passing file pointers will disrupt this feature.
    +--------------------------------------------------------------+
*/
FILE * CurrentMasterFile;
FILE * NewMasterFile;
FILE * TransactionFile;

int EndOfMasterFile = 0;
int EndOfTransactionFile = 0;
int MoreData = 1;

int main(void)
{
    struct TransactionRecordLayout masterRecord;
    struct TransactionRecordLayout transactionRecord;
    struct ControlListingStatistics stats;
/*
    +--------------------------------------------------------------+
    +   The following function opens the master and transaction files
    +   and reads the first record from both files.
    +--------------------------------------------------------------+
*/
    Initialization(&masterRecord, &transactionRecord, &stats);

    while (MoreData)
    {
        CompareAndUpdate(&masterRecord, &transactionRecord, &stats);
    }
    Termination(&stats);

    fclose(CurrentMasterFile);
    fclose(NewMasterFile);
    fclose(TransactionFile);
    return 0;
}

void Initialization(struct TransactionRecordLayout * masterRecord,
    struct TransactionRecordLayout * transactionRecord,
```

```
   struct ControlListingStatistics * stats)
{
   char inputBuffer[INPUT_BUFFER_SIZE + 1];

/*
   +-------------------------------------------------------------+
   + void *memset (void *s, int c, size_t n);
   + memset sets the first n bytes of the array s to the character c.
   + in our case, we initialize the entire structure to 0.
   +-------------------------------------------------------------+
*/
   memset(masterRecord, 0, sizeof (struct TransactionRecordLayout));
   memset(transactionRecord, 0, sizeof (struct TransactionRecordLayout));
   memset(stats, 0, sizeof (struct ControlListingStatistics));

   printf("Enter the name of the transaction file: ");
   gets(inputBuffer);
   TransactionFile = fopen(inputBuffer, "r");
   if (NULL == TransactionFile)
   {
      printf("acech14.exe cannot open \"%s\" for input\n", inputBuffer);
      return;
   }

   printf("Enter the name of the current master file: ");
   gets(inputBuffer);
   CurrentMasterFile = fopen(inputBuffer, "r");
   if (NULL == CurrentMasterFile)
   {
      printf("acech14.exe cannot open \"%s\" for input\n", inputBuffer);
      return;
   }
   printf("Enter the name of the new master file: ");
   gets(inputBuffer);
   NewMasterFile = fopen(inputBuffer, "w");
   if (NULL == NewMasterFile)
   {
      printf("acech14.exe cannot open \"%s\" for input\n", inputBuffer);
      return;
   }

/*
   +  Read from both the transaction and current master files as a
   +  prime read. These reads start the process. Subsequent reads are
   +  performed according to the dictates of the logic, which is based
   +  on the value of the key of the records read.
*/

   ReadMasterFileRecord(masterRecord);
   if (EndOfMasterFile)
   {
      printf("The current master File is empty. Therefore, the\n");
      printf("new master file will consist entirely of the\n");
      printf("current transaction file records\n");
   }

   ReadTransactionFileRecord(transactionRecord);
   if (EndOfTransactionFile)
   {
      printf("The current transaction File is empty. Therefore, \n");
      printf("the new master file will consist entirely of the\n");
```

```
         printf("current master file records unless it is also empty\n");
   }
}

void ReadMasterFileRecord (struct TransactionRecordLayout * masterRecord)
{
   char inputBuffer[INPUT_BUFFER_SIZE + 1];
   char * moreData;
   int toFloat;

   moreData = fgets(inputBuffer, INPUT_BUFFER_SIZE + 1,
      CurrentMasterFile);

   /* Now, parse the data into their respective fields. */
   if (moreData)
   {
      sscanf(inputBuffer, "%3d%8c%5d%4c%3c", &masterRecord->itemNumber,
         masterRecord->transactionDate, &toFloat, masterRecord->memberId,
         masterRecord->storeId); masterRecord->charge = toFloat / 100.0;
   }
   else
   {
      EndOfMasterFile = 1;
      if (EndOfTransactionFile)
      {
         MoreData = 0;
      }
      else
      {
/*
   +----------------------------------------------------------+
   + Set the masterRecord->memberId to the highest possible
   + value so as to force the reading and processing of the
   + transaction file until the end of the transaction file
   + is reached.
   +----------------------------------------------------------+
*/
         memset(masterRecord->memberId, 255, MEMBER_ID_SIZE);
      }
   }

   return;
}

void ReadTransactionFileRecord (
   struct TransactionRecordLayout * transactionRecord)
{
   char inputBuffer[INPUT_BUFFER_SIZE + 1];
   char * moreData = 0;
   int toFloat;

   moreData = fgets(inputBuffer, INPUT_BUFFER_SIZE + 1,
      TransactionFile);

   /*   Now, parse the data into their respective fields.   */
   if (moreData)
   {
      sscanf(inputBuffer, "%3d%8c%5d%4c%3c", &transactionRecord->itemNumber,
         transactionRecord->transactionDate, &toFloat, transactionRecord->memberId,
         transactionRecord->storeId); transactionRecord->charge = toFloat / 100.0;
   }
```

```
      else
      {
         EndOfTransactionFile = 1;
         if (EndOfMasterFile)
         {
            MoreData = 0;
         }
         else
         {
         /*
         +----------------------------------------------------------+
         + Set the transactionRecord->memberId to highest possible
         + value so as to force the reading and processing of the
         + transaction file until the end of the transaction file
         + is reached.
         +----------------------------------------------------------+
         */
            memset(transactionRecord->memberId, 255, MEMBER_ID_SIZE);
         }
      }
      return;
}

void CompareAndUpdate (struct TransactionRecordLayout * masterRecord,
      struct TransactionRecordLayout * transactionRecord,
      struct ControlListingStatistics * stats)
{
      stats->newMasterFileRecordCount++;
      if (strcmp(transactionRecord->memberId, masterRecord->memberId) == 0)
      {
         stats->currentMasterFileRecordCount++;
         stats->transactionFileRecordCount++;
         stats->memberIdCountInBothFiles++;
         RegularUpdate(masterRecord, transactionRecord);
      }
      else
      {
         if (strcmp(transactionRecord->memberId, masterRecord->memberId)
            < 0)
         {
            stats->transactionFileRecordCount++;
            NewMember(transactionRecord);
         }
         else
         {
            stats->currentMasterFileRecordCount++;
            NoUpdate(masterRecord);
         }
      }
      return;
}

void RegularUpdate (struct TransactionRecordLayout * masterRecord,
      struct TransactionRecordLayout * transactionRecord)
{
      long temp;

      masterRecord->itemNumber = transactionRecord->itemNumber;
      strcpy(   masterRecord->transactionDate, transactionRecord->transactionDate);
      masterRecord->charge += transactionRecord->charge;

      temp = 100.0 * masterRecord->charge;
```

```
      fprintf(NewMasterFile, "%3d%s%05ld%4s%3s\n", masterRecord->itemNumber,
         masterRecord->transactionDate, temp, masterRecord->memberId, masterRecord->storeId);

      ReadMasterFileRecord(masterRecord);
      ReadTransactionFileRecord(transactionRecord);
      return;
   }

   void NoUpdate (struct TransactionRecordLayout * masterRecord)
   {
      long temp = 100.0 * masterRecord->charge;

      fprintf(NewMasterFile, "%3d%s%05ld%4s%3s\n", masterRecord->itemNumber,
         masterRecord->transactionDate, temp, masterRecord->memberId, masterRecord->storeId);

      ReadMasterFileRecord(masterRecord);
      return;
   }

   void NewMember(struct TransactionRecordLayout * transactionRecord)
   {
      long temp = 100.0 * transactionRecord->charge;

      fprintf(NewMasterFile, "%3d%s%05ld%4s%3s\n",
         transactionRecord->itemNumber,
         transactionRecord->transactionDate, temp,
         transactionRecord->memberId, transactionRecord->storeId);

      ReadTransactionFileRecord(transactionRecord);
      return;
   }

   void Termination(struct ControlListingStatistics * stats)
   {
      printf("\t|                                                             |\n");
      printf("\t|                                                             |\n");
      printf("\t|    Program Name: acech14.EXE                 Page:  1       |\n");
      printf("\t|      Run Date: 12/10/2000           Ace Billing            |\n");
      printf("\t|                                                             |\n");
      printf("\t+-------------------------------------------------------------+\n");
      printf("\t|     No. of records in Current master file: %3d             |\n",
         stats->currentMasterFileRecordCount);
      printf("\t|         No. of records in New master file: %3d             |\n",
         stats->newMasterFileRecordCount);
      printf("\t|        No. of records in transaction file: %3d             |\n",
         stats->transactionFileRecordCount);
      printf("\t|            No. of member ids in both files: %3d            |\n",
         stats->memberIdCountInBothFiles);
      printf("\t|_____|"
         "\n\n");
   }
```

[The acech14.c and acech14a.c programs differ only in two functions. The other functions, and the header file, acech14.h, have been omitted due to space considerations. All files are included on the attached disk.]

```
/*
   +----------------------------------------------------------------+
   +    Program Name: acech14a.c
   +       Author(s): Austell-Wolfson and Otieno
   +          Date: 12/10/2000
```

```
+   Purpose:
+   This program performs an update of the master file by the data
+   from the transaction file. It is assumed that the both master
+   file and the transaction file are sorted by the memberID, which
+   is the primary key. This solution also assumes that there are
+   multiple records with the same key in the transaction file
+   and unique key records in the master file.
+
+   Process:
+
+   Here is a summary the mechanics of processing transaction records,
+   where there may be multiple records with the same key
+   field value. (In other words, member 2223 can have more than
+   one charge added to the master record file.)
+
+      Case A: Transaction-Key = Master-Key, do the following:
+         A.1 Copy the old master record to the new master record
+         A.2 Add the values from the transaction record onto the
+             new master record for all the transaction records
+             having the same key as the master record
+         A.3 Write the updated record to the new master file
+         A.4 Read from both files
+      Case B: Transaction-Key < Master-Key, do the following:
+         B.1 Copy the first Transaction record to the New Master
+                Record from a Transaction Record
+         B.2 Add the values from subsequent transaction records
+             onto the new master record for all the transaction
+             records having the same key as the master record.
+         B.2 Read from Transaction File Only
+      Case C: All other conditions, do the following:
+         C.1 Write a new Master Record from the old master Record
+         C.2 Read from the Master file
+
+   What follows is the pseudocode that is implemented:
+
+   Initialization
+   while (not EOF on either file)
+      CompareAndUpdate
+   end while
+   Termination
+
+   Initialization Function
+      Open the master and transaction files
+      ReadMasterFileRecord
+      ReadTransactionFileRecord
+
+   ReadMasterFileRecord Function
+      ReadMasterFile and parse it into its respective fields
+
+   ReadTransactionFileRecord Function
+      ReadTransactionFile and parse it into its respective fields
+
+   CompareAndUpdate Function
+      If TransactionMemberId = MasterMemberId
+         RegularUpdate
+      else
+         If  TransactionMemberId < MasterMemberId
+            NewMember
+         else
+            NoUpdate
+         end if
```

```
    +        end if
    +
    +    RegularUpdate Function
    +        Update and Write the master record
    +        ReadmasterFileRecord
    +        ReadTransactionFileRecord
    +
    +    NewMember Function
    +        Write a new Master Record from the Transaction Record
    +        ReadTransactionFileRecord
    +
    +    NoUpdate Function
    +        Write a New master Record from an Old Master Record
    +        ReadMasterFileRecord
    +
    +    Termination Function
    +        Close files
    +--------------------------------------------------------------+
*/
```

[All but two function definitions are omitted.]

```c
void RegularUpdate (struct TransactionRecordLayout * masterRecord,
    struct TransactionRecordLayout * transactionRecord,
    struct ControlListingStatistics * stats)
{
    long temp;

    masterRecord->itemNumber = transactionRecord->itemNumber;
    strcpy(masterRecord->transactionDate,
        transactionRecord->transactionDate);

    while(strcmp(transactionRecord->memberId, masterRecord->memberId)
        == 0)
    {
        stats->transactionFileRecordCount++;
        masterRecord->charge += transactionRecord->charge;
        ReadTransactionFileRecord(transactionRecord);
    }
    temp = 100.0 * masterRecord->charge;
    fprintf(NewMasterFile, "%3d%s%05ld%4s%3s\n", masterRecord->itemNumber,
        masterRecord->transactionDate, temp, masterRecord->memberId, masterRecord->storeId);

    ReadMasterFileRecord(masterRecord);
    return;
}

void CompareAndUpdate (struct TransactionRecordLayout * masterRecord,
    struct TransactionRecordLayout * transactionRecord, struct ControlListingStatistics *
    stats)
{
    stats->newMasterFileRecordCount++;
    if (strcmp(transactionRecord->memberId, masterRecord->memberId) == 0)
    {
        stats->currentMasterFileRecordCount++;
        stats->memberIdCountInBothFiles++;
        RegularUpdate(masterRecord, transactionRecord, stats);
    }
    else
    {
```

```
        if (strcmp(transactionRecord->memberId, masterRecord->memberId)
            < 0)
        {
            stats->transactionFileRecordCount++;
            NewMember(transactionRecord);
        }
        else
        {
            stats->currentMasterFileRecordCount++;
            NoUpdate(masterRecord);
        }
    }
    return;
}
```

```
#ifndef acech14b_H
#define acech14b_H
/*
    +-------------------------------------------------------------------+
    +    Program Name: acech14b.h
    +        Author(s): Austell-Wolfson and Otieno
    +             Date: 12/10/2000
    +    Purpose:
    +        This file has all the manifest constants or macros needed
    +        by the acech14b.c program.
    +
    +-------------------------------------------------------------------+
*/

#define MEMBER_ID_SIZE        4
#define STORE_ID_SIZE         3
#define INPUT_BUFFER_SIZE     256
#define DATE_SIZE             8
#define FILENAME_SIZE         50

struct ControlListingStatistics
{
    int currentMasterFileRecordCount;
    int transactionFileRecordCount;
    int newMasterFileRecordCount;
    int memberIdCountInBothFiles;
};
struct TransactionRecordLayout
{
    int     itemNumber;
    char    transactionDate[DATE_SIZE + 1];
    float   charge;
    char    memberId[MEMBER_ID_SIZE + 1];
    char    storeId[STORE_ID_SIZE + 1];
};

void Initialization (struct TransactionRecordLayout * masterRecord,
    struct TransactionRecordLayout * transRecord, struct ControlListingStatistics * stats);
void ReadBFileRecord (struct TransactionRecordLayout * masterRecord);
void ReadAFileRecord (struct TransactionRecordLayout * transRecord);
void CompareAndUpdate (struct TransactionRecordLayout * masterRecord,
    struct TransactionRecordLayout * transRecord, struct ControlListingStatistics * stats);
```

```
void RegularUpdate (struct TransactionRecordLayout * masterRecord,
    struct TransactionRecordLayout * transRecord);
void NoUpdate (struct TransactionRecordLayout * masterRecord);
void NewMember(struct TransactionRecordLayout * masterRecord);
void Termination(struct ControlListingStatistics * stats);
#endif
```

```
/*
    +---------------------------------------------------------------+
    +    Program Name: acech14b.c
    +        Author(s): Austell-Wolfson and Otieno
    +             Date: 12/10/2000
    +    Purpose:
    +    This program consolidates all the transaction files from all
    +    stores into a single transaction file.
    +
    +    Process:
    +    The name of the transaction files is stored in a file called
    +    trans.fil. Therefore, the program opens this file, trans.fil,
    +    for input, reads a record from it, and then gets a file pointer
    +    for the name just obtained from trans.fil. The contents of this
    +    file is merged in an interleaving fashion so as to produce a
    +    combined file that is still sorted by the memberId.
    +
    +    Pseudocode:
    +
    +        Remove oldTemp & newTemp files (just in case they exist)
    +        Open trans.fil for reading
    +        Read first filename from trans.fil and store in fileA
    +        Open fileA for reading and point AFile to stream
    +        while (more records remain in trans.fil)
    +            Read next filename from trans.fil & store in fileB
    +            Open fileB for reading and point BFile to stream
    +            if not first time in loop
    +                Open oldTemp for reading & point AFile to stream
    +            end if
    +            Open newTemp for writing and point CFile to stream
    +            Merge new file and oldTemp into newTemp (A+B->C)
    +            Close all three files
    +            Remove oldTemp file
    +            Rename newTemp oldTemp (for next loop)
    +        end while
    +        Remove newtrans (just in case it exists)
    +        Rename oldTemp newtrans
    +        Remove oldTemp and newTemp
    +
    +---------------------------------------------------------------+
*/
#include <stdio.h>
#include <string.h>
#include <stdlib.h>
#include "acech14b.h"

/*
    +---------------------------------------------------------------+
```

```
   +    We have used external variables for file pointers because these
   +    file pointers are used by several files. These functions depend
   +    on the pointers pointing to the next record to be read remaining
   +    unchanged. Passing file pointers will disrupt this feature.
   +------------------------------------------------------------------+
*/

FILE * AFile;
FILE * BFile;
FILE * CFile; /* new file from A & B merged */

int EndOfBFile = 0;
int EndOfAFile = 0;
int MoreData = 1;

int main(void)
{
    struct TransactionRecordLayout BRecord;
    struct TransactionRecordLayout ARecord;
    struct ControlListingStatistics stats;
    char fileA[FILENAME_SIZE + 1], fileB[FILENAME_SIZE + 1];
    char newTemp[FILENAME_SIZE + 1] = "c:\\temp\\newTemp",
    oldTemp[FILENAME_SIZE + 1] = "c:\\temp\\oldTemp";
    int firstTime = 1;

    FILE *fileList = fopen("c:\\temp\\trans.fil", "r");
    if (NULL == fileList)
    {
        printf("acech14b.exe cannot open \"%s\" for reading\n",
            "c:\\temp\\trans.fil");
        return 0;
    }

    /* make sure temp files don't really exist */
    remove(newTemp);
    remove(oldTemp);

    fgets(fileA, FILENAME_SIZE, fileList);
    if (strrchr(fileA, '\n'))
    {
        *strrchr(fileA, '\n') = 0;
    }
    while (fgets(fileB, FILENAME_SIZE, fileList))
    {
        if (strrchr(fileB, '\n'))
        {
            strrchr(fileB, '\n') = 0;
        }
        if (firstTime)
        {
            AFile = fopen(fileA, "r");
            firstTime = 0;
        }
        else
        {
            AFile = fopen(oldTemp, "r");
        }
        BFile = fopen(fileB, "r");
        if (NULL == AFile ¦¦ NULL == BFile)
        {
            printf("acech14b.exe cannot open \"%s\" for reading\n",
                AFile? fileB : fileA);
```

```
            return 0;
        }
        CFile = fopen(newTemp, "w");
        if (NULL == CFile)
        {
            printf("acech14b.exe can't open newTemp file for output\n");
            return 0;
        }

/*
    +------------------------------------------------------------------+
    +  The following function opens file A and file B,
    +  and reads the first record from both files.
    +------------------------------------------------------------------+
    +
*/

        Initialization(&BRecord, &ARecord, &stats);
        MoreData = 1;
        while (MoreData)
        {
            CompareAndUpdate(&BRecord, &ARecord, &stats);
        }

        fclose(AFile);
        fclose(BFile);
        fclose(CFile);
        remove(oldTemp);
        rename(newTemp, oldTemp); /* newTemp now becomes oldTemp */
    } /* end while fgets */

    fclose(AFile);
    fclose(BFile);
    fclose(CFile);
    remove("c:\\temp\\newtrans");
    rename(oldTemp, "c:\\temp\\newtrans");
    remove(oldTemp);
    remove(newTemp);
    Termination(&stats);
    return 0;
}

void Initialization(struct TransactionRecordLayout * BRecord,
    struct TransactionRecordLayout * ARecord,
    struct ControlListingStatistics * stats)
{
/*
    +------------------------------------------------------------------+
    + void *memset (void *s, int c, size_t n);
    + memset sets the first n bytes of the array s to the character c.
    + in our case, we initialize the entire structure to 0.
    +------------------------------------------------------------------+
*/
        memset(BRecord, 0, sizeof (struct TransactionRecordLayout));
        memset(ARecord, 0, sizeof (struct TransactionRecordLayout));
        memset(stats, 0, sizeof (struct ControlListingStatistics));

    /*
        Read from both the transaction and current master files as a
        prime read. These reads start the process. Subsequent reads are
        performed according to the dictates of the logic, which is based
        on the value of the key of the records read.
    */
```

```
      ReadBFileRecord(BRecord);
      if (EndOfBFile)
      {
         printf("The current master File is empty. Therefore, the\n");
         printf("new master file will consist entirely of the\n");
         printf("current transaction file records\n");
      }

      ReadAFileRecord(ARecord);
      if (EndOfAFile)
      {
         printf("The current transaction File is empty. Therefore, \n");
         printf("the new master file will consist entirely of the\n");
         printf("current master file records unless it is also empty\n");
      }
}

void ReadBFileRecord (struct TransactionRecordLayout * BRecord)
{
   char inputBuffer[INPUT_BUFFER_SIZE + 1];
   char * moreData;
   int toFloat;

   moreData = fgets(inputBuffer, INPUT_BUFFER_SIZE + 1,
      BFile);

   /* Now, parse the data into their respective fields. */
   if (moreData)
   {
      sscanf(inputBuffer, "%3d%8c%5d%4c%3c", &BRecord->itemNumber, BRecord->transactionDate,
         &toFloat, BRecord->memberId, BRecord->storeId);
      BRecord->charge = toFloat / 100.0;
   }
   else
   {
      EndOfBFile = 1;
      if (EndOfAFile)
      {
         MoreData = 0;
      }
      else
      {
      /*
         +----------------------------------------------------------+
         + Set the BRecord->memberId to the highest possible
         + value so as to force the reading and processing of the
         + transaction file until the end of the transaction file
         + is reached.
         +----------------------------------------------------------+
      */
         memset(BRecord->memberId, 255, MEMBER_ID_SIZE);
      }
   }

   return;
}

void ReadAFileRecord (
   struct TransactionRecordLayout * ARecord)
{
   char inputBuffer[INPUT_BUFFER_SIZE + 1];
   char * moreData = 0;
```

```
      int toFloat;

   moreData = fgets(inputBuffer, INPUT_BUFFER_SIZE + 1, AFile);

   /* Now, parse the data into their respective fields */
   if (moreData)
   {
      sscanf(inputBuffer, "%3d%8c%5d%4c%3c", &ARecord->itemNumber, ARecord->transactionDate,
         &toFloat, ARecord->memberId, ARecord->storeId);
      ARecord->charge = toFloat / 100.0;
   }
   else
   {

      EndOfAFile = 1;
      if (EndOfBFile)
      {
         MoreData = 0;
      }
      else
      {
      /*
      +----------------------------------------------------------+
      + Set the ARecord->memberId to the highest possible
      + value so as to force the reading and processing of the
      + transaction file until the end of the transaction file
      + is reached.
      +----------------------------------------------------------+
*         /
         memset(ARecord->memberId, 255, MEMBER_ID_SIZE);
      }
   }
   return;
}

void CompareAndUpdate (struct TransactionRecordLayout * BRecord,
   struct TransactionRecordLayout * ARecord, struct ControlListingStatistics * stats)
{
   stats->newMasterFileRecordCount++;
   if (strcmp(ARecord->memberId, BRecord->memberId) == 0)
   {
      stats->newMasterFileRecordCount++;
      stats->currentMasterFileRecordCount++;
      stats->transactionFileRecordCount++;
      stats->memberIdCountInBothFiles++;
      RegularUpdate(BRecord, ARecord);
   }
   else
   {
      if (strcmp(ARecord->memberId, BRecord->memberId)
         < 0)
      {
         stats->transactionFileRecordCount++;
         NewMember(ARecord);
      }
      else
      {
         stats->currentMasterFileRecordCount++;
         NoUpdate(BRecord);
      }
   }
   return;
}
```

```c
void RegularUpdate (struct TransactionRecordLayout * BRecord,
   struct TransactionRecordLayout * ARecord)
{
   long temp; = 100.0 * BRecord->charge;
   fprintf(CFile, "%3d%s%05ld%4s%3s\n", BRecord->itemNumber, BRecord->transactionDate, temp,
      BRecord->memberId, BRecord->storeId);
   temp = 100.0 * ARecord->charge;
   fprintf(CFile, "%3d%s%05ld%4s%3s\n", ARecord->itemNumber, ARecord->transactionDate, temp,
      ARecord->memberId, ARecord->storeId);

   ReadBFileRecord(BRecord);
   ReadAFileRecord(ARecord);
   return;
}

void NoUpdate (struct TransactionRecordLayout * BRecord)
{
   long temp = 100.0 * BRecord->charge;

   fprintf(CFile, "%3d%s%05ld%4s%3s\n", BRecord->itemNumber, BRecord->transactionDate, temp,
      BRecord->memberId, BRecord->storeId);

   ReadBFileRecord(BRecord);
   return;
}

void NewMember (struct TransactionRecordLayout * ARecord)
{
   long temp = 100.0 * ARecord->charge;

   fprintf(CFile, "%3d%s%05ld%4s%3s\n", ARecord->itemNumber, ARecord->transactionDate, temp,
      ARecord->memberId, ARecord->storeId);

   ReadAFileRecord(ARecord);
   return;
}

void Termination(struct ControlListingStatistics * stats)
{
   printf("\t|_____|\n");
   printf("\t|                                                |\n");
   printf("\t|    Program Name: acech14b.EXE          Page:  1 |\n");
   printf("\t|       Run Date: 12/10/2000        Ace Billing   |\n");
   printf("\t|                                                |\n");
   printf("\t|                                                |\n");
   printf("\t|    No. of records in Current master file: %3d   |\n",
      stats->currentMasterFileRecordCount);
   printf("\t|       No. of records in New master file: %3d   |\n",
      stats->newMasterFileRecordCount);
   printf("\t|       No. of records in transaction file: %3d   |\n",
      stats->transactionFileRecordCount);
   printf("\t|          No. of member ids in both files: %3d   |\n",
      stats->memberIdCountInBothFiles);
   printf("\t|_____|"
      "\n\n");
}
```

```c
#ifndef acech14c_H
#define acech14c_H
```

```
/*

    --------------------------------------------------------------
    +    Program Name: acech14c.h
    +       Author(s): Austell-Wolfson and Otieno
    +            Date: 12/10/2000
    +    Purpose:
    +       This file has all the manifest constants or macros needed by the
    +       acech14c.c program.
    +
    +-------------------------------------------------------------------+
*/

#define MEMBER_ID_SIZE        4
#define STORE_ID_SIZE         3
#define INPUT_BUFFER_SIZE     256
#define DATE_SIZE             8
#define LAST_NAME_SIZE        20
#define FIRST_NAME_SIZE       15
#define CITY_SIZE             18
#define STATE_SIZE            3
#define ZIP_CODE_SIZE         5
#define ZIP_CODE_BREAK        0
#define CITY_BREAK            1
#define STATE_BREAK           2
#define FINAL_BREAK           3
#define NUM_OF_HOLD_AREAS     5
#define PAGE_SIZE             50


#define TOP_LINE      fprintf(ReportFile,\
    "\t┌──────────────────────────────────────────────┐\n");


#define MID_LINE      fprintf(ReportFile,\
    "\t├──────────────────────────────────────────────┤\n");
#define BOTTOM_LINE fprintf(ReportFile,\
    "\t└──────────────────────────────────────────────┘\n");
#define BLANK_LINE fprintf(ReportFile,\
    "\t│                                                │\n");

struct CustomerRecordLayout
{
    char    lastName[LAST_NAME_SIZE + 1];
    char    firstName[FIRST_NAME_SIZE + 1];
    char    initial;
    char    city [CITY_SIZE + 1];
    char    state[STATE_SIZE + 1];
    char    zipCode[ZIP_CODE_SIZE + 1];
    char    memberId[MEMBER_ID_SIZE + 1];
    float   bill;
    float   discount;
    int     numberOfCharges;
    char    storeId[STORE_ID_SIZE + 1];
};

struct SummaryControls
{
    float   bill;
    float   discount;
    int     numberOfCharges;
    char    city [CITY_SIZE + 1];
    char    state[STATE_SIZE + 1];
```

```
   char    zipCode[ZIP_CODE_SIZE + 1];
   char    firstRecord;
};

char * Initialization (struct CustomerRecordLayout * customerRecord,
   struct SummaryControls * holdAreas);

char * ProcessCurrentRecord(struct CustomerRecordLayout * customerRecord,
   struct SummaryControls * holdAreas);

void Termination(struct CustomerRecordLayout * customerRecord,
   struct SummaryControls * holdAreas);

char * ReadCustomerFileRecord(struct CustomerRecordLayout * customerRecord);

void StateBreak(struct CustomerRecordLayout * customerRecord,
   struct SummaryControls * holdAreas);

void CityBreak(struct CustomerRecordLayout * customerRecord,
   struct SummaryControls * holdAreas, int breakInd);
void ZipCodeBreak(struct CustomerRecordLayout * customerRecord,
   struct SummaryControls * holdAreas, int breakInd);
void PrintHeadings(struct CustomerRecordLayout * customerRecord);
void Termination(struct CustomerRecordLayout * customerRecord,
   struct SummaryControls * holdAreas);
#endif
```

```
/*
 +-------------------------------------------------------------------+
 +    Program Name: acech14c.c
 +       Author(s): Austell-Wolfson and Otieno
 +           Date: 12/10/2000
 +    Purpose:
 +            This program takes the customer file and produces a three-level
 +      control break on state, city, and zip code. It also produces the
 +      totals for each level: state, city, and zip code.
 +
 +    Process:
 +
 +       What follows is the pseudocode implemented:
 +
 +-------------------------------------------------------------------+
 +
 +
 +       Initialization
 +       while (not EOF)
 +          ProcessCurrentRecord
 +       end while
 +       Termination
 +
 +-------------------------------------------------------------------+
 +
 +       Initialization Function
 +          Open the input as well as report files
 +          ReadCustomerFileRecord
 +
 +-------------------------------------------------------------------+
 +
 +       ProcessCurrentRecord Function
```

```
+        if (FirstRecord)
+        {
+            Assign control fields to hold areas
+            print the heading
+            Turn off First Record Flag
+        }
+        else
+        {
+            if (State break)
+            {
+                StateBreak
+            }
+            else
+            {
+                if (City Break)
+                {
+                    CityBreak
+                }
+                else
+                {
+                    if (Zip Code break)
+                    {
+                        ZipCodeBreak
+                    }
+                }
+            }
+        }
+        if (lineCount > PageSize)
+        {
+            Heading()
+        }
+
+        Write Detail Record
+        Sum up Zip Code Amounts
+
+----------------------------------------------------------------+
+
+    Termination Function
+        StateBreak
+        CityBreak
+        ZipCodeBreak
+        GrandTotalsLine
+      Close files
+
+----------------------------------------------------------------+
+
+    ReadCustomerFileRecord Function
+      Read a record from CustomerFile and parse it into its
+          respective fields
+
+----------------------------------------------------------------+
+
+      Headings Function
+         Write headings
+         Initialize lineCount
+
+----------------------------------------------------------------+
+
+         StateBreak Function
+           CityBreak()
```

```
+           Roll Up State Totals to Grand totals
+        Write State totals
+           Initialize State Hold areas
+           Initialize State totals
+
+--------------------------------------------------------------+
+
+        CityBreak Function
+           ZipCodeBreak()
+           Roll Up City Totals to State totals
+        Write City totals
+           Initialize City Hold areas
+           Initialize City totals
+
+--------------------------------------------------------------+
+
+        ZipCodeBreak Function
+           Roll Up ZipCode Totals to City totals
+        Write ZipCode totals
+           Initialize ZipCode Hold areas
+           Initialize ZipCode totals
+--------------------------------------------------------------+
*/
#include <stdio.h>
#include <string.h>
#include <stdlib.h>
#include "acech14c.h"

FILE * CustomerFile;
FILE * ReportFile;
int LineCounter;
int PageNo;
int FirstTime = 1;

int main(void)
{
   struct CustomerRecordLayout customerRecord;
   struct SummaryControls holdAreas[NUM_OF_HOLD_AREAS];
   char * moreData;

   moreData = Initialization(&customerRecord, holdAreas);

   while (moreData)
   {
      moreData = ProcessCurrentRecord(&customerRecord, holdAreas);
   }

   Termination(&customerRecord, holdAreas);

   return 0;
}
/*
 +
 +--------------------------------------------------------------+
 +
 */

char * Initialization (struct CustomerRecordLayout * customerRecord,
   struct SummaryControls * holdAreas)
{
```

```
      char inputBuffer[INPUT_BUFFER_SIZE + 1];
      char * moreData;
      /*
       +---------------------------------------------------------------+
       + void *memset (void *s, int c, size_t n);
       + memset sets the first n bytes of the array s to the character c.
       + in our case, we initialize the entire structure to 0.
       +---------------------------------------------------------------+
       */
      memset(customerRecord, 0, sizeof (struct CustomerRecordLayout));
      memset(holdAreas, 0, sizeof (struct SummaryControls) * NUM_OF_HOLD_AREAS);

      printf("Enter the customer file name: ");
      gets(inputBuffer);

      CustomerFile = fopen(inputBuffer, "r");
      if (NULL == CustomerFile)
      {
         printf("acech14c.exe cannot open \"%s\" for input\n", inputBuffer);
         return NULL;
      }

      printf("Enter the Report file name: ");
      gets(inputBuffer);

      ReportFile = fopen(inputBuffer, "w");
      if (NULL == ReportFile)
      {
         printf("acech14c.exe cannot open \"%s\" for output\n", inputBuffer);
         return NULL;
      }

      moreData = ReadCustomerFileRecord(customerRecord);
      if (!moreData)
      {
         printf("The customer File is empty. Therefore, the\n");
         printf("report will not be produced\n");
      }
      else
      {
         PrintHeadings(customerRecord);
      }
      return moreData;
}

/*
 +
 +---------------------------------------------------------------+
 +
 +
 */

char * ProcessCurrentRecord(
   struct CustomerRecordLayout * customerRecord,
   struct SummaryControls * holdAreas)
{
   char fullName[FIRST_NAME_SIZE + LAST_NAME_SIZE + 2];

   /* Place a null character at the first space in the last name */
   *(strstr(customerRecord->lastName, " ")) = '\0';
```

```c
      *(strstr(customerRecord->firstName, " ")) = '\0';

      sprintf(fullName, "%s, %s", customerRecord->lastName, customerRecord->firstName);

      if (holdAreas[ZIP_CODE_BREAK].firstRecord == '\0')
      {
         strcpy(holdAreas[ZIP_CODE_BREAK].zipCode, customerRecord->zipCode);
         strcpy(holdAreas[CITY_BREAK].city, customerRecord->city);
         strcpy(holdAreas[STATE_BREAK].state, customerRecord->state);
         holdAreas[ZIP_CODE_BREAK].firstRecord = 'N';
      }
      else
      {
         if (strcmp(holdAreas[STATE_BREAK].state, customerRecord->state) != 0)
         {
         StateBreak(customerRecord, holdAreas);
      }
      else
      {
         if (strcmp(holdAreas[CITY_BREAK].city, customerRecord->city) != 0)
         {
            CityBreak(customerRecord, holdAreas, CITY_BREAK);
         }
         else
         {
            if (strcmp(holdAreas[ZIP_CODE_BREAK].zipCode, customerRecord->zipCode) != 0)
            {
               ZipCodeBreak(customerRecord, holdAreas, ZIP_CODE_BREAK);
            }
         }
      }
   }

if (LineCounter > PAGE_SIZE)
{
      PrintHeadings(customerRecord);
   }
   LineCounter ++;

   holdAreas[ZIP_CODE_BREAK].bill += customerRecord->bill;
   holdAreas[ZIP_CODE_BREAK].numberOfCharges += customerRecord->numberOfCharges;
   holdAreas[ZIP_CODE_BREAK].discount += customerRecord->discount;

   fprintf(ReportFile,"\t|     %s %-30.30s %4d %8.2f %8.2f     |\n", customerRecord->memberId,
      fullName, customerRecord->numberOfCharges, customerRecord->discount,
      customerRecord->bill);

   return ReadCustomerFileRecord(customerRecord);
}

/*
 +
 +----------------------------------------------------------------+
 +
 */

char * ReadCustomerFileRecord (struct CustomerRecordLayout * customerRecord)
{
   char inputBuffer[INPUT_BUFFER_SIZE + 1];
   char * moreData;
   int toFloat;
   int toFloat1;
```

```
        moreData = fgets(inputBuffer, INPUT_BUFFER_SIZE + 1, CustomerFile);

    /* Now, parse the data into their respective fields. */
    if (moreData)
        {
            sscanf(inputBuffer,
            "%20c%15c%c%*1c%*1c%*26c%17c%2c%5c%*10c%*3c%4c%*3c%2d%4d%5d", customerRecord->lastName,
                customerRecord->firstName, &customerRecord->initial, customerRecord->city,
                customerRecord->state, customerRecord->zipCode, customerRecord->memberId,
                &customerRecord->numberOfCharges, &toFloat1, &toFloat);
            customerRecord->bill = toFloat / 100.0;
            customerRecord->discount = toFloat1 / 100.0;
        }
    return moreData;
}

/*
 +
 +----------------------------------------------------------------+
 +
 */

void StateBreak(struct CustomerRecordLayout * customerRecord,
    struct SummaryControls * holdAreas)
{
    CityBreak(customerRecord, holdAreas, STATE_BREAK);

    holdAreas[FINAL_BREAK].bill += holdAreas[STATE_BREAK].bill;
    holdAreas[FINAL_BREAK].numberOfCharges += holdAreas[STATE_BREAK].numberOfCharges;
    holdAreas[FINAL_BREAK].discount += holdAreas[STATE_BREAK].discount;

    fprintf(ReportFile,"\t    State Totals  %*s%4d %8.2f %8.2f      |\n", 24, " ",
        holdAreas[STATE_BREAK].numberOfCharges, holdAreas[STATE_BREAK].discount,
        holdAreas[STATE_BREAK].bill);
    BLANK_LINE
    MID_LINE
    BLANK_LINE
    fprintf(ReportFile,"\t|     State: %-55s|\n", customerRecord->state);
    fprintf(ReportFile,"\t|      City: %-55s|\n", customerRecord->city);
    fprintf(ReportFile,"\t|  Zip Code: %-55s|\n", customerRecord->zipCode);
    BLANK_LINE
    LineCounter += 8;

    /*  Reset the hold areas for the state  */
    holdAreas[STATE_BREAK].bill = 0.0;
    holdAreas[STATE_BREAK].numberOfCharges = 0;
    holdAreas[STATE_BREAK].discount = 0.0;
    strcpy(holdAreas[STATE_BREAK].state, customerRecord->state);
}

/*
 +
 +----------------------------------------------------------------+
 +
 */

void CityBreak(struct CustomerRecordLayout * customerRecord,
    struct SummaryControls * holdAreas, int breakInd)
{
    ZipCodeBreak(customerRecord, holdAreas, CITY_BREAK);

    /*
```

```
   +  Update the state totals. In other words, roll the city totals
   +  to state totals.
   */

   holdAreas[STATE_BREAK].bill += holdAreas[CITY_BREAK].bill;
   holdAreas[STATE_BREAK].numberOfCharges += holdAreas[CITY_BREAK].numberOfCharges;
   holdAreas[STATE_BREAK].discount += holdAreas[CITY_BREAK].discount;

   fprintf(ReportFile,"\t|    City Totals  %*s%4d %8.2f %8.2f      |\n", 25, " ",
      holdAreas[CITY_BREAK].numberOfCharges, holdAreas[CITY_BREAK].discount,
      holdAreas[CITY_BREAK].bill);
   LineCounter++;

   if (breakInd == CITY_BREAK)
   {
      BLANK_LINE
      fprintf(ReportFile,"\t|        City: %-55s|\n", customerRecord->city);
      fprintf(ReportFile,"\t|    Zip Code: %-55s|\n", customerRecord->zipCode);
      BLANK_LINE
      LineCounter += 4;
   }

   /*   Reset the hold areas for the City   */
   holdAreas[CITY_BREAK].bill = 0.0;
   holdAreas[CITY_BREAK].numberOfCharges = 0;
   holdAreas[CITY_BREAK].discount = 0.0;
   strcpy(holdAreas[CITY_BREAK].city, customerRecord->city);
}

/*
 +
 +-------------------------------------------------------------------+
 +
 */

void ZipCodeBreak(struct CustomerRecordLayout * customerRecord,
   struct SummaryControls * holdAreas, int breakInd)
{
   /*
   +  Update the city totals. In other words, roll the zip code
   +  totals to city totals.
   */

   holdAreas[CITY_BREAK].bill += holdAreas[ZIP_CODE_BREAK].bill;
   holdAreas[CITY_BREAK].numberOfCharges += holdAreas[ZIP_CODE_BREAK].numberOfCharges;
   holdAreas[CITY_BREAK].discount += holdAreas[ZIP_CODE_BREAK].discount;

   BLANK_LINE
   fprintf(ReportFile, "\t|  Zip Code Totals  %*s%4d %8.2f %8.2f     |\n", 21," ",
      holdAreas[ZIP_CODE_BREAK].numberOfCharges, holdAreas[ZIP_CODE_BREAK].discount,
      holdAreas[ZIP_CODE_BREAK].bill);
   LineCounter += 2;

   if (breakInd == ZIP_CODE_BREAK)
   {
      BLANK_LINE
      fprintf(ReportFile,"\t|    Zip Code: %-55s|\n", customerRecord->zipCode);
      BLANK_LINE
      LineCounter += 3;
   }

   /*   Reset the hold areas for the zip code   */
   holdAreas[ZIP_CODE_BREAK].bill = 0.0;
```

```
      holdAreas[ZIP_CODE_BREAK].numberOfCharges = 0;
      holdAreas[ZIP_CODE_BREAK].discount = 0.0;
      strcpy(holdAreas[ZIP_CODE_BREAK].zipCode, customerRecord->zipCode);
}
/*
 +
 +----------------------------------------------------------------+
 +
*/

void Termination(struct CustomerRecordLayout * customerRecord,
   struct SummaryControls * holdAreas)
{
   StateBreak(customerRecord, holdAreas);

   MID_LINE
   BLANK_LINE
   fprintf(ReportFile, "\t|      Final Total: %*s %4d %8.2f %8.2f      |\n", 23, " ",
      holdAreas[FINAL_BREAK].numberOfCharges, holdAreas[FINAL_BREAK].discount,
      holdAreas[FINAL_BREAK].bill);
   MID_LINE
   BLANK_LINE
   BOTTOM_LINE
}

/*
 +
 +----------------------------------------------------------------+
 +
*/

void PrintHeadings(struct CustomerRecordLayout * customerRecord)

{
   if (!FirstTime)
   {
      BOTTOM_LINE
      fprintf(ReportFile, "\f\n");
   }
   FirstTime = 0;

   TOP_LINE
   BLANK_LINE
   fprintf(ReportFile, "\t|    Program Name: acech14c.EXE        Page: %2d  |\n", ++PageNo);
   fprintf(ReportFile, "\t|       Run Date: 12/10/2000       Ace Billing              |\n");
   BLANK_LINE
   BLANK_LINE
   MID_LINE
   BLANK_LINE

   fprintf(ReportFile, "\t|   Summary Report By State, City, Zip Code, and Last Name   |\n");
   BLANK_LINE
   MID_LINE
   BLANK_LINE
   fprintf(ReportFile,"\t|      State: %-55s|\n", customerRecord->state);
   fprintf(ReportFile,"\t|       City: %-55s|\n", customerRecord->city);
   fprintf(ReportFile,"\t|   Zip Code: %-55s|\n", customerRecord->zipCode);
   BLANK_LINE

   LineCounter = 17;
   return;
}
```

14.19.4   Output

Figures 14.8 to 14.10 show sample output of a couple pages of acech14c.exe.

Figure 14.8   acech14c.exe — *Sample Output (p.1)*

```
Program Name: acech14c.EXE                             Page:    1
    Run Date: 12/10/2000           Ace Billing


  Summary Report By State, City, Zip Code, and Last Name


      State: AZ
       City: Globe
  Zip Code: 85233

     3215 Adenauer, Konrad              21     20.00     190.00
     3215 Addison, Joseph               21     20.00     190.00
     3215 Goodall, Jane                 21     20.00     190.00

  Zip Code Totals                       63     60.00     570.00

  Zip Code: 85234

     3215 Tubman, Harriet               21     20.00     190.00
     3215 Daimler, Gottlieb             21     20.00     190.00

  Zip Code Totals                       42     40.00     380.00
  City Totals                          105    100.00     950.00

       City: Phoenix
  Zip Code: 85283

     3215 Daubigny, Charles-Francois    21     20.00     190.00
     3215 Earhart, Amelia               21     20.00     190.00
     3215 Milaud, Darius                21     20.00     190.00

  Zip Code Totals                       63     60.00     570.00

  Zip Code: 85284

     3215 Darwin, Charles               21     20.00     190.00
     3215 Delacroix, Eugene             21     20.00     190.00
     3215 Planck, Max                   21     20.00     190.00
     3215 Forssmann, Werner             21     20.00     190.00

  Zip Code Totals                       84     80.00     760.00
  City Totals                          147    140.00    1330.00
  State Totals                         252    240.00    2280.00


      State: GA
       City: Atlanta
  Zip Code: 30330
```

Figure 14.9 `acech14c.exe`—*Sample Output (p.2)*

```
   Program Name: acech14c.EXE                         Page:    2
      Run Date: 12/10/2000           Ace Billing



   Summary Report By State, City, Zip Code, and Last Name



     State: GA
      City: Atlanta
 Zip Code: 30330

     6532 Franco, Francisco             17     70.00       80.00
     6532 Longfellow, Henry             17     70.00       80.00
     6532 Ledbetter, Huddie             17     70.00       80.00
     6532 Schick, Bela                  17     70.00       80.00

 Zip Code Totals                        68    280.00      320.00

 Zip Code: 30340

     6532 Scarlatti, Alessandro         17     70.00       80.00
     6532 Santa Anna, AntonioLopez      17     70.00       80.00
     6532 Schiller, Friedrich           17     70.00       80.00
     6532 Sandburg, Carl                17     70.00       80.00

 Zip Code Totals                        68    280.00      320.00

 Zip Code: 30350

     6532 Rommel, Erwin                 17     70.00       80.00
     6532 Roosevelt, Eleanor            17     70.00       80.00
     6532 Rickover, Hyman               17     70.00       80.00
     6532 Richter, Jean                 17     70.00       80.00

 Zip Code Totals                        68    280.00      320.00
 City Totals                           204    840.00      960.00

      City: Augusta
 Zip Code: 34993

     3228 Romanov, Michael              20     10.00       50.00
     3228 Schelling, Friedrich          20     10.00       50.00
     3228 Sardou, Victorien             20     10.00       50.00
     3228 Samuelson, Paul               20     10.00       50.00

 Zip Code Totals                        80     40.00      200.00

 Zip Code: 34994
```

Figure 14.10 acech14c.exe—*Sample Output (p.3)*

```
Program Name: acech14c.EXE                        Page:   3
    Run Date: 12/10/2000           Ace Billing


Summary Report By State, City, Zip Code, and Last Name


      State: GA
       City: Augusta
  Zip Code: 34994

      3228 Schonberg, Arnold          20    10.00     50.00
      3228 Segovia, Andres            20    10.00     50.00
      3228 Selden, John               20    10.00     50.00
      3228 Steinbeck, John            20    10.00     50.00
      3228 Stanton, Elizabeth         20    10.00     50.00

  Zip Code Totals                    100    50.00    250.00

  Zip Code: 34995

      3228 Beyle, Marie               20    10.00     50.00
      3228 Stevenson, Robert          20    10.00     50.00
      3228 Truman, Harry              20    10.00     50.00

  Zip Code Totals                     60    30.00    150.00
  City Totals                        240   120.00    600.00

       City: Savannah
  Zip Code: 30001

      3432 Thatcher, Margaret         11    10.00     20.00
      3432 Gorbachev, Raisa           11    10.00     20.00
      3432 Ghandi, Indira             11    10.00     20.00

  Zip Code Totals                     33    30.00     60.00

  Zip Code: 30002

      3432 Maimonides, Moses          11    10.00     20.00
      3432 Mayo, Charles              11    10.00     20.00
      3432 Mazarin, Jules             11    10.00     20.00
      3432 McCarthy, Eugene           11    10.00     20.00

  Zip Code Totals                     44    40.00     80.00

  Zip Code: 30003
```

Chapter Summary

1. Reading from a file means taking data from a file and placing a copy of it in the computer's primary memory.

2. Writing to a file means taking data from the computer's RAM and placing a copy of it into a file. Placing the data just after the end of the existing data in the file can be referred to as appending.

3. In a file, data is always stored on a byte level only. What is stored in the file are the character representations of values 0 to decimal 255, according to whatever character-encoding system the computer uses.

4. Generally, reading and writing are buffered.

5. The text functions read and write characters as such. The binary functions treat the characters written to or read from a file as only a graphic way of expressing the byte values the characters represent.

6. The text functions are `fprintf()` and `fscanf()`, `fputs()` and `fgets()`, and `fgetc()` and `fputc()` for formatted, string, and character writing and reading.

7. We can place numerical data as well as text into the file with the text functions, but the numerical data is simply stored in character form.

8. The binary functions are `fwrite()` for writing and `fread()` for reading.

9. We open a file by calling `fopen()` and setting a pointer of type FILE to `fopen()`'s return value. The first argument is the name of the file to be opened; the second is the file-opening mode.

10. You must use the FILE pointer returned by `fopen()` as an argument in all operations relating to the file, not the filename.

11. The file-opening mode dictates whether the file is opened for reading, writing, or appending (or reading and writing or appending) and is in text or binary: `r`, `w`, `a`, `rb`, `wb`, `ab`, `r+`, `w+`, `a+`, `rb+`, `wb+`, `ab+`.

12. Standard C requires that when your C program starts, three text-stream FILE structures be automatically opened: standard output, standard input, and standard error (`stdout`, `stdin`, and `stderr`).

13. You close the file with `fclose()`, which takes a single argument, the FILE pointer.

14. The `freopen()` function attempts to close the file currently associated with the current stream and to open another file, pointing the FILE pointer to the new file. It can be used to redirect a file to `stdin` or redirect `stdout` to a file, or redirect `stderr` to an error log file for future review.

15. The `fprintf()` and `fscanf()` functions work the same way as `printf()` and `scanf()`, with the addition of a FILE pointer argument.

16. The `fgets()` and `fputs()` functions also add a FILE pointer argument to the `gets()` and `puts()` char pointer argument. The `fgets()` function adds another argument, the maximum number of characters to be read, making `fgets()` safer to use than `gets()`.

17. The `gets()` function discards the newline and the `puts()` function adds one. The `fgets()` function retains the newline and the `fputs()` function does not add one.

18. The `fgets()` function stops at the earlier of reading a newline or when it has read one character less than the maximum number of characters specified as its second argument. This allows it always to store the NULL character at the end of the string.

19. The `fgetc()` and `fputc()` functions operate the same way as `getchar()` and `putchar()` do for the standard input stream. Each takes a FILE pointer as an additional argument.

20. You can use `ungetc()` to place a character into the associated input stream ahead of what is already there. You can be guaranteed of placing only a single character without an intervening read function call.

21. The character placed into the stream by `ungetc()` will be read on the next call to `fgetc()` or any other read operation function on the same stream.

22. For `fwrite()`, the first argument is the starting address in RAM of where we are copying from. For `fread()`, the first argument is the starting address in RAM of where we are copying to.

23. In each case the pointer is of type pointer to `void`, so that we may use the address of any type of variable to copy from or assign to without having to use a type cast for the first argument.

24. These two functions write or read in a specified number of blocks of a specified byte size at a time. We typically use devices such as `sizeof()` or `strlen()` to help us copy the correct number of bytes we want to copy.

25. Use the text functions when you want to write text to the file, including numerical data you find more convenient to store as text and when portability is paramount.

26. Use the binary functions when you want to write numerical data as such to a file and when you want to store text or text and numerical data en masse, as large data objects.

27. Writing data in order in the file and reading it back in the same order is called sequential access. Jumping about in the file during reading or writing is known as random access.

28. The `ftell()` function lets you know how many bytes from the beginning of the file you are; `fseek()` lets you move a specified number of bytes after the beginning, before the end, or before or after the current position in the file.

29. Except for returning to the point when `ftell()` was last called, using `fseek()` in text mode is implementation defined and will not always produce meaningful results.

30. A binary stream need not meaningfully support `fseek()` calls with a mode of SEEK_END.

31. The `rewind()` function not only moves the file position to the beginning of the file, but it also clears the error indicator.

32. One convenient way to mark your place between write or read statements so that you can return there is the combination of `fgetpos()` and `fsetpos()`.

33. These functions are meant to handle two situations—files too large for their positions to be representable by a `long`, and system file structures where file position is

more complex than simply a matter of a fixed number of bytes from the beginning.

34. The r+, w+, and a+ update modes allow for both reading and writing to a file.

35. The buffer for the file must be flushed between read and write calls to the same file.

36. One way to flush the buffer expressly is to call fflush() with the name of the FILE pointer as the argument. You can flush the buffers for all files with fflush(NULL);

37. Another way to flush the buffers is to call one of the file-positioning functions, fsetpos(), fseek(), or rewind().

38. The clearerr() function clears both the error indicator for a stream and its end-of-file indicator.

39. The feof() function tests whether the end-of-file indicator for the stream is on; the ferror() function tests whether the error indicator is set.

40. You alter the default buffer size for a particular file by calling setvbuf(). You can also set the type of buffering: fully buffered, line buffered, or no buffering.

41. If you call setvbuf() with a second argument of NULL, the function assigns the file a buffer on its own.

42. You must call setvbuf() immediately after opening the file.

43. Standard C permits implementations to add, alter, or delete characters on input and output to conform to system conventions for representing text.

44. Standard C guarantees that data read in from a text stream will be the same as data earlier written out to that stream only if the data consists of printable characters (as defined by isprint()), horizontal tab characters, and newline characters.

45. Some systems have trouble with a last line in a text file that does not terminate in a newline character.

46. Some systems limit text lines to a specific length.

47. For binary files, Standard C requires that data read in match data written earlier, but this is only guaranteed for the same implementation on both the writing and reading end.

48. Alignment, significant byte storage and bit evaluation mechanism, type size, character encoding, and other differences make reading and writing in binary across systems a risky business.

49. You can delete a file with the remove() function; you can rename a file with rename().

50. The tmpfile() function opens a temporary binary file in the current working directory in wb+ mode. At normal termination of the program or explicit closing of the file, the file is automatically deleted.

Review Questions

1. When a file is opened for reading and writing, generally reading and writing take place directly from one location in the file to another without involving primary memory (True or False).

2. In a file, values are stored on a bit level, as in primary memory (True or False).

3. The first argument to fopen() must be a literal string (True or False).

4. None of the three text streams normally automatically opened, is opened if your program uses no file operations at all (True or False).

5. If an attempt is made to open a file in r+ mode for reading and writing, the file will be automatically created if it does not now exist (True or False).

6. Any filed opened during a program will be left open after normal program termination unless explicitly closed by fclose() or another file-closing function (True or False).

7. Closing a file automatically closes any associated output stream (True or False).

8. It is not possible to send output from putchar(), printf(), and puts() to a file instead of the standard output device; the related file output functions must be used (True or False).

9. It is possible to write the value 75.375 to a file either as a binary value or as text characters (True or False).

10. Unlike gets(), fgets() has a built-in feature that guards against array overflow (True or False).

11. If you call fseek() between reads and writes to the same file, there is no need to explicitly flush the buffers (True or False).

12. The character placed into the input stream by ungetc() must have been previously read in from the input stream (True or False).

13. The first arguments to both fread() and fwrite() represent file locations (True or False).

14. Calls to fread() and fwrite() advance the file position by the number of bytes read or written; the calls return the number of bytes read or written (True or False).

15. What is the output of the following:

```
FILE *fp = fopen("c:\\junk", "w+");
float a;
fputs("125.25", fp);
rewind(fp);
fscanf(fp, "%f", &a);
printf("%.2f\n", a);
```

16. What does the following print, assuming the characters A and B have encoded values of 65 and 66, respectively, and assuming the computer stores least significant byte first?

```
FILE *fp = fopen("c:\\junk", "w+");
unsigned long numeric = 66UL + (65UL << 8)
    + (65UL << 16) + (65UL << 24);
```

```
int i;
static char alpha[5];
fwrite(&numeric, sizeof(unsigned long), 1,
   fp);
rewind(fp);
for (i = 0; i < 4; i++)
   alpha[i] = fgetc(fp);
puts(alpha);
```

17. Since floating point numbers are complex, the binary reading and writing functions work more slowly than the text functions (True or False).

18. Since fseek() and ftell() are not completely reliable indicators of byte position in text mode, the following is not guaranteed to get back to the same place in a file opened in text mode even if a long is perfectly adequate to specify file position in all cases (True or False):

```
long position = ftell(fp);
fread(&record, sizeof(record), 1, fp);
fseek(fp, position, SEEK_SET);
```

19. The rewind() function is guaranteed to get back to the very beginning of the file even if the file is opened in text mode (True or False).

20. The fgetpos()-fsetpos() combination is more portable than the ftell()-fseek() paired calls (True or False).

21. The setvbuf() function can be called successfully for one stream more than once in a program, provided a different buffer address is used each time (True or False).

22. All operating systems distinguish between binary and text files and treat them differently (True or False).

23. Since implementations are given wide latitude in text mode to add or delete characters, binary files tend to be more portable (True or False).

24. You cannot remove or rename a file from your C program with Standard C functions; C leaves such operations to the operating system (True or False).

25. Given the following declarations, complete the code fragment that would write the values of myself to the file with a single statement; read those values back into I; and convert the string in I.date to an unsigned long and store that value in I.numdate. (Assume no padding or other alignment considerations.)

```
FILE *fp = fopen("c:\\junk", "wb+");
struct me {char name[30], ssn[10],
   date[7];} myself =
   {"Kris Kringle", "346404059",
   "991225",};
struct and
{
   char name[30], ssn[10], date[7];
   unsigned long numdate;
} I;
```

Programming Exercises

The specifications of the programming assignments were introduced in Chapter 1, at which time you were to

- think through the solution to these problems.
- identify the modules that, once implemented, will solve the problem.
- prepare a hierarchy chart of all the modules.
- prepare a pseudocode/flowchaart for each module in the hierarchy chart.
- write the program stubs the same way we did with the ACE Billing system application.

This chapter has added coverage of files to our C knowledge. We urge you to continue developing what you started in Chapter 1. If you have not started, we recommend that you start by applying the methodology presented in that chapter. We have helped you get started with some of the programming assignments by specifying only what can be done by this time.

Modify all the programming assignments you did in Chapter 13 to use file operations rather than reading data from standard input. See Section 14.19 for the acech014.c program.

Additional enhancements and modifications for each programming assignment are specified accordingly.

Programming Assignment 14.1: Billing

Program Description

There are now two input record layouts; see Tables P14.1A and P14.1B. Create a Part Reference File that has at least 10 parts and an Order Activity File that has at least 25 entries. Write a program to read both files in and create a bill showing each transaction, with each field plus an extended price for each transaction, and a total. The transactions for any one part should be consolidated (in other words, if you have 10 parts, there will be no more than 10 transaction lines).

Table P14.1A   *Order Activity Record Layout*

Order Activity File			
Field Name	**Size**	**Type**	**No. of Decimal Positions**
Order Date	8	Alphanumeric (MM/DD/YY)	
Product Number	6	Alphanumeric	
Quantity	5	Alphanumeric (up to 32,000)	

Table P14.1B   *Past Reference Record Layout*

Part Reference File			
Field Name	**Size**	**Type**	**No. of Decimal Positions**
Product Number	6	Alphanumeric	
Product Description	25	Alphanumeric	
Cost per item	8	Alphanumeric (up to 999,999.99)	2

Programming Assignment 14.2: Payroll

Program Description

The new input record layouts are shown in Tables P14.2A and P14.2B.

Table P14.2A   *Time Card Record Layout*

Time Card Record Layout			
Field Name	**Size**	**Type**	**No. of Decimal Positions**
Payroll Date	8	Alphanumeric (MMDDYYYYY)	
Start Time	4	Alphanumeric (HHMM: 24-hour clock)	
Ending Time	4	Alphanumeric (HHMM: 24-hour clock)	
Social Security No.	9	Alphanumeric (digits)	

Table P14.2B   *Personnel File Record Layout*

Personnel File Record Layout			
Field Name	**Size**	**Type**	**No. of Decimal Positions**
Employee Name	25	Alphanumeric	
Social Security No.	9	Alphanumeric (digits)	
Employee Title	15	Alphanumeric	
Employee Hourly Pay Rate	4	Alphanumeric (up to 99.99)	2

Create a Personnel File that has at least 10 employees and a file for the week's time cards for each employee (five-day week). Write a program that reads the files and generates a gross paycheck amount for each employee for the week.

Programming Assignment 14.8: Science and Engineering (Chemical Engineering)

Program Description

Take the record layout specified in Programming Assignment 1.8. Create at least three files with data in the specified layout. Assume that the data for specific volume, enthalpy, and entropy are the same for a given combination of temperature and pressure (in inches of mercury). Make sure you have several entries for each temperature (with different pressures). The files should be in order by temperature and within temperature by pressure.

Combine all entries into a single report in the following manner. Merge the files by interleaving the entries in the various files according to temperature and pressure. There should be only one entry for each combination of temperature and pressure in the final file. Print a report.

Programming Assignment 14.11: Distribution/Packaging/Shipping

Program Description

Use the record layout from Programming Assignment 1.11. Write a program to read each record and, if the back-order date is more than six months before today's date, to delete the record from the file. All deleted records go into a separate file to be used to generate letters to the customer advising of the company's inability to fill the order.

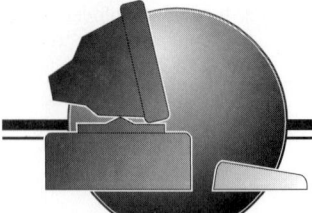

CHAPTER **15**

Dynamic Data Structures and Memory Allocation

OBJECTIVES

- To appreciate the resource management advantages that dynamic memory allocation has over arrays and structures
- To learn how to allocate, reallocate, and free memory dynamically
- To understand how to use pointers to manage dynamic data structures
- To learn how to create indexed files of records
- To see how to use key files to order, search for, add, delete, and edit records
- To learn fixed- and variable-length record storage techniques and examine the relative advantages of each approach

- To become familiar with Standard C functions for binary searches and ordering
- To create your own binary functions and data structures
- To be able to create and edit various forms of linear and binary linked lists of dynamically reserved structures
- To be able to create more sophisticated menus and message boxes

NEW TERMS

binary search
binary tree
circular linked list
double-linked list

dummy node
key
linked list
memory leakage

nodes
perfectly balanced tree
root

Programs not infrequently must manage vast amounts of data, often in the form of records—employee records, customer records, sales records, inventory records. Using a unique variable name for each piece of data would obviously be a poor way to manage the data. So far, we have looked at two methods of data management: arrays and structures.

We first examined arrays as a more organized method of storing like bits of data, but there we found three key drawbacks:

1. All data must be of the same type. If we want to store names, addresses, salaries, years of service, and grade, we need a number of separate arrays.
2. The bits of data must all be of the same size—or at least, we must allocate the same amount of room. If we have 1000 personnel records and the longest name is twice as many characters as the next longest, we must size our array to fit the longest one. If fitting "Rushing North Wind of the Everlasting Willow under the Full Moon Smith" requires 73 characters, and the average name is only 20 letters, we waste 53,000 bytes.

3. The number of elements in the array must be determined at compile time by a constant rather than interactively filled in by a variable value at run time. If we do not know precisely how many records the user will be entering or we will be reading from a file of uncertain contents, we have to either allocate massive amounts of memory by making more elements than we reasonably expect to use or run the risk of running out of array space.

Next, we took a look at structures. Structures allow us to group diverse but related bits of data into one variable. We can, for example, maintain a customer database with each customer's data residing in a separate element of an array of structure variables and each element containing separate members of the appropriate data types for the customer's name, address, city, state, zip code, home and work telephone numbers, social security number, income level, birth date, dates and amounts of purchases, shipping preference, and so on. By using pointers or subscripts, we can easily move from record to record. But structures still do not alleviate the twin memory problems that plague arrays—making the structure members large enough to fit the largest expected pieces of data and compile-time sizing.

The way we overcome these problems is with a combination of dynamic data structures and Standard C run-time memory allocation functions. Dynamic data structures are informal groupings of records that have no system-defined type or variable name. They are accessible through chains of pointers that our program manages. Remember that arrays and structures are just contiguous bytes in memory that the compiler *treats* as related in specified ways. With dynamic data structures, we essentially do the same job the compiler does in this regard by marshaling, viewing, and manipulating bytes in memory in ways *we* dictate.

Our strategy will be to use the function `malloc()` to request memory in tailor-made chunks just large enough to accommodate the data we need to store. We will use a dynamic data structure known as a ***linked list*** to allow us to keep track of these memory chunks as we request them. The linked list will consist of a series of structure variables. Each structure variable will be composed of one or more members that store data and a member that will store the address of the next of our structure variables. The structure variables will not have variable names, nor will there be an array of them—to use these would defeat our aim of run-time creation of just as many of them as we need. Our only access to them will be through the series of pointer members. In effect, the variables are anonymous.

15.1   THE `malloc()` FUNCTION

We call `malloc()` to request a block of memory and receive a pointer to the start of that block. The memory block will be in the heap on the PC (see Appendix B regarding the heap).

You pass to `malloc()` as its sole argument the number of bytes of memory you want. If there is enough memory available, `malloc()` returns the address of the start of the memory block; if not, it returns NULL. To keep track of that address, so that we can access the memory thus reserved for us, we assign the return value to a pointer:

```
char *name;
name = malloc(11);
strcpy(name, "Andre Gide");
puts(name);
```

The prototype for `malloc()` is found in `stdlib.h`. The type of its return value is a pointer to void, so we can set a pointer of any type to its return value without having to use a type cast:

```
void *malloc(size_t bytes);
```

The argument type, `size_t`, is a `typedef` (a nickname or alias for a defined C type; see Chapter 13) for an unsigned integer type defined in `stddef.h` as the type of the value returned by the `sizeof` operator. The allocated memory block is not initialized in any way, so you cannot depend on its contents.

Generally, unlike the last example, we will use `strlen()` or `sizeof()` to make the byte allocation more convenient and amenable to run-time interactive sizing—which is, after all, the chief purpose of this exercise. We will also make use of a dummy variable of large size to temporarily house the interactive input before creating memory space just large enough so that we can then copy the input to a pointer to the memory space.

Listing 15.1 `malloc.c`

```c
/* malloc.c */

/* simple use of malloc to reserve space for a small record */

#include <stdio.h>
#include <stdlib.h> /* malloc */
#include <string.h> /* strlen, strcpy */

int main(void)
{
    char temp[81];
    struct record
    {
        char *name;
    } *ptr;

    ptr = malloc(sizeof(struct record));
    puts("Enter name");

    gets(temp);
    ptr->name = malloc(strlen(temp) + 1);
    strcpy(ptr->name, temp);

    printf("name is %s\n", ptr->name);
    printf("ptr: %p, &ptr: %p, name: %p, &name: %p\n", ptr, &ptr, ptr->name, &ptr->name);
}
```

We have now reserved enough memory for a structure and we have a pointer, `ptr`, rather than a structure variable name to show us the start of that memory. That memory location contains a pointer to another reserved memory area just large enough to house a name we obtained interactively. (Actually, a request to `malloc()` may be rounded up to some power of 2 convenient to the implementation. Also, memory reserved by `malloc()` is generally aligned just as we have seen earlier with structure variables, so there may be some unused memory between the areas reserved by successive calls to `malloc()`.)

Note that `ptr` does not point to the name; nor does the structure pointed to by `ptr` house the name. The structure is but 2 bytes in size. This structure, pointed to by `ptr`, contains merely a pointer that points to our name data. Take a sample run:

```
Enter name
Paul Claudel
name is Paul Claudel
ptr: 05BC, &ptr: FFF4, name: 05C4, &name: 05BC
```

Figure 15.1 shows what we have in memory.

Figure 15.1 *Pointer to Structure Housing Pointer to Data*

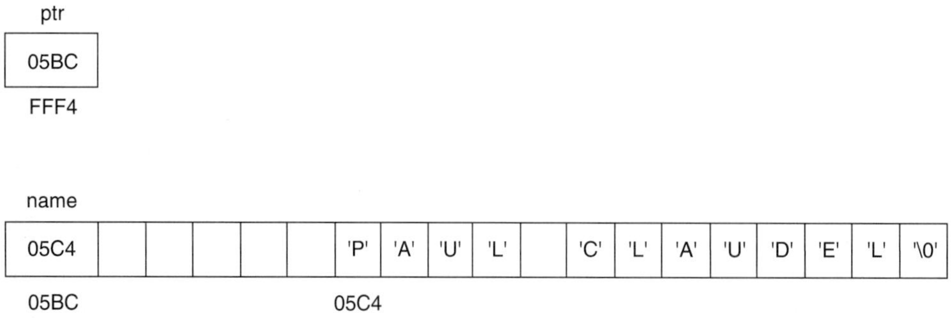

15.1.1   Solving a char Pointer Memory Problem

For the char pointer portion of this example, the construction solves the memory-overwriting problem characteristic of pointers. If we initialize a char pointer on declaration, the compiler assigns sufficient space to the address pointed to for the initializing string:

```
char *name = "Andre Gide";
```

The variable name now points to an 11-byte memory area. However, depending on the length of the input, the following may now overwrite some program data:

```
gets(name);
```

The malloc() construction we've just used makes sure there is sufficient space. At the same time, it ensures that we do not use more space than is needed, as might be the case with the following:

```
char name[81];
gets(name);
```

15.1.2   Alternative Formulations

As is often the case in C, we can make our memory allocation construction more compact. Instead of

```
gets(temp);
ptr->name = malloc(strlen(temp) + 1);
strcpy(ptr->name, temp);
```

we can write:

```
gets(temp);
strcpy(ptr->name = malloc(strlen(temp) + 1), temp);
```

or, even more compact:

```
strcpy(ptr->name = malloc(strlen(temp) + 1), gets(temp));
```

However, the less compact versions are easier to follow.

15.1.3   Making Sure There Is Sufficient Memory Available

It is good practice to check the return value of the call to malloc() to make sure we have sufficient space available. Otherwise, we run the risk of writing over other data already stored by the program.

 **Listing**   **15.2 mal_chk.c**

```
/* mal_chk.c */

/* do error-testing on malloc calls */

#include <stdio.h>
#include <stdlib.h> /* malloc */
#include <string.h> /* strlen, strcpy */

int main(void)
{
    char temp[81];
    struct record
    {
        char *name;
    } *ptr;

    puts("Enter name");
```

```
    gets(temp);

    if ((ptr = malloc(sizeof(struct record))) == NULL ¦¦
        (ptr->name = malloc(strlen(temp) + 1)) == NULL)
        puts("malloc(): not enough memory");
    else
    {
        strcpy(ptr->name, temp);
        puts(ptr->name);
    }
}
```

15.2   ALLOCATING MEMORY AND INITIALIZING TO ZEROS: `calloc()`

If we want to initialize all bytes allocated dynamically to 0, we can use `calloc()` rather than `malloc()`. Apart from this initialization difference, `calloc()` uses two arguments to specify the number of bytes to reserve instead of `malloc()`'s one: the number of blocks of bytes we want and the size of each block (this latter most commonly furnished by the `sizeof` operator):

```
void *calloc(size_t num_blocks, size_t bytes_per_block);
```

A simple example:

```
int *ptr;
int blocks;
puts("How many ints do you need?");
scanf("%d", &blocks);
ptr = calloc(blocks, sizeof(int));
```

This construction achieves roughly the same result as we would have if we had known the number of `ints` needed and declared a static `int` array that size. The memory location would be different, and we would have an array name, however.

Indeed, we can treat our homemade structure as if we *had* declared an array of `ints`:

```
*(ptr + 1) = 5;
ptr[2] = 10;
```

The second of these two statements is allowed because, as we learned earlier, we can use array *notation* for a pointer and vice versa.

We also could have achieved precisely the same result with `malloc()`:

```
ptr = malloc(blocks * sizeof(int));
memset(ptr, 0, blocks * sizeof(int));
```

We simply take the first of `calloc()`'s arguments and multiply it by the second. Then we set the entire block of bytes to zeros.

Actually, `calloc()` turns off all bits in the reserved memory area. On nearly all systems (including the PC and all others that use the IEEE Standard for Binary Floating Point Arithmetic; see Chapter 12), that will have the effect of value zeroing even if the area is considered a block of floating point variables. However, some systems declaring a static array of `floats` (where each element of the array will have values of zero) will produce a different result from a bit-zeroed memory area reserved by a call to `calloc()`. It is simple enough to check:

```
long double *ptr = calloc(1, sizeof(long double));
printf("%Lf\n", *ptr);
```

15.2.1   Changing the Memory Block Size: `realloc()`

If we want to increase or decrease the size of the block of memory created by `malloc()` or `calloc()`, we can do so with `realloc()`. The arguments to `realloc()` are the pointer to the existing memory block and the new number of bytes, expressed as a single number of bytes, as for `malloc()`:

```
void *realloc(void *ptr, size_t bytes);
```

A simple example:

```
int *p2;
long *p4;
p2 = malloc(sizeof(int));
*p2 = 234;
p4 = realloc(p2, sizeof(long));
*p4 = 232323L;
```

The `realloc()` function returns a pointer to the newly adjusted memory block if the call is successful. On failure (there is insufficient available memory or the size argument evaluates to zero), `realloc()` returns `NULL`. If insufficient memory is a possibility at any given point and you don't want to lose track of a pointed-to memory area, you might consider assigning the return value of a call to `realloc()` to a temporary pointer variable and only making a reassignment if the call does not return `NULL`:

```
char *s1 = "I need my space", *s2 = "I need even more space than that";
char *string, *temp;
if ((string = malloc(sizeof(s1))) != NULL)
    strcpy(string, s1);
if ((temp = realloc(string, sizeof(s2))) != NULL)
{
    string = temp;
    strcpy(string, s2);
}
```

The address returned by a successful call to `realloc()` may be different from that of the start of the original block of memory. The new block will still consist of contiguous bytes in memory. However, if necessary in situations where the block is being enlarged, `realloc()` will "move" the earlier block to another location. Actually, of course, the memory block doesn't move anywhere; it is the values of each byte within the block that must be copied to another location. Repeated calls to `realloc()` of that nature can be time consuming. If a call to `realloc()` returns a different address from the one passed, you should assume that the old memory block has been deallocated and should not be used any longer.

The `realloc()` function preserves the contents of the previously allocated memory block—for the first part of the block if the reserved area is shrunk and for the entire old block if the block is enlarged, with the new part being of undetermined garbage contents, just as for an original call to that new part by `malloc()`.

You can assign the newly expanded or shrunken memory block to the same pointer or a different one.

 Listing **15.3 `realloc.c`**

```
/* realloc.c */

/* illustrate realloc reassignment to same pointer
   and to a new pointer */

#include <stdio.h>
#include <stdlib.h>

int main(void)
```

```
{
   struct employee
   {
      char *name;
   } *p1, *p2;

   p1 = calloc(5, sizeof(struct employee));

   /* reassign to same pointer */

   p1 = realloc(p1, 7 * sizeof(struct employee));

   /* assign to new pointer */

   p2 = realloc(p1, 9 * sizeof(struct employee));
}
```

Note that we have, in each case, made the pointers point to what in effect amounts to an array of structures of type struct employee.

If the pointer passed as an argument to realloc() does not match one earlier returned by malloc(), calloc(), or realloc(), or the pointed-to space has been deallocated by an earlier call to free() (see below) or realloc(), the behavior is undefined.

On the other hand, if the first argument (the pointer to the existing memory area) happens to have a value of NULL, a call to realloc() will still work, provided, of course, that there is enough memory available to honor the new request. The call to realloc() in such a case operates just like a call to malloc(). For instance:

 **Listing** **15.4 realloc0.c**

```
/* realloc0.c */

/* shows realloc will work even if its first argument is NULL */

#include <stdio.h>
#include <stdlib.h>

int main(void)
{
   struct record
   {
      char *name;
   } *ptr;
   int orig_records, new_records;

   puts("Number of records to be entered; enter 0 if none");
   scanf("%d", &orig_records);

   /* if records is 0, ptr will be NULL after this */
   ptr = malloc(orig_records * sizeof(struct record));
   printf("before realloc(): ptr = %p\n", ptr);

   puts("Number of records to be added; enter 0 if none");
   scanf("%d", &new_records);

   /* call will work even if ptr is NULL: becomes like malloc() */
   ptr = realloc(ptr, (new_records + orig_records) * sizeof(struct record));
   printf("after realloc(): ptr = %p\n", ptr);
}
```

Here's a sample run:

```
Number of records to be entered; enter 0 if none
0
before realloc(): ptr = 0
Number of records to be added; enter 0 if none
3
after realloc(): ptr = 079C
```

If the bytes argument to `realloc()` happens to be zero (generally, of course, this will occur as a result of passing a variable the value of which works out to zero at the time of the call), `realloc()` returns a NULL pointer and the old region is deallocated. Such a call would have the same result as a call to `free()`, to which we now turn.

15.3   FREEING A MEMORY BLOCK

If you declare a nonstatic array inside a function, the memory allocated to that array is automatically released once the function call ends. In the homemade structure we've described to this point, this is one more task you must do on your own.

The memory allocated by `malloc()` or `calloc()` remains after the function call in which the memory blocks were assigned ends. We free these memory blocks with `free()`:

```
void free(void *ptr);
```

The `free()` function takes but a single argument: a pointer to the start of the memory block. You do not need to indicate the size of the existing memory block, even if you readjusted the block size with `realloc()`:

```
float *ptr;
ptr = malloc(100 * sizeof(float));
ptr = realloc(ptr, 200 * sizeof(float));
free(ptr);
```

A call to `realloc()` with a second argument of zero will have the same effect as `free()`, as would be the case if the second input below is zero:

```
int *ptr;
int records;
puts("Number of records: ");
scanf("%d", &records);
ptr = malloc(records * sizeof(int));
. . .
puts("Total records to remain outstanding: ");
scanf("%d", &records);
ptr = realloc(ptr, records * sizeof(int));
```

Watch for "dangling" pointers left behind by a call of `free()`:

```
int *p, *q;
p = malloc(sizeof(int));
q = p;
free(p);
. . .
*q = 7; /* oops! memory area may be allocated to something else now*/
```

As you will see later in the chapter, where you have a group of dynamically created structure variables linked by a series of pointers to memory areas reserved by `malloc()`, it is easy to lose track of the reserved memory areas. In fact, even with a simpler framework, it is not difficult to misplace a reserve memory area:

```
char *ptr = malloc(sizeof(char));
*ptr = 'a';
ptr = malloc(sizeof(char));
*ptr = 'b';
free(ptr);
```

Here, by reserving memory twice and pointing the same pointer there both times, we have lost track of the first memory block. If you do not explicitly release memory you have allocated with one of the standard allocation functions, it remains allocated for the balance of the program despite its being inaccessible. In fact, whether memory is freed even on program termination depends on the machine, the system, and the compiler. If a huge amount of memory is allocated and not freed—a process sometimes referred to as inadvertent *memory leakage*—the user may have to reboot the system to unallocate the memory.

Failure to free previously dynamically reserved memory is a common cause of problems, even with commercially sold programs. Whenever we code a construction with braces, we put the open and close braces before we even fill in what goes between them:

```
while (ways < means)
{

}
```

 That way we don't forget about the closing brace later on. The same goes for `malloc()` calls. *Whenever you write a call to `malloc()`, write a companion call to `free()` at the same time, even before you finish the `malloc()` construction.*

If the argument to `free()` happens to be a NULL pointer, the call has no effect (generally, this would happen dynamically in the course of running your program, where depending on what transpired before the call, the pointer passed might or might not be NULL). The argument passed to `free()` must either be the start of a memory area previously reserved by one of the allocation functions (`malloc()`, `calloc()`, or `realloc()`) or NULL; otherwise the behavior of a call is unpredictable. Attempting to `free()` the same memory area more than once would also have unpredictable results.

15.4   LINKED LISTS

We now know how to requisition a tailor-made chunk of memory, how to assign a pointer to mark the start of the memory block, and how to fill that memory block with data. We also know how to free the memory once we're through using it. Our next task is to figure out how to keep track of the pointers to the various memory blocks and how to declare enough of them to accommodate interactive requests for data storage.

We could declare an array of pointers. But that would be inconsistent with our goal of creating just what we find we need at run time. We would not know how large an array to declare. In addition, putting the pointers into an array would make it clumsy to delete or add a record whose memory location is marked by a pointer in the middle of the array. For instance, if we have 500 records and we want to delete the 203rd record, we would first find the pointer to the record, free the memory space, and then wipe the pointer out of the array by copying the address of pointer 204 into 203's slot, 205 into 204's slot, and so on down to the last pointer element—a messy business.

We can manage this matter efficiently by using structures of a slightly different configuration from what we've used as examples in this chapter. We first declare a structure template. We will declare a member for each record field we need to store and an extra member to house the address of the memory starting point of *another* record. To simplify matters for now, let's assume, as we did in our prior examples, that the only field in each record is a name:

```
struct record
{
    char *name;
    struct record *next;
};
```

15.4.1   Overview of Linked-List Creation

To create a linked list, we will proceed this way:

1. Request a structure's worth of memory through `malloc()` (that is, enough to house a pointer to `char` and a pointer to a structure).

2. Record the address of this first block of memory.

3. Obtain a name interactively through `gets()` or noninteractively by reading from a file with `fgets()` or `fread()`, and store it in a temporary buffer.

4. Use `malloc()` to reserve a block of memory just large enough to house the input, set the structure's `char` pointer to the beginning of the memory block, and copy the input to that location.

5. Get another structure's worth of memory. Assign its starting address to the structure pointer member of the *previous* structure variable.

6. Repeat steps 3 to 5. Each time a new record is added, the structure pointer member of the *previous* structure is reset to the memory address of the *current* record's structure.

7. Stop when the user tells us to, or if we are reading from a file, when we reach the end of the file.

8. Set the structure pointer in the current structure to `NULL` to mark the end of the list of records. This assignment will act as a sentinel value, enabling us to stop at the end of the linked list as we traverse it from one point.

To move through these steps, we just need to declare a few pointers to the structure:

```
struct record
{
   char *name;
   struct record *next;
} *start, *current, *previous;
```

15.4.2 Creating and Traversing a Simple Linked List

We will record the address of the first structure in `start`. This is our anchor. Without it, we have no way to start through the maze of structure pointers and the successions of records they point to. We need `current` to access the current record's structure for data storage. We need `previous` to access the previous record's structure so that we can store the address of the current record's memory area.

Because of the dynamic creation of these structure variables, we cannot use variable names for member access. Our only access is through pointers. The unnamed structure variables in a linked list are often called ***nodes***.

Here is a simple program that illustrates the linked-list approach. We had originally thought of a list of honest politicians. After diligent research, we concluded that such a list constitutes what is known in mathematics as a null set, so we decided on famous painters instead.

 **Listing** **15.5 records.c**

```
/* records.c */

/* create and traverse simple linked list */

/*
   Interactively enter names of painters until user signals quit. As
   the names are input, they are stored in a linked list, which is
   printed to the screen at the end.

*/

#include <stdio.h>
#include <stdlib.h> /* malloc */
#include <string.h> /* strcpy, strlen */

struct record
{
   char *name;
   struct record *next;
};

int main(void)
```

```
{
   char temp[81];
   struct record *previous, *current;
   struct record *start = NULL;

   puts("Enter the name of a painter");
   gets(temp);
   while (1)
   {
      /* get space for structure and name at same time */
      if (!(current = malloc(sizeof(struct record))) ||
         !(current->name = malloc(strlen(temp) + 1)))
      {
         puts("malloc(): not enough memory");
         break;
      }
      strcpy(current->name, temp);

      /* the first time through, record the address of the starting node */
      if (!start)
         start = current;

      /* otherwise, point the "next" member of the previous node to this node */
      else previous->next = current;
      /* current node becomes the previous node in the next loop iteration */
      previous = current;
      puts("\nEnter the name of a painter\n"
         "Press [enter] first to quit");
      gets(temp);

      /* stop when user presses enter key without entering a name */
      if (!strcmp("", temp))
         break;
   }

   /* mark end of linked list with sentinel */
   current->next = NULL;
   puts("\nList of painters in database\n");

   /* reset current to marked first address */
   current = start;

   /* traverse linked list, printing out each name pointed to */
   do
   {
      puts(current->name);
      current = current->next;
   } while (current);
}
```

The program uses interactive input to obtain a series of names. It then stores the names in a linked list in the manner we described above. Once the user signals the end of input, we reset current to start. Having thus moved to the start of the linked list, we then traverse the list, printing each name along the way.

We traverse the list in a simple while loop. At each iteration, we print the name member of the structure current points to and then advance current by setting it to the address of the next structure in the list, current->next.

Figure 15.2 *Single-Linked List*

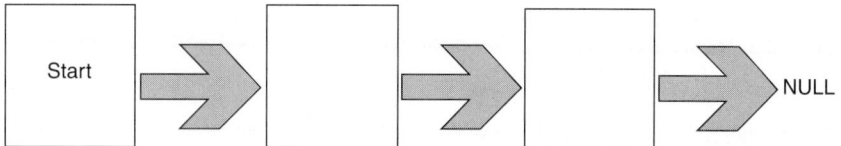

We stop when the postprinting increment of current to current–>next results in current having a value of NULL. The arbitrary sentinel device we employed—setting the last structure's pointer member to NULL—allows us to traverse the list with a loop that stops automatically when

```
while(current);
```

is false.

We end up with a list that you can visualize as in Figure 15.2.

15.5   DATABASE FILES—FIXED-SIZE RECORD STORAGE

It is probably more common to store records in a file than to simply print them to the screen. Then too, most records will consist of more than just the one field records.c permitted us to enter.

The task of storing records in a file—particularly multifield records—gives rise to a problem. Once we read them in, how do we separate the records from one another and the fields from one another to read them back out?

The simplest way is to store records of uniform size. We can read our data into a structure whose members contain a char array for each field we need. We can then use fwrite() to write a structure's worth of data into a database file with a single statement. At the same time, we can place the record into a linked list with the method used by records.c. Later, we can retrieve the same records with fread()—again a structure's worth at a time.

The next program, rec_fixd.c, reads records made up of a name, address, city, state, and zip code from a text function-created file. (It is assumed the text file stores each field of a record on a separate line.) Those records are placed into a linked list. After the records are read into the list, they are written to a binary function-created database file the user designates. If the database file exists, the user is given the choice of wiping out the existing records before adding the new ones or of appending the new records from the text file to the binary database file.

The data from the input file, as placed into the linked list, is then printed. If the selected database file was an existing file, and the user chose to append the new records to the existing ones, we free up all memory reserved for the linked list of records and rewind the database file. Then we load the entire database file into a linked list and print the list out. We have omitted some error-checking to simplify the program.

 **Listing   15.6 rec_fixd.c**

```
/* rec_fixd.c */

/*
   Uses fixed-length records, written to file a structure at a time.

   Reads in records consisting of name, address, city, state, and zip
   from a text file and puts them into a linked list.

   The user first specifies an input file and a database file. The
   input file is a text file; the database file will be a binary
   file. If the database file already exists, the user is given the
   option of overwriting or appending the new records.
```

```
    In a loop, for each record:
    1. A record is first read into a temporary storage structure
    by reading the input file with 5 homemade fgets()
    calls. The fgets() calls are done through t_read(), which
    passes a pointer to the temporary storage structure, temp,
    calls fgets, and then stores a NULL over the newline
    fgets stores. The temp structure has arrays for the 5 data
    field members.
    2. We copy temp into the structure we use for the linked list.
    This structure has char pointers rather than arrays.
    3. We use fwrite() to write what's in the temporary structure
    to the database file. We write a structure at a time. Since
    temp contains arrays, not the pointers the linked list
    structure contains, we get fixed-size records.
    4. We use malloc to get a structure's worth of memory (of type
    record, which contains 5 char pointers) and then to get
    the memory where the pointers point to, for the record's
    fields themselves. Then we use a series of strcpy()
    statements to copy temp to the new structure. This is
    done by fill_record()

    The input file records are printed to the screen by traversing the
    linked list.
    If the database already existed and the user chose "append":
    1. We free up the linked list. We free the pointed to memory
    first and then free up the structure containing the pointers
    to that now-freed memory.
    2. We rewind the database file, which now contains the old
    and new records.
    3. We create a new linked list by a loop of calling fread() for
    a structure at a time until it returns 0. We must be careful
    to fread() before the malloc() call for a new structure.
    Otherwise, we are left with an empty structure for the last
    node.
    4. We print the new linked list to the screen.
*/

#include <stdio.h>
#include <stdlib.h> /* malloc */
#include <string.h> /* strcpy, strlen, strrchr */

#define COLS 81
#if 1 /* change to 0 if stdprn is a predefined stream */
#define stdprn stdout /* or change to another facility */
#endif

struct record
{
    char *name;
    char *address;
    char *city;
    char *state;
    char *zip;
    struct record *next;
};

struct storage /* used for temporary storage */
```

```c
{
    char name[22];
    char address[25];
    char city[13];
    char state[10];
    char zip[6];
} temp;

FILE *read_only, *read_write;

void free_up(struct record *start), print(struct record *start);
int t_read(char *field);
struct record *fill_record(struct record *current);

int main(void)
{
    char in_file[COLS], db_file[COLS];
    char mode[3] = "w+";
    char ch;
    struct record *previous, *current;
    struct record *start = NULL;

    puts("Specify name of input file [Enter]");
    gets(in_file);
    puts("Specify name of output file [Enter]");
    gets(db_file);
    puts("Type \"a\" to add to existing output file\n"
        " or \"n\" to start new one");
    if ((ch = getchar()) == 'a' || ch == 'A')
        *mode = 'a';
    /* open input file in read mode */
    if (!(read_only = fopen(in_file, "r"))
        || !(read_write = fopen(db_file, mode)))
    {
        printf("Error opening %s", !read_only ? in_file : db_file);
        exit(0);
    }

    /*
        read in ordinary text file a record at a time

        first read each field into the temporary structure temp with
        fgets modified to eliminate newline
    */

    while (t_read(temp.name) && t_read(temp.address) &&
        t_read(temp.city) && t_read(temp.state) && t_read(temp.zip))
    {
        /*
            Use malloc to reserve memory for various string fields in
            a record as well as a structure of type record containing
            pointers to those memory areas. Then copy from temp to the
            various pointers for
            each member.
        */

        if (!(current = fill_record(current)))
```

```
       break;

    /* write the temporary structure to a file with a binary function */
    fwrite(&temp, sizeof(temp), 1, read_write); /* fixed-size record */

    /* first time through, mark the first node in the linked list */
    if (!start)
       start = current;

    /* set the structure pointer in the prior structure to the current one */
    else previous->next = current;

    /* for the next iteration, make the current structure the prior one */
    previous = current;
}

/* mark the end of the linked list */
current->next = NULL;

/* close input file; data is now in linked list */
fclose(read_only);

fputs("  INPUT FILE LIST\r\n\r\n", stdprn);

/* pass the first node to print the list out */
print(start);

/*
   If specified database file existed and user just appended
   records to it, free up linked list and make new one
   consisting of both old and newly added records in the database
   file.
*/
if (*mode == 'a')
{
   /* free up memory for entire linked list */
   free_up(start);
   rewind(read_write);
   start = NULL;

   /*
      Create new linked list by reading a record at a time
      from the database file containing old & new records
   */
   while(fread(&temp, sizeof(temp), 1, read_write))
   {
      /*
         Use malloc to reserve memory for various string
         fields in record as well as a structure of type
         record containing pointers to those memory areas.
      */

      if (!(current = fill_record(current)))
         break;

      /* first time through, mark the first node in the linked list */
      if (!start)
```

```
                  start = current;

              /* set structure pointer in the prior structure to the current one */
              else previous->next = current;

              /* for the next iteration, make the current structure the prior one */
              previous = current;
          }

          /* mark the end of the linked list */
          current->next = NULL;
          fputs("   DATABASE LIST\r\n\r\n", stdprn);

          /* pass the first node to print the list out */

          print(start);
      } /* end if mode is 'a' */
      fclose(read_write);
      free_up(start);
}


/* +------------------------------------------------------------------+
   +  FILL_RECORD
   +
   +  Use malloc to reserve memory for various string fields in record
   +  as well as a structure containing pointers to those memory areas
   +
   +  The struct members stored into the reserved memory locations
   +  are in a global structure variable temp.
   +
   +  Argument: pointer to a struct record variable
   +
   +------------------------------------------------------------------+
*/
struct record *fill_record(struct record *current)
{
    if (!(current = malloc(sizeof(struct record))) ||
        !(current->name = malloc(strlen(temp.name) + 1)) ||
        !(current->address = malloc(strlen(temp.address) + 1)) ||
        !(current->city = malloc(strlen(temp.city) + 1)) ||
        !(current->state = malloc(strlen(temp.state) + 1)) ||
        !(current->zip = malloc(strlen(temp.zip) + 1)))
    {
        puts("malloc(): not enough memory");
        return NULL;
    }

    strcpy(current->name, temp.name);
    strcpy(current->address, temp.address);
    strcpy(current->city, temp.city);
    strcpy(current->state, temp.state);
    strcpy(current->zip, temp.zip);

    return current;
}


/* +------------------------------------------------------------------+
```

```
   +   FREE_UP
   +
   +   Free up entire linked list. We free the pointed to memory first
   +   and then free up the structure containing the pointers to that
   +   now-freed memory.
   +
   +   Argument: pointer to first node
   +
   +----------------------------------------------------------------+
*/
void free_up(struct record *start)
{
    struct record *previous;
    struct record *current = start;

    /*
        We don't need to free the current->next member; although it
        has a value assigned to it, we did not reserve any memory for
        the area it points to other than the structure it points to
        (the release of which is handled separately).
    */

    do
    {
        previous = current;
        current = current->next;
        free(previous->name);
        free(previous->address);
        free(previous->city);
        free(previous->state);
        free(previous->zip);
        free(previous);
    } while (current);
}

/* +----------------------------------------------------------------+
   +   PRINT
   +
   +   Print out records in linked list by traversing linked list
   +
   +   Argument: pointer to a first node in linked list
   +
   +----------------------------------------------------------------+
*/
void print(struct record *start)
{
    struct record *current = start;
    int rec_count = 0;

    puts("\nPrinting: please wait");
    do
    {
        fprintf(stdprn, " %-21s %-24s %-12s %-9s %5s\r\n", current->name, current->address,
            current->city, current->state, current->zip);

        /* eject page and restart record counter when reach 50 */
        if (++rec_count > 50)
        {
            fputc('\f', stdprn);
```

```
            rec_count = 0;
        }


        /* advance to next node in linked list */
        current = current->next;

        /* stop when we reach end of list (i.e., when current->next is NULL) */
    } while (current);
    fputc('\f', stdprn);
}


/* +--------------------------------------------------------------+
   +  T_READ
   +
   +  Read in a text field terminated by a newline, deleting newline
   +  retained by fgets()
   +
   +  Argument: pointer to the start of the field
   +
   +  Return 1 if successful; 0 if end of file reached
   +
   +--------------------------------------------------------------+
*/
int t_read(char *field)
{
    /* fgets returns NULL on end of file or error */

    if (!fgets(field, COLS, read_only))
        return 0;

    /* delete newline, which fgets retains */
    if (strrchr(field, '\n'))
        *strrchr(field, '\n') = 0;
    return 1;
}
```

If the database file already exists, users are asked whether they wish to add to the file or overstore and start afresh. Depending on the response, we open the database file in either read-write or read-append mode.

In a `while` loop, we read in the name, address, city, state, and zip code with a series of `t_read()` calls. This function uses `fgets()` to read from the input file. The `fgets()` function stores the newline character into the string. We remove the newline this way:

```
if (strrchr(field, '\n'))
    *strrchr(field, '\n') = 0;
```

The results are stored in a structure variable, `temp`, which contains arrays large enough to hold lengthy entries. This structure variable is used as a temporary holding area. We overstore it each time we read in a new record.

The linked-list structure, `record`, contains pointers to `char` instead of the arrays `temp` has. This allows us to requisition just as much memory as we need to house the entries.

In the same loop, we call `fill_record()`. First, we use `malloc()` to obtain memory for a new linked-list structure variable and for each of its members. After the memory is obtained, the data is copied from the temporary arrays in `temp` to the newly allotted structure and then written to the database file. We write to the database file with `fwrite()`, writing the entire `temp` structure in a single statement. Since `temp` contains arrays, we end up with fixed-size records.

The new records are placed into the linked list (and from there to the database file) in the order they appear in the input file. In later programs in this chapter, we will learn to insert new records into an existing list in alphabetical order.

The records are printed by traversing the linked list. Printing is set to stdout, but if the environment is DOS or another system with a similar printer facility, it is easy to make the switch:

```
#if 1 /* change to 0 if stdprn is a predefined stream */
#define stdprn stdout /* or change to another facility */
#endif
```

Following printing of the linked list formed from the input file's data, and assuming the "overstore" option was chosen, we call free_all() to free up the memory we had commandeered earlier. This function traverses the linked list from the structure pointed to by start until we reach NULL, in much the same manner as we did when we printed. Instead of using a printf() statement, we utilize free(current). Before we release the memory pointed to by current, we first release the memory pointed to by each of its members. We don't need to free the next member—although this pointer has been assigned a value, we do not reserve any memory for the area it points to other than the structure pointed to, the release of which is handled separately.

We then rewind the database file, which now contains the old and new records. We create a new linked list by calling fread() in a loop to read in a record at a time. The new list is then printed by traversing the new linked list.

15.6   VARIABLE-SIZE RECORDS— FIELD-LENGTH SEPARATOR

The chief drawback to the fixed-size record file storage approach is that we waste disk space. Squandering disk space is not as serious as wasting RAM during the running of the program (note that in rec_fixd.c, even though we used fixed-size records in the file, we used variable-length records in RAM), but with large databases, it can be a concern. The advantage of the fixed-size record approach is its simplicity and speed. We can use a single statement to read or write a structure's worth of data to or from the file in one fell swoop.

There are two basic approaches to storing variable-size records. One approach stores the length of each field just before the field itself, so that we know how many bytes to read before reaching the next field. The other approach uses a nontext character to act as a separator between fields; we read until we encounter the character.

We have reworked records.c slightly to produce a program that illustrates the technique of storing the field size as a road map to reading the following field. The program, rec_size.c, creates a linked list interactively. At the same time that we create a node and fill it, we use fwrite() to store the record length and then the record into a file. After the user signals the end of input, we print the linked list, free up all the linked list's memory, rewind the file, and read the records into a new linked list. We read each record with fread(), first reading the record size we stored and based on this size, the record itself.

We have left out error-checking and multiple fields to simplify the program.

 **Listing**   **15.7 rec_size.c**

```
/* rec_size.c */

/* Uses field size to separate fields */

/*
    1. Creates linked list interactively and at the same time
    fwrites the record length and then the record
    2. Prints list.
    3. Frees up memory.
    4. Rewinds file and reads records into linked list by reading
    the record length and then the record based on this length,
    using fread().
    5. Prints list.
*/
```

```
#include <stdio.h>
#include <stdlib.h> /* malloc */
#include <string.h> /* strcpy */

struct record
{
    char *name;
    struct record *next;
};

void free_up (struct record *start);
void print(struct record *start);

int main(void)
{
    char temp[81];
    unsigned char recsize;
    struct record *previous, *current;
    struct record *start = NULL;
    FILE *pfile;

    /* error-checking omitted */
    pfile = fopen("c:\\temp\\input", "w+");

    puts("Enter name");

    /* input names until user presses enter key */
    while (gets(temp) && temp[0])
    {
        /* reserve and fill memory for one record */
        current = malloc(sizeof(struct record));
        recsize = strlen(temp) + 1;
        current->name = malloc(recsize);
        strcpy(current->name, temp);

        /* write record size */
        fwrite(&recsize, sizeof(unsigned char), 1, pfile);

        /* now write record itself */
        fwrite(current->name, recsize, 1, pfile);

        /* first time through, mark the first node in the linked list */
        if (!start)
            start = current;

        /* set the structure pointer in the prior structure to the current one */
        else previous->next = current;

        /* for the next iteration, make the current structure the prior one */
        previous = current;
        puts("\nEnter name\nPress [enter] first to quit\n");
    }

    /* mark the end of the linked list */
    current->next = NULL;

    /* print the entire list by passing a pointer to starting node */
    puts("List as input");
    print(start);
```

```
      free_up(start);
      rewind(pfile);

      start = NULL;

      /* read in records until we reach end of the file, starting with rec size */

      while (fread(&recsize, sizeof(unsigned char), 1, pfile))
      {
         /* based on size just read in, reserve and fill
            memory for one record */
         current = malloc(sizeof(struct record));
         current->name = malloc(recsize);

         /* read a name in from the file using the size read in above */
         fread(current->name, recsize, 1, pfile);
         if (!start)
            start = current;
         else previous->next = current;
         previous = current;
      }
      current->next = NULL;

      puts("\nList as read in from file");
      print(start);
      free_up(start);
      fclose(pfile);
   }

   /* +------------------------------------------------------------+
      +   FREE_UP
      +
      +   Free up entire linked list. We free the pointed-to memory first
      +   and then free up the structure containing the pointers to that
      +   now-freed memory.
      +
      +   Argument: pointer to first node
      +
      +------------------------------------------------------------+
   */
   void free_up(struct record *start)
   {
      struct record *previous;
      struct record *current = start;

      do
      {
         previous = current;
         current = current->next;
         free(previous->name);
         free(previous->next);
         free(previous);
      } while (current);
   }

   /* +------------------------------------------------------------+
      +   PRINT
      +
```

```
    +   Print out records in linked list by traversing linked list
    +
    +   Argument: pointer to a first node in linked list
    +
    +---------------------------------------------------------------+
*/

void print(struct record *start)
{
    struct record *current = start;

    do
    {
        puts(current->name);
        current = current->next;
    } while (current);
}
```

15.7   VARIABLE-SIZE RECORDS—CHARACTER SEPARATOR

In rec_size.c, we have a single-field record. Where we have quite a number of fields in each record, as will be the case in any real-life example, the field-size method becomes messy. The character-separator method is probably the more widely used variable-size record method. The character-separator method is used in rec_pick.c. (To save space, Listing 15.8—rec_pick.c—is included on disk only.)

15.7.1   Menu Screen

The rec_pick.c program, which stores a name, address, city, state, and zip code for each record, is slightly more sophisticated in appearance and substance than the earlier versions we've looked at. It offers a menu of choices, as shown in Figure 15.3. We use a structure to house the menu choices, with

Figure 15.3 *Menu of User Choices*

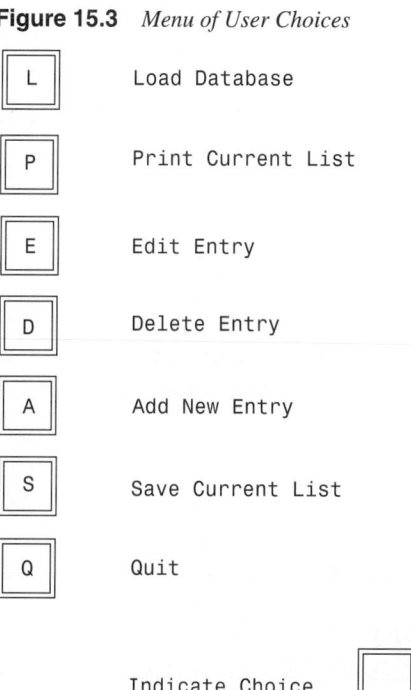

L	Load Database
P	Print Current List
E	Edit Entry
D	Delete Entry
A	Add New Entry
S	Save Current List
Q	Quit

Indicate Choice ☐

one member holding the character to be pressed by the user and the other member storing the corresponding heading:

```
struct
{
   char ltr;
   char heading[25];
} options[7] =
   {
      {'L', "Load database"},
      {'P', "Print current list"},
      {'E', "Edit entry"},
      {'D', "Delete entry"},
      {'A', "Add new entry"},
      {'S', "Save current list"},
      {'Q', "Quit"}
   };
```

To paint the menu, we call screen(), which in turn calls paint_choice() repeatedly in a for loop, passing it options[i].ltr and options[i].heading each loop. The paint_choice() function contains a single printf() statement:

```
printf("\t⌐\n\t‖%c‖\t%s\n\t∟⌐\n", option, string);
```

15.7.2   Message Printing

We also use a more attractive screen for asking the user for input or signaling an error in input. We use a function called message(). The message() function is a variable-argument list function. (See Chapter 8 for an explanation of the mechanics of such a function.) If the first argument—its fixed argument—is WAIT, the function waits for the user to press a key; this allows the user to read what is on the screen. If the argument is NO_WAIT, the function does not wait before proceeding with program execution. Instead, there is another function call, such as a call to getch() or gets(), following the message() call, that operates to halt program operation.

The variable arguments, terminated by a NULL, are pointers to message strings. As arguments, we can use a literal string, a pointer to a char array, a string (for instance, one we gave a value to with sprintf()), or the name of a char array.

In a for loop, for each message string, the message() function centers the passed string in a char array of a size equal to the width of the box the function draws. We set the entire array to the space character with a memset() statement:

```
memset(line, ' ', sizeof(line));
```

We mark the end of the array by setting the last element to NULL. Then we copy the passed string to a centered location in the array:

```
memcpy(line + (BOX_WIDTH/2 - strlen(ptr) / 2),
   ptr, strlen(ptr));
```

We use memcpy() rather than strcpy() to avoid copying the NULL character at the end of each string. Figure 15.4 depicts the result. Both the error-message routine and the menu screen we use here, however, pale in comparison to the elegance of the screens we introduce in Appendix C.

15.7.3   Program Mechanics

If the user presses L, for loading in a database file, we first check to see whether a file has already been loaded into a linked list. We keep track of this state of affairs by the flag variable loaded. If a file has already been loaded in, we take this selection as a command to replace it with a new file and free up the memory allocated to the linked list with the free_all() function we saw earlier.

After we ask the user to specify a database file to be loaded in, we use access() to make sure the file exists. If it exists, we open it in read mode and set the global stream variable read_write to point to the file. If not, or if we are unable to open the file, we signal an error and continue to the next menu screen loop.

Figure 15.4 *Automatically Centered Message Strings*

```
                    Type "S" to list one state
                 Press any other key for all entries
                 Press ESC key to return to menu
```

Assuming the file exists and has been successfully opened, we call the load-choice managing function, load(). There, we first ask the user whether the file to be read is a text function-created file, in the form we saw in rec_fixd.c, or a binary file previously created with this program.

The binary file we create with this program uses ASCII 1, the happy-face character, to separate the fields. In the write_record() function, we first use fwrite() to write this single separator byte to the file and then use it to write the field itself.

Though we do not do so here, we could also use another similar nonalphanumeric character, such as ASCII 2, to separate the records as well. The file looks like this, in one row without the newline character between the two rows we depict:

```
DEGAS,  EDGAR    888 AVENUE DE SEINE PARIS FRANCE 75383
DURER,  ALBRECHT  888 PLATZ FENSTER  NUREMBERG  GERMANY  98383
```

15.7.4 Filling a Node with File Data

We use a function called b_read() to read each field if the file has been written with binary functions and a function called t_read() if the file has been written with text functions (see Chapter 14 for the distinction between these two categories of functions). Both take a pointer to char and return an int, namely, 1 if there is a successful read and 0 if not. We can set a function pointer, fptr, to whichever of the functions is appropriate:

```
int(*fptr)(char *field);
if (getch_upper() == 'B')
   fptr = b_read;
else
   fptr = t_read;
```

In place of the field-reading statement

```
if (!fptr(temp.name) || !fptr(temp.address) ||
   !fptr(temp.city) || !fptr(temp.state) || !fptr(temp.zip)
      break;
```

we could have cycled through each field in a record with a for loop:

```
int end_reached = 0;
. . .
for (ptr = temp.name, i = 0; i < NUM_FIELDS; i++,
   ptr += sizeof(temp.name))
      if (!fptr(ptr))
      {
         end_reached = 1;
         break;
      }
if (end_reached)
   break;
```

At the beginning of the loop, ptr would be set to the first member array of temp. That pointer would be passed to either b_read() or t_read(). Following each loop iteration, ptr would be advanced to the next array member of temp.

Although this alternative coding is about the same length as the code in the listing, in a real-life example, with far more fields for each record, the alternative formulation would be considerably shorter. However, this alternative method might run into trouble with a compiler that uses byte alignment rather than word alignment for structures. Also, this pointer device would not work if the field arrays were of different lengths unless you stored the size of each member in an array and incremented the pointer by those sizes in a loop (We write to the file from the linked list, not from `temp`, so it doesn't matter here that `temp`'s elements are longer than they need to be.)

The `b_read()` function starts at the passed address and, in a loop, uses `fgetc()` to read the next character in the file, character by character, until it reaches the separator character. At that point, it stores a `NULL` character in the string to close it off. The `t_read()` function uses `fgets()`, then deletes the newline that `fgets()`, unlike `gets()`, stores:

```
*(field + strlen(field) - 1) = 0;
```

After each of the five fields is read in to the respective members of `temp`, we call for a structure's worth of memory and assign its address to the structure pointer `new`. Then we call `fill_node(new)` to get memory allotted for `new`'s members and copy `temp` into those locations.

15.7.5   Converting Input Format

All input is converted to uppercase before storing by `gets_upper()`. We also use this function for name input in the add, edit, and delete choices. Conforming all data to the same format will simplify data searches and updating.

The name field is further converted to "last, first" format so that the alphabetical searching and inspection we do elsewhere in the program makes sense:

```
last_first(gets_upper(temp.name));
```

The `last_first()` function must take the possibility of suffixes into account. It must handle four possible cases:

1. last, first ("Brown, Tom")
2. last, first suffix ("Brown, Tom Jr.")
3. first last ("Tom Brown")
4. first last, suffix ("Tom Brown, Jr.").

If we pass a string that happens to be in one of the first two formats, we can return the string as is. To test for these two cases, we first determine whether the name as input contains a comma. If it does and if we can eliminate the fourth case, we can simply return the passed string.

If there is no comma, or if the name contains a comma and we find a suffix after the comma, the name is in format "first last" or "first last, suffix" and we must switch the name order. We start by copying the passed name string to a temporary holding buffer `temp`.

If we have a comma and hence a suffix, we copy from the space before the suffix (which we locate by setting a pointer to the comma) to the array `suffix` for later use. Our pointer `ptr` is now pointing to the comma just after the last name. We close off the last name by assigning a `NULL` character at this point.

If there is no suffix, we point to the last character in the last name, which will be just before the terminating `NULL`. Whether there is a suffix or not, we then move `ptr` back to the space just before the last name:

```
while (*--ptr) != ' ')
   continue;
```

We advance one character to the first letter of the last name and copy from that point in `temp` to `name`, the pointer to the passed string. On the chance that the last name has a prefix such as "VON", we check each possible prefix with `strstr()` (see Chapter 9). If we find a prefix, we copy from that point to `name`, overstoring what we had copied there earlier. In either case, we add a comma and a space to `name`, which now contains a last name only.

Our pointer `ptr` is now on the first letter in the last name. By backing up one, and setting that location to `NULL`, we have closed off the first name or first name–middle name or first name–initial combination. We can concatenate the resulting first name to `name` and do the same for any suffix.

We next discuss how to alter nodes—by inserting, deleting, or editing. In insertion and deletion routines, it is critical to keep a pair of pointers to consecutive nodes. If we use only the current note, then by the time we've found the location we seek, we have lost its link to the earlier part of the list. In our experience, among the most common errors students and novice programmers make in linked-list programs are those that disconnect the list or in some way leave dangling references.

15.7.6   Inserting a New Node

To place the new structure variable into the linked list in alphabetical order by name, we call `insert(start, new)`, passing it a pointer to the newly filled structure variable and the starting address of the linked list. We traverse the linked list until we either find a node where the name comes after the new node's name or we run out of nodes. The function must handle three separate cases:

- The new structure variable goes before the first structure in the linked list. We set `new->next` to `start` and reassign `start` to `new`.
- The new node is to be inserted in the middle somewhere. We set the node prior to the current comparison node in the loop, `previous->next`, to `new` and `new->next` to `current`.
- The new node is to be placed after the last node. We set `current->next` to `new` and `new->next` to `NULL`, with `new` thereby becoming the last node.

Figures 15.5A to 15.5D depict the three cases.

Figure 15.5A *Starting Address*

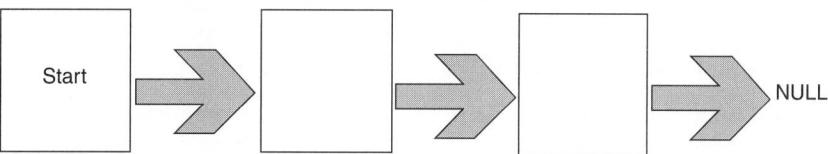

Figure 15.5B *Insertion Before First Node*

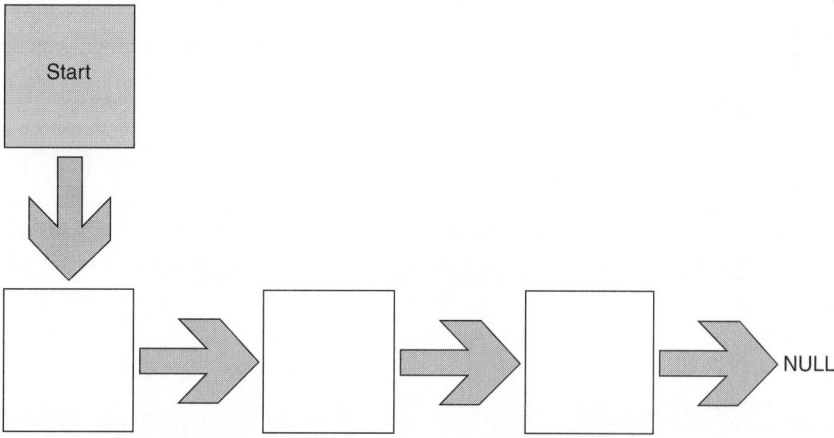

Figure 15.5C *Insertion Between Nodes*

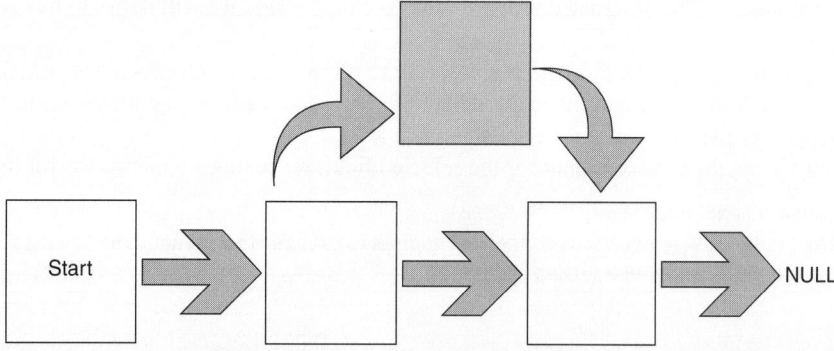

Figure 15.5D *Insertion After Last Node*

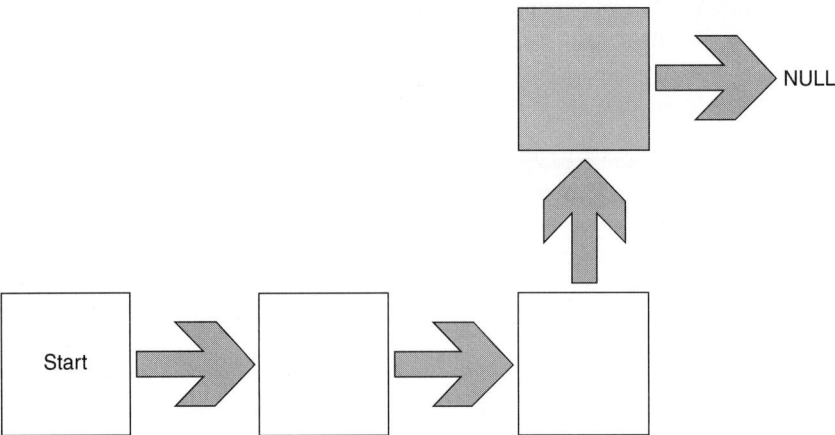

15.7.7   Deleting a Node

We have the same three cases to handle if the user selects "Delete entry". The function that handles deletion, delete(), first prompts the user for a name. We traverse the linked list in typical fashion, setting previous to current and then advancing current to current->next until we either get a match or reach the end of the list. The three cases:

- The first node is to be deleted. We set a temporary dummy structure pointer to start, advance start to the next node, and free the memory pointed to by the dummy.
- A middle node is to be deleted. We simply set previous->next to current->next and free current.
- We have reached the last node. If there is no match, we signal an error.

Otherwise, we simply set previous->next to NULL and free the truncated node's memory.

15.7.8   Dummy Nodes

Inserting or deleting nodes could be simplified by adding a dummy node at both the beginning and end of the linked list—at only a minor memory cost. Figures showing various dummy node configurations are given later in this chapter. With the dummy node method, there is, in effect, one case—"insert after." Keeping track of two consecutive nodes, "current" and "previous," is all you need to make everything work out right.

15.7.9   Editing a Node's Data

If the user selects the "Edit entry" option, we ask for a name and traverse the linked list until we find the record. If the name is not found, we issue an error message. If the record is found, the program gives the user the choice of editing any of the record's fields other than the name.

We have used a particular field—here, the name—to search through and to order the records. This usage is common. The designated ordering field is called a ***key***. We will return to this concept when we cover binary trees.

You could, if you wish, enhance the program to allow for behind-the-scenes "editing" of the name field as well. You would automatically delete the record and add a new record with the altered name field whenever the user chose to "edit" the name field.

After we obtain new user input for the selected field, we reallocate memory—for instance,

```
gets_upper(temp.address);
current->address = realloc(current->address, strlen(temp.address) + 1);
strcpy(current->address, temp.address);
```

If you greatly favor compactness over ease of reading your code, you could accomplish input, re-allocation, and copying in one step:

```
strcpy(current->address = realloc(current->address,
    strlen(temp.address) + 1), gets_upper(temp.address));
```

We definitely do not recommend this style. We mention it only because we've encountered it and if you do, you should be able to see what's going on.

15.7.10 Adding a Node

If the user selects "Add a record", we first determine whether there is a database file loaded in. If not, we give the user the choice of starting a new list or going back to the menu to load a database in with the L option.

If there is a file loaded in or if the user wishes to start a new list, we call hand_fill() to reserve memory space for a new node and to fill the node with entries interactively from the keyboard. That accomplished, we call insert() to place the new record in the linked list in order.

The hand_fill() function first solicits user input for each field and stores the user input in the temp structure. As with data read in from a file, all user input is converted to uppercase before storage in RAM, and the name field is converted with last_first().

We could have avoided all this name switching business if we had made the name two separate fields. However, you may be confronted with reading names in from a file where the format may not be "last, first", so the exercise here is useful.

15.7.11 Printing the Linked List

The print option causes the currently loaded linked list to be printed either to the screen or to the printer. The currently loaded list could differ from the one originally loaded in if the user has added, deleted, or edited records.

Users are asked whether they want to list all records or only those records from a designated state. The coding for printing to the screen is similar to that in records.c and rec_fixd.c, with the addition of (1) a conditional test where we check to see either that the state member of the structure current points to matches the designation, or users have elected to list all records, and (2) a line counter that lets users view a screen's worth of records at a time.

15.7.12 Saving the List to a File

Users can also choose to save the currently loaded linked list to a file. This could overstore the currently loaded file or create a new one. After checking to make sure a list is in memory, we call the handling function for this choice, save(). As we traverse the linked list, we call write_record(), passing it the current node in the list.

In write_record(), we set a pointer to pointer to char, ptr, to the address of the name member of the current structure. In a for loop, we alternately write a separator character to the file to be saved and the value of what the pointer points to, namely, a member of the current structure. We increment ptr with each iteration, so that it moves from pointing to the name member to the address member, and so on:

```
char **ptr = &current->name;
int i;

for (i = 0; i < NUM_FIELDS; i++, ptr++)
{
    fwrite(&separator, 1, 1, read_write);
    fwrite(ptr, 1, strlen(*ptr), read_write);
}
```

By calling fwrite() with a byte size of strlen(*ptr), we eliminate storing the NULL character at the end of each field.

Note that `ptr` is a pointer to pointer to `char`. The first structure member `current->name` points to the memory location that holds the first field of the current node. We want to be able to write each string pointed to by the other structure members. If we set a simple pointer to `current->name` and increment it by 1, we will accomplish only pointing to the second letter of the name field. If, on the other hand, we set a pointer to pointer to the pointer `current->name` and increment, we will move to the next structure member and by decrementing (`*ptr`), access the next field.

Instead of using pointers, we could have adopted a more laborious but more straightforward approach:

```
fwrite(&separator, 1, 1, read_write);
fwrite(current->name, 1,
    strlen(current->name), read_write);
fwrite(&separator, 1, 1, read_write);
fwrite(current->address, 1, strlen(current->address), read_write);
fwrite(&separator, 1, 1, read_write);
fwrite(current->city, 1,
    strlen(current->city), read_write);
fwrite(&separator, 1, 1, read_write);
fwrite(current->state, 1, strlen(current->state), read_write);
fwrite(&separator, 1, 1, read_write);
fwrite(current->zip, 1, strlen(current->zip), read_write);
```

However, if we had 30 or 40 fields, this longer approach would be very tedious to code, though a macro would help somewhat. For example, given the macro

```
#define WRITE(field) \
fwrite(&separator, 1, 1, read_write); \
fwrite(current->##field, 1, \
    strlen(current->##field), read_write)
```

the statement

```
WRITE(name);
```

expands to

```
fwrite(&separator, 1, 1, read_write);
fwrite(current->name, 1, strlen(current->name), read_write);
```

See Chapter 11 regarding the `##` device.

We use the same pointer to pointer to `char` device when we delete a record. We pass `free_record()` a pointer to the node to be deleted.

15.8   DOUBLE-LINKED LIST

In some cases, it is useful to be able to traverse a linked list backward as well as forward. For example, with word processing programs, which generally use linked lists to process documents when they are in active memory, it is essential to be able to move in both directions. Otherwise, when the user on page 100 of a lengthy document moves the cursor to the preceding paragraph, the program would have to go all the way back to the start of the list and work forward a considerable distance.

The way to accomplish dual-direction traversal is to add another member to our node structure. This new member will be a pointer to the *prior* node:

```
struct record
{
    char *name;
    char *address;
    char *city;
    char *state;
    char *zip;
    struct record *next;
    struct record *prior;
};
```

Figure 15.6 *Double-Linked List*

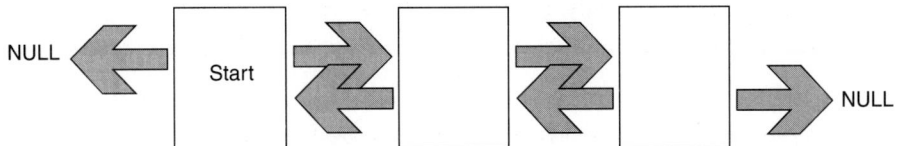

Figure 15.7 *Sample Screen Output of* `rec_two.c`

```
Type "+" [enter] to page down
     "-" [enter] to page up
 Number [enter] to select
```

1	TINTORETTO, MARIETTA	22 BELL DI	CARAVAGGIO	ITALY	21929
2	DEGAS, EDGAR	888 AVENUE SEINE	PARIS	FRANCE	75383
3	FONTANA, LAVINIA	19 BUONA NOTTE	SIENNA	ITALY	39395
4	KAUFFMANN, ANGELICA	888 PLATZ FENSTER	NUREMBERG	GERMANY	83831
5	GOYA, FRANCISCO DE	3 CALLE BUENO	ARAGON	SPAIN	38939
6	BRACQUEMOND, MARIE	4 RUE SANS SOUPIRS	PARIS	FRANCE	75018
7	INGRES, DOMINIQUE	12 AVENUE MARS	MONTAUBAN	FRANCE	69282
8	BONHEUR, ROSA	393 RUE DE CHAMPS	PARIS	FRANCE	23939
9	ANGUISSOLA, SOFONISBA	999 VIA VENETO	CAPRESE	ITALY	33939
10	PEETERS, CLARA	233 EBEN STRASSE	SIEGEN	HOLLAND	29292
11	DE AYALA, JOSEFA	88 CALLE BUONO	PIEVE	ITALY	69599
12	VELASQUEZ, DIEGO	18 AVENIDA DOMINGO	SEVILLE	SPAIN	39393
13	WATTEAU, ANTOINE	3 RUE PETIT PRINCE	VALENCES	FRANCE	75005

The resulting dynamic data structure is known as a ***double-linked list*** (see Figure 15.6).

In `rec_pick.c`, when users select "Edit record", they are asked to type the name for the record they want to change. We can use the double-linked list to make the selection of the record to edit more sophisticated. Users will be given a choice of specifying the name as before, or of selecting from a list the program sends to the screen a handful of records at a time. Each of the records on the screen will be numbered starting with 1. Users can select a record by typing in its corresponding number or can ask to see the next or previous screenful of records by typing a '+' or a '–' (see Figure 15.7).

In Appendix A, you will see how to have the program recognizes presses of the [Page Down] and [Page Up] keys.

To `edit()`, we have added a call to a new function, `list()`.

 **Listing 15.8 `rec_two.c`** *(excerpt—entire listing on disk)*

```c
/* rec_two.c */

/* double-linked list: variable-length records; can scroll
   up & down */

/* +--------------------------------------------------------------+
   + EDIT
   +
   + Change a field in a record specified by name.
   +
   + Traverse list until find match; then ask user which field to
   + change
   +
   + Argument: a pointer to the starting node
   +
   +--------------------------------------------------------------+
*/
void edit(struct record *start)
```

```
{
   struct record *current;
   char ch;

   message(NO_WAIT, "Type \"S\" to specify name or",
      "any other key to select from name list", NULL);

   /* specify name chosen */
   if ((ch = getch_upper()) == 'S')
   {
      message(NO_WAIT, "Type name to edit", NULL);

      /* put input in format "last_first" if not already */
      last_first(gets_upper(temp.name));

      /* traverse linked list and find node or give error message if not found */
      current = start;
      while(strcmp(current->name, temp.name))
      {
         current = current->next;
         if (!current)
         {
            message(WAIT, "Error: Name not found", ANYKEY, NULL);
            return;
         }
      }
   }

   else if (ch == ESC)
      return;

   /* select from list chosen */
   else current = list(start);

   /* return if NULL pointer returned as a result of
      ESC/Enter being pressed */
   if (!current)
      return;

   /* if record is found, ask user which field
      to change (can't change name) */
   message(NO_WAIT, "Type the following to change:", "\"A\" address", "\"C\" city,
      \"S\" state, \"Z\" zip", NULL);

   do
   {
      ch = getch_upper();

      switch(ch)
      {
#define DO(field) \
         message(NO_WAIT, "Current record:", \
            current->name, current->address, current->city, \
            current->state, current->zip, \
            "Type new " #field, NULL); \
            gets_upper(temp.##field); \
            current->##field = realloc(current->field, \
            strlen(temp.##field) + 1); \
            strcpy(current->##field, temp.##field);
```

```
            case 'A':
                DO(address)
                break;
            case 'C':
                DO(city)
                break;
            case 'S':
                DO(state)
                break;
            case 'Z':
                DO(zip)
                break;
        }
    } while (ch != 'A' && ch != 'C' && ch != 'S' && ch != 'Z' &&
    ch != ESC);
}
```

The last part of `edit()` is unchanged in substance. We simply inserted a macro to show you an alternative way of writing the code. The preprocessor expands

```
case 'A': DO(address)
```

to

```
case 'A':
    message(NO_WAIT, "Current record:", current->name, current->address,
        current->city, current->state, current->zip, "Type new " "address", NULL);
gets_upper(temp.address);
current->address = realloc(current->address, strlen(temp.address) + 1);
strcpy(current->address, temp.address);
break;
```

Note from the expansion of the `message()` call that string concatenation works in our own functions as well as in `printf()` or `puts()`. "Type a new" and "address" (the latter, as replaced by `##field`) are concatenated into a single-string argument.

The only real addition to `edit()` is the statement

```
else current = list(start);
```

The `list()` function handles both the screen-painting and name selection. Until the user makes a name selection, it continues to repaint the screen with every key press. If a '+' is selected and we are not yet at the end of the list, it advances down the linked list before repainting. If a '−' is pressed and we are not yet at the start of the list, it moves up the list before repainting.

```
/* +----------------------------------------------------------------+
   +  LIST
   +
   +  Allows the user to scroll up and down a list of names and select
   +  one.
   +
   +  Argument: pointer to starting node
   +
   +  Returns pointer to selected node, unless user ESCs out, in which
   +  case, returns NULL
   +
   +----------------------------------------------------------------+
*/
struct record *list(struct record *start)
{
    struct record *top, /* record at top of screen */
        *current;
```

```
        int i;
        int selection;
        int last_rec;

    top = current = start;
    do
    {
        message(NO_WAIT, "Type \"+\" [enter] to page down",
            "\"-\" [enter] to page up", "Number [enter] to select",
            NULL);
        for (i = last_rec = 0; i < ROWS; i++)
        {
            if (current)
            {
                printf("%2d  %-20s %-20s %-15s %-10s %-5s\n", i + 1, current->name,
                    current->address, current->city, current->state, current->zip);
                current = current->next;

                /* note # of last rec on page; ignore higher user presses below */
                last_rec++;
            }

            /* if no more records, fill page with blank lines */
            else putchar('\n');
        }

        /* stop & return selection if user presses # between 1 & last rec */
        if ((selection = atoi(gets(response))) >= 1 && selection <= last_rec)
            break;

        /* if user presses ESC or enter key without making response, return NULL */
        if (strcmp("", response))
            return NULL;

        /*
            Position ourselves to repaint the very same set of records
            by resetting the current node (where the for loop above
            starts painting) to the top node unless either the users
            press the plus key or, even if they press the plus key,
            there are no more records.
        */

        if (*response != '+' || !current->next || !current)
            current = top;

        /*
            If minus sign is pressed, back up a screen's worth of recs,
            stopping if we have reached the start (i.e.,
            current->prior is NULL); reset top to that record.

            Note that the last statement just reset the current node
            to the node at the top of the screen.
        */

        if (*response == '-')
            for (i = 0; i < ROWS && current->prior; i++)
            current = current->prior;
        top = current;
    } while(1);
```

```
/*
    Figure out which node is the selected node by going back to the
    node at the top of the screen and working down to the selected
    node.
*/
current = top;
for (i = 0; i < selection - 1; i++)
    current = current->next;

return current;
}
```

We use a do while loop to handle screen painting until the user makes a selection by typing a number in. At each loop we print the user message and 13 records (ROWS is defined as 13), starting with the node that current points to. If we have reached the end of the list, we print a newline instead, so that we move the message to the top of the screen. We preserve the location of the top node on the screen by storing its location in the structure pointer top.

Unless the user has made a selection or types a "+" (or unless we are already at the end of the linked list), we reset current to top. That way, if the user types a nonresponsive key, we simply reprint the same screen. If the user has typed a "–", we also move backward in the list a screen's worth of records. We stop, however, if we have reached the starting node, where

```
current->prior
```

would have a value of zero (our sentinel concept) and hence the for loop's evaluation condition

```
i < ROWS && current->prior
```

would evaluate to false.

Once a selection is made, we break out of the do while loop and initially set current to the first record on the screen, the address of which is preserved in top. To get the selected record, we move down the list by whatever number selection is.

15.8.1   Node Deletion and Insertion

The only other changes we need to make to rec_pick.c for the double-linked list are to modify delete() and insert() to reflect the double-pointer mechanism. We must take the prior node as well as the next node into account.

```
/* +---------------------------------------------------------------+
   +  DELETE
   +
   +  Delete a record the user designates by name.
   +
   +  Traverse linked list until find a match. If a match is found,
   +  determine if the record to be deleted is the first, a middle, or
   +  the last node in the list. Readjust the structure pointers
   +  accordingly and then call free_record() to bring about the deletion.
   +
   +  Argument: a pointer to the starting node
   +
   +  Returns a pointer to the starting node (as possibly changed)
   +
   +---------------------------------------------------------------+
*/
struct record *delete(struct record *start)
{
    struct record *previous, *current;

    message(NO_WAIT, "Type name to delete", NULL);
```

```
      last_first(gets_upper(temp.name));
      current = start;

      /* keep traversing until find a match or get to end of list */
      while(strcmp(current->name, temp.name) && current->next)
      {
         previous = current;
         current = current->next;
      }

      /* match in first node */
      if (current == start)
      {
         /* set a temporary marker to start */
         previous = start;

         /* move start to next node (to where start's structure pointer
            points) */
         start = start->next;

         /* mark new start of list sentinel */
         start->prior = NULL;

         /* delete the former start node, as temporarily marked by
            previous */
         free_record(previous);
      }

      /* in last node */
      else if (!current->next)
      {
         /* match in last node? */
         if (!strcmp(current->name, temp.name))
         {
            /* chop off current node from list with sentinnel in previous node */
            previous->next = NULL;
            free_record(current);
         }
         else message(WAIT, "Error: Name not found", ANYKEY, NULL);
      }

      /* match found in middle */
      else
      {
         /* chop current node from list by pointing previous node to next node */
         previous->next = current->next;
         previous->next->prior = previous; /* previous->next: new following node */
         free_record(current);
      }
      return start;
}

/* +----------------------------------------------------------------+
   +  INSERT
   +
   +  Traverse the linked list until find a match with a new name.
   +  Then determine if the new name is the first, a middle, or the last
   +  node and change the list's existing pointers accordingly.
   +
   +  Argument: a pointer to the starting node and the node to be
   +  inserted
```

```
        +
        +  Returns a pointer to the starting node (as possibly changed)
        +
        +---------------------------------------------------------------+
*/
struct record *insert(struct record *start, struct record *new)
{
    struct record *previous;
    struct record *current = start;

    /*
        Keep traversing the linked list until we either reach the end
        or the name in the current node is alphabetically after the
        node to be inserted (e.g., if we have "able, charlie, dog"
        and the name is "baker", we would stop at "charlie").
    */
    while((strcmp(new->name, current->name) > 0) && current->next
        != NULL)
    {
        previous = current;
        current = current->next;
    }

    /*
        If we are still on the first node and it is after the new node,
        make the new node the start node and point its structure pointer
        to the former start node and vice versa. Also, set the prior
        member of the new start node to NULL to mark the beginning of
        the list.
    */
    if (current == start && strcmp(new->name, current->name) < 0)
    {
        new->next = start;
        new->prior = NULL;
        start->prior = new;
        start = new;
    }

    /*
        If we are at the last node and the new node is still after it,
        add the new node to the end of the list by pointing the
        current node's next structure pointer to the new node and
        the new node's prior structure pointer to the current node.

        Also point the new node's structure pointer to NULL to mark
        the end of the list.
    */
    else if(!current->next && strcmp(new->name, current->name) > 0)
    {
        current->next = new;
        new->prior = current;
        new->next = NULL;
    }

    /*
        Otherwise, just insert the new node before the current node
        and after the previous node; make the previous node point to
        the new node and vice versa; and make the current node point
        to the new node and vice versa.
    */
    else
```

```
    {
        previous->next = new;
        new->prior = previous;
        current->prior = new;
        new->next = current;
    }

    return start;
}
```

If you find the formulation

```
previous->next->prior
```

in `delete()` confusing, you can instead declare a structure pointer variable `following`, set it to `previous->next`, and then use `following->prior`. The more complex formulation we have used is legitimate, as would be something even more complex, like

```
start->next->next->next->next->next
```

assuming we had sufficient nodes by that time. You would not likely use such a formulation, but you should understand the concept. Incidentally, you can look up or down the chain like this in Borland C with the inspect feature. For instance, if you inspect `start`, you will see the values and addresses of all the members of the structure `start` points to. If you cursor down to `next` and press Enter , you will get another window with the same information for the structure the `next` member of `start` points to. You can cursor down to `next` again and again press Enter , and so on all the way to the end of the list.

15.9   LINKED-LIST VARIATIONS

In addition to the forms of single- and double-linked lists we have examined, there are several variations. For example, instead of having the last node point to `NULL`, you can have it point to a *dummy node*. You would create the node with `malloc()`, as with other nodes. However, you would not place any record data into it. You would assign the node's address to a structure pointer `end` and keep track of that address just as we have done for `start` (see Figure 15.8). You would know when a search for an item had not found a match or when you otherwise had come to the end of the list by comparing the `current` structure to `end` rather than comparing its pointer member to `NULL`. This method will also allow you to quickly move to the end of the list without having to traverse it node by node.

Some programmers find it more convenient to code linked lists with a dummy node at the beginning of the list as well as at the end (see Figure 15.9).

As still another alternative, you could fill the last node with data and assign `NULL` to its pointer member, as we did in `rec_pick.c`, and then keep track of the last node by setting a structure pointer `end` to that node, as we do with `start`. That way you can move directly to the last node when you want to do so, or in another context keep traversing the linked list until you get to `end`.

Figure 15.8   *Dummy End Node in Linked List*

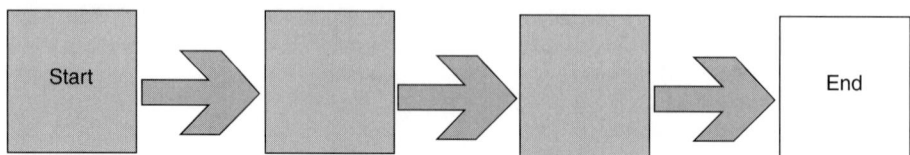

Figure 15.9   *Dummy Start and End Nodes in Linked List*

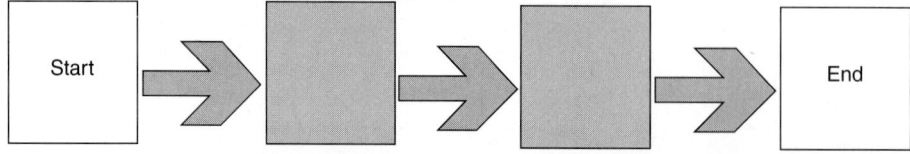

Figure 15.10 *Circular Linked List*

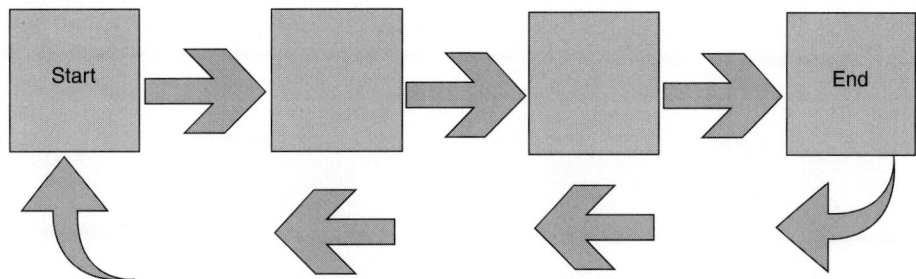

In an appropriate programming context, you might also find a circular list useful. In a ***circular linked list***, the pointer member of the final node points to start instead of to NULL or to a dummy node. If you use a dummy start node, the final node would point to the first nondummy node instead of start (see Figure 15.10). Any of these variations—as well as any others you can create—can be used with double-linked lists as well as single.

15.10 BINARY TREES: NONLINEAR LINKED LISTS

The linked-list structures we've examined so far are all linear. That is, to add, delete, or modify a record, we must traverse the linked list by moving one by one from the very first node until we come to the desired location. These linear structures work fine for a few hundred modest-size records. But for larger jobs, we need to find a more efficient method. Otherwise moving through thousands of records to insert records toward the end of the alphabet could bog the program down.

Let's assume we have seven records, with the following names given in Figure 15.11. If we want to add "Wit", we will end up making seven comparisons if we move from left to right a record at a time. Let's look at a new method.

15.10.1 Binary Search

Say we could proceed as follows: go right to the middle record, record 4, and make a comparison. The new record is alphabetically after record 4, so we go to the middle record among the three records to the right of record 4—record 6—and make a comparison. We would proceed in this fashion, continually splitting the remaining group in two until we find a record that comes after the new record, as Figure 15.12 shows.

We have cut the job down to three passes instead of seven. This method of searching, by repeatedly splitting the records into two groups, is referred to as a ***binary search***.

The following program, bin_seek.c, illustrates a simple binary search of an array of integers arranged in ascending order.

Figure 15.11 *Alphabetically Sorted Name Records*

| Alan | Bob | Sam | Tim | Tom | Will | Zoey |

Figure 15.12 *Divide and Conquer*

Alan	Bob	Sam	Tim	Tom	Will	Zoey
Alan	Bob	Sam	Tim	Tom	Will	Zoey
Alan	Bob	Sam	Tim	Tom	Will	Zoey

 **Listing** **15.9 bin_seek.c**

```c
/* bin_seek.c */

/* simple binary search */

#include <stdio.h>

int bin_search(int val, int *array, int num_elements);

int main(void)
{
    int list[]= {2, 4, 7, 21, 34, 123, 135, 1234, 2234, 32341};
    int num, position;
    int elements = sizeof(list) / sizeof(list[0]);

    printf("Enter an integer: ");

    /* determine position in array of input number */
    scanf("%d", &num);
    position = bin_search(num, list, elements);
    if (position != -1)
        printf("%d is element %d\n", num, position + 1);

    else
        puts("This integer does not occur in the array");
}

int bin_search(int val, int *array, int num_elements)
{
    int middle;
    int left = 0, right = num_elements - 1;

    /* before first element or after last: return -1 */
    if (val <= array[left] || val > array[right])
        return -1;

    while (right - left > 1)
    {
        /* keep splitting in two */
        middle = (left + right) / 2;
        if (val <= array[middle])
            right = middle;
        else left = middle;
    }

    if (val == array[right])
        return right;
    else return -1;
}
```

If you find you need to search for a string instead of a numerical value, you would simply use `strcmp()` at the appropriate points in `bin_search()`.

15.10.2 The Standard Function bsearch()

Generally, you will search through a series of records, each consisting of a number of fields, rather than something as simple as an array of integers. This is usually done by selecting one field and searching through the records for a match in that field. The selected field is referred to as a *key*.

There is a Standard C function, bsearch(), that allows us to search through elements of an array. The array elements can be simple scalar variables or complex data types such as structures. Because of this generality, the format of bsearch() is somewhat complex. The prototype, found in stdlib.h, looks like this:

```
void *bsearch(const void *key, const void *start_address, size_t num_elements,
    size_t bytes_per_element, int (*compare_function)(const void *p1, const void *p2));
```

Say we had an array of structures, with each element housing a name, address, city, state, and zip code field. We now want to search through these records to find the element that contains a specified name. In other words, the name is the key.

In this example, the starting address of the name string is the key argument; the starting address of the array of structures is the start_address argument (a pointer to void, as was the key argument, so we don't need any type cast); the number of elements in this array of structures is the num_elements argument; and the number of bytes in each structure array element is the bytes_per_element argument.

You have to make up the comparison function yourself. Note that it must take two pointers to void and return an int. What gets passed to your comparison function are the key and a pointer to an element of the array. Since the type of each of these arguments is pointer to void, you will have to type cast within the guts of the function itself when you are comparing the key with the passed element or a member or element of the passed element.

All this is done in bsearch.c. In keeping with recent learning, and to make the application more generalized, we have the structure elements each contain char pointers to areas we reserve through malloc(). Records are read in from a preexisting binary file, bname.out, previously created with Listing 15.6, the rec_fixd.c program. The user inputs a name and the program responds with the corresponding record data, assuming the name is in the database.

 **Listing 15.10 bsearch.c**

```
/* bsearch.c */

/* illustrate bsearch() on list of names and addresses */

#include <stdio.h>
#include <stdlib.h>
#include <string.h>
#include <ctype.h>

#define MAX_SIZE 1000


int compare(const void *p1, const void *p2);
char *strUpr(char *string);

struct
{
   char name[22];
   char address[25];
   char city[13];
   har state[10];
   char zip[6];
} temp;

struct record
{
   char *name;
   char *address;
   char *city;
   char *state;
```

```
      char *zip;
} rec_list[MAX_SIZE], *sptr;

int main(void)
{
    FILE *fp;
    char namebuf[81];
    int rec_num = 0;
    fp = fopen("c:\\temp\\bname.out", "rb"); /* binary file created with rec_fixd.c */
    if (fp == NULL)
    {
        puts("Unable to open c:\\temp\\bname.out for reading");
        exit(1);
    }

    /* fill rec_list structure array with record data from file */
    /* stop at end of file */
    while (fread(&temp, sizeof(temp), 1, fp))
    {
        if (rec_num == MAX_SIZE)
        {
            puts("Database too large");
            exit(2);
        }

        /* point to next structure array element */
        sptr = &rec_list[rec_num++];
        if (!(sptr->name = malloc(strlen(temp.name) + 1)) ||
            !(sptr->address = malloc(strlen(temp.address) + 1)) ||
            !(sptr->city = malloc(strlen(temp.city) + 1)) ||
            !(sptr->state = malloc(strlen(temp.state) + 1)) ||
            !(sptr->zip = malloc(strlen(temp.zip) + 1)))
            puts("malloc(): not enough memory");

        strcpy(sptr->name, temp.name);
        strcpy(sptr->address, temp.address);
        strcpy(sptr->city, temp.city);
        strcpy(sptr->state, temp.state);
        strcpy(sptr->zip, temp.zip);
    } /* end of reading in file */

    /* get record that matches user's name input with
       bsearch() & then print */
    while(1) /* keep locating recs until user says to stop */
    {
        printf("Enter \"last name, first name\" "
          "(or ENTER key to stop): ");
        strUpr(gets(namebuf));
        if (namebuf[0] == 0)
            break;

    /* bsearch returns ptr to item if found;
       if not, returns NULL */
        sptr = bsearch(namebuf, rec_list, rec_num, sizeof(struct record), compare);
        if (sptr == NULL)
            puts("Not found");
        else printf("  %-21s %-24s %-12s %-9s %5s\n", sptr->name, sptr->address, ptr->city,
            sptr->state, sptr->zip);
    }
```

```
}

/*
    Note that function MUST return int and take two pointers to void.
    First one passed will be key; second will be an entire element. We must
    make the appropriate type casting inside the called function.

    void *bsearch(const void *key, const void *base, size_t nelem,
        size_t width, int (*fcmp)(const void*, const void*));
*/

int compare(const void *p1, const void *p2)
{
    return strcmp((char *)p1, ((struct record *)p2)->name);
}

char *strUpr(char *string)
{
    char *ptr = string;
    while(*ptr)
    {
        *ptr = toupper(*ptr);
        ptr++;
    }
    return string;
}
```

Note the type casting in the comparison function:

```
return strcmp((char *)p1, ((struct record *)p2)->name);
```

Observe that the following, without an extra set of parentheses in the second argument, will *not* work:

```
(struct record *)p2->name
```

For the bsearch() function to work properly, the array elements must be arranged in order (by the key, if the elements are not scalar variables). Here, we have assumed the records are in ascending order by last name (A before B). We could accommodate records in descending order by simply reversing the logic of our comparison function.

What if the records are not in order? Funny you should ask.

15.10.3   Binary Sorting

We can employ a binary algorithm for sorting as well as for searching. Let's take the same array we had in bin_seek.c and shuffle the element values so they are no longer in order. The bin_sort.c program uses a binary method to arrange the values in order.

 **Listing**   **15.11 bin_sort.c**

```
/* bin_sort.c */

/* simple binary sort */

#include <stdio.h>

void bin_sort(int *array, int num_elements);

int main(void)
{
    int list[]= {21, 1234, 2, 2234, 4, 123, 7, 135, 34, 32341};
```

```
      int elements = sizeof(list) / sizeof(list[0]);
      int i;

      bin_sort(list, elements);
      for (i = 0; i < elements; i++)
         printf("list[%d]: %d\n", i, list[i]);
}

void bin_sort(int *array, int num_elements)
{
   int temp;
   int left = 0, right = num_elements - 1;
   int middle = array[right/2];

   do
   {
      /* on left half, stop when get to element > middle */
      while(array[left] < middle)
         left++;

      /* on right half, stop when get to element < middle */
      while(array[right] > middle)
         right--;

      /* swap to get bigger to right of middle
         and smaller to left */
      if (left < right)
      {
         temp = array[left];
         array[left] = array[right];
         array[right] = temp;
      }

         /* stop when all swapped */
   } while (left > right && ++left <= --right);

   /* recursive sorts of left and right halfs */
   if (right > 0)
      bin_sort(array, right + 1); /* left half */
   if (left < num_elements - 1)
      bin_sort(array + left, num_elements - left); /* right half */

}
```

We pass to the binary sorting function, `bin_sort()`, the starting address of the array and its number of elements. Within the function, we start by assigning the local variables, `left`, `middle`, and `right` to the subscript number of the first, middle, and last array elements. This effectively splits the array in two.

We then move `left` toward `middle`, looking for an element with a value greater than `middle`'s value, and move `right` toward `middle`, looking for an element with a value less than `middle`'s value. When we find such values, we swap them.

We repeat the process, each time incrementing `left` and decrementing `right` until `right` < `left` and there is a set on the left with elements not greater than those of `middle` and a set on the right with elements not less than those of `middle`. The same method is applied to each set, and so on, recursively.

15.10.4   The Standard Sort Function `qsort()`

Like the Standard C function `bsearch()`, there is an equally general Standard C function, `qsort()`. This function also uses a binary algorithm.

The prototype is similar to that of `bsearch()`:

```
void qsort(void *start_address, size_t num_elements, size_t bytes_per_element,
    int(*compare_function)(const void*p1, const void *p2));
```

An interesting exercise would be to take the same file we used in `bsearch.c`, except with the records out of order. We can sort the records prior to calling `bsearch()`, with the addition of a single statement immediately after reading the file

```
qsort(rec_list, rec_num, sizeof(struct record), sort_compare);
```

and the addition of a new function, `sort_compare()`:

```
int sort_compare(const void *p1, const void *p2)
{
    return strcmp(((struct record *)p1)->name, ((struct record *)p2)->name);
}
```

15.10.5   Our Own Binary Searching and Sorting: Binary Trees

The Standard C functions `bsearch()` and `qsort()` are useful as far as they go. But because they are necessarily crafted to apply to a variety of different situations, they are relatively slow.

Nor do they take control of the process and do more than simply sort and search. For example, we need the ability to add and delete records without having to resort to the whole works. We need the ability to traverse a list of records from a given point, examining each record individually along the way. For large numbers of records, we need the ability to sort externally—that is, to rearrange the records in a file instead of in an array in RAM. We can do this and more with binary trees.

To construct a binary tree initially, we need two things:

- The records must be in order.
- We need to know how many records there are in total.

When those two conditions are met, we can build a variant of our double-linked list—a ***binary tree***. The middle record is the starting point of the list. It is called the ***root***. Each node contains two pointers, one pointing to a record whose key is alphabetically (or if the key is a number rather than a string, numerically) prior to the node's key, and one pointing to a record alphabetically (or numerically) after. Each of those nodes, in turn, contains similar pointers. As with our linear lists, the end of the list is signaled by setting a pointer to `NULL`.

Figure 15.13 illustrates how the structure we create can be visualized. You can see why the structure is referred to as a tree. (Of course, the data is stored linearly, in contiguous memory locations; this figure is merely a way to visualize the data structure, just as we think of arrays as being made of rows and columns.) To traverse the tree, we start at the root, so we need to preserve its address.

There are many data structure books that contain lengthy treatments of binary trees. Our purpose here is not to treat binary trees in great depth. Rather, we seek to present a relatively simple binary tree construct that will demonstrate dynamic data structures. More complex methods are not necessarily constrained by our self-imposed twin constraints of ordered records and advance knowledge of the number of nodes.

Figure 15.13   *Binary Tree*

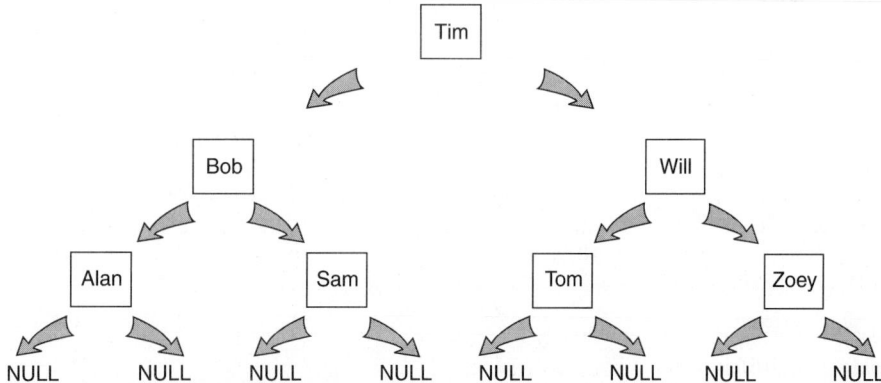

15.10.6   Creating a Balanced Tree

The following recursive function, make_tree(), places an ordered list into a binary tree:

```
struct record *make_tree(int entries)
{
    int entries_to_left, entries_to_right;
    struct record *ptr;

    if (!entries)
       return NULL;
    entries_to_left = entries / 2; /* to speed up: entries >> 1 */
    entries_to_right = entries - entries_to_left - 1;
    if(!(ptr = malloc(sizeof(struct record))))
    {
       puts("Error: Insufficient memory");
       return NULL;
    }
    ptr->left = make_tree(entries_to_left); /* if no entries to left, returns NULL */
    if (!fread(&temp, sizeof(temp),
       1, fp) || !fill_node(ptr)) /* see below for fill_node */
          return NULL;
    ptr->right = make_tree(entries_to_right);
    return ptr;
}
```

You can speed the function up somewhat by using bit manipulation in place of division (see Chapter 12):

```
entries_to_left = entries >> 1;
```

The procedure of successively splitting the remaining list in two, as we do in make_tree(), produces what is called a ***perfectly balanced tree***. In a perfectly balanced tree, all levels except for the bottom level are completely full. The tree that Figure 15.14 illustrates is perfectly balanced: The tree depicted in Figure 15.15 is not perfectly balanced.

Keeping the tree perfectly balanced reduces the work the program must do when searching for records.

15.10.7   A Binary Tree Program

You will generally use a binary tree where you have great numbers of records. In that case, speed usually becomes a concern. Since speed by hypothesis is critical, we will use a fixed record size to store records to disk. Our overall plan will be as follows:

- Load in a database file.
- Use fread() to read a record at a time, reading a structure's worth of data into temp.
- Build a binary tree with the records. After using malloc() to secure space for a new node and its members, copy the record from temp to the node's members. As in the linear linked-list fixed-size record programs, temp will contain arrays rather than pointers to char.

Figure 15.14   *Perfectly Balanced Binary Tree*

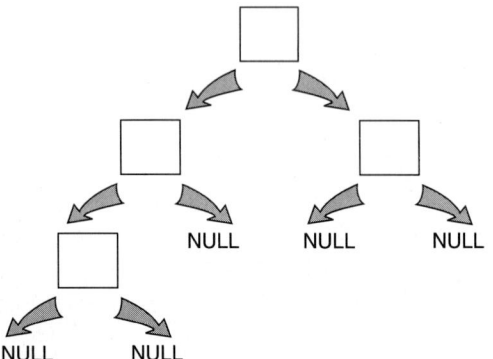

Figure 15.15 *Imbalanced Binary Tree*

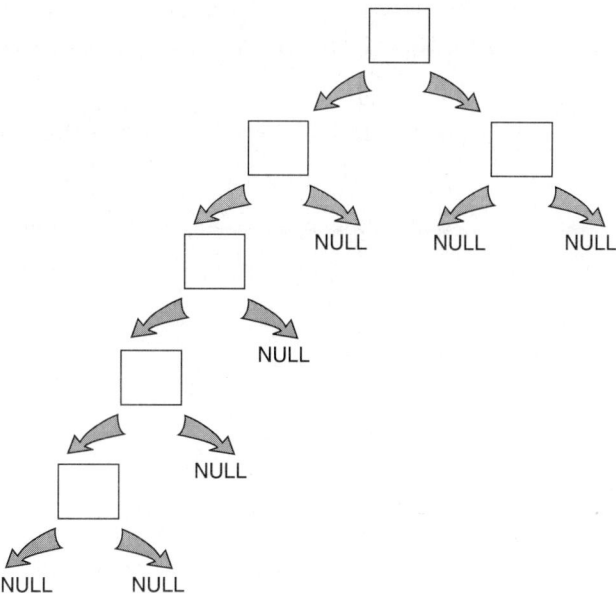

■ Add, delete, or modify records. Any added records will be placed in order.
■ Use fwrite() to write a record at a time to file in alphabetical order.

In the program we are about to review, rec_tree.c, we will use structures similar to those you have already seen in the linear linked-list examples, except that the record structure will contain pointers left and right instead of next or next and prior. We will also add a char member, delete, to assist in deleting records. (To save space, Listing 15.13—rec_tree.c—is included on disk only.)

15.10.8 Recursive Node Insertion

After we load a database file into a binary tree, we can add records interactively. To do so, we call add(). The add() function in the listing is nonrecursive. We could have made the function recursive:

```
struct record *add(struct record *ptr)
{
    if (!ptr) /* finally at bottom of tree: insert */
    {
        if (!(ptr = malloc(sizeof(struct record))) || !fill_node(ptr))
            return NULL;
        ptr->left = ptr->right = NULL; /* mark as bottom of tree */
        recnum++;
    }
    else /* not yet at bottom of tree: keep looking */
    {
        if (strcmp(temp.name, ptr->name) < 0)
            ptr->left = add(ptr->left);
        else if (strcmp(temp.name, ptr->name) > 0)
            ptr->right = add(ptr->right);
    }
}
```

We first pass this recursive add() a pointer to the root node. We compare the name in the new record with the name in the root node. If the new name is before the root name, we make the recursive call add(ptr->left); otherwise, we recursively call add(ptr->right), in this first case, ptr pointing to the root. We persist in these recursive calls until we reach a NULL. At that point, we have finally reached the bottom of the tree. We allocate memory for a new node and its members and copy data into the field members of the node by calling fill_node().

Figure 15.16 *Node Insertion Example*

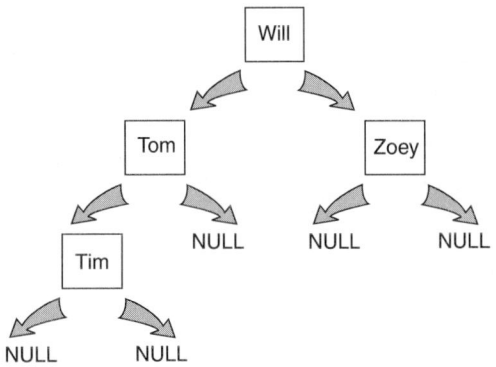

Figure 15.17 *Node Insertion Example—Adding Sam*

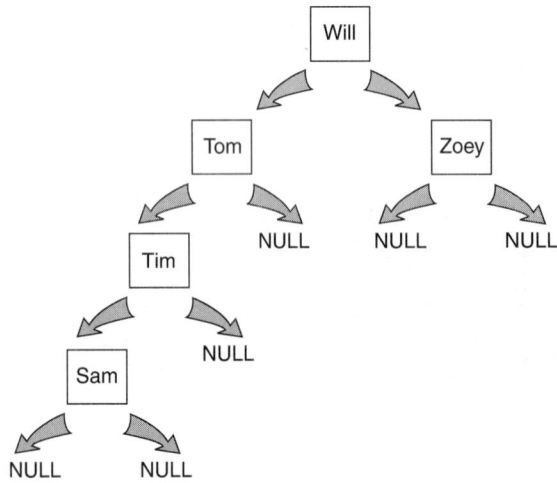

Let's take an example to see how this works. Say we had the names given in Figure 15.16 in our binary tree after loading in a database file. Now we add the record for the name "Sam". After the user interactively enters data for each of the fields in the new record, we start by calling add(root). On the first call, ptr is not NULL, so we drop down to make a string comparison with the name in the root node. Since "Sam" comes before "Will", we make a recursive call add(ptr–>left) to access the node that contains "Tom". Since ptr still has a value and since "Sam" comes before "Tom", we again call add(ptr–>left) to access the node containing "Tim". Again, the same result and the same call. This time, however, ptr is NULL, since that is the value of ptr–>left in the "Tim" node. At that point, we allocate memory, fill the node, and set the node's left and right pointers to NULL to mark the bottom of the tree (see Figure 15.17).

Notice that the distribution is no longer as even as before the addition. If we add other names prior to "Sam", the imbalance becomes even more pronounced (see Figure 15.18). The result is that some additions will require more comparisons. The imbalance will be cured, however, once the tree is saved to a file and loaded again. The make_tree() function will see to that. Our method is not necessarily the most efficient way to balance an unbalanced tree, but—in line with stated chapter goals—it is simple.

15.10.9 Nonrecursive Node Insertion

The nonrecursive add() function in the listing is somewhat more difficult to follow than its recursive counterpart, so we've chosen to discuss it second. The methodology is similar to the methodology we used for linear linked lists. We traverse the tree until we find where the new record fits, just as we traversed the linear linked lists. With linear linked lists, once we found a record whose name came after the new record alphabetically, we simply made the prior node's next member point to the new record and the new record's next member point to the following record.

Figure 15.18 *Node Insertion Example—Further Unbalancing*

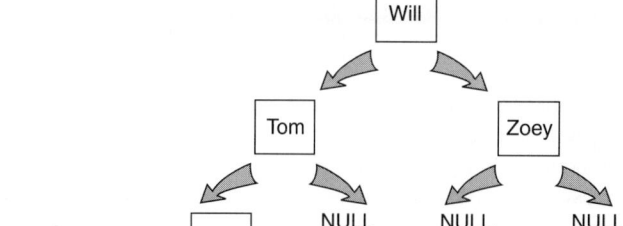

The process is not so simple here. With binary trees, the problem is mechanical. We keep going further down the tree until we get to a NULL, indicating the bottom of the tree. We replace the NULL with the new node. However, we do not know whether to set the left or right pointer of the node above the new node to point to the new node. We could use a flag variable to keep track of the direction in which we move on every movement further down the tree, assigning l if we move left or r if we move right. When we finally reach the bottom, we could do something like this:

```
if (direction == 'l')
   prior.left = new;
else prior.right = new;
```

But that method is a little messy.

A more efficient method is to use a pointer to a pointer to struct record:

```
/* nonrecursive method */
void add(void)
{
   struct record **pptr;
   struct record *new;

   if (!(new = malloc(sizeof(struct record))) || !fill_node(new))
      return;
   if (recnum)
   {
      pptr = &root;
      while(*pptr)
      {
         if ((strcmp(temp.name, (*pptr)->name) < 0))
            pptr = &(*pptr)->left;
         else if ((strcmp(temp.name, (*pptr)->name) > 0))
            pptr = &(*pptr)->right;
      }
      *pptr = new; /* right or left member of parent node */
   }
   else root = new;
   new->left = new->right = NULL; /* mark as bottom of tree */
   recnum++;
}
```

We start out by setting this pointer to pointer, `pptr`, to the address of the root node. (This assumes the root has already been assigned; if instead we are on the first record in the tree, we have a much simpler case.) We loop until the node `pptr` points to points to `NULL`:

```
while(*pptr)
```

Inside the loop, we traverse the tree by setting `pptr` to the address of where the current node points (that is, where the node `pptr` points to points). Once we reach a `NULL`, we automatically get the correct pointer member of the current node—either `right` or `left`—by setting the decremented value of `pptr` to the new node. This is so because `pptr` will have been set to the address of either the `left` or `right` member in the last loop iteration.

The nonrecursive `add()` is somewhat more complex than the nonrecursive method. However, where it is possible to accomplish the same task recursively or nonrecursively, a nonrecursive method should generally be favored.

15.10.10   Saving the Tree to a File

When the user selects "Save current list", `save()`, after opening a file, first writes the number of records to the file. It then makes a call to the recursive function `file_write()`, passing the address of the root node first. The `file_write()` function first checks to see that the passed structure pointer does not point to `NULL`. If it does not, the next step is a recursive call: `file_write(ptr->left)`. In this way we traverse the tree all the way to the left-most node.

We then check to see whether the `delete` member of that node is set to d. This member was initialized to n at the time the record was added to the tree. If the user selected the "Delete a record" option, the member was reset to d. If the current node's `delete` member is set to d, we simply skip writing the node's record to the file. Otherwise, we copy the data members into `temp` and write the entire structure to the file:

```
fwrite(&temp, sizeof(temp), 1, fp);
```

This method of marking records for deletion, rather than actually chopping the node from the tree as we did with the linear linked lists, accomplishes the deletion far more quickly. We use the same trick to skip records marked for deletion in the `print()` function.

After writing the record to the file, we call `file_write(ptr->right)`. In this way, we write the record to the left of each node and the record to the right of each node, if any.

15.10.11   Searching the Tree

To find the correct node for deleting a record or editing a record, we call `search(root)`. The `search()` function uses essentially the same mechanism as the linear linked lists. As with `add()`, we can make a recursive version of `search()`:

```
/* recursive method */
struct record *search(struct record *ptr)
{
   if (!ptr)
      return NULL;
   if (strcmp(temp.name, ptr->name) < 0)
      return search(ptr->left);
   if (strcmp(temp.name, ptr->name) > 0)
      return search(ptr->right);
   if (ptr->delete == 'd') /* from here down: match found */
      return NULL;
   return ptr;
}
```

Chapter Summary

1. Dynamic data structures are informal groupings of records—called nodes—that have no system-defined type or variable name. The nodes are accessible through chains of pointers—called linked lists—that our program manages.

2. We call `malloc()` to request a block of memory and receive a pointer to the start of that block.

3. If there is enough memory available, `malloc()` returns the address of the start of the memory block; if not it returns `NULL`.

4. To initialize all bytes allocated dynamically to zero, use `calloc()`.

5. To increase or decrease the size of the block of memory created by `malloc()` or `calloc()`, use `realloc()`. The arguments to `realloc()` are the pointer to the existing memory block and the new number of bytes.

6. The address returned by a successful call to `realloc()` may be different from that of the start of the original block of memory.

7. The `realloc()` function preserves the contents of the previously allocated memory block.

8. Memory allocated by `malloc()` or `calloc()` remains allocated after the function call in which the memory blocks were assigned ends. The memory blocks must be explicitly freed with `free()`.

9. Failing to release dynamically allocated memory is referred to as inadvertent memory leakage.

10. There are two basic approaches to separating records and fields from one another after reading them into a file: storing records of uniform size (the simplest approach, but it squanders disk space and RAM) and storing variable-size records—either by storing the length of each field just before the field itself, or by using a nontext character to act as a separator between fields.

11. In the simplest form of linked list, each node has pointers to memory reserved for each field as well as a pointer to house the address of the next node. By keeping track of the starting node's address, we can move from node to node until we encounter a NULL address for the next node, marking the end of the list.

12. All memory—for the node pointers and the data pointers—is reserved dynamically through calls to `malloc()`.

13. We can traverse the list for storing information, or editing, or adding or deleting nodes. Adding or deleting nodes requires different handling depending on whether the new node or the node to be deleted is at the beginning, in the middle, or at the end of the linked list.

14. Searching through a series of records, each consisting of a number of fields, is usually done by selecting one field and searching through the records for a match in that field. The selected field is referred to as a key.

15. Nodes in a linked list are ordered and searched according to such a selected key field.

16. To create more complex and flexible structures, we can mark the end node as well as the starting node, and we can add a pointer to the previous as well as the next node, so that we can traverse the list in either direction, the resulting data structure being referred to as a double-linked list. We can also use dummy, nondata housing nodes to mark the beginning or end of the list, or make the last node point to the first node, this structure being called a circular linked list.

17. The most sophisticated form of linked list—called the binary tree—is binary rather than linear. To add, delete, or modify a record, we do not traverse the linked list node by node. Instead, we jump to the middle of an ordered set of records and move recursively right or left from the middle depending on whether the key field we are looking for is before or after the new middle.

18. The `bsearch()` function allows us to make a binary search on a key field through elements of an array. The array elements can be simple scalar variables or complex data types.

19. For the `bsearch()` function to work properly, the array elements must be arranged in order—by key, if the elements are not scalar variables.

20. The `qsort()` function uses a binary algorithm to order records.

21. Because the Standard C functions `bsearch()` and `qsort()` are made to apply to a variety of different situations, they are relatively slow and inflexible.

22. To construct a binary tree initially, the records must be in order, and we need to know how many records there are in total.

23. The middle record, called the root, is the starting point of a binary tree. Each node contains two pointers, one pointing to a record whose key is alphabetically or numerically prior to the node's key, and one pointing to a record alphabetically or numerically after.

24. In a perfectly balanced tree, all levels except for the bottom level are completely full. Keeping the tree perfectly balanced speeds up record searches.

25. Any imbalance created by adding records to the binary tree is cured once the tree is saved to a file and loaded again.

26. We can speed up the record deletion process by marking records for deletion rather than deleting nodes. The marked records are simply not written back to the file.

Review Questions

1. Dynamic data structures are accessible by variable name (True or False).

2. The only difference in effect between `malloc()` and `calloc()` is that the latter also sets the dynamically reserved memory to binary zeros (True or False).

3. The `malloc()` function always allocates exactly the number of bytes requested, assuming sufficient memory is available (True or False).

4. The address returned by a successful call to `realloc()` will always be the same as the start of the original block of memory (True or False).

5. If a call to `realloc()` successfully increases memory reservation from 512 to 1024 bytes, and a completely different memory area is reserved, the values in the original 512 are copied to 512 of the bytes in the newly reserved area (True or False).

6. The return value of `realloc()` must be assigned to the same pointer that the originally reserved memory area was pointed to (True or False).

7. The pointer passed to `realloc()` for reallocation must have been one returned earlier by `malloc()`, `calloc()`, or `realloc()` (True or False).

8. If a call to malloc() is made inside a function, the allocated memory is freed when the function terminates (True or False).

9. A call to realloc() with a second argument that happens to work out to zero is the same as a call to free() (True or False).

10. It is possible to create a linked list without the use of pointers (True or False).

11. Variable-size records will take up less storage space than fixed-size records (True or False).

12. If records are stored in a file as fixed-size, when read back from the file, they must be placed into primary memory as fixed-size (True or False).

13. Records in a linked list are nearly always written to or read from a file with binary I/O functions, but it is possible to use text functions (True or False).

14. It is possible to order a file of records without designating one field as a key field (True or False).

15. A binary search will always be faster than a linear search (True or False).

16. A binary search is generally faster than a linear search (True or False).

17. The records to be searched with bsearch() must be elements in an array (True or False).

18. It is not possible to use bsearch() to search through an array of union variables (True or False).

19. A binary tree can have many roots (True or False).

20. It is not possible to search through a binary tree that is not perfectly balanced (True or False).

21. In a perfectly balanced binary tree, all levels are completely full with nodes (True or False).

Programming Exercises

This chapter has added coverage of dynamic memory allocation and linked lists to our C knowledge. Modify all the programming assignments you did in Chapter 14 to use dynamic memory allocation and linked lists, if applicable.

Additional enhancements and modifications for each programming assignment are specified accordingly.

Programming Assignment 15.1: Billing

Program Description

Take Programming Assignment 14.1. Modify the program so that the data is loaded in from the file to a single-linked list. Print the report by traversing the linked list.

Programming Assignment 15.2: Payroll

Program Description

Take Programming Assignment 14.2. Modify the program so that the data is loaded in from the file to a double-linked list. Print the report by traversing the linked list.

Programming Assignment 15.8: Science and Engineering (Chemical Engineering)

Program Description

Take Programming Assignment 14.8. Modify the program so that the data is loaded in from the file to a binary tree. Print the report by traversing the tree.

CHAPTER **16**

Working with the System

OBJECTIVES

- To become familiar with Standard C library function error-checking
- To learn how to run operating system commands from your C program
- To learn how to process command-line arguments
- To learn how to manage premature program termination
- To see how to connect your programs automatically to files through operating system commands

- To learn about operating system environmental variables and how to have your program change them
- To learn how to tell the computer how to do something or delay program execution for an arbitrary length of time
- To learn how to determine real-clock time and date

NEW TERMS

command line
command-line argument
environmental variable

environmental variable string
redirection

16.1 LIBRARY FUNCTION ERROR-CHECKING: errno

Errors that arise from the use of certain Standard C library functions not only cause a return of the value the function is coded to return upon error, but also set errno to a particular value. Generally, errno is a system global variable. However, the C Standard permits an implementation to define it as a macro.

The value errno is set to correspond to an implementation-defined set of messages in the system global char pointer array variable sys_errlist. The total number of elements in this array for a given implementation is contained in the system global variable sys_nerr.

With all this information, we could print out an implementation's list of strings corresponding to its various possible values of errno.

 Listing **16.1 err_list.c**

```
/* err_list.c */

/* print out list of system error messages corresponding to errno values */

#include <stdio.h>
#include <errno.h>
```

```
int main(void)
{
    extern int sys_nerr;
    extern char *sys_errlist[];
    int i;

    for (i = 0; i < sys_nerr; i++)
        printf("%d: %s\n", i, sys_errlist[i]);
}
```

Here's the output for Borland C:

```
0: Error 0
1: Invalid function number
2: No such file or directory
3: Path not found
4: Too many open files
5: Permission denied
6: Bad file number
7: Memory arena trashed
8: Not enough memory
9: Invalid memory block address
10: Invalid environment
11: Invalid format
12: Invalid access code
13: Invalid data
14:
15: No such device
16: Attempted to remove current directory
17: Not same device
18: No more files
19: Invalid argument
20: Arg list too big
21: Exec format error
22: Cross-device link
23:
24:
25:
26:
27:
28:
29:
30:
31:
32:
33: Math argument
34: Result too large
35: File already exists
36: Possible deadlock
```

Two Standard C error codes, defined in errno.h, are

```
#define EDOM   <some positive integer value>
#define ERANGE <some different positive integer value>
```

The EDOM macro indicates a domain error; that is, a value passed is not of a type acceptable to a mathematical function—for instance, passing a negative value to log(), log10(), or sqrt(). The ERANGE macro indicates that the result of a mathematical function is valid but out of range—for example; pow(MAX_DBL, 2.0);

At the commencement of any program, errno will have a value of zero. A library function error will result in it being set to some positive nonzero value. (Also, a library function will never set errno to zero, whether or not there has been an error.) Since, on a library function error, the value of errno will be set to a positive nonzero value that will linger until a further library function error, and since a further error will reset its value: *You should zero out* errno *before testing its postlibrary function call value. You should test its value immediately after using the library function the correct working of which you want to check. Assuming you have zeroed out* errno *immediately before a call to a library function, there is no point printing any error message after calling the function unless* errno *is not then zero.*

```
errno = 0;
root = sqrt (hypotenuse);
if (errno)
    printf("Error calling sqrt function: %s", sys_errlist[errno]);
```

If you neglect to check errno's value right after calling a library function, you might get the value set by subsequent call to another function; if you forget to zero out its value before calling a library function, you might get a positive value from a prior function call even though the function in question worked fine:

```
double natural, root, hypotenuse;
errno = 0;
root = sqrt(-1.0);
if (errno)
    perror("sqrt failed");
root = pow(3.14159, 0.5);
if (errno)
    perror("pow failed");
errno = 0;
hypotenuse = pow(DBL_MAX, 2.0);
natural = log(-8.375);
if (errno)
    perror("pow failed");
```

Here's the output:

```
sqrt failed: Math argument
pow failed: Math argument
pow failed: Math argument
```

The first call to sqrt() is invalid since it passes a negative number; the message reflects the error. The call to pow() is fine, but since we failed to clear errno, a call is made to perror(), still reflecting the error in the prior call to sqrt(). We do then clear errno, and we call pow() with a value-power combination that will produce an out-of-range error. However, before checking errno after the call, we make an erroneous call to log(), with a negative number. Therefore, perror() incorrectly reports the pow() call problem as a an invalid argument rather than an out-of-range problem.

16.1.1   Automated Error-Checking: `perror()`

If you are interested in ascertaining the precise cause for an error in calling a library function, the simplest method is to use perror(). The perror() function, the prototype for which is contained in stdio.h, allows us to automatically print to stderr (generally, the screen) the sys_errlist string corresponding to the current value of errno.

The perror() function takes a single argument, a pointer to char. What gets printed to the screen is the string we pass as an argument, a colon, a space, the sys_errlist string corresponding to the current value of errno, and finally, a newline. For instance, in lieu of this from a previous example

```
root = sqrt (hypotenuse);
if (errno)
    printf("Error calling sqrt function: %s", sys_errlist[errno]);
```

we could use the somewhat simpler

```
if(errno)
    perror("Error calling sqrt function");
```

Instead of testing the value of errno, you can call perror() if the function returns its failure value:

```
FILE *fp;
if ((fp = fopen("nosuchfile", "r")) == NULL)
    perror("Error opening nosuchfile");
```

If you don't feel the need to precede the system error message with one of your own, you can simply use a null string as an argument to perror():

```
if ((fp = fopen("nosuchfile", "r")) == NULL)
    perror("");
```

This prints to the screen:

```
No such file or directory
```

At the other extreme, you can use a message plus __LINE__ and __FILE__ directives to show you not only precisely what went wrong but where in your code the problem occurred. See Chapter 11.

```
char msg[81];
. . .
if ((fp = fopen(file, "r")) == NULL)
{
    sprintf(msg, "Error opening %s in line %d of %s", file, __LINE__, __FILE__);
    perror(msg);
}
```

```
Error opening test in line 57 of . . \TC\BSOURCE\PERROR.C: File already exists
```

Again, since a further library function error will reset errno, you need to make sure to call perror() immediately after an error occurs.

16.1.2   Creating an Error Log

The key limitation to perror() is that it prints to stderr. If you wish to create an error log file to preserve the causes of library function errors, you can use errno directly. You can do this by incorporating sys_errlist[errno] into a file printing statement, or you can use the Standard C library function strerror(), the prototype for which is in string.h:

```
char *strerror(int error_num);
```

This function returns the implementation-defined message string that corresponds to whatever error_num value you pass.

The following program will print

```
Error with fopen(): No such file or directory
```

both to stderr and to an error log file (twice, once with each of the methods described above).

 **Listing** 16.2 err_log.c

```
/* err_log.c */

/* create library function error log in a file */

#include <stdio.h>
#include <errno.h>

int main(void)
{
    FILE *fp, *log;
    extern char *sys_errlist[];
```

```
    log = fopen("err_log", "w");

    if (!(fp = fopen("nonesuch", "r")))
    {
        perror("Error with fopen()");
        fprintf(log, "Error with fopen(): %s\n", sys_errlist[errno]);
        /* a slightly simpler approach */
        fprintf(log, "Error with fopen(): %s\n", strerror(errno));
    }
    return 0;
}
```

If you have a lot of such message points in your file, you might want to create an error log function:

```
if(!(fp = fopen("nonesuch", "r")))
    err_log("Error opening nonesuch", __LINE__, __FILE__);
. . .
void err_log(char *err_msg, int line, char *src_file)
{
    char msg[127];
    sprintf(msg, "%s in line %d of %s", err_msg, line, src_file);
    perror(msg);
    /* assumes log is global & error file is opened early in main */
    fprintf(log, "%s: %s\n", msg, strerror(errno));
}
```

Assuming you have included errno.h in your program, you can also watch the value of errno as you step through the program in debug mode.

16.2   RUNNING SYSTEM COMMANDS FROM YOUR PROGRAM: system()

The system() function allows you to execute an operating system command from your program. The system() function takes a single argument, a pointer to char that points to the operating system command you want to use. For instance, rather than use one of the file-copying programs we created, f_copy_b.c or f_copy_t.c (Listings 14.5 and 14.3), you could do this:

```
system("copy c:\\data\\test c:\\data\\test.bak");
```

Just as with any function—a library function or your own—that takes a pointer to char as an argument, you can use a literal string, as we did above, or a pointer to char or an array name as an argument.

 **Listing**   **16.3 sys_copy.c**

```
/* sys_copy.c */

/* use system() to copy a file in DOS */
#include <stdio.h>
#include <process.h> /* system */
#include <string.h> /* strchr */

int main(void)
{
    char filename[45], temp[81];
    char *ptr;

    printf("Specify file to be copied\n");
```

```
    gets(filename);

    /* truncate any extension */
    ptr = strchr(filename, '.');
    if (ptr)
        *ptr = 0;

    sprintf(temp, "copy %s %s.bak", filename, filename);
    system(temp);
}
```

The `system()` function returns a 0 on successful execution and a –1 in case of error. By successful execution, we mean that whatever command that was to be passed on to the operating system was in fact passed on. If your command contains a typographical or syntax error, but the defective command is actually issued to the operating system, `system()` will return a 0, indicating success even though the operating system generates an error message.

Although the `system()` call in `sys_copy.c` is at the end of the program, your `system()` calls may be anywhere in the program. Control temporarily passes from your program to the operating system and then back again once the command has been executed.

One important point about `system()` calls: you must run the program that contains them from an operating system prompt, not from your compiler's editor.

16.2.1 Temporarily Exiting Your C Program

You can call `system()` with a NULL pointer:

```
system("");
```

This call invokes the command processor in such a way that its command prompt is displayed. The user can then type in one or more commands (for instance, commands to list directories, copy files, and so on).

To return to the C program, the user types in a special system command (in DOS, you type "exit"). You are probably already familiar with this process from your C editor. You might want to precede your NULL `system()` command with a message that tells the user how to get back to the C program.

 **Listing** **16.4 detour.c**

```
/* detour.c */

/* use system() to temporarily exit program and go to DOS */

#include <stdio.h>
#include <process.h> /* system */

int main(void)
{
    puts("Type EXIT to return to C program");
    system("");
    puts("Now back in C program");
}
```

16.3 PREMATURE PROGRAM TERMINATION: abort() AND exit()

Sometimes, in the case of error or other circumstances in your program, you will want to terminate the program prematurely. You can do so either with `exit()` or with `abort()`. Both prototypes are found in `process.h` and `stdlib.h`.

The `exit()` function takes an `int` as an argument.

 **Listing**   **16.5 ex_check.c**

```
/* ex_check.c */

/* find cause of file-opening error & call exit with appropriate integer */

#include <stdio.h>
#include <sys\stat.h> /* S_IFDIR, stat */
#include <io.h> /* access */
#include <stdlib.h> /* exit */

int main(void)
{
   char filename[45];
   FILE *fp;
   struct stat file;

   puts("Specify filename");
   gets(filename);

   if (!(fp = fopen(filename, "r+")))
   {
      /* returns 0 (success) if filename OR directory */
      if (access(filename, 0))
      {
         printf("Error: file %s does not exist\n", filename);
         exit(4);
      }
      if ((!stat(filename, &file)) &&
          ((file.st_mode & S_IFDIR) == S_IFDIR))
      {
         printf("Error: %s is a directory, not a file\n",
            filename);
         exit(3);
      }
      if (access(filename, 2))
      {
         printf("Error: file %s is read-only\n", filename);
         exit(2);
      }
      printf("Unknown error opening file %s\n", filename);
      exit(1);
   }

   return 0;
}
```

After the program terminates, the low-order byte of whatever `int` value you passed as an argument is made available to the operating system. For this to work properly, you have to make sure to return a value (by convention a 0 is returned) on successful completion. We did that here by making `main()` return 0 at the end.

In this particular program example, where `exit()` is called from `main()`, we could have achieved the same result by substituting `return` statements in lieu of the respective `exit()` calls. For example:

```
printf("Error opening file %s\n", filename);
return 1;
```

16.3.1   More on `exit()`'s Argument Value

The `exit()` function also makes its argument value available to the parent process where `exec()` or `spawn()` is being used. (The parent-child process is covered in Appendix L.)

You may also just ignore the value passed to `exit()`. In some instances, you may want to prematurely terminate the program, but you don't really care about passing any value to the operating system or a parent process. In that case, it really doesn't matter what value you place in the `exit()` call.

By convention, a zero indicates success of some operation and a nonzero integer indicates failure. If you have more than one potential `exit()` call in a program and want to use the values passed as arguments, you can pass a different value to each `exit()` call, as we did in `ex_check.c`, but there is no requirement that the values passed be different from one another. You can also use either of the macros `EXIT_SUCCESS` or `EXIT_FAILURE`, both defined in `stdlib.h`.

16.3.2   Preexit Cleanup: `exit()` vs. `abort()`

Just before the program terminates, `exit()` causes all file buffers to be flushed and then all open files to be closed. Implementations are not required by Standard C to do the same thing with `abort()`. Generally, the `abort()` function terminates the program without flushing file buffers or closing files:

```
if (!(fp = fopen(filename, "r+")))
   abort();
```

This behavior may cause loss of data or file corruption. Generally, therefore, `exit()` is to be preferred over `abort()`. Calling `abort()` generally causes a message such as "Abnormal program termination" to be written to the screen.

16.3.3   More Preexit Cleanup: `atexit()`

You may want to engage in certain cleanup or message-generating work just before terminating the program with `exit()`. For example, although calling `exit()` flushes all buffers and closes all files, the call will not necessarily free memory allocated dynamically with `malloc()`. Whether memory is freed depends on the machine, the system, and the compiler.

If you have only one `exit()` call in the program, you can place these bookkeeping matters in statements to be executed just before you call `exit()`. If, however, you have several potential `exit()` calls, or if you have different bookkeeping requirements, depending on how far into the program the user got before an `exit()` call was encountered, you can make use of `atexit()`.

You pass `atexit()` the name of a function you wish to have called once an `exit()` call is made. Each function passed to an `atexit()` call is placed into a queue. Once `exit()` is finally called, the functions in the queue are called in reverse order. The functions are called prior to the buffer flushing and subsequent file closing `exit()` causes to occur before program termination.

The functions passed to `atexit()` must not return a value and may not take any arguments. The inability to pass arguments greatly limits the function's usefulness.

You do not need to create a pointer to the function being passed. You pass `atexit()` the function name itself, without the following parentheses.

 **Listing   16.6 `at_exit.c`**

```
/* atexit.c */

/* illustrate atexit() call */

#include <stdio.h>
#include <stdlib.h> /* atexit */

void do_nothing(void);

int main(void)
```

```
{
   char buffer[BUFSIZ]; /* defined in stdio.h */

   /* make stdout buffered (normally unbuffered) */
   setbuf(stdout, buffer);
   atexit(do_nothing);
   puts("Just after atexit call & before exit");
   exit(0);
   puts("Oops! This line is never reached");
   return 0;
}

void do_nothing(void)
{
   puts("I'm a do-nothing");
}
```

The do_nothing() message appears *after* the puts() message from main() even though the atexit() call that invokes the do_nothing() message precedes it by order of execution:

```
Just after atexit call & before exit
I'm a do-nothing
```

Here's a simple program that illustrates atexit().

 **Listing** **16.7 exit_que.c**

```
/* exit_que.c */

/* illustrate atexit() order */

#include <stdio.h>
#include <stdlib.h> /* atexit, malloc */

struct record
{
   char name[81], address[81], city[35], state[15], zip[12];
   char ssn[12], home_phone[13], office_phone[13];
} *sptr[500];

void count_women(void);
void free_heap(void);
void tell_record(void);

int records;

int main(void)
{
   FILE *fp = fopen("employee.dat", "rb"); /* assumes this file exists */

   atexit(free_heap); /* note this one is first, since we want to call it last */
   atexit(count_women);
   atexit(tell_record);

   while(1)
   {
      /* exit if run out of heap memory */
      if (!(sptr[records] = malloc(sizeof(struct record))))
      {
         printf("Out of heap memory: %d records\n", records);
```

```
        exit(1);
    }

    /* stop if reach end of file */
    if (!fread(sptr[records++], sizeof(struct record), 1, fp))
        break;
    }
}

void tell_record(void)
{
    printf("Left off with record %d: %s\n"
        "Make a note of the record number and name in the log\n",
            records, sptr[records - 1]->name);
}

void count_women(void)
{
    int women = 0;
    int i;

    for (i = 0; i < records; i++)

    /* count Mrs. and Ms. entries */
    if (sptr[i]->name[1] == 's' || sptr[i]->name[2] == 's')
        women++;

    printf("%d females out of %d records\n", women, records);
}

void free_heap(void)
{
    int i;

    for (i = 0; i < records; i++)
        free(sptr[i]);
}
```

```
Left off with record 232: Mr. Joe Tuna
Make a note of the record number and name in the log
116 females out of 232 records
```

We have intentionally created a program that will run out of heap memory. Once that happens, exit() is called. At that point, free_heap(), count_women(), and tell_record() are called in reverse order. The order is important here. If we were to call free_heap() before the other two functions, we would no longer be able to access the pointed-to records.

Since we cannot call functions that have arguments, our cleanup functions use global variables for needed information here.

How long can your function queue be? Standard C requires implementations to support the registration by atexit() of at least 32 functions.

16.4   INVOKING main(): COMMAND-LINE ARGUMENTS

So far, we have seen the following format for main():

```
int main(void)
{
    . . .
    return 0;
}
```

As with any other function, you can terminate `main()` prematurely by another `return` statement or statements placed in the middle of the function and invoked conditionally. If you wish, you can use the manifest constant values `EXIT_SUCCESS` and `EXIT_FAILURE`, defined in `stdlib.h`, to signal normal and abnormal program termination to the invoking process (normally the operating system, but as you will see, this could be another program). If you do not include a `return` statement in `main()`, a value determined by the system will be returned to the invoking process, and the compiler will probably complain that a function declared to return an `int` should return one.

Since functions are type `int` by default, the following is perfectly legal, despite being in a style we do not recommend:

```
main()
{
    . . .
}
```

Since returning a value from `main()` generally serves no purpose, some programmers use the following formulation:

```
void main(void)
```

However, even though this formulation may make some sense and even though many compilers allow it, it is not Standard C and is not guaranteed to work on all implementations.

The other format recognized by the C Standard involves passing command-line arguments to `main()`. We now turn to that topic.

16.4.1   Command-Line Arguments

You can run a C program from the C editor with some compilers or from a system prompt. In DOS, executable files have a `.exe` or `.com` extension. You run the program from the system prompt by typing the name of the program, either with or without its `.exe` or `.com` extension.

What you type after the system prompt is referred to as the *command line*. What you type in on the command line are referred to as *command-line arguments*. A space on the command line marks the end of one argument and the start of the next. For instance:

```
cpy_file
```

has a single command-line argument and

```
cpy_file  c:\data\test  reports
```

has three. In UNIX, but not in DOS, you can lump more than one word into a single argument by enclosing it in double quotes:

```
"this is a single argument"
```

16.4.2   Passing Command-Line Arguments to a C Program

You can pass these command-line arguments as strings to a C program. You can do this by declaring `main()` with an `int` argument and a pointer to pointer to `char` argument:

```
int main(int argc, char **argv);
```

or

```
int main(int argc, char *argv[]);
```

When `main()` contains these arguments, C does the following at program inception:

- Assigns the number of command-line arguments to `main()`'s `int` argument.
- Establishes an array of pointers to `char`, with as many elements as there are command-line arguments.
- Assigns the starting address of each of the string arguments to the respective elements of the `char` pointer array.
- Assigns the starting address of the array to `main()`'s pointer to pointer to `char` argument.

You may use any variable names for the two arguments.

```
int main(int num_args, char **arg_addresses);
```

but argc and argv (standing, respectively, for argument count and argument vector) are used as a convention by nearly all programmers.

You can run programs with command-line arguments from the Borland C editor. Then you run or step through the program from the editor in the normal way.

16.4.3   Mechanics of argc and argv

Here's a program that will show us how command-line arguments are handled in memory.

 Listing   **16.8 argv_mem.c**

```c
/* argv_mem.c */

/* show how command-line arguments are placed in memory */

#include <stdio.h>

int main(int argc, char **argv)
{
    int i;

    for (i = 0; i < argc; i++)
    {
        printf("argv[%d] points to %s, starting at %p\n", i, argv[i], argv[i]);
        printf("\t&argv[%d]: %p\n", i, &argv[i]);
    }

    /* 1 past array end */
    printf("argv[argc] points to %p\n", argv[argc]);
    printf("argv: %p &argv: %p\n", argv, &argv);
}
```

With the following command line:

```
argv_mem one two
```

we get the following output (we usually store our executable files in c:\bc\out, but to simplify the output, we copied the executable file to c:\):

```
argv[0]: C:\ARGV_MEM.EXE at FFE4
   &argv[0]: FFDC
argv[1]: one at FFF4
   &argv[1]: FFDE
argv[2]: two at FFF8
   &argv[2]: FFE0
argv[argc] points to 0000
argv: FFDC &argv: FFD8
```

As Figure 16.1 shows, the pointers to the argument strings are stored contiguously in memory with the strings themselves (though for visual clarity, we have split them). The end of the pointers is marked by a NULL pointer. That would allow us to substitute the following loop for the one we had above in the listing if we wished:

```c
i = 0;
while (argv[i])
{
    printf("argv[%d] points to %s starting at %p\n", i, argv[i], argv[i]);
    printf("\t&argv[%d]: %p\n", i, &argv[i]);
    i++;
}
```

Figure 16.1 *Memory Location of Command-line Arguments*

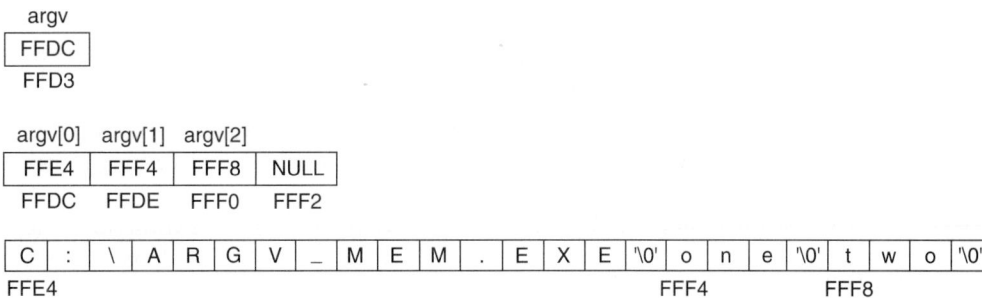

16.4.4 Application: Multiple-File Copying

We can now modify one of our file-copying programs, Listing 14.5, `f_copy_b.c`, to allow us to make backup copies of several files at once.

 **16.9 mult_cpy.c**

```
/* mult_cpy.c */

/* make backup copies of many files at a time with command-line arguments */

#include <stdio.h>
#include <string.h> /* strcpy, strcat */
#include <stdlib.h> /* exit */

void file_copy(char *file);

int main(int argc, char **argv)
{
   int i;

   if (argc < 2)
   {
      puts("Must have at least one filename");
      exit(1);
   }

   /* start at 1: 0 is the executable file itself */
   for (i = 1; i < argc; i++)
      file_copy(argv[i]);
}

void file_copy(char *file)
{
   FILE *original, *copy;
   int blocks;
   char temp[BUFSIZ];

   strcpy(temp, file);
   if (strchr(temp, '.'))
      *strchr(temp, '.') = 0; /* truncate any extension */
   strcat(temp, ".bak");
   original = fopen(file, "rb");
   copy = fopen(temp, "wb+"); /* error-checking omitted */

   while((blocks = fread(temp, 1, BUFSIZ, original)) > 0)
      fwrite(temp, 1, blocks, copy);
}
```

Note that we started with element 2 (i=1), not 1. The executable file itself, mult_cpy[.exe], is argv[0].

16.4.5   Application: Interactive Print Options

One common use of command-line arguments is to give users various options. To minimize the chance of user error, users are generally allowed to include as many of these options as they wish and to place them in any order.

The following program, pick_cl.c, allows users to specify a text file to be read, processed, and printed. Printing can be directed to a file, the screen, or the printer. Users can specify double-spaced printing or any other number of spaces between lines.

Users can also choose to indent each line a specified number of spaces. This last option is useful for those times you want to put a hard copy of files into a notebook and you don't want to punch holes in text. In the DOS environment, you might incorporate the executable version of the following program in a single-line batch file to print an indented copy automatically:

```
call pick_cl %1 _P _I  3
```

If the output is to the printer, users can specify multiple copies.

 **Listing   16.10 pick_cl.c**

```c
/* pick_cl.c */

/*
   command-line program to allow users to specify device,
   lines space and copies; also to have each line indented
   a specified number of spaces
*/

#include <stdio.h>
#include <string.h> /* strupr, strcmp, strcpy, strcat, strlen */
#include <stdlib.h> /* exit */

int main(int argc, char **argv)
{
   char temp[81], newlines[20] = "\n", skip[3] = "\n";
   int lines = 1, copies = 1, indent_spaces = 0;
   int i;
   FILE *in, *out;

   /* check # of args; issue format directions if insufficient #
      or user requests format */
   if (argc < 2 || !strcmp(argv[1], "?") || !strcmp(argv[1], "\/?"))
   {
      puts("Format: pick_cl <filename> _S(creen) _P(rinter) "
         "_F(ile) <filename> _C(opies) <#> _L(ines space) <#> "
         "_I(ndent each line x spaces) <#>");
      puts("\nExample: pick_cl _P _C 2 _L 2 _I 3");
      exit(2);
   }

   /* open designated file for reading */

   in = fopen(argv[1], "r");
   if (!in)
   {
      printf("Unable to open %s file\n", argv[1]);
      exit(1);
   }
```

```
/* process command-line arguments one by one */

for (i = 2; i < argc; i++)
{
    /* underscore or hyphen signals option start */

    if (argv[i][0] == '_' || argv[i][0] == '-')
    {
        strupr(argv[i]);
        switch(argv[i][1])
        {
            case 'S': out = stdout; break;
            case 'P':
                out = stdprn;

                /* need carriage return as well as newline for printer */
                strcpy(newlines, "\r\n");
                strcpy(skip, "\r\n");
                break;
            case 'F': out = fopen(argv[++i], "w"); break;
            case 'C': copies = atoi(argv[++i]); break;
            case 'L': lines = atoi(argv[++i]); break;
            case 'I': indent_spaces = atoi(argv[++i]); break;
            default: break;
        } /* end switch */
    } /* end if */
} /* end for */

/* adjust line spacing, if appropriate */

while(--lines)
    strcat(newlines, skip);

for (i = 0; i < copies; i++)
{
    /* read line at a time into temp */
    while (fgets(temp, 81, in))
    {
    /* omit newline; replace in next line */
        temp[strlen(temp) - 1] = 0;
        fprintf(out, "%*s%s%s", indent_spaces, "", temp, newlines);
    }

    /* multiple copy option is for the printer only */

    if (out != stdprn)
        break;
    rewind(in);
    fputc('\f', stdprn);
}
}
```

If the user types fewer than two arguments in addition to pick_cl, or if the user has forgotten the format and types pick_cl ? or pick_cl /?, the program prompts:

```
Format: pick_cl <filename> _S(creen) _P(rinter) _F(ile)
<filename> _C(opies) <#> _L(ines space) <#>
_I(ndent each line x spaces) <#>

Example: pick_cl _P _C 2 _L 2 _I 3
```

The program sets defaults of printing to the screen, single-line spacing, no indenting, and a single copy.

We loop through the argument strings, checking to see whether the first character is a '_' or '–', indicating that we have an option rather than a filename. If we encounter an option, we use a `switch` on the character following the underscore or hyphen, `argv[i][1]`, to determine the proper course of action. If the character is S, P, or F, we set the `FILE` pointer accordingly.

The string `newlines`, printed at the end of each line, is initialized to a single newline character. If the output is to be sent to the printer, we add a carriage return. If there is to be more than a single space between lines, we add a newline (or, for the printer, a carriage return–newline) for each extra space:

```
while (--lines)
   strcat(newlines, skip);
```

16.5   THE ENVIRONMENT *(OPTIONAL)*

The operating system maintains a set of so-called *environmental variables*. These variables are used by the operating system and by applications programs running under the operating system.

In DOS, the environmental variables can be set upon bootup in the `autoexec.bat` file or set or reset from the command line with the `SET` command:

```
SET LIB=C:\BC\LIB
```

If you type `SET` alone, DOS gives you a whole list of the current environmental variables—for example, on our system:

```
COMSPEC=C:\DOS\COMMAND.COM
PATH=C:\PCTOOLS;C:\DOS;C:\;C:\WP61;C:\BC\BIN;C:\EXECUTE;
C:\NU;C:\123;C:\TAPE
PCTOOLS=C:\PCTOOLS\DATA
PCTV=/nr
LIB=c:\qc2\lib
INCLUDE=c:\qc2\include
PROMPT=$p$g
```

Each line is referred to as an *environmental variable string*. The object to the left of the equal sign is the environmental variable. Some of these have specific functions. `COMSPEC` tells DOS where to find the command-processing program, `command.com`. `PATH` determines which directories will be searched, and in what order, for `.exe`, `.com`, and `.bat` files. The next four environmental variables in our example are used by two commercial applications to find the locations of or to place certain types of files used by those applications.

You can also use environmental variables to tell the computer where to find various files for other applications, including your own, or for other tasks, such as determining the local time zone for the computer's clock and customizing certain system commands.

16.5.1   Using Environmental Variables in a C Program

You can use environmental variables in your C program. You can use them as is, or you can add new environmental variables or alter the existing ones. Unless you do so with a `system()` call, however, any additions, deletions, or alterations you make last only for the duration of your program.

The scheme for accessing the environmental variable strings is similar to that used to store command-line strings. Recall that with command-line arguments, a pointer to pointer to `char` you declare as an argument to `main()` holds the address of a pointer to the first argument string.

When a C program starts, the address of a pointer to the first environmental variable string is assigned to the global system variable `environ`. As with command-line argument strings, the environmental variable strings are stored consecutively in memory, separated by the terminating `NULL` of each individual string. The addresses of the first element of each of these strings are stored in an array of pointers to `char`, the first address of which is assigned to `environ`.

With command-line arguments, `argc` can be used to allow us to loop through the strings. It gives us a stopping point. As an alternative, you can use the fact that the end of the array of pointers to the strings is marked by a NULL pointer. With environmental variable strings, this second method is the only method available. The pointer array element after the element that points to the last environmental variable string points to NULL. We can do something similar to argv_mem.c to see graphically how the environmental variable strings are arranged in memory in our C program (we've used %u specifiers instead of the more normal %p because we thought this might be easier to visualize with decimal notation rather than hex).

 **Listing 16.11 env_list.c**

```
/* env_list.c */

/* show how environmental variable strings are stored in memory */

#include <stdio.h>

extern char **environ;

int main(void)
{
    int i = 0;

    while (environ[i]) /* go until NULL */
    {
        printf("environ[%d] points to %s starting at %u\n", i, environ[i], environ[i]);
        printf("\t&environ[%d]: %u\n", i, &environ[i]);
        i++;
    }
    printf("environ[%d] points to %u\n", i, environ[i]); /* 1 past array end */
    printf("environ: %u &environ: %u\n", environ, &environ);
}
```

The output on our system:

```
environ[0] points to COMSPEC=C:\DOS\COMMAND.COM starting at 1964
    &environ[0]: 2156
environ[1] points to PATH=C:\PCTOOLS;C:\DOS;C:\;C:\WP61;
C:\BC\BIN;C:\EXECUTE;C:\NU;C:\123;C:\TAPE starting at 1991
    &environ[1]: 2158
environ[2] points to PCTOOLS=C:\PCTOOLS\DATA starting at 2068
    &environ[2]: 2160
environ[3] points to PCTV=/nr starting at 2092
    &environ[3]: 2162
environ[4] points to LIB=c:\qc2\lib starting at 2101
    &environ[4]: 2164
environ[5] points to INCLUDE=c:\qc2\include starting at 2116
    &environ[5]: 2166
environ[6] points to PROMPT=$p$g starting at 2139
    &environ[6]: 2168
environ[7] points to 0
environ: 2156 &environ: 860
```

Of course, while Figure 16.2 shows the various bytes on separate lines, in RAM, the whole works, other than environ, is stored in contiguous memory locations.

16.5.2 Altering the Environment: putenv()

What if we want to change one of the environmental variables? Say we wanted to change the PATH we showed above to

```
PATH=c:\temp
```

Figure 16.2 *Memory Location of Environmental Variable Strings*

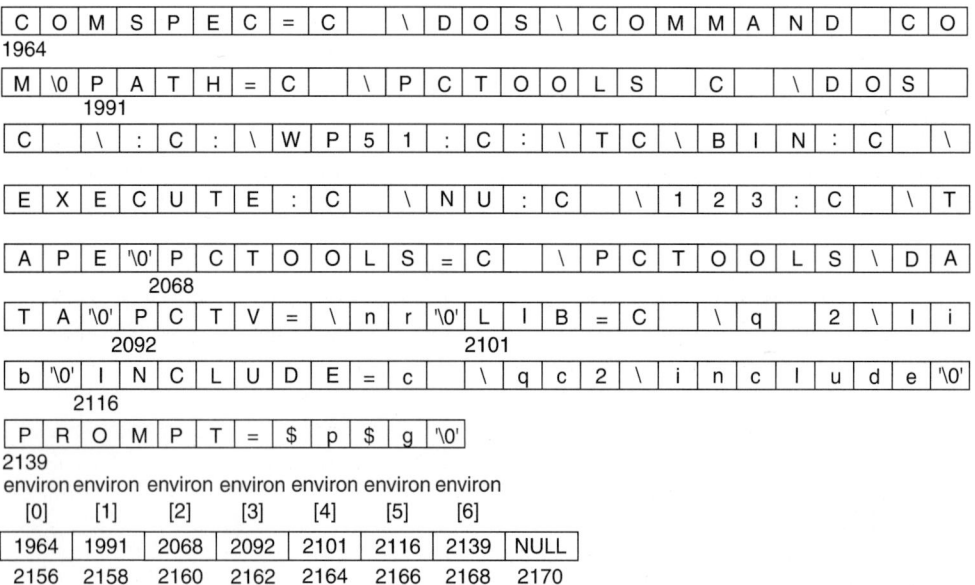

We could do the following.

 **16.12 new_path.c**

```
/* new_path.c */

/* use environ to alter PATH */

#include <stdio.h>
#include <string.h> /* strncmp, strlen, strcpy */

extern char **environ;

int main(void)
{
   int i = 0;

   while (environ[i])
   {
      if (!strncmp(environ[i], "PATH", 4))
         break;
      i++;
   }

   if (!environ[i])
      printf("PATH not found\n");
   else
   {
      strcpy(environ[i] + strlen("PATH="), "c:\\temp");
      printf("environ[%d]: %s\n", i, environ[i]);
   }
}
```

We just locate the environmental variable string containing PATH and alter it with `strcpy()`. Since we wanted to shorten an environmental variable string, the task was not difficult.

But what if our modified string would be longer than the original string? Or still worse, what if we wanted to add a brand-new environmental variable? Given the scheme of storing strings and pointers to those strings in contiguous memory locations, we would have to reshuffle the whole business, being careful in the process not to write over already-allocated memory space.

Fortunately, there is a function that carries out that messy job for us, `putenv()`. We pass `putenv()` the full environmental variable string we want to exist after the call. If the environmental variable exists, the call will change the string:

```
putenv("PATH=c:\temp");
```

If not, the call will add a new string. If we call `putenv()` with nothing after the = following the environmental variable, the environmental string is deleted:

```
putenv("TEMP=");
```

Any changes to the environmental variables, whether on your own or through `putenv()`, last only for the duration of your program. Once the program terminates, the system has whatever environmental variables it had before you ran the program. The process is analogous to passing a structure variable to a function. The function gets only a copy of the structure members' values. Any changes made in the function are local only. The same holds true here. However, any process launched by your program through `exec()` or `spawn()` gets the environmental variables as revised by you or `putenv()`. See Appendix L.

The `putenv()` function prototype is contained in `stdlib.h`. It returns a 0 if successful, or a −1 if not. However, this function is a DOS/UNIX function only; it is not Standard C.

16.5.3 Determining the Environment: `getenv()`

The `putenv()` function updates the global system variable `environ` and its pointed-to array of `char` pointers. Consequently, after we alter the environment with `putenv()`, we can always be confident that we can find the value of an environmental variable merely by looping through the array pointed to by `environ` and then calling `strncmp()` at each iteration, just as we did in `new_path.c`. (Note that if you use `strstr()` instead of `strncmp()`, you run the risk of finding the string on the wrong side of the equal sign.)

However, as is the case with altering our copy of the environment, there is also a function we can use that does all the work of determining the environmental variables—`getenv()`, that is, at least provided we know what environmental variable we're looking for. The `getenv()` function, a Standard C function, also found in `stdlib.h`, takes as its argument a string containing the environmental variable without the = or its value:

```
getenv("PATH");
```

It returns a pointer to the starting address of the value portion of the environmental variable string corresponding to the environmental variable passed. That is,

```
puts(getenv("COMSPEC"));
```

will print something like

```
C:\DOS\COMMAND.COM
```

not

```
COMSPEC=C:\DOS\COMMAND.COM
```

If there is no such variable, `getenv()` returns `NULL`.

16.6   REDIRECTION

In Chapter 14, we learned that C automatically opens three files when you run a program: `stdin`, `stdout`, and `stderr`. By default, `stdin` takes its input from the keyboard, and `stdout` sends its output to the screen.

With a technique called *redirection*, however, you can cause stdin to take input from another device, such as a magnetic tape, or from a file. Likewise, you can cause stdout to redirect output to a device such as the printer, or to a file. You cannot redirect the other automatically opened files.

Redirection is available in both DOS and UNIX. Since we can redirect stdin or stdout to a file, we can get input from a file or send output to a file without having to bother explicitly opening a file in our C program for that purpose. These files are automatically opened and closed for us.

Redirection is accomplished from the system command line. You redirect input from a file or device with the < operator; you redirect output to a file or a device with the > operator. Say you had the following little program.

 **Listing 16.13 sir_echo.c**

```
/* sir_echo.c */

/* illustrate redirection */

#include <stdio.h>

int main(void)
{
    char temp[81];

    while(gets(temp) && temp[0])
        puts(temp);
}
```

The program takes input a line at a time from standard input (the keyboard in the absence of redirection), and sends it back a line at a time to standard output (the screen in the absence of redirection). We might have input and output like this:

Two lines.
Two lines.
That's all I feel like typing.
That's all I feel like typing.

We can create a file that contains the same input. Let's call it echo.dat:

Two lines.
That's all I feel like typing.

If we type the following at the system prompt

sir_echo < echo.dat

we get the following on the screen:

Two lines.
That's all I feel like typing.

The program takes input from echo.dat just as though you had typed echo.dat's contents from the keyboard character by character.

If we type the following

sir_echo > echo.out

and type the same two lines in from the keyboard, the echo.out file will contain just what would have been sent to the screen:

Two lines.
That's all I feel like typing.

If you do this instead

sir_echo > prn

the output would be sent to the printer rather than to the screen.

16.6.1   Simultaneous Input and Output Redirection

We can redirect both input and output at the same time:

```
sir_echo < echo.dat > echo.out
```

The following syntax works just as well

```
sir_echo > echo.out < echo.dat
```

although the first formulation may appeal to your intuitive sense that input comes before output. In any case, the executable program comes first on the command line.

16.6.2   Mechanics of Redirection

By redirecting input, we are essentially opening the redirected file for reading. If the file does not exist, the command is meaningless. By the same token, redirecting output is equivalent to opening a file for writing. If the file does not exist, it will be created. If it exists, it will be truncated to zero length before any writing takes place. Nor will redirecting output to a write-protected file work. If no_write.out is a read-only file, all you will get from

```
sir_echo < echo.dat > no_write.out
```

will be the message "file creation error".

Since redirecting output to an existing file will truncate it to zero length, you cannot use the same file for input and output using these two redirection operators. This will not work:

```
sir_echo < somefile > somefile
```

The first thing that happens when the program starts running is that somefile's contents get sent to oblivion. If you want to read input from a file, alter it, and write the updated records back to the same file, you have to use file-opening and reading and writing operations.

You can, however, add data to the end of an existing file by redirecting output with the >> operator:

```
echo < echo_one > echo.out
echo < echo_two >> echo.out
```

This second operation is equivalent to opening a file in the append mode.

Some redirection rules:

- The executable program must come first on the command line.
- The < operator redirects input from a data file to an executable program and the > and >> operators redirect output from an executable program to a data file. You cannot use these three operators to connect one data file to another or one executable program to another.
- Input cannot be redirected from more than one file, nor can output be redirected to more than one file.
- You cannot use the same data file for both input and output (at least not with redirection operations).
- If you redirect output with the > operator and the file exists, its original contents will be lost.

16.6.3   Redirecting Program Output as Input for Another Program

There is a way to accomplish what the second rule says you can't do. The pipe operator, |, lets you use the output of one program as the input for another program. Say we have two simple programs. One reads name records a record at a time and changes each character to uppercase. The other reads name records a record at a time and reverses the order of the first and last names and prints the altered records out.

 **Listing**   **16.14 cap_name.c**

```
/* cap_name.c */

/* capitalize name records: output piped into shift.c */

#include <stdio.h>
```

```
#include <string.h> /* strupr */
#include <ctype.h> /* toupper */

int main(void)
{
   char name[81];
   char *ptr;

   while(gets(name) && name[0])
   {
      ptr = name;
      while(*ptr)
      {
         putchar(toupper(*ptr));
         ptr++;
      }
   }
}
```

 **Listing** **16.15 shift.c**

```
/* shift.c */

/* capitalized name output from cap_name.c piped into here to shift first/last */

#include <stdio.h>

int main(void)
{
   char first[20], last[20];

   while(scanf("%s%s", first, last) == 2)
      printf("%-20s %-20s\n", last, first);
}
```

We can feed the output from the first program directly to the second program. We can do so without having to store the output in a file and have the second program read the file:

cap_name ¦ shift

Furthermore, if we don't feel like typing in the names in the first place, we can use redirection to read them in from a file:

cap_name < name.dat ¦ shift

16.7   TIME AND DATE

In this section, we will examine date and real-time functions, as well as relative-time functions.

16.7.1   Date and Real Time

We can use Standard C functions to give us the current date and time. Prototypes for these functions are found in time.h. An example is found in timedate.c.

Listing **16.16 timedate.c**

```
/* timedate.c */

/* determine current date and time with Standard C functions */
```

```
#include <stdio.h>
#include <time.h>

int main(void)
{
    time_t now;
    struct tm *split_time;

    /* get the number of seconds elapsed since midnight 1/1/70 */
    time(&now);

    /* convert that # to a string & print */
    printf("Current date and time: %s\n", ctime(&now));

    split_time = localtime(&now);

    /* day of month, secs/mins 1-based; hr is 0-based so all ok as is;
       year is actual yr - 1900 so ok as is;
       day of yr and month are 0-based, so must adjust */
    printf("Time: %02d:%02d\n", split_time->tm_hour, split_time->tm_min);
    printf("Date: %02d/%02d/%02d\n", split_time->tm_mon + 1,
        split_time->tm_mday, split_time->tm_year % 100);
}
```

The starting point is a function, time(), which takes the address of a time_t variable (defined in time.h—typically just a typedef for long) as its argument, and stores at that address the number of seconds between midnight January 1, 1970, and the time of the call. The time() function also returns that same value as a time_t, so the following two calls achieve the same result:

```
time_t now;
time(&now);
now = time(NULL);
```

We can use ctime() to convert that number of seconds into a string in the format "Fri Mar 06 17:50:32 1999". We simply pass ctime() the address of the time_t value filled by time(). Earlier, we saw a method for parsing that string into more useful components with a for loop and sprintf().

As an alternative to parsing the ctime() string, we can use localtime(). The localtime() function takes the address of the time_t variable that houses the number of seconds and returns a pointer to a variable of type struct tm. That structure's template looks like this:

```
struct tm
{
    int tm_sec; /* seconds after the minute */
    int tm_min; /* minutes after the hour */
    int tm_hour; /* hours since midnight (24-hour basis) */
    int tm_mday; /* day of the month (1st day is 1, not 0) */
    int tm_mon; /* month of the year (Jan is 0, Feb is 1, etc.) */
    int tm_year; /* years since 1900 */
    int tm_wday; /* days since Sunday (e.g., Sunday is 0, Monday is 1) */
    int tm_yday; /* days since January 1 of current year
        (Jan. 1 is 0, Jan. 2 is 1, etc.) */
    int tm_isdst; /* daylight savings time flag */
};
```

In timedate.c, we use particular members of a pointer to such a structure variable to put together the date and time print-outs we want.

16.7.2 Relative Time

It would be simple to use successive calls to time() and a pair of struct tm variables to determine elapsed time to the nearest second (the smallest time member in struct tm), or to delay program execution for a specified number of seconds. Alternatively, you can use a Standard C function that does all the work for you, `difftime()`, the prototype for which is found in `time.h`. All the function does is to take two `time_t` values representing seconds and subtract one from the other and return the result as a `double`. The following simple program illustrates this function.

 **Listing   16.17 delay.c**

```
/* delay.c */
/* delay program execution with Standard C functions */

#include <stdio.h>
#include <time.h>

int main(void)
{
   time_t start;

   time(&start);   /* or start = time(NULL): Get system time */
   while(difftime(time(NULL), start) < 3.) /* delay for 3 seconds */
      continue;
   printf("Time elapsed: %d seconds\n", (int)difftime(time(NULL), start));
}
```

Despite the fact that `difftime()` returns a `double`, since it takes two integers representing seconds as arguments, it obviously returns only an integer value in double-precision floating point format. If you need something more precise, you can use `clock()`, also located in `time.h`. This function returns the number of the computer's clock-ticks from the start of program execution to the function's being called. The number returned is of type `clock_t`, again generally just a `typedef` in `time.h` for a `long`. There is also a macro in `time.h`, `CLK_TCK`, that defines how many times per second that is.

Armed with this information, you can conveniently learn just exactly how much time it took your program to run, by simply calling `clock()` just before you exit. That will let you optimize your code by seeing the effect of tinkering with this or that code structure. By calling `clock()` and assigning the return value to a variable at some point in the program and then doing the same thing later in the program, you can determine the time between two events. You can also easily delay program execution for a specified amount of time. The following program does all three.

 **Listing   16.18 clock.c**

```
/* clock.c */

#include <time.h>
#include <stdio.h>

/* To determine the time in seconds, divide the value returned
   by clock() by the value of the macro CLK_TCK. */

void wait_secs(double secs);

int main(void)
{
   clock_t start, pause;
   start = clock();
   printf("%f seconds so far (this had better be zero)\n", start / CLK_TCK);
   wait_secs(2.2);
   pause = clock();
   printf("That took %f seconds\n", (pause - start) / CLK_TCK); wait_secs(.1);
   printf("This program took %f seconds to run\n", clock() / CLK_TCK);
   printf("This should be the same: %f\n", (clock() - start) / CLK_TCK);
   printf("Incidentally, this thing clicks %f times a second\n", CLK_TCK);
```

```
    }

    void wait_secs(double secs)
    {
        clock_t begin;  /* usually a typedef for long */
        begin = clock();
        while (clock() < begin + (clock_t)(secs * (double)CLK_TCK))
            continue;

    }
```

16.7.3   Application: An Intelligent ID Number

We can utilize a couple of the date and time functions we've constructed to create a unique string from a combination of the current date and time. We might use such a function to have our program automatically create a unique invoice number or form ID number. The function returns a string in the format YYMMDD-HHMM, where the hour is a number between 0 and 24:

```
/* return as a string combo date/time in format YYMMDD-HHMM */

char *date_time_str(void)
{
    static char date_string[22];
    int month, day, year, hr, min;

    /* store current month, day & yr (e.g., 99 for yr) in 3 separate variables */

    get_date_split(&month, &day, &year);

    /* same for hour and minute (hr is 24-hour clock: e.g., 22 for 10 p.m.) */

    get_real_time_split(&hr, &min);

    /* stick them all together in string in format YYMMDD-HHMM */

    sprintf(date_string, "%02.2d%02.2d%02.2d-%02.2d%02.2d", year, month,
        day, hr, min);
    return date_string;
}
```

Since the first six characters represent YYMMDD, this string can also be converted to a numerical value and used to sort data chronologically or to retrieve data from records dated between those two dates. Of, if an application calls for more precise sorting, you could omit the hyphen between the day and hour. See if you can create the subfunctions called for.

Chapter Summary

1. Errors that arise from the use of certain Standard C library functions set the system variable or macro errno to a value that corresponds to an implementation-defined set of messages in the system global char pointer array variable sys_errlist.

2. Two Standard C error codes are EDOM, indicating that a value passed is not of a type acceptable to a mathematical function, and ERANGE, indicating that the result of a mathematical function is valid but out of range.

3. At the commencement of any program, errno will have a value of zero. A library function error will result in its being set to some positive nonzero value. You should zero out errno before testing its postlibrary function call value, and you should test its value immediately after using the library function you want to check.

4. The perror() function allows us to automatically print to stderr the sys_errlist string corresponding to the current value of errno. Make sure to call perror() immediately after an error occurs.

5. If you wish to create an error log file to preserve the causes of library function errors, you can use errno directly by using strerror(). This function returns the implementation-defined message string that corresponds to errno.

6. The `system()` function allows you to execute an operating system command from your program. The `system()` function takes a single argument, a pointer to `char` that points to the operating system command you want to use.

7. If you call `system()` with a `NULL` pointer, the call invokes the command processor in such a way that its command prompt is displayed, allowing the user to type in system commands before returning to the C program.

8. Premature program termination can be accomplished with `exit()` or `abort()`.

9. Just before the program terminates, `exit()` causes all file buffers to be flushed and all open files to be closed.

10. You may pass `atexit()` the name of a function you wish to have called once an `exit()` call is made. Each function passed to an `atexit()` call is placed into a queue, and when `exit()` is called, functions in the queue are called in reverse order prior to `exit()`'s buffer flushing and file closing.

11. The functions passed to `atexit()` must not return a value and may not take any arguments.

12. You can pass command-line arguments from the system prompt as strings to a C program by declaring `main()` with an `int` argument (that C sets to the number of arguments) and a pointer to pointer to `char` argument (that C uses to house an array of pointers to the various arguments): `int main(int argc, char **argv);`

13. When a C program starts, the address of a pointer to the first operating system environmental variable string is assigned to the global system variable `environ`. The environmental variable strings are stored consecutively in memory, separated by the terminating `NULL` of each individual string. The end of the array of pointers to the strings is marked by a `NULL` pointer.

14. The work of determining the environmental variables can be done for us with `getenv()`, but only if we know what environmental variable we're looking for. The `getenv()` function takes a string containing the environmental variable and returns a pointer to the value portion of the corresponding environmental variable string.

15. With redirection, you can cause `stdin` to take input from a device other than the keyboard or from a file, and you can cause `stdout` to redirect output to a device other than the screen or to a file, in each case without explicitly opening the file.

16. Redirection is accomplished from the system command line: input is redirected with the < operator, and output is redirected with the > operator.

17. You can redirect both input and output at the same time. The executable program comes first on the command line.

18. Redirecting input is equivalent to opening the redirected file for reading; redirecting output is equivalent to opening a file for writing.

19. Since redirecting output to an existing file will truncate it to zero length, you cannot use the same file for input and output by employing the two redirection operators.

20. You can add data to the end of an existing file by redirecting output with the >> operator.

21. The pipe operator, ¦, lets you use the output of one program as the input for another program. You can combine a pipe operation with redirected input.

22. The `time()` function returns the number of seconds between midnight January 1, 1970, and the time of the call.

23. We can use `ctime()` to convert the number of seconds returned by `time()` into a readable date and time string, or `localtime()`, to produce in structure form all the individual date and time components that `ctime()` produces in string form.

24. Successive calls to `time()` can be used to determine elapsed time or to delay program execution for a specified period of time, or the Standard C function `difftime()` can be used instead.

Review Questions

1. How would you use the `system()` function to cause the program to temporarily exit, until an appropriate command is entered from the operating system?

2. If you redirect output to a file that already exists, the operation will fail and the existing file will not be impaired (True or False).

3. Error messages for various values of `errno` are dictated by Standard C (True or False).

4. At program commencement, `errno` has a zero value (True or False).

5. Since `errno` is reset with every Standard C function call, as long as you check the value of `errno` immediately after such a call, you will get the accurate `errno` result for the function call in all cases (True or False).

6. You must append an error message to a `perror()` call (True or False).

7. If the operating system command contained within a `system()` call has a syntax error (insofar as the operating system is concerned), the call to `system()` will return a –1, indicating an error (True or False).

8. Calling `exit(NULL)` is the same as calling `abort()` (True or False).

9. Buffers for all files will be flushed and all files closed prior to program termination occasioned by a call to either `exit()` or `abort()` (True or False).

10. Functions passed to `atexit()` are called in the order in which they are passed.

11. It is possible to invoke `atexit()` by calling `abort(NULL)` (True or False).

12. When attempting to process command-line arguments, the arguments to `main()` must be called `argc` and `argv`, respectively (True or False).

13. The first argument on the command line *after* the program execution name itself is processed by a program that accepts command-line arguments as the first argument—that is, the program name itself is not considered a command-line argument (True or False).

14. For a program to correctly process a command-line argument, the user must type NULL after the last argument (True or False).

15. It is not possible to redirect both input and output at the same time with the same operating system command (True or False).

16. It is not possible to use the same file for both redirected input and output (True or False).

17. The >> redirection operator can be used with either input or output (True or False).

18. The redirection operators cannot be used to connect one data file to another (True or False).

19. You can use the redirection operators to redirect input from more than one file to an executable program (True or False).

20. With the pipe operator, ¦, you can redirect the output of one executable program to serve as the input to another executable program (True or False).

21. Since difftime() returns a double, and clock() returns an integer value, the former is a more precise way of measuring elapsed time (True or False).

22. There is no Standard C function that could tell us the number of days today is from January 1 of the current year; we would have to derive the number mathematically after calling a Standard C function (True or False).

Programming Exercises

This chapter has added command-line arguments to our C knowledge. Modify all the programming assignments you did in Chapter 15 to use command-line arguments to designate the input and output files.

This chapter has also added date and time and disk utilities to our C knowledge. Take the programs you wrote for Programming Assignments 14.1, 14.2, and 14.11. Write a program that will scan all record files and report on all files that are over six months old for potential deletion at management's direction.

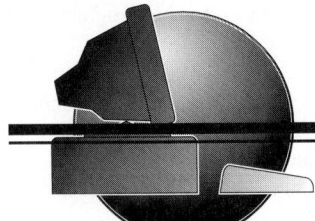

CHAPTER 17

Projects and Program Chaining

OBJECTIVES

- To see the advantages of multiple-source code programs and learn how to put them together
- To learn how to group your own functions and create your own libraries from them
- To see how program control can be transferred permanently or temporarily to another program

- To understand how information can be transferred from program to program
- To learn how to create a master executable module that serves as a menu for various programmer-created and commercially created programs

You have seen throughout this book how the efficiency of your program is enhanced by dividing it into a number of functions instead of lumping all the code into one monstrously long main(). As your programming progresses, and you increasingly tackle more lengthy and complex jobs, you will find that having a single source code packed with a multitude of different functions becomes unwieldy, albeit far better than one long function thousands of lines long. In this chapter, we will investigate techniques for further efficiencies: projects consisting of more than one source code, libraries of functions, and chaining of executable files.

17.1   AN OVERVIEW OF PROJECTS AND LIBRARIES

After you've been programming in C for a while, you will likely have developed many of your own functions. As you move from one programming job to another, you will find that you use many of the same functions over and over.

You can place each of the functions in its own separate source code. Then when you develop a new program, you can include each of the functions you need by placing the respective source codes into a project file. A *project* is a listing of source codes, one of which contains a main() function. It may also include your own or a third-party vendor's libraries. The compiler links the object modules for those source codes together with such libraries and the Standard C library for whatever memory model you have selected, into the executable code.

17.1.1   Grouping Source Codes

The process of first determining just which of dozens of source codes to include and then placing them into a project file would be tedious and time consuming, however. A far better alternative might be to group related functions together and split your functions into a number of source codes. For instance, from functions we've created to this point and in the appendixes, we could make the groupings shown by the header files cursor.h, datetime.h, paint.h, response.h, and status.h found on disk.

You will find that the same increase in efficiency as between a long hodgepodge of statements and a carefully organized set of functions can be achieved by

1. Organizing the commonly used functions into conceptually related groups—database, cursor control, time and date, screen painting, memory status, string handling, file operations, and so on—and making a separate master source code file (without a `main()` function) for each.
2. Linking the source code for a particular programming job, containing `main()` and functions unique to the job, with these master source codes for the commonly used functions by means of a project file.

In the source code containing `main()`, we would include header files for each of the master source codes. We can even create a header file, `all.h`, that would consist solely of include directives for each master source code header file, and include `all.h` in the `main()` source code for each new program. To speed up project file creation, we can copy the project file for an existing program with the name of our new program and then just delete the nonmaster source codes and add the new program's source codes.

17.1.2   Libraries

This alternative system is a good deal simpler and quicker to put together. The drawback is that we needlessly increase the size of our executable code by including code for some functions our program does not use.

The solution is to create your own library. A library efficiently manages a collection of C functions. When you link your program with a library—whether it be the library that comes with your compiler, a third party's library, or your own—the linker searches through the functions in the library and includes only those used by the program. Using a library also speeds up the linking process, because only one object file is opened, instead of several.

You would make your library functions available to the job-specific source code with a project file. This time, the project file would contain the library object code rather than the source codes for each group of commonly used functions.

17.1.3   Program Chaining

For extremely large programming jobs, we can take one final step. We can create a master source code module that mainly serves as a menu to allow the user to select one of the working modules. The main module uses `exec()` or `spawn()` to move back and forth from the menu to a working module, back to the menu, on to another working module, and so forth.

17.2   ADVANTAGES

There are a number of advantages to splitting the collective source code into separate source code modules. First, it makes programming each of the modules much simpler. It is far easier to code five separate source code files of 1500 lines than one source code of 7500 lines. The longer source code has to be in a workable whole, and your mind has a harder time grasping the whole picture at once.

Second, if you work as part of a team—even just you and your partner in a budding software development or consulting company—splitting your code allows each team member to work on a separate module, for later integration.

Third, making a project consisting of a number of separate source codes speeds up compiling time. When you make a change to just one source code module in your project, you can recompile just the one changed source code. If, as you should, you keep a hard copy of your source code, you need only reprint the changed module. If you have created a library out of the commonly used functions, you will not need to compile those modules at all. If you use a library, the compiler will include in the final executable code only those functions actually used by your program.

Fourth, there are computer memory considerations. On the PC, even in the large code memory models (see Appendix B), where your source code is allotted more than one 64K segment, no *one* source code file can exceed 64K. If your compiled source code exceeds 64K, you have no choice but to split the source code.

There are system memory considerations as well. Use of the large code memory models does nothing to expand RAM. If you have only a relatively small amount of RAM, or your program is destined for clients who have such systems, you may find that a very large program simply cannot be run on the system without using spawn() or exec() to overlay one module over another in memory.

We can also use exec() to assist us in linking our programs with a third party's executable program. Say you were writing an electronic mail program. The user is to type a message that your program will then transmit to another site. Rather than incorporating an editor feature into your program, you could simply have the user enter and edit the message with a commercially available editor.

One of the user selections in your e-mail program would be "create a message". When this choice is selected, the commercial editor program is run. When the message has been created, your program would again take control.

17.3   PROJECT FILE MECHANICS

Assuming your compiler has a project file mechanism, the project file must contain a list of all source codes and libraries—other than the Standard C library—to be linked together. Only one of the source codes may contain the function main().

Each source code on your project list is compiled separately, in the order you have them listed in the project file (if this is the first time you have processed this project, all source codes will be compiled; otherwise, only those that have changed since the last processing are recompiled). If errors are encountered in any source code, the compiler stops and gives you the error and warning messages before compiling the succeeding source codes. Thus, each source code must be separately compilable.

17.3.1   Header File Contents

The most efficient way to handle a project is to put all the prototypes for the functions in any one source code into a header file with a base name the same as that of the source code, with a .h extension. The header file should be included in its related source code as well as in all other source codes in the project list that use one or more of the header's functions.

The header file should also contain define directives and structure and union templates, but it may *not* contain variable declarations. If it did, you would generate a redeclaration error in the second source code that included this header file. The proper procedure for a variable shared by more than one source is to declare the variable with the word extern before it in any subsequent source codes that use it. The initial declaration reserves memory space; the subsequent extern declarations do not.

17.3.2   Structure Pointers in Prototypes

If any of the prototypes in the header file contain pointers to structures, you must declare the structure in the header *before* declaring the functions containing the pointers. Having the structure declaration included in more than one source code by inclusion of the header file will not lead to a redeclaration error, since the declaration of the structure does not by itself reserve RAM. Be careful not to declare a variable of the structure type in the header file, however, or you will get a redeclaration error; only the structure template goes in the header.

Though we can define a structure template in more than one source code module, we can't define it more than once in a single source code. If we have two source code modules in the same project that each use functions from one another and both have functions with a pointer to the same structure, we can run afoul of this rule. Take as an example the following fragments from response.h and paint.h, found on disk. Both source codes include paint.h and response.h:

```
/* paint.h    master module header */

#if !defined MENUCOLOR
    struct menucolor
    {
        unsigned char primary, reverse, highlight, window,
            border, b_rev, b_high, b_bord;
```

```
    }
#endif
#define MENUCOLOR

void paintmenu(struct vertical *sptr,
    struct menucolor *colors, char line_type);

/* response.h   master module header */

#if !defined MENUCOLOR

    struct menucolor
    {
        unsigned char primary, reverse, highlight, window,
            border, b_rev, b_high, b_bord;
    };

#endif
#define MENUCOLOR
void choice_horiz(struct horizontal *hpt, char choice, char choices,
    struct menucolor *mpt);
char move_vert_menu(char ch, char choice, char line_type, struct vertical *vptr,
    struct menucolor *mptr);
```

But for this define trick, we would have the menucolor structure defined twice in the same source code in both cases.

17.3.3   A Simple Project Example

The following source codes represent a very simple project example.

 **Listing**   **17.1 ext_main.c**

```
/* ext_main.c */

#include <stdio.h>
#include "ext_sub1.h"
#include "ext_sub2.h"

int i = 2; /* global i */

int main(void)
{
    int i, j; /* local i */

    /* set local i to global i's (in ext_main.c) value */
    i = echo_main();
    for (j = 0; j < 2; j++)
    {
        printf("local i = %d; main's global i = %d; "
            "sub1's global i = %d; main's local j = %d\n",
            i, echo_main(), echo_sub1(), j);
        printf("after plus2_sub1(), sub1's global i = %d\n", plus2_sub1());
        printf("after times2_sub1(), sub1's global i = %d\n", times2_sub1());

        /* sum of local i & local j gets passed in next call */
        printf("after add_to_j(), sub1's local j = %d\n", add_to_j(i + j));
        printf("after plus2_main(), main's global i = %d\n", plus2_main());
    }
}
```

 **Listing** **17.2 ext_sub1.c**

```
/* ext_sub1.c */
#include "ext_sub1.h"
static int i = 5; /* global i limited to this file */

int echo_sub1(void)
{
   return i;
}

int plus2_sub1(void)
{
   return i += 2; /* uses global i in this file */
}

int times2_sub1(void)
{
   return i *= 2; /* uses global i in this file */
}

int add_to_j(int i)
{
   static int j = 3; /* local j; unconnected to j inside main
      retains value from call to call since static */

   return (i = j += i); /* local i; value passed as parameter
      Assignment to i has no real effect */
}
```

Listing **17.3 ext_sub2.c**

```
/* ext_sub2.c */
extern int i; /* makes ext_main.c's global i available to this file */
int echo_main(void)
{
   return i; /* this is main's global i */
}

int plus2_main(void)
{
   return i += 2;
}
```

```
/* ext_sub1.h */

int echo_sub1(void);
int plus2_sub1(void);
int times2_sub1(void);
int add_to_j(int);
```

```
/* ext_sub2.h */

int echo_main(void);
int plus2_main(void);
```

The project file would contain `ext_main.c`, `ext_sub1.c`, and `ext_sub2.c`. It would *not* contain `ext_sub1.h` or `ext_sub2.h`. The combination of these files would produce a single executable file with a `.exe` extension added onto whatever you named the project file (for example, a Borland C project file of `ext.prj` would produce `ext.exe`). Here's the output:

```
local i = 2; main's global i = 2; sub1's global i = 5; main's local j = 0
after plus2_sub1(), sub1's global i = 7
after times2_sub1(), sub1's global i = 14
after add_to_j(), sub1's local j = 5
after plus2_main(), main's global i = 4
local i = 2; main's global i = 4; sub1's global i = 14; main's local j = 1
after plus2_sub1(), sub1's global i = 16
after times2_sub1(), sub1's global i = 32
after add_to_j(), sub1's local j = 8
after plus2_main(), main's global i = 6
```

There are actually four different variables named `i`: a global one declared and initialized to 2 in `ext_main.c`; a local one declared inside `main()` in `ext_main.c`; a global one, declared as `static` (and hence limited to the file in which it is declared) and initialized to 5 in `ext_sub1.c`; and a local `i` declared by way of being a parameter to `add_to_j()` in `ext_sub1.c`. Of course, such a profusion of variables with the same name would hardly be a recommended practice; its only purpose here is for illustration of scope across multiple source code files.

The first output line simply reflects the two separate initializations to the global `i` variables, as well as the assignment of `ext_main.c`'s `i` variable to the local `i` in `main()`. The value returned by `echo_main()` is the value of the `i` variable made available to `ext_sub2.c` by virtue of the referencing declaration there:

```
extern int i;
```

The value returned by `echo_sub1()` reflects the value of the global `i` variable in `ext_sub1.c`—that global variable being restricted to that file by the initializing declaration:

```
static int i = 5;
```

The next two statements respectively add 2 and then double the `i` variable that it is restricted to `ext_sub1.c`.

In the next statement, we pass the `i` and `j` variables local to `main()`, which now have the values 2 and 0, respectively, as a total to `add_to_j()`. That function adds that passed value to the value of the local `static` variable `j` (initialized to 3) and also assigns the new value of `j` to the local `i` variable. Since this `i` variable is local only, the final assignment (remember, assignment is made from right to left) has no real effect. Since `j` is `static`, its new value will be preserved for the next call; it will not be reinitialized.

The value of the global `i` variable declared in `ext_main.c` is increased by 2 in the final statement in the loop. Since none of the earlier calls affected this variable, it now has a value of 4.

Make sure you can follow how the values in the next iteration are derived.

17.4 CONSISTENCY AND INITIALIZATION OF EXTERNAL VARIABLES IN MULTIPLE FILES

Where several source codes use the same variable (as in the last example for the `i` declared in `ext_main.c` and made available to `ext_sub2.c` by an `extern` declaration), a couple of questions arise: Which occurrence constitutes the variable's definition (where storage is allocated for the variable), and which are only referencing declarations? How do we ensure consistent declarations across files, and what happens if we make inconsistent declarations?

Assume a variable is declared without the storage class specifier `extern` in one file and also initialized there. Assume further that in all other files, the variable is declared with `extern` and not initialized at the same time and is declared with the same type as the non-`extern` initializing occurrence. Under these assumptions, there are no concerns at all. But if all this is not adhered to, there can be a devil of a

Table 17.1   *External Variable Declaration as Definition or Reference*

Declaration	Interpretation
`int var = 0;`	Definition
`int var;`	Reference, *unless* no other initialization elsewhere, in which case is a Definition
`extern int var;`	Reference
`extern int var = 0;`	Definition

problem.

If a variable is declared outside any function and is initialized, and if there is no other such initializing declaration in any other file, the declaration is the definition.

That is so irrespective of which of the declarations use or do not use the `extern` storage class specifier. If an external variable is declared without an initialization and without the keyword `extern`, and no other declaration of the same variable in other files has an initialization, the former is the definition. The Standard C rules on declarations are summarized in Table 17.1.

To avoid any potential problems, first be sure there is a single instance in which a variable is declared without the `extern` keyword, and be sure to initialize it at that point, even if it is just set to 0, the default value it would have in absence of initialization anyway.

Second, in every other location, use `extern` and do not initialize.

Third, make certain all the instances of declaration use the same type. Unfortunately, the C compiler has no way of checking type consistency across files for the same variable. So if you declare the same variable as an `int` in one file and as a `double` in another, the result may be erratic behavior at run time. You will get no warning about the inconsistency.

Most UNIX compilers include the `lint` program, which can do the required across-file checking. There are also commercial utilities for both DOS and UNIX systems that will do the same job.

17.5   CREATING A LIBRARY IN BORLAND C *(OPTIONAL)*

Most compilers have library creation utilities. With Borland C, you create a library with `tlib.exe`. The `tlib` utility must be run from the command line. The syntax is as follows:

tlib [library name] + [object code 1] + [object code 2] + . . .

For instance, to create a library called `master.lib` from the modules found on disk:

tlib master + btree + cursor + datetime + paint + print + response + status

The `tlib` utility will add a `.lib` extension to the library and will assume a `.obj` extension for each of the object code modules to be included.

17.6   CHAINING AND OVERLAYING PROGRAMS

To promote modularity, we first learned to split our source code into functions that perform discrete tasks. Another step in that direction was splitting our code into separate source codes and linking them together in a project file. In the process, we learned that if some of those source code modules handle programming tasks that we can use in several of our programs, we can compile those modules into libraries. We can go even further.

17.6.1   Splitting a Job into Separate Executable Programs: An Example

We can split a programming task into separate programs. Suppose we were designing a software package for a hair salon. The salon carries an inventory of several dozen products and offers a couple dozen different services. The hair stylists the shop employs work partly on salary and partly on a commission paid both on services and on the products their customers buy. The salon keeps a database of its customers. Shortly before a customer's birthday, the shop sends the customer a letter offering a free haircut.

The software package you write for the shop might contain the following program modules, each with its separate executable file:

- *A product and services database program.* Here, the shop could add to, delete, or modify its products and services and the prices charged for each. Minimum quantities for each product could be set or reset. The quantity of each product in inventory would be maintained in a file. A report showing the current products and services in the database and their prices and the quantity in inventory and minimum quantities for each product could be printed out. Inventory quantities could also be manually adjusted in case of such things as theft or spoilage.
- *A stylist compensation database program.* As with the products and services program, stylists could be added or deleted or their salaries or commission levels and rates modified.
- *A customer database program.* Each customer's name, address, stylist, birth date, and home and work telephone numbers would be stored. Customer records could be added, deleted, or modified manually. Selecting a purging feature would delete customers who have not been back to the shop for a stated length of time. Each month, birthday announcements for customers with birthdays the following month would be printed out, along with envelopes. A list of all customers in a particular zip code, with a particular telephone prefix, who had been in to the shop within a designated time period, who are male or female, above or below a certain age could be printed out.
- *A bill calculation and printing program.* This program would open the stylist commission database file and the customer database file (to update the last-time-in field and to make any address or telephone number changes). In cases where a customer bought a product, the program would also open the inventory database file. Inventory would be reduced accordingly, and if the quantity fell below the specified minimum for the product, a warning to order more would be printed out.
- *A payroll program to calculate salaries and commissions.* It would determine the proper amount of withholdings and would write checks. The program would use the compensation database file to make its calculations and on completion reset accrued commissions to zero.
- *A check-writing program for expenses other than payroll.*
- *An accounting program that would calculate profits and losses and print a report.* Profits and losses could be calculated on a monthly, quarterly, or annual basis. The annual profit-and-loss statement would be used by an accountant to prepare the shop's income tax return.

The billing program could be run by any staff member. The other programs could be run only by management. In addition, there could also be a menu program whose sole function would be to allow automated selection of one of the working modules. At the end of each module, the menu program would be run.

The materials in Appendix L show how exec() and spawn() can be used to link all those various executable programs together.

Chapter Summary

1. Multiple source codes, only one of which contains main(), can be linked together, along with programmer-created function libraries, in a single program.
2. Prototypes for a source code's functions should be placed in a header file with the same base name as the source code's, along with define directives and structure and union templates.
3. The header file should be included in all source codes in the program that use any of the header's functions.
4. To avoid any conflict in external variables used in mul-

tiple source codes in the same program:
- Make sure there is a single instance in which a variable is declared without the extern keyword.
- Initialize it at that point, even if just to 0.
- In every other location, use extern and do not initialize.
- Make certain all the instances of declaration use the same type.

Review Questions

1. In a multiple source code program, each source code must have a `main()` function (True or False).
2. If the memory required for the executable code and data to solve a particular programming problem exceeds the computer's primary memory, the only way to solve the problem is to buy another computer or move to another platform (True or False).
3. You must make a global variable in one source code of a multiple-source code program explicitly available to another source code by notation in that other source code in order for that other source code to have access to the variable (True or False).
4. You must make a function in one source code of a multiple-source code program explicitly available to another source code by notation in that other source code in order for that other source code to have access to the function (True or False).
5. You must make a function in one source code of a multiple-source code program explicitly available to another source code by notation in that other source code in order for the compiler to do argument-checking on calls in that other source code to the function (True or False).
6. All header files must have a `.h` extension (True or False).
7. Normally, global variables that will be used by several source codes in a multiple-source code program are placed into a header file (True or False).
8. A variable's definition reserves memory; a declaration is not always a definition (True or False).
9. If you define a global variable, `confused`, in one source as `int` and make the following declaration in another source code, the compiler will catch the error, since not only are the types different, the number of bytes is different (True or False):

   ```
   extern double confused;
   ```

10. Unlike the case with Standard C libraries, including your own library of functions in a program will result in all functions in the library being part of the executable code whether the program calls them or not (True or False).

Programming Exercises

This chapter has added projects and program chaining to our C knowledge. Take the programs you wrote for Programming Assignments 14.1 (billing), 14.2 (payroll), 14.11 (distribution and shipping), and 9.12 (invoicing). Make a master program that contains a user menu with each of these programs as choices. Create a single executable program with each of these subtasks as separate source codes and the master program file as the one that houses the main menu and the `main()` function.

Now do the same programming task by creating a separate *program* for each of the choices. Now your choice program would call the other tasks by `spawn()` calls to the various programs. (See Appendix L.)

Now do the same programming task this time with `exec()` calls to the various programs. (See Appendix L.) Be sure to include an `exec()` call back to the master menu program with an additional argument that alerts the master program to who is calling it and where it left off.

APPENDIX **A**

Controlling the PC Console—Escape Sequences

Thus far, when we've used `printf()`, we've simply allowed whatever is currently being printed to the screen to be placed directly after what is already there. Once the screen is filled, what's printed next is placed on the screen at the bottom row, with each previous row moving up one row to make room (this is called *scrolling*). The top row vanishes.

What may appear a haphazard process is really quite orderly. As we will see in much greater detail when we learn how to use direct memory access in Appendix D, in our computer's normal video mode on a PC, the ASCII values and the colors and attributes of each character we see on the screen are contained in pairs of bytes at specific locations in RAM. The character is stored in one byte, and the color and attributes for that character are stored in the next byte. (The attribute dictates whether the character is blinking or not, whether the foreground colors are light or dark, and for monochrome monitors, whether the character is underlined or in reverse video.)

For example, the screen character in row 0, column 1 is stored at a memory location 2 bytes higher than the 2 bytes for the screen character in row 0, column 0; the screen character in row 1, column 0 is stored at a memory location 160 bytes higher than the screen character in row 0, column 0 (80 columns per row times 1 row times 2 bytes per character display box); and so forth.

When a line is scrolled up, the character-color/attribute combinations move up in memory location, with the bytes for the top row's characters and color/attributes being lost unless we've made other arrangements to store the crowded-out information elsewhere just before we scroll. This process is analogous to what takes place with the end bits lost in a bit shift operation. (See Chapter 12.)

We can take control of this process and write wherever on the screen we want and in whatever available color we want. We can do this in one of three ways:

- Escape sequences embedded in `printf()` statements' control strings
- BIOS interrupts that access subroutines built into the computer's ROM
- Direct memory access (DMA)

The first method, which we will cover in this appendix, is the simplest and, with one possible exception, the most portable. The escape sequence method, however, is more limited in what it can do. BIOS interrupts are more flexible and also faster performing than the escape sequence method; DMA is far quicker than either of the other methods. All three methods ultimately access the computer's RAM. The question is how far down the chain of higher-level command to direct memory access we choose to break in and issue instructions.

A.1　SETTING UP ESCAPE SEQUENCES

The computer transforms escape sequences into subroutine calls through a device driver file called *ansi.sys*. This file is loaded into memory by the following line in the `config.sys` file:

```
device=ansi.sys
```

DOS can work by itself in a rudimentary fashion with ordinary computer devices such as disk drives, printers, keyboards, and monitors. Using other kinds of peripherals or making more sophisticated use of the common ones requires additional software, called *device drivers*. The `ansi.sys` file enhances standard DOS screen output and keyboard input.

The ansi.sys driver looks for a special 2-byte code that identifies commands for the driver to send for processing. The ansi.sys driver strips out the special codes from a printf() statement so that they go to the command processor for evaluation rather than show up on the screen.

The first byte of the code is the escape character, ASCII decimal 27 (octal 033, hexadecimal 0x1B); the second is the left-bracket character [, ASCII decimal 91. Following the 2-byte code are an integer parameter or parameters and then a letter that represents the command itself. The final letter is case sensitive—for example, h is not the same as H.

Tables A.1 and A.2 list some of the escape sequences for cursor movement, screen and line erasing, and colors and attributes. As advertised, each begins with the escape character and the [character. The # represents an integer to be selected by the programmer. If no number is substituted for #, the computer inserts a 1 by default. Thus, \33[A will move the cursor up one row, just as \33[1A would. (Incidentally, remember that, unlike notation for octal and hexadecimal constants, where we precede the digits by 0 or 0x, respectively, we write octal and hexadecimal escape sequences \ooo and \xhhh.)

There are two exceptions to this default rule. If you do not specify a number with \33#m (that is, \33m), all attributes will be turned off and the colors reset to the default gray on black. If you do not specify a number with \33#;#H or \33#;#f (that is, \33H or \33f), the cursor moves to the home position (row 0, column 0). (Actually, as you will see, for purposes of console control with escape sequences, the home position is 1,1 and the lower-right corner is 25,80, rather than the more usual 0,0 and 24,79 notation.)

Table A.1 *Escape Sequences*

Escape Sequence	Meaning	Escape Sequence	Meaning
\33[2J	Clear the screen and home cursor	\33[#D	Move left # columns
\33[K	Erase from cursor through end of row	\33[#;#f	Move to specified row and column
\33[s	Save cursor position	\33[#;#H	Same as f (move to specified row/column)
\33[u	Move to saved cursor position		
\33[6n	Read current cursor position by sending string to stdin in format \33[%02d;%02dR\r	\33[7h	Turn line wrap on
		\33[07l	Turn line wrap off (last character is lower case L)
\33[#A	Move up # rows	\33[#m	Change screen attributes and colors *(see Table A.2 for integer values)*
\33[#B	Move down # rows		
\33[#C	Move right # columns		

Table A.2 *Attributes and Colors*

	Integer	Meaning	
Screen Attributes	0	All attributes off	
	1	Light foreground colors (bold for monochrome monitors)	
	4	Underline (monochrome only)	
	5	Blink	
	7	Reverse video (monochrome only)	
		Light Attribute Off	*Light Attribute On*
Foreground Colors	30	Black	Light Black
	31	Red	Light Red
	32	Green	Light Green
	33	Brown	Yellow
	34	Blue	Light Blue
	35	Purple	Light Purple
	36	Cyan	Light Cyan
	37	Grey	White
Background Colors	40	Black	
	41	Red	
	42	Green	
	43	Brown	
	44	Blue	
	45	Purple	
	46	Cyan	
	47	Grey	

A.2   MECHANICS OF ESCAPE SEQUENCES

To effectuate an escape sequence in a C statement, you insert the escape sequence as a string inside `printf()`. You may include the escape character and the balance of the escape sequence inside the format string or in the argument list. Any of the following formats will do (we use moving the cursor down one row as an example):

```
char *format[] = "\33[B";
printf("%c%s", '\33', "[B");
printf("%c[B", '\33');
printf("\33%s", "[B");
printf("\33[B");
printf(format);
```

Where the escape character is included in the argument list, as in the first or second statement examples, you may use the decimal, octal, or hexadecimal 27, 033, or 0x1B, or the octal or hexadecimal string equivalents, \33 or \x1B, to represent the escape character. Where, however, the escape character is placed directly in the format string, you may use only \33 or \x1B. Of course, you could replace the escape character by macro:

```
#define ESC '\33'
printf("%c[B", ESC);
```

or

```
#define SEQ "\33["
printf("%sB", SEQ);
```

or still more compact

```
#define PRT(sequence) printf("\33[" #sequence)
PRT(B);
```

(The # operator causes the macro's argument to be replaced by the argument enclosed in double quotes. See Chapter 11.)

Your `printf()` statement does not have to be limited to escape sequence commands. For example, the following statement

```
printf("\33[BI just moved down one line\n");
```

would move the cursor down one line and print "I just moved down one line" at the new location. Also, as long as you include an escape-bracket combination for each separate command, you may include as many separate commands in one `printf()` statement as you wish:

```
printf("\33[6;11H\33[07l  MENU  \33[5B");
```

This statement moves the cursor to row 5, column 10, turns line wrapping off, prints " MENU " at the cursor location, and then moves down 5 rows.

A.3   POSITIONING THE CURSOR

You can position the cursor with either of the two following commands

```
printf("\33#;#H");
printf("\33#;#f");
```

where the # is replaced by an integer between 1 and 25 for the row and 1 and 80 for the column. The first number is the row, and the second is the column. Either the row or the column or both may be omitted, but the semicolon is retained:

```
printf("\33[5;Hgo to row 4, col 0");
printf("\33[;5Hgo to row 0, col 4");
```

If both are omitted

```
printf("\33[Hgo home");
```

the cursor is moved to the home position.

The starting row and column on the screen are generally referred to as row 0, column 0, rather than row 1, column 1. This is the same numbering system we use for specifying array elements. This zero-based scheme is followed when you use interrupts or direct memory access for writing to the screen. However, when you use escape sequences, the home cursor position is row 1, column 1. We will convert this rogue notation to the more normal 0 offset scheme in our discussions and in our programs.

A.4   READING THE CURSOR POSITION

You can read the cursor position with the following command:

```
printf("\33[6n");
```

This command places a string in `stdin` in the following format

```
"\33[%02d;%02dR\r"
```

where each `%02d` represents a two-digit integer, the first for the row and the second for the column. The first digit is a 0 if the number is less than 10. Thus, using the above command to read the cursor's position when it is at the home position would place the following string in `stdin`:

```
"\33]01;01R\r"
```

To read the cursor position, you must read the string placed in `stdin` immediately after issuing the command (or at least before anything further is sent to or read from standard input). Something along the following lines would do the job:

```
void get_curs(int *row, int *col)
{
    char temp[81];
    int i;

    /* send cursor position string to stdin */
    printf("\33[6n");
        /* current cursor position string format is ESC[%02d%;02dR\r */
        i = getch(); /* gobble up ESC */
        i = getch(); /*  gobble up '[' */
        for (i = 0; i < 7; i++) /* read rest of input */
            temp[i] = getch();
        temp[5] = 0; /* cut off R and carriage return */
        sscanf(temp, "%d%*c%d", row, col); /* row & col are pointers, so no & */
        /* unlike with interrupts & DMA, home is row 1/col 1, not 0/0 */
        (*row)--;
    (*col)--;
}
```

The trick is to read the string without echoing any part of it to the screen. The following will not work because part of the string gets printed to the screen:

```
scanf("%*c%*c%d%*c%d%*c%*c", row, col);
```

The same would result from a call to `gets()`. That's why we used a series of `getch()` statements to quietly place the string into a temporary holding array where we can examine and parse it with `sscanf()`. We use `int` pointers for the row and column rather than `int`s so that we can effectively "return" both values to the calling function.

You can also record the current cursor position without bothering to determine precisely which row and column it is at. You can then later replace the cursor at that recorded position. This saving and restoring is done through a pair of commands that work in tandem:

```
printf("\33[s"); /* save current cursor position */
. . .
printf("\33[u"); /* move cursor to
    position most recently saved by "\33[s" */
```

A.5 LINE WRAPPING

The DOS default is line wrapping. With *line wrapping*, the cursor moves to column 0 of the next row if a character is printed while the cursor is on the right-most column. If the cursor is at the last row as well as at the last column, the cursor is moved to the home position. To turn line wrapping on if it's been turned off:

```
printf("\33[7h");
```

If line wrapping is turned off, the cursor will not advance past the last column. Unless the cursor position is manually changed or line wrapping is turned on once again, new characters will just overprint the current character in column 79. To turn line wrapping off:

```
printf("\33[7l");
```

A.6 COLORS AND ATTRIBUTES

With colors and attributes, you may, if you wish, place more than one escape sequence in a single `printf()` statement by substituting a semicolon for each subsequent escape character. For example, to set a background color of brown and a foreground color of white (which, in turn, for a color monitor is a combination of the bold and gray foreground commands), you can use either

```
printf("\33[1;37;43m");
```

or

```
printf("\33[1m\33[37m\33[43m");
```

Note that in the compact example, m occurs only once amid the three escape sequences, at the very end of the combined sequence.

For example, all of these five commands are valid:

```
printf("\33[1;5;37;44m");
printf("\33[0;36;40m");
printf("\33[37;40m");
printf("\33[44m");
printf("\33[m");
```

The first command turns on the *high-intensity* (light foreground colors) and blink attributes and changes the screen colors to white on blue. The second command turns off all attributes and changes the screen colors to cyan on black. The third command changes the screen colors to gray on black and leaves the attributes unchanged. The fourth command changes the background color to blue and leaves the foreground color and attributes unchanged. Finally, the last command resets the attributes and colors to their default values: all attributes off and gray-on-black color combination.

The following program, `esc_colr.c`, shows all color combinations possible with escape sequences. Each writes the color combination, such as "white on brown," in the appropriate color to the screen.

 **Listing A.1 esc_colr.c**

```
/* esc_colr.c */

/* show all possible color combinations with escape sequences */

#include <stdio.h>
#include <string.h>

int main(void)
{
   int intensity, fore, bkgd;
   char *prompt[2] = {"Turn all attributes off", "Turn high intensity on"};
```

```
char *colors[8] = {"Black", "Red", "Green", "Brown", "Blue", "Purple", "Cyan", "Gray"};
char *lt_colors[8] = {"Lt Black", "Lt Red", "Lt Green", "Yellow", "Lt Blue", "Lt Purple",
   "Lt Cyan", "White"};

/* clear screen */
printf("\033[2J");

/* turn line wrap on */
printf("\033[7h");

/* for dark colors and light colors */
for (intensity = 0; intensity < 2; intensity++)
{
   /* white on gray prompt, centered */
   printf("\033[1;30;37m%*s%s\n",
      40 - strlen(prompt[intensity])/2, "", prompt[intensity]);

   /* at start of first loop turn all attributes off */
   if (intensity == 0)
      printf("\033[m");

   /* at start of second loop, turn high intensity on */
   else printf("\033[1m");

   /* now do foreground/backgrnd combinations at this intensity */
   for (fore = 0; fore < 8; fore++) /* foregrnd colors: 30-37 */
      for (bkgd = 0; bkgd < 8; bkgd++) /* bkgrnd colors: 40-47 */
         printf("\033[%d;%dm %s/%s ", fore + 30, bkgd + 40, (intensity == 0 ? colors[fore] :
            lt_colors[fore]), colors[bkgd]);
   putchar('\n');
}
}
```

A.7 DURATION OF COMMANDS

When you use escape sequences to control the colors and attributes of what gets printed to the screen, any color and attribute command you issue lasts until you change it with another command. In fact, the command lasts beyond the life of your program, unless you reset color and attributes to their default values just before program termination. You can do this by placing the following statement as the last statement in main():

```
printf("\33[m");
```

By contrast, you will see that where you use interrupts or direct memory access for cursor control, you must attend to the color and attributes separately for each and every single character you write to the screen. In other words, if your default color is gray on black and you use interrupts or direct memory access to print a character in white on red, the next character printed will be in gray on black if you fail to issue a specific color command.

A.8 SCAN CODES

Generally, we want to allow the user to enter data at various places on the screen, be able to jump from place to place on the screen by pressing the tab key or the arrow keys, make changes in the various locations, and then signal satisfaction with the data as shown on the screen by pressing a certain key. More sophisticated programs may allow the user to call up various program utilities or options by pressing special key combinations—for example, Alt M to call up a menu, Alt P to print, Esc to exit the program or a particular utility, Page Down or Page Up to jump to other screens of data, function keys to designate colors for different areas of the screen or categories of input or to call up a help screen, Alt S to save data to a user-designated file, Ctrl Alt Home followed by a number to move to a specified page of data, and so on.

To write programs that reflect user presses of some of these keys or key combinations, you must understand how the computer processes key presses. When a particular key is pressed, a keyboard processor transmits a numerical value, called a *scan code*, to the CPU. The value is not the ASCII value of the character represented by the key. Instead, it is based on the key's physical location on the keyboard. For example, the contiguous keys Q, W, E, and R have scan codes of 10, 11, 12, and 13.

For the garden variety keys—numbers, letters of the alphabet, punctuation, and a few others—the computer converts the scan codes into the corresponding ASCII values. Therefore, it is not important that you know what the scan codes for these keys are. (Note that the code generated by the Enter key is converted to 13, the carriage return character, rather than to 10, the newline character. So, if your program tests for whether the user has pressed the Enter key, it must ask whether the variable you use to store key presses is equal to \r, not \n.)

For special keys and other key combinations—the function keys F1–F12, the arrow keys, End Home Insert Page Up Page Down Alt and Ctrl in combination with other keys, and certain other keys—something different is done. Those keys are handled in two bytes, with the first byte being set to zero and the second byte being set to a number that has a relationship to keyboard position. For example, Alt A has a second-byte value of 30, Alt S has a second-byte value of 31, and Alt D has a second-byte value of 32. They are sequentially numbered because those three keys are side by side on the keyboard. A complete listing of the second-byte values for the special keys is found in Appendix G. These special keys are referred to as *extended keys*.

For example, given the following statements

```c
char first, second;
first = getch();
second = getch();
printf("first: %d, second: %d\n");
```

holding the Alt key down and pressing the S key would cause this output:

```
first: 0, second: 31
```

Pressing the F1 key would produce

```
first: 0, second 59
```

Listing A.2, concolor.c, shows how we can read in regular and extended keys and how we can use them in conjunction with escape sequences for an interactive cursor control program.

Listing A.2 concolor.c

```c
/* concolor.c */

#include <stdio.h>
#include <conio.h> /* getch */
#include <string.h> /* strcpy */
#include <stdlib.h> /* exit */
#include "keys.h" /* Appendix H */
#include "concolor.h" /* Appendix H */

/* colors for directions at top & bottom of screen in help() */
#define HIGH "\33[1;37;47m" /* white on gray */
#define NORMAL "\33[0;31;47m" /* red on gray */
#define BORDER "\33[0;30;47m" /* black on gray */

static int wrap; /* if 0, line wrap is off; if 1, line wrap is on */

void get_curs(void);
void help(void);
void return_curs(int *row, int *col);
void set_curs(void);
void wrap_toggle(void);

/* +----------------------------------------------------------------+
   +   MAIN
   +----------------------------------------------------------------+ */
```

```
int main(void)
{
    int row, col, skip_move = 0;

    /* initialize to white on red */
    int intense = 1, fore = GRAY_F, back = RED_B;

    unsigned char ch;
    char direction[4]; /* used to store string to be tacked onto ESC[ */

    printf("\33[%d;%d;%dm" , intense, back, fore); /* set color */
    printf("\33[2J"); /* clear screen */
    help(); /* draw directions */
    printf("\33[2;1H"); /* start at row 1, col 0 */

    while (1) /* loop until escape key pressed */
    {
        if ((ch = getch()) == 0) /* extended characters? */
        {
            ch = getch();
            switch (ch)
            {
                /* background colors: function keys */
                case F1: back = BLACK_B; break;
                case F2: back = BLUE_B; break;
                case F3: back = BROWN_B; break;
                case F4: back = CYAN_B; break;
                case F5: back = GREEN_B; break;
                case F6: back = GRAY_B; break;
                case F7: back = PURPLE_B; break;
                case F8: back = RED_B; break;

                /* foreground colors: shift-function: dark/ctrl-function: light */
                case SF1: case CF1: fore = BLACK_F; break;
                case SF2: case CF2: fore = BLUE_F; break;
                case SF3: case CF3: fore = BROWN_F; break; /* yellow */
                case SF4: case CF4: fore = CYAN_F; break;
                case SF5: case CF5: fore = GREEN_F; break;
                case SF6: case CF6: fore = GRAY_F; break; /* white */
                case SF7: case CF7: fore = PURPLE_F; break;
                case SF8: case CF8: fore = RED_F; break;
                case UP:
                    return_curs(&row, &col);
                    if (row > 1) /* don't write over directions */
                        strcpy(direction, "A");
                    else skip_move = 1;
                    break;
                case DN:
                    return_curs(&row, &col);
                    if (row < 23) /* don't write over directions */
                        strcpy(direction, "B");
                    else skip_move = 1;
                    break;
                case RT:
                    return_curs(&row, &col);
                    if (!wrap || col < 79)
                        strcpy(direction, "C");
                    else
                    {
```

```c
            if (row != 23) /* move down one row, at col 0 */
               sprintf(direction, "%d;%dH", ++row + 1, 1);
            else strcpy(direction, "2;1H"); /* home cursor */
      }
      break;
      case LT: strcpy(direction, "D"); break;

      /* don't erase directions */
      case HM: strcpy(direction, "2;1H"); break;

      /* move to top row, current column */
      case PGUP:
         return_curs(&row, &col);
      sprintf(direction, "%d;%dH", 1, col + 1);
      break;

      /* move to bottom row, current column */
      case PGDN:
         return_curs(&row, &col);
      sprintf(direction, "%d;%dH", 25, col + 1);
      break;

      /* clear screen with delete key */
      case DEL:
      /* for replacement after clear */
         return_curs(&row, &col);
      strcpy(direction, "2J");
      break;

      /* end key: erase from cursor to end of row */
      case END:  strcpy(direction, "K"); break;

      /* go to user-specified row & col */
      case ALTS: set_curs(); break;

      /* print cursor position at lower left */
      case ALTG: get_curs(); break;

      /* repaint directions */
      case ALTH: help(); break;

      /* turn word wrap off if on or vice versa */
      case INS: wrap_toggle(); break;
} /* end switch */

/* color commands */

if ((ch >= F1 && ch <= F8) || (ch >= SF1 && ch <= SF8) || (ch >=
   CF1 && ch <= CF8))
{
   if (ch >= SF1 && ch <= SF8)
      intense = 0;
   if (ch >= CF1 && ch <= CF8)
      intense = 1;

   /* execute the color command */

   printf("\33[%d;%d;%dm", intense, back, fore);
}
```

```
        /* movement commands */

        if (ch == UP || ch == DN || ch == RT || ch == LT || ch == HM || ch == PGUP ||
            ch == PGDN || ch == DEL || ch == END)
        {
            if (!skip_move)
                printf("\33[%s", direction);
            else skip_move = 0; /* reset skip flag */
        }
        if (ch == DEL)
        {
            help(); /* redraw directions after clear screen */

            /* replace cursor */
            sprintf(direction, "\33[%d;%dH", row, col);
            printf(direction);
        }

    } /* end if 0 first byte (extended character) */

    else
        switch(ch) /* not an extended character */
    {
        /* backspace: left, space character, left */
        case '\b': printf("\33[D \33[D"); break;
        /* convert CTRL-C to French soft c */
        case CTRL_C: putchar('ç'); break;
        /* box characters: */
        /* down & left to facilitate more vert chars */
        case CTRL_V: printf("‖\33[B\33[D"); break;
        case CTRL_Z: putchar('='); break;
        case CTRL_T:
            if ((ch = getch()) == 'l' || ch == 'L')
            putchar('╔');
        if (ch == 'r' || ch == 'R')
            putchar('╗');
        break;
        case CTRL_B:
            if ((ch = getch()) == 'l' || ch  == 'L')
            putchar('╚');
        if (ch == 'r' || ch == 'R')
            putchar('╝');
        break;

        /* <===end program with ESC key===> */
        case ESC:
        /* reset to DOS default: light gray on black */
            printf("\33[m");
        exit(0);
        default:
        /* ignore other control characters */
            if (ch >= ' ')
            putchar(ch);
        break;
    } /* end switch */

    } /* end while */
}
```

```
/* +-----------------------------------------------------------------+
   +  GET_CURS: prints the current cursor row and column at the lower
   +  left-hand corner of the screen
   +-----------------------------------------------------------------+*/


void get_curs(void)
{
   int row, col;

   /* save current cursor position */

   printf("\33[s");
   return_curs(&row, &col);

   /* move to next to bottom row to print message */
   printf("\33[24;1H");
   printf("Now at row %d, col %d  ", row, col);

   /* move back to cursor position */
   printf("\33[u");
}

/*Botttom Directions
Cursor ALT-S Set ALT-G Get Colors F#  Bkgd CTRL-F#/Shft-F# Fore DEL Clr ESC Exit
Top Directions
ALT-H Help  Lines CTRL-V/Z Vert/Horiz  CTRL-T L/R Top lt/rt CTRL-B L/R bot lt/rt*/


/* +-----------------------------------------------------------------+
   +  HELP: print directions at top and bottom of screen
   +-----------------------------------------------------------------+*/


void help(void)
{
   /* top directions */

   printf("\33[%d;%dH%s", 1, 1, NORMAL);
   printf( "ALT-H           CTRL-V/Z           CTRL-T L/R           CTRL-B L/R");
   printf("%s", HIGH);
   printf("\33[%d;%dH Lines", 1, 12);
   printf("%s", BORDER);
   printf("\33[%d;%dH Help", 1, 6);
   printf("\33[%d;%dH Vert/Horiz ", 1, 27);
   printf("\33[%d;%dH Top LT/RT", 1, 49);
   printf("\33[%d;%dH Bot LT/RT ", 1, 70);


   /* bottom directions */
   printf("\33[%d;%dH%s", 25, 8, NORMAL);
   printf( "ALT-S    ALT-G           F#      CTRL-F#/SHFT-F#    DEL    ESC");
   printf("%s", HIGH);
   printf("\33[%d;%dHCursor ", 25, 1);
   printf("\33[%d;%dHColors ", 25, 28);
   printf("%s", BORDER);
   printf("\33[%d;%dH Set", 25, 13);
   printf("\33[%d;%dH Get", 25, 23);
   printf("\33[%d;%dH Bkgd", 25, 37);
   printf("\33[%d;%dH Fore", 25, 58);
   printf("\33[%d;%dH Clr", 25, 67);
   printf("\33[%d;%dH Exit", 25, 75);
```

```
}

/* +--------------------------------------------------------------+
   +  RETURN_CURS: "returns" current cursor row and column
   +  (pass 2 pointers to int)
   +------------------------------------------------------------+*/

void return_curs(int *row, int *col)
{
    char temp[81];
    int i;

    /* send current cursor position string to stdin in format ESC[%0d%;0dR\r */
    printf("\33[6n");

    i = getch(); /* gobble up ESC */
    i = getch(); /*  gobble up '[' */

    /* store rest of string in temp */

    for (i = 0; i < 7; i++)
        temp[i] = getch();

    /* cut off 'R' and carriage return at end of stdin string */
    temp[5] = 0;
    sscanf(temp, "%d%*c%d", row, col);

    /* unlike with interrupts & DMA, home is row 1/col 1, not 0/0 */
    (*row)--;
    (*col)--;
}

/* +--------------------------------------------------------------+
   +  SET_CURS: lets user position cursor at specified row and column
   +------------------------------------------------------------+*/

void set_curs(void)
{
    int row, col;

    /* move to row 23, col 0 */

    printf("\33[24;0H type row #, a space, col # and press [enter]"

    /* move back to row 23, col 0 for input */
       "\33[24;1H");

    /* read in user input */
    scanf("%d%d", &row, &col);

    /* back to col 0, erase whole row, go to designated spot */
    /* unlike with interrupts & DMA, home is row 1/col 1, not 0/0 */
    printf("\33[24;1H\33[K\33[%d;%df", row + 1, col + 1);
}

/* +--------------------------------------------------------------+
   +  WRAP_TOGGLE: turns line wrap on if it's off and vice versa
   +------------------------------------------------------------+*/
```

```
void wrap_toggle(void)
{  /* if on, turn off */
   if (wrap)
      printf("\33[07l");

   /* otherwise, turn on */
   else printf("\33[7h");

   /* toggle between 0 and 1 */
   wrap = (wrap + 1) % 2;
}
```

First, we initialize the color to white on red and clear the screen. Clearing the screen paints the entire screen in whatever color the current background color is (effectively, we are writing 2000 space characters to the screen, so the foreground color does not show up). Then, after positioning the cursor at row 1, column 0, we read characters in from the keyboard with getch(). We do this in an infinite loop, stopping only when the [Esc] key is pressed. Remember that getch(), found in conio.h, returns whatever key is pressed without waiting for the enter key to be pressed and without echoing the character to the screen:

```
if ((ch = getch()) == 0)
```

If one of the extended keys is pressed, the statement will be true and the program will proceed to determine which of the extended keys has been pressed and what course of action to take for each relevant one. It does this by a second getch() statement. Since entering one of the extended keys sends two bytes to stdin, the second getch() does not require or permit additional user input.

We have set [F1]–[F8] to change background color, [Shift][F1]–[Shift][F8] to change foreground color to a dark color, and [Ctrl][F1]–[Ctrl][F8] to change foreground to a light color.

If we find an extended key and determine that a function key has not been pressed, we next check to see whether one of the arrow keys, the page movement keys, or the [Delete] or [End] keys have been pressed. If so, we direct appropriate action to be taken.

We have coded the arrow keys [↑] [↓] and [→] [←] to move the cursor up or down a row or right or left a column. If a [→] key is pressed, we check to see whether line wrapping is on. With line wrapping on, typing a printable character when the cursor is at the right-most column will automatically cause the cursor to move to the next row. However, sending a move-right-one-column command when the cursor is at column 79 will be ignored. It is up to the program to take care of line wrapping in this case.

We let the user toggle line wrapping by pressing the [Insert] key. Pressing the [Insert] key will call wrap_toggle(). The function uses a global variable, wrap. If wrap is equal to 1, indicating line wrapping is on, we turn it off; if wrap is equal to 0, we turn it on. We then use the modulus operator to change wrap to reflect the new state of affairs:

```
wrap = (wrap + 1) % 2;
```

This statement will change wrap's value from 0 to 1 or from 1 to 0.

We first determine the current cursor position by calling return_curs(), the mechanics of which were discussed above. If line wrapping is off, or if the cursor is not at the right-most column, we simply issue a move-right-one-column command. Otherwise—that is, if line wrapping is on and we are now at column 79—provided we are not also at the bottom row, we send the cursor one row down, at column 0:

```
if (row != 23) /* move down one row, at column 0 */
    sprintf(direction, "%d;%dH", ++row + 1, 1);
else strcpy(direction, "2;1H"); /* home cursor */
```

If the cursor is also at the last row, we home the cursor.

We have coded the [Page Up] key to move to the row 0 of whatever column the cursor is currently in and the [Page Down] key to move to row 24 of the current column. We clear the screen with the [Delete] key (and then repaint the directions at the top and bottom of the screen and replace the cursor). We erase from the cursor through the end of the current row with the [End] key. We could have coded the [Ctrl] [End] key combination to perform that latter function, just as some word processing programs do.

After the switch statement, we issue the appropriate command, having first copied the proper string into direction with either strcpy() or sprintf().

If the user presses [Alt] [H], we paint key directions at the top and bottom rows. These directions were also painted in the initial screen.

We have also created a somewhat inelegant user-specified interactive row and column position function, set_curs(), which the user accesses by pressing [Alt] [S]. We print a prompt in an out-of-the-way position at the bottom of the screen and use scanf() for row and column input. As you can see, interactive input with escape sequences is clumsy. Pressing [Alt] [G] will print the current cursor position at the lower left-hand corner of the screen. This is done in get_curs().

If a regular key is pressed, we skip all of the above. We check instead for the [BACKSPACE] key, specific control characters, the [Esc] key, or a printable character. For a backspace, we move the cursor left, print a space, and move left again. If a normal printable character's key is pressed, we just print it to the screen with putchar(). If [Esc] has been pressed, the program resets the color to gray on black and exits.

A.8.1   Key Remapping

For certain control characters, we engage in a little mnemonic *key remapping* in concolor.c. [Ctrl] [C] produces a ç (a French soft c). We facilitate interactive box drawing by setting [Ctrl] [V] to the vertical double-line character, [Ctrl] [Z] to the horizontal double-line character, [Ctrl] [T] with [L] or [R] for the top-left or right-corner double-line character, and [Ctrl] [B] with [L] or [R] for the bottom-left or right-corner double-line character.

You can accomplish this sort of keyboard remapping postprogram in DOS with the use of specific escape sequences during your program. The format for regular keys is

```
printf("\33[#;\"string\"p");
```

and that for extended keys is

```
printf("\33[0;#;\"string\"p");
```

where # is the scan code for the key to which assignment is being made. For example, to assign "Please make sure your printer is on" to the [F1] key:

```
printf("\33[0;59;\"Please make sure your printer is on\"p");
```

Remember that the changes created by escape sequences remain until undone. This is so even after termination of your program. Thus, in DOS, every time you press the [F1] key, "Please make sure your printer is on" will appear on the screen wherever the cursor is, until you either remap or reboot. Likewise, if you run a program that contains the following statement

```
printf("\33[38;\"AND\"p");
```

you will get "AND" on the screen in DOS every time you press the & key (the ASCII value of which is 38).

If the first character is not an extended key, you can use a string in place of the ASCII value:

```
printf("\33[\"&\";\"AND\"p");
```

Conversely, you can substitute ASCII values for the replacement string. The following statement will cause pressing ¦ to produce "OR":

```
printf("\33[\"¦\";79;82p");
```

You can use extended keys in the replacement string. Here, of course, you must use ASCII values. The following statement will cause pressing the [F10] key to generate an [F3] and an [Enter], causing the last DOS command to be repeated without having to press the [Enter] key as you would have to do with [F3]:

```
printf("\33[0;68;0;61;13p");
```

The ansi.sys driver is smart enough to know that it has completed processing the key to be replaced once it has encountered either an initial string or a number and a semicolon, or if the first number is a 0, then that 0, a semicolon, another number, and a semicolon. The rest of the escape sequence is then processed as the replacement string.

A.9   LOADING IN ansi.sys

If you use escape sequences, you must remember to make sure the config.sys file contains the line

```
device=ansi.sys
```

Adding ansi.sys uses up 4K of RAM, though the chances are a majority of users already have that line in their config.sys files. Also, the ansi.sys driver can be loaded into high memory rather than conventional memory, assuming the computer has that memory available.

If you plan to write a program with escape sequences for use by others, you would have to first check the config.sys file for the line's existence and add it if it is not there. The following program does that.

 **Listing A.3 ansi_sys.c**

```
/* ansi_sys.c */

/* checks config.sys for ansi.sys line & adds it if it's not there */

#include <stdio.h>
#include <string.h> /* strupr, strstr */
#include <ctype.h> /* toupper */

char *strUpr(char *string);

int main(void)
{
   char line[129]; /* large enough for max DOS command line */
   char answer;
   int found_it = 0; /* whether file has ansi.sys line */
   FILE *original = fopen("c:\\config.sys", "r+"); /* error-checking omitted */
   FILE *copy;

   while(fgets(line, 129, original))
   {
      /* check whether file line has "DEVICE" or "device" in it */
      if (!strstr(strUpr(line), "DEVICE"))
         continue;

      /* line must have "DEVICE" if we get past here */
      if (strstr(line, "ANSI.SYS")) /* strupr has already made line all caps */
      {
         found_it = 1;
         break;
      }
   }

   if (found_it)
      printf("ansi.sys driver already loaded");
   else
   {
      /* ask user before adding */
      printf("Add ansi.sys driver to config.sys? (Y/N): ");
      scanf("%c", &answer);
      if (answer == 'y' || answer == 'Y')
      {
         copy = fopen("c:\\config.noa", "w"); /* error-checking omitted */
         rewind(original);

         /* copy original to c:\config.noa */
         while(fgets(line, 129, original))
            fputs(line, copy);

         /* add ansi.sys line to config.sys only */
         fputs("DEVICE=ANSI.SYS", original);
      }
   }
}

char *strUpr(char *string)
```

```
{
    char *ptr = string;
    while(*ptr)
    {
        *ptr = toupper(*ptr);
        ptr++;
    }
    return string;
}
```

A.10   ON BEYOND ESCAPE SEQUENCES

There are several drawbacks to using escape sequences as the means of controlling console output. For example,

- You cannot move back and forth from one screen page in memory to another.
- The printing of a series of characters—to form, say, a box or to paint the entire screen with a single character repeatedly—is visibly slow.
- There is no easy way to read characters from the screen once the user has typed them in. You would have to keep track of where the cursor is and digest input when the user presses the [Enter] key, with the aid of scanf(), a messy process.
- Scrolling of a window narrower than the entire 80-column rows, or of rows other than those at the very top of the screen, is not possible.
- You cannot set the border color. The border is an inaccessible strip consisting of a single row and column around the screen. (See Appendix C.) With interrupts, you can set the border color. Otherwise it remains black, making it indistinguishable from the blank space at the outer screen edges.

All these tasks can be accomplished, or accomplished much more quickly, with interrupts. We cover interrupts in Appendix B, after first learning there how memory is treated.

A.11   APPLICATION: A MENU-DRIVEN PROGRAM

We now have everything we need to write a rudimentary menu-driven program.

 **Listing** A.4 con_menu.c

```
/* con_menu.c */

/* use escape sequences to paint a menu and sample data pages */
#include <stdio.h>
#include <conio.h> /* getch */
#include <string.h> /* strcpy, movedata */
#include <dos.h> /* segread */

#include "keys.h" /* Appendix H */
#include "concolor.h" /* Appendix H */
#include "box_chars.h" /* Appendix H */

#define CHOICES 6
#define HIGH "\33[1;37;47m" /* white on gray */
#define NORMAL "\33[0;31;47m" /* red on gray */
#define BORDER "\33[0;30;47m" /* black on gray */
#define BACKGRD "\33[0;30;44m" /* black on blue */
#define BYTES (80 * 25 * 2)
#define NONE 0
#define SINGLE 1
#define DOUBLE 2
```

```c
char buffer[BYTES];
unsigned video_seg = 0xB800 data_seg;

void box_border(int row, int col, int height, int width, char *color_str, int
   linetype);
void paint_menu(int choice) paint_page(int page) restore(void) save(void)

int main(void)
{
   int i;
   static int choice;
   unsigned char ch;
   char ltr_pick[CHOICES * 2] = "CcEePpDdLlXx"; /* don't need terminating NULL */
   struct SREGS segs;

   /* determine segment address of data segment for save & restore */
   segread(&segs);
   data_seg = segs.ds;

   /* clear screen */
   printf("\33[2J");

   /* turn line wrap on */
   printf("\33[7h");

   /* set color to black on blue */
   printf("%s", BACKGRD);

   /* fill whole screen with shade character */
   for(i = 0; i < 1999; i++)
      putchar('▓'); /* decimal 177 */

   /* turn line wrap off (last character is lowercase L) */
   printf("\33[07l");

   /* do final shade character at bottom right of screen */
   putchar('▓');

   /* home cursor and reset color to white on gray */
   printf("%s\33[H", HIGH);

   /* gray strip at top row */
   for (i = 0; i < 80; i++)
      putchar(' ');

   /* gray strip at bottom row */
   printf("\33[25;1H");

   for (i = 0; i < 80; i++)
      putchar(' ');
   paint_menu(choice);
   while (1)
   {
      if ((ch = getch()) == 0 || ch == TAB) /* extended chars? */
      {
         if (ch == TAB || (ch = getch()) ==  UP || ch == DN ||
            ch == SH_T)
         {
```

```
          switch(ch)
          {
              case UP: case SH_T: choice =
                 (choice - 1 + CHOICES) % CHOICES;
              break;

              /* "+ choice" above avoids negative #, without altering result */
              case DN: case TAB:
                 choice = (choice + 1) % CHOICES;
              break;
          }
          paint_menu(choice);
       }
    } /* end if ch is 0 */

    /* <===end program with ESC key or press of 'x'===> */
    else if (ch == ESC || (ch == '\r' && choice == CHOICES - 1)
       || ch == '0' + CHOICES || ch == 'x' || ch == 'X')
    {
       /* reset to DOS default: light gray on black */
       printf("\33[m");
       break;
    }

    /* paint page based on press of enter key, letter or # */
    else if (ch == '\r')
       paint_page(choice);
    else if (ch >= '1' && ch <= '0' + CHOICES - 1)
       paint_page(ch - '0' - 1);

    /* highlighted ltr pressed? */
    else for (i = 0; i < (CHOICES - 1) * 2; i++)
       if (ch == ltr_pick[i])
    {
       paint_page(i / 2);
       break;
    }
  } /* end while */
}


/* +----------------------------------------------------------------+
   + BOX_BORDER
   + Draw outside boundary of rectangle with single/double/no lines
   + Arguments:
   + - trow/lcol:    left corner of box
   + - height/width: height and width of box
   + - color_str:    string with escape sequence for color
   + - linetype:     lines around box (NONE, SINGLE, DOUBLE)
   +----------------------------------------------------------------+*/
void box_border(int trow, int lcol, int height, int width, char *color_str, int
   linetype)
{
   int i;
   unsigned char vert, horiz, topl, topr, botl, botr; /* box chars */

   /* set color */
   printf("%s", color_str);
   if (linetype == NONE)
      vert = horiz = topl = topr = botl = botr = ' ';
```

```
        else if (linetype == SINGLE)
        {
            topl = TL1; /* all defined in box_chars.h */
            topr = TR1;
            botl = BL1;
            botr = BR1;
            horiz = H1;
            vert = V1;
        }

        else /* double-lined box */
        {
            topl = TL2;
            topr = TR2;
            botl = BL2;
            botr = BR2;
            horiz = H2;
            vert = V2;
        }

        /* do 4 corners */
        printf("\33[%d;%dH%c\33[%d;%dH%c\33[%d;%dH%c\33[%d;%dH%c",
            trow, lcol, topl, /* top left */
            trow, lcol + width - 1, topr, /* top right */
            trow + height - 1, lcol, botl, /* bottom left */
            trow + height - 1, lcol + width - 1, botr); /* bottom right */

        /* horizontal lines */
        for (i = 0; i < width - 2; i++)
        {
            printf("\33[%d;%dH%c", trow, lcol + i + 1, horiz);
            printf("\33[%d;%dH%c", trow + height - 1, lcol + i + 1, horiz);
        }

        /* vertical lines */
        for (i = 0; i < height - 2; i++)
        {
            printf("\33[%d;%dH%c", trow + i + 1, lcol, vert);
            printf("\33[%d;%dH%c", trow + i + 1, lcol + width - 1, vert);
        }
}

/* +-------------------------------------------------------------------+
   +  PAINT_MENU
   +  Paint main menu numbers and headings.
   +  All numbers and current choice's letters are highlighted.
   +-------------------------------------------------------------------+*/
void paint_menu(int choice)
{
    int i;
    int trow = 7, lcol = 10, rcol = 17;

    /* each menu entry has a left, middle & right part */
    char *menu[CHOICES][3] = {
        {"", "C", "reate report  "},
        {"", "E", "dit report    "},
        {"", "P", "rint report   "},
        {"", "D", "elete report  "},
        {"See Report ", "L", "ist"},
```

```
        {"E", "x", "it to DOS    "}
    };
    char outside_color[15], inside_color[15];

    printf("%s", HIGH);
    for (i = 0; i < CHOICES; i++)
    {
        /* highlight all numbers */
        printf("%s\33[%d;%dH %d ", HIGH, trow + 3 * i, lcol, i + 1);

        /* designate colors */
        if (i == choice) /* highlight current choice (except middle letter) */
        {
            strcpy(outside_color, HIGH);
            strcpy(inside_color, NORMAL);
        }
        else /* nonchoice entry gets highlighted middle letter only */
        {
            strcpy(outside_color, NORMAL);
            strcpy(inside_color, HIGH);
        }

        /* paint number and heading */
        printf("\33[%d;%dH   %s%s%s%s%s%s    ", trow + 3 * i, rcol,
            outside_color, menu[i][0], inside_color, menu[i][1],
            outside_color, menu[i][2]);
    }
}

/* +-------------------------------------------------------------------+
   +  PAINT_PAGE
   +  Paint data page for each of the choices once selected from main menu
   +-------------------------------------------------------------------+*/
void paint_page(int page)
{
    char *titles[5] =
    {"   CREATE REPORT    ", "   EDIT REPORT    ", "   PRINT REPORT    ",
        "  DELETE REPORT    ", "   SEE REPORT LIST    "};
    int i, len = strlen(titles[page]) / 2;

    /* save menu page */
    save();

    /* clear screen in blue */
    printf("%s\33[2J", BACKGRD);

    /* draw a blank box around screen */
    box_border(1, 1, 25, 80, BORDER, 0);

    /* within that box draw a double-lined box */
    box_border(2, 2, 23, 78, BORDER, 2);
    printf("\33[%d;%dHfor next page", 1, 8);

    /* put directions at screen bottom */
    printf("\33[%d;%dH%s", 25, 2, NORMAL);
    printf("F1        ESC        ALT-S            ALT-P        ALT-V");
    printf("\33[%d;%dHPGDN", 1, 3);
    printf("%s\33[%d;%dHPage 1", HIGH, 1, 73);
    printf("%s", BORDER);
    printf("\33[%d;%dH Help   ", 25, 4);
```

```
      printf("\33[%d;%dH Exit    ", 25, 15);
      printf("\33[%d;%dH Save file    ", 25, 28);
      printf("\33[%d;%dH Print report    ", 25, 46);
      printf("\33[%d;%dH View report", 25, 67);

      /* do title box: title, then top & bottom half box, then drop shadow */

      /* position cursor & draw title */
      printf("\33[%d;%dH%s", 5, 41 - len, titles[page]);

      /* do top half of box with bottom 1/2 char (top of char is background) */
      printf("\33[0;%d;%dm\33[%d;%dH", GRAY_F, BLUE_B, 4, 41 - len);
      for (i = 0; i < len * 2; i++)
         putchar('▄');
      /* do bottom half of box & drop shadow with top 1/2 char (bottom is black) */
      printf("\33[0;%d;%dm\33[%d;%dH", GRAY_F,
         BLACK_B, 6, 41 - len);
      for (i = 0; i < len * 2; i++)
         putchar('■');

      /* a little touchup */

      printf("\33[0;%d;%dm\33[%d;%dH%c", GRAY_F, BLUE_B, 6, 41 - len,'■');
      printf("\33[0;%d;%dm", BLACK_F, BLACK_B);
      printf("\33[%d;%dH \33[%d;%dH ", 5, 41 + len, 6, 41 + len);

      /* these pages are just dummies; nothing is done here */
      if(!getch())
         getch();

      /* restore menu page */
      restore();
}
/* +------------------------------------------------------------------+
   +   RESTORE
   +   Write from RAM buffer back to video memory
   +------------------------------------------------------------------+*/
void restore(void)
{
   movedata(data_seg, (unsigned)buffer, video_seg, 0, BYTES);
}
/* +------------------------------------------------------------------+
   +   SAVE
   +   Write video memory to buffer in RAM for later use of restore()
   +------------------------------------------------------------------+ */
void save(void)
{
   movedata(video_seg, 0, data_seg, (unsigned)buffer, BYTES);
}
```

A.11.1   Painting the Screen

We first paint the entire screen with one of the shaded full-box characters, '▓', ASCII decimal 177, in black on blue. To do this, we first make sure line wrapping is on. This allows us to print 1999 characters with putchar(), without having to worry about repositioning the cursor. If line wrapping were off, we would have to do the following instead:

```
for (row = 1; row < 26; row++)
   for (col = 1; col < 81; col++)
      printf("\33[%d;%dH▓", row, col);
```

Before printing the 2000th character, we must first turn line wrapping off. Otherwise, printing a character at the bottom right of the screen would cause the screen to scroll up one line, and we would lose our top row and be left with a blank bottom row.

Next, we home the cursor, set the color to white on gray, and paint two 80-column strips at the top and bottom of the screen. We do this by printing the space character 80 times.

A.11.2   Menu Selection

To paint the menu itself, we call paint_menu(), passing it the current proposed menu selection (the one we want highlighted and the one the user can select by pressing [Enter]). The paint_menu() function declares a two-dimensional array of pointers to char. We have six arrays, each containing an array of three pointers. Each of the six master arrays matches one of the six menu headings. Splitting each menu heading into three components allows us to highlight part of each heading and leave the balance unhighlighted. The function effectuates the following color scheme: paint a number and a heading for menu selection. The numbers are all highlighted (white on gray). The proposed menu selection is all highlighted, except for a single letter. The rest of the menu selections are just the opposite—only the single letter is highlighted.

In this way, the user is signaled that a choice may be made in one of three ways: by typing 1 to 6, by typing any of the highlighted letters, or by pressing [Enter] when the desired menu selection is highlighted (see Figure A.1).

An infinite loop in main() handles moving the proposed menu selection if the user presses an up- or down-arrow key or [Tab] or [Shift] [Tab]. When [↑] or [Shift] [Tab] is pressed, we decrement choice, the variable representing the number of the currently proposed menu selection; when [↓] or [Tab] is pressed, we increment choice. Then we call paint_menu() with the altered choice value.

We use the modulus operator to cycle choice from a value of 0 to 5 and back again to 0. For example, where choice is 2, setting choice to

```
(choice - 1 + CHOICES) % CHOICES
```

will produce 1—that is, (2 – 1 + 6) % 6—and setting it to

```
(choice + 1) % CHOICES
```

will produce 3—that is, (2 + 1) % 6. We need to include

```
+ CHOICES
```

Figure A.1   *Sample Menu Screen*

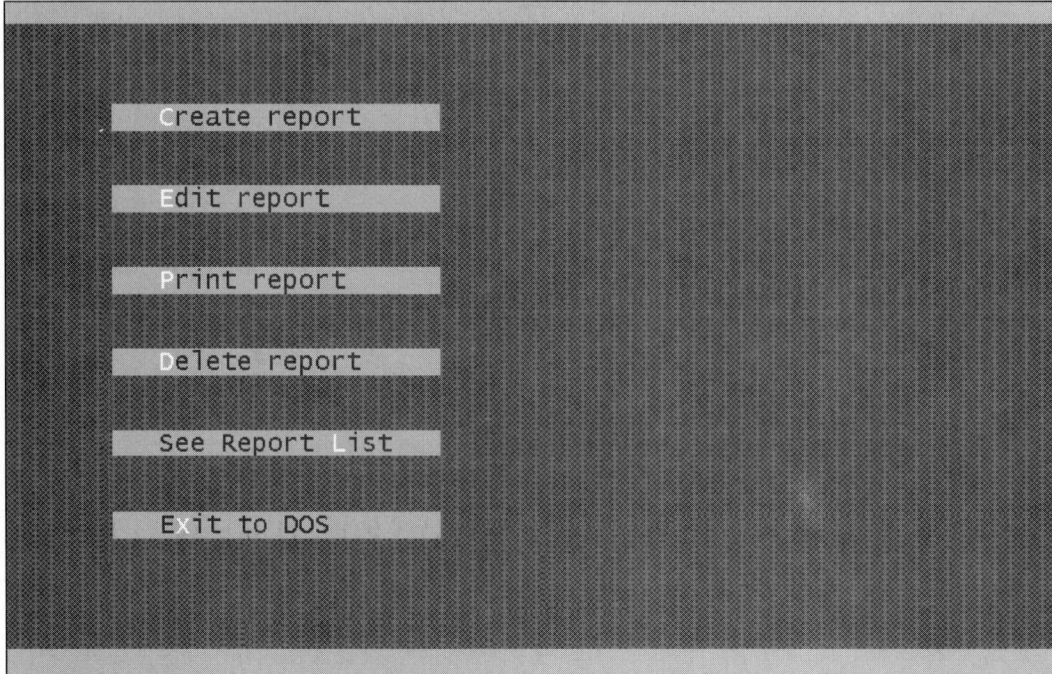

in the first statement's first expression to prevent a 0 choice from becoming negative if a ⬆️ or Shift Tab is pressed:

```
(choice - 1) % CHOICES /* (0 -1) % 6 = -1 */
(choice - 1 + CHOICES) % CHOICES /* (0 - 1 + 6) % 6 = 5 */
```

If we determine the key pressed is not one of those we've coded to alter choice and repaint the menu, we check to see whether one of the highlighted numbers or letters has been pressed. If the user has pressed Esc or has pressed a 6 or an X or x, we reset the colors and attributes to their defaults and break the while loop, terminating the program:

```
else if (ch == ESC || (ch == '\r' && choice == CHOICES - 1) || ch == '0' + CHOICES
    || ch == 'x' || ch == 'X')
{
    printf("\33[m");
    break;
}
```

If Enter is pressed, we call paint_page(), the data page printing function, with the current value of choice as an argument:

```
else if (ch == '\r')
    paint_page(choice);
```

Remember that we test the pressing of the Enter key against \r, not \n.

If a number between 1 and 6 is pressed

```
else if (ch >= '1' && ch <= '0' + CHOICES - 1)
```

we call

```
paint_page(ch - '0' - 1);
```

For instance, if 2 is pressed, ch has a value of 2 and we would call

```
paint_page(1); /* '2' - '0' - 1 = 1; */
```

To see whether a letter selection has been made, we loop through ltr_pick, an array that contains all the relevant letters, in both uppercase and lowercase. If we find a match, we call paint_page(), with the loop counter divided by 2 as the argument. For instance, pressing E or e would leave the loop counter at 2 or 3 and give us, by virtue of integer division, an argument of 1.

A.11.3   Painting the Data Page

The paint_page() function paints the data page corresponding to the menu choice that has been selected. Before we paint the data page, we call save() to preserve the current menu page in a buffer with memmove(). We use a technique explained in Appendix D.

After clearing the screen, we proceed to paint the data page. First, we draw a blank border around the screen's edge and within that border, a double-lined box. Both are done by calling box_border().

We pass box_border() the top-left corner's row and column, as well as the box's height and width, a color string, and an integer representing a line type: 0 or NONE for no lines, 1 or SINGLE for single-lined, 2 or DOUBLE for double-lined. The box_border() function positions the cursor at each of the box's four corners and places the appropriate character there. Then we do a series of for loops to draw the two horizontal and vertical lines. If NONE is passed as linetype, all characters drawn are spaces.

Next, we position the cursor at various spots in the top and bottom rows and write user directions in red on gray (names of keys to press), black on gray (effect of corresponding key), and white on gray (page number, hard-wired to 1 here). We then draw the data page title in black on gray. For visual impact, we want to paint the title in a box that sets it off from the page background and by a *drop shadow* (a row and column of black at the bottom and right of a rectangle to give the illusion of a shadow).

If we paint a solid row of spaces in gray above and below the title line, and a black row beneath that, we will have taken up four lines in all—too much space to waste and too clunky looking. Instead we will achieve the effect of drawing a half-row space above and below the title and a half-row shadow at the bottom. We do this by using the half-box characters (see Appendix F)—the lower-half character, ▄ (ASCII decimal 220), and the upper-half character, ▀, (ASCII decimal 223), respectively.

Figure A.2 *Sample Date Page*

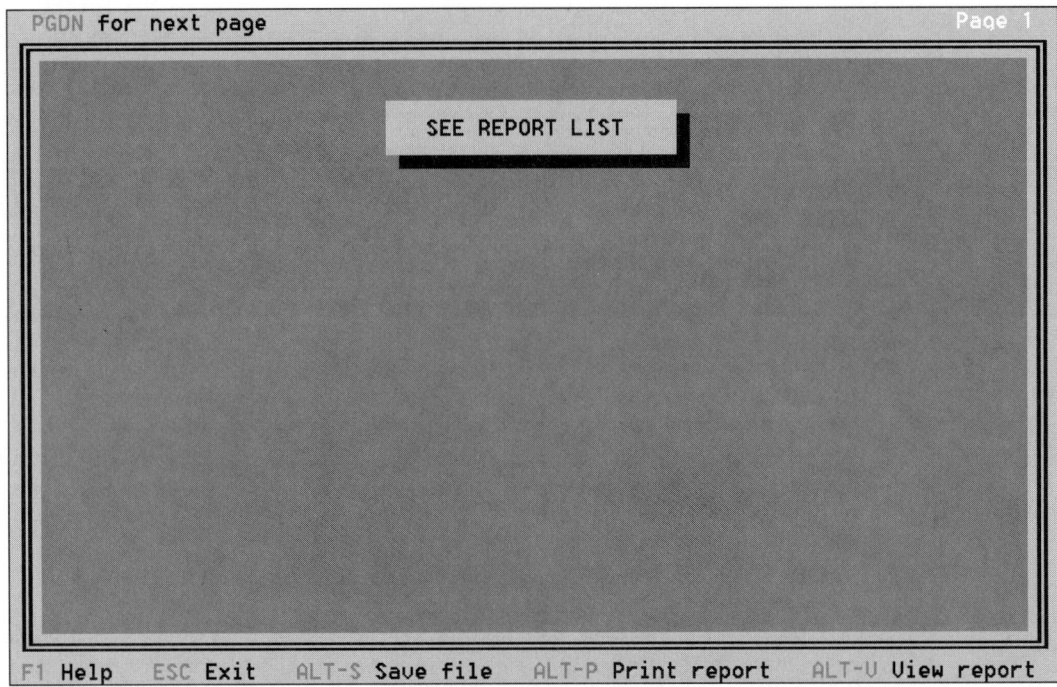

We put the lower-half character above the title, painting it in gray on blue. The blank top-half background portion of the character blends into the background. We put the upper-half character below the title, painting it in gray on black. The gray character portion becomes part of the title block and the black background portion forms a drop shadow. We then draw a black vertical line to the right of the title box (see Figure A.2).

At this point, we would call a function to carry out whatever this page is supposed to do. We've left that for you. Here, after a key press, we restore the menu screen previously saved by save(). That gets us back to the main menu loop.

Memory and
Interrupts on the PC

Disregarding expanded memory procedures and the larger memory addressing capabilities of the 8086 family from the 286 upward, the PC accesses memory by a 20-bit address mechanism. Under this scheme, the highest possible memory address is the value resulting from each of the 20 bits being turned on. That would be 1,048,576, or stated another way, 1024 kilobytes or 1 megabyte.

However, again disregarding the 32-bit register capability of the 386 upward, the 8086 processors have only 16-bit internal registers for storing these 20-bit memory addresses. Since a single 16-bit register cannot hold a 20-bit address, a different lowest-common-denominator scheme for accessing RAM locations had to be found.

If we start from the beginning of random access memory and work our way up to 1 megabyte, stopping every 16 bytes, we will have stopped 65,535 times. If we want to store any of these stopping point numbers (that is, numbers between 0 and 65,535), we find that we can just fit the very largest number, 65,535, in our 16-bit register. (Stated mathematically, the relationship between the 20-bit address and the stopping points at 16-bit intervals: $2^{20} / 2^4 = 2^{16}$.)

Having stored the stopping point number in one register, we can store in another register the distance in bytes from that stopping point to a particular memory address. This would allow us to specify an address anywhere from 0 to 65,535 bytes from the stopping point. In hex notation, this maximum distance would be 0xFFFF bytes, with each of the four hex digits corresponding to four binary digits. The true address of any memory location in this bifurcated dual register system would be the stopping number (stored in one register) times 16, plus the distance in bytes from the stopping point to the memory location (stored in another register).

We refer to the maximum possible 64K range from a stopping point as a *segment*. The number of the stopping point is called its *segment address*. For example, the stopping point 32 bytes from the beginning of memory would have a segment address of 2.

The distance from the start of the segment to a particular memory address is referred to as the *offset*. We commonly combine the segment address and offset in writing them as follows: SSSS:HHHHh or SSSS:HHHH, with the S's representing hexadecimal segment address digits, the H's representing hexadecimal offset digits, and the final h denoting hexadecimal notation. This format, without the trailing h, is the format that prints out for a `%Fp` specifier in a `printf()` statement.

This somewhat convoluted PC memory addressing scheme is referred to as a *segmented memory model*, for obvious reasons. Nearly all other computers use a *flat memory model* (that is, just a specific number of bytes from the beginning of memory for a certain address). Most other computers load local variables onto a stack frame, as the PC does; virtually all computers have registers, as the PC does. However, the particular stack mechanism, the number and size and function of registers we deal with in this appendix, as well as the discussion of memory models and many other concepts (particularly `near` and `far` pointers, which are not part of Standard C at all) relate solely to the PC.

For example, as you will see, you have to worry about the size of the stack in the DOS environment. By contrast, most UNIX implementations use some form of virtual memory for the stack. If a process runs out of primary memory, secondary storage is used as a temporary extension of primary memory.

B.1   SEGMENTS: NONUNIQUENESS AND OVERLAP

The address notation 0005:0003h would represent a true address 93 bytes from the start of memory (5 * 16 + 3). But so would 0000:005Dh. Because of the scheme of designating 64K segments the starts of which are separated by only 16 bytes (referred to as a *paragraph*), we find that a single true memory address can be described by a number of segment-offset combinations. On the other hand, given a designated segment address, a memory location can be described only by a unique offset.

How can we apply these principles to the data in a C program? Let's assume that all the data in our program (that is, the variables at various memory locations and the values they contain) must fit into a single 64K segment. (This is the case in C's default memory configuration, the *small memory model*.) We will call this segment the *data segment*. Assuming our compiler and the operating system assign and keep track of the segment for us (and they do), we can manipulate all our data by reference to the offset alone.

B.1.1   Three Methods for Placing Values in RAM

There are several ways to manipulate data. Generally, we simply assign values to variables' names (the names merely representing memory locations to the computer):

```
char ch;
ch = 'A';
```

We can also point pointers to those variables and assign values by dereferencing:

```
char ch;
char *ptr = &ch;
*ptr = 'A';
```

Though much less commonly done, we can even assign the offset of a variable as a numerical value—directly to a pointer—and then assign a value to the variable pointed to by dereferencing. In fact, though even less commonly done, we can assign a numerical value directly to a location in memory. For instance, the following uses the first of these two assignment methods to print an A to the screen:

```
char ch;
unsigned offset;
offset = (unsigned)&ch;
*(char *)offset = 'A'; /* store 'A' at that offset address */
putchar(ch);
```

And the following will print the A in white on a red background at the top-left corner of the screen of a PC (assuming you have a color monitor, of course):

```
*((int far *)0xB8000000) = 'A' ¦ (0117 << 8);
```

(We will discuss far pointers later in this appendix—here, we had to specify both the segment and offset addresses, since video memory lies outside the data segment, and indeed outside the 640K user RAM area; see Appendix D.)

If we do use a pointer, it normally need only be a 16-bit object. It is C's job to keep track of the segment address for most purposes. We can determine what the segment address is if we wish, but except in limited though not altogether rare instances (see, for example, save() and restore() in Appendix D), we need not trouble ourselves with knowing what it is.

Assuming that (1) the data segment address is established at the outset of running the program, (2) the address remains the same throughout the life of the program, and (3) the address is preserved in a readily accessible spot for the program to use (and all these are true for the default memory model), the manipulation of values in the course of running the program is speeded up by the fact that the computer need only concern itself with loading the variables' offsets in order to access their respective memory locations.

B.2   DATA SEGMENT

On the PC, the compiler allows you to select from among several different configurations for placement of data and code into primary memory. These configurations, referred to as *memory models*, are discussed in detail later in the appendix.

In the small memory model, C actually stores data in three separate locations within the data segment. One area is used to for static and global variables (*static memory*); one is used for automatic variables declared within a function (the *stack*); and one is used for memory requested at run time (the *heap*, also called the *near heap*) through calls to `malloc()` and similar functions and by such procedures as opening files, where heap memory is automatically appropriated.

The size of static memory is known at the outset of the program. Indeed, it is known at compile time. C assigns a fixed portion of the data segment to this data. The balance is allocated to the stack and the heap. Figure B.1 shows what the resulting data segment look like.

We will see below how memory is divided between the stack and the heap.

Figure B.1   *Data Segment*

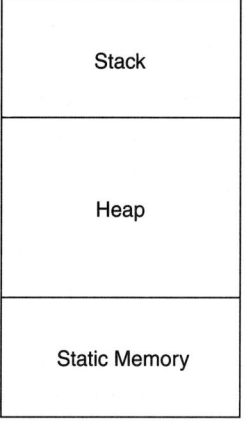

B.3   CODE SEGMENT

In the small memory model, the entire set of program instructions (that is, the running version of the executable file) is contained within a single segment, called the *code segment*. The data segment begins at the start of the paragraph immediately after the last code instruction. This is so even if the code does not fill an entire segment (see Figure B.2). Technically, the code segment extends into the data segment. But there is no significance per se to this overlap. The segment notion is not a memory reservation mechanism, but rather a memory access scheme. Unless the code takes up the entire segment, we use only the bottom portion of the code segment for code.

Figure B.2   *Code and Data Segments*

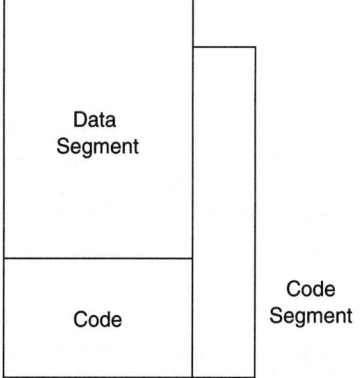

B.4   STACK SEGMENT

Automatic variables are created at run time and last only during the time the function in which they are declared is active. As these automatic variables are declared upon the call of a function, they are "placed on the stack." At the termination of a function, its variables are "taken off the stack" in a last-in, first-out order, just as one would remove dishes or books from a stack (hence its name).

We have just spoken of placing variables onto, or removing variables from, the stack. This commonly used terminology, however, does not reflect the true mechanism of the processing of local variables. When variables are placed on the stack, we reserve specific locations in memory in the stack segment. When values are assigned to those respective variables, the values get stored at those reserved locations. We start the reservation process from the point where the last such variable reservation on the stack left off.

When the function is terminated and the variables "taken off the stack," neither the reserved memory locations nor even the values at those locations disappear or change in any way. All that happens is that we move our place markers back. Then, the next time variables are "placed on the stack," they start at that new place marker, thereby overstoring data in the memory locations that previously had been reserved for other variables with values assigned to the current function's variables.

Locations in the stack can be accessed by offset from the start of the data segment. In addition, to assist in the orderly addition and removal of variables to and from the stack, another method of accessing stack locations is maintained. Offsets from the start of the paragraph after the end of static memory are measured, this beginning being known as the *stack segment*. We will discuss the stack segment in greater detail below.

B.5   REGISTERS AND SEGMENTS

The segment addresses—for the code segment, the data segment, and the stack segment—and various offset place markers are maintained in some of the computer's registers designated for those purposes. All in all, the 8086 family has (at least viewing the matter from its least common denominator) fourteen 16-bit registers—four *segment registers* and five *offset registers*, as well as four general-purpose (also called *scratch-pad*) registers and one flags register. We will discuss the general-purpose registers later in this appendix, when we treat interrupts (see Figure B.3).

B.5.1   Segment Registers

The segment registers are cs, ds, ss, and es. The cs register holds the code segment address, where the program being executed is stored. The ds register holds the data segment address. The ss register holds the stack segment address. The es register is used in combination with the ds register in string comparing, copying, and concatenation. It is also to hold the segment address of an item of data outside the program's data segment, as discussed in Section B.8.

You can determine a segment register address through the segread() function. That function places the register addresses in members of a variable of structure type SREGS.

The SREGS structure is found in dos.h:

```
struct SREGS { unsigned int es, cs, ss, ds; };
```

You pass segread() the address of the SREGS variable you declare. Following the call, the various segment addresses are contained in that variable's members:

```
struct SREGS segs;
segread(&segs);
printf("cs: %#X   ds: %#X\n", segs.cs, segs.ds);
printf("ss: %#X   es: %#X\n", segs.ss, segs.es);
```

B.5.2   Pointer and Index Registers

Of the five offset registers, three are alternatively referred to as *pointer registers* and two as *index registers*. These registers keep track of offsets within the memory segments.

The index registers, si (for *Source Index*) and di (for *Destination Index*) can be used for general-purpose addressing. Typically, they are used by C in conjunction with the ds and es segment registers. In any string copy, concatenation, or comparison, ds:si point to the source string and es:di point to the destination string.

Figure B.3 *IBM 8086 Registers*

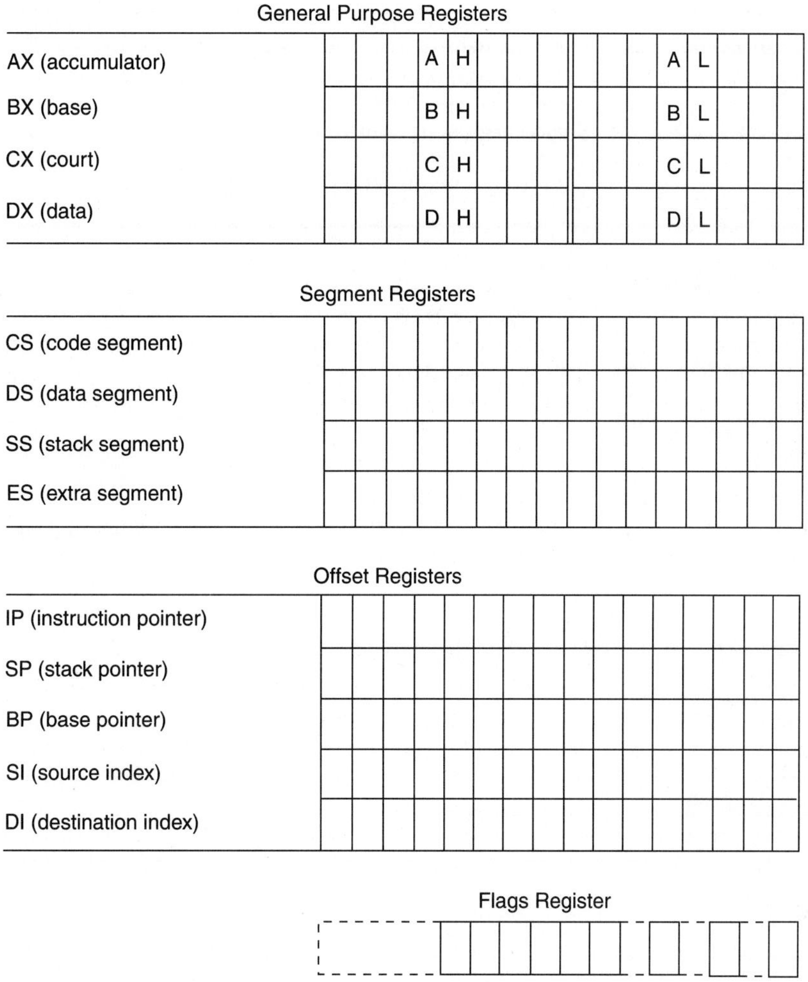

General Purpose Registers

AX (accumulator)			A	H						A	L		
BX (base)			B	H						B	L		
CX (court)			C	H						C	L		
DX (data)			D	H						D	L		

Segment Registers

| CS (code segment) |
| DS (data segment) |
| SS (stack segment) |
| ES (extra segment) |

Offset Registers

| IP (instruction pointer) |
| SP (stack pointer) |
| BP (base pointer) |
| SI (source index) |
| DI (destination index) |

Flags Register

The `ip` register (for *Instruction Pointer*) holds the offset address from the segment address in `cs` of the next code instruction to be executed. The value of `ip` is incremented by the CPU after each program statement finishes executing.

Both the `sp` register (for *Stack Pointer*) and `bp` register (for *Base Pointer*) are used by C in conjunction with the stack segment. The `sp` register holds the offset of the last variable placed on the stack—referred to as the "top" of the stack. Despite this terminology, used by virtue of the dish or book stack analogy, on the PC and most other computers, variables added to the top of the stack are added at successively lower memory addresses. The `sp` register is updated with each addition or removal of a variable to or from the stack.

B.5.3   Flags Register

The *flags register* is a collection of 6 individual status and 3 control bits. Some of the rest of the bits are used to support protected-mode operation (where a process is confined to a specific area in memory). Table B.1 specifies the status and control bits.

The carry flag is used by a number of interrupts (see later in this appendix) to indicate whether an error has occurred. See Section K.3 for an example.

B.5.4   Register Pseudovariables

Borland C maintains *register pseudovariables*. These are continually updated throughout the program to contain what the registers of the same name hold at any point in the program. Borland C has register pseudovariables for each of the registers other than the `ip` register. Each is in uppercase and preceded by an underscore (see Figure B.4). So as

Table B.1   *Flags Register*

Flag Name	Control Flag – Indicates:	Status Flag – Controls:
Carry flag	Arithmetic carry	
Overflow flag	Signed arithmetic overflow	
Zero flag	Zero result or equal comparison	
Sign flag	Negative result or unequal comparison	
Parity flag	Even number of bits	
Auxiliary carry flag	Adjustment required in binary coded arithmetic operation	
Direction flag		Increment direction in string operations
Interrupt flag		Whether interrupts are enabled
Trap flag		Single-step operation used by Debug

Figure B.4   *Borland C Register Pseudovariables*

General Purpose		
_AH	_AL	_AX
_BH	_BL	_BX
_CH	_CL	_CX
_DH	_DL	_DX

Segment
_CS
_DS
_ES
_SS

Offset and Flag	
_BP	_SP
_DI	_SI
_FLAGS	

an alternative to declaring a SREGS variable and calling segread(), we can simply do the following to determine the segment addresses:

```
printf("code segment: %#x\n", _CS);
printf("data segment: %#x\n", _DS);
printf("stack segment: %#x\n", _SS);
printf("extra segment: %#x\n", _ES);
```

Using segread() would be more portable, however.

B.5.5 Stack Mechanism—A Closer Look

Both the sp and bp registers initially start at the bottom of the stack—that is, at the memory location in the area allocated for the stack furthest removed from the start of the stack segment address. The stack grows downward toward the beginning of the stack segment (see Figure B.5).

The following occurs when a function is called. First, the function's arguments are placed on the stack—that is, memory is reserved and values assigned commencing at the former top of the stack, as pointed to by the sp register. With most compilers, these are placed in reverse order, from right to left. (For example, in

```
add(one, two, three);
```

first three is placed on the stack, then two, then one.)

However, Standard C does not require compilers to place parameters on the stack in any particular order, so depending on a specific order would not be portable. Likewise, a compiler might place a parameter in a register to be able to access and process it faster. Nothing in Standard C prohibits this. In the examples below, we assume that parameters are placed on the stack from right to left and that none are sent to a register.

Next goes the address (in the small memory model on a PC, the 2-byte offset value) of the code the call is to return to. The bp register is assigned the address of the next 2 bytes. Into these bytes goes the address that—until this new bp register assignment—the bp register held as a value prior to the call of the currently active function.

Finally, the variables declared within the function are placed on the stack, in the order in which they are declared.

Figure B.5 *Two Snapshots of the Data Segment*

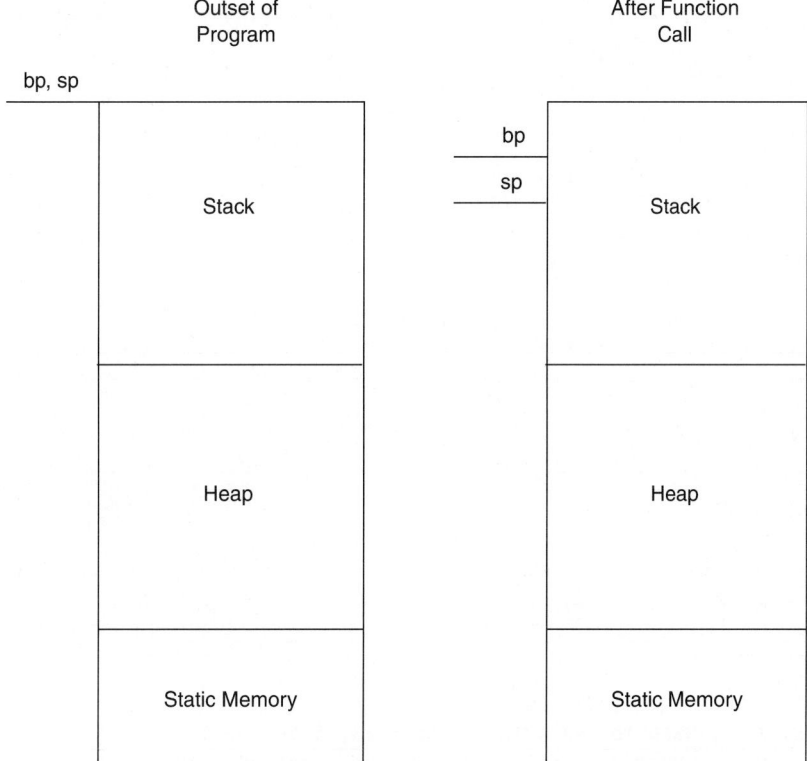

B.5.6   A Stack Example

The following listing, `stk_mech.c`, illustrates the stack mechanism:

 **Listing** **B.1 stk_mech.c**

```c
/* stk_mech.c */

/* see stack variable creation mechanism */

#include <stdio.h>

void first(int arg_1a, int arg_1b, int arg_1c);
void second(int arg_2a, int arg_2b, int arg_2c);

int main(void)
{
    printf("main: _BP, _SP: %#x, %#x\n", _BP, _SP);

    /* first calls second() */
    first(1, 2, 3);
}

void first(int arg_1a, int arg_1b, int arg_1c)
{
    int var_1a = 4, var_1b = 5, var_1c = 6;

    /* & operator stops variables from going to register instead of stack */
    printf("first:  &arg_1c, &arg_1b, &arg_1a, &var_1a, &var_2a, &var_3a:"
       "\n\t%#7x %#8x %#8x    %#8x %#8x %#8x\n", &arg_1c, &arg_1b, &arg_1a, &var_1a,
       &var_1b, &var_1c);
    printf("_BP, _SP: %#x, %#x\n", _BP, _SP);
    printf("values at _BP, _BP + 2: %#x %#x\n", *(unsigned *)_BP, *((unsigned *)_BP
       + 1));
#if defined __MEDIUM__
    printf("_CS, value at _BP + 4: %#x %#x\n", _CS, *((unsigned *)_BP + 2));
#endif
    second(21, 22, 23);
}

void second(int arg_2a, int arg_2b, int arg_2c)
{
    int var_2a = 24, var_2b = 25, var_2c = 26;

    /* & operator stops variables from going to register instead of stack */
    printf("second: &arg_2c, &arg_2b, &arg_2a, &var_2a, &var_2b, &var_2c:"
       "\n\t%#7x %#8x %#8x    %#8x %#8x %#8x\n", &arg_2c, &arg_2b, &arg_2a, &var_2a,
       &var_2b, &var_2c);
    printf("_BP, _SP: %#x, %#x\n", _BP, _SP);
    printf("values at _BP, _BP + 2: %#x %#x\n", *(unsigned *)_BP, *((unsigned *)_BP
       + 1));
#if defined __MEDIUM__
    printf("_CS, value at _BP + 4: %#x %#x\n", _CS, *((unsigned *)_BP + 2));
#endif
}
```

Here's the output:

```
main: _BP, _SP: 0xfff6, 0xfff6
first: &arg_1c, &arg_1b, &arg_1a,    &var_1a, &var_1b, &var_1c:
        0xfff4   0xfff2   0xfff0    0xffea   0xffe8   0xffe6
_BP, _SP: 0xffec, 0xffe6
```

Table B.2 *A Stack Example*

Address	Variable	Value	Represents
0xfff6			*starting BP & SP*
0xfff4	arg_1c	3	first argument evaluated
0xfff2	arg_1b	2	second argument evaluated
0xfff0	arg_1a	1	third argument evaluated
0xffee		0x2e0	first()
0xffec		**0xfff6**	*BP after first call:* points to original BP
0xffea	var_1a	4	first local variable declared
0xffe8	var_1b	5	second variable declared
0xffe6	var_1c	6	*SP after first call:* last local variable
0xffe4	arg_2c	23	first argument evaluated
0xffe2	arg_2b	22	second argument evaluated
0xffe0	arg_2a	21	third argument evaluated
0xffde		0x347	second()
0xffdc		**0xffec**	*BP after second call:* points to BP after first call
0xffda	var_2a	24	first local variable declared
0xffd8	var_2b	25	second variable declared
0xffd6	var_2c	26	*SP after second call:* last local variable

```
values at _BP, _BP + 2: 0xfff6 0x2e0
second: &arg_2c, &arg_2b, &arg_2a,    &var_2a, &var_2b, &var_2c:
        0xffe4   0xffe2   0xffe0      0xffda   0xffd8   0xffd6
_BP, _SP: 0xffdc, 0xffd6
values at _BP, _BP + 2: 0xffec 0x347
```

Graphically, we could show the relevant portion of the stack as in Table B.2.

Note the method by which we learn the value at the location pointed to by the bp register:

```
*(unsigned *)_BP
```

There is no need to declare a separate pointer variable, assign it _BP's value, and dereference. Likewise,

```
*((unsigned *)_BP + 1)
```

gives us the value stored in the memory location 2 bytes beyond where the bp register points.

Note that the value found at offset 0xffdc (where the bp register points after the second call) is 0xffec, the value stored in the bp register after the *first* call. There is, in effect, a linked list of base pointer values that can be used to move back to the calling functions in order.

B.6   MEMORY MODELS

In many cases, the program's code or its variables will not fit within a single 64K segment, the constraint imposed on us by the default small memory model. In that case, you must use a different memory model.

The compiler allows you to preselect a memory model—tiny, small, medium, compact, large, or huge. Figures B.6 to B.12 depict the overall space these memory models operate in as well as a breakdown of that memory area.

Figure B.6   *Program Memory in RAM*

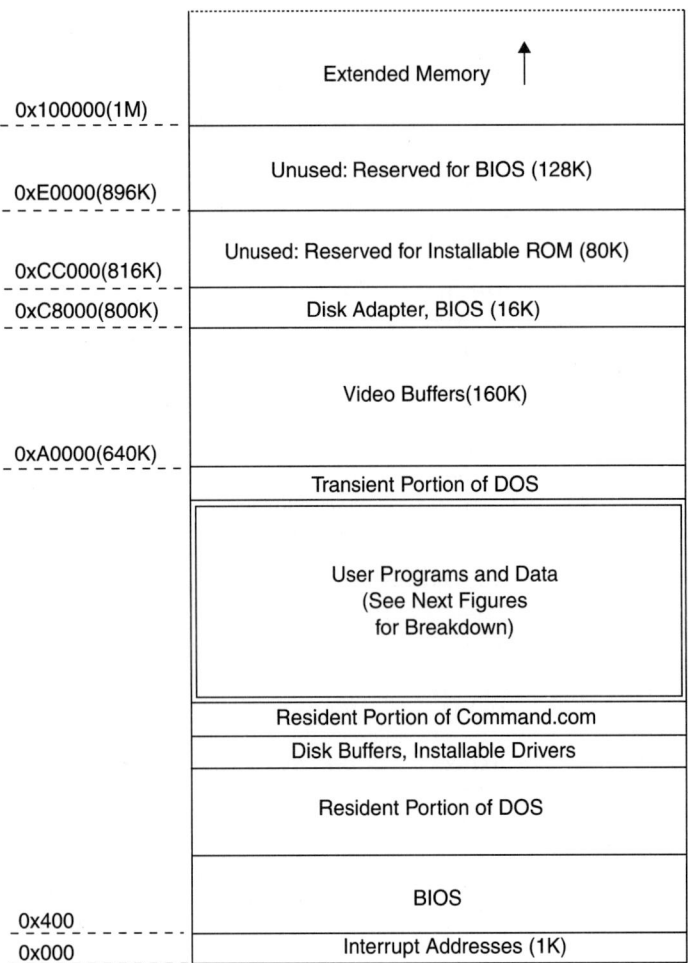

Figure B.7   *Tiny Memory Model*

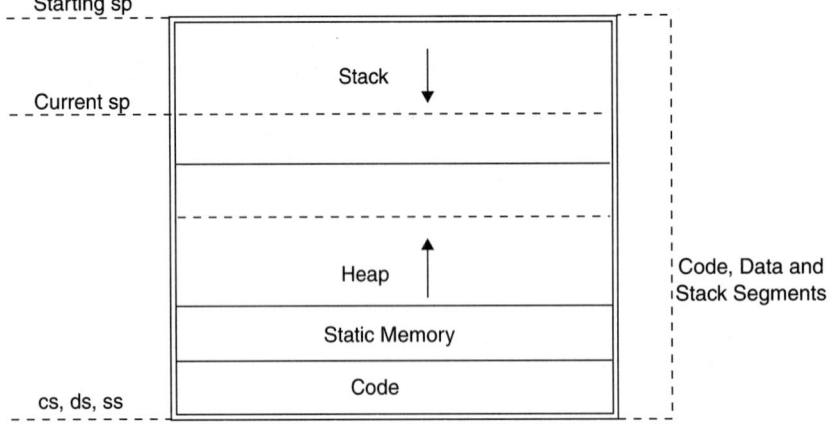

Figure B.8   *Small Memory Model*

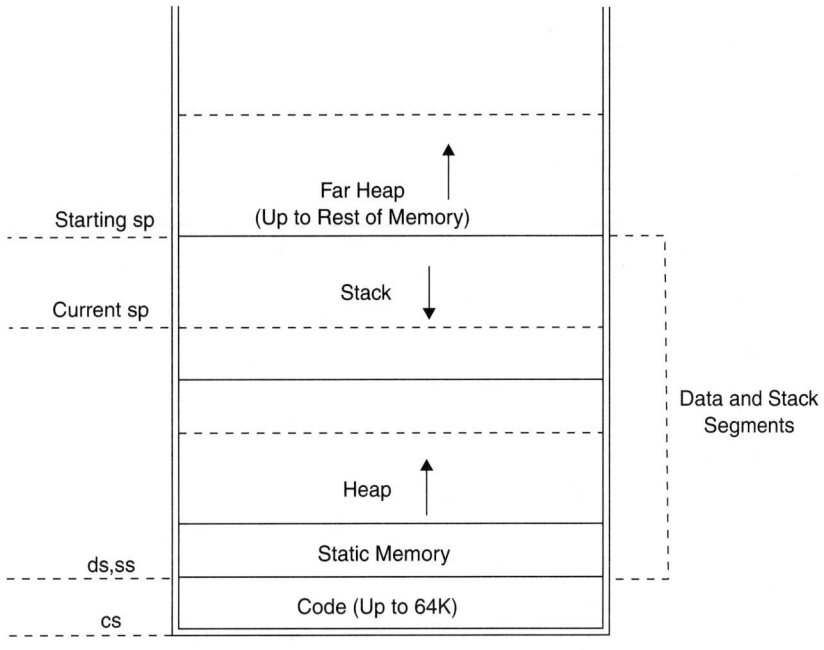

Figure B.9   *Medium Memory Model*

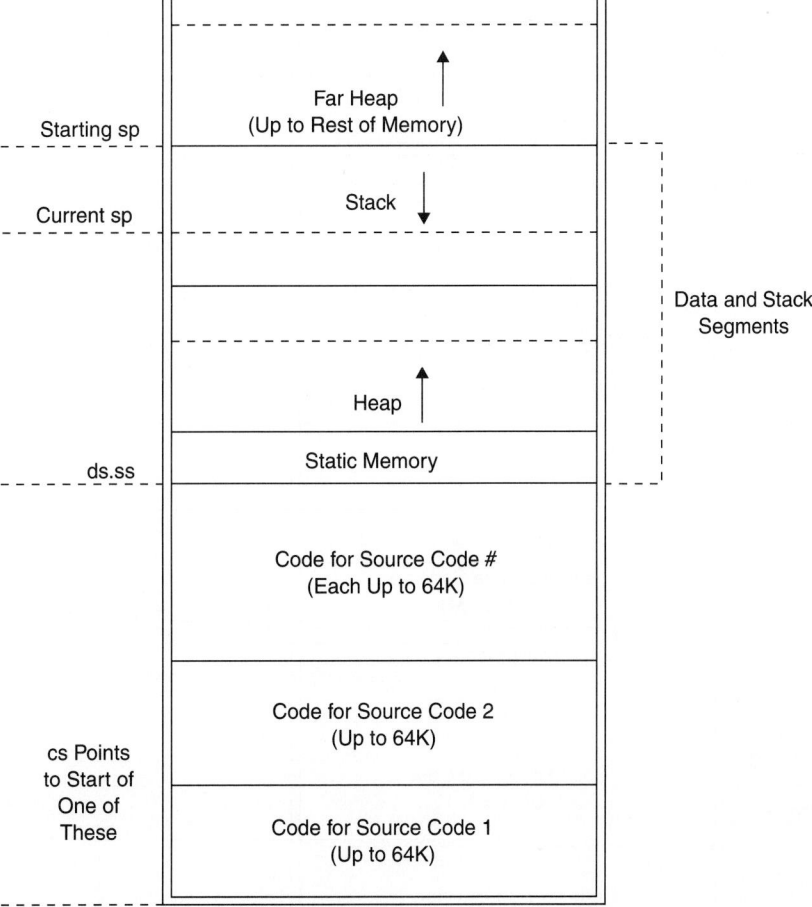

Figure B.10 *Compact Memory Model*

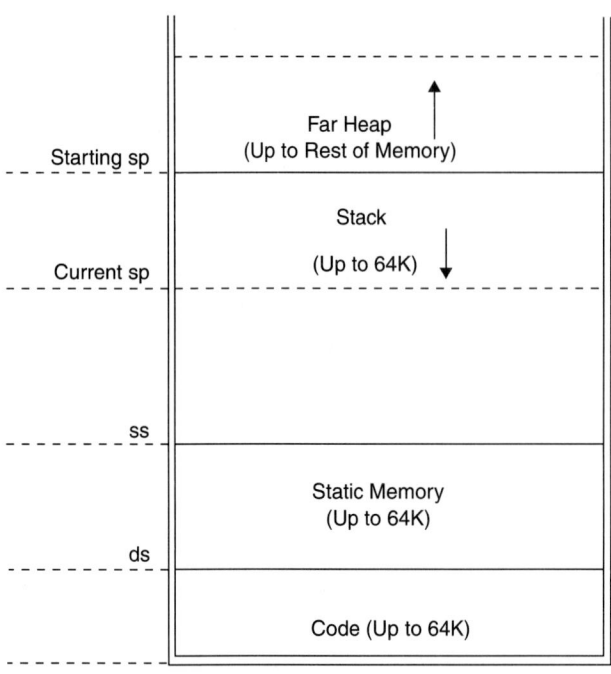

Figure B.11 *Large Memory Model*

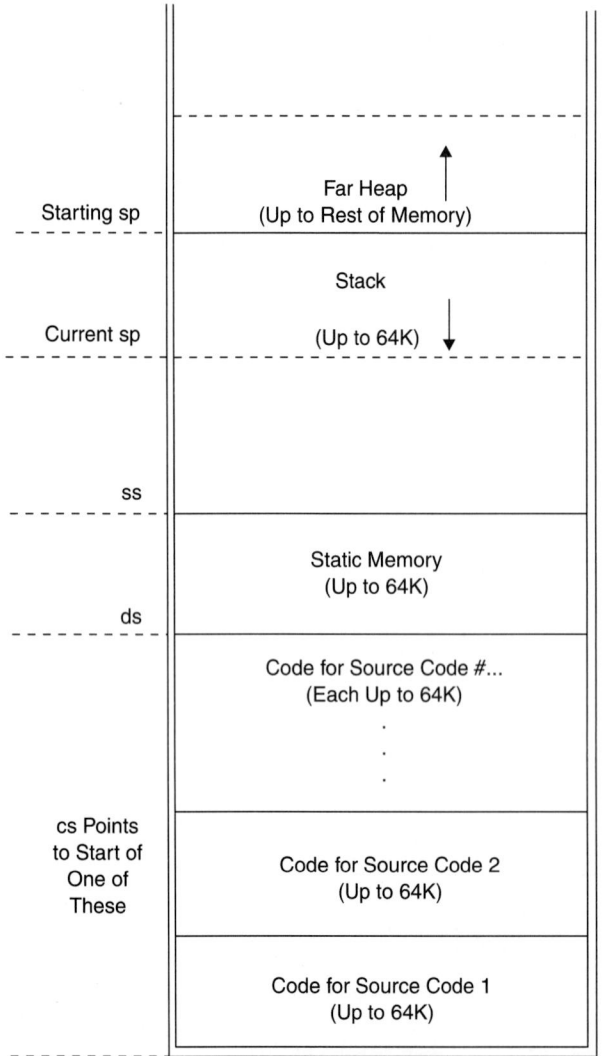

Figure B.12   *Huge Memory Model*

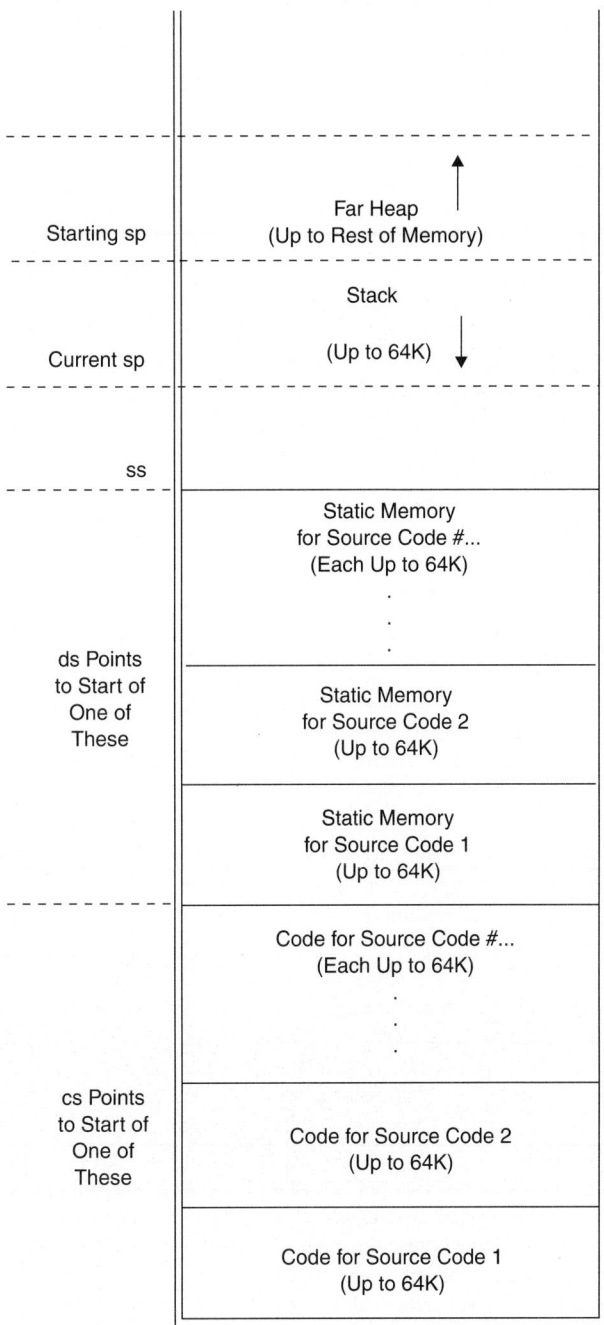

B.7   TINY AND SMALL MEMORY MODELS

The tiny memory model allows only 64K for both code and data. The cs, ds, and ss segments are completely contiguous. The overlap presents no problem. Only the very bottom portion of the code segment is used to store code; only the portion of the data segment commencing where the code leaves off is used to store static and global data; only the top portion of the stack segment and data segment is used to store stack variables.

In the tiny and small memory models, the stack and heap areas start at no individually predefined sizes. In the small memory model, the heap and stack are collectively allocated the balance of the data segment not used for static and global data (the size of which static and global data is known at compile time). In the tiny memory model, the heap and stack are collectively allocated what is left over in the program's single 64K segment after both the code and static and global data are given the space they require.

The area between the "top" of the stack (the memory location allotted to the last variable "placed" on the stack) and the top of the heap (the highest allocated area in the heap) is essentially a no-person's land. This free area is available to the stack or the heap on a first-come, first-served basis. The following listing, `stk_heap.c`, illustrates this "free space" concept.

 **Listing** **B.2 `stk_heap.c`**

```
/* stk_heap.c */

/* show how stack and heap interact in small memory model */

#include <stdio.h>
#include <alloc.h>

void test(void);

char *p1, *p2;

int main(void)
{
    test();
    if (!(p1 = malloc((unsigned)62000)))
        perror("p1 in main");

    test();

    if (!(p2 = malloc(1)))
        perror("p2 in main");
    free(p1);
    test();
}

void test(void)
{
    char buffer[62000];
    buffer[(unsigned)61099] = 1;
    if (!(p1 = malloc(4000)))
        perror("test");
}
```

There is no problem having declared a 62,000-byte array locally. The subsequent call to `malloc()` for 4000 bytes fails, however, because at that point 62,000 bytes of free space have been reserved for the stack.

Once the call to `test()` has concluded, a call to `malloc()` for 62,000 bytes from `main()` meets with success since the stack space reserved for the large local `char` array has now been released. The subsequent call this time to `test()` results in a stack overflow being signaled.

If, on the other hand, we free the heap space before calling `test()` a second time, there is no stack overflow:

```
free(p1);
test();
```

Allocations are initially made on the heap from lowest memory locations up. In other words, in the small memory model, the heap grows toward the stack just as the stack grows toward the heap. The end of the highest allocated block in the heap is referred to the *top of the heap*.

Say we reserve 1 byte on the heap after having first reserved 62,000 bytes there and then free the first large block:

```
if (!p2 = malloc(1)))
    perror("p2 in main");
free(p1)
test();
```

We find that we have a stack overflow on subsequently calling `test()`. Since the 1 byte we last reserved is at the highest memory address and hence closest to the top of the stack, the stack cannot grow past this point.

B.8   THE FAR HEAP AND far POINTERS

In the small memory model, we can also access the memory area above the data segment. This area is referred to as the *far heap*. The heap area within the data segment is sometimes referred to as the *near heap* to distinguish it from the far heap. We can reserve far-heap space in the small memory model through calls to `farmalloc()`.

The available space in the far heap would be the amount reported by the DOS `mem` command. It is the balance of available memory in the 640K system RAM area. The amount would depend on what drivers are loaded within, as opposed to above, the 640K system RAM area, what TSR programs are in memory, how much RAM your C program consumes, and so on.

When all our data is within a single segment, we can use 2-byte pointers to access data. The pointer holds the offset from the beginning of the data segment as its value. The computer knows enough to look at the value in the `ds` register to determine the memory location pointed to. However, the far heap is, by hypothesis, outside the data segment. Therefore, we cannot rely on this convenient system of data access to the extent that we want to use the far heap in our program. We must use 4-byte pointers for this purpose. The high-order 2 bytes will hold the segment address, and the low-order 2 bytes will hold the offset.

B.8.1   Using far Pointers

In the tiny, small, and medium memory models (called collectively the *small data memory models*), all pointers we declare are by default 16-bit objects. However, C permits us to expressly declare 32-bit pointers, called *far pointers*, by using the keyword `far`:

```
char far *ptr;
int far *int_ptr;
long far *long_ptr;
```

The keyword becomes part of the pointer variable's type, so that if we declare a function that passes a `far` pointer to `int` and wish to omit the variable name designation in the prototype, we would do so this way:

```
void function(int far *);
```

The syntax is a little different from the normal syntax. The following prints 4 and 2, not 4 and 4:

```
unsigned char far *fptr, *ptr;
printf("fptr: %d ptr: %d\n", sizeof(fptr), sizeof(ptr));
```

Like the `*` itself, the `far` keyword does not carry over in the declaration as `unsigned char` does. We end up with `ptr` being a `near` pointer to `unsigned char`, not `far`, unless you declare it this way:

```
unsigned char far *fptr, far *ptr;
```

Using the keyword `far` tells the compiler to use an explicit segment address when generating code that accesses a specific data item, rather than assume the default data segment value. The `es` segment register is used to hold the segment addresses of such data items.

B.8.2   Reserving Memory in the Far Heap

In the small data memory models, we can reserve memory in the far heap through calls to `farmalloc()`. For instance, to reserve a 100-byte area:

```
int far *ptr = farmalloc(100L);
```

Note the difference between `farmalloc()` and `malloc()`: for `farmalloc()`, we pass a `long` value as the number of bytes requested and use a `far` pointer to the allocated heap area. Also note that `farmalloc()`, like `malloc()`, starts memory allocation on paragraph boundaries.

B.8.3   Introduction to Direct Memory Access

We can also use `far` pointers to access memory locations completely outside our program's memory area. That process is referred to as *direct memory access* or *DMA*; we cover its practical applications in Appendix D. On a PC we can, for instance, place the letter A in white foreground on a red background at the top-left corner of a color monitor by inserting values at the first 2 bytes of video memory:

```
#include <dos.h>
int main(void)
{
    char far *ptr = MK_FP(0xB800, 0x0000);
    *ptr = 'A';
    *(ptr + 1) = 0x4F; /* white on red color byte */
}
```

The MK_FP macro is defined in dos.h as

```
#define MK_FP(segment,offset) \
    ((void _seg *)(segment) + (void near *)(offset))
```

This macro takes a segment address and an offset and produces a far pointer. Though this accepted macro formulation is more elegant for that job, the following will do every bit as well:

```
char far *ptr = 0xB8000000;
```

The true address of the start of color video memory is decimal 753,664 (0xB800 * 16 + 0x0000). But 0x8000000 is only decimal 47,104. How then does this simplified formulation work?

The answer is that the treatment of far pointers is the same as we saw with the use of segment and offset registers to derive a true memory location. The value in the segment register gets multiplied by 16 and added to the value in the offset register. With far pointers, the value in the high-order 2 bytes gets multiplied by 16 and added to the value in the low-order 2 bytes. Rather than reading the 4 bytes as a long, each pair of bytes is in effect treated and read as an unsigned int. Taking advantage of the fact that 4 hexadecimal digits represent 16 binary bits or 2 bytes, we can assign a segment and offset value to a far pointer by combining the two sets of 4 hexadecimal digits. This is so even though the value of the 8 digits as an entity has no meaning in this context.

So much for deriving a far pointer from a segment address and offset. What about the converse? From a given far pointer, you can derive the segment address component with the FP_SEG macro and the offset component with the FP_OFF macro, both as unsigned values:

```
int far *ptr = farmalloc(2L);
printf("ptr segment: %#X\n", FP_SEG(ptr));
printf("ptr offset: %#X\n", FP_OFF(ptr));
printf("data segment: %#X\n", _DS);
```

On our machine, in the small memory model, we get the following output:

```
ptr segment: 0X9D79
ptr offset: 0X4
data segment: 0X8D79
```

The data segment and the segment for ptr, in the far heap, are 4096 paragraphs apart (0x9D79 or decimal 40,313 – 0x8D79, or decimal 36,217). Multiplying by 16 bytes per paragraph, we get 65,536 bytes apart. This, of course, is just what we expected: in the small memory model, the far heap is located just after the data segment.

Both macros, like MK_FP, are found in dos.h:

```
#define FP_SEG(fp) ((unsigned)(void _seg *)(void far *)(fp))
#define FP_OFF(fp) ((unsigned)(fp))
```

B.9   MEDIUM MEMORY MODEL

The medium memory model allocates memory for data in the same way as the small memory model. The difference between the two memory models lies in the treatment of memory for code. In the medium memory model, each separate source code that is part of the program (made part of the program through a project; see Chapter 17) has its own separate code segment.

The code for the second source code commences at the start of the paragraph right after the code for the first source code in the project file and so on. The data segment follows at the start of the paragraph after the code for the last source code. Except in the rare case where the code for one source code takes up precisely 64K, there will be overlap among at least some of the various code segments, and between one or more of the code segments and the data segment.

Note that:

 Although the program code in the medium memory model can exceed 64K, no one source module's code can exceed 64K.

In practice, this is no impediment. It would be unusual for that much code not to be broken up into more than one source code.

 If you are using the small memory model and, on linking, receive the error message "Error: Segment _TEXT exceeds 64K", you will know it is time to switch memory models.

B.9.1 Using far Code Pointers

Because the program in the medium memory model will have more than one code segment (otherwise, there's no reason to use it, though theoretically you could do so), the program must reload the cs register as it switches from code module to code module during program execution. In the small memory model, the code segment address is loaded into the cs register only once, at the outset of program execution. *The need to continually reload the code segment address in the large code memory models slows execution of the program slightly, just as using far pointers for data will do.*

 Also, the necessity of distinguishing among various code segments requires that when a function is called, not only the offset to the calling function's code is placed on the stack, but also in a contiguous 2 bytes, the segment address as well. This same procedure is followed for the other large code memory models—the large memory model and the huge memory model.

B.10 COMPACT AND LARGE MEMORY MODELS

 The compact memory model is appropriate where the code does not exceed 64K and where the data cannot fit within one segment. (Note that if you use the small or compact memory model for a multiple–source code program, all the source modules' code will be placed in the single code segment. In the medium memory model, each source code in a project is accorded a separate memory segment.)

There is no heap (that is, no "near heap") in the compact memory model, only a far heap. Nor is the amount of space allocated to the stack dynamically changeable at run time as it is in the small and medium memory models.

By default, there is 4K (4096 bytes) allocated to the stack in the compact memory model for Borland C and 2K for Microsoft C. In Borland C, you can change this to a size no less than 2K bytes and no greater than 64K by placing the following statement above main():

```
extern unsigned _stklen = <number of bytes>;
```

For Microsoft C, you can specify the stack size as a linker parameter. The parameter

```
STACK:bbbb
```

instructs the linker to reserve bbbb bytes for the stack.

Static and global data are placed in the single data segment. Immediately after this data (or at least, at the start of the next paragraph), which may be up to 64K, comes whatever amount of space is allotted to the stack. The stack and data segments are not, as they are in the small data memory models (tiny, small, medium), contiguous.

 The large memory model simply uses the same data allocation scheme as the compact memory model and the same code allocation scheme as the medium memory model.

Since neither the compact memory model nor the large memory model has a near heap, calls to malloc() and farmalloc() will produce the same results:

```
char far *p1 = farmalloc(1L);
char far *p2 = malloc(1);
printf("p1: %Fp, p2: %Fp\n", p1, p2);
printf("_DS: %X\n", _DS);
```

On our machine, we get this output:

```
p1: 8EE2:0004, p2: 8EE3:0004
_DS: 8D81
```

B.11   HUGE MEMORY MODEL

The huge memory model uses the same code allocation scheme as the medium and large memory models. It differs from the large memory model by using a separate data segment for the static-global data of each source module in the program's project. Its static-global data memory allocation approach is similar to the code memory allocation approach taken by the medium and large memory models as well as its own memory model.

We noted earlier that in the large code memory models, although total memory allocated to code can exceed 64K, the code for a single source module is limited to 64K. The same restriction holds for the static-global memory allocation in the huge memory model. Even though total memory allotted to static and global data can exceed 64K, each source code module is limited to 64K.

B.12   USING huge POINTERS

What if you have a data object larger than 64K? We have seen that even in the huge memory model, no data segment can exceed 64K. The only way to accommodate such a data object is by using the far heap.

Still, we have a problem accessing and manipulating this massive data object. With near pointers, we measure an offset from the start of the data segment. When we increment a near pointer, we increment the offset only. Eventually, if we increment far enough, we have the same odometer overflow effect we have through incrementing variables past their range. The offset goes from 0xFFFF (decimal 65535) to 0.

The same problem exists with far pointers. When we increase past a 0xFFFF offset, the offset moves to 0 without the segment address incrementing.

There is a pointer type, huge, designed specifically to address this problem. The *huge pointer* is, like the far pointer, a 4-byte data object. However, the segment and offset addresses are *normalized* in a huge pointer. This process involves converting the segment and offset so that the offset is no more than 15 bytes away from the segment. For example, if the address is 0000:0010 (16-byte offset from the segment address), the normalized address would be 0001:0000. All that is done is to move the left three hex digits from the low-order byte and add them to the high-order byte. So, 0040:0056 becomes 0045:0006, and 0009:0010 becomes 000A:0000.

The pointer will now wrap every 16 bytes instead of every 65,536. At the same time, the segment value will be incremented every time we move from a 15-byte to a 0-byte offset.

B.12.1   Pointer Value Comparisons

In addition to allowing us to manipulate large data objects, using huge pointers also allows us to circumvent another problem we have with far pointers: pointer value comparisons. With near pointers, comparing one pointer address value to another presents no problem: the segment address is the same and we are comparing the offset address only.

With far pointers, however, one absolute address can be represented by 4096 (that is, 65,536/16) different segment-offset pairs (provided the absolute address is high enough). Comparing two different addresses can lead to incorrect results. With far pointers, the >, >=, <, and <= operators use only the offset for comparison purposes. The == and != operators use the full 32-bit value, but as an unsigned long, not as a combination of segment and offset in two separate 2-byte packages.

With huge pointers, normalization ensures that there is only one possible segment-offset combination for a given absolute address. Thus pointer comparisons are valid.

B.12.2   Disadvantages of huge Pointers

The drawback to using huge pointers is that the normalization process and the use of special subroutines for huge pointer arithmetic significantly slow processing down.

You may use huge pointers in any memory model but the tiny memory model. Contrary to what you might see in some otherwise reliable C texts, the huge pointer is *not* the default pointer in the huge memory model, and the huge memory model does not per se allow us to utilize data objects larger than 64K.

B.13   MIXED MEMORY ADDRESSING

Table B.3 shows the default size of the data pointers you declare and code pointers in the various memory models.

For data, we can explicitly declare a pointer to be of a type other than the default for the particular memory model. In the small or medium memory model, this declaration,

```
char *ptr;
```

Table B.3 *Pointer Size*

Memory Model	Code	Data
Tiny	2-byte	2-byte
Small	2-byte	2-byte
Medium	4-byte	2-byte
Compact	2-byte	4-byte
Large	4-byte	4-byte
Huge	4-byte	4-byte

would produce a 2-byte pointer. However,

```
char far *ptr;
```

would yield a 4-byte pointer. In other words, the expression `sizeof(ptr)`, would have a value of 4, not 2.

As we have seen, we can then use such a pointer to reserve and access memory locations that are in the far heap or that are outside our program's allotted memory area altogether.

B.13.1   Using **near** Pointers in Large Data Memory Models

In the large data memory models, where the declaration

```
char *ptr;
```

will produce a 4-byte object, we can use the keyword `near` to produce a 2-byte object:

```
char near *ptr;
```

 This keyword is not as commonly used as the `far` modifier. *Near pointers can be useful in the compact or large memory models to speed up the processing of functions that make heavy use of pointers to access data, all of which is known to be located within the program's data segment.*

B.13.2   Creating **near** Functions

We can also use the `near` keyword with functions. For example, in a large code memory model (medium, large, or huge), the declaration

```
int near factorial(int num);
```

would create a *near function*. When this function was called, the computer would not have to load the `cs` register. Nor would 4 bytes have to be placed on the stack for the code address. This would speed up the code and reduce stack usage. The reduced overhead would be handy if the function is repeatedly called or if it is recursive.

There are some limitations to this device, however.

 You can correctly call a near function only from the source code module where the function is defined.

 For that reason, you should declare the function as static, so that the function would not be available outside the proper module. Also, a near function must be declared before the first time it is used.

B.14   INTERRUPT PROGRAMMING

If there are ready-made C functions that can perform essentially the same tasks we show you how to accomplish with interrupts or direct memory access, why bother with the latter business at all? There are several reasons.

First, the aim here is to gain the most comprehensive and in-depth understanding of the computer and its operating system possible insofar as programming is concerned. A code-by-rote education will no more adequately prepare you for creative and efficient programming work than a diploma-mill law school will prepare its students for the practice of law simply by having them memorize material expected to appear on the bar exam without any real understanding of the legal concepts involved.

Second, creating your own functions gives you a great deal more control and flexibility. Canned functions generally take a vanilla least-common-denominator approach to a task. If what the functions provide is not completely suitable for your task, you're out of luck.

Third, the farther down the chain we get of application programming interface–canned function–interrupt–direct memory access with higher-level language–DMA with assembly language–DMA with machine language, the faster our code performs. Now, if we have a simple, nonrepetitive task such as determining the printer status or determining the current directory, speed is not of critical importance. But if we have to assign values to thousands of bytes of memory at once, as we must do in graphics programming, nothing less than direct memory access will perform a satisfactory job.

Fourth, in some cases, the interrupt or DMA programming is actually more uniform. For instance, the graphics functions for one compiler are generally specific to that compiler and completely different from compiler to compiler. Borland C's graphics functions bear little resemblance to Microsoft's, for example.

Finally, in some cases, there is no canned C function to handle the matter—for example, creating or removing a subdirectory, clearing the keyboard buffer; or changing the current directory. For such a task, you must either use interrupts or invoke the operating system's command processor through a system() call (see Chapter 16).

B.14.1   Interrupts

An *interrupt* on a PC is a signal to the central processing unit that something has occurred that requires immediate attention. When the CPU receives an interrupt, it makes a sort of bookmark to preserve its place in and the state of whatever process is running, and then "interrupts" the process to handle the signaled request.

There are two software interrupt types: *ROM BIOS interrupts* and *DOS interrupts*. What are the ROM BIOS?

There are programs written into the computer's read-only memory that handle the computer's input-output operations. These programs are called the ROM BIOS (for *Basic Input-Output System*). The ROM BIOS control the computer's peripheral devices such as the printer, monitor, keyboard, and disk drives and also direct tasks essential to the computer's operation, such as measuring time and keeping track of the time of day.

The ROM BIOS translate a command such as "open a file" or "read some data from the disk" or "print these words" into all the steps needed to carry out the command. When an operating system command such as "copy" a file is issued, when a printf() statement in a C program is executed, or when escape sequences are used to move the cursor or change colors, it is the ROM BIOS that ultimately do the work.

On a PC, the ROM BIOS can be invoked directly by programs executing in RAM—including your C program, as well as DOS and any applications software—through a combination of an interrupt number, which identifies the general service requested, and a service or routine number, which identifies the specific task desired. The principal general ROM BIOS services are video services, disk services, keyboard services, and time-of-day services. Each of these services has separate routines. Within time-of-day services, for example, are routines to read and set the current clock count, read and set the real-time clock time and date, and read, set, and reset the alarm.

The same mechanism is used for the DOS interrupts, which generally deal with process management, memory management, file operations and file system, and I/O. The DOS interrupts handle such tasks as creating and removing subdirectories; opening and closing files; reading from and writing to files; creating, deleting, and renaming files; getting and setting file dates and times; getting the default drive and the current directory for the current or another specified drive; getting file allocation table information; getting file size; getting the number of sectors per cluster, bytes per sector, and available and total clusters on the default or another specified drive; and so on.

In C, interrupts are invoked by functions whose prototypes are found in dos.h. Generally, we will use int86() or, less often, int86x(). Prior to calling this function, we must place specific values in certain of the computer's registers to identify the particular routine we want and to provide parameters—for example, we want the cursor setting routine of the video services interrupt and we want the cursor moved to row 1, column 8, page 2.

The first kilobyte of RAM contains 256 4-byte "interrupt vectors." These are far pointers to the interrupt handler itself, with 2 bytes housing the segment address and 2 bytes containing the offset. (Actually, a few of these 256 4-byte slots are pointers to tables rather than code—such as vector 43h, the graphic character bitmap table pointed to by interrupt 1Fh.)

These interrupt handlers are simply functions in compiled object code form—generally written in assembly language. By calling int86(), with the interrupt number as the first argument, we call these functions. We pass parameters to these interrupt handler functions by placing them in certain of the CPU's registers appropriate to the particular interrupt prior to calling the functions. The interrupt handler functions return values by placing them in certain registers, which we can then read after the calls. In other words, the whole process is just like our normal C function calls, except that there are a couple of extra steps involved in passing and returning values. The int86() function operates essentially as a function pointer in this process.

B.15   SCRATCH-PAD REGISTERS AND THE REGS UNION

We have visually depicted the scratch-pad registers in Figure B.3. The scratch-pad registers are commonly referred to as the ax, bx, cx, and dx registers. Each of these 16-bit scratch-pad registers can be accessed either as a 16-bit entity or as a set of two 8-bit registers, with the x replaced by an h for the *High*-order 8 bits (ah, bh, ch, and dh) and by an l for the *Low*-order 8 bits (al, bl, cl, and dl).

C accesses the scratch-pad registers to store and retrieve values for interrupt calls. It does this with the aid of a union that contains two structures—one of which contains chars and the other of which contains ints. The union is the REGS union, the template for which is found in dos.h. Here are the union and its related structures:

```
struct WORDREGS
{
    unsigned int ax, bx, cx, dx; /* scratch-pad registers */
    unsigned int si, di; /* index registers */
    unsigned int cflag, flags; /* flags register */
};

struct BYTEREGS
{
    unsigned char al, ah, bl, bh, cl, ch, dl, dh;
};

union REGS
{
    struct WORDREGS x;
    struct BYTEREGS h;
};
```

The WORDREGS structure member of the REGS union contains 16-bit members, corresponding to the 16-bit registers, and the BYTEREGS structure member of the REGS union contains 8-bit members, corresponding to the 8-bit views of the registers. Say we created two union of REGS type called in and out for storing values we put in and read out, respectively:

```
union REGS in, out;
```

We could store values in BYTEREGS members like this

```
in.h.ah = 6;
in.h.al = 25;
```

since h, a member of the REGS union, in, has as two of its members ah and al.

We could achieve the same result in a single statement with a WORDREGS member:

```
in.x.ax = 6 + (25 << 8);
```

Note that in addition to the four scratch-pad registers, the WORDREGS but not the BYTEREGS structure contains the two index registers si and di, as well as the flags register (a collection of individual status and control bits called *flags* that are normally tested or set on a single-bit basis). None of these three elements has an 8-bit counterpart in BYTEREGS. Most of the ROM BIOS calls use only the 8-bit BYTEREGS structure.

B.15.1   Syntax for int86() Calls

When we create functions that contain int86() calls, we first establish two union variables of type REGS. We then store values in the appropriate register by assignment statements that access either the WORDREGS x structure members or the BYTEREGS h structure members. Finally, we make the int86() call, in the following format:

```
int86(0x10, &in, &out)
```

The second and third arguments are the addresses of the REGS union variables we would have declared to house, respectively, the register values we must first establish before making the int86() call and the register values we can read after the call. (Actually, you could declare a single variable and pass its address as both the first and second arguments, if you wish.)

The first argument is the interrupt service number. The interrupt in the example here is the video services interrupt. Interrupts are almost universally referred to by hexadecimal notation, using the assembly-language version of the notation: the number in hex digits followed by an h. In the following appendix, we will be dealing with the video services interrupt. We will refer to this interrupt as interrupt 10h. However, when we write the interrupt statement in our code, we will use Standard C hexadecimal notation

```
int86(0x10, &in, &out)
```

though decimal or octal notation will work just as well:

```
int86(16, &in, &out);
int86(020, &in, &out);
```

What will *not* work is our nonprogram reference

```
int86(10h, &in, &out) /* error! */
```

For the DOS interrupt (interrupt 21h), we can use another function, intdos(). The call would be the same as using int86(), except that you would omit the first parameter, the interrupt number. That parameter is, in effect, hard-wired to 0x21. For instance, the following two calls would be identical:

```
int86(0x21, &in, &out);
intdos(&in, &out);
```

For the sake of uniformity, we will use int86() in all our DOS interrupt examples.

B.15.2   Interrupt Service Subsets

With interrupt 10h, the video service interrupt, we can, among other things, set or read the video mode, set the cursor size, set the cursor position, read the cursor position, set the active display page, scroll a window up or down, read a character and its color, write one or more of the same character and its color to the screen, or write a character string to the screen. Each of these tasks is differentiated by the value that must be placed in the ah register before int86() is called to invoke the interrupt. For example, to set the video mode, we must first set the ah register to 0. By convention, we say that setting the video mode is "routine," "function," "service" 0h (again, generally expressed in books and manuals in assembly-language hexadecimal notation) of interrupt 10h.

Each of the various services of an interrupt requires us to set other registers to specified values prior to invoking the interrupt. In addition, certain of the services return one or more values to registers after invocation of the interrupt.

Let's take an example. To clear the screen by invoking the window scroll-up routine of the video services interrupt, we set the ah register to 0x6, then we place the number of lines to scroll in the al register and the corners of the window in the ch, cl, dh, and dl registers:

```
void clearscreen(void)
{
    union REGS in, out; /* two REGS union variables */

    in.h.ah = 0x6; /* scroll-up routine */
    in.h.al = 25; /* number of lines to scroll */
    in.h.ch = 0; /* top row of window to scroll */
    in.h.cl = 0; /* left-most column */
    in.h.dh = 24; /* bottom row */
    in.h.dl = 79; /* right-most column */
    int86(0x10, &in, &out) /* call video services interrupt */
}
```

In this case, we do not make use of any values placed in the registers after the int86() call. In other cases, we do—for instance, where we want to ascertain the character and color attribute located at the current cursor position (see Appendix C):

```
void get_char_color(int active_page,
unsigned char *character, unsigned char *attribute)
{
    union REGS in, out;

    in.h.ah = 0x8; /* read character and attribute routine */
    in.h.bh = active_page;
    int86(0x10, &in, &out); /* call video services interrupt */
    *character = out.h.al;
    *attribute = out.h.ah;
}
```

Figure B.13 *Registers Before and After Interrupt 0x10/0x8 Call*

Scratch-pad Registers

0	8	X	X	AX(AH/AL)	0	79	0	65
0	0	X	X	BX (BH/BL)	X	X	X	X
X	X	X	X	CX (CH/CL)	X	X	X	X
X	X	X	X	DX (DH/DL)	X	X	X	X

Offset and Pointer Registers

X	X	X	X	SP	X	X	X	X
X	X	X	X	BP	X	X	X	X
X	X	X	X	SI	X	X	X	X
X	X	X	X	DI	X	X	X	X
X	X	X	X	IP	X	X	X	X

Segment Registers

X	X	X	X	CS	X	X	X	X
X	X	X	X	DS	X	X	X	X
X	X	X	X	SS	X	X	X	X
X	X	X	X	ES	X	X	X	X

Figure B.13 shows what the scratch-pad, segment, and offset registers look like before and after the `int86()` call, assuming we call the function with a parameter of 0, and the values of the character and attribute are 65 (A in ASCII) and 79 (0x4F: white on red), respectively.

The character and color-attribute values the `ax` register is filled with by invoking interrupt 10h, after having stored 0x8 in the `ah` register and 0 in the `bh` register, are placed into the `al` and `ah` members of the `h` member of the `REGS` variable we declare.

B.15.3 Summary Interrupt List

The interrupts we will examine in this and following appendixes are shown in Figure B.14.

For the various precall and postcall register values for each interrupt and service listed above, see Appendix C for the video interrupt (interrupt 10h), later in this appendix for the extended memory manager interrupt (interrupt 67h), and Appendix K for the rest.

B.15.4 Segment and Offset Registers

A limited number of interrupts require that we set a segment register or a segment register and one or more offset registers in addition to setting one or more of the scratch-pad registers.

You access the segment registers by declaring an `SREGS` variable. `SREGS`, like `REGS`, is declared in `dos.h`:

```
struct SREGS {
    unsigned int es, cs, ss, ds; };
```

You load values into the `SREGS` variable you declare by calling `segread()`:

```
struct SREGS segs;
segread(&segs);
```

The `segread()` function copies the current values of the segment registers to the respective members of the `SEGS` variable whose address you pass it. After the call here, `segs.es` will hold the address of the start of the es segment, `segs.cs` will hold the start of the code segment, `segs.ss` will hold the start of the stack segment, and `segs.ds` will hold the start of the data segment.

Figure B.14 *Summary of Interrupts*

Type	Interrupt	Description	Service	Description
BIOS	10h	Video	00h	Set video mode
			01h	Set cursor type
			02h	Set cursor position
			03h	Read cursor position and configuration
			05h	Set active display page
			06h	Scroll window up
			07h	Scroll window down
			08h	Read character and color-attribute
			09h	Write character and color-attribute
			0Ah	Write character at cursor
			0Ch	Write graphics pixel
			0Dh	Read graphics pixel
			0Fh	Get current display mode
BIOS	17h	Get printer status		
BIOS	1Ah	System timer/Real-time clock services		
DOS	19h	Get current drive		
DOS	23h	Get file size		
DOS	2Ah	Get date		
DOS	2AC	Get time		
DOS	33h	Mouse	00h	Determine whether mouse is present, and initialize mouse cursor
			01h	Show mouse cursor
			02h	Hide mouse cursor
			03h	Determine mouse button status and mouse position
			04h	Set mouse position
			07h	Set mouse X (column) limits
			08h	Set mouse Y (row) limits

Figure B.14 *(continued)*

Type	Interrupt	Description	Service	Description
DOS	35h	Get interrupt vector		
DOS	36h	Get free disk space		
DOS	39h	Create subdirectory		
DOS	3Bh	Set directory		
DOS	47h	Get current directory		
DOS	57h	File time and date	00h	Get file date and time
			01h	Set file date and time
DOS	67h	Extended memory manager	0x40	Get status
			0x41	Get page grame address
			0x42	Get number of expanded memory pages
			0x43	Allocate pages
			0x44	Map expanded aemory page
			0x45	Release pages

The function to use for an interrupt that requires loading of a segment register is int86x(). The format of a call to int86x() is the same as that for a call to int86(), except that you add as a third argument the address of the SREGS variable you declare.

An example is service 47h of the DOS interrupt (get current directory service), which requires us to establish a 65-byte buffer and point ds:si to this buffer before the interrupt call (that is, assign this buffer's segment address to the ds register and the buffer's offset address to the si register). We determine the segment and offset address with the FP_SEG and FP_OFF macros (found in dos.h), respectively:

```
char buffer[65];
union REGS in, out;
struct SREGS sreg;

in.h.ah = 0x47; /* get-current directory service of DOS interrupt */
in.h.dh = 0; /* current drive */
sreg.ds = FP_SEG(buffer); /* or: = (unsigned)(void_seg*)(void far *) buffer */
sreg.si = FP_OFF(buffer); /* or: = (unsigned) buffer */
int86x(0x21, &in, &out, &sreg);
```

See Appendix K for a more extensive discussion of this example and for a function that sets the current directory.

As with int86() and intdos(), there is a DOS-specific interrupt function for int86x() calls, intdosx(). A call to intdosx() is identical to a call to intdos(), except that the first argument—the interrupt number—is omitted:

```
intdosx(&in, &out, &sreg);
```

B.16 PROGRAMMER MEMORY UTILITIES

As we saw in Chapter 15, if your program allocates memory dynamically, it is easy to determine *when* you've run out of heap memory. But if you find your program unexpectedly runs out of memory, you may need to find out *why*.

Likewise, assuming you have set the proper option, if you are overflowing the stack, your program will terminate, with the message "Stack overflow!" appearing on the screen. Getting a feel for how close you come to overflowing the stack at various points in your program will give you a better idea of which functions' arrays or structures you should make global or of which other steps would best cure the problem. Also, stack overflow is not implemented within a Standard C library function. So a monitoring of the stack size may lead you to find an unreported stack overflow.

B.16.1   Running Out of Heap Memory

A possible cause of running out of memory is what we could characterize as memory leakage—because of some flaw in your formulation of requests for memory or freeing of memory, you either request more memory than you intend or you fail to free as much memory as you suppose.

One way to home in on the cause of the glitch is to look at the amount of heap memory remaining immediately after the various calls to `malloc()` or other memory request functions and to `free()` or `realloc()`.

Borland C has a function, `coreleft()`, that, in the small data memory models, returns the number of bytes between the top of the heap and the stack. In the large data memory models, `farcoreleft()` returns the number of bytes between the highest allocated block and the end of available memory.

But neither function tells the whole story—some C texts that incorrectly describe the two functions as returning the amount of unused heap memory to the contrary notwithstanding. In either case, if you reserve some of the heap and then free less than all reserved heap memory, neither `coreleft()` nor `farcoreleft()` will give you a true indication of total remaining memory unless you just happen to have freed memory in precisely the reverse order in which it was reserved. Figures B.15 and B.16 show how we can reserve and then free memory in the same order. The code to reserve it:

```
int i;
char *buffer[10];
for (i = 0; i < 10; i++)
    buffer[i] = malloc(1024 * 2);
```

And the code to release it:

```
for (i = 0; i < 10; i++)
    free(buffer[i]);
```

To determine how much available memory lies below the highest allocated heap block, you can use `heapwalk()` to "walk through the heap." We use a structure variable of type `heapinfo` to assist us in moving from one of the blocks of heap memory we reserved to another. At each point, we determine whether the block is free.

The `heapinfo` template is found in `alloc.h`:

```
struct heapinfo
{
    void *ptr;
    unsigned int size;
    int in_use;
};
```

Figure B.15   *Reserving 10 Blocks of Memory*

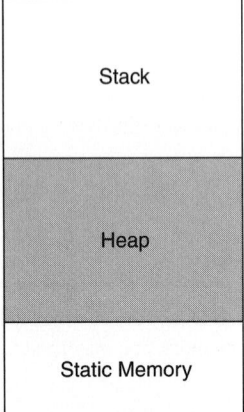

Figure B.16 *Freeing Blocks of Memory in the Order Reserved*

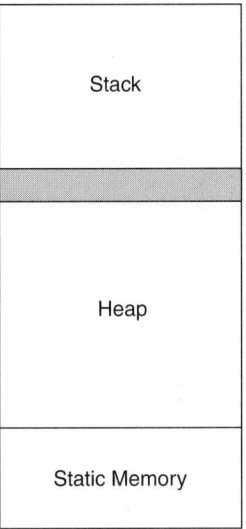

By setting the `ptr` member of the `heapinfo` variable we declare to NULL, and then passing the variable to `heapwalk()`, we instruct `heapwalk()` to start with the first entry in the heap. We then proceed to call `heapwalk()` repeatedly in a `while` loop, each time passing it the address of the `heapinfo` variable.

After each call to `heapwalk()`, the `ptr` member will have the address of the next entry in the heap. If the value of the `in_use` member of the `heapinfo` variable is 0 following an iteration's call, we add the block's size, assigned to the `size` member of the `heapinfo` variable, to an accumulating total byte count.

Once a call to `heapwalk()` returns a value other than the manifest constant _HEAPOK, the end of the heap has been reached. We then terminate the loop and add the accumulated total to the amount we first determined from `coreleft()`:

```
/* +----------------------------------------------------+
   +   MEM_FREE
   +   Determines and returns how much heap left by
   +      walking through the heap entry by entry and
   +      adding the amount of free memory to the value
   +      returned by coreleft().
   +   For small data memory models
   +----------------------------------------------------+*/
unsigned long mem_free(void)
{
   int i;
   unsigned long size = coreleft();
   struct heapinfo info;
   /* Setting the ptr member to NULL tells heapwalk() to start
         with the first entry in the heap.
      After each call to heapwalk(), the ptr member will have
         the address of the next block of memory. */

info.ptr = NULL;

while((i = heapwalk(&info)) == _HEAPOK)

   /* if this block of heap is free, the .in_use member will be set to 0 */

   if (!info.in_use)

   /* .size member has the size of this block of memory */

      size += info.size;
```

```
/* values returned by heapwalk():
   _HEAPOK: block of memory we're looking is valid
   _HEAPEMPTY: no heap
   _HEAPEND: end of the heap reached */

if ((i != _HEAPEMPTY) && (i != _HEAPEND))
   return -1L; /* can't use 0 because that could be a correct return value */
   return size;

}
```

The function to use for the large data memory models is similar:

```
/* +-------------------------------------------------------+
   +    FAR_MEM_FREE
   +    Determines and returns how much heap left by
   +       walking through the heap entry by entry and
   +       adding the amount of free memory to the value
   +       returned by farcoreleft().
   +    For large memory model.
   +-------------------------------------------------------+ */
unsigned long far_mem_free(void)
{
   int i;
   unsigned long size = farcoreleft();
     struct farheapinfo info;
   info.ptr = NULL;
   while((i = farheapwalk(&info)) == _HEAPOK)
      if (!info.in_use)
         size += info.size;
   if ((i != _HEAPEMPTY) && (i != _HEAPEND))
      return -1L;
   return size;
}
```

B.16.2   Stack Checking

When your program begins execution, the sp register holds the address of the start of the stack. This address changes as variables are "placed on the stack." If we record and preserve the initial address and later compare it to the current stack address, we then know how much of the stack is being used at any given point in the program.

The following function, stack_test(), tells you how much of the stack has been used at the point of the call:

```
/* +-------------------------------------------------------+
   + STACK_TEST
   + test for stack usage at intervals throughout
   +    the program
   + Argument:
   + - function: name of function calling this function
   + NOTE: following statement must appear at start
   +    of main():
   + start_stack = _SP; /* this will be off to extent
   +    main() has local variables */
   +-------------------------------------------------------+ */
void stack_test(char *function)
{
   unsigned temp_used =
      start_stack - _SP; /* start_stack & _SP are globals */

   fprintf(stdprn, "stack_used - function %s: %u\n\r",
      function, temp_used);
   if (temp_used > stack_used) /* stack_used is global */
```

```
        {
            stack_used = temp_used;
            fprintf(stdprn, "MAX STACK USAGE so far - %s: %s\n\r",
                function, temp_used);
        }
    }
```

B.17   EXPANDED MEMORY ON THE PC

We will see in Appendix D how the computer and the video board utilize a portion of RAM within the upper 384K of conventional memory. The video board is "mapped" to a designated portion of this memory area we have called video memory. That is, when we alter values within video memory, the changes show up on the monitor controlled by the video board. We can make those changes directly with `far` pointers, or we can make changes within our program's data segment and move them en masse to video memory with `movedata()`.

We can use similar techniques to access memory above the 1M conventional memory area and hence above the physical addressing of the computer. An expanded memory board will be mapped to a 64K block in the same 384K upper-memory area. This 64K block is referred to as the *page frame*.

The page frame is divided into four *pages* of 16K each, numbered from 0 to 3. Since the page frame is exactly one segment large, once we know the segment address of the page frame, we can access any location within the page frame by offset from that address. The offset to the beginning of any page will be 16K times the page number.

To access expanded memory, we must map 16K areas of that memory to one of the pages that are in turn mapped to the expanded memory board. These 16K areas are also called *pages*. They are logical pages, as opposed to the four physical pages within the page frame. Numbering also commences at 0 for these logical pages.

We can map no more than four logical pages to the page frame at one time. Accordingly, if our program requires more than 64K of expanded memory, it must provide for swapping in and out of logical pages of expanded memory to the page frame. In Figure B.17, we see logical pages 0, 3, 5, and 9 mapped to the four pages of the page frame.

Figure B.17   *Page Mapping*

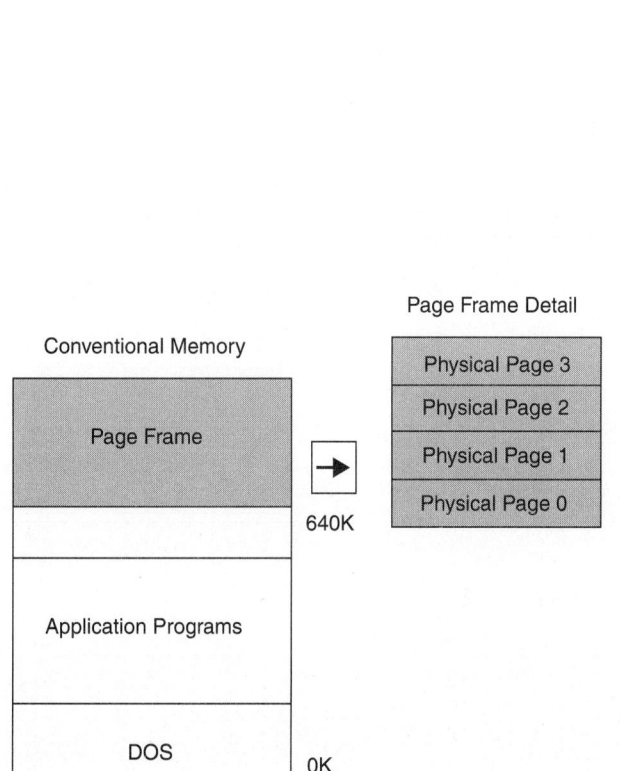

B.17.1   Expanded Memory Interrupt 67h

A software interface called an *expanded memory manager* (*EMM*) keeps track of which expanded memory pages are in use, which pages may be used by a particular application, and which pages are currently accessible. It is up to the application itself to call the manager to request the number of logical expanded memory pages it needs, to make its expanded memory pages available within the page frame as necessary, and to release its expanded memory pages before the application terminates.

All this is done by the application with interrupt 67h. Table B.4 summarizes the most commonly used functions of that interrupt. All the functions indicate success by returning 0 in the ah register, or failure by returning an error code in that register.

Table B.4   *Expanded Memory Interrupt Functions*

Function	Call Values	Return Values
Get Status	ah = 0x40	ah = status
Get Page Frame Address	ah = 0x41	ah = status bx = page frame segment
Get Number of Expanded Memory Pages	ah = 0x42	ah = status bx = available pages dx = total pages
Allocate Pages	ah = 0x43 bx = number of pages	ah = status dx = handle
Map Expanded Memory Page	ah = 0x44 al = physical page bx = logical page dx = handle	ah = status
Release Pages	ah = 0x45 dx = handle	ah = status

B.17.2   Programming Example

The following listing, expanded.c, illustrates the use of these expanded memory interrupt functions. We altered Listing A.4, con_menu.c, to write the five data screens produced by that program to separate files, named page_0 through page_4. In expanded.c, we place the contents of those files into expanded memory and utilize the data by transferring it to video memory as needed.

 **Listing B.3 expanded.c**

```
/* expanded.c */

#include <stdio.h>
#include <stdlib.h> /* exit */
#include <dos.h> /* int86, intdosx, segread */
#include <string.h> /* strcpy */
#include <conio.h> /* getch */

#define IN 1
#define OUT 2
#define PAGES 5
#define PAGE_LEN (16 * 1024) /* 16K */
#define BYTES 4000
```

```c
void emm_free(void), get_page_seg(void);
unsigned emm_malloc(int pages), page_status(void);
char emm_present(void), emm_status(void);
void map_page(int logical_page, int board_page);

unsigned emm_seg, ds_seg, handle;

int main(void)
{
    int i;
    int board_pg = 0; /* physical page #: here hard-wired to 0 */
    char buffer[BYTES], filename[12];
    FILE *fp;
    struct SREGS segs;

    /* determine segment address of data segment */
    segread(&segs);
    ds_seg = segs.ds;

    /* if EMM software/hardware not present or if not enough memory, exit */
    if (!emm_present() || !emm_status() || page_status() < PAGES
        || (handle = emm_malloc(PAGES)) == 0)
    {
        puts("Not enough available memory");
        exit(4);
    }

    /* determine segment address of the page frame used by the EMS */
    get_page_seg();
    /* write to each of the pages from files generated by con_menu.c */
    for (i = 0; i < PAGES; i++)
    {
        /* open file and write it to buffer */
        sprintf(filename, "c:\\tc\\ver\\page_%d", i);
        fp = fopen(filename, "rb");
        fread(buffer, BYTES, 1, fp);
        fclose(fp);

    /* Map 1 of the logical pages assigned to the handle to
       1 of the 4 physical pages on the memory board. board_page is hard-wired to 0:
       we only use first board page here */
    map_page(i, board_pg);

    /* now move from RAM to that page (again, hard-wired to 0 for first page) */
    movedata(ds_seg, (unsigned)buffer, emm_seg, board_pg * PAGE_LEN, BYTES);
}

/* read them back in and recover the test string */
for (i = 0; i < PAGES; i++)
{
    map_page(i, board_pg);

    /* move from memory board directly to video memory */
    movedata(emm_seg, board_pg * PAGE_LEN, 0xB800, 0, BYTES);

    /* pause for next page */
    if (!getch())
```

```
      getch();
   }

   /* close the handle and return the memory for use by other processes */
   emm_free();
}
/* +---------------------------------------------------------------+
   +   EMM_FREE
   +   Close the handle and return the memory for use by other processes
   +---------------------------------------------------------------+ */
void emm_free(void)
{
   union REGS in, out;

   /* deallocate handle and memory function of EMM interrupt */
   in.h.ah = 0x45;
   in.x.dx = handle;
   int86(0x67, &in, &out);
}


/* +---------------------------------------------------------------+
   +   EMM_MALLOC
   +   Get handle and allocate memory
   +   Argument: pages: number of logical pages to allocate
   +   Returns handle & associates it with a specified number of pages
   +---------------------------------------------------------------+*/
unsigned emm_malloc(int pages)
{
   union REGS in, out;

   /* get handle/allocate memory function of EMM interrupt */
   in.h.ah = 0x43;
   in.x.bx = pages;
   int86(0x67, &in, &out);
   if (out.h.ah != 0) /* returns 0 in ah if successful */
      return 0;
   else return out.x.dx; /* handle gets returned in dx */
}


/* +---------------------------------------------------------------+
   +   EMM_PRESENT
   +   Determine whether expanded memory board is installed
   +---------------------------------------------------------------+ */
char emm_present(void)
{
   char far_strncmp(char far *str1, char far *str2, int num_chars);

   union REGS in, out;
   struct SREGS segs;
   char far *emptr, far *nameptr = "EMMXXXX0";

   /* get interrupt vector function of DOS interrupt */
   in.h.ah = 0x35;
   in.h.al = 0x67; /* interrupt number (EMM interrupt) goes here */
   /* address of interrupt handler goes into es:bx */
   intdosx(&in, &out, &segs);

   /* set a far pointer to access the EMM driver */
   emptr = MK_FP(segs.es, 10);
```

```
    /* see if first 8 characters are EMMXXX0 */
    if (far_strncmp(emptr, nameptr, 8))
        return 1;
    return 0;
}

char far_strncmp(char far *str1, char far *str2, int num_chars)
{
    /* could also use _fstrncmp */
    while (*str2 && num_chars)
    {
        if (*str1 != *str2)
        {
            printf("EMM not installed\n");
            return 0;
        }
        num_chars--;
        str1++;
        str2++;
    }
    return 1;
}

/* +-----------------------------------------------------------------+
   +  EMM_STATUS
   +  Test whether expanded memory board (if installed) is functional
   +-----------------------------------------------------------------+ */
char emm_status(void)
{
    union REGS in, out;

    in.h.ah = 0x40; /* get manager status function of EMM interrupt */
    int86(0x67, &in, &out);
    if (out.h.ah == 0) /* 0 in ah if functioning properly */
        return 1;
    if (out.h.ah == 0x80)
        printf("EMM not functioning properly\n");
    return 0;
}

/* +-----------------------------------------------------------------+
   +  GET_PAGE_SEG
   +  Determine the segment address of the page frame used by the EMS.
   +  We set a far pointer to an address comprised of that segment and a 0 offset
   +-----------------------------------------------------------------+ */
void get_page_seg(void)
{
    union REGS in, out;

    /* get page frame segment function of EMM interrupt */
    in.h.ah = 0x41;
    int86(0x67, &in, &out);
    if (out.h.ah != 0) /* 0 in ah if functioning properly */
    {
        printf("Error getting page frame segment\n");
        exit(3);
    }

    emm_seg = out.x.bx;
```

```
}

/* +-------------------------------------------------------------+
   +  MAP_PAGE
   +  Maps one of the EMS logical pages assigned to the handle
   +  to 1 of the 4 physical pages in RAM mapped to the memory board
   +-------------------------------------------------------------+ */
void map_page(int logical_page, int board_page)
{
   union REGS in, out;

   in.h.ah = 0x44; /* map memory function of EMM interrupt */
   in.h.al = board_page; /* physical page number (0-based) */

   /* logical page # of those pp assigned to handle */
   in.x.bx = logical_page;
   in.x.dx = handle;
   int86(0x67, &in, &out);
   if (out.h.ah != 0)
   {
      printf("Error mapping page\n");
      exit(2);
   }
}


/* +-------------------------------------------------------------+
   +  PAGE_STATUS
   +  Determine currently available number of expanded memory logical pages
   +-------------------------------------------------------------+ */
unsigned page_status(void)
{
   union REGS in, out;

   in.h.ah = 0x42; /* get page count function of EMM interrupt */
   int86(0x67, &in, &out);
   if (out.h.ah != 0)
   {
      printf("Error getting page count\n");
      exit(1);
   }

   return out.x.bx; /* can also get total pp. from dx if wish */
}
```

B.17.3   Determining Whether Software and Hardware Are Present

The first step in using expanded memory is to determine whether the EMM is present. We do this in emm_present().
The EMM is installed when the system is booted, with a DEVICE= directive in the config.sys file. The device
has a logical device name that is always EMMXXXX0. This device name will be found starting at an offset of 10
bytes from the entry point of interrupt 67h.

Therefore, to determine whether the EMM is present, we need to inspect the address value at the interrupt 67h
vector location and then examine the 8 bytes starting 10 bytes from that address. We use function 35h, the get interrupt vector function, of the DOS interrupt to determine the address at the interrupt location. We set the ah register to 0x35 and the al register to the interrupt number—here, 0x67. The function returns the interrupt handler
address for the specified interrupt in es:bx.

We then set a far pointer to the returned segment at an offset of 10 bytes. This is done with the MK_FP macro.
Finally, we use this pointer in far_strncmp() to compare the 8 bytes found starting at that location. (In lieu of
the homemade character-by-character comparison accomplished in far_strncmp(), we could have used the library function _fstrncmp(). However, that function is not available in early versions of some compilers.)

After we determine that an EMM is present, we then must verify that the expanded memory hardware is installed and is functioning properly. We do this in `emm_status()`, using function 40h of interrupt 67h.

B.17.4 Determining Whether Enough Expanded Memory Is Available

Next, we must compare the amount of expanded memory our program needs to the amount on the user's system. Our `page_status()` does this with function 42h of the EMM interrupt. That function returns both the total number of logical pages in the system and an indication of how many of those pages have not already been allocated to this or other programs. Assuming we call this function at the outset of our program, the two page number totals will be equal, except to the extent that our program is running in a multitasking environment or unless TSRs or device drivers that use expanded memory are currently loaded.

Since we are only concerned with the number of pages available, our `page_status()` function returns only this value. If you need both, you can alter the function, passing it two pointers to `unsigned`.

B.17.5 Dealing with No or Insufficient Expanded Memory

If you find there is no expanded memory or not enough available, you must decide on a course of action to handle the deficiency. The simplest solution is to issue an error message and terminate the program, as we do here. And, if there is no expanded memory available at all and your application positively requires it, you have no other choice.

Otherwise, you can choose to run the program without any expanded memory at all. You can use files or some other slower process in lieu of expanded memory. You might, if you do that, warn the user of this degradation.

Assuming expanded memory is available but not as much as your program needs ideally, there are all sorts of middle grounds between terminating the program and using no expanded memory at all. For instance, if your program needs 50 pages of expanded memory to work best and there are only 10 available, you may be able to have your program just swap pages in and out more frequently than would be optimal.

B.17.6 Allocating Expanded Memory

Assuming there is enough expanded memory available for your program, the next step is to reserve it for your application. The reservation process is a cross between reserving heap memory and opening a file for low-level I/O. With heap memory, you reserve a specified amount of memory with a function such as `malloc()` and you record the starting address of that memory in a pointer declared for that purpose. When you open a file, you are given a handle to allow you to access the file and do what you want to it with the various I/O functions.

To reserve expanded memory, we use function 43h of interrupt 63h. In addition to setting the `ah` register to 0x43, we set the `bx` register to the number of logical pages of expanded memory we wish to reserve. The function returns a handle to these memory pages in the `dx` register. The process is accomplished in `emm_malloc()`. We will use this handle in mapping expanded memory pages to the page frame and in freeing expanded memory.

This simple program uses a single handle to access the five logical expanded memory pages the program needs. We have made `handle` a global variable. In another application, of course, you could call `emm_malloc()` several times and receive different handles to reserve expanded memory areas, just as you could with `malloc()` and the heap.

B.17.7 Page Mapping and Usage

To use a logical page of expanded memory, we must map the page to one of the four physical pages in the page frame. We do this with function 44h of the EMM interrupt. This mapping can be done only a page at a time for each interrupt call. In addition to setting `ah` to 0x44, we set `al` to the physical page number (from 0 to 3), `bx` to the logical page number of those pages assigned to the handle we pass (again 0-based), and `dx` to the handle.

This process is accomplished in `map_page()`. You can map up to four logical expanded memory pages at one time. In `expanded.c`, we made use of physical page 0 only. However, the `map_page()` function and the other functions in the program will accommodate a four-page process.

With a page mapped to one of the pages of the page frame, we can manipulate the data in that memory area with `far` pointers or with `movedata()`. (See Appendix D for a description of the mechanism for this function.) First, however, we need to know the segment address of the page frame.

Video memory is assigned a universally agreed on area in upper memory. For instance, as we have seen, monochrome memory begins at 0xB0000000. The page frame, however, is set at some nonuniform location that does not conflict with video memory or with other hardware's mapped areas, such as those for a network card. We use function 41h of interrupt 67h to determine the segment address of the page frame. The segment is returned in the `bx` register. The process is handled in `get_page_seg()`.

We read the various screen page files into a buffer in the program's data segment, and from there we move the screen data into the physical page with `movedata()`. Again, though we use only physical page 0 in this program, the code will accommodate a multipage approach:

```
movedata(ds_seg, (unsigned)buffer, emm_seg,
   board_pg * PAGE_LEN, BYTES);
```

(The data segment was determined early in the program with a call to `segread()`.) If we were using a large data memory model, we could have read data directly from the file into the physical page, bypassing the file–data segment/ data segment–physical page data transfers.

When we want to retrieve data, we bring the logical page with the new data back to the physical page with `map_page()` and then use `movedata()` to transfer the data from the physical page directly to video memory:

```
movedata(emm_seg, board_pg * PAGE_LEN, 0xB800, 0, BYTES);
```

Note that we didn't have to do anything to preserve the data in the logical page, as stored there at the time it was mapped to a physical page within the page frame. When another logical page is mapped to that same physical page, we don't lose any data in the logical page that makes way for another in the page frame.

B.17.8   Releasing Expanded Memory

You must free expanded memory at the termination of your program or whenever your program is finished using expanded memory. If not, the expanded memory will not be available for use by other programs until the system is rebooted.

We free expanded memory with function 45h of interrupt 67h. We set the `dx` register to the handle for the expanded memory we wish to free. The process is accomplished in `emm_free()`.

APPENDIX **C**

Video Services Interrupts on the PC

In Appendix A, we saw how to use `printf()` and escape sequences to control the printing of characters on the screen. Now we will tackle more sophisticated methods. We will look first at BIOS interrupts and later at direct memory access (DMA). In this appendix, our focus will be the video services interrupt, interrupt 10h. We will examine colors here in text mode. In Appendix E, we will look at colors in graphics mode, in text as well as in non-text applications.

C.1 VIDEO MODE AND DISPLAY

There are two types of video modes: text modes and graphics modes. In text modes, you may depict any of the 255 ASCII characters within a character display box. In the most commonly used text modes—mode 3 for CGA and VGA monitors and mode 7 for monochrome monitors—there are 25 rows and 80 columns of these character display boxes to cover the entire screen. The characters are formed by individual pixels within the character display boxes, but you do not access the pixels directly. That is done on a hardware level by a character generator.

Certain of the characters allow you to create boxes, shading and drop shadows, and other professional effects. See, in particular, the single- and double-lined box characters and full- and half-box characters shown in Appendix F.

 In graphics modes, you work with the individual pixels. For that reason, programming in graphics mode is more complex and graphics modes applications operate more slowly than text mode applications. Also, when deciding whether to use a text or graphics mode for your program, remember that not all users have graphics output capabilities.

Table C.1 lists the most common text and graphics display modes. Note that insofar as the display is concerned, most vendors call any display that has a greater resolution than the VGA display adaptor's native 640 × 480 resolution "Super VGA," but this is really a marketing concept, without any standard for what constitutes "Super," rather than a different display type.

Table C.1   *Video Display Modes*

Mode		Type	Resolution	Colors	Pages	Display	Memory Start
Hex	**Decimal**						
01h	1	Text	40 x 25	16	8	CGA VGA	0xB8000000
03h	3	Text	80 x 25	16	4 8	CGA VGA	0xB8000000
04h	4	Graphics	320 x 200	4	1 2	CGA VGA	0xB8000000
06h	6	Graphics	640 x 200	2	1	CGA VGA	0xB8000000
07h	7	Text	80 x 25	Mono	1 8	MDA VGA	0xB0000000
0Dh	13	Graphics	320 x 200	16	8	VGA	0xA0000000
0Eh	14	Graphics	640 x 200	16	4	VGA	0xA0000000
0Fh	15	Graphics	640 x 350	Mono	2	VGA	0xA0000000
10h	16	Graphics	640 x 350	16	2	VGA	0xA0000000
11h	17	Graphics	640 x 480	2	2	VGA	0xA0000000
12h	18	Graphics	640 x 480	16	1	VGA	0xA0000000
13h	19	Graphics	320 x 200	256	1	VGA	0xA0000000
6Ah	106	Graphics	640 x 400	16	1	VGA	0xA0000000
100h	256	Graphics	640 x 480	16	1	VGA	0xA0000000
101h	257	Graphics	640 x 480	256	1	VGA	0xA0000000
102h	258	Graphics	800 x 600	16	1	VGA	0xA0000000
103h	259	Graphics	800 x 600	256	1	VGA	0xA0000000
104h	260	Graphics	1280 x 768	16	1	VGA	0xA0000000
105h	261	Graphics	1280 x 768	256	1	VGA	0xA0000000
106h	262	Graphics	1280 x 1024	16	1	VGA	0xA0000000
107h	263	Graphics	1280 x 1024	256	1	VGA	0xA0000000

C.2   SETTING THE VIDEO MODE

Function 00h (decimal 0) sets the video mode. In addition to placing 0 in the ah register, you set the al register to the desired video mode before invoking int86(). The following function sets the video mode:

```
/* +---------------------------------------------------+
   + SET_MODE
   + Set the video mode and clear the screen.
   + Argument: - mode: mode to set to
   +---------------------------------------------------+ */
```

```
void set_mode(int mode)
{
    REGS in, out;

    in.h.ah = 0;
    in.h.al = mode;
    int86(0x10, &in, &out);
}
```

Mode 3 is the DOS default color text mode. If you want larger characters, you can use mode 1, though mode 3 is far more commonly used.

By default, setting the video mode also clears the screen. If you want to set the video mode without clearing the screen, you must turn bit 6 of the `al` register on. You can do this by ORing

```
in.h.al = mode | 0x80;
```

or by simply adding 0x80 (decimal 128) to the video mode number you specify in the `al` register.

Switching from a text mode to a graphics mode without clearing the screen would produce bizarre results. Even moving from one graphics mode to another or one text mode to another without clearing the screen may not produce the results you expect.

C.2.1   Determining and Preserving the Current Video Mode

 Prior to setting the mode, you should test for the current video mode. That way, at the program's termination, you can reset the mode to its original state. Function 0Fh (decimal 15) reads the current video mode. The current video mode is returned in the `al` register:

```
/* +------------------------------------------------------+
   + GET_MODE
   + Determine the current video mode. Returns current
   + video mode.
   +------------------------------------------------------+ */
int get_mode(void)
{
    union REGS in, out;

    in.h.ah = 0xF;
    int86(0x10, &in, &out);
    return out.h.al;
}
```

C.2.2   Display Pages

In the most commonly used video mode, color text mode 3, there are eight video pages. As you will see in greater detail in Appendix D, each page is a reflection of a separate 4000-byte area in the video memory portion of RAM. The pages are numbered from 0 to 7.

 Each of the 2000 character display boxes on the screen reflect a 2-byte pair. The first of these 2 bytes contains the character; the second contains the color.

What shows up on the user's screen are a reflection of the 4000 bytes of whatever video page is the *active page*.

The default active page is page 0. This is the active page when you are in DOS, for example. At the outset of your C program, the page will be 0.

To determine the active page number at any point during the running of your program, you use function 0Fh (decimal 15) of the video services interrupt. Function 0Fh (decimal 15), which we've already looked at, returns not only the display mode in the `al` register, but also the active page in the `bh` register:

```
/* +------------------------------------------------------+
   + GET_PAGE
   + Determine active page. Returns active page.
   +------------------------------------------------------+ */
int get_page(void)
{
```

```
   union REGS in, out;

   in.h.ah = 0xF;
   int86(0x10, &in, &out);
   return out.h.bh;
}
```

We can change the active page with function 05h (decimal 5). We set the al register to the desired page:

```
/* +-------------------------------------------------------+
   + GOTO_PAGE
   + Change active page to designated page.
   + Argument: page: page to change to
   +-------------------------------------------------------+ */
void goto_page(int page)
{
   union REGS in, out;

   in.h.ah = 5;
   in.h.al = page;
   int86(0x10, &in, &out);
}
```

You will probably find more use for functions that move the page up or down a single page at a time in response to the user pressing [Page Up] or [Page Down] instead of moving to a designated page. These functions would ignore requests to move before page 0 or beyond the last page of video memory for the particular mode (you need to declare a variable for the last page and assign a value):

```
/* +-------------------------------------------------------+
   + PAGEDN
   + Increment active video page, but not past last video
   + page (assumes this last page is a global variable that
   + has been set already). Calls get_page()
   +-------------------------------------------------------+ */
void pagedn(void)
{
   union REGS in, out;

   in.h.ah = 5;
   in.h.al = get_page() + 1;
   if (in.h.al < last_page + 1)
      int86(0x10, &in, &out);
}
/* +-------------------------------------------------------+
   + PAGEUP
   + Decrement active video page, but not below 0.
   + Calls get_page()
   +-------------------------------------------------------+ */
void pageup(void)
{
   union REGS in, out;
   int page;

   if ((page = get_page()) < 1)
      return;
   in.h.ah = 5;
   in.h.al = page - 1;
   int86(0x10, &in, &out);
}
```

C.2.3   To Page or Not to Page

When the user is presented with separate screens or "pages," those screens or "pages" may or may not correspond to separate pages of the computer's memory. For example, as a programmer, you might use only one of the computer's memory pages and yet create several different screens for the user. You may even foster the notion of "pages" by putting a page designation at the top or bottom of each screen and by having the user press the ⌨ and ⌨ keys to move from "page" to "page."

If the user has several screens of data to fill in or there are several menu and data screens, restricting the program to one active page slows the program operation down somewhat. If the user switches back and forth from one data screen to another, the ability to preserve each screen in memory once drawn avoids having to completely redraw a screen for each time after the first. On the other hand, once you learn to use direct memory access, you will see that with today's computer speeds, the drawing appears virtually instantaneous.

     A multipage program can appear more seamless to the user, even the first time a screen is drawn. When the user presses a key to signal moving from screen to screen, the program keeps the current screen visible until the new screen is completely drawn and only then makes the new screen visible to the user by moving to the memory page that contains the new screen. This gives the screen switch a more seamless appearance than the flashing or popping appearance of moving to a blank screen and seeing the blank screen instantaneously written on. The multipage approach adds somewhat to the program's complexity.

     If you are working in a graphics mode, you can rapidly cycle through images drawn on different video pages to create the illusion of motion.

C.3   CURSOR SIZE AND PLACEMENT

Function 01h (decimal 1) sets the text mode cursor size. In text modes, the computer displays a blinking cursor. The default cursor appears as one or two blinking scan lines at the bottom of the character box.

For monochrome video modes, you can display a cursor that has up to 14 scan lines, numbered *from top to bottom*, 0 to 13. The default setting is a bottom cursor scan line of 12 and a top scan line of 11. For color video modes, you can display a cursor that has up to 8 scan lines, numbered from 0 at the top to 7 at the bottom. The default setting is a bottom cursor scan line of 7 and a top scan line of 6.

Cursor size in text mode is controlled by specifying a top scan line in the ch register and the bottom scan line in the cl register prior to invoking the interrupt. The following program allows the user to interactively set the size of the cursor:

 Listing **C.1 cur_size.c**

```
/* our_size.c */

/* interactively set cursor size */

#include <stdio.h>
#include <dos.h> /* regs, int86 */

#define MONO 7

void set_curs_size(int topline);

int bottom;

int main(void)
{
    int top, input;
    union REGS in, out;

    /* first determine whether we have mono or color mode */
    in.h.ah = 0xF; /* get-video-mode routine */
    int86(0x10, &in, &out);
```

```
    /* set bottom scan line accordingly */
    bottom = (out.h.al == MONO) ? 13 : 7;

    /* set top scan line interactively */
    while(1)
    {
        puts("\n\nPress any letter to quit or\n");
        printf("Type a number from 0 (smallest) to %d (largest)"
            " for cursor size:  ", bottom);

        if (!scanf("%d", &input))
            break;

        top = bottom - input;

        /* adjust erroneous user input > maximum */
        if (top < 0)
            top = 0;

        set_curs_size(top);
    }

}

void set_curs_size(int topline)
{
    union REGS in, out;

    in.h.ah = 1; /* cursor-size routine */
    in.h.cl = bottom; /* bottom scan line */
    in.h.ch = topline;
    int86(0x10, &in, &out);
}
```

The program first determines the video mode, so that we can specify a maximum number of scan lines for the user. The user is then prompted to type in a number from 0 to that largest number. The program positions whatever size cursor the user wants at the bottom of the character display by setting the bottom scan line to the maximum possible value and adjusting the top scan line according to how big a cursor the user specifies.

The lower a number we assign to the top scan line, the bigger the cursor. However, since a smaller number for a smaller cursor would seem to make more sense to the user, we invert the relationship:

```
top = bottom - input;
```

The cursor change survives program termination.

C.3.1   Application: Toggling Cursor Size with the  Key

Many programs distinguish between an insert and a noninsert mode. In the insert mode, any letter typed in at the keyboard writes over the character at the cursor; in noninsert mode, the character at the cursor is pushed to the right of the cursor to make room for the new character typed in. The ⌷ key is generally used as a toggle for this purpose. Many programs that use the two modes change the cursor size to indicate which mode is currently selected. A large cursor generally indicates the insert mode is on and a small one indicates the insert mode is off. The following program toggles the cursor from big to small on the pressing of ⌷. The program terminates when ⎋ is pressed.

Listing **C.2 curs_tog.c**

```
/* ours_tog.c */

/* toggle cursor size on press of ins key */

#include <stdio.h>
```

```c
#include <conio.h> /* getch, kbhit */
#include <dos.h>

#define INS 82
#define ESC 27
#define MONO 7
int main(void)
{
    int top, bottom;
    char ch;
    union REGS in, out;

    in.h.ah = 0xF; /* get-video mode routine */
    int86(0x10, &in, &out);


    in.h.ah = 1; /* cursor-size routine */

    /* bottom scan line */
    in.h.cl = bottom = (out.h.al == MONO) ? 13: 7;

    top = bottom - 1; /* start small */

    while(1) /* loop until ESC key pressed */
    {
        if(kbhit()) /* returns 0 until a key is pressed */
        {
            if (!(ch = getch())) /* check for extended keys */
            {
                if (getch() == INS)
                {
                    /* if big, make small */
                    if (!top)
                        top = bottom - 1;

                    /* otherwise, make big */
                    else top = 0;

                    /* change cursor size */
                    in.h.ch = top;
                    int86(0x10, &in, &out);
                }
            }

            /* terminate program if ESC pressed */
            else if (ch == ESC)
                break;
        }
    } /* end of while loop */
}
```

The kbhit() function checks to see whether a key has been pressed. If no key has been pressed, kbhit() returns 0; otherwise, it returns a positive integer. If a key has been pressed, we first check to see whether it is an extended key. If so, we check for the key: if that key has been pressed, we toggle the value of the top scan line from 0 to its maximum value or vice versa and then call int86(). If the character pressed is not an extended key, we check for the [Esc] key; if we find that key has been pressed, we terminate the program.

Although each page of video memory has its own cursor, you cannot set a different cursor size for the various display pages. If you want the cursor to have a different size on different video pages of your program, you need to keep track of the active page the cursor is on and adjust the cursor size programmatically.

C.3.2   Turning Off the Cursor

In some cases, you will want to turn off the cursor altogether. For instance, say your program presents the menu illustrated in Figure C.1.

Figure C.1   *Sample User Menu Screen*

```
Create New Report

Edit Report

See List of Reports

Print a Report

Exit
```

You would most likely want to highlight the current choice by making the background or foreground color, or both, different from the other choices. Since you are asking the user to press the ⌈Enter⌋ key rather than type in input, a blinking cursor on the screen would look unprofessional.

Turning the cursor off altogether presents somewhat of a problem because of differences in video adapters. In some adapters, setting the ch register to a greater value than the cl register value will disable the cursor. In others, however, it just makes the cursor wrap around the inside of the character box, creating a two-piece cursor.

    Probably the most widely used method is to hide the cursor rather than disable it. You can simply move the cursor to row 25, column 0 (see the next section for how to move the cursor). There is a 96-byte buffer in video memory between pages (representing 48 characters) that is never displayed on screen. Placing the cursor in row 25, column 0 places the cursor in this buffer.

You could even place the cursor at row 26 or greater. That would move the cursor past the buffer to the next video page. That cursor would not show up on the following page if you were to make that page active; you would only see that page's cursor. However, if you started printing characters at that cursor location, they would show up on the following page at the now hidden cursor position, and you would see them if you made that page active.

C.3.3   Setting the Cursor Position

You can move the cursor to a designated row, column, and page. The cursor position is set by routine 02h (decimal 2):

```c
/* +-------------------------------------------------------+
   + SET_CURS
   + Move the cursor for a video page to designated
   +    row, column
   + Argument: row/col/page: designated row, column and
   +    video page for cursor
   +-------------------------------------------------------+ */
void set_curs(int row, int col, int page)
{
    union REGS in, out;

    in.h.ah = 2;
    in.h.bh = page;
    in.h.dh = row;
    in.h.dl = col;
    int86(0x10, &in, &out);
}
```

In addition to setting the ah register to 2, we put the desired row in the dh register, the desired column in dl, and the page in bh. As usual with computer numbering, numbering starts with 0, so row choices are 0–24, columns 0–79, and pages 0–7 (for VGA; CGA has pages 0–3, and a monochrome MDA video adapter has only page 0). When we first start executing a program, by default we are placed in page 0.

C.3.4   Reading the Cursor Position

On first setting the video mode, the cursor starts at row 0, column 0 on *each* page in video memory. That is so whether you clear the screen or not. The active page—the page of video memory made visible to the user—starts at page 0. The computer keeps track of where the cursor is on each of the pages in memory. Say, for example, at the very beginning of the program, you move the cursor on the initial active page, page 0, down to row 10, column 5, and then you change the active page to page 1. If you later reset the active page to page 0, the cursor on that page will appear at row 10, column 5, not at row 0, column 0.

Function 03h (decimal 3) allows us to determine the cursor's position on any page. After setting the ah register to 3 and the bh register to the desired page, we invoke int86(). The cursor's row and column are returned in the dh and dl registers. (Also, the starting and ending scan lines are returned in ch and cl.)

```
/* +----------------------------------------------------+
   + GET_CURS
   + Determine cursor position on specified video page.
   + Arguments:
   + - prow/pcol:   pointers to cursor row and column
   + - page:        video page for cursor
   +----------------------------------------------------+ */
void get_curs(int *prow, int *pcol, int page)
{
   union REGS in, out;

   in.h.ah = 3;
   in.h.bh = page;
   int86(0x10, &in, &out);
   *prow = out.h.dh; /* row # */
   *pcol = out.h.dl; /* col # */
}
```

Since we can return only a single value and we require two, we pass pointers to the row and column and assign values with the decrement operator. Alternatively, we could have returned out.x.dx, the 16-bit view of this register, and taken a separate look at its two 8-bit components in the calling function by bit manipulation or by incrementing a type-cast char pointer and dereferencing at each of the two bytes. For example:

```
row_col = get_curs(page);
col = (row_col << 8) >> 8; /* right byte */
row = row_col >> 8; /* left byte */
```

We do not believe this alternative method is preferable, but as usual, we point it out so that you can use this understanding in another instance where is it helpful.

Instead of passing the page number as the third argument in the set_curs() function above, we could have restricted the program to a single memory page by hard-wiring in.h.bh to 0 and eliminating the page argument:

```
void set_curs(int row, int col)
{
   union REGS in, out;

   in.h.ah = 2;
   in.h.dh = row;
   in.h.dl = col;
   in.h.bh = 0; /* page hard-wired to 0 */
   int86(0x10, &in, &out);
}

void get_curs(int *prow, int *pcol)
{
   union REGS in, out;

   in.h.ah = 3;
   in.h.bh = 0; /* page, hard-wired to 0 */
   int86(0x10, &in, &out);
   *prow = out.h.dh; /* row # */
   *pcol = out.h.dl; /* col # */
}
```

C.4   WRITING A CHARACTER IN A DESIGNATED COLOR

In color text mode (mode 3), the screen consists of 25 rows and 80 columns. Each character is represented by two bytes, the first byte for the character itself and the second byte for its foreground color, background color, and what's called the character's *attributes*—whether it blinks or not, whether the foreground color is light or dark, and, for the monochrome mode, whether the character is bold, underlined, or in reverse video.

We write a specified character in a specified color attribute to the screen at the current cursor position of a designated page with function 09h (decimal 9). In addition to setting the ah register to 9, we set the al register to the character, the bh register to the selected page, the bl register to the color attribute, and the cx register to how many of this same character and same color attribute we want to write starting at the cursor. Generally, you will want to write only one of a particular character to the screen, so we've hard-coded the function that way. If you want to leave open the possibility of a multicharacter write, make the number a third argument to the function:

```
/* +------------------------------------------------------+
   + PRINT_CHAR
   + Print character at cursor on current video page
   + and move right.
   + Arguments:
   + - ch:      character to be printed
   + - color:   color for character
   + This version calls get_page(), get_curs() and set_curs()
   +------------------------------------------------------+ */
void print_char(unsigned char ch, unsigned char color)
{
    union REGS in, out;
    int row, col, page;

    in.h.ah = 9;
    in.x.cx = 1; /* print just 1 of designated character */
    in.h.al = ch;
    in.h.bl = color;
    page = in.h.bh = get_page();
    int86(0x10, &in, &out); /* print character */
    /* move cursor one to the right */
    get_curs(&row, &col, page);
    set_curs(row, col + 1, page);
}
```

The interrupt call with the character-printing routine does *not* move the cursor. You have to program that yourself—hence the calls to get_curs( ) and set_curs( ). Alternatively, we can omit the cursor-moving component of print_char() and have that accomplished elsewhere in our code. In some situations, we will not even wish to move the cursor after printing a character.

In some cases, you will want to write a number of the same character to the screen. For example, to fill the entire screen with"▓", after first moving the cursor to row 0, column 0, you can place set the cx register to 2000 and the al register to 177 before the int86( ) call. Once the writing gets to the last column in any row, it jumps down to the next row to print the next character.

In fact, if you set the cx register to 2048 times 8, you would write this character to all 8 video pages in memory. (The interrupt ultimately writes to video memory; there is a buffer of 96 bytes between pages in video memory; hence 2048 instead of 2000.) Writing a character to all 8 pages in this way is so fast it would seem virtually instantaneous. By contrast, writing a character at a time in a for loop for even a part of a single page would be visibly slow on an older machine (486 or older).

 This multicharacter device will work for large areas only where you want to fill in an area extending across all columns. If you want to paint an rectangular area in a solid color (that is, with the space character) over fewer than all columns, use the scrolling feature.

C.5   SCROLLING A WINDOW

Function 06h (decimal 6) is the window-scrolling function. You can use function 06h to scroll up one or more rows—either the entire 80-column screen or a window less than 80 columns wide. When we speak of "scrolling up" a row, we mean that the top row of our window disappears, every other row moves up one, and the vacated row is rewritten in blank with space characters (ASCII 32).

The color for the blank row or rows is placed into the bh register. Normally, the color you put there will be the same as whatever color you already have in your window, but this need not be so. Whatever color you choose, note that the foreground color when you print spaces is irrelevant. We cover colors in the next section.

The number of rows you want to scroll up is placed into the al register. However, if you put 0 there or a number at least equal to the number of rows in the window, all rows in the window will be scrolled up, making all rows on the screen vanish and be replaced by blank lines. Incidentally, despite a suggestion to the contrary in one text, we found no difference in time whatever between a scroll-up call with the al register (where the number of lines to be scrolled up is specified) being set to 25 as opposed to 0.

The top row, left column, bottom row, and right column of the top-left and bottom-right corners of the window go in the ch, cl, dh, and dl registers, respectively. You can make the "window" equal to the entire screen by putting 0, 0, 24, and 79 in those registers. You can use such a full-screen window in combination with a 0 or a row number of at least 25 to effectively create a screen-clearing function:

```
/* +----------------------------------------------------+
   + CLEAR_SCREEN
   + Clear screen with window scrolling function
   + Argument: color: color screen is to be painted when cleared
   +----------------------------------------------------+ */
void clear_screen(unsigned char color)
{
   union REGS in, out;

   in.h.ah = 6; /* scroll-up function */
   in.h.al = 25; /* # of rows to scroll up */
   in.h.bh = color;
   in.x.cx = 0; /* top-left row and column of window in ch and cl */
   in.h.dh = 24; /* bottom row */
   in.h.dl = 79; /* right-most column */
   int86(0x10, &in, &out);
}
```

A simpler and faster way to clear the screen is to call the video mode setting function. However, this leaves you with a black screen rather than a color screen.

Setting the mode clears all video memory pages, if that is of interest to you in a particular application. But you can do the same thing in color with window scrolling. Like the cursor setting and character-printing functions, the scrolling function recognizes rows below the current video page. If you are on page 0 and set the dh register to 205 in the clear_screen() function example above, you will paint all eight video pages in whatever color is passed as an argument. (The extra five rows are to cover the 96-byte buffers between video memory pages.) Likewise, if you are on page 1 and set dh to 51, you will paint pages 1 and 2 with the designated color, effectively erasing anything else on those pages.

The window-scrolling function works from the current active video page down. If you want to scroll on an earlier page, you must change the active page first.

You can scroll a window down as well as up. The bottom rows of the window are pushed into oblivion; each row of the window moves down; and the vacated top rows are written in blank with space characters—just the opposite of the scroll-up function. We use function 07h (decimal 7) to scroll down. Apart from placing 7 instead of 6 in the ah register, there is no difference between a scroll-up call and a scroll-down call.

C.6 COLOR-ATTRIBUTE BYTE

Of the 8 bits that make up the color-attribute byte, bits 0–2 are used for foreground color. Bit 3 is for foreground intensity: if it is on, the foreground color will be light; if not, it will be dark. The lighter colors tend to be on the garish electric side, rather than soft pastels. Figure C.2 shows what the foreground part of the attribute byte looks like.

Tables C.2A and C.2B show the available foreground colors in mode 3 using all possible bit patterns.

As you can see, brown is made by turning on red and green, purple by turning on red and blue, and cyan (as in cyanide, computer talk for blue-green) by turning on green and blue. Note also that "light brown" is really yellow and "light gray" is really white.

Bits 4–6 are used to represent background color. The same red-green-blue order is observed for the background as for the foreground. The key difference is that there is no easily accessible intensity bit for the background; the background colors are only the dark versions of the colors. This is a limiting factor in creating attractive screens. There is no simple way to create a yellow, white, or light red, light green, light blue, or light purple background.

Figure C.2   *Foreground and Intensity Bits*

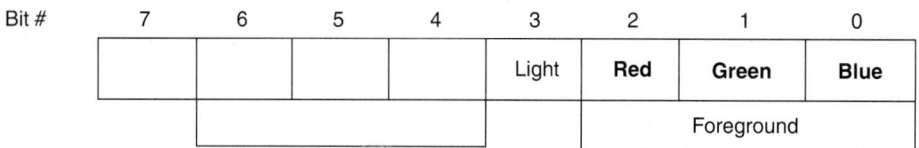

Table C.2A   *Dark Foreground Colors*

I	R	G	B	Color
0	0	0	0	black
0	0	0	1	blue
0	0	1	0	green
0	0	1	1	cyan
0	1	0	0	red
0	1	0	1	purple
0	1	1	0	brown
0	1	1	1	gray

Table C.2B   *Light Foreground Colors*

I	R	G	B	Color
1	0	0	0	light black
1	0	0	1	light blue
1	0	1	0	light green
1	0	1	1	light cyan
1	1	0	0	light red
1	1	0	1	light purple
1	1	1	0	yellow
1	1	1	1	white

Bit 7 is the blink bit: if it is on, the character will flash on and off; if it is off, the character appears without flashing. The geniuses who thought this color scheme up chose to allocate that last precious bit to the maddening attribute of flashing characters, with no easy way to tell the computer to use that bit for background intensity instead. See Section C.6.1 for a discussion of disenabling the blink attribute and substituting intense background.

Figure C.3 shows what the entire color-attribute byte looks like.

With the exception of the screen border color, which we'll discuss below, colors must be expressed as a foreground-background combination. Some pleasing combinations are shown below by way of a header file. The header file also includes all colors individually. All colors are listed as hexadecimal values:

```
c_combo.h

/* alphabetical color combination list - by background color */

#define   GY_BK    0x7      /* gray on black    000  0  111 */
```

Figure C.3 *Color, Intensity, and Blink Bits*

Bit #	7	6	5	4	3	2	1	0
	Blink	**Red**	**Green**	**Blue**	Light	**Red**	**Green**	**Blue**
		Background				Foreground		

```
#define   WH_BK    0xF    /* white on black   000 1 111 */
#define   Y_BK     0xE    /* yellow on black  000 1 110 */

#define   BK_BL    0x10   /* black on blue    001 0 000 */
#define   GY_BL    0x17   /* gray on blue     001 0 111 */
#define   WH_BL    0x1F   /* white on blue    001 1 111 */
#define   Y_BL     0x1E   /* yellow on blue   001 1 110 */

#define   WH_BR    0x6F   /* white on brown   110 1 111 */
#define   Y_BR     0x6E   /* yellow on brown  110 1 110 */

#define   BK_CY    0x30   /* black on cyan    011 0 000 */
#define   BL_CY    0x31   /* blue on cyan     011 0 001 */
#define   R_CY     0x34   /* red on cyan      011 0 100 */
#define   WH_CY    0x3F   /* white on cyan    011 1 111 */

#define   BK_GN    0x20   /* black on green   010 0 000 */
#define   R_GN     0x24   /* red on green     010 0 100 */
#define   WH_GN    0x2F   /* white on green   010 1 111 */
#define   Y_GN     0x2E   /* yellow on green  010 1 110 */

#define   BK_GY    0x70   /* black on gray    111 0 000 */
#define   BL_GY    0x71   /* blue on gray     111 0 001 */
#define   LBK_GY   0x78   /* lt blk on gray   111 1 000 */
#define   R_GY     0x74   /* red on gray      111 0 100 */
#define   WH_GY    0x7F   /* white on gray    111 1 111 */

#define   BK_PU    0x50   /* black on purple  101 0 000 */
#define   WH_PU    0x5F   /* white on purple  101 1 111 */

#define   BK_R     0x40   /* black on red     100 0 000 */
#define   GY_R     0x47   /* gray on red      100 0 111 */
#define   WH_R     0x4F   /* white on red     100 1 111 */
#define   Y_R      0x4E   /* yellow on red    100 1 110 */

/* single colors alphabetically */

#define   BK    0    /* black  */
#define   BL    1    /* blue   */
#define   BR    6    /* brown  */
#define   CY    3    /* cyan   */
#define   GN    2    /* green  */
#define   GY    7    /* gray   */
#define   PU    5    /* purple */
#define   R     4    /* red    */
```

Table C.3 lists the decimal values of all possible color combinations.

Rather than bothering to calculate the decimal, octal, or hexadecimal value of each color combination, however, a simpler approach is to specify separate values for foreground and background colors, shift the background color 4 bits to the left, and add the shifted value to the foreground color. This macro does just that:

```
#define C(fore, back) ((back << 4) + fore)
```

Table C.3   *Decimal Values for Foreground/Background Combinations*

background ⊟ ⊡ foreground	Black (0)	Blue (1)	Green (2)	Cyan (3)	Red (4)	Mgnta (5)	Brown (6)	Gray (7)
Black (0)	0	16	32	48	64	80	96	112
Blue (1)	1	17	33	49	65	81	97	113
Green (2)	2	18	34	50	66	82	98	114
Cyan (3)	3	19	35	51	67	83	99	115
Red (4)	4	20	36	52	68	84	100	116
Magenta (5)	5	21	37	53	69	85	101	117
Brown (6)	6	22	38	54	70	86	102	118
Gray (7)	7	23	39	55	71	87	103	119
Light Black (8)	8	24	40	56	72	88	104	120
Light Blue (9)	9	25	41	57	73	89	105	121
Light Green (10)	10	26	42	58	74	90	106	122
Light Cyan (11)	11	27	43	59	75	91	107	123
Light Red (12)	12	28	44	60	76	92	108	124
Lt Magenta (13)	13	29	45	61	77	93	109	125
Yellow (14)	14	30	46	62	78	94	110	126
White (15)	15	31	47	63	79	95	111	127

Then you can use the shorter header file, `colors.h`:

```
/* colors.h */

#define   BK   0   /* black */
#define   BL   1   /* blue */
#define   BR   6   /* brown */
#define   CY   3   /* cyan */
#define   GN   2   /* green */
#define   GY   7   /* gray */
#define   PU   5   /* purple */
#define   R    4   /* red */
```

For example, to express white letters on a red background:

```
C(WH,R)
```

Still another approach to simple color creation would be to use bit fields. For instance, to print an A in bright red on gray at the cursor:

```
#include "colors.h"

struct color_bits {
    unsigned fore: 3, intensity: 1, bkgd: 3, blink: 1; };

union color
{
    unsigned color_byte;
```

```
        struct color_bits color_bits;
    } color;
    color_bits.fore = R;
    color_bits.intensity = 1;
    color_bits.bkgd = GY;
    print_char('A', color.color_byte); /* code above */
```

Or, if you know what combination of red, green, and blue make the colors you want:

```
struct color_bits
{ unsigned red_fore: 1, green_fore: 1, blue_fore: 1, intensity: 1,
    red_bkgd: 1, green_bkgd: 1, blue_bkdg: 1, blink: 1; } color;
```

C.6.1 Intense Color Background

To use bit 7 of the attribute byte for high-intensity background color rather than for blinking, you employ subservice 3 of service 10h (decimal 16) of the video services interrupt. If you set the bl register to 0 before making the int86() call, turning on bit 7 of the attribute byte will produce a bright background color in characters written to the screen. If you set the bl register to 1 before making another subservice 3 interrupt call, writing characters to the screen with bit 7 turned on will again cause the character to blink. Blinking is the default mode.

Characters already written to the screen that have bit 7 of their attribute bytes turned on will switch from blinking to intense background or vice versa, as you toggle the bl register with this subservice.

The following program, bright.c, illustrates writing to the screen with intense background characters. Some of the functions are discussed later.

 Listing **C.3 bright.c**

```
/* bright.c */

/* enable bright background color by disenabling blink bit */

#include <stdio.h>
#include <dos.h> /* int86, REGS union */
#include <conio.h> /* getch */

#define LT_R_WH 0xFC/* bright red on white */
#define LT_R 0xC0 /* bright red */
#define BLINKING 1
#define BRIGHT 0

#include <colors.h>

void blink_bright(char mode), blink_off(void), getcurs(char *prow, char *pcol);
int get_mode(void);
void paint_block(unsigned char color, char trow, char lcol, char height, char width);
void print_char(unsigned char ch, unsigned char color);
void print_string(char *string, unsigned char color);
void setcurs(char row, char col);

int main(void)
{
    if (get_mode() == 3)
    {
        /* turn blink off */
        blink_bright(BRIGHT);

        /* paint entire screen in bright red */
        paint_block(LT_R, 0, 0, 25, 80);

        /* paint small centered box in white */
        paint_block(LT_R_WH, 8, 25, 10, 30);
```

```
      setcurs(13, 30);
      print_string("bright red on white", LT_R_WH);

      /* pause for key press */
      if (!getch())
        getch();

      /* observe effect of what's already on screen when blink is back on */
      blink_bright(BLINKING);
   }

   else
   {
      blink_off();

      /* reverse video bold */
      print_string("reverse video bold", 0xF0);
   }
}

/* +----------------------------------------------------------------+
   +  BLINK_BRIGHT
   +  Turn blink off & substitute bright background or vice-versa
   +  Argument: mode: BLINK (1) to turn blink; BRIGHT (0) to use bit 7
   +              for bright background instead
   +----------------------------------------------------------------+ */
void blink_bright(char mode)
{
   union REGS in, out;

   in.h.ah = 16; /* blink routine */
   in.h.al = 3; /* background intensity/blink subroutine */
   in.h.bl = mode; /* 0 turns blink off & light bkgd on; 1 is opposite */
   int86(0x10, &in, &out);
}
/* +----------------------------------------------------------------+
   +  BLINK_OFF
   +  Turn blink off & substitute reverse video bold. The enable-blink
   +  bit is bit 5 of the register at port 0x38B, so we AND value at
   +  0040h:0065h with value having all 1's except in bit 5;
   +  (0x3B8 is monochrome monitor's mode display register address)
   +----------------------------------------------------------------+ */
void blink_off(void)
{
   int far *attrib_ptr = (int far *)0x00400065;
   outportb(0x3B8, *attrib_ptr & 0xDF); /* Microsoft: use outp() */
}

/* +----------------------------------------------------------------+
   +  GETCURS
   +  Determine the row and column of the cursor's current position.
   +  There is a cursor position on each video page; this function
   +  hard-wires the one read to page zero.
   +  Arguments: prow/pcol: pointers to variables housing the cursor
   +  row & col
   +----------------------------------------------------------------+
*/
void getcurs(char *prow, char *pcol)
{
```

```
   union REGS in, out;

   in.h.ah = 3;
   in.h.bh = 0; /* video page, hard-wired at zero */
   int86(0x10, &in, &out);
   *prow = out.h.dh; /* row # */
   *pcol = out.h.dl; /* col # */
}
/*
   +----------------------------------------------------------------+
   +  GET_MODE: determine video mode
   +----------------------------------------------------------------+ */
int get_mode(void)
{
   union REGS in, out;

   in.h.ah = 15;
   int86(0x10, &in, &out);
   return out.h.al;
}

int get_page(void)
{
   union REGS in, out;

   in.h.ah = 15;
   int86(0x10, &in, &out);
   return out.h.bh;
}

/* +----------------------------------------------------------------+
   +  PAINT_BLOCK
   +  Paint a rectangular block in a color with window scrolling.
   +  interrupt
   +  Arguments:
   +  - color        : color to paint block (only background color matters)
   +  - trow/lcol    : top left box corner
   +  - height/width: box height and width
   +----------------------------------------------------------------+
*/
void paint_block(unsigned char color, char trow, char lcol, char height, char width)
{
   union REGS in, out;

   in.h.ah = 6; /* window-scrolling function */
   in.h.al = height;
   in.h.bh = color;
   in.h.ch = trow;
   in.h.cl = lcol;
   in.h.dh = trow + height - 1;
   in.h.dl = lcol + width - 1;
   int86(0x10, &in, &out);
}

/* +----------------------------------------------------------------+
   +  PRINT_CHAR
   +  Puts a character in color on the screen at the cursor and
      advances the cursor. Called by print_string()
   +  Arguments:
```

```
+  - ch:    character to be written
+  - color: color it is to be written in
+----------------------------------------------------------+ */
void print_char(unsigned char ch, unsigned char color)
{
   char row, col;

   union REGS in, out;

   in.h.bh = 0; /* video page number, hard-wired at 0 */
   in.h.ah = 9;
   in.x.cx = 1; /* print just 1 of the designated character */
   in.h.al = ch;
   in.h.bl = color;
   int86(0x10, &in, &out);

   /* the interrupt doesn't advance the cursor by itself; we have to do that. */
   getcurs(&row, &col);
   setcurs(row, col + 1);
}

/* +----------------------------------------------------------+
   +  PRINT_STRING
   +  Print a string to the screen at the cursor by calling print_char
   +  Arguments:
   +  - string:    string to be written
   +  - color :    color it is to be written in
   +----------------------------------------------------------+ */
void print_string(char *string, unsigned char color)
{
   while(*string)
      print_char(*string++, color);
}

/* +----------------------------------------------------------+
   +  SETCURS
   +  Set the cursor at the row and col passed as arguments.
      Assumes the cursor is for page 0 of video memory
   +  Argument: row/col: where cursor is to be placed
   +----------------------------------------------------------+
*/
void setcurs(char row, char col)
{
   union REGS in, out;

   in.h.ah = 2;
   in.h.dh = row;
   in.h.dl = col;
   in.h.bh = 0; /* video page number hard-wired at 0 */
   int86(0x10, &in, &out);
}
```

C.6.2   Monochrome Attributes

Table C.4 lists our range of choices for the attribute byte in mode 7

To achieve high-intensity reverse video in monochrome, we have to disable the blink attribute (bit 5 of the 8-bit register mapped at I/O port 0x3B8). We do this by modifying the value sent to the video adapter's mode display register. You must read the value stored by the BIOS at location 0040h:0065h (the register's value is stored at this

Table C.4 *Monochrome Attribute Byte Values*

Attribute	Hex Value	Decimal Value
normal	0x7	7
high intensity	0xF	15
reverse video	0x70	112
high intensity reverse video	0xF0	240
underlined	0x1	1
high intensity underlined	0x9	9

location), AND that value with a value having all 1s except in bit 5 (0xDF, decimal 223) to turn off the blink bit, and send the resulting value to port 0x3B8 (0x3D8 for disabling the blink bit and turning on intense background for the CGA monitor):

```
int far *attrib_ptr = (int far *)0x00400065; outportb(0x3B8, *attrib_ptr & 0xDF);
    /* Microsoft: use outp() */
```

C.7   SETTING THE SCREEN BORDER TO A COLOR

The border is a 1-row by 1-column strip around the four edges of the 25 × 80 area in which we are able to place characters. We cannot access the border to write characters. We can set the border color with function 0Ch (decimal 11). In addition, the ah register is set to 11, bh is set to 0, and bl is set to the desired color:

```
/* +----------------------------------------------------+
   + SET_BORDER
   + Set the border around the screen to a designated color.
   + Argument: color: color (from 0 to 15) border is to be set to
   +----------------------------------------------------+ */
void set_border(unsigned char color)
{
    union REGS in, out;

    in.h.ah = 0xB; /* set color palette service */
    in.h.bh = 0; /* set border color subservice */
    in.h.bl = color;
    int86(0x10, &in, &out);
}
```

We set the border with a single color only, not a color combination. The border color stays in effect until we call set_border() again. It stays in effect even as we flip from page to page. Clearing the screen does not alter the border color.

If the border is left black, its default starting value, the user cannot distinguish the border from the black screen edge, nor is the size difference occasioned by the loss of two rows and columns really noticeable. It is probably more common for a program to leave the border black than it is to use it for color.

 If the border color is set to something other than black, it may look a little odd unless the background color of the area immediately adjacent to the border is the same color, but try it yourself in colorrun.c below with a different color and see what your opinion is.

At least on our monitor, the following border colors did not match what was supposedly the same color painted over the entire screen with the char_fill() function described later in this appendix: light blue (9), light green (11), light red (12), light purple (13), brown (6), yellow (14), white (15). You can test yours with Listing C.5, brdrtest.c.

C.8   A TEST-DRIVE SCREEN-BUILDING PROGRAM: `colorrun.c`

Initially, we will put characters on the screen just by typing them in wherever we want and in whatever colors. This we do with `colorrun.c`. Later in the appendix, we'll see how to insert characters and strings from our source code for preprogrammed output to the screen, and how to read characters and strings placed at various locations on the screen by the user.

 **Listing**   C.4 `colorrun.c`

```c
/* colorrun.c */
/* - Cycle through all 256 color combos with each successive keystroke, or lets
   user fix color.
   - Lets user page up or down.
   - Allows user to repeat same keystroke with ALT-R and to keep color the same or
   cycling with INS as the toggle.
   - Allows box drawing with CTRL characters.
   - Allows user to select own color & border color & clear screen.
   - Handles monochrome as well as color. */

#include <stdio.h>
#include <dos.h> /* int86 */
#include <conio.h> /* getch */

#include "keys.h"
#include "colors.h"

#define LASTCOL 79
#define BOTROW 24
#define C(foreground,background)\
color = foreground + (background << 4); break;
#define MONO 7
#define COLOR_TXT 3
#define NORMAL "\33[0;31;47m" /* red on gray */
#define BORDER "\33[0;30;47m" /* black on gray */

void backspace(unsigned char color), clear_screen(unsigned char color),
    curs_move(char direction), get_curs(int *prow, int *pcol, int page);
int get_mode(void), get_page(void), void help(void), pagedn(void), pageup(void),
    print_char(char ch, unsigned char color), set_border(unsigned char color),
    set_curs(int row, int col, int page), set_mode(int mode);

int last_page;

int main(void)
{
    unsigned char ch, oldch, color = 0;
    int ins = 0, skip = 0, original_mode, mode;

    /* preserve original mode for later restoration */
    original_mode = get_mode();

    /* set last page to 0 for monochrome, 7 for VGA (use 3 if CGA) */
    last_page = (original_mode == MONO) ? 0: 7;

    /* set mode to 3 unless originally monochrome */
    set_mode(mode = (original_mode == MONO) ? MONO : COLOR_TXT);
```

```
      /* display instructions */
    if (mode == COLOR_TXT)
       help();

set_curs(1, 0, 0);

while (1)
{
    if ((ch = getch()) == 0) /* extended keys? */
    {
       ch = getch();
       skip = 1;
       if (mode == COLOR_TXT)
          switch(ch) /* color only */
          {
             /* change colors with function, SHIFT-function, & CTRL-function keys */

             /* function keys */
                case F1: C(GY,BK) /* black background */
                case F2: C(WH,BK) case F3: C(Y,BK)
                case F4: C(BK,BL) /* blue background */
                case F5: C(GY,BL) case F6: C(WH,BL) case F7: C(Y,BL)
                case F8: C(WH,BR) /* brown background */
                case F9: C(Y,BR)

             /* SHIFT-Function keys */
                case SF1: C(BK,CY) /* cyan background */
                case SF2: C(BL,CY) case SF3: C(R,CY) case SF4: C(WH,CY)
                case SF5: C(BK,GN) /* green background */
                case SF6: C(R,GN) case SF7: C(WH,GN) case SF8: C(Y,GN)

             /* CTRL-Function keys */
                case CF1: C(BK,GY) /* gray background */
                case CF2: C(BL,GY) case CF3: C(R,GY) case CF4: C(WH,GY)
                case CF5: C(BK,PU) /* purple background */
                case CF6: C(WH,PU)
                case CF7: C(BK,R) /* red background */
                case CF8: C(GY,R) case CF9: C(WH,R) case CF10: C(Y,R)

             /* set border with ALT-function keys */
                case AF1: set_border(BK); break;
                case AF2: set_border(BL); break;
                case AF3: set_border(BR); break;
                case AF4: set_border(CY); break;
                case AF5: set_border(GN); break;
                case AF6: set_border(GY); break;
                case AF7: set_border(PU); break;
                case AF8: set_border(R); break;
                case ALTH: help(); break;
          }
          else
             switch(ch) /* mono only */
             {
                case F1: C(0x7,0) /* normal */
                case F2: C(0xF,0) /* high intensity */
                case F3: C(0x70,0) /* reverse video */
                case F4: C(0x1,0) /* underlined */
                case F5: C(0x9,0) /* high intensity underlined */
             }
```

```
        switch(ch) /* color or mono */
          {
            case DEL: clear_screen(color); break;
            case HM: set_curs(1, 0, get_page()); break;
            case UP: curs_move('u'); break;
            case DN: curs_move('d'); break;
            case LT: curs_move('l'); break;
            case RT: curs_move('r'); break;
            case PGUP: pageup(); break;
            case PGDN: pagedn(); break;

            case ALTR: /* repeat prior keystroke */

            /* repeat in same color or in new colors */
               print_char(oldch, ins ? color: color++);
               ch = oldch;
               break;

            /* toggle between 0 and 1 for printing chars in same or new colors */
            case INS: ins = (ins + 1) % 2;
          }
} /* end of extended keys */

else if (ch == '\b')
   backspace(ins ? color: --color);

else if (ch == CTRL_V) /* vertical box character */
{
   print_char('‖', color);
   curs_move('d');
   curs_move('l'); /* down 1, left 1 to facilitate move vertical chars */

}


/* horizontal box character */
else if (ch == CTRL_Z)
   print_char('=', color);

/* top left & right corner of box */
else if (ch == CTRL_T)  /* top . . . */
{
   if ((ch = getch()) == 'l' ¦¦ ch == 'L')
      print_char('╔', color); /* . . . left corner */
   if (ch == 'r' ¦¦ ch == 'R')
      print_char('╗', color); /* . . . right corner */
}

/* bottom left & right corner of box */
else if (ch == CTRL_B) /* bottom . . . . */
{
   if((ch = getch()) == 'l' ¦¦ ch == 'L')
      print_char('╚', color); /* . . . left corner */
   if (ch == 'r' ¦¦ ch == 'R')
      print_char('╝', color); /* . . . right corner */
}

/* print ordinary characters */
else if (ch >= ' ')  /* ignore other control characters */
   print_char(ch, ins ? color: color++);
```

```
      /* <===end program with escape key===> */
      else if (ch == ESC)
         break;
      if (!skip)
         oldch = ch; /* store char for repeating with . . */
      skip = 0;    /* . . ALTR unless it's an
         extended key like cursor up */
   } /* end while */

   /* return to preprogram mode */
   set_mode(original_mode);
}


/* +---------------------------------------------------------------+
   +  BACKSPACE: move cursor left, print space in designated color,
   +  cursor back left
   +  Argument: - color: color to print space in
   +---------------------------------------------------------------+ */
void backspace(unsigned char color)
{
   curs_move('l');
   print_char(' ', color);
   curs_move('l');
}


/* +---------------------------------------------------------------+
   +  CLEAR_SCREEN: use scroll-up routine to clear screen in color
   +  Argument: - color: color to paint entire screen in
   +---------------------------------------------------------------+ */
   void clear_screen(unsigned char color)
   {
   union REGS in, out;

   in.h.ah = 6;
   in.h.al = 0; /* normally # lines to scroll; 0 = blank window */
   in.h.bh = color;
   /* top left row (1: leave directions in row 0) */
   /* & col (0) in ch and cl */
   in.x.cx = 0x0100;
   in.h.dh = BOTROW - 1; /* leave directions at bottom row */
   in.h.dl = LASTCOL;
   int86(0x10, &in, &out);
}


/* +---------------------------------------------------------------+
   +  CURS_MOVE: move cursor up, down, right, or left
   +  Argument: - direction: letter to indicate direction of move
   +---------------------------------------------------------------+ */
void curs_move(char direction)
{
   int row, col, page = get_page();

   get_curs(&row, &col, page);
   switch(direction)
   {
      case ('r'):
         if (col < LASTCOL)
         set_curs(row, col + 1, page);
      else if (row != BOTROW - 1)
```

```
                    set_curs(row + 1, 0, page);
                else set_curs(1, 0, page);
                break;
                case ('l'):
                    if (col)
                    set_curs(row, col - 1, page);
                else if (row)
                    set_curs(row - 1, LASTCOL, page);
                break;
                case ('u'):
                    if (row > 1) /* don't write over directions in row 0 */
                    set_curs(row - 1, col, page);
                break;
                case ('d'):
                    if (row < BOTROW - 1) /* leave directions in row 24 */
                    set_curs(row + 1, col, page);
                break;
        }

/* +--------------------------------------------------------------------+
   +  GET_CURS: determine row and column of cursor on designated page
   +  Arguments:
   +  - prow, pcol: pointers to row and column of cursor
   +  - page:        video page of cursor
   +--------------------------------------------------------------------+ */
void get_curs(int *prow, int *pcol, int page)
{
    union REGS in, out;

    in.h.ah = 3;
    in.h.bh = page;
    int86(0x10, &in, &out);
    *prow = out.h.dh; /* row # */
    *pcol = out.h.dl; /* col # */
}

/* +--------------------------------------------------------------------+
   +  GET_MODE: determine video mode
   +--------------------------------------------------------------------+ */
int get_mode(void)
{
    union REGS in, out;

    in.h.ah = 15;
    int86(0x10, &in, &out);
    return out.h.al;
}

/* +--------------------------------------------------------------------+
   +  GET_PAGE: determine active video page
   +--------------------------------------------------------------------+ */
int get_page(void)
{
    union REGS in, out;

    in.h.ah = 15;
    int86(0x10, &in, &out);
    return out.h.bh;
}
```

```
/*Top Directions
PGUP/DN UP/DN/RT/LT HOME Move  F#/  SHFT-F#/CTRL-F# Bkgd Colors  ALT-F# Border

Bottom Directions
ALT-H Help ALT-R Repeat CTRL-V/Z/T/B  Lines DEL Clr INS Vary/Fix Color ESC Exit*/

/* +-----------------------------------------------------------------+
   + HELP: print directions at top and bottom of screen
   +-----------------------------------------------------------------+ */

void help(void)
{
   /* top directions */

   printf("\33[%d;%dH%s", 1, 1, NORMAL);
   printf( "  PGUP/DN UP/DN/RT/LT HOME        F#/SHFT-F#/CTRL-F#"
           "                ALT-F#");
   printf("%s", BORDER);
   printf("\33[%d;%dH Move", 1, 27);
   printf("\33[%d;%dH Bkgd Colors", 1, 52);
   printf("\33[%d;%dH Border  ", 1, 72);

   /* bottom directions */
   printf("\33[%d;%dH%s", 25, 1, NORMAL);
   printf( " ALT-H      ALT-R         CTRL-V/Z/T/B       DEL      INS"
           "                ESC");
   printf("%s", BORDER);
   printf("\33[%d;%dH Help", 25, 7);
   printf("\33[%d;%dH Repeat", 25, 18);
   printf("\33[%d;%dH Lines", 25, 38);
   printf("\33[%d;%dH Clr", 25, 48);
   printf("\33[%d;%dH Vary/Fix Color", 25, 56);
   printf("\33[7l"); /* line wrapping off */
   printf("\33[%d;%dH Exit ", 25, 75);
   printf("\33[7h"); /* line wrapping on */
}

/* +-----------------------------------------------------------------+
   + PAGEDN: move to next video page, but not past last page
   +-----------------------------------------------------------------+  */
void pagedn(void)
{
   union REGS in, out;

   in.h.ah = 5;
   in.h.al = get_page() + 1;
   if (in.h.al < last_page + 1)
   int86(0x10, &in, &out);
}

/* +-----------------------------------------------------------------+
   + PAGEUP: move to prior video page, but not past first page
   +-----------------------------------------------------------------+ */
void pageup(void)
{
   union REGS in, out;
   int page;

   if ((page = get_page()) < 1)
```

```
        return;
    in.h.ah = 5;
    in.h.al = page - 1;
    int86(0x10, &in, &out);
}


/* +----------------------------------------------------------------+
   +   PRINT_CHAR: print specified character in specified color at
   +   cursor and move cursor right
   +   Arguments:
   +   - ch:    character to be printed
   +   - color: color to print character in
   +----------------------------------------------------------------+ */
void print_char(char ch, unsigned char color)
{
    union REGS in, out;

    in.h.ah = 9;
    in.x.cx = 1; /* print just 1 of the designated character */
    in.h.al = ch;
    n.h.bl = color;
    in.h.bh = get_page();
    int86(0x10, &in, &out);
    curs_move('r');
}


/* +----------------------------------------------------------------+
   +   SET_BORDER: set border to designated color
   +   Argument: - color: color to set border to
   +----------------------------------------------------------------+ */
void set_border(unsigned char color)
{
    union REGS in, out;

    in.h.ah = 11;
    in.h.bh = 0;
    in.h.bl = color;
    int86(0x10, &in, &out);
}


/*
   +----------------------------------------------------------------+
   +   SET_CURS: set cursor on designated page to designated row & col
   +   Arguments:
   +   - row, col: row and column of cursor
   +   - page:    video page of cursor
   +----------------------------------------------------------------+ */
void set_curs(int row, int col, int page)
{
    union REGS in, out;

    in.h.ah = 2;
    in.h.dh = row;
    in.h.dl = col;
    in.h.bh = page;
    int86(0x10, &in, &out);
}


/* +----------------------------------------------------------------+
   +   SET_MODE: set video mode
```

```
     +  Argument: - mode: mode to set to
     +--------------------------------------------------------------+ */
void set_mode(int mode)
{
    union REGS in, out;

    in.h.ah = 0;
    in.h.al = mode;
    int86(0x10, &in, &out);
}
```

We read characters in from the keyboard with `getch()` and distinguish and deal with regular keys and extended keys in the same way as in Listing A.2, `concolor.c`. Characters are actually placed on the screen by our `print_char()` function, which uses service 09h. Note that we get to apply `print_char()` to write a character to the screen only if the first byte is not 0 (a special key has not been pressed), or if the `Enter` key, `BACKSPACE` key, or certain control keys have not been pressed.

C.8.1   Moving the Cursor after Character Printing

After we call `int86()` in the `print_char()` function itself, we advance the cursor by calling the `set_curs()` function. We didn't have to advance the cursor if we didn't want to; the computer would be happy writing new characters on top of the old ones. The function 09h video services interrupt call just puts a character on the screen at the designated row and column in the designated color; it does not move the cursor. We've done that by design by following the function 09h call with paired `get_curs()` and `set_curs()` calls. After `get_curs()` determines the cursor's current row and column, `set_curs()` increments the column by 1, unless we're in column 79, in which case we go to column 0 of the next row—unless we're already in the last row, in which case we just home the cursor.

There's nothing magic or mandatory about the cursor advance scheme adopted here. We could have just as easily provided that if the cursor is at column 79, it stays where it is after printing a character, or that it is placed in column 0 of the same row, instead of the row below. In fact, were we, in a different program, to have the user enter data into a defined field, we normally would set our function up so that if the cursor is at the right-most boundary of the field, the next key press would either just overprint what's already there without moving the cursor or would be ignored.

C.8.2   Color Selection

In terms of color, we have started by initializing the variable `color` to 0 (black on black). If we are printing a nonextended character, we increment the color by 1 with every such keystroke. In this manner, we will cycle through each of the possible 256 color background-foreground combinations every 256 keystrokes. To accommodate this range, we've used an `unsigned char` for `color`. Once we pass 256, there is an overflow and our odometer-like variable resets to 0.

If the key is pressed, we toggle the variable `ins` back and forth between 0 and 1. The use of %, the modulus operator, to toggle back and forth between two values or to move up or down within a defined range is common. In Listing A.4, `con_menu.c`, for instance, we use % in conjunction with ↑ or ↓, or `Tab` or `Shift` `Tab` user key presses to move from, say, choice 0 through choice 5 of a menu selection screen:

```
switch(ch)
{
    case UP: case SH_T: choice = choice - 1 + CHOICES) % CHOICES; break;
    case DN: case TAB: choice = (choice + 1) % CHOICES; break;
}
```

If `ins` is not 0, we do not change the color with succeeding keystrokes; otherwise we do:

```
print_char(ch, ins ? color: color++);
```

Note the use of ?, the conditional operator. We could have written the same statement in less compact form like this:

```
{
    if (ins)
        print_char(ch, color);
    else
        print_char(ch, color++);
}
```

And we could have written the first statement of that less compact code like this:

```
if (ins != 0)
   print_char(ch, color);
```

Rather than letting the computer choose the color combination, the program lets us select our own by pressing one of the function keys, either by itself or in conjunction with `Shift`, `Ctrl`, or `Alt`. Pressing `Alt` and a function key will set the border color.

C.8.3   Programming Special Functions

We have programmed the backspace key to cursor left, print a space, and cursor back left again. (Incidentally, when we print a space—ASCII decimal 32—it doesn't matter what the foreground color is: all we see is the background color.) You can see a more sophisticated backspace function in `cursor.c` on diskette.

Pressing `Alt` `R` allows the user to repeat the previous key without having to press that key again. This repeating device is useful for ASCII characters beyond 127 (see Appendix F). Those characters can be entered by holding the `Alt` key down, punching in the three digits of the ASCII value *on the number keypad* (`NUM LOCK` needn't be on), and then releasing the `Alt` key. Try running `colorrun` and using this repeat capability to draw a box on the screen, with the last two pages of Appendix F as a guide. We have repeated the same keyboard remapping we used in `concolor.c`, so if you want to draw the double-lined box character, you can use the appropriate `Ctrl` keys as a simpler alternative. We have also repeated the top and bottom key directions and help function.

C.8.4   A Sample Screen

Try the following. Put an 80-column strip of spaces in any color on gray both in row 0 and row 24 as follows: press `Home`; press `Insert` to stop the color from advancing; press `Shift` `F8` for black on gray; press the space bar once; hold down `Alt` `R`; do the same for the bottom row. Put a double-lined row (ASCII character 205) in white on blue (`F6`) or black on blue (`F4`) in rows 1 and 23. Fill the rest of the page in with ASCII character 176, 177, or 178 in the same color. Remember that the way we've set up `print_char()`, character writing wraps from row to row, so just keep holding down `Alt` `R`. Then sprinkle ASCII character 250 in white on blue here and there.

Now move somewhere in the middle of the page and try a message box. Change the color to white on red (press `Ctrl` `F6`). Paint a 25-column rectangular box with six rows of spaces. From the second column of the top row of the rectangle to the next-to-last column of the bottom row, draw in a double-lined box, using the appropriate `Ctrl` key combination. Type a message on the third row inside the rectangle (something like "Error: file not found"). Switch colors to red on gray (`Shift` `F10`), and type another message one row below that (for example, "Any key to continue"). Go to the row below the rectangle and move in two columns from the left-most column. Switch to anything on black (for example, press `F1`) and draw a row of spaces extending two columns beyond the right-most column of the rectangle. Move to the third row from the top of the rectangle, the column to the right of the rectangle. Draw two columns of spaces there and in the column to the right, extending each one down to the rows of spaces you've just drawn below the rectangle. Voilà: a message box with a drop shadow. To get even fancier, assuming you've put ASCII character 176, 177, or 178 around the rectangle, go back and see how it looks to replace the solid black drop shadow with 176, 177, or 178 in black on blue.

If you don't like what you've drawn on the screen, you can press either `Page Up` or `Page Down` to move to another page or you can "erase" what's on a page by pressing the `Delete` key, which we've programmed to call `clear_screen()`. Finally, to exit from the program, just press the `Esc` key, which breaks the otherwise infinite `while(1)` loop.

C.9   READING A CHARACTER AND COLOR

Function 08h (decimal 8) reads a character from the screen at the cursor position. In addition to setting the `ah` register to 8, you set the `bh` register to the page whose cursor position you want to read. After making these settings, an `int86()` video services interrupt call returns the ASCII value of the character in the `al` register and the color attribute of the character in the `ah` register. The following function returns the character at a designated row and column:

```
/* +----------------------------------------------------+
   + READ_CHAR
   + Read character at designated row and column
   + on video page 0.
   + Arguments: row/col: row and column to read at
   +----------------------------------------------------+ */
```

```
char read_char(int row, int col)
{
    union REGS in, out;

    set_curs(row, col);
    in.h.ah = 8;
    in.h.bh = 0; /* assumes a single-page approach */
    int86(0x10, &in, &out);
    return out.h.al;
}
```

As an alternative to passing the row and column of the character display box you want to read, you could precede the read_char() call with a set_curs() call and make read_char() a no-parameter function.

We can use the same video services interrupt function to read the color at the cursor position. The only thing we must change from read_char() is to return the value placed in the ah register after the int86() call rather than the value placed in the al register:

```
/* +------------------------------------------------------+
   + READ_COLOR
   + Reads and returns a color of character at a specified
   + row and col on page 0.
   + Interrupt called only works where cursor is, so we move
   + the cursor to the designated spot, and when we're done,
   + we move it back.
   + Argument: row/col: row and column to read at
   +------------------------------------------------------+ */
char read_color(char row, char col)
{
    char oldrow, oldcol;
    union REGS in, out;

    /* preserve current cursor location */
    getcurs(&oldrow, &oldcol);
    setcurs(row, col);
    in.h.ah = 8;
    in.h.bh = 0; /* hardwired to page 0 */
    int86(0x10, &in, &out);
    /* move cursor back to old location */
    setcurs(oldrow, oldcol);
    return out.h.ah;
}
```

We used a slightly different approach here. Since the interrupt works only where the cursor is, we preserved the current cursor location, moved the cursor to the designated spot, and when we were done reading, moved it back to its original location. This same approach could be incorporated into read_char().

You will have occasion to read a color far less often than a character.

C.10   WRITING A STRING

In the last appendix, we showed you a cumbersome, nonportable string-writing interrupt, function 13h (decimal 19) of the video services interrupt. The simplest method of writing strings in color at designated locations is to make use of the print_char() function we already have and create our own string-writing function. The following four functions allow us to print a character or string either at the cursor (place_char() and place_string()) or at a designated location (print_char() and print_string()). All of them assume we use video page 0 only:

```
/* +------------------------------------------------------+
   + PLACE_CHAR
   + Prints a character in color at a specified row and col
   + on video page 0. Does not advance cursor.
   + Arguments:
   + - ch:      character to be printed to screen
```

```
      + - color:     color of character
      + - row/col:   row and column to place character
      +------------------------------------------------------+ */
void place_char(char ch, unsigned char color,
   int row, int col)
{
   union REGS in, out;

   set_curs(row, col);
   in.h.ah = 9;
   in.h.al = ch;
   in.h.bh = 0; /* page #, hardwired to 0 */
   in.h.bl = color;
   in.x.cx = 1; /* # of characters to print */
   int86(0x10, &in, &out);=
}
/* +----------------------------------------------------+
   + PLACE_STRING
   + Prints a string in color at a specified row and col
   + by repeatedly calling place_char and incrementing
   + the column.
   +   Arguments:
   +   - ptr:    starting address of string
   +   - color:  color to print string
   +   - row/col: row and column (on video page 0) to
   +             start printing string
+------------------------------------------------------+ */
void place_string(char *ptr, unsigned char color, int row, int col)
{
   while(*ptr)
      place_char(*ptr++, color, row, col++);
}


/* +----------------------------------------------------+
   + PRINT_CHAR
   + Prints a character in color at cursor (on video page 0)
   + and advances cursor by calling get_curs and set_curs
   + Arguments:
   + - ch:      character to be printed
   + - color:   foreground/background color for character
   +
+------------------------------------------------------+ */
void print_char(char ch, unsigned char color)
{
   union REGS in, out;
   int row, col;

   in.h.ah = 9;
   in.h.al = ch;
   in.h.bh = 0; /* page # */
   in.h.bl = color;
   in.x.cx = 1; /* # of characters to print */
   int86(0x10, &in, &out);
   get_curs(&row, &col);
   set_curs(row, col + 1);
}
/* +----------------------------------------------------+
   + PRINT_STRING
   + Prints a string in color at cursor (on video page 0) by repeatedly calling
   + by repeatedly calling print_char
```

```
    + Arguments:
    + - ptr:     starting address of string to be printed
    + - color:   foreground/background color for string
    +--------------------------------------------------+ */
void print_string(char *ptr, unsigned char color)
{
   while(*ptr)
      print_char(*ptr++, color);
}
```

C.11   READING A STRING

In the previous section, we saw how you can use repeated calls to a character-printing function to print a string. We can use the same sort of approach to reading a string, repeatedly using the read-character function of the video services interrupt:

```
/* +--------------------------------------------------+
   + READ_STRING
   + Read string from screen at cursor on page 0 by reading
   + a character at a time to
   + a char pointer and adding NULL at the end.
   + Arguments:
   + - field_len:   number of characters to be read
   + - string:      starting address of where to store
   +                characters read
   +--------------------------------------------------+ */
void read_string(int field_len, char *string)
{
   union REGS in, out;
   int row, col;
   int i;

   get_curs(&row, &col);
   in.h.ah = 8; /* read-character function */
   in.h.bh = 0; /* page number */
   for (i = 0; i < field_len; i++)
   {
      int86(0x10, &in, &out);
      *(string + i) = out.h.al;
      set_curs(row, ++col);
   }
   *(string + field_len) = 0;  /* add null character at end of string */
}
```

Since there is no NULL character to tell us where to stop reading, we have to pass the number of characters we want read in as an argument. For the same reason, we have to tack on a NULL character to the string after we have concluded our reading task.

You will see in our more sophisticated programs later in this appendix that we will allow the user to make several entries on a page. We will limit each entry—which we can think of as a field in a record—to a designated length. The lengths of the various fields will be stored in an array. We will use the designated length to read the entire field in, trailing blank spaces and all. If we use a fixed-length record approach, we will store the terminating spaces. For variable-length records, we will create a function that, after reading the entire field in, truncates the field just before the first space at the end of the entry.

We could have inserted a read_char() call in our read_string() function instead of incorporating the int86() character-reading call in read_string().

```
void read_string(int field_len, char *string)
{
   int row, col;
   int i;

   get_curs(&row, &col);
```

```
    for (i = 0; i < field_len; i++)
    {
        *(string + i) = read_char();
        set_curs(row, ++col);
    }
    *(string + field_len) = 0;
}

char read_char(void)
{
    union REGS in, out;

    in.h.ah = 8;
    in.h.bh = 0;
    int86(0x10, &in, &out);
    return out.h.al;
}
```

Every time we create a function to perform a certain task, we enhance the organization and modularity of our program. At the same time, however, we slow down the program slightly, because it takes extra time to make the call. This tradeoff is something you should carefully consider, particularly in programs such as the ones we will create in this appendix, where speed is important. When we move from interrupts to direct memory access for most screen operations in later appendixes, you will find that speed becomes less of a consideration, however.

In both of these alternative formulations, we read from wherever the cursor is. We could expand either version to add row and column arguments. Then our function would start with a set_curs() call. If appropriate, we could also have the function preserve the current cursor position before moving the cursor to the designated spot, then move it back when we've finished reading:

```
void read_string(int field_len, char *string, int row, int col)
{
    int old_row, old_col, row, col, i;
    get_curs(&old_row, &old_col);
    for (i = 0; i < field_len; i++)
    {
        set_curs(row, col++);
        *(string + i) = read_char();
    }
    *(string + field_len) = 0;
    set_curs(old_row, old_col);
}
```

C.12   SOME RECTANGLE-FILLING FUNCTIONS

We've seen how you can use the window-scrolling functions to paint a window with spaces. We can generalize this ability into a function that paints a rectangular area in a designated color. All we need to pass the function is the top-left corner, the height and width, and the color:

```
/* +----------------------------------------------------+
   + BOX_FILL
   + Uses scroll-up interrupt to paint, in a specified color,
   + a rectangle of a specified height and width, starting
   + at a specified top-left corner. When height is 1,
   + paints a line of spaces of designated length.
   + Arguments:
   + - trow/lcol:     top-left corner of box
   + - height/width:  height and width of box
   + - color:         color of box
   +----------------------------------------------------+ */
void box_fill(int trow, int lcol, int height, int width, unsigned char color)
{
    union REGS in, out;
```

```
    in.h.ah = 6; /* scroll window up function */
    in.h.al = 0; /* scroll whole window */
    in.h.bh = color;
    in.h.ch = trow; /* top row */
    in.h.cl = lcol; /* left-most column */
    in.h.dh = trow + height - 1; /* bottom row */
    in.h.dl = lcol + width - 1; /* right-most column */
    int86(0x10, &in, &out);
}
```

C.12.1   Drop Shadow

With only a little more effort, we can create a function that, by calling box_fill() twice, places a *drop shadow* in black one row deep and two columns wide under and to the right of the box. We first paint a black box of the same size as the colored box we want, starting at a top-left corner one row and two columns from the top-left corner of our box; then we paint the colored box on top of it, obliterating all but the shadow:

```
/* +-------------------------------------------------------+
   + SHADOW_BOX
   + Paints a rectangle in a designated color as well as a
   + drop shadow at the bottom and right. Paints a box in
   + black at an offset of 1 row and 2 columns, then a box
   + in color, both by calls to box_fill.
   + Arguments:
   + - trow/lcol:      top-left corner of colored box
   + - height/width:   height and width of main colored box
   + - color:          color of box
   +-------------------------------------------------------+
*/
void shadow_box(int trow, int lcol, int height, int width, int color)
{
    box_fill(trow + 1, lcol + 2, height, width, 0); /* 0: black */
    box_fill(trow, lcol, height, width, color);
}
```

C.12.2   Rectangles with Characters and Bright Rectangles

Since all the scroll-up function does is to paint an area with the space character, our scroll-up-based box_fill() function limits us to painting a blank area in one of the background colors. If we want to paint an area in another character—say one of the shaded box characters, ▒, ▓, or █, ASCII 176, 177, or 178—we need another function. We have to be able to pass this function a designated character, and we need a different mechanism from the scrolling function.

One efficient means of handling this task is to paint the area a row at a time by using the character-printing function of interrupt 10h. We can create a place_chars() function identical to the place_char() function above, except that we would pass it the number of characters to print and would set the cx register to that number instead of to 1:

```
/* +-------------------------------------------------------+
   + CHAR_FILL
   + Fills a rectangle whose top-left corner and height
   + and width are specified with a specified character
   + in a specified color. Calls place_chars() for each row.
   +   Arguments:
   +   - ch:           character to comprise box
   +   - color:        color of character
   +   - row/col:      top-left corner of box
   +   - height/width: height and width of box
   +-------------------------------------------------------+ */
void char_fill(char ch, unsigned char color, int row, int col, int height, int
    width)
{
    int i;
```

```
    for (i = row; i < row + height; i++)
        place_chars(ch, color, i, col, width); /* paint a row at a time */
}
/* +----------------------------------------------------+
   + PLACE_CHARS
   + Print a specified character in a specified color at a
   + specified row, starting at a specified column.
   + Arguments:
   + - ch:        character to be printed
   + - color:     color of character
   + - row/col:   row and column of first character
   + - times:     number of characters to be printed
   +----------------------------------------------------+ */
void place_chars(char ch, unsigned char color,
int row, int col, int times)
{
    union REGS in, out;

    set_curs(row, col);
    in.h.ah = 9; /* print character function */
    in.h.al = ch;
    in.h.bh = 0; /* page # */
    in.h.bl = color;
    in.x.cx = times;
    int86(0x10, &in, &out);
}
```

If we pass char_fill() the full-box character, ▮, ASCII 219, we can paint an area in a light color. Whereas writing a space character to the screen operates to fill the character display box with the background color only, writing the full-box character fills the character display box with the foreground color only. See install.c, on disk, where we paint a small rectangle in white, for an example.

As long as we don't need to paint characters on a bright background, using char_fill() is a simpler alternative to disabling the blink bit and using bit 7 for intense background colors.

C.12.3   Lined Box Border

Once you have painted a box, you can put a lined border around it with the following function:

```
/* +----------------------------------------------------+
   + BOX_BORDER
   + Draw a double-lined box of specified height and width
   + and in a specified color at a specified top-left corner.
   +    Arguments:
   +    - trow/lcol:    top-left corner of box
   +    - height/width: height and width of box
   +    - color:        color for box (background) and
   +                    lines foreground/background)
   +----------------------------------------------------+ */
void box_border(int trow, int lcol, int height, int width, int color)
{
    place_char('╔', color, trow, lcol);
    place_char('╗', color, trow, lcol + width - 1);
    place_char('╚', color, trow + height - 1, lcol);
    place_char('╝', color, trow + height - 1, lcol + width - 1);
    place_chars('=', color, trow, lcol + 1, width - 2);
    place_chars('=', color, trow + height - 1, lcol + 1, width - 2);
    char_fill('║', color, trow + 1, lcol, height - 2, 1);
    char_fill('║', color, trow + 1, lcol + width - 1, height - 2, 1);
}
```

You could incorporate a call to box_fill() or shadow_box() to draw the interior and border at the same time. You could also generalize the function by adding an additional argument to indicate whether you want to use a single- or double-lined box.

C.12.4   Testing Border Colors against Rectangles

You can use the char_fill() function to run a test on your monitor to see which border colors match the corresponding screen colors.

 Listing   C.5 brdrtest.c

```
/* brdrtest.c */

/* test the border colors against the corresponding screen colors */

#include <stdio.h>
#include <dos.h>
#include <conio.h> /* getch */

void char_fill(char ch, unsigned char color, int row, int col, int height, int width);
void place_chars(char ch, unsigned char color, int row, int col, int times);
void setborder(unsigned char color), set_curs(int row, int col);

int main(void)
{
   int i, j, color;
   char *color_names[2][7] =
   {   /* dark colors */
      {"blue", "green", "cyan", "red", "purple", "brown", "gray"},
      {"light blue", "light green", "light cyan", "light red",
      "light purple", "yellow", "white"} /* intense colors */
   };

   for (i = 0; i < 7; i++) /* for each color */
      for (j = 0; j < 2; j++) /* dark and light within each color */
      {
         color = i + 1; /* first color is blue (value of 1) */
         if (j == 1) /* light colors */
            color += 8; /* 8 is for intensity bit (bit 3) */
         setborder (color)

      /* print name of color at col 30 of top row */

         printf("\033[H %30s%-20s", "", color_names[j][i]);

      /* fill screen, except top row */

         char_fill('█', color, 1, 0, 24, 80);

      /* await user key press before seeing next color */

         if (!getch())
         getch();
      }
}

void setborder(unsigned char color)
{
   union REGS in, out;
```

```
   in.h.ah = 11;
   in.h.bh = 0;
   in.h.bl = color;
   int86(0x10, &in, &out);
}

void set_curs(int row, int col)
{
   union REGS in, out;

   in.h.ah = 2;
   in.h.bh = 0; /* page # */
   in.h.dh = row;
   in.h.dl = col;
   int86(0x10, &in, &out);
}

void place_chars(char ch, unsigned char color, int row, int col, int times)
{
   union REGS in, out;

   set_curs(row, col);
   in.h.ah = 9; /* print character function */
   in.h.al = ch;
   in.h.bh = 0; /* page # */
   in.h.bl = color;
   in.x.cx = times;
   int86(0x10, &in, &out);
}

void char_fill(char ch, unsigned char color, int row, int col,
   int height, int width)
{
   int current_row;

   /* paint row at a time */
   for (current_row = row; current_row < row + height; current_row++)
      place_chars(ch, color, current_row, col, width);
}
```

C.13   SAMPLE SCREENS

The following listing, screen.c, contains samples of introductory screens you might want to use as models for incorporation into your programs. Figures C.4A to C.4C show what the screens look like.

 **Listing** **C.6 screen.c**

```
/* screen.c */

/* uses single-page approach to paint three sample screens */

#include <stdio.h>
#include <dos.h>
#include <conio.h> /* getch */
#include <string.h> /* strlen */
#include "keys.h"
#include "colors.h"

#define C(foreground,background) foreground + (background << 4)
```

Figure C.4A *Sample Screen: Program Intro*

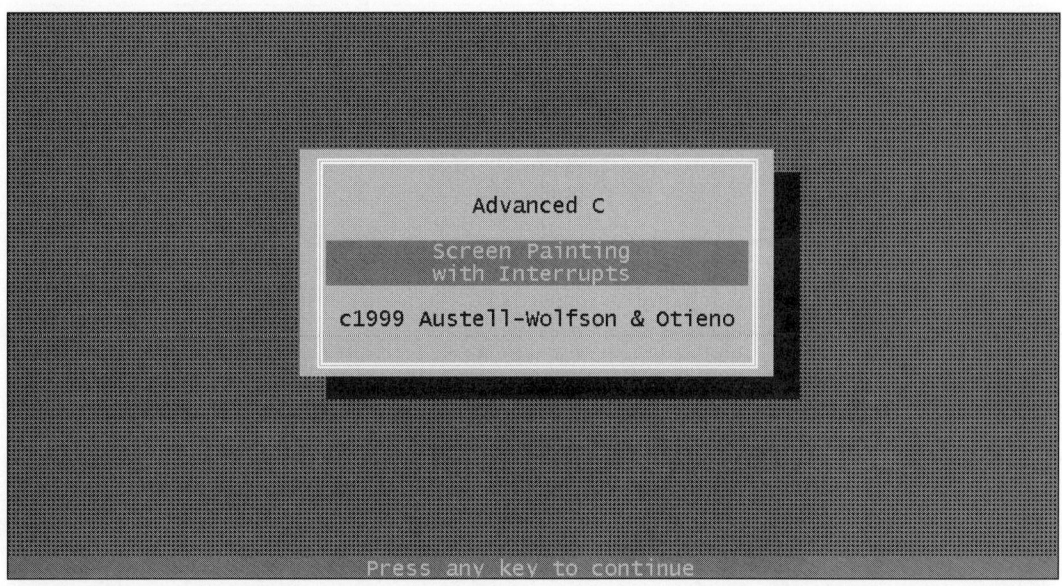

Figure C.4B *Sample Screen: Another Program Intro*

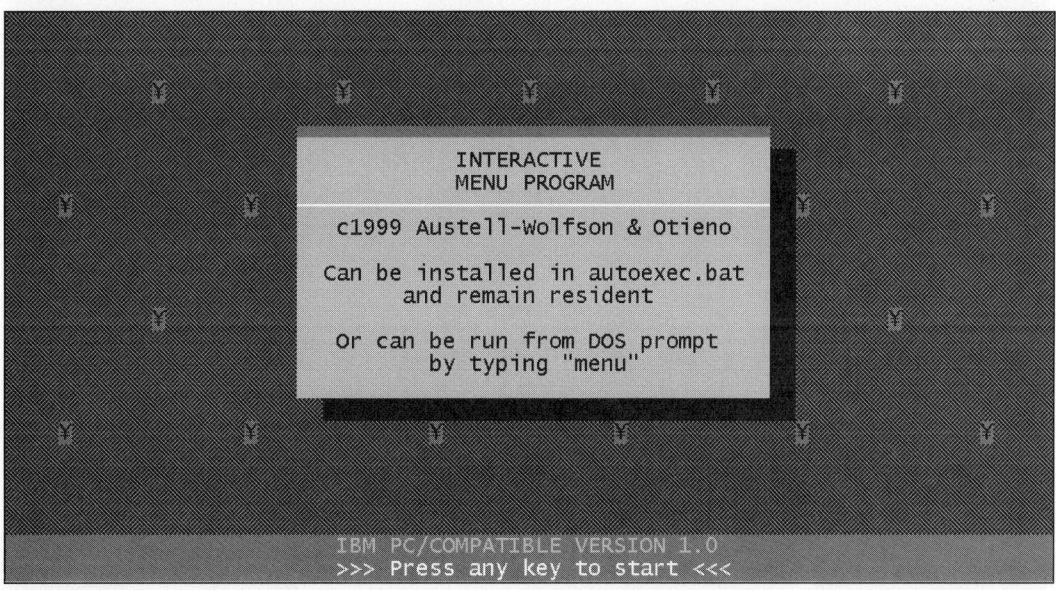

Figure C.4C *Sample Screen: User Menu*

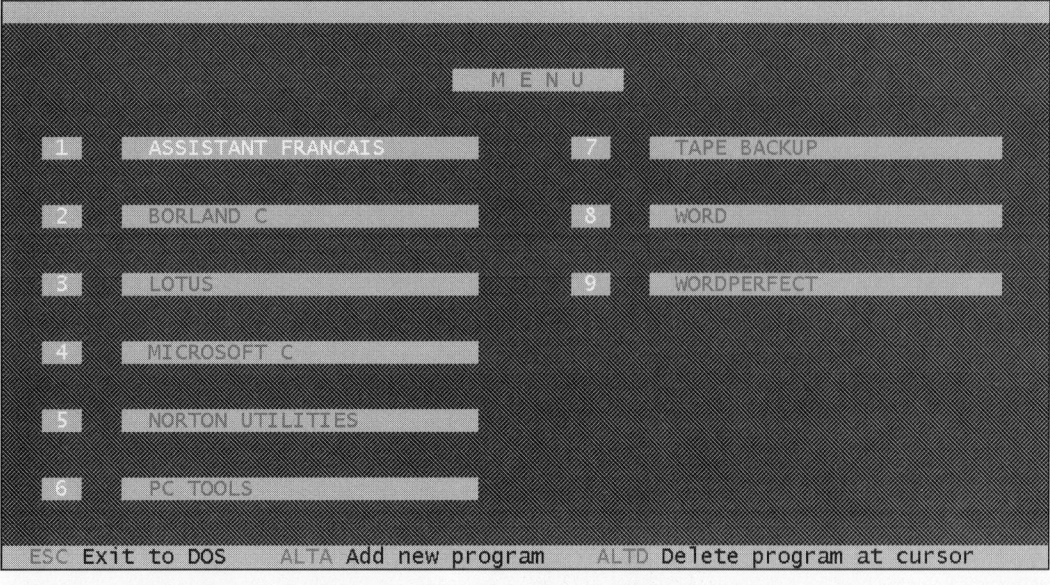

```c
#define COLS 80
#define ROWS 25
#define MAX_CHOICES 12
#define MONO 7
#define COLOR_TXT 3


void box_border(int trow, int lcol, int height, int width, unsigned char color);
void box_fill(int trow, int lcol, int height, int width, unsigned char color);
void char_fill(char ch, unsigned char color, int row, int col, int height, int width);
void choice_paint(int choices, int choice), get_curs(int *row, int *col);
int get_mode(void);
void menuselect(int choices), mono(void), pinholes(unsigned char color);
void place_char(unsigned char ch, unsigned char color, int row, int col);
void place_chars(unsigned char ch, unsigned char color, int row, int col, int times);
void place_string(char *ptr, unsigned char color, int row, int col);
void print_char(unsigned char ch, unsigned char color);
void print_string(char *sptr, unsigned char color);
char read_char(void);
void screen1(void), screen2(void), set_curs(int row, int col), set_mode(int mode),
   start_menu(void);
void shadow_box(int trow, int lcol, int height, int width, unsigned char color);

struct
{
   unsigned char normal, menu_normal, highlight, reverse, background, border_high, shadow;
} colors =
{ C(BK, GY), C(R, GY), C(WH, GY), C(GY, BL), C(BK, BL), C(WH, BL), BK, };


/* +---------------------------------------------------------------+
   +                             MAIN
   +---------------------------------------------------------------+ */
int main(void)
{
   int original_mode = get_mode(), mode;

   set_mode(mode = original_mode == MONO ? MONO : COLOR_TXT);
   if (mode == MONO)
      mono();
   screen1();
   screen2();
   start_menu();
   menuselect(9);
   set_mode(original_mode);
}

void box_border(int trow, int lcol, int height, int width, unsigned char color)
{
   place_char((unsigned char)'╔', color, trow, lcol);
   place_char((unsigned char)'╗', color, trow, lcol + width - 1);
   place_char((unsigned char)'╚', color, trow + height - 1, lcol);
   place_char((unsigned char)'╝', color, trow + height - 1, lcol + width - 1);
   place_chars((unsigned char)'=', color, trow, lcol + 1, width - 2);
   place_chars((unsigned char)'=', color, trow + height - 1, lcol + 1, width - 2);
   char_fill('║', color, trow + 1, lcol, height - 2, 1);
   char_fill('║', color, trow + 1, lcol + width - 1, height - 2, 1);
}


void box_fill(int trow, int lcol, int height, int width, unsigned char color)
{
```

```
   union REGS in, out;

   in.h.ah = 6;
   in.h.al = 0;
   in.h.bh = color;
   in.h.ch = trow;
   in.h.cl = lcol;
   in.h.dh = trow + height - 1; /* bottom row */
   in.h.dl = lcol + width - 1; /* right-most column */
   int86(0x10, &in, &out);
}

void char_fill(char ch, unsigned char color, int row, int col, int height, int width)
{
   int i;

   for (i = row; i < row + height; i++)
      place_chars((unsigned char)ch, color,
         i, col, width); /* paint a row at a time */
}

/* +----------------------------------------------------------------+
   +  CHOICE_PAINT: paint main menu choices
   +----------------------------------------------------------------+ */
void choice_paint(int choices, int choice)
{
   int trow = 6;
   int row, wordcol, numcol;
   int i;
   char *program[MAX_CHOICES] =
   {
   "ASSISTANT FRANCAIS     ",
   "BORLAND C              ",
   "LOTUS                  ",
   "MICROSOFT C            ",
   "NORTON UTILITIES       ",
   "PC TOOLS               ",
   "TAPE BACKUP            ",
   "WORD                   ",
   "WORDPERFECT            "
   };
   char temp[COLS];
   unsigned char color;

   for (i = 0; i < choices; i++)
   {
      row = trow + (3 * (i % 6));
      if (i < 6)
         numcol = 4;
      else numcol = 44;
      wordcol = numcol + 5;
      color = (i == choice) ? colors.highlight: colors.menu_normal;
      sprintf(temp, " %d ", i + 1);
      place_string(temp, colors.highlight, row, numcol - 1);
      sprintf(temp, "  %s  ", program[i]);
      place_string(temp, color, row, wordcol);
   }
   set_curs(ROWS + 1, 0);
}
```

```
void get_curs(int *row, int *col)
{
   union REGS in, out;

   in.h.ah = 3;
   in.h.bh = 0; /* page # */
   int86(0x10, &in, &out);
   *row = out.h.dh;
   *col = out.h.dl;
}

int get_mode(void)
{
   union REGS in, out;

   in.h.ah = 15;
   int86(0x10, &in, &out);
   return out.h.al;
}

/* +------------------------------------------------------------+
   +  MENUSELECT: lets you cursor up and down through 6 menu choices.
   +  Current choice has verbiage and number in highlight; other
   +  locations are normal color. Choices are made by pressing enter
   +  key, the number of the first letter of a choice. Going up
   +  past 1, gets you to 6 and down past 6 gets you to 1.
   +------------------------------------------------------------+ */
void menuselect(int choices)
{
   char ch;
   int choice = 0;

   while (1)
   {
      ch = getch();
      if (ch == ESC)
         return;
      if (ch == '\r')
         ch = choice + 1;
      if (ch >= '1' && ch <= '0' + choices) ch -= '0';
      if (ch >= 1 && ch <= choices)
      {
         /* COMPLETE */
      } /* end if ch is between 1 & choices */
      if (ch == '\t' || (ch == 0 && ( (ch = getch()) == DN || ch == UP || ch == SH_T ||
         ch == ALTA || ch == ALTD)))
      {
         if (ch == ALTA)
         {
            /* COMPLETE */
         } /* end if ch is ALTA */
         else if (ch == ALTD)
         {
            /* COMPLETE */
         } /* end if ch is ALTD */
         else
         {
            if (ch == '\t' || ch == DN)
               choice = (choice + 1) % choices;
```

```
              else choice = (choice - 1 + choices) % choices;
              set_curs(ROWS, 0);
              choice_paint(choices, choice);
          }
      } /* end if ch is tab or 0 */
   } /* end while */
}


/* +----------------------------------------------------------------+
   +  MONO: Convert all colors to monochrome scheme
   +----------------------------------------------------------------+ */
void mono(void)
{
   colors.normal = colors.menu_normal = 0x7;
   colors.reverse = 0x70;
   colors.border_high = colors.highlight = 0xF;
   colors.background = colors.shadow = 0x70;
}


/* +----------------------------------------------------------------+
   +  PINHOLES
   +  Place ASCII 157 characters at various spots on the screen for looks
   +----------------------------------------------------------------+ */
void pinholes(unsigned char color)
{
   int startrow = 3, endrow = 18, spaces = 5, startdot;
   int row, col;
   char dot = '¥'; /* ASCII 157 */

   for (row = startrow; row <= endrow; row += spaces)
   {
      if ( (row + 2) % 2 == 0 ) startdot = 4; /* even rows */
      else startdot = 11; /* odd rows */
      for (col = startdot; col < COLS; col += 14)
         place_char(dot, color, row, col);
   }
}

void place_char(unsigned char ch, unsigned char color, int row, int col)
{
   set_curs(row, col);
   print_char(ch, color);
}

void place_chars(unsigned char ch, unsigned char color, int row, int col, int
   times)
{
   union REGS in, out;

   set_curs(row, col);
   in.h.ah = 9; /* print character function */
   in.h.al = ch;
   in.h.bh = 0; /* page # */
   in.h.bl = color;
   in.x.cx = times;
   int86(0x10, &in, &out);
}


void place_string(char *ptr, unsigned char color, int row, int col)
```

```
{
   while(*ptr)
      place_char(*ptr++, color, row, col++);
}

void print_char(unsigned char ch, unsigned char color)
{
   union REGS in, out;
   int row, col;

   in.h.ah = 9;
   in.h.al = ch;
   in.h.bh = 0; /* page # */
   in.h.bl = color;
   in.x.cx = 1;
   int86(0x10, &in, &out);
   get_curs(&row, &col);
   set_curs(row, ++col);
}

void print_string(char *sptr, unsigned char color)
{
   while (*sptr)
      print_char(*sptr++, color);
}
/* +----------------------------------------------------------------+
   +  SCREEN1
   +----------------------------------------------------------------+ */
void screen1(void)
{
   int i, trow = 6, lcol= 22 , height = 10, width = 36;
   unsigned char color;
   char *line[6] =
   { "Advanced C", "", "Screen Painting", "with Interrupts", "",
      "c2000 Austell-Wolfson & Otieno" };

   char_fill('▓', colors.background, 0, 0, ROWS, COLS); /* ASCII 177 */
   shadow_box(trow, lcol, height, width, colors.normal); /* center box */
   box_border(trow, lcol + 1, height, width - 2, colors.highlight); /* lines around box */
   box_fill(10, lcol + 2, 2, width - 4, colors.reverse); /* middle strip in box */
   for (i = 0; i < 6; i++)
   {
      if (i == 2 || i == 3 )
         color = colors.reverse;
      else
         color = colors.normal;
      place_string(line[i], color, 8 + i, lcol + 3 + ((width - 6) -
         strlen(line[i]))/2); /* center string */
   }
   box_fill(ROWS - 1, 0, 1, COLS, colors.reverse); /* bottom strip */
   place_string("Press any key to continue", colors.reverse,
      ROWS - 1, (COLS - strlen("Press any key to continue"))/2);
   set_curs(ROWS + 1, 0); /* hide cursor */
   if (getch() == 0)
      getch();
}


   +----------------------------------------------------------------+
   +  SCREEN2
   +----------------------------------------------------------------+ */
```

```
void screen2(void)
{
   unsigned char boxcolor = colors.normal;
   int i, height = 12, width = 36, trow = 5, lcol = 22;
   char *line[11] =
      {
         "------------------------------------", "INTERACTIVE", "MENU PROGRAM",
         "_____", "c2000 Austell-Wolfson & Otieno",
         "", "Can be installed in autoexec.bat", "and remain resident", "",
         "Or can be run from DOS prompt", "by typing \"menu\""
      };

   char_fill('▓', colors.background, 0, 0, ROWS, COLS); /* ASCII 176 */
   pinholes(colors.background);
   shadow_box(trow, lcol, height, width, colors.normal);
   place_string(line[0], (unsigned char)(colors.menu_normal
      | (1 << 3)), trow, lcol); /* light red strip */
   for (i = 1; i < 11; i++)
      place_string(line[i], boxcolor, i + 5, lcol +
         (width - strlen(line[i]))/2); /* center string */
   place_string(line[3], colors.highlight, 8, lcol);
   box_fill(ROWS - 2, 0, 2, COLS, colors.background); /* 2-row strip at bottom */
   place_string("IBM PC/COMPATIBLE VERSION 1.0", colors.reverse,
      ROWS - 2, (COLS - strlen("IBM PC/COMPATIBLE VERSION 1.0"))/2);
   place_string(">>> Press any key to start <<<", colors.border_high, ROWS - 1,
      (COLS - strlen(">>> Press any key to start <<<"))/2);
   set_curs(ROWS + 1, 0); /* hide cursor */
   if (getch() == 0)
      getch();
}

void set_curs(int row, int col)
{
   union REGS in, out;

   in.h.ah = 2;
   in.h.bh = 0; /* page # */
   in.h.dh = row;
   in.h.dl = col;
   int86(0x10, &in, &out);
}

void set_mode(int mode)
{
   union REGS in, out;

   in.h.ah = 0;
   in.h.al = mode;
   int86(0x10, &in, &out);
}

void shadow_box(int trow, int lcol, int height, int width, unsigned char color)
{
   box_fill(trow + 1, lcol + 2, height, width, colors.shadow);
   box_fill(trow, lcol, height, width, color);
}

/* +----------------------------------------------------------+
   +  START_MENU: draws background of screen for main menu
   +----------------------------------------------------------+ */
```

```
void start_menu(void)
{
    char_fill('▓', colors.background, 0, 0, ROWS, COLS); /* ASCII 177 */
    box_fill(0, 0, 1, COLS, colors.normal); /* top row strip */
    box_fill(ROWS - 1, 0, 1, COLS, colors.normal); /* bottom row strip */
    place_string("  ESC                   ALTA                   ALTD",
        colors.menu_normal, ROWS - 1 , 0);
    place_string("Exit to DOS", colors.normal, ROWS - 1, 6);
    place_string("Add new program", colors.normal, ROWS - 1, 26);
    place_string("Delete program at cursor", colors.normal, ROWS - 1, 50);
    place_string("  M E N U  ", colors.menu_normal, 3, 40 - strlen("  M E N U  ")/2);
    choice_paint(9, 0);
}
```

C.14   USING 50 ROWS PER SCREEN

If you have a VGA monitor, you can convert the display to 50×80 rather than 25×80. To convert the screen's depiction, we have to alter both the number of scan lines per screen and the number of lines per character. We will set the number of scan lines per screen to 400, the maximum number of scan lines supported by the VGA monitor. Given these 400 scan lines, the VGA monitor can do 25 rows at 16 scan lines per character ($25 \times 16 = 400$) or 50 lines at 8 scan lines per character ($50 \times 8 = 400$).

Here is a function that allows the program to switch to 50- or 25-row mode:

```
/* +--------------------------------------------------+
   + CHANGE_ROWS
   + Make screen 80 x 50 or 80 x 25 according to what
   + variable rows is.
   +--------------------------------------------------+ */
void change_rows(int rows)
{
    union REGS in, out;

    in.h.ah = 0x12; /* alternate select service of int 10h */
    in.h.bl = 0x30; /* select scan lines subservice */
    in.h.al = 0x2; /* 400 scan lines/screen */
    int86(0x10, &in, &out);

    in.h.ah = 0x0; /* set mode service of int 10h (to effectuate scan lines) */
    in.h.al = 0x3; /* 3: 80x25 color text mode */
    int86(0x10, &in, &out);

    in.h.ah = 0x11; /* character generator interface service of int 10h */
    if (rows == 50)
        in.h.al = 0x12; /* 8 scan lines/character */
    else
        in.h.al = 0x14; /* 16 scan lines/character */
    int86(0x10, &in, &out);
}
```

To set the number of scan lines, we use the scan lines subservice, subservice 30h, of the alternate select service, service 12h, of the video services interrupt. The subservice value is placed into the bl register. We set the al register to the appropriate value for the number of scan lines we want: 0 for 200 scan lines per screen, 1 for 350, and 2 for 400.

Prior to setting the number of scan lines per character display box, we must first reset the mode (even if we reset it to what it already is). That being done, we use the character generator interface service, service 11h, of the video services interrupt. This time, we set the al register to the appropriate value for the number of scan lines per character: 0x12 for 8 per character, 0x11 for 14 per character, or 0x14 for 16 per character.

If you want to experiment further with combinations of scan lines per screen and scan lines per character, you might find Table C.5 useful. The table gives the resulting rows per screen based on different combinations.

Table C.5 *Rows Per Screen*

Scan Lines Per Screen	Scan Lines per Character Display Box		
	8 (Default CGA)	14 (Default EGA)	16 (Default VGA)
200 (default CGA)	25	14	12
350 (default EGA)	43	25	21
400 (default VGA)	50	28	25

C.15   APPLICATION: A COLOR SELECTION UTILITY

The color section utility contained in `select.c` allows the user to interactively alter the colors utilized to depict the program screens. There are three different screen types: a menu screen and two different data page screens. The program is lengthy enough to take up to 35 pages of text, so we have included it on disk only.

The color selection screen contains a scaled-down version of the screen currently being changed so that the user can see proposed alterations before they are actually made. The user can also restore any or all of the original colors.

Just as a preview, we have included a few direct memory access functions: `box_fill()`, `char_fill()`, `place_char()`, and `place_string()`. You can replace them with the interrupt versions in this appendix, if you wish.

Each screen has 10 foreground-background color combinations. The colors are stored in two files, `colors.org`, for the original color selections, and `colors.cur`, for the current user-selected colors. The first time the program is run, both files are created. Before the user has made any changes, the files are identical.

C.15.1   Color Variables

While the program is running, the colors are maintained in RAM in global structure variables. For the menu screen:

```
struct menucolor
{
   unsigned char primary, reverse, highlight, window, border, b_rev, b_high, b_bord;
} menucolor =
{ C(R, GY), C(WH, R), C(WH, GY), C(WH, BL), C(BK, GY), C(WH, R), C(R, GY),
   C(BK, BL) };
```

For the data screens:

```
struct datacolor
{
   unsigned char primary, reverse, highlight, window, border, b_rev, b_high,
      b_intense, keys, b_bord;
} datacolor[2] =
   {
      { C(GY,BL), C(WH,R), C(WH,BL), C(BK,GY), C(WH,GY), C(GY,BK), C(WH,BK),
           C(WH,GY), C(R,GY), GY },
        { C(BK,GY), C(Y,R), C(WH,GY), C(GY,BL), C(Y,BL), C(Y,GN), C(BK,GN),
           C(WH,BL), C(Y,BL), BL }
      };
```

These assignments are made only as a precaution in case there is a problem reading `colors.cur`:

```
if ((colors_cur = fopen("c:\\junk\\colors.cur", "rb+")) != NULL)
{
   fread(&menucolor, sizeof(menucolor), 1, colors_cur);
   fread(datacolor, sizeof(datacolor), 1, colors_cur);
}

if ((colors_org = fopen("c:\\junk\\colors.org", "rb")) != NULL)
{
```

```
        fread(&menucolor_org, sizeof(menucolor_org), 1, colors_org);
        fread(datacolor_org, sizeof(datacolor_org), 1, colors_org);
}
```

Within the function, select_colors(), we declare local variables of struct menucolor and datacolor. We copy all current color selections from the global structure variables into these local variables. Thus, the colors in colors.cur are read into menucolor and datacolor and those in colors.org are read into global menucolor_org and datacolor_org variables. The latter set of variables are used only if the user chooses to restore the original color scheme after having made an alternative selection.

Next, we paint the color selection screen (see Figure C.5).

Figure C.5 *User Color Selection Screen*

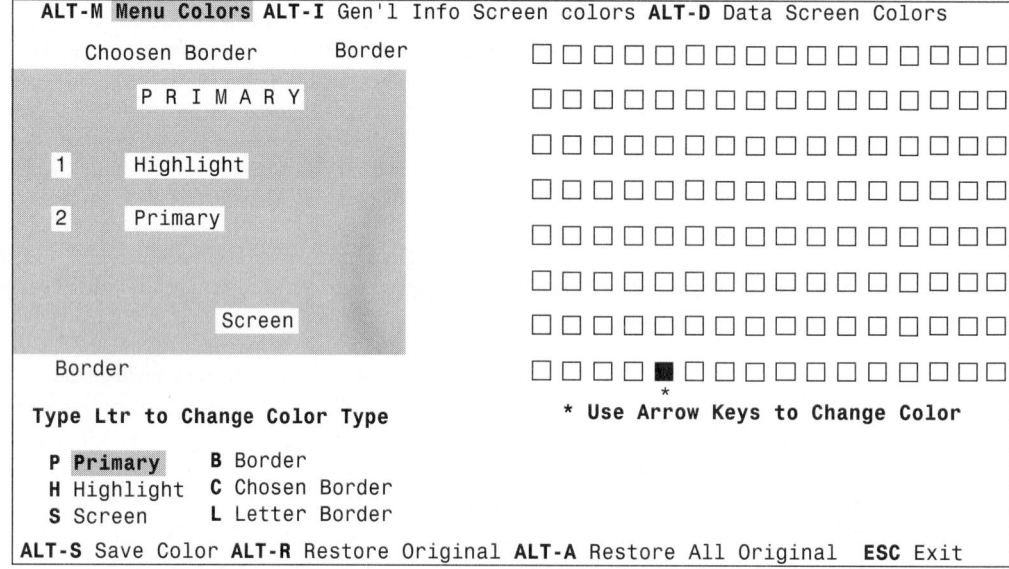

C.15.2   The Color Selection Process

Color selection is a three-step process. First, the user selects one of the three screens; then the user selects a color type; then the user picks a foreground-background color combination for this color type in this screen. A blinking white asterisk shows where the user is in this process. The current menu and color type selection is also highlighted.

The color selection table itself is created by table(). Here, we use a nested for loop to paint all the possible color combinations in 8 rows of 16 colors each. We alternate the space character with the full box character for each iteration.

The first step in the process is commenced by the user's pressing `Alt` `M` (for the menu page), `Alt` `I` (for one data screen), or `Alt` `D` (for the other data screen). Here, I stands for general information page and D for data page. You should change the letter according to your particular application. You may also want to eliminate a data page type or add one if appropriate.

Once this selection is made, the asterisk is moved from the top-page type selection line to the color type selection area to show the user the next step. At the same time, the page type selection is highlighted on the top line and a miniscreen is painted in the current colors.

The user now makes a color type selection by pressing a letter that corresponds to the particular color type. These letters are highlighted.

We use a switch statement to assign the current color for the selected color type to the variable picked_color. To place the asterisk in the color table at the location corresponding to this color, we first isolate the color's foreground and background components by bit shifting.:

```
/* get rid of background color to isolate foreground */

fore = picked_color << 4;

/* move foreground back to its bits */
```

```
fore >>= 4;

/* lop off foreground color to get shifted background color */

back = picked_color >> 4;

/* place current color selection in table with blinking */

place_char('█', C((fore + (1 << 7)),back),
    page_start_row + back * 2, table_lcol + fore * 2 + 1);
place_char('*', C(WH,CY), page_start_row + back * 2 + 1,
    table_lcol + fore * 2 + 1);
```

At this point, the user has a number of choices:

- Jump back two levels to start a new page type, by pressing Alt M, Alt I, or Alt D.
- Save the current color by pressing Alt S.
- Restore the currently selected color type to its original color by pressing Alt R.
- Restore *all* color types for the current screen page type to their original colors by pressing Alt A.
- Continue to change the color for the currently selected color type with the arrow keys.

C.15.3 Changing the Color

If the ↑ arrow is pressed, we decrement the local variable that temporarily holds the background color, back:

```
if (ch == UP)
    back = (back + 8 - 1) % 8;
```

This formulation ensures that the number cycles from 7 to 0 and then back to 7—or, in other words, from the top row to the bottom row and then back to the top row. We increment if the ↓ arrow is pressed.

The same approach is taken for ← and → arrow key presses. Here the local variable fore is used for temporary storage. We cycle from 0 to 15 and then back to 0 for the → arrow and from 15 to 0 and then back to 15 for the ← arrow.

We then move the position of the blinking asterisk by repainting the entire table and replacing the asterisk in the appropriate place. Based on the new combination of fore and back, we show the change in the miniscreen page itself. We do this by setting the appropriate member of mtemp or dtemp, the temporary color storage structure variable, to the newly selected color combination. This storage variable allows us to alter the color combination in advance of the user's choosing to save the color. A pointer to this variable is passed to the function that paints the sample screen, mini_menu() or mini_data().

C.15.4 Saving or Restoring Colors

Saving a color is simple. All we do is copy the mtemp or dtemp values into the permanent menucolor or datacolor:

```
menucolor = mtemp;
```

If Alt R is pressed, we use a switch statement to copy the values of the appropriate member of menucolor_org or datacolor_org into both the global menucolor or datacolor variable member and the local mtemp or dtemp variable. Assigning this original color to a menucolor member is necessary to restore any previous alteration that had been saved; altering mtemp is necessary to restore any color change that had not yet been saved.

If Alt A has been pressed, we copy menucolor_org or datacolor_org in its entirety into menucolor or datacolor.

If Alt S, Alt R, or Alt A is pressed, we set the global flag variable changed_colors to 1, so that on leaving select_colors(), we call change_file_colors() to effectuate any changes by altering the appropriate files.

C.16 VIDEO SERVICES INTERRUPT FUNCTION SUMMARY

Table C.6 summarizes the video services functions we covered in this appendix.

Table C.6   *Selected Video Services Interrupt Functions*

Function	Call Values	Return Values
Set Video Mode	ah = 0x00 al = video mode	
Set Cursor Size	ah = 0x01 ch = starting scan line cl = ending scan line	
Set Cursor Position	ah = 0x02 dh = row dl = column bh = display page	
Get Cursor Position and Size	ah = 0x03 bh = display page	dh = row dl = column ch = starting scan line cl = ending scan line
Set Active Display Page	ah = 0x05 al = active page	
Scroll Window Up/Down	ah = 0x06 (up) / 0x07 (down) al = lines to scroll bh = color ch = upper row cl = left column dh = bottom row dl = right column	
Read Character and Attribute	ah = 0x08 bh = display page	ah = attribute al = character
Write Character and Attribute	ah = 0x09 al = character bl = color bh = display page cx = times to write this character	
Set Border Color	ah = 0x0B bh = 0x00 bl = color	
Get Current Video Mode and Active Display Page	ah = 0x0F	al = current mode bh = display page

Set Scan Lines per Character	ah = 0x11
	al = 0x12 (8 scan lines)
	    0x11 (14 scan lines)
	    0x14 (16 scan lines)	

Set Scan Lines per Screen	ah = 0x12
	bl = 0x30
	al = 0x00 (200 scan lines)
	    0x01 (350 scan lines)
	    0x02 (400 scan lines)	

Direct Memory Access on the PC

So far we've explored two methods of screen control on a PC: first, having `ansi.sys` act as a buffer to filter and convert escape sequences into requests to the BIOS to perform certain tasks (Appendix A), and second, activating the BIOS routines directly through the use of interrupts (Appendix C). Each of these two methods ultimately involves setting bytes in video memory to certain values. In this appendix, you will see how to short-circuit the process by placing values directly into the appropriate bytes of video memory, bypassing both `ansi.sys` and the BIOS. This third method is referred to as *direct memory access,* or *DMA*. Later in the chapter, we will turn to other DMA applications.

D.1   VIDEO MEMORY

The starting address of video memory depends on the video mode. The starting address for the 80×25 color text mode, mode 3h is B800:0000h; that of the 320×200 color graphics mode, mode 13h, discussed in Appendix E, is A000:0000h.

As we saw in Appendix B, this address does not represent the absolute memory address 0xB8000000 bytes from the start of RAM. Rather, it represents an address with a zero-byte offset from the 0xB800th segment, each of whose starting addresses are spaced 16 bytes apart in RAM. Nevertheless, we can assign the address in that concatenated form to a `far` pointer as a `long` constant:

```
int far *fptr = ((int far *)0xB8000000LU;
```

The starting address for the 80 x 25 monochrome mode, mode 7, is B000:0000h.

A table of the starting address for each video mode is contained in Table C.1. Note that the starting addresses are a function of the mode, not the monitor. The statement, found in a few texts, that memory for monochrome *monitors* starts at B000:0000h and that for color *monitors* starts at B800:0000h, is not accurate. For example, video memory for a system with a VGA monitor operating in mode 7 would start at B000:0000h, not B800:0000h.

The character representation of the value stored at the first byte of video memory shows up at row 0, column 0 of the screen. That character's foreground and background color and its attributes are determined by the value stored in the second byte. (See Appendix C for a discussion of the color-attribute byte.) The character and color attribute for row 0, column 1 are determined by the next 2 bytes. The character and color attribute for row 1, column 0 are determined by the 2 bytes starting 160 bytes from the start of video memory—80 character display boxes per row times 2 bytes per character display box.

Generalizing, we can identify the address of the first byte of a character display box in a particular row and column as being

```
screen_mem + (row * 80 + column) * 2
```

where `screen_mem` represents the start of video memory.

This formula works fine for page 0, the first page of video memory. However, for subsequent pages, there is a wrinkle. Between video pages is a 96-byte block. For instance, the character for row 0, column 0 on page 1 is determined by the byte 4096 bytes from the start of video memory, not 4000. The result is that we have exactly 4K per video page. We can refine our formula:

```
screen_mem + (row * 80 + column) * 2 + page * 4096
```

So far, then, we know that we can place characters in specific colors at designated locations on the screen by altering video memory and we have a formula to find the proper video memory locations to do this. Now we need to see how we can access those locations and place values there.

D.2   ACCESSING VIDEO MEMORY

We have already seen how to place values at specific locations in memory—with pointers.

```
char ch;
char *ptr = &ch;
*ptr = 'A';
```

We generally don't bother to determine the address of the bytes into which we place values; we leave that to the computer. In the preceding example, the computer assigns an address to the variable ch; we assign that address to a pointer; we store a value into the pointed-to address with the dereferencing operator.

However, we *could* determine the address if we wanted to:

```
char ch;
printf("ch is located at %p\n", &ch);
```

More important for the purposes of this discussion, we can assign that address or any other specific address to a pointer directly.

```
char temp[6];
char ch;
char *ptr;
sprintf(temp, "%u", &ch); /* use %u for atoi below */
ptr = (char *) atoi(temp); /* assign ch's address to ptr */
ptr = (char *) 65224; /* assign another address to ptr */
```

The pointers we have been using so far have only 16 bits. The largest address value they can hold is 65,535 (0xFFFF). These pointers, called near pointers, hold only the number of bytes from the start of the program's data segment. (See Appendix B.) To alter video memory, we need to access addresses outside our program's data segment.

One method of accomplishing this is to use the large, compact, or huge memory model. In those memory models, pointers are, by default, 32 bits. Because these 32-bit pointers allow the program to access memory locations outside the program's data segment, they are called far pointers.

The segment portion of the address contained in a far pointer is stored in the es register. Having to stop to calculate the segment portion of the address and store it in a segment register slows the program down. Also, the compiler must generate code to load the segment register, so the executable code is larger for programs that use these larger memory models.

Fortunately, there is an alternative. C allows us to explicitly declare a 32-bit far pointer in the smaller memory models (conversely, in the larger memory models, we can explicitly declare near pointers). We simply use the keyword far for this purpose:

```
char far *p1;
int far *p2;
```

For a more extensive discussion of far pointers and memory models, see Appendix B.

D.3   USING far POINTERS TO ACCESS VIDEO MEMORY

If we initialize a far pointer to the start of video memory, we can increment the pointer to wherever in video memory we want. For example, to write " Error opening file " in white on red (see Appendix C regarding colors) starting at row 10, column 25 of page 0:

```
char far *ptr = (char far *) 0xB8000000LU + ((10 * 80) + 25) * 2;
char *message = " Error opening file ";
unsigned char color = 0x4F;
while (*message) /* loop through string character by character
    until we get to NULL */
```

```
{
    *ptr++ = *message++; /* set first byte of pair to character */
    *ptr++ = color; /* set second byte to color */
}
```

We can make this somewhat quicker and more compact by treating the 2-byte character color-attribute pair as a unit:

```
int far *ptr = (int far *) 0xB8000000LU + (10 * 80) + 25;
char *message = " Error opening file ";
unsigned char color = 0x4F;
while (*message)
    *ptr++ = (int) *message++ ¦ (color << 8);
```

Since we have made ptr a pointer to int, every time we increment, we move it 2 bytes. Each time we do that, we move color into the more significant of the 2 bytes by bit shifting.

D.3.1   Speed Check: Escape Sequence vs. Interrupts vs. DMA

Is direct memory access noticeably faster than escape sequences or interrupts? Let's see. Listing D.1, scrn_spd.c, conducts two tests. First, we write the alphabet repeatedly over an entire screen, cycling through all the color combinations along the way. We do the same task with escape sequences, then with interrupts, then with DMA. In the second test, we fill the entire screen with a single character in a single color.

 **Listing**   **D.1 scrn_spd.c**

```
/* scrn_spd.c */

/* compare speed of escape sequences, interrupts, DMA */
/* compare screen painting, first with different characters; then with same */

#include <stdio.h>
#include <dos.h>
#include <conio.h>

int main(void)
{
    void pause(void);
    int i, row, col;
    unsigned char color;
    union REGS in, out;
    int far *farptr;
    unsigned long screen_mem = 0xB8000000LU;

    /* FIRST TEST: do A - Z over entire screen, cycling through colors */

    /* Escape Sequences */

    printf("\033[m\033[2J\033[7h"); /* clear attributes and screen */
    for (i = 0; i < 1999; i++)

    /* intensity: change every 8 times, cycling from 0 to 1
       foreground: change every 8 times, rotating between 30 & 37
       background: change every 16 times, rotating between 40 & 47 */

    printf("\033[%d;%d;%dm%c", (i  / 8) % 2, 30 + (i % 8), 40 + ((i / 16) % 8),
        'A' + (color % 26));
    pause();
```

```
/* Interrupts */

   color = 0;
   in.h.bh = 0;  /* page */
   for (row = 0; row < 25; row++)
      for (col = 0; col < 80; col++)
      {
         in.h.ah = 2; /* set cursor function */
         in.h.dh = row;
         in.h.dl = col;
         int86(0x10, &in, &out);
         in.h.ah = 9; /* print character function */
         in.x.cx = 1; /* print just 1 of the designated char */
         in.h.al = 'A' + (color % 26);
         in.h.bl = color++; /* will cycle back to 0 by itself */
         int86(0x10, &in, &out);
      }
   pause();

   /* DMA */

   color = 0;
   farptr = (int far *) screen_mem;
   for (row = 0; row < 25; row++)
      for (col = 0; col < 80; col++, farptr++)
      {
      /* ch ¦ (color << 8) puts color in left byte, leaves character in right */
         *(farptr) = (int) ('A' + (color % 26)) (color++ << 8);
      }
      pause();

      /* SECOND TEST: fill screen with a single character in the same color */

      /* Escape Sequences */

      printf("\033[1;37;41m"); /* set color to white on red */
      for (i = 0; i < 1999; i++)
         putchar('E');
      pause();

      /* Interrupts */

   in.h.bh = 0; /* page */
   in.h.ah = 9; /* print character function */
   in.x.cx = 2000; /* print 2000 of the designated character */
   in.h.al = 'I';
   in.h.bl = 0x4F; /* white on red */
   int86(0x10, &in, &out);
   pause();

      /* DMA */

   color = 0;
   farptr = (int far *) screen_mem;
   for (row = 0; row < 25; row++)
      for (col = 0; col < 80; col++, farptr++,
         *(farptr) = (int) 'D' ¦ (0x4F << 8));
   pause();
}
```

```
    void pause(void) /* wait for key press and then clear screen */
    {
        if (!getch())
            getch();
        printf("\033[2J"); /* clear screen */
    }
```

The chain of graphics processing—or any I/O—from most indirect to most direct runs from Windows application programming interface to canned C functions to escape sequences to interrupts to direct memory access to assembly-language programming. Until recently, speed was a critical consideration in graphics work, particularly in graphics mode, where virtually all work was done in assembly language.

Windows code gets larger and more bloated as time passes, so that Windows-based programs do not seem to run much faster today than they did several years ago, despite dramatically more powerful machines. The performance difference shows up in DOS-based applications, however.

On a 486 machine, in the first test, the escape sequence method performs quite slowly. Using interrupts works more than twice as fast, but you can still see the screen being written. With DMA, screen writing seems instantaneous.

In the second test, where we fill the screen with a single character, the escape sequence method still produces unsatisfactorily slow results. Here, interrupts move into the instantaneous category. The interrupt screen painting is accomplished by a single function call. Since both the interrupt and DMA methods produce screens at a speed faster than the screen refreshes itself, it really doesn't matter which method is faster.

With even a 166-MHz Pentium, however, all but the very first escape sequence test is virtually instantaneous. On a machine 450-MHz or faster, all would appear instantaneous.

Nevertheless, if you have users some of whom might have older machines, and you are writing a series of characters to the screen, DMA is the favored approach. This is especially true for graphics modes, where assembly routines might be called for in some cases still—although less and less as time goes on and CPUs get more powerful.

On the other hand, for small, one-time tasks, such as setting the graphics mode or clearing the screen, escape sequences (used for clearing the screen in scrn_spd.c) or interrupts are just fine.

Before we leave scrn_spd.c, we should take a look at one statement:

```
for (i = 0; i < 1999; i++)
    printf("\33[%d;%d;%dm%c", (i  / 8) % 2, 30 + (i % 8), 40 + ((i / 16) % 8),
        'A' + (i % 26));
        /* arguments: intensity, foreground, background */
```

Because of the way integer division works, truncating any remainder using the / operator will allow us to make a value alteration every *n*th loop, where *n* is the number to the right of the division operator. Use of the % operator will allow us to cycle from 0 through 1 less than the number to the right of the modulus operator.

As you see, we can combine both principles to produce a periodic change that results in a cycling. The intensity will change every 8 loops, cycling from 0 to 1 and back; the foreground will change every 8 loops, cycling from 30 through 37 and back (30 plus 0 to 7); the background will change every 16 times, cycling from 40 to 47 and back (40 plus 0 to 7); the letter will change every 26 times, cycling from A to Z.

D.4   DMA FUNCTIONS

We now can recode for DMA some of the screen control functions we saw in Appendix C. We show you both versions for comparison. The following DMA examples assume that we have an external variable set as follows:

```
int far *screen_mem (int far *)0xB8000000LU;
```

Here are the rectangle-filling functions:

```
/* +------------------------------------------------------+
   + BOX_FILL: paints a box of specified size at a designated
   + location with a specified color; when row is 1, just
   + paints a single line of spaces of designated length.
   +------------------------------------------------------+ */
void box_fill(char trow, char lcol, char rows, char cols, unsigned char color)
{
    union REGS in, out;
```

```
      in.h.ah = 6; /* scroll up window function */
      in.h.al = rows; /* # of lines to scroll up */
      in.h.bh = color;
      in.h.ch = trow; /* top row */
      in.h.cl = lcol; /* left-most column */
      in.h.dh = trow + rows - 1; /* bottom row */
      in.h.dl = lcol + cols - 1; /* right-most column */
      int86(0x10, &in, &out);
}


/* +----------------------------------------------------+
   + BOX_FILL: (DMA Version)
   +----------------------------------------------------+ */
void box_fill(char trow, char lcol, char height, char width, unsigned char color)
{
   char row, col;

   for (row = trow; row < trow + height; row++)
      for (col = lcol; col < lcol + width; col++)
         *(screen_mem + row * COLS + col) = (int) ' ' ¦ (color << 8);
}


/* +----------------------------------------------------+
   + CHAR_FILL: fill a rectangular area of specified top-
   + left corner and height and width with a specific
   + character in a designated color
   +----------------------------------------------------+ */
void char_fill(char trow, char lcol, char rows, char cols, unsigned char ch,
   unsigned char color)
{
   char i;
   union REGS in, out;

   in.h.bh = 0; /* page number */

   in.h.ah = 9;
   in.x.cx = cols;
   n.h.al = ch;
   in.h.bl = color;
   for (i = trow; i < trow + rows; i++)
   {
      setcurs(i, lcol);
      int86(0x10, &in, &out);
   }
}


/* +----------------------------------------------------+
   + CHAR_FILL: (DMA version)
   +----------------------------------------------------+*/

void char_fill(char trow, char lcol, char height, char width, unsigned char ch,
   unsigned char color)
{

   char row, col;

   for (row = trow; row < trow + height; row++)
      for (col = lcol; col < lcol + width; col++)
      *(screen_mem + row * COLS + col) = ch ¦ (color << 8);
}
```

Note that for all these DMA functions, we set memory to `screen_mem`. We use page 0 only. This limitation would make programs using the functions simpler and more portable. Otherwise, we would need to expand our formulation. For instance,

```
*(screen_mem + row * 80 + col) = ch ¦ (color << 8);
```

would become

```
*(screen_mem + getpage() * 4096 + row * 80 + col) = ch ¦ (color << 8);
```

to paint something on the current video page. Or you could add a page argument to `box_fill()` and `char_fill()`.

The same would apply to the following character and string reading and writing functions:

```
/* +-------------------------------------------------------+
   + PLACE_CHAR: puts character in color on screen at
   +    designated row/col.
   + Does NOT advance the cursor—this is not for user input.
   +-------------------------------------------------------+ */
void place_char(unsigned char ch, unsigned char color, char row, char col)
{
    union REGS in, out;

    setcurs(row, col);
    in.h.bh = 0; /* page number */
    in.h.ah = 9;
    in.x.cx = 1; /* print just 1 of the designated character */
    in.h.al = ch;
    in.h.bl = color;
    int86(0x10, &in, &out);
}


/* +-------------------------------------------------------+
   + PLACE_CHAR: (DMA Version)
   +-------------------------------------------------------+ */
void place_char(unsigned char ch, unsigned char color, char row, char col)
{
    /* ch ¦ (color << 8) puts color in left byte, leaves character in right */
    *(screen_mem + row * COLS + col) = ch ¦ (color << 8);
}


/* +-------------------------------------------------------+
   + PLACE_STRING: prints a string in color at a specified row and col
   +-------------------------------------------------------+ */
void place_string(unsigned char *ptr, unsigned char color, char row, char col)
{
    while (*ptr)
        place_char(*ptr++, color, row, col++);
}


/* +-------------------------------------------------------+
   + PLACE_STRING: (DMA version)
   +-------------------------------------------------------+ */
void place_string(unsigned char *ptr, unsigned char color, char row, char col)
{
    int far *farptr = screen_mem + row * COLS + col;

    while(*ptr)
        *farptr++ = *ptr++ ¦ (color << 8);
}
```

```
/* +--------------------------------------------------+
   + READ_STRING: reads in a specified # of screen characters
   + starting where the cursor is and puts them into a string
   + after storing a null character at the end
   +--------------------------------------------------+ */
void read_string(char row, char col, char field_len, char *string)
{
    union REGS in, out;
    char i;

    in.h.ah = 8;
    in.h.bh = 0;  /* page number */
    for (i = 0; i < field_len; i++)
    {
        int86(0x10, &in, &out);
        *(string + i) = out.h.al;
        setcurs(row, col++);
    }
    *(string + field_len) = '\0';  /* add null character at end of string */
}


/* +--------------------------------------------------+
   + READ_STRING: (DMA version)
   +--------------------------------------------------+ */
void read_string(char row, char col, char field_len, char *string)
{
    char i;
    int far *farptr = screen_mem + row * COLS + col;

    for (i = 0; i < field_len; i++)
        *(string + i) = *farptr++ & 0xFF;  /* zero out high byte with 0xFF */
    *(string + field_len) = '\0';  /* add null character at end of string */
}
```

In the DMA version of read_string(), the far pointer farptr points to an int. We want only the first of the two bytes it points to, the byte containing the character. We zero out the high-order byte by ANDing with a number that has 1s in all low-order byte bits and 0s in all high-order byte bits, 0xFF (decimal 255).

D.4.1   Speed Comparison

Note that in the DMA version of read_string(), it is not necessary to repeatedly call setcurs() within the function, as it is in the non-DMA version. That difference alone would make the DMA version quite a bit faster.

We wrote the string "Søren Kierkegaard" (19th-century Danish philosopher) in white on red 25,000 times with escape sequences, with interrupts, and with DMA. We likewise read in the same string from the screen 25,000 times with interrupts and with DMA (you can't read from the screen with escape sequences). In both cases, we used a "low-end" 166-MHz machine. Here are the results in seconds:

Writing	
Escape sequences	2.91
Interrupts	3.78
DMA	0.16
Reading	
Interrupts	4.23
DMA	0.33

Quite a difference between DMA and the other two. Note, however, that since the escape sequence version consists of a single function call per string, it is actually faster than interrupts in this context.

D.5 SAVING AND RESTORING THE VIDEO SCREEN WITH `movedata()`

In Listing A.4, `con_menu.c`, we saw two related functions, `save()` and `restore()`, whose purpose was to save the current video screen prior to plopping a window down in the middle of the screen, and, when we no longer need the window, restoring the saved screen. The following versions of these functions not only save and restore the screen; they also replace the cursor at its former position in the saved screen. These functions assume that the following global variables exist, and values have been assigned to them as follows:

```
#define BYTES 4000
#define MONO 7
#define COLOR_TXT 3
struct SREGS segs;
char buffer [BYTES];
int oldrow, oldcol;
unsigned video_seg;
int mode;

int main(void)
{
    segread(&segs);
    mode = get_mode()
    set_mode(mode == MONO ? MONO : COLOR_TXT);
    video_seg = mode == MONO ? 0xB000 : 0xB800;
    . . .
}
```

Here are the functions (the text for the `setcurs()` and `getcurs()` functions called here, and the `get_mode()` and `set_mode()` functions in the code fragment above is found in Appendix C).

```
/* +----------------------------------------------------+
   + RESTORE: writes from array in program's data segment,
   + previously saved with save() from page 0 of video memory,
   + back to video memory.
   +----------------------------------------------------+ */
void restore(void)
{
    struct SREGS segs;

    setcurs(oldrow, oldcol);
    movedata(segs.ds, (unsigned)buffer, video_seg, 0, BYTES);
}
/* +----------------------------------------------------+
   + SAVE: writes page 0 of video memory to array in program's
   + data segment for later use of restore().
   +----------------------------------------------------+ */
void save(void)
{
    struct SREGS segs;
    getcurs(&oldrow, &oldcol);
    movedata(video_seg, 0, segs.ds, (unsigned)buffer, BYTES);
}
```

The `movedata()` function allows us to copy the value of bytes in one memory segment into bytes in another segment:

```
void movedata(unsigned source_segment, unsigned source_offset, unsigned
    destination_segment, unsigned destination_offset, unsigned num_bytes);
```

The technique is to use an external array in our program's data segment as a buffer. In `save()`, we transfer data from page 0 of video memory to the buffer; in `restore()`, we transfer it back. We determine the program's data segment address by the use of the SREGS structure (the S standing for segment register). The SREGS structure template, found, like that for REGS, in dos.h, contains the following members:

```
struct SREGS {
    unsigned int es, cs, ss, ds; };
```

When we call segread() with the address of an SREGS variable, the current values of the segment registers (that is, the addresses of the extra, code, stack, and data segments) are placed into the variable's corresponding members.

D.5.1   Using Another Video Page as a Buffer

There are at least two alternative methods for accomplishing the same objective of saving and restoring the screen (in addition to the clumsy device of simply redrawing the original screen with the various screen-drawing functions that created the screen in the first place). One would be to use page 1 of video memory as the buffer instead of an external array in the program's data segment (as in the first method, these functions assume the existence of a global variable video_seg, which has been set to the address of the segment in which video memory is found):

```
/* copy page 0 of video memory to page 1 */
void save_video(void)
{
    movedata(video_seg, 0, video_seg, BYTES + 96, BYTES);
}

/* restore screen by copying page 1 of video memory back to page 0 */
void restore_video(void)
{
    movedata(video_seg, BYTES + 96, video_seg, 0, BYTES);
}
```

The external array technique eats up 4000 bytes of memory (a screen's worth) that might be needed for other purposes. The video page method eliminates this potential problem. But what if your program uses a multipage approach and all video pages are spoken for? Or what about a monochrome monitor, where there is only a page of video memory? This latter concern makes the video page-swapping method somewhat nonportable.

D.5.2   Using a File as a Buffer

A third approach is to use a temporary file to act as a buffer:

```
/* copy page 0 of video memory to file */
void save_file(void)
{
    char local_buffer[BYTES];

    movedata(video_seg, 0, segs.ds, (unsigned)local_buffer, BYTES);
    rewind(screen_file);
    fwrite(local_buffer, BYTES, 1, screen_file); /* write from buffer to file */
}

/* copy from buffer back from file to video memory */
void restore_file(void)
{
    char local_buffer[BYTES];

    segread(&segs);
    rewind(screen_file);
    fread(local_buffer, BYTES, 1,
        screen_file); /* read from file to buffer */
    movedata(segs.ds, (unsigned)local_buffer,
        video_seg, 0, BYTES);
}
```

Here, we assume the existence of a global FILE pointer variable that points to the file we plan to use to temporarily house the screen data. We would create and delete the file in something like the following manner:

```
screen_file = fopen("tempfile",
    "wb+"); /* error-checking omitted */
save_file();
. . .
restore_file();
fclose(screen_file);
unlink("tempfile");
```

The unlink() function deletes the file just as a del command in DOS would do.

This third approach is slower and messier than the first two. Also, note that with the file approach, we have to make an intermediate stop at a local array; we cannot transfer data directly from an area outside our program's data segment to a file or vice versa. So, while we do not have a 4000-byte external array overhanging the program at all times, as we do with the first method, we still need to have 4000 bytes of room on the stack for a short period of time. Watch out for potential stack overflow.

If you don't mind some slight file operation delay, you could reduce the size of the local buffer as small as you like and read the video page in chunks. For example, if you declare a 500-byte local buffer:

```
for (i = 0; i < 8; i++)
{
    fread(local_buffer, 500, 1, screen_file);
    movedata(segs.ds, (unsigned)local_buffer,
        video_seg, i * 500, 500);
}
```

You can write directly between video memory and a file if you use a large data memory model (see Appendix B):

```
/* write directly to file from video memory (LARGE DATA MEMORY MODELS ONLY) */
void save_video(void)
{
    rewind (screen_file);
    fwrite(video_mem, 1, BYTES, screen_file);
}


/* read directly from a file to video memory (LARGE DATA MEMORY MODELS ONLY) */
void restore_video(void)
{
    rewind(screen_file);
    fread(video_mem, 1, BYTES, screen_file);
}
```

APPENDIX **E**

Graphics Mode and the Mouse on the PC

In this appendix, we will cover graphics mode on the PC. In text mode, the screen consists of a grid of rows and columns—80×25 in the most commonly used modes, including mode 3, the default PC display mode. Actually, the hardware uses individual pixels to write each character in text mode, but even with direct memory access, we access only the character display boxes, not the individual pixels. Each of these boxes is controlled by 2 bytes in RAM.

In graphics mode, we work on a pixel basis. Treatment of memory for the representation of the pixels on the screen varies considerably from graphics mode to graphics mode. In some graphics modes, memory for pixel rows is interleaved. For instance, in the two-color mode 6, pixels for even-numbered rows are stored starting at B800:0000h and those for odd-numbered rows are stored starting at the second half of the video buffer, at B800:2000h. In others, the structure is even more complex. In some 16-color modes, each pixel is a concatenation of 4 separate bits in parallel memory maps.

The video services interrupts would permit us to ignore the pixel-memory complexity and write a pixel in a specified color at a specified location. However, in graphics mode, using interrupts for the thousands or tens of thousands of pixels we must write would be impossibly slow. For speed's sake, we must use direct memory access, and therefore we must deal with the different memory configurations of the various graphics modes.

We will use a graphics mode that has a relatively simple configuration. In the mode we will select, mode 13h, there is the same sort of linear pixel-to-memory byte correspondence as we saw in text mode for character-to-memory byte.

E. 1   VIDEO BUFFER STRUCTURE IN MODE 13h

In video mode 13h, you can visualize the video buffer as a cell table or two-dimensioned array with 200 rows and 320 columns. Each cell is a single byte, with the cell at $x = 0$, $y = 0$ being at the start of video memory (see Figure E.1).

Every cell of this array contains the color of a pixel on the screen—or more accurately, a color reference. The value of a cell is an index to a 255-byte *color palette* table. For instance, if the value of a pixel is 3, it will have whatever color the fourth element of the palette table contains. Each element of the palette table contains 3 bytes—one each for the red, green, and blue color components (see Figure E.2).

Only 6 bits of each component byte are used by a standard VGA card for color in mode 13h. Therefore, the red, green, and blue components can range from 0 to only 63 (the maximum value when all 6 bits are on). For example, in Figure E.2, palette element 15 will produce white since it has the maximum value for each color component, 63. Palette element 0 will produce black: it is at the other extreme, with a value of 0 for each color component. Palette element 1 is a medium-high intensity blue with RGB values of 0, 0, 42; palette elements 2 and 4 are medium-high intensity green and red, respectively; and element 3 is medium-high intensity cyan (computer-speak for blue-green). All the default RGB palette values are shown in Figure E.3.

Figure E.1   *Depiction of Video Memory for Mode 13h*

Figure E.2   *The Video Memory–Palette Registers Connection*

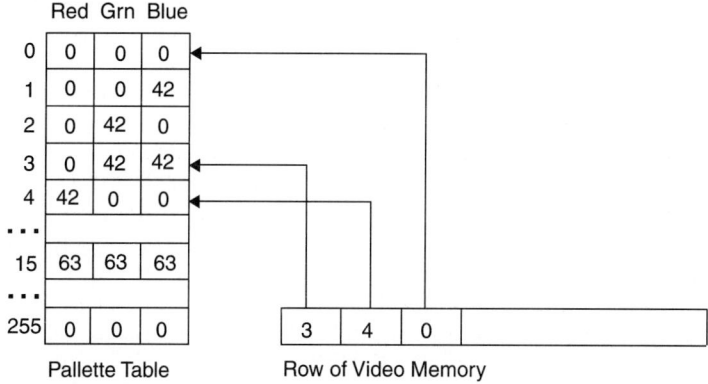

To set video mode 13h, we will use the `setMode()` function we have already used for text mode graphics in Appendix C, with a parameter value equal to 0x13. You can find the function in `graphics.c:` on disk:

```c
#include <dos.h> /* int86() */
/* +--------------------------------------------------------+
   +   setMode
   +   Use video interrupt 10h and the C interrupt function to
   +   set the video mode.
   +--------------------------------------------------------+ */
void setMode(int mode)
{
   union REGS inregs, outregs;
   inregs.h.ah = 0; /* set video mode subfunction */
   inregs.h.al = (unsigned char)mode; /* mode to change to */
   int86(0x10, &inregs, &outregs);
}
```

Now that we are in the mode, let's see how to draw lines by writing pixel color values to video memory.

E.2   LINE DRAWING

As we have seen in Figure C.1, video memory in most graphics modes, including mode 13h, starts at 0xA0000000L. We set a `far` pointer to the start of graphics mode video memory, where the first "cell" is found, this way:

```c
unsigned char far *video_buffer =
   (unsigned char far *) 0xA0000000L;
```

First, we will write a function that draws a horizontal line. We will get the color of the line and the color of other geometric shapes from the global variable, curColor. For the time being, we will hard-code the color to palette index 3:

```
#include <mem.h> /* _fmemset */


int curColor = 3;


/* Draw horizontal line from point (x1, y) to point (x2, y) */
void lineH(int y, int x1, int x2)
{
   int length = abs(x2 - x1) + 1;
   int startX = min(x1, x2);
   _fmemset(video_buffer + y * 320 + startX), curColor, length);
}
```

Since the bytes corresponding to a horizontal row of pixels are found sequentially in video memory, to set a line's worth of them to the same value of the global variable curColor, we can do the whole job at one stroke by using the far memory analog to the memset() function we discussed in Chapter 9, _fmemset():

```
void far * far _fmemset(void far *farBuffer, int value, size_t numBytes);
```

Each of the buffer functions, memset(), memcmp(), memchr(), and memcmp(), has a far cousin function that takes a far pointer to void instead of a pointer to void. The prototypes for all these functions are found in mem.h.

We can use the same _fmemset() function for screen clearing with the current color or rectangle filling. For example, clearing the screen is simple:

```
void clearScreen(void) { _fmemset(video_buffer, curColor, 320 * 200); }
```

These functions are all found in the file on disk, drawing.c.

As we saw earlier, the 320 number in lineH() and clearScreen() represents the screen width for video mode 13h. For example, the memory location for the pixel in the second row, left-most column ($x = 0$, $y = 1$) will be 320 bytes from the beginning of video memory.

Now, it is a slightly more complicated function to draw vertical lines. Since the bytes for cells in different rows are not sequential in video memory, we will have to use a looping mechanism rather than a simple _fmemset() call:

```
#define SCREEN_WIDTH 320;
#define SCREEN_HEIGHT 200;


/* Draw vertical line from point (x1,y1) to point (x1,y2) */
void lineV(int x1, int y1, int y2)
{
   int step = SCREEN_WIDTH;
   int n = abs(y2 - y1) + 1, y = min(y1, y2);
   int k;
   for (k = 0; k < n; k++)
      video_buffer[x1 + (y + k) * step] = curColor;
}
```

We use the macro SCREEN_WIDTH to shift our video memory pointer to next line of the screen with the same x (horizontal) position.

With the lineH() and lineV() functions, we can now write a drawRect() function and a fillRect() function. Before peeking in draw.c, see whether you can write one for fillRect(). You can either call lineH() repeatedly in a loop or, to save the overhead of function calls and speed the process up, you can use a loop with lineH()'s operative code embedded. The drawRect() function is merely a combination of two lineH() and two lineV() calls.

The next step is drawing a line in an arbitrary direction. For this we will write the function line(), using the *J. E. Bresenham* algorithm. This algorithm does not use any multiplication or division operations:

```
/* Draw line from point (x1,y1) to (x2,y2) */
void line(int x1, int y1, int x2, int y2)
{
```

```
int x = 0, y = 0, sx, sy, dx, dy, k, d;

sx = x2 - x1;
sy = y2 - y1;

if (sx > 0)
   dx = 1;
else if (sx == 0)
   dx = 0;
else if (sx < 0)
   dx = -1;

if (sy > 0)
   dy = 1;
else if (sy == 0)
   dy = 0;
else if (sy < 0)
   dy = -1;

sx = abs(sx);
sy = abs(sy);
d = max(sx, sy);

for (k = 0; k <= d + 1; k++)
{
   *(video_buffer + SCREEN_WIDTH * y1 + x1) = curColor;
   x += sx;
   y += sy;
   if (x > d) { x -= d; x1 += dx; }
   if (y > d) { y -= d; y1 += dy; }
}
}
```

The essence of this algorithm is moving from one point to a second point on crossed or graph paper. This paper has equally spaced vertical and horizontal lines in a grid from end to end. We increment x or y by 1 as our line crosses vertical or horizontal lines on the paper, nearest the point of vertical- or horizontal-line intersection.

E.3 HOW TO SET THE COLOR FOR DRAWING

All the drawing functions we have written so far make use of the global variable curColor variable. As an alternative, you could eliminate this global variable and just add color as an additional argument to each of the drawing functions.

Assuming we keep the global variable approach, we should have a function to set a new value for the variable. It is quite simple:

```
void setColor(unsigned char color)
{
   curColor = color;
}
```

The function must be called before any drawing with this color. You can any color number from 0 to 255. As we have seen, the color number corresponds to an element of the palette register, to which we now turn in greater detail.

E.4 THE COLOR PALETTE

The palette registers are the keys to understanding the color depiction process in this mode. We'll start by examining the default state of affairs.

E.4.1   The Default Color Palette

If you do not change the contents of the palette registers, the default color values are used. Let's look at the default values. We create a color table with 16 rows and columns. Every color cell corresponds to the palette index. Our table grows from left to right at first and then from top to bottom as we traverse the palette index:

```
/* +----------------------------------------------------------+
   +   colorDemo
   +   Draw all 256-color default palette colors as a 16*16 color
   +   table. Then draw frame for the table with the color (frameColor).
   +----------------------------------------------------------+ */
void colorDemo(unsigned char frameColor)
{
   int color = 0, x = 0, y = 0,
      size = 10; /* length & width in pixels for each color */

   for (color = 0; color < 256 color++)
   {
      x = 80 + (color % 16) * size;
      y = 20 + (color / 16) * size;
      setColor(color);
      fillRect(x, y, x + size, y + size);
   }

   setColor(frameColor);
   drawRect(80, 20, 240, 180);
   waitKey();
}
```

The default color elements from 0 to 15 are same ones used for 16-color video modes. Elements from 16 to 31 are gray colors with growing intensity (equal values of RGB produce black when all 0 and white when all 63). Other colors smoothly cover the colors of the rainbow. Figure E.3 shows all the palette color values.

Figure E.3 *Default Palette Color Values*

	R	G	B		R	B	B		R	G	B		R	G	B
0	0	0	0	64	63	31	31	128	14	14	28	192	0	16	0
1	0	0	42	65	63	39	31	129	17	14	28	193	0	16	4
2	0	42	0	66	63	47	31	130	21	14	28	194	0	16	8
3	0	42	42	67	63	55	31	131	24	14	28	195	0	16	12
4	42	0	0	68	63	63	31	132	28	14	28	196	0	16	16
5	42	0	42	69	55	63	31	133	28	14	24	197	0	12	16
6	42	21	0	70	47	63	31	134	28	14	21	198	0	8	16
7	42	42	42	71	39	63	31	135	28	14	17	199	0	4	16
8	21	21	21	72	31	63	31	136	28	14	14	200	8	8	16
9	21	21	63	73	31	63	39	137	28	17	14	201	10	8	16
10	21	63	21	74	31	63	47	138	28	21	14	202	12	8	16
11	21	63	63	75	31	63	55	139	28	24	14	203	14	8	16
12	63	21	21	76	31	63	63	140	28	28	14	204	16	8	16
13	63	21	63	77	31	55	63	141	24	28	14	205	16	8	14
14	63	63	21	78	31	47	63	142	21	28	14	206	16	8	12
15	63	63	63	79	31	39	63	143	17	28	14	207	16	8	10
16	0	0	0	80	45	45	63	144	14	28	14	208	16	8	8
17	5	5	5	81	49	45	63	145	14	28	17	209	16	10	8

Figure E.3 *(continued)*

	R	G	B		R	B	B		R	G	B		R	G	B
18	8	8	8	82	54	45	63	146	14	28	21	210	16	12	8
19	11	11	11	83	58	45	63	147	14	28	24	211	16	14	8
20	14	14	14	84	63	45	63	148	14	28	28	212	16	16	8
21	17	17	17	85	63	45	58	149	14	24	28	213	14	16	8
22	20	20	20	86	63	45	54	150	14	21	28	214	12	16	8
23	24	24	24	87	63	45	49	151	14	17	28	215	10	16	8
24	28	28	28	88	63	45	45	152	20	20	28	216	8	16	8
25	32	32	32	89	63	49	45	153	22	20	28	217	8	16	10
26	36	36	36	90	63	54	45	154	24	20	28	218	8	16	12
27	40	40	40	91	63	58	45	155	26	20	28	219	8	16	14
28	45	45	45	92	63	63	45	156	28	20	28	220	8	16	16
29	50	50	50	93	58	63	45	157	28	20	26	221	8	14	16
30	56	56	56	94	54	63	45	158	28	20	24	222	8	12	16
31	63	63	63	95	49	63	45	159	28	20	22	223	8	10	16
32	0	0	63	96	45	63	45	160	28	20	20	224	11	11	16
33	16	0	63	97	45	63	49	161	28	22	20	225	12	11	16
34	31	0	63	98	45	63	54	162	28	24	20	226	13	11	16
35	47	0	63	99	45	63	58	163	28	26	20	227	15	11	16
36	63	0	63	100	45	63	63	164	28	28	20	228	16	11	16
37	63	0	47	101	45	58	63	165	26	28	20	229	16	11	15
38	63	0	31	102	45	54	63	166	24	28	20	230	16	11	13
39	63	0	16	103	45	49	63	167	22	28	20	231	16	11	12
40	63	0	0	104	0	0	28	168	20	28	20	232	16	11	11
41	63	16	0	105	7	0	28	169	20	28	22	233	16	12	11
42	63	31	0	106	14	0	28	170	20	28	24	234	16	13	11
43	63	47	0	107	21	0	28	171	20	28	26	235	16	15	11
44	63	63	0	108	28	0	28	172	20	28	28	236	16	16	11
45	47	63	0	109	28	0	21	173	20	26	28	237	15	16	11
46	31	63	0	110	28	0	14	174	20	24	28	238	13	16	11
47	16	63	0	111	28	0	7	175	20	22	28	239	12	16	11
48	0	63	0	112	28	0	0	176	0	0	16	240	11	16	11
49	0	63	16	113	28	7	0	177	4	0	16	241	11	16	12
50	0	63	31	114	28	14	0	178	8	0	16	242	11	16	13
51	0	63	47	115	28	21	0	179	12	0	16	243	11	16	15
52	0	63	63	116	28	28	0	180	16	0	16	244	11	16	16
53	0	47	63	117	21	28	0	181	16	0	12	245	11	15	16
54	0	31	63	118	14	28	0	182	16	0	8	246	11	13	16
55	0	16	63	119	7	28	0	183	16	0	4	247	11	12	16
56	31	31	63	120	0	28	0	184	16	0	0	248	0	0	0
57	39	31	63	121	0	28	7	185	16	4	0	249	0	0	0
58	47	31	63	122	0	28	14	186	16	8	0	250	0	0	0
59	55	31	63	123	0	28	21	187	16	12	0	251	0	0	0
60	63	31	63	124	0	28	28	188	16	16	0	252	0	0	0
61	63	31	55	125	0	21	28	189	12	16	0	253	0	0	0
62	63	31	47	126	0	14	28	190	8	16	0	254	0	0	0
63	63	31	39	127	0	7	28	191	4	16	0	255	0	0	0

E.4.2   Setting a Palette Register

We are not restricted to the default palette. We can make our own colors for the palette. If we need one color only, we can simply use the BIOS interrupt designed to alter a designated palette index element:

```
/* +-------------------------------------------------------------+
   +  setPalette
   +  Set new color value for i-th palette register.
   +  Arguments:
   +   i     - palette register index
   +   red   - intensity for red component of the color
   +   green - intensity for green component of the color
   +   blue  - intensity for blue component of the color
   +-------------------------------------------------------------+ */
void setPalette(unsigned char i, unsigned char red, unsigned char green,
   unsigned char blue)
{
   union REGS inregs, outregs;

   inregs.h.ah = 0x10;
   inregs.h.al = 0x10;
   inregs.h.bl = i;
   inregs.h.dh = red; * intensity of red, with 0-63 possible */
   inregs.h.ch = green; /* same for green . . .*/
   inregs.h.cl = blue; /* . . . and for blue */

   int86(0x10, &inregs, &outregs);
}
```

E.4.3   Saving the Default Palette

If you want to preserve the default value of the palette register, you can first save the value with the following function before calling setPalette():

```
/* +-------------------------------------------------------------+
   +  getPalette
   +  Get color value from i-th palette register.
   +  Arguments:
   +   i     - palette register index
   +   red   - pointer to intensity for red component of the color
   +   green - pointer to intensity for green component of the color
   +   blue  - pointer to intensity for blue component of the color
   +-------------------------------------------------------------+ */
void getPalette(unsigned char i, unsigned char *red,
   unsigned char *green, unsigned char *blue)
{
   union REGS inregs, outregs;
   inregs.h.ah = 0x10;
   inregs.h.al = 0x15; /* read one video card register service */
   inregs.h.bl = i;
   int86(0x10, &inregs, &outregs);
   *red   = outregs.h.dh;
   *green = outregs.h.ch;
   *blue  = outregs.h.cl;
}
```

E.4.4   Resetting the Entire Palette

This personalized color setting will work fine if you need to set only a few new colors. If you want to reset the entire color palette, you need a function that changes all colors at once. Our setPaletteAll() function will do the job:

```
/* +-------------------------------------------------------------+
   +  setPaletteAll
   +     Set all 256 colors of current palette from (palette) array.
```

```
      +   Argument: palette - the array must have 256*3-byte size.
      +                       Each color - red, green, and blue - has own byte
      +--------------------------------------------------------------+ */
void setPaletteAll(char *palette)
{
   union REGS inregs, outregs;
   struct SREGS segregs;

   inregs.h.ah = 0x10;
   inregs.h.al = 0x12;
   inregs.x.bx = 0;
   inregs.x.cx = 256; /* number of registers to update */
   segregs.es  = FP_SEG(palette);
   inregs.x.dx = FP_OFF(palette);
   int86x(0x10, &inregs, &outregs, &segregs);
}
```

The update block of video card color registers service, service 12h, sends a table of values to the buffer pointed to by `es:dx`. The `FP_SEG` and `FP_OFF` macros we use to assist us were covered in Appendix B.

Again, if we want to preserve the default palette values before calling this function, we may do so. Our `get-PaletteAll()` function can be used for this purpose:

```
/* +--------------------------------------------------------------+
   +   getPaletteAll
   +       Get all 256 colors of current palette to (palette) array.
   +   Argument: palette - the array must have 256*3-byte size.
   +                       Each color red, green, and blue has its own byte.
   +--------------------------------------------------------------+ */
void getPaletteAll(char *palette)
{
   union REGS inregs, outregs;
   struct SREGS segregs;

   inregs.h.ah = 0x10;
   inregs.h.al = 0x17; /* read block of video card registers */
   inregs.x.bx = 0;
   inregs.x.cx = 256;
   segregs.es  = FP_SEG(palette);
   inregs.x.dx = FP_OFF(palette);
   int86x(0x10, &inregs, &outregs, &segregs);
}
```

As you can see, the mechanism is the same as the flipside function, `setPaletteAll()`.

Now we are ready to change all palette registers. But we can make our job easier still. We can create a structure for more convenient access to the three color components. We used a pointer to this structure already in `set-PaletteAll()` and `getPaletteAll()`:

```
typedef struct palette_type
{
    unsigned char red, green, blue;
} palette, *palette_ptr;
```

See if you can now go back and rework `setPalette()` and `getPalette()` to make use of a pointer to this new structure type. We will also need a work array, `savedPalette`, for saving and restoring palette registers:

```
palette savedPalette[256];
```

The useful functions `savePalette()` and `restorePalette()` can now easily be written:

```
/* Save current palette. */
void savePalette(void)
{
   getPaletteAll(&savedPalette);
}
```

```
/* Restore previous palette. */
void restorePalette(void)
{
   setPaletteAll(&savedPalette);
}
```

E.4.5 A Palette Demo

We can view all 64 intensity values that each of the colors red, green, blue, and gray can accept. The palette-Demo() function shows them to us. First, we declare another global 256-element structure array, rgbPalette:

```
/* +----------------------------------------------------------+
   +   paletteDemo
   +   Draw all possible color intensities (64 values) for red, green,
   +   blue, and gray colors.
   +----------------------------------------------------------+ */
palette rgbPalette[256];

void paletteDemo(void)
{
   int k;
   unsigned char intensity;

   /* 1. Set all red colors */
   intensity = 0;
   for (k = 0; k < 64; k++)
   {
      rgbPalette[k].red   = intensity++;
      rgbPalette[k].green = rgbPalette[k].blue  = 0;
   }

   /* 2. Set all green colors */
   intensity = 0;
   for (k = 64; k < 2 * 64; k++)
   {
      rgbPalette[k].red = rgbPallette[k].blue = 0
      rgbPalette[k].green = intensity++;
   }

   /* 3. Set all blue colors */
   intensity = 0;
   for (k = 2 * 64; k < 3 * 64; k++)
   {
      rgbPalette[k].red   = rgbPalette[k].green = 0;
      rgbPalette[k].blue  = intensity++;
   }

   /* 4. Set all gray colors */
   intensity = 0;
   for (k = 3 * 64; k < 4 * 64; k++, intensity++)
   {
      rgbPalette[k].red = rgbPalette[k].green = rgbPalette[k].blue = intensity;
   }

   /* Save old palette */
   savePalette();

   /* Set new palette */
   setPaletteAll((char*) &rgbPalette);
```

```
    /* Draw all palette registers contents in white frame and wait for key press */
    colorDemo(255);

    /* Restore old palette */
    restorePalette();
}
```

E.5   GRAPHICS IMAGES

We have used a function we have already seen, colorDemo(), that draws a 16 × 16 color table. However, in this case, we have prepared our own color palette beforehand. The color palette we have used shows only the various possible intensity levels for each color, without combining red, green, and blue in a single color. Of course, we could combine them in quite a number of different ways. In fact, the total color combinations would be 64 to the third power, or 262,144 different possible colors. That gives quite a range of colors to work with.

How do we select colors? We could do so manually. Any inexpensive commercial graphics software such as PhotoFinish, Photoshop, or even the Paint accessory that comes with Windows will let us assign three RGB values and see the resulting color in a little box in the screen.

Normally, however, we look through the other end of the telescope. We take an already-created graphics image in one of the recognized formats (TIFF, or .tif; bitmap, or .bmp; PCX, or .pcx; JPEG, or .jpg; GIF, or .gif; Windows metafile, or .wmf; and so on) and use the palette the graphics image has used. We will show you how to do that with PCX images.

If you open a graphics file in PhotoFinish, for instance, you will see not only the graphics image itself, but also a 256-grid palette. How does the program get the colors? Well, it could look at each pixel and make an array of structures as we did and fill it, keeping track to make sure it does not duplicate any one color. As you will see shortly, the mechanism is much simpler than that.

E.5.1   Drawing a PCX File

We will now try to draw an already-existing graphics image saved in a file that has a PCX format. The PCX format was developed by the ZSoft firm for PC Paintbrush. We will use two versions of the PCX file format. The first is version 2.5, with a fixed EGA palette, which we will use to draw black-and-white images. The second is version 3.0, which allows us to draw 256-color images with a palette saved at the end of the file with the image (aha, so that's the secret!).

PCX file images are compressed, but we will start with an easier job. Our first program will draw an arbitrary noncompressed image that is placed in a buffer table named bitmap. We will draw the bitmap contents on the screen. Before doing so, we can save the image currently on the screen to a bitmap if we wish.

These functions can be useful for other purposes as well, not only for drawing a graphics image in PCX file format. They would be useful in drawing complicated images that have several image layers, for example. Each layer is saved as a separate bitmap and drawn in the order you need.

After we can draw a simple bitmap, we will decompress an image of a PCX file to a bitmap and draw it. Our bitmap will have following structure:

```
typedef struct bitmap_type
{
    unsigned int x, y; /* Position of bitmap: top left corner */
    unsigned int width, height; /* Size of bitmap */
    unsigned char far *buffer; /* Buffer containing image */
} bitmap, *bitmap_ptr;
```

To draw this bitmap we will use the function bitmap_put():

```
/* +--------------------------------------------------------------+
   +    bitmap_put
   +    Draws a bitmap in the destination buffer
   +    image       - pointer to bitmap image
   +    destination - pointer to destination buffer.
   +    transparent - 0: clear image background if image pixel == 0.
   +                 - 1: don't clear image background if image pixel == 0.
   +--------------------------------------------------------------+ */
```

```c
void bitmap_put(bitmap_ptr image, unsigned char far *destination, int transparent)
{
   unsigned x, y, width, height, /* Size of bitmap */ minWidth, minHeight;

   unsigned char far *bitmap_data; /* Pointer to bitmap buffer */
   unsigned char far *dest_buffer; /* Pointer to destination buffer */
   unsigned char pixel; /* Current pixel value being processed. */

   /* Compute offset of bitmap in destination buffer.
      Note: all buffers must be 320 bytes wide */
   dest_buffer = destination + SCREEN_WIDTH * image->y + image->x;

   /* create aliases to variables so the structure doesn't need to be
      dereferenced continually */
   width       = image->width;
   height      = image->height;
   bitmap_data = image->buffer;

   minWidth  = min(SCREEN_WIDTH,  width);
   minHeight = min(SCREEN_HEIGHT, height);

   /* Test whether transparency is on or off */
   if (transparent)
   {
      /* Use version that will draw a transparent bitmap */
      /* (slightly slower) draw each line of the bitmap. */
      for (y = 0; y < minHeight; y++)
      {
         /* Copy the next row into the destination buffer */
         for (x = 0; x < minWidth; x++)
         {
            /* test for transparent pixel, i.e., 0; */
            /* if not transparent then draw */
            if ((pixel = *(bitmap_data + x)) != 0)
               *(dest_buffer + x) = pixel;
         }

         /* Move to next line in destination buffer and in bitmap buffer */
         dest_buffer += SCREEN_WIDTH;
         bitmap_data += width;
      } /* end for y */
   } /* end if transparent */
   else
   {
      /* Draw each line of the bitmap; note how each pixel doesn't need
         to be tested for transparency, so memcpy can be used */
      for (y = 0; y < minHeight; y++)
      {
         /* Copy the next row into the destination buffer using fmemcpy
            for speed. */
         _fmemcpy(dest_buffer, bitmap_data, minWidth);

         /* Move to next line in destination buffer and in bitmap buffer */
         dest_buffer += SCREEN_WIDTH;
         bitmap_data += width;
      }
   } /* end else nontransparent version */
} /* end bitmap_put */
```

E.5.2   Transparency

As you can see in the comments to `bitmap_put()`, we do not necessarily clear the background for our bitmap. Our bitmap may be *transparent* in areas where the pixel value is 0. We give ourselves the option of using register index 0 for a pixel value of 0 (which will usually be black), or not writing anything for a pixel if we encounter a 0 value, thus leaving the background color of our screen to show through since we will not have written anything there. Figures E.4A and E.4B show the difference in treatment between transparency and nontransparency. If you are afraid to lose an image already on the screen, you can save it beforehand to a bitmap structure with the `bitmapGet()` function:

```
/* +---------------------------------------------------------+
   +   bitmap_get
   +   Function to extract a bitmap from a source image buffer.
   +   image  - pointer to resulting image
   +   source - pointer to destination buffer
   +---------------------------------------------------------+ */

void bitmap_get(bitmap_ptr image, unsigned char far *source)
{
   unsigned int source_off, /* Offsets into destination and source buffers. */
      bitmap_off;

   int y, width, height; /* Size of bitmap. */
   unsigned char far *bitmap_data; /* Pointer to bitmap buffer */

   /* Compute offset of bitmap in source buffer.
      Note: destination buffer must be 320 bytes wide */
   source_off = SCREEN_WIDTH * image->y + image->x;

   bitmap_off = 0;

   /* Create aliases to variables so the structure doesn't need to be
      dereferenced continually */
   height = image->height;
```

Figure E.4A   *Transparent Image*

Figure E.4B   *Nontransparent Image*

```
    width  = image->width;
    bitmap_data = image->buffer;

    /* Draw each line of the bitmap; note how each pixel doesn't need
       to be tested for transparency hence memcpy can be used  */
    for (y = 0; y < height; y++)
    {
        /* Copy the next row into the bitmap buffer using memcpy for speed. */
        _fmemcpy(&bitmap_data[bitmap_off], &source[source_off], width);

        /* Move to next line in source buffer and in bitmap buffer. */
        source_off += SCREEN_WIDTH;
        bitmap_off += width;
    } /* end for y */
} /* end bitmap_get */
```

E.5.3   File Decompression

Now we are ready to decompress a PCX file image. But how are the images compressed? The PCX files use a simple compression method called *run-length encoding*. If some bytes in the image are repeated in sequence (as will often occur), the number of times in the sequence and then the byte value repeated are placed in the PCX file. Often our images have "empty" areas (transparent, as we have discussed), and this method works fine for these areas.

How can we differentiate a byte repeater from the repeated byte? We will assume that all bytes that have both bits 6 and 7 set to 1 are repeater bytes. Why? Remember that only the first 6 bits are used for color. ZSoft made use of that fact and zeroed out the 2 most significant bits where the byte represents a color (actually, for the purpose of representing color, the video card register ignores the two most significant bits, so it doesn't matter what value they have) and turned them both on where the byte represents a repeater. Since the repeater byte's 2 most significant bits are sentinel bits only, we must look only at the other 6 bits for the number of times to repeat the succeeding color byte when we find such a repeater byte. We can do this by subtracting 192, or hex 0xC0 (the value represented by bits 6 and 7 being on) or we can AND with a mask having bits 6 and 7 off (thus zeroing out those bits) and all other bits on (thus leaving them as is). See Chapter 12 for a refresher.

Before the actual color bytes, however, there are a number of bytes in what is called the header that give general information about the image. Here's how the PCX file starts:

```
typedef struct pcxHeader
{
    char identifier; /* Always 0Ah for PCX format            */
    char version;    /* Version number                       */
    char encoding;   /* Only one method now = 1              */
    char bitsPerPixel;/* How many pixels used for pixel value */
    int  x1;         /* Left edge of image                   */
    int  y1;         /* Top edge of image                    */
    int  x2;         /* Right edge of image                  */
    int  y2;         /* Bottom edge of image                 */
    int  hResolution;/* Horizontal resolution               */
    int  VResolution;/* Vertical resolution                 */
    char palette[48];/* Palette for 16-color video mode     */
    char reserved;   /* Always 0                             */
    char nPlanes;    /* Number bit planes (for 16-color mode) */
    int  bytesPerLine; /* Bytes used for one image line      */
    int  palinfo;    /* 1 - color palette 2 - gray palette   */
    int  hScreenSize;/* Horizontal screen resolution         */
    int  vScreenSize;/* Vertical   screen resolution         */
    char reserve[54];/* Always 0                             */
} PCXHEADER;
```

Our program will decompress files with 2-color and 256-color images. These images are saved as one bit plane. The file attribute nPlanes must be equal to 1. If our image has two colors only, the file attribute bitsPer-Pixel will equal 1. If the image has 256 colors, bitsPerPixel will equal 8.

Now we can write the decompressing function:

```
/* +-----------------------------------------------------------------+
   +  PCX_loadBitmap
   +      Decompress and load the image to bitmap structure.
   +  Arguments:
   +      fileName - file with image
   +      bmp      - bitmap to save file image
   +-----------------------------------------------------------------+ */
int PCX_loadBitmap(char *fileName, bitmap_ptr bmp)
{
   FILE *fp;

   unsigned int k, i, x, bytesLeft, planesLen, repeatCount,
      headerLen = sizeof(PCXHEADER);
   PCXHEADER header;

   unsigned long y;

   unsigned char *readBuffer, far *bmpBuffer, far *rb, far *planes, color,
      byteValue;

   fp = fopen(fileName, "rb");
   if (fp == NULL)
      return -1;

   fread(&header, headerLen, 1, fp);

   /* Make buffer for compressed plane values */
   readBuffer = malloc(BUFFER_LEN);
   rb = readBuffer;

   /* Make buffer for decompressed plane values */
   planesLen = header.nPlanes * header.bytesPerLine;
   planes = farmalloc(planesLen);

   bmp->x      = header.x1;
   bmp->y      = header.y1;
   bmp->width  = header.x2 - header.x1 + 1;
   bmp->height = header.y2 - header.y1 + 1;
   bmp->buffer = farmalloc(bmp->width * bmp->height);
   bmpBuffer   = bmp->buffer;

   /* Read first part of compressed image bytes */
   bytesLeft = fread(readBuffer, 1, BUFFER_LEN, fp);
   rb = readBuffer;

   if (header.nPlanes == 1)  /* This is 2-color or 256-color image */
   {
      for(y = 0; y < bmp->height; y++)
      {
         /* Decompress one image line to line buffer */
         for (k = 0; k < header.bytesPerLine; k += repeatCount)
         {
            if (bytesLeft == 0) /* Get next byte portion */
            {
               bytesLeft = fread(readBuffer, 1, BUFFER_LEN, fp);
               rb = readBuffer;
            }
```

```
                        /* Get byte: pixel repeater or pixel itself */
                        byteValue = rb[0]; rb++; bytesLeft--;

                        if ((byteValue >= 0xC0) && (header.encoding == 1))
                        {
                            /* Byte repeater was read */
                            repeatCount = byteValue - 0xC0;

                            if (bytesLeft == 0) /* Get next byte portion */
                            {
                                bytesLeft = fread(readBuffer, 1,
                                    BUFFER_LEN, fp);
                                rb = readBuffer;
                            }

                            /* Get repeated pixels */
                            byteValue = rb[0]; rb++; bytesLeft--;
                        }
                        else repeatCount = 1;

                        /* Put decompressed bytes to plane buffer */
                        for (i = 0; i < repeatCount; i++)
                            planes[k + i] = byteValue;
                    } /* byte decompress */

                    if (header.bitPerPixel == 1)
                    /* Convert black and white bytes to bitmap bytes */
                        for (x = 0; x < bmp->width; x++)
                    {
                        color = planes[x >> 3] & (0x80 >> (x & 0x7));
                        *(bmpBuffer + x) = (color == 0 ? 0x1 : 0x0);
                    }
                    else if (header.bitPerPixel == 8)
                    /* Convert 256-color bytes to bitmap bytes */
                        for (x = 0; x < bmp->width; x++)
                            *(bmpBuffer + x) = *(planes + x);

                    bmpBuffer += bmp->width; /* Shift to next bitmap line */
            } /* Line decompress */
    } /* 2-color or 256-color image */
    free(readBuffer);
    farfree(planes);
    fclose(fp);

    return 0;
}
```

All done. But if we drew the image now, it wouldn't be correct. The PCX file holds its own palette values, and we must load them before drawing. The 256-color image has its palette not in the file header, but, as we pointed out earlier, at the very end of the file—the last 768 bytes (256 * 3 = 768). We will write a function to find the bytes and load the palette:

```
palette PCXPalette[256];


/* +----------------------------------------------------------------+
   +  PCX_loadPalette
   +       Load file palette to PCXPalette array.
   +  Argument: fileName - file with image palette.
   +----------------------------------------------------------------+ */
int PCX_loadPalette(char *fileName)
{
```

```
        FILE *fp;
        int k;
        char *palette;
        PCXHEADER header;

        fp = fopen(fileName, "rb");
        if (fp == NULL)
          return -1;

        fread(&header, sizeof(PCXHEADER), sizeof(char), fp);

        if (header.bitPerPixel == 1)
        {
           /* Read palette from file header */
           setPalette(0, header.palette[0], header.palette[1], header.palette[2]);
           setPalette(1, header.palette[3], header.palette[4], header.palette[5]);
        }
        else
           if (header.bitPerPixel == 8)
        {
           /* 256-color image palette is loaded from the file end */
           fseek(fp, -256 * 3, SEEK_END);
           palette = malloc(256 * 3);
           fread(palette, 256 * 3, 1, fp);
           for (k = 0; k < 256; k++)
           {
              PCXPalette[k].red   = palette[3 * k] >> 2;
              PCXPalette[k].green = palette[3 * k + 1] >> 2;
              PCXPalette[k].blue  = palette[3 * k + 2] >> 2;
           }
           setPaletteAll((char*) &PCXPalette);
           free(palette);
        }

        fclose(fp);
        return 0;
}
```

Now we can draw the correct PCX image with this simple miniprogram, using the image on disk, `color1.pcx`, as an example:

```
savePalette();
PCX_loadPallete("color1.pcx");
PCX_loadBitmap("color1.pcx", &bmpColor1);
bmpColor1.x = 0;
bmpColor1.y = 0;
bitmap_put(&bmpColor1, video_buffer, 0);
if (getch() == 0)
   getch();
setColor(0);
clearScreen();
restorePalette();
```

E.6   TEXT DRAWING

Now that we have mastered graphics images, we will turn to drawing text. For our text drawing to be most useful, we must be able to use whatever font and font size we wish. How can we do this? There are hundreds of true-type fonts, used by Windows, that we can utilize. We will show you how to select a font type and size and draw a font set from the selected type and size in a black-and-white PCX file.

E.6.1   Creating a Text File of Printable Characters

We will draw all printable characters from the standard ASCII symbol set in standard order as one very long symbol column and then save it, first as a text file. The following simple program, makechar.c, does that:

```
/* makechar.c */
/* for making pcx symbol-set files, create file with all printable
   ASCII characters in one long strip (character, newline, character,
   newline, etc.) */

#include <stdio.h>
#include <ctype.h> /* isprint(z) */

int main(int argc, char **argv)
{
    int ch;
    FILE *fp;

    if (argc < 2)
    {
        puts("Format makechar <filename>");
        return 1;
    }

    fp = fopen(argv[1], "w");

    for (ch = 33; ch < 127; ch++)
        if(isprint(ch))
            fprintf(fp, "%c\n", ch);
    return 0;
}
```

A copy of this file, which we've named symbols.txt, is found on the accompanying disk.

E.6.2   Creating a PCX File of Text as Graphics Images

We can use this symbols file to create PCX files for any combination font and font size we wish. To do this, it is easiest to use a commercial graphics program, such as PhotoFinish or Photo Shop. These programs are inexpensive. You can do the same thing with the Windows accessory, Paint, but it's a little more cumbersome.

Whichever you choose, you must create a new file. Select black-and-white or 1-bit mode. Select a size that is about 25 pixels wide × 2500 pixels long (remember, we have nearly 100 characters in one long vertical strip)—wider and longer the larger your font size. Open symbols.txt in any text program (Word, WordPerfect, NotePad, WordPad, and so on) and copy the entire text to the clipboard: Ctrl A Ctrl C. Switch back to the graphics program and select create text (in most programs, you click on the letter A or T in the toolbox). Select the font and size you want from the font list. Paste the clipboard buffer: Ctrl V. Save the file as a PCX file.

In Paint, the process is more difficult because you cannot draw a text area large enough to fit all characters vertically. You have to do the pasting job in four or more chunks vertically with portions of our text file each time. If you find this too difficult, we have included sample font PCX files on the accompanying diskette.

E.6.3   Making a Lookup Table

Now that we have created the PCX file for a font, we will proceed as follows:

- Select several font PCX files; we will decompress each PCX file and load it into a bitmap using the PCX_loadBitmap() function we have discussed.
- Parse each bitmap into the 93 individual printable characters and create a lookup table in which each entry contains the following information about the character: the number of bytes from the start of the bitmap to the character (called the *shift*), the height of the character (how many lines or rows of the bitmap), the left-most pixel in the character, and the width (that is, the difference between the right-most pixel in the character and the left-most).
- Select a particular font.
- Draw text with the font.

We will use a `typedef` for the lookup table element structure:

```
typedef /* Lookup table element for a letter in bitmap */
struct LookUpTable
{
   unsigned int x, width, shift, height;
} lookup, *lookup_ptr;
```

We will declare a global 256-element array of such structure variables for each font as well as corresponding bitmap pointers (see the discussion above for the `bitmap` structure `typedef` and the structure's members):

```
lookup_ptr lookupTable;
lookup normalLookup[256], boldLookup[256], italicLookup[256], comicLookup[256];
bitmap_ptr fontBitmap, normalFont, boldFont, italicFont, comicFont;
```

The top-level mechanics of the process are managed by the `loadFonts()` function. We have chosen four true-type fonts—Arial Normal, Arial Bold, Arial MT Italic, and Comic—and assigned them arbitrary unique symbolic constant values to distinguish them in a `switch` statement:

```
/* +------------------------------------------------------------+
   + loadFonts
   +       Load font letters images from pcx file to bitmap
   +------------------------------------------------------------+ */
void loadFonts(void)
{
   normalFont = malloc(sizeof(bitmap));
   PCX_loadBitmap("normal.pcx", normalFont);
   normalFont->x = normalFont->y = 0;
   makeLookupTable(normalFont, (lookup_ptr) &normalLookup);

   boldFont = malloc(sizeof(bitmap));
   PCX_loadBitmap("bold.pcx", boldFont);
   boldFont->x = boldFont->y = 0;
   makeLookupTable(boldFont, (lookup_ptr) &boldLookup);

   italicFont = malloc(sizeof(bitmap));
   PCX_loadBitmap("italic.pcx", italicFont);   italicFont->x = 0;
   italicFont->y = makeLookupTable(italicFont, (lookup_ptr) &italicLookup);

   comicFont = malloc(sizeof(bitmap));
   PCX_loadBitmap("comic.pcx", comicFont);
   comicFont->x = comicFont->y = 0;
   makeLookupTable(comicFont, (lookup_ptr) &comicLookup);

   setFont(COMIC_FONT);
}
```

The `setFont()` function allows us to select the current font before actually doing text drawing:

```
int cur_font;
/* +------------------------------------------------------------+
   + setFont
   +       Set current font for text drawing.
   +  Argument: font - standard font number
   +------------------------------------------------------------+ */
void setFont(int font)
{
   cur_font = font;

   switch(font)
   {
      case NORMAL_FONT:
         fontBitmap  = normalFont;
         lookupTable = normalLookup;
```

```
            break;

        case BOLD_FONT:
            fontBitmap  = boldFont;
            lookupTable = boldLookup;
            break;

        case ITALIC_FONT:
            fontBitmap  = italicFont;
            lookupTable = italicLookup;
            break;

        case COMIC_FONT:
            fontBitmap  = comicFont;
            lookupTable = comicLookup;
            break;
    }
}
```

Now we are nearly ready for the function that makes a lookup table. There are at least two basic approaches. The simplest is to assume that each character in the file is given equal vertical space and that within the equal number of bitmap lines for each character, the character is placed vertically at the appropriate place—thus, an ascending character such as b is placed starting higher within the character's vertical space than one that does not ascend above the character baseline, such as a, and other characters such as "_" are placed even lower within the character's total vertical space. This assumption should hold true for PCX files created with most commercial graphics programs.

With this approach, we will make two passes through the PCX file. On the first pass, we will simply determine the line numbers for the very first pixel for the very first character and the very last pixel for the very last character. We will then divide the difference between the first and last lines by the total number of characters to give us the height of each character. This height will include some spacing above and below the character (less above for ascenders and less below for descenders such as y). The "shift" for the first character will be the first line as determined above and that for each subsequent character will be the shift for the first character plus the height times the number of characters between the first and the character under investigation.

On the second pass, we will move from shift line to shift line and within the resulting character space determine the left-most and right-most pixels. If we have this information, we know the width (right-most pixel minus left-most pixel plus 1). Since the height is the same for all characters, we have that value from the first pass. We then store the values of the height, right-most pixel, left-most pixel, and width into their proper elements.

```
/* +---------------------------------------------------------------+
   +   makeLookupTable
   +   Make lookup table that contains for each letter:
   +       - first letter's byte number in the bitmap
   +       - first letter's pixel in the letter's line
   +       - the letter's width
   +       - the letter's height
   +       Arguments:
   +          fontBitmap  - pointer to decompressed image
   +          lookupTable - calculated lookup table
   +---------------------------------------------------------------+ */
void makeLookupTable(bitmap_ptr fontBitmap, lookup_ptr lookupTable)
{
    int letter_number = 0;
    int letter_x1 = fontBitmap->width; /* Letter image */
    int letter_x2 = 0; /*       horizontal limits */
    int bitmap_width = fontBitmap->width, bitmap_height = fontBitmap->height;
    int first_line = 0, last_line = 0, num_letters = 16 * 6 - 2, letter_height;
    unsigned char far *fb = fontBitmap->buffer;

    int k, i;

    /* determine very first and last lines in graphic with pixels */
    for (k = 0; k < bitmap_height; k++) /* row by row in graphic */
```

```
    {
        for (i = 0; i < bitmap_width; i++) /* whole row's bytes */
            if (*fb++ != 0)
            {
                if (first_line == 0)
                    first_line = k;
                last_line = k;
            }
    }
    /* letter height # lines between first & last / # of characters */
    letter_height = (last_line - first_line + 16) / num_letters;

    /* reset to point to start of graphics image again */
    fb = fontBitmap->buffer + first_line * bitmap_width;
    for (k = first_line; k <= last_line; k++)
    {

        /* after last line in character, store left col and width */
        if (((k - first_line) % letter_height == 0 && k > first_line)
            ¦¦ k == last_line)
        {
            lookupTable[letter_number].x = letter_x1;
            lookupTable[letter_number].width = letter_x2 - letter_x1 + 1;
            letter_number++;
            /* reset for next character */
            letter_x1 = bitmap_width;
            letter_x2 = 0;
        }

        for (i = 0; i < bitmap_width; i++)
        {
            if (*fb++ != 0)
            {
                letter_x1 = min(letter_x1, i);
                letter_x2 = max(letter_x2, i);
            }
        }
    }

    /* determine bytes from start of image for each character and height of each
       character (the height will be the same for all characters with this method) */
    for (i = 0; i < num_letters; i++)
    {
        lookupTable[i].shift  =
            (first_line + letter_height * i) * bitmap_width;
        lookupTable[i].height = letter_height;
    }
}
```

If we use the Windows utility Paint, where we must make the PCX file in several chunks, we may have trouble with this uniform-space approach. In that case, we can take a more precise but somewhat more complex approach. With this approach, we will scan the PCX file line by line. We will assume a character starts whenever we find a line with a pixel and stops when we next find a blank line. One exception to this methodology—certain characters are two-part: !, :, ;, =, ?, i, and j. For those characters, we will assume the character ends only after we have found the first line with pixels, the first line after that without pixels, another line after that with pixels, and finally another line without pixels.

Note that this second approach will not work for fancy fonts that have multipart characters for most characters:

```
/* +---------------------------------------------------------------+
   +  makeLookupTableTwo
   +  Complex version of makeLoopup: corresponds to drawTextTwo.
   +  Make lookup table that contains for each letter:
   +     - first letter's line in the bitmap
```

```
+       - first letter's pixel in the letter's line
+       - the letter's width
+       - the letter's height
+     Arguments:
+        fontBitmap  - pointer to decompressed image
+        lookupTable - calculated lookup table
+------------------------------------------------------------+ */
void makeLookupTableTwo(bitmap_ptr fontBitmap, lookup_ptr lookupTable)
{
   int has_point; /* Is two-part character? */
   int is_empty;  /* Is line in letter's bitmap empty? */
     int in_letter; /* Is letter image parsed? */

   int letter_number;
   int letter_x1; /* Letter image           */
   int letter_x2; /*        horizontal limits */
   int letter_y1; /* Letter image start      */
   int letter_y2; /*        and end shifts    */

   int point_x, point_shift, point_width, point_saved;
   int x, shift, width, height; bitmap_width, bitmap_height;
   unsigned char far *fb;

   int k, i;

   bitmap_width  = fontBitmap->width;
   bitmap_height = fontBitmap->height;
   fb            = fontBitmap->buffer;

   has_point   = point_saved = 0;

   is_empty  = 1;
   in_letter = 0;

   /* Set default limits for next letter */
   letter_number = 0;
   letter_x1 = bitmap_width; /* To minimize it later */
   letter_x2 = 0;            /* To maximize it later */
   letter_y1 = letter_y2 - 0;

   for (k = 0; k < bitmap_height; k++)
   { /* Find the letter line width limits */
      is_empty = 1;
      for (i = 0; i < bitmap_width; i++)
         if (*fb++ != 0)
         { /* Change the letter limits */
            is_empty  = 0;
            letter_x1 = min(letter_x1,i);
            letter_x2 = max(letter_x2,i);
         }

      /* two-part character? */
      switch ('!' + letter_number)
      {
         case '!': case ':': case ';': case '=': case '?': case 'i': case 'j':
            has_point = 1; break;
         default:
            has_point = 0;
      }
```

```
      if (in_letter && !is_empty)
      /* The letter is continued */
         letter_y2++;
      else if (in_letter && is_empty)
      {
         /* The letter is ended for all letters except i and j */
         x      = letter_x1;
         shift  = letter_y1 * bitmap_width;
         width  = letter_x2 - letter_x1 + 1;
         height = letter_y2 - letter_y1 + 1;

         if (has_point)
            if (!point_saved)
         {
            /* Save point sizes */
            point_x     = x;
            point_shift = shift;
            point_width = width;
            point_saved = 1;
            in_letter   = 0;
            continue;
         }
         else
         {
            point_saved = 0;
            x = min(x, point_x);
            width  = max(width, point_width);
            height += (shift - point_shift + 1) / bitmap_width;
            shift  = point_shift;
         }

         lookupTable[letter_number].x      = x;
         lookupTable[letter_number].shift  = shift;
         lookupTable[letter_number].width  = width;
         lookupTable[letter_number].height = height;

         letter_number++;

         /* ASCII symbols from ! to ~ */
         if (letter_number >= 16 * 6 - 2)
            break;
         in_letter = 0;

         /* Set default limits for next letter */
         letter_x1 = bitmap_width; /* To minimize it later */
         letter_x2 = 0;            /* To maximize it later */
      }
      else
         if (!in_letter && !is_empty)
      {
         /* New letter starts for all letters except i and j */
         in_letter = 1;

         letter_y1 = letter_y2 = k;
      }
      /* Else skip space between letters - do nothing */
   }
}
```

E.6.4   Drawing Text

Now our lookup table is prepared. How we can draw anything? We will write a function that draws a symbol string. For each character in the string, we will simply determine the element number in the lookup table; load in the appropriate shift, height, left-most pixel position, and width; move to the appropriate line of the bitmap according to the shift; and finally read as many bitmap lines as the height dictates and write them to video memory:

```
/* +------------------------------------------------------------------+
   +   drawText
   +    Shift symbols from lookup table
   +   Arguments:
   +        x    - left of the symbol string
   +        y    - top of the symbol string
   +        text - symbol string for drawing
   +        len  - how many symbols are used for drawing
   +------------------------------------------------------------------+ */
void drawText(int x, int y, char* text, int len)
{
   int k, i, j, letter_number, letter_height, letter_width, int bitmap_width =
      fontBitmap->width;

   unsigned char pixel;
   unsigned char far *fb, far *vb, far *fbs = fontBitmap->buffer;
   unsigned char far *vbs = video_buffer + SCREEN_WIDTH * y + x;

   /* draw no more symbols that really exist */
   len = min(len, strlen(text));
   if (len <= 0)
      return;

   vb = vbs;
   for (k = 0; k < len; k++)
   {
      /* For blank symbol draw nothing */
      if (text[k] == ' ')
      { vb += 5; continue; }

      /* Get letter number for the font bitmap */
      letter_number = text[k] - '!';
      letter_height = lookupTable[letter_number].height;
      letter_width  = lookupTable[letter_number].width;

      /* Shift font buffer pointer to first letter pixel to letter's
         byte # and then to the letter's pixel */
      fb = fbs + lookupTable[letter_number].shift lookupTable[letter_number].x;

      /* Copy the letter pixels from buffer to screen */
      for (i = 0; i < letter_height; i++)
         for (j = 0; j < letter_width; j++)
         {
            pixel = *(fb + i * bitmap_width + j);
            if (pixel)
               *(vb + i * SCREEN_WIDTH + j) = curColor;
         }

      /* Shift video memory pointer to next letter screen position */
         vb += letter_width + 2;
   }
}
```

With our alternative approach, we must bear in mind that our cropped symbols are adjusted by top edge. In the first approach, the relative adjustment vis-à-vis the printing baseline is self-contained within the character's vertical space. In the second approach, we must shift the symbol to correct the size vertically:

```
/* +--------------------------------------------------------------+
   +  drawTextTwo
   +   More complex approach than drawText; does not assume equal
   +   vertical spacing between symbols in PCX file; special
   +   treatment of two-part symbols such as i, j, =, ; (hence the
   +   "two" on the end of the name of the function).
   +   Shift symbols from lookup table
   +  Arguments:
   +       x    - left of the symbol string
   +       y    - top of the symbol string
   +       text - symbol string for drawing
   +       len  - how many symbols are used for drawing
   +--------------------------------------------------------------+ */
void drawTextTwo(int x, int y, char* text, int len)
{
   int k, i, j, d, h2, h1,

   int letter_number, letter_height, letter_width, bitmap_width = fontBitmap->width;

   unsigned char pixel, far *fb, far *vb,
   unsigned char far *fbs = fontBitmap->buffer;
   unsigned char far *vbs = video_buffer + SCREEN_WIDTH * y + x;

   /* draw no more symbols that really exist */
   len = min(len, strlen(text));
   if (len <= 0)
      return;

   vb = vbs;
   for (k = 0; k < len; k++)
   {
      if (text[k] == ' ') /* For blank symbol draw nothing */
      { vb += 5; continue; }

      /* Get letter number for the font bitmap */
      letter_number = text[k] - '!';
      letter_height = lookupTable[letter_number].height;
      letter_width  = lookupTable[letter_number].width;

      /* Get height difference for small and long letters */
      /* Use as example: the letters (a) and (b) */
      h1 = lookupTable['b' - '!'].height - lookupTable['a' - '!'].height;

      /* Get shift size for symbols with lowest position */
      /* Period and comma are examples of the symbols */
      h2 = lookupTable['1' - '!'].height - lookupTable['.' - '!'].height;
      d = 0;
      switch (text[k])
      {
         /* Symbols are not shifted down */
         case 'b': case 'd': case 'h': case 'i': case 'j': case 'k':
            case 'l': case 'f': case '\'' : case '@': case '?': case '/':
            case '<': case '=': case '>': d = 0; break;

         /* Symbols are shifted down */
         case '.': case ',': case '_': d = h2; break;
```

```
          case 't': d = 1; break;

          /* Symbols are shifted to middle line of all letters */
          case '+': case '-': case '*': case ';': case ':': d = h2 / 2; break;

          default: /* Set shift size for groups of symbols */
             if (('0' <= text[k]) && (text[k] <= '9'))
             d = 0;
          else if (('A' <= text[k]) && (text[k] <= 'Z'))
             d = 0;
          else if (('a' <= text[k]) && (text[k] <= 'z'))
             d = h1;
       }

       /* Shift font buffer pointer to first letter pixel to letter's line and then
          to the letter's pixel */
       fb = fbs + lookupTable[letter_number].shift lookupTable[letter_number].x;

       /* Copy the letter pixels from buffer to screen */
       for (i = 0; i < letter_height; i++)
          for (j = 0; j < letter_width; j++)
          {
             pixel = *(fb + i * bitmap_width + j);
             if (pixel)
                *(vb + (i+d) * SCREEN_WIDTH + j) = curColor;
          }

       /* Shift video memory pointer to next letter screen position */
       vb += letter_width + 2;
    }
```

Now we will draw all possible text symbols. The function drawTextTable() draws them:

```
/* +--------------------------------------------------------------+
   +    drawTextTable
   +    Draw all acceptable symbols in 16*16 text table.
   +    Then draw frame for table with the color (frameColor).
   +--------------------------------------------------------------+ */
void drawTextTable(unsigned char frameColor)
{
    int dx = 16, /* Sizes of box for          */
        dy = 12, /*          current symbols.  */
        x, y,    /* Current letter position.   */
        tw, th,  /* Symbols table sizes.       */
        x1, y1,  /* Left top of table.         */
        x2, y2;  /* Top bottom of table.       */
        char c;      /* Current symbol.         */

    tw = 16 * dx;
    th = 16 * dy;

    x1 = (SCREEN_WIDTH  - tw) / 2;
    y1 = (SCREEN_HEIGHT - th) / 2;
    x2 = (SCREEN_WIDTH  + tw) / 2;
    y2 = (SCREEN_HEIGHT + th) / 2;

    setColor(126);
    fillRect(x1, y1, x2 + dx, y2);
    setColor(frameColor);
    drawRect(x1, y1, x2 + dx, y2);
```

Figure E.5 *Text Demo with Comic Font*

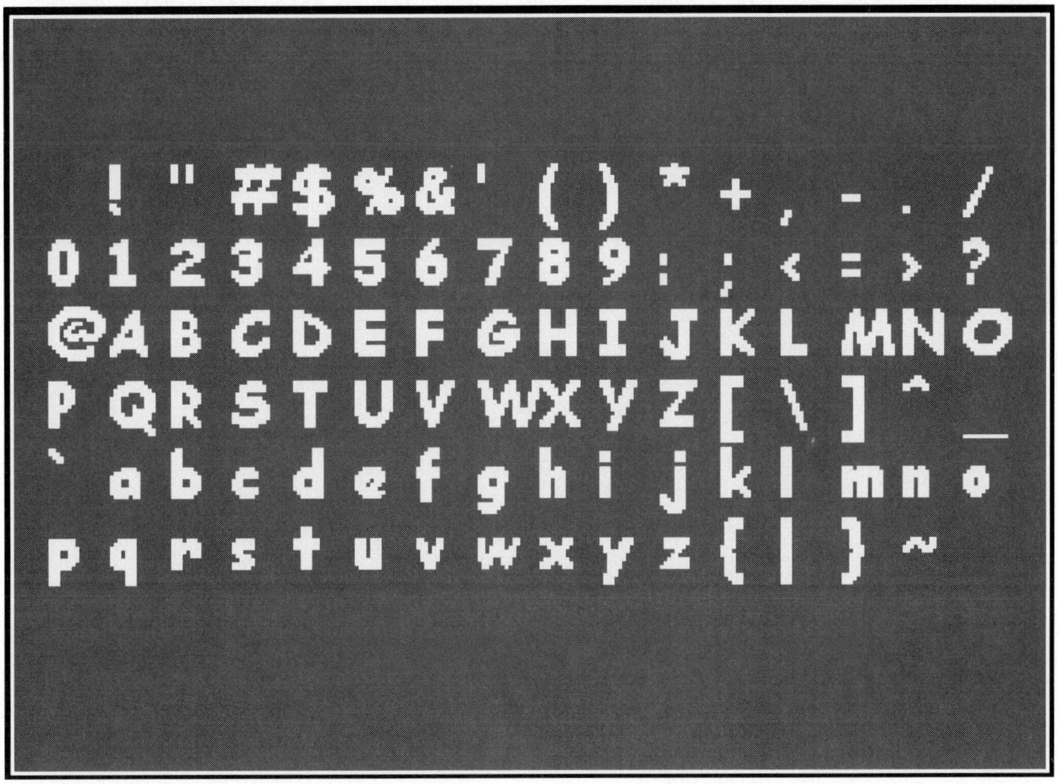

```
    setColor(15);
    for (c = '!'; c <= '~'; c++)
    {
        x = x1 + (c % 16) * dx;
        y = y1 + (c / 16) * (dy + dy / 2);
        drawText(x + 5, y + 2, &c, 1);
    }
} /* end of function drawTextTable */
```

Let's draw all symbols with a comic font. We will make a white frame around the symbol table (as we have seen, palette index number 15 is white: 63, 63, 63 RGB):

```
setFont(COMIC_FONT);
drawTextTable(15);
```

Figure E.5 shows what results.

E.7   MENU DRAWING

If we can draw text, lines, and rectangles, we can draw a menu for a dialog with our user. We start with a simple menu with which the user can select menu alternatives by keyboard. Then we will progress to allow menu selection by mouse instead.

If we want to make a properly spaced and sized menu that includes text, we need to know text size in pixels beforehand. The getTextHeight() and getTextWidth() functions are used to calculate these sizes:

```
/* +-------------------------------------------------------------+
   +  getTextWidth
   +      Get text string width in pixels.
   +  Arguments:
```

```
   +      text - string of symbols
   +      len  - count of symbols are used to calculate width
   +----------------------------------------------------------------+ */
int getTextWidth(char* text, int len)
{
    int letterNumber, letterWidth, textWidth, k;

    len = min(len, strlen(text));
    if (len <= 0)
        return 0;

    textWidth = 0;
    for (k = 0; k < len; k++)
    { /* For blank symbol draw nothing */
        if (text[k] == ' ')
        { textWidth += 5; continue; }

        /* Get letter number for the font bitmap */
        letterNumber = text[k] - '!';
        letterWidth  = lookupTable[letterNumber].width;

        /* Shift video memory pointer to next
           letter screen position */
        textWidth += letterWidth + 2;
    }
    return textWidth;
}
/* +----------------------------------------------------------------+
   +  getTextHeight:
   +      Get text string height in pixels
   +----------------------------------------------------------------+ */
int getTextHeight(void)
{
    return lookupTable[0].height; /* all letters are same height */
}
```

Again, the alternative approach is more complex:

```
/* +----------------------------------------------------------------+
   +  getTextHeightTwo
   +      Get text string height in pixels. (find max height of symbols)
   +  Arguments:
   +      text - string of symbols.
   +      len  - count of symbols are used to calculate height
   +----------------------------------------------------------------+ */
int getTextHeightTwo(char* text, int len)
{
    int k, h1, h2, d, letterNumber, textHeight, letterHeight;

    len = min(len, strlen(text));
    if (len <=0)
        return 0;

    textHeight = 0;
    for (k = 0; k < len; k++)
    {
        /* For blank symbol draw nothing */
        if (text[k] == ' ')
        { textHeight = max(textHeight,2); continue; }

        /* Get letter number for the font bitmap */
        letterNumber = text[k] - '!';
        letterHeight = lookupTable[letterNumber].height;
```

```
    /* Get height difference for small and long letters */
    /* Use as example the letters (a) and (b) */
    h1 = lookupTable['b' - '!'].height -
       lookupTable['a' - '!'].height;

    /* Get shift size for symbols with lowest position */
    /* Period and comma are examples of the symbols */
    h2 = lookupTable['1' - '!'].height -
       lookupTable['.' - '!'].height;
    d = 0;
    switch (text[k])
    {
        /* Symbols not shifted down */
        case 'b': case 'd': case 'h': case 'i': case 'j': case 'k':
           case 'l': case 't': case 'f': case '\'' : case '@':
           case '?': case '/': case '<': case '=': case '>':
           d = 0; break;

        /* Symbols shifted down */
        case '.': case ',': case '_': d = h2; break;
        /* Centered symbols */
        case '+': case '-': case '*': case ';': case ':': d = h2 / 2; break;

        default: /* Get shift size for groups of symbols */
           if (('0' <= text[k]) && (text[k] <= '9'))
           d = 0;
        else if (('A' <= text[k]) && (text[k] <= 'Z'))
           d = 0;
        else if (('a' <= text[k]) && (text[k] <= 'z'))
           d = h1;
    }

    /* Shift video memory pointer to next letter screen position */
    textHeight = max(textHeight, letterHeight + d);
    }
    return textHeight;
}
```

For drawing menu text, we will use an array of pointers to char, pointing to NULL-terminated strings. We will use a NULL string as the final element to act as a sentinel to let a looping mechanism know where to stop. For example, the main menu items for our demo program will be these:

```
char *menuItems[] =
{
    "Exit", "Text demo", "PCX file demo", "Palette demo", "Drawing demo",
    "Color demo", NULL
};
```

To calculate the menu size, some service functions will be useful. The functions are menuCount(), which calculates the number of menu items; menuWidth(), which calculates the width of the widest menu item; and menuHeight(), which calculates the total heights of all menu items combined:

```
/* +------------------------------------------------------------+
   +  menuCount
   +  Calculate menu string count.
   +  Arguments:
   +    menuStrings: array of pointers to menu strings, with last as NULL
   +  Returns:        menu string count.
   +------------------------------------------------------------+ */
int menuCount(char **menuStrings)
{
    int n = 0;

    while (*menuStrings) /* keep going until hit NULL sentinel */
```

```
   { menuStrings++;
      n++; }
   return n;
}


/* +----------------------------------------------------------------+
   +  menuWidth
   +  Calculate menu width.
   +  Argument: menuStrings: array of pointers to menu strings, with last as NULL
   +  Returns:       menu width in pixels.
   +----------------------------------------------------------------+ */
int menuWidth(char **menuStrings)
{
   int w = 0, ws;

   while (*menuStrings) /* keep going until hit NULL sentinel */
   {
      ws = getTextWidth(*menuStrings, strlen(*menuStrings));
      w = max(w, ws);
      menuStrings++;
   }
   return w;
}


/* +----------------------------------------------------------------+
   +  menuHeight
   +  Calculate menu height
   +  Arguments: menuStrings: array of pointers to menu strings,
   +            with last as NULL
   +  Returns:       menu height in pixels.
   +----------------------------------------------------------------+ */
int menuHeight(char **menuStrings)
{
   int h = 0;

   while (*menuStrings) /* keep going until hit NULL sentinel */
   {
      h += getTextHeight();
      /* for alternative formulation:
      h += getTextHeight(*menuStrings, strlen(*menuStrings)); */
      menuStrings++;
   }
   return h;
}
```

Now a function that draws a menu would not be much effort:

```
/* +----------------------------------------------------------------+
   +  menuChoice
   +  Paints menu choices and gets user key press.
   +  Arguments:
   +    x, y:        start position of first menu item
   +    menuStrings: array of pointers to menu strings, with last as NULL
   +  Returns:       key choice converted to 0-based number (key - '0')
   +----------------------------------------------------------------+ */
int menuChoice(int x, int y, char **menuStrings)
{
   int key; /* to store user key press */
   int numStrings = 0; /* calculated number of menu items */
   int w, h;
```

```
    /* Calculate extent of menu & draw */
    w = menuWidth(menuStrings);
    h = menuCount(menuStrings) * MAX_SYMBOL_HEIGHT;
    drawMenu(x, y, w, h, GRAY, LIGHT_GRAY, DARK_GRAY);
    /* Draw menu text */
    setFont(NORMAL_FONT);
    setColor(1);
    while(*menuStrings) /* keep going until hit NULL sentinel */
    {
        /* text.c: top left corner, string, length */
        drawText(x + 5, y + 5, *menuStrings, strlen(*menuStrings));

        /* move down 20 pixels for the next menu item */
        y += MAX_SYMBOL_HEIGHT;
        menuStrings++;
        numStrings++; /* keep track of how many strings */
    }

    for (;;)
    {
        if ((key = getch()) == 0) /* in case extended key pressed */
            key = getch();
        key -= '0'; /* convert key press to 0-based # */

        if (1 <= key || key <= numStrings)
            return key;
    }
}


/* +--------------------------------------------------------------+
   +  drawMenu
   +  Draws menu background and lines.
   +  Arguments:
   +    x, y:               start position of first menu item
   +    w, h:               max height and width of menu
   +    bkgd, left, right:  menu colors: back, left/top & right/bottom
   +--------------------------------------------------------------+ */
void drawMenu(int x, int y, int w, int h, unsigned char bkgd,
    unsigned char left, unsigned right)
{
    setColor(bkgd);
    clearScreen();

    /* Draw menu background */
    fillRect(x, y, x + w + 10, y + h + 10);

    /* Light left and top sides */
    setColor(left);
    lineH(x,     y,     x + w + 10);
    lineV(x,     y,     y + h + 10);
    lineH(x + 1, y + 1, x + w +  9);
    lineV(x + 1, y + 1, y + h +  9);

    /* Dark right and bottom sides */
    setColor(right);
    lineH(x + w + 10, y + h + 10, x + 1);
    lineV(x + w + 10, y + h + 10, y + 1);
    lineH(x + w +  9, y + h +  9, x + 2);
    lineV(x + w +  9, y + h +  9, y + 2);

}
```

To check to see how the menu works, you can use the interactive text demo program below:

```
/* +--------------------------------------------------------------+
   +   textDemo
   +   Draw text with normal, bold, italic. and comic fonts.
   +--------------------------------------------------------------+ */
void textDemo(void)
{
   char *menuItems[] =
   {
      "Exit text demo", "Normal text", "Bold text", "Italic text",
      "Comic text", NULL
   };

   int menuKey;

   do
   {
      menuKey = menuChoice(100, 50, menuItems);
      switch(menuKey)
      {
         case 0: continue;
         case 2: setFont(NORMAL_FONT); break;
         case 3: setFont(BOLD_FONT);   break;
         case 4: setFont(ITALIC_FONT); break;
         case 5: setFont(COMIC_FONT);  break;
         default: return;
      }

      drawTextTable(15);
      waitKey();
   }
   while (menuKey != 1);
}
```

Now we will see how we can implement the same thing with a mouse instead of a key for menu selection. First, we will make a considerable digression to investigate the mouse thoroughly.

E.8   THE MOUSE

The mouse interrupt is 33h. We will take a look at the functions of the mouse interrupt listed in Table E.1.

Table E.1 *Mouse Functions*

Function	Purpose
0h	Determine whether mouse is present and initialize mouse cursor
1h	Show mouse cursor
2h	Hide mouse cursor
3h	Determine mouse button status and mouse position
4h	Set mouse position
7h	Set mouse X (column) limits
8h	Set mouse Y (row) limits

E.8.1 Initializing

We use function 0h to determine whether a mouse is present—that is, whether a mouse is physically connected to the computer and whether a mouse driver (generally `mouse.com`, `mouse.sys`, or `amouse.com`) is installed:

```
/* +------------------------------------------------------------+
   +   mouse_init
   +   determine whether mouse is installed.
   +   if installed, establishes these default conditions:
   +   - sets cursor range to entire screen (x = 0 to 639, y = 0 to 199)
   +   - position mouse cursor at center of screen (x = 320, y = 100)
   +   - sets cursor to full character box/reverse video
   +   - sets display page to 0
   +   - sets speed threshold to 64 mickeys per second (mickey = 1/200 inch)
   +   returns 0 if mouse installed; -1 if not
   +------------------------------------------------------------+ */
int mouse_init(void)
{
    union REGS in, out;

    in.x.ax = 0x0;
    int86(0x33, &in, &out);
    return out.x.ax;
}
```

The `int86()` call returns 0 in the `ax` register if no mouse is installed. Assuming a mouse is installed, the call also initializes the mouse cursor in the manner described in the comment block above. Be sure your program checks the return value and if it is zero, issues a message to the user about running a mouse driver (see the one we have in `graphic.c` on disk) and exits.

If this is of importance to your particular application, the `bx` register returns the number of buttons on the installed mouse. We will use the left mouse button only.

E.8.2 Displaying and Hiding the Mouse Cursor

Initializing the mouse cursor will not cause the mouse cursor to be shown. That you must do expressly with function 1h:

```
/* +------------------------------------------------------------+
   +   show_mouse
   +   Display mouse cursor.
   +------------------------------------------------------------+ */
void show_mouse(void)
{
    union REGS in, out;

    in.x.ax = 0x1;
    int86(0x33, &in, &out);
}
```

To hide the mouse cursor, either at the end of the program or intermittently at various points in the program when it is not appropriate to show it, you use function 2h:

```
/* +------------------------------------------------------------+
   +   hide_mouse
   +   Hide mouse cursor.
   +------------------------------------------------------------+ */
void hide_mouse(void)
{
    union REGS in, out;

    in.x.ax = 0x2;
    int86(0x33, &in, &out);
}
```

You might, for example, display the cursor at the outset of your program and then hide it if the user relies on the arrow or tab keys instead of the mouse to make selections. Then if your program perceives that the mouse has changed position, you can make the mouse reappear.

Actually, neither of these functions is an absolute function. Function 1h increments an internal counter flag, but not past 0; function 2h decrements the same flag. Initially, the flag is set to –1.

The mouse will appear only when the flag is set to 0. Accordingly, since the flag can never exceed 0, calls to hide_mouse() will always hide the mouse cursor. However, multiple calls to hide_mouse() without paired calls to show_mouse() will mean that a single subsequent call to show_mouse() will not increment the flag high enough to cause the cursor to be shown. Therefore, you should always be sure to pair your calls to these two functions.

Note that even if the cursor is hidden, the mouse is still active, assuming one is installed. These two functions do not turn the mouse on or off; they merely determine whether the cursor is visible.

E.8.3   Determining Whether a Button Has Been Pressed or Released

To determine whether a mouse button is being pressed, we use function 3h. The function 3h call to int86() returns the button status in the bx register. If the left button is pressed, the value will be 1 (bit 0 on); if the right button is pressed, the value will be 2 (bit 1 on); if the middle button is pressed, the value will be 4 (bit 2 on); if no button is pressed, the value will be 0 (no bits on):

```
/* +------------------------------------------------------------+
   + mouse_button
   + Determine whether mouse button is pressed and if so, which one.
   + bit 0 = left button, bit 1 = right, bit 2 = middle (1 if pressed,
   +    0 if not)
   +------------------------------------------------------------+
*/
int mouse_button(void)
{
   union REGS in, out;

   in.x.ax = 0x3; /* get-mouse position/button status */
   int86 (0x33, &in, &out);
   return out.x.bx;
}
```

To determine whether a button has been released, and if so, which one and where it is at the time of release, we use function 6h. This time, before calling int86(), we must set the bx register to 0, 1, or 2 to check on the left, right, or middle buttons, respectively. We will check on the left button, so we will always pass 0. The number of times the selected button has been pressed since the last call is returned in the bx register, and the x and y coordinates of the mouse at the time this button was last pressed are returned in the cx and dx registers:

```
/* +------------------------------------------------------------+
   +    mouse_getReleaseStatus
   +    Determine whether specified mouse button has been released
   +    since last call and if so, where it was at its last release.
   +    Arguments:
   +    button: which button's status is determined.
   +       (0 = left button, 1 = right, 2 = middle)
   +    x and y coordinates at time of last release
   +    Return: presses of this button since last call
   +------------------------------------------------------------+ */
int mouse_getReleaseStatus(int button, int *x, int *y)
{
   union REGS in, out;

   in.x.ax = 0x6; /* get-mouse position/button status */
   in.x.bx = button; /* button whose status we want */

   int86 (0x33, &in, &out);
```

```
   *x = out.x.cx;
   *y = out.x.dx;
   /* # of presses of this button since last call */
   return out.x.bx;
}
```

E.8.4   Determining the Mouse's Location

We can also use function 3h to tell us where in this matrix the mouse currently is. The horizontal position is returned in the cx register, and the vertical position is returned in the dx register:

```
/* +------------------------------------------------------------+
   +    mouse_location
   +    Determine mouse position (in pixels)
   +    Arguments: pointers to vertical and horizontal pixel count
   +------------------------------------------------------------+ */
void mouse_location(int *x, int *y)
{
   union REGS in, out;

   in.x.ax = 0x3; /* get-mouse position/button status */
   int86 (0x33, &in, &out);
   *x = out.x.cx;
   *y = out.x.dx;
}
```

Of course, we could have combined mouse_button() above with this function into a single function.

For most video modes, the mouse driver divides the screen into a matrix of 640 horizontal points and 200 vertical points. If the number of pixels horizontally or vertically for a particular graphics mode is higher than 640 or 200, the matrix will be made large enough to accommodate the larger number of pixels. For graphics modes with a 640×200 pixel configuration or greater, we can simply use the values in the cx and dx registers directly for mouse position. For other graphics modes and all text modes, we need to convert the values there to normalized pixel locus or to row and column position. Table E.2 shows any required conversion.

For text modes 3 and 7, with 25 rows and 80 columns, the 200×640 minimum mouse-pixel screen means that there is an 8-to-1 correspondence between the character display boxes your program uses and the mouse position interrupt 33h will report. For text mode 1, with 25 rows and 40 columns, there would be an 8-to-1 vertical correspondence and a 16-to-1 horizontal correspondence. For instance, if you are using mode 3 and you have a menu item that covers row 10 from columns 10 through 25, you would have to check whether the mouse, if pressed, is within the vertical pixel range 80 through 87 and the horizontal range 80 through 207. See play_mou.c, on disk, for an example.

Another solution would be to have the function return normalized row and column values:

```
*row = out.x.dx / 8;
*col = out.x.cx / 8;
```

In a program, you will normally be polling the mouse position repeatedly in a loop, as you wait for the user to click a mouse button. Since bit shifting is faster, in lieu of dividing, you could shift left 1 in cases where dividing by 2 is required (as in our mode 13h programs), 3 in cases where dividing by 8 is required, and 4 in cases where dividing by 16 is required:

```
*row = out.x.dx << 3; /* mode 3 conversion */
*col = out.x.cx << 3;
```

E.8.5   Restrict Mouse Movement

We can limit the range of mouse movement to a rectangular area we specify with functions 7h and 8h. Function 7h controls the vertical range and function 8h controls the horizontal range. In each case, we set cx to the lower limit and dx to the upper limit desired. The function we have created to set a range takes the upper-left row and column and lower-right row and column of the area as arguments. Thus, we assume a text mode in this case for illustration.

Table E.2 *Mouse-Pixel Conversion Chart*

Mode	Type	Resolution	Column or x Coordinate	Row or y Coordinate
01h	Text	40 x 25	cx / 16	dx / 8
03h	Text	80 x 25	cx / 8	dx / 8
04h	Graphics	320 x 200	cx / 2	dx
06h	Graphics	640 x 200	cx	dx
07h	Text	80 x 25	cx / 8	dx / 8
0Dh	Graphics	320 x 200	cx / 2	dx
0Eh	Graphics	640 x 200	cx	dx
0Fh	Graphics	640 x 350	cx	dx
10h	Graphics	640 x 350	cx	dx
11h	Graphics	640 x 480	cx	dx
12h	Graphics	640 x 480	cx	dx
13h	Graphics	320 x 200	cx / 2	dx
6Ah	Graphics	640 x 400	cx	dx
100h	Graphics	640 x 480	cx	dx
101h	Graphics	640 x 480	cx	dx
102h	Graphics	800 x 600	cx	dx
103h	Graphics	800 x 600	cx	dx
104h	Graphics	1280 x 768	cx	dx
105h	Graphics	1280 x 768	cx	dx
106h	Graphics	1280 x 1024	cx	dx
107h	Graphics	1280 x 1024	cx	dx

The function converts the row and column values into pixels. Since restriction is typically done only once, we eschew bit shifting for simple multiplication:

```
/* +--------------------------------------------------------------+
   + mouse_cage
   + Restrict where mouse can go
   + Arguments: top left and bottom right screen row and column
   +    coordinates
   +--------------------------------------------------------------+ */
void mouse_cage(int y1, int x1, int y2, int x2)
{
   union REGS in, out;

   in.x.ax = 0x7; /* set mouse x limits */
   in.x.cx = x1;
   in.x.dx = x2;
   int86(0x33, &in, &out);
```

```
    in.x.ax = 0x8; /* set mouse y limits */
    in.x.cx = y1;
    in.x.dx = y2;
    int86(0x33, &in, &out);
}
```

Rather than restrict where the mouse can go, we can allow unfettered movement but ignore mouse presses unless the mouse is within a designated area. The sound-generating and mouse programming example on disk, `play_mou.c`, illustrates both methods. In the graphics mode menu illustrations in this chapter, we will use the latter method only.

E.8.6   Setting the Mouse Position

At the beginning of the program, you may want to set the mouse cursor at a location other than the default center position. For example, you may want to set the mouse cursor on the first of several menu selection items.

You use function 4h to set the mouse cursor position. You place the *x* coordinate in the `cx` register and the *y* coordinate in the `dx` register. To be generic, our function, `position_mouse()`, uses pixel coordinates rather than hard-wiring to rows and columns for a particular text mode. For a text mode application, you would either have to adjust the calls (for instance, in mode 3, pass `row * 8` or `row >> 3` and `col * 8` or `col >> 3`), or else hard-wire the function assignments accordingly (for example, `in.x.cx = col * 8`):

```
/* +-------------------------------------------------------------+
   +    position_mouse
   +    Set mouse position to specified row and column coordinates.
   +    Arguments: x and y coordinates
   +-------------------------------------------------------------+ */
void position_mouse(int x, int y)
{
    union REGS in, out;

    in.x.ax = 0x4; /* set mouse screen position */
    in.x.cx = x;
    in.x.dx = y;
    int86(0x33, &in, &out);
}
```

E.8.7   Mouse Interrupt Function Summary

Table E.3 summarizes the mouse interrupt functions we covered in this appendix, as well as some we did not discuss.

Table E.3 *Selected Mouse Interrupt Mouse Functions*

Function	Call Values	Return Values
Determine whether mouse is present and initialize mouse cursor	ax = 0x0	ax = status (0: not installed) (−1: installed) bx = number of buttons
Show mouse cursor	ax = 0x1	
Hide mouse cursor	ax = 0x2	
Determine mouse button status and mouse position	ax = 0x3	bx = button status (0 = up) bit 0: left button bit 1: right button bit 2: middle button cx = x coordinate (col) dx = y coordinate (row)

(continued on next page)

Table E.3   *(continued)*

Function	Call Values	Return Values
Set mouse position	ax = 0x4 cx = x coordinate (col) dx = y coordinate (row)	

Get information for most recent button press	ax = 0x5
	bx = button
	    0 = left
	    1 = right
	    2 = middle
		ax = button status
		    (same as function 3h)
		bx = number of button
		    presses since last call
		    of this function
		cx = y coordinate (col)
		dx = x coordinate (row)

Get information for most recent button release	ax = 0x6 bx = (same as function 5h)	(same as function 5h, with bx returning the number of releases since last call)
Set mouse x coordinate (column) limits	ax = 0x7 cx = minimum dx = maximum	
Set mouse y coordinate (row) limits	ax = 0x8 cx = minimum dx = maximum	
Hide mouse cursor within rectangular area (restore with call to function 1h)	ax = 0x10 cx = left dx = top si = right di = bottom	
Set video display page	ax = 0x1D bx = display page	
Determine display page	ax = 0x1E	bx = display page

E.8.8   Using the Mouse in Your Graphics Mode Program

Now, being familiar with all the required basic mouse functions, all we have to do is make a menu to be selected by the mouse. In `menuIconChoice()`, we will draw a menu somewhat as we have in `menuChoice()`.

To significantly enhance the menu's appearance, however, we will use two graphics icons for each menu choice. One will be displayed only when the mouse is positioned over the corresponding menu choice. Otherwise, the other icon will be displayed. In other words, as the user moves the mouse over a particular choice the icon for that menu item changes and the color of the text for that choice also changes. Figures E.6A and E.6B show how the menu looks when the mouse is not on any choice and when it is.

Figure E.6A   *User Menu—No Selection*

Exit

Text Demo

PCX Demo

Palette Demo

Drawing Demo

Color Demo

Figure E.6B *User Menu—Exit Choice Selected*

Text Demo
PCX Demo
Palette Demo
Drawing Demo
Color Demo

We will add to our menuIconChoice() function two parameters, menuIcons and menuIconsSelected. They are each a pointer to an array of strings housing the PCX filenames for the various menu icon items.

We have made the function versatile enough to be able to draw a menu with text only or with icons and text for each item. If we want text only, we just pass NULLs for the menuIcons and menuIconsSelected, then we code menuIconsSelected() to ignore all statements relating to bitmaps if that happens. If you create an application that uses icons and no text, you can use the same device of passing NULL for the menuStrings argument and slightly modifying the function to ignore text drawing statements in that case:

```
/* +------------------------------------------------------------+
   +   menuIconChoice
   +   Paints menu choices and gets user mouse selection.
   +   Each choice is represented by graphic icon and text.
   +   Arguments:
   +     x, y:        start position of first menu item
   +     menuStrings: array of pointers to menu strings, with last
   +                  as NULL
   +     menuIcons:   array of pointers to menu icon names, with last
   +                  as NULL
   +              NOTE: if **menuIcons is NULL, no icons are to be painted
   +   Returns:       selected item number.
   +------------------------------------------------------------+ */
int menuIconChoice(/*int startX, int startY,*/ char **menuStrings,
   char **menuIcons, char **menuIconsSelected)
{
  int startX, startY; /* start position of first menu item */
  int item = -1;       /* Default selected alternative */
  int oldItem = -1;    /* Item selected previously */
  int x, y, w, h;      /* Menu left, top, width & height */
  int mouseX, mouseY; /* Current mouse position */
  int button;          /* Pressed mouse button    */
  int itemsCount = menuCount(menuStrings); /* Items in menu */
  int itemHeight;      /* Maximum item height     */
  int iconWidth = 0;   /* Maximum icon width      */
  int iconHeight = 0;  /*             and height  */
  int icons = 1;       /* whether text only or icons also */
  int k;               /* Icon counter            */
  bitmap_ptr *bmps,    /* Bitmaps for menu icons' unselected state */
      *bmpsSelected;       /* and selected state */

  unsigned char far *video_buffer = (unsigned char far*) 0xA0000000L;

  if (menuIcons == NULL)
    icons = 0;

  if (icons)
  {
    bmps          = malloc(itemsCount * sizeof(bitmap_ptr));
    bmpsSelected = malloc(itemsCount * sizeof(bitmap_ptr));
```

```
        for (k = 0; k < itemsCount; k++)
        {
            bmps[k] = malloc(sizeof(bitmap));
            PCX_loadBitmap(menuIcons[k], bmps[k]);
            iconWidth  = max(iconWidth,  bmps[k]->width);
            iconHeight = max(iconHeight, bmps[k]->height);

            bmpsSelected[k] = malloc(sizeof(bitmap));
            PCX_loadBitmap(menuIconsSelected[k], bmpsSelected[k]);
            iconWidth  = max(iconWidth,  bmpsSelected[k]->width);
            iconHeight = max(iconHeight, bmpsSelected[k]->height);
        }
    }
    itemHeight = max(iconHeight, MAX_SYMBOL_HEIGHT);

    setFont(COMIC_FONT);
    w = menuWidth(menuStrings) + iconWidth + 5;
    h = itemsCount * itemHeight;
    x = startX = (320 - w) / 2;
    y = startY= (200 - h - 10) / 2;

    drawMenu(x, y, w, h, GRAY, LIGHT_GRAY, DARK_GRAY);

    /* Now place icons (if icons are to be used) and text */
    setColor(1);
    for(k = 0; menuStrings[k] != NULL; k++)
    {
        if (icons)
        {
            /* Set bitmap drawing position */
            bmpsSelected[k]->x = bmps[k]->x = x + 5;
            bmpsSelected[k]->y = bmps[k]->y = y + 5;

            /* Draw bitmap for states of items not selected */
            bitmap_put(bmps[k], video_buffer, 1);
        }
        /* text.c: top-left corner, string, length */
        drawText(x + 10 + iconWidth, y + 5, menuStrings[k], strlen(menuStrings[k]));

        /* move down to menu item height */
        y += itemHeight;
    }

    show_mouse();
    for(;;)
    {
        mouse_location(&mouseX, &mouseY);

        /* Mouse x range is 0 to 639. See mouse_init in mouse.c.
           Correct x position for our video mode, with only 320 */
        mouseX >>= 1;
        /* Just continue if mouse not within menu, whether button pressed or not */
        if (mouseY < startY || mouseY > startY + h) continue;
        if (mouseX < startX || mouseX > startX + w) continue;

        /* Past this point, mouse is within menu area */

        /* Determine menu item mouse is now on */
        item = abs(((mouseY + 5 - startY) / itemHeight));
        item = min(item, itemsCount-1);
```

```
        if ((item >= 0) && (oldItem != item)) /* don't bother if hasn't moved */
        {
            hide_mouse();
            setColor(15); /* White color for selected state */
            /* draw text & paint icon in selected state for item */

            drawText(startX + iconWidth + 10, startY + 5 + itemHeight * item,
                menuStrings[item], strlen(menuStrings[item]));
            if (icons)
                bitmap_put(bmpsSelected[item], video_buffer, 1);

            if (oldItem >= 0)
            {
                /* draw text & paint old item in unselected state */
                setColor(1); /* Blue color for unselected state */
                drawText(startX + iconWidth + 10, startY + 5 + itemHeight * oldItem,
                    menuStrings[oldItem], strlen(menuStrings[oldItem]));
                if (icons)
                    bitmap_put(bmps[oldItem], video_buffer, 1);
            }
            show_mouse();
        }
        oldItem = item;

        /* has left button been released since last call & where was it when it was
            last released */
        button = mouse_getReleaseStatus(0, &mouseX, &mouseY);
        if (button != 0) /* has been released */
        {
            /* Hide mouse before drawing anything */
            hide_mouse();
            mouse_init();

            /* Clear screen after menu drawing */
            setColor(0);
            clearScreen();

            item++;
            break;
        }
    }

    if (icons)
    {
        /* Free memory of icon bitmaps */
        for (k = 0; k < itemsCount; k++)
        {
            farfree(bmps[k]->buffer);
            free(bmps[k]);
            farfree(bmpsSelected[k]->buffer);
            free(bmpsSelected[k]);
        }
        free(bmps);
        free(bmpsSelected);
    }

    return item;
}/* end of menuIconChoice function */
```

First, we show the mouse cursor with the show_mouse() function. Then we start the loop of mouse button reading with mouse_button(). If the mouse has been pressed outside the menu, we reject the mouse position and continue the loop. If a mouse press and release occurs within the menu, we calculate the selected item number by seeing where the mouse was when the left button was released.

We follow the same process for each submenu. For example, with textdemo(), we replace the menu-Choice() call shown above with

```
menuKey = menuIconChoice(menuItems, NULL, NULL);
```

and we add a mouse-position statement after the choice is concluded so the mouse is replaced in the same spot as where it left off when the choice was made:

```
position_mouse(320, 100 + (menuKey - 3) * 21 - 10);
```

APPENDIX F

ASCII/EBCDIC Characters

F.1   ASCII/EBCDIC CHART

Table F.1   *Control Characters*

Decimal	Octal	Hex	Binary	ASCII Keys/ Action	ASCII Character
0	00	0x0	00000000	Ctrl 1	
1	01	0x1	00000001	Ctrl A	(
2	02	0x2	00000010	Ctrl B	)
3	03	0x3	00000011	Ctrl C	
4	04	0x4	00000100	Ctrl D	,
5	05	0x5	00000101	Ctrl E	♣
6	06	0x6	00000110	Ctrl F	♠
7	07	0x7	00000111	Ctrl G *Beep*	•
8	010	0x8	00001000	Ctrl H *or* BACKSPACE	3
9	011	0x9	00001001	Ctrl K *or* Tab	○
10	012	0xA	00001010	Ctrl J *Newline*	4
11	013	0xB	00001011	Ctrl K *Vertical Tab*	%
12	014	0xC	00001100	Ctrl L *Form Feed*	&
13	015	0xD	00001101	Ctrl M *or* Enter *Carriage Return*	*
14	016	0xE	00001110	Ctrl N	+
15	017	0xF	00001111	Ctrl O	'
16	020	0x10	00010000	Ctrl P	▶
17	021	0x11	00010001	Ctrl Q	◀
18	022	0x12	00010010	Ctrl R	ø

(continued on next page)

Table F.1 *(continued)*

Decimal	Octal	Hex	Binary	ASCII Keys/ Action	ASCII Character
19	023	0x13	00010011	Ctrl S	.
20	024	0x14	00010100	Ctrl T	¶
21	025	0x15	00010101	Ctrl U	§
22	026	0x16	00010110	Ctrl V	′
23	027	0x17	00010111	Ctrl W	0
24	030	0x18	00011000	Ctrl X	↑
25	031	0x19	00011001	Ctrl Y	↓
26	032	0x1A	00011010	Ctrl Z	
27	033	0x1B	00011011	Esc	†
28	034	0x1C	00011100	Ctrl \	2
29	035	0x1D	00011101	Ctrl]	⅃
30	036	0x1E	00011110	Ctrl =	
31	037	0x1F	00011111	Ctrl -	

Table F.2 *Noncontrol Characters*

Decimal	Octal	Hex	Binary	ASCII Character	EBCDIC Character
32	040	0x20	00100000	SPACE	
33	041	0x21	00100001	!	
34	042	0x22	00100010	"	
35	043	0x23	00100011	#	
36	044	0x24	00100100	$	
37	045	0x25	00100101	%	
38	046	0x26	00100110	&	
39	047	0x27	00100111	'	
40	050	0x28	00101000	(	
41	051	0x29	00101001	)	
42	052	0x2A	00101010	*	
43	053	0x2B	00101011	+	
44	054	0x2C	00101100	,	
45	055	0x2D	00101101	–	

Table F.2   *(continued)*

Decimal	Octal	Hex	Binary	ASCII Character	EBCDIC Character
46	056	0x2E	00101110	.	
47	057	0x2F	00101111	/	
48	060	0x30	00110000	0	
49	061	0x31	00110001	1	
50	062	0x32	00110010	2	
51	063	0x33	00110011	3	
52	064	0x34	00110100	4	
53	065	0x35	00110101	5	
54	066	0x36	00110110	6	
55	067	0x37	00110111	7	
56	070	0x38	00111000	8	
57	071	0x39	00111001	9	
58	072	0x3A	00111010	:	
59	073	0x3B	00111011	;	
60	074	0x3C	00111100	<	
61	075	0x3D	00111101	=	
62	076	0x3E	00111110	>	
63	077	0x3F	00111111	?	
64	0100	0x40	01000000	@	SPACE
65	0101	0x41	01000001	A	
66	0102	0x42	01000010	B	
67	0103	0x43	01000011	C	
68	0104	0x44	01000100	D	
69	0105	0x45	01000101	E	
70	0106	0x46	01000110	F	
71	0107	0x47	01000111	G	
72	0110	0x48	01001000	H	
73	0111	0x49	01001001	I	
74	0112	0x4A	01001010	J	¢
75	0113	0x4B	01001011	K	.

(continued on next page)

Table F.2 *(continued)*

Decimal	Octal	Hex	Binary	ASCII Character	EBCDIC Character
76	0114	0x4C	01001100	L	<
77	0115	0x4D	01001101	M	(
78	0116	0x4E	01001110	N	+
79	0117	0x4F	01001111	O	¦
80	0120	0x50	01010000	P	&
81	0121	0x51	01010001	Q	
82	0122	0x52	01010010	R	
83	0123	0x53	01010011	S	
84	0124	0x54	01010100	T	
85	0125	0x55	01010101	U	
86	0126	0x56	01010110	V	
87	0127	0x57	01010111	W	
88	0130	0x58	01011000	X	
89	0131	0x59	01011001	Y	
90	0132	0x5A	01011010	Z	!
91	0133	0x5B	01011011	[	$
92	0134	0x5C	01011100	\	*
93	0135	0x5D	01011101	]	)
94	0136	0x5E	01011110	^	:
95	0137	0x5F	01011111	_	¬
96	0140	0x60	01100000	`	-
97	0141	0x61	01100001	a	/
98	0142	0x62	01100010	b	
99	0143	0x63	01100011	c	
100	0144	0x64	01100100	d	
101	0145	0x65	01100101	e	
102	0146	0x66	01100110	f	
103	0147	0x67	01100111	g	
104	0150	0x68	01101000	h	

Table F.2   *(continued)*

Decimal	Octal	Hex	Binary	ASCII Character	EBCDIC Character
105	0151	0x69	01101001	i	
106	0152	0x6A	01101010	j	^
107	0153	0x6B	01101011	k	,
108	0154	0x6C	01101100	l	%
109	0155	0x6D	01101101	m	_
110	0156	0x6E	01101110	n	>
111	0157	0x6F	01101111	o	?
112	0160	0x70	01110000	p	
113	0161	0x71	01110001	q	
114	0162	0x72	01110010	r	
115	0163	0x73	01110011	s	
116	0164	0x74	01110100	t	
117	0165	0x75	01110101	u	
118	0166	0x76	01110110	v	
119	0167	0x77	01110111	w	
120	0170	0x78	01111000	x	
121	0171	0x79	01111001	y	'
122	0172	0x7A	01111010	z	:
123	0173	0x7B	01111011	{	#
124	0174	0x7C	01111100	¦	@
125	0175	0x7D	01111101	}	'
126	0176	0x7E	01111110	~	=

Table F.3   *Characters in Nonstandard Set*

Decimal	Octal	Hex	Binary	ASCII Character	EBCDIC Character
127	0177	0x7F	01111111	–	A
128	0200	0x80	10000000	Ç	
129	0201	0x81	10000001	ü	a

(continued on next page)

Table F.3 *(continued)*

Decimal	Octal	Hex	Binary	ASCII Character	EBCDIC Character
130	0202	0x82	10000010	é	b
131	0203	0x83	10000011	â	c
132	0204	0x84	10000100	ä	d
133	0205	0x85	10000101	à	e
134	0206	0x86	10000110	å	f
135	0207	0x87	10000111	ç	g
136	0210	0x88	10001000	ê	h
137	0211	0x89	10001001	ë	i
138	0212	0x8A	10001010	è	
139	0213	0x8B	10001011	ï	
140	0214	0x8C	10001100	î	
141	0215	0x8D	10001101	ì	
142	0216	0x8E	10001110	Ä	
143	0217	0x8F	10001111	Å	
144	0220	0x90	10010000	É	
145	0221	0x91	10010001	æ	j
146	0222	0x92	10010010	Æ	k
147	0223	0x93	10010011	ô	l
148	0224	0x94	10010100	ö	m
149	0225	0x95	10010101	ò	n
150	0226	0x96	10010110	û	o
151	0227	0x97	10010111	ù	p
152	0230	0x98	10011000	ÿ	q
153	0231	0x99	10011001	Ö	r
154	0232	0x9A	10011010	Ü	
155	0233	0x9B	10011011	¢	
156	0234	0x9C	10011100	£	
157	0235	0x9D	10011101	¥	
158	0236	0x9E	10011110	Pt	

Table F.3 *(continued)*

Decimal	Octal	Hex	Binary	ASCII Character	EBCDIC Character
159	0237	0x9F	10011111	ƒ	
160	0240	0xA0	10100000	á	
161	0241	0xA1	10100001	í	~
162	0242	0xA2	10100010	ó	s
163	0243	0xA3	10100011	ú	t
164	0244	0xA4	10100100	ñ	u
165	0245	0xA5	10100101	Ñ	v
166	0246	0xA6	10100110	ª	w
167	0247	0xA7	10100111	º	x
168	0250	0xA8	10101000	¿	y
169	0251	0xA9	10101001	⌐	z
170	0252	0xAA	10101010	¬	
171	0253	0xAB	10101011	½	
172	0254	0xAC	10101100	¼	
173	0255	0xAD	10101101	¡	
174	0256	0xAE	10101110	«	
175	0257	0xAF	10101111	»	
176	0260	0xB0	10110000	░	
177	0261	0xB1	10110001	▒	\
178	0262	0xB2	10110010	▓	{
179	0263	0xB3	10110011	│	}
180	0264	0xB4	10110100	┤	[
181	0265	0xB5	10110101	╡	]
182	0266	0xB6	10110110	╢	
183	0267	0xB7	10110111	╖	
184	0270	0xB8	10111000	╕	
185	0271	0xB9	10111001	╣	
186	0272	0xBA	10111010	║	
187	0273	0xBB	10111011	╗	

(continued on next page)

Table F.3 *(continued)*

Decimal	Octal	Hex	Binary	ASCII Character	EBCDIC Character
188	0274	0xBC	10111100	⅃	
189	0275	0xBD	10111101	⅃	
190	0276	0xBE	10111110	⅃	
191	0277	0xBF	10111111	¬	
192	0300	0xC0	11000000	∟	
193	0301	0xC1	11000001	⊥	A
194	0302	0xC2	11000010	⊤	B
195	0303	0xC3	11000011	├	C
196	0304	0xC4	11000100	–	D
197	0305	0xC5	11000101	+	E
198	0306	0xC6	11000110	╞	F
199	0307	0xC7	11000111	╟	G
200	0310	0xC8	11001000	╚	H
201	0311	0xC9	11001001	╔	I
202	0312	0xCA	11001010	╩	
203	0313	0xCB	11001011	╦	
204	0314	0xCC	11001100	╠	
205	0315	0xCD	11001101	=	
206	0316	0xCE	11001110	╬	
207	0317	0xCF	11001111	╧	
208	0320	0xD0	11010000	╨	
209	0321	0xD1	11010001	╤	J
210	0322	0xD2	11010010	╥	K
211	0323	0xD3	11010011	╙	L
212	0324	0xD4	11010100	╘	M
213	0325	0xD5	11010101	╒	N
214	0326	0xD6	11010110	╓	O
215	0327	0xD7	11010111	╫	P
216	0330	0xD8	11011000	╪	Q

Table F.3 *(continued)*

Decimal	Octal	Hex	Binary	ASCII Character	EBCDIC Character
217	0331	0xD9	11011001	⌐	R
218	0332	0xDA	11011010	⌐	
219	0333	0xDB	11011011	█	
220	0334	0xDC	11011100	▄	
221	0335	0xDD	11011101	▌	
222	0336	0xDE	11011110	▐	
223	0337	0xDF	11011111	▀	
224	0340	0xE0	11100000	α	
225	0341	0xE1	11100001	ß	
226	0342	0xE2	11100010	Γ	S
227	0343	0xE3	11100011	π	T
228	0344	0xE4	11100100	Σ	U
229	0345	0xE5	11100101	σ	V
230	0346	0xE6	11100110	μ	W
231	0347	0xE7	11100111	τ	X
232	0350	0xE8	11101000	Φ	Y
233	0351	0xE9	11101001	Θ	Z
234	0352	0xEA	11101010	Ω	
235	0353	0xEB	11101011	δ	
236	0354	0xEC	11101100	∞	
237	0355	0xED	11101101	ø	
238	0356	0xEE	11101110	ε	
239	0357	0xEF	11101111	∩	
240	0360	0xF0	11110000	≡	0
241	0361	0xF1	11110001	±	1
242	0362	0xF2	11110010	≥	2
243	0363	0xF3	11110011	≤	3
244	0364	0xF4	11110100	⌠	4
245	0365	0xF5	11110101	⌡	5

(continued on next page)

Table F.3 *(continued)*

Decimal	Octal	Hex	Binary	ASCII Character	EBCDIC Character
246	0366	0xF6	11110110	÷	6
247	0367	0xF7	11110111	≈	7
248	0370	0xF8	11111000	O	8
249	0371	0xF9	11111001	°	9
250	0372	0xFA	11111010	•	
251	0373	0xFB	11111011	√	
252	0374	0xFC	11111100	ⁿ	
253	0375	0xFD	11111101	²	
254	0376	0xFE	11111110	■	
255	0377	0xFF	11111111	(blank)	

F.2   SINGLE-PAGE HEX-CHARACTER ASCII CHART

Table F.4 *Hexadecimal Numbers with Corresponding ASCII Characters*

	0–	1–	2–	3–	4–	5–	6–	7–	8–	9–	A–	B–	C–	D–	E–	F–
–0		►		0	@	P	`	p	Ç	É	á	▒	└	╨	α	≡
–1	☺	◄	!	1	A	Q	a	q	ü	æ	í	▓	┴	╤	ß	±
–2	☻	↕	"	2	B	R	b	r	é	Æ	ó	█	┬	╥	Γ	≥
–3	♥	‼	#	2	C	S	c	s	â	ô	ú	│	├	╙	π	≤
–4	♦	¶	$	2	D	T	d	t	ä	ö	ñ	┤	─	╘	Σ	⌠
–5	♣	§	%	5	E	U	e	u	à	ò	Ñ	╡	┼	╒	σ	⌡
–6	♠	▬	&	6	F	V	f	v	å	û	ª	╢	╞	╓	µ	÷
–7	•	↨	'	7	G	W	g	w	ç	ù	º	╖	╟	╫	τ	≈
–8	◘	↑	(	8	H	X	h	x	ê	ÿ	¿	╕	╚	╪	Φ	O
–9	○	↓	)	9	I	Y	i	y	ë	Ö	⌐	╣	╔	┘	Θ	°
–A	◎	→	*	:	J	Z	j	z	è	Ü	¬	║	╩	┌	Ω	•
–B	♂	←	+	;	K	[	k	{	ï	¢	½	╗	╦	█	δ	√
–C	♀	∟	,	<	L	\	l	¦	î	£	¼	╝	╠	▄	∞	ⁿ
–D	♪	↔	-	=	M	]	m	}	ì	¥	¡	╜	=	█	ø	²
–E	♫	▲	.	>	N	^	n	~	Ä	₧	«	╛	╬	█	ε	■
–F	☼	▼	/	?	O	_	o	⌂	Å	ƒ	»	┐	╧	■	∩	

F.3 SINGLE-PAGE DECIMAL-CHARACTER ASCII CHART

Table F.5 *Decimal Numbers with Corresponding ASCII Characters*

	0–	1–	2–	3–	4–	5–	6–	7–	8–	9–	10–	11–	12–	13–	14–	15–	16–	17–	18–	19–	20–	21–	22–	23–	24–	25–
–0	4	¶			(	2	<	F	P	Z	d	n	x	é	î	û	á	¬	┤	╛	╚	╥	■	µ	≡	•
–1	(	⅜	§		)	3	=	G	Q	[	e	o	y	â	ì	ù	í	½	╡	┐	╔	╙	▌	τ	±	√
–2	)	&	,		*	4	>	H	R	\	f	p	z	ä	Ä	ÿ	ó	¼	╢	└	╩	╘	▐	Φ	≥	ⁿ
–3	*	0		!	+	5	?	I	S	]	g	q	{	à	Â	Ö	ú	¡	╖	┴	╦	╒	■	Θ	≤	²
–4	,	+	↑	"	,	6	@	J	T	^	h	r	¦	å	É	Ü	ñ	«	╕	┬	╠	╓	α	Ω	⌠	■
–5	♣	'	↓	#	-	7	A	K	U	_	i	s	}	ç	æ	¢	Ñ	»	╣	├	═	╫	ß	δ	⌡	
–6	♠	▶		$	.	8	B	L	V	`	j	t	~	ê	Æ	£	ª	░	║	─	╬	╪	Γ	∞	÷	
–7	•	◀	†	%	/	9	C	M	W	a	k	u	-	ë	ô	¥	°	▒	╗	┼	╧	┘	π	ø	≈	
–8	3	ø	2	&	0	:	D	N	X	b	l	v	Ç	è	ö	Pt	¿	▓	╝	╞	╨	┌	Σ	ε	°	
–9	○	.	⅟	'	1	;	E	O	Y	c	m	w	ü	ï	ò	ƒ	⌐	│	╜	╟	╤	█	σ	∩	∙	

F.4 ASCII CHARACTER LINE BOXES

Figure F.1 *Single-Line Box Characters*

```
218 ┌     196 ─     194 ┬     191 ┐

179 │

195 ├                197 ┼    180 ┤

192 └                193 ┴    179 ┘
```

Figure F.2 *Double-Line Box Characters*

```
201 ╔     205 ═     203 ╦     187 ╗

186 ║

204 ╠                197 ╬    185 ╣

200 ╚                202 ╩    188 ╝
```

Figure F.3   *Complete Single-Line Box*

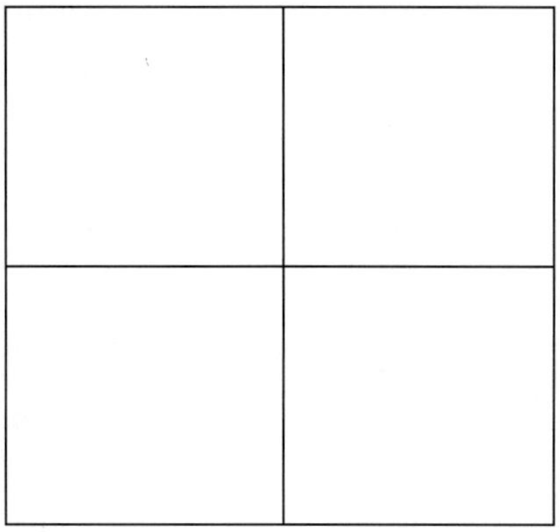

Figure F.4   *Complete Double-Line Box*

Figure F.5   *Outline Single-Line Box*

Figure F.6 *Outline Double-Line Box*

Figure F.7 *Box Characters: Double-Line Vertical/Single-Line Horizontal*

214	196	210	183
╓	─	╥	╖
186			
║			
199		215	182
╟		╫	╢
211		208	189
╙		╨	╜

Figure F.8 *Box Characters: Single-Line Vertical/Double-Line Horizontal*

213	205	209	184
╒	═	╤	╕
179			
│			
198		216	181
╞		╪	╡
212		207	190
╘		╧	╛

Figure F.9 *Complete Double-Line Vertical/Single-Line Horizontal Box*

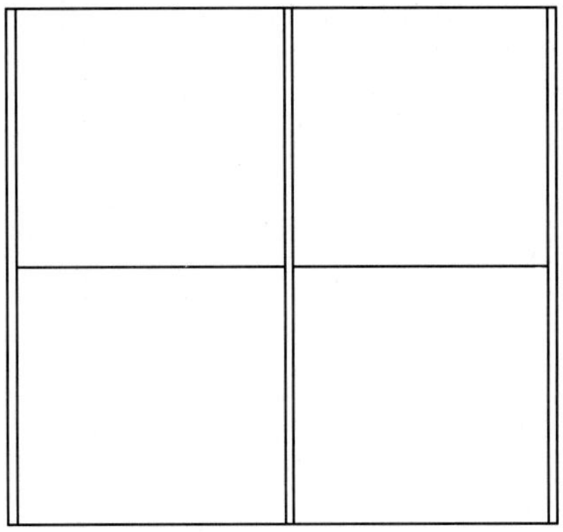

Figure F.10 *Complete Single-Line Vertical/Double-Line Horizontal Box*

Figure F.11 *Outline Double-Line Vertical/Single-Line Horizontal Box*

Figure F.12 *Outline Single-Line Vertical/Double-Line Vertical Box*

F.5   ASCII FULL- AND HALF-BOX CHARACTERS

Table F.6 *Solid Full- and Half-Box Characters*

Full-box Characters	ASCII Value	Character	Half-box Characters	ASCII Value	Character
solid	219	■	top half	223	▬
dark shade	178	▓	bottom half	220	▬
medium shade	177	▒	left half	221	▐
light shade	176	░	right half	222	▐

APPENDIX **G**

Extended
Keyboard Codes

Table G.1 *Extended Keyboard Codes (by Key)*

	Key	Shift	Ctrl	Alt
F1	59	84	94	104
F2	60	85	95	105
F3	61	86	96	106
F4	62	87	97	107
F5	63	88	98	108
F6	64	89	99	109
F7	65	90	100	110
F8	66	91	101	111
F9	67	92	102	112
F10	68	93	103	113
F11	133	135	137	139
F12	134	136	138	140
Home	71		119	151
End	79		117	159
Insert	82		146	162
Delete	83		147	163
Page Up	73		132	153
Page Down	81		118	161
↑	72		141	152
↓	80		145	160
←	75		115	155
→	77		116	157
A				30

Table G.1 *Extended Keyboard Codes (by Key)*

	Key	Shift	Ctrl	Alt
B				48
C				46
D				32
E				18
F				33
G				34
H				35
I				23
J				36
K				37
L				38
M				50
N				49
O				24
P				25
Q				16
R				19
S				31
T				20
U				22
V				47
W				17
X				45
Y				21
Z				44
1				120
2				121
3				122
4				123
5				124
5 keypad			143	

(continued on next page)

Table G.1 *(continued)*

Key	Shift	Ctrl	Alt
6			125
7			126
8			127
9			128
0			129
Esc			1
BACKSPACE			14
Tab	15	148	165
RETURN			28
RETURN keypad			166
[			26
]			27
:			39
'			40
"			41
,			51
.			52
\			43
/			53
/ keypad		149	164
* keypad		150	55
-			130
- keypad		142	74
+ keypad		144	78
=			131

APPENDIX **H**

Header Files— Define Directives

```
/* box_chars.h */

#define TL1   218     /* top-left single line */
#define TR1   191
#define BL1   192
#define BR1   217
#define H1    196
#define V1    179
#define ML1   195     /* cross-shaped line at middle left */
#define MR1   180
#define MT1   194
#define MB1   193
#define TL2   201     /* top-left double line */
#define TR2   187
#define BL2   200
#define BR2   188
#define H2    205
#define V2    186
#define ML2   204
#define MR2   185
#define MT2   202
#define MB2   203




/* colors.h */

#define   BK    0     /* black */
#define   BL    1     /* blue */
#define   BR    6     /* brown */
#define   CY    3     /* cyan */
#define   GN    2     /* green */
#define   GY    7     /* gray */
#define   PU    5     /* purple */
#define   R     4     /* red */




/* concolor.h */

/* colors for printf escape sequences

   colors are dark background/light foreground only */
```

```
#define GRAYB  "[47m"
#define CYAN_  "[46m"
#define PURPLE_  "[45m"
#define BLUE_  "[44m"
#define BROWN_  "[43m"
#define GREEN_  "[42m"
#define RED_  "[41m"
#define BLACK_  "[40m"
#define WHITE_  "[1;37m"
#define GRAYF  "[0;37m"
#define LCYAN  "[36m"
#define LPURPLE  "[35m"
#define LBLUE  "[34m"
#define YELLOW_  "[33m"
#define LGREEN  "[32m"
#define LRED  "[31m"
#define LBLACK  "[30m"
#define BK_GRAY  "[7m"
#define GRAY_BK  "[0m"


/* keys.h */

#define TAB 9 /* byte 1 */
#define SH_T 15
#define CR 13 /* byte 1 */
#define ESC 27 /* byte 1 */

#define LT 75
#define RT 77
#define UP 72
#define DN 80
#define PGUP 73
#define PGDN 81

#define INS 82
#define DEL 83
#define HM 71
#define END 79

#define ALTA 30
#define ALTB 48
#define ALTC 46
#define ALTD 32
#define ALTE 18
#define ALTF 33
#define ALTG 34
#define ALTH 35
#define ALTI 23
#define ALTJ 36
#define ALTK 37
#define ALTL 38
#define ALTM 50
#define ALTN 49
#define ALTO 24
#define ALTP 25
#define ALTQ 16
#define ALTR 19
#define ALTS 31
```

```
#define ALTT 20
#define ALTU 22
#define ALTV 47
#define ALTW 17
#define ALTX 45
#define ALTY 21
#define ALTZ 44

#define CTRL_B 2
#define CTRL_C 3
#define CTRL_T 20
#define CTRL_V 22
#define CTRL_Z 26

#define F1 59
#define F2 60
#define F3 61
#define F4 62
#define F5 63
#define F6 64
#define F7 65
#define F8 66
#define F9 67
#define F10 68
#define F11 133
#define F12 134

#define SF1 84
#define SF2 85
#define SF3 86
#define SF4 87
#define SF5 88
#define SF6 89
#define SF7 90
#define SF8 91
#define SF9 92
#define SF10 93
#define SF11 135
#define SF12 136

#define AF1 104
#define AF2 105
#define AF3 106
#define AF4 107
#define AF5 108
#define AF6 109
#define AF7 110
#define AF8 111
#define AF9 112
#define AF10 113
#define AF11 139
#define AF12 140

#define CF1 94
#define CF2 95
#define CF3 96
#define CF4 97
#define CF5 98
#define CF6 99
#define CF7 100
```

```
#define CF8 101
#define CF9 102
#define CF10 103
#define CF11 136
#define CF12 137

#define ALT_PGUP 153
#define ALT_PGDN 161
#define ALT_UP 152
#define ALT_DN 160
#define ALT_RT 157
#define ALT_LT 155

#define CTRL_PGUP 132
#define CTRL_PGDN 118
#define CTRL_UP 141
#define CTRL_DN 145
#define CTRL_RT 116
#define CTRL_LT 115

#define ALT_HM 151
#define ALT_END 159
#define ALT_INS 162
#define ALT_DEL 163
#define ALT_TAB 165
#define ALT_CR 166

#define CTRL_HM 119
#define CTRL_END 117
#define CTRL_TAB 148
```

Standard C Functions

Table I.1 *Standard C Functions Grouped by Task Type*

String Copying, Combining, Comparing, Length		
`char *strcpy(char *string1, const char *string2);`	Places a copy of `string2` starting at `string1`.	string.h
`char *strncpy(char *string1, const char *string2, unsigned num_characters);`	Same as `strcpy` for specified number of characters in `string2`.	string.h
`char *strcat(char *string1, const char *string2);`	Places copy of `string2` starting at NULL character in `string1`, thus combining the strings.	string.h
`char *strncat(char *string1, const char *string2, unsigned num_characters);`	Same as `strcat`, but only for specified number of characters in `string2` if `string2` is longer than num_characters. Adds terminating NULL.	string.h
`int strcmp(const char *string1, const char *string2);`	Checks whether `string1` is identical to `string2`. Returns 0 if they are.	string.h
`int strncmp(const char *string1, const char *string2, unsigned num_characters);`	Same as `strcmp` for specified number of characters.	string.h
`int strcoll(const char *string1, const char *string2);`	Same as `strcmp`, except characters in both `string1` and `string2` are compared according to locale-specific collating conventions (setlocale(LC_COLLATE)).	string.h

(continued on next page)

Table I.1   *(continued)*

`size_t `**`strxfrm`**`(char *destination_string, const char *source_string, size_t max_chars);`	Transforms `source_string` and places up to `max_chars` of resulting string at `destination_string`. The transformation is such that if the `strcmp` function is applied to two transformed strings, it returns a value greater than, equal to, or less than zero, corresponding to the result of the `strcoll` function applied to the same two original strings.	string.h
`size_t `**`strlen`**`(const char *string_start);`	Returns the number of bytes from `string_start` to first `NULL` byte, including spaces and other punctuation characters, and control characters such as newline, tab, and formfeed.	string.h
Character and Substring Locators and Parsers		
`char `**`*strchr`**`(const char *string, int character);`	Returns address of first occurrence of specified `character` in `string`.	string.h
`char `**`*strrchr`**`(const char *string, int character);`	Same as `strchr`, except *last* occurrence.	string.h
`char `**`*strstr`**`(const char *string, const char *substring);`	Returns starting address of `substring` inside `string`.	string.h
`size_t `**`strcspn`**`(const char *string1, const char *string2);`	Returns zero-based position # of first occurrence in `string1` of any character in `string2`. Returns the position number of `NULL` in `string2` if no match.	string.h
`size_t `**`strspn`**`(const char *string1, const char *string2);`	Returns zero-based position # of first occurrence in `string1` of any character *not* in `string2`. Returns length of `string1` if all its characters are found within `string2`.	string.h
`char `**`*strpbrk`**`(const char *string1, const char *string2);`	Same as `strcspn`, except returns a pointer to the first matching character rather than its position number (or `NULL` if there is no match).	string.h
`char `**`*strtok`**`(char *string, char *delimiters);`	Parses `string` into substrings or "tokens" by placing `NULL` characters wherever in `string` any characters in `delimiters` string appear. Completely parsing `string` requires successive `strtok` calls. In the first call, `string` and `delimiters` are passed. On each successive call, `NULL` and `delimiters` are passed.	string.h

Table I.1   *(continued)*

Character Classification and Case Conversion		
`int isdigit (int character);`	Is `character` a digit? ('0'–'9')	ctype.h
`int isalpha (int character);`	Is `character` a letter?	ctype.h
`int isalnum (int character);`	Is `character` a digit or a letter?	ctype.h
`int isxdigit (int character);`	Is `character` a hexadecimal digit character? ('a'–'f' and 'A'–'F')	ctype.h
`int islower (int character);`	Is `character` a lowercase letter?	ctype.h
`int isupper (int character);`	Is `character` an uppercase letter?	ctype.h
`int isspace (int character);`	Is `character` a white-space character? ([space], '\t', '\n', '\v', '\f', '\r')	ctype.h
`int iscntrl (int character);`	Is `character` a control character? (white-space or decimal 0–8, 14–31, 127 in ASCII)	ctype.h
`int ispunct (int character);`	Is `character` a printing character other than a space, a digit, or a letter? (!"#$%&'()*+,.=/:;<=>?@[\]^_`{¦}~)	ctype.h
`int isprint (int character);`	Is `character` a printing character, including space? (digit, letter, punctuation, or space)	ctype.h
`int isgraph (int character);`	Is `character` a printing character other than space?	ctype.h
`int tolower (int character);`	If `character` is an uppercase letter, returns character as a lowercase letter; otherwise, returns the argument unchanged.	ctype.h
`int toupper (int character);`	If `character` is a lowercase letter, returns character as an uppercase letter; otherwise, returns the argument unchanged.	ctype.h
Reading and Writing		
`char *gets(char *string);`	Reads `string` from standard input: copies characters to first newline, places them starting at `string`, adds a terminating `NULL`, and discards newline. Returns `NULL` on read error or end of file.	stdio.h
`int puts(const char *string);`	Writes `string` to standard output and adds newline.	stdio.h

(continued on next page)

Table I.1   *(continued)*

`char *fgets(char *string,`
`int max_chars, FILE`
`*stream);`
	Reads from a file *through* earlier of one character less than `max_chars` or first newline, places them starting at `string`, and adds `NULL`. Returns `NULL` on read error or end of file.	stdio.h

`int fputs(const char` `*string, FILE *stream);`	Same as `puts`, except writes `string` to file and does not add terminating newline.	stdio.h
`int getchar (void);`	Reads the next character from standard input. Returns `EOF` on end of file or read error. Equivalent to `getc(stdin)`.	stdio.h
`int putchar (int` `character);`	Writes `character` to standard input.	stdio.h
`int fgetc(FILE *stream);`	Same as `getchar`, except reads a character from file associated with `stream` instead of from standard input. Returns `EOF` on end of file or read error.	stdio.h
`int getc(FILE *stream);`	Equivalent to `fgetc`, but usually implemented as a macro. Returns `EOF` on end of file or read error.	stdio.h
`int fputc(int character,` `FILE *stream);`	Same as `putchar`, except writes to file associated with `stream` instead of to standard output.	stdio.h
`int putc(int c, FILE` `*stream);`	Equivalent to `fputc`, but usually implemented as a macro.	stdio.h
`int ungetc(int character,` `FILE *stream);`	Places a character into the associated input `stream` ahead of what is already there, to be read by the next read operation on the stream.	stdio.h
`int printf(const char` `*format, . . .);`	Writes `format` to standard output character by character until conversion specifier is encountered, at which point, the value of the next variable, constant ,or expression in the argument list is printed, in the format indicated by the conversion specifier. The process continues in the same way until the end of the format string.	stdio.h
`int scanf(const char` `*format_string, . . .);`	Reads from standard input and with the aid of conversion specifiers in `format_string`, converts the character groups read into values to be stored in variables in memory, the addresses of which are in the argument list.	stdio.h

Table I.1   *(continued)*

`int` **`sprintf`**`(char *string, const char *format_string, . . .);`	Like `printf`, except writes to an array in memory instead of standard output. Adds terminating `NULL`.	stdio.h
`int` **`sscanf`**`(const char *string, const char *format_string, . . .);`	Like `scanf`, except reads from string in memory instead of standard input.	stdio.h
`int` **`fprintf`**`(FILE *stream, const char *format_string, . . .);`	Same as `printf`, except writes to file associated with stream.	stdio.h
`int` **`fscanf`**`(FILE *stream, const char *format_string, . . .);`	Same as `scanf`, except reads from file associated with stream.	stdio.h
`int` **`vprintf`**`(const char *format_string, va_list arg);`	Same as `printf`, except that instead of using an argument list, it uses a `va_arg` variable to move through another function's variable argument list.	stdio.h
`int` **`vsprintf`**`(char *string, const char *format_string, va_list arg);`	Same as `sprintf`, except that instead of using an argument list, it uses a `va_arg` variable to move through another function's variable argument list.	stdio.h
`int` **`vfprintf`**`(FILE *stream, const char *format_string, va_list arg);`	Same as `fprintf`, except that instead of using an argument list, it uses a `va_arg` variable to move through another function's variable argument list.	stdio.h
`size_t` **`fwrite`**`(void *ptr, size_t bytes_per_block, size_t number_of_blocks, FILE *fp);`	Writes specified number of bytes (`number_of_blocks *` `bytes_per_block`) starting at address in primary memory, `ptr`, to file associated with `stream`.	stdio.h
`size_t` **`fread`**`(void *ptr, size_t bytes_per_block, size_t number_of_blocks, FILE *fp);`	Reads specified number of bytes (`number_of_blocks *` `bytes_per_block`) from file associated with `stream` and copies them to primary memory starting at `ptr`.	stdio.h
Number-String Converters		
`int` **`atoi`**`(const char *number_string);`	Converts `number_string` to an `int`. Skips over leading whitespace. Recognizes leading sign; no type suffix, or octal or hexadecimal characters recognized. First inappropriate character halts conversion.	stdlib.h

(continued on next page)

Table I.1 *(continued)*

`long `**`atol`**`(const char *number_string);`	Converts `number_string` to a `long`. Skips over leading whitespace. Recognizes leading sign; no type suffix or octal or hexadecimal characters recognized. First inappropriate character halts conversion.	stdlib.h
`double `**`atof`**`(const char *number_string);`	Converts `number_string` to a `double`. Skips over leading whitespace. Recognizes leading sign, decimal point, and characters appropriate for exponential notation; no type suffix recognized. First inappropriate character halts conversion.	stdlib.h
`double `**`strtod`**`(const char *number_string, char **stop);`	Converts `number_string` to a `double`. Recognizes same characters as `atof`. Address of first inappropriate character is stored in `stop`.	stdlib.h
`long `**`strtol`**`(const char *number_string, char **stop, int base);`	Converts `number_string` to a `long`. Recognizes same characters as `atol` plus characters appropriate to specified `base` (which can be from 2–36). Address of first inappropriate character is stored in `stop`.	stdlib.h
`unsigned long `**`strtoul`**`(const char *number_string, char **stop, int base);`	Converts `number_string` to an `unsigned long`. Recognizes same characters as `atol` plus characters appropriate to specified `base` (which can be from 2–36). Address of first inappropriate character is stored in `stop`.	stdlib.h
Buffer Manipulation		
`void `**`*memset`**`(void *buffer, int value, unsigned num_bytes);`	Sets each byte in block of memory (`num_bytes`, starting at `buffer`) to same specified value.	string.h
`void `**`*memmove`**`(void *destination, const void *source, unsigned num_bytes);`	Copies byte values from one memory location to another (copies `num_bytes` starting at `source` to `num_bytes` starting at `destination`). Buffers may overlap.	string.h
`void `**`*memcpy`**`(void *destination, const void *source, unsigned num_bytes);`	Same as `memmove`, except no overlapping buffers allowed.	string.h
`int `**`memcmp`**`(const void *buffer1, const void *buffer2, unsigned num_bytes);`	Same as `strcmp`, except comparison for specified # of bytes rather than until `NULL`.	string.h

Table I.1 *(continued)*

`void *memchr(const char *buffer, int character, unsigned num_bytes);`	Same as `strchr`, but searches specified # of bytes starting at `buffer` instead of stopping at `NULL`.	string.h
File Operations		
`FILE *fopen(const char *filename, const char *mode);`	Opens `filename` in file-opening `mode`, which dictates whether the file is opened for reading, writing, or appending (or reading and either writing or appending) and is in text or binary: `r`, `w`, `a`, `rb`, `wb`, `ab`, `r+`, `w+`, `a+`, `rb+`, `wb+`, `ab+`. Returns pointer to stream.	stdio.h
`int fclose(FILE *stream);`	Closes file associated with `stream`.	stdio.h
`FILE *freopen(const char *new_filename, const char *mode, FILE *existing_stream);`	Closes file associated with `existing_stream` and opens `new_filename` in specified `mode`, pointing FILE pointer to the latter. Can be used to redirect a file to `stdin`, redirect `stdout` to a file, or redirect `stderr` to an error log file.	stdio.h
`long ftell(FILE *stream);`	Returns number of bytes from the beginning of file.	stdio.h
`int fseek(FILE *ptr, long offset, int mode);`	Moves `offset` bytes after the beginning, before the end or before or after the current file position, depending on whether `mode` is `SEEK_SET`, `SEEK_END`, or `SEEK_CUR` and `offset` is positive or negative. Except for returning to the point when `ftell()` was last called, will not always produce meaningful results in text mode; a binary stream need not meaningfully support calls with a mode of `SEEK_END`.	stdio.h
`void rewind(FILE *stream);`	Moves the file position to the beginning of the file and clears the error indicator.	stdio.h
`int fgetpos(FILE *stream, fpos_t *position);`	Marks file `position` for subsequent `setpos` call.	stdio.h
`int fsetpos(FILE *stream, const fpos_t *position);`	Goes to file location previously stored by `fgetpos` in `position`.	stdio.h
`int fflush(FILE *stream);`	Flushes buffer for `stream`. To flush buffers for all open streams, call `fflush(NULL)`.	stdio.h
`void clearerr(FILE *stream);`	Clears both the error indicator for `stream` and its end-of-file indicator.	stdio.h

(continued on next page)

Table I.1 *(continued)*

`int `**`feof`**`(FILE *stream);`	Tests whether the end-of-file indicator for `stream` is on.	stdio.h
`int `**`ferror`**`(FILE *stream);`	Tests whether the error indicator for `stream` is on.	
`int `**`setvbuf`**`(FILE *stream, char *buffer, int buffer_type, size_t size);`	Alters `stream`'s default buffer size and location to `size`, starting at `buffer`, and alters its default `buffer_type` to `_IOFBF` (fully buffered), `_IOLBF` (line buffered) or `_IONBF` (no buffering). If buffer is `NULL`, assigns the file a buffer on its own. Must be called immediately after opening the file.	stdio.h
`void `**`setbuf`**`(FILE *stream, char *buffer);`	Establishes buffer of `BUFSIZE` for `stream` starting at `buffer` instead of at the location automatically assigned on opening the file.	stdio.h
`int `**`remove`**` (const char *file);`	Deletes `file`.	stdio.h
`int `**`rename`**`(const char *oldname, const char *newname);`	Renames file from `oldname` to `newname`.	stdio.h
`FILE *`**`tmpfile`**`(void);`	Opens a temporary binary file in the current working directory in `wb+` mode, and at normal program termination or explicit file closing, automatically deletes the file.	stdio.h
`char *`**`tmpnam`**`(char *filename);`	Generates a string that is a valid and unique file name and stores it starting at `filename` (or as an internal static object if `filename` is `NULL`). Does this each time it is called, up to at least `TMP_MAX` times.	stdio.h
Dynamic Memory Allocation, Reallocation, and Deallocation		
`void *`**`malloc`**`(size_t bytes);`	Reserves a block of memory of `bytes` size and returns the address of the start of that block.	stdlib.h
`void *`**`calloc`**`(size_t num_blocks, size_t bytes_per_block);`	Reserves a block of memory of a specified number of bytes (num_blocks * bytes_per_block), returns the address of the start of that block, and initializes all bits in block to 0.	stdlib.h

Table I.1   *(continued)*

`void *realloc(void *ptr, size_t bytes);`	Increases or decreases to `bytes` the size of a block of memory, starting at `ptr`, previously reserved by `malloc` or `calloc`. Address returned may be different from `ptr`. Preserves the contents of the previously allocated memory block to the extent possible.	stdlib.h
`void free(void *ptr);`	Unreserves memory block starting at `ptr` previously allocated by `malloc` or `calloc`.	stdlib.h
Binary Searching and Sorting		
`void *bsearch(const void *key, const void *start_address, size_t num_elements, size_t bytes_per_element, int (*compare_function)(const void *p1, const void *p2));`	Makes a binary search on a key field through elements of an array, where the elements are either scalar variables or complex data types. Array elements must be arranged in order—by key, if the elements are not scalar variables.	stdlib.h
`void qsort(void *start_address, size_t num_elements, size_t bytes_per_element, int(*compare_function) (const void*p1, const void *p2));`	Uses a binary algorithm to order records.	stdlib.h
Error Checking		
`char *strerror(int error_num);`	Prints to standard error the `sys_errlist` string corresponding to `error_num`.	stdio.h
`void perror(const char *string);`	Prints to standard error the `sys_errlist` string corresponding to the current value of `errno`.	stdio.h
Operating System and the Environment		
`char *setlocale(int category, const char *locale);`	Changes locale-specific features of the Standard C library for specified `category` (e.g., character handling, money formatting, decimal point/comma characters) to specified `locale`.	locale.h
`struct lconv *localeconv(void);`	Determines conventions for formatting numeric and monetary values in the current locale.	locale.h

(continued on next page)

Table I.1   *(continued)*

`int system(const char *command);`	Executes operating system `command`. If called with `NULL`, invokes the command processor in such a way that its command prompt is displayed, allowing the user to type in system commands before returning to the C program.	stdlib.h
`char *getenv(const char *env_variable);`	Takes string containing the environmental variable and returns a pointer to the value portion of the environmental variable.	stdlib.h
`void (*signal(int signal_num, void (*function)(int)))(int);`	Chooses one of three ways in which receipt of `signal_number` is handled, depending on the value of `function`: `SIG_DEF`: default handling; `SIG_IGN`: signal is ignored; otherwise, `function` points to a signal handling function to be called when signal occurs. In the last case, when a signal occurs, the equivalent of `signal(sig, SIG_DFL)` is executed or an implementation-defined blocking of the signal is performed; and then the equivalent of `(*func)(sig)` is executed. The `function` may terminate by executing a return statement or by calling `abort`, `exit`, or `longjmp`. The program generally resumes execution at the point it was interrupted.	signal.h
`int raise(int signal);`	Sends `signal` to the executing program; returns zero if successful, nonzero if unsuccessful.	signal.h
`int setjmp(jmp_buf environment);`	Saves its calling environment in implementation-defined array `environment` for later use by `longjmp`.	setjmp.h
`void longjmp(jmp_buf environment, int status);`	Restores the environment saved by the most recent invocation of `setjmp`.	setjmp.h
Program Termination		
`void exit(int status);`	Terminates program prematurely. Causes all file buffers to be flushed and all open files to be closed. Returns `status` to the host environment.	stdlib.h
`void abort(void);`	Terminates program prematurely.	stdlib.h
`int atexit(void (*func)(void));`	When `exit` is called, calls functions passed to it in reverse order prior to `exit`'s buffer flushing and file closing.	stdlib.h

Table I.1 *(continued)*

Time and Date		
`time_t` **`time`**`(time_t *seconds);`	Stores at the address of a `time_t` variable the number of seconds between midnight January 1, 1970, and the time of the call. Also returns that same value.	time.h
`char` **`*ctime`**`(const time_t *seconds);`	Converts number of seconds (generally returned by `time` function) into a string in format "Fri Mar 06 17:50:32 1999".	time.h
`struct tm` **`*gmtime`**`(const time_t *seconds);`	Same as `localtime()` below, except that converts results to Greenwich mean time (GMT) based on environmental variable for difference between local time and GMT.	time.h
`struct tm` **`*localtime`**`(const time_t *timer);`	Converts number of seconds (generally returned by `time` function) into broken-down time and date components in a variable of type `struct tm`, which contains members for seconds after the minute, minutes after the hour, hours since midnight, day of the month, years since 1900, days since Sunday, days since January 1, and a daylight savings flag.	time.h
`char` **`asctime`**`(const struct tm *timeptr);`	Converts the broken-down time and date (generally returned by `localtime`) into a string in format "Fri Mar 06 17:50:32 1999".	time.h
`double` **`difftime`**`(time_t time1, time_t time0);`	Takes two `time_t` values representing seconds (and generally returned by the `time` function) and subtracts one from the other and returns the result as a `double`.	time.h
`clock_t` **`clock`**`(void);`	Computes the number of the computer's clock ticks from the start of program execution to the function's being called. Macro `CLK_TCK` defines how many times per second the clock ticks.	time.h

(continued on next page)

Table I.1   *(continued)*

`time_t` **`mktime`**`(struct tm *timeptr);`	Constructs a value of type `time_t` (number of seconds) from the `tm` structure data pointed to by `timeptr` (ignoring the days since Sunday and since January 1 members). For instance, determine the number of seconds between an arbitrary time and date and current time and date by calling `difftime(time(NULL), <return value of mktime call>);`	time.h
`size_t` **`strftime`**`(char *time_string, size_t max_chars, const char *format_string, const struct tm *timeptr);`	Places characters into `time_string` as controlled by `format_string`, which consists of conversion specifiers and ordinary characters. All ordinary characters (including the terminating null character) are copied unchanged into `time_string`, just as with `printf`. No more than `max_chars` are placed into `time_string`. Each conversion specifier is replaced as described in the following list and as determined by the values contained in the structure pointed to by `timeptr` for the current locale. %a/%A: abbreviated/full weekday name; %b/%B: abbreviated/full month name; %c: date and time representation; %d: day of the month #; %H/%I: hour # (24-hr/12-hr); %j: day of year #; %m: month #; %M: minute #; %p: equivalent of the AM/PM designations 12-hr clock; %S: second #; %U/W: week # of year (first Sun/Mon as the first day of week 1); %w: weekday # (Sun = 0); %x/X: date/time representation; %y/Y: yr # without/with century; %Z: time zone name or abbreviation.	time.h
Math		
`double` **`acos`**`(double angle);`	Calculates arc cosine of `angle`.	math.h
`double` **`asin`**`(double angle);`	Calculates arc sine of `angle`.	math.h
`double` **`atan`**`(double angle);`	Calculates arc tangent of `angle`.	math.h
`double` **`atan2`**`(double y, double angle);`	Calculates arc tangent of the `angle` formed by drawing a straight line from point x=0, y=0 on a Cartesian coordinate system to x and y.	math.h
`double` **`cos`**`(double angle);`	Calculates cosine of `angle`.	math.h
`double` **`sin`**`(double angle);`	Calculates sine of `angle`.	math.h

Table I.1 *(continued)*

`double ` **`tan`**`(double angle);`	Calculates tangent of `angle`.	math.h
`double ` **`cosh`**`(double angle);`	Calculates hyperbolic cosine of `angle`.	math.h
`double ` **`sinh`**`(double angle);`	Calculates hyperbolic sine of `angle`.	math.h
`double ` **`tanh`**`(double angle);`	Calculates hyperbolic tangent of `angle`.	math.h
`double ` **`exp`**`(double exponent);`	Computes e to the `exponent` power.	math.h
`double ` **`log`**`(double floating_pt_number);`	Computes the natural logarithm of `floating_pt_number` (i.e., `floating_pt_number` is e to what power?)	math.h
`double ` **`log10`**`(double floating_pt_number);`	Computes the base-ten logarithm of `floating_pt_number` (i.e., `floating_pt_number` is 10 to what power?)	math.h
`double ` **`pow`**`(double floating_pt_number, double floating_pt_exponent);`	Computes `floating_pt_number` to the `floating_pt_exponent` power.	math.h
`double ` **`ldexp`**`(double floating_pt_number, int whole_exponent);`	Multiplies `floating_pt_number` by 2 to the integer `whole_exponent` power.	math.h
`double ` **`frexp`**`(double floating_pt_number, int *whole_exponent);`	Splits `floating_pt_number` into a fraction of between 1/2 and 1 and 2 to the `whole_exponent` power. Returns fraction; stores power at address of `whole_exponent`.	math.h
`double ` **`modf`**`(double floating_pt_number, double *integer);`	Splits `floating_pt_number` into a fraction and an integer with the same sign as `floating_pt_number`. Returns fraction; stores integer at address of `integer`.	math.h
`double ` **`fmod`**`(double floating_pt_dividend, double floating_pt_divisor);`	Computes modulus of two floating point numbers.	math.h
`double ` **`sqrt`**`(double floating_pt_number);`	Computes square root of the positive value, `floating_pt_number`.	math.h
`double ` **`ceil`**`(double floating_pt_number);`	Rounds up to the next integer.	math.h
`double ` **`floor`**`(double floating_pt_number);`	Rounds down to the next integer.	math.h

(continued on next page)

Table I.1 *(continued)*

`double` **`fabs`**`(double floating_pt_number);`	Returns absolute value of `floating_pt_number`.	math.h
`int` **`abs`**`(int integer);`	Returns absolute value of `integer`.	math.h
`long` **`labs`**`(long big_integer);`	Same as abs, except that argument and return value are `longs`.	math.h
`div_t` **`div`**`(int numerator, int denom);`	Computes integer `quotient` and `remainder` of `numerator` by `denom`. Returns a structure of type `div_t`, with two members, `quot` and `rem`.	stdlib.h
`ldiv_t` **`ldiv`**`(long numerator, long denom);`	Same as `div` function, except arguments and structure members of `ldiv_t` are longs.	stdlib.h
`int` **`rand`**`(void);`	Returns a pseudo-random number.	stdlib.h
`void` **`srand`**`(unsigned seed);`	Uses the argument as a seed for a sequence of pseudo-random numbers to be returned by subsequent calls to `rand`.	stdlib.h

Operator Precedence and Associativity

Table J.1 *Precedence and Associativity of C Operators*

Operators in descending order of precedence	Associativity
( ) [ ] . ->	→
! ~ ++ -- + - * & *(type)* sizeof	←
* / %	→
+ -	→
<< >>	→
< <= > >=	→
== !=	→
&	→
^	→
|	→
&&	→
||	→
? . . . :	←
= += -= *= /= &= |= ^= <<= >>=	→

Notes:

The – and + operators in line 2 are the unary sign operators: the – and + in line 4 are the binary addition and subtraction operators.

The * in line 2 is the unary decrement operator; the * in line 3 is the binary multiplication operator.

Low-Level I/O and Other File and Disk Operations

K.1 LOW-LEVEL I/O

Low-level I/O parallels the method the system uses to read and write to disk. For that reason, and because there are fewer layers of functions to go through, low-level I/O is faster and more efficient than standard I/O. Also, the low-level I/O functions have smaller code, so executable programs that incorporate them rather than standard I/O functions are smaller.

Low-level I/O is essentially limited to programmers writing code for very small systems, such as motorized wheelchairs and other computerized medical devices. In such systems, the need to save the space and overhead required for the FILE data object may be paramount despite the cost in performance. Note that the low-level functions, though available on all DOS and UNIX compilers, are *not* part of Standard C.

Low-level file operations are not only unbuffered but unformatted. You will use only the low-level counterparts to fwrite() and fread() to write to and read from a file. The functions used for unbuffered low-level I/O are similar in format to those used for buffered standard I/O. In fact, in most cases, the name is the same, with just the f left off.

K.1.1 Opening a File

To open a file, you use open(). The open() function is more complex than fopen(). The prototype looks like this:

```
int open(char *filename,
    int current_mode[, int permanent_mode]);
```

The prototype for open() is found in io.h, as are the prototypes for the other low-level functions discussed below: close(), lseek(), tell(), read(), and write().

As with fopen(), the filename argument may be a literal string or a string variable. An fopen() call returns a pointer to a FILE structure. One member of the structure is the file handle—sort of an identification number attached to the file by the operating system. The open() function returns only a file handle.

If the call is not successful, it returns –1; errno is set to one of the following values (see Chapter 16 for a discussion of errno): ENOENT (no such file or directory), EMFILE (too many open files), EACCES (permission denied), or EINVACC (invalid access code).

The second argument to open() determines the mode for opening the file with the current open() call. The third argument allows you to restrict future calls to the file. We have put the third argument in brackets because you use a third argument only if you indicate by your second argument that you are opening a new file. This third argument determines the limits of future access to this new file.

K.1.2 File-Opening Modes

You must use one, and only one, of the following mandatory file-opening modes for the current opening-mode argument in opening a file with open(). The modes are manifest constants defined in fcntl.h (see Table K.1).

You may combine a mandatory file-opening mode with one or more of the optional mode modifiers listed in Table K.2.

Table K.1 *Mandatory File-Opening Modes*

Mode	Meaning
O_RDONLY	reading only
O_WRONLY	writing only
O_RDWR	reading and writing

Table K.2 *Optional File-Opening Mode Modifiers*

Text or Binary	
O_TEXT	text mode
O_BINARY	binary mode
File Creation	
O_CREAT	requires third argument: create a new file; if the file exists, ignore this modifier
O_EXCL	used only with O_CREATE: if file exists already, do not open
Write-Mode Options	
O_APPEND	allows writing to occur only at end of file
O_TRUNC	used only when file is opened for writing: truncate file to zero length, destroying its current contents

Note that the mode argument in open() is an int, in contrast to the string mode argument required by fopen(). Each of the constants listed in the two preceding figures has a value that affects different bits in the mode int. You combine them by ORing (see Chapter 12). For example, to open a file for writing in binary mode:

```
int fh; /* file handle */
fh = open("data", O_WRONLY | O_BINARY);
```

As is the case with standard I/O, the default is text mode. With some implementations, you can globally change the default by setting a global system variable generally called _fmode, to O_BINARY, as described earlier.

With fopen(), if you specify a write or append mode, the file contents are destroyed if the file already exists. Not so with open(); you must specify truncation explicitly if that's what you want to happen. For example, to open a file in binary for appending and to destroy the existing file contents:

```
fh = open("data", O_WRONLY | O_BINARY | O_APPEND | O_TRUNC);
```

The same holds true for file creation. With fopen() in the write or append mode, the file is created if it does not already exist. With open(), if the file does not already exist, you will get an error unless you have included O_CREAT as part of the mode.

K.1.3 Permission Modes

When and only when you include O_CREAT in the file-opening mode, you must include a third argument. This argument specifies the read-write permission for *subsequent* openings of the same file. Again, we use manifest constants, this time defined in stat.h (see Table K.3).

Under DOS, all files are readable, so using S_IWRITE alone would be equivalent to using S_IREAD | S_IWRITE; it would not stop future attempts to open the file for reading. Making a file read-only prevents its unintentional deletion as well as preventing attempts to write to it.

Table K.3 *Subsequent Permission Modes*

Mode	Meaning
S_IWRITE	writing only
S_IREAD	reading only
S_IREAD ¦ S_IWRITE	reading and writing

If O_CREAT is part of the file-opening mode, and the file already exists, the O_CREAT portion will simply be ignored. However, if you include O_CREAT and O_EXCL, and the file already exists, the file will not be opened. Thus, the following open() call will return –1 instead of a file handle if the file already exists:

```
fh = open("data", O_CREAT ¦ O_EXCL ¦ O_WRONLY, S_IWRITE);
```

K.1.4　Closing a File

To close a file opened with open(), you use close(). It takes a single argument, the file handle. The close() prototype is found in io.h.

K.1.5　Reading and Writing

With low-level I/O, we use write() to copy data from RAM to a file and read() to copy data from a file to RAM. Compare the formats of fwrite() and fread() to those of the low-level functions, write() and read():

```
size_t fwrite(void *ptr, size_t bytes_per_block,
   size_t number_of_blocks, FILE *fp);
size_t fread(void *ptr, unsigned bytes_per_block,
   unsigned number_of_blocks, FILE *fp);

int write(int handle, void *ptr, unsigned number_of_bytes);
int read(int handle, void *ptr, unsigned number_of_bytes);
```

We use the file handle rather than a FILE pointer, and this argument is first here, not last. The address of the area we are copying from (with write()) or to (with read()) is moved to the second argument. The two arguments we use in fread() and fwrite() to specify the number of bytes to be written or read are now combined into one argument.

Of course, we can still make use of sizeof and strlen() to facilitate the specification of the correct number of bytes to be written or read, even if it means making the number_of_bytes argument the product of a size and quantity:

```
int num[5] = {13, 2343, 34, 333, 322};
write(fh, num, sizeof(int) * 5);
```

And in most cases, you will find that one or the other of the bytes_per_block or number_of_blocks arguments to fwrite() or fread() is a 1, so that combining the two arguments will not prove much of an inconvenience:

```
write(fh, num, sizeof(num));
```

To show you an example of reading and writing with low-level I/O, we have reworked our file copying programs:

 **Listing K.1 f_cpy_1.c**

```
/* f_cpy_1.c */

/* simple file-copying program with low-level I/O */

#include <stdio.h>
#include <io.h>
#include <fcntl.h>
```

```
#include <sys\stat.h> /* read-write permission manifest constant */
#include <stdlib.h> /* exit */

#define MULT 48 /* 2, 10, 48 */

#define BUFSIZE BUFSIZ * MULT

int main(void)
{
    char buffer[BUFSIZE];
    int orig_handle, copy_handle;
    unsigned bytes_read;
    unsigned bytes = BUFSIZE;

    if ((orig_handle = open("c:\\atlas5\\nameshap.dat",
        O_RDONLY | O_BINARY)) < 0)
    {
        puts("Error! Unable to open \"nameshap.dat\" for reading");
        exit(1);
    }

    if ((copy_handle = open("c:\\temp\\junk",
        O_CREAT | O_WRONLY | O_BINARY, S_IWRITE)) < 0)
    {
    puts("Error! Unable to open file for writing");
    exit(2);
    }

    while((bytes_read = read(orig_handle, buffer, bytes)) > 0)
        write(copy_handle, buffer, bytes_read);
    close(orig_handle);
    close(copy_handle);
}
```

We ran the program using the same file we used with f_speed.c, Listing 14.11, nameshap.dat, containing 11,261,553 bytes. Its speed compares favorably to that of f_speed.c at all buffering sizes.

On the other hand, with a different application from this file-copying example, low-level I/O can present a more complex coding task. If our program were to read a file character by character, stopping and doing something whenever it got to a certain character, the coding in standard I/O is fairly simple. However, with low-level I/O, unless we wanted a very slow program, we would need to set up a complete buffering system of the sort standard I/O does for us. We would have to read a block of bytes at once into the buffer. Then we would have to examine the bytes in the buffer. When we reached a target character, we would have to back up a certain calculated distance in the file for the next read—all matters automatically handled with standard I/O.

K.1.6   Random Access Functions with Low-Level I/O

The functions lseek() and tell() work essentially the same way as their standard I/O relatives, fseek() and ftell(), except that you use the file handle in place of a FILE pointer argument. However, whereas fseek() returns 0 on a successful call, lseek() returns the number of bytes from the beginning of the file to the position moved to by the call, if the call is successful:

```
long lseek (int handle, long offset, int fromwhere);
long tell (int handle);
```

As a result, the following two calls are identical in effect:

```
long position;
position = tell(fh);
position = lseek(fh, 0L, SEEK_CUR);
```

Both lseek() and tell() return a –1 in the case of error.

```
if ((position = tell(fh)) == -1)
   printf("error calling tell()\n");
if (lseek(fh, (long)BUFSIZ, SEEK_CUR) == -1)
   printf("error calling lseek()\n");
```

K.1.7   Changing File Permission: chmod()

There are times when you may want to change the file permission you originally assigned on creation of the file. This change may be permanent (at least until you change your mind again): the file you wanted to safeguard against deletion or modification no longer needs that protection, for instance. Or it may be temporary. For example, you may want to keep a file that contains certain records read-only but allow modification in the course of running a program designed to update the records, and then at the end of the program, change the permission back to read-only. That would allow modification by that specific program but would prevent deletion or modification of the file at any other time.

You may also want to write-protect a file created with fopen(). While the open() function allows you to create a read-only file, there is no such option with fopen().

The way to alter the file permission through a C program (as opposed to command-line arguments in your operating system's shell, such as attrib in DOS, or the corresponding system() call in a C program, as discussed in Chapter 16) is through chmod(). The chmod() function, the prototype for which is found in io.h, akes two arguments, a char pointer to the name of the file and one of the permission modes listed in Table K.3. The filename argument is the same argument as the one used to open a file with open() or fopen(); it is *not* the FILE pointer or the file handle:

```
int chmod(const char *filename, int permission_mode);
```

The chmod() function is *not* part of Standard C. You do not have to open a file in order to call chmod(). The chmod() function returns a 0 if successful; otherwise, it returns a –1.

K.1.8   Determining File Existence and Permission: access()

The access() function allows us to ascertain whether a specified file exists or to determine what sort of read-write permission it has. The access() function takes two arguments. The first is the filename. The same rules for using filenames with fopen()'s first argument apply. This function is *not* part of Standard C:

```
int access (const char*filename, int mode);
```

The second argument is an integer specifying what we want to test for. The function returns a 0 if the test is met and a –1 if not (see Table K.4). Under DOS, every file has read permission. Therefore, under DOS, tests 2 and 6 are identical, and test 4 would do no more than report what test 0 would report.

We may want to use these tests to determine what course of action to take in our program, or to ascertain the precise reason for a failure to open a file. As an example of the former, suppose we want to revise the data in a file. We may first want to determine whether the file is a read-only file. If so, we can call chmod() before updating to give it read-write permission, and again following updating, restore the file to read-only:

```
int read_only = 0;
char filename[45];

printf("Specify file to update");
gets(filename);
```

Table K.4 access() *Test Values*

Value	Tests Whether File . . .
6	has read and write permission
4	has read permission
2	has write permission
0	exists

```
if (access(filename, 6)) /* test read-write permission;
   permission only if returns 0 */
{
   read_only = 1;
   chmod(filename, S_IWRITE | S_IREAD);
}
. . . /* open file and update */
if (read_only) /* change back if it was read-only */
   chmod(filename, S_IREAD);
```

You might create database files that have some initial bookkeeping matters stored at the start of the file, just before the series of records. If you are opening such a file to insert records, you might do something like the following:

```
char mode[4];
FILE *fp;

printf("Specify name of database file");
gets(filename);
if (access(filename, 0)) /* test existence of file */
{
   strcpy(mode, "wb");
   . . . /* add bookkeeping matters to file */
}
else strcpy(mode, "ab");
fp = fopen(filename, mode);
```

K.1.9   Ascertaining Read Error Causes with `access()`

We saw earlier how to check for a file's being successfully opened:

```
if (!(fp = fopen(filename, mode))
   printf("Error opening file %s\n", filename);
```

However, this check tells us nothing about the cause of the error. With `access()`, we can pin down a couple potential causes of error:

```
if (!(fp = fopen(filename, "r+")))
{
   if (access(filename, 0))
      printf("Error: file %s does not exist\n", filename);
   else if (access(filename, 6))
      printf("Error: file %s is read-only\n", filename);
   else printf("Error opening file %s\n", filename);
}
```

In Sections K.2 and K.3, we will see how to test for error occasioned by the supposed filename's being a directory name instead (`stat()`) or by various hardware problems.

K.2   FILE INFORMATION AND ERROR-CHECKING: `stat()`

Earlier in this appendix, we saw how to test whether a file exists and whether the file is write-protected prior to attempting to open the file. The `stat()` function lets us add one more test and also gives us a good deal more information. The various pieces of information are assigned to members of a structure of type `stat`, the template for which is declared in `stat.h`. Some of the members are included in Table K.5.

We call `stat()` with two arguments: a file or directory name and the address of the variable of type `stat` we declare. Whether we specify a filename or a directory, we need to include the full path unless the file or directory is in the path from which we run the program. The `stat()` function returns a 0 if the call is successful and a –1 if the file or directory does not exist.

Note that, like the `access()` function we reviewed earlier, `stat()` is a DOS/UNIX function; it is not in the Standard C library.

Table K.5   stat *Members*

Member	Type	Meaning
st_mode	unsigned	file mode information
st_dev	int	drive number of disk containing file
st_size	long	file size in bytes
st_mtime	long	time file was last modified

The following program illustrates the use of stat() to obtain information about a file.

 **Listing K.2 fileinfo.c**

```
/* fileinfo.c */
/* get file size, drive and time last modified */

#include <stdio.h>
#include <sys\types.h>
#include <sys\stat.h>
#include <time.h> /* ctime() */

int main(void)
{
   char filename[45];
   struct stat info;

   puts("Specify filename");
   gets(filename);
   if (stat(filename, &info) == 0) /* returns 0 on success */
      printf("%s: \n\t%ld bytes\n\tfound in %c drive\n"
         "\tlast modified: %s\n", filename, info.st_size, info.st_dev + 'A',
         ctime(&(info.st_mtime)));
   else puts("error calling stat");
}
```

The st_mtime member gives you the number of seconds from midnight January 1, 1970, to the call. The ctime() function, the prototype for which is contained in time.h, converts that long value into a string holding the date and time in the following format:

```
Sat Jan 25 11:34:23 1992\n
```

We pass ctime() the address of the s_mtime member.

The st_mode member is interpreted on a bit level. The stat.h file contains manifest constants for the various bits. In addition to the S_IREAD and S_IWRITE constants we discussed earlier in this appendix to show whether the file has read permission or write permission, there is S_IFDIR, to show whether the first argument to a stat() call is a directory rather than a file.

With the st_mode information, we can expand the file testing we saw previously in this appendix.

 **Listing K.3 file_err.c**

```
/* file_err.c */

/* ascertain cause of error in opening file */

#include <stdio.h>
#include <sys\stat.h> /* S_IFDIR, stat */
#include <io.h> /* access */
```

```
int main(void)
{
    char filename[45];
    FILE *fp;
    struct stat file;

    puts("Specify filename");
    gets(filename);

    /* if file opening fails, examine cause */
    if (!(fp = fopen(filename, "r+")))
    {
        /* does it exist? (access returns 0 (success)
           if filename OR directory) */
        /* 0 as arg checks for existence of file */
        if (access(filename, 0))
            printf("Error: file %s does not exist\n", filename);

        /* exists, but is "file" a directory rather than a file? */
        /* make sure stat variable has value before
           testing in 2nd line */
        else if ((stat(filename, &file) == 0)
            && ((file.st_mode & S_IFDIR)
            == S_IFDIR)) /* if yes, is directory */
            printf("Error: %s is a directory, not a file\n",
                filename);

        /* exists, and is a file, but is file read_only? */
        /* with arg of 2, access returns 0 if has write permission */
        else if (access(filename, 2) != 0)
            printf("Error: file %s is read-only\n", filename);

        else printf("Unknown error opening file %s\n", filename);
    }

    else printf("File %s successfully opened for reading and writing\n",
        filename);
}
```

When we call access() with a 0 second argument, it returns a 0, indicating success, if the first argument represents a file or a directory. If the access() call returns a number other than 0, we know the filename passed does not exist. If the call returns a 0, we next have to test whether the purported filename is really a directory. We do that with stat().

A stat() call will fail if the file argument is not a file or a directory. In such a case, no value will be placed into the stat variable we declared, leaving it with whatever garbage value it had on declaration. To avoid an invalid test of the stat variable value, we make the test only if the call to stat() is successful, in which case stat() returns zero.

```
if ((!stat(filename, &file)) &&
    ((file.st_mode & S_IFDIR) == S_IFDIR))
```

Actually here, by the time we call stat(), we already know what we're testing is a file or a directory; otherwise, the prior call to access() would have failed. However, we wanted to show you how you would normally use stat().

The expression

```
file.st_mode & S_IFDIR
```

turns off all bits in file.st_mode except the one indicating that the name is a directory or subdirectory (see Chapter 12).

K.3   DISK AND FILE INFORMATION

Earlier in this appendix, we saw how to use the stat() function to obtain certain information about a file. We pass to stat() the name of the file and the address of a structure variable of type stat.

One of the members of the stat variable, st_size, gives us the number of seconds since the time the file was created or last revised. We can use the Standard C function ctime(), the prototype for which is found in time.h, to convert this number in seconds to a more intelligible format: Fri Mar 06 17:50:32 1999. We can, in turn, use our own function to further simplify this format. The following program prints out the size of a file and when it was last revised.

 **Listing   K.4 filespec.c**

```c
/* filespec.c */

/* print out # of bytes and time last revised for specified file */

#include <stdio.h>
#include <sys\stat.h> /* stat */
#include <time.h>

FILE *fp;

int main(int argc, char **argv)
{  /* error-checking on # of args omitted */
   struct stat fileinfo; /* for file size & date/time last revised */
   struct tm *split_time;

   /* fill stat variable; no need to open file */
   stat(argv[1], &fileinfo);

   split_time =
       localtime(&fileinfo.st_ctime); /* fill tm structure */

   printf("%s: %ld bytes  Revised: %02d/%02d/%02d %02d:%02d\n",
       argv[1], fileinfo.st_size, split_time->tm_mon,
       split_time->tm_mday, split_time->tm_year % 100,
       split_time->tm_hour, split_time->tm_min);
}
```

Here, we have used the localtime() function to convert to various int members of a struct tm variable the number of seconds since midnight January 1, 1970, placed into the st_ctime member of our struct stat variable. As an alternative, we could have used ctime(), either with or without the convert_time() function we made. The localtime() and ctime functions, are covered in Chapter 16.

K.3.1   Ascertaining Available Disk Space

We can use service 36h of the DOS interrupt (interrupt 21h) to determine the remaining free space on a designated drive, whether the drive be a hard drive or a diskette in a floppy drive. We set the dl register to the drive we want to check: 0 represents the current or "default" drive, 1 represents the A drive, 2 represents the B drive, 3 represents the C drive, and so on. Note that if, for example, the C drive is the current drive, passing 0 or 3 will yield the same result.

Here's a function that implements this interrupt:

```
/*
+------------------------------------------------------+
+ DISK_FREE
+
+ Returns free space on disk on specified drive
+   passed as argument.
+
+ Drive passed can be a letter or number
+   (0: current drive; 1: A; 2: B, 3: C, etc.)
+
+------------------------------------------------------+
```

```
*/
unsigned long disk_free(int drive)
{
   union REGS in, out;

   if (drive > 10)
      drive = toupper(drive) - 'A' + 1;
   in.h.ah = 0x36; /* get free disk space function */
   in.h.dl = drive;
   int86(0x21, &in, &out);

   /* bx: # of free clusters, ax: sectors/cluster, cx: bytes/sector */
   return (unsigned long)out.x.bx * (unsigned long)out.x.ax *
      (unsigned long)out.x.cx;
}
```

After the int86() call, the bx register will contain the number of clusters, the ax register will contain the number of sectors per cluster, and finally, the cx register will hold the number of bytes per sector.

See install.c, on the diskette, for a programming example where we make more extensive use of the disk_free() function.

K.3.2 Determining the Letter of the Current DOS Drive

You can use service 19h of the DOS interrupt to determine the current DOS drive. The interrupt returns the current drive in the al register, again with 1 representing the A drive, and so on. You can add A to convert this value to a letter:

```
/*
+--------------------------------------------------------+
+
+ GET_DRIVE_NUM and GET_DRIVE_LTR
+
+ Returns the number / letter of the current DOS drive
+
+--------------------------------------------------------+
*/
char get_drive_num(void)
{
   union REGS in, out;

   in.h.ah = 0x19; /* get current disk service of
                      DOS interrupt (0x21) */
   int86(0x21, &in, &out);
   return out.h.al;
}

char get_drive_ltr(void)
{
   return get_drive_num() + 'A';
}
```

K.3.3 Determining the Current DOS Directory

You can use service 47h of the DOS interrupt to determine the current directory for the current or a specified drive. This process is a little more complicated. You must establish a 65-byte buffer and then point the ds register and si register to the segment and offset, respectively, to that buffer. To access the ds register, you must use int86x(), rather than int86(), and you must add a SREGS variable (see Appendix B). Again, you must set the dl register to the desired drive, with 0 for the current drive.

After the call, the buffer is filled with the directory. The directory does not include the drive portion (for example, BORLANDC\BIN, not C:\BORLANDC\BIN). You can add that yourself with a call to our `get_drive_ltr()` function.

```
/*
+------------------------------------------------------+
+
+ GET_DIRECTORY
+
+ Returns the current directory on the specified
+    or default drive.
+
+ Drive passed can be a letter or number
+   (0: current drive; 1: A; 2: B, 3: C, etc.)
+
+------------------------------------------------------+
*/
char *get_directory(int drive)
{
    static char path[68];
    char buffer[65];
    union REGS in, out;
    struct SREGS sreg;

    if (drive > 10)
        drive = toupper(drive) - 'A' + 1;

    in.h.ah = 0x47; /* get-current directory service */
    in.h.dl = drive;
    in.x.si = FP_OFF(buffer);
    sreg.ds = FP_SEG(buffer);
    int86x(0x21, &in, & out, &sreg);

    sprintf(path, "%c:\\%s", get_drive_ltr(), buffer);
    return path;
}
```

If you specify an invalid drive number or letter, the carry flag is set to 1 and the `ax` register is set to 0xF. If you wish, you can modify the above function to incorporate such error-checking. The `cflag` member of the WORDREGS structure member of the REGS union variable we declare will house the carry flag register value after the interrupt call.

K.3.4   Setting the Current DOS Directory

Function 3Bh of the DOS interrupt sets the current directory to a specified string. We must point `ds:dx` to the string where we have the desired directory before the interrupt call. After the call, the carry flag in the flags register (see Appendix B for an explanation of the flags register) is set to 0 if the call was successful; otherwise the carry flag is set to 1 and the `ax` register is set to 3, indicating the specified path was not found:

```
int set_directory (char *new_dir)
{
    union REGS in, out;
    struct SREGS sreg;

    in.h.ah = 0x3B; /* set current directory service of DOS
    interrupt */
    in.x.dx = FP_OFF(new_dir);
    sreg.ds = FP_SEG(new_dir);
    int86x(0x21, &in, &out, &sreg);
    if (in.x.cflag)
        return in.x.ax;
    return 0;
}
```

If your program changes the current DOS directory, you should generally first call the `get_directory()` described above, so that you can politely restore the original directory when your program finishes.

In conjunction with the `set_directory()` function, you can use function 39h of the DOS interrupt to create a subdirectory if none exists:

```
int main(void)
{
    char orig_dir[65], program_dir[] = "c:\\invoice";
    strcpy(orig_dir, get_directory(0));
    if (set_directory(program_dir) != 0)

        /* may be nonzero above if already in program_dir;
           test for that first */

        if (access (program_dir, 0) != 0)
        {
            printf("%s directory does not exist.\n"
                " Do you want to create it?", program_dir);
            if (toupper(getch()) == 'Y')
            {
                create_subdirectory(program_dir);
                set_directory(program_dir);
            }
            else exit(1);
        }
    . . .
    set_directory(orig_directory)
}

int create_subdirectory(char *new_dir)
{
    union REGS in, out;
    struct SREGS sreg;

    in.h.ah = 0x39; /* create subdirectory service
                        of DOS interrupt */
    sreg.ds = FP_SEG(new_dir);
    in.x.dx = FP_OFF(new_dir);
    int86x(0x21, &in, &out, &sreg);
    if (out.x.cflag != 0)
        return out.x.ax;
    return 0;
}
```

The interrupt call will return an error code in the `ax` register and not create the requested directory if the directory already exists, if any element of the pathname does not exist, or if the directory is in the root and the root is full (maximum of 512 files or directories in the root directory). In a network environment, you must have create-access rights to create a subdirectory. The possible error codes are 3 (path not found) or 5 (access denied).

The create-subdirectory function works just like a DOS `mkdir` or `md` command. You can specify a full path (for example, `c:\\invoice`), or you can specify a subdirectory name only, in which case a subdirectory will be created in whatever directory you are now in (for instance, if the current directory is `c:\`, passing "invoice" will create `c:\invoice`). It is generally safest to pass the full path.

APPENDIX **L**

Program Chaining with exec() and spawn()

The exec() function allows control of the program to be passed to another program. If the call to exec() is successful, the calling program (referred to as the *parent*) ceases to run and the called program (referred to as the *child*) takes over in memory.

Calling spawn() causes control to be temporarily transferred to the child. When the child program terminates, control passes back to the parent directly after the point of the call. This is analogous to program flow being transferred from a calling function to the function called. Both the parent and the child exist simultaneously in memory. (They have different code and data segments, however.)

The exec() functions are available in DOS or UNIX. The spawn() functions are available only in DOS. However, you can often achieve the same effect as spawn() with a system() call, with exec() embedded in the call. The prototypes for both exec() and spawn() are found in process.h.

L.1   VERSIONS OF exec() AND spawn()

Actually, you never use the exec() or spawn() function name alone. You *must* add either l or v to indicate how command-line arguments are passed from the parent to the child. You *may* add p or e or both, to allow exec() or spawn() to use the PATH environmental variable of the parent to find the name of the child executable file, and to furnish a new environment to the child, respectively. Table L.1 lists the possible calls.

Any files opened in the parent and not closed at the time the exec() or spawn() call is made remain open in the child. In addition to inheriting all open files of the parent, the child also inherits the parent's environment. However, if the e form of exec() or spawn() is used, the child has only the environment expressly passed to it rather than the parent's environment.

L.2   THE FIRST ARGUMENT TO spawn()

The spawn() functions take one more argument than the corresponding exec() functions. This is a manifest constant passed as the first argument. There are three possibilities, defined in process.h:

P_WAIT	suspend parent until child execution is completed
P_NOWAIT	execute parent and child simultaneously
P_OVERLAY	terminate parent, and transfer control completely to child

However, only the first choice, P_WAIT, is of much use. The P_NOWAIT choice has not been implemented in DOS. In fact, using it will generate an error. Using P_OVERLAY turns spawn() into an exec() call. There really is no reason to call spawn() with a first argument of P_OVERLAY rather than simply using the corresponding exec() function—unless perhaps you are using a conditional expression and you call spawn() with a first argument of either P_WAIT or P_OVERLAY depending on the results at that point:

```
spawnv(filecount > 2 ? P_WAIT : P_OVERLAY,
   "c:\\tc\\out\\data", arg_list);
```

Table L.1   exec() *and* spawn() *Variations*

	List of command-line arguments passed (l)	Pointer to command-line arguments passed (v)	PATH used to find child executable file (p)	Pointer to array of new environment strings passed (e)
execl	x			
spawnl	x			
execv		x		
spawnv		x		
execlp	x		x	
spawnlp	x		x	
execvp		x	x	
spawnvp		x	x	
execle	x			x
spawnle	x			x
execve		x		x
spawnve		x		x
execlpe	x		x	x
spawnlpe	x		x	x
execvpe		x	x	x
spawnvpe		x	x	x

L.3   THE CHILD-EXECUTABLE FILE ARGUMENT

The first argument to an exec() call, and the second argument to a spawn() call, is the name of the executable program you want to run in place of the currently executing program (that is, the child program's name). If the function call contains a p, exec() or spawn() will search the various directories specified in the PATH environmental variable for the executable file specified as the exec() call's first or spawn()'s second argument. Otherwise, no search is made; if the full path is not specified and the program is not located in the current directory, the call will fail.

Just as when you type the name of an executable file from the command line, you may include or not include the .exe extension in this argument.

L.4   ARGUMENT LIST—exec() AND spawn()

With execl() or spawnl(), each command-line argument is written out separately. Each is separated by commas. These arguments can be literal strings, enclosed in double quotes, or they can be pointers to strings. You must add a NULL at the end of the argument list. For example:

```
char *program = "print.exe";
execl("c:\\master\\vendor.exe", "c:\\master\\vendor.exe", program, "P", NULL);
```

Since the name of the child program will generally be passed as the first argument to the child program, the first two arguments to an execl() call and the second and third arguments to a spawnl() call will generally both be the name of the child program.

The length of all the arguments together, including the terminating NULLs, cannot exceed the maximum specified by the operating system (for example, 128 characters in DOS). Executable file arguments will contain the .exe extension when passed, even if we do not include the extension in the call's argument. Thus, if we had written "c:\\master\\vendor" above, "c:\\master\\vendor.exe" gets passed anyway.

Now let's look at an example. Say we have a data-compilation program. Once the data is compiled, the data-compilation program calls a separate program to print out a report. Assume further that the user can, from the data-compilation program, specify that printing be to a file, to the printer, or to the screen. If printing is to be to the screen, the print program will in turn call a screen browsing program once it has created the file to browse.

We have omitted error-checking for fopen() and execl() errors and for invalid user input. The data-compilation program is called execl.c; the report-printing program is called execl_p.c. Both programs use a header file, profit.h, that contains the template for the structure used to house the data. The program used to print to the screen, scan.c, is included on disk.

 **Listing** **L.1 execl.c**

```
/* execl.c */

/* execl with child reading file opened and closed by parent */
#include <stdio.h> /* unlink, perror */
#include <process.h> /* execl, exit */
#include <string.h> /* strcmp */
#include "profit.h"

char filename[45];
struct profit profit; /* template in profit.h */

int main(int argc, char **argv)
{
    static char print_mode[2];
    char *datafile = "c:\\temp\\data";
    char *print_prog = "c:\\tc\\out\\execl_p";

    /* if being called by exec from print program, argc will be > 1; */
    /* if just being started from command line, argc will be 1 */
    if (argc > 1)
    {
        /* if printing was to file or screen, ask if now want to send to printer */
        if (*argv[1] != 'P')
        {
            /* if print to screen specified, delete temporary file used by scan */
            if (*argv[1] == 'S')
                unlink("tempfile");

            if (get_response("Print to printer also (Y/N)? ") == 'Y')
                execl(print_prog, print_prog, datafile, "P", NULL);
        }

        /* do another office or quit? */
        if (get_response("Another office (Y/N)? ") != 'Y')
        {
            unlink("c:\\temp\\data"); /* delete temporary data file */
            exit(1);
        }
    }

    /* ask user whether to print to screen, file or printer & then exec */
    * print_mode = get_print_mode();
```

```c
   /* open data file & get data for it interactively */
   write_data(datafile);
   if (*print_mode == 'F')
      execl(print_prog, print_prog, datafile, "F", filename, NULL);
   else
      execl(print_prog, print_prog, datafile, print_mode, NULL);

   /* don't reach here unless call failed */
   perror("Call to execl failed");
}

/* derive data interactively */
void get_data(void)
{
   printf("Office number: ");
   scanf("%s", profit.office);
   printf("Revenues: ");
   scanf("%ld", &profit.revenues);
   printf("Expenses: ");
   scanf("%ld", &profit.expenses);
}

/* determine whether user wants to print to screen, file, or printer */
char get_print_mode(void)
{
   static char mode[2];

   *mode = get_response("Print to file (F), printer (P), "
      "or screen (S), or quit (Q): ");

   /* ask for file name if user wants to print to file */
   if (*mode == 'F')
   {
      printf("Name of file (include full path): ");
      scanf("%s", filename);
   }
   if (*mode == 'Q')
      exit(1);
   return *mode;
}

/* get user response of yes or no */
char get_response(char *msg)
{
   char response[81];
   puts(msg);
   scanf("%s", response);
   return toupper(*response);
}

/* open data file and get data for it interactively */
void write_data(char *write_file)
{

   FILE *fp = fopen(write_file, "wb"); /* error-checking omitted */
   get_data();
```

```
        /* write data to file and close data file */
        fwrite(&profit, 1, sizeof(profit), fp);
        fclose(fp);
    }
```

Listing L.2 execl_p.c

```
/* execl_p.c */

/* print program for execl.c */

#include <stdio.h>
#include <string.h> /* strcpy */
#include <process.h> /* execl */
#include "profit.h"

char nl[3] = "\n";
FILE *fp, *data;
struct profit profit; /* template in profit.h */

int main(int argc, char **argv)
{
    /* argv[1]: datafile, argv[2]: print mode, argv[3]: file name if to file */
    char print_mode = *argv[2];
    char *main_prog = "c:\\tc\\out\\execl";

    switch(print_mode)
    {
        case 'P': /* print to printer selected */
            fp = stdprn;
            strcpy(nl, "\r\n");
            break;

        /* if print to file selected, open file designated */
        case 'F': fp = fopen(argv[3], "w"); break;

        /* if print to screen selected, open temporary file to send to screen */
        case 'S': fp = fopen("tempfile", "w"); break;
    }

    /* open file with data and read it into profit structure */
    data = fopen(argv[1], "rb");
    fread(&profit, 1, sizeof(profit), data);

    /* print the results to the appropriate stream */
    form_head("EXECL_P", 1);
    print_form();

    /* call the main program back, telling it which print mode had been chosen */
    switch(print_mode)
    {
        case 'P':
        case 'F':
        /* argv[2] is print mode */
            execl(main_prog, main_prog, argv[2], NULL);
```

```
        case 'S': /* scan will execl parent program */
            execl("c:\\tc\\out\\scan", "c:\\tc\\out\\scan", tempfile, main_prog, "S", NULL);
        default: perror("Call to execl failed");
    }
}


/* print heading at top of each page */
void form_head(char *program, char page_no)
{
    fprintf(fp, "%s%s%s%s%s%s%s", nl, nl, nl, TOP, nl, BLK, nl);
    fprintf(fp,"%c   PROGRAM: %9s%11s OFFICEWIDE SYSTEM"
        " %10s PAGE: %6s%2d  %c%s",
        VERT, program, "", "", "", page_no, VERT, nl); /* head line 1 */
    fprintf(fp, "%c  %s%9s%s%9sDATE: %s  %c%s",
        VERT, "VERSION:       1.0", "", "Office Profit Statement", "",
        get_date(), VERT, nl); /* head line 2 */
    fprintf(fp, "%s%s%s%s%s%s%s%s%s%s%s", BLK, nl, BOT, nl, nl, nl, nl, nl, nl);
}


/* for heading, return date string in format MM/DD/YY */
char *get_date(void)
{
    static char date_string[L];
    time_t num_secs;
    struct tm *time_struct;

    /* get the number of seconds elapsed since midnight 1/1/70 */
    time(&num_secs);

    /* convert that # to a structure */
    time_struct = localtime(&num_secs);
    sprintf(date_string, "%02.2d/%02.2d/%02.2d", time_struct->tm_mon + 1,
        time_struct->tm_mday, time_struct->tm_year % 100);
    return date_string;
}


/* print text of form */
void print_form(void)
{
    fprintf(fp, "Office No. %s%s%s", profit.office, nl, nl);
    fprintf(fp, "Revenues: %8ld%s", profit.revenues, nl);
    fprintf(fp, "Expenses: %8ld\r            _____%s%s", profit.expenses, nl, nl);
    fprintf(fp, "Profit:   %8ld%s\f", profit.revenues -profit.expenses, nl);
}
```

```
/* profit.h */

#include <time.h> /* time, localtime */
#include <ctype.h> /* toupper */
#define TOP "╒════════════════════════════════════════╕"
#define BOT "╘════════════════════════════════════════╛"
#define BLK "║                                        ║"
#define VERT '║'


void form_head(char *program, char page_no), get_data(void);
```

```
char *get_date(void), get_print_mode(void), get_response(char *msg);
void print_form(void), void write_data(char *write_file);

struct profit
{
   char office[6];
   long revenues, expenses;
};
```

When `execl.exe` is initially run, we skip over the first 17 lines in the body of `main()`, since `argc` will only be 1. After opening the data file, having the user input data and writing to the data file, we call `execl()`. We pass the name of the print program, the name of the data file, the print mode (P for print to printer, F for print to file, and S for print to screen), and if the print mode is F, the name of the file the report is to be written to. Note the `NULL` that terminates the argument list.

The print program, `execl_p`, opens both the data file and a file for printing. Using a series of `fprintf()` statements, we print to `stdprn` if printing is to the printer, to the designated file if printing is to a file, and to a file we name "tempfile" if we are to print to the screen. Whichever we choose, Figure L.1 shows what the page, file, or screen will look like.

Figure L.1   *Output for* `execl_p.c`

```
PROGRAM:   EXECL_P            OFFICEWIDE SYSTEM              PAGE: 1
VERSION:   1.0            Office Profit Statement        DATE:06/03/00
```

```
Office No. 2

Revenues:   632562
Expenses:   321231

Profit:     311331
```

If printing is to the printer or to a designated file, we do an `execl()` back to the data-compilation program. If printing is to the screen, we do an `execl()` to `scan.exe`. The `scan` program, after letting the user browse through the file passed to it, does an `execl()` call to `execl.exe`, also passing it an argument of S. Executing `execl.exe` with an argument (which will be F, S, or P) gives the user the opportunity of also printing to the printer if the print-to-a-file option or the print-to-screen option had just been chosen, and then of continuing with another round of input and printing or quitting the program.

L.5   ARRAY OF POINTERS TO ARGUMENT STRINGS—execv() AND spawnv()

With `execv()` or `spawnv()`, the argument that follows the child-executable file argument is an array of pointers to char. All of the pointers in the array point to a command-line argument. These pointers and the strings they point to can be set at run time. We effectively designate the number of command-line arguments by setting the pointer after the pointer to the last argument to NULL.

The v version is more appropriate where the number of arguments to be passed is determined at run time. The l version is more appropriate when the number of arguments is fixed and known in advance.

The `spwnv.c` and `spwnv_p.c` programs illustrate `spawnv()`. In these and all following programs to illustrate `exec()` and `spawn()`, we have omitted the code for functions other than `main()`, since they are identical to those in `execl.c` and `execl_p.c` above.

 Listing   **L.3 spwnv.c**

```
/* spwnv.c */

/* spawnv with child reading data in parent's data segment */
```

```
#include <stdio.h>
#include <process.h> /* spawn */
#include <alloc.h> /* malloc */
#include <string.h> /* strcmp */
#include "profit.h"

char filename[45];
struct profit profit, *sptr; /* template in profit.h */
int main(void)
{
    static char *arg_list[5]; /* static, so set to all NULLs */
    static char print_mode[2];
    char struct_locus[18];
    char *print_prog = "c:\\tc\\out\\spwnv_p";

    sptr = &profit;

    /* this data will not be in child's data segment: pass on segment & offset */
    sprintf(struct_locus, "%Fp", (void far *)sptr);

    /* ok for large memory model */
    /* sprintf(struct_locus, "%p", (void *)sptr); */

    /* put print program, struct address, print mode in arg string pointer list */
    arg_list[0] = print_prog;
    arg_list[1] = struct_locus;
    arg_list[2] = print_mode; /* to be filled in below */

    while(1)
    {
        /* get data from user interactively and have user select print location */
        *print_mode = get_print_mode();
        get_data();

        if (*print_mode == 'F')
            arg_list[3] = filename; /* set in get_print_mode */

        spawnv(P_WAIT, print_prog, arg_list);

        /* blank out filename argument for subsequent printing to printer */
        arg_list[3] = NULL;

        /* if user specified screen or file, ask if also wants to printer */
        if (*print_mode != 'P')
        {
            if (get_response("\nPrint to printer also (Y/N)? ") == 'Y');
            {
                *print_mode = 'P';
                spawnv(P_WAIT, print_prog, arg_list);
            }
        }

        /* do another office or quit? */
        if (get_response("\nAnother office (Y/N)? ") != 'Y')
            exit(0);
    }
}
```

 **Listing** **L.4 spwnv_p.c**

```c
/* spwnv_p.c */

/* print program for spwnv.c */

#include <stdio.h>
#include <string.h> /* strcpy */
#include <process.h> /* spawn */
#include "profit.h"

FILE *fp;
char nl[3] = "\n";
struct profit profit, far *sptr; /* template in profit.h */
/* struct profit *sptr; // ok for large memory model */

int main(int argc, char **argv)
{
    char print_mode = *argv[2];
    char *scan_prog = "c:\\tc\\out\\scan";

    /* data is in parent's data segment: address passed is segment & offset */
    sscanf(argv[1], "%Fp", (void far *)&sptr);
    /* ok for large memory model */
    /*   sscanf(argv[1], "%p", (void *)&sptr); */

    /* copy data from parent into local structure variable */
    profit = *sptr;

    switch(print_mode)
    {
        /* if printer selected, add carriage return & point to stdprn */
        case 'P':
            fp = stdprn;
            strcpy(nl, "\n\r");
            break;

        /* if print to file selected, open designated file */
        case 'F':
            fp = fopen(argv[3], "w");
            break;
        /* if screen, open temporary file for scan program to read */
        case 'S':
            fp = fopen("tempfile", "w"); /* error-checking omitted */
            break;
    }

    /* print data to appropriate stream */
    form_head("SPWNV_P", 1);
    print_form();

    /* call scan program if print to screen selected */
    if (print_mode == 'S')
    {
        spawnl(P_WAIT, scan_prog, scan_prog, "tempfile", NULL);

        /* delete temporary file read by scan.exe */
        unlink("tempfile");
    }
}
```

In this program, we have chosen a different method of accessing data input in the parent. Since, with `spawn()`, the parent is in RAM at the same time as the child, we can access directly the structure we use in the parent to store our data rather than using a file. Even though the parent and child are in memory at the same time, however, they have different data segments. Consequently, to access from the child the `profit` structure variable declared and filled with data by the parent, we have to implement a way to let the child know `profit`'s segment as well as offset address. In the parent, we determine the address with `sprintf()`:

```
sprintf(struct_locus, "%Fp", (void far *)sptr);
```

The `%p` specifier is a special specifier for pointer addresses. The `%Fp` specifier is the far-pointer version. (If we were using a large data memory model, we could omit the F, since all pointers are `far` by default.) The array `struct_locus`, which is the first argument passed to the print program other than the print program's name, will look something like 8D51:055EE.

When we get to the child, we reverse the process with `sscanf()`:

```
sscanf(argv[1], "%Fp", (void far *)&sptr);
```

Note that `sptr` is declared as a far pointer to a `profit` structure variable.

L.6   A PATH EXAMPLE

As we can see from the following example, the argument format for the p version of `exec()` or `spawn()` is no different from the non-p counterparts. (Functions other than `main()` are omitted.)

 Listing **L.8 execlp.c**

```c
/*   execlp.c */

/*   execlp with child reading file opened & closed by parent */

/*   shows that PATH used by execlp() is parent's PATH, even as temporarily
     altered by putenv() */

#include <stdio.h>
#include <process.h> /* execl */
#include <string.h> /* strcmp */
#include <stdlib.h> /* putenv */
#include "profit.h"

char filename[45];
struct profit profit; /* template in profit.h */

int main(int argc, char **argv)
{
    static char print_mode[2];
    char *datafile = "c:\\temp\\data", *print_prog = "c:\\tc\\out\\execlp_p";

    putenv("PATH=c:\\tc\\out");

    /* if being called by exec from print program, argc will be > 1 */
    if (argc > 1)
    {
        /* if printing was to file or screen, ask if now want to send to printer */
        if (*argv[1] != 'P')
        {
            /* if print to screen specified, delete temporary file used by scan */
            if (*argv[1] == 'S')
                unlink("tempfile");
            if (get_response("Print to printer also (Y/N)? ") == 'Y')
                execlp("execlp_p", print_prog, datafile, "P", NULL);
        }
```

```
            /* do another office or quit? */
            if (get_response("Another office (Y/N)? ") != 'Y')
            {
                unlink("c:\\temp\\data"); /* delete temporary data file */
                exit(0);
            }
        }

    /* ask user whether to print to screen, file, or printer & then exec */
    *print_mode = get_print_mode();

    /* open data file & get data for it interactively */
    write_data(datafile);

    if (*print_mode == 'F')
        execlp("execlp_p", print_prog, datafile, "F", filename, NULL);
    else
        execlp("execlp_p", print_prog, datafile, print_mode, NULL);

    perror("Call to execl failed"); /* only get here if failed */
}
```

Listing L.9 execlp_p.c

```
/* execlp_p.c */

/* print program for execlp.c */

/* In the program calling this with an execlp() call, PATH was changed to
   c:\tc\out, a directory not in autoexec's DOS path. This program makes
   an execlp() call, passing as the first argument, the file name only,
   demonstrating that the child inherits the parent's environment. */

#include <stdio.h>
#include <string.h> /* strcpy */
#include <process.h> /* execl */
#include "profit.h"

char nl[3] = "\n";
FILE *fp, *data;
struct profit profit; /* template in profit.h */

int main(int argc, char **argv)
{
    /* argv[1]: datafile, argv[2]: print mode, argv[3]: file name if to file */
    char print_mode = *argv[2];
    char *main_prog = "c:\\tc\\out\\execlp";

    switch (print_mode)
    {
        case 'P': /* print to printer selected */
            fp = stdprn;
            strcpy(nl, "\r\n");
            break;

        /* if print to file selected, open file designated */
        case 'F':
            fp = fopen(argv[3], "w");
            break;
```

```
        /* if screen selected, open temporary file
           to send to screen */
        case 'S':
            fp = fopen("tempfile", "w");
            break;
    }

    /* open file with data and read it into profit structure */
    data = fopen(argv[1], "rb");
    fread(&profit, 1, sizeof(profit), data);

    /* print the results to the appropriate stream */
    form_head("EXECLP_P", 1);
    print_form();

    /* call the main program back, telling it which print mode had been chosen */
    switch(print_mode)
    {
        case 'P': case 'F':
            execlp("execlp", main_prog, argv[2], NULL);
            break;
        case 'S': /* scan will execl parent program */
            execlp("scan", "c:\\tc\\out\\scan", "tempfile", main_prog, "S", NULL);
            break;
    }

    perror("Call to execl failed");
}
```

At the beginning of execlp.c, we alter the PATH environmental variable with putenv() (the putenv() and getenv() functions are discussed in Chapter 16):

```
putenv("PATH=c:\\tc\\out");
```

(We have assumed that this subdirectory was not already in the PATH and that the child-executable file is found there.) This allows us to pass execlp_p as the child-executable file argument, rather than c:\\tc\\out\\execlp_p.

Note that the calls from execlp_p.c to either scan.exe or back to execlp.exe likewise omit the full path. It was not necessary to include another putenv() call in execlp_p.c: the child inherits the environment of the parent. The exception to this rule is where we use the e version of either exec() or spawn(). In that case, the child's environment is only what is expressly passed by the parent. We turn now to that case.

L.7   POINTER TO ENVIRONMENT STRINGS

When we use the e version of exec() or spawn(), the final argument is a pointer to an array of pointers to strings containing environmental variables. The end of the list of strings must be marked by setting the pointer after the last environment string to NULL, just as we place NULL after the argument list with the l version, and just as we set the pointer after the pointer to the final command-line argument to NULL with the v version.

We do this in the following example by declaring the array of pointers to char as static, thus initializing all pointers to NULLs. We have to make sure to create our array so that there is at least one more element than we will have pointers to environment strings. Then we can just assign addresses to the first elements of the array.

Normally, the child inherits the parent's environment. However, when we use the e version of exec() or spawn(), that environment is totally supplanted, not supplemented, by what is passed in the call. The only exception is that if the first pointer in the environment string pointer array is NULL, the child inherits the parent's environment. (Normally, of course, such an occurrence would take place in a situation where the first pointer might be NULL or not, depending on some run-time set of circumstances. Otherwise, there would be no point using the e version at all for this case.)

In the following example, execle.c and execle_p.c, we pass a single environment string. This will be the handle for the file we use to store the user data, in the format

```
HANDLE=#
```

where # is the file handle number.

In execlp.c, we had the child read a file opened and closed in the parent. Here, we have the child read a file opened and not closed in the parent. The file handle is passed through the environment. (Functions other than main() are omitted.)

Listing   **L.7 execle.c**

```
/*   execle.c */

/*   execle with child reading file opened & not closed in parent:
     file handle passed through the environment */

#include <stdio.h>
#include <io.h> /* open, write */
#include <fcntl.h> /* open flags */
#include <sys\stat.h> /* open permissions */
#include <process.h> /* exec */
#include <string.h> /* strcmp */
#include "profit.h"

char filename[45];
struct profit profit; /* template in profit.h */

int main(int argc, char **argv)
{
    static char print_mode[2];
    char handle_str[22];
    static char *env_list[2]; /* both start out as NULL; 2nd will stay NULL */
    char *print_prog = "c:\\tc\\out\\execle_p", *datafile = "c:\\temp\\data";
    char handle;

    unlink(datafile);

    /* if being called by exec from print program, argc will be > 1 */
    if (argc > 1)
    {
        /* if printing was to file or screen, ask if now want to send to printer */
        /* argv[1] will be file handle */
        if (strcmp(argv[1], "P"))
        {
            /* if print to screen specified, delete temporary file used by scan */
            unlink("tempfile");

            if (get_response("Print to printer also (Y/N)? ") == 'Y')
            {
                sprintf(handle_str, "HANDLE=%s", argv[1]);
                env_list[0] = handle_str;
                execle(print_prog, print_prog, "P", NULL, env_list);
            }
        }

        /* do another office or quit? */
        if (get_response("Another office (Y/N)? ") != 'Y')
        {
            unlink(datafile);
            exit(0);
        }
    }

    else
    {
```

```
      /* open data file for reading and writing */
      if ((handle = open(datafile, O_RDWR | O_CREAT | O_TRUNC |
          O_BINARY, S_IWRITE | S_IREAD)) == -1)
          perror("error opening c:\\temp\\data");

      /* determine file handle and write it into a string */
      sprintf(handle_str, "HANDLE=%d", handle);
      env_list[0] = handle_str;
   }

   /* write data to file; don't close */
   write(handle, (char *)&profit, sizeof(profit));
   get_data();
   /* ask user whether to print to screen, file or printer & then exec */
   *print_mode = get_print_mode();
   if (*print_mode == 'F')
      execle(print_prog, print_prog, "F", filename, NULL, env_list);
   else
      execle(print_prog, print_prog, print_mode, NULL, env_list);

   perror("Call to execl failed");
}
```

Listing L.8 execle_p.c

```
/* execle_p.c */

/* Print program for execle.c

   Note the 3rd argument to main, env, which is a local variable assigned
   the address of the address of the first environmental string.

   By adding the following to the code, we can see that the parent's
   environment is completely replaced by the environmental strings
   created in the parent.

   char i;
   char **env_ptr;
   for (i = 0, env_ptr = env; *env_ptr; env_ptr++, i++)
      printf("env[%d]: %s\n", i, *env_ptr); */

#include <stdio.h>
#include <io.h>
#include <string.h> /* strcpy */
#include <process.h> /* execl */
#include <stdlib.h> /* atoi */
#include "profit.h"

struct profit profit; /* template in profit.h */
FILE *fp;
char nl[3] = "\n";

int main(int argc, char **argv, char **env)
{
   /* args: 1: print mode, 2: filename if print to file */
   char handle;
   char print_mode = *argv[1];
   char *main_prog = "c:\\tc\\out\\execle", *scan_prog = "c:\\tc\\out\\scan";
   char handle_string[3];
```

```
      /* get handle from passed enviornment string: copy from char after '=' */
      strcpy(handle_string, strchr(env[0], '=') + 1);
      handle = atoi(handle_string);

      switch(print_mode)
      {
         case 'P': /* print to printer selected */
            fp = stdprn;
            strcpy(nl, "\r\n");
            break;

         /* if print to file selected, open file designated */
         case 'F':
            fp = fopen(argv[2], "w");
            break;

         /* if screen selected, open temporary
            file to send to screen */
         case 'S':
            fp = fopen("tempfile", "w");
            break;
      }

      /* go the the beginning of the file already opened in parent & read */
      lseek(handle, 0L, SEEK_SET);
      read(handle, (char *)&profit, sizeof(profit));

      /* print the results to the appropriate stream */
      form_head("EXECLE_P", 1);
      print_form();
      fclose(fp);

      /* call the main program back, telling it which print mode has been chosen */
      switch(print_mode)
      {
         case 'P': execl(main_prog, main_prog, "P", NULL);
         case 'F': execl(main_prog, main_prog, handle_string, NULL);
         case 'S': /* scan will execl parent program */
            execl(scan_prog, scan_prog, "tempfile", main_prog, handle_string, NULL);
            break;
      }
      perror("Call to execl failed");
}
```

We declare a two-element array of pointers to char. We fill the first one this way:

```
handle = open("c:\\temp\\data", O_RDWR ¦ O_CREAT ¦ O_TRUNC ¦ O_BINARY,
   S_IWRITE ¦ S_IREAD));
sprintf(handle_str, "HANDLE=%d", handle);
env_list[0] = handle_str;
```

After writing to the file, we execute the print program:

```
execle(print_prog, print_prog, print_mode, NULL, env_list);
```

The environment strings are passed to the child in the same way command-line arguments are (see Chapter 16), by an additional argument to main():

```
int main(int argc, char *argv[], char *env[])
```

In this case, env[0] would point to the string HANDLE=5 (the first five handles, 0–4, would be for stdin, stdout, stderr, stdaux, and stdprn). We isolate the handle portion itself with strchr():

```
strcpy(handle_string, strchr(env[0], '=') + 1); /* copy from char after '=' */
handle = atoi(handle_string);
```

If you add the following code to execle_p.c, you can see that the parent's environment is completely replaced by the environment strings created in the parent:

```
int i;
char **env_ptr;
for (i = 0, env_ptr = env; *env_ptr; env_ptr++, i++)
  printf("env[%d]: %s\n", i, *env_ptr);
```

L.8 POINTER TO ENVIRONMENT STRINGS WITH POINTER TO ARGUMENT STRINGS

The following examples, spwnve.c and spwnve_p.c, show the format of the v and e versions together. In this example, we also see yet another method for accessing data created in the parent. In exec1.c and execlp.c, the child opened a file opened and closed by the parent; in spwnv.c, the child read data directly from the parent's data segment; in execle.c, the child read a file opened and not closed in the parent, through a file handle passed through the environment. Here, the child reads data from a file opened and not closed in the parent, through a file pointer passed through the environment. (Functions other than main() are again omitted.)

 Listing **L.9 spwnve.c**

```
/* spwnve.c */

/* spawnve with child reading file opened & not closed in parent:
   file pointer passed.
   Compile with large memory model. */

#include <stdio.h>
#include <process.h> /* spawn */
#include "profit.h"

char filename[45];
struct profit profit; /* template in profit.h */

int main(void)
{
    static char *arg_list[3], *env_list[2]; /* set to all NULLs */
    static char print_mode[2];
    char parent_stream[20]
    char *print_prog = "c:\\tc\\out\\spwnve_p";
    FILE *fp;

    fp = fopen("c:\\temp\\data", "wb+"); /* write here, read in child */

    /* address pointed to will not be in child's data segment: pass on seg/off */

    /* sprintf(parent_stream, "STREAM=%Fp", (void *far)fp); */
    sprintf(parent_stream, "STREAM=%lu", (FILE *far)fp);

    /* put parent stream string in environment string pointer list */

    env_list[0] = parent_stream;
```

```
   /* put print program and print mode in argument string pointer list */
   arg_list[0] = print_prog;
   arg_list[1] = print_mode;

   while(1)
   {
      /* get data from user interactively & write to data file */
      get_data();
      rewind(fp);
      fwrite(&profit, 1, sizeof(profit), fp);

      /* ask user where to print data */
      *print_mode = get_print_mode();

      /* if print to file selected, ask user to specify filename */
      if (*print_mode == 'F')
         arg_list[2] = filename;

      spawnve(P_WAIT, print_prog, arg_list, env_list);

      /* blank out filename argument for subsequent printing to screen */
      arg_list[2] = NULL;

      /* if user specified screen or file, ask if also wants
         to printer */
      if (*print_mode != 'P')
      {
         if (get_response("\nPrint to printer also (Y/N)? ") == 'Y')
         {
            *print_mode = 'P';
            spawnve(P_WAIT, print_prog, arg_list, env_list);
         }
      }

      /* do another office or quit? */
      if (get_response("\nAnother office (Y/N)? ") != 'Y')
         exit(0);
   }
}
```

Listing L.10 spwnve_p.c

```
/* spwnve_p.c */

/* Print program for spwnve.c: compile with large memory model. */

#include <stdio.h>
#include <string.h> /* strcpy */
#include <process.h> /* spawn */
#include <stdlib.h> /* atoi */
#include "profit.h"

FILE *fp, *data;
char nl[3] = "\n";
struct profit profit; /* template in profit.h */

int main(int argc, char **argv, char **env)
{
   /* arguments: argv[1]: print mode, argv[2]: filename if there is one */
   char print_mode = *argv[1], *scan_prog = "c:\\tc\\out\\scan";
```

```
    /* get FILE pointer passed through environment string by parent */

    /*  sscanf(strchr(env[0], '=') + 1, "%Fp", (void *)&data); */
    /* from 1 after = */
    data = (FILE *far)atol((strchr(env[0], '=') + 1));

    /* rewind file and read data */
    rewind(data);
    fread(&profit, 1, sizeof(profit), data);

    switch(print_mode)
    {
        case 'P': /* if printer selected, add carriage return & point to stdprn */
            fp = stdprn;
            strcpy(nl, "\r\n");
            break;
        case 'F': /* if print to file selected, open designated file */
            fp = fopen(argv[2], "w");
            break;
        case 'S': /* if screen, open temporary file for scan program to read */
            fp = fopen("tempfile", "w");
            break;
    }

    /* print data to appropriate stream */
    form_head("SPWNVE_P", 1);
    print_form();

    /* call scan program if print to screen selected */
    if (print_mode == 'S')
    {
        spawnl(P_WAIT, scan_prog, scan_prog, "tempfile", NULL);

        /* delete temporary file read by scan.exe */
        unlink("tempfile");
    }
}
```

We "encode" the file pointer environment string in spwnve.c this way:

```
sprintf(parent_stream, "STREAM=%ld", (FILE *far)fp);
```

and we "decode" in the following manner in spwnve_p.c:

```
data = (FILE *far)atol((strchr(env[0], '=') + 1)); /* from 1 after = */
```

We could have used the following alternative formulations with the same result:

```
sprintf(parent_stream, "STREAM=%Fp", (void *far)fp);

sscanf(strchr(env[0], '=') + 1, "%Fp", (void *far)&data); /* from 1 after = */
```

Note that we have compiled both programs in the large memory model. (See Appendix B.) Here, we are using a file pointer and standard I/O, rather than a file handle and low-level I/O as we did in execle.c. Using the large memory model allows use to use a far FILE pointer for fread().

L.9   RETURN VALUES AND ERROR HANDLING

In the sample programs above, we have omitted error-checking code for the calls we make to exec() and spawn(). In your actual programs, of course, you should include extensive error-checking. On error, exec(), and spawn() return a –1 and the global variable errno is set to one of the manifest constants given in Table L.2.

Table L.2   `errno` *Values on* `exec()` *and* `spawn()` *Errors*

Manifest Constant	Perror Message	Meaning
E2BIG	Arg list too long	Total length of the argument strings is greater than 128 characters (or the environment strings total more than 32K).
EACCES (exec only)	Permission denied	File-sharing is enabled and the child executable file specified is either locked or not set up for sharing.
EMFILE (exec only)	Too many open files	DOS's file limit has been exceeded
ENOENT	No such file or directory	Either the path or the file specified as the child executable file was not found
ENOEXEC	exec format error	File specified as child is not an executable file
ENOMEM	Not enough memory	Insufficient memory to execute the child or available memory is corrupted
EINVAL (spawn only)	Invalid argument	The first spawn argument is invalid

The simplest way to determine the error is to use `perror()`. For instance:

```
execl("no_such_file", "no_such_file", "data", NULL);
perror("execl");
```

The output would be

```
execl: No such file or directory
```

See Chapter 16 for a discussion of `perror()` and `errno`.

When a call to `exec()` is successful, there is no return value. A successful call to `spawn()`, on the other hand, returns the child's exit status. This would be 0 for a normal termination or the value assigned with an `exit()` call made in the child or the return value of its `main()` function.

L.10   CHOOSING exec() OR spawn()

In some cases, it will be clear whether `exec()` or `spawn()` is the function to be used. If you need to execute program B from program A and program C from program B and program D from program C, without ever having to return to program A, then `exec()` is appropriate.

By contrast, say you have a program that creates a report. You then need to edit the report manually and return to the report-generating program at the same point you left it. Here, the preferred function is `spawn()`. This is particularly true if the editor program is a third-party vendor's. Unlike the program examples above, where we executed the `scan.exe` program through an `exec()` call and had `scan.exe` in turn reexecute the original program with another `exec()` call, we would not have the luxury of being able to call back our own original program from the commercial program through `exec()`.

Nevertheless, memory considerations may prevent our using `spawn()`. Keep in mind that with `spawn()`, both the parent and child are in memory at the same time. At some point, we will run out of RAM. This is especially so if the programs are each large, if the users may be running some TSRs, or if we have a series of `spawn()` calls: program A calls program B, program B calls program C, and so on.

But what do we do if we have a situation that calls for `spawn()`—for instance, our program calls a commercial program and we want to return to our program in the spot we left it after the user is done with the commercial program—but memory or other considerations prevent us from using `spawn()`? Here, we can use a batch file in conjunction with `exec()` to achieve nearly the same effect as using `spawn()`.

The following DOS batch file is taken from the 60,000-line VendoRiter program package written by the authors for about 10,000 users at AT&T:

```
:vendor.bat
@echo off
echo off
c:
cd\vend
cls
vend
goto levtest
:ret98
scan tempfile
goto ret100
:ret99
protilt tempfile
:ret100
vend 1
goto levtest
:ret49
protilt tempfile
:ret50
vend 2
:levtest
if errorlevel 100 goto ret100
if errorlevel 99 goto ret99
if errorlevel 98 goto ret98
if errorlevel 50 goto ret50
if errorlevel 49 goto ret49
:end
cls
```

The main executable program is vend.exe. If vend.exe is run without command arguments, an introductory screen is painted. When the user presses any key, the main menu appears. If the program is run with a command-line argument, the introductory screen is skipped. If the argument is 1, the main menu appears; if it is 2, the program jumps to the form-printing submenu.

We have already seen one of the other two programs called by the batch file, scan.exe. The other, protilt.com, is a driver we created that transforms an ASCII file into a graphics image and rotates it for printing in landscape mode on a dot-matrix printer.

If the user chooses to print the vendor database list—either to the screen, to the printer, or to a file—the work is done by vnd_lst.exe. Here's the code in vend.c used to access vnd_lst.exe:

```
if (mode == PRINTF) /* print to file */
   execl("vnd_lst", "vnd_lst", signer_str, mode_str, filename, NULL);
else /* print to printer or screen */
   execl("vnd_lst", "vnd_lst", signer_str, mode_str, NULL);
```

And here's the code in vnd_lst.c that gets us back to vend.exe:

```
if (print_mode == PRINTS) /* print to screen */
   exit(98); /* call scan tempfile, then restart vend with arg of 1 */
else
   exit(100); /* restart vend with arg of 1 */
```

The exit() function passes on its argument to the batch file. If we exit vnd_lst.exe with a passed value of 98, we move in this fashion in the batch file:

```
goto levtest
:levtest
if errorlevel 98 goto ret98
:ret98
```

```
scan tempfile
goto ret100
vend 1
```

Thus, we call scan.exe with a file argument of "tempfile", this file having been created by vnd_lst.exe. When the user is done browsing through the file and scan terminates, we call vend.exe with an argument of 1. If the user has chosen to print to the printer or a file instead, a value of 100 is passed instead of 98 and we get to the same place in the batch file, skipping over the "scan tempfile" line, however.

If the user chooses to print a vendor invoice, the work is done by vnd_p301.exe. The user can print a completed form, selected from a database list or from the screen, or a blank form of one of several types. This is the code in vend.c (all error-checking code for calls to exec() and system() is omitted here and in all following examples):

```
if (blank)
   execl("vnd_p301", "vnd_p301", "0", form_string, NULL);
else
{
   if (mode != PRINTF) /* print to file */
      execl("vnd_p301.exe", "vnd_p301.exe", form_name, formnum, mode_str, NULL);
   else
      execl("vnd_p301.exe", "vnd_p301.exe", form_name, formnum, mode_str, filename,
         NULL);
}
```

The corresponding termination code in vnd_p301.c:

```
/* print to screen & not blank forms */
if (print_mode == PRINTS && !blank)
   exit(98); /* call scan tempfile, then restart vend with arg of 1 */


/* print to dot-matrix printer: cause vendor.bat to execute protilt, then vend */

else if (print_mode == PRINTP && dot_matrix)
{
   if (blank)
      exit(49); /* call protilt, then restart vend with arg of 2 */
   else
      exit(99); /* call protilt, then restart vend with arg of 1 */
}


/* cause vendor.bat to reexecute vend, without protilt first */

else
{
   if (blank)
      exit(50); /* print blank form: restart vend with arg of 2 */
   else
      exit(100); /* restart vend with arg of 1 */
}
```

Since all programs chained by vend.exe are in-house programs, it is really not necessary to use a batch file. Either exec() or, if a particular user's machine has sufficient memory, spawn() could be used. Providing a batch file option allows the company to switch to commercially created screen browsing and dot-matrix graphics printing programs (such as "Sidekick") in the future.

Meanwhile, both the exec() and spawn() options are available by way of conditional directives. For example, in vend.c's call of vnd_mgmt.exe, used to create and print management report compilations of the vendor invoices, we have our choice of using a system call or exec():

```
#if defined SYS_WAY
   sprintf(testbuf, "%s %s %s %s %d %d ", "vnd_mgmt.exe", sdate,
      edate, mode, form_type, print_mode);
   if (print_mode == PRINTF)
      strcat(testbuf, filename);
   system(testbuf);
```

```
#else
   if (print_mode == PRINTF)
      execl(temp, temp, sdate, edate, mode_str, form_type,
         print_mode_str, filename, NULL);
   else
      execl(temp, temp, sdate, edate, mode_str, form_type, print_mode_str, NULL);
#endif
```

(The system() call here is identical in effect to a spawn() call.) The corresponding termination code in vnd_mgmt.c:

```
if (print_mode == PRINTS) /* print to screen */
{
   #if defined SYS_WAY
      system("scan.exe tempfile")

   #elif defined EXEC_WAY
      execl("scan.exe", "scan.exe", "tempfile", "vend.exe", "1", NULL);

   #elif defined BATCH_WAY
      exit(98); /* call scan tempfile, then restart vendor with arg of 1 */

   #endif
}

else /* print to file or printer;
         printing already done by this point */
{
   #if defined BATCH_WAY
      exit(100); /* restart vendor with arg of 1 */

   #elif defined EXEC_WAY
      execl("vend.exe", "vend.exe", "1", NULL);

   #endif
}
```

Index

A